THE OXFORD COMPANION TO

Italian
Food

THE OXFORD COMPANION TO

Italian
Food

Gillian Riley

OXFORD
UNIVERSITY PRESS
2007

OXFORD
UNIVERSITY PRESS

Oxford University Press, Inc., publishes works that further
Oxford University's objective of excellence
in research, scholarship, and education.

Oxford New York
Auckland   Cape Town   Dar es Salaam   Hong Kong   Karachi
Kuala Lumpur   Madrid   Melbourne   Mexico City   Nairobi
New Delhi   Shanghai   Taipei   Toronto

With offices in
Argentina   Austria   Brazil   Chile   Czech Republic   France   Greece
Guatemala   Hungary   Italy   Japan   Poland   Portugal   Singapore
South Korea   Switzerland   Thailand   Turkey   Ukraine   Vietnam

Published by Oxford University Press, Inc.
198 Madison Avenue, New York, NY 10016

www.oup.com

Oxford is a registered trademark of Oxford University Press

Library of Congress Cataloging-in-Publication Data
Riley, Gillian.
The Oxford companion to Italian food / Gillian Riley.
p.   cm.
Includes bibliographical references and index.
ISBN 978-0-19-860617-8
1. Cookery, Italian—Dictionaries
2. Food habits—Italy—History.   I. Title.
TX723.R5265 2008
394.1'20945—dc22
2007012080

1 3 5 7 9 8 6 4 2
Printed in the United States of America
on acid-free paper

To the memory of
Emilio Lancellotti 1954–2001
generous host, kind friend,
loyal son and brother,
who did so much
to encourage enthusiasm
for the food
of Italy

Contents

Foreword

I'm still hungry for Italy. By this of course I mean not only the food and drink, along with all of their associated tastes and smells, but also the weather, the landscape, places, people, and their way of life, too. Helping my parents cook meals during my childhood in Seattle produced this appetite, and stories from my relatives as well as writers like Angelo Pellegrini caused it to grow over the years. Even before I decided to become a chef, Italy held a special significance in my life, and I knew I wanted to visit someday. I was right. Since my first trip I've been back as often as possible.

Whenever I'm there, I'm always a little surprised to learn that the countless varieties of the peninsula's dishes are able to evoke memories that I hardly knew I had. For so many reasons Abruzzo, where my grandparents grew up, can only be described as heavenly, and I honestly don't think I'll ever be convinced that a better Italian saffron exists outside of L'Aquila. If I learned anything while living in the Po Valley and working at La Volta, however, it's that the food of Emilia-Romagna represents the absolute culmination of what the country can offer. From rapturous helpings of *bollito misto* I've enjoyed there to the indisputable superiority of the region's Parmigiano, I've been convinced over and over—in Emilia-Romagna especially, but also elsewhere in Italy—that food and culture are very closely intertwined. A particularly fine infusion made with the passage of time.

An appreciation of this relationship is precisely what appealed to me about the *Oxford Companion to Italian Food*. I didn't know Gillian Riley when I first learned of the project, but as I read her manuscript I quickly saw that she understands the essence of these things and writes with passion, knowledge, and an ever-important pinch of humor. Writing about Modena, she states that "the city is famous as the home of a sports car and an opera singer, but its *aceto balsamico tradizionale di Modena* surpasses them both." Anyone who's tried the real thing would have to agree. Consult this book for answers to questions great and small about Italy's rich culinary history, but do so also to remind yourself that the best food is most often prepared in a simple fashion, with readily available ingredients. It defines who we are. So if the best food is what makes us healthiest, and happiest, then let us follow Gillian in hot pursuit.

Mario Batali, New York, April 2007

Introduction

Those of us who have encountered and come to love the food of Italy become obsessed with trying to find out more about it. We experience both the thrill of the chase, and despair and frustration at the immensity of the task. We press our noses against the misted-up window pane trying to glimpse what lies beyond, hardly daring to venture in search of the pleasures within. Italians do not have this problem; they know it all, they seem to be born with an innate sense of their national gastronomic heritage, and deep knowledge of their own local traditions. They are justified in being dogmatic, didactic, sometimes quite noisily. We dare not behave like this, we totter and fumble our way towards understanding— questioning, listening, reading, shopping, cooking, and eating. Only rare souls have the tenacity to adopt and write about a region or a topic with authority; the rest of us advance step by step, and this work hopes to be a kindly guide to these first attempts. No book on Italian food can cover all the ground or answer all the queries, but we hope to convey the delights and excitement of the pursuit, and lead the reader towards other sources and authorities. This is not a recipe book, although recipes are described with enthusiasm, but if it points the way to happy cooking and eating of what is probably the best cuisine in the world, it will have been worth the efforts of everyone involved.

Acknowledgements

Alan Davidson and Pam Coote of Oxford University Press had the idea in the first place, and Pam, Joanna Harris, and Judith Wilson guided and helped the book in its early stages; Benjamin Keene and Sara Lieber brought the project to a conclusion, helped by the production expertise of Joellyn Ausanka and the design skills of Rachel Perkins. Helen Saberi brought order and discipline to the task, and without her kind and unstinting help there would have been no end to the project. Many generous friends and advisors contributed information and advice, corrected blunders, filled in gaps, and suggested improvements. Andrew Dalby shared his erudition with entries and wise comments; Carol Field was a constructive contributor and advisor; Anna del Conte gave generous guidance right from the beginning, and her books were a constant source of knowledge; Ann and Franco Taruschio gave expertise and inspiration; the late Alan Davidson generously offered books from his library; June di Schino provided the fruits of her recent work on Scappi; Robin and Caroline Weir filled me with ice cream and its history; Jig Patel gave me a new left knee and the strength to carry on; and the Lancellotti family cooked their wonderful food. There are many more friends whose help made the book possible, including Michele Mori of Gallo Nero, Philip and Mary Hyman, Charles Perry, Giovanni Ballarini, Faith Willinger, John and Nichola Fletcher, Giovanni Lussu, and Paola Cirioni, along with the Italian Trade Centre in London, and of course the many people who fed me in Italy and patiently answered questions.

My greatest debt is to James Mosley, who got me to Italy in the first place and has been inspiring and supportive throughout this project.

Contributors

Author
Gillian Riley
London

Assistant Editor
Helen Saberi
London

Advisory Editors and Contributors
Unsigned entries are written by the author

Anna del Conte
Dorset, England

Andrew Dalby (AKD)
Saint-Coutant, France

Carol Field (CF)
San Francisco

Ann and Franco Taruschio (T)
Abergavenny, Wales

June di Schino (JdS)
Rome

Notes on Using This Book

The book was written with the intention that browsing through it should be a pleasure. However, most readers are likely to use it in the first instance to find information on a particular topic pertaining to the cuisine of Italy.

To look something up, the first step is to determine if it is in fact a headword. The headwords, printed so that they stand out clearly on the page, are in alphabetical order. If the topic sought is not a headword, the next step is to look for it in the index at the back of the book.

The index caters for synonyms and provides help in a situation where there is an English name for something but a name in Italian has wide currency (e.g., a reader looking for *dado* is directed to **bouillon**, but pesto or ciabatta have their own entries, while **vinegar** is where to look for *aceto*, but **balsamic vinegar** is where to look for *aceto balsamico tradizionale*). Finally, it provides cross-references for readers who are looking for topics which are actually presented as subtopics within entries of larger scope (e.g., a reader looking for *pollo alla romana* will be directed to **chicken**).

Another way of using the book would be to start with the subject index, a thematic listing of headwords which shows at a glance the whole range of entries in a particular field of interest such as fruits, fish, baked goods, and regional cuisine.

Cross-references are indicated by small capitals. They appear only where they are likely to be helpful to the reader, and normally only once within an entry. Thus, an entry about offal might contain the word liver numerous times, but only the first occurrence in that entry is in small capitals.

Bibliographic references in the standard form (author's last name, date, page number if needed) direct the reader to an item in the bibliography at the end of the book. If a book is referred to in a less specific way, it will probably not be in the bibliography.

Entries by Subject

ART AND CULTURE

Accademia della Crusca; Accademia Galileiana del Cimento; Accademia Italiana della Cucina; artists; Bimbi, Bartolomeo; Bronzini, Agnolo; Campi, Vincenzo; Camporesi, Piero; Caravaggio, Michelangelo Merisi di; Carpaccio; Crivelli, Carlo; Empoli, Jacopo Chimenti da; food in art; Garzoni, Giovanna; Giovanni da Udine; Italian food literature; Maestro di Hartford; Mantegna, Andrea; Michelangelo, Buonarroti; Mitelli, Giuseppe Maria; Munari, Cristoforo; myths; Pinelli, Bartolomeo; Pontormo, Jacopo Carucci, il; Rajberti, Giovanni; Ruoppolo, Giovan Battista and Giuseppe Recco

BAKED GOODS (BREADS, CAKES, ETC.)

amaretti; amaretto di saronno; babà; baci di dama; bagel; baicoli; bignè; biscotti, biscotto; bocca di dama; bocconotto; bread; bread and butter pudding; bread rolls; breads, braided or knotted; breads, ring-shaped; breads, rustic; bruschetta; cantucci; ciambelli; cirola romana; colomba; companatico; cornetto; crescentini, cresia; crostini, crostoni; crumiri; dolci; flatbreads; flour; focaccia; grissini; michetta; millet; pandoro; pane di genzano; pane di ramerino; pane e coperto; panettone; panforte; panini (o); panmelato; panpepato; pasticceria; pastry; piada, piadina; pizza; pretzel; rosetta (e); rye; savoiardi; spelt; sugar; tarallo; tart; wheat; yeast

BIOGRAPHIES

Aldrovandi, Ulisse; Arcimboldo, Giuseppe; Artusi, Pellegrino; Bassano, Jocopa da Ponte; Belli, Guiseppe Gioachino; Bimbi, Bartolomeo; Bockenheim, Giovanni; Boni, Ada; Bonvesin de la Riva; Bracciolini, Poggio; Bronzino, Angnolo; Calvino, Italo; Camilleri, Andrea; Campi, Rossana; Campi, Vincenzo; Camporesi, Piero; Caravaggio, Michelangelo Merisi di; Carpaccio; Casanova, Giacomo; Castelvetro, Giacomo; Cavalcanti, Ippolito; Cervio, Vincenzo; Christina of Sweden; Corrado, Vincenzo; Crivelli, Carlo; Dante; Della Verde, Suor Maria Vittoria; Empoli, Jacopo Chimenti da; Evitascandalo, Cesare; Felici, Costanzo; Fusoritto da Narni, Reale; Garzoni, Giovanna; Giovanni da Udine; Giegher, Mattia; Guerrini, Olindo; Lampedusa, Giuseppe di; Landi, Giulio; Latini, Antonio; Liberati, Francesco; Ligozzi, Jacopo; Maestro di Hartford; Mantegna, Andrea; Marinetti, Filippo Tommaso; Martino de Rossi; Massonio, Salvatore; Mattioli, Pier Andrea; Medici, Caterina de'; Messisbugo, Cristofaro; Michelangelo Buonarroti; Mitelli, Giuseppe Maria; Munari, Cristoforo; Nebbia, Antonio; Petronilla; Pinelli, Bartolomeo; Pisanelli, Baldassare; Platina, Bartolomeo Sacchi; Pontormo, Jacopo Carucci, il; Rajberti, Giovanni; Romoli, Domenico (Panunto); Rosselli, Giovanni de; Rossetti, Giovanni Battista; Ruoppolo, Giovan Battista and Giuseppe Recco; Scappi, Bartolomeo; Stefani, Bartolomeo; Vasselli, Giovan Francesco

CHEESE AND MILK PRODUCTS

asiago; bagòss; bel paese; bettelmatt; bitto; bocconcino; bra; branzi; bruss; burrata; burrino; butter; cacio; caciocavallo; cacioricotta lucano; caciotta; canestato pugliese; casciotta d'urbino; casieddu; casolet della val camonica; castelmagno; cheese; cream; crema; crema fritta; dairy products; EEC dairy products regulation; fior di latte; fiore sardo; fonduta; fontina; formaggio di fossa; formai de mut; formaio embriago; gelato; gorgonzola; grana padano; marzolino; mascarpone; milk; montasio; Monte Veronese; mozzarella di bufala; murazzano; paglierina di rifreddo; Pantaleone da Confienza; parmesan; pecorino; pecorino romano; pecorino sardo; pecorino toscano; prescinsoeua; pressato; provatura; provola; provolone; provolone del monaco; provula di floresta (casafloresta); quartirolo lombardo; ragusano; raschera; rennet; ricotta; robiola; salato morbido friulano; scamorza molisana; silter; taleggio; toma; whey; yoghurt; zuccotto

CULINARY TERMS

agresto; amario; bitterness; brasato; civet; dente, al; drizzle; fernet branca; food words and their origins; funghetto, al; graters; lesso; musk; pestle and mortar; scapece; sourness; timballo; tofeja; trifolati; umami; zimino

DRINKS AND BEVERAGES

alchermes; aperitivi; chocolate; coffee; digestivi; fernet branca; granita; mistrà; nocino; ratafia; rosolio; sambuca (o); sorbet; spremuta; strega; tea; water; wine

FISH AND SEAFOOD

acciuga; amberjack; anchovy; angel shark; angler fish; anguilla; arsella; astice; baccalà; bianchetti; bivalves; bleak; bogue; bonito; bream; burrida; cacciucco; calamaro; cappa santa ventagli; carp; carpione; chub; cockle; cod; comber; conger eel; corb; coregone, corrigone; cozze; crab; cuttlefish; dentex; eel; fish and seafood; fish, freshwater; fish, preserved; fish sauce; fish soup; flounder; frog; gambero; gar-fish; gilt-head bream; goby; granchio; grey mullet; grouper; gurnard; hake; herring; John Dory; lamprey; langoustine; latterini; linguattola; lobster; lumache; mackerel; meagre; monkfish; moray eel; mussel; octopus; ombrine; ostrica; oyster; palourde; pandora; perch; pesce persico; pesce spada; pesce San Pietro; pike; rana; ray; razza commune; red mullet; roach; rombo; rospo, coda di; saddled bream; salt cod; salt fish; sand smelt; saor; sar; sardine; sardine, freshwater; scallop; scampi; scorpion fish; sea bass; sea bream; sea urchin; shad; sharks; sheepshead bream; shellfish and crustaceans; shrimp; skate; smooth hound; snail; sole; spigola; squid; stoccafisso; stockfish; sturgeon; swordfish; tench; trout; tunny; turbot; twaite shad; two-banded bream; vongola (e); wedge shell; weever; whitefish; zimino

FRUITS, VEGETABLES, AND NUTS

acorn; agrumi; alexanders; almond; apple; apricot; artichoke; arugula; asparagus; aubergine; azarole; barley; bergamot orange; bilberry; bitter orange; blackberry; broad bean; broccoli; buckwheat; cabbage; capsicum; cardoon; carrot; castagna; cauliflower; cavolo nero; celery; cherries, cornelian; cherry; chestnut; chickpeas; citron; citrus fruits; coconut; concentrato (tomato paste); cornel; cucumber; currant and raisin; cynar; dried fruit; eggplant; elderflower and berries; emmer wheat; fave dei morti; fico d'India; fig; gooseberry; grape; gianduia; hazelnut; hops, wild; jerusalem artichoke; juniper; lamb's lettuce; lemon; lentil; lettuce; lime; limoncello; lupin; macco; maize; mandorle; maraschino;

marrone; marrow; mastic; medlar; melon; millet; mostarda di frutta; mulberry; mushrooms; must; nettles; nut; oats; olive; olive oil; orange; orange flower water; orzata; ossi da morta; panissa; parsnip; pea; peach; peanut; pear; pepperoni; peppers; persimmon; pine nuts; pinzimonio, al; pistachio; plum; pomegranate; poppy; porcini; potato; prickly pear; primizie; prune; pumpkin; purslane; quince; radish; rampion; raspberry; rhubarb; risi e bisi; rye; salad; sorb apples; spelt; spinach; strawberry; sunflower; sweet or bell pepper; tomato; truffle; turnip; valerianella; vegetarianism; verdura; walnut; watermelon; wheat; wild asparagus; wild greens; zucca; zucchini

HERBS, SPICES, AND CONDIMENTS

agliata; agretti; allspice; angelica; anise; asafoetida; bagna cauda; balsamic vinegar; barba di frate; basil; battesimo; bay leaves; bergamot; borage; bugloss; calamint; camomile; cannabis; capers; caraway; cardamom; cassia; catalogna; chervil, chicory; chilli pepper, chives; cinnamon; cloves; coriander; costmary; cren; cubeb; cumin; dandelion; dill; dittany; elderflower and berries; endive; fennel; feverfew; flowers; galangal; garlic; geranium; ginger; grains of paradise; gremolata; hemp; herbal infusions; herbs; horehound; horseradish; hyssop; impatiens; jasmine; lampascione; lavender; lemon balm; lemon verbena; licorice; long pepper; lovage; mallow; marjoram; mentuccia; micromeria; mint; must; mustard; myrtle; nasturtium; nepitella; nutmeg; olive oil; onion; oregano; parsley; pennyroyal; pepper; pepperoncino; poppy; preboggiòn; puntarelle; radicchio; rocket; rose; rosemary; rue; safflower; saffron; sage; salad burnet; salsa verde; salsify; salt; samphire; savoury; senape; sesame; shallot; silphium; sorrel; southernwood; spices; sugar; sweet cicely; tansy; tarragon; thyme;

vanilla; verdura; verjuice; vinegar; violet; wallflower; wild garlic; wild greens; wormwood; zucchero

HISTORY AND SOCIETY

Abruzzo; Accademia della Crusca; Accademia Galileiana del Cimento; Accademia Italiana della Cucina; agriturismo; Anonimo Meridionale; Anonimo Toscano; Anonimo Veneziano; Arab influence; banquet; Basilicata; brigata spenderecccia; Calabria; Campania and Naples; cookbooks; cookery schools; cucina dele nonne; cucina povera; Della Verde, Suor Maria Vittoria; DOC, DOP, IGP, and SGT; DOP, Denominazione di Origine Protetta; eating out; ecological movements and food; egg; Emilia-Romagna; fast food; fast, lenten or lean; Felici, Costanzo; festivity and food; food words and their origins; Friuli–Venezia Giulia; gastro-legends; Greek gastronomy, influence of; hemp; home cooking; Italian food abroad; Italian food literature; Jewish gastronomy; kitchen equipment; Latini, Antonio; Lazio; *liber de coquina*; Ligozzi, Jacopo; Liguria; literature and food; Lombardy; Maestro di Hartford; Manna; Marche, the; Marinetti, Filippo Tommaso; Marsala; Martino de Rossi; Massonio; Mattioli, Pier Andrea; meals and patterns of eating; Medici, Caterina de'; Mediterranean diet; Messisbugo, Cristofaro; Michelangelo Buonarroti; Molise; myths; nuova cucina; osterie; pane e coperto; pasta, history of; Petronilla; Piedmont; Pisanelli, Baldassare; Platina, Bartolomeo Sacchi; precepts and prohibitions; Puglia; Rajberti, Giovanni; Roman food; Rome; Rossetti, Giovanni Battista; saffron; salt; Sardinia; Scappi, Bartolomeo; Sicily; slow food; Stefani, Bartolomeo; street food; sugar; table manners; Tiella; Trentino–Alto Adige; Tuscany; Umbria; Valle d'Aosta; vegetarianism; Veneto; Vincisgrassi; walnut

MEAT AND MEAT PRODUCTS

abbacchio; agnello; ambergris; bacon; beef; blood; boar, wild; bollito; bologna; brain; brasato; bresaola; brodo lardiero; capocollo; cappello da prete; capriolo (roe buck); caul fat; chicken; ciccioli; colonnata; coppa; coratella; cotechino; cotechino cremonese; cotechino modena; cotenna di maiale; culatello; cured meats; deer; donkey; dormouse; drippings; duck; ears; egg; fegatelli; fegatini; fegato; finocchiona; fiocchetto; free range; garofolato; goat and kid; goose; guanciale; guinea fowl; guinea pig; ham; hare; head; hearts; horse; intestines; kid; kidneys; lamb; lard; lardo; lattonzolo; liver; lucanica; lungs; maiale; meat; meatballs; mortadella; mule; mutton; nervetti; offal; ossobuco alla milanese; oxtail; pajata; pancetta; Parma ham; partridge; peacock; pheasant; pig; pigeon; pig's extremities; pig's fat; pig's head; pig's offal; polpette; porchetta; pork products; poultry; prosciutto; quail; rabbit; rennet; ruspante; salama da sugo; salame; salame di fabriano; salame di Napoli; salame di varzi; salame d'la duja; salame d'oca; salame felino; salame "gentile"; salame Milano; salame Toscano; salsiccia; saltimbocca alla romana; salume; sanguinaccio; sausages, fresh and cured; sheep; small birds; soppressata; speck; spezzatino; spleen; stracotto; stufato; sucking pig; sweetbreads; tails; testicles; tongue; tripe; trotters and feet; turkey; udders; veal; venison; violino di capra; vitello tonnato; water buffalo; wild boar; zampone modena

PASTA AND RICE

arancini; cuscusu; dente, al; fettucine; flour; Lampedusa, Giuseppe di; lasagne; maccheroni; passatelli; pasta; pasta alimentare; pasta aromatizzata; pasta, baked; pasta, cooking it; pasta, dried; pasta, dried, artisan; pasta, fresh; pasta, history of; pasta sauces; pasta shapes; pasta, stuffed; pirciati; rice; riso al forno; risotto; supplì; tortellini; vermicelli

PREPARED FOOD AND DISHES

acquacotta; amaretti; amaretto di saronno; amatriciana,all'; antipasto; Apician flavour; arancini; battuto; biancomangiare; bollito; bouillon cubes; brodetto; brodo lardiero; broth; bruschetta; buridda; burrida; cacciucco; capocollo; chicken; chickpeas; chilli pepper; cibreo; civet or civé; coda alla vaccinara; convenience foods; cotechino; cotechino cremonese; cotechino modena; crostini, crostoni; dado; dumplings; egg; emmer wheat; fegatelli; fish soup; fonduta; frico; frittata; fritter; garofolato; gnocchi; goose; guincate; head; lasagne; lesso; liver; lucanica; marzipan; meatballs; migliaccio; minestra; minestrone; mischianza; mortadella; ossobuco alla milanese; pajata; panada; pancotta(o); panforte; panmelato; panna cotta; panpepato; panzanella; pappa al pomodoro; parmigiana; passatelli; pasta sauces; pasta, stuffed; pastella; pasticcio; peacock; pearà; peperata; peposo; pesto; pevarada; pizza; polenta; polpette; potacchio; pudding; ragù; ribollita; salad; salama da sugo; salam d'la duja; salmoriglio; saltimbocca alla romana; sformato; soffritto; sottaceti; soup; spezzatino; stew; stracciatelle; stracotto; stufato; suppli; verjuice; vignarola; violino di capra; zuppa

PREPARING, SERVING, AND EATING

antipasto; banquet; brasato; casalinga; casareccio; Cervio, Vincenzo; Christina of Sweden; Christmas foods; companatico; cucina delle nonne; dente, al; DOC, DOP, IGP, and SGT; DOP, Denominazione di Origine Protetta; drizzle; duck; Easter foods; EEC dairy products regulations; Evitascandalo, Cesare; fast food; fast, lenten or lean; fennel; festivity and food; fritto misto; funghetto, al; Giegher, Mattia; home cooking; honey; kitchen equipment; lardo; leftovers; *liber de coquina;* Liberati, Francesco; meals and patterns of eating; musk; nuova cucina; osterie; panini (o); pestle and mortar; pigeon; precepts and prohibitions; quail; Romoli, Domenico (Panunto); Rossetti, Giovanni Battista; salt; salume; saor; scapece; schiacciata; slow food; speck; street food; table manners; trifolati; trionfi; Vasselli, Giovan Francesco; zampone modena; zimino

pomodoro; Parma ham; parmigiana; pearà; peposo; pevarada; Piedmont; prescisoeua; Puglia; quartirolo Lombardo; ribollita; Roman food; Rome; salame di fabriano; salame di Napoli; salame di varzi; salame felino; salame "gentile"; salame Milano; salame Toscano; Sardinia; Sicily; silter; Tiella; toma; tortellini; Trentino–Alto Adige; Tuscany; Umbria; Valle d'Aosta; Veneto; vignarola; Vincisgrassi

REGIONAL CUISINE

Abruzzo; agliata; arsella; Basilicata; buridda; burrida; cacciucco; Calabria; Campania and Naples; cannolo; cantucci; capocollo; cibreo; coda alla vaccinara; confortini; coppa; coratella; Emilia Romagna; fish soup; flatbreads; formaggio di fossa; formai de mut; Friuli–Venezia Giulia; garofalato; grana padano; Lazio; Liguria; Lombardy; Manna; Marche, the; Marsala; mascarpone; Molise; Nebbia, Antonio; pajata; pancotta(o); pane di ramerino; panzanella; pappa al

SWEETS AND CONFECTIONERY

candied fruit; cannolo; cannoncino; caramel; cassata; cenci; chocolate; colomba; confetti; confortini; crema; crema fritta; crostata; crumiri; custard; dolci; gelato; Granita; gubana; honey; ice cream; jam; jelly; junkets; Macedonia di frutta; marzipan; moscardini; mostacciolo; mosto cotto; must; panna cotta; pasticceria; pie; pudding; saba, sapa; savoiardi; sherbet; sugar; tart; tiramisù; torrone; torta; trifle; wafer; zabaglione; zeppole; zucchero; zuccotto; zuppa inglese

THE OXFORD COMPANION TO

Italian
Food

a

ABBACCHIO. *See* LAMB.

ABRUZZO is located in the middle of the Italian peninsula, and borders the regions of the MARCHE, LAZIO, and MOLISE and to the east, the ocean. It has a varied geography and a varied cuisine, reflecting the contrasts between the highest mountain ranges in Italy and the pleasant, diverse coastline, from the Gran Sasso to the Adriatic. A great national park protects a huge area of Abruzzo, along with parts of Lazio and Molise. In living memory a schoolboy coming home in winter darkness would be scared by a wolf, hungrier and more terrified than he, scavenging in the streets of one of the ancient hillside towns. Protected now, along with the timid brown bear, the even more timid lynx, the chamois, and the golden eagle, wolves and many other wild animals and birds are an attraction for eco-tourists; where the wild and lawless charcoal burners once toiled and the shepherds trudged with their flocks in laborious transhumance, there are monitored walks and park rangers, outdoor sports and gastronomic experiences.

Regional Flavours

The national parks and nature reserves in Abruzzo have rejuvenated the economy, generating a recent influx of tourists from abroad, bringing euros and stimulating wider outlets for local produce. The soil and climate are ideal for making high-quality wines and OLIVE OIL, and a new generation of young growers is moving on from making decent stuff for local consumption to scientifically managed products, using both traditional and high-tech methods, which impress the gastro-tourists and are increasingly sold abroad. Old vines are grubbed up and new stock are brought in to complement indigenous varieties. The results are deep, dark, young wines that go perfectly with the robust local food, and subtle olive oils with a powerful after-kick, which hold their own with all that *peperoncino* (CHILLI PEPPER).

Readers accustomed to the profusion of chilli and garlic in Oriental cuisines are aware of how these flavours can enhance the qualities of the other ingredients, and so welcome their generous use in the food of Abruzzo, a region cut off politically and geographically from the polite worlds of courts and cookery manuals, where the *uso e abuso* of these seasonings still occasions much moralistic discourse from refined gastronomes. Both the cuisines of coast and mountain use plenty of hot chilli peppers, *diavolicchio*, and strong seasonings. But the lavish use of chillis begs a few questions. When were they first introduced into Abruzzo? And what did people use before then? Might they even be becoming something of a tourist attraction? Their use in traditional salami and cheeses implies a genuine delight in their fiery flavour. The entry on chilli gives information about its appearance in Italy, first as a botanical curiosity, then as an ingredient, with early sightings in seventeenth- and eighteenth-century recipes, leaving some puzzlement about its common and unrecorded use. The strong-flavoured herbs and plants of Abruzzo, wild and cultivated—SPINACH, PENNYROYAL, MINT, MARJORAM—would for centuries have given a sharp peppery kick to go with bland pulses and roots, and plain boiled or roasted meat, and the newcomers, dried or fresh chillis, would have been a cheap alternative to them, useful to shepherds and mariners, on the move, and needing portable seasonings.

SAFFRON is grown as a cash crop in the microclimate around the plain of Navelli in the province of Aquila, and because of its cost is used less frequently than the cheaper herbs and chillis, but nevertheless now appears in many local dishes, contrary to the assertion that it is only used in SCAPECE, fried fish marinated in white wine and vinegar and saffron.

Regional Cooking

Game and fish, and the products of meadows, terraces, and upland pastures, inspire an inventive range of dishes. The coast has a profusion of fish recipes similar to those up and down the Adriatic, made with as big a selection of fish and crustaceans as available, all carefully prepared, but in Abruzzo distinguished by robust seasonings and a variety of cooking methods. All restaurants and cooks have their own recipes; the cooking medium of most versions is a sauce made with olive oil and chopped garlic, sometimes onion, celery, herbs, often dried sweet peppers, tomatoes, chillis, and occasionally saffron. Some of the ingredients are added one by one to the—usually terracotta—pot, according to the time needed to cook them, as with the BRODETTO of Vasto, and cooked with the lid plonked firmly down and never lifted until the dish is done, or otherwise chucked in all at once and boiled vigorously in an open pan. Most have in common a seasoning of hot chilli and garlic; some include tomatoes, sweet peppers, onions, or other

vegetables; some have herbs (sage, thyme, bay leaves) as well as parsley; some add vinegar and wine; some are served on thick slices of local bread fried crisp in olive oil, and some on toasted bread rubbed with garlic.

In the province of Pescara, *brodetto* is usually made with SQUID, SKATE, MONK-FISH, rascasse (*see* SCORPION FISH), dogfish, mussels, cockles, prawns and langoustines, sometimes with colour and flavour from fried onions pounded with dried hot sweet peppers, instead of tomatoes. Anna del Conte gives a workable version of *brodetto Abruzzese* in her *Gastronomy of Italy* using monkfish, rascasse, John Dory, hake, red and grey mullet, and mussels. The mountains offer game and meat from sheep, goats, and pigs, with many dishes using OFFAL and cheaper cuts, like *'ndocca 'ndocca* and *mazzarelle*.

Ham and Salumi

Grazing for pigs on the margins of woods and forests produces tasty material for the local ham and SALUMI; of these, *fegato dolce* from the province of Aquila is made from the livers and lights of pigs which have lived this semiwild existence, seasoned with salt, pepper, and honey, sometimes with the addition of pistachios, pine nuts, and candied peel, first smoked, then matured in a cool damp place. The *fegatazzo di Ortona* in the province of Chieti is again a mass of entrails and fatty cuts coarsely minced and seasoned with garlic, chilli, salt and orange peel. *Ndoc ndoc* shares its ingredients and name with a stew made from the bits left over after curing the nobler parts of the pig—ears, snout, liver, spleen, and so on. The name probably does not derive from the French *andouille* (a cooking sausage made from pig's intestines); some think it is from the Latin *inductilis*, meaning something stuffed into, in this instance, a casing of intestines, so an Italian rather than imported name. Local usage is more likely—*'ndocca* means crazy, all mixed up, which is what this is. These sausages are matured for a few days and then eaten in various ways—grilled, or stewed with vegetables, or simmered and finished off with fresh greens and herbs. One made from fine cuts, especially the shoulder, is the *mortadellina di Campotosto*, matured in a microclimate in a small area of Aquila, exposed to a smoky kitchen fire and then the drying rigour of the *tramontana*.

A salami, *salamella di tratturo*, made from lean mutton and some pork fat, is a recent revival of old traditions, transforming the flesh of a mature and unprofitable animal into a product worth a lot more than the carcass, which in the past was literally thrown to the wolves (for a small payment from forestry officials). According to an old recipe, the minced meats are flavoured with red wine, salt, pepper, coriander and fennel seeds, and juniper berries, and are matured for two and a half months, a profitable and delicious way of recycling an unfashionable meat. Another esteemed salumi is *ventricina*: that from Crognaleto is made from plenty of pork fat and the lesser cuts of lean meat, seasoned with mild and fierce chilli, slightly smoked, and matured for as long as a year in the animal's stomach, or less if put up in the bladder. The result is a pungent spreading salami, the qualities enhanced by the benign bacterial activity of the natural casings. The *ventricina di Guilmi* includes fennel seeds and orange peel, and finer cuts of meat; it is a dry cure, depending on the local microclimate. The *salsiciotto di Guilmi* is so esteemed locally that it hardly ever gets on the market, as it is part of a complex social web of gifts and obligations. It is made from local pigs and seasoned only with salt and pepper, and its excellence is due to the skills of the *norcino* (the craftsman who processes the meat immediately after it is slaughtered) and the environment where it is matured—in pork fat or olive oil in ancient structures where resident microbes and the local climate reinforce the traditional skills of the maker.

Cheese

The cheeses of the region include many kinds of PECORINO traditionally made from the milk of sheep grazing in wild places, with variations in production that produce numerous versions. That from the mountain community of Farindola is coagulated with the RENNET from pigs' stomachs and contributes enzymes that seem to bring out in the cheese the aromas of the wild grasses and herbs on which the sheep grazed. There are CACIOCAVALLO, CACIOTTA, MOZZARELLA DI BUFALA, and *giuncatella*, a delicate freshly coagulated cheese which is sold and eaten the same day. Other fresh cheeses include a goat's cheese wrapped in vine leaves, *pampanella*, and *caciofiore aquilano*, from cows' milk, known and loved in Rome, according to Gioachino Belli, who mentions it in a sonnet in praise of the robust appetites of the *minente*, a certain stratum of Roman society who (then as now), without being all that low, rejoice in the robust speech and cuisine of the populace: "*Ce funno peperoni sott'asceto / Salame, mortatella e casciofiore*" (There were pickled sweet peppers / Salami, mortadella and *casciofiore*). It was sold by the shepherds, who came down from the hills in their sheepskin jerkins, with wicker baskets of pots and baskets of junkets for sale. For the rest of the sonnet, *see* LAZIO.

Pasta

PASTA is made commercially, and there are fresh home-made kinds, notably *maccheroni alla chitarra*, made from sheets of home-made pasta pushed with a roller through an instrument made of rows of thin steel wire to make short, square section lengths of pasta similar to *fettucine*, seasoned with a meat sauce lively with chillis and garlic, sometimes with little meatballs.

Traditional Abruzzo Feasts

The food of Abruzzo is essentially a rustic cuisine, recently enriched by unprecedented prosperity. It is sometimes enhanced by legends, like the story of a folklorique nature. The seven virtuous and lovely maidens who each contributed an ingredient to the famous dish *le virtù* are probably a figment of some antiquary's imagination, for the beauty of this recipe from Teramo lies in making good come of necessity, not in number crunching. Traditionally made on 1 May, it celebrates the end of the lean and anxious period when the comforting winter stores were dwindling and the new crops were not yet ready. (Winter was a time of rest and plenty, not hardship, when ample stores were enjoyed; the dried pulses, jars of lard, hams and sausages, vegetables pickled in oil, and grain were used generously, perhaps improvidently, and by early spring were often used up.) So into *le virtù* would go the last dried peas, beans, lentils, and chickpeas, soaked and cooked, while a bone from the last of the ham (trimmed of rancid bits), a salted pig's ear, some trotters, the treasured *cotenne* (strips of skin), and any other cheap cuts were soaked and then simmered to make a rich broth. Meanwhile, the long-awaited fresh vegetables and wild plants and herbs, products of the fertile slopes and terraces of Abruzzo, were prepared and cooked separately—the tender young peas, broad beans, wild asparagus and mushrooms, baby artichokes, and so on all done to perfection—and then a mixture of chopped garlic, onion, celery, carrot, and herbs was fried in lard and added to the pulses and the broth. One by one, the different ingredients were brought together, along with various kinds of pasta, dried from the store cupboard and freshly made. The whole was seasoned with fresh herbs, particularly pennyroyal and marjoram. This magical fusion of textures and flavours in perfect balance is a lovely paradigm of the gastronomy of Abruzzo.

Another less subtle gastronomic event is the *panarda* of Aquila, a vast meal of at least 30 to 40 courses with seven dishes to each course, of which guests are expected to eat the lot. A distinguished journalist who attempted to quit halfway through was threatened at gunpoint by his host: "*O continui a magnà, o te sparo!*" "Eat up or I shoot!" Although gross overindulgence as a tourist attraction can be depressing, the alternation of plenty and want, scarcity and profusion is a more natural way of eating than the balanced diet of nutritionists. The contrast between occasional abundance and the necessary frugality of everyday eating has always been a normal way of eating in Italy.

Huge feasts for special occasions, or the ritual consumption of products of the slaughterhouse that will not keep, are part of a rural tradition of frugal eating—a stark contrast to the bleakness of everyday meals. A stew made at pig-killing time from cheap cuts and extremities, *'ndocca 'ndocca*, would be eaten in copious helpings. Snout, ears, trotters, a few ribs, some strips of skin, maybe the cheek, are first washed and soaked in water and a little vinegar for some hours, then cooked very slowly in water with herbs and chilli for four to five hours until the cooking liquid is reduced and unctuous, and served with homemade bread.

Mazzarelle are made in Teramo from lamb's or kid's *coratella*, or pluck: the heart, lungs, and offal, together with the cleaned intestines, are carefully sliced and cut into strips, which are then rolled up in substantial beet or lettuce leaves or in lengths of the intestines, with plentiful seasoning, including herbs and chilli, and cooked first in oil and garlic, then with small quantities of wine and water; each addition of liquid is absorbed before the next is put in, a long slow process that yields tender bundles of melting softness. The dish is called *marro* in Aquila and *tuncenelle* in Chieti. A traditional shepherds' dish is lamb stewed slowly in a huge copper cauldron, *a cotturo*, with herbs and wild plants.

ACCADEMIA DELLA CRUSCA

was founded in 1583 to investigate and safeguard the purity of the "Italian" language, as it was spoken and written in Tuscany, purging it of the impurities of long-winded pedantry and coarse vulgarity, separating the refined white flour of civilised speech from the rough chaff of debased usage. But the chaff, *crusca*, could also be seen as a refining force in its own right, used to polish tarnished metal, preserve fruit and dried foods, feed farmyard animals and fowl, and stuff cushions. Bread as well as literature was the most important product of this refining process; the magic of its making, the technology and the many uses to which it was put were a metaphor for the refining and purification of language. Since everyday usage was an important aspect of living language, everyday objects and occupations were worthy of consideration.

All these practical and emblematic aspects of flour power were to be seen on the *pale*, the devices of the members of the academy, in the form of bakers' peels (shovels), decorated with complex iconography and punning mottoes often linked to the name of the member. The 152 surviving *pale* date from the late 16th to the 18th century and are a wonderful source of visual information about bread, baking, and the state of milling and baking technology.

What at first appears to be a burger—a *panino* stuffed with some unidentifiable cured meat—turns out to be tarnished silver gilt lace placed inside a freshly baked bread roll to brighten it up, with the motto of the member Francesco Ridolfi, known as Rifiorito, "Brightened anew"—"*Perchè la sua bontà si disconda*" (That its beauty might be revealed). The shock of this visual pun is heightened by the realism of the painting, possibly by Lorenzo Lippi, and is a reminder of the brilliant fillings hidden away in buns that can still be enjoyed in bars all over Italy today. The vocabularies published by the Accademia della Crusca are a useful source of culinary words, where their first use can be traced, or their absence remarked.

A *pala* by Cesare Bandini shows a neat little mound of ricotta, turned from its reed basket onto a blue and white dish, with a "soldier" of stale bread stuck into it, to help preserve it by absorbing surplus liquid, with the motto "*Per me non basto*" (This is not for me) of Baldassarre Suarez, who was known as Mantenuto, "Preserved."

A glass still, similar to the equipment used by the Accademia del Cimento, is seen in an apothecary's establishment, reminding us of the ubiquity of grain-based spirits. A stale loaf, reduced to crumbs on a stout metal grater, would have been used to thicken a sauce or stew. *Cantucci* are dunked in a shallow bowl of *vin santo*. Many varieties of bread and biscuit are shown—a festive loaf made up of small lozenge-shaped bits, various fancy breads. An implement for making *cialde*, a kind of wafer, is shown in action, and an all-purpose wooden screw press can be seen churning out coils of fine vermicelli, an early sighting of pasta-making technology.

As the work of discussing and defining words engendered tense feelings, and many procedural squabbles, there was often a need to lighten the atmosphere, so very welcome *stravizzi* were organised, with members contributing both food and entertainment. This group therapy for jaded intellectuals involved a mock-serious discourse on some trivial topic, with a recital of imaginary complaints and some light verse, and much guttling. On one occasion, on 24 September 1656, with 42 notables and six guests at the top table, they sat down to a first course of cold dishes, including various pies made to resemble the various kinds of strainers used in milling and baking, and two turkeys served on a winnowing sieve; a second course of hot dishes from the kitchen included pies of stuffed pigeons with partridges, pistachios, prunes, and testicles, roast sweetbreads, and a subtle roast, *un arrosto sottile*. Then came more hot food—stewed pigeons served with stuffed lettuce leaves, partridges simmered covered with *cavolo nero*, mature turkeys cooked in wine, stuffed calves' heads, and celery thickened with eggs and perfumed with truffles. A course of noble roasts came next, each one adorned in some way, the pheasant with its tail feathers, capons covered in vermicelli of different colours, the smaller game decked with a fretwork of extruded pastry, and the turkeys decorated with lemons cut in patterned slices. The final course included fruit, cheeses (marzolini and raveggioli and the inevitable chunks of Parmesan), some pastries, and welcome pieces of raw celery, fennel, and artichokes to clear the palate, anise seed comfits, and boxes of quince paste. This feast cost the academicians 46 scudi each, but there were lavish contributions from the ducal family of much wine, 80 fat pigeons, two roe bucks, and six joints of roast venison, not forgetting the four loads of ice from the ducal ice-house.

ACCADEMIA GALILEIANA DEL CIMENTO (1657–1667) was

founded by Ferdinando II de' Medici, grand duke of Tuscany, and his brother Prince Leopoldo, to promote scientific experiments at the court in Florence, tip-toeing cautiously around the areas of controversy which had led to the condemnation by the Catholic Church of Galileo and his theories. Always a staunch protector of Galileo, Ferdinand applied his ideas about experimentation and accurate observation of the natural world to areas carefully selected to avoid more trouble. The Medici rulers desired the international prestige due to them as patrons of advanced scientific ideas, whilst nervously shunning the taint of heresy attached to their hero, Galileo.

The members of the Accademia, more or less sensitive to these issues, were busy finding out how the natural world worked and explaining this in simple prose and diagrams. Their pioneering work in the development of measuring instruments, telescopes, lenses, and thermometers was published at the end of their 10-year period of intense activity, and later summarised by Giovanni Tarzoni Tozzetti in 1780.

Gastronomy, sadly for us, did not impinge on their preoccupations, but glimpses of daily life can be discerned in both the manuscript and published versions of these experiments, and historians of ICE CREAM can find some fascinating insights into its origins in the descriptions of investigations into freezing various liquids. Flavoured waters (orange blossom, myrtle, cinnamon, lemon juice), enjoyed as chilled drinks or frozen to a soft slush as *sorbetti*, got quite a lot of attention, and experiments with different ways of freezing liquids to produce vapours which looked like smoke were recorded in some beguiling sketches, looking very much like whipped sorbets, presented in the same goblets and containers that must indeed have held ice cream at the sumptuous Medici banquets. These visual puns may perhaps have been a reflection of Prince Leopoldo's somewhat capricious direction of the experiments.

Their preoccupation with examining and recording the natural world made the Medici rulers enlightened patrons of the arts, of particular interest to us because of developments in botanical illustration and still life painting. Details of fruit and vegetables esteemed and enjoyed in 17th-century Florence can be seen in the works of BIMBI, LIGOZZI, MUNARI, and many others and tell us a lot about the practical encouragement the Medici regime was giving to the horticulture and agriculture of Tuscany. The golden balls, *palle*, of the Medici crest, which glimmer in the orange groves in Uccello's *Battle of San Romano*, painted over 200 years earlier for Lorenzo de' Medici, indicate a concern for the profitable cultivation of citrus fruit. They later become blown glass globes in the engraved chapter headings of the Accademia's experiments, with a chubby *putto* offering the muse an optical lens, neatly sliced off one of the glass balls. At first sight this seems, but is not, a typical Florentine cookie.

ACCADEMIA ITALIANA DELLA CUCINA was founded in

1953 at the prestigious Restaurant Diana in Milan by a select group of professional men, representative of Italy's intelligentsia, distinguished in their own fields and united in a love of Italian gastronomy, not just in response to the dry *"La cucina italiana muore!"* but to celebrate Italy's living food heritage, and to foster an appreciation of the *civiltà della tavola*, an untranslatable concept that might perhaps be rendered as *the refinement of civilised dining*. The founder members included the architect Gio Ponti, the publisher Arnaldo Mondadori, and the journalists Orio Vergani and Vincenzo Buonassisi. This association still flourishes half a century later, offering awards for merit, prizes for outstanding achievement, a list of distinguished publications, and conferences and events world-wide, designed to foster the original aims of the Accademia. The great and the good are proud and pleased to belong, and now that since 2003 the Accademia has acquired the status of a national institution on a par with the great academies of the past (recognised officially as an *istituzione culturale della Repubblica Italiana*), membership (by invitation) is one of the highest accolades available to food lovers in Italy and beyond. Italians have a genius not just for gastronomy but for the rhetoric that surrounds it, and the mellifluous flow of phrase-making that accompanies much of the self-praise of Italian gastronomes is an acquired taste, but once acquired can afford much quiet and affectionate enjoyment. In the context of fine dining, it contributes to a mood of well-being, like the music and perfumes of a baroque banquet, and the virtuosic deployment of fine words enhances the appreciation of fine foods and wines. This should not obscure the importance of the contribution of the Accademia Italiana della Cucina to essays on food history. Many of today's giants in this field were in their infancy at the time of its foundation, and contributors to the first *convegno* in Venice in 1967 set the tone for many series studies to come. For example, Maxime Rodinson's essay on the Venetian spice trade was a model of lucidity, ending with a reminder that it is in the study of the past that we come to appreciate and understand our gastronomic future.

ACCIUGA. *See* ANCHOVY.

ACORN, *ghianda*, is the nut of the oak tree, of which there are many varieties. The beautiful evergreen holm oak or ilex bears agreeable acorns, probably enjoyed by Cosimo when he fled from the constraints of the family dinner table to a life of independence in the tree tops (Calvino, 1957, p. 19). Sweet acorns are indeed the best to eat, as they have a lower tannin content. Their low fat and high carbohydrate content make them a suitable food for both humans and animals; pounded and washed in running

The low fat and high carbohydrate content of these wild acorns make them a suitable food for both humans and animals. (Shutterstock)

water, boiled or roasted, they can be quite pleasant. When ground they provide a flour, used in times of hardship, which has given this benign food a bad name. As a substitute for coffee or food for starving peasants, acorns are despised and rejected, but when it comes to pigs, they acquire a glow of virtue, and we seek out pork products from semi-wild creatures who have rummaged in woods, devouring acorns, which give their flesh a lean sweetness. *See* PARMA HAM.

ACQUACOTTA. *See* ZUPPA.

AGLIATA. *See* GARLIC.

AGNELLO. *See* SHEEP.

AGRESTO. *See* SOURNESS.

AGRETTI look like grass or chives (but not hollow) and have a slightly acid, almost bitter flavour, eaten raw in a mixed salad, or lightly cooked and served with salt and pepper, oil and vinegar. They are the young leaves of SALSIFY or *scorzonera*, *Tragopogon pratensis* and *Tragopogon porrifolius*. *Agretti* appear in the markets in spring. Confusion arises around the various names for this plant, since a plant of the cress family, or *Lepidium sativum*, is also called *agretto* in some parts of Italy, and to confuse us even more, *agretto* is also called *barba di frate* or *barba di becco*. So in the market forget the names, look out for bundles of plump grassy crunchy green leaves, take them home, cook quickly in salted water, and enjoy with oil and salt and pepper or butter. This advice applies to buying and cooking most foodstuffs; a name is easily forgotten, but a kindly explained recipe will be remembered forever.

AGRITURISMO is a recent development. The explosion of interest in Italian regional food has brought visitors from all over the world seeking out specialities and recipes in an authentic setting, and what better place to find them than a farmhouse kitchen? Many farms and small agricultural enterprises that would otherwise have withered and perished have been reborn as an aspect of the tourist industry. Villas and farmhouses offer accommodation and outdoor activities, or the ever popular cookery schools, where local or nationally famous experts show how to prepare and enjoy local ingredients in ways not possible for commercial restaurants. This movement is good for both the tourist industry and the organic movement, *agricoltura biologica*, and initiatives to foster and preserve indigenous livestock and plants. Products like cheese and salami that would have difficulty reaching commercial outlets are sold in local outlets, to everyone's advantage. However, authenticity and gullibility make congenial bedfellows, and one needs to remember that the length and breadth of the peninsula would have to be honeycombed with subterranean rock caves to meet the demand for *formaggio di fossa*, or the entire Apennines riddled with cellars full of marble troughs to give us all the *lardo di Colonnata* we crave. Some landscapes that are not picturesque or appealing in their own right, like that of Emilia, now pull in busloads in search of its renowned cuisine, searching out cookery schools, restaurants, small producers of perhaps parmesan from the *razza bruna* fed on natural forage, or ham and salami from rare-breed animals, made in small units using slow and costly procedures, or learning from an almost extinct breed of old lady how to make the glorious egg pasta of the region. Meanwhile the beaches of Romagna teem with the less discriminating, happy with industrial ICE CREAM and less subtle versions of the local cuisine. Italians too have become gastro-tourists, and now that many city dwellers have few ties with the land, they come looking for good things, giving a boost to growers of special kinds or rice, pasta made from flour grown from rare strains of wheat, cheeses made and sold on the spot, and the many dried pulses and legumes that the new vegetarianism appreciates.

AGRUMI. *See* CITRUS FRUITS.

ALCHERMES is a sweet, spicy

liqueur, with low alcohol and a pleasant flavour, taken on its own as an after-dinner drink, or during the day, but interesting in gastronomy for its use in colouring desserts. The ZUPPA INGLESE of EMILIA-ROMAGNA (versions can be found all over Italy) includes sponge cake soaked in this lurid red liquid, very different from the sherry-flavoured English version, which with its whipped cream makes a more enjoyable pudding, not a thing one could often say about our desserts. Artusi uses *alchermes* in a Tuscan *zuppa inglese*, alternating alchermes-soaked SAVOIARDI biscuits with some dunked in a white *rosolio* (see APERITIVI). Ada Boni uses it, alternating with rum, in her Roman versions of *zuppa inglese*. She states with authority, but without naming her source, that *alchermes* was created for the Medici family in Florence and taken to France by the young Maria de' Medici; probably another myth.

The name derives from the Arabic *kirmiz*, the name for an insect, *kermes*, *Coccus ilicis*, which attaches itself as a parasite to a certain kind of oak tree, becoming a fat round thing more like a dried berry than a beetle. This was used to make a crimson red food colouring, hence the name *cremisi* or *chermisi*, later superseded by the even brighter cochineal from a different insect from the New World.

Other ingredients of *alchermes* include cinnamon, nutmeg, cloves, and bay leaves. The one available in the Farmacia di Santa Maria Novella has quite an impact; it is made by distillation and gives a delicate balance of flavours as well as the bright colour. Ada Boni gives a recipe for *alchermes*, among many others for liqueurs and elixirs of various kinds, which involves macerating spices and vanilla with cochineal in 90 proof alcohol, then diluting with water, sugar, and rosewater.

It is possible that the red glop that can be seen decorating ice creams in early Neapolitan prints, referred to in early recipes as *alacca*, was some kind of *alchermes*, derived from another insect, *lac*, of the same family. It must have tasted good on a light lemon *sorbetto* or rich cream ice, and is weirdly echoed in the red tomato that can also be seen on top of the pyramids of grated cheese in prints of street maccheroni sellers.

ALDROVANDI, ULISSE

(1522–1605) was born in Bologna to a comfortably off family, and in spite of his father's death at an early age and his own precocious restlessness (he kept running away from home—once to Rome, at the age of 12, and later, at 16, to go on the pilgrimage to Santiago de Compostela, where robbery and violence attended him), he studied diligently, learning mathematics and bookkeeping at 14. He went on to excel in law and jurisprudence, and enjoyed a distinguished career as lecturer, naturalist, botanist, and collector, leaving at his death many publications, and a mass of notes and illustrations, specially executed at his own expense, by some of the finest artists of the time, many the result of contacts with the Medici rulers of Florence, including Bartolomeo and Jacopo Ligozzi.

Of the 8,000 colour illustrations Aldrovandi had commissioned by 1598, today 2,832 survive, in 18 volumes preserved in Bologna University Library. (They can be seen, postage-stamp size, on the Web.) They were the models for the woodcuts in his *Storia Naturale*, 10 volumes of which were published between 1603 and 1667. He was one of the early natural scientists who exploited the virtue of the printing press to produce multiple copies of reference works, whose woodcut illustrations conveyed more accurate information than earlier heavy, sometimes archaic Latin texts, which carried the tedious burden of references to ancient authors and a jumble of alchemical and mythological misinformation. But Aldrovandi realised that his engravers, as well as working directly from nature, needed references from which to make their images of perishable plants and rare and exotic creatures; hence the enormous expenditure on coloured portraits of everything in the natural world that had to be described and classified.

Later naturalists wrote with a more scientific rigour, but an aspect of Aldrovandi's work, irritating to scientists but endearing to the layperson, is the conversational, anecdotal quality of some of it. *Cercopithecus*, the guenon monkey, is portrayed sitting on a red silk cloth, clutching an artichoke in its elegant, prehensile fingers, with the comment that it "often gets drunk on wine ... and imitates all kinds of voices.... It especially hates deformed old women. Finally it has such an elegant bearing that it looks like a creature endowed with reason." The artichoke may have been a "prop" to indicate that the little monkey was part of an aristocratic menagerie, a treasured possession, like the fashionable vegetable.

Aldrovandi's energy floods into his writing, sometimes verbose but always enthusiastic, and into correspondence with friends and colleagues. He travelled a lot, visiting other naturalists and botanists, exchanging samples of plants, minerals, insects, fish, and fossils, and he devoured information about everything. This urge to observe, record, and analyse contributed to the intellectual atmosphere in which Linnaeus developed the scientific classification of plants we know today. Before that the accurate observation and description of the natural world was an uncertain and painstaking task, fraught with confusion and misunderstandings, and it is greatly to Aldrovandi's credit that he avoided and in many cases damped down the quarrels that ensued, unlike his contemporary MATTIOLI, who seemed to enjoy them.

Aldrovandi's massive work on birds, *Ornithologia, hoc est de Avibus Historiae*, first published in 1599, includes a section on chickens, in which every possible fact and observation is conveyed, shedding some helpful light on the status of the GUINEA FOWL, and delighting us with a really down-to-earth discourse on the nutritional and therapeutic value of cockerels, capons, and chickens, with little-known material from medical as well as gastronomic handbooks. The restorative power of chicken broth was universally acknowledged, and Aldrovandi's overview of theories and recipes shows a thorough understanding of kitchen matters. He distinguishes between broth made from an old, worn-out fighting cock, a young cockerel, a capon, and a hen or young chicken, and quotes recipes from sources from Apicius to Platina, listing all the spices and herbs used, and the effects on patients and their ailments of these various brews. Chicken soup with barley turns out to have an ancient and honourable history, soothing the convalescent and restoring the moribund for centuries. Aldrovandi writes with a hands-on understanding of cooking, and although he quotes other authors frequently, he also paraphrases ancient and contemporary writers with a complete understanding of what is going on.

It is hardly surprising that a fellow naturalist and botanist, COSTANZO FELICI, composed for Aldrovandi his *Letter on Salads*, which blossomed into a list of all the edible plants known at the time, with notes on how they were prepared. Their correspondence gives some idea of Aldrovandi's gift for friendship, of the enthusiasm with which he welcomed and encouraged collaborators, from this relatively obscure doctor in the MARCHE to naturalists of international renown like Ghini and Michiel.

Aldrovandi married late in life, after the death of his mother, and his wife's tragic death after only a short time brought messages of sympathy from Felici and his wife, who had chosen them as godparents to one of their many daughters. The warmth and kindness of Felici's letter of condolence give some indication of the affection Aldrovandi inspired in his correspondents. He married again, happily, and the friendship between the two families lasted until Felici's death in 1585.

Lecturing (Aldrovandi gave more than 700 lectures in ten years), writing, travelling, and organising his collections, creating Bologna's botanical gardens, establishing a structure for and control of the *speziali* responsible for making up medical prescriptions, kept him busy until retirement at the age of 80, on full salary, and he died in 1605 aged 85. A wood engraving, frontispiece to one of his works shows Aldrovandi at the age of 78, a merry-looking old man with bright, inquisitive eyes, a neat white beard and moustache, and the appearance of someone about to smile or talk or both.

ALEXANDERS, *Smyrnium olusatrum, macerone, smirnio,* is one of the umbelliferae and similar to CELERY and LOVAGE, which are different genera, both sometimes referred to as *apio.* The leaves, stem, and root were enjoyed for their bitterness, and the seeds and roots were used in medicine and to flavour liqueurs, imparting that much-loved aromatic bitterness. Mattioli described how the tender young shoots are eaten raw, or cooked, in SICILY. Its strong aromatic flavour has been superseded by the gentler blandness of celery, and the less pungent lovage.

ALLSPICE, *Pimenta dioica, pimento, pepe della Giamaica,* is used more commercially than in the domestic kitchen. Its pleasant aroma, like a mixture of bayleaf, nutmeg, cinnamon, and cloves, is used to flavour stews and sometimes when cooking freshwater fish.

ALMOND, *Prunus amygdalus, Prunus dulcis, mandorla,* is common all over the Mediterranean, wherever the climate is kind to the early-flowering blossoms. The fruit when fresh is a leathery, greenish thing, a drupe, without the juicy flesh of apricots or cherries of the same family. Gathered and eaten fresh, they are a delicacy of late spring, and sometimes appear in still-life paintings cut in half to reveal the immature nut. When the shell is hard, the outer skin removed, and the nut dried in the sun, or mechanically, almonds are a useful and not easily perishable source of proteins and oil, and are a delicious addition to both sweet and savoury dishes. They have been widely used in the cuisines of the Middle East, and the Arab presence in Spain and southern Italy left a lasting heritage of confectionary and sauces based on ground almonds. Some survive in the *cubbaita* of Sicily, and the *copeta* of Valtellina (although often made with walnuts); the recipe, if not the name, is close to medieval Arab sweetmeats. (For the origins of the name, *see* WALNUT.) Pounded almonds are stirred into a syrup of sugar or honey, often perfumed with musk and rosewater, and, being sticky, rolled into a flat layer enclosed in thin wafers or flat bread, for ease in handling.

Sauces made of a base of ground almonds are the culinary legacy left by the early Arab presence in Southern Italy. (Shutterstock)

This rich, sweet, absorbent pastry or bread was used as a sort of Yorkshire pudding in the cook shops of Baghdad, put to soak up the juices underneath a fat saffron-flavoured chicken or lamb turning on the spit. Echoes of this survived in the Italian medieval kitchen; Martino recommended scattering over a roasting larded chicken a mixture of salt and breadcrumbs to take up the fat and juices and form a rich crust.

Many sauces were thickened and flavoured with almonds, pale and mild when they were combined with peeled nuts and flavoured with powdered ginger, sugar, and rosewater, or powerful when roasted and ground with bread toasted brown or black and with dark spices like cloves, black pepper, cinnamon, and mace, with dried fruit to give density and sweetness.

Almonds were often an important ingredient in BIANCOMANGIARE, an ambiguous dish of pounded and sweetened chicken breasts; the skinned and pounded almonds gave texture and flavour to this pure, white, and aristocratic concoction. This was nutritious food for invalids and convalescents; the ground almonds provided body, protein, and vitamins and contributed to the delicate, enigmatic flavour. When combined with chicken, whose therapeutic properties were venerated by the medical profession and the domestic cook, the dish was prepared to comfort and restore women in childbirth. Sugared almonds, CONFETTI, were traditional presents for the new mother and her guests—as expensive as they were nourishing. When Caterina, the wife of Ser Girolamo da Colle, gave birth in 1473 to their son Giovanni, her husband, a comfortably off but prudent Florentine notary, kept a detailed account of the expenses involved in the pregnancy and birth, including several pounds of sugared almonds. It is likely that the covered box visitors are shown bringing to the mother on a *desco da parto* (a wooden childbirth tray), decorated by Masaccio,

would have contained these expensive sweetmeats.

Peeled, pounded, softened with water, and pushed through a sieve, almonds were used in a stuffing made of soft cream cheese, eggs, and chopped herbs and spices that was inserted between the skin and flesh and stuffed into the cavities of chickens before roasting, as described in a 14th-century cookery manuscript. The same work has a recipe for a soup made from the broth from some stewed chicken, thickened with ground almonds thinned with rosewater and VERJUICE, and seasoned with cloves and ginger, to be served with the cut-up chicken sprinkled with sugar.

Almond milk was a substitute for cows' milk on the Lean or Lenten days when eating dairy produce was prohibited, used in a thick, creamy form or as a light liquid, often to thicken the cooking juices of fish. The milk could be reduced by boiling with sugar and kept as the basis for a cooling drink, similar to the Spanish *horchata*, made with tiger nuts.

Almond butter was also used when dairy and meat products were forbidden; it was made by diluting pounded, peeled almonds with water, bringing the mixture to the boil, straining through a cloth, and cooling until the fat could be taken up and used instead of butter or lard.

Almond oil had medicinal rather than gastronomic uses: to relieve headaches and soothe sores. Five or six peeled nuts, eaten before a festive occasion, were thought to help prevent drunkenness, while sugar-coated almonds, taken at the end of a banquet, would promote digestion while induce a healthy slumber. The sugared almonds still offered today to celebrate weddings and christenings are a reminder of the comfits, nuts, and seeds of all kinds, coated with sugar, which were prepared and sold by the apothecaries, who supplied that expensive spice, sugar.

Sweet almonds are mild and gentle; bitter almonds are smaller with a much more distinct flavour, which can be overwhelming if not used with discretion. Overwhelming, too, in their capacity to release prussic acid (as a result of enzymic reactions when in contact with water), which is mercifully destroyed by heat, and so cannot harm us in baked confectionary flavoured with bitter almonds. Having been heated thoroughly, bitter almonds can be added to dishes where a stronger taste is needed, but not eaten raw. When Mattioli said that half a dozen can help avoid drunkenness, one cannot help feeling that to be dead drunk is preferable to being dead from such a massive dose of poison. *Bitter Almonds* is the title Mary Taylor Simeti gave to the book she based on the experiences of her friend Maria Grammatico, who escaped from a harsh, restrictive upbringing in an enclosed Sicilian orphanage with the skills to become a pastry cook and confectioner of world renown. The exquisite recipes learnt in the convent were made with sweet almonds, but the memories left a bitter taste. Shelled and skinned almonds were ground by hand and worked with sugar syrup into a fine paste that was the basis of many convent specialities. *Frutta di Martorana*, lifelike almond paste fruits, formed in moulds and carefully coloured, were traditionally made on November for the Feast of All Souls but are now a tourist attraction all year round. The same almond paste, with the addition of egg whites, honey, and lemon zest, is the basis for cooked sweetmeats such as *sospiri e désirs*, *belli e brutti*, and *cuscinetti*. When recreating these recipes at home, it is best to buy good-quality almonds and take the trouble to skin and grind them, by hand or in a food processor, to make the most of the evanescent flavour and texture. AMARETTI are mostly made with sweet and bitter almonds, sugar, and white of egg, but those we buy as *amaretti di Saronno* include bitter apricot kernels, with a strong flavour, which makes them ideal to use, crumbled, in very discreet quantities, in recipes using bland

ingredients that need something of a boost, like the pumpkin paste that is the traditional filling for the *tortelloni* associated with Mantua. But it is as well to be wary of cheap *amaretti* made with synthetic flavouring, which can be extremely unpleasant. Other almond-based biscuits are CANTUCCI, *brutti ma buoni*, and *fave dolci*, a sweet almond biscuit traditionally associated with the commemoration of the dead (*see* BROAD BEANS). Combined with other nuts, dried fruit, spices, and honey, almonds are the main ingredient in PANFORTE, today a speciality of Siena but in the past found all over Italy, from convents to court kitchens.

A *budin alla moda* (pudding à la mode) described by Vincenzo Corrado could be sweet or savoury, depending on the balance of ingredients, and so serve as a dessert or an accompaniment to a delicate roast, for he combines blanched almonds pounded with candied orange blossoms, eggs, cream, milk, veal suet, sugar, pulverised dried sponge fingers, and grated parmesan, flavoured with cinnamon and nutmeg, wrapped in pig's caul and baked in the oven. *See also* MARZIPAN.

AMARETTI, *amaretto di Saronno*, are biscuits made from sweet and bitter almonds ground or chopped, mixed with egg whites beaten well with sugar, made into little balls the size of a walnut, and baked in a moderate oven. There are many variations, some crisp and friable, and some with soft centres. They can be crumbled and used to flavour other dishes, both sweet and savory. The *amarettus* of SARDINIA are made with pulverised almonds stirred into beaten egg whites, forming a lighter, meringue-like biscuit. A Sicilian recipe from Maria Grammatico (Simeti, 1994) uses unpeeled almonds and a little flour processed to a fine powder with sugar and a pinch of salt, then mixed with the egg whites.

There is a somewhat sickly liqueur, *amaretto di Saronno*, which includes bitter almonds among other aromatics, and is also used to impart a sweetish bitter almond flavour to desserts and drinks.

Crumbled *amaretti* are a flavouring in the squash filling for *tortelloni* in Emilia, and the bittersweetness is a subtle corrective to the stodginess of the squash, but if overdone, or using commercial *amaretti* flavoured with synthetic almond flavour, the effect is far from subtle.

The elegant, thin paper wrappings of the *amaretti di Saronno* decorated with an intricate 19th-century engraving of a ship in full sail make a beguiling party piece, rolled up neatly but not too tight, placed upright on a flame-proof saucer or dish, then set alight at the top; this creates sufficient updraught to waft the burning paper roll heavenwards, to fall back as fragile charred fragments on the upturned faces of the assembled company. (CF)

AMARI(O). *See* BITTERNESS.

AMATRICIANA, ALL'. *See* PASTA SAUCES.

AMBERGRIS, *ambra grigia,* is a greyish substance found in the intestines of sick sperm whales; usually washed up on the seashore, like amber (which is a resin of vegetable origin), and much prized for its pervasive perfume, a sort of musky violet, which is long-lasting and valued in perfumery and confectionary. The term *amber* was used rather loosely, and could mean either of these. Ambergris and MUSK were used to flavour creams, delicate savory dishes, and perfumed waters. Vincenzo Corrado has a recipe for a perfume made of musk and ambergris dissolved in spirits of wine, which could be sprinkled on the fire, diffusing an aroma of sweet musty violets. He also has a *rosolio* (see APERITIVI) of ambergris and cinnamon,

steeped in spirits of wine and sweetened with syrup, and another one made with spirits, red wine, sugar, ambergris, and mace. A cordial called *acqua di francipane* was made by infusing jasmine blossoms in syrup, diluting with spirits of wine, and flavouring with ambergris. His recipe for *confortini di cacao,* a kind of chocolate fondant, involves boiling a sugar syrup to soft ball stage, cooling it, beating it until pale and light, then beating in pounded chocolate solids flavoured with ambergris, leaving the mixture to cool, and into shapes.

Musk and ambergris became increasingly popular during the 17th century, used in perfumery as well as cooking, in a move away from the range of spices used in past centuries.

AMBERJACK, *ricciola, Seriola dumerili* (confusingly *leccia* in Liguria), is a fish of the order of Perciformes, related to bluefish; it is pinkish bluish grey with a firm flesh and is good fried, grilled, or baked, cut in slices if it is a big fish. Another related fish called *leccia,* or *Lichia amia,* is similar to but not the same as amberjack—it is a stronger blue—also has firm flesh which can be cooked in the same way as SWORDFISH. Pompano, *leccia stella,* a smaller fish with firm flesh, is good grilled or fried.

ANCHOVY, *acciuga, alice,* is one of the most versatile of the *pesce azzuro* (a very broad term—not to be translated as "bluefish," which is something else— covering many fish of the Clupeid family, all well-flavoured and with a high proportion of oils). Fresh, it is cooked in a variety of ways, after a long-drawn-out and fiddly preparation, needing deft fingers. Taking the anchovy in one hand, use the thumb of the other to slit open the belly and then, grasping the head firmly between finger and thumb, detach it, together with the guts; then all that remains to do is to prise away the spine and flatten the little fish, ready for the next stage. A mixture of chopped herbs, garlic, and breadcrumbs can be spread on the flattened fishes—which can then be rolled up—or it can be used as stuffing, or strewn over layers of anchovies in an oiled, oven-proof dish. Then, rolled up, flat or whatever, they can be anointed with more olive oil and lemon juice, and baked; the timing will depend on the size of the fish and the method chosen. There are many regional variations on this; one from CAMPANIA uses parsley and a little oregano; one from PUGLIA includes grated pecorino and adds basil and mint to the herbs. From LIGURIA comes a firm stuffing of egg, breadcrumbs, parmesan, salt, pepper, and flavourings which might include garlic, chopped cooked spinach beets, and pine nuts. The anchovies are filled with this, dipped in egg white and then breadcrumbs, and fried in oil. There are many layered dishes, using prepared anchovies layered with sliced potatoes, onions, and tomatoes, often seasoned with mint and basil, as well as the breadcrumb mixture. Scappi marinated whole anchovies or sardines in a mixture of oil, verjuice, reduced must, salt, pepper, and fennel, threaded them on a thin metal rod passed through the eyes, and grilled them, basting with the marinade. The same marinade could be poured over fried sardines, together with gooseberries in season, and perhaps later fresh verjuice or dried fruit and spices. He made a *pottaggietto* of boned and cleaned anchovies simmered in wine, water, olive oil, and salt, with chopped herbs, mint, marjoram, and salad burnet added at the end, and thickened, if needed, with ground almonds. Corrado softened chopped spring onion, garlic, mushrooms, parsley, and oregano in butter, seasoned with spices, and cooked the prepared anchovies in this with some white wine.

Anchovies are preserved in salt, brine, or oil. This can be done at home, using the freshest possible fish, but it is often more convenient to buy a few at a time from the large tins of anchovies in salt which most good food stores should have. (These are getting harder to find, and you may have to buy the small glass jars of anchovies in salt, which are not as good). The whole anchovy is salted, and it is the activities of enzymes on its guts that creates the characteristic colour and flavour. Before use, these salted anchovies have to be cleaned of the salt with which they are encrusted, the bones, head and guts removed, and the fillets washed in milk or water; they can then be crushed with oil and garlic, pounded to a paste with herbs, or used in a variety of ways. They add saltiness and flavour to many sauces, stuffings, and relishes, like the BAGNA CAUDA of PIEDMONT. The cleaned salt fillets can be canned or put up in jars of oil, draped whole over salads and vegetable dishes, or rolled round pickled or salted capers and eaten as part of an ANTIPASTO Strong views are held on the superiority of anchovies in salt to those in brine or oil. It must depend on what you are using them for.

ANGEL SHARK (sometimes also called angel fish). *See* MONKFISH.

ANGELICA, wild parsnip (*angelica, Angelica archangelica*), is known today mainly for its candied stems, used in confectionary, but the seeds and root are used to flavour liqueurs and GRAPPA. and the young leaves can be added to salads, or cooked as a *contorno*. Thinly sliced young stems, tossed with slivers of Parma ham and a little tomato, are part of a delicate sauce for home-made *farfalle* devised by Angelo Lancellotti. The leaves are sometimes used in fish cookery.

ANGLER FISH. *See* MONKFISH.

ANGUILLA. *See* EEL.

ANISE (*anice*) (*Pimpinella anisum*), of the Umbelliferae family, has a pleasant sweet flavour, less harsh than fennel, and less powerful than star anise. All these are used in liqueurs; as Tom Stobart put it in his *Herbs, Spices, and Flavorings*, "Anise drinks are a convenient way of introducing the flavour of anise into cooking as well as into the cook." The digestive properties equal the enjoyable flavour. Anisetta Meletti is one of many, made from the anise of the region round Ascoli Piceno in the MARCHE, where Silvio Meletti adapted his mother's personal recipe to large-scale production, while keeping her special secrets. (For a discussion of Sambuca, the Italian sweet anise liqueur, *see* DI-GESTIVI.)

The gentle perfume of anise is also good in breads and confectionery. Maria Vittoria DELLA VERDE, a nun in 17th-century Perugia, scribbled in her personal notebook full of jottings about cookery and embroidery and convent matters a not very coherent account of some *biscottini* made with eggs and sugar beaten to a froth and thickened with a little flour, flavoured with anise, first hardened in a hot oven, then baked some more with a glaze of rosewater and sugar. She also has some exquisite little almond biscuits made with finely pounded almonds, diluted with rosewater and flavoured with anise. Another recipe for *ciabelle in aqua* is a classic bagel recipe; the dough flavoured with crushed anise, sugar, or salt, formed into rings, cooked first by chucking into boiling water and removing when they bob to the surface, and then baked in a hot oven. (*See* BREADS, RING-SHAPED.) Anise is used in festive breads and buns, like the *mescuotte* of BASILICATA, which is made from *farina di grano duro*, durum hard grain flour (the best explanation of the different kinds of flour used in baking in Italy is by Carol Field, *The Italian Baker*, pp. 34–39), lard, sugar, salt, and anise worked to a smooth dough, formed into rings or knots, and cooked in the same way as *ciabelle in aqua*. Originally a keeping bread used by shepherds, *mescuotte* is now an Easter speciality.

From Cantiano in the MARCHE come sweet buns, *ungaracci*, made with maize flour, raisins, and anise, a local delicacy, and a reminder of the use of maize flour when wheat was scarce.

Anise is one of the mild spices used in PANFORTE, and like fennel is used in comfits (see CONFETTI) eaten at the end of a meal to sweeten the breath and help digestion. Dried figs are sometimes prepared with anise, its gentle flavour enhancing the fig; together with bay leaves in the container, anise acts as preservative and insect repellent.

ANONIMO MERIDIONALE. *See* LIBER DE COQUINA.

ANONIMO TOSCANO. *See* LIBER DE COQUINA.

ANONIMO VENEZIANO. *See* LIBER DE COQUINA.

ANTIPASTO is the first event in a restaurant meal, after the arrival of bread and wine, and is usually served from a display that greets customers as they enter. It might include special creations of the chef, as well as standard items like olives, *affetati* (sliced salami), prepared seafood, stuffed vegetables, artichokes, wedges of *frittata*, and so on and on. The aim is to excite rather than fill diners, who will then be inspired to choose yet more delicacies from the menu. The "self-service" procedure of helping oneself from the antipasto display is disgusting, an "all you can eat" orgy, which is a negation of the intended benign titillation of the palate with only a few delicacies. The idea of antipasti is not new; medieval and Renaissance banquets presented morsels to sample before the main offering of course after course from *credenza* and kitchen, sometimes sampled standing round a flower-strewn table, before the ritual of washing the by then slightly sticky hands in perfumed water and drying them on embroidered linen towels. There was then no differentiation between sweet and savoury, as Scappi's menus show—with sweet spiced *mostaccioli* from Naples, slices of salt tongue cooked in wine, slivers of cooked ham with capers and raisins and sugar, and fresh grapes out of season, for a winter menu. As spring approached, salads of raw and cooked vegetables came on stream, to refresh the palate and "open the stomach" as physicians advised, but reinforced with hunks of wild boar pasty to sustain the starving. Later came little pots of clotted cream strewn with sugar, *bianco mangiare* in puff pastry, trimmed stalks of cardoons dipped in salt and pepper, and sugared nuts or fennel seeds, which were both stimulating and digestive.

Today, tidbits are sometimes offered for clients to nibble on while they pore over the menu, maybe cubes of mortadella or *ciccioli*— the crispy salty fragments left after rendering pork fat down to make lard—that are a prelude to meals in Emilia (some might think a meal in themselves, but not in Modena). Local specialities might be on offer, like the large stuffed and deep-fried green olives of Ascoli in the MARCHE, dried and salted fish, and BRUSCHETTA or *crostini*, delicate morsels on toasted or fried bread, which are now quite widespread.

APERITIVI, like many agreeable Italian beverages, often have a herbal or bitter note, due to their medicinal origins, hence the

name *amari*, "bitter." The use of flavoured alcohol or syrups to make sick people feel better by stimulating digestion, gentle purging, and sedation goes back to ancient theories of medicine. The doctor and the cook worked together to assure a balance of the humours, dosing to match the patient, the affliction, and the remedy, unique to each individual. Starting a meal with something to "open up" the stomach and stimulate the appetite was as desirable as closing the meal with a *digestivo (see* DIGESTIVI) to help everything settle. The monastic tradition of dosing the sick and selling products to generate revenue was another source of pleasant and medicinal elixirs. The *teriaca* or theriac of the physicians was a useful universal medicine, a mixture with enough therapeutic ingredients to alleviate most conditions, and a close relative of the recreational potions. GARLIC was described as the poor man's theriac, for its multitudinous uses and wholesome effects. Its association with vulgar usage might well account for its avoidance by many scrupulous culinary writers today.

Tonics and pleasant drinks were prepared in the home, and family cookery notebooks as well as printed texts used to have a variety of these. A *rosolio* in an anonymous late 18th-century notebook from the Albini family in Saludecio on the borders of Romagna and the Marche was made by macerating anise, cloves, cinnamon, vanilla, the peel of citron, some bitter almonds, and roast and ground coffee in equal weights of sugar and spirits of wine for at least 48 hours. In 18th-century Naples, Corrado listed 49 potions and ratafias under the heading *Delli rosoli*, describing them as "bevanda di molto spirito e gusto," "very lively and tasty drinks," pleasure rather than health being the Neapolitan preoccupation. A distilled *acqua d'oro* was made from cinnamon, cloves, anise, angelica root, orange peel, and bitter almonds, sweetened, coloured with saffron, filtered, and bottled with tiny sparks of gold leaf glimmering in the clear liquid. Corrado gives a couple of recipes for juniper berries macerated in spirits of wine with orange blossom or spices. His *verdolino do moscovia* has sage, mint, and rue as well as cinnamon, mace, and cubebs. A distilled *acqua stomatica* has a terrifying mix of wormwood, mint, nard, cinnamon, cloves, nutmeg, and anise, coloured with cochineal and alum. These low-alcohol sweetened liquids, distilled or infused, could be taken neat or diluted to make refreshing long drinks. They are the ancestors of the commercial products of today, but with the advantage of being made with natural rather than synthetic flavourings.

It was in the 19th century that domestic production of *aperitivi* was overtaken by industrial manufacturers, mainly in the north of Italy, many of whose names passed to the product—Cinzano, Campari, Carpano, Martini, Fernet Branca, and many more. Others, like Strega, Vermouth, Sambuca, and Cynar, are named after an ingredient. Herbs and spices familiar to the kitchen and stranger ones known to the pharmacy were used by these pioneering *liquoristi*. Many dry *aperitivi* can be used in small amounts to flavour food, and sweet ones have their uses in desserts.

APICIAN FLAVOUR, if it can

be identified at all, is surely to be found in the dishes called "Apician" in the Roman cookbook *Apicius*. They are clearly named after Apicius, the famous 1st-century gourmet; perhaps he invented them, but that is anybody's guess.

What can be made of *Minutal Apicianum*? Begin with olive oil, fish sauce, wine, chopped leeks, mint, little fish, little meatballs (apparently), sucking-pig sweetbreads, and the testicles of which capons have been deprived. Cook all this, seasoning with pepper, lovage, and green coriander or coriander seed. Add fish sauce again and not too much honey, and "its own juice," whatever that may mean, adjusting for flavour with wine

and honey. Bring to the boil, thicken with noodles (possibly) or crumbled pastry (possibly), stirring as it thickens. Sprinkle with pepper when serving. If *minutal* is a soup, which is uncertain, this is certainly a rich and recherché one.

And what of *Sala Cattabia*, a mixed dressed salad incorporating bits of bread? The special *Sala Cattabia Apiciana* begins with the grinding and mixing of a dressing: celery seed, dried pennyroyal, dried mint, ginger, fresh coriander, seeded raisins, honey, vinegar, olive oil, and wine. Then you put in a serving dish pieces of Picentine bread (very light and dry), chicken meat, kids' sweetbreads, Vestine cheese (probably a goat's cheese), pine nuts, cucumber (sliced?), and onions chopped very small, and you pour the dressing over. Just before serving, you sprinkle with snow, a luxury not unknown in the early second century AD (for example) when the younger Pliny wrote to chide a friend who had missed a modest dinner party, complete with snow-sprinkled salad, and had foolishly gone elsewhere for the promise of dancing girls. (AKD)

APPLE, *Malus pumila*, *Malus communis*

(crabapple), *mela*, is one of the oldest domesticated fruits, along with QUINCE, and shines brightly in legend and history, from the Song of Songs to the wanton Galatea tossing one at Virgil. An apple may have been the Golden Apple of the Hesperides, but quinces and oranges are candidates, too. In Christian iconography, apples can signify the Fall of Man, but as the fruit of the Tree of Knowledge, they can also imply the benefits of learning as a path to understanding of the divine, and are thus used in religious paintings to stand for both sin and redemption. The Christ Child holding an apple is reminding us of our innate sinfulness and our capacity, mediated by his sacrifice, to attain salvation. So apples in still life paintings can celebrate fruitfulness, wickedness, and goodness, as well as

Apicius is the name attached to a collection of recipes made during or after the first century AD and may have little to do with the person or persons of that name who lived at that time. The reputation of Marcus Gavius Apicius, 14–37 AD, gourmet and glutton, probably got attached long after his death to recipes he had not written. The recipes need to be put in the context of surviving information about Roman ingredients and eating habits to be found in literature and the arts, or we might get a false picture of what the ancient Romans really ate—probably an austere and much simpler diet than the luxurious dishes of the wealthy. These recipes may have been compiled by slave cooks for other slave cooks, in a sort of shorthand, described by Grainger as "blue-collar Latin," with no need to spell out procedures, quantities, or timing—convenient for them but confusing for us. Dalby has pinpointed the characteristics of Apician gastronomy (see APICIAN FLAVOUR), and described the pleasures of Roman gastronomy throughout the Empire (Dalby, 2000). A growing interest in historic food and the cuisines of the Near and Far East leads us to a better understanding of Apicius, and a recent accurate translation (the first ever) and an adaptation of Apician recipes for modern cooking (Grocock and Grainger, 2006; Grainger, 2006; Dalby and Grainger, 1996) give us insights and practical help in "cooking Apicius." Well worth the effort. Surviving manuscripts of Apicius have been known for centuries, and pored over by scholars and gourmets. In the Renaissance, their interest was part of a general search for the knowledge of classical antiquity, an enthusiasm that led Platina and his friends in the Roman Academy to dress up in togas and re-enact Roman banquets and, more seriously, explore the catacombs for links between early Christian culture and its classical background. Platina found references in ancient authors to ingredients and their properties, and added them to the recipes of his friend Martino in his work *De honesta voluptate et valetudine*. Later writers were less analytical, and by the 18th and 19th centuries often downright silly in their ooh-ing and ah-ing over things like dormice in honey, and rotten fish condiments. In fact, the compilation contains some lovely recipes, far from outlandish, like mushrooms simmered in *nam pla*, honey and pepper, or a pork and apricot *minutal* in which the salty sweet/sour mix of fruit and meat is delicious and totally acceptable today.

the corruption of innocence, demonstrated by the outer blemishes and the worm within; we see this in the apparently innocuous basket of fruit in Caravaggio's *Supper at Emmaus*, where in art as in life, imperfection and original sin await divine intervention and redemption; and in genre scenes where a modest market maiden holding or offering an apple can be seen to be virtuous or quite the reverse.

Of the many hundreds of different apples that grew in Italy yesterday, a diminishing number of regional and historic varieties, as commercial cultivation ousts the less productive kinds, is today available in markets supplied by small domestic orchards. The old, the ugly, the irregular, and the unusual are giving way to the bland and beautiful fruit relentlessly specified by supermarkets the world over. The varieties grown today, in order of importance, are Golden Delicious, Red Delicious, Gala, Granny, Braeburn, Morgenduft, Fuji, Jonagold, Pink Lady, Renetta, Stayman, Idared, and Elstar. Over half this production is exported to Germany, with the United Kingdom not far behind. A consumer group recently complained in the *Corriere della Sera* that Italian apples cost half as much in Finland as at home. A conference of the major Italian apple producers in Bolzano in 2003 stressed that quality, appearance, and price are of course a major preoccupation, but did not feel the need to mention flavour, whereas MATTIOLI in 1568 said that of the many varieties produced in Tuscany the *mele appie* and the *mele rose* had "apart from a pleasing and delightful aroma, a most delicious flavour in the mouth." Castelvetro wrote of a "paradise apple" with a yellow skin speckled with little red spots, with such an intense sweet smell that it was used to scent linen sheets, and the peel would perfume a room when thrown on the fire. Perfumed apples were used to make cosmetic creams and ointments (pomades).

When Bartolomeo Bimbi recorded the fruit produced for Grand Duke Cosimo III of Florence in the late 17th century on huge canvases—now displayed at Poggio a Caiano, outside Florence—over 100 varieties of apple were presented as a group portrait, with each fruit numbered and named in a cartouche below. Many of these were curiosities produced from grafts, but many more were intended to be produced commercially to increase prosperity in the dukedom. Italy then led the world in advanced fruit-culture, and we shall never know if Cosimo is turning in his grave or applauding the flourishing agribusiness of his native land. By-products of mass production include alcohol made from substandard fruit, pulp for use in confectionary, and juice for soft drinks.

On the last day of February, Carnival time, Scappi surpassed himself with a massive feast for 50 guests during which apples of various kinds were served cooked and raw.

APRICOT, *albicocca, Armeniaca vulgaris* or *Prunus armeniaca,* one of the drupe family, is grown all over Italy. Although these fruits have been known in the Mediterranean since their introduction in the time of Alexander the Great, their origins are in ancient China, not Armenia, and their Italian name today, *albicocca,* is said to derive from the Arabic, although the Arabic word is *mishmish.* That is the word used by Al-Baghdadi in the 13th century for a dish similar to one in Apicius that uses apricots in a complex combination of cooked meat, finished in a mixture of spices, fish sauce, honey, fruity must, apricots, and vinegar. Mattioli in the 16th century recorded many regional names, as did Felici—*armeniache, moniache, briccocole, albercocche, armenini, precocie*—with no connection with areas of Arab influence. *Albaricoque* is the Spanish name, and might have prevailed in areas under Spanish rule, and got to Italy that way. Apricots have a high content of vitamins A and C and minerals—potassium, magnesium, iron, calcium—and a unique combination of acidity and sweetness, with a perfumed flavour. This makes them particularly good in desserts and pasties, and also as jams and candied fruit. Their kernels have a strong almond-like flavour and are often used instead of bitter almonds, as in AMARETTI. Since the kernels contain a small amount of cyanide, it is for once no hardship to accept a substitute. The fragrant bitterness of apricot kernels can be added to sweet and savoury dishes by crumbling a few *amaretti* into the mixture or adding a few drops of the liqueur *amaretto di Saronno.* Too much is usually disastrous, overpowering everything else, as in the case of the pumpkin filling for *tortelli,* where only a little is needed to give the bland pumpkin a lift. Corrado has a recipe for a ratafia, *rattafè reale,* made with apricot kernels and white mulberries, flavoured with cinnamon, coriander, and AMBERGRIS. Apricot oil had medicinal uses, as well as being a pleasant flavouring. It was used for skin infections and was good for haemorrhoids, according to Mattioli; a baby massage oil on the market today might make you want to eat your infant, we are warned.

ARAB INFLUENCE on Italian

gastronomy has been discussed by various authorities, not always unanimous, but it is safe to say that early Arab occupation in the south, and later trading links with Venice in the north, and then the Crusades, brought contacts with oriental civilisation and culture that can be detected in recipes and writing about food. Many Arabic words—like *limonia, romania, sommachia*— survive in the names of 14th-century recipes, although cooks and consumers were unaware of the connection. *Romania* is derived from *rummān*, the Arabic word for pomegranate. This and other examples were investigated by Maxime Rodinson (Perry, 2001, p. 168). It is hard to tell if this filtered down from the earlier Arab presence in Sicily and the south of Italy, or is an indication that Arabic culinary texts were known to western writers on food and dietetics. Arab scholarship assured the survival of much of the medical and scientific culture of Greece and Rome, and brought improved agriculture and the arts of civilised living to countries the Arabs conquered and settled in around the Mediterranean. From the 9th century onwards, Arab writers translated the medical and botanical works of Greek and Roman writers and incorporated them into their own treatises on health and agriculture, while peasant wisdom and practical experience put these ancient theories into practise. The Galenic approach to health and food was preserved and passed down by them, and the benign idea of the cook adjusting ingredients and their seasoning to the physical and mental condition of the diner—not so much "you are what

you eat" as "eat according to what you are"—is with us still.

The diligence with which Arab horticulturalists preserved the heritage of the ancient world, was similar to the attitude of Renaissance humanists, who, in their search for classical knowledge, developed a sophisticated culture of their own. The fertile land around the kingdoms of Seville, Cordoba, and Granada blossomed for centuries under this intensive but always ecologically balanced system, where agronomists matched soil quality with irrigation systems and complex methods of tillage and manuring to suit the terrain and crop. And so landowners in Sicily enjoyed plump artichokes while Charlemagne could only use his scrubby thistles for teaselling cloth. This mixture of erudition and ingenuity was also behind the establishment of botanical gardens in Europe during the Renaissance, when gardeners and collectors cherished plants from the New World alongside specimens described by the classical writers Dioscorides and Columella, and experimented with selective breeding and grafts, exchanging cuttings and seeds as they would antique cameos or modern portrait busts. The rapacious Isabella d'Este collected classical fragments and commissioned works of art from the uncompromisingly modern Mantegna and hoarded with equal enthusiasm seeds of a new kind of cabbage which she sent to her brother with instructions on how to cook and serve it. Mantegna incorporated into many of his devotional paintings the glowing oranges and lemons of northern Italy's agribusiness (*see* CITRUS FRUITS); he had enjoyed their classical associations, and there they are glowing like jewels in the canopy above the Virgin and Child in the altarpiece of *La madonna della Vittoria*, anticipating the secular display of citrus fruits painted by Bartolomeo Bimbi for the Medici rulers of Florence centuries later. This enthusiasm for rediscovered edible plants of the ancient world brought asparagus and artichokes onto the dinner tables of the rich in northern Europe; how they got there from the infidel south of Spain by way of southern Italy is not entirely clear; the interesting thing is that they were part of this culture of innovation and discovery.

The art of distilling, particularly for the production of perfumed waters, was brought to the West by the Arabs. The use of rosewater and orange blossom water for both cooking and ritual hand washing before meals and between the succession of courses was one of many aspects of civilised dining that Europe owed to the Arab world. Cleanliness in the preparation and serving of food, the ritual wiping the rim of a dish with rosewater, or sprinkling some over the food, along with sugar and cinnamon, added sensory delights to the pleasures of taste and texture. Taking up food in the fingers was a tactile sensation that enhanced the others, an aspect of civilised eating, not messiness, so that the use of forks and today's prim strictures on touching food seem almost a negation of the hedonism of Arab eating.

But medieval Italian food culture developed its own identity, and it would not do to make too much of names of recipes and ingredients, spices in particular, that seem to prove a direct Arab connection. These are survivals, part of a fusion of tastes that developed over centuries. The use of spices, and spice mixtures, is derived from Arab gastronomy, but developed a dynamic of its own in Europe over the centuries; spices were enjoyed as an exotic and very expensive luxury, until changes of taste in the 16th and 17th centuries led to the use of milder seasonings.

Thanks to the work of Maxime Rodinson, and later Charles Perry, we can study translations of Arabic culinary texts, and recognise with pleasure similarities between historic and modern Italian food. Rodinson traced connections between the court cuisine of France and the Angevins in Naples, perhaps through a translation—by the possibly mythical Jambobino of

Cremona—of an Arabic text on dietetics, and compares Arab and Italian recipes for *limonia, romania,* and *sommachia,* in which the Arab influence is clear. But the surviving Italian cookery manuscripts in which these Arab-influenced recipes are embedded consist of many recipes which are plainly indigenous Italian and owe little to direct Arab influence. Charles Perry is far too nice to put the boot in, but the tunnel vision of Arberry and Rodinson oversimplifies and obscures the much more complex realities of the development of Italian cuisine, and the Arab contribution to its complex multicultural evolution.

The *Vivanda detta limonia* in the 14th-century *Libro di cucina* is a spiced dish of chickens, first simmered in broth, then taken out and fried in lard, and served with a sauce made of ground almonds, spices, dates, and prunes, with a sweet/sour effect achieved by the addition of sugar and the juice of bitter oranges. The many Arab versions of this, known as *laymūnīiya,* are all so different from each other that the only common factor is the use of a souring element, usually lemon or, as in the Italian, bitter orange or citron. Pomegranate juice, to add colour and acidic perfume to a meat or chicken dish, is used in *rummāniyya mukhaththara,* in *The Description of Familiar Foods* (Perry, 2001, p. 307), a 14th-century compilation of recipes using material from al-Baghdādī: pieces of meat, probably lamb, are cooked with a very little water until simmering in their buttery juices, then thickened with pomegranate juice crushed with rose petals, and ground pistachios, flavoured with mint, coloured with saffron, and served with a sprinkling of rose water. Italian cooks had similar ideas, but not necessarily related. *Hisrimiyya,* a dish of chicken joints in a sauce of verjuice, ground almonds, and herbs, reminds us of Martino's simple *chicken with verjuice,* but it is hard, and hardly necessary, to suppose a direct connection. Something neither he nor his patron Ludovico Trevisan, the scourge of the infidel Turks, would have wished to contemplate.

Scappi had a recipe for *succussu*, couscous, made in the traditional way from semolina, which he describes with great accuracy. By then it was a familiar dish and not a foreign one.

ARANCINI

ARANCINI are well known as a bar snack, eaten freshly cooked and hot, so that the soft filling contrasts with the crisp outside. A small ball of rice, cooked as a RISOTTO, or plain rice mixed with beaten egg and grated parmesan, is given a filling of a rich RAGÙ and perhaps some cubes of cheese. A hole is made in a small handful of rice and some of the filling put in, then the rice is folded over and shaped into a ball. This is then floured and dipped in beaten egg, coated in breadcrumbs, and deep fried. In a version called *supplì*, or *supplì al telefono*, the *ragù* is incorporated into the enclosing rice, with cubes of MOZZARELLA inside it, and the eater has to contend with telephone wires of melted cheese. Made at home, *arancini* get more complicated. They have been immortalised in a story by Andrea Camilleri, in which Montalbano narrowly escapes diverting the course of justice in order to enjoy a feast of *arancini* cooked by the mother of two young villains to celebrate their short-lived release from jail (Camilleri, 1999). The recipe takes two whole days to make, during which the delinquents teeter on the brink of reincarceration, while their old mother, Adelina, makes a risotto, cools it, and mixes in some raw eggs, then makes the *ragù*, of equal parts veal and pork cooked very slowly in a BATTUTO of onion, celery, parsley, and basil, with tomatoes and some chopped salame; and then a béchamel sauce, then cooks some sweet young peas, and finally mixes the finely chopped meats with the peas and béchamel to make the filling for these superlative *arancini.*

ARCIMBOLDO, GIUSEPPE

ARCIMBOLDO, GIUSEPPE (1527–1593) was born and trained in Milan and worked for much of his life in Prague in the service of the Austrian emperors Maximilian II and Rudolph II. Although a versatile and gifted artist, Arcimboldo is notorious today for his slightly creepy portrait heads composed of mainly natural objects—fruit, vegetables, flowers, and bits of wood and vegetation, representing the four elements or the four seasons, or sometimes a particular type, such as a gardener, librarian, or cook. Whatever the theoretical basis for these compositions, we treasure them for the accurate depictions of fruit and vegetables, and knowing that the artist also organised festivities and banquets for the Hapsburgs (though no records of the banquets survive) we can assume that they are accurate representations of things known at the imperial court. Both feasts and theatrical events were full of symbolic imagery, so it is not surprising that Arcimboldo's contemporaries enjoyed the concepts of cosmic unity and imperial hegemony, along with taking pleasure in the fruitfulness of the changing seasons that we find in his strange and beautiful works. *Summer*, in the Louvre, is a jovial, smiling side view composed of fruit and vegetables, including the newly introduced eggplant, some corn on the cob, various gourds, a bursting melon, ripe apples and pears for plump cheek and chin, with cherries for lips and an open pea pod revealing shiny teeth, a garland of cherries and plums with a raspberry glowing in the middle, and a single blackcurrant as a bright eyeball between the fleshy lids of tiny pink pears.

After returning to Milan, Arcimboldo continued to work for the emperor; his *Vertumnus*, a portrait of red-nosed Rudolph as the god of fruitfulness and the changing seasons, bringer of peace and harmony, virile, voluptuous, and brimming over with good humour, carries its burden of symbolism gracefully, at a time when the empire and Europe were threatened by the Ottoman Turks and solidarity and harmony were indeed desperately needed. The flowers are both symbolic and edible—the lily, rose, and carnation of devotional works jostle with zucchini blossoms, cabbages, and an artichoke, while the eyes, a mulberry and a cherry, twinkle above the ruddy apple and peach that form the cheeks. Immediately recognisable as an irreverent but accurate likeness without any distortion of the component parts, the double meanings rather crudely emphasised in an accompanying poem by Gregorio Comanini, this portrait was a great success with the emperor.

Another form of *trompe l'oeil* painting was equally strange and diverting—a bowl of humble root vegetables, turnips, radishes, carrots, skirrets, a parsnip, some with their leaves, and a cluster of nuts, and a large onion, when turned upside down, becomes the portrait of a somewhat uncouth rustic character, usually described as a gardener. A dish containing roast sucking pig, a large and a small roast bird, and what might be a chunk of filled pie or some other kind of meat, when reversed becomes a debonaire cook, the traditional slice of lemon on the rim of the pewter plate now seen as a decoration pinned to the brim of a hat, the cook's beady eyes formed by the head of the big fowl neatly tucked under its wing.

Whether comic or cosmic, the significance of Arcimboldo's images for us is the realistic portrayal of the fruit and vegetables, as vivid as the market scenes and still lifes his contemporaries were painting in northern Italy, giving us an insight into the products his patrons enjoyed in Italy and the Austrian empire.

ARSELLA. *See* WEDGE SHELL, PALOURDE.

ARTICHOKE, *carciofo, Cynara scolymus,* comes in many varieties, the main division being with spines and without. The most common are: *spinoso di Palermo, spinoso sardo, spinoso di Liguria,* and *violetto di Toscana, precoce di Chioggia, romano* or *mammola.* Artichokes are a seasonal crop, and enjoyed all the more for that reason, from the earliest babies, the size of a walnut, which appear in winter, to the fat plump artichokes which last through spring into early summer. The fleshy base of the leaves (which are not really leaves, but bracts protecting the interior flower heads, which as they mature become the inedible choke) and the heart to which they are attached can be delicate or dull and stodgy, and the cooking methods evolved to bring out the best in the different varieties show great inventiveness and imagination. It is rare in Italy to see the laborious and thoroughly unsatisfactory procedure of eating an overboiled artichoke leaf by leaf, with congealed melted butter dripping inexorably from lips to wrist, to elbow, to armpit, with debris piling up around in ever-growing heaps. Italian cooks do the hard work for us, serving the heart (*fondo*) or the edible flower head with its leaf base (*cuore*) in a variety of inventive dishes, from frittatas to pasta sauces. When young, before the unpleasantly hairy and inedible choke has developed, whole baby artichokes can be eaten raw, *al pinzimonio,* with salt, pepper, and olive oil. *Carciofi alla giudia,* a speciality of the Jewish community in Rome, uses a less compact variety; trimmed and with the leaves splayed out like a chrysanthemum, they are deep fried to give a soft melting interior surrounded by crisp, charred outer leaves, all edible. The best recipe for this is given with meticulous authority by Ada Boni (Boni, n.d., p. 540). In *carciofi alla romana,* young artichokes have the tough outer leaves cut away, leaving just the heart and leaf base, which are stuffed with chopped garlic and *mentuccia* (PENNYROYAL, not the same as *menta romana*) and cooked slowly in a little water and olive oil, stalks upwards, until the liquid has evaporated and the artichokes are meltingly tender and aromatic. The prepared, trimmed

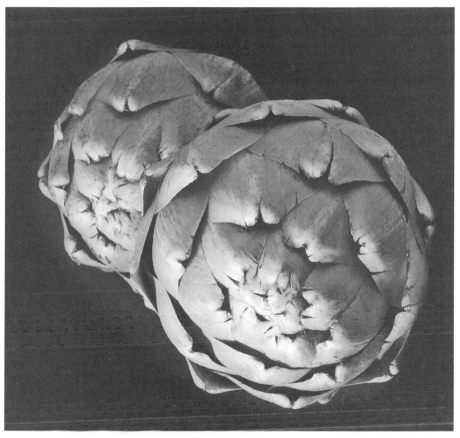

These mature artichokes will need to be trimmed of their outer "leaves" and choke before cooking, but tender young "baby" artichokes can be sautéed and eaten whole. (Shutterstock)

heads can be bought in most markets, and are well worth the extra cost, for the market women work with a rapid skill the domestic cook can rarely match, rubbing the cut surfaces with lemon to stop them browning, and will throw in a bunch of the indispensable pennyroyal. Artichokes come to market in huge bundles with the decorative leaves attached to the stems, a welcome display, celebrated in Pinelli's engravings of Roman street life.

Artichokes were known to the Greeks and Romans; they were developed from the wild cardoon (*Cynara cardunculus*) which probably originated in the Mediterranean, but, as with asparagus, it is not easy to plot their route from antiquity to the tables of the princely courts of the Renaissance, whence they passed to France and the rest of Europe. We are told that their cultivation declined during the Dark Ages, and evidence of their use before the 16th century is hard to find. We do know that artichokes were cultivated with great sophistication in Andalusia during the centuries-long Arab occupation, so the connection with Italy may have been through Sicily and the south, or from Byzantium and Venice in the north.

Visual evidence of pride in this improved species comes from a still life painting by Vincenzo Campi, in 1580, in which the decorative leaves and heads of artichokes mingle with fresh young broad beans, partly shelled, nestling in baskets adorned with pink roses, and bowls of tender little garden peas, bright red cherries, and blushing pears, echoing the complexion of a buxom fruit-seller. In 1607, Cardinal Scipione Borghese shrewdly grabbed the art collection of the Cavalier d'Arpino, the patron of Caravaggio, thus preserving a painting which is an important link with northern Italian horticulture. This anonymous painting in the Galleria Borghese—now known as the Hartford still life, executed some time in the 1590s—shows an elegant array of fruit and vegetables, including both artichokes and asparagus. But there is some even earlier documentary evidence. On 26 February 1519, Isabella d'Este sent some "novelties" (*qualche stranieze*) to her brother in Ferrara to refresh his jaded appetite after a long and exhausting journey—a little basket of fresh young peas, and some artichokes: "and I would say they were from my own garden in the country, if I thought you as gullible as I was over those pickled fennel bulbs you sent me from Spain." Two years later, she rejoiced in a present from him—so many artichoke plants that she feared they might lose their scarcity value, but which she nevertheless had planted in her garden in Mantua, following his careful instructions. By 16 November 1529, Isabella's son, Duke Federico of Mantua, received 300 artichoke plants from a correspondent in Genoa. Demands for plants and seeds, from as far away as Rome, indicate a growing interest in this hitherto rare and exotic vegetable, treasured and exchanged by wealthy collectors, as they would antique coins and jewellery. A plump artichoke appears as illustration in a songbook manuscript, probably originating in the Mantuan court, of *composizioni profane* from the end of the 15th century, an exotic illustration to a sophisticated version of secular songs.

Writing in 1611, Baldassare Pisanelli claimed that artichokes originated in Sicily, and mentions fine varieties grown there and in Naples. By the mid–16th century, Costanzo Felici described them as well known: "*Tanto

la gola vi ha industriato sopra che gli ha fatto familiarissimi a tutti et in gran reputatione appresso de' grandi*" (Gluttony has led to their exploitation to such an extent that they are now most familiar to all and have a high reputation amongst the great). In the mid-16th century, Scappi was serving tiny artichokes in early February—raw, with salt and pepper, and cooked, with oil and pepper—at banquets for nobles and prelates at the papal court in Rome. A few decades later, Castelvetro was telling the British ingenious recipes for this, to them, newly fashionable vegetable (bake trimmed artichokes in a pie with oysters, bone marrow, and sweetbreads—delicious). At the same time, one hot April night in Rome, the tempestuous painter Caravaggio threw a plate of artichokes at the head of an insolent waiter, an episode that implies that by then they were popular tavern food, but still prepared and discussed with passionate discrimination.

In 18th-century Naples, Corrado treated artichokes, trimmed, with choke removed, and precooked in salted water with a little lemon juice, as vehicle for his daring combinations of flavours—simmered in olive oil, seasoned with pepper, parsley, and *bottarga*, and served in a prawn *coulis* decorated with shelled prawns; or floured, dipped in beaten egg, deep fried, and served with a sauce of bitter orange zest and sugar diluted in vinegar.

A modern recipe from LIGURIA, *al funghetto*, has prepared and sliced artichokes browned in oil with cubed potatoes and chopped garlic, and then moistened with stock and cooked covered until soft, served with a scattering of chopped oregano, thyme, and parsley.

"*Contro il logorio della vita moderna*" used to be an advertising slogan for Cynar, a bitter Italian aperitif based on artichokes, and indeed their nutritional content is impressive, rich in minerals (potassium, calcium, iron, phosphorous) and folic acid, with diuretic and laxative properties, and with a useful fibre content, all of which might well help us overcome the stresses of modern life.

ARTISTS are included in this work if we know something about their food preferences that helps to illustrate the story of Italian food; MICHAELANGELO and PONTORMO are in this category. Other artists are of interest because they provide evidence in their paintings of foodstuffs and eating habits of their time; of course these have to be seen in an art historical context, or an uninformed and overly literal interpretation of things like fruit and bread and wine (whose symbolism is important) might lead to blunders and false assumptions. (Conversely, the gastronomic contents of a painting can, or should be, useful tools for art historians.) Still lifes, genre scenes showing kitchens, markets, weddings, bible stories (the marriage at Cana, the meal at Emmaus, the prodigal son, Christ in the house of Martha and Mary), historic scenes (Cleopatra's feast) all contain food, and are sometimes the only source of information about what dishes for which we have recipes may have looked like—the ornate pies, peacocks in their plumage, roast fowl larded with bacon or cloves, and piles of cheeses and fruit.

This is a somewhat arbitrary selection, to give some idea of the huge amount of material that is available to illustrate the story of Italian food. Recent exhibitions of Italian still life paintings bring more and more treasures to light, which can be scrutinised for gastronomic insights. Glimpses of fruit and things to eat in devotional works can tell much about the appearance and variety of things like apples, cucumbers, oranges, bread, and wine, although they are included for symbolic purposes. The solitary cucumber and apple in CRIVELLI's *Annunciation with Saint Egidius* are real earthy products, as are the slightly blemished fruit in CARAVAGGIO's painting *The Meal at Emmaus*, and the glorious canopies of citrus fruits in MAN-TEGNA's *Madonna of the Victories*; while the golden oranges glimmering in the background of Uccello's *Battle of San Romano* remind us of the *palle*, the round balls of the Medici crest, and are a punning reminder of both apothecaries' pills and health-giving fruit. Tiepolo's rapid little sketch *The Banquet of Cleopatra* shows little food but conveys the bustle and paraphernalia of a courtly banquet: the procession of servants bringing food and drink (vinegar for the notorious pearl), musicians, pet dogs, entertainers, and the costly appurtenances of a table set with an oriental carpet, covered by a starched lace-trimmed cloth, in a cool, airy courtyard in a modern (c. 1740) Venetian palace.

The Italian still life paintings known to the public at present are a valuable resource for food historians, and as interest in this genre grows, more and more material is becoming available through exhibitions, catalogues, and monographs, and although it is regrettable that the two disciplines are not working together more closely, it is possible that a closer look at content, as well as style and technique, might be to everyone's advantage.

ARTUSI, PELLEGRINO

(1820–1911) published in 1891, at his own expense, a little work written to divert himself in his retirement—*La scienza in cucina e l'arte di mangiar bene*. Advised by friends that it had no future, he dedicated it to his two white cats, Biancani and Sibillone, and took care of sales and distribution himself. By 1909, it had expanded from the initial 475 recipes to 790 in the 13 edition, and so great was the demand that he handed the business side over to the publisher Benporad, while keeping control over the contents himself. It went on to become a best-seller, with more than 90 reprints and several deluxe editions, and is still a much-loved kitchen companion. The 14th edition of 1910, Artusi's final version of his text, has been edited by Piero

Camporesi, with extensive footnotes and an introduction (Artusi, 1970); this is the version to get, for the wealth of historical and gastronomic information in the footnotes and Camporesi's perceptive assessment of Artusi's importance.

Artusi's avuncular, encouraging tone of voice and sensible, easy to understand recipes were just what the emerging urban middle class needed. *Igiene, economia, buongusto*—hygiene, economy and good taste—were the watchwords on the title page, indicating a sober, genteel approach that won hearts and minds for generations. A cuisine that is decent, nourishing, and in no way showy fitted the frugal, though comfortably off readership; the virtues of thrift, the reassurance of doing the right thing, the sense of being part of a national consensus gave this in fact quite narrow section of society a sense of security, of belonging to a wider national entity.

It was not just the contents but the language that was to be so influential. Camporesi reminds us that this, and Manzoni's novel *I promessi sposi,* were the two books most likely to be found in every middle-class household, from the top to the toe of the peninsula. Artusi's book made a greater contribution to the unification of Italy than all the efforts by politicians and linguists to bring a country of separate entities with their own languages and dialects into a coherent nation. While the *questione della lingua* was being debated by academics, innocent housewives throughout the land were consulting their "Artusi" every day, and his literate, slightly colloquial, Florentine version of Tuscan, tinged with Romanguolo (he came from Forlimpopolo—Forlì—near Bologna) became reassuringly familiar. A generation later, Ada Boni, in somewhat bad taste, wrote slightingly of Artusi's "*umoristico capolavoro della incompetenza culinaria*" (that jokey masterpiece of culinary incompetence), unkindly mocking a style that by her time had already achieved so much, and which she her-

self was to benefit from, and at times emulate. (Something there of the usual scorn of the hands-on cook—she tested all her recipes herself—for the gentlemanly theorist who relied on cook and housekeeper to implement his work.) Artusi was one of a group of scholarly gastronomes who investigated food history, and it is to them (they included Olindo Guerrini and Ludovico Frati, and the lexicographer Fanfani) that we owe much of our knowledge of early Italian cookery texts. So when Artusi said "*La cucina e una briconcella*" (Cooking is frippery), he was being characteristically ironic and self-deprecating. His own knowledge of Italian food, its past and present, was extensive; he had travelled much in his youth as a businessman, and then, having retired from a prosperous career in banking in Florence, with leisure in which to pursue his interests in gastronomy and the evolution of his country's language, he had further opportunity to digest and present his findings.

La scienza was the first cookery book in more than two centuries to discard the pretentious gobbledegook of aristocratic, French-influenced texts and present in a clear, modern style a compendium of traditional Italian food—up to date, but reflecting the author's interest in history, and for some readers perhaps a thought-provoking introduction to a world beyond the home, for Artusi's anecdotes, jokes, and historical titbits, designed to entertain and amuse, were artfully dispersed among the practical instructions, and so read by generations of women, opening the book for a particular recipe, and ending up reading for pleasure for perhaps the first time in their lives.

This was, as Artusi intended, a new book about Italian food, in a new version of the Italian language, for a new nation, or at least the social class that was to represent it, written in a clear, user-friendly culinary language, explaining modest, unthreatening dishes—an engaging narrative rather than an authoritarian step-by-step set of instructions. Camporesi reminds us of Artusi's deliberate exclusion of the cuisines of many of the regions of Italy, and his affectionately condescending inclusion of a pasta sauce at the request of a widowed friend, whose Sicilian husband used to make it. He was anxious to avoid antiquarianism, and his well-bred diffidence, to quote Camporesi, about *"suggestioni folkloriche e nell'evitare piatti troppo municipali o communque limitati a un certo ambiente o ceto sociale"* (any dishes with a whiff of folklore, and the avoidance of those that were too localised, or at any rate limited to particular environments or social levels). (No need to remind ourselves of the poor or vulgar . . .) Artusi is apologetic about his recipe for *Pollo in porchetta* (p. 466): *"Non e piatto signorile, ma da famiglia"* (Family food, not a refined dish). This when the *Inchiesta Jacini* was investigating and publishing the harrowing details of the life and work of the poor in the regions, where a chicken in the pot was an unobtainable, almost unimaginable luxury. (The *Inchiesta sulle condizioni della classe agricola in Italia* was set up in 1877 under the direction of Stefano Jacini to investigate conditions of life in rural areas throughout the newly united nation of Italy.)

It is difficult to appreciate the impact of this work when our enthusiasms and methodology are so different. We crave regional, authentic, preferably endangered *cucina povera*, and the *cucina delle nonne*, and pursue rare and peculiar ingredients, complex obsolete procedures, at the same time demanding that they be spelled out in the gobbledegook of the professional "recipe writer." We regret Artusi's blandness, his avoidance of excess or exaggeration, his dumbing down of the robust regional food he knew and enjoyed; we regret, too, his narrow class outlook, his indifference to the illiterate and badly fed masses that in his time formed the greater part of the population of Italy, and for that the introduction by Cam-

poresi, ever sensitive to the plight of the underdog, provides a sympathetic and generous corrective.

ARUGULA. *See* ROCKET.

ASAFOETIDA,

one of the umbelliferae, *Ferula assafoetida, asafetida,* is mentioned briefly here because it is the nearest we can get to the ancient, and now extinct, plant silphium, used by the Romans to flavour and tenderise food. Apicius *see* APICIAN FLAVOUR suggested that one could use asafoetida instead of silphium, which by the time of Pliny had practically disappeared, the last specimen having been presented to the emperor Nero, before supplies vanished as a result of overcropping. Anyone working from ancient Roman recipes can try asafoetida, which is easily available in stores selling spices used in Indian cookery; it is best freshly ground, and in spite of its horrible smell—rather like stale, rank garlic—it is a delicious flavouring. Sally Grainger (Dalby and Grainger, 1996, p. 108) has a simple dish from Apicius which may have originated in Parthia, in which chicken pieces are baked in a sauce of black pepper, red wine, fish sauce (*nam pla*), asafoetida, chopped fresh lovage, and caraway seeds.

ASIAGO

is a cow's cheese from the VENETO, named for the high rich pastures of the Asiago uplands above Vicenza, traditionally producing wool and cheese from sheep, but now milk from Pezzata nera and Bruno alpina cattle. There are two types—*asiago d'allevo*, which is sold as *mezzano, vecchio,* or *stravecchio,* depending on the length of aging, and *asiago pressato*, made using a recent method producing a less pungent cheese. As the name *d'allevo* implies, the cheese needs much individual care, cooking the curds twice after coagulation, and turning frequently when the cheeses are drained, salted, and maturing in their moulds. It has higher protein and lower fat content and is easier to digest than the younger pressed version, which is nonetheless popular for its milder, sweeter flavour. The pale straw colour and irregular holes are characteristic of both. As it ages, *asiago* can be used as a grating cheese and goes well with POLENTA, PASTA, and local dishes.

ASPARAGUS, *asparagi, Asparagus officinalis*, is one of the best loved vegetables in the Italian cuisine. The spears are eaten raw, grilled or fried, boiled and dressed with olive oil and lemon or butter and parmesan, or deep fried in batter as part of a FRITTO MISTO. Asparagus is cultivated all over Italy, each region having its own much-prized varieties, the best known perhaps the fat, pale, slightly tinged with pink asparagus from Bassano, in the VENETO. That from Ravenna was prized in classical times, and it was said to be excellent in Verona. Two bundles of asparagus sit neatly in their containers in a mosaic from Antioch, part of a snack of boiled eggs, bath chops (cured pig's cheeks), and a dipping sauce. We are told that cultivation declined during the Middle Ages, but was flourishing again during the Renaissance. Evidence for this is not easy to find, perhaps because what seemed like a new interest in asparagus is merely due to the availability of more information, particularly printed cookery texts, at that time. An early sighting comes from the Po valley during the last decades of the 14th century in an illuminated manuscript, *Tacuinum Sanitatis*, produced for the Ceruti family; the page devoted to asparagus shows two men, heads protected from the sun, cutting the young spears and packing them neatly into baskets. This is a cash crop in a large field protected by a thorn hedge, but does it depict late medieval agriculture in the north of Italy, or in 11th-

One of the most beloved vegetables in Italian cuisine. The spears are most commonly eaten raw, grilled or fried, boiled and prepared with a simple dressing of olive oil and lemon or butter. (Shutterstock)

century Baghdad, where Ibn Botlan, the author, came from? Asparagus was listed, and sometimes illustrated, in versions of this text that are based on its first translation into Latin in SICILY in the 13th century, which circulated throughout medieval Europe. Perhaps we should look south, to the fertile plains of Andalucia, where sophisticated Arab horticulture flourished while northern Europe was sunk in the gloom and recession of the Dark Ages. The rich landowner Ibn al Awam grew asparagus in the valley of the Gaudalquivir in the 12th century, and contemporary Arabic cookery manuscripts give elaborate recipes in which the spears are (unbelievably) stuffed with a spiced meat mixture. Pliny wrote of some from Ravenna weighing three spears to a Roman pound, monsters certainly big enough to stuff, or cut into lengths and added to stewed lamb and chickpeas, flavoured with herbs and spices. This was (most likely) just one agreeable vegetable among many, whose cultivation was managed with elaborate care, and whose uses, gastronomic and medicinal, were chronicled by Arab writers and eventually translated and diffused in the West. It is difficult to find out how the asparagus plant might have been reintroduced into northern Italy from Spain or Sicily, probably through political contacts between wealthy aristocratic courts, avid for expensive luxuries from afar.

On the fifth of April 1466, Barbara of Brandenburg, wife of the duke of Mantua, received a gift of asparagus spears with a note: "*Item* one bunch of asparagus. Your ladyship must forgive me for sending so few, but they are a novelty." Later the rapacious Isabella d'Este exchanged seeds and plants with friends and relatives, and by 29 January 1530 a peremptory note from her son the hedonistic duke of Mantua demanded two wagon loads, as much as possible, of the delicacy, to be sent to him at the Palazzo del Te (Malacarne, p. 110).

An anonymous Tuscan author gives a simple recipe for asparagus at the end of the 14th century: it is first given a boil in water, then finished in olive oil, chopped onion, salt, saffron, and spices. Bartolomeo Platina, in the second half of the 15th century, mentions both wild and cultivated asparagus in his work *De honesta voluptate et valetudine*. A century later, Costanzo Felici described the different regional varieties, along with wild shoots of various plants, in his *Letter on Salads*, while at about the same time Bartolomeo Scappi listed asparagus salads in his menus for April and May, and gave a rich recipe for tender asparagus spears cooked in a meat broth with slivers of ham, finished with fresh herbs chopped with pepper, cinnamon, and saffron, sharpened with verjuice or gooseberries.

A few decades later, Castelvetro berated the English for not making more of the commercial possibilities of asparagus; he thought the weedy specimens the English brought to market were pathetic compared with Italian crops. (Though by the end of the 17th century the English had mended their ways, and were even experimenting with forced varieties.) He says the landowners around Verona had given up growing flax and wheat 20 years earlier (that would be about the 1580s), making a much better living from asparagus, sending consignments as far away as Venice, and he describes the usual ways of serving them, including this: "Take the plumpest spears of asparagus and having oiled them well, roll them on a plate in salt and pepper to season them thoroughly, and roast them over a grid. Lavishly sprinkled with bitter orange juice this makes a most delicate dish." He was right; the charred outside and the soft interior of the spears are delicious with the olive oil and bitter orange juice.

The pervasive influence of Italian culture during the 16th and 17th centuries probably accounted for improved horticulture in many European countries; peas and asparagus were some of the fashionable luxuries that were enjoyed along with the art, calligraphy, and literature of Italy. Visual evidence is found in many still life and genre scenes, in northern Italy and the Low Countries, where bunches of asparagus grace market stalls and kitchens, and life-sized portraits of plump asparagus spears were by then something you hung on the walls as well as enjoyed on the plate.

Wild asparagus is still enjoyed in Italy today; its thin, straggly-looking spears are more bitter than the cultivated variety but are delicious on their own, or in FRITTATAS and RISOTTOS. They look like, and so can be confused with, wild HOPS.

The only disadvantage attached to this delectable vegetable is the strong, unmistakable odour imparted to urine by the amino acid methionine, creating the sulphurous methyl mercaptan. Artusi's benevolent antidote to this was a few drops of turpentine in the chamber pot, converting the pong into the sweet smell of violets.

ASTICE. *See* LOBSTER.

AUBERGINE. *See* EGGPLANT.

AZAROLE, *Crataegus azarolus, azzerola,* is one of the Rosaceae family (which includes rowan and QUINCE) and was enjoyed in the past for its bittersweet flavour, eaten as a refreshing fruit, fresh or bletted, made into jellies, or dried. Similar to hawthorn berries, the fruit or drupe comes in various sizes, colours, and flavours. The red ones were common in Italy in the 17th century, and Castelvetro boasted of how he had introduced them to Sir Henry Wotton, the British ambassador in Venice, who developed quite a craving. Their high vitamin content and thirst-quenching properties made them helpful for those with a high fever. Mattioli recommended them for pregnant women, to subdue nausea and stimulate appetite; he pointed out how they resemble hawthorn berries, with their pretty flowers and sweet/sour pulpy drupes, and have much in common with MEDLARS. Azeroles were cultivated around Naples and in Liguria and are still appreciated for their visual appearance as much as for their use as a table fruit.

b

BABÀ is a rich yeasted sponge, strongly flavoured with liqueurs, in particular rum, often made with candied fruits and sultanas, and usually reinforced by soaking after cooking in a syrup containing much rum. Usually cooked in individual moulds, *babà* could also be made as one big cake. *Babà* is said to have been invented for Stanislas Leczinski in exile in Lorraine after the War of the Polish Succession, needing to mitigate the rigours of the local *kugelhupf* with a rich syrup. Some say it was a Slav invention, the name *babà* being a derogatory term for an old lady, which is what these cakes might look like. Others prefer the exiled king's enthusiasm for Ali Baba in *The Arabian Nights*. Lesley Chamberlain makes a good case for the 16th-century Italian princess Bona Sforza, who brought Italian fashions to the Polish court at Cracow and may have introduced this aromatic sponge, so similar to today's Milanese PANETTONE.

BACCALÀ, salt cod, is codfish, *merluzzo*, which has been split down its length, salted, and dried, and—although smelling horrible in this state—can be made into a huge variety of delicious dishes. Strong feelings, of delight or revulsion, are more common than indifference to such an addictive commodity, and the range of recipes round the world for this widely distributed and highly nutritious food is enormous. Those from Italy are some of the best. We think of fish as perishable and beautiful, a local,

ephemeral food to be enjoyed fresh and simply cooked. Salt cod and STOCKFLSH are the complete opposite, as old as the rocks on which they are dried and sometimes bashed, they carry a heavy baggage of history, politics, commerce, religion, and linguistics. The name *baccalà* comes from the Spanish *bacalao*, which comes with a bit of twitching from the Dutch *kabeljauw*, close to *cabillaud*, the French for fresh cod. *Stoccafisso* seems to come from the Dutch *stokvisch* or German *Stockfisch*, perhaps because it was so dry it seemed like a stick, or was hung to dry on sticks or rods.

Baccalà can be seen hanging in food shops, where there is usually an implement, a sort of hinged blade attached to a board, for slicing off pieces large or small, as customers require. It then has to be taken home, washed of surplus salt, and put to soak, changing the water often, for anything from 12 to 24 to 48 hours, depending on the size and saltiness of the fish, bearing in mind that too much soaking can make the flesh soggy and tasteless, and too little leave it desperately salty and stringy. Baccalà can also be bought ready soaked from great tubs, which used to stand brim full outside the shops on Fridays for strict observers of the Church's dietary laws. Once a cheap staple food, it is now something of an expensive luxury, when handled with care, and expensive restaurants all over Italy offer smooth, sophisticated versions of what in the past was sometimes a dish of doubtful appeal. Misunderstandings can arise in the VENETO and FRIULI—VENEZIA

GIULIA, where stockfish is confusingly called "bacalà," but since various kinds of dried white fish known as stockfish are now hard to come by outside of Italy, many fall back on *baccalà* when trying out the many entrancing stockfish recipes of the region. The method for cooking *Baccalà alla vicentina* of Verona (*see* STOCKFISH) can be adapted to salt cod, reducing the soaking and cooking times.

Venice has *baccalà mantecata*, similar to *brandade de morue*, but patriots and purists see the Venetian recipe as superior in every way. Soaked *baccalà* is pounded with a little garlic and olive oil in a mortar to make a smooth thick paste; this is transferred to a pot and beaten with a wooden spoon, gradually adding a light olive oil drop by drop, until the fish has taken up what it can handle, which can sometimes be diluted in the process with warm milk, to make a light but pungent cream, sometimes with finely chopped garlic added at the end. (Stockfish gives a smoother, almost fibreless mixture.)

The traditional Roman recipe *Baccalà al' agro dolce* is bright with tomatoes, cooked in wine and vinegar moderated with sugar, and flavoured with pine nuts, sultanas, and pepper, sometimes spices and *peperoncino* (*see* CHILLI PEPPER) as well. Naples has a simple dish, *Baccalà alla pizzaiola*, in which prepared salt cod is simmered a short while with black peppercorns and bay leaves, drained and dried and put in a dish, covered with breadcrumbs, chopped parsley, capers, peeled and diced fresh tomatoes, a good amount of dried oregano, and plenty of pepper, covered with olive oil and left to mature in a medium oven for half an hour or so.

BACI DI DAMA

are summed up by Carol Field: "button-shaped buttery cookies fused with a spot of chocolate from Tortina in PIEDMONT, where sweets with somewhat frivolous, evocative names were served in the mid-19th century to men seriously at work creating a united Italy." These are small enough to pop into a mouth pursed for a kiss, as are many other little cookies with the name *baci*, like the well-known commercial chocolate cookies *baci Perugina*. They are not to be confused with BOCCA DI DAMA, a large light sponge cake made with almonds.

BACON.

See LARDO, PANCETTA, PIG'S FAT.

BAGEL

is a strange term to find in a book on Italian food. But although bagels are loved the world over as a manifestation of New York deli gastronomy, and have become the American national bread, it is by no means certain that they are Jewish or German or Polish in origin. (Balinska, 2006). How they got to New York and triumphed there is only the last, and quite recent, stage in their history. The name *bagel* is said to derive from *beugel*, a German dialect word for ring or bracelet, looking somewhat like a stirrup— the irregular shape of a hand-rolled bagel. We are asked to believe that 17th-century Viennese bakers, already working overtime to produce their celebratory croissants, were also commemorating the defeat of the Turks by the Polish Jan Sobiesky by offering up facsimiles of his stirrups, though it is hard to believe how a stirrup shaped like a bagel could function effectively. Stirrup-shaped bread was described by Maria Vittoria della Verde quite a while before the final defeat of the Turks (*see* BREADS, BRAIDED). In Italy, ring-shaped breads have been made in a variety of shapes and flavourings for centuries, many of them with the techniques we associate with bagels—a ring of yeasted dough first dunked in boiling water, dried, then baked in the oven. Leaving aside the symbolic aspects of its circular form, the ring shape is handy for storage, display and eating, as many images of Italian street vendors show. (*See* BREADS, RING-SHAPED.)

BAGNA CAUDA (*caôda*) is a hot sauce made with salt anchovies, garlic, butter, and olive oil, in which prepared, mainly raw, vegetables are dipped and eaten as an ANTIPASTO. This Piedmontese speciality can be made in many different ways, sometimes with garlic tamed by cooking first in milk, but the basic method is to soften the chopped or sliced garlic in the butter, without browning, then add three times as much light olive oil, preferably Ligurian, and some salt anchovies, cleaned and trimmed, gently stirring all together on the lowest possible heat until all dissolves in a dense aromatic sauce. This needs to be kept hot at table with a spirit lamp or a night-light under its earthenware pot. The prepared vegetables can be fennel, cardoons, celery, sweet peppers, raw young artichokes, radishes, and white cabbage, depending on what is in season. Their fresh bitterness makes a wonderful contrast to the rich mellow tangy sauce.

BAGÒSS is produced in Brescia in LOMBARDY in an area of high pastures rich in grass and herbs where cattle graze in the summer months and the herdsmen make the cheese on the spot, with traditional methods and equipment, tending each form daily, dry salting for several months, turning constantly, brushing off the mould and anointing the crust with oil, a labour of love that produces a mellow aromatic cheese, sometimes coloured with saffron. The custom of letting the cheeses mature under a layer of dried cow's dung is said to enhance the flavour, but this may be a myth (a neat way of concealing the precious cheeses from invading barbarians) or an invention to tease the health police.

BAICOLI are a Venetian biscuit made from a yeasted buttery dough which is sliced, after a preliminary baking, with a serrated knife to look like little ears of corn. They are taken with coffee and chocolate, and dipped into wine.

BALSAMIC VINEGAR, *aceto balsamico*, is a loaded name. It implies a precious substance, a spice, an aromatic plant, a perfume, a medicine, a cordial—in other words, an exceptional vinegar with all of these attributes. But it is not a vinegar, and is not produced in the same way, even though in the early stages of its manufacture a vinegar mother may or may not be used. The genuine product—recognized by the precise wording of its name, *aceto balsamico tradizionale di Modena*, and the characteristic shape of the flask in which it is bottled—is a dense, aromatic condiment. In the past, a superfluity of grapes produced a year's supply of fresh young wine, a plentiful amount of vinegar, and much must to boil down to the thick sweet fruity syrup, *sapa*, or *saba*, which was used as a universal sweetener or a filling for tarts. The discovery of the complex changes which turn this reduced must into an extraordinary condiment remains a mystery, but references in classical literature have been interpreted as evidence that something like it has been known for centuries. Virgil (*Georgics*, I, 295–296), quoted in Benedetti, 1999) evokes a simple peasant couple in Padania (*balsamico*'s territory today):

> *aut dulcis musti Vulcano decoquit umorem*
> *et foliis undam trepidi despumat aheni.*
> the fire concentrates the essence of
>   the sweet must,
> and [the peasant] skims with leaves
>   the froth from the boiling
>   cauldron.

The condiment we know is made mainly from must of the white *Trebbiano di Castelvetro* grape, which is traditionally boiled slowly down to one-half or a third of its original volume in huge vats over open fires. This concentrated sweet yet acidic must is then allowed to rest for a year in demijohns or barrels, scrupulously rinsed with boiling vinegar, where initial fermentation takes place. In the course of the following years, the *balsamico* comes to maturity, and after this an ageing process sets in. After the first year, the concentrated must is transferred to the first of a series of wooden barrels, where it will be left to work for another year and subsequently siphoned off, year after year, into barrels of diminishing size, made from a variety of different woods, including cherry, chestnut, mulberry, ash, pear, and oak, each contributing to the aroma of the finished product. The set of barrels is known as a *batteria*. They are housed, not in a cellar, but on their sides in attics or specially constructed lofts, where they experience the truly gruesome changes in climate characteristic of the region, from the oppressively hot humid summers to the unpleasantly cold damp foggy winters. The barrels have a hole in the topmost side, big enough for the *acetaio* to be able to sample the aromas and peer inside and monitor conditions as the liquid matures over the years. Covered with a fine linen cloth or a smooth stone, this aperture also allows the product to evaporate and breathe, exposed to micro-organisms in the atmosphere, which mingle with the yeasts and bacterial acids within, to contribute to the evolution of this rich and complex brew. As the years pass, the liquid becomes more and more concentrated and more and more aromatic, controlled by the judgment of the *acetaio*, who continuously checks and evaluates the contents of the barrels, topping them up from younger barrels or with fresh must, until his or her experience pronounces the *balsamico* ready for use. It is then submitted for evaluation and authentication by the panel of experts of the organization which administers the production of the genuine *aceto balsamico tradizionale*. (This entry is based on information supplied by the Consorzio tra produttori dell'aceto balsamico tradizionale di Modena, who, together with a similar or-

ganization at Spilamberto, maintain and defend, with considerable heroism and expertise, the integrity of their product).

As we have seen, the terrain, within the geographical limits of what was the Dukedom of Modena, the variety of grape (which is mainly *Trebbiano di Castelvetro*, from the mountain slopes of the region but can also include *Lambrusco Graspa Rossa* from the plains and *Ancellotta, Occhio di Gatta, Berzemino, Spergola,* and *Ciocchella* from the central region), and the microclimate of the area all contribute to the factors which make this product unique. The process is not labour intensive, but the expense of the specially made and carefully maintained barrels and the cost of the ever-diminishing liquid they house makes for an inevitably expensive product, retailing at anything from $100 to $500 for a small bottle. The sensitivity and expertise of the producer is based on years of experience, but an error of judgment or a bacteriological misfortune might mean the loss of a costly batch and all the capital locked up in it. The profits are not huge, given the time and materials involved, but the need to protect the integrity of the product is critical. Inferior or fraudulent versions can be offered to a gullible public, to the detriment of the consumers and producers of the genuine article. Hence the need for an extremely rigorous blind tasting and evaluation, and the spate of technical and scientific investigations by chemists and microbiologists, to ensure the quality of the authentic, DOC-protected product.

The blind tastings are conducted on the premises of the Consorzio, where the anonymous samples from members are independently evaluated by a panel of segregated experts, under a vast range of headings, totted up and scrutinized; only then can the submitted batches, if up to the desired standard, be bottled and labelled on the premises, using the Consorzio's equipment and labels, and handed back to the producer to keep for his or her own use or for sale.

By the time this expensive liquid has reached our kitchen cupboards, the problem of what to do with it needs to be addressed. Certainly not to be splashed promiscuously over a wide range of things, as happens with what we can only suspect is not the real thing. Genuine *aceto balsamico tradizionale di Modena* is best treated with restraint, taken on its own as a liqueur or tonic, a few drops dribbled over a home-made vanilla ice cream, added to a salad of sliced pears, crushed raspberries and rocket, salt and olive oil (this recipe is from the restaurant Lancellotti near Modena), as a last-minute condiment to a plainly grilled steak, or the voluptuous local usage, *battesimo*, of pouring some over chunks of Parmesan cheese at the end of a meal.

BANQUET, *banchetto*, is still a feature of Italian life; in the past the Italian banquet was synonymous with wealth, luxury, and

---

Official definition of *Aceto Balsamico di Modena*; from the Maestri Assaggiatori della Consorteria, Camera di Commercio di Modena, 1976, subsequently officially recognised by the Ministero dell'Agricoltura e delle Foreste by means of a "decreto" and a "disciplinare" of 5 April 1983:

> *Il vero aceto balsamico naturale (tradizionale) è prodotto nell'area degli antichi domini estensi.*
>
> *È ottenuto da mosto cotto, maturato per lenta acetificazione derivata da naturale da naturale fermentazione a da progressiva concentrazione mediente lunghissimo invecchiamento in serie di vaselli di legni diversi, senza alcuna addizione di sostanze aromatiche.*
>
> *Di colore scuro bruno, carico, lucente, manifesta la propria densità in una corretta, scorrevole sciropposità.*
>
> *Ha un profumo caratteristico e complesso, penetrante, di evidente, ma gradevole ed armonica acidità.*
>
> *Di tradizionale ed inimitabile sapore dolce e agro, ben equilibrato, si offre generosamente pieno, sapido, con sfumature vellutate in accordo con i caratteri olfattivi che gli sono propri.*

The true natural (the term now used is "traditional") balsamic vinegar is produced within the area of the historic domains of the Este family. It is produced from cooked grape must, matured by a slow acidification derived from natural fermentation and from a progressive concentration by means of very long ageing in a series of vessels of different woods, without the addition of any aromatic substances. A shiny dark brown in colour, its correct density is indicated by a certain fluid viscosity.

It has a characteristically complex perfume, somewhat powerful but pleasing, with an agreeable and harmonious acidity. With its traditional and well-balanced sweet/sour flavour, it is generously full-bodied, with a velvet texture in accordance with its appropriate olfactory qualities.

refinement throughout Europe; today it is a way of celebrating weddings, anniversaries, birthdays, and all the life events that provide an excuse for a family celebration. Banquets go on for many hours, with a leisurely succession of dishes, often prepared by the extended family, although there are many establishments that specialise in banquets, serving treasured local specialities and wines.

In the past, banquets were a means of cementing political and dynastic arrangements, celebrating weddings, reconciliations, births, and victories, as well as a good way of luring an enemy to his destruction with the promise of a feast, as happened in Rimini in 1323 when one of the nastier Malatesti, Ramberto, invited Umberto, count of Ghiaggiuolo, who was conspiring a take-over of the City of Rimini, to a banquet where he was assassinated at the start of the meal. *"Andare a tavola con i Malatesti"* came to mean risking life and liberty.

Ostentatious display and conspicuous consumption were what banquets were about, as well as eating, and often in the Middle Ages the food was plentiful but gross, and the displays—hefty table decorations in the form of wooden castles full of warriors, or a roast stag put back in its skin, displayed in a mock forest—were spectacular but somewhat crude. The Renaissance brought refinement and more delicate manners, with a move away from big roasts and towards carefully made dishes, beautifully arranged on silver, gold, and the decorative new ceramics that were being developed, with elegant glass and beautifully woven and embroidered tablecloths and napkins, changed throughout the meal, and with music and dancing rather than the rugged references to hunting and battles. These banquets have been chronicled by observers, and many ambassadors' reports fill in the details omitted in the accounts to be found in cookery texts and works on carving and household management. We have two contemporary accounts

of a feast held to welcome members of the Medici family to Rome in the 15th century, at the end of which—what with the heat in an enclosed space, a wooden structure arranged like an amphitheatre for lesser guests to view the diners—things got out of hand, and the ritual distribution of leftovers became a mêlée of cooked chickens and rabbits flying through the air. The marriage of Costanzo Sforza to Camilla of Aragon in Pesaro in 1475, an affair of splendour, was chronicled in detail in an account circulated in manuscript, with miniatures in colour of mythical beings taking part in the ceremonies, including the resplendent peacock in his plumage.

Information can be found in paintings, of banquet scenes in their own right, or Bible stories involving feasting, like the marriage at Cana, or genre scenes in which details of pies, cakes, roasts, and table settings can be glimpsed; and still lifes show luxury items like decanters and glasses, fruit, slices of ham and *salame*, and cooked dishes. VERONESE and his contemporaries painted huge, larger-than-life–sized canvases showing biblical feasts in modern settings and with contemporary dress, with all the bustle, noise, and confusion of servants and pages coming in and out with food and drink, bringing Scappi's static menus to life. The worldly secular atmosphere of these paintings got Veronese into trouble with the Inquisition, which he side-stepped by renaming *The Last Supper* as *Feast in the House of Levi*.

The new sensibility could not do away with old favourites like the peacock in his plumage who could be set up to strut down the table belching forth flames, or the very large pie full of live birds or baby rabbits, who would frolic among the guests, who duly pretended to be startled. Later these displays became more ingenious, with machinery lowering surprises from above or lowering tables down to the room below. Perhaps the ultimate banquets were those arranged for Christina of Sweden in 1668, on one of her visits to Rome, where hopes of converting a Protestant of royal blood to Catholicism were an incentive to lavish displays of hospitality. The wayward Christina was no gourmet; her complex personality rose above mere food and drink, and she was more concerned with the symbolism and design of the ornate table settings than the dishes prepared for her. She ate little, but treasured the watercolour sketches Sévin made showing the *trionfi*—elaborate sugar sculptures, perfect works of art commissioned from artists of the calibre of Bernini—displayed among the other elements of the meal.

French fashions in dining spread inexorably among the nobility, and Corrado's menus show the changed sequence of courses, designed to be served on a table laid according to a beautifully engraved diagram indicating the place settings and the position of every dish, bowl, and tureen. It is a pleasure to note his subversive use of French terms for defiantly Neapolitan dishes.

The influence of the Italian banquet throughout Europe has been described in many works which give details of menus, ceremonies, and recipes, by writers as diverse as Sir Roy Strong, Claudio Benporat, Nichola Fletcher, Carolin Young, Ken Albala and many more. They are the ones to turn to for more detail than this work can give.

BARBA DI FRATE. *See* AGRETTI.

BARLEY, *orzo*, was used in the ancient world, but by Roman times it was mainly cooked to make a nourishing mush for the lower orders, soldiers or animals, or made into a medicinal potion, *tisana*, which survives in our *orzata* or "barley water," a refreshing drink, which can also be made with ground almonds or other nuts, sweetened and diluted with water to taste. It is similar to the *horchata* of Spain, which is usually made with tiger nuts.

Polenta was the name for the mush of grains and vegetables, which was later transferred to the POLENTA we know today, made with corn meal. Roasted and with the outer husk removed, "pearl" barley is used today in regional soups and stews, like one from Altoaltesino in which the barley is cooked in a light meat broth or water seasoned with garlic, onion, parsley, and carrot together with sliced leeks, potatoes, and celery, and some chopped SPECK. The flour is low in gluten and so does not make good bread, but is sometimes used in FLATBREADS and biscuits.

An ancient bread, survival food for shepherds living for months on end with their flocks in alpine regions, is still made in LIGURIA today: *carpesina* or *pan d'ordiu*, a fermented bread made from stone-ground barley, formed into long loaves which are then cut with a cord into slices which are baked slowly in a low oven, turned over and baked some more; long-keeping and hard as rocks, these are intended to be soaked in water, wine, or milk and dressed with herbs, oil, or tomato. They are similar to the *friselle* or *friselle* of PUGLIA and CAMPANIA, which are hard and crispy, made usually with barley and wholemeal flour, looking like *ciambelle*, sliced horizontally, then baked again; they keep a long time and are destined to be soaked for a short while in water and then dressed with oil, aromatics, and whatever fragrant things are to hand, to make a refreshing and filling salad. The soaking should be rapid, so that some crunch remains. Legends from Puglia would have us believe that Aeneas brought these loaves to Italy in his baggage—something every sensible mariner or shepherd would have with him on long journeys.

A version of the *farinata* of Liguria can be made today with barley flour rather than the usual chickpea flour. Based on ancient Greek and Roman practises, the batter is mixed with linseeds and ground coriander, and the

Though a sprig of fresh basil is now a welcome addition to any kitchen, it was once controversial in Italy due to its ability to both attract scorpions and sometimes counteract the venom of a scorpion bite. (Shutterstock)

resultant pancake or flatbread is served with herbs and olive oil, as explained by Nico Valerio (Valerio, 1989, p. 213).

BASIL, *basilico, Ocimum basilicum* of the Labiatae family, originated in tropical Asia and needs warmth and sunlight, flourishing wherever it finds them. Several varieties are commonly cultivated in Italy: the broad-leaved variety, which is usually commercially produced, especially around Genoa, and bought in bunches as required; the beautiful Dark Opal and various kinds which do well in pots; and the small-leaved little bush basil, *O. minimum,* which has a particularly intense aroma. Pots of this basil appear in art and literature as handy receptacles for the heads of murdered lovers (Bocaccio and later Keats told the tale of Isabella, who mournfully concealed the head of her murdered lover in a plant-pot) or more usefully as insect repellent. Legend connects the herb with fertility and divine and regal status. The Virgin in CRIVELLI'S painting *The Annunciation with Saint Emidius*—executed in 1486 to celebrate the political independence of Ascoli Piceno in the MARCHE—has a pot of basil on the windowsill of her modern town house, where it has both symbolic and prac-

tical use, celebrating her holiness and fecundity while perfuming the air and keeping the flies out. A century later, the great botanist Mattioli, in his commentary on the *Materia Medica* of Dioscorides, tells how basil is so well loved in Italy that every house, particularly in towns and cities, has a pot of it on the windowsill or veranda, or growing in the garden. The connection with scorpions generated much controversy—it was said to attract them, or mitigate the venom of their bite; if for "scorpion" we understand any insect bite or skin infection, this seems reasonable, the pot of basil on the windowsill keeping away insects (the "scorpions" that lurked under the pot might have been slugs or earthworms), while the perfume of the leaves "comforted the heart" (reducing stress), and a poultice made with the leaves macerated in vinegar soothed the inflammation of insect bites and was good for cardiac troubles. Medical theory during the Renaissance was confusing; some agreed with ancient physicians who held that basil could upset the stomach, cloud vision, and drive one mad, while others agreed with Pliny that it did nothing of these things, but had medicinal uses. Platina dismissed most of the superstitious stuff about scorpions and sanctioned moderate use of a delicious herb that everyone was apparently using in abundance, regardless of theory.

It is a long way in space and time from the Marche to 18th-century Naples, where Corrado used basil with pigeons, birds which figure prominently in Crivelli's painting. Perhaps the worthy citizens of Ascoli Piceno cooked the domestic pigeons in the dovecotes high up in the top left-hand corner with basil from their window pots. Corrado suggested stewing the pigeons in good meat broth and butter with celery and an onion stuck with cloves and bits of cinnamon, the finished dish perfumed with basil. He describes a sauce to go with pigeons made of finely chopped basil stirred into spiced melted butter and thickened with the yolks of hard-boiled eggs.

Basil has an affinity with cloves, and the clove-scented pink or carnation (*garofano*) has holy associations, too. The nail-like form of the spice reminds us of the nails used to crucify Christ. This was not lost on Crivelli, who placed pots of carnations in meaningful relationship to his images of the Virgin, but the worldly cleric Corrado was less likely to be motivated by anything other than gastronomy in his use of basil with pigeons.

In another recipe Corrado fries jointed pigeons in butter with basil and spices, degreases the pan with broth, and thickens the sauce with cream. He made a basil soup using broth from pigeons stewed with basil; which is then thickened with the flesh of roast pigeon pounded with soaked bread and pine nuts and then passed through a sieve and mixed with chopped basil. The resulting soup is then poured over sippets of toast previously soaked in the broth. A modern salad of tomatoes, mozzarella, and basil, bathed in extra virgin olive oil, is a classic only worth making with first-class ingredients. Rubbery cheese, tasteless tomatoes, and flaccid basil will not do.

In the classic *Pasta alla Norma*, the pungency of Sicilian basil joins with garlic, tomato, fried eggplant, and salted dried ricotta in a sauce for rigatoni or *maccheroni*; the best recipe for this is in Simeti 1989, p. 39; we begin to understand the impact this substantial dish had on Andrea Camilleri's wayward Sicilian cop, Salvo Montalbano. Reluctant to prolong an interview with a frail old lady whose diet he felt sure would consist of pallid invalid food, he found himself pressed to stay to lunch and regaled with *Pasta alla Norma* followed by a hearty *stuffatino* (Camilleri, 1998, p. 51).

An uncooked pasta sauce, also from Simeti, is made by pounding garlic cloves, salt, dried red *peperoncino* (see CHILLI), and plenty of basil leaves in a mortar until smooth, then gradually incorporating olive oil bit by bit, adding this to some skinned and chopped ripe tomatoes and stirring with dried ricotta into the pasta. With more oil this mixture becomes *ammogghiu*, a wonderful dressing for grilled meat or fish, or fried eggplants (Simeti, 1989, p. 170).

Basil is perhaps too well known as the main ingredient of *pesto genovese*, where its sweet and beautiful fragrance is often overcome by the conflicting elements of this traditional Ligurian sauce (*see* PESTO). A more subtle use of basil in a sauce is Pietro Leemann's: he pounds (or liquidizes) fresh basil with peeled walnuts and olive oil, passes the resultant purée through a sieve, and uses it to dress a dish of freshly made *tagliolini* and tiny green beans (Leemann, 1991, p. 100).

Some maintain that basil leaves should always be torn, never cut with a knife, as contact with metal causes browning. In fact, browning, the result of action by enzymes in the plant itself, happens, according to Harold McGee, regardless of whether the leaves are cut or torn (McGee, 1992, p. 55). His agonies over the discolouration of pesto can be avoided by making it at the last minute, bunging it onto the freshly cooked pasta, stirring in rapidly, and eating with speed and concentration, as all good Italians do. That way the browning remains a theoretical problem. (The wider question of whether to tear, cut up, or pound salad leaves or herbs or vegetables is a matter of aesthetics as well as dogma; you choose the method to give the results you want—herbs pounded to a purée for a sauce, or herbs finely or coarsely chopped to scatter over a finished dish, or finely sliced vegetables softened in a flavoured oil.)

BASILICATA, also known as Lucania, is sandwiched between CAMPANIA and PUGLIA, with CALABRIA in the south, and with coastlines on the Tyrrhenian and

Mediterranean seas. It has a shared gastronomic heritage with it neighbours and the distinction of giving its name to an ancient and much loved sausage, LUCANICA. History and climate dealt harshly with this mountainous region, where the fertile soil, when watered, produces incomparable vegetables. But waves of settlers who drove out the original inhabitants had abrasive and hostile relations with the Romans, and Lucania had none of the advantages of neighbouring Apulia, with its gentler terrain and two main roads for smooth connections to Rome, with a traffic of trade and travellers who brought prosperity and outside contacts. Lucania was stuck for millennia in versions of the feudal system (long before its invention), getting the worst of all worlds, exploitation without protection, and a legacy of grasping absentee landlords, ferocious bandits, and rebellious peasants. The wild beauty of the landscape was celebrated by Horace, whose birthplace, Venusia, was situated on the border between Apulia and Lucania. His love of the Italian countryside was formed there, and he remembered a happy childhood playing in the woods on Mount Voltur (Dalby, 2000, p. 63), where as a "brave baby and divinely favoured" he fell asleep outside his wet nurse's cottage, and was saved from marauding vipers and bears by protective woodpigeons who strewed bay and myrtle over him. Game, good wines, and excellent bread, wool from the famous flocks, and long periods of peace made this a happier time than later centuries, when squabbles between church and state and the complexities of European politics brought misery to what could have been a more prosperous area. Neither trade nor industry nor the princely courts of more settled regions were able to make an impact on Lucania/Basilicata. The cooking is consequently a peasant cuisine, based on self-sufficiency and an inventive use of local products— cured and fresh meat from pigs and sheep; cheeses, pasta and bread from the local hard wheat flour; and a wide variety of wild and cultivated herbs and vegetables. This food has a character and integrity formed by past hardships. Many Italian writers describe the generous use of chillies with a mixture of horror and regret, but their arrival is relatively recent, and their intense flavour and bite have to be appreciated in the context of a long history of seasoning bland foodstuffs like pulses and grains with cheap substitutes for the expensive spices like those used in the famous Apician *lucanicae.* Bitter and strong-tasting wild herbs enlivened bread and grain porridges, so when a cheap, easy-to-grow plant bearing a range of hot and piquant flavours arrived from the New World, it met a long-felt need, and has flourished ever since. Flavour plus heat is not unsubtle, and those who denigrate the uses of chillies could learn a lot from the refined use of them in the cooking of the New World.

The nurture, and cult, of the pig as a source of survival foods was widespread. It was said that in the 3rd century BC, Roman soldiers from the north took *lucanicae* back home with them, but these well-spiced, strong flavoured sausages (*see* LUCANICA) were probably known throughout the ancient world long before the compilation of the collection of recipes associated with the somewhat nebulous glutton Apicius.

Other pork products from Basilicata, like the *soppressate* of Lagonegro and Sasso di Castalda, are made locally by small producers for their own consumption, using the nobler parts of the local black breed of pig, running semiwild among woodland and farmyard, with a delicate seasoning of salt and black pepper and sometimes fennel: luxury products that resist industrialisation, a prized heritage of the years of uninterrupted hardship. And the uses made of the OFFAL and less appealing parts are equally splendid—the *pezzenta* of mountainous areas is made of head meat and the less prized organs, all cut up with a knife and well seasoned with salt, wild fennel, and chopped chillies, matured for a while, and eaten grilled or boiled with local vegetables. A similar version, *vecchiareddra*, is made in Rotonda in the province of Potenza, using lungs and lights and the bits and pieces unsuitable for the finer salami or sausages, together with skin and cartilaginous stuff that gives the cooked sausage the glutinous qualities of COTECHINO. *Ventresca di Rionero* is a version of PANCETTA, fatty pork belly seasoned with a generous amount of garlic and chilli and eaten as a titillating antipasto rather than used in cooking.

The cheeses of Basilicata are among some of the finest in the south; the *caciocavallo podolica della Basilicata* is made from the incomparable milk of the *podolica* race of cows (*see* CHEESE). These intelligent, semiwild creatures flourish on rugged Apennine terrain, and do not take to domestication, so in spite of the increasing demand for this legendary cheese, it is an uphill task for the SLOW FOOD Presidio to get protection for the artisan processes, supply appropriate help to the producers, come to grips with the tyranny of EEC milk quotas, and establish commercial outlets. *Burrino* is a soft cheese based on milk fats extracted from the whey of *podolica* milk and matured in a skin of *caciocavallo*; it is sometimes made with a piece of *sopressata* inserted in the middle, the salty *salame* contrasting with the buttery sweetness of the cheese. Most parts of the region produce ricotta, to be eaten very fresh or, salted and matured, to be used as a grating cheese and condiment for many dishes. There are many creamy young sheep's and goat's cheeses, in particular *casieddu di Moliterno*, a soft cheese of goat's milk strained through ferns, flavoured with *nepitella*, and matured wrapped in the same foliage.

Meat from animals reared for their wool or milk was a rare treat, but the pig, which ran wild with the sheep and goats, was venerated in life and in death, for the way every bit of its carcass could be used, fresh and pre-

served. LARD (rendered pork fat), seasoned with chilli, is used as appetiser, as a spread on bread, and to flavour many cooked dishes.

Pigneti is a dish of lamb or mutton, cut into chunks and cooked in a sealed pot along with potatoes, onions, tomatoes, pieces of salami, and *pecorino*, and seasoned with chilli; starting in a very hot oven after the bread baking, it cooked slowly in the dying heat. There are many robust dishes using chopped innards, seasoned and put into the intestines of sheep and lamb, *gnomirelli* or *gnumariddi*, and fried in lard with onion and garlic.

Bread from the local wheat is famous for its quality and keeping powers. It used to be made in huge round or horseshoe-shaped loaves, cooked in communal wood-fired ovens, and each household had a wooden stamp to press into the dough the initials of the head of the household. These *marchi* were in common use but are now museum pieces, their primitive beauty loaded with symbolism (*see* BREAD). In the area around Matera, a loaf that can weigh from one-half to 20 kilos is made from hard durum wheat and a sourdough from the previous batch. The long slow rising process and the large size of the loaf produce intense flavours. With large loaves, the organisms in the centre of the dough are not destroyed by the heat of the oven and continue working away, contributing to the flavour and the nutritional content of the bread. From the province of Potenza comes *mescuotte*, a dough made with lard, sugar, and anise seeds, shaped into rings, knots, or shapes like the letter *M*, briefly plunged into boiling water, dried, and then baked in the oven until hard (*see* BREADS, RING-SHAPED). A FLATBREAD or FOCACCIA, *ruccul* or *ruccolo*, is flavoured with olive oil, garlic, oregano, chilli, and a pinch of salt.

Scarcedda, a traditional sweet preparation, is ricotta in a short pastry with a hard-boiled egg concealed within, bringing good luck to the person who finds it in his or her portion.

Vegetables from the fertile soil go into dishes like *ciaudedda*: potatoes, young artichokes, and broad beans sweated slowly with onions mixed with chopped *pancetta* or lard and olive oil. For *ciammotta*, sliced aubergines, diced potatoes, and sweet peppers are fried in oil separately and then finished slowly together with chopped tomatoes, garlic, and salt. A special bright red aubergine, *Solanum Aethiopicum*, a late-comer (arriving probably from Africa centuries after the dark purple version came to Europe) is grown in Rotonda on the edge of the Pollino national park.

BASSANO, JACOPO DA PONTE

(c. 1510–92), and his sons belonged to a family of artists working in Bassano in the VENETO. Much of their work combines religious subjects with genre scenes, and from them we can learn about daily life, markets, kitchens, and banquets. This wealth of detail must reflect the desire of patrons for a naturalistic, if sometimes idealised, representation of their own affluent lives. Leandro Bassano's *Feast of Anthony and Cleopatra* in the National Museum in Stockholm shows the feast itself in the middle distance, with part of the busy kitchen in the foreground. This feast was the ultimate competitive dinner party, in which the couple vied with each other to see who could spend the most, with Cleopatra compounding this silliness by dissolving a priceless pearl earring in vinegar and swallowing the lot. The banquet food is sketched in, but the table setting is of great interest, with a lace-trimmed linen cloth over an oriental carpet and the succession of gold and silver dishes close together and overlapping, some balanced on each others' rims, with yet more being borne ceremoniously in from the kitchen, showing with accuracy the presentation of many of the festive meals Scappi and his contemporaries describe. A harassed seated cook keeps a watchful eye on the succession of dishes, while preparing a fowl which is being fixed on a spit by a servant maid and her assistant. He is trimming the gizzard and liver, which will be tucked under the wings and in the crook of the thighs, just as we observe in genre scenes from the Netherlands. We note how the head and neck of the creature (a wild duck?) are retained, to be wrapped round the spit and then twisted under a wing, to secure the bird as it roasts. The final course (*ultimo servzio di credenza*— the term "dessert" from the French *deservir* only came into use much later) is waiting to be brought on: frosted cookies shaped like stars and mushrooms, a bowl of comfits (sugared almonds, fennel or anise seeds) and a decorative open tart, with tall thin upright comfits (sugar-coated sticks of cinnamon or eringo root) standing up, looking a bit like candles, which they are not. This is not great art, but a treasure trove of visual references.

Another Bassano painting, more characteristic, shows the meal at Emmaus, with Christ and his guests relegated to a table in the distance, on an open terrace, the last light of a lurid sunset illuminating the interior of the inn's kitchen in the foreground. The cook, exhausted at the end of a hot, busy day, is slumped on a chair before the dying fire, while the ever-busy womenfolk toil over the pots and pans and food for the newly arrived guests. The same cook, probably painted from the same model, lords it over a laid table in another painting, *Christ in the House of Martha and Mary*; the cook instructs a woman busy cooking over an open fire, while in the foreground are displayed the fish, fowl, and pots and pans of the kitchen, and the household pets supping from their dishes. There is plenty of scope here for painters and their clients to moralise about the active and contemplative life, reinforced by the pastoral scene in the background, and at the same time enjoy realistic scenes from daily life, and the moody atmospherics of a north Italian sunset.

A big market scene is full of noise, bustle, and confusion: a butcher's stall, a poultry woman plucking a fowl, a variety of flatbreads, bagels, and rolled wafers on a white cloth, junk stalls, and kitchen equipment, with fruit and vegetables in carefully composed still lifes in the foreground. The symbolism is there for the asking (a sinister owl brooding over the butcher's meat, performing monkeys, faithful dogs, feral cats), but we value this crowded canvas as a companion to the crowded pages of Scappi and Messisbugo, a display of the products listed in their recipes.

BATTESIMO. *See* BALSAMIC VINEGAR.

BATTUTO is a mixture of LARDO, chopped cured pork fat or bacon, and finely chopped vegetables, usually celery, onion, carrot, garlic, and herbs pounded together to make a paste, which can be used to season many dishes, either as a SOFFRITTO— melted or lightly coloured in the pan at the start of a dish—or added at the end, perhaps to a hearty soup or a pot of beans, for extra flavour. Many recipes start with getting you to prepare a *battuto*, often specifying the vegetables and herbs to use, and any additions, like cubed ham. The basic mixture can sometimes be bought from the butcher ready made. Ada Boni uses the Roman version of a *battuto* in some characteristically robust recipes, where it would be hard to draw too fine a line between this and a *soffritto*, which she also calls a *pesto*. Her hearty *minestre* start with frying a *battuto* of chopped *lardo*, fatty ham or *guanciale* and chopped vegetables in *strutto* (lard), adding tomato and enough liquid to cook the main vegetable, which might be broccoli, peas, or endive, to which can then be added short pasta or rice, to finish cooking. She points out that a *battuto* is an alternative to a meat broth, which might not

have been to hand in the average Roman kitchen, a good example of the inventive richness of CUCINA POVERA.

BAY LEAVES, *Laurus nobilis*, of the Lauraceae family, should not be confused with laurel (*Prunus laurocerasus*), on account of one of its Italian names, *lauro*. (The alternative name is *alloro*.) The fragrant and decorative leaves crowned the brows of victors in war and those who excelled in athletics and the arts. Their association with Apollo is deftly handled in the statue by Gianlorenzo Bernini; at the precise moment when the face of the beautiful young god shows his hurt and surprise at Daphne's unexpected rejection, while the hapless nymph vibrates with anguish and horror at the impending rape, the leaves crushed beneath her left foot become the fronds and branches of the protective tree into which she is transformed with the timely help of the Earth Mother. Bay leaves deftly twitched from victor's reward to victim's defence, their fragrance soothing both the vanquished hero and the despairing maiden Bernini was a multimedia artist; he arranged our response to the perfume of those crushed leaves in the way he orchestrated the aromas and flavours of the banquet sugar sculptures designed for the delectation of prelates and princes (*see* BANQUETS). If, however, the nymph had been ingesting

Worn in wreaths on the heads of Roman warriors, bay leaves have since settled into their role as a savory addition to soups and sauces. (Shutterstock)

laurel leaves, with their highly hallucino-genic hydrocyanic acid content, the hapless Apollo, according to Robert Graves, would have been tangling with a wacky Maenad priestess, who "chewed laurel leaves as an intoxicant and periodically rushed out at the full moon, assaulted unwary travellers, and tore children and young animals in pieces."

A more restrained use of bay leaves both fresh and dry, is widespread today, mainly in savoury dishes; they are also used to perfume and preserve dried figs and fruit pastes, and flavour beer. Fresh bay leaves are pungent, with a bitterness which diminishes after dry-ing, but stale dried leaves are not much use. Bay leaves are used to flavour roasts, grilled and spit-roast meat and poultry, and used in stews, both fish and meat, and in marinades and pickling fluids. Recreations of classical Roman cooking deploy bay leaves under bread dough and pies before putting them in the oven, or cooking over hot coals, to stop them from sticking to the surface of the pot or baking tin.

Plentiful in a pumpkin risotto, they give added flavour to the other ingredients, and look decorative among the bright flesh of the *zucca* and the pale rice, served in the decora-tive hollowed-out shell of the pumpkin. Platina recommended fresh bay leaves, first softened in lard or oil, then dipped in spiced batter and fried, as being good for flatulence as well as delicious.

BEANS, *fagioli, Phaseolus vulgaris,* were brought to Italy from the New World in the early 16th century, to join *Vigna unguiculata, fagioli dall'occhio,* black-eyed peas (or beans) or cowpeas, which had been cultivated since Roman times, sometimes confusingly known as *Phaseolus sinensis* or *fagiolo dolico.* (Another kind of bean is the *Vicia faba, fava,* fava bean or BROAD BEAN.) These early black-eyed beans originated in Africa and spread to both the Far East and the Mediterranean,

were enjoyed by the ancient Egyptians and Greeks, and became a staple food for the Ro-mans, later to be immortalised by Annibale Carracci in his *Mangiafagioli* of 1583. Here a dish of beans is being eaten by an uncouth character in a fine linen shirt, at a well-appointed table. His unsophisticated man-ners, and the humble food, in a setting well above his station, create a dissonance that is like the *frottola* at a court banquet: a rustic theme, often with vulgar words, is performed by musicians at the cutting edge of modern refinement. Carracci was a bit late on the scene for Isabella d'Este, who promoted *frot-tolle* and was also fond of her food, but he hit the right note—enjoyment by the pampered rich of CUCINA POVERA. So his painting of a dish of beans, hanging on the wall of a rich patron, might have had the same impact as Munari's still life of fried eggs and hunks of parmesan; a celebration of the qualities of idealised peasant food, a theme that can be found all the way through the history of Italian gastronomy. The double-entendres and coarse themes of the *frottole* were sung by famous singers in peasant costume, just as beans and pulses could be seen as coarse food or a delicacy, depending on how they were prepared and presented.

The new beans from the New World were a useful and prolific plant; they enriched earth that had been depleted by other crops and filled in the gaps between slower grow-ing ones. They were more subtle and versatile than the older legumes. Good when young and green, the thin pods of *fagiolini,* cooked until just soft (but never ever underdone and crunchy!) and simply dressed with oil, salt, and pepper, have been a delicacy for cen-turies. When the pods are dry but the beans within still slightly moist they cook quickly, and are delicious. When dry, beans of all va-rieties keep well; if not too old they can be cooked without soaking, though just about all Italian recipes tell us to soak them to re-duce cooking time. In Mexico, their country of origin, they are often neither soaked nor drained, thus retaining flavour and nutrients. Many of the good things in beans get leached out into the soaking and cooking water, and are lost when they are drained. In fact, as they absorb water during cooking, and exude nutrients, the liquid they are cooked in gets more and more dense, as the beans "make their own sauce," as Harold McGee eloquently puts it, adding their own flavour and concentrating that of the dish—something it would be silly to throw away. The protein, vitamin, carbohydrate, and starch content of beans makes them an ideal complementary ingredient to pasta, maize polenta, or vegetable soups. Most regions have dishes with this enhanced nutritional value, and sometimes it works the other way round, with bacon fat, tomatoes, oil, or herbs giving a boost to the beans. The admonition not to add salt at the start is something of a myth, since it does not in fact harden the beans or slow down cooking. Old, stale beans will be hard and refuse to soften, whatever you do to them. Salt or baking soda actually speed cooking, but they can alter the texture and mouth feel, which you might wish to avoid. Long slow cooking is the best way to cook beans, with salt added whenever you please, and it has the advantage of getting rid of the substances that cause flatulence. The inclusion of acids, sugar, and calcium can help beans keep their shape during this lengthy process. The Tuscan bean pot or flask seems to meet all these requirements, and in *fagioli all'uccelletto*, the beans, soaked or unsoaked, with their traditional seasoning of garlic and sage, with olive oil, salt, and freshly ground pepper added before serving, are superb. The hearty *pisarei e fasò* of Emilia combines chewy little *gnocchetti* with *borlotti* beans finished in a rich sauce of *pancetta*, onions, garlic, and parsley, with a little tomato paste. The bean soup of Romagna is made with mature but not yet dry beans cooked in pounded cured pork fat (LARDO), parsley, and garlic, sometimes with the lovely glutinous addition of *cotiche* or *cotenne*, pork rind,

which also enriches the *fagioli con cotiche* of Lombardy, where the beans are first cooked with onion and celery, then added to a rich mixture of onion, celery, and carrot softened in chopped bacon and butter, seasoned with spices, garlic, and tomato paste, and finished slowly with cooked *borlotti* beans. RIBOLLITA is another Tuscan dish, in which *cannellini* or *toscanelli* beans join vegetables in a hearty soup served over slices of the hard salt-free bread of the region. There are variations on *pasta e fagioli* from all over Italy, some particularly sumptuous ones from Veneto in which the beans and accompanying vegetables can be sieved to thicken the broth, which is then enriched with herbs and garlic fried in oil, and the pasta cooked in the final brew. Potatoes can be a thickener, or flour can be added to the fried garlic and herbs, and the kinds of pasta will vary, from rich egg to plain flour and water. *Panissa is* a soup of beans and shellfish from Lazio, and in Campania there is a risotto from the Vercellese using fresh *borlotti* beans and rice. The rice is started off in a BATTUTO of PANCETTA and onion, then with red wine, and finished cooking with the bean liquid, to which the beans are finally added. A more complicated version from the Novarese includes vegetables (cabbage, celery, carrot, and tomato) which are cooked with the fresh beans, and the risotto is started in a *battuto* of *pancetta*, onion, butter, and some flavourful local salami, begun with red wine, and finished with the bean liquid. Sardinia has *fagioli alla gallurese*, in which dried beans are cooked until almost done, then finished with finely sliced cabbage and wild fennel and chopped onion. Chopped fresh tomatoes are put in towards the end, and the final touch is a dollop of pounded garlic and *lardo*. We know of *macco* as a purée of dried broad beans, mainly enjoyed in the south, but Scappi has a version, *minestra di fagioli secchi*, made from dried beans, finished with oil and cloves of garlic, seasoned with sage, pepper, cinnamon, and saffron, which he said was called *macco* in Lombardy, and sometimes also made with the addition of rice or yellow turnips. The expression *a macco*, or *a macca*, can mean an abundance, but may also connect with *ammacare*, which is about bashing or damaging something, which is what cooking does to the beans, a dish to be enjoyed in abundance.

By the early 17th century, Castelvetro was writing of beans and their versatility with affectionate nostalgia. He recalled how the women of Venice could gaze unseen at passers-by from behind a screen of green beans growing up white trellises set in window-boxes. He also wrote knowledgably of their uses, from the fresh green pods to dried beans cooked in a good meat broth, or simmered in several changes of water and seasoned with oil, salt, and pepper, "il suo ver condimento" (Mattioli had recommended GALANGAL, sugar, and long pepper to enhance their aphrodisiac properties) or cooked with shelled and peeled chestnuts, or puréed and seasoned with honey and spices as a filling for tarts or fritters.

BEEF, *bovino* or *carne bovina,* is now designated either VEAL, *vitello,* or beef, *bovino adulto,* but in the past there were more subdivisions—*vitello, vitellone, manzo, bue, vacca,* and *toro* (roughly: milk-fed veal, calf, young beef, mature beef, cow, and bull). *Bue,* both the animal and the meat, that of a male, castrated animal aged four years or more, is now falling out of use, and its flavourful, marbled flesh hard to come by. *Manzo* is the generic name for different cuts of beef of different races and ages, and there are regional variations which can be confusing, as can the different names for all the different cuts. Diagrams of the various regional cuts show 14 different detailed ways of dividing up a carcass. This is partly due to the different kinds of cattle reared in Italy today, all producing varying kinds and qualities of meat. The *cinque erre,* the five land races, are

chianina, marchigiana, maremmana, podolica, and *romagnola,* with the *piemontese* forming another group. There are other lesser races as well as the five main ones, and breeds from Great Britain and France have also been introduced and merged with local animals, so it would now be difficult to find a direct descendant of the primitive cattle, some wild and some domesticated, from which these races developed. Perhaps the *chianina* race is one of the purest and most ancient—great white beasts over two yards high, with beautiful heads, neat short legs, and strong feet, adaptable to hard work on harsh terrains. They originated in the Val di Chiana and are found in the provinces of Arezzo, Tuscany, Livorno, Pisa, Siena, and Perugia, and are valued for their strength and tender, marbled meat; a prime cut best known is *bistecca alla fiorentina.* They were known in Roman times; the snow-white cattle of Falerii, who grazed on the fertile green meadows and were brought to Rome to take part in sacrificial processions, were probably of the *chianina* race, and revered for their beauty and strength rather than for gastronomic reasons, so we have practically no evidence about the fate of the meat of the sacrificial beasts. There is only one beef recipe in Apicius, and few for veal. Mindful of the Mesopotamian hymn "Give the Gods a roast, a roast," one might speculate that this meat became the diet of the priesthood. The heads of horned cattle decorate the frieze round the outside of the Temple of Vesta in Tivoli, a reminder of the sacred role of these great white bulls. They can be seen in London at Tivoli Corner, part of the massive Bank of England complex designed in 1828 by Sir John Soane, who had made a pilgrimage to Tivoli to draw the temple and its inscription. White cattle in the backgrounds of works by Bellini and Carpaccio, tended by minders in vaguely classical drapery, could be references to antiquity as well as scenes from 15th-century daily life.

The combustion engine and developments in genetic manipulation have almost eliminated some of the all-purpose races of cattle that were used for work, meat, and milk. (For the role of high-milk-yield Friesians, see PARMESAN). However, the particular characteristics of a land race can be consolidated in breeds which are documented and regulated, with the help of genetic data banks, and the different races which developed in the regions of Italy to meet different geographical and climatic conditions are now being cherished, modified, and preserved. Looking at the DNA of animals and comparing it with information from archaeological studies opens up interesting speculations about the migration of humans; evidence from a recent study tentatively suggests that further research might show that the Etruscans, about whom we know so little, might have migrated by sea to Italy from the Fertile Crescent, bringing with them cattle whose DNA persists only in autochthonous bovines in Tuscany and Liguria.

The cattle in the background of Bellini's *Madonna of the Meadow* (in the National Gallery in London) resemble the kind now known as *piemontese*, descended from aurochs, *bos primigenius,* who roamed from the steppes of Central Asia over 30,000 years ago and came contentedly to a halt in the remote landlocked alpine valleys where they settled and later merged with zebu, *zebu primigenius* drifting in from northern India and later bred with cattle brought by waves of human migrants. This animal had the advantage of being a sturdy worker in the fields, a good milk producer, with tasty meat, a pleasant disposition, and useful longevity. In the parts of the Veneto painted by Bellini, the cattle were reared in lowland areas where these cherished beasts were watched over by attendants and kept in pens and enclosures, then driven into the surrounding hills and mountains for the summer pasture. In winter they shared their stalls during the *veglia* or *filò* with the peasant families who on cold nights would leave the chilly kitchen, the fire frugally put out after cooking, to crowd together with the animals for warmth, knitting, gossiping, receiving visits, and sipping grappa in a companionable animal and human fug, a means of social cohesion and good husbandry common in many agricultural areas until quite recently.

Today animals are reared in various ways—in free-range conditions, or partly loose and partly in stalls but fed with locally produced fodder, and in sophisticated modern "industrial" arrangements where hygiene and nutrition are strictly controlled. The use of growth hormones is now illegal, but enforcement is difficult. The cost of producing rare-breed, free-range, organic (*biologico*) meat is high, but a growing market exists, encouraged by *agriturismo,* in which people enjoy the pleasures of visiting and staying at an *azienda agricola* and eating and purchasing its products. But not all peasant cultures are kind to animals, and not all intensive conditions are cruel, so between the polarities of agribusiness and *agriturismo* lies a variety of pleasant and unpleasant possibilities, with an international demand for an abundance of cheap meat balanced by an expensive gourmet market for exquisite regional produce.

Where a recipe book says *manzo,* a general word for beef, you might have to consult a butcher if the name of the cut is uncertain. The meaning of *manzo* varies from one region to another; in Milan it can mean the meat of a mature animal, but in other parts of the north it is a young animal, three or so years old, with the tender cuts used for quick cooking, and the other parts for the renowned meat dishes of Lombardy, Piedmont, and the Veneto.

The tradition of rearing cattle as beasts of burden whose meat is sacrificed to the pot only when unable to work has provided a range of recipes for tough but tasty cuts, like the *brasato* of Piedmont and Genoa, where a whole piece of beef is cooked slowly in a good red wine. Rome also has meat dishes in which a tough cut is reduced to melting tenderness, with a similar concentration of wine and aromatics: CODA ALLA VACCI-NARA, *stufato*, and *garofolato*. The extreme treatment is the *lesso*, in which meat is cooked slowly with aromatics to extract every whiff of flavour, leaving the meat in a fairly boring state, but creating a wonderful broth. *See also* BOLLITO MISTO.

BEL PAESE is a bland industrial cow's milk cheese with a mild flavour and pleasant melting texture, inspired by Port Salut and Saint Paulin, and astutely named for the title of a best-seller by a cleric, Antonio Stoppani, by its inventor, Egidio Galbani, in the early 19th century. It is better to cook with than poor-quality MOZZARELLA, for those of us who cannot get the real thing.

BELLI, GIUSEPPE GIOACHINO (1791–1863), born in Rome, had a far from tranquil childhood; his family had a bad time during the political upheavals caused by the Napoleonic Wars, and periods of poverty and relative affluence ensued. Gioachino's studies were curtailed by the need to earn a living, but he became a prolific poet at an early age, and his skill in languages extended to fluency in the Roman dialect, Romanesco, really more a language than a dialect, which was spoken on the streets, regardless of class and income, and to some extent still is. He wrote thousands of sonnets in it, scurrilous, funny, and obscene, many of them to do with food. They are the audible background to the engravings of his contemporary Bartolomeo Pinelli, who portrayed the Roman street life Belli immortalised in his sonnets. Belli mourned his premature death in 1835, probably from alcoholism, with a sonnet, "La morte der zor Meo."

The papacy was going through a period of disrepute under Gregory XVI, and Belli,

a devout Christian, lacerated the self-indulgence and laxity of the Church to such an extent that later in life he wanted all his dialect sonnets destroyed. His family and friends made sure this did not happen, so we can enjoy the cheerful recital of a lush meal in preparation in the papal kitchen:

La cucina der Papa

Co' la cosa che er coco m'è compare
m'ha voluto fa vede' stammatina
la cucina santissima. Cucina?
Che cucina! Hai da di' porto de mare.

Pile, marmitte, padella, callare,
cosciotti de vitella e de vacina,
polli, ovi, latte, pesce, erbe, porcina,
caccia e ogni sorta de vivanne rare.

Dico: "Prosite a lei sor Padre Santo!"
Dice: "Eppoi nun hai visto la dispenza,
che de grazia de Dio ce n'è altrettanto."

Dico: "Eh, scusate, povero fijolo!
Ma cià a pranzo co lui quarch'
Eminenza?"
"Nòo," dice, "er Papa magna sempre solo."

The Pope's Kitchen

The cook wanted to show me,
this morning, all the stuff he bought
for the most holy kitchen. Kitchen?
Some kitchen! You'd think it was a
    sea-port.

Piles of things, pots and pans and
    cauldrons,
haunches of veal and beef,
chickens, eggs, milk, fish, veg, pork,
game and all kinds of choice cuts.

So I says: "Your Holy Father does
    himself all right!"
He says: "You've not seen the
    sideboard,
where praise be there's as much
    again."

I says: "Pardon me, mate!
There must be someone grand for
  dinner then?"
"Come off it," he says, "the Pope
always eats on his own."

His sonnet in praise of lard, once the chosen cooking medium in the Roman kitchen, was quoted by Ada Boni. One of the many uses of lard was to baste grilled lamb chops, as they cooked over, or in front of, a brazier or bed of charcoal, to be eaten at once, "*a scottadito*":

Una spiegazzione

*Pe' capì mejo, tu guarda Cremente
quanno, incartato er lardo, ce pilotta
l'abbacchio, er porco o l'altra carne ghiotta,
perchè se coci en resisti ar dente.*

*Er lardo acceso sbrodola e borbotta
mannanno in giù tante goccette ardente,
che, una qua, una là, tutte uguarmente
vanno a investi' la carne in sin che è cotta*

*Questa è una cosa chiara più del vetro,
e nun ce vo er cervello d'un oracolo
pe' sciferalla e nun rimane addietro.*

*Be', lo Spirito Santo pe' miracolo
se ne ascenze accusì sopra a San Pietro
e all'Apostoli sui drento ar Cenacolo.*

What you have to understand,
  Clementina,
is that when you've smothered your
  meat—lamb, pork or whatever—
in lard, you baste the meat with the
  drippings,
so that it cooks nice and tender.

The burning lard sweats and mutters
Throwing off so many scorching
  drops
that they anoint the meat evenly all
  over until it is cooked.

This is clear as day

and you don't have to have second
  sight
to guess that it will all get eaten up.

Well, the Holy Ghost would enjoy
  this miracle,
floating above St. Peter's, with all his
  Apostles
down below in their refectory.*

A selection of these sonnets, with appropriate recipes, most of them derived from Ada Boni, was published by Vittorio Metz, and is a light-hearted account of Roman gastronomy a century ago. Much has changed, however, and although many trattorias still offer traditional Roman food, it comes at a price, and is still best searched out in places like Testaccio, away from the centre. This reflects all too accurately the changes in the historic centre; where once ordinary Romans lived and worked are now boutiques, international fast food outlets (yes, McDonald's opposite the Pantheon), and expensive restaurants. In those days, most people went home for lunch, and those who could not looked for a simple *bottiglieria* for a flask of draught wine from the Castelli Romani to wash down a bread roll . . .

Belli is still worth reading for what he tells us about everyday life and food in 19th-century Rome.

BERGAMOT, *monarda*, is a plant of the mint family from North America, with fragrant leaves and flowers that can be used to flavour drinks, or make herbal tea, sometimes called bee balm or Oswego tea. Bergamot was a patriotic substitute for unloved British tea at the time of the Boston Tea Party. It has calming and digestive properties. To some it has a similar perfume to the BERGAMOT ORANGE.

*Cenacolo can mean shrine or refectory.

BERGAMOT ORANGE, *berg-amotto*, *Citrus bergamia Risso*, a fruit of the citrus family (see CITRUS FRUITS), possibly a cross between a fruit similar to lime, *limoncello*, and bitter orange, is harsh and unpleasant to eat, but its peel yields a delicate oil used to flavour confectionary, liqueurs, and cordials, and above all cosmetics and perfumes, and a much loved brand of tea, Earl Grey. Bergamot oranges are cultivated in the south of Italy, particularly Reggio Calabria, for extraction of the essential oil, where a friendly microclimate and a protective consortium promote this DOP product with its worldwide market. A biscuit from Piedmont, *pazientino*, is made of flour, sugar, and egg whites, flavoured with bergamot, patiently formed in little strips, crisp and long keeping. In the past, a small round pear, juicy and with a strong bergamot flavour, was greatly esteemed, and some say that the name *berg-amotto* derives from the Turkish *beg-armusi*, the master's pear.

BETTELMATT might get its name from the Bettelmatt Alps in Piedmont, on the border with Switzerland, or the Alps of the same name in the commune of Formazza in the province of Novara. This is a relatively recent codification of a name which varied from place to place for several alpine cheeses, sometimes called *fontina* or *toma*, or *ossolano* in the Val d'Ossola (now seeking autonomy), and depends for its melting texture and delicate flavour on the cows (*razza bruna*) and the aromatic alpine pasture where they feed; one of the many fragrant herbs, *Ligusticum mutellina*, mountain lovage, with the local name *mottolina*, or *mattolina*, contributes to its colour and slightly bitter aromatic flavour. The cheese is produced from July to September and ripens for a year or more, often on layers of hand-harvested hay or straw. It has had a reputation for quality since the early 19th century.

BIANCHETTI is one of the names for very small larval fish, usually of the Clupeidae—tiny SARDINES, ANCHOVIES, or TWAITE SHAD, white or transparent.

BIANCOMANGIARE, a "white dish" with a long and distinguished history, was by the end of the 14th century an inevitable item in European banquet menus. Versions of it were prepared in Italy, France, Catalonia, Germany, and England, having nothing at all to do with the horrible "blanc-mange" of Victorian and modern nursery food, a bland, cornflour-thickened, gelatinous wodge. The key to the popularity of *biancomangiare* is its unearthly and expensive whiteness, a quality hard to achieve in everyday cooking, where much food, however tasty, can appear sludge-coloured. Brightly coloured dishes abounded, transforming the sludge into vivid shades of red, green, blue, yellow, between the extremes of black and white. Using white meat, usually chicken breast, carefully prepared to retain its pallor, and white forms of starch and sugar, *biancomangiare* would have glowed with the luminosity of a full moon among the sombre stews and sauces, the deep browned roasts, decorated with gold and silver, and the brightly coloured tarts, pies, and sauces of the banquet table. Like white linen and the ethereal pale complexion of a pampered princess, this delicate dish speaks of conspicuous consumption and a flagrant use of costly commodities. And it was a health food as well (*see* CHICKEN).

Apart from white meat or fish, *biancomangiare* might contain ground almonds, rice, expensive clarified white sugar, white breadcrumbs, and a delicate flavouring of cinnamon or ginger, the paleness accentuated by a decoration of pomegranate seeds, embedded in their globules of glowing red juice. It was eaten as a delicacy in its own right or as a dressing to other dishes, perhaps coating a boiled fowl or as filling in an open tart or little pastries. The ingredients were pounded together in a mortar and simmered with carefully clarified broth until thickened; but since this could result in a sticky gloop, many recipes tell us to shred the cooked chicken breasts into hair-like filaments, which gives a more interesting texture. Perfumed with rosewater and a hint of ginger or cinnamon, this was far from bland, providing a subtle contrast to the more strongly flavoured and garish banquet food. Invalids could enjoy it, too: nutritious, easy to digest, and potent with that prized medicinal substance SUGAR. It has been suggested that *biancomangiare* may have once been invalid food, and the main ingredients, chicken and sugar, were both held to be medicinal. Scappi has two delicate recipes for *biancomangiare* in his section on food for the sick. The qualities of chicken—moderately moist and moderately warm—were ideally balanced for the human frame, and rice and almonds, given the right treatment, together with sugar (also moderately moist and moderately warm) were indeed suitable for the sick.

The alleged Arab origins of *biancomangiare* are something of a gastronomic myth. The ingredients were widely available all over the Mediterranean, and surviving Arabic cookery texts do not reveal any recipes to substantiate this claim. The important point is that regardless of a possible origin in Arab Spain, or direct transmission from the Middle East as part of the trade in expensive luxuries, this dish had by the late Middle Ages become part of the international style of aristocratic eating.

We find a recipe in Platina in which two pounds of soaked and peeled almonds are pounded in a mortar, moistened to prevent oil forming, and added to the breast of a capon, also pounded, and some breadcrumbs soaked in verjuice or broth. These are passed through a fine sieve and cooked slowly on a low heat, stirring all the time, until the mixture thickens. Just before serving, it is perfumed with rosewater.

A Catalan version, also from Platina, uses rice flour cooked in goat's milk into which sugar and the breast of a partly cooked, newly killed capon, separated into fine threads, is mixed, after being softened by two or at most three thumps in the mortar; the resultant mixture, simmered slowly for what ought to be a quarter of an hour (though Platina says four hours—possibly a scribe's error), is seasoned with rosewater and a sprinkling of sugar.

For Lent, *biancomangiare* is made with pounded almonds and cooking water from dried peas (the standard nonmeat stock) or the broth made from boiling white bread in water, mixed with the flesh of cooked fresh or salt water white fish, and flavoured with an improbable amount of ginger (half a pound—even half an ounce would be pushing it), sugar, rosewater, and verjuice or bitter orange juice. Bartolomeo Scappi, in his *Opera* of 1570 (bk. 2, p. 67r, sec. 157) gives a meticulous account of how to make *biancomangiare* which explains both its appeal and the perfectionism needed to achieve a successful result.

BIGNÈ are little morsels like profiteroles made from choux pastry; they puff up hollow when cooked, and can be filled with cream or custard. This name is sometimes applied to the *rosetta* (*see* MICHETTA) or hollow BREAD ROLLS of Milan, when it gets as far as Rome.

BILBERRY, *mirtillo*, *Vaccinium myrtillus*, is one of the *Ericaceae*. It grows wild on alpine and subalpine moors and in woodland, and the small black berries are harvested as a local crop rather than a commercial one. The larger, less tasty variety is cultivated in

North America, on bushes from which harvesting is easier than the chore of stooping over low-growing plants in the wild. The concentrated flavour and agreeable acidity of bilberries are good in cooked desserts and sauces to go with game and meat, and they feature in breads and ice cream.

BIMBI, BARTOLOMEO,

(1648–1723) was a young unknown Florentine artist when a flower painting of his was drawn to the attention of Grand Duke Cosimo III, who saw his genius at once and employed Bimbi for the rest of his life. His dazzling skills went way beyond the accuracy required for botanical illustration, but it is the combination of the two which endears Bimbi to food historians, for his depictions of fruit and vegetables illustrate the sophisticated horticulture encouraged by the Medici rulers in their domains, and give us a good idea of both everyday and rarified plant cultivation.

A shy person with a modest view of his own skills, Bimbi always undercharged, and once infuriated Cosimo by asking such a low fee for a painting of a monster squash that the duke paid him double the amount. The duke was right; the hazards of depicting these perishable specimens, which must have survived long journeys from their donors, involved working at speed before the monsters deliquesced, and a painter who could immortalize an ugly big vegetable on a shelf, transforming it into a heroic personality, draped in shot silk, against a dramatic sky, glowing in a tormented evening light, was more than a mere botanist to his enthusiastic patron.

Cosimo commissioned many of these individual "portraits" of extraordinary plants, vegetables, and natural phenomena which make the prize-winning bloated vegetable marrows of our agricultural shows seem rather small beer. A giant squash from a garden in Pisa, weighing in at *libri 160* (close to 160 pounds), was immortalised, life-sized, against a distant landscape with the *duomo* and leaning tower of Pisa small and insignificant in the far distance. A huge horseradish of just over eight pounds is quite dwarfed by a massive 18-pound cauliflower, with its halo of dark green leaves, veined with white, on a drape of rich red silk against a lowering evening sky, the huge things filling most of the canvas, giving an impression of menacing immensity. Were they edible? Highly unlikely, with the exception of a giant watermelon which was first painted whole; then the next day Cosimo sent Bimbi a 30-pound chunk to be added to the composition, chilled and ready to eat, showing the juicy inside with its gleaming black seeds, a little bonus on top of the fee.

Bimbi also executed a series of huge panels showing every variety of fruit cultivated in the Tuscan principality during the late 17th and early 18th centuries. The subjects were painted with skill and virtuosity, each fruit numbered and named in a cartouche, providing a permanent record for Cosimo of his gardens and orchards, with their espaliered ranks of fruit trees onto which grafts of amazing and improbable varieties were made by his team of gardeners. Bimbi's success in producing "portraits" of every plant and fruit is astonishing; each one seems to have a vibrant personality of its own. In the four panels devoted to citrus fruits, each of the 116 individual fruits hangs amid rustling fronds of leaves and blossoms; the artist conjures up the bruised peel of the fruit, the aroma of the crushed leaves, and the perfume of the flowers. He shows various types of cherries tumbling out of a huge basket, while pears are piled each on a separate platter.

Cosimo was inclined to vegetarianism, and this may explain his interest in the cultivation and depiction of fruit and vegetables. His sympathetic physician, Francesco Redi, encouraged this. He, too, was interested in the lifelike depiction of plants, and had lessons in drawing from Giovan Carlo da Remigio Cantagallina, paid for with linen handkerchiefs, two brace of chickens, and a dozen flasks of wine. The botanist Pier Antonio Michele was another protegé of the Grand Duke, sharing his modest vegetarian meals, and encouraged to make a list of all the fruit and vegetables enjoyed at the ducal table. This list includes 126 varieties of melon, cucumbers, watermelons, zucchini, peas, and beans; 10 kinds of strawberry, walnuts, hazelnuts, almonds, and over 40 kinds of chestnut; blackberries, raspberries, gooseberries, apricots, peaches, cherries, jujubes, sorbs, medlars, pomegranates, apples (as many as 56 varieties), pears (over 200), quinces, apricots, peaches, and cherries. Most of these would come into season at different times, many could be stored for winter use, and some would have been rushed from the sun-warmed espalier straight to Cosimo's table, ensuring a healthy diet all the year round and reassuring us that the ducal passion for horticultural novelties was put to immediate practical use. This ferment of horticultural and botanical activity also had a wider significance, proclaiming the wealth and fertility of the Tuscan territories, and the prestige of the Medici as patrons of scientific enquiry. The golden globes of Uccello's battle scene lived on in the trim gardens of Poggio a Caiano and Castello.

Bimbi's reputation has increased over the past two decades, as art historians have moved away from centuries of obscurantism towards still life painting, concerned as it often is with mundane matters like food, and as a result more and more of his work is being restored and exhibited, and provides a remarkable resource for the study of late 17th- and early 18th-century horticulture in Tuscany.

BISCOTTI, BISCOTTO,

cookie, means twice cooked, like the French *biscuit*, from which comes the British *biscuit*. Many Italian versions are made by first cooking the mixture in a narrow loaf shape, then letting it cool and cutting it into diagonal slices which are then cooked again in a much lower oven, to become dry and crisp. Others are piped or dropped on baking sheets and cooked only once. Yet others are shaped with cutters from a rolled-out sheet of dough or pastry. Some have butter or oil in the mixture, others do not, and eggs appear in some, all affecting flavour and texture. Starting out as the sugared, spiced banquet food of the rich in the Middle Ages and Renaissance, biscuits became traditional treats for everyone, and are now everyday pleasures, often eaten for breakfast with coffee, or dunked in chocolate or wine. There are many possible flavourings and ingredients, and regional variations. Most confectioners and bakers produce their own specialities, some kinds are often still made at home, and industrial production is massive, but responsive to critical consumer preferences, and so of a higher quality than commercial cookies elsewhere. (Some biscuits, if not named *biscotti*, have their own entry, like CANTUCCI; others are listed here.)

Biscotti al latte are made with butter, eggs, and milk, sweetened with honey and sugar, flavoured with lemon and orange zest and vanilla, made into wreath shapes, and baked with a light covering of ground almonds. These are dismissed by some as dry and boring, and liked by those who appreciate them with a cup of tea or coffee.

Biscottini all'anice come in different versions. In one from Sicily, once made by the nuns of the Istituto San Carlo in Erice, they are made by whipping sugar and eggs to a pale froth, folding in flour, baking powder, and anise seeds, piping the mixture into lengths a bit like sponge fingers, and baking until golden. They can then be cooled, sliced diagonally, and cooked again until hard and crisp. A version of this from Sardinia includes lemon zest and vanilla, and a higher proportion of egg to flour, with a lighter result; these also can be sliced and baked a second time to become crunchier. A richer version includes butter and condensed milk, the anise seed flavour reinforced by anise seed liqueur, cooked once only in little rounds. (CF)

BITTER ORANGE AND BITTER ORANGE JUICE.
See CITRUS FRUITS.

BITTERNESS, *amaro*, is a character-istic quality much prized in Italian drinks and food. Salad herbs like sorrel, endive, dandelion, and *rucola* (*see* ROCKET) are less bitter than the ones used in liqueurs and aperitifs, such as wormwood, southernwood, rue, quinine, gentian, and many more. Distilled or infused, secret combinations of these plants, and also various bitter roots (angelica, rhubarb, liquorice, galangal, artichoke) and spices (cinnamon, cloves, coriander, cardamom, etc.) go into many well-known APERITIVI, *amari*, and DIGESTIVI, names which imply a certain medicinal virtue—rightly, since they all contain herbs and spices which in the past were used to stimulate appetite and promote digestion or act as a tonic to jaded minds and bodies. *Amari* are only mentioned here as examples of the Italian taste for bitterness in food and flavourings. We get some idea of preindustrial uses of bitter flavours in Corrado's work *Il credenziere di buon gusto* of 1778, in which, among the various spirits, essences, *rosolios*, ratafias, tinctures, and waters are many combinations with varying degrees of bitterness. His *Aqua stomatica*, stomachic water, a distillation of spirits of wine, water, cinnamon, cloves, nutmeg, anise, wormwood, mint, spikenard, alum, and cochineal, sweetened with sugar syrup, is a domestic version of later commercial *digestivi*. *Acqua di Mandorle Amare* is made with bitter almonds and anise seed, distilled

with spirits of wine and water; a *Ratafé di Noci* is a version of the *Nocino* we associate today with Modena in EMILIA-ROMAGNA: unripe, shelled walnuts macerated in spirits with cinnamon, anise, and cloves, then strained and sweetened with syrup (*see* WALNUTS).

The industrial products we know so well today are mostly 19th-century versions of these comforting and healthy potions that were made in the home or by apothecaries. Ferro-China Bisleri, full of iron and the stimulating properties of the Peruvian bark *china*, quinine, was invented by Felice Bisleri, one of Garibaldi's veterans, after prolonged chemical experiments in a little workshop in Milan. The slogan *"Volete la salute? Bevete Ferro-China Bisleri"* (You want good health? Drink Ferro-China Bisleri) promoted its consumption by all ages; in 1845, Bernardino Branca concocted a sort of universal panacea which soon became a liqueur in its own right—Fernet Branca, with its dark, bitter taste, due to rhubarb, aloes, gentian, and zedoary, as well as herbs, is taken either on its own or with a generous slug in some strong coffee, a weird and wonderful way of mitigating a robust meal. From their famous café in the Galleria in Milan, the Campari family dispensed bitter aperitifs and digestives, a custom soon to become universal.

Bitter flavours can be used in cooking by adding a dry vermouth, or a few drops of a chosen liqueur, sometimes a more subtle use of the bitter herbs like southernwood which might otherwise overwhelm a dish in their raw state. AMARETTI, or the liqueur of the same name, with a pronounced flavour of bitter almonds, can be used to give liveliness to bland dishes like pumpkin soup.

The bitterness in the peel and pith of some citrus fruits is enjoyable when countered with sugar, salt, and rosewater or orange blossom water, in the salads included by Scappi in many of his rich and copious menus. Bitterness in olive oil is a factor in the very complex sensations released as warm oil is tasted on the tongue, and the characteristic delay in development of this flavour is one of the pleasures in using extra virgin olive oil.

BITTO is an alpine cheese made in the Valtellina, in LOMBARDY, where the orientation and microclimate create a unique terrain, with maximum sunlight and protection from the harsher extremes of weather, where animals in the summer are led to graze on high mountain pastures, and to the intensive work of conducting them in rotation from one meadow to another is added the task of preparing, tending, and maturing the cheese. This is made with the addition of a small percentage of goat's milk, is coagulated with veal or lamb RENNET, and the heating and subsequent stirring, straining, salting, and turning needs constant care. All this intensive work in remote and sometimes inaccessible isolation from early June to September is repaid with a product whose excellence commands high prices; once a delicacy for local consumption, *bitto* is now in much demand. A protective DOC is helpful here, to maintain and enforce standards.

BIVALVES. See CLAM, COCKLE, MUSSEL, OYSTER, PALOURDE, WEDGE SHELL.

BLACKBERRY, *mora, Rubus fruticosus,* is the fruit of the bramble or *rovo*, which grows wild and is also cultivated. In the past, the young shoots were boiled and eaten with oil and vinegar, or pickled. The fruit were used to colour food, particularly sweet and savoury jellies. Mattioli writes of a gentler kind, growing wild on Monte Ida, which is pink and fragrant, ancestor of our raspberry. Martino has a sauce made of almonds pounded with a few white breadcrumbs, added to crushed blackberries, passed through a sieve, and flavoured with cinnamon, ginger, and nutmeg. He also has a *sapor celeste de estate,* a brighter blue sauce for summer.

BLEAK, *alborella*, perhaps better known to anglers than gastronomes, is a small fish of the Cypridinae. It is useful as bait and is part of the diet of larger predatory fish, so many of the Italian lakes have restocked with it, as a commercial and environmental benefit. It can be eaten, floured and deep fried, or cooked in the oven in a BATTUTO of parsley, garlic, salted anchovies, oil, and rosemary.

BLOOD. *See* PIG'S BLOOD.

BOAR, WILD. *See* WILD BOAR.

BOCCA DI DAMA is a light eggy sponge cake made with finely pulverised dried or toasted ALMONDS and only just enough flour or cornstarch to keep the mixture together, beaten into egg yolks whipped with sugar to a pale froth, folded into beaten egg whites, and baked in a buttered mould. It can be flavoured with lemon zest and vanilla. A light version of the much heavier, strongly flavoured almond cakes and cookies of the past, this sort of baking might be associated with the mind-cast that produced the Enlightenment.

BOCCONCINO is a small mouthful, sweet or savoury. The name is applied to the small, round, baby MOZZARELLA cheeses, and to little balls of fresh, not pasteurized, ricotta, flavoured in various ways, coated in breadcrumbs and fried.

BOCCONOTTO is a little round pastry, baked in a mould, made of *pasta frolla* (*see* PASTRY) and filled with a soft paste of ALMONDS and biscuit crumbs, flavoured with cinnamon, lemon zest, and an appropriate liqueur.

BOCKENHEIM, GIOVANNI. *See* MARTINO DE ROSSI.

BOGUE, *boga, vopa, boba,* a species of bream and one of the Serranidae family, *Boops boops* (a cheerful name which is perhaps the best thing about this fish) is pleasant enough if it has fed on good things, and is usually very fresh. The variant names can be traced back to ancient Greek, in which the original term *box* (whence Latin *boca*, Italian *voga*) was reinterpreted by inventive lexicographers as *bops* or *boops,* "ox-eyed," or *boba, vopa,* in Italian. Like the fish salema (*sarpa* or *salpa* in Italy) bogue is best enjoyed fried.

BOLLITO, *bollito misto,* is the familiar "boiled dinner," a dish made from one or more pieces of meat, simmered rather than boiled, sometimes also known as *LESSO.* In the *bollito misto,* various meats are cooked, some together and some separately, and brought together as a sumptuous amalgam of flavours in a broth which has added as much to the meats as it has taken away. Beef is an important element in both these recipes; in the *bollito* it is so good that the tradition is to eat a slice with no other condiment than some coarse unrefined salt sprinkled over at the last minute. The lavish, almost gross, array of a *bollito misto* in a restaurant, wheeled to the table in a covered trolley, is a reminder that it was once festive food, a rare indulgence to be made the most of, and remembered with nostalgia until the good times came round again. It can include beef, veal, pork, chicken, sausages of various kinds, *cotecchino, zampone,* or *capello del prete,*

and pig's trotters, or NERVETTI, to give extra unctuousness. In Piedmont many different cuts of beef are used, a reminder of the times when beef cattle had a long hard life before ending up in the pot. In Lombardy the selection is less rich.

BOLOGNA. *See* EMILIA-ROMAGNA.

BONI, ADA (1891–1973), born into a comfortable upper-middle-class Roman family, was cooking for fun from the age of 10, and went on to cook enthusiastically for family and friends for the rest of her life. Her paternal uncle Adolfo Giaquinto was a chef and published a cookery magazine, and her husband, the music critic Enrico Boni, was a keen cook, so it is not surprising that Ada, too, started a cookery magazine—*Preziosa,* which ran from 1915 to 1959—and published in 1927 *Il talismano della felicità* (The talisman of happiness), perhaps the most influential Italian cookbook of its time. She also gave cookery classes to the grand ladies of Rome, who were impressed by the fond embrace publicly bestowed on Ada one night at a concert by Queen Margherita (she of the pizza). Ada is described by her nephew as "a sweet little lady, totally dedicated to her family, in a way hardly possible in today's society. A lady who I can never remember ever seeing out of doors during the summer without her faithful parasol and her white outfit, like a Belle Epoque print." This unbelievable image can only be fully appreciated in the context of the Rome of Federico Fellini and Pier Paolo Pasolini, who overlapped Ada's long and privileged life.

Boni wrote a work on the gastronomy of Rome, *La cucina romana,* in 1930, broadcasted frequently, and collaborated with the magazine *Arianna* in a series on the regional food of Italy. The *Talismano* went into many editions, and it is not now at all clear to what extent Boni's original text has been altered and amplified by the publisher (researchers found information hard to come by). Like Isabella Beeton's work, it became a culinary bible, and was modified during Boni's lifetime to adapt to changing tastes. But unlike *Household Management*, the *Talismano* preserved living traditions and characteristically robust national and regional dishes, without, at least in the earlier editions, the stultifying gentrification of Beeton's work.

La cucina romana, Boni's best book, was a labour of love, which to us today is an evocative mixture of some almost obsolete and some happily still familiar Roman ways of cooking, a record of a cuisine that was on the way out when she realised the need to write about it. The *Talismano* has a broader appeal, and in spite of later editorial additions of fashionable or foreign recipes which had only a small part in the original concept (the 882 recipes in the first edition of 1927 had been expanded to 2,245 by 1976) it remains a classic compendium of the cooking of an aspiring middle class, striving for aristocratic gentility—characteristic of its times, though, and very different from today's search for vanishing peasant and rural food and ingredients. It still sells around 20,000 copies a year, we are told; perhaps the title, not the contents, still make it the ideal wedding present (to give rather than to receive). But the *Talismano* is still a helpful work of reference.

This gentrification of Italian food follows on from Artusi's book *La scienza in cucina e l'arte di mangiar bene* of 1910, a work which met the needs and aspirations of a predominantly urban middle class. Ada Boni, or her advisors, must have seen this as a fruitful terrain, but shrewdly appealed to the would-be aristocratic middle classes, with social and gastronomic pretensions that Artusi's humbler readership would never have countenanced. A recent bibliographical study by Cristina Carpegna, in *Le cucine della memoria* (1995), reveals the changes made during and after the author's lifetime. In the first edition of 1927, the role of offal and extremities was greater than that of beef, 28 percent compared with 25 percent. This reflects a change of attitude between 1570, when Scappi was cooking luxurious dishes of offal for princely banquets, and 1970, when it was hardly visible on the radar. Like most Romans of every social class (did she speak with a Roman accent? she certainly had no problems with Belli's ribald sonnets in Romanesco), Boni seems to have had an earthy appreciation of characteristic Roman food, which shows in her typically Roman recipes; *Piselli al prosciutto* (Peas with cured ham), a typically Roman creation, is "una vera leccornia" (a finger-licking treat), and her long, hands-on explanation of how to prepare *Carciofi alla giudia* (Jewish-style ARTICHOKES) insists that we use an earthenware pot (*terraglia*) in which to fry them, to get "that characteristic dark gold colour" of this chrysanthemum-like delicacy; and she advises a perilous but essential splash of water into the pan of boiling oil, just at the end, to get a final crispness outside and tenderness within. When it comes to *la pagliata* (*see* PAJATA), her graphic description of how to clean and prepare the intestines of cow or calf for this robust Roman dish is not for the squeamish—"so easy, no need to get the butcher to do it for you," she said blithely.

An emphasis on the simple pleasures of putting excellent food before an appreciative family, rather than laying on pretentious, but economical, dinner parties is more apparent in *La cucina romana* than in the *Talismano*, where *fare bella figura*, but without undue expense, was what her aspiring readers wanted. In *La cucina romana*, she expressed robust views on economy—a good bargain had to be the best possible quality for a sensible price. A typical Roman "would never be led astray by notions of 'penny-pinching,' convinced, rightly, that economy with ingredients was a false economy; being always ready to pay that much more to be sure of really first-class, prime quality material." And furthermore, capable of noisy battles with fraudulent shopkeepers: *"Questo, ber fijo, ve lo magnate voi!"* roughly translated as "You know where you can put that, mate!"

Boni's work on Roman food was written at the point when centuries-old traditions of gastronomy were disappearing under the influence of demographic changes, pressure from the international food industry, and the demands of tourism. The robust simple fare that Platina and Martino noisily championed in the taverns of Trastevere was getting harder and harder to find, and the relaxed lifestyle of the laid-back Roman *buongustaio* was being eroded by the work ethic of the pallid northern Piedmontese, ruining both the environment and the ethos of what used to be an easygoing backwater. Augustus Hare, writing in the 1870s, lamented the decision to move the new nation's capital from Turin to Rome, and the partial destruction of this beautiful, slightly seedy, quiet provincial city. Quiet, that is, in its orchards and gardens and overgrown ruins, but not the narrow streets and raucous markets, portrayed in the sonnets of Gioachino Belli and the engravings of Bartolomeo Pinelli. Boni quoted Belli's sonnet of 1837 "Li connimenti," in which he enthuses over the traditional uses of oil and lard in cooking:

Si, è bbona la cucina co' lo strutto;
anzi lo strutto er barbiere m'ha detto
ch'è un connimento che ffà bbene ar petto
come fà er pepe ch'arifresca tutto.

S'adatta a li grostini cor presciutto. . . .
ar pollame . . . all'arrosto de lommetto . . . ,
a lo stufato . . . all'ummido . . . ar
   guazzetto . . . ,
ma adoprallo ner fritto è un uso brutto.

Voi frigge er pesce co' lo strutto?! Eh zitto,
er pesce fritto in nell'ojjo va cotto:
l'ojjo è la morte sua p'er pesce fritto.

Yes, cooking with lard is good;
and the barber* told me
that it's a condiment good for the
   chest
the way pepper is, so invigorating.
It goes with crostini and ham.
poultry, roast loin of veal.
stew, casserole, braised meat;
but frying with it is a horrid thing.
You'd fry fish in lard?! For shame,
fried fish has to be cooked in oil:
oil is its chosen fate.

Although things have changed, and lard is no longer the cooking medium and flavouring of choice, Boni's summary of the uses of pig fat is still valid:

Roman cooking is simple, healthy, nourishing, and tasty. Its essential condiment is *strutto* (lard), that is, pig fat processed at home and preserved for years for use in the kitchen. To this one should add *lardo* (cured pork fat), *guanciale* (cured pig's cheek), *ventresca* (*pancetta*, streaky bacon, smoked or unsmoked), and the fat of cured ham, all of which can go into what we call the *battuto*. Oil is used for dressing raw vegetables and, less frequently, for strictly nonmeat, lean, dishes. It is also used for frying and especially fish, though many prefer lard for frying other things (p. 13).

There was a time, before nutritionists put us right, when pasta was considered both gross and fattening; and now the virtues of animal fat are likewise undergoing a rehabilitation. Meanwhile, a *battuto*, pork fat in any of these forms, finely chopped to a creamy paste, with a variety of aromatics—celery,

---

*As well as dealing with hair and beards, the barber would draw teeth and give advice or even remedies for all kinds of ailments, to those unable to afford the fees of a conventional doctor.

onion, garlic, carrot, parsley—is still used as the starting-off point for many dishes, not just in Rome. In Boni's recipes, chopped onion and the *battuto* are cooked in lard until golden, then some tomato, tinned, fresh, or concentrated, is added; the mixture, diluted with water, is now ready for cooking rice, pulses, or a mixture of things, to achieve a dense, not too runny *minestra*, something between a soup and a stew.

BONITO, *palamita*, one of the bluefish, the same family as MACKEREL and TUNNY, was known and appreciated in the ancient world. The two earliest known Sicilian gastronomes, the playwright Epicharmus (c. 480 BC) and the poet Archestratus (c. 350 BC), provide brief recipes for bonito. Epicharmus suggests (in a description of the good life in the mythical land of the Sirens) splitting young bonito down the middle and grilling them. Archestratus deserves quoting: "Use fig leaves and season with oregano, but not very much of it, no cheese, no nonsense. Just do the fish up nicely in fig leaves fastened above with string, then hide it under hot ashes, keeping a watch on the time when it will be baked. Don't overcook it" (Athenaios 276f).

Today it is usually sliced, floured, and fried, and can also be pickled, *in carpione*, with onions, garlic, thyme, bay leaves, and chilli cooked in the oil it has been fried in, and some vinegar.

(AKD)

BONVESIN DE LA RIVA
lived and wrote during the last decades of the 13th and into the early 14th century. He belonged to the third order of the Umiliati, a religious sect which lived and worked in the secular community, and has sometimes mistakenly been classed as heretic, which it was not. Bonvesin taught in his own school and wrote in Latin and the vernacular. He may

have lived near the *riva* or canal basin not too far from the centre of Milan, one of the *navigli* close by the Porta Ticinese, and until as recently as 50 years ago it would not have been difficult to imagine him busy teaching and caring for his neighbours in this environment of fields and open spaces, docks, warehouses, and small-scale commercial activities, with quiet courtyards of trees and the small workshops of the many craftsmen who made up Milan's population of 200,000. (Inner city pressures have recently driven the craftsmen away and lured in the property developers; farewell to trees and quiet spaces.) The ancient Romans had done a lot to improve the natural waterways of the region, connecting them with canals, to bring produce and commodities into and out of Milan. More was done in Bonvesin's time, expanding the Ticino into a waterway affectionately known as the Ticinello, used for irrigation as well as commercial traffic and also as a defensive barrier, and linking up with a whole network of other hydraulic undertakings, elaborated over the centuries, earning Milan the name of *città acquatica*. Bonvesin saw the need for a real port, for seagoing vessels, as did Napoleon, but attempts over the centuries succumbed to the vagaries of local and national politics, and withered away with the coming of large steam-powered vessels, too big for the narrow waterways. The historian of the *navigli*, Paolo Colussi, quotes Bonvesin's crisp and perceptive comment: "If I might venture to say, this city is lacking in two particular things—civic harmony and a seaport; the first can be achieved through wise counsel, but the port will never happen whilst the rich and powerful waste their powers destroying their enemies and their fellow citizens and extorting money for their wretched schemes," thus summarising in advance the long-drawn-out story of the port that never was.

Two of Bonvesin's many writings are of interest to us; first, a set of verses in the vernacular, *De quinquaginta curialitatibus ad mensam* (Fifty rules for good behaviour at table), illuminate with startling clarity many of the undesirable habits he advises us to avoid—slurping, spitting, sneezing, and coughing spittle all over the table, filling the mouth too full, then attempting to talk, criticising the food. The verses give advice on the etiquette of shared bowls, spoons, and glasses (wiping them clean before proffering to your neighbour), on how to hold a shallow goblet of wine with both hands to avoid spilling, how to present oneself at table "cortese, adorno, alegro e confortoso, e fresco, no stà cuintoroso ni gramo ni travacao, ni con le gambe incrosae ni torto ni apodiao" ("courteous, well-dressed, cheerful and good-humoured, lively, not melancholy, nor preoccupied and vacant, nor with legs crossed, twisted, or waving around"). The ritual of hand washing before and after a meal demanded a restrained performance, with great care at the end to remove all grease and mess.

Bonvesin's other work is *De magnalibus Mediolani* (The marvels of Milan), written in 1288, a panegyric to his city, fulsome in its praise, but careful neither to placate nor irritate the Visconti, at present in power, with a wealth of descriptive detail that was unlikely to be pure hyperbole. This genial author writes with an endearing mixture of *campanalismo* and statistics; one might raise an eyebrow at his round sums and adulation, but Bonvesin's listings are totally convincing. He enumerates all the professions and crafts of Milan, including the fishmongers:

Pischatores cuiusque maneriei piscium, tructarum, denticum, capitonum, tencharum, timulorum, anguilarum, lampredarum, cancrorum, demum cuiusque reliqui generis tam grossorum quam minutorum copiam quasi cotidie a lacubus comitatus nostri, pluribus xviii; et a fluminibus, pluribus lx; et ab infinitis quasi montium rivulis ad

civitatem portantes, plures CCCC pro firmo se esse fatentur.

Just about every day our fishermen, who claim that they certainly number more than 400, bring into the city copious quantities of every kind of fish, trout, dentex, chub, tench, grayling, eels, lampreys, crayfish, and every other kind, both great and small, from our lakes of our county, 18 in number, and our rivers, over 60 of them, and the almost infinite number of mountain streams.

Bonvesin has a nice word, "glorious," for the well over 1,000 taverns, and we note with interest the 40 scriptoria in which books were copied by diligent scribes, who were allowed bread as well as their daily expenses. There were 300 civic bakeries, not counting the ovens in monastic establishments, and 440 butchers did a fine job of slaughtering the cattle which were brought daily to the city: 70 beef cattle, on meat days, as well as sheep, lambs, goats, and others; then there were quantities of fowl, capons, hens, geese, ducks, peacocks, pheasants, squabs, thrushes, quail, partridges, and other birds. On meatless days, a stream of honey, milk, junkets, ricotta, butter, cheese, eggs, and crayfish flowed into the city. The crayfish were measured by the *modius*, a unit which contained eight *sextarios*, each the weight a man could just about carry. A 15th-century pencil sketch for a *Tacuinum Sanitatis* shows a man weighing them by the bucketful, and a market woman peeling cooked crayfish for a customer, just as Bonvesin must have seen in the fish markets of Milan.

A prosperous city surrounded by fertile countryside, tilled by 300,000 pairs of oxen, with cartloads of grain, pulses, green vegetables, fruit, and nuts pouring into the markets, with a generous surplus for export. The market gardens of the city provided fresh vegetables and herbs all year round—many kinds of cabbage, beets, spinach, lettuce, celery, fennel, garlic, onions, parsnips, turnips; the fragrant potherbs basil, parsley, mint, savory, marjoram; and other plants, to eat raw or cooked, like mallow, borage, rue, poppies, and others no longer in use.

Fruit was enjoyed throughout the year—from the sweet and sour cherries, ripe from May until July, to an almost infinite quantity of various kinds of plums, from July until October. At the same time come early apples and pears, figs, even a few almonds, cornel berries, jujubes, apricots, wild hazelnuts, an incredible amount of walnuts (eaten at the end of a meal all the year round, and also shelled, skinned, and pounded with cheese, egg, and pepper to use as a stuffing for meat); later come winter apples, pears and quinces, pomegranates, and an enormous number of different kinds of grape, which last through July to December. Then chestnuts, both kinds (he lists all their uses), medlars, and even some olives and bay berries, but not, Bonvesin is happy to say, dates and all the spices that need a searingly hot dry environment. He praises the benign climate of LOMBARDY, mild and warm nearly the whole year round, with fresh clear streams and lush meadows, and notes the constant supply of fresh pure drinking water. Climate change and industrialisation have tarnished this ideal image, but Bonvesin's description remains an endearing account of civic life in medieval Milan.

BORAGE, *borragine, borrana, Borago officinalis*, grows wild all over the Mediterranean. It is loved for its pretty blue edible flowers and delicate flavour, which is also found in the tender young leaves. The flowers are used to decorate food and in salads, which together with its hairy leaves, edible when cooked to get rid of the prickles, have a mild cucumber taste. They can be used to stuff pasta or eaten with oil and lemon, and

are used a lot in LIGURIA, part of the PRE-BOGGIÒN. Scappi used the flowers in a lettuce salad, or to brighten up monochrome dishes like a stuffed breast of veal, or boiled chickens. He also used them to decorate a delicate dish of stewed young kid.

They were good for you as well, as Pisanelli pointed out; "*infusa nel vino genera grandi allegrezza nell'animo, e conforta potentemente il cuore, levando via ogni melanconia e disponendo l'huomo sempre a pensieri piacevoli e giocondi*" (infused in wine, they generate great cheerfulness of spirit, comfort the heart mightily, removing all traces of melancholy and disposing one to pleasant and cheerful thoughts), which sheds a whole new light on Pimms.

Corrado describes the flowers as decoration for cold meats and fish, and used the health-giving leaves in soups or chopped in a *torta* of ricotta. They are still used this way in Liguria. In his *Cibo Pitagorico* he has many recipes for borage: the *pottaggio alla rustica* parboils the leaves briefly, and then turns them in oil with garlic, anchovies, wild fennel, salt, and pepper; or he dips borage leaves, folded round a boneless salt anchovy, in batter and deep fries them, to eat with a tart apple sauce.

BOTARGO, *bottarga*, is the salted and cured roe of GREY MULLET, which is the best, although the roe of other fish can also be used. It is made in large amounts in SARDINIA, where grey mullet are plentiful. Thin slices are usually eaten with toast, after softening for a short while in oil and lemon juice. *Bottarga* can also be shaved into aromatised oil as a pasta sauce, or soaked a little while, then pounded to a paste with oil, lemon, and pepper, and spread on *crostini* (*see* BRUSCHETTA). A cheap version of this is a widely known travesty of *taramasalata* made with smoked cod's roe, which works well enough if homemade, but the synthetic pink commercial version is disappointing

and is no substitute for that made with real *bottarga*, which is more subtle. In SICILY it is made from TUNNY roe. In Sardinia it is melted in oil as a source for pasta. Its modern name can be traced via Arabic and Coptic to Hellenistic Greek.

BOUILLON CUBES, *dadi,* fall in

and out of favour. There is no substitute for a good, home-made stock, but the convenience and novelty, when they first appeared in the early 20th century, led many respectable writers to specify them in recipes. In the past, in the kitchens of large establishments, where boiled foods were part of everyday eating, there would always have been good chicken and beef BROTH to add to other dishes, and vegetable stock, from dried pulses, as well as fish stock, to use on nonmeat days. In restaurants in EMILIA-ROMAGNA, where the BOLLITO MISTO is prepared with loving care (the meats are not boiled together in the same pot, but given different treatments) there is a ready supply of full-bodied or subtle broth to use, for example, in *tortellini in brodo.*

Cubes have the advantage of including various herb and vegetable flavours, and also flavour-enhancing things like yeast and MSG; which is fine in some dishes, but can be obtrusive and overpowering in others. The pervasive aroma of LOVAGE in a particular brand has led to a change of name for this herb in some countries, where it is often referred to as the Maggi plant.

BRA is the name for a cheese produced in

PIEDMONT in the province of Cuneo and the commune of Villafranca Piemonte in the province of Turin, not in the small town whose name it bears, which is where alpine cheeses were brought down from the mountains by nomadic herdsmen to mature and ripen before distribution. It comes in two varieties—*duro,* hard, and *tenero,* soft, the latter

being lighter, with a gentler flavour; the hard version is used as a seasoning rather than a table cheese, particularly in LIGURIA, where it can replace the more expensive PECORINO in making PESTO, which seems a good idea, though frowned on. This DOC- and DOP-designated cheese used to be the local cheese of the area, *nostrale,* and although some is made on lowland farms, the definition requires that the cows, preferably the indigenous Piedmontese race, feed on fresh alpine grass or hay, not silage or artificial cattle feed.

BRACCIOLINI, POGGIO. *See* PLATINA.

BRAIN, *cervello,* is a delicacy best known

today as part of a FRITTO MISTO, or served in various ways after a preliminary simmering in an aromatic broth. Brains can then be turned quickly in butter, or dipped in flour, then beaten egg, then breadcrumbs, fried in butter or oil, and served with wedges of lemon. Cleaned and washed brains can be incorporated into fillings for pies, tarts, and pasta. In the past, they were added to pies and tarts, often along with SWEETBREADS, and today can be used in the more luxurious versions of brawn, *coppa di testa (see* COPPA). The preliminary soaking and trimming of blood and membrane is essential for a pleasant appearance. (*See also* VEAL.)

BRANZI is an alpine CHEESE made in

an area around Bergamo, centred on the little town of Branzi in the Valle Brembana, where the herdsmen used to come down from the mountains in September to sell their summer cheeses, fragrant from the lush grazing; since it is now also made on lowland farms during the winter, using different techniques to produce a fresh young table cheese, it takes discriminating customers appreciative of both versions to save the winter cheese from being stifled in the DOC strait-jacket which defines them both.

BRASATO is a way of slow cooking, a sort of pot roast, in which a large piece of meat or game, sometimes fish or fowl, is cooked very slowly in a hermetically sealed pot, with very little liquid. The meat can be marinated beforehand, with aromatic herbs, spices, and vegetables, then browned in fat or oil, and, as in the classic *brasato al Barolo*, allowed to absorb a whole bottle of some very good-quality full-bodied red wine, Barolo or Nebbiolo being the obvious choice in Piedmont. When the wine has vanished, the pot is sealed and cooked very slowly for three hours or more. The Genoese version includes dried mushrooms, some ham, and a mixture of wine and broth, and can be used with pork instead of beef. The name comes from the hot coals, or *brace*, over which this sort of dish would have been cooked in the past, sometimes with more hot coals placed on the concave lid.

BREAD, *pane*, has been both a luxury and a staple in Italian life since earliest times. The first and last words about Italian bread come from Carol Field, whose indefatigable research and accurate recipes tell us how it was and how it still can be:

> Do they really exist, those mahogany-coloured wheels of country bread with creamy interiors, crackly crusted chewy loaves that still taste intensely of the grains of the fields? The question can only be answered both yes and no.

Corrado Barberis supplies, in the INSOR publication *Atlante dei prodotti tipici, Il Pane* (INSOR, 2000), many of the answers to Field's question and a detailed and witty overview of bread-making in Italy today. Both authors tell an amazing story, unexpected and comforting—how thousands of intrepid Davids with hands-on approach and small resources are vanquishing the Goliaths of the international bread industry. Small artisan bakeries that were in decline a few decades ago are now flourishing, they have discriminating clients who are happy to pay the higher prices, and what is even more encouraging, for every picturesque bread boutique in tourist areas, with intricate decorative breads of all kinds, there will be as many serious small bakers supplying local needs in the form of craggy loaves and fresh light pastries. Home bread-making has declined with changing patterns of rural life and urban employment, but it is more than a nostalgia for old ways that fuels the demand for good honest bread from bakers in town and countryside. Regional specialities have either survived or been revived, and people now seek them out.

Today bread is essential to all main meals, and in spite of the international trade in grain and flour, widespread industrial production, and the dire effects of "improvers" of various kinds in both milling and baking, an appreciation of good bread is fundamental to Italian gastronomy. Bread goes with every kind of food and is eaten at every meal, brought to welcome eaters when they arrive, and as much as is needed flows with the succession of courses, as essential as potatoes or rice in other cuisines. No messing about with special knives and plates and bits of butter; bread is balanced on the edge of the plate it accompanies, or sits in fragments on the table cloth, at hand's reach, to guide food onto the questing fork, mop up juices, enjoy on its own between bites, and be dunked in broth. But the weird custom of putting a saucer of oil on the table to dip bread in at the start of a meal is an aberration found only in the more pretentious Italian restaurants abroad. An offering of BRUSCHETTA anointed with oil would be more likely.

Today we can choose from a bewildering variety of different breads, innovative new breads, and recently revived ancient breads. This variety depends on the kind of grain used, how it was harvested and milled, what sort of leavening makes it rise, how much and what kind of salt gets put in, and how it is baked (in what oven, using what kind of fuel); add to this the water, the climate, the touch of a particular baker, and the microorganisms in the atmosphere which get to work on the leavening process, and a delightful complexity is inevitable. Then there are all the different shapes and sizes of breads—an exhaustive list would be over 1,500, but the *Atlante* whittled it down to 200 main types, with about 50 well-known regional products, with the reservation that similar breads with different names would clog up the listing. Field's list of some basic shapes and kinds includes *azimo*, unleavened, *casareccio*, home-made, *ciabatta*, slipper, *ciambella*, wreath or ring, *corolla*, crown, *manini*, little hands, *pagnotta*, round loaf, *panino*, small roll, *piadina*, flat thin disk, *quattrocorni*, four horns, *ruota*, wheel, *schiacciata*, flattened, *sfilatino*, long thin thread, *stella*, star, *tegola*, tile, *treccia*, braid.

Large loaves, round, domed or oblong, some light with a crisp crust, others solid and built to last, improving with keeping, yet others chewy and full of holes, then little rolls of innumerable sizes and textures, fancy shapes, festival breads, breads for special occasions, loaves made with additions to the flour, with flavourings of herbs and seeds, both inside and out—there are as many pungent and enticing varieties as there are languages and dialects in Italy.

There is a risk of becoming soft-centred when writing about the symbolism and mythology connected with bread-making. This is a hard trade, with long exhausting hours, sleep deprivation, and punishing working conditions, with a low profit margin, strictly hemmed in with regulations, and the gruelling necessity to start over again every day of the year. The enthusiastic amateur home bread-maker loves the sounds, smells, and rhythms of the task, is moved by the sense of a living organism responding to touch and feel, by the continuity of a task performed by women since the beginning of time—we are all great earth mothers in the kitchen—and pagan superstitions and Christian rituals seem to us endearing rather than tyrannical and obscurantist. But the harsh realities of bread-making, the prevalence of shortages and want, have always been more immediate than pretty legends and symbolism.

An example of the theoretical/romantic approach to bread is the interpretation of the stamp or *marchio* used to impress makers' initials on bread before it was put in the communal oven. These can be seen as a primitive functional tool with crude letters and a stout handle for grasping, or as a symbol of male supremacy and female subjugation. Rituals surrounding the use of these tools reinforce this attitude; the *marchio*, carefully guarded by the woman of the house, handled with protective care before being thrust by the baker into the about-to-be-baked bread, moulded into the shape of female genitalia, is carrying a heavy load of anthropological obfuscation. Given that it is difficult for a stamp with a handle suitable for grasping to avoid looking phallic, and that a tired woman in a hurry has no time for musing on crude symbolism, we are tempted to see these useful objects as tools and no more; simply a convenient way for a housewife to identify her bread when it comes out of the communal oven.

Marking a loaf with a cross can be a link with the sacramental role of bread, a gesture to assure success in baking, or simply a means of getting it to rise better. Bread was never wasted; scraps, crusts, even crumbs were saved and used in a range of imaginative ways, to thicken soups and stews, to give body to sauces, in dumplings, soaked in oil or wine, then dressed with something liquid like tomatoes or cucumbers. This was respect for an elemental, indispensable source of life, a necessary frugality, and a need to make the most of something delicious in itself, for good bread has texture and flavour that enhances everything it is put with, while bad, poor-quality bread on the other hand has no redeeming qualities at all, and cannot be improved whatever is done to it. "Stale bread" with its unhappy associations with stale fish, stale news, or even socks, is a misleading translation of *pane raffermo*, implying a deterioration and unpleasantness. The Italian expression means firmed-up, hardened, matured, the reverse of freshly baked, but in no way inferior; in fact it is the bread of choice for many dishes where fresh bread would not give the best results. This is explained by Harold McGee (2004, p. 541); briefly, when freshly baked bread cools, the starch molecules change their structure, and the bread slowly hardens, a process called "starch retrogradation," moving water from one part of the structure to another, a process that can be reversed by heating, which obliges the water to go back where it came from in the starch granules, giving an admirable firmness to the bread. So when this "stale" bread is toasted, then allowed to soak up broth, it keeps its shape beautifully and tastes good as well, and so is used for preference in many dishes where fresh bread would disintegrate and not taste so good.

Pane raffermo goes into Tuscany's RIBOLLITA, where reused bread and the re- or twice-cooked vegetable- and bean-based soup make an unforgettable combination. It is used in PAPPA AL POMODORO, another Tuscan soup, a delicious soft pap of bread cooked with tomatoes, where in this case the bread is simmered until it forms a creamy soft mass. PANZANELLA, a salad of soaked bread and tomatoes; is another Tuscan speciality now enjoyed everywhere. PANCOTTO is perhaps the most basic of the bread soups, and every region has its version, sometimes simply bread cooked in water flavoured with whatever comes to hand, herbs, vegetables, and pungent olive oil. The PANADA or *pancotto* of the VENETO is made with slices of

dry bread soaked in beef broth flavoured with cinnamon and good olive oil, then cooked some more until it becomes a loose mass, to be served with plentiful parmesan and sometimes beaten egg. In LOMBARDY a *panada*, once a special Easter dish, is made with breadcrumbs first soaked then simmered in broth with a little butter, and served thickened with beaten egg and parmesan, flavoured with pepper and nutmeg.

Breadcrumbs are used in many dishes, to thicken stews and sauces, and sometimes to create dumplings, like the *minestra mariconda* of Brescia, north of Milan, where stale breadcrumbs, softened in milk, then cooked dry again in butter, are made into dumplings with eggs and PARMESAN, and cooked in beef or chicken broth. A version from Mantova includes finely chopped left-over meat or chicken in the dumplings. *Canederli* are bread dumplings from the Trentino region, enriched with fried pancetta and salame, onion, garlic, and parsley cooked in chicken broth.

There are mixtures of breadcrumbs, cheese, and egg which can be swirled into broth, giving it body and texture, like STRACCIATELLE, or the variations on *panada* that abound. A *minestra del paradiso* is a more sophisticated delicacy, consisting of stiffly beaten egg whites into which the yolks, some dry breadcrumbs, parmesan and nutmeg are folded, after which it is either tossed straight into simmering broth or dropped in deftly by the spoonful to make ethereal little dumplings.

A fairly stiff mixture of breadcrumbs, eggs, and parmesan is forced through a sieve to make *passatelli*, which look like little worms of short pasta.

Bread got equal respect in the past; Martino has several recipes for grated breadcrumbs mixed with cheese and eggs and stirred into a meat broth yellow with saffron, one for a version cooked in a broth coloured green with herbs, and some exquisite little dumplings made with white breadcrumbs, ground almonds, and whites of egg into a stiff mixture which is dropped in small spoonfuls into chicken broth. Artusi has a version of this enriched with ham and beef marrow, and bound with a little flour, made into balls the size of walnuts and cooked in broth, called *minestra di pane angelico*, an angelic bread dish. Equally heavenly is his *minestra del paradiso*, described earlier. Martino also had a sweet dish, *suppa dorata*, made of carefully trimmed slices of white bread, toasted in the oven then soaked in eggs beaten with sugar and rosewater, and fried in butter.

Cristofaro di Messisbugo has a far from frugal use of slices of fine white bread, *pan boffetto*, toasted, layered in a baking dish and sprinkled with sugar, grated parmesan, and cinnamon, with slices of roast chicken, then more sugar, cinnamon, and cheese, and so on for several layers, alternating chicken and bread, then pouring hot veal or capon broth over everything and putting it in the oven to finish, covered, until served. He follows this rich dish with a recipe for what we might call "summer pudding"—slices of toasted bread in the bottom of a dish, soaking up the juices of cherries and pears cooked in red wine and sugar, with cinnamon and rosewater.

Scappi's recipes for invalids include *panata*, made from diced stale white bread softened in water or broth, and finished in a concentrated chicken broth, enriched with egg yolks or in summer with milk of melon seeds. He is characteristically careful to explain why the bread is soaked—to soften it and make it more tasty, before cooking it longer. When making a *panata* with almond milk, he explains, the cubes of day-old white bread need to be first soaked in boiling water, to make them more absorbent, so that the almond liquid will be completely taken up as it cooks. A lighter dish is made by passing grated hardened bread through a coarse sieve directly into boiling meat or capon broth, simmering gently for half an hour, then thickening with egg yolks. Scappi's

vivarole is made of beaten eggs mixed with breadcrumbs and cheese, stirred into a broth of finely chopped spinach, beets, marjoram and mint simmered in water, butter, saffron, and cinnamon.

Maria Vittoria della Verde made convent soups using slices of bread simmered in broth and enlivened with chopped meat (maybe leftovers too). Another recipe, *panpina stufata*, layers thin slices of bread with chopped meat, cinnamon, and sugar, soaked in broth and simmered in a pan deep enough to allow room for the bread to expand.

Bread was also used in sweet dishes; the capacity of breadcrumbs to absorb flavours and bind ingredients makes them the basic ingredient in *panmelato priora*, the prioresses' spice bread, a version of PANFORTE; they are first soaked in water and sweet wine to soften and expand them, then tipped into a huge vat of boiling grape must and honey, spiced with pepper and cloves, and flavoured with candied orange peel and walnuts (Casagrande, 1989, p. 180). The huge quantities imply production on an industrial scale, sweetmeats as a source of revenue for the convent. This is just one of many versions of *panforte*, a long-keeping sweetmeat thick with nuts and dried fruit, heavy with honey and spices, once made all over Italy and now renowned in Sienna.

The positive virtue of stale breadcrumbs is emphasised by Maria Vittoria della Verde when she specifies in another recipe that the bread rolls must be baked a week before starting to make the *panmelato*, and grated on a cheese grater the day before starting the task. They need to have the strength and absorbency to hold together this heaving mass of honey, spices, and fruit.

Other sweet dishes using bread are similar to our BREAD PUDDINGS; in the *torta nicolotta* of Venice, cubes of rough rustic bread, crusts removed, are soaked in warm milk, sugar, and butter, mixed with eggs, raisins soaked in rum, some lemon zest, and chopped candied citron, flavoured with cinnamon and vanilla, sometimes fennel seeds, and baked until golden.

The use of breadcrumbs as the binding element in puddings or other things cooked in a bag in water, or baked in the oven, is not unique to the English *pudding*, popular from the 17th century onwards, and even the name may not be English in origin, possibly derived from the Italian *budella* or *budello* (casings using the intestines or stomachs of animals) or the French *boudin*. *Budin* is the word used by Corrado for 15 totally different recipes, only six of which involve breadcrumbs, and only two are boiled in a cloth. Some are more like custards, some are like what we know as trifles, some use crumbled stale sponge cake, or sponge fingers, and two are a delicious mixture of blood, cream, and aromatics, cooked in the intestines of the animal concerned, what we now call "black puddings" (*see also* PUDDING) and "white puddings" made from the white meat of chicken. In these far from frugal recipes, breadcrumbs bind the ingredients together, before boiling them in a bag, thickening them in a pan, or baking them in the oven. Corrado gives a green *budin*, coloured with spinach juice mixed with breadcrumbs and rice flour soaked in egg and milk, slightly sweetened and flavoured with cinnamon, grated citron peel, and chopped pistachios, thickened in a saucepan, then baked in the oven. *Semplice* is a rich mixture of eggs, cream, butter, and crumbled sponge fingers, flavoured with cinnamon and vanilla, and boiled in a buttered cloth, served with a cream sauce. Present-day usage is to call such a savoury dish a *sformato* and the sweet ones *pudding* or *flan*. See also FLATBREADS.

BREAD AND BUTTER PUDDING

is one of many ways of using left-over bread which became a luxury dish in its own right. Scappi describes layered slices of bread, sometimes toasted or fried, with butter, soft cheese, sometimes chicken and slices of cooked meat or sausage, soaked in not too salty broth, and baked gently in the oven, seasoned with sugar and cinnamon, and there is not much difference between this and Scappi's many almost solid soups based on bread under soup, *zuppa* (Scappi, book 2, p. 83 r, recipe 225).

BREAD ROLLS,

to eat with meals or on their own, with or without fillings, come in many shapes, sizes, and textures, with countless regional variations; some are now made nationwide, while others have a strong local identity. *Rosette* or MICHETTE are a northern speciality but are enjoyed in central Italy as well. They are made of a dense, stiff *pasta dura* which is so stiff that before mechanical ways of doing the work arrived, a primitive wooden machine was used, with a lever driving a hammer down on the unyielding mass, demanding skill and care on the part of the users. This can then be shaped and knotted in many complex ways, producing hard dry rolls much loved by the initiated: *copiette,* two crescents intertwined, a scroll shape, and *montasu,* or *carciofi,* with slashed strips of dough like artichoke leaves. *Semelle* from Florence are round with a cleft in the middle; *biovette* are soft plump rolls from Piedmont. (*See also* CIROLA ROMANA.)

BREADS, BRAIDED OR KNOTTED,

are made in such a variety of shapes and textures that is perhaps confusing to link them too closely with the PRETZELS of New York, with their Germanic origins. They appear in many cultures throughout history. Perhaps the defining characteristic is a twisted, knotted shape, baked in various ways. In Spain and the Low Countries in the 16th and 17th centuries they were elaborate constructions, in the spirit of the ornate parterres and strapwork of formal gardens and embroidery. The game children played in the Low Countries in the 17th century, hooking a little finger through the loops of an *s* or *krakeling*, then tugging it till it broke, was said to symbolise the frailty of the young, both physical and moral, and the importance of a sound moral education. Knotted and tressed breads are also part of a tradition of offerings to placate the Great Earth Mother, be she Demeter or Ceres, and later Christian saints, to whom pagan fertility rites were adroitly transferred. Easter breads share many of these characteristics.

Maria Vittoria della Verde, a nun in 17th-century Perugia, also had a recipe for *staffette di pasta, ciambelle,* which described in bewildering detail how to knot strips of a yeasted dough into a "stirrup" shape. Maria Vittoria jotted down recipes and embroidery patterns, practical hints and pious thoughts, in a notebook she kept from the 1580s until her death in 1622, which indicate that she had hands-on experience of the intricacies of both disciplines. Sometimes her rough wild sketches look as if they could be for either cookies or applique work, both sources of revenue for the convent. Her *zuccarini* look very like the ornate filled, slashed, and crimped sugared cookies in paintings by Clara Peters, in Antwerp.

Another 17th-century woman with a sweet tooth was the Portuguese painter Josefa de Obidos, deeply religious, with a private income and considerable professional skills, who was thus able to avoid marriage and pursue an independent career. Her rather sugary devotional paintings were surpassed by her renderings of pastries and sweetmeats, equally sugary, and are mentioned here because they illustrate the way convent breads and pastries were common all over Europe at a time when religious orders were like huge multinational corporations today. Some of her works show Easter bread, plaited and shaped, often enclosing whole eggs in their shells in a web of twisted and braided strips of dough. The symbolism of the eggs, the cross-shaped pastry, spring flowers, and early

broad beans and peas seems to be a celebration of rebirth and renewed growth. In a companion painting, the cakes, comfits, pressed sugar sweets, ribbons, blossoms, and luxury objects might imply the vanity of ephemeral pleasures or be a celebration of the convent's earning power. These resemble the *pupi cu l'ova* of Sicily, bread dough rolled in strips and fashioned into an amazing variety of decorative shapes, usually incorporating whole eggs, made to celebrate the springtime solstice, and part of our Easter celebrations. The *cavagneddo* of Cassaro in Sicily is a sweet bread made in various shapes, often baskets containing eggs, decorated with fruit and flowers of coloured marzipan and multicoloured confetti (comfits).

BREADS, RING-SHAPED,

ciambelle, bracciatelle, have been around in Europe for a long time; one version, the BAGEL, is loved the world over. Ring-shaped breads can be divided into two main categories—those meant to keep, long-lasting, hard as rocks, used by soldiers and mariners as subsistence food on long journeys, needing to be softened in water, wine, or oil. The ring shape makes them easy to store (on poles or branches), and they are winsomely referred to as bracelets, though the unhygienic practice, by vendors or gluttons, of wearing them on the arm is not appealing. They were a cheap, popular food. Then there are the short-lived, sometimes luxury products, often made with eggs, some kind of shortening, and sugar.

A characteristic of some of these ring-shaped breads that are similar enough to what are now called bagels to claim kinship, though known by different names in different countries, is that they are a dough formed in rings or twisted garlands like bracelets (as indeed are many other breads and biscuits), and some of them, the ones known in some cultures as bagels, are cooked first by plunging the risen rings into boiling water, from which they are quickly removed and left to cool and dry, and then baked in an oven, sometimes brushed with a shiny glaze of egg or sugar. The result is a firm, chewy, portable object, which can be filled with cheese or cured meat, taken on journeys or to the workplace, easy to carry and eat, being more compact and less friable than other breads. Claudia Roden quotes the definition of bagel: "a doughnut with rigor mortis," and stresses the need to eat them hot and fresh, or indeed the toughness will have to be mitigated by cutting them in half and toasting them.

This dunking in a pot of boiling water before drying out and baking in the oven might be to give a firmer texture to the dough, or cause the surface starch to gelatinise (McGee, 1984, p. 310) into a thin transparent coating, which when dried will create the characteristic glossy surface of the ring once baked; a way of enhancing flavour and maybe retarding or to some extent preventing the staling process. Well worth the trouble.

There were round bread rolls with a hole in the middle in Roman times, glimpsed in a relief in Ostia, and to be seen in a mosaic pavement in Algeria, while the eye of faith might discern a basket of twisted circular rolls among the bread on offer in a mural of a baker's shop in Pompeii. As *buccellatum*, from the Greek *boukellaton*, ring-shaped twice-cooked wheat biscuits were familiar as military provender, so much so that by the 4th century, soldiers in private armies were known as *buccellarii*. Twice-baked ring-shaped breads and biscuits have quite a bit in common. They are found in many countries and many cultures, and a firmly antidiffusionist approach might indicate that making breads and buns in a circular form with a hole in the middle could have been a spontaneous way of handling both dough and symbolic forms, not something "brought" from region A to region B. This twice-cooked ring bread did not have to originate in a specific place; it was simply a common item throughout Europe. The *obarzanki* of medieval Poland were being made some time before Jewish immigrants arrived in the 14th century. Dara Goldstein describes how in Russia in the 1920s, when street trading became a possibility, itinerant bakers sold delectable *bubliki*, sweet rich ring-shaped buns flavoured with mace and boiled in milk and vanilla before baking.

Ciambelle is only one of the names for ring breads and biscuits, and not all of them get a preliminary dunking in boiling water. They bob to the surface in a Perugian nunnery in the 17th century, in the court of the Este dukes of Ferra in the early 16th century, in the papal kitchens a few decades later, in rural Lazio today. Costanzo Felici wrote in breathless detail in the 1560s about wheat and bread; he says, "There is also a twice-cooked bread, circular or ring or other shaped, made with a fairly hard dough, with salt, anise or fennel seeds, first cooked in boiling water and then in the oven." He goes on to mention other ring breads, not all precooked in water, but made to titillate the industrious palate with many varieties that we might call "reinforced" breads, with a wide range of additions to the flour or dough according to the changing tastes of mankind, among these breads made in various shapes commonly known as *bricuocoli* or *ciaramilie* or *bracciatelli* or *braciatelletti*, made with flour mixed and kneaded with eggs (although some still make them without eggs) and cooked in the oven, sometimes twice cooked, or in copper pans; some of these are light and very spongy, some covered with powdered sugar, called *berlingozzi* in Rome, others without sugar, some smoother, some harder, some low and flattened, large or small in shape, and among these last one often sees little *biscotelli* mixed with milk and sugar, or just sugar, or without. Of the same form, but made with much thinner strips of dough, are other ones—*bracciatellini* or *zuccarini*, as they call them, made with eggs and sugar (1986, p. 115).

Suor Maria Vittoria della Verde's convent cookery notebook has some *ciabelle in aqua* first given a boil, then baked. Messisbugo gives a recipe for *brazzatelle* made with a rich dough of flour, eggs, butter, sugar, milk, and rosewater, plunged into boiling water before baking. Scappi gave a recipe for *ciambelloni*, a dough of flour, eggs, rosewater, sugar, and goat's milk, sometimes flavoured with anise seeds or fennel, formed into rings and first cooked in boiling water, then baked in the oven (Book 5, p. 371v, recipe 148). A young Medici prince, the three-year-old Francesco Maria, poses for a portrait in the long pleated silk skirts of the time, sweet natured, round eyed, firmly clutching in his left hand a *ciambellina*, no doubt a bribe for good behaviour, while crumbled cookies are scattered on the red brocade tablecloth on his left. Giovanna Giusti (2001, p. 14), who sees in these ephemeral treats a prefiguration of the luxurious tastes of the future cardinal, also points out a painting in Florence by Lorenzo Lippi in which the infant Christ holds a *ciambella*, and a *Carità* by Cesare Dandini where a podgy infant grasps a *ciambella* while reaching up to his mother. Giusti goes on to point out how *ciambelle* had a universal appeal to all classes, hawked in the streets of Bologna and engraved by Mitelli, with an explanatory caption:

"*Il comprar le ciambelle è buona usanza, / d'aniso d'oglio di botiro e d'uova. / Non solo il companatico s'avanza, / ma il comprator l'economia ritrova.*" (Buying ciambelle is a good habit, / aniseed, oil, butter and eggs. / It doesn't just make the food go further, / the buyer finds it an economy.)

Ciambelle can be seen in many Italian still life paintings, often in the context of luxury items, and selections of fancy breads. A painting by Evaristo Baschenis of a sad little boy with a basket of rolls and cookies, from mid-17th-century Bergamo, might imply that as a page he had the melancholy task of offering these forbidden sweetmeats to his elders and betters. Among the sponge fingers, flaky pastries, and decorative biscuits are some *ciambelle*, or *braciatelle* as they were sometimes called, rough circles of dough with their characteristic glaze. Cristoforo Munari in Reggio Emilia painted these among Venetian glasses, musical instruments, and fragile blue and white china, luxurious snacks rather than the rough crisp rolls and coarse breads seen in his compositions of salami and cheese. One still life shows broken *ciambelle* with their crisp texture that look like something between our bagel or pretzel. They are sometimes painted along with the delicate cups and bowls associated with drinking chocolate, and frequently with sponge fingers dunked in wine in ethereal goblets.

The *pane del marinaio* from Fano in the MARCHE is a yeasted dough including lard, formed into rings and baked in the oven, then dried and matured for a week, taken by fishermen on long journeys and gratefully dunked in wine on their return. Giusti shows a detail from a Claude Lorrain landscape in which mariners disembarking in a refulgent sunset are greeted with a dish of welcoming *ciambelle*.

A traditional recipe from Lazio, *ciambelle affogatelle*, is for a fairly soft mixture of flour and eggs and a pinch of salt, shaped into rings and first dropped into boiling water, then dried and finished in the oven.

The dough for the *mescuotte* of BASILICATA is made with lard and flavoured with sugar and anise. The rings, knots, or M shapes are first cooked in boiling water, dried, then baked in the oven after the bread is taken out. Now Easter specialities, they used to be strung on strings and worn by shepherds round their necks, or kept as long-lasting treats in the linen chest.

A delicate version from the Veneto, *brasadèle broè*, is an Easter speciality of Pazzon di Caprino on the slopes of mount Baldus, made to a secret recipe which is said to include flour, eggs, butter, and a pinch of sugar, worked together, left to mature, then made into rings decorated like laurel wreathes. These *ciambelle* are dunked in boiling water and then baked in the oven until crisp. The final touch is to thread them onto boughs of cherry blossom (Da Mosto, 1969, p. 371).

The *taralli* of Avellino in Campania are flavoured with fennel seeds, boiled, and then baked. Puglia has its *scaldatelli* flavoured with fennel, black peppercorns, or *peperoncino* and cooked in the same way. *See also* BREADS, BRAIDED OR KNOTTED; FESTIVITY AND FOOD.

BREADS, RUSTIC, *pani rustici*,

are made in a variety of shapes and sizes, with the basic ingredients flour, yeast, salt, and water. Differences due to the local microclimate, the kinds of grain used for the flour, the starter sourdough mixture, kept from batch to batch, and passionately held regional preferences make for a huge range of delicious breads. Most are listed in the INSOR publication (INSOR, 2000), and how to make many of them is explained in Carol Field's book *The Italian Baker*. Some of the main kinds are *pane di Como*, which comes in two sorts, a white bread with a strong crust; *pane Toscano*, a saltless bread from TUSCANY, where it is said that the well-salted cured meats of the region make salt unnecessary in bread; *pane di Terni* from UMBRIA, made using some wholemeal flour, and with a texture honeycombed with holes; *pane di Genzano*, a bread from Genzano, a small town outside Rome, made with an acidic starter from the previous baking,

and a quality of flour which has earned it the protection of an IGP (*indicazione geografica protetta*). The *pane di Altamura* of PUGLIA is made from the hard durum wheat flour of the region, using malt and a sourdough starter as well as fresh yeast, and has a hard crust and chewy interior; like many very large loaves it keeps well, and the interior, not totally sterile from the heat of the oven, continues to develop in flavour. In SICILY, the large *casareccio*, keeping loaves, sometimes known as *vastedda*, made with strong flour and still often cooked in wood-fired ovens, taste better after several days. This flour, milled from durum wheat, *semola di grano duro*, comes as coarse semolina, or more finely ground silky golden *farina di semola rimacinata*, to make the golden breads of Sicily. A version of *vastedda* made with elderflowers is a speciality of Ragusa. As well as the large rustic loaves, bread appears in many shapes—the *mafalda*, a rolled-out length of bread twisted or braided into a serpent shape or one vaguely resembling a pair of spectacles, for Santa Lucia who looks after our eyesight; or a length of bread rolled to a half-moon shape then slashed part way so that it opens out like a crown seen from the side; *cucciddatu*, a round circle of bread with decorated outer edges, often of considerable splendour, like a sunburst, all sprinkled with sesame seeds before baking. At this point the dividing line between rustic and refined gets blurred, for so many of the traditional festive and symbolic breads have skills and elegance that are both rustic and sophisticated. The intricate breads prepared for the feast of San Giuseppe on 19 March are bread sculpture, with floral, animal, figurative, and topical themes that relate to pagan practises and modern icons—wreathes for Ceres and motorbikes—and decorate the festive altars created for the saint, as the new crops start to appear and the food stored for the winter months can now be eaten up in the form of stewed pulses along with the new green stuff appearing in the fields. The Easter braided bread enclosing eggs is still a living tradition, a pagan symbol of creation and a Christian emblem of rebirth and renewal.

A modern venture in the Valle del Dittaino in the province of Catania in Sicily, *il pane del Dittaino*, is a thoroughly industrialised bread produced by a cooperative of 54 local wheat growers who have heroically realised the dream of combining improved yield, hence greater profits, with improved nutritional and gastronomic value, by getting all the processes together under one roof and making a bread with indigenous wheat, grown with a minimum of chemical intervention, processed in their own plant, using methods that make it possible to omit fungicides and insecticides.

Pane bigio is made from a mixture of wholewheat flour and unbleached plain white flour, worked with fresh yeast and a starter to make a really runny, sloppy dough which after long fermentation becomes a crusted loaf with a moist, well-flavoured interior full of holes. Variations on this are made all over Italy, now that more and more bakers and their clients want to return to the hefty breads of the past, happy to be able to enjoy rusticity without the hardship and scarcities that drove the poor to add anything to hand to bulk out the wheat flour, harrowingly documented by Camporesi.

Corn bread is made in the north of Italy where maize is grown, and is regarded with the same affection as POLENTA. Made with a mixture of wheat flour and maize flour fermented with fresh yeast, it is hearty and heavy, keeps well, and goes with hearty local dishes. A version is made in the Marche without yeast, and in Lazio with maize and soft wheat flour, where its popularity increases with a growing nostalgia for the robust food of the region.

Rye bread, *pane di segala*, is made with a mixture of wheat and rye flour, and is found mainly in northern areas where rye grows better than wheat, and where the cultural influences of Alpine and northern Europe are prevalent. These heavy breads (there is precious little gluten in rye flour to help it rise) can be made for immediate use or long keeping, and the strong sour flavour matches local food, game, and pungent cured meats, often enhanced with caraway or cumin seeds. In the province of Sondrio, rolls based on a rich mixture of rye and wheat flour with butter or lard and eggs, formed into rings you could wear as bracelets, *brazadei* or *brazzadele*, are found in valleys of Valchiavenna and Valtellina. *See also* BREADS, RING-SHAPED; BREADS, BRAIDED OR KNOTTED.

BREAM belong to the Sparidae family, and there are a lot of them. A selection of the best known in Italian cuisine have entries here: DENTEX, *dentice*; gilt-head bream, *orata*; PANDORA, *fragolino*; SEA BREAM, *pagro*. There are several striped bream, including salema, *salpa*; sar, *sarago maggiore*; striped bream, *marmora*; sheepshead bream, *sarago pizzuto*; two-banded bream, *sarago fasciato*; and bogue, *boga*; red bream, *occhialone*; saddled bream, *occhiata*. This is confusing enough without the different regional names. Most of them can be cooked in the same way as sea bream or gilt-head bream; when in doubt, marinate the fish, whatever it is, in a mixture of salt, oil, and lemon before grilling or baking.

BRESAOLA is one of many SALUMI not derived from the pig. It is made from five permitted cuts of beef. including fillet, *girello*, or *fesa*, from the buttock, which is carefully trimmed of all fat and stringy bits and dry salted in a tub with spices (pepper, cinnamon, cloves, and crushed garlic), then dried and agitated to ensure deep penetration of the salt, then left to recover in a dry place before the final period of hanging for two to three months, during which time it loses moisture and weight and takes on an intense and beautiful deep red colour and an incomparable flavour. After a long cure, *bre-*

saola is best marinated before eating for an hour or so in olive oil, a drop or two of lemon juice, and black pepper. The lighter cure can be enjoyed straight away. Both industrial and artisan *bresaola* is made almost everywhere, but that from Valtellina and Valchiavenna in the province of Sondrio in LOMBARDY is exceptional, due to the mountain air and the verdant pastures, where graze cattle imported from Argentina and Brazil, who can sometimes be heard mooing gently in Latin American accents. These semi-wild creatures, grass fed on their native pampas, here enjoy traditional alpine fodder and grazing, and so the product could be said to have more *tipicità* than intensively reared and industrially produced *bresaola* from elsewhere.

Bresaola is also made from HORSE and venison (*see* DEER), which traditionally might have been the origin of the product, and is still made today with animals imported from afar.

BRIGATA SPENDERECCIA.

See TUSCANY; CLOVES.

BROAD BEAN, *fava, Vicia faba,* has been around for longer than all the other beans we know today. The ancient Egyptians

Pythagoras prohibited his followers from consuming these versatile legumes, as a way of protesting democracy. (The beans were cast in urns as votes.) (Shutterstock)

ate broad beans, and the Greeks must have liked them enough for Pythagoras to prohibit their use, although Aristotle thought this might have been a coded way of advising his followers to stay clear of politics (beans were cast into urns as a way of voting). Broad beans were associated with the dead until recent times, cooked and offered up at the tombs of relatives and ancestors in the ancient world, and later left overnight on the eve of the Day of the Dead, 2 November, in a bowl on the kitchen table, as solace for their visiting souls, a reminder of family joys and sorrows, and also offered liberally to the poor folk of the neighbourhood. Castelvetro wrote of this custom with some asperity as mere papist superstition, but it goes further back to pre-Christian times. More recently the *fave dei morti* evolved into sweet biscuits, sometimes also called *ossi da morto*, made of almonds and dusted with icing sugar, looking a bit like little bones or beans, a more suitable treat for children, who still enjoy these seasonal cookies.

The best overview of the history of the broad bean in Italian food is hidden away in two footnotes to Camporesi's edition of Artusi's *La scienza in cucina* (Artusi, 1970, p. 380 n. 1; p. 543 n. 1). Here Camporesi quotes writers with inventive, and tasty, ways of dealing with windiness, the scourge of bean-eaters, which may have been behind the otherwise irrational prohibitions. It is not so much the flatulence as the distension and thus the acute discomfort which provokes nightmares and mental agony, "sogni orribili e opprimenti, che i Latini chiamano incubi," personified in Fuseli's *Nightmare,* in which the *incubus,* a grotesque monster, squats on the chest of a young woman sprawled in discomfort and abandon over a disordered bed, useless bottles of tinctures and potions discarded on the bedside table. She would have done better to follow the advice of Castor Durante by cooking dried broad beans, without the outer skins, with fennel and oregano, leeks or onions, pounded and seasoned with oil and spices (saffron, pepper, cinnamon, and cumin) to help digestion. A reminder that Carraci's uncouth peasant, eating beans with a bunch of spring onions, was simply applying sound dietetic principles. These can be found at work in the compilation associated with the name of Apicius, in two recipes in which legumes (dried peas, black-eyed beans, or broad beans could all take the place of his enigmatic Baian beans). *Fabaciae virides et Baiani*, green beans and those of Baia, were cooked until soft and then pounded and seasoned with crushed mustard seeds, honey, pine nuts, cumin, and vinegar. Or the beans, fresh or dried, were crushed or chopped and served in a sauce of chopped or pounded rue, celery leaves (or lovage), leeks, vinegar, oil, *liquamen* (Thai fish sauce), *caroenum* (a mystery liquor perhaps similar to genuine traditional BALSAMIC VINEGAR), *defrutum* (probably the same as *saba*); just the brew to banish Boreas.

Scappi's menus for springtime banquets include *scafetti teneri con la scorza*, young broad beans in their pods, a delicacy then as now. Today fresh young beans are eaten raw from the pods, with a sharp young cheese, either as a snack or at the end of a meal; they can be cooked in broth and seasoned with chopped herbs and ham or bacon. When more mature they can be boiled to get rid of the tough outer skin, a chore well worth doing. Artusi has a lovely recipe in which they are turned in a SOFFRITTO of chopped onion and diced fatty ham, then finished cooking in broth with coarsely chopped lettuce leaves. The dried beans either come in their hard outer skins, which if cooked long enough can add a pungent chewiness, or they can be bought without them, sometimes cracked, for boiling to a mush or purée, as in *macco*. This dish of puréed dried beans is a descendant of the ancient Roman *puls*, or polenta, the elemental "porridge" of grains or pulses or legumes that has sustained peasants and farmers for millennia. Lovers of Middle Eastern food will recog-

nise *houmous* and *ful medamès* as direct survivals, seasoned as well and effectively as in the effete Apician tradition, and close relatives of the Sardinian *favata* or the *'ncapriata* of Basilica and Puglia.

Castelvetro reminded us of other uses of bean purée, as a savoury or sweetened filling for tarts and turnovers, or a cosmetic, using bean flour to make a frothy foam in the bath.

BROCCOLI, *cavolo broccolo, broccoletti, Brassica oleracea* var. *cauliflora,* can be confused with CAULIFLOWER, since they are both the inflorescence of some plants of the CABBAGE family, and are cooked the same way. Kinds of broccoli to look out for are the beautiful greeny-yellow *romanesco,* a bewitching cluster of closely packed florets grouped in an intricate architectonic spiral formation; the violet, pink, and green broccoli of Naples and Sicily; the white ones from both south and north; and then the kind we are more familiar with, *broccoletti,* the small cluster of flower heads on little stems of their own, the best of which can be compared with asparagus. Writing of these, Castelvetro said: "Some prefer to cook them with a few cloves of garlic, which gives them a wonderful flavour." This is true, though I don't understand how the garlic (plenty of it, coarsely chopped) boiled up with the broccoli in a small amount of salted water, gets rid of the "cabbagey" pong, as well as tasting so good. Serve the broccoli, cooked so that all liquid has evaporated, tepid, with extra virgin olive oil and a squeeze of lemon and freshly ground black pepper. This works well with the other kinds of broccoli, too. Nico Valerio, writing of *"i piatti ricchi della cucina povera"* (the rich dishes of the cuisine of the poor) tosses parboiled *broccoletti* in a pan with oil, garlic, and dried chilli, with a glass of dry white wine added halfway through cooking. Broccoli and the various kinds of cauliflower are often combined with sausages as a sauce for pasta, seasoned with garlic and chilli. In PUGLIA, the chewy orec-

chiette go well with tender broccoli and are often cooked together in the same pot of boiling water and seasoned with a sauce made of garlic and salted anchovies melted in oil, sometimes with chilli.

BRODETTO is a diminutive of *brodo*, BROTH, and in the past was applied to different recipes; today it is either an Easter soup, *brodetto di Pasqua*, made of chicken broth thickened with eggs and lemon, well known in Florence and Lazio, or the name given to many different fish soups made all along the Adriatic coast, from Trieste right down to Vasto. Originally a quickly cooked dish, made by fisherman to use up the catch they had not managed to sell earlier in the morning, seasoned with whatever came to hand, these *brodetti* evolved into rich and complex recipes differing from port to port, influenced by the availability of fish and local tastes. The important thing is to have a wide range of fishes, with different textures and flavours, cooked so that they give up enough of their goodness to enhance the whole, without losing any of their essential character. This calls for nice judgment and sensitive timing, careful preparation of all the different fish, and a neat hand with the seasonings. Some recipes have a lot of fresh tomatoes and tomato paste, some are made with saffron, some involve a SOFFRITTO of chopped onion, celery, and carrot to start off the cooking; some must have garlic, others exclude it; some add wine vinegar, others wine. One or two are boiled rapidly, many are simmered slowly, but with each one, timing has to be a matter of personal judgment, depending on the size and nature of each fish. The range of essential fishes includes scorpion fish, *scorfano*, goby, *ghiozzo*, squid or octopus, stargazer, *pesce prete* or *lucerna (bocca in capo)*, greater weever, *tracina*, angler fish, *rana pescatrice (see MONKFISH)*, red mullet, *triglia di fango*, turbot, *rombo*, grey mullet, *cefalo*, razor-shell, *canolicchioi*, scampi. Some additional ones, which can only improve the result, are smooth hound, *palombo*, hake, *nasello*, John Dory, *pesce San Pietro*, flying squid, *totano*, a large prawn called *mazzancolla*, sea bass, *spigola*, skate, razza, gurnard, and *capone*. In the MARCHE, the magic number of 13 fish, one for each person at the Last Supper, is desirable.

The *brodetto* from Fano in the Marche begins by making a broth from the fish trimmings, celery, carrot and onion, seasoned with a bay leaf. In a *soffritto* made by frying chopped garlic and spring onion in olive oil, cook the squid or octopus, then add dry white wine, chopped tomatoes, and the strained broth. In this simmer the chosen fish, starting with the bigger, firmer fleshed pieces and adding the red mullet and hake right at the end.

When attempting any regional recipes for *brodetto*, you have to aim at a selection from the foregoing lists, and be both resigned and imaginative in what you do with them. A helpful recipe from Ann and Franco Taruschio's *Leaves from the Walnut Tree* (Taruschio, 1993, p. 181) uses fish they used to get up at dawn and buy from Welsh fishermen on the Pembrokeshire coast, and includes monkfish, red mullet, sole, gurnard, whiting, mussels, and Dublin Bay prawns.

Something to agonise over are the bones; however delicious the little fishes, if they present the eater with a mouthful of pins and needles, the *brodetto* looses its charms. So where possible trim and bone the fishes, retaining heads and edible parts, and make a stock with these bits and pieces and well-flavoured creatures like scorpion fish, which can be strained and the flesh pushed through a sieve to thicken the final cooking liquid, in which the prepared fillets and slices can be poached and eaten with carefree abandon. This is something like the Venetian *broeto*, made with a big grey mullet, gently poached, and in its cooking liquid a few small fish— goby and gurnard and the heads of scorpion fish—are poached, the small fish removed, the heads and bits all boiled up, and strained, while the flesh of the small fish is pounded in a mortar with garlic, butter, and oil, forced through a sieve, and used to thicken the broth, which is poured over the pieces of grey mullet, laid on slices of fried bread, sprinkled with parmesan and parsley.

BRODO. *See* BROTH.

BRODO LARDIERO, a medieval

favourite, is made from venison (*see* DEER) cooked in white wine with diced bacon and SAGE leaves, flavoured with mixed spices and the broth thickened with dried bread and hard-cooked egg yolks, and the pounded liver and other organs. Before cooking the meat is rinsed in the wine, which is then strained and the liquid used in the cooking. Martino has a version of this which is lighter and less heavily spiced than his *civero* or CIVET, which is dark with well-toasted bread and dried fruit, and the meat is enriched by frying it after cooking in water and wine vinegar.

BRONZINO, ANGNOLO

(1503–1572) was a pupil and lifelong friend of Pontormo, interesting to us because of the references in Pontormo's "diary" to the good food and drink he offered his old master, and for gastronomic references in his poetry (Nigro, pp. 81–111). Bronzino, with a network of supportive male friendships, had no inclination to marry, but his benevolent disposition found him caring for and maintaining a large dependent household of widows and orphans, which became a sort of surrogate family for the solitary Pontormo. Bronzino was of humble origins, and although his position as court painter to the Medici dukes brought him money and patronage, his responsibilities were a drain on his income. The food Pontormo ate in his home on Sundays sounds good but not

lavish, and we note that the parsimonious old man would contribute, sometimes with wine, or some fish, to these family meals.

BROTH, *brodo* or *bouillon*, is preferred home-made by most writers on traditional and regional Italian food. Our preoccupation with authenticity now overrides commercial pressures and notions of convenience, but horses for courses—a busy Italian housewife will use BOUILLON CUBES, *dadi*, with discrimination; a "foreigner" seeking insights into an unfamiliar cuisine will probably prefer to follow instructions for a good meat or chicken stock in any classic Italian cookery book, very different from classic French procedures. Petronilla knows we should all have a pot of meat simmering away for "real" broth, and speaks guiltily of *falso brodo di falsi carne* (false broth from false meat, made from a cube), knowing that by then, 1937, both options were being used.

Artusi gives clear and brief instructions for a tasty broth: using the cheaper cuts of meat (which will not be eaten as a separate course, having given up all their substance to the liquid, later to be used as a base for soups and stews), start with cold water and cook very slowly, so that all the flavour goes into the broth. For a dish of boiled meat, to eat as a course on its own, with a sauce, or a simple dressing of olive oil, but whose broth might be used for other purposes, start with a pan of boiling salted water into which the meat is tossed—the heat and salt will help it retain flavour and texture—then carry on with the long, slow simmering. Bones might help the flavour but have little nutritional value. The stems of celery, parsley, basil, and some carrot and onion are put in for flavouring, and caramel (browned sugar diluted in water) for colouring. Ada Boni goes into more detail, stressing that "broth is a fundamental preparation in the kitchen."

Brodo ristretto, or *consumato*, has to be made from a good meat or chicken broth in which more carefully prepared cuts of meat are cooked slowly to yield a dense, concentrated liquid. Boiling down an everyday broth would have a less pleasant result, becoming rank and oversalty rather than dense and rich. Boni is pragmatic about skimming: a carefully cooked domestic broth would not need it, but where a clear liquid is required it is worth the trouble.

Scappi's *brodo consumato* is described in the section on invalid food; the basic recipe needs a nice plump capon, neither young nor decrepit, killed the same day by cutting its throat to whiten the flesh, and cooked slowly, cut in pieces, in a sealed pot covered with four fingers of water, until the meat is soft and the liquid reduced to one-third. This is strained, sweetened with sugar and whatever else the physician prescribes, and given the patient to drink. Other recipes flavour the broth with cinnamon and a slice of cured ham; a particularly tempting version thickens it with egg yolks, and flavours it with sugar, cinnamon, and bitter orange juice—"di gran sustanza," say the medics. (*See* CHICKEN.)

Anna del Conte gives the best recipe in English (Del Conte, 1998, p. 324). This produces a lighter broth than the traditional French method, just what is needed for risottos and thick pasta and vegetable dishes, where too powerful a flavour would be intrusive.

BRUSCHETTA, *crostoni, crostini,* are

slices of toast with things on them, depending for success on the quality of the bread and olive oil. Their popularity has grown with the recent revival of good authentic regional breads. At their most elemental, *crostini* can be made by rubbing a peeled clove of garlic into a hefty slice of toasted country bread until it disappears, then carefully pouring over it enough extra virgin olive oil to anoint the whole, and sprinkling with salt. In the past, FLATBREADS or toasted slices from a loaf several days old used to be eaten by farmworkers or manual labourers as a substantial snack to relieve the exhaustion of heavy outdoor work, spread with salt, oil, salame, or cheese, but today the concept has been turned upside down, and small, exquisitely put-together morsels are served with wine to stimulate jaded appetites in anticipation of the meal to come. Definitions are best not agonised over; the little *crostini* that make pretty canapés and the *crostoni,* slabs of bread big enough to carry a fat pork chop, speak for themselves. *Bruschetta* was known and loved in Lazio before its current popularity, as well as in Tuscany and Umbria, sometimes known as *fett'unta* or *panunta.* Now whole books are devoted to the topic, bringing together, in the case of the Taruschios, traditional recipes and wildly innovative ideas (Taruschio, 2000).

BRUSS, *brôs, brüs, bruzzu,* is a creamy

spreading cheese, made in the past from leftover bits of ROBIOLA-type sheep's cheese, or ricotta, left to ferment with milk, sometimes with the addition of pepper, chilli, herbs, olive oil, or vinegar. When the effect gets too much even for addicts, the activity is slowed down by stirring in some GRAPPA or other spirit, which usually gives the mixture a greyish hue, but can vary from green to yellow. There are as many versions as there are names for this cheese spread. Packed in attractive ceramic pots with pretty fabric covers, this pungent delicacy can travel well beyond the Langhe in Piedmont, or the Apennine valleys between Piedmont and Liguria, where it is made; the smell was once said to be a deterrent to invaders, but barbarians of all nations now carry these pots away in triumph. A version whose *tipicità* (special and unique qualities) merits protection is from the provinces of Cuneo (*bruss di Castelmagno*), Asti, Valle Argentina, and Arroscia in the province of Imperia, made with cheeses from the milk of cows, sheep, and goats and treated with traditional techniques which give the resultant *bruss* special and unique qualities. Traditionally made in terracotta pots called *toupini*, it can also be matured in plastic containers. The *Bruz d'Murazzan* is made from the *robiola* of Murazzano. The *Bruss di Fabrosa* uses the whey and residues from making RASCHERA cheese. It is an indication of the future for regional cheeses that this at one time domestic product, recycling leftovers, is now made with good-quality ingredients by small commercial producers for a growing market. It is enjoyed as a spread, on bread or BRUSCHETTA, and as a condiment for polenta and boiled pulses.

BUCKWHEAT, *grano saraceno, Fagopyrum sagittatum* or *esculentum,* is a seed, not a cereal grain, and was introduced into Italy in the late 14th and early 15th centuries. It grows well in cold mountain regions, and was and still is used, whole, in soups and stews, and as flour in breads, pasta, and versions of polenta. With protein content almost as high as wheat, and with good amounts of carbohydrate and oils, it is a nourishing ingredient, easy to grow on poor land and with a distinctive, slightly bitter flavour appreciated by many, including Mattioli, who wrote with enthusiasm of its use in northern Italy: "Peasants who live in the area between Germany and Italy make a polenta with the flour, and divide the cooked mass into thin slices with a cord, then serve them on a dish seasoned with cheese and butter, which they devour with gusto, and rightly, I think, for it is not unpleasant to eat, and does not weigh on the stomach like the polenta made with millet, eaten by charcoal burners and wood cutters." In the Valtellina today, buckwheat is made into *sciatt*, delectable fritters made with two-thirds buckwheat flour and one-third white wheat flour, mixed together to a soft batter with lo-

cal cheese (*scimud* or fresh *bitto*) and a slug of GRAPPA, then fried in lard and eaten very hot. Also from the Valtellina comes a homemade pasta, *pizzoccheri*, made with white wheat and buckwheat flour, which is traditionally cooked in a broth made from sliced waxy potatoes and sliced cabbage, into which some chopped onion softened in butter is added, and the final dish layered in a soup tureen with sliced local cheese (*scimud* or *casera*) and anointed with garlic and sage leaves browned in butter. *Polenta taragna* from the same region is made with a mixture of buckwheat (*fraina*) and maize flour cooked and stirred for an hour, and served with plenty of butter stirred in, and just before serving some sliced cheese, fresh *bitto* or *scimud,* mixed in until almost melting. In the Trentino, a FOCACCIA made with buckwheat flour and milk, mixed with sliced onions and sausage, cooked in the oven in a pan anointed with lard, has the evocative name *smacafam,* "hunger buster." A long way from the health-conscious use of buckwheat noodles in oriental vegetarian cuisine.

BUGLOSS, *buglossa, Anchusa azurea* or *officinalis,* grows wild and has a pretty purple flower which like BORAGE can be used to decorate salads. The leaves are edible and are eaten in salads or cooked in soups and stews.

BURIDDA is one of the two main soups or stews of Liguria, in which a variety of prepared fish are cut up and either stewed in a SOFFRITTO or mixture of chopped garlic, onion, celery, and carrot softened in olive oil, cooked down to make a pleasant sauce in which the fish are simmered until done, or sometimes layered with the vegetables in a terracotta pot and cooked for several hours, often with the addition of salted anchovies, dried mushrooms, pine nuts, and capers, usually some tomatoes as well, maybe white wine instead of water. All this could take hours, ending up with mature squid and octopus nice and tender and the other fish disintegrated; or the fish could be added in sequence according to their cooking time. These might include angler fish, rascasse, gurnard, weevers or stargazers, dogfish, octopus, and squid, mussels, shrimp, and razor clams. (The name *buridda* is similar to the Provençale *bourride*, but the method is not— a *bourride* is cooked quickly with the raw sauce ingredients and thickened to a velvety softness with aïoli and egg yolks. *Buridda* is not to be confused with BURRIDA, a way of cooking fish with aromatic vegetables and finishing with a sauce.)

BURRATA a speciality of PUGLIA, is a MOZZARELLA to which the addition of cream gives a lush buttery flavour and texture. A fresh ephemeral delicacy, that from Martina Franca and Andria in particular, *burrata* is made from the milk of the *razza poldolica*, grazing on fragrant herbs and grasses. It is made now on a semi-industrial scale by the family who first exploited the possibility of using "offcuts" of pulled mozzarella to make this much appreciated tourist attraction, whose ample rotund shape is said by some to evoke the comforting maternal belly.

BURRIDA is a Sardinian way of serving fish like skate (*see* RAY) and dogfish or smooth hound shark (or any firm fleshed fish, like SWORDFISH or halibut), which are first sliced and simmered in water flavoured with onion, celery, carrot, and lemon and then dressed with a sauce made of garlic cooked in olive oil and mixed with pounded pine nuts or walnuts, chopped parsley, and a little vinegar, and served cold after absorbing the sauce for a few hours.

BURRINO is a kind of butter or ghee made in MOLISE and BASILICATA from cow's milk whey; the butter fat is extracted from it, and water and air expelled, then it is enclosed in a skin of pulled MOZZARELLA, and salted and matured for a short time, after which it is fresh and creamy, and for longer, to get a more piquant effect.

BUTTER, *burro, manteca,* as cooking medium or condiment, is not restricted to the north of Italy. The popular generalisation which assigns butter to the north, OLIVE OIL to the south, and LARD to roughly the middle does not do justice to a more complex reality. Throughout history tastes have changed, as Capatti and Montanari have explained (Capatti and Montanari, 1999, pp. 120–26), tracing the evolution from the preference for oil in the ancient world to pork fat arriving with the erosion of Roman gastronomy by barbarian Germanic influences, and the growing taste for butter during the Renaissance, giving way to a sort of pluralism, where oil, butter, or lard are specified "according to taste or availability, to the situation in the 20th century in which butter showed signs of moving on, leaving behind its elitist connotations and reaching a wider range of consumers. But the story does not end here, for now olive oil is staging a comeback, thanks to the discovery (or possibly invention) of the "Mediterranean diet" by American doctors and journalists."

Taste as well as locality determines choice; in many dishes a touch of butter adds flavour, richness, and texture. Risottos have butter stirred in just before serving, a delicate dish of home-made egg and flour *linguine* or *tagliolini,* or whatever name they go by, is often dressed with a walnut-sized lump of unsalted butter and a powdering of finely chopped fresh herbs (an austere selection of one or two mild young herbs such as chives and marjoram).

In the past, butter was squeezed and pounded to get rid of excess water, then beaten and forced through a syringe to make decorative patterns, and served sprinkled with powdered sugar. Hardened in ice, lumps of butter were sculpted into figures to grace banquet tables, their ephemeral quality being a great part of their charm.

C

CABBAGE, *cavolo, Brassica oleracea,* has been around for thousands of years, and many of the types we recognize today were known to the ancient Romans. A large brassica family, which has been divided into many groups, also includes CAULIFLOWER and BROCCOLI, which can easily be confused, though this state of affairs is not serious, for pedantry has no place in a situation where recipes are virtually interchangeable for the many different varieties of *Brassica oleracea* var. *cauliflora.*

Another group of brassica contains the many kinds of headed, or hearted, cabbage, some with close-packed tight leaves, others with looser foliage, bred to make themselves available from winter to autumn, and appearing in a huge variety of shapes and colours. Castelvetro suggests cooking a finely sliced cabbage in good meat broth, and halfway through adding some hard PIG'S FAT chopped to a cream with garlic and herbs (borage, parsley, thyme), and serving with parmesan and freshly ground pepper. He describes a simpler way to cook a whole cabbage head in salted water, drain it, cut it into pieces, pour on melted butter, and let it sweat away, seasoned with salt and pepper, covered, until needed.

The *cavolo nero,* much loved in the cuisine of TUSCANY, belongs to the group which produces leaves from a heartless base. It is one of the main ingredients in the Florentine RIBOLLITA, where its clear dark green colour is as important as its pronounced flavour. Finely sliced, it is also cooked slowly for an hour or so with the fine pale polenta of Tuscany, a loose, sloppy, mixture, perfumed with parmesan and some extra virgin olive oil.

Odour, rather than flavour, can be a problem with this vast cabbage family. Harold McGee explains that this is due to sulphur-containing compounds, including hydrogen sulphide, which get released as the cabbage is cooked; the longer the cooking, the more powerful the effect. So when Castelvetro advises us to take a leafy green cabbage by the stem, plunge it briefly into boiling water two or three times, and eat the chopped leaves as a cooked salad with oil and vinegar, he is intuitively responding to the presence of vitamins and trisulphides that he could never have imagined.

A contemporary of Caravaggio, Tommaso Salini (Rome, 1575–c. 1625), might well have painted his *Ragazzo con fiasco e natura morta* (Boy with flask and still life), at the same time Castelvetro was writing out his cabbage recipes. Perhaps too much has been made of the nubile youth, mildly décolleté, holding aloft a wicker-covered flask of wine and smiling beguilingly at an unseen companion, to the neglect of the flamboyant cabbages in the foreground, which here find their apotheosis in a swirl of baroque splendour, quite eclipsing the somewhat ordinary allure of the boy.

CACCIUCCO is the Tuscan answer to Italy's other fish soups, and is said to have originated in Livorno, influenced by contacts with Turkey (the name is derived from the Turkish *küçük*, which means tiny, referring to the small fish used). It is strongly flavoured with garlic and *peperoncino* (*see* CHILLI PEPPER), called *zenzero* in Tuscany, which is confusing, since ginger does not come into it. If you include appropriate quantities of all the fishes specified by tradition, there will be enough to feed eight or ten people: *scorfano nero* and *rosso, capone gallinella, grongo, mureno, gattuccio, palombo, seppie e polpi piccoli, canocchie, granchi di scogli,* as well *pesce lucerna, rana pescatrice, ombrina, triglia, ghiozzo,* and plenty more. First cook a SOFFRITTO of finely chopped onion, celery, and carrot in oil with some whole cloves of garlic and hot chilli pepper and a handful of chopped parsley, then add the squid, octopus, and shellfish, fry a bit, put in a tablespoon of strong red wine vinegar and let it evaporate, then add a glass of good red wine and a bay leaf and about two pounds of chopped tomatoes. Cook everything together until the sauce is dense and the squid done, then add the other fish according to size and firmness of flesh. This is traditionally eaten over slices of bread dried in the oven and rubbed with garlic and washed down with plenty of young red wine.

A version from Viareggio omits the vinegar, adds water as well as wine, and cooks the heads and trimmings, together with the smaller fish, in the *soffritto* and tomatoes, then rescues the squid and shellfish, and passes the lot through a sieve to thicken the soup before adding the other prepared fishes.

Artusi, with his dual loyalties, born in Romagna but Tuscan by adoption, saw the two words for fish soup, *cacciucco* and *buridda,* not as an indication of regional variety, but more as showing the need for a uniform language for a newly united kingdom.

CACIO is another word for cheese, used mainly in southern and central Italy; in the north FORMAGGIO is used. From *cacio* or *cascio* are derived names like CACIOTTA, CACIOCAVALLO, and so on. It was used by writers in the past, particularly in central and southern Italy, until overtaken by *formaggio,* now in general use.

CACIOCAVALLO has a perplexing name, for its literal meaning, horse cheese, is hardly credible for a product made from the milk of an exceptional race of cow, the *podolica.* The cheeses are traditionally hung to mature in pairs over a pole, *a cavallo,* as if on horseback, say some; others think the word's possible origins were with some nomadic tribe who slung skins filled with milk over their saddles and discovered cheese at the end of the journey, or that there was even a shared origin with a range of similar cheeses throughout the Mediterranean, with its epicentre in Bosnia, perhaps under the influence of Catholic monastic settlements. The cows themselves may be an ancient indigenous race, descendents of *Bos primigenitus,* the uro, or part of prehistoric migratory movements, or even brought along by the ever obliging Lombards; whatever its origins, this amiable animal is perfectly adapted to the harsh terrain of the Mezzogiorno (Campania, Basilicata, Puglia, Calabria) and deftly picks its way in a semiwild state over the barren rocks and parched outcrops of areas like Sila in Calabria, its silvery grey form glimmering in the first light of dawn among the rocks and shrubs, or glowing palely as it chews cud on the rare green patches. They munch on acorns, nuts, bark, bits of wood, and lichens in the winter, enjoying the springtime roots and shoots of aromatic plants like wild roses, juniper, blueberries, hawthorn, and damsons and their berries and fruits in summer, taking particular pleasure in the wild strawberries which stain their hooves and muzzles a pretty pink after a day's grazing. Wild herbs add their aromas to the milk—thyme, oregano, summer savory, manzanilla, curry plant (*elicriso*, *Helichrisum italicum*)—and also have useful preservative properties. Connoisseurs claim to recognise the terrain and time of year from the flavour of even a well-aged cheese. The *podolica* cow has the additional virtue of being a good mother, giving birth to and rearing its young unaided, and only with difficulty being persuaded to share its low yield of milk with the patient cowherd, up by 4 a.m. to milk the animals who have been grazing all night, before they flee to the woods to escape the flies and heat of daytime.

The *massaro* who tends the cows also supervises the cheese-making, a complicated process, in which the milk is coagulated with calves' or goats' RENNET, heated, the curds stirred, partly drained, left in the warm whey, then drained again, cooled, later worked and pulled in very hot water until elastic, then shaped by hand into the characteristic pear shape, salted, and finally hung up in pairs for a few months. They can later be left to ripen for months longer. Something unique, a round, butter-filled *caciocavallo*, is a traditional product of Calabria under the names of BURRINO and *butirro*. It is made in spring and early summer, after the cattle reach their mountain pastures, and the butter will vary in colour depending on the season. George Gissing evidently heard the name *butirro*, whence his puzzled observation that "the so-called butter, by a strange custom of Cotrone, was served in the emptied rind of half a spherical cheese—the small *caccio cavallo*, horse-cheese."

The low yield of milk, labour-intensive production, and special qualities of the DOC and DOP versions of *caciocavallo* make it both rare and expensive, hardly to be found on the open market, changing hands in a typically Italian way, as a gift or token of esteem, in a clandestine way that makes it difficult to apply the regulatory norms that would maintain high standards and high prices for the benefit of both producer and consumer.

CACIORICOTTA LUCANO

is made in Lucania in BASILICATA. It is a version of PECORINO made with goat's milk, sometimes with the addition of sheep's milk—testimony to the importance of the goat in the rural economy, where local breeds abound, in spite of attempts to banish them in favour of sheep. Heated to just under boiling point, the milk gives a rich curd rather like ricotta. It is enjoyed young and fresh, or after maturing for several months.

CACIOTTA

is another word for cheese, a name derived from CACIO, itself derived from the Latin *caseus*. This affectionate diminutive is a survival of regional and historic usage, and is applied to so many soft, semi-ripened cheeses that it would be confusing to try to describe them all. There are many kinds of *caciotta* in production, mostly made on an industrial scale, rustic-sounding but fairly run of the mill, but there are also some unique to a particular area, with distinct individuality; the *Atlante* (INSOR, 2001) lists over a dozen of these. *Caciotta toscana* is a fresh cheese made from the milk of sheep and cows grazing on local pastures and hay. It is eaten fresh, and has a mild creamy taste. *Caciotta sarda* is made in SARDINIA from the milk of native sheep, grazing on local pastures, pasteurised, acidified, coagulated, put in moulds and drained in a warm atmosphere; it ripens in a month in a warm humid place, to produce a mild, soft, delicate cheese. A version of this is confusingly now blessed with its DOP under the name *pecorino sardo*, as is the Sardinian *semicotto ovino*, thus conferring both protection and loss of identity at the same time. An unusual *caciotta* from Montemauro in the commune of Brisighella in EMILIA-ROMAGNA is made with a mixture of water buffalo's, sheep's, and goat's milk, with a delicate soft freshness even when ripened for some months. A fresh unripened *caciotta* is made in UMBRIA, delicately flavoured with truffles. One from the area around Fermo in the MARCHE is prepared by warming the milk in a *bain-marie*, draining and salting quickly, ready to eat in about 10 days. The *casciotta di Montefeltro* and the *casciotta d'Urbino* are similar, though the latter has its DOP, both made from mixed sheep and cow's milk. These cheeses sometimes spend time under walnut and chestnut leaves, which gives them a characteristic flavour. An artisan *caciotta* is made in the province of Viterbo, of cow's milk, sometimes with the addition of sheep's, sold either fresh or matured.

Caciotta genuina romana is made in the Roman Campagna, the Agro Romano, and even now, in places infested not with the *malaria* but motorways, light industry, and satellite housing, there is still to be found excellent pasture for the sheep whose milk, pasteurised, cooked twice as curds, pressed, and salted can be enjoyed fresh or matured. LAZIO provides a dozen other interesting *caciotta* cheeses. CAMPANIA has a *caciotta* made from mixed cow's and sheep's milk in the same way as the PECORINO, without pasteurisation, but zapping undesirable bacteria by boiling the cheeses, in their moulds, in hot whey for 10 minutes; both are eaten fresh or matured. Versions of *caciotta foggiana* known as *caciofiore* and *caciogargano* are made in Foggio and Manfredonia in PUGLIA; they are light, soft, buttery fresh cheeses made from the milk of local sheep grazing on natural pasture.

CALABRIA is the long, narrow peninsula that forms the toe of Italy, the southern extremity of the mainland. The valley of the river Crathis separates it from Lucania. South of this are two successive mountain masses, Sila and Aspromonte, both partly wooded (in spite of modern deforestation), snow-capped in winter, with upland meadows that offer summer pasture.

What we now call Calabria emerges into written history with Greek colonisation in the 7th century BC. In the early period the most prosperous Greek city in the region was Sybaris. It was famous for its long rivalry with neighbouring Croton, whose citizens, eventually successful, destroyed Sybaris entirely (in 510 BC) and diverted the waters of the Crathis (Crati) over the site. Sybaris gave its name to the sybaritic pursuit of luxury, setting a standard of hedonism (gastronomic and otherwise) that Calabria has never since attained. Setting an example of elaborate preparations for religious festivals, the Sybarites ruled that sacrifices in their city should be announced a year ahead. To favour gastronomic luxury, they exempted eel-sellers from taxation, and for the benefit of any cooks who invented a new dish, they decreed a one-year protection from imitators, an ancient patent.

Croton, by contrast, is famous as the city where, in the late 6th century, the mysterious Pythagoras first established a community that followed his curious rules and beliefs. Surviving information about these is doubtful and contradictory. Did he forbid the eating of broad beans, or did he eat them avidly? Did he rule out fish, or only sea anemones? The Pythagoreans, as a functioning community, were eventually driven out of the south Italian cities in a series of violent upheavals within two centuries of the master's death.

In the 2nd century BC, the Romans established their rule over the Bruttii of the mountainous interior, as well as the Greeks and Oscans of the coastal cities; they called the region ager Bruttius or, more briefly, Bruttium. Not long after the end of the Roman Empire, the toe of Italy lost its political link with Rome and the north, a link that was not to be restored until the modern kingdom of Italy was established in 1860. Meanwhile, throughout medieval and early modern times, southern Italy and Sicily were tossed among rulers of Gothic, Byzantine, Arab, Norman, German, Angevin, and

Aragonese origin. The region was often fought over and seldom benignly governed. Under Byzantine rule the name Calabria, which had earlier belonged specifically to the southeastern peninsula, the heel of Italy—the nearest district to Greece—began to be used for the whole reconquered zone; eventually it became the name of the southwestern peninsula formerly called Bruttium.

In view of the region's exciting history, it is no surprise that the everyday speech of Calabria is quite distinct from standard Italian but very close to Sicilian, of which it is usually considered to be a dialect. Italian, however, is commonly used, and names given in this article are generally in Italian, not Calabrian. The major long-established minorities are the Greeks, whose ancestors are generally thought to have arrived during a period of Byzantine rule in the 9th century, and the Albanians, the first wave of whom came in the 15th century, escaping the Ottoman conquest of Albania. As exemplified in the discussion that follows, Greek (ancient and medieval) has loaned several food terms to the Calabrian dialect that are quite unknown in standard Italian.

Calabria is a food producer and proud of it. The region is rich in citrus fruits, including citrons, oranges, lemons, and clementines (the latter have a local appellation). There are also various more unexpected fruits, including the arbutus or tree-strawberry (*corbezzola*) and the ELDERBERRY (*sambuco*), here used, among other things, as a flavouring for bread. The CHESTNUT, here as in some other parts of Italy, has in the past served as a dietary staple; chestnut bread is still found, and so are fresh and dried chestnuts used in other ways. Calabria (especially the district of Rossano) produces a good deal of Europe's LIQUORICE. Its vegetables are proudly displayed in *licurdia*, the traditional vegetable soup, properly made with potatoes, onions, greens, and bread (stale bread, naturally). Wild greens, a very healthy dietary item in theory, are not quite so

healthy when fried in egg batter and served as an Easter dish, *frittata pasquale*. Among the regions of Italy, Calabria is the second largest producer of OLIVE OIL. Oil is used not only as dressing, cooking medium, and culinary ingredient but also in conserving local products: tomatoes, mushrooms, aubergines, chillies, not to mention *pesce azzurro*.

Local food festivals are numerous and getting more numerous every year; many of them are recent inventions, such as the Sagra della Cipolla Rossa di Tropea, dedicated to a local variety of red onion. The CHILLES of Calabria (which attain a high academic level at the Accademia Italiana del Peperoncino) are particularly important as a culinary ingredient and a flavouring in local products.

The best known cheese of Calabria is CACIOCAVALLO, also familiar in Sicily, in southern Italy in general, and across the Balkans. The local MOZZARELLA of Sila was traditionally made during the spring migration to the high plateau of Mount Sila. *Musulupu*, said to have Albanian origins, is a fresh, unsalted, spring and summer cheese of mixed sheep's and goat's milk, made on the eastern slopes of Aspromonte, not far from Reggio Calabria.

Calabria is most famous, perhaps, for simple dishes such as *sursuminata* (scrambled eggs with tomatoes) and *ova chi curcuci* (fried eggs with pork crackling), both confidently said to have been enjoyed by Edward Lear during his walking tour of Calabria in 1847. It is not famous for its meat, but there are good local foods based on OFFAL. *Murseddu* or *morzeddu* is a favourite of Catanzaro: lamb or kid offal cooked with tomato in a pie-like bread container. Another typical local dish, *mazzacorde*, is made from lamb or kid entrails wrapped around offal. There are several local types of sausage, with flavourings including fennel seeds, chilli, and sweet pepper. The *nduja* of which Spilinga boasts is no longer a chitterling sausage, like the French *andouille* from which it gets its name, but a chitterling sauce or spread containing lip-smarting quantities of chilli.

The Greeks and Romans praised the MORAY EELS of Reggio Calabria; in the Ionian Sea, it was said, these big fish lay basking on the surface, waiting to be caught, and earned the nickname *plotai*, floaters. Nowadays moray eel is less heard of, but TUNNY and SWORDFISH, already enjoyed in ancient times, are still on the menu. In Calabrian cuisine, swordfish may be accompanied by SALMORIGLIO, a sauce based on olive oil, lemon (or vinegar), and garlic. A well-known local speciality, also familiar in Sicily, is stuffed swordfish rolls (*involtini di pesce spada*). Small fry, consisting of baby sardines and anchovies and sometimes other species, generally called *neonata* or *bianchetto* in standard Italian, will be found fresh—in Calabrian coastal towns—and also as a conserve called *rosa marina*, smarting with chilli; this can be spread on bread and is used on locally made pizzas. There are alternative names to look for: *nunnata*, *nudilla*, *mustica*. Another conserve is *sardella cirotana*, made from pilchard roe, anchovy, and chilli. In spite of the good supply of fresh fish, dried salt cod (Calabrian *piscistoccu*) remains popular; *ghiotta* is one of several local dishes based on this.

Calabria has its own forms of PASTA. A type of lasagna is locally called *lagani*, a name that comes straight from one of the Hellenistic Greek names for pasta. There are also *schiaffettoni*, big macaroni typically filled with pork and other ingredients in the dish *schiaffettoni calabri*. The spiral *fileja* is served with a chilli-flavoured sauce of tomatoes and PECORINO. Another spiral shape is *fusilli*. *Pasta chijna* ("filled pasta") is a local variant of the cooked dish best known as lasagne: it is likely to incorporate minced meat, sliced hard-boiled egg, salami, and cheese.

The ices, said Norman Douglas, are "excellent at Cotrone." So is *torrone gelato*, which, in spite of its name, is neither iced nor a nougat but a sweetmeat of candied fruits and nuts coated in chocolate. Dried figs are a favourite base for sweets: they will be found chocolate-covered or stuffed with nuts and spices, under various names, including *crocette* and *pallone*. Many sweets are in origin festival foods (and here real religious festivals are meant, not touristic food festivals), like the honeyed *mostaccioli* (*mustazzuli* or sometimes *nzudda* in Calabrian), the *zeppoli di S. Giuseppe*, and *cuculi*, typical of Easter. These sweet delicacies are formed from pastry carefully shaped like newborn children wrapped in swaddling clothes, and may be seen garnished with little chocolate eggs and with an olive branch. Other Easter sweets are *cuzzupe*, *cuzzughi*, and *nepitelle*, little tarts filled with raisins, chocolate, and almonds. *Pignolata*, too, flavoured with honey and orange zest, may be a Carnival treat. *Pitta 'mpigliata* and honey-soaked spiral *scalille* are eaten at Christmas; so are the sweet "ravioli" known as *chinulille* (variously spelt) and the sweet gnocchi called *turtiddi*. *Cuddura*, an elaborate sweet loaf with a Greek name, belongs to New Year (*see* FESTIVITY AND FOOD).

Perhaps the wines of Sybaris were once as excellent as the other luxuries of that legendary city. Unfortunately, no one happens to say so. In the judgment of classical Romans, wines from Calabria reached no higher than the third class, with the single exception of the vineyards of Thurii, a later Greek settlement that stood very close to the site of Sybaris.

Nowadays, it must be admitted, Calabrian wines are most appreciated by those drinking them *in situ*. Norman Douglas, habitually by no means lavish in his praises, described the wine of Cirò as "purest nectar," but he makes it clear that when he reached this view he was sitting outside a restaurant at Crotone (15 miles south of Cirò) having already taken a glass of Strega "to ward off the effects of overwork," meanwhile "imbibing alternately ices and black coffee" and preparing to uncork the day's last bottle of *vino di Cirò*. The red wine now called Melissa, from just south of Crotone, is approved by Douglas but by no one else; his claim that Pliny liked it cannot be substantiated. The modern wines most praised by others are two sweet whites: *moscato di Saracena* from slopes south of Castrovillari, which George Gissing thought possibly "worthy of Sybaris," and *Greco di Gerace*, from the far southeastern coast, described as "really distinguished" by Cyril Ray. These wines can still be found, though neither has a DOC. *Greco di Bianco*, which does have one, claims to share the reputation of its rarely encountered neighbour. Calabria is known for liqueurs of unusual flavours, lemon (*limoncello*), citron (*cedrata*), liquorice, wild fennel, and bergamot orange.

Calabrian food shows some unexpected survivals from that of the ancient Mediterranean. The bulbs known to northern gardeners as grape-hyacinths are eaten with relish (southern Italian LAMPASCIONI, Calabrian *cipudduzzi*), as they were by classical Greeks. Lupin seeds (*lupini*), once praised as the staple of an ascetically flatulent diet by ancient philosophers, are produced in Calabria and are marketed as a relish all over Italy; some local recipes demand lupin flour, but that is now difficult to buy. An even more unusual ingredient is the sea anemone, locally known as *jùjime* (literally "jujubes"); this creature, plentiful around Diamante, forms the basis of the traditional sea anemone fritters. Calabria is the major producer of the sweet medicinal substance known as manna, the exudate of the manna ash (*Fraxinus ornus*), long prized in therapeutics and still in demand in alternative medicine. The real uniqueness of Calabrian gastronomy is found in its sweets, its sweet pastas, and its festival foods. (AKD)

CALAMARO. *See* SQUID.

CALAMINT, *calaminta, nepitella, Calamintha nepeta*, one of the many Labiatae, is described as *mentuccia* in Sotti and Della

Beffa (1989, p. 48), which is confusing, since *mentuccia* as we know it is usually the name for PENNYROYAL. This pungent herb is indeed similar to pennyroyal, and can be used in the same way. Apart from its affinity with artichokes, it is used in stuffings and marinades, and in TUSCANY has been used for centuries as a medicinal herb, antispasmodic, tonic, and stimulant, with the power to calm gastric sufferings and soothe upset nerves, as well as flavouring food and cordials.

CALVINO, ITALO (1923–1985), used food sparingly but with effect in his short stories and novels (Biasin, 1993, p. 97) and has vivid evocations of the landscape of Liguria in *Il barone rampante*, including a horrendous episode with a kitchen full of captive snails, which is the catalyst for the hero's flight from his stultifying family life to one of freedom in the tree tops. *See* CHESTNUT, COOKBOOKS, LIGURIA, SNAILS

CAMILLERI, ANDREA. *See* ARANCINI, BASIL, CHILLI PEPPER, PASTA.

Camomile (see next page) is used mainly for tisanes and poultices, making a pleasant, calming alternative to coffee at the end of an evening meal. (Shutterstock)

CAMOMILE, *camomilla romana, Anthemis nobilis, camomilla comune, Matricaria camomilla, Chamaemelum nobile*, and *Chamomilla aurea*, are plants of the Compositae family and are used mainly for tisanes and poultices, making a pleasant, calming alternative to coffee at the end of an evening meal. Their use as a flavouring for wine has virtually died out, but is a reminder of the overlapping of medicinal and gastronomic potions, and the benefits to be derived from both.

CAMPANIA AND NAPLES.

Politics and geography combined have shaped the cuisine of Campania, where one region and many nations have contributed products and traditions to create cooking of rich and joyful abundance. The Apennine ridges inland, beneath them fertile slopes and plains, then the coast, with its beautiful bays and gentle climate, have for centuries been described as an earthly paradise, where scenery, climate, fruit, vegetables, olives, and wine from the fertile volcanic soil, and fish from the sea, delighted body and soul.

Etruscans, Greeks, and Italic peoples settled and enjoyed the amenities of land and sea, with Capua as an early centre for trade and commerce inland, and coastal ports and roads developed by the Romans. After the Romans came Lombards, Byzantines, Arabs, Normans, and later Spanish conquerors, or despots by other means, who rolled in and ruled, imposed by treaties and dynastic marriages, all too confusing to enumerate, until the Bourbons held sway in the 18th century, more or less universally despised, and then regretted when replaced by worse tyrants. It took a long time for the Kingdom of the Two Sicilies (Sicily and parts of southern Italy) to join a united Italy.

Strategic roads led from Rome, with the Via Appia, begun by Appius Claudius Caecus in 312 BC, hugging the coast, then branching off to join the Via Latina at Capua and across to Brindisi on the Adriatic, point of departure for Greece, or continuing as the Via Aquilia along the coast right down to

Naples, with Mount Vesuvius in the background, has attracted foodies for centuries. (Shutterstock)

what is now Pozzuoli, through Naples and Pompeii and across the peninsula of Sorrento to Salerno and beyond. Rich Romans had holiday villas on the Bay of Naples, and even the catastrophic eruption of Vesuvius in AD 79 did not deter later visitors and settlers.

The ruins of Pompeii and Herculaneum have yielded much information about daily life, from charred and fossilised remains of food to elegant still life renderings of fruit and vegetables, and *trompe l'oeil* mosaic pavements using leftovers and the debris of messy eating as decoration. We have discovered bakeries, fast food outlets, *garum* factories, wine and olive presses, repositories for the renowned olive oil, and the remains of cellars of fine wines on a commercial scale; historians have combined this evidence with references in literature, and material compiled by Apicius, to reveal a lot about food and cooking in classical times. In *Empire of Pleasures*, Andrew Dalby brings all this together with imaginative insight, taking us on a voluptuous journey from Rome to Baia and beyond, passing through the land of the fabled Falernian wines, enjoying the smooth new road constructed by the emperor Domitian, skirting the sulphurous depths of Lake Avernus, and hitting the seaside towns of Campania, with a coastline verdant with villas, holiday resorts, and pleasure gardens. Seafood was good, and fish farmed in the Lucrine lake even better, especially the range of shellfish. Apicius has a basic recipe for shellfish, which are cooked in a sauce made from pounded pepper, cumin, chopped fresh lovage, parsley, mint, and seasoned with honey and wine vinegar, bay leaves, and cinnamon, mixed with fish sauce. Horace could not resist satirising the foodies and their arcane arguments over preferences for different kinds of these delicacies, but he might have enjoyed this simple recipe in Baia, in which oysters, chopped if big, mussels, and sea urchins are cooked in a sauce of sweet white wine and fish sauce with chopped rosemary,

rue, celery, and coriander, thickened with lightly toasted and ground pine nuts and a few chopped dates.

From Baia the gastro-tourist could progress to Naples, stopping to admire the big modern port of Pozzuoli, and the unloading of luxuries, spices, and staple foods from all over, especially cargoes of grain from Africa. The climate as well as the accessibility of wheat flour made the area ideal for the manufacture of PASTA. Sophia Loren, whose love of pasta and exuberant temperament were in perfect symbiosis, had a harsh childhood in wartime Pozzuoli and later Naples, so comfort food was important; as a successful diva, she travelled everywhere with packets of pasta, and when the effects became ponderous, she mitigated this by cheerfully running up and down stairs instead of using the lift. She was quoted as saying "I owe everything you see to spaghetti."

Naples had been an early Greek settlement, *nea polis*, but centuries later became a relaxed holiday resort for rich Romans when Greek implied *docta, facunda, otiosa*— cultivated, diverting, leisured, and often licentious (Dalby, 2000, p. 54). These refined, and vulgar, hedonists enjoyed the fish reared in artificial ponds, especially the parrot wrasse (*Euscarus cretensis*), an imported creature prized more for its expense and beauty than its gastronomic qualities. Perhaps dressed with one of the vibrant Apician sauces they would taste good anyway. Dalby and Grainger (1996, p. 62) give a recipe quoted by Athenaeus for fish poached in white wine and oregano and rue, and served in a sauce of mulberries stewed in the cooking liquid and red wine, mixed with honey, fish sauce, vinegar, and asafoetida, which would cheer up any dull fish, or guest. Many private villas had fishponds more costly than the living quarters, where, according to Pliny, favourite fish were kept as pets rather than food; they came when called and were sometimes adorned with earrings. Many of the prized fish and crustaceans were immortalised in mosaic pavements; one shows a basket from which fish, so fresh they seem alive, appear to be levitating, helped by the vertical stripes of the pavement on which they are superimposed. Another, from Pompeii, has a massive writhing octopus at the centre of a composition which includes bass, lampreys, red scorpion fish, sea urchin, baby squid, a red mullet *di scoglio*, a massive ombrine, and a red gurnard.

Something of this profusion is celebrated in an 18th-century popular song, "La canzone del Guarracino," sung to the music of a tarantella, an epic tale of piscine strife in which the doomed and ugly *guarracino*, *coracino nero*, or *castagnola* (according to Davidson, a small bream-like fish not interesting enough to be listed in his *Mediterranean Seafood*), enamoured of the fresh and vivacious little sardine, is attacked by a rival, the *alletterato*, one of the tunny family, a squabble that merits a mention because of the cheerful listing in the song of most of the fish in the Bay of Naples, with the exception of *spigola*, *red mullet*, and *pesce lovero*:

*A meliune correvano a strisce
de sto partito e de chillo li pisce
Che bediste de sarde e d'alose!
De palaje e raje petrose!
Sarache, dientece ed achiate,
scurme, tunne e alletterate!*

*Pisce palumme e pescatrice,
scuorfene, cernie e alice,
mucchie, ricciole, musdee e mazzune,
stelle, aluzze e storiune,
merluzze, ruongole e murene,
capodoglie, orche e vallene,
capitune, auglie e arenghe,
ciefere, cuocce, traccene e tenghe.*

*Treglie, tremmole, trotte e tunne,
fiche, cepolle, laune e retunne,
purpe, secce e calamare,
pisce spate e stelle de mare,
pisce palumme e pisce prattielle,*

*voccadoro e cecenielle,
capochiuove e guarracine,
cannolicchie, ostreche e ancine,*

*vongole, cocciole e patelle,
pisce cane e grancetielle,
marvizze, marmure e vavose,
vope prene, vedove e spose,
spinole, spuonole, sierpe e sarpe,
scauze, nzuoccole e co le scarpe,
sconciglie, gammere e ragoste,
vennero nfino co le poste,*

*capitune, saure e anguille,
pisce gruosse e piccerille,
d'ogni ceto e nazione,
tantille, tante, cchiu tante e tantone!
Quanta botte, mamma mia!*

This merry account has the same liveliness as the fish-scapes of Giuseppe Recco and Giovan Battista Ruoppolo, in which the fish quiver with a similar combative freshness.

In the 19th century, Ippolito Cavalcanti (1847, p. 156) had a recipe which takes us back, if not to ancient Rome, at least to Rome of the popes, in which OMBRINE, a big noble fish, is parboiled in water with sliced lemons and oranges, salt, cloves, cinnamon, marjoram, mint, parsley, salad burnet, and bay leaves, then cooled in the cooking liquid, and finished off in a rich sauce of almond milk and butter, eventually thickened with egg yolks, and seasoned with lemon juice tempered with sugar. Scappi has similar recipes, but without the egg yolk thickening, which use the same subtle combination of herbs and spices, sweet and sour (Scappi, bk. 3, p. 103v, recipe 3).

Modern fish recipes are less complicated, with a stuffing or garnish of chopped herbs (usually thyme, parsley, oregano, and mint) and chopped garlic, seasoned with salt and pepper and dressed with oil and lemon juice.

Westwards in the hinterland beyond Vesuvius between Pompeii and Sorrento were the fertile pasture lands of Mons Lactarius, and their produce is there in a wall painting in Pompeii—a *trompe l'oeil* scene of a rustic interior with the sun on two fresh cheeses in little reed baskets, sitting to drain on recessed window ledges, a blue spring sky beyond, and between the two windows a basket of fresh asparagus—a mural evoking a calm country meal, fresh air, and silence, the simple things of life, in the narrow confines of raucous city street. A 4th-century mosaic shows a contented goat at rest, contemplating a basket of fresh young cheeses, a rustic idyll which survives today in the making of the *caprino degli Alburni*, a mildly fermented and coagulated cheese from the milk of goats grazing on the fertile pastures of the Alburnine hills. FIOR DI LATTE *campano*, from the Sorrentine peninsula, is a fresh pulled cheese from the rich low-yield milk of the indigenous Agerolese breed of cow, with an acidulated sweetness and characteristic texture. A less complicated recipe from Athenaeus is typical of the Mediterranean love of cheese and honey: the fresh creamy milk is mixed with honey before the addition of rennet, giving a delicate sweetness, and the warmth of the sun on the Pompeian windowsill might have helped coagulation, and encouraged a slightly tangy fermentation.

Today Campania has a distinguished range of matured cheeses from the milk of cow, sheep, goat, and water buffalo, including the CACIOCAVALLO *podolico*, a CACIORICOTTA, CACIOTTA, PECORINO, PROVOLA *affumicata*, and BURRINO *in corteccia*, a butter base, enclosed in a pouch of pulled curds, salted and matured, to give a rich creamy cheese, based on ancient traditions of keeping the butter of spring and summer until the autumn.

Fruit trees flourished, and new varieties were introduced from the east. Cato wrote of 15 varieties of apples, pears, and figs, but by the 1st century AD Pliny could describe over 100. Lucullus brought sweet cherries from Asia, peaches from Persia, apricots, and quinces, and they all flourished in the fertile

soil of Campania, their beauties celebrated in mosaics and murals. A painting of hard green peaches on a branch, with a detached one from which a hearty bite has been taken, is puzzling, for this crisp fruit might not have been much of a pleasure to eat. Patience Gray has a recipe for a preserve made from hard wild green peaches (1986, p. 311), and Ada Boni explains how to pickle hard yellow peaches in white wine vinegar. We are reassured by other murals from the villa of Poppaea, where ripe peaches are among the fruit keeping cool in a glass bowl of water, apparently on a ledge, a simulated glimpse of everyday life, against a rich red background, like the wall painting from the same villa of fruit piled in a tall elegant wicker basket, protected by a wisp of transparent gauze from birds who might have mistaken them for the real thing. *Xenia*, or still life, in the aesthetic theories of illusion and reality in Roman art, explains some of these images, but to us a covering of cotton net seems common sense rather than intellectual conceit, and illusionistic murals an ingenious response to urban overcrowding.

After the austere realism of these seemingly factual Roman representations, it is something of a relief to turn to the fruit and vegetables of Campania in the overblown baroque canvases of painters in 17th-century Naples, who moved on from the gritty realism of Caravaggio and his followers to the lush ripe fruit of Paolo Porpora and Giovan Battista Ruoppolo. Conrad Berentz, a painter from the Low Countries who settled in Italy, produced a stunning example in a huge, bright painting, now in the Capodimonte museum in Naples. A larger-than-life peasant maiden, bearing on her head a shallow basket of fruit, amidst a wealth of flowers and classical architecture, against an eternal summer's sky, the air perfumed with roses and the aromas of ripe fruit, cooled by the fountain in which an urchin has dipped a bunch of grapes, is an intoxicating blend of realism and artifice, luxury and natural abundance. Both Pietro Navarra and Bartolomeo Spadino included transparent glass bowls in their still lifes, with peaches, plums, and grapes in chilled water, more a reference to everyday life than to the ancient world. The profusion of these works, treasured by patrons in Naples and hanging in the homes where the lavish menus of Vincenzo Corrado would later be served, show a delight and pride in local produce, as in the cascade of fruit in a Ruoppolo still life, with over six different kinds of grapes, apples, quinces, peaches, pomegranates, a rugged melon, and a cut-open watermelon, one of many canvases owned by Don Giuliano Colonna in Naples in 1688. Abraham Breughel, who worked in Naples towards the end of his life, set a profuse pile-up of fruit in a dramatic landscape with a blowsy peasant girl among seven kinds of grapes, peaches, apricots, apples, figs, pomegranates, and the melons he was said to have burst open by dropping from a height, to show their colourful flesh. Everyday life on a humbler level was another theme of Neapolitan artists, and here we can see details of less exotic things to eat. Tomaso Realfonso's piece of bread and a hunk of very rustic salame or *mortadella*, with its huge gobbets of fat, is a down-market version of the elegant slices of cured ham painted for patrons in Rome by Berentz.

The owners of these lush still lifes would have enjoyed the more formal presentation of their contents in the Baroque banquets staged by Antonio LATINI, described in his book *Lo scalco alla moderna*, published in Naples in 1694. His account of the duties of the *scalco* or steward and his subordinates in a noble household is detailed and illuminating, and together with the menus of some of these banquets, and recipes for the dishes served up, gives an idea of Neapolitan pleasure-seeking in the late 17th century. The Spanish rulers intermarried with the nobilty of Europe, and ceremonial visits spawned formal banquets and more light-hearted events. The landscape and climate made a

perfect backdrop for the tables covered in crimson damask and diaphanous white linen, with elaborate *trionfi*, often of sugar or gilded pastry. A typical outing to the countryside was in April, when the Conte di San Stefano and his consort and their daughter the Marchesa d'Aytona invited the regent to their country estate at Torre del Greco, where the table was laid on a terrace with views of Capri and Vesuvius and a bosky vista of verdant trees and bushes. A modest meal was followed by a prudent period of rest before a hunt party set about the profusion of animals in the game reserve, while the ladies sang and danced amongst the verdant groves. Refreshments were served—iced chocolate, pyramids of chilled fruit, *sorbetti*, in such profusion that what was left was distributed among the servants, even the lowest of the low: well over 300 of them, including huntsmen, coachmen, grooms, mariners, and others, who dutifully cried out *Huzza* and *Viva* in praise of the absent regent, sadly confined to bed and unable to be present. Piling fruit in a formal pyramid was a convention of banqueting, and freezing them in an obelisk of ice created table decorations of great beauty, cooling the air as they melted, releasing the fragrant fruit. The *sorbetti* are mentioned with considerable caution by Latini in his recipe section, anxious to avoid any infringement of the rights of the professional ice cream makers, whose creations are discussed in the entry on ICE CREAM. Another hidden clue to Neapolitan food habits is the mention of tomatoes in a recipe for *cassuola alla spagnola* which included breast of veal, stuffed chicken necks, pigeons, ham, and cocks' combs and testicles, the sauce thickened with eggs and served with little veal patties and decorated with sliced lemons. The Spanish influence, in the early use of chilli and tomato, is discussed in the entries for these items.

This theme of the pleasures of common food and ordinary life was taken up by the Spanish painter Luis Meléndez during his years in Naples, and appreciated by patrons there and later in Madrid, where his compositions were of simple ingredients for modest dishes, or light meals of cheese, fruit, and wine. Meléndez was perhaps influenced by the views of Antonio Genovesi, one of the pioneers of Enlightenment thought in Italy, who abandoned theology and philosophy for economics, and lectured on ways of improving the well-being of state and citizens within the framework of enlightened despotism and conventional religion; hardly the stuff of revolution, but it had a knock-on effect. Genovesi saw that the health and education of the masses were of the first importance, and that to change "quello strano impasto di ragazzesco e di malvagio, di violento e di molle" ("that strange amalgam of boyishness and villainy, violence and lethargy") required improvements in the law and land tenure and education. Vincenzo Corrado was likely to have been of the same cast of mind, as his writings about farming and improved food production show. But progress was slow; the *lazzaroni*, impatient with the corrupt and self-indulgent Bourbon regime, and inflamed by revolutionary ideas wilder by far than Genovesi's theories, got caught up in movements of considerable complexity, and the Parthenopean Republic, without an adequate power base, collapsed in confusion. But something about the shared enjoyment of popular food and drink in a benign climate and beautiful setting rubbed off on the Bourbon monarch Charles III, who—recalled to Madrid on the death of his brother—missed the *joie de vivre* of Naples, and hung the simple food paintings of Meléndez on the walls of his country retreat as a reminder of past pleasures.

The vegetables enjoyed by Vincenzo Corrado were so delicious that meat rarely seemed a necessity, and the cheeses from the hilly or low-lying areas of Campania—the creamy fresh ricotta, newly made mozzarella, and the variety of cured cheeses—are sufficient on their own, or combined with vegetables or pasta to make incomparable meals. It was not an aberration of the Enlightenment that inspired Corrado's book of vegetable recipes, *Del cibo pitagorico*, for unlike Rousseau's insipid Julie, with her pale creams and soups, washed down with buttermilk, Corrado had a passionate enthusiasm for robust local vegetable dishes, which he infiltrated subversively into the aristocratic French banquet menus of his time. A soup of cabbage and puréed chickpeas, another of fennel and lentils, a dish of lightly cooked borage leaves and flowers, drained and turned in olive oil with garlic, anchovies, salt, pepper, and fronds of wild fennel, or a dish of stuffed cabbage leaves sat comfortably amidst the rococo appurtenances of rich and costly dinners. In the first service of the menu for April, tender young artichokes appeared in a soup with veal broth, alongside a plain pottage of green chicory, and some fried baby zucchini. The second service listed peas in cream; cooked and seasoned spinach encased in a light yeasted batter and deep fried; asparagus in butter; endive *al parmigiano*, parboiled, stuffed with cheese, egg yolks, and herbs and fried in butter; artichokes trimmed and cooked in acidulated water then finished in a rich meat broth and thickened with egg yolks; borage leaves fried in a light yeasted batter; hop shoots in a prawn sauce; and lettuce, parboiled, stuffed with a rich thick cheese sauce, rolled in flour, then egg, then breadcrumbs, and fried in butter. August brought that novelty, a tomato soup, and one of celery thickened with egg. Then among the lighter chicken and fish dishes, undemanding in the summer heat, come eight little *entremets*—a savoury tomato pudding, spinach dressed with pine nut milk, endive cooked in butter, tomatoes hollowed out and stuffed with ricotta (probably enlivened with garlic, anchovies, and herbs), another savoury pudding of eggplant, spinach, beets with cream, celery braised in broth and sprinkled with herbs, and slices of eggplant, fried and baked with chopped basil, grated *provatura*, crumbled *mostaccioli* or spiced biscuits, and a little veal broth.

A summer's *pranzo pitagorico* is neither austere nor abstemious, with 18 vegetable dishes in the first course and 16 in the second, many of them rich with cream, meat broth or coulis, and cheese and eggs. Reaching back from the menus in Corrado's *Il cuoco galante* to the recipes in *Cibo pitagorico*, one can savour an extraordinary mélange of fashionable frenchified dishes and wonderfully robust Neapolitan food, parsnips for example dressed with delicate sauces of cream and butter, or a local version, with a vibrant garnish of chopped chilli, anchovies, capers, olives, oregano, and mint in vinegar. Traditional Italian dishes of elderflower fritters or spinach gnocchi served with butter hold their own among recipes for cauliflower *alla pampadur*, parboiled then baked in a rich buttery cheese sauce, while asparagus or hop shoots prepared *alla contadina*—parboiled then seasoned with chopped garlic, parsley, anchovies, oil, salt, and pepper, wrapped in paper, and grilled—use many of the powerful seasonings of Campania.

Today vegetable markets all over Italy display fruit and vegetables from Campania: San Marzano tomatoes, little *pomodorini*, six kinds of artichoke, apples—especially an ancient variety with a sweet crisp acidity, *mela annurca campana*, looking very like apples painted on a wall in Herculaneum, with a name probably derived from Pliny's mention of apples grown in Orcole near Pozzuoli; lemons from Amalfi and Sorrento, possibly known to the Romans, but certainly cultivated intensively by the Arabs, their fresh fragrance captured today in *limoncello*.

The tarnished image of the now universally loved and loathed pizza and pasta, strident with tomato sauce, is best dealt with rapidly. Street food for the poor enjoyed as a diverting tourist attraction leaves a slightly bitter taste; the 18th- and 19th-century travellers who got cheap entertainment by tossing a coin to street urchins who then performed

the ritual consumption of long strands of spaghetti straight from the pot, held high in grubby fingers, could also buy cheap prints of this amusing spectacle. Ice cream sellers offered a more refined product, also depicted in prints, in which the red of tomatoes was replaced by the *alacca* or dense fresh fruit syrup anointing the summits of ice cream cones, like molten lava on Vesuvius.

Slices of bread flavoured with olive oil and whatever comes to hand are one of the glories of Italian regional cooking, and have always been sold on the street fresh from bakers' ovens. It was only after this became debased by industrial production worldwide that the cult of the perfect pizza led to the claims and counter-claims of countless experts, but the Neapolitan pizza at its best, made in Naples in the classic, simple versions, depending on climate, ingredients, and skills that cannot be mass produced, frozen, shipped all over, and zapped in a microwave, is—or can be—superb.

Foreign writers who commented on the benign climate and cheap food which sustained the homeless *lazzaroni* might have been unaware of the potential menace of the mob. Francesco de Bourcard, in *Usi e Costumi di Napoli* (1857, p. 232) wrote with affectionate condescension of the easy ways of these "ragamuffins and lazybones":

> Summer, therefore, is carnival time for our populace—in these months they regain their usual feckless cheerfulness, with enough of life's sufficiencies, and are happy, completely happy, thinking little of the morrow, knowing that they'll never want for their princely feast, a dish of vermicelli with tomato sauce, a carafe of thin white wine, and fruit by the handful; and all this for a small coin that they can earn from one of the thousands of jobs that summer gives them the chance to do. Nor should you think that they give themselves much trou-

ble choosing a preference from the jobs on offer; anything goes that meets their need to provide for a day's sustenance. A *carlino* and he's rich, very rich indeed; this coin is enough for a meal, and for the day's amusements; 3 *grana* for maccheroni, 1 *grano* for the wine, 3 *grana* for the gods at the Sebeto theatre. Ask someone who spends 10 piastres a day, if he goes to bed at night as happy and content as our Neapolitan, the bed of course having the bare earth as mattress, with the heavens and their arabesque of stars for a coverlet.

Not many milords would buy that one. And the *lazzaroni* were not so easygoing, as the violent history of republican movements in Naples has shown.

But freshly cooked pasta with simple seasonings of grated hard cheese and a very little tomato sauce vindicates the behaviour of those corrupted urchins; for together with fruit and ice cream, this is indeed nutritionally adequate. Neapolitan immigrants to the United States brought with them traditions of this CUCINA POVERA and nostalgic memories of luxury food; the ubiquitous spaghetti and meat balls is a version of the latter, and in its original version has little to do with modern meat balls made frugally from raw minced meat of doubtful origin. It is helpful to relate them to Neapolitan traditions, including the so-called *genovese*, which has no connection with Genoa, and the classic *ragù*, which has nothing to do with Bologna. *Genovese* is based on a classic meat glaze, *carne alla glassa*, made by reducing a prime cut of beef, after hours of slow cooking with onion, carrot, celery, and parsley, together with oil, butter, lard, and ham, moistened with white wine, to achieve a succulent tender piece of meat in a reduced liquid which when strained makes a sauce for various kinds of pasta. In the version called *genovese*, the ingredients include, besides a prime cut of meat,

various *salami* and sausages and a lot of onions, which are all softened, then browned, and cooked down with wine to make a dense dark sauce which is used as a condiment for *maccheroni* and *timpani* (pasta baked in moulds); the meat is served as a rich dish on its own.

CAMPI, ROSSANA. *See* ITALIAN FOOD ABROAD.

CAMPI, VINCENZO

(c. 1536–1591), was painting genre scenes, overflowing with the produce of orchard and market garden, at the time that Castelvetro was pining for the fruit and vegetables of his native Emilia. Born into a family of painters, Vincenzo set up his own studio in Cremona in 1574 and soon became renowned for these works. He might have been influenced by the work of Aertsen and Beuckelaer in the Low Countries, many of whose genre scenes were in collections in the north of Italy. But where their work was heavy with guilt-ridden symbolism, Campi's canvases radiate a joyful cheerfulness, celebrating the profusion and enjoyment to be found in kitchen and marketplace, whilst also providing enough material for moralists to have a good time, too, with examples of sexual innuendo, allegory (the four elements), and the coarse expressions and vulgar behaviour of the market folk. Noise and mayhem as well as patient, painstaking work goes on in the crowded kitchen scene in the Brera Accademia in Milan, where at least 10 people fill the entire space with the preparation of meat, poultry, and pasta, but still making room for objects—pots, pans, bowls, dishes, and a huge stone pestle and mortar.

In the companion piece, *The Fruit Seller*, the scene is static: a single figure, a comely and virtuous young woman holding a bunch of grapes (in the Netherlands a symbol of chastity and at the same time fecundity, not to mention its Eucharistic associations), is surrounded by plates, bowls, baskets, and tubs of fruit and vegetables, each one a perfect still life. A blue and white Chinese bowl is full of red cherries, while two other varieties are piled into plain white majolica bowls (an innovation which allowed cooks to display food on a lighter background than the usual metal or earthenware). This makes a stunning background to a handful of mulberries, leaking their dark juices over the white glaze. Broad beans, some of them ready shelled (as in vegetable markets today), sit in a big wicker container, decorated with pale pink roses, which may be there to mitigate, in their freshness and purity, the earthy vulgarity of the beans. The painting spans the seasons, with artichokes and asparagus (recent but popular newcomers) in one corner, and an autumnal cabbage, almonds and hazelnuts, and the pumpkins, peaches, apricots, and pears of summer, with a pile of fresh young peas, several kinds of cherries, and late and early figs all arranged more as a celebration of the fertile countryside than the raucous recreation of a market. This pile-up of bowls and dishes resting on other containers is characteristic of table settings in which food was brought in from the kitchen or sideboard with much ceremony and placed apparently at random but in fact with the more luxurious dishes nearest the guests of honour. So here the modest maiden is presiding over a feast for the senses, inviting us to share Italy's cornucopia.

Another version of this scene was commissioned in 1580 by the international banker Hans Fugger for his castle in Kirchheim; here the maiden is peeling a fruit, probably a peach, a theme used later by Caravaggio, whose symbolism is still far from clear. (Castelvetro quotes the saying "A l'amico monda il fico, e il persico al nemico," "Peel a fig for a friend, and a peach for an enemy," which he guessed might refer to the alleged unwholesomeness of peaches, many of which he claimed did not need peeling anyway.) The prominent white lily, a suspended bunch of grapes, and the young woman's coral necklace might indicate the vulnerability of innocence, teetering on the brink of ripeness and temptation, but the array of life-sized overlapping dishes and baskets offer pure uncomplicated visual delight. To the list of products in the Brera version, Campi has added eggplants (long known in the south but still regarded with suspicion in the north), fennel stalks, eaten raw when young and fresh at the end of a meal.

A painting by Campi now in the Fine Art Museum in Lyon shows a group of peasants devouring a mound of freshly made ricotta, enjoying this ephemeral delicacy at its peak.

Campi's "fruit portraits" must have been a response to the taste for accurate depictions of the natural world, in a climate of opinion that fostered the beginnings of scientific research, as well as influencing the fine arts for centuries to come.

CAMPORESI, PIERO. *See* CHEESE.

CANDIED FRUIT, *canditi*, are beautifully prepared in Italy, and can be bought loose or packaged. The whole fruit are encrusted with sugar on the outside and are soft and almost translucent within. There is a wide variety, from cherries and plums to chestnuts and marrow, or pumpkin (*zuccata*). They can be eaten on their own, whole or sliced, often served in glass goblets to show off the brilliant colour. They can be used to decorate confectionary, like the rich cake *certosina*, added to biscuits and spiced cakes like *panforte*, even to SALAME and other cured meat products. Candied CITRON has long been used, diced, in ICE CREAM, where the perfumed skin and pith of this versatile fruit add flavour add a contrasting texture. Edible FLOWERS can also be candied—rose petals,

violets, rosemary, and geranium blossoms. *See also* CASSATA.

CANESTRATO PUGLIESE

is a sheep's cheese made in PUGLIA, in the province of Fogia and parts of Bari, and to qualify for the DOC awarded in 1985, the milk must be from the breeds Merino or Gentile di Puglia only. After bringing to a low heat, the curds are drained and aged in baskets woven from local reeds, and matured for up to a year, imprinting their pattern on the rind of the cheese. This hard, crumbly cheese is rich and pungent.

CANNABIS. *See* HEMP.

CANNOLO is a classic Sicilian deli-

cacy, once made as a Carnival speciality but now enjoyed throughout the year. Deep-fried cylinders made with a rich dough of lard and flour flavoured with vanilla and honey, filled with sweetened creamed ricotta, sometimes enriched by bits of CANDIED FRUIT, *zuc-cata*, or chocolate, are known worldwide, but the rich creamy sheep's milk ricotta of Sicily has no substitute. The name comes from the cylindrical wooden tube round which the dough is wrapped.

CANNONCINO is a delectable

pastry made with a strip of puff pastry wound in a spiral round a metal tube, baked in the oven, and filled with whipped cream or *crema pasticciera* (*see* CUSTARD).

CANTUCCI, *cantuccini, biscottini di*

Prato, are twice-cooked biscuits made of toasted, peeled, and chopped almonds mixed with flour and egg yolks, beaten to a froth with sugar; small flattened logs are baked, cooled, sliced diagonally, and baked again in a hot oven to dry and crisp them. They are a typically Tuscan end to a meal, dunked in *vin santo.* Some versions have whole eggs, add baking powder, and can be flavoured with vanilla, or made using hazlenuts instead of almonds.

CAPERS, *Capparis spinosa, cappari,* are

the flower buds of a plant that flourishes in hot dry climates. There are many varieties—bushes, trees, and climbing plants; the most renowned in Italy come from the south, and those preserved in salt are the best to use in sauces, and as a garnish, especially the ones from the island of Pantellaria. A preliminary soaking of the prepared and cleaned buds in brine or vinegar is followed by a period of preservation in jars, layered with coarse sea salt, in brine, or in vinegar. This pickling produces capric acid, which enhances the flavour. The capers need to be soaked or rinsed, then dried, before use, but cooking

Tart and savory, the most renowned capers in Italy originate in the south. The fruits have a mild pungency. Those preserved in salt are the best to use in sauces and as a garnish. (Shutterstock)

them destroys the flavour, so they are best used as a garnish to fish or meat, or in sauces, scattered on or added at the last minute. Preserved in vinegar, capers work well with dishes where the acidity cuts the richness, but the salted ones seem to keep more freshness of flavour.

In the past, capers had medicinal uses: good for the spleen, helpful for sore joints, driving out worms, and stimulating a jaded appetite, if taken at the beginning of a meal. They sometimes figure as salads at the start of Scappi's banquets, and Platina describes how to dress them, soaked to remove the salt, then served with plenty of oil and a little vinegar, and seasoned with chopped mint. Mattioli writes of the sight of them flourishing all over the ruins in Rome, especially around the Temple of Peace.

The fruit of the caper plant, not as pungent as the buds but with a pleasant taste and texture, are also used, pickled, as garnishes, and in salads.

CAPOCOLLO is made from a cut of pig similar to *coppa*, the shoulder and back of the neck, and is produced in UMBRIA, PUGLIA, and CALABRIA using fatter pigs, to give a less fatty, more lightly cured salame. In Puglia, the area round Martina Franco in Taranto has a microclimate benefitting from breezes from the Ionian and Adriatic seas mingling around its hilltop site, and a local expertise in preparing the *capocollo martinese*—salted, washed with *vino cotto*, dried, put into natural casings, rested, lightly smoked with oak bark, then hung in a ventilated but not too dry spot for several months. In Calabria, *capocollo* is made with a fatty cut from the top of the loin, massaged in dry salt, rinsed in wine vinegar, rolled up with whole peppercorns, wrapped in peritoneum casing, perforated, and hung to dry for three months or more.

CAPON. *See* FESTIVITY AND FOOD.

CAPPELLO DA PRETE, or *cappello del prete*, is special to Sassuolo in Emilia. It has a filling similar to ZAMPONE MODENA, sewn into a casing of skin, stitched into the shape of a tricorne hat. Traditionally it was a spin-off from CULATELLO, using the remains of the ham from which the interior muscle had been removed and other trimmings from the finer cuts, ground up with some body fat and skin from the spinal area. Industrial versions use boned head meat as well. This rich, unctuous mixture is hung for five to six hours in a warm spot, and then cooked and eaten, the fresher the better. Bologna has a similar version called *bondiola*, stitched up in a rhomboidal packet of skin. Confusingly, *cappello da prete* is also the name for a shoulder cut of beef used for stews.

CAPRIOLO (roe buck). *See* DEER.

CAPSICUM. *See* SWEET PEPPER.

CARAMEL. *See* SUGAR.

CARAVAGGIO, MICHELANGELO MERISI DI (1573–1610), arrived in Rome with an expertise in the depiction of fruit and flowers learnt in his youth in Lombardy, where pioneering developments in still life painting were going on. He was later to say that it took as much skill and talent to paint a still life as it did to make a religious or history painting. We can only regret that commissions from his worldly ecclesiatical patrons, or his own vocation, prevented Caravaggio from doing more in that genre. The Counter-

Reformation brought the teaching of the worried and renewed church home to congregations seduced by the dangerous new Protestantism, commissioning artists to show ordinary people experiencing the message of the Gospels: realism rather than arid dogma inspiring religious emotion. Caravaggio's *Supper at Emmaus* in the National Gallery in London shows contemporary people about to enjoy a meal that might have been found in any Roman tavern, and at the same time struck by the thunderbolt of revelation as the disciples recognise the young stranger in their midst as the resurrected Christ. A jug of wine, a flask of pure water, a glass half full of the golden *vino dei castelli*, bread, fruit (grapes and apples), and a guinea fowl, plainly cooked, with the soft glow that might indicate a pot roast, are painted with a naturalism that echoes that of the clothing of the apostles and the waiter.

It was in another Roman tavern that an incident took place which found its way into the tempestuous painter's police record. On 24 April 1604, Caravaggio threw a plate of artichokes at the head of a waiter. Sometimes quoted as an example of his murderous rage, it strikes a chord with all of us who have cravenly endured the behaviour of a less than civil waitperson. Caravaggio called for artichokes; when asked if he wanted them served with butter or oil, he asked for some of both, which is not unreasonable, but objected when they came on the same dish, to which the waiter replied that if Caravaggio couldn't tell the difference, he would have to sniff them and see. After this provocation the resulting mayhem was inevitable.

The point to note is that by then artichokes, young and plentiful, were no longer luxuries but tavern food, cooked in various ways—stewed to a melting tenderness with pennyroyal, garlic, and oil, as in *carciofi alla romana*, or parboiled then finished with oil, fat, or butter, or grilled, roasted, and dressed with oil, salt, and pepper (*see* ARTICHOKES).

A survey of the fruit and vegetables in Caravaggio's work by Jules Janick, available on the Web, shows that they were "portraits" rather than idealised subjects, even allowing for the possible symbolism (the spots of rust and decay on the apples indicating the corruption of beauty and innocence by the worm of evil within, and so forth; *see* APPLE). The painter's work does give an idea of what products were available in early 17th-century Rome. Janick has located a surprising number of still lifes by Caravaggio and his contemporaries, and we can see how his realism is in direct contrast to the idealised fruit of other painters, just as his saints and martyrs are portraits of the rough companions of his scurrilous social life and not the bland images of conventional devotion.

CARAWAY, *Carum carvi, carvi* or *comino dei prati*, are the dried fruit, not seeds, of one of the umbelliferae; it grows wild in northern and central Italy. Caraway was used a lot in the past, but not so much now, though it appears in liqueurs and perfumery. It is specified by Apicius in many of his recipes, and it must have been a shift in tastes that replaced caraway with the equally cheap and widely available fennel, both wild and cultivated, which has now almost completely supplanted it. Mattioli writes of caraway as a popular wild plant, in common use, its leaves eaten raw and boiled, its bitter roots treated like wild parsnips, and its seeds used to flavour bread and cooked food, "the way we use anise in Tuscany," noting its wide use as a flavouring in Germany.

CARDAMOM, *Elettaria cardamomum, cardamomo*, was little known in Roman times, mainly used in medicine or perfumery, though it does occur in a recipe in Apicius (*see* APICIAN FLAVOUR) for a fairly pungent *oxygarum digestibilem*, a digestive sauce or

Cardamom appears alongside cloves and cinnmon in many medieval Italian recipes. (Shutterstock)

relish made of dried herbs (including mint and parsley), pepper, cumin, and cardamom, all ground up in a mortar and diluted with honey, *liquamen*, and vinegar. Various kinds and qualities were known in the ancient world. It seems to have been one of those spices that did not get written about, but was useful to both cooks and chemists, appearing in medicines and cordials and various spice mixtures. This was so in medieval Italy, where it appears in several recipes; for example, a sauce in an anonymous 15th-century manuscript from southern Italy uses cardamom, cinnamon, long pepper, and galangale, ground and diluted with lemon juice, vinegar, and sugar (Bergström, 1985, p. 28). The same manuscript has a sauce for beef, verjuice mixed with saffron, cinnamon, nutmeg, cloves, and cardamom, thickened with hard egg yolks, and a green sauce including cardamom and garlic; and cardamom figures in one for boiled meats. In Italy today, car-

damom is virtually unheard of, except in the context of exotic foreign food, though it may appear as a flavouring in industrial products.

CARDOON, *cardo, gobbo, Cynara cardunculus* var. *altilis,* is a cultivated version of the wild cardoon, *Cynara cardunculus* var. *silvestris,* from which cultivated artichokes also derive. With the fleshy leaf stems, spines, and strings removed, cardoons can be eaten raw, with various sauces, or cooked in different ways. In the past, raw cardoons were held to make a healthy end to the meal, dipped in salt and pepper, freshening the mouth and improving the taste of wine, as well as having aphrodisiac properties. Seasoned with the BAGNA CAUDA of Piedmont, they would nowadays be eaten raw at the beginning of a meal. Their mild bitterness can be enhanced with butter and parmesan, or olive oil, after parboiling in water, or the prepared stems

can be stewed in stock. They can be enriched with a sauce of lemon juice and egg, or cooked, according to Artusi, first in boiling water, then sweated in some butter and finshed with a little cream and béchamel, flavoured with parmesan; a nice accompaniment to a rich, dark meat dish.

The tender tips of leaves and shoots come into the category of edible shoots, and the flower heads are used instead of rennet to coagulate milk.

The rugged appearance of the curved stems of cardoons, ribbed and spiny, add an almost architectural element to many Italian still life paintings, reminiscent of Borromini's idiosyncratic mouldings. Cristoforo Munari painted some around 1703, in the context of a loaf of bread, ham, salame, a sharp knife, and a covered cooking pot, suggesting a simple meal or snack in the northern tradition, though we shall never know if the pot contained *bagna cauda* or not.

CARP, *carpa, carpo* (sometimes called *regina*), is one of the big Cyprianidae family, originating in the rivers that flow into the Black Sea. Danube carp were known to the rich and powerful in Italy even in late Roman times. The Gothic king Theoderic, for example, around AD 500, was supplied with carp from the Danube. More recently the species has been bred and fished in Italy.

Although originating in rivers such as the Danube that ran into the Black Sea, the carp is now bred and fished in Italy. (Shutterstock)

Platina remembered its local name in Mantua, *bulbari*, used as a term of abuse by the Veronese when quarrelling with the Mantuans. If its living conditions and food are wholesome, it is a good food fish, but living in crowded, unhygenic, muddy ponds and tanks, it can acquire an unpleasant muddy taste, since the plankton on which carp feed can flourish on unwholesome things like sewage and various kinds of waste. Carp, anyway, like lounging in the ooze, and although excited and competitive when fed, if left to themselves usually scavenge quietly at night time. A recipe from Lake Trasimeno, *Regina in porchetta*, takes a fine specimen, scrapes off the scales, pierces the fish along the sides and back, and fills the gashes and the interior with a pounded mixture of fatty pancetta, garlic, rosemary, wild fennel, salt, and pepper, which after 12 hours absorbing the flavours is roasted in the oven, basted the while with the traditional *unzione*, unction, of lemon juice or vinegar, oil, salt, and pepper, applied with a sprig of rosemary, and later served as a sauce.

CARPACCIO. *See* VENETO.

CARPIONE is not a carp; it is a freshwater fish of the Salmonidae, the salmon, esteemed as good as trout caught in fastflowing streams, but found only in Lake Garda, where it is carefully protected yet remains endangered today. Baldassare Pisanelli has the highest praise for *carpioni* in his *Trattato della natura de'cibi e del bere* of 1611, p. 111: "*da ottimo nutrimento, e di esquisitissimo e delicatissimo sapore*" (the finest food, with the most exquisite and delicate flavour). Scappi praised them, and described how around Lake Garda they first gut and then salt the freshly caught fish, then cook them in hot oil, take them out and plunge them into hot, salted vinegar, take them out after 10 minutes or so, let them cool, then pack in boxes layered with leaves of bay or myrtle. In this light cure they will keep for some days, so this luxury could be transported all over Italy. This method is called *in carpione* and is used with many kinds of sea and freshwater fish. Luca Pacioli, another enthusiast of classical letterforms, perhaps like Mantegna drawn to Benaco, Lake Garda, in search of inscriptions, wrote enthusistically of this *"unico carpionista laco; amenissimo sito"* (this unique home of the carpione, loveliest of sites). It seems that carpione were not known to classical writers.

CARROT, *carota, Daucus carota* var. *sativa*, has a long history, growing wild throughout Europe and the Mediterranean area, where the leaves and seeds were used by the ancient Greeks, and the roots cultivated by the Romans. Alan Davidson offers a global summary of the ebb and flow of the culture of the carrot worldwide, with the possible conclusion that Arab expertise in southern Spain led to improved cultivation in the rest of Europe by the 14th and 15th centuries.

In Italy today, carrots are used in the preliminary BATTUTO of vegetables (usually celery, carrots, onions, garlic), herbs, particularly parsley, and pork fat or bacon which is chopped finely together almost to a paste, and used, cooked or raw, in many dishes. Carrots also make a fine *contorno* in their own right, cooked in a very little salted water and when tender seasoned with a fruity olive oil and a few drops of *aceto balsamico tradizionale di Modena* (see BALSAMIC VINEGAR). Ada Boni gives three distinctive carrot recipes: turned in butter, sprinkled with flour, seasoned with a pinch of sugar, covered with broth, and cooked in a moderate oven until tender; cut in four lengthwise, woody heart removed if necessary, cooked in water, then matured for a day in a marinade of oil, vinegar, garlic, salt, *peperoncino*, and oregano (this

is similar to a version by Mary Contini of a recipe from her husband's Neapolitan great-grandmother), and finally hollowed out and stuffed with a mixture of tinned tunny, breadcrumbs, and parsley and cooked slowly in a tomato sauce seasoned with oil and garlic, until the sauce is reduced and the carrots tender.

CASALINGA. *See* MEALS AND PATTERNS OF EATING.

CASANOVA, GIACOMO. *See* OYSTER, SALAD.

CASARECCIO. *See* MEALS AND PATTERNS OF EATING.

CASCIOTTA D'URBINO got a DOP in 1996 and at the same time acquired a letter *s*, distinguishing it from *caciotta*. It must be made from mainly sheep's milk, of the Sardinian and Bruna Alpina breeds, fed on nature pasture and fodder, with the permitted addition of no more than 25 percent cows' milk, in the province of Pesaro, in the MARCHE, in the area around Urbino. It is made, like its twin sister, CACIOTTA del Montefeltro, by coagulating the milk before heating, and then only up to 44 degrees (compare the PECORINO *marchigiano*). The curds are drained and then dry salted and are ready to eat in a month or less. The gentle flavour and texture were appreciated by Michelangelo, who insisted on a regular supply. His friend and collaborator Francesco Amatori, known as Urbino, was from Casteldurante, now Urbania, and his wife's family had farms and property there. After Urbino's death in 1556, they sent him propitiatory hams and cheeses (Michelangelo was ward to Urbino's children and controlled their inheritance, secure in a Roman bank). This may have been the cheese that Costanzo Felici's wife sent to his friend Ulisse Aldrovandi in 1570, *"una mano di formaio de queste nostre bande"* (a cheese from these parts), his estate in the remote little hamlet of Piobico in the hills above Rimini, where the cheese is still made today.

CASIEDDU

CASIEDDU is a goat's cheese made in the commune of Moliterno in BASILICATA. It is similar to CACIORICOTTA from the same area, but has a distinctive flavour derived from the ferns through which the milk is filtered, and the nepita or CALAMINT (*Calamintha nepeta savi*) which is added to the milk as it is heated; this is an antibacterial herb as well as a strong-flavoured one and, together with the techniques of production, makes for easier digestibility and higher nutritional value.

CASOLÈT DELLA VAL CA-MONICA

CASOLÈT DELLA VAL CA-MONICA is one of many mountain cheeses from the valleys of Trentino and Lombardy, especially the Val Camonica, which winds its way up from the Lago d'Iseo to the mountains of Ponte di Legno and over into Capo di Ponte in Brescia.

In the times before cheese-making on a large scale was possible, families made their own, and this might be the origin of the name *casolet*—made in the house, *casa*. Traditionally it was made from the milk of cows and goats grazing together, the goats exploiting marginal land, and the rock art of the area seems to indicate that the use of animals for ploughing and massed in herds goes back to Paleolithic times, when forbidding mountain passes seemed no obstacle to friendly and warlike exchange between neighbours. Today *casolet*, a soft mild cheese with irregular eyes or holes, is an artisan production,

round, triangular, or shaped like a clover leaf, perhaps inspired by all that rock art (*see also* SILTER).

CASSATA

CASSATA, *Cassata siciliana* (not the same as the ice cream called *cassata*), is a cake made from a voluptuous mixture of creamed and sweetened ricotta, layered with slices of liqueur-soaked sponge cake and set in a tin or pan with sloping sides also lined with the sponge and thin layers of green-tinted almond paste, its sweetness then enhanced by a layer of sugar icing, decorated with CANDIED FRUIT. Mary Taylor Simeti describes it to perfection, and also gives a detailed recipe:

> A proper *cassata* is spectacularly decorative: the cake, striped with marzipan coloured pale green in memory of the days when one could afford to use pistachio paste, is glazed with white icing, and then crystallized wedges of oranges and pears are placed on top, spread out like the petals of a flower within curving ribbons of translucent squash.

Then she brings us back down to earth with a bump with aspersions on its extreme sweetness.

The name might derive from the Latin for cheese, *caseus*, or the Arabic for a large kettle or container, *qas'at*. But no need to quibble, for both civilisations must have contributed ingredients, the Romans the ancient milk product, and the Arab world the cane sugar and almond paste, while the candied fruits, especially the *zuccata*, the chocolate, the light sponge, and the baroque decoration all derive from layer on layer of Sicily's complex history.

The ice cream *cassata* is also made in a mould, lined with a rich ice cream, which is filled not with ricotta, but possibly whipped cream, or sponge, or different-coloured and –flavoured ice creams, and maybe fruit and chocolate, so that when unmoulded and sliced, there is a richly decorative effect.

CASSIA. *See* CINNAMON.

CASTAGNA. *See* CHESTNUT.

CASTELLUCCIO. *See* LENTILS.

CASTELMAGNO, a hard, pressed, semifat cheese, is from Castelmagno, Pradleves, and Monterosso Grana, in the Valle Grana of the province of Cuneo in PIEDMONT (Piemonte). Its quality has been appreciated for over a thousand years, so much so that it was used as currency, and until recently was a useful commodity for barter in rural communities; the unique blend of milk from cows, sometimes also a small amount from sheep and goats, which have fed on fragrant local grass and hay, aged and ripened in cool conditions which give it a distinctive character, gives this cheese a renown which needs the protection of its DOP of 1996, for imitations abound. It is mild when young but becomes piquant and marbled with blue when aged.

CASTELVETRO, GIACOMO, was born in Modena in
1546 and died in London in 1616. He is known to us because of his short work *Brieve racconto di tutte le radici, di tutte l'erbe e di tutti i frutti che crudi o cotti in Italia si mangiano* (A brief account of all the roots, all the green stuff and all the fruit that are eaten, raw and cooked, in Italy), which he wrote in an attempt to persuade the British to eat less meat and sweet things and more fruit and vegetables. But at the time of writing, in London, between 1613 and 1614, he was also old, impoverished,

homesick, and dependent on precarious patronage, so his need to secure a position and an income was more pressing than concern, however genuine, for Great Britain's national nutritional status, as worrying then as it is now. The manuscript, which he rewrote and polished, survives in several copies, circulated among those he needed to impress. It was written with considerable tact and discretion, emphasising the positive aspects of Italian vegetable cookery rather than the negative aspects of ours, with its gross consumption of meat and sweet things, and our habitual disregard of the finesse involved in cooking tender young *primatici* and preparing seasonal salads. His tone of voice is deceptively modest, chatty, almost rambling, and without any literary pretensions. This choice of style was deliberate. Castelvetro included no tedious references to classical authorities, no quotations from dead old men, no long-winded moralising (customary in contemporary writers like Mattioli and Pisanelli). He wrote without pedantry in the here and now, for sophisticated readers with an enthusiasm for the language and culture of Italy and for new developments in horticulture, who might have resented being preached at and would not have enjoyed being talked down to—a delicate balance to aim for.

Castelvetro's work was never published in his lifetime, and although copies of the manuscript were passed around (one wonders if John Evelyn ever saw it and enjoyed the section on salads) it remained unknown except to a few scholars until its publication in Italian by Luigi Firpo (1974) and a later version by the Lancellotti family in Soliera, and its translation into English in 1989 (Castelvetro, 1989). The patron he had hoped so much of, Lucy Countess of Bedford, was in big financial trouble and could not even support her friend John Donne, and so Castelvetro died poor, unhappy, and alone, and we never had the benefit of his tactful message. But things were already changing, and it could be that Castelvetro had sensed this, and could have made a perfectly timed contribution to a growing enthusiasm in Great Britain for a lighter, less rich cuisine (long before the French were alleged to have invented it), based on the kitchen gardens and estates of the lesser country gentry, who exchanged cookery notebooks with recipes for light creams, fruit possets, vegetable potages, and light meat dishes, a reaction against the rich court cookery of an earlier generation (Spurling, 1986).

Castelvetro's narrative, starting in the spring, runs through the products of each season, with suggestions on how to prepare and serve them; not a recipe book, not a botanical or health handbook, just a gently informative account of fruit and vegetables and herbs in common use in his native land. A typical entry for broad beans: "when broad beans start to become hard we cook them in water to loosen their skins, which we remove. Then we put the beans in a little pot with oil or fresh butter, and sweet herbs chopped very fine, and salt and pepper, and stew them gently, to make a really tasty little dish." Or sprouting broccoli: "Next come the tender shoots which grow on the stalks of cabbage or cauliflower plants left in the garden over winter. They are cooked and served cold with oil and salt and pepper, as I described for hops. Some prefer to cook them with a few cloves of garlic, which gives them a wonderful flavour." This is a good way of dealing with the rank, "cabbagey" pong of broccoli; tossing a lot of coarsely chopped garlic into a pan of broccoli florets, cooked in just a little water, and finishing with oil and freshly ground pepper produces an unexpectedly mild dish. Later versions use CHILLI, which was starting to get known in Castelvetro's time, although he does not mention it.

Apart from a factual line-up of fruit and vegetables in common use, Castelvetro gives us some charming vignettes of daily life in the parts of Italy he knew well, EMILIA-ROMAGNA and Venice. A screen of climbing beans on a Venetian windowbox, behind which unseen women ogled passers-by, little boys learning to swim in the canals round Modena on empty dried gourds (Felici mentions this, too, a common sight, and by no means grounds for accusations of plagiary, which are just plain daft), market women preparing artichoke bottoms, as they still do today, and fraudulent Venetian innkeepers passing round morsels of raw fennel to disguise their awful wine. The lightness of touch barely conceals a poignant homesickness, for by then Castelvetro knew that he would never return to his native land. He was obliged to leave Venice after being arrested by the Inquisition in 1611 and rescued from the state prison by the British ambassador, and ended up in England in 1613, after wandering around Europe, dining out on his horrendous experience, as Casanova was to do later.

This short manuscript remains as relevant today as it did in 1614; seasonal produce cooked and served with simplicity and affection is what we still seek and enjoy in Italy; our current enthusiasms are a belated vindication of Castelvetro's aspirations.

CATALOGNA. *See* ENDIVE.

CAUL FAT, *rete, omento,* is a lacy layer of membrane marbled with fat enclosing the intestines of an animal. That from the pig is most commonly used. It can be wrapped round meat balls, portions of lean meat intended for grilling or roasting, or used to cover lean meat like rabbit, hare, or wood pigeon. It has the virtue of enclosing mixtures of meat and other ingredients to keep them together during cooking, and at the same time basting as the fat melts, and eventually turning an appetising brown.

CAULIFLOWER, *cavolo fiore, Brassica oleracea* var. *botrytis,* are grown to be available from spring to autumn, in a variety of shapes and colours, from snowy white to pink, purple, and bright green. They can be treated in the same way as broccoli florets, simply cooked quickly until just tender and eaten at room temperature with oil, salt, pepper, and a squeeze of lemon, or parboiled and finished in good broth or butter and nutmeg. Sometimes the stems of the florets benefit from being peeled of their outer layer, or the heads will be boiled to a mush before they are done, and as Stefani said, "*sta vigilante nella cottura, perchè si cuocono molto presto, e quando son troppo cotti, sono poco stimati*" (when they are overdone they are not much liked) Artusi must have had this in mind in his recipe *Cavolfiore all'uso di Romagna*, in which they are cooked without a preliminary boil, in a BATTUTA of garlic, oil, and parsley which, when nicely browned, is moistened with a little water and tomato paste, and finished with plenty of parmesan, recommended with COTECCHINO. Like broccoli, cauliflower florets combine well with PASTA, often with the bite of CHILLI and garlic to offset the blandness. Though blandness is not a problem for Simeti, who gives the ultimate Sicilian recipe for pasta and broccoli or cauliflower, in which the cauliflower sprigs are cooked lightly in plentiful water, then removed and finished with olive oil, anchovies, onion, pine nuts, raisins, and saffron to make a creamy sauce for *bucatini*, which are cooked in the cauliflower water, a pungent brew, and served topped with toasted breadcrumbs. A dish whose success depends on the quality of the cauliflower.

CAVALCANTI, IPPOLITO,

Duca di Buonvicino, was born into a noble Neapolitan family in 1787 and died in Naples in 1859. His work *Cucina teorico-pratica* was first published in 1837 and was amended by him on several occasions, running to nine different editions, two of them posthumous. The first part consists of menus throughout the year with their corresponding recipes, 600 in all. This is followed by a part entitled "*tutti i Pranzi di uso della nostra Bella Napoli espressi in dialetto Napolitano, esprimentino la vera cucina casareccia*" (all the meals in common use in our Bella Napoli rendered into the Neapolitan dialect, explaining our real home cooking). This use of the vernacular is not as jokey as it seems, for every social class used the Neapolitan language and pronunciation, and it was as natural to his readers as the limpid Tuscan of Artusi was to the Florentine bourgeoisie later in the century. The cuisine is the predictable mixture of foreign, particularly French influences, but the Neapolitan accent is strong. A soup made from pigeons stewed with a calf's foot, bacon, celery and parsnips, herbs, cloves, and cinnamon, then the flesh pounded, sieved, and mixed with a purée of green peas and basil, diluted with the clarified broth and served over cubes of toasted bread reminds us of Corrado's inventiveness, but there is nonetheless a creeping gentility in the dumbing down of some dishes, the absence of chillis and garlic, fewer herbs and spices, and sometimes the comfortable, reassuring tone of the author can become cloying. However, we can enjoy the trickle-down of sophisticated recipes and the upward mobility of popular food—pasta in many forms, tomato sauce, the fried street food, *zeppoli,* and *pizza.* Today's obsession with *cucina povera* leaves us disappointed with some of Cavalcanti's bland versions of traditional dishes, and even in the section in Neapolitan dialect, written at the request of middle-class ecclesiastical *bon viveurs,* and reflecting their tastes rather than that of the street urchins and *lazzaroni,* we find lively local dishes alongside some rather dull frenchified recipes.

Cheap coloured engravings, the equivalent of tourist postcards, showed a picturesque rabble devouring spaghetti with their fingers, straight from the pot, sometimes with a slug of tomato sauce and some grated cheese. Cavalcanti's recipes are more sophisticated, with versions of the TIMBALLO and baked pasta dishes, many different sizes and shapes of pasta, and many sauces. He usually cooked his pasta *verde, verde*—extremely *al dente*—and let it finish cooking in its sauce, "turning every five minutes," something we rarely do now.

A brief outburst in a delicate and possibly original recipe for a *minestra di frutti tagliati* (a stew of fruit and vegetables) gives a touching insight into the elderly writer at work. After describing with some firmness how to choose the best kind of squash for the job, depending on your knowledge and skill, he vaunts his own—"since I can assure you from my own huge experience and enjoyment of cooking, beginning at the age of ten, and now as I write this fifth edition, on Wednesday 21 October 1864, a beautiful autumn day, well into my seventieth year, that the best *cocozelle* are indeed the straight ones." A tetchy old man soothed by the autumn sunshine and a sense of his own worth. The stew in question is a delicate combination of diced squash or pumpkin of an excellent local variety, cooked in a rich tomato broth with peeled, cored, and sliced pears and apples, and diced turnips and onions. He is insistent that each be cooked separately in the broth, rather than all together, and brought together at the end.

The few sightings of TOMATOES in 17th-century Naples in Latini's recipes indicate that a popular product was starting to infiltrate aristocratic kitchens, but in Cavalcanti, nearly 200 years later, they are becoming mainstream; out of over 600 recipes, we find tomatoes in at least 30. His recipes for tomato sauces were not the first to appear in print, but they show the use of tomatoes of many kinds and in different ways, fresh, dried, as cooked sauces and *passato*, as a reduced *coulis*, or as a vegetarian broth, for use with pasta, rice, and other ingredients. A delicious version of STRACCIATELLE has the egg and parmesan mixture swirled into a tomato broth with finely chopped parsley.

Vermicelli are served with shelled PALOURDES in a reduced sauce made of tomatoes simmered until reduced in their cooking liquid.

Cavalcanti was wary with garlic and chillies, with that bourgeois fear of violent seasonings that is so irritating in Artusi, and is still sometimes met with today. Anglo-Saxon gastro-tourists, denied garlic in their distant youth, seek out with a desperate hunger the pungent recipes of rural grannies, and feel let down by the mildness of some published versions of traditional recipes. This is how we tend to react to Cavalcanti, which is perhaps unfair, for his upbringing exposed him to a corrupt frenchified cuisine, and when he rails, as he sometimes does in passionate italics, at the awfulness of modern cooks and their lack of understanding, he is demanding a return to and a respect for local ingredients and methods, though probably without having experienced himself the rigours of street life or the pleasures of street food. When, in later editions of his book, Cavalcanti lets his imagination rip, we do get some vibrant dishes; he tells how, desperate in his search for nice egg recipes, he flung together a sauce made of capers, olives, black and green, anchovies, and several brightly coloured pickled chillies, chopped with mint or parsley, and briefly cooked in oil and vinegar, seasoned with salt, pepper, and a little sugar, thickened with flour (for shame) to form a base for quartered hard-boiled eggs. These pickled chillies are mysterious; he never mentions the fresh ones, but their use was probably more widespread in popular cooking. Cod or a similar whole fish is cooked in water with salt, vinegar, sliced lemons, and bay leaves and served with a piquant sauce of chopped onions softened in oil, then simmered with pickled gherkins and chillies, chopped parsley and mint, passed through a sieve, and seasoned with salt and pepper and some lemon juice. Cavalcanti's recipe for stuffed tomatoes implies a choice—select the round fat ones, he says—empty them of seeds and juice, and fill with a stuffing of either the meat mixture for POLPETTE or a lean one of parmesan, breadcrumbs, chopped parsley and basil and egg, bake them in the oven, and serve with a sauce made of chopped pickled chillies, gherkins, capers, green olives, parsley and marjoram, lean ham, all cooked together and thickened with flour and seasoned with salt, pepper, and dark sugar. (Today the flour-based sauces of France seem alien to the Italian tradition, and even here in a truly local dish they add an unnecessary complication to what might have been a crisp raw condiment.)

The only mention of sweet peppers is for yellow ones, first roasted to remove the outer skins, then the tops and the core of seeds removed, next stuffed with a mixture of breadcrumbs, oregano, chopped olives, green and black, deboned anchovies, parsley, and, if you like, some chopped cloves of garlic. They are then covered with their tops, like lids, sprinkled with more breadcrumbs, anointed with olive oil, and baked in the oven.

A traditional dish of sliced and fried EGG-PLANTS layered with parmesan and mozzarella, spread with tomato sauce and chopped basil, covered with breadcrumbs and baked in the oven has the unnecessary name *gattò*.

Recipes *alla cittadina*, a term that might imply either the cuisine of the urban middle-class housewife or that of a lower social level, use garlic as well as tomatoes—red mullet are simmered in a sauce of finely chopped shallots, spring onions, garlic, and parsley softened in olive oil into which some salt anchovies are sieved, together with tomato sauce and fish broth, to which raisins and pine nuts can be added. The *cittadina* cooked prepared cuttlefish in a sauce of chopped onions, a clove of garlic on a toothpick for easier removal, plenty of parsley and good oil and white wine, boiled up fast at first to reduce the sauce, then simmered slowly with a little tomato sauce. But Cavalcanti's fear of garlic fades away in his dialect menu for

Christmas Eve. The traditional first course of a *minestra* of broccoli, *vruccoli*, still a popular classic, needs and gets plenty of garlic (five cloves) and what he calls *pepe sovierchio* which might mean strong pepper or chilli, as well as boned salt anchovy dissolved in olive oil; carefully trimmed and blanched tufts of broccoli are cooked slowly in this pungent mixture.

Tagliariell' e boncole is a dish of *tagliolini* first given a quick boil, *vierd', vierd',* then finished in the strained and reduced broth in which *palourdes* have been cooked, fragrant with finely chopped parsley, pepper, and good olive oil.

True to his promise, Cavalcanti offered his hungry clerics a succession of traditional lean menus and recipes for Holy Week, followed by some for various feast days, some *d'oglio*, meat free, and some quite rich, like the first course of the menu for the last day of Carnival, a *timpano de maccaruni*, a rich short pastry lining a big container, filled with layer on layer of the local *maccaruncielli*, lightly done, with cooked meat balls, chicken livers and giblets, mushrooms, parmesan, slices of caciocavallo, mushrooms, peas, all bathed in a *brodo russo*, a dark sauce, and since Carnival is the time for frugality as well as excess, add all the ends of salami, bits of ham, and mozzarella that have to be eaten up before Lent. Getting this huge pie, for 12 people, out of its *timpano* or *timballo* was always tricky, and he thoughtfully explains a way of up-ending it that preserves the luscious crust.

Cavalcanti is a good read, in spite of the dumbing down, the facetiousness, and the unavoidable French terminology, which he sends up rotten by spelling it like Italian. He cared passionately about food and cooking, about the traditions of his region, and deplored the decadence of the previous two centuries. Good Italian cooking depended on using first-class ingredients and handling them well, with careful restraint in seasoning, he said, and he maintained that professional skill, imagination, and humility were essential qualities in the cook. He wrote when the poor were always hungry and the rich had lost their gastronomic sense of direction, while the classes in between were either trying, disastrously, to ape the rich or, lower down the scale, quietly getting on with producing and cooking what they could afford. Far away from the north of Italy, where geographical and political ties with France meant that their cuisines had a lot in common, the Kingdom of Naples, with its strong links with Spain, had a happy way, as we see in the works of Vincenzo Corrado, of combining French culture and manners with the lively local gastronomy. One has only to look at the ill-digested, and indigestible, mishmash of Italian and French terminology and recipes in *La cuciniera Piemontese*, published anonymously in Turin in 1798, to realise how fortunate Naples was in its traditions and its three great cookery writers. Cavalcanti, like Latini and Corrado, accepted Spanish and French customs while deploying local ingredients. He seemed bemused at the success of his work, which seems to have responded to a need, and was happily busy on revisions and additions to each new edition until his death in 1859.

CAVOLO NERO. *See* CABBAGE.

CELERY, *sedano, Apium graveolens,* of the Umbelliferae family, has been used since prehistoric times, wild and cultivated—sometimes popular, as with the ancient Romans, sometimes eclipsed by CARDOONS and FENNEL, as it almost is today, when it is rarely used in its own right, except as accompaniment to certain rich meat dishes like *stufatino alla romana*, where its watery mildness is a fitting contrast to the rich stew of shin of beef perfumed with garlic and marjoram.

Celery stems and leaves are used a lot, though, in the various mixtures of chopped vegetables, including onion and carrot, which are often fried with oil or PANCETTA at the start of cooking; it goes into soups and stews, and is one of the things eaten raw with BAGNA CAUDA. In the past, the leaves with their pungent bitterness were more medicinal than gastronomic, but their decorative qualites inspired Hercules to weave them with olive fronds and willow into a victor's crown, according to Pliny, though we cannot help wishing he had told us more about this plant's role in the kitchens of Greece and Rome. Apicius used the leaves, stems, and roots of what he called *apium*, but it is not easy to be sure whether he meant those other pungent umbelliferae, parsley, LOVAGE, or ALEXANDERS. These wild things, when tamed and domesticated, loose their aggressive pungency, and can become mild and bland, like the celery of European agribusiness, but their distinct flavours, along with those of *silphium, see* ASAFOETIDA, a plant that has now become extinct, were once widely used in the cuisine of the ancient world.

Artusi gives some nice recipes, in which, after a preliminary short blanching in salted water, pieces of prepared celery are finished in butter and a little broth and served sprinkled with parmesan; or with an aromatic sauce made of chopped onion and lean and fatty ham cooked in butter with two cloves, simmered in a little broth, and passed through a sieve, in which the celery has its final cooking, served with freshly ground pepper.

Vincenzo Corrado, inventive as ever, has 14 recipes, including a *pottaggio* in which prepared celery is simmered in chicken or meat broth with chopped sorrel and tarragon, thickened just before serving with egg yolks; or *alla nobile*, first cooked in broth, then finished in a sauce of cream, ground coriander seeds, cinnamon, and butter, served on slices of bread, though triangles of bread fried in butter would make an even richer foil, particularly to accompany lean ham or plain boiled fowl.

CENCI are little deep-fried biscuits made from a rich eggy pastry, flavoured with grappa or rum, rolled out, cut into strips which are sometimes knotted, or into shapes which puff up enticingly, and drained and sprinkled with sugar. They are traditionally made at the start of Carnival, and will last right through Lent. *See also* FESTIVITY AND FOOD.

CERVIO, VINCENZO, first

worked for Guidobaldo II of Urbino and by the 1540s was *trinciante* or carver to Cardinal Alessandro Farnese in Rome, in whose service he worked in papal legations in France, Germany, and the Low Countries. He wrote a treatise on his art, *Il trinciante*, which was improved, enlarged, and perfected in manuscript by his colleague Reale Fusoritto da Narni, who took over Cervio's job on his death. Fusoritto had the work published by Tramezzini in Venice in 1581 and later in 1593, and an edition in Rome of the same date. By this time Cervio was an old man, retired on a pension from his employer, and may have been already dead by 1582. He mentions that he was himself of humble origin; carvers and chief stewards were expected to be of noble birth, with the graces and demeanour of aristocrats, but in spite of this, Cervio held an honoured position in the cardinal's household, provided by his master with the gentlemanly attributes, lodgings, fine clothing, horses, and salary to keep up an appearance that could only reflect well on his employer.

Fusoritto contributed extra material to Cervio's book, including a dialogue with his colleague Cesare Pandini, Farnese's *maestro di casa*, as well as descriptions of banquets and some additional carving instructions, and observations on the various household officials. For this he drew on a longer and more detailed manuscript by another friend and colleague, Cesare Evitascandolo, who also worked in Rome, as *maestro di casa* to many nobles and prelates. Fusoritto's dialogue has a colloquial tone, like a verbatim transcript of a conversation, and a sort of sceptical realism mitigates the idealised descriptions of these upright and incorruptible officials:

Q *"Dunque questo maggiordomo potria, se non volesse esser fidele, rubbare assai?"* (So this *maggiordomo*, if disposed to be dishonest, could steal a fair amount?)

A "Well not all that much, for when the prince comes to look at the accounts he can check them against those of the *computista*." (Cervio, 1593, p. 149)

And these accounts, drawn up by the accountant from the lists submitted to him by the various household officials, could be cross-checked, but really everything depended on the relationship between the master and his *maggiordomo*, a good companion, not a mere servant: *"Questo mi piace bene, perché gli uomini non si conoscano se non si mangia molto sale insieme"* (I like that, for it is only by sharing the salt [eating together at the same table] that one can really get to know someone).

Il trinciante is full of such insights into the organisation of life in a grand household in Rome in the 16th century. This was the city where ambitious youngsters might find an apprenticeship and employment, with hopes of advancement and foreign travel (cardinals went on missions abroad, where they needed to show a *bella figura*), and it was in this melting pot of competitive skills, with refined aesthetes and ruthless hustlers fighting for position, that the young artist Caravaggio bubbled to the surface. The innkeeper he depicts in his *Supper at Emmaus*, with his clean linen, a respectful pose, and long white napkin over his left shoulder, for covering food before presenting it at table, is a humble version of the *scalco* or *maestro di casa* that he might have encountered in the household of Cardinal Montalto, Fusoritto's employer.

Caravaggio's patron, Cardinal Del Monte, employed a household of over 200, whose functions were described by Fusoritto and Evitascandalo in their manuals of household management. The painter was able to move effortlessly between these circles of worldly power and secular hedonism, from watching the absurdity of carving an artichoke with flashing blade and fork at a refined banquet to the tavern in which he threw a dish of artichokes at a waiter's head and then went on to get arrested for carrying unauthorised weapons after dark. The weapons turned out to be compasses, measuring instruments that indicated the painter's and his patron's concern with scientific realism, and we note the same concern for precision in Cervio and Fusoritto's description of the choice of carving implements, and their maintenance. A generation later the young Antonio Latini got caught up in this world of sleaze, skills, and ambition and survived by taking his hard-won professionalism back to the provinces and working there until he was mature enough to cope with the Roman scene.

Apart from being a performance art, carving was a skill that enhanced the qualities of the food, as the diagrams in Mattia GIEGHER's treatise show. Cervio is scornful of servants who hack meat up on a dish like a carcass in a slaughterhouse. Carving "in the air" was not just showing off, but a way of demonstrating the integrity of the food; the distance between the carver, the high table, and the other servants meant that there was no possibility of contamination or poison being introduced. The *credenza* or ritual of tasting (which gave its name to the sideboard or dresser where food was placed before serving) might by then have become a formality, but the rituals of carving showed a respect for the ingredients and the cook, as well as the guests. Even a pie could be carved with a show of precision, the pastry top severed and discarded and the contents, if whole birds or large pieces of meat, cut up and ready for eating. Still life paintings from the Low Countries at that time often show the silver spoon used to serve those with loose contents of meat, dried fruit, nuts, and other things tumbling out of an opened pie.

Properly carved, meat could be handed round and eaten with the fingers, or a knife, all the hard work having been done by the *trinciante*. Cervio describes with great clarity how to impale a joint, a leg of lamb or a loin of veal, on a stout two-pronged fork so that it is quite rigid and does not twist and turn when handled. It is then lifted high in the air above the serving dish, all six pounds of it, and the impassive carver, perfectly poised, and with no visible signs of strain, proceeds first of all to remove the outer crust of browned meat or fat in slices which he arranges round the rim of the dish; then he slices first vertically, then horizontally in the opposite direction, and finally detaches the resultant small morsels from the bone to drop in a shower into the centre of the platter, which he then anoints with some of the gravy and sprinkles with salt from the point of his knife. The standing carver balances his own weight against that of the meat rotated in his left hand, so that the sharp blade he wields in his right uses torsion and gravity to make the desired cuts. Only the highly skilled manage this without getting gravy all over sleeves and shoes, the sort of mishap Cervio says you can avert by altering the angle of the impaled meat as you work. Mattia Giegher admits that in an imperfect world you might need to pass this off with a merry quip or appropriate proverb, which takes a certain amount of nerve. Cervio greatly dislikes the histrionics of the show-off school of carving—he will have none of it, the gestures and grimaces and crowd-pleasing performance. He writes calmly of the skills and dexterity that should be deployed with a cool head and steady hands, without any fuss of flourishes.

Cervio's comments on roast beef are revealing—veal was plentiful and popular, but mature cattle became beasts of burden and only appeared on the table when too old to work and after long cooking. He says that young beef can be surprisingly good, if well hung and properly cooked, and that it needs to be served with some of the very finely sliced fat, "*perché invero la carne di vaccina non vale niente se con la magra trinciata non vi è un poco di grasso*" (for indeed beef is worth nothing at all unless the carved lean portions have a little fat with them). If you can carve beef successfully, he says, you can handle anything.

A small chicken can be carved in 15 cuts, three for each limb, another two to sever each breast from the carcass, and a final blow to detach the neck. Larger birds like goose, or peacock, need a more complex treatment, to produce at least six serving dishes of assorted cuts.

The descriptions of BANQUETS, *banchetto stupendo, banchetto bellissima, banchetto reale*, come with a useful entry on *l'ordine di levar la confusione da ogni gran convito*, "how to avoid confusion in all large entertainments," a way of dealing with the crowds of servants, onlookers, and hangers-on who came in droves to watch the spectacle and grab what they could of the leftovers. The solution was to usher the crowds towards a buffet meal in adjoining rooms, from which there was no returning to the banqueting area, with generous provision for all the servants involved in the smooth running of the event, and refreshments also provided for the rabble at even safer distance, and then an orderly distribution of the remaining food. This makes the bustle of the great VERONESE banquets seem quite restful.

CHEESE.
Italian cheeses are among the best known in the world; what is more to their honour, they are among the best. They embody the evidence of many centuries of thought and experimentation, all directed towards the utilisation of that ephemeral product, milk, to give a food that is nourishing, digestible, infinitely flavoursome, and (in some cases) extremely long-lasting.

The group of very hard cheeses known as GRANA PADANO is the most enduring of all. This includes PARMESAN (now officially labelled Grana Parmigiano-Reggiano) as well as the formerly well-known and still estimable Lodigiano and Piacentino. Their medieval fame throughout western Europe is evidence of the crucial importance to the premodern economy of the Po Valley of a product that would triumphantly survive the rigours of slow transport and long storage. At the other end of the spectrum are the cream cheese MASCARPONE, originating from Lodi, like one of the varieties of *grana*; and the whey cheese RICOTTA, so named ("recooked") because it is the product of a second heating of whey, from which curd has previously been separated. Lightly pressed, crumbly fresh ricotta is eaten as a dessert, with salt or sugar; other kinds are firmly pressed, salted, and dried.

Origins, styles, colours, flavours, and shapes vary astonishingly. *Grana, mascarpone* and (usually) *ricotta* are made from cow's milk. So is CACIOCAVALLO, the oldest and most familiar cheese of the south, also made in the Balkans under names such as *kashkaval*. So is FONTINA, which has been the pride of the Val d'Aosta for many centuries; so is the soft, creamy blue cheese GORGONZOLA, a more recent development. *Caprino* and PECORINO are general names for sheep's and goat's milk cheeses, of which there are many regional types; MARZOLINO is a historic sheep's cheese, made near Florence and Siena and originally the speciality of Sardinian shepherds who came to Tuscany in the spring, but now less special than it used to be. MOZZARELLA is the best known water buffalo's milk cheese, though the name is also used for a cow's milk cheese of similar type.

Cheese has been made in Italy and Sicily from the earliest historic times, and even in those times it could claim a legendary pedigree and many centuries of prehistoric development. In the 5th century BC, Sicily—studded with Greek colonies—was famous for its cheese, treated in Greek literature as the island's typical product. All we can say of ancient Sicilian cheese is that it was made from a mixture of sheep's and goat's milk. When grated, it would make a tasty crust over grilled fish, a recipe that was typically Sicilian but (according to the culinary poet Archestratus) suited only to coarse fish such as skate or ray. Cheese is used in this way in the very oldest surviving Sicilian recipe, attributed to the celebrity chef Mithaecus (c. 400 BC), for the ribbon-like fish *cepola*: "Gut, discard the head, rinse, slice; add cheese and oil."

Such cheeses could have been made in many places, but there was something about the Sicilian kind that made them worth the considerable cost of sea transport. Moreover, it was universally believed that the land of the monstrous Cyclops, visited by Odysseus in the Homeric *Odyssey*, was Sicily. The Cyclops was a man-eater but also a cheese-maker; this mythical Sicilian, like his human successors, kept both sheep and goats and mixed their milk. His story develops in later poetry from Greek Sicily: like many another literary shepherd, he is seen offering freshly made cheeses to his hoped-for bride, in this case the nymph Galatea.

Five centuries later, by which time there was a home-grown gastronomic tradition in Roman Italy, the cheeses of the peninsula played a full role. Cow's milk cheese was familiar but goat's and sheep's milk cheeses were more common. The basic Latin term was *caseus*, whence Italian *cacio*, "cheese." Columella, the most systematic of Roman authors on farming, writing in the 1st century AD, describes several methods of cheese-making depending on whether the cheese is to be eaten within a few days or slowly drained, pressed, and matured. Cheese-makers used animal RENNETS, from lambs'

or kids' stomachs, or sometimes vegetable rennets such as fig sap or thistle flowers. The emperor Augustus was described by Suetonius as "very sparing as regards food, almost plebeian, with a liking for brown bread, whitebait, soft, spongy hand-pressed cheese, and green figs from a twice-bearing tree," and Columella tells us how this hand-pressed cheese (something like a rich ricotta) was made: when the milk is just curdling in the pail, it is broken up, hot water is poured over it, and then it is shaped by hand or pressed into boxwood moulds; the mould is Latin *forma*, source of Italian *formaggio*, "cheese," by way of French *fromage*. Columella also recommends brined cheese that has afterwards been smoked over apple-wood or burning stubble; Rome was actually the first known civilisation to develop smoked cheese. The farming calendar of Palladius, compiled during the 5th century, also gives instructions for the cheese-maker. As the milk curdles, it is gradually pressed to expel the whey. The solidifying cheese is placed in a dark, cool room and pressed again using weights. After several days, the firm, fresh cheeses are placed on reed mats to mature in a draught-free room. Some makers combined fresh pine nuts, or chopped thyme, with the cheese as it began to solidify; it might be rolled in black pepper or other spices for added flavour.

Fresh local cheeses, drying on rush mats, are among the delicacies offered at an imaginary country tavern in the anonymous poem "*Copa*" (The bar-girl). In the *Georgics*, Virgil describes how a mountain shepherd would make cheese, from morning and evening milkings, and sell it himself at the nearest market; excellent mountain cheeses of this kind were brought to Rome from the nearby territory of the Vestini in modern Abruzzo Vestine cheese is once specified as an ingredient in the cookery book *Apicius*, in a recipe for "Apician dressed salad" (*see* APICIAN FLAVOUR.) The finest mature cheeses travelled over much longer distances than this. Several became famous, including the *meta* (pyramid) of Sassina in northern Umbria, and the smooth, round, white cheeses of mount Sila, southeast of Naples. The cheese of Luna, in northwestern Tuscany, was stamped with a crescent moon (*luna*) as an easily read designation of origin. The best smoked cheese was matured in the Velabrum district of the city of Rome.

The typical Roman breakfast was bread, which might well be eaten with cheese, if cheese had not already been added to the dough before baking. Cheese also served as flavouring with *puls*, EMMER WHEAT porridge, in the rich version known as *puls Punica*, "Phoenician or Carthaginian porridge." Cheese with bread and green vegetables, alongside wine or water, made a good simple meal; it is a principal ingredient in the peasant farmer's midday meal, with abundant garlic and green herbs in a fiery paste to be eaten with bread, as described in the poem "Moretum," written in the late 1st century BC by a contemporary of Virgil. Cheese and nuts were served by wine-makers at tastings to mask the poor quality of their wine. In more elaborate meals, cheese was served as a dessert, eaten with honey and bread while one was drinking wine after dinner. What kind of cheese? We are not told, but any cheese kept in brine (as ancient cheeses often were) and washed before serving is likely to be good with honey. At some meals, goat's milk or sheep's milk cheese was fried in slices to be served as a starter. Cheese was also a culinary ingredient, used in sauces and in various dishes called *patina*, which, if they can be compared with anything, were like quiches or tarts without the pastry base. Cheese lent its Greek name, *tyros*, to *tyrotarichos*, a fish *patina* mentioned by Cicero, and *tyropatina*, an egg custard, though the latter contained no cheese.

Palladius had listed cheese-making as an activity for the month of May. This was an oversimplification. The fact it was based on was that farm animals give most milk in the spring; however, the cheese-making season lasted much longer than one month, as is hinted in the medieval farming manual and calendar by Piero de' Crescenzi (or Petrus de Crescentiis), *Liber Commodorum Ruralium* (1309), which gives full instructions and adds the month of June to the list. It is certainly true that at certain times of year animals give little or no milk; fresh, young cheese would therefore sometimes have been rare or unavailable. Yet no text tells us of a period of the year when there was no cheese; moreover, we know that some cheeses were marketed over long distances, in spite of the slowness of transport. Thus medieval cheeses, like Roman ones, must often have been carefully matured.

An early medieval landmark is the introduction to Italy in the 6th century AD of the WATER BUFFALO, domesticated in China long before, but not originally used for milking; its milk is the classic source for mozzarella cheese. A second landmark is the revived fame of Sicilian cheese during the Arab domination of Sicily, when Sicilian cheese is specifically named as culinary ingredient in recipes from the Arab world. Finally, in the early 14th century, comes the first literary mention of a specific cheese still known by the same name today—the *Parmigiano*, or PARMESAN, of which an imaginary mountain is constructed in one of the stories of Boccaccio's *Decamerone* (c. 1360). In literature of later centuries, parmesan appears more frequently than any other named cheese in the world, from John Ford's play *'Tis Pity She's a Whore* (1633), in which a young rake is said to love his mistress "almost as well as he loves Parmasent" to Robert Louis Stevenson's *Treasure Island* (1883), in which Doctor Livesey observes: "In my snuff-box I carry a piece of parmesan cheese—a cheese made in Italy, very nutritious." The grain of parmesan, unmistakeable even in the medium of oil painting, is celebrated also in Italian still lifes by the local artist Cristoforo Munari.

It was in 1477 that Pantaleone da Confienza published in Turin his remarkable survey of European cheeses and cheese-making. He called it *Summa Lacticiniorum* (Survey of milk products) in allusion to venerable works such as the vast *Summa Theologiae* of Thomas Aquinas; Pantaleone is asserting that his book, too, is definitive in its limited field. He discusses the nature of milk and cheese and the potential variety of cheeses; then he catalogues the regional and local cheeses he considers important. This impressive survey begins with northern Italy, from the *marzolino* of Tuscany to the cheeses of the Alpine valleys; it includes an early mention of ROBIOLA, now better known as a cheese of Lombardy but particularly linked at this date with the marquisate of Monferrato (Montferrat) in Piedmont. Pantaleone insists that the cheese of Piacenza is better than that of Parma, though he admits that the two are often grouped together. Southern Italy is entirely excluded; instead the cheese itinerary continues through Savoy and across France, moving on to England, Flanders, and the Rhine Valley. Part 3 discusses the nutritional value of different cheeses in accordance with medieval dietary theories.

This needed some discussion, because Galen, Oribasius, Avicenna, and other early medical authorities generally advise their readers against cheese. Sometimes they make an exception for soft, fresh cheese, because that is not heating and not putrescent (hence ricotta features in the medieval dietary text *Tacuinum Sanitatis*). Thus, in speaking up for the dietary qualities of cheese, Pantaleone was attacking received medical opinion. Sixty years later, a whimsical book, *Formaggiata di Sere Stentato*, appeared. This "Cheesery," by an imaginary Sere Stentato, was in fact written by Giulio Landi, member of a society of gastronomes in Piacenza. Landi takes up the defence of cheese, and in particular the wonderful hard cheeses of Parma and its region, against all kinds of detractors, using all kinds of arguments—some of them so scurrilous or indecent that the censor deleted them from later editions. Landi compared *provatura* unfavourably with an old man's testicle and *caciocavallo* with an old woman's sagging breast. The argument begun by Pantaleone and taken up by Landi is triumphantly concluded by Ercole Bentivoglio in the first poem devoted entirely to cheese (published 1557), firmly asserting the nutritional benefits of cheese, with light-hearted attention to its aphrodisiac effect. In two recent historical essays, Piero Camporesi, focusing on texts of the late medieval and early modern period, explores the early dieticians' suspicions of cheese, counterpointed as they were by the growth of a gastronomic tradition. Camporesi concludes each essay by quoting municipal instructions from the 17th and 18th centuries for making the *marzolino* cheese familiar at Florence—early evidence of the public importance already accorded to cheese and its quality as a matter of public policy.

(AKD)

CHERRIES, CORNELIAN,

dogwood cherry or cornel, *Cornus mas, corniola*, are rather too acid and bitter to eat raw, but make a delicious fruit paste and a jelly, both of which were made a lot in the past. Martino boiled crushed ripe cornelian berries with fresh must, salt, and pepper, which strained makes a relish that will keep well and can be added to other sauces. They are still used in a sauce for boiled meats in the north of Italy. They are just one of many wild and cultivated berries which are still used locally but are disappearing from commercial outlets, and so from the conventional repertoire of recipes. Arbutus or *corbezzolo, Arbutus unedo*, is used in jellies and preserves and to flavour liqueurs. There is the internationally fashionable cranberry, which, like cultivated wild rocket is everywhere, but we miss out on many pungent fruit and herbs which many Italians can still find in regional markets and shops.

CHERRY, *ciliegia,* is one of the *Rosaceae,* a genus that includes plums, peaches, and apricots; they are subdivided into *Prunus avium,* the sweet fruit, and *Prunus cerasus,* sour cherry. There are subdivisions within these groups, and hybrids of the two. The sweet ones are *tenerine* or *duracine,* with soft or firm flesh; the sour ones *amarene, marasche, visciole,* again in many varieties. They are grown today mainly in Campania, Emilia-Romagna, Puglia, and Veneto. Their uses in the past were many, not just as a dessert fruit but preserved, dried, and eaten medicinally; when astringent and underripe, they could stimulate digestion, regulate the bowels, and quench thirst, and ripe ones had the reverse effect, accordingly to Pisanelli. Cherries brought out the best in Mattioli, the sometimes tetchy botanist, who wrote with affection of the many varieties, so well adapted to Italian conditions and tastes, though he admits that as a dessert, fruit cherries, staining the fingers and mouth, were not best suited to formal dinners. Today they are enjoyed fresh, and used, lightly cooked, in tarts, tartlets, cakes, and desserts and as glazes and syrups, and when candied their bright colour makes them a popular if garish decoration for many dishes.

Giovanna GARZONI painted for her Medici patrons in the 1650s several versions of a bowl of cherries with wayward stems giving a sense of uncanny movement and freshness. Bartolomeo BIMBI later in the century produced a glowing painting of 34 varieties, tipping out of a massive wicker basket in a stormy landscape lit by the setting sun.

CHERVIL (*Anthriscus cerefolium, cerfoglio, erba stella*), one of the Umbelliferae, has leaves resembling parsley, with a mild and fragrant flavour, used raw in salads or added to stews, FRITTATAS, and stuffings. The dried leaves have more pungency and are used in soups, or to flavour stewed pulses.

CHESTNUT, *castagna,* is the fruit of the sweet chestnut, *Castanea sativa,* a tree which exists in Italy in as many as 300 varieties, the main division being between *castagna* and *marrone,* the latter being larger, heart-shaped, with a streaked light and dark brown outer skin—a version perfected by grafting onto indigenous wild trees. The fruit or nut of both is encased, singly or with several others, in a prickly outer covering or burr which splits open when ripe to expose the contents. This is the easy bit, when it comes to cooking chestnuts; the hard work is all in peeling off the outer shell or skin, then tackling the tenacious inner one, which has a bitterness that makes its removal essential. Dried chestnuts, ready to cook, and chestnut flour can be bought in most food stores, but it is acknowledged that fresh ones are more delicious in both sweet and savoury preparations. Once an essential part of the basic subsistence diet of dwellers in Apennine woodlands and alpine regions, chestnuts, *castagne,* are now almost a luxury, for depopulation and deforestation have made their daily use less common than it was. The association of chestnuts with the coarse subsistence fare of underprivileged woodlanders accounts for the absence from the 19th-century classics of many traditional chestnut recipes, except when they became gentrified and were called *marroni* and used in luxurious French recipes with French names, *marrons glacés,* or in desserts like *mont blanc,* or combined with cream and meringue, an altogether more aristocratic cuisine than the rustic preparations of CUCINA POVERA. There is, however, a rustic pedigree for *monte bianco* which may have originated in Cuneo, a frugal dish, cooking the ubiquitous chestnuts in milk, mixing them with honey, and forcing the mixture through an old-fashioned horsehair sieve, then topping with unsweetened whipped cream. Castelvetro mentions this as a typical peasant dish, sometimes using ricotta instead of cream. He reminds us how chestnut flour keeps well (with its low moisture content) and so is a useful for provisioning fortresses. Dried and smoked chestnuts were shelled by putting them in a sack and bashing them, he tells us, and became a delicacy when put to soften in baskets of fragrant rose petals. In a 16th-century banquet menu for late May, Scappi served chestnuts, roasted, peeled, and still hot, wrapped in towels to steam and soften with rose petals, seasoned with salt, pepper, and sugar. The custom of cooking chestnuts over the coals in a perforated roasting pan, then eating them with salt and pepper, or dowsed in wine or GRAPPA, was widespread, and when part of the *ventura*, when the new wines were sampled on the Feast of San Martino, their absorbent qualities must have helped mitigate the festivities, which still left many reeling. The 15th-century health handbook *Tacuinum Sanitatis* produced for the Ceruti family has an illustration of two countrymen roasting chestnuts under the tree from which they had fallen, one of them lifting his skirts to enjoy the warmth of the fire. Martino has a nice recipe for chestnuts as a tart filling, enriched with cheese, soft and grated, eggs, spices, and saffron. Costanzo Felici also writes of their widespread use, and universal appeal, their presence in so many dishes; it is not clear when they came to be regarded as fit only for animals and peasants, a fate which also overtook the equally esteemed and versatile parsnip, with its similar sweetish flouriness. Memories of wartime hardship might account for both disdain and nostalgia in a later generation.

Castelvetro (p. 125) summed up another use for chestnuts: "Peeled chestnuts are used with prunes, raisins and breadcrumbs in a stuffing for roast chicken, goose or turkey." This continues to this day.

Chestnut and potato GNOCCHI go well with game, like the recipe from the restaurant The Walnut Tree in which they are served with a dish of pheasant cooked with tiny onions and chestnuts in a wine sauce (Taruschio, 1993, p. 164). Chestnut fettuccine, from

the same book, are good with winter game dishes (p. 86).

Apicius (*see* APICIAN FLAVOUR) has some recipes for *Lenticulam de castaneis* (Grocock and Grainger, 2006, p. 209), which is a purée of chestnuts, pounded with a sauce of herbs and spices, honey, vinegar, oil, and fish sauce; which seems a not very appealing combination, but one of them mercifully omits the implied lentils, and the strong seasoning gives the bland chestnuts quite a kick; peeled and skinned, they are parboiled with crushed peppercorns, coriander seeds, cumin, mint, rue, asafoetida, honey, vinegar, and broth, then pounded in a mortar and passed through a coarse sieve; then, he says, "taste to see if anything is missing and if so put it in" and serve with a fresh, fruity extra virgin olive oil.

One of the best of the rustic recipes is to cook chestnut flour like polenta, stirring constantly to stop it getting lumpy or sticking to the pan, and the result is a tasty accompaniment to sausages or a roast. The flour goes into bread, to eke out the more expensive wheat flour, but since it contains no gluten, it has to be used sparingly. Pasta is made using boiled and sieved chestnuts or chestnut flour; sometimes, as in Emilia, freshly made *maltagliati* are added to boiled chestnuts as they finish cooking, then seasoned with grated parmesan. Perhaps the best loved survival of these rustic dishes is *castagnaccio*, a sort of sweet flatbread made by mixing chestnut flour with salt, water, sugar, and olive oil to make a batter, into which can be stirred some previously soaked sultanas. This is then spread on an oiled baking tin, sprinkled with rosemary leaves and pine nuts, baked in a moderate oven for 45 minutes, and enjoyed tepid or cool. This batter can also be fried like pancakes. A simpler version, called *baldino*, is described by Elizabeth Romer in *The Tuscan Year* (1984, p. 149), and her evocative description of the now neglected chestnut plantations and overgrown pathways in a secret valley between

Tuscany and Umbria touches on their association with hard times: "This [chestnut flour] together with other grains was made into an unappetizing bread which the Cerottis call castagnaccia, a poor food that still brings back memories of deprivation." A useful way of dealing with rodents is revealed by Romer—when they attack the sacks of chestnuts in the loft is the time to set a nasty trap: a wooden tub of water is sprinkled with chestnut flour, and the aroma tempts the creatures onto what seems like a solid surface and so leads them to their doom.

Calvino's evocative description in *Il barone rampante* of the last survivor of a land, the Gulf of Ombrosa, where it was said a monkey could travel from Rome to Spain in the tree tops, gives some idea of the heavily wooded valley in which his hero, Cosimo Piovasco di Rondò, lived without ever touching the ground, where the now deserted arid slopes were green with trees and undergrowth, crisscrossed with footpaths and tracks, among the chestnut woods. He describes the way the wood clothed the steep valley sides, stretching up from the coast and port below, with fruit orchards and nut trees and shrubs giving way to olive groves, followed by larch and oak among the enveloping pines, and then the chestnuts.

Eric Newby must have collided with chestnut groves in his time on the run in the Apennines during the German occupation, dodging among the unfrequented footpaths, like tunnels through the woods, and there is a telling detail of a meal of the mushrooms he had unwisely gathered, unaware that they were a cash crop leased to the *fungaio* who paid for the rights, which all the same were cooked by the family who sheltered him, in a huge iron pan kept specially for chestnuts and mushrooms.

CHICKEN, *pollo,* but also known as *gallo, gallina,* is so widely available today that we are losing sight of its historic role—as invalid food, or as an important part of a vanished rural economy. The pale, delicate flesh is easily digestible and was cooked in a variety of subtle ways for the sick and elderly and for women in childbirth. A *brodo consumato* or *ristretto* was prepared for invalids by cooking a chicken or capon in water until only a cup or so of liquid remained. Other meats and flavourings were permitted, on the advice of the physician. Scappi dosed the ailing cardinal Andrea Cornaro in 1551 with a jelly made from four capons, chopped small, covered with water, skimmed and simmered in a sealed pot until reduced to one-third, then seasoned with sugar and a stick of cinnamon or some quince, the fat skimmed off, the liquid clarified with egg whites and strained, then coloured with saffron or pomegranate juice. In his old age, Pietro Bembo was cherished by Scappi with the liquid obtained by cooking slices of chicken breasts suspended by crimson silk threads in a tall sealed jar or flask standing in a pot of water, bubbling over carefully controlled heat (for a shorter version, *see* BROTH).

Women in childbirth were cared for with care and affection; the processions of friends and neighbours visiting the confinement room appear in so many paintings of the birth of the Virgin or her mother, St. Anne, that we can conjecture the nature of the comforting cordials and food, and sometimes recognise the stewed chickens that were often budgeted for by caring husbands (Musacchio, 1999, p. 40). In 1473, Ser Girolamo da Colle invested in a pen of chickens to sustain his wife Caterina during pregnancy and the birth of their son Giovanni. This was typical of the time.

Also typical was the way chickens and other fowl were part of the domestic economy of country women; the poultry yard was a source of income as well as food, and many families would eat vegetables and pulses while the woman of the house sold eggs and chickens for cash, the family only getting to eat these delicacies on special occasions.

Today there is a wide choice, with farmyard, industrially reared, and free range chickens available in shops and markets. The scrawny, tasty *pollo ruspante* (free range) is the best for traditional recipes, and dishes that benefit from long cooking. The traditional nomenclature embraces the varieties of chicken at different stages of growth available in the past, very different from the uniform product of today—to *pollastro, pollo do grano, galletto, gallina*, and the fattened *cappone* and *pollanca*.

Pollo alla romana is typical—the chicken joints are fried with pancetta or ham, preferably in lard, until golden, then finished with garlic and marjoram and some dry white wine which is allowed to evaporate, and finally cooked for a short while more with some chopped tomatoes, to give a dense, not runny, sauce. To this can be added red or green peppers, scorched, peeled, and finished in olive oil. *Pollo alla cacciatora* used to be a cliché in London in the 1960s, immortalised by Iris Murdock in *The Italian Girl*. There are many versions of this; the important thing is that the chicken joints are cooked first *in padella*, in a frying pan, and the aromatic additions—vegetables, herbs, olives, anchovies, garlic, wine, or vinegar—are all added later, then the joints are cooked, covered, to obtain a dry result, the joints bathed in a very little concentrated aromatic sauce. *Pollo in porchetta* is a pot roast chicken flavoured with wild fennel or fennel seeds, the typical seasoning for roast piglet.

CHICKPEAS, *ceci, Cicer arietinum,* get

their Latin name from *aries*, ram, as the dried peas were said to ressemble a ram's head complete with horns. And the orator Cicero is said to have got his family name from this humble pulse, already well known and eaten, both fresh and dried, after thousands of years of cultivation. The floury texture and nutty, slightly musty, taste of chickpeas is agreeable on its own, but becomes delicious in a uniquely versatile way when cooked or finished with different seasonings, and has the additional virtue of being both filling and nutritious. The main kinds are ochre or brown, red and black—the last two now used only for animal food, although in the past the red were considered the most healthy. Martino gives a recipe for red chickpeas which involves washing them in hot water, drying them, and rubbing in a mixture of flour and ground cinnamon and black pepper, salt and oil, then adding plenty of water, parsley root, sage, and rosemary, and simmering slowly until almost done, finishing off cooking with more oil. He advises omitting the oil and spices if intended for invalids. But both the sick and the well would benefit from "the healthiest of vegetables," as Castelvetro described chickpeas; he says that the red ones were the most wholesome and recommends cooking them in water with plenty of oil and serving with lemon juice. He remembers fondly how "on summer evenings after supper, our good ladies sit around in droves on their doorsteps, and when they see the countrywomen coming home from the fields with baskets full of tender young chickpeas, they buy quantities of them, to nibble raw just for fun" (1989, p. 102). He recommended soaking tough chickpeas overnight with some charcoal or ashes in a clean linen bag. (The alkali would soften them and incidentally might enhance the nutritional content, as in the nixtamalistion of corn, which loosens the outer skin and by great good chance also releases the amino acid niacin, a form of protein we cannot live without.)

Platina said of chickpeas:

There are many differences in shape, and colour and flavour. The chickpea looks something like a ram's head. The red ones have more heat (referring to the Humoral Theory) than the black or white; the black ones are considered milder. The water in which they have been soaked and cooked is good for the lungs, removes obstructions from liver and spleen, breaks up kidney stones, purges the kidneys and bladder, makes the voice clearer, arouses lust, and gets rid of stomach worms. Fresh chickpeas harm the stomach and intestines and make the mouth smell bad. (Platina, 1998; my translation of "cicer," bk. 7, item 11, p. 310)

Mattioli went so far as to call the red chickpeas *venerei*, a tribute to their aphrodisiac powers, and quotes classical writers who recommended feeding them to stallions. The cooking water was used with other ingredients to make poultices and dressings for skin infections.

Although a humble legume, chickpeas appear in many recipe books from the 14th century onwards. Messisbugo cooked them in water, topping up with broth, together with *una buona pestata di lardo* (cured pork fat pounded with herbs), and served them with *cotiche* (*cotenna*, prepared pig's skin), blanched then simmered slowly with aromatics to release its glutinous properties and flavour, cut into squares, and finished off with the chickpeas and some chopped herbs, with a final sprinkling of mint on top. This is similar to the Roman *fagioli con le cotiche*, made with dried beans and the trimmings of outer skin from *prosciutto crudo*, which most delicatessens will give away with the ham you purchase.

Scappi also soaked red chickpeas in a mild lye, or with some charcoal in a linen bag, to soften them before cooking. They then had to be rinsed well in tepid water, mixed with a little flour, and cooked with rosemary, sage, whole garlic cloves, and pepper and served with chopped herbs.

Recipes created by Vincenzo Corrado for the affluent society of 18th-century Naples included a rich and meaty stew of chickpeas, ham, and sausage, and a more interesting vegetarian one in which the washed and cleaned chickpeas are simmered in plain water, and halfway through cooking some whole chilli peppers, peeled garlic cloves, bay leaves, thyme, chopped parsley and olive oil are added. The stew is served with a purée of anchovies. His brief paragraph on chickpeas in *Il cuoco galante* of 1778 is worth quoting in full because it is typical of the Italian genius for taking basic subsistence-level ingredients and turning them, in subtle and not necessarily extravagant ways, into gastronomic delights:

Chickpeas are very good both fresh and dry. When green they can be used in the ways I have just described for peas; when dried they delicious in stews for lean [when meat and some dairy products are forbidden] as well as meat days, but they need to be well seasoned. On meat days they are flavoured with ham, pork sausages, and *cervellato* [a spiced sausage coloured yellow with saffron]; on lean days with good fish broth, rosemary, garlic, thyme, and spices. When cooked in broth then pounded with candied citron, sugar, and cinnamon, they make a filling for tarts and pasties; this mixture is also used for fritters. They can be puréed for soups, and stewed in various ways. Chickpea flour makes excellent polenta. (Corrado, 1778)

Corrado's vegetarian *Cibo Pitagorico* enlarges on these suggestions—a lean recipe cooks them first in water, then finishes in fish broth flavoured with chervil and marjoram, with short macaroni added towards the end, and served with a lobster sauce. His fritters are made from cooked chickpeas pounded with bone marrow, passed through a sieve, flavoured with *provatura* cheese and cinnamon, floured and rolled in beaten egg yolks, then fried— aristocratic ancestors of today's Neapolitan *panelle*.

There are many modern recipes for

hearty stews or soups made with chickpeas and pasta; a Roman version given by Ada Boni, *minestra di pasta e ceci*, involves cooking *cannolicchi* (short tubular pasta) with chickpeas and their cooking liquid, flavoured with rosemary and enriched with a garlicky sauce of anchovies and chopped garlic dissolved in oil, and a little tomato sauce.

A Tuscan recipe cooks chickpeas in the usual way until soft, flavoured with garlic and rosemary, then enriched with garlic, rosemary and tomatoes cooked in oil, thickened with some of the chickpeas passed through a sieve, finished cooking with some home-made *tagliatelle*, and served with more olive oil and pepper.

Livorno, a rough, independent "frontier town" created by Cosimo I de' Medici in 1565 as a new port, free from fiscal and political restrictions, had a mixed population, more or less without roots, and no hallowed gastronomic traditions. The poor ate as best they could, and within living memory food shops in the popular quarter would put out notices every Thursday: *"Domani baccalà e ceci"* (Tomorrow salt cod and chickpeas).

They were cooked separately, aromatised with celery, carrot, and onion, and served together, anointed with fragrant olive oil, the neutral flouriness of the chickpeas contrasting with the concentrated saltiness of the fish and the richness of the oil. In two separate marble basins the salt cod and the chickpeas were soaked overnight.

Ceci con la tempia di maiale is a Milanese speciality which is traditionally prepared for All Souls' Day—the Day of the Dead, 2 November—using meat from a pig's temples, though any head meat, or the rich and fatty cheek or jowl, can be used. This might be derived from the ancient Roman practise of offering bowls of beans and chickpeas to the dead, though many hold that this recipe was brought to Italy, perhaps, during times when dynastic policies put parts of Italy under Spanish rule, and is derived from the *cocido* of Madrid, a suggestion that would be roundly rejected by any right-thinking *madrileño*. (The complexity of the many versions of the sophisticated urban *cocido madrileño* cannot be compared to this simple peasant dish.) The chickpeas are simmered slowly with a bunch of sage leaves, then finished off with the pork meats, previously cooked for an hour, with celery, carrots, and onion, in unsalted water and drained. When both are nicely done, the chickpeas are served first in their broth, and the meat is cut up and eaten separately with *sottaceti*. The local poet Giovanni Rajberti wrote:

gh'è finna el dì di Mort
ch'el porta tempia e scisger per confort,
e la sira, per compì l'indigestion.
gh'è el Rosari e I marron

and then comes along the Day of the
    Dead
with comforts of chickpeas and pigs
    head,
much later, indigestion is complete
with chestnuts and some cordial
    sweet.

Quite apart from their nourishing and curative powers, dried chickpeas keep well, and can be made into a flour which can be used in many ways. The *farinata*, *panissa*, and *frittelle* of Liguria are typical, while Sicily has its *panelle*. *Farinata* is made by mixing a smooth batter of chickpea flour and water and letting it sit for an hour or so, then pouring a very thin layer of it into a shallow baking tin with plenty of oil and baking in a hot oven for about 10 minutes until golden; it is eaten hot. This is best made in a really hot wood-fired oven, and eaten freshly cooked as a street snack. Livorno has its own version—*torta di ceci*, now sadly displaced by the ubiquitous pizza, but once a popular street food, the basis of *cinque e cinque*: five centesimi of *torta* inside five centesimi of *baguette*.

Panissa (or *paniccia* or *panizza*) is made like a polenta with chickpea flour, and after stirring continuously for half to three-quarters of an hour can be tipped out of the pan, formed into a sort of loaf shape, and eaten hot, or cut into slices which can be fried in oil and enjoyed with chopped spring onions and salt. This is popular in various forms all over Liguria, but especially in the region round La Spezia, now more as a street food than home cooking. *Panelle* is a Sicilian version, flavoured with parsley, which is cooked with the flour; the mixture is then spread thin, cut into to pieces, and deep fried, and is often eaten between slices of bread, seasoned with a squeeze of lemon juice. *Semenza e càlia* is another Sicilian treat: roasted chickpeas and pumpkin seeds, street food similar to the universal seeds and nuts of the Middle East, without which a stroll or outing would never be complete. In Livorno, a polenta of maize flour is enriched with the thick dark liquid from cooking red beans, the appearance as it is stirred in giving the dish the name *bordatino*, after the striped cotton fabric of granny aprons, and in Pisa this robust dish was made with, instead of maize, chickpeas—a staple food of mariners before the port silted up in the 15th century.

CHICORY. *See* ENDIVE.

CHILLI PEPPER, *Capsicum annuum* and *Capsicum frutescens*, *peperoncino*, have been cultivated since time immemorial in the New World. Samples were brought back by Columbus in 1492, and probably came to Italy in the early 16th century, where they were at first regarded with suspicion, as were TOMATOES, regarded as decorative pot plants, probably poisonous novelties, and took some time to work their way from the BOTANIC garden to the kitchen. Once there, chillies became indispensible, and are now grown, and consumed, in Italy in many varieties. They may have become popular in Italy long before this was acknowledged in the cookery books of the upper classes. Mattioli described them in 1568 in a rather confused and tetchy section on cardamoms, and also illustrates the plant in a woodcut illustration drawn from life with the name *pepe d'India*, which he said was brought to this country and is "hormai fatto del tutto volgare," "and by now thoroughly well-known." He described several varieties and remarked how much hotter they were than any other kind of pepper. He would not have known about endomorphins, said to be behind the addictive pleasure derived from the pain of the burn, but Mattioli was already using ground-up chillies as a poultice to relieve sciatic pains, in the same way that chilblain ointment, rich in menthol and capsaicin, soothes to this day the discomfort of arthritic knees. In a letter of 1572 to Ulisse Aldrovandi, Costanzo Felici explains that he is sending seeds of an unknown plant, with leaves a bit like those of of the eggplant, but with fruit rather like the *pomo d'oro*, the red, not the yellow one, clearly segmented, and would like his opinion. (Perhaps a *peperone* or sweet pepper?) In his *Letter on Salads*, written during the 1560s, Felici mentions the *pevere d'India* or *pevere rosso* as being agreeable to those who enjoy the heat of black peppercorns, and notes how they are often seen growing in pots on windowsills. We see chilli peppers lurking in the bottom right-hand corner of a still life by the MAESTRO DI HARTFORD, probably painted in Rome at the end of the 16th century, but this seems to be a rare sighting in early still life paintings. This work, showing fruit and vegetables and foodstuffs in common use, would hardly have included things nobody cooked with, so historians have assumed that chillies and tomatoes were perhaps part of a kitchen subculture, used and enjoyed some time before they got into recipe books. Chillies were easy to grow, cheap, and thus totally unlike the expensive, elitist spices imported from faraway places, enjoyed only by the privileged few. Like garlic, chillies perhaps became the

markers of crude peasant eating, something to enliven the boring fodder of the poor. Lacking more documentary evidence, this has to remain a hypothesis.

By 1781, Vincenzo Corrado, in his *Cibo Pitogorico*, is condescending: "*Sono i Peparoli anche di rustico volgar cibo, ma sono però a molti di piacere*" (chillies, even though a rustic common food, are still enjoyed by many; 1781, p. 32). It is not always clear if he means sweet peppers or hot chillies, but his recipe for pickling them in vinegar with mint, tarragon, sage, fennel, and garlic would work well with chillies. Another recipe, in which the outer skin is removed by singeing over coals, and then the *peparoli* are stuffed with a mixture of chopped olives, anchovies, garlic, parsley, and oregano, is similar to the very hot stuffed chillies of Calabria, but would also work well with milder ones. In his *Cuoco Galante*, Corrado mentions *peparoli* in his list of ingredients, and it is significant that they are used with garlic (another rustic flavouring) and tomatoes, in a very early version of a pungent tomato sauce, which also includes thyme, rue, spices, and juices from roast lamb. His *salsa al tornagusto*, a sauce to revive the jaded palate, includes green chillies, oregano, peppermint, green fennel and fennel seeds, garlic, and anchovies all pounded up with vinegar, lemon juice, and oil, to be served with olives. He used powdered red chilli to season blanched white cabbage cooked with lard, ham, and garlic, finished in meat broth with basil, and served with a purée of chickpeas—a sophisticated treatment of humble ingredients.

An earlier cook in Naples, Antonio Latini, writing in 1694, has a section on how to season food without using expensive spices; he recommends fresh herbs, particularly parsley and thyme, but also a whole range of dried herbs, ground to a powder, each one stored in airtight containers; one of these is *peparoli*. His sauce *alla Spagnola* is the only one in the book to use tomatoes and chillies; these are chopped fine with a little onion,

peppermint, salt, and oil and served as a relish in little dishes. Another recipe described as *alla Spagnola* is for a marinade for stoned, mild olives incudes sugar, garlic, fresh chillies, oregano, mint, and fennel seeds, pounded in a mortar and diluted with oil and vinegar. For a salad of cooked cucumbers, Latini offers a sauce of garlic, chilli, salt, and pepper pounded together in a mortar, diluted with vinegar, with dried oregano sprinkled on top—"refreshing, healthy and tasty," he said. It seems as if the Spanish presence in the Kingdom of Naples might account for the gradual acceptance of chillies and tomatoes in polite society. (Velázquez showed chillies and garlic about to be pounded in a mortar in his *Kitchen Scene with Christ in the House of Martha and Mary*, painted around 1618.)

Artusi's seasonings are discreet: little garlic and no chillies at all. Ada Boni, writing about the robust cuisine of Rome, hardly mentions them, though a little is allowed in the pungent BACCALÀ *in agro-dolce* (sweet/sour salt cod); the soaked, fried fish fillets are finished in a sauce of fried onions, garlic and parsley, white wine and vinegar, cooked until the liquid evaporates, topped up with a tomato sauce, with the addition of prunes, sultanas, sliced apple, pine nuts, grated lemon peel, and some sugar. Her version of *Spaghetti con aglio e olio* (spaghetti with olive oil and garlic, often known as *spaghetti al oglio, aglio, peperoncino*) shows a genteel moderation, which almost defeats the purpose of the dish, where the pungent fried garlic should perfume the oil, and is often reinforced with a few very hot small chillies, which can be removed or not, according to taste. Was our Ada dumbing down a popular dish for her middle-class readers? Later collections of Roman recipes have *peperoncino* in *spaghetti all' Amatriciana*, and of course in *penne all' arabiata*, and they are a necessary seasoning in *broccoletti strascinati*, in which tender young broccoli florets are quickly preboiled and finished in oil, garlic, and chilli.

Another characteristic Roman dish is *spaghetti con le vongole,* in which clams are cooked in hot oil with garlic and chillies, to which white wine is added, served with a sprinkling of chopped parsley. The glow of chilli and the flavour of the almost browned garlic seems to enhance the flavour of the pasta and clams.

From CAMPANIA, where hot red chillies are used more frequently, comes a recipe for large green chillies, seeds and pith removed, fried in oil until soft, and finished off with some smashed cloves of garlic, pitted olives, and capers, and served hot garnished with chopped parsley. A similar dish was familiar to Corrado centuries ago.

The important thing to remember about chillies is that the flavour is more interesting than the heat, so the codification in Scoville heat units tells us little about the taste, and is only a rough guide to the heat, which varies a lot even in the same plant. Italians do not have the rather silly macho attitude to chillies of Anglo-Saxon countries, and use them with moderation, even in the south, where they are more pervasive. The episode in Andrea Camilleri's novel *La forma dell'Aqua* (*see* PIRCIATI), makes this point; the heat is shocking, but what counts for the Sicilian cop, Salvo Montalbano, is the intensity of flavour.

CHIVES, *erba cipollina, Allium schoenoprasum,* are the grass-like cylindrical leaves of a plant of the ONION family, and are used chopped in many dishes, to impart a more delicate flavour than onions or garlic. Sprinkled with chopped marjoram over homemade egg *tagliolini,* with a little butter but no parmesan, chives enhance the delicate flavour of the pasta. They can be chopped into salads and *frittatas.*

CHOCOLATE, *cioccolata,* the beverage, *cioccolato,* in solid form, is made from the seeds of *Theobroma cacao,* brought to Europe

from the New World in the early 16th century. Its value and uses in Central and South America have been chronicled in fascinating detail (Coe and Coe, 1996). Cacao products were valued for their stimulatory powers and their rich flavour, and were the prerogative of Maya rulers and warriors, who, according to some authorities, reached towards communion with the gods in a hallucinatory state brought on by blood-letting, pain, and the use of psychotropic substances, of which cacao was one. The Aztecs valued cacao beans as currency, and a prestigious drink, not at first appreciated by the boorish conquerors. When cacao beans arrived in Spain, they were probably brought by conquistadors or members of religious orders who had experienced their use in Mexico and eventually become enthusiastic about the pleasures of cocoa as a drink, and of chocolate as a seasoning for other foods. Spain seemed to lead the way in this, and sauces for game and meat using a small amount of chocolate among many other spices might have been dim echoes of the "fusion" sauce *mole poblano,* combining ingredients from the Old and the New Worlds. This survives in Italy today in one or two dishes, where bitter chocolate adds to the sombre, dark qualities of a sauce, often for GAME or WILD BOAR, which of course should never taste of chocolate, or have any sweetness, just an indefinable enigmatic richness. A survival from the time when distinctions between sweet and sour were blurred is the variety of recipes combining blood and bitter chocolate, tarts, cakes, and various preserved blood puddings, *migliaccio.* These recipes often include spices and dried fruit, and are an inspiring link with imaginative early uses of chocolate. A family recipe from Milan, described by Anna del Conte, marinates hare and its innards in wine, herbs, and spices and cooks it in the marinade with its blood and only one ounce of bitter dark chocolate. The *caponata* of Sicily sometimes includes chocolate in its *agrodolce* version. Bits of chocolate are often mixed into creamed ricotta in Sicilian pastries.

Chocolate as a drink was popular in Spain and Portugal before it was taken up in Italy, but it is not certain how it got there. An early mention is by Francesco Redi, scientist, poet, and physician at the court of Cosimo III de' Medici in Florence; his poem "Bacco in Toscana" of 1685 has his own copious commentaries, and among them we find acknowledgement of the unpublished notes of Francesco Carletti, an explorer and businessman, who wrote a firsthand, accurate description in the early 1600s of cacao preparation and consumption in Mexico. Another Italian, Pietro Martire d'Anghiera, living in Spain, who became official historian of the Spanish New World, had written an equally detailed account 80 years earlier, and Girolamo Benzoni, a Milanese traveller, described in 1575 a murky brew "more a drink for pigs than for humanity." A Roman physician, Paolo Zacchia, wrote of the warming powers of chocolate in 1644, implying that it was a novelty. But by the time Redi was writing in 1665, he could claim that chocolate prepared in Florence had a *squisita gentilezza* (an exquisite refinement) which surpassed that of Spain, with its subtle additions of fresh citron and lemon peel, the sweet perfume of jasmine, and the aromas of cinnamon, vanilla, ambergris and musk. As with the uncertain documentation of early ice cream making, there is a big gap between the abstract assessments of men of letters and the pragmatic practises of cheerful hedonists. The Medici court encouraged both scientific rigour and unbridled gluttony, and Redi balanced the two with tact and wit. A contemporary, Tommaso Rinuccini, described how chocolate was sold by a Florentine tradesman in little ceramic beakers, hot or cold. It was catching on. Forty years later, these little pots were replaced in aristocratic households by Chinese porcelain, delicate fragile bowls and beakers of different shapes and sizes, displayed among collections of luxury goods, or safe in glass-fronted cupboards, in still life paintings commissioned by the Medici rulers of Florence. Cristoforo Munari gave them what they wanted, an elegant mixture of expensive items, fine wines in crystal glasses, hothouse fruit, and the homely comforts of everyday life, eggs fried in a humble terracotta dish, cured ham, huge wedges of parmesan, a chunk of salami. Showing off conspicuous consumption and pride in their roots, the rulers of Tuscany got the best of both worlds. And one of these flaunted luxuries was chocolate, to be seen clearly in a work dated 1714, where *rosolio* (*see* APERITIVI) or a fine wine is shown in a virtuoso

From *"Bacco in Toscana"* (v. 184)

non fia già, che il cioccolatte
v'adoprassi, ovvero il tè,
medicine così fatte
non saran giammai per me:
beverei prima il veleno,
che un bicchier che fosse pieno
dell'amaro e reo caffè.
colà tra gli Arabi
e tra i Giannizzeri
liquor sì ostico,
sì nero e torbido
gli schiavi ingollino.

That chocolate might not yet
be taken up, or even tea,
medicines like this
would never do for me:
I would rather take poison
than a glass brim full
of bitter harmful coffee,
a brew for Arabs
and Janissaries
so repulsive
dark and turbid
that even slaves choke on it.

depiction of precious glass on a silver salver alongside *ciambelle* (*see* BREADS, RING-SHAPED) and sponge fingers to dunk in the chocolate which is going to be made from the dark brown slabs spilling out of their paper wrapping. Another work from 1705 displays the same assortment of glass and porcelain, with the *ciambelle* and a metal pot on its side, for coffee or chocolate. Other paintings show delicate cups together with a traditional round Chinese teapot, with hinged wicker handles and chained lid. Other props that occur in Munari's paintings show different pots, jugs, and pitchers which give us an idea of a range of novel, nonalcoholic drinks, matched with musical instruments, books with fine bindings, shells, and costly textiles. Redi might not have had room for them in a dithyramb devoted to Bacchus, but they were all around him.

CHRISTINA OF SWEDEN.
See BANQUETS, SUGAR.

CHRISTMAS FOODS. *See*
FESTIVITY AND FOODS.

CHUB, *cavedano,* is another rather boring member of the Cyprinidae family, enjoyed by anglers all over Italy, in lakes, ponds, and streams. The resourceful inhabitants of Montisola in Lake Iseo salt and dry it, which improves the flavour, eaten with the local olive oil as an antipasto.

CIABATTA means slipper, flat, floppy footwear, and is one of the few genuine "inventions" to have a date of birth and a fixed place of origin, according to the INSOR publication *Atlante dei prodotti tipici—il pane* (INSOR, 2000). Similar artisanal breads are made around Como, but the action now is in Adria, Rovigo. What is being imitated all over the world is described as the brainchild of Arnaldo Cavallari, who in 1982 abandoned the world of car racing for his family's flour mills in Adria, in the VENETO, where he set up an experimental bakery to establish the methodology and authentication of the product *ciabatta Italia,* made industrially with his special version of soft flour, *tipo 1 italia.* Whatever method is used, the dough needs to be very soft, almost fluid, and is hard to handle—as Carol Field puts it, "utterly unfamiliar and probably a bit scary" (1985), made with a sourdough starter and fresh yeast, and with a long rising period producing a fragrant interior and a good crust.

Many versions of this late-comer seem to have become, to foreigners, a sort of iconic Italian national bread. Over a decade ago the food department of a department store in north London tentatively put on sale on Saturday mornings a few *ciabatta,* and the ensuing scrum involved this writer in hand-to-hand combat with some pretty tough characters (Italian); and now bakeries the world over produce innumerable versions of *ciabatta,* with varying degrees of success, although it is unlikely that the microclimate and the quality of flour around Adria and Lake Como will ever be equalled.

CIAMBELLI. *See* BREADS, RING-SHAPED.

CIBREO is a Tuscan speciality, given in a refined version by Artusi using only poultry livers, combs, and testicles, prepared, first fried together in butter, and then simmered in broth, and when done thickened with egg yolks and lemon.

Martino had a recipe in the 1460s for a *pastello de creste ficatelli et testiculi di galli,* which seems to be a tart or pie filling or a dish on its own, using cocks' combs, livers, and testicles, cut up (the testicles left whole) and cooked in a mixture of chopped bacon and bone marrow and dried bitter cherries, seasoned with ginger, cinnamon, and sugar, thickened with egg yolks and verjuice and coloured with saffron.

Scappi has some recipes for chicken livers, and an entry on using necks, wings, and feet and gizzards of fowl—similar to a *cibreo*—which are cooked in lard with bacon and sauces in a sort of *fricassea* or stewed and the broth thickened with egg yolks, saffron and verjuice. In his section on invalid food, Scappi has a recipe for a *pottaggietto*, which cooks chicken testicles in a strong chicken broth with mint, marjoram, sorrel, verjuice, ground almonds, and breadcrumbs. Cooks at that time used cockscombs to decorate other dishes; when cooked and—if necessary—peeled of the outer skin, they could be arranged round the outer rim of a serving dish to make a pretty frilly border. Robert May did this a lot in 17th-century England.

The Florentine Francesco Gaudentio, in his *Il panunto toscano* of 1705, gives three versions of *civreo*, specifying *entragne*, poultry innards cooked in white wine, then finely chopped and finished in good broth with spices, lemon juice, capers, and anchovies, and served on slices of toasted bread. Another way was to cook the chopped innards in *vin greco* with chopped candied fruits, crumbled spiced biscuits, a chopped lime, salt, and spices. A more complicated version uses a calf's head (ears, tongue, etc.), feet, tail, and udder, all cooked in water until falling off the bone; then the chopped flesh and fat is mixed with cooked fowl, celery, cabbage, and fried chopped onions, simmered together with cloves and saffron, thickened with beaten egg and lemon juice; the whole is browned rapidly on top before being served hot.

A version from Mugello starts the crests, hearts, and gizzards in chopped onion cooked in butter and sage, then adds broth and, when they are tender, the livers and testicles, then some "unborn" eggs, and finally

the thickening of lemon juice and egg yolks. The derivation of the name is uncertain, probably nothing to do with the French *civet*, but it has acquired lustre from the restaurant of the same name near Santa Croce in Florence, which combines high gastronomy with robust local specialities.

There is no documentary evidence that CATERINA DE' MEDICI brought the recipe with her to France; it is likely that similar delicious dishes already existed.

CICCIOLI. *See* PIG'S FAT.

CINNAMON, *Cinnamomum zeylanicum*, and cassia, *Cinnamomum cassia, cannella, cinnamomo*, are the bark of two shrubs, with a similar aroma. Cassia includes the hard outer bark, more woody, with a less subtle flavour; cinnamon is sold in rolled up "quills" and is papery and friable, with a more delicate perfume. In most dishes they are interchangeable, but cinnamon is preferable when used on its own in desserts and as a last-minute condiment. It is always more fragrant if ground just before use; powdered cinnamon loses its flavour quickly, and might have been adulterated. A whole piece can be added to flavour sweet and savoury dishes, and then removed when the taste seems right.

Cinnamon has been used for thousands of years, enveloped in legends and anecdotes, entertaining but inaccurate, about its origins, which we now know to be Southeast Asia, borne along the spice routes, or Ceylon via southern India, coming to Arabia on monsoon-borne craft, and then on, laboriously, to Europe, getting more and more expensive by the mile (Dalby, 2000, p. 36). It seemed most unfair to Mattioli, at a time when botanists were searching out exotic and faraway plants, and tending them in hothouses and gardens in Italy, that the origins and nature of the plants from which cinnamon came should be so totally obscure.

"Sono state create della sagace natura in questo nostro mondo alcune piante implacabili, che quantunque loro sieno state fatte infinitissime carezze, e servitù; nondimeno e stato impossibile di ritenerle appresso à noi" (Nature in her wisdom has created in this world of ours some implacable plants that, in spite of the caresses and homage lavished unendingly upon them, there is no way of persuading them to settle amongst us.) Nobody knew anything about the plant or where it came from. The classical authors were anecdotal and confusing, and unfortunately the one person who knew exactly what cinnamon looked like and how it was harvested, Leonhardt Fuchs, the founder of modern botany, who had actually talked to the Portuguese traders who were importing the stuff from Ceylon, was rubbished by Mattioli, along with several other eminent botanists unfortunate enough to disagree with him.

Valued by the ancient Romans as perfume, aphrodisiac, and medicine, it was much loved during the Middle Ages and went on being used, mixed with sugar as a flavour enhancer, long after heavy spicing was no longer fashionable. Today it is probably the most used and best loved spice in the Italian kitchen, mainly in desserts, but also lingering on in dishes like the Roman recipe for *maccheroni* with ricotta, in which the pasta is dressed with a sauce made of fresh ricotta beaten up with sugar and powdered cinnamon and loosened with some of the salted water in which the *maccheroni* were cooked. "Children love it," said Ada Boni, somewhat condescendingly. But it is a reminder of the catalytic effect of sugar, salt, and cinnamon that is a thread running through the story of Italian seasonings. This can be experimented with today by whizzing sugar, cinnamon quills or bark, and a little salt in an electric grinder and storing it in an airtight jar. A very little of this "Renaissance stardust" can then be sprinkled over sweet or savoury dishes in homeopathic doses, together with pepper, to enliven fried chicken pieces, baked

fish, or vegetables. This is how so many medieval and Renaissance dishes were seasoned just before serving, perhaps with the addition of rosewater or bitter orange juice.

Cinnamon was also used in most spice mixtures in the past (*see* SPICES) both strong and mild (*spezie forte, spezie dolce*) and might be behind the name of a sauce, *camelino*, with its brownish colour, more familiar to anyone cooking with spices than would have been that exotic unknown animal the camel— almonds were ground with raisins, toasted bread soaked in red wine, cinnamon, cloves, and nutmeg, then moistened with verjuice or vinegar, and sweetened to taste.

In a delicate food like BIANCOMANGIARE, a stick of cinnamon was used to perfume the liquid used to dilute a mixture of pounded chicken breasts and ground almonds, and then powdered cinnamon was sometimes sprinkled with sugar over the dish just before serving, together with some drops of rosewater.

Cinnamon is used today mostly in confectionery—the hard almond biscuits from Sicily, *mostaccioli di Erice*, flavoured with cinnamon and cloves (Simeti, 1994, p. 168), or the softer, orangey *mostaccioli di vino cotto*, made with grape must, biscuits in which cinnamon, cloves, and black pepper give a spicey tang (p. 180). PANFORTE, not confined to Sienna in the past but made all over Italy, was one of the many spiced cakes of the past which used a spice mixture in which cinnamon predominated.

Cinnamon is not so widely used in savoury dishes, but the historian Dino Coltro, writing on the cuisine of the VENETO, remembers with nostalgia the unusual taste of cinnamon in a RISOTTO prepared by his mother for special occasions. A recipe from the Isola della Scala, *risotto all'isolana*, using the local *vialone nano* rice, is seasoned towards the end of cooking with the rich, golden juices from pieces of veal and/or pork, browned in butter and simmered in meat broth with salt, pepper, rosemary, and cinnamon. Powdered cinnamon is stirred in with parmesan and butter before its final rest.

Little slivers of cinnamon bark coated in sugar, along with comfits (*see* CONFETTI) of fennel, ginger, orange peel, almonds, and other healthy things, were served at the end of a meal. Cinnamon's digestive properties were appreciated as much as the delightful aroma, and its capacity to settle a disturbed stomach, and "comfort the heart," and help coughs and respiratory problems made it a spice of universal appeal.

CIRIOLA ROMANA, a robust bread roll from Lazio much loved in Rome, is an elongated strip of dough, somewhat thicker in the middle, not very much like the eel from which its affectionate local name derives (a reminder of the Roman delicacy of young eels stewed with herbs). It has more body than the lighter *rosetta*, and makes a good *panino*.

CITRON, *Citrus medica, cedro*, may have originated in India, found growing in Persia by Alexander the Great's botanists, and was the first of the CITRUS FRUITS to be introduced into Europe. It was known in Italy by the 4th century BC, but was not seriously cultivated until the time of the Arab presence in the south. The fragrant blossom and aromatic peel are enjoyable in themselves, are also used in perfumery and medicine and have many gastronomic uses—the fruit can be sliced thinly and dressed as a salad, sprinkled with sugar, salt, and rosewater, as listed in Scappi's menus in 1570; the fresh, fragrant acidity would have been a perfect foil to his more sumptuous dishes. The peel of this fruit, larger than most lemons, is nobbly and ridged and highly perfumed, reminiscent of the cedars of Lebanon, hence the Italian name *cedro*. A version of the citron, known as *etrog*, is important in the Jewish Feast of the

Tabernacles; when held in the hand, its aroma, along with fragrant fronds of palm, myrtle, and willow, creates a sumptuous atmosphere reminiscent of the origins of this ritual in celebrations of harvest and fertility. The juice helped withstand the pains of childbirth.

Citrons are an important element in "candied peel," although their flavour is usually drowned in sugar. The fresh fruit can be found in Italian markets and is well worth seeking out. Contrary to popular belief, the white pith (*albedo*) of citrus fruits is not to be shunned; there are times when its slight bitterness gives an edge to a dish, for example, the chopped lemon, parsley, and garlic mixture used to stuff baked fish. Candied citrons are used in both sweet and savoury dishes; in the past, some chopped candied citron would liven up a stuffing for meat or fish.

Citrons were praised—especially those from Lake Garda—for their wonderful aroma, sweetening the breath, warding off the plague, and keeping moths out of clothes. The irascible Mattioli enthused about the small citrons grown round Lake Garda; he said they were the best to eat, and noted how from having limited use in Roman times, citrus fruit, "*per ispetiale arte, & nuova diligenza*" (through special skills and new diligence) were cultivated, and enjoyed, all over Italy, especially on the Genoese Riviera, in the Kingdom of Naples, and in Sicily. He recommended eating them candied, which we do today, often in confectionery like the mildly flavoured *panettone* or the densely spiced *panforte*. Scappi decorated roasts and boiled dishes with sliced citrons and served them candied in the last course, along with other sweet things, to aid digestion. Vincenzo Corrado describes a ratafia (*see* APERITIVI) of rasped citron peel, steeped for a day in spirits of wine with some sticks of cinnamon, filtered and sweetened with sugar syrup; and another less subtle syrup, coloured red with sandalwood and flavoured with cloves, cinnamon, and nutmeg as well as citron peel, which he calls *Labbro di Rubino* (Ruby Lips). He gives a citron-flavoured vinegar, an unsweetened spirits of citron, various marmalades, and a recipe for candied citron peel.

There are many varieties of citron today, including the *cedrone* from Calabria, *cedratello* of Florence, *col picciolo* or *degli Ebrei*, used in the Jewish ritual of the Feast of the Tabernacle (mentioned earlier), the *cucurbitato*, *cornuto*, *coststo*, and *striato*.

CITRUS FRUITS, *agrumi*, are

fruits of the citrus family. The main ones cultivated in Italy are *Citrus aurantium*, *arancia amara*, bitter orange (sometimes known as Seville orange, known to North American readers as *naranja agria*); *Citrus sinensis*, *arancia dolce*, sweet orange; *Citrus bergamia*, *bergamotto*, BERGAMOT; *Citrus medica*, *cedro*, CITRON; *Citrus bigaradia*, *chinotto*, blood orange; *Citrus aurantifolia*, *limetta acida*, lime, both sweet and sour; *Citrus limonia*, *limone*, lemon; *Citrus nobilis*, *mandarino*, mandarin. Most varieties are well known outside Italy, except citrons.

Although it is more or less agreed that citrus fruits were first cultivated in China or India about 2200 BC, it is not clear how and when they came to Italy. Perhaps from China via Persia to Greece, probably in the wake of Alexander the Great, who encouraged botanists and collectors of medical plants to collect and bring home specimens, and from there to Italy; but when, how, and under what name? The Golden Apples of the Hesperides may have been oranges, citrons, or quinces. Citrus fruits do not appear in Roman gastronomy, although citrons were used for ritual purposes by the Jews of Roman Palestine, and there have been sightings of what might be citrus fruit in Roman wall paintings. A floor mosaic in Tunisia depicts the foodstuffs of a comfortably off household, with fragrant flowers, fruit, and nuts, and

what looks like a citron on its stem with two leaves attached. Perhaps its perfume was more important than its gastronomic uses. Lemons were known in the Arab world and with its expansion came to Spain and Italy, possibly before the first mention of them in the 11th century. By the time Platina was writing his *De honesta voluptate et valitudine* in the 1460s, there were several varieties of lemon, citron, and orange, and he describes how they could all be eaten as salads, sliced, with salt, oil, and vinegar, or as seasoning. The peel provided pungent aromatic oils, the pith a welcome astringency, and the juice a refreshing acidity. Although their antiscorbutic properties were not understood at that time, citrus fruit were known to have curative powers, stimulating the appetite, aiding the digestion, soothing pregnant women, keeping moths out of clothes, cheering the melancholy heart; and they were also esteemed for their beauty. The glossy evergreen foliage, the glowing fruit, and the perfumed flowers, flourishing simultaneously throughout most of the year, were valued by artists for their symbolic and aesthetic power. The pale, fragrant flowers signified the purity of the Virgin Mother, the fruit her fecundity, and the evergreen leaves the immortality of her son. Mantegna and his contemporaries portrayed fruit in swags and garlands, in imitation of classical themes, but also with reference to the local agribusiness, for the orange and lemon groves around Lake Garda, where in October 1464 they frolicked in search of classical inscriptions, were not a natural phenomenon, but the product of sophisticated cultivation, with a complex system of terracing to make the most of the sunshine, and protective constructions to protect from the dangerous northern frosts. But earlier still, in the 1450s, Paolo Uccello had deftly placed the golden balls of the Medici (a pun on his patron's name and escutcheon) in the orange trees that are part of the bosky background to the Battle of San Romano. At the same time, a couple of rich expats in the Low Countries, the Arnolfini, had a wedding portrait painted by Jan van Eyck, in which that rare luxury object, an orange, glows on the windowsill—symbol of fruitfulness, memories of home, or status. This imported luxury appears among other expensive commodities in still life paintings in the Low Countries: oriental carpets, Chinese porcelain, lobsters, and exotic pies jumbled together in displays of worldly goods, often with a curl of lemon peel adding aroma to a goblet of wine. Costanzo Felici wrote succinctly of the varieties of orange and citron, and the many uses of lemons, finely chopped as a relish with roasts, and the blossoms, when plentiful, eaten in salads. He also describes how the shops in Venice are full of little green limes put up in jars, pickled in salt and vinegar, leaving us wondering whether they were imported from the Middle East or a Venetian speciality. By the time Pisanelli was describing foodstuffs in 1611, he mentioned the uses of sweet, bitter, and medium sweet oranges, known as *melangoli* in Rome and *citrangoli* in Naples, and wrote of the virtues of lemons, distilled as a cosmetic water, or the juice dissolved in syrup, perhaps a harbinger of the now very popular *limoncello*, a liqueur which at its best has a fresh taste of both blossom and peel. He strayed from his strictly medical brief to enthuse about the Genoese and Neapolitan custom of serving with meat and fish a sauce of lemons chopped fine and dressed with salt and rosewater. This is indeed delicious, and a pleasant way of introducing historic food into everyday eating. By the 17th century, Bartolomeo Bimbi painted three huge panels recording the 116 varieties of lemons, limes, and citrons cultivated by the gardeners of Grand Duke Cosimo III of Tuscany with their ingenious horticultural skills, both to satisfy the duke's passion for invention and to encourage the commercial activities of his dukedom. Each fruit was numbered and described in an ornate cartouche, and these and other fruit portraits by Bimbi can now be seen at the Medici villa at Poggio a Caiano, just outside Florence.

CIVET or civé is a term probably derived from the french *civet* but in common use in medieval and Renaissance Italy. The name might refer to the onions which traditionally were used to thicken any sauce, along with breadcrumbs and hard egg yolks, but by the time this had become a recipe for game on international menus, the sauce was almost black with the animal's blood and liver and bread toasted black and soaked in vinegar. Corrado in 18th-century Naples had a more delicate recipe for venison (*see* DEER) in civet, simmered in water and white wine with bay leaves, whole spices, and the peel of limes or green lemons, served with a sauce of crushed almond biscuits simmered with lime juice, vinegar, sugar, herbs, and spices and passed through a sieve. *See also* MUSK, ONION.

CLAM. This bivale has many different varieties, carpet shell, PALOURDE, *vongola verace*, as well as the common *vongola*, the *vongola gialla*; the Venus (warty venus, *tartufo di mare*, *caparozzoli*, and smooth venus, *cappa liscia*), WEDGE SHELL, *tellina*. There is also the razor shell clam, *cannolicchio*, *capa longa*.

CLOVES, *Syzygium aromaticum* (*Eugenia aromaticum*), *chiodi di garofano*, are the dried flower buds of an aromatic tree, known and greatly prized since antiquity, probably spreading to Europe from Egypt, used by Apicius, and by the Renaissance—thanks to explorers and merchants who broke through centuries of secrecy—were known to have come from the Moluccas. Eugenol is what gives the essential oil its pungent and agreeable aroma. Cloves are carminative and digestive and help with respiratory conditions, are good in ointment and poultices, especially for the bites of scorpions, and so have been used in medicine as well as in the kitchen, and are one of the few spices which have gone on being used in the Italian kitchen today in the preparation of cured meats and in confectionary. "Best below the level of recognition" said Tom Stobart in uncharacteristic puritanical mode, suggesting the lightest possible touch in adding just one clove or less to certain dishes. But some delight in the sense of overload in PANFORTE or other spiced biscuits and cakes, and historians have attempted to make a close connection between the unknown author of a 14th-century cookery manuscript originating in Sienna with the *brigata spendereccia* of Niccolò de' Salibeni, so priggishly reviled by Dante:

> *E Niccolò che la costuma ricca*
> *del garofano prima discoperse*
> *nell'orto, dove tal seme s'appicca . . .*

And Niccolò who first discovered the lavish use of cloves, there in his garden where these seeds clustered . . .

This cheerful hedonist was suffering in Dante's *Inferno* for the crime of having decided, along with 11 equally rich and self-indulgent companions, to devote their entire fortune to gastronomic excess, involving a conspicuous consumption of the costliest spice on the market. It is perhaps too neat to link what little we know about the hapless Niccolò with the anonymous cookery manuscript, with recipes for 12 people, and assume that there is any coherent connection. Dante the austere Florentine was probably just having a swipe at the sybaritic Siennese and using cloves as a symbol of excessive luxury, rather than giving precise information for investigative food historians, some of whom imagined that these guys were growing cloves in their backyards or, worse still, burning them on bonfires.

An onion stuck with cloves goes into many broths and meat dishes; cloves are included in the seasoning of stews and casseroles, particularly the Roman *garofolato*, in which *girello*, a cut of beef from the back of the thigh—thick flank or topside—is cooked very slowly, larded with seasoned pancetta, in a dense sauce of red wine and the usual aromatics: celery, onion, carrot, garlic, parsley, chopped and fried pancetta, a pinch of spice, and two cloves.

Mattioli, even in his embittered old age, got much pleasure from the strong scent of carnations, very like the aroma of cloves; he kept these flowers around him everywhere, in pots on window-sills and in vases indoors, perfuming rooms, as a cheap alternative to cloves, and at the same time a delight to the eye. The *Impanatiglie modicane* from Sicily are a survival from the past, when there was no clear distinction between sweet and savoury dishes. These little pasties are a bit like British mince pies—a sweet pastry made with lard and marsala, with a filling of minced veal, crushed almonds, walnuts, sugar and chocolate, seasoned with cinnamon and cloves.

COCKLE, *Cerostoderma edule, cuore edule, cocciola, cuore di mare*, is a name we associate loosely with mussels—"cockles and mussels alive, alive oh"—but what we eat with *spaghetti cozze e vongole* are *vongole veraci*, PALOURDES or carpet shell clams, which have a better flavour. Cockles can go into pasta sauces and fish soups.

COCONUT, *noce di cocco*, fruit of the palm *Cocos nucifera*, is not a native of Italy, but the nuts in their hairy shells are imported and used in confectionary and ICE CREAM. In hot weather, segments of the nut, neatly arranged on vine leaves, kept cool and fresh with a little fountain of water, are refreshing street food. It is not certain when this versatile nut came to Italy. Marco Polo might well have seen them on his travels, but it could have been later explorers who found out about their uses and traded in them. Arab adventurers probably brought them from the Far East to East Africa, and thence to Spain and Portugal, where the name *coco*, meaning funny or grotesque face, might have originated. A huge coconut, larger than life, is pictured on the table of an apothecary selling nutmegs in a treatise on spices and herbs illuminated in Modena in the 15th century. One peers out at us from the early 16th-century frescoes in the Loggia di Psiche, in the Farnesina in Rome, executed for Agostino Chigi by Raphael and Giovanni da Udine; the "eyes" on the hairy outside of the nut become human features in the face of a hairy old man. The same humanoid features are clear in the life-size illustrations to Mattioli, who comments that in his time (second half of the 16th century) *noci d'India*, as they were called, were available to most apothecaries. The oil was good for haemorrhoids, and relieved pain in the lower back and knees. The flesh, when the nut was still fresh, with liquid still inside it, was pleasant to eat, and ideal for those who needed to put on weight. Costanzo Felici, writing about the same time, knew of coconuts' gastronomic uses in their country of origin, but dismisses them as being of little importance except in medicine.

COD, *merluzzo* (*Gadus morhua callarias* or *Gadus morhua morhua*), the fresh, not salted, fish, is not found in Italy, but is much loved in its dried and salt states. *See* STOCKFISH and BACCALÀ. *Merluzzo* is, confusingly, also the name for HAKE, also known as *nasello*.

CODA ALLA VACCINARA,

oxtail stew, is a speciality of Rome, where there is a tradition of recipes made with the tougher cuts of BEEF from cattle too old to work. In the engravings of Pinelli, we can see these great horned beasts being driven to the slaughterhouse, rampaging through the narrow streets, goaded on by wild young men

on horseback with classical profiles. Pinelli also engraved the massive carcasses hanging in the butchers' shops, with women, also with classical profiles, shopping noisily and with determination as they do today. Oxtail was good value, cooked according to the traditional Roman recipe; *lardo*, carrots, parsley, onion, and garlic are pounded together and browned in lard or dripping, the cut-up oxtail and ox cheek are added and cooked until golden, a glass or two of red wine added and, when it has evaporated, tomato purée or fresh tomatoes, along with just enough water to cover, and the dish is simmered slowly and eaten served with celery, which has been added towards the end or cooked separately. Some recipes include sultanas, pine nuts, and dark chocolate, as well as herbs (marjoram, thyme, and bay leaves) and spices (cinnamon and nutmeg), and recommend using the dry white wine of the Castelli Romani. The cartilage and connective tissues give this dish an unctuousness, and the long slow cooking— at least six hours, according to Boni—makes the meat fall from the bone, and the finished result should be bathed in a dense, dark sauce, not as liquid as a stew.

COFFEE, *cafè*, *coffea arabica*, *coffea canephora (robusta)*, and *coffea liberica* are the main kinds of coffee bush from which the "berries," in fact the seeds enclosed within drupes, are harvested. The plant originated in Ethiopia; it spread to the Near East and thence to Europe from the 16th century onwards, probably entering Italy through Venice. It is hard to imagine a time when the preparation and partaking of coffee, so central to Italian life today, was unknown. The aroma pervades the streets of towns and villages, wafts over airports and train stations, and the social rituals of drinking it—alone, with a group of friends, or with a chance acquaintance—are some of the vital threads in the fabric of Italian society. Like other late arrivals, the tomato and the combustion engine, coffee seems to outsiders to define Italy. Italy is where you get the best coffee, and where the best way of making it developed. *Espresso* coffee is not "express," though it is fast, but means "especially," that is, made specially for you, on demand. Forcing water under pressure through freshly roasted and ground coffee beans extracts oils as well as aroma, which gives a smoothness of texture and richness of flavour, *crema*, which lingers in the mouth. Coffee provides the burst of adrenaline, from its 1 to 2 percent

---

In the 1930s, an anonymous Futurist wrote an evocative poem which survives on the back of a publicity postcard for the Caffè Bar 900 in Turin, and conveys the mixture of modernity and slight raffishness of the early coffee bars:

I vassoi planano decisi su aeroporti di marmo.
Ne discende un americano.
Una vecchia zitella vuole un cappucino.
La macchina espresso piange.
Tante bocche vanno a consolarla.
Una zolla di zucchero si veste a lutto.
Qualche mano caritatevole lascia anche due soldi.
Un direttore senza testa va in giro con la visiera.
Un limone si toglie il vestito e rimane in camicia.
Un plotone di bottiglie schierate di fronte sta sull'attenti.
Due mosche aristocratiche prendono il fresco su di una pasta.
Ad un ventilatore gira forte la testa.
Due cassate vanno al mattatoio.
Un fiero panettone commette il karakiri.
Un cucchiaio batte un bicchiere.
Tutti s'accorgono che è fesso.

The crockery hovers decisively over the marble airport.
An American disembarks.
An old maid wants a cappucino.
The espresso machine laments.
Many voices offer consolation.
A sugar-lump goes into mourning.
Some kind hand even leaves a couple of pennies.
A headless director wanders around in a mask.
A lemon removes its coat and sits in its shirt sleeves.
A platoon of bottles stands to attention in battle array.
Two aristocratic flies take the air on a pastry.
A ventilator's head is in a whirl.
Two cassatas go for slaughter.
A proud pannetone commits harakiri.
A spoon hits a glass.
Everyone can see this is crackers [cracked].

caffeine content, that fuels the benign social expression of the Italian temperament, dynamism without intoxication, and vivacity without aggression. If Caravaggio could have fuelled his need for adrenalin with double espressos, he might not have needed to quarrel and kill, and he might cheerfully have transferred his urges for mayhem to the noise and speed of a *motorino*. But this romantic view of coffee applies only to postwar Italy, where the espresso bar was one of the first symptoms of economic recovery after the depression following World War II, when a young urban middle class with pocket money and leisure played tennis and sought the modernity and sociability of this familiar form of refreshment in a new milieu. The espresso machine had been invented much earlier, and was part of the café society of Milan from the early decades of the century, but it was only during the 1950s that it created a "movement" both in Italy and abroad. In Britain, the espresso bar was both modern and exotic; it presented the face of Italy and the taste of good coffee to many of us who were hitherto ignorant of both. Coffee in the United States had a history in some ways independent of Italy, stimulated perhaps in 1773 when tea drinking became an unpatriotic act, until the present wave of coffee drinking establishments with a vast spectrum of Italian-style versions of coffee, some good and some horrible, now familiar to all of us. Like the late arrival of other novel and agreeable substances—TEA, CHOCOLATE, and ICE CREAM—coffee provoked polemics about its use from the 17th century onwards. Disapproval and condemnation on moral and health grounds flowed from the pens of physicians and philosophers, while popular and often unrecorded consumption went on regardless. The myth about the pragmatic Pope Clement VIII who, when faced in the early 17th century with demands to condemn that dangerous infidel brew coffee, tasted it and decided to baptise it instead, at least embodies the essential realities of the situation. While academics raged, ordinary people were probably quietly enjoying the stuff, as with chocolate and ice cream. By the late 18th century, Corrado wrote of a coffee cream, a *sorbetto*, a coffee icing, *naspro*, and *confortini*, coffee fondant, confetti made by creating fake coffee beans with powdered roast coffee worked with gum arabic, dried, and then coated with sugar in the usual way; among his *rosoli* is a brew of strong coffee distilled with alcohol to make an essence to use as a beverage or flavouring; a similar infusion of strong coffee is mixed with syrup and alcohol to make a sweet *crema*. An extraordinarily rich coffee ice cream is made with strong coffee and milk, mixed with 24 egg yolks, cooked until thick and then frozen. Coffee today is a flavouring in cakes, biscuits, and ice creams less alarming than Corrado's. Perhaps the most refreshing is the *granita di caffè* (*see* GRANITA), very strong sweetened coffee frozen to a mush rather than solid, and often served with *panna montata*, whipped cream, a wonderful contrast of textures on a hot summer's day.

COLOMBA. *See* DOLCI, FESTIVITY AND FOOD, PANETTONE.

COLONNATA. *See* LARDO.

COMBER, *perchia*, *sciarrano*, a fish of the Serranidae, is best as part of a fish soup. One species called *scrittura*, because of its hieroglyphic markings, is good floured and fried. In English, this fish is also known as lettered perch.

COMPANATICO, something to eat with your bread, is a word that says a lot about the importance of bread in Italian life, for it is the bread that counts, and the bit of cheese or salami or handful of olives or home-made pickles are meant to enhance the pleasures of a fresh roll or loaf. Sometimes Andrea Camilleri settles his fictional Sicilian cop, Montalbano, on the terrace overlooking the sea at Marinella, with the fresh bread brought that morning by Adelina, his cleaning lady, a few *sottaceti*, some olives, and a glass or two of his father's wine. A moment to enjoy, while brooding on a case, or Livia's latest intransigence—a moment of tranquility, where the bread is as potent as the light and the sea.

CONCENTRATO (tomato paste).
See TOMATO.

CONFETTI (comfits in English) are
nuts or seeds or spices with a coating of hard sugar. The best known in Italy today are probably the sugared ALMONDS which are sent to relatives and friends to celebrate weddings and similar joyful life events. The little circles of coloured paper tossed over the bride at weddings are a substitute for the ancient custom of scattering seeds and ritual breads, symbols of fertility and renewal, which predate Christian ceremonies. The combination of seeds and sugar was quite potent, and apart from their symbolic value, *confetti* were made and used by apothecaries as both medicine and treats; they were offered at the end of lavish banquets, as exquisite morsels and soothing digestives, and brought in to offer visitors coming to pay the ritual congratulatory visit to women after childbirth. In Florence in 1473, Ser Girolamo di Ser Giovanni di Ser Taddeo da Colle, a comfortably off notary, paid a large sum of money for *confetti* (also known as *treggea* or *manuscristi*) as his wife Caterina went into labour. The birth of their son Giovanni was celebrated by family and friends who visited over the next few days, bearing gifts and being treated to refreshments, including the *confetti*. The sweetmeats brought by guests would have in-

cluded *confetti*, and the covered bowls and boxes depicted on birth trays, on which ritual food and ceramics were presented, might well have contained them. Sometimes the proud but harassed father would have to renew supplies, as his wife and guests nibbled their way through pounds of them. Jacqueline Marie Musacchio (1991, p. 41) describes the uses of these ritual sweetmeats in her work on childbirth in Renaissance Italy.

The making of *confetti* was slow and laborious, the seeds or nuts to be coated were put into a sugar syrup at the *manuscristi* stage (*see* SUGAR) and swirled and tossed in a concave metal tray suspended over a low heat. The constant motion had the same function as a cement mixer, keeping the material free flowing without sticking. But unlike cement the *confetti* went through this treatment over and over again, each layer of sugar had to dry out completely before the next coating, and many coatings were needed. The gob-stopper of old fashioned sweet shops was made this way, needing up to a thousand different coloured coats. The aniseed balls of my remote childhood had aniseed in the centre and a powerful flavour as one sucked though the reddish brown outer layers to the white centre, an unimagined link between rural Yorkshire and quattrocento Florence.

CONFORTINI are today little keeping biscuits, cat's tongues, *lingue di gatto*, now a speciality of Piedmont, flavoured with vanilla and lemon zest, made of butter and sugar creamed together until fluffy, with egg whites beaten in, flour added, baked until golden round the edges, and shaped while still warm over a bottle or rolling pin to get the characteristic curved shape. A version called *lingue di suocera*, mother-in-law's tongue, sandwiches some melted bitter chocolate between two still-warm *lingue di gatto* and curves them in the same way. Some recipes whip the egg whites to a foam and cool the biscuits flat. There are many variations. In

Sicily there is a version made with *pasta frolla* filled with lemon or citron marmalade.

In the past, the name was given to what we now call fondant candies, a sugar syrup boiled to the soft ball stage; as it cools it starts to revert to sugar crystals, and is then beaten or pounded vigorously to turn the developing crystals into a soft melting candy, similar to fudge, Kendal mint cake, or the sugar mice of old-fashioned sweet shops. This is what Vincenzo Corrado was doing in 18th-century Naples, with a dazzling range of flavours and textures. He made sugar syrup to the stage of *cottura di maturatura*, the same as *manuscristo*, then worked it with a wooden spoon or roller to a soft paste, incorporating flavours like candied citron, ambergris, and cocoa, pistachios and orange flower water, or coffee. This paste could then be shaped in little metal moulds, or spread out in paper containers to dry, then cut up into shapes and wrapped in fancy paper. These are domestic versions of the more complex lozenges and pastilles made by apothecaries, for medicinal use as well as pleasure. Corrado's sweets seem designed solely for hedonistic purposes.

CONGER EEL, *grongo*, is another
creature in the eel family, though not as delicate and delicious. It is best in fish soups and stews, like the CACCIUCCO of Livorno, where its strong flavour can be modified and enhanced by slow cooking with wine, herbs, and tomatoes. A concentrated sauce made with conger eel makes a good pasta sauce.

CONVENIENCE FOODS are
an inescapable part of cooking today. Pre-prepared food or ingredients which have been treated "to save trouble" are as common in the Italian kitchen as they are elsewhere. A fundamentalist condemnation of all of them would exclude some freeze dried or vacuum packed delicacies that are not

without merit, and a whole range of products, often based on traditional methods, which shed a new, or rather old, light on the concept of FAST FOOD. Tinned food, *in scatola*, or vacuum packed, *sotto vuoto*, or cured and matured in a casing, *insaccati*, or things preserved in jars, in oil or vinegar, *sott'olio, sott'aceti*, have always been used to get a meal together fast. The SLOW FOOD movement was born in protest against the flood of meretricious pre-prepared industrial horrors, travesties of real cooking, that were infiltrating Italy. Slow Food has encouraged the survival of the genuine preserved foods that are part of the traditional fast food culture. Many of Italy's preserved foods are for rapid use in a variety of circumstances. In the past ships' biscuits, like pasta, could be taken on long journeys and used in many ways, as were salt cod (*see* BACCALÀ) and dried fruit. Travellers in the past could carry with them little balls of dried mustard, all ready to dilute with vinegar and deploy on the boiled meats of roadside taverns.

The huge range of commercially prepared sauces for PASTA, using fresh ingredients in perfect condition, are in the same tradition as the home-made jars of tomatoes, seasoned to suit the family's tastes, made in many homes in the past. It can be argued that you can get an impromptu sauce together in the time it takes for the pasta to cook without recourse to tins or jars, but the products that promise fresh country ingredients made by a granny are usually too beguiling to resist. PESTO, a summer sauce made from fresh basil, depends on ephemeral aromas that fade soon after making; we know this, but we still buy it in jars, and enough people do the same to create and sustain a year-round cultivation of basil and the making of pesto on an industrial scale. There are risotto mixes that do everything you could have done in the 20 minutes it takes to make a risotto from scratch, but do not really save you much time. Instant polenta saves the hour of arduous stirring, but does not have the flavour and texture of the slower method (though many recipes for cooking it in the oven, equally slowly, really do work). Pasta cooks so quickly (10–12 minutes, or less) that it ranks as an early convenience food in its own right. A passage in a story by Leonardo Sciascia tells of the sheer incomprehension and bewilderment of a rural Sicilian family, emerging from wartime misery, over the arrival of gift parcels from the United States, including tinned spaghetti and canned orange juice. To Sicily of all places. Fresh egg pasta has traditionally been made by rolling the dough wafer thin by hand, a long and exhausting task—but with incomparable results—then going on to the equally slow business of cutting, folding, stuffing, and twisting, and now you can either buy a little domestic machine that does it all, or freeze-dried packs, or soft vacuum packs, or go out and spend an arm and a leg to eat the real thing prepared in one of the restaurants that still do this.

COOKBOOKS are used more in Italy today than they were in the past. Until recently, women learnt to cook, and men to criticise and evaluate, from their mothers and grandmothers. Family recipes and traditions were passed on by word of mouth, not in writing. But now the cook is bombarded with regional and national recipe books, works of reference, books by famous chefs or from renowned restaurants, books about products, books by local food historians, and facsimiles of historic works. It has been argued that the irreversible decline of traditional cooking created an interest in something it was too late to save, and that studies of regional food were too little and too late. On the other hand, it is claimed that the invention of the pedal cycle and the combustion engine allowed hungry travellers to collide with cuisines they had not met before, and inspired them to search and record local delicacies, instigating a healthy curiosity about

unfamiliar cuisines, which continues to this day. Olindo Guerrini, who was born in Forlì in 1848 and worked as university librarian in Bologna, is typical of these intrepid cyclists: on one expedition he absentmindedly bought a book to get rid of an importunate street vendor, it turned out to be a cookery book, which he added to his solitary copy of his friend Artusi's work, and from this grew a large library. He and his fellow academics in Bologna shared an interest in the evolution of both the Italian language and the cuisines of the peninsula, and old cookery texts and manuscripts were a fascinating source of information about nonliterary usage and the food of the past. This erudite literary tradition was continued in Bologna by Emilio Faccioli, and it is his *Arte della cucina* that many of us owe our first introduction to the literature of Italian gastronomy. Now "food culture and society" is a multidisciplinary area in which academics, sociologists, art historians, linguists, botanists, chefs, and restaurateurs add depth to our understanding of Italian gastronomy. Putting food in its cultural context, with rigorous academic discipline, helps us get charming myths and received wisdom into perspective. Italy is unique in having many small publishers who somehow manage to print and sell modest volumes by local historians that are unique, and often transient, treasures, books to search out and snap up. There are many food magazines, television programmes, and cookery schools, catering for both tourists and native Italians.

Writers about Italian food in the English language, in Great Britain and North America, come in various shapes and sizes. Some are English-speaking enthusiasts for Italian life and food who read, travel, and write in a sometimes chaotically endearing attempt to understand the food and themselves. Some are more focussed, sometimes verging on authoritarian, for example, Elizabeth David, who has been the role model for many since she wrote her pioneering *Italian Food* in 1954, although it is now acknowledged that there were others not far behind. Among Italians living and working in England, Anna del Conte is perhaps the most thorough and knowledgeable writer of recipes. There are moving accounts of Italian immigrants to Great Britain who revived their peasant family traditions with spectacular success in a luxury food emporium. Of the Italian cooks and restaurateurs who have become famous in Britain, the most modest and original is one Franco Taruschio from the Italian Marche, operating in the Welsh Marches, whose *Leaves from the Walnut Tree* is a classic record of an individual interpretation of Italy. Another Italian who has a successful restaurant and a chain of shops and cheap food outlets, Antonio Carluccio, brings good basic Italian food to many who had hitherto had no chance to experience it, and his books reinforce his impact. Some restaurateurs have met a different need, with glossy colour photography and elaborate presentation, to respond to the tastes of customers who want to see the luxury and expense of the restaurant mirrored in the appearance of the book. It is no criticism of the food portrayed to feel that the sublime simplicities of Italian cooking are not always best served by these elaborate publications. The paradox here is that the success of these prestigious restaurants is due to their fidelity to the essentials of Italian cooking, but the hype surrounding the success can be destructive of it. Take the classic example of two small grilled lamb cutlets alone on a plate with a dribble of olive oil and a wedge of lemon; and absolutely nothing else. No sprig of marjoram crossing swords with three chives, no asymmetric squiggles of different coloured *jus*, and no tastefully grouped seasonable vegetables. It takes courage and is not photogenic. Few do it.

The continuing enthusiasm for Italian food in the United States has created a receptive market for books by Americans drawn to Italy—some to live there, and some, like Fred Plotkin, Faith Willinger, Carol Field, and Lynne Rosetto Casper, going back to their Italian roots with a deft sense of what their readers want—an encyclopaedic coverage of the subject, accuracy, precision, and foolproof recipes. Martino and most grannies (and me) would be hard put to meet the standards of these deities. But it must be said that this American literal-mindedness can have the great virtue of re-enforcing a concern for authenticity, and encouraging the sourcing of genuine ingredients. Mary Taylor Simeti, an American settled in Sicily, writes with the advantages of an outsider—curiosity and the desire to find out—and the assurance of the native and brilliantly presents today's food in the context of the island's history.

Then there is a class of popular bestselling writers, on both sides of the Atlantic, who with impeccable timing produce their own book on Italian food, and because their renown is due to a sensitive feeling for what their readers want, and a trustworthy presentation of recipes, success follows. Delia Smith, Jamie Oliver, and many others have mastered this art. Some specialise in other areas, like the Middle East, and bring new perspectives to perceptions of Italy, for example, Claudia Roden.

There are other books that are illuminating, where food is used as a marker, or to give local colour, or highlight character. Calvino's novel *Barone rampante* starts with a dire meal of snails, symbolising many horrid things about the family life. Andrea Camilleri uses food shamelessly to create local colour and join the "food in fiction" genre. Donna Leon intertwines Venetian family food and police procedure in her dark novels.

COOKERY SCHOOLS. *See* AGRITURISMO.

COPPA, a speciality of Emilia, is made from meat and its accompanying fat from the back of the neck of the PIG and the top of the shoulder, handled in different ways in different parts of the province. Dry salted and seasoned, the whole cut is then hung in a cool dry place for about six months. A similar cut is used for *CAPOCOLLO* in central and southern Italy and *l'ossocollo* in the north.

Coppa di Parma is different, in that the meat is massaged with salt, manually or by machine, and kept in a cold dry place for some days, then shaped and put into the thick large intestine of cow or pig, and hung in a warmer place for two or three weeks, then a final period of two to three months in a gradually decreasing temperature. The initial dehydration and the subsequent biochemical activity gives it a unique aroma and flavour.

Coppa Piacentina develops special characteristics from the diet of the pigs and the climate of the area round Piacenza. The same cut of meat is wrapped in the peritoneum, or abdominal lining, of cow or pig (*bondeana*) and tied up in an intricate web of string so that it keeps its shape when drying out after massaging in salt and spices (cinnamon, cloves, nutmeg, and bayberries). It starts off in chilled conditions and, after drying out in a warm place, is put to hang where it gets natural light and ventilation, some of the time below ground, the entire process lasting about six months. Always a luxury product, *coppa Piacentina* used to be a delicacy offered to farm workers during the arduous harvest times, and a prestigous gift accompanying political negotiations, a treasure and a reward for good behaviour.

Coppa di testa is a very different product, made in central and southern Italy, a sort of brawn made out of all the parts of the head, cooked with aromatics and spices, taken off the bone, cooled, pressed, then sliced and eaten cold.

CORATELLA is the offal of SHEEP or lamb, or baby lamb, and sometimes kid, consisting of the heart, lungs, liver, windpipe, and sometimes sweetbreads. These are a delicacy in central Italy and Lazio, where they are cooked, fried in lard, with artichokes or onions. The preparation and timing ensure that the different organs are each cooked to perfection, and the resulting somewhat khaki-coloured mixture is a delicate as well as robust balance of textures and flavours, with the bitterness of the artichokes offsetting the slight sweetness of the various meats.

CORB, *corvina, corvo, corbo*, a fish of the Perciformes, can be cooked like OMBRINE or SEA BASS. Corbs were already familiar to the classical Roman farming author Columella. He regarded the species as native to Italy and as one of those especially suitable for farming in artificial ponds (Columella 8.16.7).

COREGONE, CORRIGONE. *See* WHITEFISH.

CORIANDER (*coriandolo, Coriandrum sativum*) is a plant of the Umbelliferae family. Native to Greece and the eastern Mediterranean, it was known in ancient Egypt. It seemed rather old-fashioned in Greece in the 3rd century BC, when exotic

Most people find they have a strong opinion about coriander, one way or the other, due to its distinctive, pungent odor. (Shutterstock)

new spices were coming in from the East. Spreading slowly to Italy, it was used a lot by the Romans. The seeds are not used much in Italy today in domestic cooking, but are included in the flavouring of some industrial products and confectionary, and in certain cured meats and SALUMI. The pungent leaves are hardly used at all, although the ancient Romans liked them, and both appear in recipes from Apicius (*see* APICIAN FLAVOUR). Coriander leaves are abhorred by those who dislike them, frequently quoting Mattioli's remark that they had an unpleasant smell a bit like bedbugs—a slur not easy to corroborate or deny.

Coriander seeds have a slightly orangey, musky pungency, which is enhanced by gentle dry-roasting. Combined with orange juice and peel, they are used to flavour some of the salumi made from organs and entrails or the less prestigious cuts, which need all the help they can get. The *mortadella di Prato* is made from cheap cuts and diced fat, with a flavouring of pepper, cinnamon, and coriander, with the unusual addition of ALCHERMES (a sweet spicey liqueur mostly used in desserts), matured, then cooked and eaten fresh. From Lazio comes the *salsiccia di Monte S. Biagio*, the innards of local pigs—liver, heart, spleen, fatty cheeks, and muscle fat, flavoured with salt, chilli, garlic, bay leaves, pine nuts, raisins, coriander, and orange peel, prepared for the feast of S. Antonio Abate and Carneval, in the towns of S. Biaggio and Fondi in the province of Latina. From the same area comes another salame sometimes called *saracena*; prime cuts of pork are flavoured only with sea salt, a little chilli, and toasted coriander seeds, marinated in white wine, then dried over a slow heat perfumed with twigs of lentisk, before maturing for a fortnight or so. The seasoning of coriander is said to be a survival from the Saracen presence, when devout warriors used large doses of coriander to disguise the flavour of the forbidden pig, or more likely flavour the alternative meat, mutton; and historians with a poetical imagination claim to perceive in the coriander seeds a touching memento of the tears of Christian virgins taken weeping into captivity. This Middle Eastern flavour is also detected in a goose salame from Venice, a Jewish speciality, where lean meat and fat are flavoured with a coriander and pepper and stuffed into the neck, a tradition revived by a prestigious company, Jolanda di Colò, in Palmanova that is admirably preserving local traditions whilst keeping the recipes shrouded in mystery (*see* GOOSE) and even, according to some authorities, giving birth to new ones.

Coriander, or *pitartamo*, as he called it, was used by Scappi in subtly flavoured recipes, but not as much as cinnamon, cloves, and the various forms of fennel. He flavours pork or veal chops with ground coriander and salt; it is one of the spices he used in seasoned and rolled strips of veal, but this seems to be a way of producing a different effect, using a flavour not in common use.

Messisbugo, in 16th-century Ferrara, has a complex recipe for preparing cured hams: after dry salting for nearly a month, they are plunged several times into boiling wine, then drained and covered with a thick crust of crushed coriander, kept under a weight, then covered again with a mixture of coriander, fennel, and cloves, and finally smoked. Mattioli confirms that coriander seeds do indeed make a good preservative, and insect repellent.

Elizabeth David, in her pioneering *Italian Food*, gives a lovely recipe for loin of pork cooked slowly in milk, with diced pancetta, chopped onion, garlic and fresh marjoram, and basil or fennel, flavoured with coriander seeds; a fragrant dish which needs care and attention, but is well worth the trouble. Her inimitable prose conveys in a few lines the complexity and aromas of this dish— "Gradually a golden web of skin begins to form over the top of the meat while the milk is bubbling away underneath," and so on (1987, p.143).

The digestive and carminative properties of the seeds made them a delicious and therapeutic end to a banquet served in the form of sugar-coated comfits. In Mattioli's time, physicians squabbled, quoting ancient and modern writers, over whether the seeds were harmfull or healthy, to which he tetchily replied that it was common sense to take them in moderation—an understandable reaction to all those arid controversies around the humoural theory.

CORNEL. *See* CHERRIES, CORNEL-LIAN.

CORNETTO, *croissant*, is a light, ethereal version of the sometimes stodgy French croissant, often with a sweet or savoury filling. Its origins are unknown, though the pretty legends that connect this delicate bread with the Turkish invasion of Vienna in the 17th century, or later, are not likely to be the only explanation. We are told that the Polish king Jan III Sobieski defeated the Turks in 1683, and these delicate pastries were invented by a Viennese pastry cook in his honour. Using the emblem of a vanquished invader who had terrorised Europe for centuries as a symbol of national survival seems a bit odd. The crescent-shaped roll, *rogal*, had been made in Poland since medieval times, and is unlikely to have been a novelty in Vienna. The croissant is sometimes described as French in origin, although the history of the croissant in France is a 19th- and 20th-century story. *Chiffel,* from the German *Kipfel,* is a crescent-shaped bread or puff pastry roll traditional in northern Italy. What makes the dough or pastry nice and flaky is the business of rolling it out flat, brushing it with softened butter or lard, folding it up into a long roll, then rolling it out again, with more fat, and so on, using the stuff to wrap round a filling to make a pie or pasty, or treating this *pasta sfogliata* as a delicacy in its own right. However, or whenever, a square or triangle of this dough or pastry got rolled up and then curved to make a crescent or half moon shape is not recorded. Since early times, bread has been made in shapes that can be offered to the deities of the sun and the moon, using their form as symbols of sacrifice and renewal, growth and fertility. Scappi was writing about a *pasta sfogliata* in 1570 as something commonly made by professional pastry cooks, taking their separate activities very much for granted, and so, to our frustration, not describing what they did.

CORRADO, VINCENZO

(1738–1836), wrote about food with joyful inventiveness in his three collections of recipes: *Il Cuoco Galante* of 1778, *Il Credenziere di Buon Gusto* of 1778, and *Del Cibo Pitagorico* of 1781. He was born in Oria, in the province of Salento, in 1738 and lived to the ripe old age of 98. At 17 he entered the Benedictine order of Celestins in Naples (a sound move for a youth of humble origins); he received a good education there and accompanied the grand master on travels all over Italy. Corrado's curiosity about food and cooking was fed and stimulated, and he was able to follow up an interest in the products and agriculture of the region. His many other writings include propaganda for that useful but little known vegetable, the potato, a work on beekeeping, and, later in life, during the turbulence of the Napoleonic invasion and the traumas of occupation by a less congenial regime than that of the gross Bourbons, a list of daily menus in a style that reflects the austerity of life under the new regime.

At a time when the tyranny of French fashion in all the arts seemed to have most of Europe in its grip, he wrote within the structures of French cuisine, but in the spirit of traditional Italian gastronomy. The elements of classic French cooking—ingredients, methods, vocabulary—are deployed by this *cuoco galante* in a subversive, imaginative, and endearingly individual way. He never pontificates, never lays down the law or scolds, or boasts. A fresh flow of ideas springs at us off every page, in a generous but controlled profusion. Corrado can convey a complex recipe in three or four lines, giving us the essence of a dish, but without anything at all in the way of method, quantities, weights, or timing. This is exhilarating for an experienced cook, but might baffle a beginner. It does give us a clue as to Corrado's readership—professional cooks or heads of households, erudite gourmets, and the fun-loving, frivolous society of 18th-century Naples, the pleasure capital of Europe.

The sort of food enjoyed there is laid out in 20 menus at the end of *Il Cuoco Galante*, which accompany two beautifully engraved table plans in the French style, showing the table settings for the first and second services. Over 30 dishes in each service, ranging from French-inspired *bisca*, *budin*, *gattò*, and *bignè* to thoroughly Italian *calamaretti fritti*, *cardoni alla Parmegiana*, *torta alla Bolognese*, and the new and innovative *zuppa di pomodoro al basilico*.

The recipes flesh out the menus, but in a shorthand that, as we have seen, implies a professional competence beyond the reach of many. A simple chicken dish is given in a few lines: he prepares capons in milk with some sticks of cinnamon and twists of lemon peel, and serves them on a bed of spinach, finely chopped and finished with butter and cream.

Pheasants, he tells us, are in season from winter through spring, but best in winter when "they are persecuted and murdered by hunters," a discreet aside which hints at his views of the sport of kings, enjoyed by the idle and illiterate Bourbons. Best stuffed with a veal forcemeat and wrapped in bacon, and spit roasted, he says, and then gives other versions—pot roast slowly with bacon, butter, thyme, and bay leaves, moisten with a full-bodied red wine, and serve with shallots softened in butter. Or cover with slices of bacon, wrap in a clean cloth, stew in a pot with white wine and water, bay leaves, juniper berries, salt, and crushed peppercorns, degrease, and serve with a lemon sauce.

Corrado's *Cibo Pitagorico* was influenced by the fashionable cult of vegetarianism in 18th-century Europe, but his voluptuous vegetable recipes have little in common with the bleak philosophy of plain living and high thinking proposed by Jean-Jacques Rousseau, whose frugal and dyspeptic life-style had little in common with that of Corrado and his patrons (*see* VEGETARIANISM). Enriched with bacon, meat stock, bone marrow, and chicken, his recipes exploit Italy's profusion of vegetables with a hedonistic disregard for current interpretations of Pythagorean theory, and no apparent concern for the Church's dietary proscriptions. Eggplants *alla Corradina* are sliced, salted, squeezed dry, and fried, and each slice is covered with a stuffing of grated *provatura*, chopped basil, egg yolks, cream, and a little sugar, rolled up, and finished in a cream sauce. Fresh green beans can be served in a sauce of anchovies pounded with pine nuts, horseradish, tarragon, and garlic, diluted with olive oil, vinegar and lemon juice, and seasoned with salt and pepper. Still life painters of the time displayed the voluptuous piles of fruit and vegetables of CAMPANIA, and the Spanish ruler of Naples Charles VII returned unwillingly to Madrid to rule as Charles III, consoling himself with the paintings of Meléndez (who had lived and worked in Naples) which reflected the popular food he had once enjoyed.

Unlike the shrill chauvinism of writers in 18th-century England, Corrado's implicit rejection of French gastronomic hegemony was tactically adroit, reflecting the complex alliances and treacheries of Neapolitan politics. The reason he gets so much space here, apart from his sublime recipes, is that his books spearheaded the movement in Italy away from the dominance of French cuisine. The tide had turned, French fashions were no longer trickling down, and Italian regional food was seeping inexorably upwards, and in the dark days of French political domination, would triumph as part of the expression of a changed political awareness.

COSTMARY, *erba di San Pietro, erba di Santa Maria, Balsamita major, Tanacetum balsamita,* is a tall plant of the Compositae family with large, pungent leaves, used sparingly in *frittatas, salads,* stuffings, and the flavouring of liqueurs and tonics—one of the many ways of conveying a fragrant bitterness to food and drink. It is the characteristic flavouring of the *casônsèi* of Val Camonica in Brescia, a stuffed fresh pasta with spinach, beets, cabbage, parsley, and a little *erba di San Pietro,* with parmesan and eggs. It used to be used, in infusion, as a hair conditioner, and every writer on herbs repeats that the leaves were said to have made agreeable bookmarks in Bibles.

COTECHINO is made with a mixture of ground lean and fat pork meat combined with ground pork skin (COTENNA), pounded together to create a glutinous, rich, and meaty filling, in natural or artificial casings, then dried and sold cooked or raw. Versions are made all over Italy, but those from EMILIA-ROMAGNA are best known. The cooking time obviously varies according to which you buy, and although enthusiasts proclaim the superiority of the uncooked product, the standard precooked industrial *cotechino,* after 30 to 40 minutes heating in barely bubbling water, is delicious.

COTECHINO CREMONE-SE, or *ciüta,* in its artisan production, is made of the meat and fat left over from other procedures, with the throat meat (*guanciale*) and skin, seasoned with pepper and red wine infused with spices and herbs. This is put

into natural casings and hung to dry near a wood-fired stove, then hung for a month in a dry place. It is eaten after long slow cooking. A version, *testeüs,* including meat from the head is exceptionally delicious.

COTECHINO MODENA, in spite of much wrangling over whether or not it originated in Cremona in Lombardy or Modena in Emilia, with local poets muddying the water with their effulgent *campanilismo,* is now made in an area stretching from Modena to Milan, Verona, and Ravenna. Its DOP lays down requirements for both ingredients and method, pork meat marbled with fat, pork fat, skin, of course, salt and pepper, and other permitted natural flavourings, and how to prepare it, either precooked, or ready for cooking by the customer.

COTENNA DI MAIALE, *cotica,* is the fresh skin or cured rind of pork. Scrubbed clean and shaved of its bristles, this is a wonderful combination of flavour, fat, and glutinous material which adds unctuousness to stews and bean dishes. Long slow cooking gives it a soft chewiness that also has a place in the various cooked sausages— *cotechino, capello del prete,* and *zampone*—that rely on long cooking to become really soft and melting. Most serious delis will give away to worthy customers the rind trimmed off cured hams before slicing—a gift to treasure and use in soups and stews.

COZZE. *See* MUSSEL.

CRAB, *granchio,* is the generic name for many creaturers, of which the *granciporro,* edible crab, is perhaps the best known, often imported, though once plentiful round Venice, whence comes a recipe for serving freshly cooked crab meat doused in garlic-flavoured butter and parsley, similar to Scappi's version, in which the meat is flavoured with pepper, cinnamon, and sugar, mixed with egg yolks and grated cheese, and heated up in its shell, then finished under a hot grill.

The best loved crab, the spider crab, *granceola, granseola, grancevola*, is plentiful in the lagoons of Venice: a spiny hairy creature, reddish brown and in season from mid-December to the end of February, when it is at its fullest and most tasty. After a good scrub to get rid of the flora and fauna and briefly cooking in salt or flavoured water, the delicate flesh is best treated with discretion; a dressing of light olive oil, lemon, salt, and pepper is amalgamated with the soft substances within the shell and used as a dressing for the firm flesh extracted from the carapace. The carcass and bits, along with mantis shrimp, *canocchie*, can be made into broth for a risotto into which are incorporated the meat from the creatures.

The shore crab, *granchio comune*, is cultivated for harvesting at the exact moment before its soft shell begins to harden.

CREAM, *panna*, is the fat content of MILK which rises to the top and can be removed or left with the milk used for cheese making. *Crema* is not cream; it means CUSTARD or *crème patissière*. Traditionally, the flavour and consistency of cream depended on the breed of cow, its pasture, and the time of year. Now it is a more consistent product, often given long life heat treatment, and is available in varying degrees of fattiness, to have with coffee or use in sweet and savoury preparations. Being so perishable, cream benefits from various treatments—fermentation, acidification, coagulation, and cooking or heating. *Panna montata* is whipped cream, often enjoyed on its own or served with ice cream. PANNA COTTA might have originated in Piedmont: cream whipped with sugar is brought to boiling point and thickened with gelatine dissolved in milk; it can

be flavoured with coffee or liqueurs, and then put into little pots or moulds to cool. Clotted cream, which rises to the top of slowly heated milk, and can then be removed and laid on a dish in wrinkled layers like cabbage leaves, or put into pots, figured in Scappi's menus as *capi di latte*, along with junkets or *gioncate* (sometimes called *raveggioli*), made from milk set in little reed containers, and served quivering gently on fresh vine leaves, soothing to the eye and the palate amongst the vibrant banquet food. These creamy, milky concoctions were part of the heritage of Italian milk and cheese culture long before the French fashion for cream-based sauces and "creamed" soups emerged from the 17th century onwards. They were served at the beginning of meals, with other cold dishes from the *credenza*, not as desserts at the end, where a *neve di latte* made from the froth from whipped milk was offered among the candied fruits and sugared almonds. Two centuries later, Rousseau's soppy Julie sipped milky drinks and ate creams and junkets and mild cheeses, a fashionable diet, but hardly a French innovation. What was alien to Italian cooking was the French use of cream in sauces for pasta and meat or fish. Cream does have the virtue of amalgamating butter and cheese and other flavours, as in a certain over-the-top sauce for fettucine (*see* PASTA), but the way it dumbs down flavour and texture is not appropriate to the subtle taste and consistency of pasta, and quite out of keeping in a recipe like *spaghetti alla carbonara* where the amalgam of GUANCIALE, and its rich fat, with eggs and pecorino aims at creaminess without cream.

CREMA. *See* CUSTARD.

CREMA FRITTA. *See* CUSTARD.

CREN. *See* HORSERADISH.

CRESCENTINI, CRESIA. *See* FLATBREADS.

CRIVELLI, CARLO (active c. 1457–1495), was a Venetian painter who, after a scandal involving the wife of a sailor, lived and worked in the MARCHE, where his work was in great demand for the churches of this prosperous region of independent small hilltop cities and coastal towns. He combined the modern, classical realism of his contemporary MANTEGNA with a wealth of decorative surfaces in the tradition of the ornate international gothic, and as well as the richly embroidered textiles, encrusted with jewels, we note with pleasure the realistic depiction of the symbolic fruit—apples standing for the fecundity and virtue of the Virgin Mother, cucumbers for the purity of her son—with the nuts, pears, flowers, and birds of the region. One painting is of special interest: *The Annunciation with Saint Emidius*, painted in 1486 to celebrate the granting of civic independence to the small hill town of Ascoli Piceno. Crivelli gave the city fathers what they wanted, the image of a prosperous, modern, successful little town, with its paved streets and elegant civic spaces, well-maintained city walls, and prosperous citizens going about their business, while the spiritual content of the painting dovetailed comfortably with the profane. In fact, doves abound, including the carrier pigeon, which brought the political news; its cage, and the recipients of the message, are on a balcony in the distance. The Holy Dove zooms in through an aperture in the decorative freize around the Virgin's elegant town house, to illuminate the chamber, furnished in the latest fashion, and, what interests us, a shelf of good things—quince paste, preserved fruits, and a flask of cordial water. And up in the sky, in a virtuoso display of perspective, domestic pigeons flit in and out of their dovecote. A peacock, symbol of both imperial power and the immortality of

Christ, perches on the upstairs *loggia*, close to herbs in pots. The traditional cuisine of the Marche is lurking within this painting, and the products of mountain, coast, and plain would have figured in Ascoli Piceno's kitchens.

CROSTATA. *See* PIE.

CROSTINI, CROSTONI. *See* BRUSCHETTA.

CRUMIRI are traditional half-moon-shaped biscuits from PIEDMONT, made with fine corn meal and plain flour in varying proportions, folded into butter beaten with sugar, eggs, or egg yolks, sometimes flavoured with vanilla, and—in a version from Sicily—baked with a covering of sesame seeds.

CUBEB, *Piper cubeba, cubebe,* from Indonesia, grows on a climbing vine similar to pepper, producing greyish peppercorns with stalks attached. Another kind, *Piper clusii,* or *Piper guineense,* comes from Africa. Cubebs were used in the Middle Ages for both medicine and cookery. Mattioli describes them as having a "fragrant aroma with something of a sharp bitterness" and medicinal uses which include calming the stomach, dealing with wind, clearing congested lungs, and, chewed with MASTIC, clearing a stuffed head. In the section of his great work, his commentaries on Dioscorides, dealing with ailments and conditions and their remedies, he gives a spice mixture to use with food to encourage good digestion—galangal, cubebs, cloves, nutmeg, mace, saffron, and cinnamon. This is a reminder that gastronomic recipes really need to be seen in the context of health, and that spices have this dual role of delicious and expensive status symbols and useful medicines. Cubebs, which seem today less appealing than cinnamon and cloves, had curative proper-

ties which justified their now diminuished use, though its pungent, camphorous bitterness still has its uses in the Italian liqueur industry.

CUCINA DELLE NONNE,

granny food, is another endearing concept which needs to be taken with a pinch of *peperoncino* (*see* CHILLI). Every Italian knows that his grandmother's cooking was the formative gastronomic influence of his life, and every granny knows that her remembered culinary exploits were the visible tip of a mountain of careful making do and scraping by with whatever came to hand. The traditional festive foods of the past, enjoyed perhaps two or three times a year on special days, can now be eaten twice daily at vast expense in artfully rustic trattorias throughout the land—CUCINA POVERA for the seriously rich.

The *tortellini in brodo* of EMILIA-ROMAGNA used to be prepared with ingredients saved for and hoarded all year round, for certain festivals during the year. They are a luxury dish, and at the same time an essential part of the *cucina povera*. The egg and flour pasta was not an everyday preparation, and the filling, a mixture of Parma ham, *mortadella*, veal or beef, some fatty pancetta, parmesan cheese, with perhaps a light spicing, chopped up and amalgamated by hand, was wrapped with deft skill in small squares of the transparently thin pasta and curved round the forefinger of the left hand to make tiny pockets, to be cooked in an aromatic *brodo* (*see* BROTH) of meat and chicken stock.

Granny food as a category of cooking is about old-fashioned, often rustic food prepared and remembered by an older generation, and in spite of a fog of journalistic nostalgia, something we are glad to have rescued from oblivion by scrupulous writers, recording methods and recipes that would soon have vanished.

CUCINA POVERA

has been around for millenia, but the concept is now a concerned response to the health problems of an affluent urban society—too much fatty meat, sugar, and processed foods and not enough exercise all contributing to a range of unpleasant diseases and conditions. According to one writer,

> Modern dietetics and the science of nutrition have reaffirmed that our "poor" cuisine of the past is the ideal preventive medicine for the many serious afflictions of the "affluent society"—from obesity to heart disease, diabetes, and cancer, with the advantages to health of a diet low in fat, based on wholegrain cereals, fresh green vegetables, olive oil, pulses, the good bread of olden times, and fish. This was clearly, for a long period, the alimentary regime, natural or holistic as one might say, that has sustained for centuries the work and leisure, the intelligence and art, of our ancestors. (Valerio, 1988, p. 9)

Grains, pulses, raw and cooked vegetables, seasoned with herbs and olive oil, eaten with good honest bread, and washed down with moderate quantities of honest wine, with milk, cheese, butter, meat, and meat products serving as garnishes rather than staples, and fresh fish where possible, are the essentials of *cucina povera*. The fact that this has been the basis of rural diet around parts of the Mediterranean for some time has given rise to the comfortable journalistic myth of a "Mediterranean diet," which has spawned cookbooks and life-style projects well beyond the bounds of historical and geographical credibility.

But it is as well not to idealize the situation; historians of rural life in Italy have documented the deficiency diseases and poor life expectation associated with povery and malnutrition, and their insights are a necessary corrective to the rosy picture of hardy bronzed peasants living to a ripe old age on messes of potage and slugs of cheap plonk. Reports on rural and urban poverty from the 18th century onwards show how living conditions and diet were neither healthy nor enjoyable—something nobody would want to return to. Perhaps this idealization of *cucina povera* is a way of looking at diet that might be a reaction to the good living during the postwar years of the Economic Miracle, when Italy enjoyed a wave of prosperity that did not last. A response to this wave of easy living (followed by austerity) and a feeling of revulsion towards the fast food spawned by agribusiness and multinational food industries has made many people think hard about what they eat and where it comes from. The idealistic urban young who turn from the comforts of their parents' lifestyles to the tales of hard times and basic food told by rustic grandparents want a return to organic, sometimes vegetarian, ingredients and traditional recipes. The urbanisation of Italian society, the drift from the countryside to work and live in towns and cities, has made this return to the past an almost unattainable ideal, but it persists, helped by the growth of agritourism and perhaps even by new directions offered by self-reform in the food industries. A family-run trattoria, in what was once a poor rural area in Emilia, used to sell a breakfast of *gnocco fritto*, salame, and Lambrusco to manual labourers and farm workers, but had to change direction when a new kind of client drove up in a sports car asking for cappuccino; moving with the times, it eventually went on to get a Michelin star for a combination of innovative and old-fashioned dishes. Decades later, a London-based restaurateur offers *gnocco fritto* to City gents, and Japanese bankers revel in *lardo di Colonnata* on hot toast. Thus can urban wealth rescue rural crafts (production of *lardo di Colonnata* has trebled in the past decade) and captains of industry can pleasurably raise their cholesterol levels without getting their hands dirty.

Enthusiasm from abroad may have helped small organic producers to find wider markets for grains like spelt and some varieties of wheat, pulses, genuine olive oil, cheeses, salami, hand made pasta, and different kinds of rice; and changes in our own eating habits have made the recipes of *cucina povera*, however idealised, a healthy option for more and more urban cooks and consumers.

CUCUMBER, *cetriolo, Cucumis sativus,* is one of the cucurbits, and was around in the ancient world, but since it looked like the chate melon, an elongated gourd, and textual references do not distinguish between them, calling them both *cucumeres*, we cannot be sure if it was the same as the modern sweet salad cucumber. Apicius (*see* APICIAN FLAVOUR) had a salad recipe, *sala cattabia*, in which bread soaked in sour wine or vinegar, and raw and cooked delicacies, including *cucumeres*, were dressed with a mixture of herbs and seeds ground with fish sauce, honey, and liquamen. This can be made with modern cucumbers, and the concept is close to some of the modern bread-based salads, like the *capon magro* of LIGURIA. Commerce has discouraged the writhing serpentine forms of early cucumbers, the delight of painters and engravers; they are now uniform and often bland and watery, but small, hard, unripe cucumbers grown organically have a good flavour. The varieties grown are thin, plump, rounded, nobbly, or smooth. They are usually salted to expel some of the water, drained, and used in salads.

CULATELLO gets its name from *culo*, a mildly improper word, diminutive of backside or bum; and indeed "smooth as a baby's bottom" is an apt description of this silky soft, rosy delicacy. The poet Alfredo Zerbini praised the melodious local dialect of Parma as fragrant with *malvasia, grana, culatello*, and violets. It is a prime pear-shaped cut, a muscle detached from the middle of a ham, the rest of which is discarded and has to be put to some other use, often *fiocchetto*, which makes it expensive, and its cure is a very different from that needed for ham. The DOP is applied to *culatelli* made in Busseto, Polesine Parmense, Zibello, Soragna, Roccabianca, San Secondo, Sissa, and Colorno in the province of Parma, from pigs reared in LOMBARDY and EMILIA-ROMAGNA and cured in specified climatic conditions. There is also a considerable industrial production, which misses out on the fog, as I will explain, and so does not rate a DOP.

Traditionally, *culatello* was made in small quantities for the private use of the producers, and very limited distribution. It is now much sought after, and production doubled between 1998 and 2000, while industrial production was 10 times that.

Ham, swathed in its own rich fat, needs a different cure from this tasty fragment, which is detached from the flesh and bone of the pig's buttock immediately after slaughter, with only a thin covering of fat, first rubbed in a little salt for a day or two, put in a cold place to absorb it, drained and allowed to rest, seasoned with pepper and garlic, then wrapped in natural casings, usually the bladder, and tied up firmly in a tight, intricate net of string to exclude unwanted air as it dries out for a month or so. It was then traditionally hung in a cellar or outhouse, the opposite of the light airy sheds where Parma or Modena ham is cured, throughout the dank, humid, horrible winters for which this region is renowned. The foggy bottoms of the Bassa Parmense, on marshy land reclaimed from the flood plains of the Po, have the murk and microorganisms that over 12 or more months transform this precious bundle into a very expensive delicacy. Before serving, the *culatello* has to be carefully rinsed and cleaned, the by now loose and tangled strings removed, and given a soaking for a day or so in dry red or white wine, then sliced very thin and eaten on its own or with a bit of butter.

Industrial production which qualifies for the use of the *marchio* or trademark and legal protection afforded the name *Culatello di Zibello* have to replicate the climatic conditions and temperature specified in the official definition of the product. One of the many problems facing those preoccupied with the survival of traditional salumi, the protection of the environment, and the demographic changes in the area, is how to meet a growing demand for an authentic product, and try to return to the more traditional ways of rearing a pig more suitable for this. The big fat pigs that have large hams suitable for PROSCIUTTO *crudo* are not so good for *culatello*, which needs the presence of fat in the tissues of the muscle removed from the ham of a different breed, fed in different ways.

CUMIN, *comino or cumino, Cuminum cyminum*, a plant of the Umbelliferae, was used more in Italy in the past than it is now. Apicius (*see* APICIAN FLAVOUR) used it in sauces and relishes for fish, and indeed it was a common and cheap flavouring all over the Ancient World, mentioned in the Linear B tablets, and known to the Mesopotamians. Its distinctive flavour is now associated with the cuisines of the Middle East and North Africa, but it was one of the flavourings enjoyed in medieval Italy, and Platina writes of it as in common use, especially by followers of Hippocrates, who wished to acquire a pallor that might indicate assiduous attention to study and brainwork, when this was not the case—"hypocrites," he called them. But Platina and his contemporaries were anxious to find continuity of use with their heroes in ancient Rome, and may have given the impression of a use that was not as widespread as they imagined. Mattioli describes *cimino* as being readily available, interchangeable with ANISE, CARAWAY, DILL, and FENNEL, used medicinally and in cooking. It flourished around Siena and Rome, so it may well have been used since classical times.

CURED MEATS. *See* SALUMI.

CURRANT AND RAISIN, *uva passa, uvetta,* are just two of several different varieties of dried GRAPE—*Sultanina,* pale gold, soft and seedless, *uva di Corinto,* small, bluish-black, and seedless, and the larger *uva di Smirna* and *uva di Malaga.* When dried they keep well, and the concentration of flavour and sweetness makes them a good addition to both sweet and savoury dishes. Naples and Sicily in particular use them together with pine nuts, a reminder of the Arab legacy, a combination found in stuffings and pasta sauces, often with anchovies and capers as well.

CUSCUSU. *See* ARAB INFLUENCE.

CUSTARD, *crema.* Scappi gave a detailed, sensitive account of its preparation back in 1570, pointing out that the name *crema* is French in origin. He also explains the making of custard tarts, *pasticci di latte,* using a rich egg custard flavoured with rosewater, sugar, and cinnamon. A century earlier, Martino gave a recipe for a custard tart using a filling of eggs, milk, sugar, and cinnamon, put into a precooked pastry case, agitated gently during cooking, stirred occasionally with a spoon, and sprinkled with rosewater just as it starts to set. "It should tremble like a junket," he said. He called it a *diriola,* which might derive from the French *dariole,* a custard tart made in a little metal tin or mould, already known as *darioles de cresme* in 14th-century Paris. The name is now applied to the mould alone. An exquisite survival of this tradition, which flourishes in Spain and Portugal, are the very eggy little custard tarts, *natas,* to be found in the recipes of Portuguese and Latin American pastry cooks.

Messisbugo has a *tartara* enriched with butter, sugar, saffron, raisins, and pine nuts, baked in a pastry case; his *tartarette alla francese* were smaller cheesecakes, rich with ricotta and fresh cream cheese, eggs, butter, rosewater, and sugar, which seems to reinforce the French connection. This kind of rich custard mixture would have been part of the international repertoire of rich banquet food, and known to European heads of state, and their cooks, so was most likely common to most countries, rather than attributable to one nation.

This custard filling or addition to cakes and pastries gradually superseded the BIAN-COMANGIARE of medieval court cookery, less laborious to prepare, and more "modern" in style. By the early 17th century, English country house kitchens were making similar light creams, and whipped-up syllabubs, and in 18th-century France we find Rousseau's Julie enjoying a pure and somewhat insipid diet of light creams and custards, fresh delicate cheeses, and cool spring water in her informal *jardin anglais.* A long long way from the refinements of city life in contemporary Naples, where Vincenzo Corrado's *Cuoco galante* was making similar creams for more worldly clients. Corrado had a profusion of more than 20 custards, made from a basic mixture of milk, egg yolk, and rice flour mixed carefully together, strained and cooked until thick, stirring in the same direction, together with a stick of cinnamon and a length of lemon peel, which are eventually removed. The variations include a bright green one, where the flavouring of candied limes is enhanced with a colouring of spinach juice, or a version of *crème brulée* flavoured with caramelised almonds, candied citron, and a little oil of cinnamon, with a topping of sugar burnt with a red-hot shovel. Other variations include sieved strawberries, grated orange zest, candied orange peel, and a wonderful mixture of blanched and ground bitter almonds, mixed with milk, strained, stirred into whipped egg whites, cooked until thick, and served with sugared bitter almonds.

Today the main custards are *crema pasticciera,* thickened with flour as well as eggs, often flavoured with lemon zest, and some-times lightened with whipped cream. It is used more frequently than whipped cream but in some regions, like Sicily, creamed and flavoured ricotta is used in many pastries and desserts. *Crema inglese* is made with egg yolks and milk only; *crema frangipane* is made with milk, egg yolks, and flour flavoured with vanilla and blanched almonds pounded in mortar, or pulverised AMARETTI. These *creme cotte* are not the same as the traditional PANNA COTTA, which is made to set with gelatine. *Panna cotta* should also not be con-fused with PANCOTTO, the name for various ways of using up stale bread. *Crema fritta* is a solid custard cut when cold into rectangles of strips, floured, coated in egg and bread-crumbs, and fried in lard—in Emilia—or butter, in Milan, and traditionally served with a FRITTO MISTO.

cephalopods. It can be up to about 25 cen-timeters long; although the size is not always an indication of age, the smaller ones are usually preferred. They can be grilled, roasted or fried, the art being to time the cooking so that they remain tender. The "ink" sac of the cuttlefish was used in the past by artists, and gave its name to the colour and substance sepia. It can be used to give a dramatic black hue to risottos and pasta dishes. There is a Venetian dish in which cuttlefish are stewed in their own ink, with wine and aromatics, and served with polenta.

A smaller related creature is the *seppiola*, and care needs to be taken to distinguish an old, tough *seppiola* from a tender young cut-tlefish. The *seppiola* has no stiff internal shell or bone, but has two little members project-ing towards its rear.

CUTTLEFISH, *seppia* (*see also* OCTO-PUS and SQUID) is a sea animal of the

CYNAR, a bitter aperitif flavoured with artichokes. *See also* ARTICHOKES.

d

DADO (stock cube). *See* BOUILLON.

DAIRY PRODUCTS include MILK, CREAM, BUTTER, CHEESE, whey, and yoghurt. They are defined and regulated internally and by European Economic Commission rules and directives. These are not entirely compatible with traditional methods of milk production and use, and the survival of many local products is a matter for concern—a point that crops up in several entries here.

DANDELION, *dente di leone, tarassaco, Taraxacum officinale,* is one of the huge daisy family, sharing some of the properties of LETTUCE and ENDIVE, and like them sometimes cultivated for both roots and leaves. It has many medicinal and gastronomic virtues, is good for the liver and kidneys, and has diuretic properties which account for the alternative name, *piscialetto.* The young leaves are good both raw and cooked, their bitterness reduced by lightly boiling. A salad of fresh young dandelion leaves, together with cubes or strips of PANCETTA fried until golden, is seasoned with the cooking fat and some good red wine vinegar, and to complete the already potent impact, sometimes cubes of bread fried in lard with garlic can be added.

DANTE. *See* TUSCANY.

DEER is the name we apply specifically to all members of the Cervidae family. Their meat, venison, which originally meant the flesh of any hunted animal, is covered by the word for GAME, *selvaggina,* or *cacciagione.* In Italy, a clear distinction is made between roe deer, *capriolo,* fallow deer, *daino,* and red deer, *cervo.* Chamois, *camoscio, Rubicapra rubicapra,* are Bovidae, not Cervidae, although they are game. They all have dark, fine-grained meat with little fat and no marbling; in spite of the low fat, it can be juicy and tender if cooked with sensitivity. The flavour and texture depends on many factors—the age of the animal, how it was killed or hunted, skinned, hung, and butchered, and then things like marinating and seasoning also have an effect.

Red and fallow deer are easier to rear in controlled conditions, and red deer are being managed in central Italy at present. Animal welfare studies show that running about in the wild can often be more stressful than munching grass in a paddock, and subjective (human) ideas of "freedom" need to be applied with caution to wild animals, which can be as diseased, elderly, and worried about the next meal as the rest of us.

The different cuts of game can be cooked in appropriate ways: haunch, loin, and fillet quickly fried or roasted, and served rare; other cuts stewed slowly with wine and herbs. In the case of wild deer, where the age and health is uncertain, cuts like saddle, loin, and fillet are usually reliable, but there might be a risk of uncertain quality in deer damaged with shot or overwhelmed with adrenalin in the hunt. Semiwild deer have many advantages, especially the provision of healthy meat of a known age.

It is now thought that many deer preserves protected as privileged hunting grounds were also there to provide reliable meat for the table, and in the past the art of the chase involved the activities of a big staff of herdsmen and farmers. When Sicily had a lush, wooded landscape, the Norman emperor Frederick II had a deer park near Palermo, a pleasure ground with a summer palace. There are deer parks today in national parks.

Recipes from Apicius for game in all its forms (wild boar, deer, hare, and even bear) have an inventive use of herbs and spices. A sauce for stewed venison involves pounding in a mortar pepper, lovage, celery seeds, caraway, oregano, asafoetida, dry and sweet wine, and some of the broth, which is then thickened with starch. He has a green sauce for roast venison of pounded green herbs with plenty of parsley, mint, rue, and onions, pepper, cumin, honey, sweet wine, olive oil, and venison broth. A darker sauce uses pounded dates, nuts, pepper, lovage, mustard, honey, and vinegar, diluted with broth. Medieval recipes in this tradition include a PEPERATA and BRODO LARDIERO and CIVET.

Venison is at its best for roasting when the deer is a year to 18 months old, and if roasted pink will retain the juices and not need larding. Stewed and braised venison does need larding, and strips of hard back pork fat rolled in spices add to texture and flavour.

Venison pasty was a safer way of offering a present to friend than sending a perishable carcass on a long journey. Sealed into its protective pastry crust (designed not to be eaten but to contain the meat), sterilized by cooking, and preserved with spices, the pie was safe portable food long before the days of refrigerated transport.

In some areas, various cuts are cured in different ways. The *cacciatorino* of Sondrio in Lombardy is made with meat from imported roe deer (often from Britain) and pork fat, and the *salame di cervo* from the Valtellina province in Lombardy from imported leg of red deer (probably from New Zealand deer farms) and pork fat. A *bresaola* is also made in the Valtellina, and in Piedmont, from red deer meat, well spiced, which is good for anaemia, having a much greater concentration of iron than meat from domestic cattle. According to Professor Giovanni Ballarini (doctor at the Università degli Studi di Parma, expert in veterinary studies and the history of the pig and its products), diligently stitching together paleolinguistic evidence, the original *bresaola* may have been made from red deer meat, not beef, the name being derived from the Latin for salt, *sal*, and a word, possibly of Indo-European origin, common from the Baltic to the Mediterranean for red deer, *bre* or *bhre* (also connected with the name of a cheese), all of which makes it possible to surmise that red deer were domesticated before wild bovines and sheep and goats. Neolithic sites all over Europe yield bones which can be interpreted as being from semi-domesticated deer that were valued also for their hard antlers, which made versatile tools, and their velvet. Later hartshorn was used to make jellies and was also a source of ammonia for smelling salts. From clearing the ground for deer to graze it was but a short step to getting the animals to pull sledges (like Father Christmas and his reindeer) and to curing their meat with salt and eventually using their milk for cheese. Happy the inhabitants of Valtellina and Valchiavenna, on a major prehistoric salt route supplying them with what it took to do this. But strange that the long silences of history have obscured the unfolding of this quiet evolution. Little trace remains, although we know of a snack found in the digestive system of a man (today known as Ötzi) from what is now Brescia, who was provisioned for a long journey over the heights of Similaun between Italy and Austria when he stopped for a meal before struggling on upwards, and in a remote alpine pass was shot in the back with an arrow. His body was preserved in the ice for over 5,000 years, and his last meal—salt meat (mountain goat and red deer) and cereals, analysed by researchers at the University of Camerino—indicates that as early as Neolithic times, cured venison was part of an ample carnivorous diet. It may be that later, when deer were protected for the hunt, the illicit use of their salted and cured meat was surreptitious and so not documented, leaving no evidence for us to explore these uses of cured deer meat.

The large, magnificent red deer was traditionally the most esteemed spoil of the chase and the glory of the banquets of the rich and powerful. There was a distinction between the beasts of venery, hart (red deer stag), hare, boar, and wolf, and the beasts of the chase, fallow buck and doe, fox, marten, and roe deer.

The rituals of hunting and slaughter of this noble beast were equalled only by the rituals of cooking it whole and serving it forth complete with fur and antlers. But the thrill of the chase did not automatically produce gastronomic highlights; a brave and defiant creature five or six years old "would blunt the teeth of a lion," as John Fletcher puts it, and perhaps for this reason deer were some of the first wild animals to be if not domesticated at least kept around as a managed food resource.

DELLA VERDE, SUOR MARIA VITTORIA, was a nun in the

enclosed Dominican order of S. Tommaso in Perugia where she lived for most of her life, dying in 1622 at the age of 67. In 1583 she began a notebook which started as a devotional exercise but evolved into memoranda on practical aspects of convent life: the embroidery and needlework which produced revenue for the convent, as did the biscuits and confectionary made on a huge scale and the work, which she seems to have enjoyed, in the

kitchen. The archivist Giovanna Casagrande realised the significance of the notebook for food historians and published all the 170 recipes embedded in the manuscript alongside a version in modern Italian (Casagrande, 1989) which is full of interest, its spontaneous and private quality a contrast to the published cookery books of the period. The pious thoughts eventually found their home in another notebook in a neater, more regular hand. It took considerable detective skills for Casagrande to "discover" Maria Vittoria— to fit a name to the two anonymous notebooks in her distinctive handwriting and to find traces of her activities among the records of the convent. The personality that emerges is that of a sensible, cheerful woman, integrated into the communal life of the nunnery, dividing her time among devotional activities in the choir, communal activities in the workroom, and shared meals in the refectory, with periods of solitude in her private cell. She was one of the many daughters of a moderately well-off functionary of the city, fieravante della Verde, who could afford to make provision for four of his children in this way. S. Tommaso was one of the biggest convents in Perugia, and to have a part in the functioning of a kitchen feeding up to 100 nuns and convent servants, as well as visiting ecclesiastics, and supplying the table of the prioress must have taken considerable skills. Cooks were not listed in the convent archives, so Casagrande assumed that the nuns themselves would have been in charge of the kitchen, under the direction of a *camerlenga*, a rotating function. This notebook does not appear to be the official convent cookery book: its structure is wildly chaotic, a contrast to the ordered regularity of convent life. Some of the recipes are detailed and coherent, others more like hastily scribbled reminders, with crossings out and interlinear comments, but all of them have a breathless, hands-on quality that brings the convent kitchen to life and perhaps tells something of the enthusiasms and practicality of the writer. There is not a hint of the mysticism of Teresa of Avila, who sought and found God among the pots and pans (*entre los fogones*), a practical respite from her agonised devotions, or the intellectual arrogance of Sor Juana Inès de la Cruz, who explored the natural sciences and the dark night of the soul in her private convent kitchen in Mexico City, and coolly maintained that if Aristotle had been a cook he would surely have written better. Unlike San Diego of Alacalá, pictured by Murillo quietly praying, while *putti* and angels make his *manjar blanco* and *gazpacho*, Maria Vittoria needed no help from visiting angels: her matter-of-fact approach to convent life and kitchen matters seems to show a cheerful acceptance of the routines and rhythms of her world. Her vernacular remarks echo them, with repetitions that enforce the actions: "*Fa bolire un bon bolore buono*" (Give it a right good old boil), "*acaldela ben ben ben*" (cook it really really well) applied to a recipe for spinach, washed, cooked, drained, and squeezed dry, then heated really well in hot oil with salt, finished with raisins, and served with pepper and bitter orange juice. Sometimes a recipe is detailed and coherent, sometimes a run of staccato phrases, a sort of shorthand, to remind the writer of something she has just done in the kitchen, perhaps with an older colleague, transmitting an unrecorded skill; there is a sense of a wish to pass on tips and wrinkles, to augment known kitchen wisdom, to add to an existing repertoire. The recipes as transcribed could not possibly be a reliable way of finding out about the everyday diet of the convent, for there would have been no need to write them down. So a special recipe, *panmelato priora*, the prioress's PANFORTE, a rich spiced honey cake made on an industrial scale, was noted, but not how they got their bread (homemade or from a nearby bakery?) or the source of vegetables and herbs (the convent had a kitchen garden, but was it self-sufficient?) or how meat was bought and prepared. The

notebook tells us how to skin a hare, but there is no recipe for cooking it. She tells us about making lard, how to use blood in a MIGLIACCIO, but we do not know if they reared and killed their own pigs. But we can put the recipes in the context of secular food of the time, and it seems that the convent ate more or less the same as the outside world, being composed of women from the more affluent social classes. Spices are used frequently, many herbs, and large amounts of saffron, the most expensive spice of all. Some menus jotted down among the recipes describe the fare for special occasions, which, although more rich and plentiful than ordinary days, give the impression of a varied and agreeable diet. A meal to welcome a new arrival, *pranzo acettatione*, included muscat wine, salad, a bowl of broth, meat, half a pigeon and a quarter of a chicken each, and cheese.

A recipe for pot roasted PIGEONS— squabs from the dovecote, presumably—has them stuffed with prunes, unripe grapes or gooseberries, chopped bacon, pepper, cloves and saffron, fresh herbs and fennel seeds, and salt, swathed in bacon, and cooked in a dish tightly covered with paper, with just sufficient broth to create a little steam, but ending up dry, not runny. "*Mai scruprilli*," she writes (Never ever uncover them). A roast kid is stuffed with a mixture of chopped cured bacon fat, parsley, fennel and summer savoury, prunes, fresh plums, and unripe grapes; some of this *bogalglie* is inserted along with sprigs of fennel and rosemary under the skin; and when almost done is taken off the spit and laid between two dishes, to rest in its gravy and some rosewater before serving. Sugar snap peas, that is, peas in their pods, not shelled, are cooked in oil with a mixture of chopped herbs (parsley, summer savoury, basil) and unripe grapes, dried and fresh plums, and garlic, adding just enough water to keep moist, and when the peas emerge from the pods they are done and can be salted and served. A sauce similar to pesto is made from basil, and fennel, with garlic *si è per contadini* (if for peasants), pepper, and saffron suffused in hot oil, then pounded with walnuts and breadcrumbs and thinned with warm water. The recipes and the manner of telling them are perhaps more remarkable than their context. Maria Vittoria's cookery notes are inspiring and workable; we are encouraged to rush to the kitchen and recreate her simple, and complex, food.

DENTE, AL. *See* PASTA, COOKING IT; PASTA, NUTRITIONAL NOTES.

DENTEX, *dentice*, *dental*, is an oval fish often with a steel-blue back and silver sides, though the colour varies, sometimes a reddish tinge here and there to its fins or on the belly, as with the large-eyed *dentex*, *occhione*, painted by Ligozzi in the 1580s; it is good grilled or stuffed. Scappi knew them well in Venice, where they are bigger than anywhere else; he cooked both *dental(e)* and *orata* in wine, vinegar, and water, which when cold forms a surrounding jelly, tinted yellow with saffron. Since their colour varies, he remarked, as did Davidson later, that you have to examine the teeth to identify the different breams, and our *dentex* has some huge dog-teeth which are quite distinctive. A recipe from Naples involves baking a large *dentex* with a stuffing of chopped herbs—parsley, rosemary, thyme, summer savoury, garlic, salt and pepper, covered with breadcrumbs, sprinkled with olive oil and salt, and serving with lemon juice. A tasty fish that can stand up to this herbal assault can handle three or four hours in a marinade of olive oil with chopped parsley, bay leaves, oregano, marjoram, wild fennel, tarragon, and garlic, then lightly coated in flour, fried in some of the oil of the marinade, and served with a garlicky tomato sauce, cooked in some of the aromatic oil.

DIGESTIVI are alcoholic drinks intended, like *APERITIVI*, to stimulate or assist digestion, and are usually taken at the end of a meal, with and sometimes in, a cup of coffee. The mixture of herbs and spices which flavour *digestivi* do indeed have useful properties, and take us right back to the tradition of monastic and domestic preparations, designed to alleviate gastric and other problems while giving pleasure, helped by the alcoholic content, which is often quite high. The turbulent politics of 19th-century Milan, with a population deftly adapting to French and Austrian occupation, was stimulated and refreshed in the various cafés and bars, where literature and the arts were on the whole safer subjects of conversation. The taste for home-made *rosolì* and cordials, aromatics steeped in alcohol and sugar, was widespread; innocent refreshing tonics to take any time of day, while less benign potions like absinthe, *mistrà*, and *anisetto* were sold commercially, so there existed a market for products like the *amaro Felsina Ramazzotti*, invented by an enterprising wine merchant, Ausano Ramazzotti, in 1815, a liqueur with over 30 herbal ingredients, including peppermint, rhubarb, and gentian, which is popular to this day. Forty years on, a mixture of roots, spices, and herbs, including rhubarb, aloes, gentian, and zedoary, macerating in alcohol, was stirred with a red-hot poker, and so got the name *fernet* (*fer*, iron, *net*, clean). It was made commercially by the brothers Branca, and their Fernet Branca is still enjoyed as perhaps the most impressive of all *digestivi*. When you read on the label that it is *anti-colerici*, this does not mean a cure for the colic, or bad temper, but a belief once held that it could prevent cholera. The label has the prophetic image of an eagle whose outstretched wings span the world, which this bitter, herb-flavoured drink now does. Much loved in the United States, it gives a herbal kick to mixed drinks and cocktails. Sambuca is another *digestivo*, a clear liqueur flavoured with anise, sweeter and less bitter; it is much loved in

Rome, where it is sometimes served with a coffee bean set alight on its surface, giving off a baleful blue light. Strega comes from the south of Italy, a herbal *digestivo* coloured with saffron, often bottled with a sprig of some characteristically bitter herb like rue. The thought that something herbal is bound to do good after a meal, in spite of the alcohol content, is comforting, and the intense herbal flavour can round off a well-seasoned meal pleasantly. Limoncello can do the same—a lighter liqueur which is becoming increasingly popular, made with the peel only of fragrant lemons from the south of Italy, Amalfi, the Gulf of Naples, Sicily, and Sardinia. The peels are steeped in a good-quality clear alcohol, then diluted with sugar and water, to make a simpler drink with all the fragrance and none of the acidity and bitterness of the fruit.

DILL, *Anethum graveolens, aneto,* has fine, feathery leaves, and pleasant-tasting seeds, like a mixture of caraway and anise, and both can be used in stuffings and salads, to flavour vinegar and pickles, and it has considerable medicinal powers, stimulant and carminative, useful to both gladiators needing strength and infants with colic. The essential oils are used to flavour liqueurs.

DITTANY, *dittamo, frasinella, Dictamnus albus* of the Rutaceae family and *Oreganum dictamnus* of the Labiates (both get called dittany) have some of the pungency of OREGANO and PENNYROYAL but with a strong lemony aroma; the leaves are often used for infusions. Both varieties have a strongly flavoured essential oil which is exuded in such quantities that it sometimes sets on fire—hence the English name "burning bush"—and is used in the preparation of liqueurs. *Dictamnus albus,* a native of Crete but growing also in northern Italy and Tuscany, was known to Italian herbalists and de-

picted by the artists working for the Medici rulers of Florence in the 16th and 17th centuries, who collected rare and wonderful plants and flowers, for both aesthetic and therapeutic reasons. The combination of hypochondria and acute aesthetic sensibilities made the Grand Duke Francesco I the ideal patron of Jacopo Ligozzi, whose depiction of plants and herbs goes beyond the accuracy of botanical illustration into plant portraiture as a fine art. Dittany had everything the grand duke could desire—rarity, medicinal properties, and beauty—and Ligozzi's depiction shows the pale, pink-tinged flowers rising from a stem above clusters of fragrant leaves and small hairy roots whose outer layers were also used.

Dittany was used to alleviate female troubles, and as a poultice for wounds. Wild goats ate it to expel the darts of hunters, and successful hunters seasoned their catch with the fragrant leaves.

Cretan dittany, although gastronomically similar to oregano and other similar herbs, had for these botanists and physicians the glamour of antiquity and mythology, and Mattioli dwells on Virgil's evocation in book 12 of the Aeneid, of Venus, who, at a critical juncture in the battle raging for control of Latium, took off for Crete to get some dittany to cure Aeneas, wounded by a javelin. Thus did herbal medicine and divine intervention contribute to the origins of one of the world's superpowers.

Dryden's rollicking translation gives some idea of the political and medicinal importance of this fragrant herb.

> But now the goddess mother, mov'd
> with grief,
> And pierc'd with pity, hastens her
> relief.
> A branch of healing dittany she
> brought,
> Which in the Cretan fields with care
> she sought:
> Rough is the stem, which woolly leafs
> surround;

The leafs with flow'rs, the flow'rs
with purple crown'd,
Well known to wounded goats; a sure
relief
To draw the pointed steel, and ease
the grief.
This Venus brings, in clouds involv'd,
and brews
Th' extracted liquor with ambrosian
dews,
And odorous panacee. Unseen she
stands,
Temp'ring the mixture with her
heav'nly hands,
And pours it in a bowl, already
crown'd
With juice of med'c'nal herbs
prepar'd to bathe the wound.
The leech, unknowing of superior art
Which aids the cure, with this
foments the part;
And in a moment ceas'd the raging
smart.
Stanch'd is the blood, and in the
bottom stands:
The steel, but scarcely touch'd with
tender hands,
Moves up, and follows of its own
accord,
And health and vigor are at once
restor'd.

Thanks to dittany, the tide of battle turned, and Aeneas vanquished his enemies and went on to found Rome.

DOC, DOP, IGP, SGT stand for

Denominazione di origine controllata, Denominazione di origine protettata, Indicazione geografica protetta, and Specialità tradizionale garantita. The use of these initials and the logo guarantees to an establishment that has won it the legal right to protection from inferior competition and imitation of its food product, because it has been proven, after rigorous scrutiny, to fulfil an exactly specified definition. The definition is based on the territory where the food or wine originates, and the characteristic qualities, *tipicità*, of that product in its own special environment. Wine was the first to win this protection in 1963 (see *The Oxford Companion to Italian Wine*), and cheese and salami followed. In the *disciplinare di produzione*, the precise geographical area is defined, the ingredients, the techniques of production, and the organoleptic and tactile qualities of the foodstuff, specifying the race of animal from which the milk or meat comes, in the case of cheese or salami, what it has fed on, the seasonings, if any, and the conditions in which it is subsequently matured. Some products which are special to a locality but are made with material from elsewhere can be awarded an IGP. The SGT applies to foods produced by traditional methods.

This system has protected and encouraged many artisan products that would otherwise have been swamped by industrial imitations, some not even made in Italy. The name "parmesan" is rashly applied to European cheeses which might have been made with a vague imitation of the method used for *parmigiano reggiano* but do not have the benefit of the microclimate that makes this cheese unique. Even with the help of its recently acquired DOC, the genuine *aceto balsamico tradizionale di Modena* has difficulty surviving the mass ignorance of cooks and restaurateurs who ought to be able to recognise the real thing, and the disgusting fraudulent imitations foisted on us by industrial producers using a travesty of the name. The cured pork fat *lardo di Colonnata*, matured in special marble troughs in a small commune near Carrara in Tuscany, has its IGP (not DOP, for most of the pigs are imported from Padania) and needs this protection, for the now fashionable slabs of cured pork fat that are much sought after, if laid end to end, would cover more ground than the dozen or so genuine producers in Colonnata have access to but would not have the qualities conferred on the genuine product, due to the special microclimate and techniques of preparation.

But the other side of the coin is that some idiosyncratic and exceptional products that do not fit into the DOC straitjacket risk perishing for lack of protection. The fact that DOP is applied and enforced so rigorously allows the health police, or *terrorismo sanitario*, according to Corrado Barberis, to impose conditions which are a negation of the methods and a rejection of the equipment used by traditional producers. Sterile stainless steel and plastic cannot host the benign microbiological organisms that make a product unique. The good becomes the enemy of the best. A DOC or DOP guarantees prices and markets that an independent creation cannot hope for. This is where information from organisations like SLOW FOOD and ENSOR help small independent producers; their publications help to inform a public anxious to know, and willing to pay. Gastro-tourists search out rare and wonderful creations, and since there has always been a certain amount of gullibility in this area, satisfaction can be found on many levels. Meanwhile, most Italian families have connections and networks of mutual obligation, relatives, business colleagues, a friend of an aunty, the cousin of a brother in law, who can be persuaded to part with salami, olive oil, cheese, unlabelled wine—*prodotti tipici* that would probably never meet the norms of the health police but help to keep alive an awareness of excellence that flourishes alongside the legal norms.

The DOP and IGT protect and define many other products, from the saffron of Aquila and San Gemignano, the white asparagus of Cimadolmo, the capers of Pantelleria to the spelt of Garfagnana, the lentils of Castelluccio, apples from the Val de Non, and the fragrant lemons of Sorrento and Amalfi.

DOLCI can be biscuits, tarts, cakes, pastries, or sweetened breads of various kinds, especially the heavily spiced *panforte*, *certosina*, *panpepato*, the light sweet fruity breads like *panettone*, *colomba*, *pandoro*, and *dolci al cucchiaio*, to be eaten with a spoon, like *zuppa inglese*, tiramisu, zabaglione, and the sweetmeats of the past—candied fruit and peel, or fruit in syrup, or the *confetti* of nuts or seeds in a coating of hard sugar (we know them as *dragées* or sugared almonds), or the different confections of almonds or other nuts, ranging from marzipan to brittle nuts in a hard caramel, or the amazing range of ice creams. Regional variations on all these are a source of pride, even more than the breads. Industrial versions of well-known cakes and pastries are usually well made, as they have to appeal to discriminating customers with childhood memories of the real thing. There has been a tradition of convent-made confectionary for centuries, where nuns had the time and skills to produce intricate, expensive cakes, biscuits, and preserves not available in everyday households, which along with embroidery was a dependable source of revenue for the convent. Maria Grammatico learned these skills in the Istituto San Carlo in Lerice in Sicily, and Mary Taylor Simeti's account of how she used them to create a world-famous confectionery enterprise explains all the traditional recipes with considerably more clarity than the endearing cookery notes of Maria Vittoria della Verde, a 17th-century nun in Perugia, where sweetmeats for the convent, or for sale, were in a very different tradition from the almond- and sugar-based products of Sicily. Instead of cane sugar and almonds, a legacy of Arab civilization, we have honey, *sapa*, and walnuts, and a heavier use of spices, with fewer of the creams and custards that came into use later, though she does give a creamed ricotta in which ricotta beaten smooth with sugar is pushed through the concave side of a coarse cheese grater to give a decorative effect.

Bars have freshly baked pastries and cookies ready early in the morning to enjoy with the first coffee of the day, important in a culture where breakfast is taken on the hoof and whose quality sets the tone for the day.

DONKEY, *asino*, like HORSE, has not been much of a food resource in the past, and was often eaten when the pack animals were past work, and so rather tough. In Piedmont there has been a recent renewal of interest since World War II, based on stories of partisans who during the Resistance were reduced to eating donkey meat and came to enjoy it. The Sagra del Tapulon, in Borgomanero near Novara, is held in September, to celebrate a coarse, savoury sausage made with donkey meat. The flesh is used in various salami and cooked products.

DOP, Denominazione di Origine Protetta, is a legal definition of a product defined by European Union and national legislation, specifying the area of production, the techniques involved, and the organoleptic and sensorial qualities desired (the characteristic flavour, aroma, and colour). The product must have an approved and recognisable logo, usually on both the cheese and its label. The DOP status is conferred only after rigorous examination and is subject to constant inspection and control by a *consorzio* which exercises stringent quality control and also is actively involved in the promotion and marketing of the product, and prevention of fraudulent use of the name by international commercial interests.

This combination of recognition and protection can be seen as both a blessing and a curse, for the very rigidity of the definition excludes similar products, which either end up hoovered up into the DOP product, suffering undesirable changes in the process, or wither away for lack of encouragement. An alternative recognition of the *tipicità* of a cheese or salami might save some very good things from extinction. Various organisations are concerned with this issue, including INSOR (*see* INSOR, 2000, 2001, 2002) and SLOW FOOD. (*See also* DOC, DOP, IGP, SGT.)

DORMOUSE, *ghiro*, was well known and bred for its meat in ancient times. Scappi implies that they were plentiful all year round in 17th-century Rome and gives some recipes. Dormice were enjoyed in ancient Rome, carefully reared in a *glirarium* or burrow, from which they would be put into a ventilated jar called *dolium* with built-in spiral walkways, to munch happily on grain, acorns, walnuts, and chestnuts, fat and sleepy in the dark, and unaware of their impending fate—to be rolled in honey and poppy seeds and spit roasted or braised. Trimalchio served them up thus for a pretentious dinner party, but by Scappi's time they were stuffed with bacon, sour fruit like gooseberries or tart young grapes, spices, and soft cheese, and roasted or baked. Apicius mentions braised dormice stuffed with pork, pine nuts, pepper, fish sauce, and ASAFOETIDA.

DRIED FRUIT, *frutta secca*, can be nuts, almonds, walnuts, hazelnuts, pistachios, pine nuts, chestnuts, and soft fruit, apples, pears, apricots, peaches, plums, dried to get rid of the moisture, and so preserving them, as well as concentrating the flavour. *Liofilizzazione* is the name for the process that partly freeze-dries the fruit, reducing weight and water content, but retaining bulk and flavour. Both fruit and nuts, together with dried grapes (*see* CURRANT AND RAISIN) of various kinds have been used in the past to make cookies and sweetmeats that, aided by sugar and spices, will keep for considerable time, like PANFORTE and *panpepato*. Both fruit and nuts are also used in savoury recipes, and nuts as a thickening agent for sauces and stews were once common, giving a better flavour and texture than the flour-thickened sauces of today.

DRIZZLE is a noun with a precise meteorological meaning—"a fine misty rain"—and when used as verb it means "to shed or let fall in minute drops or particles." Not a comfortable or accurate way to describe pouring moderate amounts of olive oil over food, and even worse when applied to honey or balsamic vinegar. A practised hand can regulate the quantity of oil needed for a dressing or last-minute addition to a dish without the use of fancy spouts or convoluted bottles, and stop worrying about the physical impossibility of producing anything remotely resembling a fine mist. The nearest to what is going on is "dribble" which may have mildly unfortunate connotations, and so has been bowdlerized as "drizzle," but "pour" or other words serve the purpose better. *Irrorare* is the Italian verb to sprinkle or disperse drops, as in dew, sweat, or tears. Squirting or spraying a liquid over food in the form of froth is a different issue.

DUCK, *anatra* or *anitra*, is a web-footed farmyard bird, and the leaner, more gamy wild duck is cooked in various ways. These ducks streak across the sky in Carpaccio's haunting scene of sportsmen on the lagoon, shooting wild birds and fishing with the help of cormorants. A traditional Venetian recipe marinates joints of wild duck in vinegar and water, then browns them in the usual *battuto*, together with capers, anchovies, olives, rosemary, and sage, to finish cooking very slowly, covered, with white wine, lemon juice, and grappa. In the past, the wings and breast were held to be the best parts of the carcass, and today's inexorable onward march of the rubbery underdone duck breast is a response to the fact that by the time the legs and thighs are properly cooked, the breast and wings are overdone. One solution is to cook them separately. Platina felt that the breasts of roast duck were best, and the rest of the bird could be left for the cook. Scappi recommended a wide range of ways ducks could be cooked: spit roasted, oven baked, stewed, or casseroled in various ways, often with aromatic stuffing, a generous use of garlic, or sauces with a predominantly sour, fruity content. Hence the use of bitter oranges, as a sauce, or sliced as a garnish— a happy combination known in France as well as Italy, without any intervention from CATERINA DE' MEDICI. Italy has many other ways of presenting ducks, of various breeds, wild and domestic. *Anatra ripiena* is a Venetian recipe for duck, sometimes boned, stuffed with a rich mixture of breadcrumbs soaked in milk *sopressa* (a soft local *salame*), the bird's liver, parmesan, parsley, sage, rosemary, sometimes some tunny *ventresca*, and nutmeg, roasted in the usual way, and served with the stuffing sliced. This dish is prepared with loving care for the feast of the Redentore, held on the last weekend in July to celebrate Venice's survival of a disastrous visitation of the plague in 1575–1577. Palladio's great church, the Redentore, was consecrated in 1592 to commemorate the event. No pains are spared, even at the hottest time of the year, to bring this rich recipe to perfection, to be enjoyed during the feasting and carousing which accompany the fireworks display and all-night revels throughout the city. *Bigoli col'anara* is a dish of pasta made with wholewheat or buckwheat flour, cooked in the broth in which a duck has been stewed with vegetables, and eaten with a sauce made from the bird's liver and heart, chopped and cooked in butter and oil with sage leaves, sometimes sharpened with pomegranate juice. *Anatra con le lenticchie* is cooked in a casserole with a *battuto* of celery, onion, carrot, garlic, and bay leaves, in which the duck is first browned, then covered and cooked slowly with some wine, and finished with some partly cooked lentils added towards the end of cooking, surplus fat having been removed. A recipe from Genoa cuts the richness of the duck by stuffing it with slices of lemon, then browning it in the usual *trito* or *battuta*, together with parsley and bay leaves, and finishing in the oven, moistened with broth from time to time; at the end of cooking the juices are thickened with some pounded stoned olives, some chopped ones, and a handful of whole ones, and seasoned with lemon juice.

DUMPLINGS. *See* GNOCCHI.

e

EARS. *See* OFFAL, PIG'S EXTREMINES.

EASTER FOODS. *See* FESTIVITY AND FOODS.

EATING OUT in Italy is better than in most other countries because the Italians are also good at eating in; they know how good food is prepared and how it should taste, they understand about the sourcing and quality of ingredients. They discuss these things, unlike the French, without any sense of superiority, and these discussions get heated and passionate, because everyone has a mother or grandmother with a special and unique knowledge, known only to the speaker.

On the other hand, there are Italians who prefer to experience and discuss the achievements of chefs and restaurants with worldwide reputations for innovative cuisine, who are in headlong flight from *cucina della nonna*, and the virtuous stodge of *cucina povera*, and encourage the development of new ideas and new menus. Many Italian restaurants in Great Britain and North America are of this persuasion, and have done much to educate us in new possibilities and new ways of using traditional products.

Eating out is more expensive now than it used to be, and patterns of eating have changed. Those who really only need a light meal can find a choice of alternatives, from the excellent *tavola calda* or *tavola fredda* to pizzerias and snacks in bars, which run from pastries, sandwiches, *tramezzini*, which are to other sandwiches as angels to mortals, *arancini* (deep-fried balls of rice), and slices of *frittata* or *torta*, which can be followed by an excellent coffee. Many gourmet food stores sell prepared food of high quality to take away and sometimes to eat in. Restaurants are now more expensive than in the past, and gastro-tourism has done much to weed out the now despised tourist fodder. This is hard to believe, but the restaurant at Malpensa airport in Milan recently served a selection of vegetables roasted to perfection and a fresh local *mozzarella di bufala*.

At one time most people could get home for lunch, a proper family meal; those less fortunate could eat cheaply in trattorias, or *ostarie*, or workmen could eat their own food with a flask of wine in a *bottigliera*, where local draught wine was cheap and good. These have just about disappeared, replaced by upmarket wine bars and the fashionable *enoteche* where food can be enjoyed with a wide range of wines by the glass; this can be a good way of sampling local and national wines, and local specialities. Now that eating out is an expensive treat, it has become a way of enjoying characteristic dishes like the *bollito misto*, which needs to be prepared on a heroic scale, or some of the regional fish stews like the *cacciucco* of Livorno, or the many *brodetti* of the different coastal regions, which need a plentiful assortment of very fresh ingredients. Some of the humble tripe or offal recipes which are arduous to start from scratch are eaten in restaurants with a reputation for doing them well. But the story of the birth of the SLOW FOOD movement reminds us that the blight of FAST FOOD is still insidious, with international burgers and other horrors competing with Italy's own rich tradition of quick, wholesome street food.

ECOLOGICAL MOVEMENTS AND FOOD.

See AGRITURISMO.

EEC DAIRY PRODUCTS REGULATIONS. *See* DAIRY PRODUCTS.

EEL, *anguilla* (the kind discussed here), begins and ends its life in the Sargasso Sea in the Atlantic Ocean, where it spawns and dies; its offspring, when old enough to travel, find their way to rivers and lakes in most areas of Italy (and other countries as well). At first these still young creatures are tiny and transparent (but not to be confused with other tiny fish, *bianchetti*) and are a great delicacy—known as *cee* in Tuscany, where they are prepared in various ways: *alla Livornese*, washed in salt water, drained, and simmered slowly in oil with garlic and sage, their cooking juices forming a creamy emulsion with the oil, or *alla Pisana*, approved by Artusi, in which they are cooked as just described and finished with beaten eggs and parmesan, sometimes breadcrumbs as well, and put briefly into a hot oven to form a crust, or *alla Viareggina*, which is like *alla Livornese* but with the addition of tomato juice.

Ciriole are young eels, not so tiny, that used to be caught in the Tiber, and are praised in a sonnet by Belli, which reminded Vittorio Metz of a time when, not wishing to be seen in the streets of Rome attired as an angler, he dressed in white from top to toe and, his telescopic rod concealed in a walking stick, braved the ribald comments of street urchins and fished for *ciriole* in the Tiber, where once the Porto di Ripetta graced the now bleak embankments, taking home his catch of small eels to be skinned, cut in pieces, marinated in oil and lemon with herbs, and then tossed in breadcrumbs and oven roasted (Metz, 1972, p. 211). Another characteristic Roman recipe cuts the *ciriole* into lengths, after cleaning, tosses them in flour and fries briefly in some chopped garlic and spring onion, then covers with a dry white wine from the Castelli, lets it evaporate, adds some of the plump, meltingly tender young Roman peas, and enough water to cover, and simmers gently until the eels and peas are done.

After 10 to 15 years, the eels have reached maturity and are ready to go back home, reproduce, and then perish exhausted. During their journey downstream, as *calata*, they are at their best, gastronomically. Those in Lake Bolsena in northern Lazio are a great delicacy grilled, served with parsley and lemon, on hot nights at the lakeside taverns, enjoyed in spite of the mosquitoes. Scappi enjoyed them, too, but said that those found in the salt water streams and ponds around Comacchio in Lombardy are the best of all—still as true as it was. In Italy today, eels are cultivated in areas called *valli* around the Po delta, Comacchio, and the Venetian lagoon, and harvested as required, particularly for Christmas Eve. They are usually bought live, as they deteriorate quickly once dead; hence cooking the valiant young *cee* is not for the squeamish, for they will leap boldly from the pan in an attempt to escape their fate. Eels have entered into the language as slippery, which they are on the outside, but inside they are not; the flesh is soft, tender, pure white, and delicious with only a slight fishiness. The sliminess was once dealt with, after killing the eel, by rubbing it in ashes from the fire, something that used to be done to clean all slimy fish.

Eels stewed with parsley and allspice are still cheap food (eels and mash) in the eel and pie shops in London's cockney street markets, while salted and smoked eel in up-market delis just round the corner are a hugely expensive luxury, an unexplained paradox. They are enjoyed more widely in Italy, with a range of interesting recipes to choose from, and as a traditional dish for Christmas Eve are in great demand both in Italy and wherever Italians happen to be.

Skinned, cleaned, and cut in pieces eels can be simply grilled; the big fat ones need no basting. Small sharp bones are attached to the spine, and a practised eater can deal with this comfortably. Small eels can be rolled round themselves like *ciambelle* and cooked in the same way. They can also be cooked slowly in oil with salt and fennel seeds, according to Scappi, then finished in white wine with ver-juice, cinnamon, cloves, and dried fruit. In Venice, unskinned eel, *bisato*, is cut into lengths and spit roasted, the pieces inter-leaved with bay leaves, the fat under the skin sufficient to baste them as they cook. They say in Murano, where this recipe comes from, that there is something tranquillizing about eel cooked this way, putting even the grump-iest person in a suitably benevolent mood for Christmas. Be that as it may, there is in fact something highly toxic about fresh eel's blood, and extra care has to be taken to avoid cutting oneself on its teeth or bones when preparing eel for cooking. Once cooked, there is no danger. Lengths of eel, side by side on a layer of bay leaves in an oven-proof dish, seasoned with salt and pepper and baked in the oven, are another speciality of Murano, at one time cooked in or around the glass-workers' furnace. A more elaborate Venetian recipe, *bisato alla sanpoese*, fries skinned lengths of eel in oil with garlic, then adds to them a mixture of chopped onion fried sepa-rately with chopped parsley, rosemary, and bay leaves, moistened with white wine vine-gar, and carries on cooking over a moderate heat, adding fish broth or white wine from time to time to prevent it drying out.

Eels are sometimes said to have been farmed in the ancient world. This is not the case, but they fetched such a high price from gastronomes that it was well worth transport-ing them alive to market over considerable distances. Dieticians, such as the imperial physician Galen, recommended eel as nour-ishing food—provided it was tested for freshness by look and smell. Pliny reports some surprising facts and nonfacts about eels: they can live out of water for five or six days if refreshed by the north wind, but if they are kept in water, it must be running water; they are particularly lascivious; they feed at night; enormous numbers were caught every October in Lake Garda.

EGG, *uovo*, has a feminine plural, *uova*. It is as well to know this when considering recipes. The egg as symbol of cosmic mat-ters, of rebirth and new life, of Easter and pre-Christian cosmologies, has gastronomic manifestations in Easter bread and in the rit-ual meals prepared for Easter, where hard-cooked eggs are eaten with elaborate breads and simple fresh vegetables. But eggs were also a part of everyday life, and it is as such that the painter Cristoforo Munari included them in still lifes for his Medici patrons, portraying the glories of fast food in his na-tive Emilia, a craggy slab of parmesan cheese, some sliced salame and fatty cured ham, and a terracotta dish of fresh eggs fried in olive oil. These items are sometimes elements of an arrangement of expensive objects, Chi-nese porcelain, hothouse fruit, and musical instruments, perhaps indicating that the good life consists of simple local pleasures as well as imported luxuries.

These simple local pleasures were still the prerogative of the relatively affluent, for chickens and their eggs were an item of domestic economy, and in Emilia the *rezdora* or female head of the household used the products of her farmyard as a source of income, selling eggs, poultry, and rabbits for cash. The family would enjoy the egg pasta, the stuffed *tortellini*, the ribbons of *tagliatelle* and *tagliolini*, only at rare festive meals during the course of the year (*see* EMILIA-ROMANA). Today these egg-rich pasta dishes are commonplace, but the best homemade versions depend on the quality of fresh free-range eggs. Industrial products use less good material.

One of the glories of Italian egg cookery is the FRITTATA, similar to the Spanish *tortilla* or the Middle Eastern *eggah*. Beaten eggs are cooked with sliced zucchini, or wild asparagus, or artichokes, or onions, or potatoes, or chicken livers—the choice is unlimited—to make a deep, thick, circular *frittata*, which is served tepid or at room temperature, cut into wedges. The other ingredient are cooked and mixed with the beaten eggs, or the eggs are poured over them in the pan in which they cooked. Halfway through cooking the *frittata* is tossed or turned to cook right through, properly done, but still soft and moist. A long way from the sometimes pretentious procedures around the making of a French omelette. Elizabeth David once complained that Italians did not know how make a decent omelette. But centuries ago they already knew how to make *uova pesce*, a rolled omelette without the French fuss, a standby for Pontormo, the solitary artist, preoccupied with his gastrointestinal troubles, and appreciative of plain food. Scappi called this rolled egg dish, plain or filled, a *frittata*.

A single egg cooked in the ashes by Pomponio Leto was not recommended by his friend Platina, who knew that the shell might break in the heat and deprive the impoverished man of letters of his austere meal. Better to sacrifice a little oil and enjoy it fried. Or *uova da bere*, a soft-boiled egg, as described eloquently by Scappi, who saw the difficulty in trying to assess the exact moment of done-ness, and said to boil an egg laid that day for the length of the *credo*, take it out of the pan, and if it rolls around and twists and turns, it is done.

Another typically Italian use of eggs is in the SFORMATO, in which eggs give body and lightness to a mixture of chopped or puréed cooked vegetables, a stiff béchamel sauce, and cheese, which is baked to a light but firm consistency—a more pragmatic and satisfying dish than the pretentious soufflé. A *frittatina*, a small thin omelette, can be cut into strips and becomes *uova trippate* when served in a sauce characteristic of the way tripe is served in various regions, from the rich meaty tomato sauce flavoured with mint or pennyroyal of Rome, or the lighter broth with butter and sage leaves of Milan.

The Italian use of eggs in soup or broth is very different from the way they can be mixed with a cream or flour to give smooth consistency to the dishes of other European cuisines. Eggs beaten with grated parmesan, sometimes with breadcrumbs, can be swirled into a simmering broth, to give a tangle of little rags, *straccie*, to give flavour and texture to a simple soup, hence the name *stracciatella* for a well-known version. Whole eggs can enrich a simple *acquacotta*, and are often added to hearty soups, like *zuppa alla pavese*, in which chicken broth is poured over a fresh raw egg sitting on a slice of bread fried in butter, and the whole sprinkled with grated cheese. There is a myth that when the Emperor Charles V drove François I from Milan in 1525, the defeated French monarch, after the battle of Pavia, took refuge in a hovel, La Repentita, where a peasant woman succoured him with this light but sustaining soup, the recipe for which, of course, he took back with him to France to impress his subjects with.

An egg custard lies behind many versions of the classic Italian *gelato*. Other flavourings can be added to the basic vanilla custard, made of eggs, sugar, and milk or cream, which gives a rich smoothness and unctuousness not found in fashionably "light" ices.

Eggplant, also known as aubergine, is a member of the deadly nightshade family. (Shutterstock)

EGGPLANT, aubergine, *melanzana*, *Solanum melongena*, is one of the deadly nightshades, the same family as POTATO, TOMATOES, and SWEET PEPPER, but was introduced into Europe long before these arrived from the New World. Eggplants originated in tropical Asia and were cultivated in India, then spread to the Middle East, whence they were brought to Spain and the south of Italy by Arab settlers. The Middle Eastern connection was noted by Artusi in the 1910 edition of *La scienza in cucina;* he wrote that 40 years earlier eggplants had been dismissed as Jewish ingredients, but now the markets of Florence were full of them. (Camporesi notes that this remark was deleted during the Fascist regime.) They are now popular all over Italy, with a range of confusing regional names: *molignane* in Campania, the name used by Scappi, *petonciani* according to Artusi, in Tuscany, *marignani* in Rome, *milangiane* in Calabria, *mulinciani* in Sicily, where there are so many good recipes; and one which Simeti explains most plausibly as a local version of *melanzane alla parmigiana,* using a local cheese, *caciocavallo,* instead of parmesan, and named after *palmigiana,* the pattern of overlapping slats in a window shutter, or a palm-leaf roof. Simeti also quotes a recipe in which layered slices of eggplant are sprinkled with currants and pine nuts, a characteristic Sicilian touch.

Early writers like Platina do not mention eggplants, but Martino added a recipe in a later version of his cookery text, in which he boils them in salt water before going on to fry them and serve in a garlicky sauce with verjuice. Scappi has several recipes for *molignane* or *pomi sdegnosi,* a name which implies unfamiliarity with this novel fruit. *Pom* or *mela* were words often applied to a foreign or unusual fruits or vegetables, like *melarancia* or *melangole,* bitter orange, *pomodoro,* golden apple (when tomatoes were yellow as well as red), *melacotogna,* quince, or *melagrana,* pomegranate. He took the precaution of first soaking them, then cooking them in salt water, then flouring and frying the slices, which were next layered in a dish with slices of *provatura,* sprinkled with chopped herbs and spices, crushed cloves of garlic, salt, sugar, and verjuice, covered with breadcrumbs, and baked. His contemporary in the north, Costanzo Felici, thought *melanciane* were more attractive in window boxes than the kitchen, with their pretty star-shaped white flowers, but he was familiar with ways of cooking them—grilled, floured and fried, stuffed and roasted, or cubed and cooked *al funghetto.* The Milanese Arcimboldo painted them in his many versions of Summer: human faces composed of all the fruit and vegetables of the season, where small purplish eggplants made convincing earlobes—so we might infer that the painter was working typical Italian produce into compositions for his Hapsburg patrons. Mattioli was aware of the Arab origins of eggplants, and was understandably tetchy towards his contemporaries, even the great botanist Fuchs, who tried to find descriptions of them in the ancient writers of Greece and Rome, unsuccessfully—and a waste of time. Mattioli thought they were good, called them *petranciani* or *melanzane* rather than *mele insane* (unhealthy or crazy fruit, also said to be aphrodisiac), and recommended boiling, slicing, and frying in oil—*"veramente al gusto non poco aggradevole"* (not at all unpleasing to the taste). To Castelvetro, a generation later, they were already mainstream.

These early recipes show what care had to be taken to get rid of the slightly prickly bitterness, not always necessary today with improved breeds of plants, although salting the cubes or slices before getting on with a recipe, is a precaution followed by some. (Harold McGee points out that the main virtue of salting eggplants is to break down cell walls and draw out water, so that less oil is absorbed during cooking). But in recipes where seasonings are taken up to enhance the fruitiness and flavour of this versatile vegetable, its loose spongy texture becomes a virtue. There are today various kinds, with deep purple skins, firm and shiny, or spectacularly beautiful ones streaked white and pale violet, some long, some oval, and some round. It is sad to peel them and throw away the beautiful skins, revealing the dull pulp within, which will later be transmogrified into gleaming oily morsels, sprinkled with flashes of green herbs, tides of red tomato, and pale molten cheese.

ELDERFLOWER AND BERRIES, *sambuco, Sambucus nigra* (edible flower, flavouring), is neither tree nor bush. The beauty of its white, parasol-shaped sprigs of blossom is offset by the unpleasant smell of the crushed leaves and bark. The shiny black clusters of fruit have a strange flavour raw, but can be crushed,

Elderflowers, fresh or dried, have a delicate perfume, enjoyed in fritters. (Shutterstock)

strained, and simmered with sugar to make pleasant syrups and jellies. In the past, the leaves, bark, and roots, both fresh and dried, were used for their medicinal properties in poultices and tisanes, and indeed almost every part of the plant had some therapeutic value. In spite of this, elder has a bad name, being the tree on which Judas hanged himself, and the wood of Christ's cross, so superstitions abound, and may account for its disappearance from the kitchen.

One tradition which survives is the use of the flowers, fresh or dried (the perfume changes and improves when dried), in fritters and other delicate dishes. Vincenzo Corrado summarized their use with his usual concise eloquence:

> *Con I fiori di sambuco mescolati con uova e cacio se ne fanno ottime frittate. Mescolati con uova e ricotta se ne fanno frittelle. I fiori, uniti alle loro cimette, vestiti di pastella oppure infarinati e dorati, si servono in frittura. Si servono ancora per ornamento di carni, pesci lessi e insalatine.*

Elderflowers mixed with egg and cheese make excellent frittatas. Mixed with egg and ricotta they are made into fritters. The flower heads, still on their stems, can be dipped in batter, or floured and dipped in beaten egg, and deep-fried. (Corrado, 1781, p. 450)

Giacomo Castelvetro told us all about the uses of elderflowers in early 17th-century Italy:

> Towards the end of spring, the elder comes into bloom, and makes wonderful fritters. Mix the blossoms with ricotta, parmesan, egg, and powdered cinnamon, and shape the mixture into little crescent shapes. Flour them lightly and fry them in butter, and send to table sprinkled with sugar.
>
> If you put some of the dried flowers into vinegar and leave the bottle for a while in the sun, it makes the

vinegar much stronger and gives it a delightful flavour. A pinch of dried elderflowers, tied up in a piece of clean linen and left in a barrel of good sweet white wine, will give it a muscat flavour. In Italy many of our innkeepers do rather well out of this, passing the wine off as genuine muscat wine, and making quite a profit for themselves. (Castelvetro, 1989, p. 71)

Bartolomeo Scappi gives a more detailed recipe, equal quantities of fat cheese and ricotta, with breadcrumbs, sugar, saffron, and eggs, but using dried elderflowers reconstituted in milk. The mixture is made into little balls which are floured and fried in clarified butter or lard, and eaten hot sprinkled with sugar (Scappi, 1570, *Opera*, bk. 5, p. 370).

The *pan de mei* of Milan, rich buns made with maize and wheat flour, are flavoured with dried elderflowers. The *Panunto Toscano* has a recipe for buns of wheat flour, enriched with oil or butter, with a similar flavouring. It was perhaps the medicinal use of elder, with its associations with folk remedies and the soothing draughts of the old-fashioned *erborista*, that gave the name *sambuca* to a sweetish liqueur with a pronounced anise seed flavour. One can't detect the muscat aroma of elder in this likeable drink, popular around Rome and Lazio, which has become a worldwide favourite; it tastes more of the star anise, which is one of its main constituents (*see* DIGESTIVI). Traditionally served with a couple of coffee beans floating on top (but not set alight, a gimmick which scorches the coffee and wastes alcohol), this is a pleasing reminder of Italy's long tradition of helpful, and health-giving, digestives.

EMILIA-ROMAGNA straddles

the upper part of the peninsula, with an Adriatic coastline to the east and the vast plains of the Po Valley, the rolling foothills

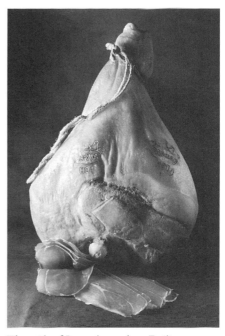

The pride of Parma in northern Emilia-Romagna, this delicacy's popularity is quite recent. (Ryman Cabannes/photo cuisine/Corbis)

of the Apennines, and the more precipitous upper slopes in the southwest. It has borders on LOMBARDY and VENETO in the north, LIGURIA and PIEDMONT in the west, and TUSCANY and the MARCHE in the south. The via Emilia, the great historic east–west route, linking ancient Rome with its northern conquests, built by Marco Aemilio Lepido in the 2nd century AD, stretches from Piacenza in the north to Rimini in the south and on down to Ancona in the east, and thence up to Rome, providing a thoroughfare for the rapid movement of armies, while traders and pilgrims had previously meandered along the more ancient via Pedemontana, in the west. Along it have marched armies, merchants, and pilgrims, bringing links with faraway places, ideas, and cultures. Towns grew up early along this route, and the railway stations sit naturally where Roman staging posts had once been. Traffic moved efficiently up and down the river Po, linked by tributaries and canals to many of these towns, and Castelvetro's memory of small boys learning to swim in the canals, buoyed up by dried hollow gourds, is part of his nostalgic recollections of his native city, Modena, where the street plan still reveals now vanished waterways.

The double-barrelled name Emilia-Romagna reflects the turbulent past, after the fall of the Roman Empire, when invading Lombards settled in the north while the east remained part of the eastern empire, hence the name Romagna, with its capital in Ravenna. Today the region is one of the most prosperous in Italy, with a comfortable economy based on modernised agriculture and light industries. The products of the plain, from fruit to high fashion, cheese and pork products, engineering and white goods, have brought an increased standard of living, but have changed many aspects of life on the plains, whose fertility is now being exploited so efficiently that new problems of pollution from pesticides and animal waste-products, the fall-out from agribusiness, are becoming increasingly urgent.

The weather systems vary from the continental climate of the plains—cold and foggy in winter, hot and humid in summer—to the alpine regions with milder winters, and the coast with its gentler climate, though exposed to harsh northeast winds.

The cuisine is as varied as the landscape and climate, but with many common characteristics, in particular a reputation for richness, which in the past could be applied only to an affluent urban minority but is now almost universally enjoyed. The floods of cholesterol-laden dishes, rich with lard, cream, cheese, and pork products, that might overwhelm enthusiastic visitors to the prosperous towns of the plain were in the past rare treats, enjoyed perhaps a few times in the year, for weddings, feast days, and family celebrations. It can be disturbing to find this special festive food on the everyday lunch and dinner menus of so many restaurants, creating a somewhat gross familiarity rather than healthy anticipation and delight felt when times were hard.

Bologna was, and still is, known as *la dotta e la grassa* (learned and rich), for the formidable reputation of its intellectual and gastronomic heritage; its university is one of the oldest in Italy, and inspired a prickly spirit of independence still apparent in its civic life. The arcaded streets of Bologna are a necessary protection from summer heat and winter wet, in a city getting on with its own busy life with little tourism but a justified pride in its heritage. The university was founded in the 11th century, famous for its law school and later for the great pioneers of work in the natural sciences Mattioli and Aldrovandi. A large covered market and many fine restaurants display the gastronomic resources of the region. The 17th-century engraver Mitelli, best known for his tarot cards, pictured some of these in 1691 on a board game called *Giuoco della cucagna che mai si perde e sempre si guadagna*, Game of the Land of Cockaigne, where nobody loses and everyone gains. A throw of the dice can land you on *mortadelle di Bologna, salccicia di Modena, investiture di Parma, buseccha di Milano, formaggio di Piacenza*, with merely a dish of broccoli for he who falls on Naples.

Moving north up the Via Emila from Bologna, the traveller comes to Modena, with its Ghirlandina, the decorative frilly gothic campanile of the Romanesque cathedral visible from afar. The city is famous as the home of a sports car and an opera singer, but its *aceto balsamico tradizionale di Modena* surpasses them both. Modena was saved from the ravages of Attila the Hun by its patron saint, Geminianus, who enveloped it in a thick protective fog, a care he continues to lavish on his city. It has the virtue of being part of the microclimate favourable to the slow process of maturing traditional balsamic vinegar.

When Giacomo Castelvetro, a native son of Modena, was living in exile in England in the early 17th century, he wrote with nostalgia of the vegetables and fruit he missed so much, with little vignettes of women coming in from the fields with baskets of fresh chickpeas, or the accidental disappearance of a melon into a vat of honey in a shop on the corner of the main square, of little children learning to swim in the canals on dried empty gourds, or the ripe grapes offered to passersby, safer by far than ditch water.

The *tortlein*, *tortellini*, of Modena and the surrounding area were made for a special meal on Christmas Eve and involved ingredients saved up for during the year: the rich filling of prime cuts of pork, cooked and finely chopped, with *mortadella*, cured ham, and parmesan—all pounded to a paste and seasoned with salt, pepper, and nutmeg—was placed in tiny pinches on a small square of transparent fresh egg pasta, which was folded over diagonally and twisted round the forefinger of the left hand into a minute bonnet shape, sometimes described as the *ombelico di venere*, Venus's belly button, said to be the inspiration of a cook who caught a glimpse of the goddess, or possibly a more earthly vision. This was once a way of making expensive ingredients go a long way—a collective task, time consuming, and a noncompetitive skill; the *tortellini* were traditionally served in the broth of the BOLLITO MISTO (simmered meats), without sauce or parmesan, so that the delicate flavours of the *tortellini* floated in the gentle aromas of the liquid, each contributing to the subtlety of the other.

Freshly made egg pasta is the preferred type of the region, and every city has its own version of strips of various sizes or filled pasta pockets, and sauces to go with them. But in winter, when the hens were not laying, a coarser pasta was made with flour and water only, often rolled out quickly in a thicker sheet and cut into square or rhomboidal shapes, cooked in salt water, and served with the simplest sauce, perhaps of onions softened in lard and coloured with preserved tomatoes mixed with some of the cooking water. This subsistence-level food was filling, and—when combined with stewed beans, dried broad beans, sometimes enriched with *coticche*, strips of cooked cured pork skin—nourishing as well; unlike polenta, of which it was said *"Presto tira, presto lenta"* (Soon eaten, soon hungry again), and which was more a product of the hills than the plain. Families had the good sense, without knowing the causes of pellagra, to be aware of the need to reinforce this nutritionally inadequate food with beans, cheese, or tomatoes and pork fat. A recipe from Romagna adds cooked beans to the polenta and serves it with a sauce of onions, bacon, sausage, and preserved tomato—a communal meal, poured from the pot onto a board and covered with the sauce on which cheese was sprinkled generously, after which all took their spoons and tucked in.

The CUCINA POVERA of the region is best understood in the context of land tenure and the agricultural practice known as *mezzadria*, a sharecropping system inherited from feudal times, in which the farmer and his family had the use of farm buildings, equipment, and land, which they worked for the owner, giving him in return a proportion, usually one-half, of the produce and the takings, together with an agreed number of animal products, hams, chickens, and so forth. In the hands of an enlightened owner, with a knowledgeable and incorruptible steward or bailiff, and an intelligent farmer, this was a benign system, providing security and protection for the family and a good return on his investment for the owner. Most of the time it seems that negative factors produced the opposite effect, with a great many families working long, hard hours, with only a meagre share of their labours at the end of the year, and consequently more and more in debt to the *padrone*, with no redress against the unfair distribution of crops and produce. It engendered habits of parsimony and secrecy, of desperate ways of scraping and saving, so that in this fertile land the good things of life were enjoyed in spite of rather than because of this system. Apologists for the *mezzadria* maintained that it supported whole extended families, giving old and young a part to play, as well as inculcating habits of hard work and thrift, and of course leaving no time or energy for dangerous political notions and activities. The *mezzadria* operated throughout most of central Italy; an example of a good landowner is Michelangelo, who ploughed his considerable earnings into land and property in his native Tuscany, and in return had shipments of beans, chickpeas, cheeses, and sausages sent to him in Rome. After the disastrous events of 1527, the failure of the Florentine republic, and the devastation of the surrounding countryside, Michelangelo was buying seed corn and restocking his farms at enormous expense. Later his hapless nephew Lionardo acted as factor of the estates, having to account for their management to his tetchy relative. The system lived on in Emilia-Romagna until the 1950s, and elderly people tell of the hardships they remember, before changes in land use and agricultural methods made things even worse and forced them off the land altogether.

The genius behind the kitchen of every farm, or *casa colonica*, was the *rezdora*, or *arzdora* as she was called in Romagna, the female counterpart of the male head of the household—the *rezdor* or *reggitore*, master and commander, to borrow a naval term. Her role depended on ability, and the need to keep a balance of power and authority within the extended family, so the *rezdora* was not always the wife of the *rezdor*; she could be sister-in-law or daughter-in-law. The power she had was absolute in the domestic domain; she ruled the poultry yard and rabbit hutches and dovecote—these were sources not so much of food as of cash, their products sold at the local market for money to spend on vital supplies of salt, sugar, and material for the family's clothes. She put

minute sums by, and often helped the *rezdor* in the regulation of accounts. She worked on average a 14-hour day, of which two-thirds was devoted to feeding the brutes—animals and menfolk—for this was what Corrado Barberis describes as a *civiltà cibocentrica*, a food-centred culture. It was a constant preoccupation for the *rezdora* to keep up a supply of nourishing, varied food from her own resources to fuel the hard physical work that went on all the daylight hours. The kitchen was her empire, and the sound of the chopping of herbs, bacon, and vegetables to season stews and pasta was part of the kitchen scene, and a pointer to the skill of the cook in getting tasty food onto plates, and clearing up afterwards, while attending to laundry, baking, darning and mending, child care, and the demands of the farmyard and kitchen garden. Even during the *filò* or *veglia*, on winter evenings, when the family relaxed in the byre, where cattle lived and hay was stored, and *"la stalla fungeva di salotto e i bovini da stufa"* (the manger was the parlour and the cattle provided the heating; Aliberti, 1995, p. 260), the *rezdora* was preoccupied with mending and knitting, and contriving snacks to go with the grappa and wine offered to visiting neighbours, and perhaps keeping on eye on the younger members of the group.

These short winter days when the weather was too bad to work out of doors were in fact frantic for the *rezdora*, who had to catch up with housework, mending, ironing, and making new clothes, neglected during the long days of summer and autumn, when she was busy out of doors. So time for cooking was limited, and since the hens were not laying, there were no long sessions rolling out fine silken sheets of egg pasta; rapid versions were made with flour and water only, rolled out at speed into thick sheets, which were then cut into rhomboidal shapes, or dumpy gnocchi, or strips which were then rolled and twisted into long ropes, *strozaprit* to those of an anticlerical disposition, or more objectively *lunghett*, boiled and eaten with cheese and a few drops of oil. The *minestra s'e squaquaron* was made in Romagna from squares of plain flour and water pasta, brought to the boil in water that would serve as their broth, into which a local fresh cheese, *squarquarone*, was stirred, its loose texture and name an earthy reminder of the realities of the farmyard midden.

Memories of those days tell us about the CUCINA POVERA of the time and place, with little sentiment, and few regrets. Ida Marverti Lancellotti remembers how when times got hard she and her husband left the countryside in the 1950s and brought up three children, working in the family tratto ria in the little town of Soliera, serving salame and *gnocco fritto* with Lambrusco to the workmen who would come in from the road works and fields for their early morning snack. She remembers the day a passing motorist asked for a *cappuccino*, so triggering the inevitable change of direction which eventually transformed the trattoria into a Michelin-starred restaurant where she found herself once again cooking the food of her young days, the *pasta e fagioli*, using the maltagliati left over from cutting the *tortelloni* wrappings, the lentils and *cotecchino*, the *tortellini in brodo*, and the sumptuous *zuppa inglese*, lurid with *alchermes*.

Moving north via Emilia towards Reggio Emilia, one comes to the hamlet of Massenzatico, where in the turbulent years of political changes after the 1860s, the first *casa de popolo* was set up in 1893. The early anarchists and socialists replaced the feast days of the Church with secular celebrations, they baptised their children with Lambrusco— Libertà, Solidario, Lenin—and this light, sharp, slightly fizzy red wine, the cheap refreshing beverage of the labouring classes, became a symbol of unity and solidarity, along with bowls of *capelletti in brodo*. At a commemorative feast in 2005 at Massenzatico, 600 bottles of Lambrusco washed down, to the strains of the Internationale, 40 kilos of *cappelletti*, a *quintale* of chicken and beef for the *bollito*, a *quintale* of tarts (red with *alchermes* no doubt) and cheese from the *vacca rossa*, in abundance. Subversive political meetings in the past were often held in taverns and unauthorised trattorias up and down the via Emilia; the first ever was in the Tre Zuchette in Piazza Nettuno in Bologna in 1871, and later *osterie senza osti* (DIY "bring your own" eating places) were a congenial way of organising clandestine gatherings, everyone bringing contributions of food and drink. It would not do to idealise these political feasts, and it is not at all clear why a time-consuming festive food like *cappelletti* should have become a symbol of grass-roots politics, but they became so early on, to such an extent that innocent consumers of *cappelletti* were often unjustly persecuted by right-wing thugs. Perhaps hijacking Christian festival food for a subversive secular purpose was a political statement in itself. The Festa dell'Unità in early autumn is another secular occasion, where the mass production of *gnocco fritto* and fried fish is enjoyed all over the area.

Cappelletti are similar in construction to *tortellini*, and are characteristic of Romagna and Reggio Emilia; in Romagna the filling is usually made of several different local cheeses, and in Reggio of prime cuts of meat and chicken, finely chopped or minced, cooked in lard or butter, seasoned with nutmeg and parmesan, and encased in twisted squares of pasta a bit bigger than *tortellini*, looking like medieval bonnets. The *anolini* (not to be confused with the *agnolini* of Lombardy) of Parma and Piacenza, at the far end of the via Emilia, have a filling made from a piece of beef, larded with pancetta, and cooked with aromatics so slowly (16 to 24 hours) that it dissolves into its own juices, which are then mixed with breadcrumbs and parmesan; the filled parcels resemble half moons with serrated edges. *Capellettacci* are large versions of the bonnet shape made in the Apennine valley of Silaro-Santerno, with a filling of cooked chestnut flavoured with chocolate and jam, eaten with a dressing of olive oil and pepper.

Parma and Reggio Emilia contribute jointly to the name *parmigiano reggiano*, made throughout the area, which to many is the finest cheese in the world. Parma is famous for its cured ham as well as parmesan cheese, and inevitably the by-products of both these large-scale activities are used in the cuisine: the whey from cheese-making makes ricotta and is also fed to the pigs, and the parts of the animal that are not used as hams figure in the *salame di Felino, spalla di San Secondo, culaccia di Fontanellato, mariola,* and *strolghino,* while there is also the more refined and considerably more expensive *culatello,* using only the prime interior cut from the buttock.

But Parma is renowned for more than hams and violets. (The perfume made from this flower, now world famous, is said to have been created for Maria Luigia, Napoleon's second wife, who ruled Parma from 1815 to 1847.) Sited where a north–south route, the via Romanea Francigena (a link with Rome and the south, threading its way through mountain passes), meets the ancient pre-Etruscan via Pedemontana (a route for pilgrims and local products winding along the Apennine foothills), parallel with the Roman via Emilia (ideal for the rapid transit of armies and large-scale commerce). Throughout history this confluence of roads has attracted settlers and rulers from afar—countless Etruscans, Romans, a multitude of tetchy Lombards and Byzantines, pilgrims from northern lands, the Farnese from Rome, Bourbons from Naples and Austria, French for much of the 18th century, then more repressive Bourbons, until in 1860 the area became part of the unified Kingdom of Italy. In the 16th century Pope Paul III Farnese had established his nephew in Parma, not as mere nepotism but to have a reliable buffer state between papal territories and the troublesome northerners. Gastronomically this was good for all concerned: products from the duchy enhanced the papal table,

and ceremonial visits required banquets and festivities masterminded by cooks and stewards of international repute. Scappi's menus show this in detail; Messisbugo served the Este in Ferrara; later writers, including Cervio, deployed their skills in the region; and by the late 17th century, the ducal table was as renowned for its splendour as were the Farnese for their great girth. Ranuccio II's cook, Carlo Nascia, from Palermo, wrote out in 1684 a manuscript of menus and recipes showing influences from all over Italy and Europe, from a rich rice pudding from Portugal to boned and stuffed pigeons from Spain, a chicken fricassee *alla francese* (similar to one of Martino's recipes), a traditional Italian sauce for roast hare, with the usual toasted nuts, spices, and bitter orange juice, but enhanced with sweetened chocolate, and a dish of stewed capons, jointed and served covered with *anolini* stuffed with breadcrumbs, chopped beef kidney, egg yolks, hard cheese, salt, and spices, cooked in meat broth.

In the 1760s, the prosperous small duchy of Parma, by then under Bourbon rule, needed to boost its political power with cultural and technological achievements; Guillaume du Tillot, the prime minister, a thoughtful protagonist of the Enlightenment, established in the ducal palace the printer Giambattista Bodoni, who first worked with French types and ornaments before his own creations brought universal fame to his adopted city. Similarly, French styles in gastronomy were assimilated into the local cuisine, which never completely succumbed to the prevailing fashion. This entrepreneurial use of local products goes on to this day, and it would be a mistake to see Parma only as the repository of mysterious artisan luxuries; for every good old boy tending his *culatelli* in dank huts in the foggy bottoms of the Bassa Parmense, there is a state-of-the-art *salumificio* run on scientific principles, where food technologists, supported by SSICA (Stazione Sperimentale per l'Industria delle

Conserve Animali) and other institutions, apply the most up-to-date principles of food hygiene and gastronomy to products destined for worldwide consumption. For every batch of sun dried tomatoes spread on a wooden board outside a picturesque farmhouse, there is a factory canning prime-quality tomatoes for mass-market distribution. From being a useful artisan crop, tomatoes became after the 1870s a heavily commercialised product, spawning massive developments in agricultural technology and new industries to supply it, while bright red sports cars come trundling off another production line. Factories, notably Barilla, began the mass production of pasta. Fruit farming is on a large scale, on the plain and in the foothills. The spirit of Du Tillot lives on in these ventures.

Further along the via Emilia is Reggio Emilia, sharing with Parma the geographical denomination of Parmigiano Reggiano that we know as parmesan cheese. This and other local products can be seen in the works of Cristoforo MUNARI, a local artist whose still life paintings influenced tastes in Rome and Tuscany. His great fatty slabs of cured ham and bacon sit alongside huge wedges of parmesan and terra cotta dishes of fried eggs and slices of salami in compositions mingling luxury items and wholesome domestic provisions. They are an invaluable source of information about the appearance in the past of many characteristic preserved meats, notable for their generous fat content.

An 18th-century cookery manuscript from the Cassoli family in Reggio Emilia gives an insight into the aristocratic cuisine of the time, influenced by the attitudes of the Enlightenment, but firmly grounded in local products and procedures. It is cheering to find among the fashionable French-influenced dishes (delicate casseroles and braised dishes with a gentle seasoning of herbs and vegetables only, with a light use of garlic and onions) robust survivals of heartier cooking, well spiced and rich. There

is a *Spungata di Modena,* a pastry crust with a filling of citrons and apples candied in honey, with chopped walnuts, dried bread-crumbs, raisins, pine nuts, spices (but no pepper), glazed, baked in the oven, and dusted with sugar, which takes one back to medieval times. This recipe follows one for *Capelletti di grasso,* with the usual filling of *cervellate* or yellow sausages, mixed with grated parmesan, eggs, spices, and cinnamon, cooked in chicken broth. No messing around with local traditions. The same goes for the recipes for *Coteghini all'uso di Modena,* using head meat, unctuous skin and fat, off-cuts from the preparation of nobler salami, with salt, pepper, cloves, nutmeg, cinnamon, and garlic in profusion. The immortal *pasticcio di macaroni,* with the usual chopped veal sauce lapped in a rich milk custard thickened with egg yolks, is redolent of truffles, spices, cheese, butter, and gobbets of bone marrow, all encased in a short pastry crust. The section on desserts, however, has a range of delicate sorbets and ice cream influenced by Neapolitan recipes from the 17th century, and those of the great *patissier* Emy in contemporary Paris. These ices are described using terminology more Spanish than French, which suggests a Neapolitan pastry cook as part of the household. A lovely ice made from chocolate, sugar, and water, beaten up with pounded pistachios and eventually frothed by vigorous whipping, is then frozen in jars or *chiccare*—a name derived from the Spanish *jícara,* a beaker or goblet, sometimes of silver, devised by the *conquistadores* for their version of drinking chocolate. (It was a poisoned *jícara* that got rid of the bishop of Chiapas when he tried to stop the highborn women in his congregation from drinking fortifying beakers of chocolate during his services in the cathedral.) The word used in the manuscript for freeze, *carapegnare,* is Spanish.

Piacenza, at the far end of the via Emilia, on the banks of the Po, is at the strategic point where the region connects with Genoa and the Mediterranean trade across the Ligurian Alps, and links with Milan in the north. An early Roman settlement, then occupied by Celts and Lombards, and later knocked about by the Visconti and Sforza, Piacenza was pacified and beautified by the Farnese after the daughter of the Emperor Charles V chose it as her home. A delicious version of the region's spinach and ricotta *tortelli* is made in a twisted form, evocatively described by Lynne Rossetto Kasper, with the light filling deftly enclosed in very thin diamond-shaped pasta, twisted and pinched to give a "rippling scalloped appearance" (Kasper, 1992, p. 153). These *turtei*, when cooked, are served simply with butter and parmesan. Piacenza shares with Cremona a talent for making musical instruments and *mostarda di frutta*, fruit preserved in a hot spicy syrup, strongly flavoured with mustard, but getting its name from the sweet grape must or *mostarda*.

Back in the opposite direction, the via Emilia eventually reached the Adriatic port of Rimini, once ruled by the Malatesti, whose hospitality was on the whole something to be avoided; between 1323 and 1327, at least three politically motivated banquets ended in the cold-blooded slaughter of the guests. A festive meal had the advantage of getting a selection of enemies and rivals together under one roof, relaxed, defences down, ripe for retribution. Consequently these opportunities for conspicuous consumption, the flaunting of wealth, were hedged with precautions, and many powerful rulers enjoyed the services of a personal staff who travelled with them, a *cuoco segreto* (private cook), often a *scalco* (steward or major-domo), and the kitchens of the mighty were organised to contain this proliferation of activities. A reputation for overweening magnificence and downright greed were behind the excommunication in 1460 of Sigismondo Malatesta, and the consequent sequestration of his wealth and property. But the delicate pagan beauty of the Tempio

Malatestiano, designed with the guidance of Alberti, indicates refined sensibilities, as does Sigismondo's enduring love for his mistress Isotta degli Atti, shown in their intertwined initials decorating the architectural details of the building. Bas-reliefs of great delicacy show *putti* and the recurrent image of an elephant, symbol perhaps of strength and gentleness. It is not surprising that the marriage of Sigismondo's son Roberto to Elisabetta da Montefeltro in 1475 was celebrated with considerable sophistication, and an official description of the festivities, intended for circulation, would have been a reassuring indication of modern and unthreatening gastronomic refinement as well as conspicuous consumption. This description lists what was spent on food and wine, all the arrangements for the event, the decoration of the banqueting hall, the entertainments, and the inevitable periods of rest after the feast. Sixteen peacocks vied with over 8,000 chickens, 890 geese, 540 ducks, and good red meat worth 4,000 lire; 40 forms of parmesan cheese, 180 cured hams, and 478 salami from Bologna were balanced by 3,896 lire spent on comfits, sugar-coated anise and coriander seeds, and almonds; marzipan and *pinochiati* cost 1894 lire; 13,000 bitter oranges and five barrels of verjuice balanced the richness; the fruit, salads and vegetables were not itemised, listed alongside sugar, rosewater, and cooked grape must. The meal itself is similar to those Scappi described in greater detail a century later, and would have been familiar to those fortunate enough to possess copies of Martino's *Libro de arte coquinaria*, written in the 1460s, which would have been passed around among gastronomes and court officials in charge of similar events, describing exactly the standard banqueting fare and the innovative modern dishes that powerful guests on this international diplomatic circuit of intrigue and gluttony had come to expect. The cooks themselves were in great demand; among those hired to create this banquet, 32 were singled out for a special reward. Giovanni and Pietro from the duke of Urbino rated 6 ducats each, while Giovanni and Bernardo from Bologna got 4, another Bolognese 3, Giuliano from Fano and three Germans 2 each, while Giovanni from Naples and one Scaramuccia who specialised in gelatine confections had 3, and six Scottish undercooks, *Schotti*, merited 1 each. Their labours produced a meal of many courses, with the usual great roasts and boiled meats following the first course of more delicate morsels, quails, sweetbreads, rabbits, and some vegetables, all with their special sauces, a high point being the peacocks roasted and then put back into their feathers, vulgar but effective, one to each table by way of overkill. After all this came the fish, which Rimini was well placed to provide: large ones, big mullet and sturgeon, roasted with bitter orange sauce and simmered with their separate relishes. A much-needed salad, many many oysters (over 4,000), fruit, and marzipan, before a change of tablecloths and the final course of sweet biscuits and comfits. The music which had been in the background throughout the meal then took over, and dancing, with pauses for rest, went on until it was time for refreshments; these were mainly from a display of ornate sugar work— imitation fruits of all kinds, chess sets made of sugar, cherubs on dolphins, models of the principal civic monuments, notably the church of S. Francesco (paganised as the Tempio Malatestiana, in its final form still incomplete), with the fountain in the piazza, surrounded by more cherubs, gushing rose-water, and the fortified castle with perfumed smoke and fire coming from its battlements. All this 200 years before the great baroque sugar *trionfi* of Bernini.

It is something of a relief to return to a more settled Rimini a century later, after Cesare Borgia had seen off the Malatesti. Costanzo Felici, a native of Piobbico, a bleak little hamlet up in the hills of the Marche, saw himself as a citizen of this prosperous modern city, with its easy communications with the rest of the world, where he could exchange scientific papers and specimens with medical colleagues up the via Emilia and further away in Europe. As a naturalist and physician Felici had an interest in food, and his long manuscript letter on salads, addressed to his colleague Aldrovandi in Bologna, expanded into an account of everything he and his contemporaries could find to eat in the natural world, a much more human document than the earlier account of the grandiose Malatesta wedding. Felici's correspondence with Aldrovandi reveals a humorous and kindly person, caring for elderly parents and unmarried sisters and a huge brood of daughters—a life of ordinary decency, in contrast to the Malatesti. He lists things that were too humble for banquets, the *piade* of Rimini, a local FLATBREAD, and the many uses of spinach, in soups and as a filling for tarts on lean days, or the wild garlic, also found in the Marche, loved by his friend Giulio Moderato, who founded Rimini's botanic gardens. The coastline of the Marche shares many dishes with Rimini, especially the different versions of BRODETTO. In the late 18th or early 19th century, one of the Albini family (possibly Basilio, whose grandson wrote a memoir of the family), living in the hilltop town of Saludecio near the border with the Marche, wrote down in a little notebook, in a neat and regular hand, over 50 recipes, which are delicious, familiar, and surprising, in that they are rooted firmly in local traditions, showing little of the predominating French influence found in published cookery books of the time. This collection of domestic recipes gives a good idea of how a family of lesser gentry used the resources of the area, sharing ingredients and vocabulary with the neighbouring Marche. The generous use of spices indicates continuity with a distant past: in a filling for *capelletti*, chicken and beef marrow are flavoured with nutmeg, cinnamon, and cloves, and a version for lean days has all these spices as well as parsley, marjoram, and thyme to season a mixture of ricotta, parmesan, and egg yolks. A delicate sauce of egg yolks, lemon juice, and sugar perfumed with candied citron is stirred in a little pot over a pan of water until thick, and a green version cooks the juice of pounded marjoram and parsley in a milk made from almonds, pine nuts, and pistachios flavoured with cinnamon—more Scappi than Artusi. The various salami are well spiced; *cotecchini*, the usual mixture of pork meat and skin, snouts, and ears, cooked to an unctuous softness, is flavoured with salt, ground pepper, cinnamon, nutmeg, and cloves. *Salami di testa di maiale* are made from a subtle mixture of boned and skinned coarsely chopped head and throat meat, with tongue and finely chopped beef, flavoured with the same spices, put into casings with strips of fat, and cooked, wrapped in hay and fresh herbs, in a mixture of wine and water, a noble version of an economical use of extremities (Bartolotti 1993).

EMMER WHEAT, *farro, Triticum turgidum dicoccum* (not the same as SPELT, although translations of Latin texts sometimes use it, which is confusing), was an early form of wheat, a staple grain in early Roman times which went on being popular during the years of imperial wealth and decadence. Dalby quotes Pliny, who said that the gods really preferred salted emmer groats from humble worshippers to the perfumed offerings of the rich. The writer Nico Valerio claims that the high protein and vitamin content of emmer bread and boiled grains were the foundation of Rome's military prowess—it was *farro* not *ferro* (the metal sword) that created the empire, with its slow release of energy reinforced with greens, fruit, and cheese, ideal for the warrior/farmers who founded the republic and went on to conquer the world.

Emmer, a "covered wheat," needed parching to get rid of the outer husks before winnowing and threshing; it then had to be pounded in a mortar, a heavy task, and eventually could be coarsely ground and cooked into a mushy *puls*, perhaps with bacon and dried broad beans, delicious enough to offer the Roman goddess Carna, she who presided over the heart on the Calends of June. In CAMPANIA it was finely ground and mixed with white chalk to make a smooth gruel called *alica*, sometimes eaten as a sweet. Starch was squeezed out of soaked whole grains of emmer, then dried to make *amylum*, starch, known as *amidon, amigdulum,* to medieval cooks; they used it to thicken sauces or make dishes like frumenty.

Today there is a revival of this pleasant-tasting grain, with its chewy, nutty texture, and the areas where it traditionally grew, UMBRIA, TUSCANY, and LAZIO, are producing it either whole or cracked, for use in sweet and savoury dishes. It cooks relatively quickly, if polished and coarsely cracked about 20 minutes to half an hour, polished and whole 40 minutes to an hour. The *faricello* of Lazio is *un piatto sensa programma*, an improvised dish, according to Nico Valerio's version, in which whole polished emmer wheat is simmered with a ham bone, and towards the end of cooking some finely chopped onion, celery, green cabbage, herbs, and whatever comes to hand in the way of light fresh things are all added to the pot, and finished with some grated PECORINO *romano*. The traditional version still cooked today uses not a ham bone but the rind of a cured ham, *cotenna*, and some of the fat (what your deli usually discards when tidying up PROSCIUTTO *crudo* before slicing), simmered in water until tender; the emmer is added to this, along with a rich tomato sauce made by cooking peeled tomatoes with garlic, pancetta, and herbs, and served with a mass of chopped parsley and basil.

Another traditional dish is made of polished emmer wheat cooked in a purée of borlotti BEANS and their cooking liquid, enriched with a SOFFRITTO of PANCETTA, herbs, and vegetables, flavoured with spices, and served with a good dollop of extra virgin oil. A sweetened open pie or tart of emmer, *torta di farro*, is made in Tuscany, with previously cooked and sweetened emmer finished on a pastry base.

EMPOLI, JACOPO CHIMENTI DA (1551–1640), painted mainly altarpieces, but loved kitchens and everything that went into or came out of them; a contemporary writer, Filippo Baldinucci, made a punning comment on his name—*"Empilo!"* (Fill him up!), referring to his manic zeal in assembling and then devouring the material for his still lifes. Patrons and apprentices flocked to his studio to enjoy the raw materials as well as the paintings. Two are in the Uffizi today; a brief summary of the contents of one of them includes a rope of garlic, a hen, some sausages, a duck, a side of bacon, a smoked cheese, a black pudding, a loin of veal, some fatty bacon, two partridges and a goose suspended over a table laden with a flask of wine, a soft cheese, some parmesan, various cooked fowl, a bread roll, squeezed lemons, roast chestnuts, a pear, a cauliflower, and some parsnips surrounding one of those ornate pies—it is a murky contrast, with warm browns and dark background, to the bright, clear food portraits of Giovanna GARZONI. The other includes a side of bacon, some wild fowl, a goose, a plucked turkey with its decorative tail still intact, a hare, a pig's head and trotters, a calf's head, a cockerel and various cheeses and sausages. There is no sense of movement here, no kitchen activity, more a well-stocked larder with a promise of feasts to come.

A work dated 1625 can be read as a well-stocked larder or a studio feast. Suspended against a warm brown background are grapes, a huge sausage, onions, a gourd, lettuce and radishes for a salad, and a newly opened ham (cut deep down into the bone, to test for quality, a fraught moment when a fault in the cure could result in considerable financial loss), a straw-covered flask of wine, a hunk of parmesan cheese, fruit and nuts, a stoppered carafe of cordial or perhaps rosewater for refreshing the sticky hands of eaters, a basket of figs, some plums, and a jug and another carafe of wine.

The contrast of Empoli's beautifully composed, elegant altarpieces and devotional works with the intense, rather brooding self-portrait, the earth-bound still lifes, and his reputation for gluttony presents us with many paradoxes, but his studies of Tuscan food at least are clear and informative.

ENDIVE, *catalogna*, is a plant of the chicory family, of which *Chicorium endivia* is known as *indivia* in Italy. The blanched version is now known as chicory or witloof in Great Britain, and as French or Belgian endive or witloof chicory in the United States; the red-leaved variety is RADICCHIO and the broad or curly-leaved variety is endive to both nations. The best overview of the confusion of names, and the profusion of plants, is in Davidson's *Oxford Companion to Food*, which gives a fascinating account of this complex profusion of fresh bitter-tasting plants. Dalby reminds us of its importance, both wild and cultivated, in the ancient world, and Mattioli came to grips with Dioscorides' description, put him right over

Usually eaten raw as a salad, endive's bitterness is more appreciated by the Italian palate. (Shutterstock)

the names, and included beautiful illustrations of 10 different kinds of chicory or endive, wild and cultivated. It was obviously a plant for which he had much affection, writing of one of the wild ones whose bright blue flowers appear among the Tuscan field crops in May and June, *"di cui fanno le contadinelle nostre ghirlande molto vaghe"* (that our country maidens make into the prettiest garlands). The bitterness so much loved in Italian cuisine is there in all of them, sometimes tempered by a preliminary blanching, then eaten as a salad or further cooked with oil and aromatics.

ESTE, D', ISABELLA (1474–1539).

"Big girls are best," wrote Leon Battista Alberti, the accomplished Renaissance man, of the role of women in his ideal household; best for child-bearing and the lower echelons of household management. Isabella d'Este met both these requirements and more, being herself an accomplished Renaissance person: attractive, intelligent, energetic, and blessed with the greatest gift of all—a first-class education. When she left Ferrara at the age of 16 to marry Francesco Gonzaga, Isabella was fluent in several languages, was an avid patron of the arts, and had all the skills needed to manage her own estates and those of the duchy she was to control for the next half century. Appetitosa—*"perchè essendo mi de natura appetitose, le cose mi sono più chare quanto più presto le havemo"* (for being by nature acquisitive, the sooner I get the things I want the more I love them)—was how she described herself: hungry for the good things in life, which she acquired with a ruthless rapacity. Many of these good things were edible, which might account for her imposing appearance.

Anything fashionable, rare, and expensive Isabella wanted at once, and at her price. She wanted a complete set of the Aldine classics, which the printer dispatched from Venice; upon which she refused to pay the going rate, complaining of poor presswork and proof-correction, and sent half of them back. When the ailing Mantegna, close to death, was constrained, through poverty, to sell her an antique statue she had long coveted, Isabella tried to beat him down to a third of his price. The painter held out, and got it, but the episode leaves a nasty taste. Her gastronomic greediness is less distasteful; the search for rare delicacies, cameos or artichokes, antique coins or cabbages, is that of the collector wishing to share enjoyment as well as show off or strike a hard bargain. Exotic spices and vegetables would grace the ducal table and add to her prestige, at a time when the banquet was a political statement and rare ingredients and costly tableware were a display of power, so messengers and relatives were constantly bombarded with special requests.

On a domestic level, we have cheerful letters from Isabella to her brother in Ferrara sending seeds of a new variety of CABBAGE and a recipe (cut away the hard stems and just blanch the tender green leaves, then eat them cold as a salad with oil, vinegar, salt, and pepper), a slightly cross letter to her husband chiding him for losing a batch of the same seeds, and much correspondence about that rediscovered novelty the ARTICHOKE, procuring plants, seeds, and experienced gardeners to cherish them. The image of an artichoke appears in a songbook manuscript of *compozioni profane*, probably originating in the Mantuan court at the end of the 15th century, an exotic illustration to a sophisticated version of secular songs. Asparagus was sought after, and delivered by the cartload to Isabella's son Federico in his luxurious palazzo del Te. PEAS, developed in the 16th century by Italian gardeners, not the field peas which were one of the staple pulses of medieval diet but the garden variety sometimes known as *rovie*, eaten young and fresh, either shelled or as a *mange-tout* variety, were a novelty.

Along with jewels, soft furnishings, fashions, and rare ingredients, Isabella collected cooks; as usual, she wanted nothing but the best, and she wanted them now. Perhaps because the results of their art were so ephemeral, for immediate consumption (apart from preserves and comfits), not for investment purposes, Isabella was kinder to her cooks than to her other artists, seeking short-term pleasure rather than long-term gain. There was the intolerable Jasone, dismissed by Isabella in the first years of her marriage, hoping to replace him with a good cook from Naples, where many were jobless due a change of regime. Much later, in 1533 she sent out searches for a good *trinciante*, master carver, whilst admitting that they were no longer fashionable. Meanwhile a really good cook, Massimino, unwisely lent to her son Ercole, a cardinal in Rome, did not want to return when told to do so, and won the battle of wills to stay where he was. In 1506, Isabella sent a talented young cook, Agreste, as apprentice to the great Christofaro Messisbugo at her father's court in Ferrara.

These and other selections made from her correspondence in the Gonzaga archives by Giancarlo Malacarne (2000) shed an agreeable light on a rather terrible personality, and also show how the position of cook, although relatively low on the scale of court officials, was held in considerable esteem.

EVITASCANDALO, CESARE. *See* CERVIO.

FAST, LENTEN OR LEAN,

magro, quadragesimale, is the term applied to days of abstinence from meat, prescribed in the liturgical calendar of the Catholic Church. There were days of real fasting, days of abstinence from certain foods, and days when the abstinence was less rigid, like the *vigilia* or eve of some religious festivals, when the light, meat-free food could include eggs and cheese. Doing without for the good of the soul, or at least cutting back on indulgences, was an aspect of lean eating. As well as Lent and Fridays, the eve of many special days, days devoted to penitence and atonement, and many saints' days, made in the past for a considerable proportion of the year when the diet had to exclude meat, and meals were built round fish, vegetables, nuts, and fruit, with eggs and dairy produce occupying a grey area, depending on current interpretations of the doctrine. There were also many humane dispensations from fasting, for the sick, the old, the young, travellers, and those doing especially hard work. Some aescetics and solitary hermits found that abstinence from food enhanced their hallucinatory experiences, a spiritual high from malnutrition, hardly to be experienced among the lean fleshpots of the great and powerful.

"Lean" cooking was with oil, not butter or animal fat, and even the many imaginative uses of eggs would have been prohibited. Almond milk, made by diluting pounded skinned almonds with water, was a fragrant substitute for milk or cream, and the use of nuts, usually walnuts, almonds, or hazelnuts, as thickening agents spilled over into the cuisine of meat days. Broth was made from fish or vegetables instead of meat or chicken, and many salads and vegetable dishes evolved, so that the term *magro* came to mean a vegetable dish eaten at any time. Dried and preserved fish were the standby for Friday food, and the expression *giovedì gnocchi, venerdì baccalà, sabato trippa* still holds good in many trattorias. Salt cod (*see* BACCALÀ) or dried STOCKFISH used to be soaked overnight in big tubs to be ready for customers on Friday morning, and a range of inventive regional recipes evolved to transform this unpromising ingredient into delicacies.

Abstinence from prohibited foods did not always achieve the intended austerity, for if a diplomatic event like a treaty or a dynastic marriage had for logistical reasons to happen on a fast day, the desired opulent banquet went ahead, with all the luxury and extravagance of a meat day, but based on fish and vegetables. In April 1536, Cardinal Lorenzo Campeggio of Bologna gave a feast in Trastevere for Emperor Charles V. The 12 guests sat down to 12 courses, five from the *credenza* or sideboard, and seven from the kitchen, a total of 198 dishes. Even allowing for the *diverse musiche con diversi suoni,* this must have been a gastronomic marathon, starting with cold things from the *credenza,* spiced sweet biscuits, and some homely chickpea fritters, moving on to roast and grilled fishes, each with its own sauce or relish, followed by a succession of potages of different fish, then different dishes made from sturgeon, pike, and trout, with the sturgeon's head *in bianco* adorned with yellow and purple pansies, and some ornate pasty constructions by way of light relief, one in the shape of the imperial arms. After this there was more from the *credenza*, then various cold fishy things, crabs, shrimp, mussel soup (nine dishes with 300 to a dish), a tart of artichoke hearts, truffles cooked in oil, orange juice and pepper, and so on. Too much to describe here, but an indication of how strict observance of dietary prohibitions was no impediment to gluttony.

FAST FOOD is not new to Italy; the
teeming tenements of urban ancient Rome did not have much in the way of cooking facilities, relying on cookshops where perishable food like offal and fish could be fried, bought, gobbled up, and enjoyed on the run, and this has happened for centuries. The "meal in a bun" is certainly not a new concept, what SLOW FOOD rightly objected to was the nature of the wretched bun and its filling, not the concept, and we can only be glad that the ideals of Slow Food persist in the new patterns of eating in urban Italy today. Until recently families ate lunch together at home, prepared by a busy housewife or parent. Most people could get back from work in time to enjoy the long lunch hour, then maybe a little siesta, and the short journey to and from office or factory was no inconvenience. Agricultural workers needed the break for a rest and a long slow meal in the cool of a farmhouse kitchen. Workmen or travellers might perforce have to eat out in trattorias, or in bottiglierias where customers could eat their own food washed down with draught wine. Now women have jobs away from home, children can eat at school, and the whole family is dispersed, reunited perhaps for a long slow evening meal, often with the television, faithful family friend, on the table, to keep everyone's mind off the food.

PIZZA has been described elsewhere; as fast food it has become a universal blessing, or curse, depending on its quality, and although the reek of gaudy tomato-smeared dough of uncertain provenance now pervades most towns and cities, the brilliance of the concept, a flat piece of flavoured bread cooked quickly and eaten on the spot, is incontestable. Claims concerning its invention are charming, plausible, and inevitably delight and entertain. Many breads qualify as fast food (for more detail, *see* BREAD and names of individual breads). In ancient Rome, flatbreads, leavened or unleavened, were cooked over convex clay domes. FOCACCIA is an alternative to sandwiches and PANINI; it can be split open and stuffed with slices of ham or/and cheese, sometimes reheated, and eaten as a snack.

Similar techniques survive in the *tigelle* of Emilia-Romagna, where a thin yeasted FLATBREAD is cooked between two decorated heated tiles to produce a crisp biscuit bread which can be cut open and filled with a *condimento* of pounded pancetta, garlic, and rosemary. *Borlengo* is a larger, thinner, more pliable version, eaten spread with a cooked version of the *condimento*. The *gnocco fritto* of Emilia is yeasted dough rolled very thin, cut into lozenges, and deep fried (at one time in lard) and was once served on demand to busy labourers wanting a rapid midmorning bite, traditionally served with salami and Lambrusco.

Flatbread pouches, or folded shapes, make containers for a mixture of herbs, vegetables and cheese, as in the stuffed "pizzas" of Umbria, and the *borlengo* and *tigella* of Emilia-Romagna, *gizzoa* of Liguria, and many more (for more detail, *see* FLATBREADS).

The *pannino* and *tramezzo* are two very different versions of fast food that can be enjoyed in most bars, eaten standing up, or taken away, and their success is because they are so good. A fresh bread roll, crisp on the outside, yielding but not soggy within, with a generous but austere filling of *prosciutto crudo, mortadella,* or salame, with its own balance of fat and lean, and the tasty pungency of well-cured meat, needs neither butter nor pickles to enhance it—a thoroughly sustaining snack. The *tramezzino* is influenced by the American sandwich, but without the overkill that can lead to floods of mayonnaise and escaped salad items cascading over the happy eater; a good selection of compatible cooked meats, fish, hard-cooked egg, artichoke hearts, asparagus, and perhaps regrettably, *salad russe,* is usually made up in square slices of a soft but not flabby bread. The buns and pastries that come fresh from the bakery into even the smallest bar make the ideal fast breakfast, with a cappuccino (only taken early in the day with *prima colazione*), eaten standing up whilst smoking and reading the papers, with only the faintest sprinkling of icing sugar descending onto your impeccably shiny shoes. In Rome and the south, ARANCINI or *supplì* make outstanding bar food. In Genoa, booths and stalls on or near the waterfront offer wonderfully fresh fried fish as snacks. The *friggitori,* vendors of fried food, in Belli's Rome, drawn by Pinelli, show passers-by enjoying, for a few *baiocchi,* freshly fried fish, cooked on improvised stoves on the streets, served in paper cones by guttering torchlight.

Many delicatessens of renown now have a take-away food section, where a whole meal of exquisite ready-prepared cold food, and some hot, can be taken home or eaten on the spot or in the street. Senators and professional men of considerable standing can be seen enjoying quality with dignity in a high-class Roman delicatessen not a stone's throw from the Vatican. In some establishments, bar seating and a cafeteria-style service are a spin-off from the deli counter, and food of high quality can be bought and eaten, allowing for haste, taste, and greed, by the busy and the discriminating.

Airports and train stations in Italy have their fair share of bad fast food, but many offer hurried travellers food of a quality unimaginable in Britain and the United States. The lasagne that used to be cried as the train drew into Bologna station, "*Lasagne, lasagne calde,*" hot in cardboard containers, was legendary.

So fast food does not have to be seen as a bad thing when it is a reallocation of traditional ingredients and methods as a response to changes in society. It can even be seen as a stimulus to local products, particularly in the case of salumi, where a well-stuffed *panino* is spearheading a vast increase in the consumption of ham and salame, and showing the world how a national treasure does not have to obliterated by the international food industry.

FAVE DEI MORTI (beans for the dead). *See* BROAD BEAN.

FEGATELLI are made from cubes of pig's liver wrapped in sheets of CAUL FAT, alternating with pieces of bread and slices of pancetta the same size as the cubes, then spit roasted or grilled. In Tuscany, they are seasoned with wild fennel, sometimes mixed with parmesan and breadcrumbs before wrapping in the caul. In Lazio, the seasoning is fresh bay leaves. Grainger has a recipe from Apicius in which cubes of liver are marinated in fish sauce, lovage seed, bayberries and pepper, wrapped in caul, and grilled or roasted, then eaten with an *oenogarum* sauce (Grainger, 2006, p. 47).

FEGATINI are the livers of domestic fowl; the name on its own will usually mean chicken livers, but those of guinea fowl, ducks, and geese are also used. They can be made into savoury mixtures to spread on *crostini* or dishes in their own right, cooked in butter with sage, or with marsala, or as a sauce for pasta. The livers of duck and goose, sometimes fattened by force-feeding, were

known in the ancient World. Scappi was impressed by the size of goose livers from birds raised by Jewish communities, where the liver was soaked in milk to make it even softer and bigger, but did not give any of their recipes, choosing to cook his goose livers, wrapped in caul, or floured, in lard and eat them with a sprinkling of sugar and bitter orange juice.

FEGATO. *See* LIVER.

FELICI, COSTANZO

(1525–1585), was born in Casteldurante in the MARCHE, but considered himself a reluctant native of Piobbico, a tiny isolated town in the hills above Rimini at the confluence of two rivers, crouching between Monte Nerone and Montiego, rich in natural phenomena but without the intellectual stimulus of a big city. Felici used to wish that his forebears had not moved there from Lucca, before he was born, for he preferred urban life, and settled in Rimini, where he lived whenever he could, although his parents retired to Piobbico and much of his adult life was spent cheerfully trying to combine his duties as only son in a large extended family, father of many, many daughters, practising physician, botanist, and writer. His correspondence with the great naturalist Ulisse Aldrovandi in Bologna reveals something of all these activities, and an essential humility and good humour. Although socially and academically inferior to Aldrovandi, Felici writes in an affectionate, egalitarian tone, glad to share his expertise in botany and medicine, and tolerant of the setbacks involved in sending fragile or perishable specimens long distances by unreliable messengers. This obscure, unknown provincial doctor had a keen eye, a talent for accurate description and a gift with words. Felici and his contemporaries were roaming the woods and fields and mountains, searching for plants and bringing them home, to draw, dry,

propagate, share, exchange, and describe. Along with the squabbles and jealousies, there was much generosity and goodwill, and it is for this that we value the correspondence that has survived, in particular the *Letter on Salads* (Felici, 1986), in which Felici's good humour and knowledge, although only a small piece in the huge jigsaw assembled by Aldrovandi in Bologna, is of such value to us.

Unknown until its publication, edited by Guido Arbizzoni in 1986, this letter on salads, *Del'insalata e piante che in qualunque modo vengono per cibo del'homo*, written at Aldrovandi's request during the 1560s and 1570s, described not only salad ingredients but all edible plants, cultivated and wild, with brief accounts of how to prepare them. It reads today as a joyful summary of everything we enjoy in Italian gastronomy, even though many of the plants described are no longer in general use, and not always easy to identify. "They also gather [for use in salads] wherever it grows, a humble little plant with long smooth leaves and seeds in a follicle like *thlaspi* smelling of garlic, hence the name *agliarino*, which Moderato uses a lot here in Rimini [in the botanical gardens]" (Felici, 1986, p. 77). Might this be wild garlic? "Artichokes . . . have lately been so improved upon for the table that they are familiar to all, and especially sought after by gentlefolk. They are eaten raw, the part where the scales [bracts] join [the receptacle] and then the bottoms, the chokes removed, with salt and pepper; and also cooked in various ways, simmered in broth, or boiled, with oil, dripping or butter, grilled or roasted in the embers" (p. 90)

Felici draws together references from classical authors, and material from modern writers and botanists, quite without pedantry, in a conversational tone of voice, and with many remarks about their everyday uses and preparation, which makes the work a joy to read. "Dwarves on the shoulders of giants" was how Anselm described the contribution of medieval philosophers to studies based on writers of the ancient World (not, maybe, of the same lofty stature, but, perched on their shoulders, having a wider view) and that is how we now see these lively, intelligent, questioning pioneers of modern botanical studies. Detailed descriptions based on firsthand observation, attempts to describe, analyse, and record natural phenomena, and a hidden, but growing and altogether healthy scepticism towards the until then unchallenged giants of classical and Arab botany and medicine, motivated this diverse network of scholars.

At one point, Felici bursts out in one of his letters, discussing a variety of laburnum: "there are so many I really don't know what to say, one could almost agree with Dioscorides (*see* MATTIOLI), but he does seem to miss out all the essential information about this plant, its seeds, or rather follicle, short and with a rounded form. I do believe they did it to drive us out of our minds, in this as in so many cases, leaving out the really vital data that would have helped to distinguish one plant from another"(Felici, 1982, p. 88).

Dioscorides was a Greek botanist and physician writing about AD 65, but his work only survived in later versions with illustrations copied, over the centuries, from earlier versions of what might have once been accurate plant drawings but had by then little relationship to the real plants. No wonder Aldrovandi spent a huge part of his income commissioning the best artists of the time to produce accurate and beautiful plant and animal portraits drawn from life (*see* LIGOZZI).

Plants were not Felici's only concern; he sent specimens and information about local birds to Aldrovandi for his work on birds, and despatched fossils and preserved fishes. Throughout the correspondence we glean bits of information about Felici's daily life, how his wife grudgingly sacrificed her knitting needles (made of terebinth, a straight, hard wood) to send as specimens and at the same time insisted that one of their special local cheeses be included in the package; how the cat got at a fine fish, drying out in ashes; and how another consignment disappeared on the way from Rimini to Bologna (only an hour or so away now on the motorway but several days' journey then); and there was news of the tempestuous little goddaughter, Florinda Elisabetta, *"la quale con la sua vivacità è il nostro trastullo"* (whose liveliness is our delight). Sometimes letters and requests for specimens got lost or were unanswered, due to family matters, *"la furia della mia vendemmia"* (my frenzied grape harvest), the death of his father, the hopes for a son, *"un altra ragazza: porrò accomodare un monastero"* (yet another girl—I could fill a nunnery).

Felici ranged way beyond salads, and when considering wheat, wrote passages on the various kinds of BREAD and PASTA which give much more information than cookery manuscripts and texts of the time (for example, on sourdough). We get an early sighting of bagels (*see* BREADS, RING-SHAPED), and a mention of today's well-known FOCACCIA and something sounding a bit like the upstart CIABATTA. He mentions the festive spiced breads, fragrant with spices and decorated with family crests, prepared for the feast of All Saints or for San Martino, the night when the season's new wine is sampled, and goes on to describe the various *cialde*, wafers, made from a liquid batter in heated waffle irons, with a sweetened version which can be eaten flat or rolled in a cylindrical shape, perhaps the ancestor of the rolled wafer which evolved into the ice cream cone centuries later.

He describes a kind of puff pastry, very thin sheets layered with fat, butter, or oil, sometimes with dried fruit and nuts; or the *cresce*, today's *crescentini*, fat- or oil-based flour and water dough, cut into diamond or rhomboid shapes and deep fried; and the mighty range of pies, pasties and tarts . . .

Here is Felici's summary of the enormous range of pasta shapes and sizes:

"They are either flat and thin as paper, or thicker, or with a round section, or long, or hollow, or made in thin filaments either finely cut or extruded, and in thin or short pieces. You will hear them called by a variety of different names in our kitchens, such as *lassagna, lassagnola tirata, maca-roni o cavadoli tirati in varie forme, strenghe, tagliatelli, vermicelli, granetti* and other names." (Felici, 1986, p. 117)

Felici has no room, though, for *farinata*, a sort of liquid mixture of flour, water and fat, which may well have been eaten in the Ancient World but seems to him like a mouthful of glue: "*al mio gusto non quadri niente perchè mi pare veramente havere in bocca una colla*" (1986, p. 117) (see *farinata* in LIGURIA). Aldrovandi and Felici were the human face of early natural history; their lack of pedantry and a certain cheerful verbosity make them a good source of information about food and ingredients, as well as the world of science.

FENNEL, *Foeniculum vulgare*, or *Foeniculum dulce* of the Umbelliferae family, is widely used in Italian cooking; the seeds as one of the mild spices, the fronds of white blossoms, fresh and dried, and the bulbous leaf base either cooked or raw.

There are several varieties of fennel—sweet, bronze, wild—whose seeds, flowers, and fronds of fine leaves are good both fresh and dried. The main difference between the kinds is that sweet fennel has a milder, more anise-like flavour, and the wild is a little more bitter, with a very different perfume. The essential oil whose main constituent is anethole (found also in the unrelated liquorice) is used as flavouring for many commercial products—babies' gripe water, liqueurs, confectionery, and so forth. Fennel calms flatulence and sweetens the breath, which explains

Fennel calms flatulence and sweetens the breath, which explains its presence at the end of Renaissance and Baroque banquets. (Shutterstock)

its presence at the end of Renaissance and baroque banquets, its seeds in sugared comfits and the crisp fresh bulbs eaten raw, which together with perfumed toothpicks and posies of fragrant flowers provided an elegant and soothing conclusion to hours of feasting. Platina had recognised this earlier and wrote of the benefits of both the flower heads and the bulbs of fennel—much sought after by serpents, improving their eyesight and longevity; they would do the same for us, as well as rectifying the humours, settling the liver, and clearing congestion in the lungs.

Fennel was used more in the past than it is today; it was one of the "sweet spices," *spezie dolce* or *spezie fine*, of spice mixtures, gentle rather than pungent like the *spezie forte* (see SPICES). Its use by Martino in the 1460s might have been a move away from the more highly flavoured dishes of earlier centuries. Crushed with salt, he rubbed it into slices of veal, or chops, before cooking. Scappi did the same a hundred years later.

Fennel is used today to flavour many different kinds of food. The feathery fronds of the leaves can be chopped and used as a stuffing for fish, or in salads. The leaves of bronze fennel chopped into a risotto made with good meat or chicken stock give a wonderful flavour. Recipes of the past mention fennel seeds and *fiori di finocchio* which are pounded with other spices for sauces and stuffings. Wild fennel, sometimes known as *finocchino*, goes well with pork, and is used, together with chopped garlic and rosemary, in the stuffing for *maialino al forno*, roast SUCKING PIG; such a characteristic combination of flavours that when used with other meats the dish is described as *in porchetta*, "like sucking pig." Artusi gives a *pollo in porchetta*—a chicken stuffed with wild fennel, fatty cured ham, salt, pepper, and two cloves of garlic, cooked in butter in a casserole, with a condescending comment that implies a rather crude "family dish" perhaps a bit pungent for his middle-class readers. When used freshly dried, but not old and desiccated, wild fennel seeds have a pleasant nutty texture which gives bite without stodginess to a stuffing. Fennel often gets into food cooked with local ingredients and herbs, picked from the wild rather than out of a commercial spice jar, like *coniglio in porchetta* from the Marche, or a pot roast guinea fowl, also from the Marche, stuffed with chopped sage, rosemary, juniper berries, and wild fennel, and cooked slowly, covered, in a garlic-rubbed earthenware pot. From Liguria comes *triglie alla genovese*, red mullet, scaled and gutted, baked slowly in the oven, covered with breadcrumbs dotted with butter, in a dense, reduced sauce of chopped onion and chopped parsley fried in olive oil, with soaked dried mushrooms, prepared salted capers and anchovies, fennel seeds, white wine, and fish broth. A similar recipe for sardines is given by Ada Boni.

Costanzo Felici gives a succinct survey of the uses of different parts of the cultivated plant, sweet fennel, mentioning the flower heads, which are used in salads (sometimes before flowering, *in scartocci*, sometimes in flower), the fresh green seeds, and the dried mature ones. Both seeds and stems are preserved in salt and vinegar; the fronds, too, are used in salads and cooked dishes. He recommends the wild plant in roasts, stews, and with fish, and says it has a particular affinity with sausages.

Today fennel is the characteristic flavouring of two versions of the salame, *finocchiona*, or *sbriciolona* (*see* TUSCANY), which is available in two forms, the conventional cylindrical shape, and a huge one with a softer texture. It is the best known of the fennel-flavoured salumi, but there are others: the *'ndoc 'ndoc* of rural Abruzzo, a sausage made with the less noble parts left over from the pig-killing—intestines, lungs, heart, parts of the snout, ears, trotters, belly fat; highly seasoned with salt, pepper, chilli, and wild fennel seeds; hung for a few days in a warm dry place; and eaten cooked, preferably as *panonta*: grilled with the juices dripping onto a slice of *bruschetta* (toasted local bread). The name *'ndoc 'ndoc* means "crazy," as in "crazy paving," made up of otherwise unusable bits and pieces, which makes sense, whereas the possibility of its being derived from the French *andouillette* seems unlikely. *Annoia* or *budellaccio di Norcia* from Umbria is a similar thing, the equivalent of our chitterlings, with carefully cleaned intestines perfumed with wine or lemon juice, flavoured with salt, pepper, and fennel, and matured for a few days before cooking.

Then there is the *salamella di tratturo* from the Valle del Sagittario in Aquila in Abruzzo, a *salame* made from pork fat and lean ewe's flesh, trimmed of fat and sinews, marinated in red wine and juniper berries, then mixed with salt, white pepper, fennel, and coriander seeds, hung for a fortnight, and matured for two months, producing a delicacy with none of the rankness one might have expected from a superannuated old sheep. In the first half of the 19th century, environmentalists persuaded the Abruzzo forestry authorities to pay a generous compensation for every ancient ewe literally "thrown to the wolves," a way of both preserving and calming the wolf population and supporting the already declining transhumance of flocks. Then a local professor of political sciences revived this traditional salame, proving that a carcass worth virtually nothing could be made to yield 6 kilos of salami, selling at 35,000 lire the kilo. Bad news for the wolves.

Fennel, wild and cultivated, is widely used in pig products using inferior cuts, often made in less prosperous regions, so from Umbria, Lazio, and Abruzzo come salumi using intestines, lungs, and other less appealing organs, things you would never think of eating, salted and spiced with pungent aromatics like orange peel, chilli, pepper, and fennel. From the Marche comes *ciarimbolo*, a fragrant preparation made from the intestines left over from casing sausages, rinsed well, marinated overnight in water and vinegar, cooked in the marinade with orange peel and basil, then seasoned with salt, pepper, garlic, and fennel seeds and matured for three days before eating. This inexpensive, thirst-provoking snack is similar to the *beverelli* of Lazio, offered in the now vanished Roman *fraschette*, along with *copiette*, to keep the punters drinking. *Copiette* were strips of lean horse meat marinated in red wine, salt, chile, lemon juice, orange peel, and wild fennel, then smoked and matured for a week or so.

The *susianella di Viterbo* is a spreading sausage made from pig fat, the finely chopped liver, tongue, heart, spleen, and pancreas, any oddments of meat, seasoned with salt, pepper, chilli, chopped garlic, and wild fennel, and eaten after it has been in a warm dry place a week.

Fennel is thus one of a selection of cheap local aromatics, like garlic, chilli, and herbs, to use up cheap parts of the pig to suit local tastes transforming them into delicacies.

The swollen white leaf base, sometimes known as Florence fennel, can be eaten raw when crisp and fresh, and has a more pungent taste than when cooked. Castelvetro, writing in the early 17th century, recalled how villainous Venetian wine-sellers would tempt punters with free morsels of raw fennel, so pleasant tasting, and such an efficacious disguise for their horrible wine. It was something to offer guests with a drink, though, or with salt at the end of meal instead of celery. The banquet menus described by Scappi in 1570 always have sweet fennel to finish, either fresh or pickled, along with comfits and preserved fruits, but fennel never seems to appear in the earlier courses, where he offered raw cardoons and artichokes as a crisp and welcome foil to richer food.

Vincenzo Corrado cooked fennel with his usual inventiveness, in good chicken broth seasoned with coriander and salt, served with a rich sauce of cream, butter, and egg yolks; or cooked in fish broth, and served with a shrimp sauce made by first blanching the shellfish, then peeling, reserving the tails, making a sauce of the shells and heads, all pounded up with breadcrumbs, bay leaves, herbs, spices, and butter, pushed through a sieve, diluted with fish broth, and garnished with the peeled tails. (Fennel seeds in the broth would enhance the flavour of the fennel.)

Martino, in the 1460s (Martino, trans. Parzan, 2005, p. 55), used fennel seeds crushed with salt to season thin slices of veal, flattened with the blade of a broad knife, and then spread over them a mixture of chopped bacon, or lard, parsley, and marjoram, and rolled them up, to be quickly spit roasted. He also used crushed fennel, or coriander, and salt to season what he called *copiette al modo romano*: joined-up kebabs—egg-sized lumps of meat (unspecified, but any tender cut of veal, beef, or pork would do), cut but remaining joined at one end—left a while to absorb the flavour of the mixture with which they have been rubbed, then spit roasted with thin slices of bacon between. Over a century later, Bartolomeo Scappi published a more sophisticated version of these recipes, with the lumps of meat marinated in *fior di finocchio* and spices, verjuice, and rose-flavoured vinegar, then spit roasted with bacon and bay or sage leaves between, and served with a sauce of the cooking juices, and any remaining marinade. His strips of veal, marinated for a couple of hours in a little vinegar, fennel, cinnamon, and salt, are covered with fat bacon, to keep them moist, and lightly grilled, or rolled up with a stuffing and fried, then finished with broth or verjuice.

Ada Boni, in her *Talismano della felicità*, has a recipe for shin of beef stewed with celery, onion, and pancetta, then finished at the end with a *trito* of finely chopped garlic, parsley, and fennel seeds, which are stirred in and given a few minutes to perfume the while before serving. The fennel here defines the dish (*Stufatino di manzo al finocchio*, Boni, *Talismano*, p. 359).

Raw fennel has a crisp pungency, at its best when the bulbs are fresh; thinly sliced and added to salads; trimmed and cut into wedges and eaten with olive oil and salt; or sliced in a salad with oranges, and black olives. There are many recipes for cooked fennel; the results, if not overcooked, are sweeter and softer; when parboiled, dipped in batter or egg and breadcrumbs and deep fried, the contrast between the soft inside and the crisp outside is delightful; quartered fennel bulbs simmered slowly, covered, with olive oil and garlic, softening in their own juices without the addition of water, are served decorated with the chopped green fronds; a similar method uses butter and a little water to stop the butter from browning and is served strewed with freshly grated parmesan.

Taralli, twice-cooked bread rings, common to most of central Italy but a speciality of Puglia and Campania, are often flavoured with fennel seeds. *Tarallini di Capri* has wild fennel among its many flavourings.

FERNET BRANCA. *See* APERITIVI, BITTERNESS.

FESTIVITY AND FOOD. In

Italy, a celebration without food is unthinkable. Whether the festival is public or private, sacred or profane, whether it is filled with the colour of folklore or the symbolic drama of religion, it always includes a ritual dish or special meal. Communities come together for *sagre* (country festivals touting a local ingredient), civic festivals exalting a city's prosperity, festivals celebrating a patron saint or agricultural rite, as well as for the major religious holidays.

Festival foods are often as rich in symbolism as they are in flavour. Fish are symbols of sanctity. Eggs symbolize the beginning of life. Grains of rice, wheat berries, and *farro* invoke the forces of fertility because they look like little seeds and promise abundance at the next harvest. Lentils resemble coins and invoke prosperity.

Dishes served on the eve of a religious festival are meant to purify the body in observance of the Church's injunction to eat lean foods (*mangiare di magro*), while the actual holiday is a gastronomic extravaganza with rich meats and fatty foods (*mangiare di grasso*). Breads for the eve of a holiday are usually made only of flour, water, yeast, and salt, while those for the following day are enriched with butter, eggs, sugar or honey, nuts, spices, and/or candied peels.

Festivals celebrating the New Year vary from region to region. Sicilians consider the end of October, when the darkness of winter takes over after all the fruit has been harvested and the wheat sown, as an alternative New Year, in Mary Simeti's words (1989, p. 13). They communicate with a feast served to ancestors returning from their graves on the night of 31 October, *I Morti* (the Day of the Dead), a time of instability between one year and the next. The departed relatives, in turn, plunder the local pastry shops and bring children gifts of marzipan fruits and vegetables; *pupi di zucchero* or *di cena*, tall brightly painted dolls made of white sugar; and *fave di morte*, dead men's cookies resembling fava beans from the plant whose leaves bear black spots, the ritual stain of death.

The Christmas season begins 6 December, the birthday of San Nicola, the original Saint Nicholas, and 8 December, the Feast of the Immaculate Conception, and it ends on 6 January, Epiphany. The real season of gift giving begins on 13 December in the Veneto and Lombardy when Santa Lucia brings presents to children, along with tiny sweets and cookies shaped like piglets, ponies, or flowers. The saint is honoured in Sicily for bringing grain to the island's famine-stricken people, the legend says in the year 1600, who were so hungry that they didn't waste time grinding grain into flour but ate the berries straightaway. As a result, everyone in Palermo observes the day by eating *cuccia*, a sweet pudding of cooked wheat berries, ricotta, and candied orange peel.

Christmas falls on 25 December, near the winter solstice, the shortest and darkest day of the year. In the pre-Christian era, the date was the birthday of Mithra, the popular pagan sun god, until the Church, responding to the competition, moved the Nativity to that day, thereby celebrating the birth of the sun and the son concurrently. Many breads made in this season of scarcity take their round shape from the sun and are meant to encourage the incremental rebirth of its warmth and to propitiate the powers governing life and death.

Christmas is a two-day feast of massive quantities and opulent dishes. Most dishes are strictly tied to local tradition, but a few have become national symbols. *Panettone*, a high-domed, buttery bread studded with candied fruit and raisins, was originally from Milan, but is now found everywhere. *Capitone*, EEL, is the traditional fish of Christmas Eve in the south, while capon is traditional on Christmas tables in the north, where stuffed pasta arrives in capon broth.

Chewy almond and honey *torrone* originated in Benevento but now is everyone's Christmas sweet.

Religious festivals have always had a special menu and none more so than Christmas. Christmas Eve, La Vigilia, ostensibly a penitential meal, is often composed of a ritual number of courses: 7 for the seven sacraments, 9 for the Trinity multiplied by itself; 12 for the disciples, 13 adds Jesus, and 21 multiplies the Trinity by the seven sacraments.

Southern Italians celebrate Christmas Eve with Il Cenone, a big dinner serving a sequence of fish courses, which always include eel, *capitone*, served grilled, spit roasted, roasted, fried, stewed *in umido*, or pickled. Almost as likely to be present on the Christmas Eve table is *baccalà*, the quintessential fasting food, served in tomato sauce in Naples, with potatoes and onions in Basilicata, and stewed in *brodetto* in the Marche.

In Apulia, the meal is composed of seven or nine fish, each cooked in a different manner, while in Abruzzo, the seven or nine courses include roasted eel and fried *baccalà* along with fish and shellfish roasted, fried, marinated, or served in broth. Once every Roman table had *pezzetti*, little pieces of broccoli, artichokes, zucchini, or cubes of ricotta, each dipped in batter and fried, while Neapolitans ate a sauté of broccoli and *frutti di mare*; "drowned" baby octopus; bass, fried mullet, and calamari; *caponata*; and *rinforzo*, a salad of cauliflower, olives, anchovies, capers, and pickled vegetables that was served daily between Christmas and Epiphany and added to or reinforced each day.

Lasagne is the pasta of choice for La Vigilia in Lombardy and Piedmont, where wide sheets of pasta evoke the swaddling clothes of the Baby Jesus and are sauced with butter and oil, anchovies, the fragrance of garlic, sage, rosemary, and bay leaves, freshly grated black pepper, and parmesan cheese. Neapolitans serve vermicelli with clams, mussels, or razor shell clams (*cannolicchi*), while Romans toss spaghetti with anchovies.

Sacred meals are experiencing change as popular taste, ingredients, and time-saving methods alter ritual dishes. Eel has definitely lost its popularity. Pastries once made by the nuns in convents are becoming as scarce as new nuns. Desserts now include *primizie*, the first fruits of the season, which may come from as far away as Hawaii and the Southern Hemisphere.

The Christmas day meal often begins with stuffed pastas floating in broth. The shape and stuffing may change—in Bologna, navel-shaped tortellini are meat-filled, and their element is capon broth, while in Mantua the *sorbir* look like half moons and the broth is spiked with Lambrusco. Ferrara's *cappellacci* look like little hats and are stuffed with pumpkin, while Emilia's *cappelletti* have the same shape but are filled with finely minced capon, eggs, ricotta, *raveggiolo*, and parmesan cheeses, grated lemon rind, and nutmeg.

Where capon was once mandated for Christmas lunch in the north, turkey is now in the ascendancy. It may be stuffed with fruit and chestnuts, as in Milan, and or with chestnuts, sausages, pork, eggs, and cheese, in Piedmont, while in Rome, breadcrumbs, eggs, and parmesan cheese fill the cavity.

Fish continue to appear on Christmas Day in the south, where, as in Calabria, the table remains set even after the diners have gone because they are waiting for the Madonna to arrive with Baby Jesus to taste the food, much as Romans believed the gods presented themselves at table.

Many breads made in this season of scarcity take their round shape from the sun. Almost every town once had its own Christmas bread made from a dough enriched with butter, eggs, sugar, or honey, dried fruits, nuts, spices, and candied peels. The *panettone* of Milan, with raisins and candied citrus peel, the star-shaped *pandoro* of Verona and *natalizia*, its denser predecessor, and *pandolce Genovese* were all originally low, dense breads whose origins scholars trace to the end of the 14th century, when Florentines first folded walnuts, dried figs, pine nuts, dates, and honey into ordinary Tuscan bread dough.

Many Christmas sweets have the word for bread in their names: *pane speziato*, spice bread; *pangiallo*, golden bread, a dense Roman sweet bursting with nuts, raisins, candied fruit, and spices; *panforte*, strong bread, today from Siena, made with honey and cloves, coriander, cinnamon, and white pepper; and *panpepato*, a peppery Tuscan bread spiced with cinnamon, nutmeg, ginger and cloves, numerous nuts, and candied fruit rinds. These are not breads at all but pastries made by chefs who were the inheritors of the tradition of *speziale*—apothecaries and herbalists who sold spices for culinary as well as medicinal purposes. Their medieval beginnings are identifiable from the spices and pepper and their invocation of abundance and fertility in the quantity of nuts and the presence of honey.

The panoply of Italian Christmas desserts is stunning. *Spongata*, a honeyed nut and raisin cake that is wrapped in two discs of pastry, like *panforte*, has been the Christmas specialty of Parma and Reggio Emilia for centuries, while in Siena spice and walnut-filled *cavallucci*, medium-hard white cookies imprinted with the image of a horse, are eaten in alternating bites with *panforte*. Romans serve *cassola*, a delicate cheesecake originally from the Jewish community, while in Campania, honours go to *struffoli*, pyramids of fried dough with a spicy honeyed glaze, *rococo*, sweet dough wreaths, Sicilian *cassata*, and *susamielle*, made with sesame seeds and honey. In Apulia, *cartellate*, curly ribbons of dough, symbolize the Baby Jesus's sheets, *calzoncielli* his pillow, and *dita degli apostoli*, tiny omelettes filled with chocolate- or espresso-flavoured ricotta, the fingers of the Apostles. Sicilians feast on *buccellato*, fig- and nut-filled Christmas ring-shaped pastries; Romans can't do without *mostaccioli*, cigar-shaped spiced nut pastries; and Calabrians eat *zeppole*, fritters which are called *zippulas* in Sardinia.

New Year's Eve celebrations have always been raucous events with emphasis on plentiful food and wine. They begin with people tossing household rejects—pots, pans, even refrigerators—out the window. Then they get down to eating dishes with lentils and raisins, symbols of money and good luck for the coming year. In most of Italy, the promise of prosperity comes with lentils, which represent coins, served with *cotechino*, a large pork boiling sausage sliced into fat coins, or *zampone*, a similar sausage encased in a pig's trotter, like a purse. In Piedmont, where grains of rice represent coins, the ritual New Year's Eve dinner is *risotto in bianco* bound with a creamy *fonduta*. In Friuli, people believe that rice grows in the pot as it cooks, and they hope money will multiply in their pockets in the same way. Until recently, Sicilians in small towns went from door to door singing *"La Strenne"* (from the Roman word for gifts), good wishes for the New Year, and asking for small gifts of raisins, dried fruit, and nuts. Once bells rang at midnight, everyone settled in for a feast of sausages, pork chops, and such local cookies as pine-nut *mustazzola* and buttery *biscotti della regina*, covered with sesame seeds.

Veneziana, the ritual New Year bread in Venice, is like *panettone* made without candied fruits; its topping is crunchy with almonds and raw sugar. The tradition in Sicily was once *cannizzu*, a two-tiered round bread connected by a small dough ladder with tiny pieces of dough shaped like grains of wheat. Neapolitans restrict their daily bites of *il croccante*, caramelized dough with tiny bits of almond, so it lasts from New Year until Epiphany, when the holiday season ends.

Ancient Romans initially marked the beginning of the New Year at the spring solstice; then in 153 BC, it was moved to 1 January. They exchanged glass jars full of dates and figs in honey so that the year would be sweet, and a bay branch so it would bring good fortune. The tradition is still honoured in Naples, where people exchange figs wrapped in laurel leaves, and in Campania and Abruzzo, where dried figs stuffed with almonds are gifts of the season. *Chiacchiere*, a traditional New Year dessert in Umbria, is made of tiny balls of dough that look like lentils and are glazed with honey so that the coming year may be sweet.

Epiphany, 6 January, the last in a 12-day cluster of holidays, is sometimes called "Little Christmas." It began when the three Magi recognized the divinity of the child born in Bethlehem and set off for a visit bearing gifts. They asked an old lady to join them, but she refused, and ever since, children have received their presents on the eve of 5 January from the Befana, a toothless old woman who fills stockings with toys and such sweets as *befanini*, sugary cookies shaped like alphabet letters. Her name comes from *befania*, a corruption of the Greek *epifania* (manifestation), referring to the first appearance of the Saviour.

Fires lit the way for the three Magi, and their light and heat became ritual blazes during the Christmas season. Some continue to burn in Friuli, where they are called *pan e vin*, bread and wine. Chestnuts, emblems of fertility, are roasted in the embers, which are then spread on the earth to encourage crops to grow. In Tarcento, a huge haystack sits on the top of the hill, and when the oldest person in town lights it, people in the flatland below light their own fires, drink *vin brule*, hot mulled wine flavoured with cinnamon and apple, and serve *pinza della Befana*, a rustic polenta *focaccia* filled with dried figs, raisins, pine nuts, and fennel seeds.

Good luck beans were baked inside cakes during raucous Roman Saturnalia celebrations, and the Church adopted the practice for Epiphany in the 14th century, when three white fava beans and a black one were baked into *focaccia*. Whoever found the dark one ruled the banquet. The custom still thrives in Piedmont, where the good luck bean may take the form of a tiny porcelain figure; but it still confers good luck.

The last day of Epiphany leads directly to the first day of Carnevale, a six-week orgy of masked balls, processions, fires, feasts, and drunken revelry. Its name, from the Latin *carne levamen*, good-bye to the flesh, is an apt definition of the last great party of the agricultural year, after which almost everything in the larder and the entire supply of meat is exhausted until spring. Like its Roman predecessors, Saturnalia, Bacchanalia, and Lupercalia, Carnevale includes buffoonery, drunken abandon, and gargantuan meals meant to invoke fertility and abundant harvests in a perilous time.

Carnevale banishes hunger, feeds everyone, and turns the world upside down by reversing social roles. In Naples, a contest of lasagna heats up. "At least once a year every family must eat it and until Ash Wednesday it's a continuous subject of discussion and eating," according to Jeanne Carol Francesconi, the expert on Neapolitan food. She explains that since the preparation requires abundant time, hard work, and expensive ingredients, and since family after family makes its own version and invites friends for the meal, by the time Carnevale is over, no one can even think about this extraordinary dish for the rest of the year.

The prototypical *dolci* of Carnevale are delicately fried pastries that change name and flavouring from region to region: they are *chiacchiare* (gossips) in Milan, *bugie* (lies) in Piedmont, *crostoli* in Alto Adige, *cenci* (rags) in Tuscany, *lattughe* (lettuces) in Emilia-Romagna, *sfrappe* in the Marche, and *nastri di suore* (nuns' ribbons) in many other places. *Frittelle*, sweetened dough fried and sprinkled with powdered sugar, are almost ubiquitous, although they are called *castagnole*, for their chestnut-like shape, in Romagna and the Marche.

Other more local *dolci* include *berlingozzo*, a sweet bread baked in Florence for Fat Thursday (Giovedì Grasso); Sicilian *cannoli*; and jam-filled *zelten*, doughnut-like sweets in friuli and Alto Adige.

The last day of Carnevale, Martedì Grasso (Shrove Tuesday) is the final culinary blowout before the arrival of Lent and Ash Wednesday. One of the last wild battles which were once common to Carnevale celebrations still takes place in Ivrea, Piedmont, where 60 tons of oranges imported from the south are thrown as weapons in gigantic battles. Not a single orange is served; instead crowds eat *tofeja*, a filling wintertime soup made of silky-textured local *saluggia* beans, *salamini* or *cotechino*, sausages, and rolled pieces of pork fat that are called *prete*, priests, much to the delight of local eaters.

Pork is the meat of the season, courtesy of the recently slaughtered pig, but it disappears the next day for the six meatless weeks of Lent. Giovanni Goria, the great authority on Piedmontese food, once cooked a traditional farewell-to-Carnevale meal that included, among many courses, *cotechino* with puréed potatoes and spinach, pigs' trotters with fried polenta, roasted pork spareribs, a *fritto misto* with pork loin, *coppa*, and sausages, and battered and fried pork shoulder—and these were only the antipasti.

Elsewhere, Verona hosts *Venerdì gnoccolar* (Gnocchi Friday), presided over by a king of gnocchi, whose sceptre is a giant fork, and Tossignano, near Bologna, serves quantities of *polenta pasticciata*, polenta layered with a bold sausage *ragu* and parmesan cheese.

The excesses of Carnevale come to an immediate halt on Ash Wednesday, the first day of Lent, Quaresima, a time of abstinence imposed by nature—food supplies were traditionally at their lowest point—as well as by the Church. A few towns treat Ash Wednesday as a continuation of Carnevale. Ivrea begins Lent with huge portions of *merluzzo e cipolle*, a lasagna-like dish of cod and onions alternating with white and red sauces, while Gradoli's six-course lunch for an immense crowd is based on fish from nearby Lake Bolsena.

Faced with the challenge of Spartan eating, Italians turn away from the fat old sausage-stuffed man representing Carnevale and are confronted by La Vecchia, a wrinkled old woman puppet, or a doll filled with dried fruits, nuts, and *cotognata* (rounds of dried quince). In rituals that fall in the middle of Lent, she is sawed open to release the treats stored inside or burned in fires to warm the earth and bring forth the food of a new season. Carnevale and Lent express the rhythm of abundance and scarcity that characterize the calendar year, with deprivation and penitence much more familiar than gastronomic exuberance until recently.

Italian ingenuity created sweets for the Lenten season made without eggs, butter, or lard. From Tuscany come chewy chocolate and orange *quaresimali*, shaped like alphabet letters, and *pan di ramerino*, rosemary-flavoured sweet buns, while Romans eat almond *quaresimali* and *maritozzi*, raisin-filled buns. Elsewhere cookies of the season are called *pazientini*, little bits of patience, precisely what's called for at Lent.

It may seem counterintuitive to throw an extravagant banquet in the middle of Lent, but the festival for San Giuseppe, Saint Joseph, the father of the Holy Family, occurs at the spring solstice, 19 March, and features quantities of bread in tribute to the fertility about to manifest itself in springtime. Once a national holiday, Saint Joseph is now celebrated only in Sicily, Apulia, and Abruzzo, always with ritual dishes that vary from community to community.

Families make a *cena di San Giuseppe*, Saint Joseph's table, to thank the saint for helping them recover from a calamity during the year. They improvise a sanctuary covered with branches, hang it with citrus fruits and ornamental breads in shapes symbolic of the products of nature and the coming season, and set before it an altar containing three huge devotional breads, one for each member of the Holy Family, as well as many smaller ones.

In Salemi, southwest of Palermo in Sicily, dozens of offerings begin with three orange slices, one for each member of the Holy Family, and end with pasta tossed with cinnamon and sugar and sprinkled with toasted breadcrumbs. In between, dozens of dishes are served to three people chosen to represent the Holy Family, as well as to neighbours and friends.

Among the offerings are fish dishes, such as *calamari ripieni*, calamari stuffed with garlic, breadcrumbs, and parsley; fried croquettes of fresh cod; *baccalà fritto*; *gamberetti fritti*; and *pasta con le sarde*. *Pesce d'uova*, little croquettes of breadcrumbs, grated cheese, and eggs, are poor man's fish.

Vegetable specialties include stuffed sweet peppers, artichokes, and tomatoes. The table is filled with *frittate* of spring vegetables ranging from wild asparagus to fava beans and peas. Silver dollar–size *polpette* are made of wild fennel; *pesci di funghi* are mushrooms dipped into egg and breadcrumbs and fried like fish. *Arancini*, fried rice croquettes, are filled with fresh spring peas and *ragù*.

Outstanding Sicilian pastries include *cassateddi*, lemon-scented, ricotta-filled turnovers, *spergi* or *pesche*, which look just like fresh peaches, and *pignolate*, fried logs of dough dipped in honey.

San Giuseppe is recognized elsewhere in Italy as the patron saint of friers. He is honored by *zeppole*, sweets made of a flour-and-water dough shaped like small wreaths, deep fried, and dusted with sugar and cinnamon or brushed with honey. *Bignè di San Giuseppe*, a more elaborate egg-enriched version, are the archetypal sweet of Naples, which are said to have been put on the culinary map when Pintauro, an 19th-century pastry chef, fried vast quantities of them on the sidewalk outside his shop. On 19 March the streets are still filled with bakers frying *bigne* that are filled with pastry cream and topped with an *amarena* cherry. These delicate fried puffs are called *sfinci* in Sicily, *tortelli* in Milan, and *bignè* and *confetti* elsewhere. *Zeppole pugliesi* are citrus-flavoured, while Sardinian *zippulas sarde* are made from dough flavoured with white wine, anise liqueur, and citrus rind, piped in spirals into boiling oil and served covered with honey.

Frittelle were made in ancient Rome on 17 March for a festival dedicated to the gods of wine. Today's creamy fritters are made with rice in Umbria, Florence, and eastern Sicily, while those in Lazio, Campania, and points south instead are based on a yeasted flour dough.

Lent ends as the penitential processions, parades, and bonfires of Easter week culminate in the celebration of the Resurrection. As spring fertility rites were the greatest celebration of the pagan year, so Easter became the climax of the religious calendar, the most solemn Christian liturgical event of the year. Unlike Christmas, Easter focuses more on rites than food, although eggs and lamb, the primary symbols of renewal and rebirth, are found in almost every observance.

When Saint Augustine said that which now takes the name of the Christian religion already existed, in certain aspects, in antiquity, he was certainly referring to Easter. Scholars trace the legends and symbols of Christian Easter to *Pasqua ebraica* (literally, Jewish Easter), Passover—a shepherd's festival before it became the event with which the Israelis celebrated their freedom from bondage in Egypt, always partaking of a ritual meal that included a roasted lamb bone, symbolizing the blood of sacrifice, and a hard-boiled egg, emblematic of life renewed. Lamb, the centrepiece of Easter eating, is both a succulent product of a pastoral people and the symbol of innocence, the sacrificial dish par excellence.

The egg, a perfect symbol of renewal and fertility, encloses the seeds of life within a delicate shell. In the 4th century, when Christianity became the state religion in Italy, believers exchanged eggs at Easter time as a symbol of hope, of the triumph of light over darkness, and of faith in rebirth. Eggs continue to be baked into multiple Easter dishes, both sweet and savoury.

Ligurians traditionally eat their savoury *torta pasqualina*, a vegetable tart once made with beet greens, now with spinach or chard, *quagliata*, a tangy curd cheese now replaced by ricotta-like *prescinseua*, onions, marjoram, and eggs. It once was made with 33 ingredients and/or 33 sheets of dough, one for each year of Jesus's life. The dough, made of flour, water, and olive oil rolled as fine as phyllo, wrapped the filling and the eggs cradled in it. Once made only at Easter, the *torta* is now found all year, although almost never with the ritual 33 layers.

For Easter lunch, Neapolitans once served *il pignato maritato*, a rich broth made with an extravagant number of meats and vegetables, but it has now been supplanted by simple pasta dishes. The traditional antipasto remains: hard-boiled eggs and *soppressata* with *casatiello*, once a rustic bread, now a spicy cheese bread flecked with salame and *ciccioli* and with eggs in their shells baked into the crust.

Easter lunch, north and south, features roast lamb and, to a lesser extent, roast kid, more rarely duck and pheasant.

Sicilians celebrate Easter with *la cassata*, cake made with alternating layers of *pan di spagna* and ricotta flavoured with candied fruit and chocolate, covered with royal icing, and garnished with candied strips of pale green squash. Other Sicilian sweets include *le pecorelle*, Paschal lambs made of almond paste with fluffy marzipan fleece, and *pane di cena*, similar to hot cross buns.

Egg-filled breads are still common in southern Italy. In Sicily, dough wrapped round hard-boiled eggs has many names which include *pupi con le uova*, *cannateddi*, and *bon hom*.

Sardinians eat *pardulas*, small golden ricotta pastries flavoured with saffron and shaped like the sun. The Neapolitan *pastiera*, a ricotta custard cake flavoured with orange-flower water, is based on white wheat berries, which were sacred to Demeter as symbols of fertility and were later used to ornament Jesus's tomb in the days before Easter.

The *colomba,* a *panettone*-like sweet bread shaped like a dove, is Italy's best known Easter bread. Originally from Lombardy, it is now mass-produced and eaten everywhere in the country. Friuli's lesser known *gubana* comes in two versions. Both are filled with raisins, multiple nuts and spices, chocolate, and jam, then laced with liqueurs; one is wrapped in puff pastry and the other in a brioche dough rolled like strudel and twisted into a snail shape. First documented in 1700, it may get its name from the Slavic *guba,* snail, or from *bubane,* Friuliani for abundance. Elsewhere *la schiacciata di Pasqua,* a risen sweet bread with many eggs in the dough, is the Easter bread of Tuscany; Umbria and Lazio claim a high domed *pizza di Pasqua* flavoured with lemon and orange.

Colored Easter eggs appeared around 1400, when Italians first wrapped hard-boiled eggs in herbs, flowers, even onion skins, to tint their shells. Eggs dyed red according to Byzantine rites still appear in Piazza degli Albanese, one of the centuries-old remaining Albanian communities. Chocolate eggs, of considerably later provenance, are objects of immense desire and come in every possible size, often at great expense.

On Easter Monday (*Pasquetta,* Little Easter), a much-loved national holiday, a picnic in the country was once imperative. Whole cities emptied out, their inhabitants celebrating in the countryside with a panoply of foods ranging from spaghetti cooked over an outdoor fire and sauced with *ragù* brought from home, to artichokes roasted in embers left by the fire that grilled lamb.

Seasonal festivals and their foods are intimately connected to the annual agrarian cycle in which crops are planted, are harvested, and then disappear, creating a long and anxious wait for the arrival of food for the new year. Romans sacrificed *primizie,* the first fruits of the season, to propitiate the gods, and later peasants and *mezzadria* workers brought them to the lords of the manor for whom they worked.

Agricultural harvests were always occasions of abundant celebratory meals. When the wheat was threshed, when the grapes were picked, and when the olives were collected, a feast was in order. Now that modern machinery can bring in the crop in hours, a neighbourly helping hand is rarely required, and the reward of a meal after immense hard work is no longer a normal part of life. The menu for the wheat harvest in the Val di Chiana in Tuscany used to include homemade charcuterie in the form of goose or duck neck stuffed like a sausage with the liver, pistachios, and parmesan cheese, and *pici,* local hand-rolled spaghetti sauced with goose or duck *ragù.*

La vendemmia, the grape harvest, occurs in many regions, but different varietals produce different wines and different *dolci.* In the Chianti area of Tuscany, *sangiovese* grapes are pressed into sweetened bread dough and covered with a blizzard of crunchy sugar to produce *schiacciata all'uva,* while the grape harvest in Quartu Sant'Elena in Sardinia focuses on sweet Muscat grapes called *zibibbo,* some of which are dried into raisins and added to a dough of chopped nuts, orange peel, anise, nutmeg, and *sapa* and baked into *pabassinas,* a delicious local sweet.

Romulus and Remus were born beneath an olive tree. Horace wrote "olives nourish me," and Virgil sang their praises. Olives are harvested in winter and brought to the *frantoio,* where the liquid pressed from them becomes the olive oil that is ubiquitous in the country's diet. The harvest is still celebrated with *bruschetta,* thick slices of grilled country bread rubbed with garlic and annointed with fresh green olive oil. The same dish is called *fettunta* (oiled slice) in Tuscany and *soma dâ'i* in Piemonte, where crisp *grissini* replace the bread. To mark the olive harvest in Chianti, a slice of *bruschetta* lies in the bottom of *zuppa frantoiana,* white bean minestrone served with a thread of new oil poured over the top.

Saints' days celebrate the protection of locally cherished saints and the salvation of the community through the offering of special foods. Some of the dishes are local, others regional or even national as the country looses its rural roots, but all celebrate the act of eating and sharing, connecting sacred and natural. Every day somewhere in Italy a saint is being celebrated, and there are often different communities celebrating the same saint with entirely different dishes.

Major saints include Sant'Antonio Abate, 17 January, whose emblem is the pig and in whose honour cuts of fresh pork are cooked and served. San Giovanni, the patron saint of Rome, is celebrated on 23 June, the eve of the summer solstice, with fire festivals and dishes featuring snails in a thick sauce of olive oil, garlic, anchovies, tomatoes, and *mentuccia,* calamint or pennyroyal.

San Martino, Saint Martin, 11 November, celebrates the end of the agricultural year, when all the crops have been brought in and the year's hard work done. The day was once a kind of New Year, when school started, leases were signed, and contracts renewed; if they weren't, San Martino meant moving day. Saint Martin is always connected with wine and the special *biscotti* made for his saint's day that are double and triple baked and meant to be dipped into the new Moscato wine.

Finally, just as there is a food for almost every festival, somewhere in the country there is a *sagra,* a country fair honouring almost every ingredient, be it rice (Villimpenta, near Mantua), truffles (Asti and Alba), or strawberries (Nemi), salame made from geese (Mortara), pecorino cheese (Pienza), boar (Capalbio), *radicchio rosso* (Veneto), and even *lardo,* which is celebrated twice, once in Arnad in Valle d'Aosta and again in Colonnata, near the marble caves of Carrara in Tuscany.

These days almost every town and fraction of a village hopes to encourage people to spend time and euros at newly invented events featuring dishes made from local ingredients. Even political parties got into the act. For years the old Communist Party celebrated the Festa dell'Unità in competition with local *sagre.* The food was delicious, more varied and plentiful and less expensive than the local offerings. Alessandro Falassi, Italy's foremost folklore expert, called these meals "the revenge of the proletariat," since Italians had done without meat for so long. *Feste* were once deeply meaningful for the poor, offering them one of their rare opportunities to eat meat or sweets, and many remain sources of close identification with their communities.
(CF)

FETTUCINE. *See* PASTA SHAPES.

FEVERFEW, *amarella, Tanacetum parthenium,* is, like tansy, a plant of the Compositae, related to pyrethrum and chrysanthemum, with the same insecticide properties. Its bitter leaves can be used to flavour stuffings, *frittatas,* stews, and game dishes, as well as figuring in many bitter herbal liqueurs.

FICO D'INDIA.
See PRICKLY PEAR.

FIG, *fico, Ficus carica,* is the fruit of a tree or shrub that has been cultivated since about 2750 BC, perhaps in Egypt or Mesopotamia. Figs and sycamore figs were depicted on the walls of Egyptian tombs, for their occupants to enjoy the fruit in the afterlife. Of the many varieties, some produce two crops a year, in early summer and autumn. The fruit is an inflorescence within which are clustered many tiny flowers which form drupelets which look like pips. Some reproduce without pollination; others rely on a little wasp to do it for them. Figs have always been a source of sweetness; when dried, they keep well, and the texture and flavour are good in cookies and sweetmeats. They were often

Figs have been cultivated since approximately 2750 BC. (Shutterstock)

used in the many versions of PANFORTE made in the past, a prudent as well as delicious way of keeping dried fruit and nuts, bound with honey and enhanced with spices, to last through the winter. This sweetness is a perfect foil to salty cheese or ham; the classic combination of figs and Parma ham is too good ever to become a cliché. Mattioli writes of figs and grapes as *"il capo e l'honore di tutti i frutti del'autunno"* (the honour and glory of all the fruits of autumn). He goes on to say that the watchmen in the vineyards eat more grapes and figs than bread at this time of year, and become plump and well fleshed (Mattioli, bk. 1, p. 312). A sign of the healthiness of figs, but a worrying insight into their diet the rest of the year.

The beauty and sweetness of the fig has endeared it to artists it as well as to gluttons; baskets of them on Pompeian murals may have inspired later painters. The juice bursting through the bloom on the blue-black flesh, and the drop of white latex sap oozing from the newly broken stem, are signs of voluptuous fecundity. Figs are the only fruit at their best when overripe.

Figs were grown in ancient times, and Dalby, and Platina before him, reminds us how a rhetorical question in the Roman senate precipitated the destruction of Carthage (Dalby, *Empire of Pleasures*, 2000, p. 109). Cato produced a fresh fig and demanded how many days it had taken to come from Africa—only three days, that is how close our enemies are. The Third Punic War was rapidly declared. Writing of the fig's medicinal qualities, Platina recalled the antidote to poison found among the possessions of the defeated Mithridate: two dried figs pounded with 20 leaves of rue, a walnut, and some salt; taken on an empty stomach, this would provide a whole day's protection.

FINOCCHIONA, or a version called *Sbriciolona*, is made all over Tuscany, both industrially and by small producers, but the best come from Chianti. This is a medium-sized salame, made of lean pork meat and fat from the cheek or shoulder, flavoured with fennel, pepper, and garlic. *Sbriciolona* is much bigger, with a softer texture.

FIOCCHETTO is made from the part of the ham remaining when the prime cut for CULATELLO has been removed, cured in the same way, but being smaller, not as long, about seven or eight months. It is not as refined as *culatello*, but its low salt and subtle flavour are much prized.

FIOR DI LATTE is a pulled cheese made in MOLISE and CAMPANIA from cow's milk, following the procedures for CACIOCAVALLO but with a different heat treatment which makes it possible to reabsorb more water and so become paler and lighter. It is sold fresh in plastic wrappings. That made in Campania is from the milk of the Agerolese cow, a low yield but with exceptional qualities; acclaim from connoisseurs has saved the race from extinction (*see* PROVOLONE DEL MONACO). It can be enjoyed as one would MOZZARELLA.

FIORE SARDO is an ancient traditional sheep's cheese that has been made since prehistoric times by shepherds all over SARDINIA. Unpasteurised, uncooked, and lovingly tended by hand at every stage in its production, this is an archetypal artisan cheese, where the skills of generations are applied even though refrigeration, modern equipment, and hygienic regulations have to some extent been introduced. From the moment of coagulation to the final anointing of olive oil as it ripens, each cheese is moulded, shaped, squeezed, turned, and wiped by hand with due attention to the development of moulds, colour, and aroma. The characteristic shape is like a squat, tubby convex barrel. The sheep in question are a native race, *razza sarda*, well adapted to the terrain; their pasture is rich in aromatic shrubs and plants, including lentisk, myrtle, wild clover, and pulses; some of these aromatic woods are used in the light smoking the cheeses get early in their career. When fresh and young, *fiore sardo* is light and fragrant, becoming less moist and more piquant as it ripens. In the past it was exported all over Europe and later to the United States, being a good eating cheese and an ideal condiment for grating over pasta and vegetable dishes, not as subtle as *grana*, but less costly, so often used in making Genoese pesto, as is another Sardinian cheese, with the confusing name PECORINO ROMANO. *Fiore sardo* is hemmed in with protective legislation and a DOP in 1996, monitored by its Consorzio at Gavoi, and watched over by SLOW FOOD, who are concerned about the way some hygienic legislation interferes with traditional methods and utensils without any appreciable benefit to the consumer.

FISH AND SEAFOOD, *pesce,*

pl. *pesci* and *frutti di mare*, are the most prized and perishable of Italian ingredients. The coastal waters are full of a huge variety, lakes and rivers inland have much to offer, and dried and preserved fish are available everywhere. Visitors are overwhelmed by the profusion and baffled by the names of fish in markets and restaurants; regional names and local varieties generate confusion; and our only comfort is in knowing that this confusion has been shared by some of Italy's greatest thinkers. When Platina came to write his *De honesta voluptate et valetudine* (On decent pleasure and good health), he was concerned to link the knowledge of classical writers to the expertise of contemporary cooks and physicians, adding words of wisdom about the properties of the ingredients he described and used. He did this with some elegance until the section on fish, which he prefaced with a disclaimer: "I had intended to speak of the nature and qualities of all fish but became totally disorientated by the confusing way their names kept changing" (Platina, 1998, p. 420, my translation). He went on to blame sloppy writing by both modern and ancient authors, a sort of deterioration of a once clear canon. We know this was not the case, for there were multiple names of fish, and disputes over identification even in classical Greek and Latin, but at least Platina was trying to get things clear, and in spite of his complaints, he could not have had a better guide than the pragmatic Martino, whose recipes he used. Martino has some sensible generalisations—fish are best cooked whole, if fried or boiled they need to be scaled and gutted, but you don't need to do this when roasting or grilling them; small fish are best fried or grilled, big ones simmered, and above all fish should be well cooked, being of a moist or wet humour and so harmful if underdone. Well, today we want our fish cooked just enough and no more, so that the muscle proteins in the connective tissues coagulate but do not dry out and get tough and stringy. But when you read Martino's recipes, you can see that he understood the practise without fretting about the theory. A sturgeon is cooked in a sufficiently large pan to accommodate the whole creature, in equal parts of white wine or vinegar and pure water, with the right amount of salt, for as long as you might cook veal or beef. A *varolo* needs a similar treatment, and if less than five pounds in weight it could be roasted, basted frequently with a *salimora* of oil, vinegar, and salt, applied with a branch of bay leaves or a sprig of rosemary.

Here I share Platina's near despair, for *varolo* or *variolo* is a Venetian dialect word for *spigola*, also known as *branzino* (*Dicentrarchus labrax*, a Perciform of the Serranidae family, *loup de mer* in French). But *spigola* is what one translator (Faccioli) uses for Platina's separate entry for *lupo*, which Martino calls *laccia*, or *lacce*, SHAD to us. (*Alosa spp.*, a genus of Clupeids, is a different family from the Serranids, to which SEA BASS belong.) Sea bass and shad are both found in streams and rivers, when they leave the sea to come and spawn, and shad was (once) called *lupus* by Pliny, although he, like the modern Genoese, usually meant sea bass by this word; anyway, *lupi* are what Platina and his friend Pomponio Leto, who called them *laccia*, used to catch "between the two bridges" over the Tiber (today's Ponte Sant'Angelo and Ponte Milvio). If you are still with me, this gives a glimpse of the confusion, mine anyway, over names. What saves one's sanity is this glimpse of two impoverished academics, fishing for their supper at the bottom of Pomponio's Trastevere garden, washed by the unruly Tiber, happy to recall that Pliny had perhaps once done the same, and enjoying the fish, sea bass or shad, whatever its name, however they cooked them. (Both kinds caught in the Tiber had a reputation of being exceptionally good, silver grey, with large scales and delicious white flesh.) *See* Laurioux 2006, p. 209.

Scappi, who was writing his great *Opera* a century later, really knew his fish, and describes them with thoughtful accuracy, comparing those he gets in Rome with those he knew in Schiavonia, along the shores of the Adriatic, and those available in Milan. His handling of GILT-HEAD BREAM, *orata*,

is concise, accurate, and reminiscent of Davidson—not preoccupied with abstract description, but giving the purchaser and cook clear information on how to recognise and handle it:

> Gilt-head bream are both large and small, the good ones have small scales and are silvery in appearance, with a line from head to tail and a transverse dark mark near the tail, a bifurcated tail, and teeth in four rows, that is two above and two below, very strong like humans' as have all fish in this family. Their season begins in November and lasts right until April. (Scappi, bk. 3, p. 113)

Then follow two recipes, for grilling and stewing. The fish to be grilled sit in a marinade of oil, vinegar, salt, and fennel for a couple of hours, which is then used to baste them as they cook slowly, turned occasionally, and served as a sauce. They can be cleaned, scaled, dipped in flour, and fried in olive oil, and eaten hot with lemon or bitter orange juice. The *pottaggio* is worth quoting in full:

> Take fresh gilt-head bream, scale and gut them, and put in an earthenware or copper dish with oil, wine, water, verjuice, salt, pepper, cinnamon, saffron, and in winter prunes and dried cherries, in summer spring onions, gooseberries, or fresh verjuice without pips; just before serving add a handful of chopped herbs, and if you want to thicken the juices add some ground almonds.

A century after Platina's attempts, the naturalist Ulisse Aldrovandi's passion for describing and naming everything in the natural world extended to fish, and he looked far and wide for specimens and employed some of the finest artists of the time to illustrate them; the problems can be imagined getting fish to his studio in Bologna, where he was professor of natural history, with their colours and shape intact. Rimini, now a short hop on the autostrada, was then several days' journey away, and his friend Costanzo Felici in the 1560s had to dry fish "in the ashes," a process sometimes sabotaged by a passing cat, before sending them on by whatever messenger he could find. He contributed all kinds of fish, mentioning their local names—"*pesce spada o falce, che noi il voliamo chiamare*," ("sword fish" or "scythe" as we like to call it) and promises in his next shipment "*una bella bizaria di pesce*" (a crazy brew of fish), one of which was a star-gazer, *pesce prete* (*see* WEEVER), which he called *pesce lucerna*, and is said by local fishermen, who call it *capo grosso*, to have eyes in the top of its head that glow like the eye in a peacock's tail, and which might or might not be the *uranoscopos* of the ancients (Felici, 1982, p. 36). Jacopo LIGOZZI painted this for Aldrovandi, who labelled it *Dracunculi speties*, and its dorsal fins do look dragon-like, though Linnaeus later classified it as *Uranoscopus scaber*. This succession of neatly labelled dried fish, with names, comments, and remarks on local names and fishermen's tales, were the raw material of Aldrovandi's life's work, and he had the curiosity and humanity to include them all— the stingray, *Pastinaca marina*, illustrated in all its greenish reddish beauty, loves music, the dance, and witty remarks; yet Aldovrandi shrewdly connects fishermen's talk of stingray as skilled hunters with Pliny's report of the observations of Aristotle, who found GREY MULLET, the fastest of fish, in the belly of the sluggish electric ray. This preoccupation with describing, drawing, and naming fish, especially the search for coherence in all the local and regional names, was already a concern of naturalists. One of them, Malatesta Fiordiano, a nobleman in Rimini, wrote in 1576 a little treatise full of poems on the subject, *Trattatello della natura e qualità de'Pesci*, listing their Latin and vernacular names, quite unfazed by the variety of local names,

with a wistful reference to his manuscript notebook with sketches of all the fish he describes, not possible in the printed book. Sadly, the poems are not gastronomic, although Fiordiano pointed out that a third of mankind's food comes from the sea.

Descriptions by naturalists and the exquisite work of LIGOZZI may have encouraged the Medici, the grand dukes of Florence, enthusiasts for scientific experiments and the cataloguing of the products of nature, to commission celebrations of the sensual as well as the scientific aspects of nature—the Neapolitan artists Giuseppe Recco and Giambattista RUOPPOLO painted the *joie de vivre* of local fishermen and the copious harvest of the sea. The fish seem to be dancing in their freshness, singing along with the idealised humans, in the bright clear light bouncing off the Bay of Naples; a work by Giuseppe Recco of 1668 shows a heroic figure (painted by his collaborator Luca Giordano) arising from the waters holding a basket of sea bass and lobsters, surrounded by a chorus of assorted fish, including the red scorpion fish, red mullet, a large red gurnard with silvery belly, weevers, *salema*, *pandora*, with others hard to identify, their last gasps heartlessly depicted as a baroque chorus. A painting in the Uffizi in Florence, Giuseppe Recco's huge fishscape of 1691, might even be a celebration of a local fish dish, the CACCIUCCO of Livorno. Against a sombre rocky background and a stormy sky are displayed a jumble of fish, tossed on shore, glistening with freshness, alongside the basket and equipment of the fishermen, artfully arranged to make the most of the bright scorpion fish, red mullet, and gurnard, with sea bass, *salema*, John Dory, *pandora*, *pagro*, a saddled bream, and many more lit by the last rays of a fitful sunset.

The grand duke Ferdinando, in Livorno not long before his premature death in 1713, persuaded the Bolognese Giuseppe Maria Crespi to execute in just two days, an incredibly short time, two paintings of fish and fowl, for which he provided the raw materials; these Crespi triumphantly transformed into a feast for his patron to celebrate the completion, on time, of the commission. Might this array of fish, and green herbs and vegetables possibly related to the Ligurian PREBOGGIÒN, have been transformed into the not-so-far-distant CIUPPIN? It would have been a neat way of dealing with the oysters, squid, a *scorfano rosso* (scorpion fish), gurnard, grouper, grey mullet and *pagro*, and several unidentified little fishes, sketched in haste with rapid flickering brushwork, to meet the deadline and a hasty lunch. So this platter of fish in the Uffizi, hard to identify, but including red mullet, sole, scorpion fish, the odd sardine, grey mullet, and others might have been gathered together not as an artistic composition but as a considered choice of fish on the way to the kitchen for one reason only—to be cooked and eaten.

There would have been no problem with fresh fish as artist's models; the ice-houses in the Boboli Gardens provided ice all the year round for cooling drinks, making ice cream, and sorbets, and for use in scientific experiments. We get some idea of this resource from a painting in the Galleria Palatino in Florence of an interior with an arrangement of foodstuffs and a wine cooler in the foreground containing a huge block of solid snow or ice surrounded by bottles of wine and liqueurs (Giusti, p. 37).

Arrangements of fruit and flowers have always been part of the décor of the wealthy, and paintings of rare blooms and hothouse fruit could only reinforce the impression of affluence, but fish, glowing like jewels and glistening with momentary perfection, could never have been appropriate interior decoration. Thanks to these talented artists, rich patrons could enjoy the catch of the day, savour the delights of them at the table, and praise the skills that immortalised them. Free, in this atmosphere of sensuous hedonism, from the complexities of symbolism which abound in fish paintings in the Low Countries, images of

fish were produced and enjoyed as a celebration of the natural world, and an appreciation of the their gastronomic value.

Although they are classified in families, and with descriptions to help punters choose and cook, it is also possible to describe fish in terms of where they feed and what they feed on, with preference given to those that come from deep waters, or have fed on nice healthy seaweed around rocks, or even have chomped on small fish and crustaceans on the sea bed; less agreeable are those that have wallowed in the muddy ooze of streams and estuaries, or cloudy ponds and fish tanks. Since some fish move around and their habitat and diet vary at different times of year, choices are difficult. A good fishmonger can help. The red mullet, *triglia di scoglio*, grilled to perfection by Don Calogero and much loved by Montalbano, would have lived in rocky waters up to 50 metres deep, feeding on smaller fish and crustaceans.

The Catholic Church's dietary regulations, which prohibited meat and eggs, and sometimes dairy produce as well, were no hardship. Fish gastronomy was nothing to do with making a virtue of necessity but a hedonistic pleasure in its own right. The variety of fish and vegetables, and the delicious dishes to be made from them, made banquets and festivities on lean days a pleasure rather than a penance. When the Emperor Charles V arrived in Rome on a diplomatic visit in April 1536 during Lent, Cardinal Lorenzo Campeggi got Scappi to prepare a sumptuous banquet. Twelve people sat down, in his palace in Trastevere, to a meal of 12 courses, with fish, fruit, vegetables and sweetmeats prepared in every imaginable way—just short of 200 dishes. The guests chose from these, as the pageant of presentation, carving, and serving pursued its splendid course: visual and olfactory delights to be admired, sampled, discussed, and enjoyed at leisure, with music between courses—a slow, well-judged sequence of events. A huge range of fish were spit roasted, baked, grilled, stewed, cooked in pies and tarts, set in coloured jelly, dressed with sauces, herbs, flowers, some teasingly elaborate and some breathtakingly simple: red mullet fried and decorated with pink pansies, slices of salted salmon set in a pale jelly to look like ham, fresh sardines in oil and vinegar with oregano, trout simmered in wine and spices and decorated with violets, a large lamprey spit roasted with a crust of basted breadcrumbs, what looked like a kid's head made in a mould from minced fish, live fish swimming in containers of transparent jelly. Apart from the usual pie full of live songbirds, the guests could choose from spring delicacies: tiny baby artichokes eaten raw with salt and pepper, a salad of asparagus, broccoli *alla Napoletana*, with oil, bitter orange juice and pepper. We know that Charles V was a pathological glutton, and so can appreciate the significance of this deployment of food in the interests of diplomacy. (At that point, he was contemplating handing Milan over to France in return for help against the infidel Turks and Protestants, while at the same time needing to establish a good relationship with the new Pope Paul III Farnese, busy rebuilding Rome after the disgraceful sack of 1527.)

The joys of fish were celebrated in another banquet masterminded in 1565 by Giovan Battista Rossetti, the *scalco* or chief steward of the duke of Ferrara. He created the illusion of eating underwater, with waves painted on the ceiling and embroidered on the tablecloth, shell-shaped majolica dishes, and footmen dressed as fish, complete with scales.

With the help of refrigeration and freezing technology, fish has today become an international commodity, with freshly caught local fish alongside products of worldwide commerce on the fishmonger's slab; with farmed salmon from Scotland in the Rialto fish market (look at the polystyrene containers behind the stalls) or farmed trout on the menu in Tivoli restaurants (the Aniene is now too polluted to fish from). Whatever the source, most fish markets and restaurants in

Italy will gladly explain, to visitors anxious to know, the best way to prepare and serve their fish—usually labelled in shops and markets, often displayed in a tank or chilled display cabinet in the restaurant—and so this steep but jagged learning curve can be negotiated with help and patience. In some ways, it is simpler to ask a stall holder or fishmonger the best way to cook a particular fish rather than ask its name, look it up when you get home, and then search for a recipe. Most Italians are both knowledgeable and generous and also quite stern about the way things should be cooked.

Present-day and historical recipes from Italy show an inventiveness that puts the pallid timidity of classic French and English fish cookery to shame; the dab of butter, squeeze of lemon, and sprinkling of parsley over plain grilled or fried fish is eclipsed by the imaginative use of herbs, spices, dried fruit, and wine, mitigating the intriguing fustiness of BACCALÀ, and enhancing the flavour of sea and freshwater fish. Regional cookery books, guides, and restaurants are full of ideas, and health preoccupations have stimulated yet more interest in this healthiest of foods. (Most fish are listed alphabetically here under their English names, except where we have the Italian name only; for an Italian name, see the index.)

FISH, FRESHWATER, *pesci d'acqua dolce*, are found in the lakes, streams, and rivers of Italy, and have also been cultivated in fishponds and artificial habitats from time immemorial. Before climate change, pollution, demographic change, new methods of fishing, and the widespread use of refrigeration, freshwater fish lived and were caught in traditional ways that until a few decades ago had changed little. Many of the Italian lakes have individual populations of fish, unique to them, which by careful management were maintained in a stable equilibrium with the environment for centuries;

now there are serious moves to combat pollution, regulate fishing, as a sport or a livelihood, and redress the imbalance by restocking lakes and rivers.

The main lakes of Italy are Garda, Maggiore, Como, Trasimene, Bolsena, Iseo, Varano, Bracciano, Lesina, and Lugano, with many smaller ones, like those in the Castelli Romani, and a wide range of fish live in them. They are a gastronomic resource both locally and now, with improved methods of distribution, in a wider area. In the past, fishermen worked extremely hard for poor rewards in conditions often overshadowed by feudal ownership of territory and equipment, restrictive fishing rights, and complex symbiotic relationships with the surrounding population, not always fruitful and supportive. The best of the catch would be sold, and often an illicit amount above the permitted quantity would be dealt with surreptitiously, but what the fisherfolk ate at home, or in the course of their work, would be of inferior quality, things they could not sell, or the more boring fish. Much of the catch would have been salted and dried, for sale or home consumption.

The fishermen of the Monte Isola, a large mountainous island rising steeply out of Lake Iseo in Brescia Bergamo, used to lie awake at night praying for daughters, whose nimble fingers made the nets on which their work depended. An independent source of work, and income, a traditional skill handed down from mother to daughter, or an inescapable fate—a lifetime of poorly rewarded toil with little hope of escape. Today these special skills are still deployed, often using synthetic materials, for making special kinds of nets sought after by specialist enthusiasts worldwide. Boat-making was another skill, and the long, flat-bottomed gondola-like craft are still made by traditional methods and exported all over to specialist anglers. The main fish in Lake Iseo were trout (*trote*), pike (*lucci*), a variety of sardine (*sarde*), and *pippie*.

Tourists can now enjoy fine local fish cooked in traditional ways in idyllic conditions, which do not perhaps reflect the harsh realities of life around the lakes. We know of early tourists, like Mantegna (though perhaps he would have called himself a a well-informed traveller) and his companions, who took to Lake Garda in a boat, complete with oriental carpets, a guitar, and other comforts, to investigate classical inscriptions, calling like Horace before them at Desenzano and Sirmione. Stopping off at riverside taverns to celebrate their discoveries might have involved some fish meals, perhaps a tasting of the *carpione*, unique to Benaco, the classical name for Lake Garda.

Lake Garda contains over 30 other kinds of fish, including trout, carp, freshwater sardines, *coregone* (whitefish), *lavarello* (pollan), tench, perch, barbell, chub, and bleak.

Monastic orders had fishponds and fishing rights and cultivated fish in managed systems of fresh water, as did the Dukedom of Parma, which excited the admiration of visitors, in particular one of the followers of Cardinal Odoardo Farnese, who wrote in 1591 of the beauties of Parma, its orangery, centrally heated in winter, and the 8 miles of aqueducts feeding its trout ponds. And not only trout; a visitor today to the little fortified town of Fontanellato might shrink from the turmoil of voracious but harmless carp in the castle moat, which figure alongside trout in a painting by Boselli in the dining room of the castle. The fish are seen flopping gasping in a rocky landscape, with crayfish, crabs, wild mushrooms nibbled by a rabbit, a pile of fat snails, and the lemons, oil, wine, spring onions, garlic, and bitter herbs to cook with them, while a marauding cat grapples with a nice fat eel.

FISH, PRESERVED, a delicacy in many forms and under many names, but originally a necessity. If food is short, but there may from time to time be a glut of one particular food item, we need to store it. Therefore, since digestibility more or less entails perishability, we need to preserve it in some way.

Freezing has at last ensured that there is now no shortage of almost-fresh fish in Italy, as in most other countries of the modern world; thus the infinitely varied flavours of seafood as preserved in more traditional ways (pickled, salted, dried, smoked, fermented) survive today less out of necessity, more because we continue to demand them as an integral part of our gastronomy. In some forms, preserved fish is so good, and so sought after, that it is more expensive than fresh. In Italy as in Greece, if restaurants use frozen fish they are obliged to own up in their menus.

Because of the annual migrations of the TUNNY and BONITO, people in Greece and Italy up to 8,000 years ago were able to predict that twice a year, they would have far more of these meaty and nourishing fish than they could eat fresh. The practice of drying fish may well be as old as that. At the other end of the spectrum, tiny fish such as gobies and anchovies are good to eat freshly caught, but they, too, are at times available in unmanageable numbers. Salted ANCHOVY, an indispensable contribution to the range of Italian flavours, must also go back some way into the prehistoric period. The early Sicilian foodies Epicharmus and Archestratus have little to say about dried or salted fish, and in fact the ancient Greek gastronomic tradition to which they belong placed high value on very fresh fish caught at the best season in the best locality. Archestratus does, however, recommend bonito, sliced and salted in barrels, from Byzantium (now Istanbul), showing that there was already a Mediterranean trade in this product in the 4th century BC.

From the beginning of the Roman period, it is possible to discover more details of the range of preserved fish available in Italy, the methods employed, and the way these products were used. This is partly owing to the wealth of written texts, partly because (apparently for the first time) the processing of fish was carried out on an industrial scale, leaving unmistakeable evidence for the archaeologist.

Latin texts tell us of a widespread trade in tunny, bonito, and mackerel; it is probable that brine, solid salt, vinegar, and olive oil were all sometimes used, but that smoking was not. Sources included southern Spain, where the business was said to have been begun by Phoenician or Carthaginian entrepreneurs, and Sardinia. This is the origin of the Latin term *sarda*, literally "Sardinian fish," a word that appears to have meant originally a large fish—mackerel or bigger—preserved in salt or oil; *sardina*, a diminutive of this, meant a pilchard, preserved in the same style. These words appear to have shrunk in their significance, so that Italian *sarda* is now a pilchard, *sardina* a young pilchard or SARDINE. The poet Martial reminds us of the smell of salted GREY MULLET from the Nile, already known to have been a local speciality in the Pharaonic period but evidently exported as far as Rome in his time (around AD 100). Apicius provides two recipes for sauce for salt mullet, *ius in mugile salso*, one of which calls for pepper, oregano, rocket leaf, mint, rue, walnut, date, honey, olive oil, vinegar, and mustard seed. There is no evidence in Roman texts of salt sturgeon, or of salt mullet roe (though at least some classical Greeks knew of these delicacies), while neither Greeks nor Romans had heard of *caviare* or of salt cod.

The most comprehensive way to use seriously unfresh fish was that famous Roman culinary ingredient *garum*, or fish sauce (*see* APICIAN FLAVOUR). It was already known to earlier Greeks, who called it *garos*, but under the Roman Empire it became a gastronomic necessity and an almost empire-wide industry, signs of which have been discovered from the Spanish coasts in the west to the Crimea in the far northeast. Either in stone vats in these industrial salteries, or in wooden barrels in a farmyard, fish or the discarded parts of fish were mixed with salt and allowed to ferment under a summer sun. Many species could be used: mackerel and tunny innards were often said to be the best. A salty, fishy liquid was drawn off after several weeks, bottled in amphorae, and marketed throughout Italy and elsewhere. The best quality, mentioned in several Greek and Latin texts and on surviving amphora inscriptions, was the sherry-coloured *garum sociorum*, partners' garum, which came from southern Spain. There is an alternate Latin name for fish sauce, *liquamen*: and Grocock and Grainger, in their translation of *Apicius*, argue that the two names represent slightly different products (2006, p. 373). *Liquamen* is required in nearly every recipe in Apicius, not excluding those for sweets. By contrast, salt is scarcely ever called for, an indication that in Roman Italy, as in modern Southeast Asia, fish sauce was actually the normal way to add salt in cooking. It would have been a powerful flavour enhancer (*see* UMAMI). Those who could not afford the proper fermented product could, instead, use a cooked version, a fishy brine called *muria*; there was also a solid paste or sauce called *allec* or *hallec*, perhaps relying largely on anchovies, for which the southern Italian name is *alice*.

Mediterranean trade declined in early medieval times, throwing Italy back on its own resources. However, the Italian trading cities were instrumental in reviving long-distance trade, and it was along their routes—by land and sea—that new flavours in preserved fish came to tickle Italian palates, cod and smoked herring (*arenga*) from northern seas, caviare (*caviale*) from far in the east. Caviare is already discussed by Platina, who tells us that it was made in Italy in his time, and that Greeks, in particular, ate it greedily.

Here, then, are the big differences, as regards preserved fish, between ancient and modern Italy. The sight, smell, and taste of Egyptian salt mullet has long vanished, sup

planted by those of dried cod or stockfish (*stoccafisso*) and salt cod (*baccalà*) from the Atlantic. Although no longer the food of the poor, no longer required by the whole of Italy as a fast-day staple, dried and salt cod remain highly popular. The ubiquitous flavour of fish sauce, unforgettable but forgotten, has given way to the much more sparing and choosy use of the salted anchovy, familiar all over Italy, to provide a rush of gustatory sensation just where and when it is wanted.

Here are some continuities: tunny is still salted and dried, now under the name *mosciame*, and is prized as much as ever. The "Sardinian fish" or *sarda*, whatever the species that once belonged to this name, retains its fame; Sicily, however, is now a better known source of sardines than Sardinia. The variously named *agone* of the northern lakes is sun-dried to make the local delicacy *missultitt*; it is probable that this practice is far older than surviving records (Platina, for example, though he mentions the species, recommends it not dried but fresh, flavoured with verjuice or bitter orange juice).

Here are some flavours unknown to ancient Italy. Salt grey mullet roe or BOTTARGA, sold wrapped in wax, is now a speciality of Sardinia and Sicily, as it has been for many centuries: it is already discussed in detail by Platina under the Latin title *ova tarycha*, which is borrowed from the original Greek but—if you look hard—visibly identical with the modern Italian *bottarga*. Smoked delicacies include smoked farmed STURGEON from Sicily (there used to be wild sturgeon in the Po, but no longer) and smoked SWORDFISH, an innovation that would surely have sent earlier gastronomes into ecstasies. Tunny is now smoked; it is also, of course, tinned, and in that form contributes its flavour and texture to salads and with pasta. So far, at least, preserved fish in its many forms has remained as popular as ever, and is even more highly valued than in the past.

(AKD)

FISH SAUCE. *See* ROMAN FOOD; FISH, PRESERVED.

FISH SOUP, *zuppa di pesce,* is more than its name implies; in Italy with its varied coastline, profusion of fish, many dialect names for them, and much *campanilismo,* fish soup has many names and ingredients and generates furious controversies. Every region has its special fish soups, with secret recipes and special ingredients, and who could be so insensitive and pig-ignorant as to suggest that a fish soup is a merely a soup made with lots of different fish? The confusion of different names stimulated Artusi back in the 1890s to think about the need, in a newly united nation, for a common spoken language, which he then deliberately deployed in his cookery book *La scienza in cucina e l'arte di mangiar bene.* The Adriatic has its BRODETTO, and Liguria its BURIDDA and *ciuppin,* Genoa has its *pesce in tocchetto,* a version of *buridda,* the Tuscan coast of the Mediterranean its CACCIUCCO, there is a *zuppa di pesce* in Sicily served with couscous, a *burrida* in Sardinia which is a sauce for cooked fish, not a soup. On the shores of Lake Trasimeno a *tegamaccio* is made from freshwater fish, eels, pike, tench, perch, in the earthenware pot from which it gets its name; Puglia has a recipe seasoned with salted anchovies and white wine, using the local sweet round tomatoes, and including squid, shellfish, and fresh fish, all added to the pot with carefully calculated timing; Taranto has a similar combination of fish and shellfish, perfumed with celery and basil; Oristano in Sardinia has a MINESTRA in which small pasta shapes are cooked in an aromatic fish broth perfumed with basil and parsley and served with the pieces of fish. There are soups made from a wide range of fish and those from one fish only. Methods vary— some involve browning the ingredients before adding liquid, which in itself can be wine, vinegar, water, or a mixture of the three; some include garlic, some not, some start with a SOFFRITTO of finely chopped aromatics fried in oil, some seem to need plenty of tomatoes, and in others saffron is considered either a necessity or a pollutant. A Sicilian recipe includes capers, stoned green olives, and sultanas. Liguria is prodigal with herbs, capers, and pine nuts. Some brews are thick and dense, others quite liquid; some are eaten with polenta, others with toast or dry bread, maybe rubbed with garlic, or fried in oil or butter. It is a relief to retreat from the red tide of tomatoes which was to engulf so many dishes, and turn to historic fish recipes where fresh green herbs and yellow saffron provide colour, and verjuice or gooseberries a fruity acidity, with dried fruit and sugar adding undertone of sweetness.

The received wisdom is that these soups were a way of enjoying the less desirable fish left over from the morning's catch, boiled up in seawater with whatever seasonings came to hand, part of the unchronicled underbelly of Italian gastronomy, and that once increasing prosperity and an interest in regional food stimulated an interest in CUCINA POVERA, these local domestic dishes were transformed by chefs in restaurants, usually for the better. This imaginative leap ignores evidence in print that although fish were cooked individually, grilled, fried, roasted, or boiled, there were also sumptuous *pottaggi* with methods and ingredients close to today's *zuppe di pesce* which were part of aristocratic cuisine and not peasant food. The continuity of this tradition seems to indicate that a spectrum of recipes based on choice not chance, not necessarily cheap, was from earliest times bridging the gap between fishermen and gastronomes. Scappi has several recipes for fish, usually one kind only, in which prepared slices, or whole fish, are cooked in a mixture of wine, water, and vinegar, with verjuice, spices and seasonings, sometimes saffron, and dried fruit, finished with ground almonds for thickening, and a handful of fresh herbs just before serving; some versions included the familiar chopped onion. Scappi knew his fish and speaks with authority of those of the Adriatic as well as those available to him in Rome; when it comes to turbot, *rombo*, he describes a *pottaggio* made from the fish whole or cut in pieces, cooked gently in oil, water, verjuice, white wine, dried fruit, and spices, with chopped onion softened in oil: "At a time when I found myself in Venice and Ravenna I heard of this from the fishermen of Chioggia and Venice who made the best *pottaggi* of anywhere along the coast, and only ever used this recipe, and I think it worked better for them than for us cooks, because they prepare the turbot the moment they catch it" (Scappi, bk 3, recipe 79, p. 120r). It is good to contemplate fishermen enjoying a carefully cooked prime fish rather than unsold odds and ends—a necessary corrective to the myths about the origins of fish soup—and encouraging to find this direct link between the grand papal kitchens of Rome and the fishermen of the Adriatic littoral. In a Venetian *pottaggio* of ombrine, Scappi simmers the prepared fish very gently in a covered pot with white wine, verjuice, a little sugar, spices, olive oil, raisins, and just enough water to cover, serving them on slices of bread to mop up the sauce. Scappi's only recipe for a selection of fish cooked together is a *pottaggio alla Francese*, in which a sweet-sour recipe for pike can also involve ombrine, trout, sea bass, and carp, cooked in wine, sugar, and vinegar well seasoned with spices, with the possible addition of dates and quince, enriched with butter or sweet almond oil, dished up on slices of toast. Scappi's contemporary Christofaro Messisbugo had some fine fish pottages; his *potaccio* of turbot, sea bass, pike, or *pandora* (*meggia*, maybe one of the bream family) cooks the prepared pieces of fish in finely chopped onion and parsley fried together, with vinegar and verjuice, seasoned towards the end of cooking with spices to taste and coloured with saffron. Another recipe simmers the fish in sweet herbs pounded in a mortar, cooked

in oil, then moistened with sweet white wine, a little strong vinegar, with raisins and spices; a pleasant sweet/sour effect, green with the herbs.

FLATBREADS, *schiaccata, piada, tigella, crescentina, crescia, borlengo,* are breads made with a mixture of flour, water, and salt, sometimes unleavened (*azzimo*, or *azimo*), sometimes made with yeast or baking powder, kneaded to a soft pliable mass, flattened or rolled out, and cooked quickly in an oven or over a very hot stone or terra cotta surface. They crop up in many parts of Italy in various forms, and with different names, with regional variations and passionate convictions about origins, ingredients, and methods. The same mixture can be rolled out, cut into round or lozenge shapes, and fried in lard or oil. Unlike traditional oven-baked bread with a very long proving time, often involving much manipulation by hand or machine, these flatbreads, pancakes, fritters, or whatever are fast food, and can be blown together at short notice.

The use of leavening is controversial—the unleavened bread of Jewish tradition is flattened by a heavy weight of symbolism, but on the simplest level it is quick bread cooked fast by people on the move, eaten with herbs and green stuff that came to hand, like the Ligurian *focaccia Genovese* (*see* FOCACCIA). Also similar to the *crescia* (or *torta*) *al testo* of Umbria, it is not possible to put them all into neat categories.

Connoisseurs observe that unleavened, unfermented fried breads and flatbreads go best with cured, fermented products like ham, salame, and cheese; so what was once a subsistence food evolves into an area of gastronomic choice and even dogma.

The *piada*, affectionately known as *piadina*, of Romagna are sold from characteristic little kiosks whose striped awnings are like unofficial road signs saying "You are now on the Romagna Riviera." In the past, they were thrown together by the *rezdora* when her good bread had run out, fast family food for hard times, using up the last of the flour, eked out with any other materials on hand; now they are an industrially produced tourist attraction, the *rezdoras* replaced by mechanised mixers and electric hotplates. The name *piada* can be linked with the pitta bread of the Middle East and with pizza. An early use of the word *piada* is in the works of Costanzo Felici, who spent much of his life in Rimini: *"hora nelli testi e panari di pietra o terra cotta o di rame non si cuoce se non piade o placente et altre vivande"* (today everything especially *piade* and flatbread and other things are cooked on disks of stone, terracotta, or copper; Felici, 1986, p. 115).

The divide between rich Emilia, with its heritage of pigs and cows and their products, derived from the Lombards, and the more austere Romagna, with an agriculture based on sheep, and a cultural connection with Byzantium, is apparent in the rich additions of lard and butter, sometimes *ciccioli* (*see* PIG'S FAT), that go into the versions from Modena in Emilia, compared with the more austere *piadina* of the east. A filling of wilted green vegetables and herbs, or cheese or *prosciutto* makes for a good nutritional balance. The uneven way the *piadina* cooks, with darker flecks highlighting the softer areas, is part of its appeal. In the period between the two world wars, many writers and antiquaries, without consciously supporting Fascism, were intent on promoting Italy's glorious past, and found in the *piada* and the myths and legends associated with it links with pagan deities and Roman heroes. Virgil has a lot to answer for; he had Aeneas and his companions disembark (in Lazio not Romagna) and settle down in the shade of a tree to a picnic of flatbread and wild fruit, and from then on his *adorea liba*, wheat flatbread, or *fatalis crusti*, fateful *focaccia*, cut into mystic quadrants, became a symbol of the mighty founding fathers. In 1909, Giovanni Pascoli took the ball and ran with it, and his devout old peasant woman's offering of humble unleavened bread, cut in four, to the wraith-like traveller in his short poem "La Piada" embodied the proud traditions and regional identity of Romagna. The gnarled workworn fingers of tired old women relinquished the fatal disk into the pale hands of poets and patriots. Today, from a mystical experience to a nice little earner, these once round, white, and pure disks, like numinous full moons, are now industrially produced, thronging the supermarket isles, murky with organic additives.

Sometimes the mixture is fried rather than baked or cooked over a hot surface. In this category we have the *gnocco fritto* of Emilia-Romagna, made in different shapes (round or rhomboidal) but with the same effect, a light, puffy fritter, both soft and crisp, and best fried in good homemade lard; the so-called healthy oils now in use just do not have the same incomparable flavour. In some places it is called *chersien*, becoming *torta fritta* in Parma, *crescentina* or *crescente* or *crescia* in the Marche (not a crescent shape but one that puffs up, from *crescere*, to grow). These are leavened or unleavened and come up crisp and puffy, to be eaten with cured ham or salame. *Spianata* is a version of the pieces of flattened dough originally used to test the heat of the oven, and are now made of bread dough enriched with eggs and ricotta.

There is a *crescentina* from the commune of Pavullo near Modena, made with lard and yeast, not fried but cooked over the *piastra*, not to be confused with *tigella*, a more domestic, less touristic product, an unleavened mixture, often enriched with lard or butter, cooked on a flat round decorated tile heated over a wood fire. The name comes from *tegola* or tile; in some areas, such as the commune of Pavullo, the flattened dough is baked between two decorated round clay disks.

The *crescia* or *torta al testo* of Gubbio in the province of Perugia in Umbria is made with

From Pascoli, "La Piada", *Vita inter-nazionale*, 1900.

Ma tu, Maria, con le tue mani blande
domi la pasta e poi l'allarghi e spiani;
ed ecco è liscia come un foglio, e grande
come la luna; e sulle aperte mani
tu me l'arrechi, e me l'adagi molle
sul testo caldo, e quindi t'allontani.
Io, la giro, e le attizzo con le molle
il fuoco sotto, fin che stride invasa
dal calor mite, e si rigonfia in bolle:
e l'odore del pane empie la casa.

But you, Maria, with your gentle hands
tame the dough and then stretch and
    flatten it;
and behold it is smooth as paper and
as big as the moon; and then you
    spread it
on my outstretched hands, and I lay it
    softly
on the hot surface, and you stand back.
Then I flip it, and with the poker
rouse up the fire beneath so that stri-
    dent heat
makes it swell with blisters:
and the smell of bread fills the house.

flour, salt, oil (sometimes with bicarbonate of soda), cooked on a ceramic *testo* made from ground-up gravel and clay, baked in a potter's oven. The thickish circles of dough are cooked on these white-hot disks, under a lid covered with cinders. They are often served split in half with a filling of salame and cheese, sausages, or cooked wild greenery. In the past, this was the sort of quick-baked bread useful at harvest time, when appetites were great and loaves in short supply. *Crescia* in the Marche are flattened disks or bread dough topped with onion, rosemary, oil, and salt, cooked in the oven, linked to charming tales of *chichiripieno*, lumps of dough given to little children to play with on baking day and cooked at the edge of the oven. There is a *crostolo del Montefeltro* in the Marche made with flour, egg, milk, lard, and bicarbonate, the worked and rested dough rolled out flat, anointed with lard, rolled up and twisted, rolled out again, and baked on a heated flat disk. Variations on this method produce a *crescia sfogliata* from Urbino, similar to rough puff or flaky pastry. The *crostoli del Montefeltro* are made of a dough enriched with lard, milk, and egg, rolled out flat, annointed with lard, then rolled or curled up on itself to make a long fat cylinder, which is then coiled into a circle, rolled out flat again, and cooked on a hot tile.

In Sardinia the *pane carasau* or *carta da musica* is the daily bread in many areas. The traditional version is made from bread dough kneaded in the *madia* using a lump of sourdough from the previous batch, left to rise for several hours (very different from the quick and easy unleavened flatbreads from elsewhere), rolled out into flat disks which puff up in the hot oven and can then be made into two disks, which are put back in to finish cooking. Industrial versions are also made, square and oblong as well as round.

PIZZA, FOCACCIA, and other flattened breads made with yeast and cooked in the oven need a longer proving time, but can be cooked fast, seasoned and flavoured in various ways, and eaten as a casual snack or street food rather than part of a serious meal. These breads have been around all over Italy since time immemorial, long before the late-comer *pizza napoletana* came along in the nineteenth century.

FLOUNDER, *passera pianuzza*, can be found all over the Adriatic and parts of the Mediterranean; when tiny, the little *passerine* can be floured and fried and eaten whole.

FLOUR, *farina,* is made from a variety of WHEAT grains, which (to summarise briefly a complex process) are freed from husks, chaff, and bran, ground in various ways, then passed through different grades of sieve to produce the types of flour available in Italy today: soft, *tenero,* flour, of which types oo and o—with lower levels of gluten, fibre, vitamins, and minerals—are used for light breads and cakes; types 1, 2, and *integrale,* wholemeal, have a higher nutritional content and are used for harder breads. We tend to use "strong flour" (explained later) for bread in Great Britain, but in Italy and the United States, soft flour is used as well.

What you lose in dietary fibre you gain in delicacy of flavour and texture. The healthy stuff in wholemeal flours is more prone to rancidity, so they need to be freshly milled and from a reliable source. Slow grinding with stone disks in the traditional way produces a different kind of flour to that made with rapid passage between revolving steel drums.

Italian bakers are mostly using a large proportion of home-grown wheat, much of it as individual as the dialect they speak, and together with the local water and the microclimate around their bakery, are producing a huge range of breads which are different for far from superficial reasons. A certain style of loaf can differ from an almost identical one in the next village, as Carol field has noted, and this is keenly understood by the consumers. Good Italian bread flourishes because of these local differences and the people who care about them.

Hard flour, *duro,* from durum wheat, is used mainly for making pasta. Home bread-makers in Great Britain use what we call strong flour, which is kneaded and put to rise, but not manipulated like Italian bread dough, where the pummelling and shaping produces an elasticity which maximizes the gluten in the soft flour and makes the bread light. Home bread-makers in the United States usually use all-purpose unbleached flour, with an 11 or 12

percent gluten content, for making Italian bread, and "bread flour," with its 15 percent gluten content, is not often used. Italian bakers also use sourdough ferments, as well as fresh yeast of various kinds, which give depths of flavour and variations in texture.

Flour made from other grains and roots, nuts or tubers, has been used throughout history—in fact the name for wheat flour, *farina,* comes, via the Latin *far,* from *farro,* emmer wheat (*Triticum turgidum,* subspecies *dicoccum,* not the same as SPELT, *triticum aestivum,* subspecies *spelta; see* EMMER WHEAT).

POLENTA was the name then for a porridge of crushed or ground BARLEY or emmer, long before the name was transferred to the disastrously inferior boiled MAIZE flour, which arrived much later from the New World, without the ancient knowledge of nixtamalisation which enhanced its nutritional value for the Maya and Aztecs.

Pulses like lentils, chickpeas, dried beans, and vetch were used to eke out wheat flour in times of shortage, as were acorns, chestnuts, and anything farinaceous that could be dried and ground to a powder. They could be delicious or horrible, depending on their condition, and survive in many rustic regional breads, flatbreads, and porridges. Although these alternative flours are a success in modern baking, in the past they were sometimes of poor quality and led to disease and in some cases mental disorientation. The periodic attacks of ergot-related diseases (*see* RYE) and mental disturbance were due to contaminated flour of various kinds, movingly described by Camporesi (1980).

FLOWERS, edible ones, have always been appreciated in Italian cuisine, from the BORAGE and BUGLOSS decorating Renaissance salads to the nasturtium, impatiens, wallflowers, pansies, rose petals, and violets of today's salad ingredients. In one of his August menus, Scappi began a light supper

A salad made with edible flowers. (Shutterstock)

with an *insalata di mescolanza con diversi fiori*, a familiar concept, and also offered an *insalata di fiori di borragine e capparetti*, a salad of borage flowers and capers. A stewed leg of lamb was decorated with borage flowers. Clusters of springtime elderflowers kept their heady perfume when dipped in batter and fried in butter, or mixed with ricotta to make little white fritters. Fresh FENNEL flowers were an alternative to the seeds which came later. Many blossoms can be crystallised—jasmine, violets, roses—and be used to decorate confectionery, as they were in the past. Jasmine flowers and their perfume figure in ICE CREAMS and sorbets, particularly in Sicily. In Naples, Corrado made preserves, syrups, and sorbets from violets and jasmine, simple, fresh ices that depended on a profusion of fragrant flowers. The extracted essences of many flowers go into perfumes and liqueurs, and were also used for medicinal purposes. Rosewater and orange or lemon flower water, made from distilled or macerated blossoms, were used to perfume food, sprinkled over dishes just before serving, usage which may derive from Arabic cuisine but was firmly entrenched in Italy during the Middle Ages, and continued into the Renaissance, until the feral perfumes of musk and ambergris ousted them by the 17th century. These waters were used to refresh guests in the ritual washing of hands before and during a meal. Flowers were strewn over the tables, as decoration and air freshener—nothing to do with unwashed bodies, for the rich and powerful could afford to be dainty in their persons and extravagant with their perfumes. Most banquets ended with the ritual presentation to each guest of bunches of scented flowers, often alongside perfumed gloves and trinkets. A portrait of Lucrezia Borgia by Bartolomeo Veneto shows her in a diaphanous see-through garment and a headdress adorned with a wreath of leaves and flowers, holding a posy of daisies in a gilt container.

Fresh edible flowers are now available all the year round, and used in equally imaginative ways. A plate of transparent slivers of cured pork fat, pink at the lower edges, sprinkled with rose petals and borage flowers, unites ancient and modern sensibilities. *See also* LAVENDER.

FOCACCIA,

known and loved in Italy and abroad, is a yeasted bread dough, often mixed or spread with oil, herbs, or onion, an ancient way of cooking bread dough quickly, possibly connected with offerings made by the Romans to the gods, *liba*, but certainly the ancestor of the PIZZA. Early versions were cooked on the hearth of a hot fire, or on a heated tile or earthenware disk, like the related FLATBREADS. Many have an inventive range of flavourings, the olive oil, rosemary, garlic or onion of the *schiacciata alla fiorentina* of Tuscany, or the herbs, sage, rosemary, oregano, onion, and *ciccioli* of the *focaccia genovese* of Liguria. The crispy *siccioli* or *ciccioli* left over from rendering chopped up pork fat into lard can be used as a topping, or worked into the bread dough with other flavourings, in the case of the *piê cun i grassul* of Romagna, and the *gnòch cun i grasô* of Modena. Artusi has a sweet version, *stiaciata coi siccioli*, in which the *ciccioli* are matched with eggs, sugar, and lemon or orange peel. The simplest *focaccia* can be an unsalted bread dough, dimpled with firm fingerprints before the final rise, anointed with olive oil and good flavoursome salt crystals, or a complex mixture, with herbs worked into the dough and

An early ancestor of pizza, focaccia usually consists of dough, baked quickly at a high heat with oil, herbs or onion. Inventive cooks can create infinite variations. (Shutterstock)

spread on top, or coverings of lightly sautéed vegetables—onions, zucchini, eggplants or peppers, olives, sunripe tomatoes. (CF)

FONDUTA is a melted cheese dish similar to the French *fondue*. The ingredients and method, however, are different. In PIED-MONT, where the dish is a speciality, FONTINA is used, of the best possible quality, preferably from Valdostana, well matured but not too elderly. The business of getting the cheese, previously diced or sliced and soaked in milk, to melt and amalgamate with the required quantity of egg yolks requires skill and patience. The result is a creamy sauce which can be eaten, messily, by dipping *crostini* into it, or with rice or polenta. The addition of slivers of white truffle makes this a sublime dish, although Artusi dismissed it as at best a starter, at worst a fallback when there was nothing better to be had. He called it by the Tuscan name *cacimperio*, which might

mean "cheese and pepper," which takes one straight back to the trattorias of present-day Rome, where *cacio e pepe* is robust dish of pasta served simply with plenty of grated pecorino and freshly ground black pepper, about as far removed as one can get from the subtlety of *fonduta*.

FONTINA is a cow's milk cheese from the mountains and valleys of the VALLE D'AOSTA, made within hours of milking from the milk of the red and black Valdostana breed of cow; high pastures produce the finest version. This sweet, rich melting cheese is unpasteurised, its quality depending on the varieties of pasture and location, and the processing of the milk with due attention to these variations by cheese-makers with centuries of skill behind them, often working hard long hours in the lonely but beautiful pastures, caring for the cheeses in dark humid ripening rooms, often underground, where the temperature and humidity contribute to biochemical modifications which add to both flavour and nutritional qualities. A disused copper mine and a World War II bunker are just some of the useful underground spaces made use of. Pantaleone da Confienza wrote in his *Summa lacticiniorum* of 1477: "The Val d'Aosta is part of the Dukedom of Savoy, where delicious cheeses are to be found; the climate is fairly temperate, the mountains are fertile, and the products of the earth are incomparable" (p. 63). The name *fontina* came later, perhaps from a geographical location, but is now firmly protected by its DOP.

Every stage of production and ripening is controlled by this rigorous DOP, and only *fontina* cheeses with the approved logo are ideal for cooking and eating. FONDUTA is the best known recipe.

FOOD IN ART is a topic explored here in entries devoted to individual artists, including CARAVAGGIO, CRIVELLI, GARZONI, MUNARI, and others, and mentioned in various entries in which they give visual confirmation of written evidence. Some produced still life paintings full of straightforward information, others included things to eat and drink in works of a religious or mythological nature, often of a ritual or symbolical nature. Historians looking for evidence of what people ate and drank have to be aware of these pitfalls; for example, apples and cucumbers, in works by Crivelli, rather than as staples of the Mediterranean diet, though common fare, hang above the throne of the Virgin or a saint to symbolise the purity of Christ and the fecundity of his mother. The blemished apples in Caravaggio's *Basket of Fruit* in Milan might have been typical of what was in the market that day or intended to make us ponder on the Fall of Man or corruption from within. Background glimpses of a kitchen or banquet table in works by BASSANO depicting Bible stories tell us a lot about cooking methods, pots and pans, and even details of tarts and pies that recipes cannot convey. This area of research is in its infancy, and there is still much to explore.

FOOD WORDS AND THEIR ORIGINS.

Italian is the modern descendant of the dialects of colloquial Latin ("Vulgar Latin") that were once the everyday speech of Roman Italy. Sardinia, Sicily, Venetia, Cisalpine Gaul (the Po Valley), and the Alpine valleys belonged to Roman provinces quite distinct from Italy; this is the primary reason why their modern dialects are vastly different from those of the peninsula, so much so that they are usually counted as separate languages.

After the empire's collapse, Italy was never again politically unified until the 19th century. In spite of the cultural prestige of Tuscan, speakers in other regions and city-states had little reason to adopt a "foreign" model in speaking, writing, or teaching. Hence the Italian dialects are very different from one another, and historically they have been far more prestigious than, say, the regional dialects of England. Word forms deriving from different dialects are often to be found side by side in the Italian dictionary, for example, Tuscan *ciriegia* and general *ciliegia*, cherry, both of which come from Latin *cerasia*; likewise *fica* and *figa*, fig, from Latin *ficus*; *mandorla* and *amandola*, almond, from Latin *amygdalus*.

Italian dialects and local languages are now in retreat in the face of national education and the mass media, but the way people speak about everyday things such as food continues to vary across Italy—just as the recipes vary.

The food vocabulary of Latin was, in part, inherited from its long-lost ancestor, proto-Indo-European. This is why some Latin words show resemblances to those in other Indo-European languages. Examples are *sal* (Greek *hals*, German *Salz*, It. *sale*, salt) and *piscis* (German *Fisch*, It. *pesce*, fish). Latin originated as the language of Rome and northern Lazio. Early speakers borrowed the names of various foods and food sources from neighbouring dialects and languages. From Sabine, to the north, came *bos*, ox, and the equally important *popina*, tavern, an etymological double of the native Latin word *coquina* (It. *cucina*, kitchen). From Greek, spoken in coastal cities from Naples to Taranto, came *castanea* (It. *castagna*, chestnut), *asparagus* (It. *asparago*), *polypus* (It. *polpo*, octopus), and many other names of fruits, vegetables, and fish. Latin eventually spread to the outlying reaches of Rome's empire, and rich Romans bought costly imports with exotic names. A north Indian language supplied *piper* (It. *pepe*, pepper), and a south Indian language *zingiber* (It. *zenzero*, ginger).

Many food words in modern Italian can be traced to Latin: *pane*, bread; *carne*, meat; *cena*, dinner. Some make it possible to reconstruct colloquial Latin words that happen not to occur in any texts (such words are called "starred forms" by linguists). For example, the Italian *nocciola*, hazelnut, must originate in spoken Latin *nuceola*, an unrecorded diminutive of *nux* (It. *noce*, walnut). In many cases, a Latin word survives only in dialects or regional languages, such as Venetian *bussolà*, the name of a cake, which comes from Latin *buccellatum*, hard tack, ship's biscuit; Friulian *rosade*, the name of a cake, from Latin *rosata*, rose-flavoured.

There are cases where dialects differ in their choice of words but both go back to Latin. For example, Italian *gallina* and Sardinian *pudda*, hen, come from different Latin words; so do Tuscan *popone* and the widespread *melone*, melon. Southern *cacio*, cheese, comes from Latin *caseus*, while northern *formaggio* is borrowed from French *fromage*—but that in turn came from spoken Latin *formaticum*, cheese made in a mould.

Some Italian words which are borrowed from neighbouring languages can be traced ultimately to Latin. French is frequently a source because of the strong influence of French culture. Even the basic word *mangiare*, eat, comes by this route; French *manger* derives from Latin *manducare*, chew, as does the older native Italian word *manicare*. Italian *cervogia*, herb beer, comes via French *cervoise* from the originally Celtic word *cerevisia*, which (like beer itself) was in daily use in the Roman northern provinces. Italian *buglione*, bouillon, broth, stew, comes from French *bouillon* and originally from spoken Latin *bullio*, formed from the verb *bullire*, boil, bubble. Medieval Greek also transmits some Latin words to Italian, such as *indivia*, endive, which came via Greek from Latin *intibus*.

But Latin is only part of the story. Italian *gigotto*, leg of lamb, comes directly from French *gigot*, ultimately from Middle High German *giga*, fiddle, and violin (because of the resemblance in shape). The common word for beer, *birra*, also comes from German. Italian *maccherone*, a kind of pasta, comes from Greek; so does *anguria*, watermelon (but there is also *cocomero*, watermelon, from Latin; and Sardinian *sindria*, watermelon, is from Arabic). *Tacchino*, turkey, is believed to come from Croatian, a Slavic language. A great number of Italian and regional words come from Arabic, and these have arrived by various routes; here are some more examples. Sicilian *zibibbu* is the name of a sweet grape variety grown on Pantelleria and Sicily, known elsewhere as *muscat d'Alexandrie*; *zibibbo* is encountered elsewhere in Italy as the name of raisins and wines from this grape. It was borrowed from Arabic *zibib*, raisins, probably in the period when the Arabs ruled Sicily. The Arabic root *sharab* is the origin of two Italian words: the older *sciroppo*, syrup, linctus, is a medieval loanword through the scholars of Salerno, who studied Arabic directly, while the younger *sorbetto*, ice cream, sherbet, arrived in the 16th century from an Arabic loanword in Ottoman Turkish. Incidentally, English *sorbet* is borrowed from Italian via French, while English *sherbet* comes directly from the Turkish word. Another important Arabic term, *alcool*, alcohol, arrived in Italian in the 16th century by way of alchemical writings.

In recent times, food words have reached Italian from many sources worldwide, often through the medium of French, Spanish, Portuguese, and (increasingly) English. *Banana* came via Portuguese from a language of central Africa. *Batata*, sweet potato, and *patata*, potato, derive from the same original word in Taino, a lost language of the Caribbean. There is confusion in several European languages (including English) about what name to give to the new foods introduced from the Americas. A good example is provided by Italian *mais*, English *maize* (a word that came via Spanish from Taino). In English, *maize* is in competition with *corn* and other terms, while in Italian there are alternatives to *mais*: *granturco*, literally Turkish grain; *granone*, literally big grain; Romagnol *furminton*, literally big wheat; Sardinian *triguindia*, literally Indian grain. A similar uncertainty can be traced, in French and Italian, about the tomato: Italian *pomodoro* (literally, golden apple) was initially rivalled by *tomate*, a now-forgotten word (borrowed via Spanish from classical Aztec), whereas in French *pomme d'or* has vanished and *tomate* reigns unchallenged.

Words change, and so do meanings. *Ciabatta*, widely familiar as the name of a kind of Italian bread, means literally a slipper or overshoe (probably Persian in origin). Latin *porcus* was a common word meaning pig, pork, while *maialis* was a specialised term for a castrated boar; in Sardinian, *procu* is still the common word, but in Italian *maiale* has taken over this role. Italian *ribes*, black currant, red currant, now known worldwide because it was adopted as the scientific name of the genus, came originally to Italian from Arabic, where *ribas* means sorrel, a salad leaf that has nothing in common with the currants except its sour and astringent flavour. Latin *ficatum* meant fattened with figs, because

pigs were fed thus to produce fine-tasting liver; *fegato* in Italian now simply means liver, and so do Sicilian *ficatu*, Neapolitan *fecata*, Venetian *figà*, Friulian *fiyat*, Lombard *fideg*, Piedmontese *fidic*, Niçois *fege*.

(AKD)

FORMAGGIO DI FOSSA is

made in Sogliano and Rubicone in EMILIA-ROMAGNA, and parts of the communes of Pesaro and Ravenna. The idea of burying a perfectly good sheep's or cow's milk cheese in a ditch for three months seems bizarre, and the results are described with consummate tact in the *Atlante*: "the aroma is *sui generis*, rich in the pungent whiff of woodland undergrowth; the flavour is delicate, almost mild, at first, with a piquant and increasingly bitter aftertaste." The ditches are in fact pits hewn out of the *tufo* or volcanic rock in the centres of these communities, in which the prepared cheeses are wrapped in clean white cloths, with the name of the owner, and put to rest in the carefully cleaned depths, which have been purified by fire, lined with fresh straw and reeds, hermetically sealed with a covering of planks of wood and a thick layer of sand, leaving the complex process of chemical, physical, and biological transformation to carry on until 25 November, the feast of Saint Catherine, when the precious bundles are disinterred and their pungent odours waft through the village, to great rejoicing. Camporesi appreciated the concept of ritual purification, death and rebirth, corruption and renewal, in this process, which legend attributes to the need to hide provisions away from the looting and pillaging of the mercenary armies that infested the area during the 15th century, but it may have been the more prosaic need to treat a glut of summer cheese so that it will last through the bleak winter months. Not only is the cheese preserved but the underground fermentation increases its nutritional qualities and makes it easier to digest.

FORMAI DE MUT is an alpine cheese from the Alta Val Brembana, above Bergamo, where the well-watered mountain pastures and benign climate provide fragrant grazing for the cows, of the *bruno alpina* breed, which spend the summer months on the heights and come down into the valley for the winter. The summer version of this rich, semi-cooked cheese is perfumed with aromatic alpine plants and grasses, perceptible even after the heating and coagulation of the milk, thanks to the careful crafting of the cheese in wide flat forms weighing from 8 to 12 kilos, where the judgment of the cheesemaker determines the draining and pressing and short ripening of each, carried out up in the mountains in traditional *casere*, built of stone, often below ground, to ensure a low, even temperature all summer. The production of this soft delicate table cheese has been protected by DOP since 1996.

FORMAIO EMBRIAGO

means "drunken cheese," and it derives its characteristic flavour from being dunked, after the usual coagulation, draining, and salting, in red grape must for 30–40 hours, which speeds up ripening and prevents deterioration. It was in the past an alternative to the olive oil with which the rind was dressed while ripening, and the strategy of hiding cheese from invading hordes, not to mention landlords and tax gatherers, in barrels of must was a typical peasant survival technique. Although the genuine version is made exclusively in the province of Treviso, it is possible to do this with other cheeses such as *montasio* and *asiago*.

FREE RANGE, applied to chickens,

is *ruspante*, from *ruspare* which means scratching about. In the past, they were scratching about in a variety of locations, barnyard, chicken coops, hen runs, and fields and meadows. These would all lead to different degrees of tenderness or palatability, and recipes would allow for this. Now we need to look out for these scrawny yellow corn-fed birds, and adjust cooking to their qualities. When it comes to animals, those reared in the wild, *bradi*, or in open but not totally wild conditions, *semibradi*, fed on wild or natural forage of the locality, have flesh with a texture and flavour, or milk, in the case of cows, sheep, and goats, quite different from the majority of animals reared in their thousands on an industrial scale, and in industrial conditions. The lean scavenging pigs in Ambrogio Lorenzetti's frescoes in Siena, the *cinta senese*, nearly died out in the face of this challenge, but are now being revived, rootling away in the woods and bosky hinterlands of the Tuscan countryside. Eggs, if mass-produced, have to conform to strict legal requirements; free range ones are called *casalinga*.

FRICO. See FRITTER.

FRITTATA is the Italian version of an

omelette, without the mystique. The base is EGG together with a precooked vegetables, asparagus, artichokes, zucchini, mushrooms— the possibilities are enormous. Pasta of various kinds, or bacon, cheese, or ham, can be incorporated into the beaten egg mixture, which is turned or flipped to cook both sides, to give a moist not runny result, about half an inch deep, often served tepid, cut into wedges. The rolled omelette has been known in Italy for centuries, immortalised by the painter PONTORMO, who found a simple *uova pesce* made a light and undemanding supper when he was feeling fragile.

FRITTER, *frittella*, is the name for a

huge range of things, either dipped in batter and fried, or consisting of ingredients stirred into the batter itself. These range from flaked soaked *baccalà*, salt cod; tiny newborn fish of the Clupeidi family, *nunnata* in Sicily (consumed in gluttonous quantities by Camilleri's Salvo Montalbano); wild fennel; or sweet versions using rice, chestnuts, or almonds. *Fritole* are fritters made of pine nuts, raisins, and candied citron to celebrate Carnevale in Venice. *Frico* is a fritter made in Friuli from a local cheese, *montasio*, aged for six months. Thin slices are fried in oil, lard, or butter in a carefully monitored sequence in which the cheese first looses its moisture, then melts, and finally becomes crisp and golden. This can be combined with apples, onions, or potatoes.

FRITTO MISTO, a selection of

ingredients coated in various ways, then fried crisp. Some are dipped in batter (*pastella*) and deep fried; others might be covered with egg and breadcrumbs; others simply floured. Many, for example, brains, sweetbreads, and other offal, are preprepared in appropriate ways, and the coating and cooking medium, lard, butter, or oil is selected to suit them. These fried foods are some of the glories of Italian gastronomy, depending on the quality of oil or fat used, the freshness and delicacy of the ingredients, and the skill of the fryer. One might rely on a restaurant to provide the full array of items in a traditional *fritto misto*, but simpler versions can be done at home, eaten straight out of the pan, as they are cooked in relays.

There are many regional variations, using different batters appropriate to the selection of these bite-sized morsels. Some need a delicate, almost transparent, crisp veil; others want a more dense protective coating. The nature of the batter and the temperature of the oil can ensure a crisp coating which absorbs the minimum of oil, gratifyingly "low fat," with nothing to perturb the health-conscious, and ensuring the retention of all the nutrients and flavour of the enclosed gobbets. These vary from artichoke hearts or asparagus tips, or delicate zucchini flowers stuffed with melting *provatura* cheese and anchovies, a speciality of the Ghetto in Rome, chronicled by Ada Boni, who lists the items in the *fritto misto* of Rome: brains, sweetbreads, calf's liver, artichokes, sliced zucchini, broccoli, cardoons, and *pezzetti*, a range of vegetables dipped in batter, the cheapest street food, described by her with nostalgia for an already vanishing way of eating (Boni, 1983, p. 61). A *friggitore* engraved by Pinelli in 1803 shows the paper-wrapped snacks being handed to a family group. Another engraving of 1815 conveys the noise and bustle of a Roman street scene: a portable stove, stoked with wood by a small child, heats a cauldron of oil in which the fryer manipulates fish from his stall, neatly laid out on fronds of green leaves, after dipping in a bowl of batter, while a woman wraps a portion into a cone of paper for a customer. An establishment in the Via dei Librari today sells fried baccalà on paper plates with something of the raucous élan of Pinelli's Rome. Boni also mentions *cuscinetti*, similar to *pandorato*, in which thick slices of bread are stuffed with ham or anchovies and cheese, floured, then left to soak in egg and milk, and finally fried in boiling lard.

Bologna has a characteristically rich *fritto misto*, with the different elements prepared in various ways, and cooked in mainly in oil. *Crema fritta* is a surprisingly delightful delicacy, a fairly thick custard cooled, cut into shapes, dipped in egg, covered in breadcrumbs, and fried in lard or oil. Florence, Naples, and Piedmont all have their special versions. Some include croquettes of chicken or potato, or the ultimate in complexity, the *stecchi* of Bologna—morsels of sweetbreads and chicken livers, precooked, and put onto toothpicks or small skewers with cubes of cheese and tongue with slivers of truffle, enclosed in a thick béchamel, dipped in seasoned egg and breadcrumbs, and fried in oil—a far cry from Pinelli's cheap vegetable fritters.

FRIULI–VENEZIA GIULIA

is northeast of VENETO, with borders on Austria and Slovenia in the northeast, a coastline on the Adriatic, and abutting on TRENTINO ALTO ADIGE to the northwest. The region shares a confusing story, with people and territories battled over for centuries, the woes of geography and history bringing conflict and misery right up to the destruction of the last two world wars. But the mixture of nations, languages, and boundaries, constantly shifting in a shared landscape and food culture, leaves much in common—cheeses, pork products, breads and cakes—while encompassing influences from the Balkans, Austria, Germany, and Hungary. After the collapse of the Pax Romana in approximately AD 180, waves of barbarians came and went, even Guelphs and Ghibellines, trampling over the territory.

By the mid-15th century, the city that has a particular resonance for food historians, Aquileia, had lost most of its territorial prestige to Venice, leaving its patriarch, Ludovico Trevisan, patron of the renowned renaissance cook Maestro Martino, with a city in decline but a fine ecclesiastical title and a reputation for successful combat against the Turks. A medal cast in 1561 commemorating an earlier battle at Anghiari liberating Tuscany and the Papal States shows a tough but humorous profile, bareheaded, with a tonsure looking more like a foot soldier's helmet. His cook, Martino de Rossi, had already worked in Milan for a soldier of fortune, Trivulzio, and would have understood the tastes and temperament of these powerful personages. Mantegna caught Trevisan's craggy ferocity in a portrait of the 1460s; one understands why Martino explains that you without question season a dish according to the tastes of your master (the warrior-priest Trevisan was a renowned gourmet as well as a collector of gems and antiquities). The esteem in which both cook and patron were held is clear in the exquisite title page of the presentation copy of Martino's cookery book, inscribed by Bartolomeo Sanvito in Rome, where Trevisan feasted and caroused with Platina and Cardinal Francesco Gonzaga in his villa at Albano. All this is a long way from Aquileia, but serves to illustrate the moral authority of the patriarchy even when its territorial power had waned. As Aquileia declined, damaged by earthquake, and its estuary silted up, Udine became the dominant city of the area.

Friuli–Venezia Giulia has areas of plains and rolling hills, with vines and fields of maize, and prealpine and woodland areas, with grazing and pasture, where transhumance is still part of the rural economy; the mountainous Carnia region behind; and the Carso, overlooking the Bay of Trieste. The cuisine, though simple, is varied, with influences from a great many races and nations that persist, as do the many dialects and languages, in spite of industrialisation and changing eating habits. Open throughout history to influences from Germany, Austria, and Slav countries, the region has been a gateway to food cultures that do not really engage with the rest of the peninsula. *Gubana*, also a speciality of Slovenia, is made in Valle de Natisone. The combination of sweet fruit and nuts and spices with meat and cheese mixtures which is characteristic of so much modern and historic European cooking was once also found in Italy, and survives here. Trieste has fine fish dishes, including a way with shellfish; in *canocie in busara*, clams are layered with breadcrumbs, parsley, garlic, salt, and pepper, dowsed with white wine, and cooked, covered, quickly. Fillets of sea bass are cooked in what sounds like filo pastry with pounded cooked shellfish. *Liptauer* relates to Austro-Hungarian recipes: salted anchovies are mixed with butter, ricotta, chopped onion, capers, mustard, paprika, parsley, kummel, and chives. Trieste was the port of the Austro-Hungarian empire, and battled over throughout its history, used as a political pawn, but receptive to many gastronomic influences, Venetian, Austrian,

Greek, Hungarian, Slav, and Jewish, with marjoram, cumin, oregano, and garlic adding a distinctive touch. The *gnocco gigante* is a huge dumpling made of breadcrumbs, flour, eggs, butter, salt, and ham, wrapped in a cloth and steamed like a traditional pudding—but this is Hapsburg, not British; it is also found in Trento and Alto Adige. Pastries similar to *strudel* and cakes like *sacher torte* and *dobos* are enjoyed in Trieste, as well as *presnitz*, similar to the *gubana* of Slovenia, and *putizza*, where the dough is made without yeast. The nutty, spicy, fruity fillings of these rolled, then coiled, serpentine creations make them a good accompaniment to ham, as well as a sweet course.

The natural grazing on hilly and mountainous terrain produces some fine cheeses. The best known is MONTASIO, now made in cooperatives and cheese factories all over the region, but there are others, like the many variations of *latteria* from independent producers, refugees from the straitjacket imposed by *montasio*'s DOP coverage—light, unpasteurised, soft, or hard, for example, *latteria di Fagagna*, a fine cheese, the product of pasture, microclimate, breed of cow, and a certain way of doing things, and *malga*, from the alpine pastures of Udine and Pordenone, milder and creamier than *montasio*, at one time made in small family units. A fresh cheese that originated in the dribbling overflow from the early stages of cheese-making, *sbrica*, is enjoyed fried or grilled, as is *frico balacin*, a fresh cheese intended to be fried in oil or grilled, reminding us of *haloumi* cheeses from Turkey and Cyprus. Ricotta, a way of using up the whey from cheese-making, to be eaten straightaway, can be made to last longer by salting, fermenting, or smoking, as with *scuete fumade*, and in these forms makes a condiment for many dishes of the region.

The small town of San Daniele, equidistant from mountain and sea, gives its name to a cured ham which is the equal of that made in the region around Parma. Its renown depends on the microclimate of the valley of the river Tagliamento in the foothills below Udine, where cold winds from the north collide with soft warm breezes from the Adriatic, and although the various stages of production are controlled by the consortium which supervises the quality of this DOP product, it is this factor above all that gives the ham its rich sweetness. The breed of pig, its food, even when sourced outside Friuli, its weight and condition are monitored before the phases of trimming, salting, pressing—some restful, some energetic—as it lumbers towards maturity; then the finished product is checked for quality and can be sold bearing the logo of the consortium. There are both industrial and artisan producers. But pigs alone are not the only source of hams; geese have been reared for centuries in the region and adjoining countries, enjoying a semiwild existence. Salted and then dried legs are prepared in Basso Friuli and in particular Palmanova, where Antonello Pessot of the establishment Jolanda De Colò is pioneering both traditional and innovative goose products. Cooked goose hams, raw and cooked salami, goose necks and skin containing mixtures of pork and fowl are seasoned, cooked, and cured, transforming a peasant product into a sophisticated luxury. Other rustic products, *pitina*, *petuccia*, and *peta*, were originally a way of using up and preserving the less palatable meat of various animals, often a mixture of pork, beef, goat, and sheep, and wild meat, but are now delicacies; the finely chopped meats are seasoned with pungent herbs and garlic, wild fennel, rosemary, cumin, juniper berries, crushed peppercorns, depending on the locality, rolled in polenta flour, and smoked. They can then be eaten raw or softened in polenta as it cooks, and thanks to a SLOW FOOD *presidio* have a local and national following. *Muset* is a cooking sausage rather like cotecchino, with a filling of some of the less amenable parts of a pig's head, the cartilaginous snout, together with chopped pork and the *cotenna* which feature in other versions, flavoured with spices and salt, and boiled gently for a long time.

FROG, *rana, ranocchio*, can be found in Italy in two varieties, *Rana esculenta*, the edible frog, and *Rana temporaria*, the common frog. Its delicate flesh is good fried in a light batter, or in a FRITTATA, or—especially in rice-growing areas—in a risotto, made with a broth from the parts of the creature discarded after removing the legs, which are cooked along with the rice. Frogs are to be had in any area with stagnant or flowing water. The area around Bologna was and still is famous for them. They need to be a decent size; unlike many cultures, Italians eat the whole animal. Scappi described how in 1564 he cooked frogs specially for Pope Pius IV—he dipped the prepared creatures in flour and fried them in oil with whole parboiled cloves of garlic and parsley and served them sprinkled with salt and pepper. They could also be served with fresh verjuice, and Scappi noted that frogs were at their best when this was available from May through October: *"mentre dura l'agresto le rane son buone."* Frogs are good while verjuice is around, meaning the tart fresh grapes from which verjuice is made (Scappi, bk. 3, p. 138r.). A more sophisticated dish, *Zuppa di rane alla monticiana*, from *Roma in Cucina*, by Luigi Carnacina and Vincenzo Buonassisi, cuts the legs off cleaned and prepared frogs and cooks the carcasses in a broth made from chopped celery, garlic, fresh herbs and a pinch of nutmeg simmered in water and white wine, then cooks the legs in the strained broth, bones them, and serves the soup over slices of country bread with some soaked *funghi porcini* cooked in butter, chopped parsley, and pecorino.

FUNGHETTO, AL, means to be "sliced as one does with MUSHROOMS," and can be applied to dishes in which artichokes, zucchini, and other vegetables are prepared thinly sliced, and fried in oil with garlic and parsley. *Trifolati* is another word used to describe vegetables, and also kidneys, cooked in this way.

FUSORITTO DA NARNI, REALE. *See* CERVIO.

g

GALANGAL, *Alpinia officinarum* (lesser galangal) and *Alpinia galanga* (greater galangal), are two of many fragrant rhizomes of the GINGER family, with a flavour reminiscent of camphor and ginger, exported from China and the Far East. Galangal is stimulant and carminative, useful for digestive problems, and was used in the past in cooking and medicine. The essential oil is still used to flavour liqueurs and bitters. Many more fragrant or bitter roots and rhizomes were used in the past, in gastronomy and medicine, some, like mandrake, deriving supposed powers from their strange anthropomorphic shape.

GAMBERO is one of the family of crustaceans, whose hard outer carapace is like that of many insects and which are not, strictly speaking, shellfish at all. The Italian term *frutti di mare* is a useful expression to cover many delicacies, from sea urchins to clams and prawns (shrimp), *gamberi*. There are many varieties of gambero, from the various kinds of *mazzancolla* or *gambero imperiale*—much loved in Lazio—whose delicate sweetness is best enjoyed grilled with garlic, olive oil, and parsley, to the two different kinds of *gambero rosso*, sometimes known as *gamberoni*, with a more pronounced flavour, making them suitable for soups and stews. There is a pink one, *gambero rosa*, a common prawn, *gamberello*, and a freshwater *gambero di acqua dolce*. The small ones known as shrimp in Great Britain are *gamberetto* or *gamberell*. SCAMPI belong to the lobster family (*see also* SHRIMP).

GAME, wild meat, is farmed, managed, and found roaming in a natural state (*brado*) in many regions of Italy. The principal game animals are WILD BOAR, *cinghiale*; red DEER (stag, hind, calf), *cervo*; roe deer (buck, doe, kid), *capriolo*; fallow deer (buck, doe, fawn) *daino*; chamois *camoscio*; wild goat, *stambecco*; moufflon (horned wild sheep), *muflone*; hare, lepre; rabbit, *coniglio*.

Over the past 20 years, various different approaches to wild meat have been discussed, from intensive rearing in enclosed areas to the management of animals in the wild. Meat for the pot is not the only issue, though; economists, ecologists, nutritionists, zoologists, hunters, and tourists all have voices, and not always in sweet harmony. A quick buck is not in it for anyone. The high costs of fencing, veterinary services, and supplementary feed see to that. Apart from being a gastronomic resource, game and its management might be a solution to the problems of the deterioration of marginal land that is no longer cultivated, to the drift of population to towns and cities, and to ecological damage of many kinds. There is an international trade in hinds for breeding purposes, and clients as far away as New Zealand, where the lush grazing is quite different from forage in the Apennines, can affect the balance of production in Europe. The distribution of game meat in Italy is usually local, and visitors

Garlic and peppers hang outside a small trattoria in Sicily. (Getty Images)

can get information from tourist offices and restaurants.

GAR-FISH, *aguglia,* with a snout like a needle or steeple, hence the name, makes fine bone-free fillets, or small ones can be fried or grilled whole.

GARLIC, *Allium sativum, aglio,* has a long history, going back to ancient Egypt and beyond; it has an ambivalent role in Italian gastronomy, where we are exhorted to exercise moderation, in the teeth of an inclination to use lots of this pungent, fragrant bulb, with its potent medicinal powers, and its wide range of uses in cooking. Anglo-Saxons and North Americans, many brought up in a climate of abhorrence of the "stinking rose," do indeed use it in extreme quantities, as a reaction to the puritanical disgust of our parents, whose exhortation to "think of others" is still trotted out as a reason for abstinence. When "others" eat garlic all the time,

we can be sure of not giving offence when we eat it ourselves, for regular eaters never seem to be incommoded by its use.

Garlic used to be described as the "theriac of the poor" (theriac was a medicament concocted as a universal remedy by physicians and less scrupulous operators), and the benign effects of garlic are considerable—apart from warding off devils and scorpions, it is good for colds, fevers, blood pressure, and digestive problems and has disinfectant and healing properties. Pisanelli describes how seafaring men used garlic in enormous quantities, to make their sometimes rancid stores less disagreeable, to give strength for their laborious tasks, and settle the stomach in rough seas. The active principle is a sulphurous compound, diallyl disulphide, which is released when the cell tissues of the bulb are damaged by chopping or crushing. This is the smell disliked by many, which is changed by cooking into something mild, sweet, and delicious. Thus garlic in the kitchen can take on many different personalities—raw and crude, it has an aggressive bite which disappears when lightly cooked in oil, or simmered in stews, when it becomes sweet and mild. Crushed with salt and other seasonings, it gives pungency to sauces and marinades; it can be mild and nutty when pickled. It gives liveliness to a salad. In Italian cooking today, garlic is used with moderation and caution, and one does sometimes wonder if this is a legacy of the well-bred, middle-class attitude of Artusi and Boni and later writers. Garlic is not thrown indiscriminately into every dish today, and it is impossible to tell if caution and moderation are really part of Italy's culinary heritage or a marker of bourgeois conventionality and insecurity. Garlic in the popular *olio aglio peperoncino* dressing for spaghetti is sometimes prepared by lightly browning the garlic and chillies in the oil used to flavour the pasta and then discarding them, but the pleasures of biting on a chunk of sweet, golden garlic or fierce chilli enhance the enjoyment of this simple sauce. A garlic-based sauce from the past is *agliata*, made from skinned WALNUTS pounded with raw garlic, white breadcrumbs soaked in water or vinegar, salt, and olive oil. The modern version is a creamy amalgam of crushed garlic and olive oil. *Agliata* today is a speciality of Liguria, similar to the Provencal *aïoli*. Garlic is used as both flavouring and preservative in many cured meats and fresh sausages.

Wild garlic, *aglio selvatico*, turns out to be the name of many wild garlic-smelling plants of the Liliaceae family, and there is a profusion of botanical and regional names to add to the confusion, *aglietta, aglio orsino, aglio giallo*. The kind with a beautiful star-like white flower and thin leaves like chives grows wild and can be cultivated easily. It is a useful addition to salads and chopped into *frittatas* or stuffings.

GAROFOLATO is typical Roman dish in which *girello*, a cut of beef from the back of the thigh—thick flank or topside—is cooked very slowly, larded with seasoned pancetta, in a dense sauce of red wine and tomatoes and the usual aromatics—celery, onion, carrot, garlic, parsley, chopped and fried pancetta, a pinch of nutmeg and pepper, and two or more cloves. It is a good example of the survival of spices in a cuisine which claims to be robust and simple.

GARUM. *See* FISH, PRESERVED; ROMAN FOOD.

GARZONI, GIOVANNA

(1600–1670), earned fame and fortune with her detailed and rather sugary portraits of the ruling Medici grand dukes of Florence and members of the House of Savoy, but her portraits of fruit and vegetables are what we value today; they have wayward personalities that she chose not to show in the images of her patrons. Garzoni was born in Ascoli Piceno in the Marche and died in Rome. She studied in Venice, where her family came from, and later worked in Naples, Rome, Turin, Paris, and Florence, returning, comfortably off and famous, to Rome, where she had always wanted to live, for the last years of her life. This remarkable, intelligent, and independent woman chose to do miniature painting, calligraphy, and painting from nature, work that she could pursue in a domestic background. She worked from home, and secured well-paid positions that made this possible; arrangements that provided a basic salary fleshed out with extras, gifts of jewellery, worldly goods, and extra cash. In return, she executed commissions, often copies of devotional works, portraits, and the studies of flowers, fruit, and vegetables that we are amazed by today. At a time when the concept "scientific method" was only just emerging, she and many of the artists employed by the Medici grand dukes of Tuscany were producing accurate representations of the visual world, painting the plants and the products of the Tuscan territories, observing, noting, recording. Garzoni's devout faith must have reinforced her usefulness to the Medici, whose support for Galileo had put them in an equivocal position with the Catholic Church. She eventually became a member of the painters' guild of Saint Luke in Rome, was on friendly terms with the Barberini family, but kept up contacts with the Medicis, sending them more fruit portraits, and continuing to draw a pension from them.

The best place to see Garzoni's work is the Galleria Palatina in the Palazzo Pitti in Florence. The small paintings (large miniatures) are executed in gouache on parchment in a delicate stippled technique. Unlike the formal, static compositions of the still life painters of the Netherlands, her work has a strangely surreal quality. The bowls of fruit are balanced on amorphous rocky surfaces, against neutral backgrounds; perspective is wild and wilful; and her rendering of the subjects goes beyond accuracy into realms of disturbing clarity. A bowl of cherries flickers with movement; they seem still to be quivering on the branch, their leaves are fresh, the stalks fleshy and upright, as fresh as the white roses in their midst. A bumblebee crawls, not flies, over the ambivalent background; a broad bean and four hazelnuts are scattered by the bowl. A dish of peas, mature, pallid, and almost dried (a reminder that field peas were a crop for keeping as a staple for lean days, when their broth, after long boiling, was a substitute for meat or chicken) is decorated with ephemeral fresh roses, pale pink and white, their delicacy and lightness contrasting with the coarseness of the peas. A dish of broad beans in an almost dried state, not the luxury dish of early spring, when they could be eaten raw, is accompanied by two carnations, perhaps a reference to the spices—cloves—needed to give savour to those dishes of boiled pulses that were the staple food of the countryside. This painting is a reminder that the Medici dukes did not

confine their interests to exotic specimens, but were active in promoting agriculture in their domains, economic prosperity and safeguards against famine being as important as rare luxuries from abroad. A blue and white bowl of artichokes shows three different varieties, still to be seen in the markets in Florence in the early spring, with a contrasting pink rose and some ripe strawberries still on the branch—always this emphasis on freshness. A monumental pomegranate, caught at the moment of bursting open to reveal its glistening seeds, towers against a sombre rock, while a fragile grasshopper twitches beside it. The parchment crackles with movement, emphasised by the static brown lumps of two chestnuts and a snail; the fruit has a presence which might have inspired Meléndez on his travels in Italy a century later.

A departure from the usual dish or bowl of fruit or vegetables is a painting done in 1648 for Don Lorenzo de' Medici, who had asked for it to include a portrait of Bencino Brugniolaio, an elderly *contadino*, who emerges from a rocky background carrying two hens, surrounded by an assortment of local products, eggs, two kinds of cheese, a cured ham, some salami, apples, grapes, chestnuts, citrus fruit, celery, artichokes, broad beans, cherries, a large melon on a dish, a straw-wrapped bottle of wine, a few birds, and a large soppy white dog waddling into the picture from the left. The composition is strange, with changing perspectives, and no consistency in the relative sizes of the objects, but their luminous colours, glowing in the unreal rugged landscape, are a celebration of the local products for the elderly prince (he died before the delivery of the painting) whose nostalgia for them must have been behind the commission.

Fruit and vegetables were not the only subjects in which surface texture and finish were desirable; the grand duke's agent reported from Rome on 18 December 1660 his frustrating search for a model: "I am looking, and have been for some time, for a spotted rabbit—there used to be plenty about, but so far all I can find are grey and white or black and white, and I would so like to find a really nice one to satisfy Garzoni" (Casale, 1991, p. 214). This might have been for a companion to a miniature listed in her account book, "A life-sized miniature of a hare for his Honour, who sent me a gold chain worth 100 scudi" (Casale, p. 216). By this time Garzoni was getting infirm—a portrait at that time shows a wise, humorous old face with red-rimmed eyes—but her skills were apparently undiminished. We appreciate her work today, not just for its artistic value, but because it tells us so much about the products of the time, and the attitudes of her contemporaries towards them.

GASTRO-LEGENDS.
See MYTHS.

GELATO. *See* ICE CREAM.

GERANIUM, *geranio odoroso, Geranium macrorrhizum, Pelargonium capitatum*, is interesting in the kitchen for the perfumed leaves of many varieties, especially the rose-scented ones, sometimes lemony, sometimes almost minty, which are used to flavour desserts, ice creams, sorbets, and summer drinks, and can sometimes be added, chopped, to salads.

GIANDUIA. *See* HAZELNUT.

GIEGHER, MATTIA, published three treatises on the art of pleating table linen, carving, and the duties of the chief steward. These were brought together in one volume and printed in Padua in 1639 by the printer Paolo Frambotto, who had purchased

the plates after Giegher's death of the plague in 1630. The volume on *scalcheria* had appeared in 1623 at the request of his students. Giegher was a Bavarian from Moosburg who had been employed by the German community in the law school of the University of Padua since 1616. We know nothing else about him; the engraved portrait in the book shows him at the age of 40, an elegantly clad man with soulful good looks and the tools of his trade, carving knife and fork, displayed in a cartouche. There is something surreal about the thought of students in one of the most prestigious universities of Europe solemnly pleating linen napkins, or carving fruit into the shape of animals and birds, and we can only conclude that the high table Giegher served in his role of steward was so renowned for elegance and luxury that the employees trained by him shared the distinction of students of weightier matters.

The first book on the creation of pleated and folded table napkins starts with simple images of the horizontally folded linen being bent into V-shaped vertical sections (to create a herringbone effect) and then twisted and curved into phantasmagorical creations like advanced origami, so that guests could discover their bread roll lurking beneath a galleon in full sail or a bishop's mitre. Fish, animals, birds, castles, and abstract geometric constructions flowed from the nimble hands of the master. Some of these linen sculptures, or *trionfi*, were conceived as table decorations in their own right, moulded and then starched in creations that rivalled the sugar sculptures or images carved in butter that were essential to the decorative scheme of the baroque BANQUET. The white card and paper decorations and pleated satin and silk structures that adorn altars for the Day of the Dead in Mexico are a survival of this art, combining Spanish traditions and native Indian design techniques. When Queen Christina of Sweden visited Rome in 1668, the artist Pietro Schor was commissioned to create her royal arms in pleated linen; she would have appreciated both the skills and the deference shown to her rank.

The art of carving was also illustrated in the *Tre trattati,* and here again the engraved plates are more illuminating than the text, with diagrams showing the sequence and direction of the different cuts, from goose to quail, sucking pig to loin of veal, with fold-out sections showing the range of carving knives and forks appropriate for each specific task. Whether held in the air or—in the case of large joints—displayed on a dish, carving was a performance art. The master carver in all his finery stood poised in front of the company, brandishing his implements, impaling and slicing with balletic flourishes, while the limbs, slivers, and juices fell neatly into the serving dish below, to be handed round to the admiring guests; a sort of parody of the arts of war and the chase, with a final consummation amidst the odours of spices and the perfumes of rosewater and musk, as pervasive as the incense of more sacred rites.

Fresh fruit did not escape this fate. Apples and pears were peeled with a narrow curved blade and a two-pronged fork in intricate patterns, while the thick-skinned citron lent itself to even more complex manipulation, transformed into animals, birds, acorns, and salamanders. Oranges, used as condiment and decoration, were slashed and sliced like the ribbons and embroidered velvets of the richly dressed guests, and perfumed like them with rosewater and spices.

The *Tre trattati* has lists of menus for the different seasons of the year, and a digression on *oglia podrida,* which, although said to be Spanish in origin, is so similar to the *gran bollito* of Padua that it merits a special description, and the comment that, served at the centre of a round table, it can be a course in itself, from which guests can select things. This indicates a mode of eating that, although rich and complex, is not as ostenta-tious as the succession of dishes in gross banquet menus. Some historians link this possible reference to the *gran bollito* of Padua to Galileo's astronomical butcher's bill for the period 11 December 1604 to 29 January 1605, when he may have been entertaining crowds of students and visiting professors with vast dishes of boiled meats.

GILT-HEAD BREAM, *orata,* was
described by Scappi in 1570: "Gilt-head bream are both large and small, the good ones have small scales and are silvery in appearance, with a line from head to tail and a transverse dark mark near the tail, a bifurcated tail, and teeth in four rows, that is two above and two below, very strong like humans' as have all fish in this family. Their season begins in November and lasts right until April." They are the most esteemed of the bream family, with a firm but delicate flesh, and can be distinguished from the others by a dark patch between the eyes. Scappi then gives some ways of cooking them: grilled, after marinating in a mixture of oil, vinegar, salt and fennel, basted with the marinade and carefully turned from time to time; or salted, floured, and fried in olive oil, and served hot with sliced lemons or bitter orange juice. In *pottaggio* they are scaled, gutted, washed, and simmered in an earthenware pot with oil, water, wine, verjuice, salt, cinnamon, saffron, prunes and dried cherries in winter, gooseberries and spring onions in summer, thickened if desired with ground almonds, and served with a sprinkling of chopped herbs.

Two hundred years later, Corrado suggests gilt-head bream simmered in water with salt, herbs and butter, served with a sorrel sauce, or—a wilfully rococo recipe—the boned fish stuffed with sweetbreads, herbs and spices, perfumed with truffles, baked doused in butter, and finished with a veal coulis.

GINGER, *Zingiber officinale, zenzero,* is the rhizome of a plant which has been used in India and Asia since the remotest times, and was one of the first spices to reach Europe. It is not clear if fresh ginger survived the long journeys of the spice routes or arrived in dried form, either with its skin still on, or peeled, blanched, and even bleached. The powdered form, like all powdered spices, can be easily adulterated, and loses its flavour rapidly. The rhizomes, when bruised, offer up their fragrance, sharper and stronger, rather musty, when dried, more vibrant when fresh, and can then be chopped or grated. Used in broth and marinades, ginger can neutralise undesirable flavours; this is one of its main functions in Chinese gastronomy. Another function is to warm and comfort those who are chilled; it has medicinal properties and is an aid to digestion, as well as a condiment. Mattioli writes in the 1560s of fresh, dried, and preserved ginger, and how the dried is inferior, as is salted or pickled ginger, which rapidly loses its aroma. It is not clear in what form it was available in the Middle Ages, where its use in spice mixtures implies a dried substance, but it was used freely in most combinations of spices. There is a recipe in the Casanatense manuscript, *Stuffà molto breve perfettissima* (a most perfect, rapid stew), in which young chickens are (jointed and) fried in lard, then finished with almond milk and verjuice, with finely chopped ginger, chopped dates, saffron, and salt. Dried ginger is not easy to chop—it would need pounding in a mortar; but preserved ginger can be cut with a knife, and must have been wonderful with the sweet fruitiness of the dates and the sharpness of the verjuice. In 1611, Baldassare Pisanelli described both fresh and dried ginger and tells how it is brought from Calcutta, fresh and preserved in sugar or honey.

In Italy today, ginger has disappeared from domestic use, and is found mainly in confectionery, usually dried, liqueurs, and sometimes, preserved in syrup, to flavour ices.

GIOVANNI DA UDINE was

born in Udine in 1487 and died in Rome in 1561. He worked in Giorgione's studio before coming to Rome to become a close friend and collaborator of Raphael. Together they enthusiastically excavated the paintings on the vaults of Nero's palace, the Domus Aurea, which had been deliberately buried from sight by his successor, Trajan, to be discovered centuries later and yield visual inspiration and technical understanding of the process of making frescoes. The swirling complexities of these decorations, which came to be known as *grottesche* (their location by then an underground cave or grotto) appealed to the sensibilities of the time, while the naturalistic details in them were congenial to Giovanni, who had drawn animals and plants with huge skill since childhood. He was thus the ideal collaborator in the ambitious execution of the paintings on the vaults of the *loggia* of the Farnesina, a villa in the countryside on the banks of the Tiber, then on the outskirts of Rome, commissioned by the rich banker Agostino Chigi. The *loggia* and its decorations were a link between the interior of the villa and the gardens and then the countryside beyond. The paintings on the vault represented the story of Psyche, but what interests us are the festoons which surround the narrative scenes, for in them Giovanni painted with wonderful accuracy and lightness of touch every known fruit, vegetable, plant, and flower of the time. For the food historian, the acres of dimpled flesh pale into insignificance beside the edible offerings. Described by Vasari as *"veramente stupendissimi"* (really stupendous), these are some of the earliest images of the products of Italian kitchen gardens, and whatever their symbolic or mythological importance, they are a rich source of information to us.

There are over 1,000 images, different views of a total of 160 subjects, accurate enough for botanists to identify most of them. We can pick out the ingredients used by Martino a generation earlier, and those Scappi would be cooking in the city for his various employers. It is exciting to see a rare representation of the elderflowers that featured in so many fritters and tarts, and the *fiori di finocchio*, the flower head, complete with blossoms and newly formed seeds of fennel; there is an early sighting of a coconut, with its humanoid features; ears of Indian corn long before they had become a staple food, and before the first printed illustration in Fuchs in 1542 and also from the New World, less than 20 years after their discovery, *Phaseolus vulgaris*, French beans, various gourds, and pumpkins (potatoes and tomatoes came later from areas of the New World not known to Columbus, and probably arrived in Italy from Spain, and so are not seen here); there are humble roots, various turnips and parsnips once common and now almost unknown; citrus fruits, including bitter oranges, ridged citrons, lemons, and little green limes; onions, garlic, spring onions, shallots; salsify, various kinds of carrot; members of the thistle family, including cardoons and artichokes; nuts—chestnuts, hazelnuts, acorns, walnuts, water chestnuts—all shown in characteristic degrees of ripeness; spinach and beets; various lettuces and cabbages, and some mushrooms.

GNOCCHI is a name for what we know as dumplings, but there is a much wider range to be found in Italy than in regional British cooking. Some gnocchi are made from potatoes, breadcrumbs, or cornmeal, with or without flour and flavourings of herbs and cheese, vegetables, or sweet things, like cocoa or prunes. They are usually cooked on their own in plenty of salted water, dressed with the appropriate sauce, often melted butter and cheese, and popped for a while into a hot oven to absorb the flavours. Sometimes the dough is rolled out, then cut into neat little shapes about the size of a

Freshly made gnocchi. Their textured surface helps hold sauce. (Shutterstock)

cork, and pressed against the ribs of a fork or a coarse cheese grater, to give a texture to hold the sauce; or they can be simply spooned or cut into lumps that go directly into the pan of boiling water. Artusi gently mocked a lady whose gnocchi disappeared completely in the pot, a vanishing act due to insufficient flour to hold the mixture together. Some gnocchi can be made from shapes of cooked polenta or semolina (*gnocchi alla romana*), which is spread out to dry, then layered with cheese and butter, and finished in the oven. Spinach gnocchi are made with potatoes, flour, and spinach, a more homogenous mixture than the *ravioli nudi* of Florence, a looser, lighter mixture of spinach, egg, parmesan, and ricotta, just dusted with flour to hold them together, put gently into a pot of gently boiling water, and fished out the moment they bob to the surface. Gnocchi are usually eaten instead of pasta as a first course, but can be served as a *contorno* to some dishes.

GOAT AND KID.

Goat, *capra*, is valued for its capacity to turn sparse grazing and poor forage into milk for cheese. The meat of an adult is tough and not very nice to eat, although there is a recipe from LIGURIA which involves a long marinade in aromatics, and very slow cooking with herbs and white wine. Where herds are big and animals can be spared, the hind legs are cured to make a ham, the VIOLINO DI CAPRA in Valtellina and Valchiavenna, which as it is sliced, appears—with a stretch of the imagination—to resemble a violin being played, or the *mocetta* of the VALLE D'AOSTA, though this is generally made with chamois or wild goat. Scappi, when describing game recipes, distinguishes between *capra*, *camozza* (female goat and chamois) and *becco*, *stambecco*, or *arcibecco* (male or castrated of the same species), referring us to recipes for mature lamb or kid.

Kid, *capretto*, is good eating, especially when milk fed, and was esteemed in the past as even better than milk-fed lamb or piglet.

The flesh is pale pink, and the flavour, even before the animal has eaten grass, is pronounced, but the meat is very low on fat, tender, and delicious, and can be cooked in all the ways you would baby lamb. A recipe from Puglia combines chunks of kid with sliced potatoes, onions, tomatoes, and a *trito* of garlic, herbs (thyme, marjoram, mint, pennyroyal, rosemary, and wild fennel), pecorino, salt, and pepper, all layered in an oven-proof dish, anointed with olive oil, and cooked slowly for several hours. A much earlier recipe from Scappi stuffs a kid with a mixture of dried fruit, sour fresh fruit, chopped ham and bacon, spices, and soft fresh cheese, spit roasts it slowly, and serves with stoned olives and bitter orange juice. The relatively strong flavour of kid lends itself to garlic, so Martino larded a quarter generously with bacon and slivers of garlic, basting it with a sauce of verjuice, egg yolks, pounded garlic, pepper, and a little good broth, and said it had to be *"ben cotto e magnato caldo caldo"* (well done and eaten really hot). Legs of kid, larded with bacon and rosemary, stewed in butter and spices, and served with that novelty a tomato sauce, delighted the aristocratic tables of 18th-century Naples. There it was considered a refined dish, but a Pinelli engraving shows a *caprarolo* in Rome a century later herding mischievous little kids through the streets, to be weighed up coldbloodedly by tough-looking proletarian housewives. Animals surplus to requirements were often sold young, rather than wasting resources fattening them up, so in Lazio and central Italy baby lamb and kid were cheap and plentiful. (Today organic kid meat is obtainable from small farmers, but when asked for milk-fed lamb, farmers laugh in your face; it is more economic for them to rear hearty fat lambs.) Elizabeth David gave a typical recipe for leg of kid cooked slowly in white wine and marsala with vegetables and garlic, flavoured with orange peel and coriander, marjoram or oregano, with orange juice added at the end.

GOBY, *ghiozzo,* is a small undistinguished fish, but Alan Davidson (Davidson, p. 154) quotes Martial, *Epigrams* 13.88, referring to the area of lagoons from which Venice was to evolve:

> At Venice, famed for dainty dishes,
> The Gobies rank the first of fishes.

This couplet may be intended, with Martial's usual irony, to express puzzlement at the Venetians' choice. More recent evidence confirms that his observation was accurate. Scappi said that Venetians cooked them in malmsey (*malvasia*), with spices and vinegar, and today there are less refined Venetian recipes which make the most of this fish, which they call *gô,* including a BRODETTO in which the prepared fishes are cooked in oil flavoured by browning onion and garlic which are then removed, continued with vinegar or wine, and finished in sea water or salted water eaten with polenta. If the *brodetto* is copious, it and the fish can be pushed through a sieve and a risotto made in the usual way with the resultant liquid.

GOOSE, *oca,* is a large, web-footed bird, reared for centuries and valued for its feathers, fat, and meat. As with the pig, nothing was wasted, and it thus had a special place in traditional Jewish gastronomy, as a substitute for pork, providing delicious and versatile fat (there is a recipe in Scappi for rendering down goose fat), cured cuts, and salami, and dishes like stuffed neck. Goose and chicken fat were the substitute for pork fat and bacon in Jewish versions of Italian food. A recipe recently revived in Mortara in Lomellina, from a surviving Jewish *salumiere,* is strips of breast meat along with rolled-up pieces of skin, salted and cured.

A young goose in the past had the same prestige as a sucking pig, with a proverb quoted by Camporesi: "*Porco d'un mese, oca di tre, è un mangiar da re*" (A piglet one month old, and a gosling of three, are food for a king). Goose used to be the traditional food for the feast of All Saints, 1–2 November, and Tassoni in his comic epic poem "*La secchia rapita*" (The stolen bucket; *secchia* is also the name of a local river) said: "*E'l giorno d'Ogni Santi al dí nascente / Ognun partí de la campagna rasa, / e tornò lieto a mangiar l'oca a casa*" (On All Saints' Day as day breaks, everyone leaves for the bleak countryside, and returns joyfully, to eat a goose at home). Artusi has an unfeeling anecdote about a comfortably-off peasant who treated his friends to a meal on the feast of San Giuseppe, every course using goose, with considerable gastric retribution.

Traditionally roasted with a stuffing of chestnuts and fruit, goose is a dauntingly massive and rich dish for those with fear of fat. Recent innovations in the rearing and processing of geese have encouraged a growing market for preserved goose in a multitude of forms, many of them reassuringly lean. Areas in Lombardy and the Veneto, where good grass grazing abounds, have seen a renaissance in goose gastronomy, and select cuts, both fresh and cured, are now more popular than the whole bird. (*See* SALAME D'OCA.)

Geese were one of the earliest creatures to be domesticated, mentioned in Homer, loved in Roman times, and said to have saved the Capitol by repulsing marauding Gauls in 390 BC. Roman gourmets wrote of the delights of goose liver, delicious in itself, and *foie gras* from force-fed creatures. Italy has thus a sound claim to be the originator of this delicacy, with a product claimed to be superior to the commercialised versions of France. The Italian for liver, *fegato* is derived from the Latin *ficatum,* meaning the liver of a goose and pig fed on figs.

GOOSEBERRY, *uva spina, uva crespina, uva marina, Ribes grossularia,* grows wild as well as being cultivated for its acidic fruit, used green or ripe. It had in the past many uses, in sauces, preserved, and as an ingredient

Ripe gooseberries on the vine. (Shutterstock)

in tarts and savoury dishes. Its fruity acidity made it a good substitute for verjuice, although Castelvetro saw verjuice as an alternative to this agreeable fruit, explaining that it was a refreshing antidote to the terrible heat of summer. Like Mattioli, he preferred them sour rather than ripe. It is now thought of as an English preference, as in the case of gooseberry sauce with a fatty fish like mackerel, but cooks used it to temper rich stews and broths, together with parsley, and its medicinal uses were many: to cure fevers, stimulate the appetite, quench thirst, and soothe pregnant women.

GORGONZOLA is a soft cheese, veined with a bluish green mould, which can be mild or piquant. It is made in PIEDMONT and LOMBARDY, including the provinces of Bergamo, Brescia, Como, Cremona, Pavia and Milan in Lombardy, and Cuneo, Novara, and Vercelli in Piedmont. Gorgonzola is a relatively recent name, that of the town which was once the centre of production, although now manufacture is based in Novara. It used to be referred to as a version of *stracchino*: *erborinato*, or "parsley-coloured." Production today is both industrial and artisan, and some traditional practises have been superseded—cold storage systems replacing the damp, cold caves, or *ghiacciaie* (ice pits), where part of the maturing process went on, and the moulds and penicillin spores are now introduced artifi-

cially, encouraged by the insertion of metal rods to give them air, rather than from the environment, partially assisted by the insertion of hardwood nails. Some versions of gorgonzola are made using morning and evening milk, *a due paste*, a "two curd" cheese, encouraging microbes from the atmosphere to get to work, and some are made from only one milking, *a una pasta*, with added RENNET, milk enzymes, and penicillin spores, producing a sweeter, milder cheese. Quality and standards are maintained by a consortium based in Novara. Rich and fatty, with a good amount of protein and vitamins A, B₁, B₂, and D, but easy to digest on account of the proteolytic action of the moulds, gorgonzola is a versatile cheese in the kitchen, as well as a superb table cheese. It is used in a risotto instead of parmesan, melted in cream as a sauce for gnocchi or pasta, and used with butter to season polenta.

GRAINS OF PARADISE, melegueta pepper, *Aframomum melegueta*, *aframomo*, is a spice from tropical West Africa, with round greyish-brown seeds, a little bigger than peppercorns, with a strong, pungent, peppery aroma, with a whiff of cardamom, which was used in the past in spice mixtures. A different spice, which looks similar, is *Afromomum granum-paradisi*. Both these can sometimes be found in North African spice mixtures like *ras el hanout*. They are both more peppery and less fragrant than allspice, which is rounder and sweeter. Costanzo Felici mentions their use in sausages, along with coriander and nigella, and today it is in the commercial production of liqueurs, confectionery, and cured meat that it is still used rather than in the home.

GRANA PADANO is a hard, long-keeping cheese made in LOMBARDY, PIEDMONT, EMILIA-ROMAGNA, and the VENETO. The official definition reads:

"produced in the entire territory of the provinces of Alessandria, Asti, Cuneo, Novara, Turin, Vercelli, Bergamo, Brescia, Como, Cremona, Milan, Pavia, Sondrio, Varese, Trento, Padua, Rovigo, Treviso, Venice, Verona, Vicenza, Ferrara, Forli, Piacenza, Ravenna and neighbouring communes in the province of Mantua and Bologna, forming a continous area." It has been protected by its DOP since 1996. Its long history of rivalry with *parmigiano reggiano* (*see* PARMESAN) need not blind us to the similarities. Both are made with partially skimmed cow's milk from morning and evening milking, as described in the entry for parmesan.

The cheese gets its name from *Padana felix*, the Pianura Padana, the vast alluvial plain of the river Po, a huge geographical and political area, with a mysterious past and a complex present. Once an area of forests and vast inland waters, the *terremare*, whose earliest inhabitants, were extinct before the arrival of the Etruscans, it looks today as different as possible from its recent past, The forests and massive inland lakes, the ponds and swamps and isolated little towns on patches of raised land have all merged into, as seen from the air, a vast patchwork of neat fields, with an almost total absence of trees, divided by symmetrical irrigation canals, crossed by an inexorable network of motorways, and slowly silting up with industrial estates, white goods factories, intensive agribusiness, and housing developments. Nothing survives of the lost lake of Gerundo, some 50 by 25 kilometres in extent, save legends of dragons and giants with pestilential breath, who terrorised the lakeside villages; huge iron rings once set into castle walls for mooring the large open-water craft, hewn from the trunks of oak trees, and the bones of long-dead mammoths or whales, that were preserved in local churches as the mortal remains of these tyrants. The dragon, beside whom the Loch Ness monster was a mere tadpole, had the head of a bison and the body of a serpent, but his pestilential breath was likely to have been the malarial scourge of a tiny winged dragon, the anopheles mosquito (Pederiali, 1985).

The Romans saw agricultural potential in this vast plain and set up drainage channels and great highways, which disappeared when the empire crumbled, to be renewed in the 10th century and then vigorously continued by the various monastic orders. The ponds and swamps of Gerundo had vanished by the 13th century, replaced by the fertile plains where *grana padana* is now produced. The lost lake and the vanished forest remain as gastronomic ghosts—a taste for plump grilled frogs, strains of pig that evoke their semiwild ancestors—and in the fogs that seep up from the inextinguished water table and the mighty and still undisciplined river to envelop the incomparable *culatello.*

The *grana padano* praised by Giulio Landi in his *Formaggiata di Sere Stentato* of 1542 is referred to as *formaggio piacentino*, using just one of the many names applied to this cheese. Readers who survive the tedium of his *dotta e faceta* (learned and facetious) discourse, padded out with smug literary references and schoolboy smut, are rewarded with rare flashes of simple description and common sense. He scorned the sententious Latin tag "*Caseus est sanus, quem dat avara manus*" (cheese is only wholesome in miserly portions), pointing out that although it might have been true of some harsh and indigestible cheeses, his *piacentino* is a benign delicacy that can be eaten in large quantities, unlike the cheeses made elsewhere, which should indeed be taken sparingly. Then, in an admirably brief account, he contrasted the brutish peasants who made *provolone* in Rome with the fragrant "shepherdesses" back home, whose white hands milked the cows and then transferred the liquid to shining clean vessels, adding nice fresh rennet, and when the milk had coagulated, slowly heated the curds in huge well-washed bell-shaped vats, half the height of a man, breaking down the mass (Landi, p. 53)."*Bisogna molta arte e cognitione in saperlo ben condurre al fine, e conoscere quando egli è bene stagionato e temperatamente cotto*" (There needs to be considerable art and experience in knowing how to achieve this end, and recognise when it is just ready and properly cooked). This is indeed the critical part of the whole process. Then the by now solid mass is removed from the vats and put into clean white hoops to drain. (At which point Landi loses the plot in a lubricious account of the maidens with their blond tresses tied back, diaphanous skirts hitched up, bending over their tasks to reveal shapely legs in red stockings, plump white arms, and massive firm bosoms . . .) Breathlessly he resumes with a description of how the milkmaids let the forms drain for four days, after which they are salted (with the special salt of Piacenza, got from deep salt water wells, pure, white, and clean), then washed, carefully dried, and anointed, with the same alluring gestures, with the best olive oil.

The cleanliness and scrupulousness of the process is one explanation for the renown of *grana padano*, then and now—a cheese which ages to a gentle maturity, keeps well, transports without loss of quality, and is versatile in its use. The version made in and around Lodi is now almost extinct; it is said to have inspired the attentions of San Bassiano, bishop in the 5th century, who detected, and punished, a little black devil who had made a pact with an unscrupulous cheese-maker, tipping the scales to his advantage. What we cannot be sure of is how close it was to the one we know today, for the breed most used now is Frisian, and the grazing and fodder have been modified to meet huge worldwide demands, putting a strain on both producers and the consortium which monitors the quality of their product. With the help of the sinister-sounding *unifeed*, it is now possible for a computer-controlled machine to trundle along state-of-the-art, concrete, temperature-controlled cowsheds, dispensing selected and carefully blended food to groups of cows with different dietary requirements, without either the cattle or their keepers getting their feet dirty. When the permitted *unifeed* is made up of organic hay and other fodder grown in the locality, and does not include silage or commercially marketed material, it can increase production of good-quality milk at lower cost and meet the criteria of *agricoltura biologica*. Romantic visions and publicity shots of black and white cattle disporting themselves like kittens in rolling green pastures are not compatible with all of today's agriculture.

GRANCHIO. *See* CRAB.

GRANITA

GRANITA is one of the great family of ices, in its simplest form a slightly slushy, grainy mass of flavoured sweetened water, frozen and crushed to produce something between a drink and a water ice. One of the best loved is *granita di caffè con panna*, in which crystals of very strong sweet coffee are topped generously with unsweetened whipped cream. Made with fresh lemon juice or fruit syrup, a *granita* is the most refreshing of summer drinks. This innocent pleasure triggered a series of violent polemics in the 16th and 17th centuries, when medical authorities extolled the virtues of chilled drinks or angrily warned of their dangers. The origins of frozen ICE CREAM might be in this use of ice, with the addition of salt, to chill beverages beyond coldness and into something more like solidity.

GRAPE

GRAPE, *uva*, *Vitis vinifera*, is a fruit grown in most parts of Italy for wine-making and eating as a dessert. Our images of Italy have been formed by the configuration of rows of vines following the contours of the land, or creating straight repetitive vistas on flat plains, giving a rhythm and pattern to the countryside and its labours. The Romans cultivated vines and brought them to northern parts of the empire, while at home there was a wide range of wines of quality, from top to toe of the peninsula, and a wide range of its uses in the kitchen. Apicius mentions the use of *defrutum*, grape juice, MUST, reduced by boiling to a sweet fruity syrup, *sapa* (today another word for MOSTO COTTO) which could then be flavoured with fruit or spices. He also used *caroenum*, a similar product, but less syrupy, possibly made from reduced wine rather than must. Then there was *passum*, a raisin wine. All of these were used in various subtle ways to flavour sauces and cooked dishes; *oenogarum* was a mixture of wine and *defrutum* and other flavourings, pepper, and fish sauce which was used as sauce or condiment and an ingredient in cooked dishes. *Sapa* in Sardinia and *saba* in Emilia is used in desserts, as tart fillings, and in ice cream.

Dried grapes of various kinds were used in savoury dishes in the past, giving a combination of sweet fruitiness and acidity that are not to today's taste, but they do get into blood puddings, the *sanguinaccio* of the south, and Emilia-Romagna's *migliaccio*. As well as sauces and relishes using fresh and dried grapes, there were stews of rich meat and fowl enlivened with fruit and spices, reminiscent of Middle Eastern food today, perhaps the legacy of Arabic cuisine, long forgotten by the time Martino gives a *civero de salvaticina* in which game is stewed in wine and vinegar, then taken out, dried, fried in lard, and finished in a sauce made from raisins and almonds pounded together, mixed with toasted bread soaked in red wine, diluted with some of the broth, and simmered with cinnamon and ginger. Scappi has a sauce or relish made from raisins and prunes simmered in equal parts of wine and vinegar, then passed through a sieve and seasoned

with sugar and finely ground cloves, cinnamon, pepper, and nutmeg. Few recipes today use these fruity combinations; one or two dishes for quail or wild birds with fresh grapes are a pale shadow of them. Verjuice gave a fruity acidity in the past, and sometimes whole unripe grapes would be added to a recipe, as in a chicken dish enjoyed by Platina in Poggio Bracciolini's household (Platina, p. 277). Italian cooks today prefer the many varieties of vinegar available, or a squeeze of lemon on a finished dish.

Cooking with wine usually involves adding it at an early stage, after meat or chicken has been browned in a BATTUTO, and allowed to evaporate completely before adding any other liquid. When cooking regional dishes, it is agreeable to use wine from the same region, if at all possible, and a little of something really good goes a long way, and adds a resonance a cheap wine could not give.

Castelvetro in exile was tactfully reticent about English beer, but there is nostalgia and humour in his memories of the profusion of wine in his native land, where thirsty travellers would be warned off water, most unsafe, and offered wine instead, and passersby would be offered grapes by workers in the vineyards, so profuse were the crops.

GRAPPA is a spirit originally distilled from the *vinace* left from the pressing of grapes for wine. It is mentioned briefly here because of its use in cooking. Now that designer grappas are all over the place, it is possible to choose a subtle flavour to splash over, say, a sea bass wrapped in Parma ham, with a few sage leaves and a dash of grated parmesan, and baked fast in a hot oven. A slug of grappa to dissolve the residues from a fried escalope or steak of venison adds a pungent whiff to a suitably robust meat. Grappa can also work well in desserts, as when poured by Franco Taruschio over Elizabeth David's persimmon *granita* (Taruschio, 1995, p. 237).

GRATERS. *See* KITCHEN EQUIPMENT.

GREEK GASTRONOMY, INFLUENCE OF.

Julius Caesar's custom during his campaigns in Gaul was to hold separate dinners for the Greeks and the Romans in his party. The separation disguises the fact that Roman food and foodways were heavily influenced by Greek. The *Deipnosophists* of Athenaios, written in Greek in Rome (c. AD 200), is a kaleidoscope of Greek culinary tradition. Romans knew this to be older and richer than their own; they both despised and imitated it.

Knowledge of Greek lifestyles first spread to Rome from the Etruscans; then directly, from contacts with Greek colonies such as Naples. Plautus's adaptations of Greek comedies were popular with Roman audiences from about 200 BC. But Roman lust for Greek luxury was specifically attributed to military victories in Asia Minor in the second century BC, when soldiers and officers were infected by the desire for Eastern foods, wines, and other pleasures. Cooks were allegedly unknown in Rome until Greek cooks arrived as prisoners of war from these campaigns. Rome was undoubtedly enriched by its eastern conquests; some of the new spending power was used on imported luxuries.

There is evidence of the fashion for Greek food and luxury even in the oldest Latin prose text, Cato's work *On Farming* (c. 175 BC), which includes recipes for cakes. These belong to the same tradition as a text on baking by Chrysippos of Tyana, which in turn shows similarities with a Greek cookery manual by Paxamos. Chrysippos and Paxamos, whose works now survive only in fragments, were perhaps the most literary among the Greek cooks who came to Rome in the 2nd century BC. The Latin poet Horace claims to report a gastronomic lecture by one of their 1st-century successors (*Satires* 2.4). Greek physicians also influenced the Roman diet.

The evidence is partly literary, partly linguistic. Historical texts depict emperors and the rich eating *à la grecque*, employing Greek names for fancy preparations (*tetrapharmacum*, a stew) and accessories (*clibanus*, baking crock, *authepta*, roughly samovar). Among technical sources, the Latin cookbook *Apicius* contains recipes with Greek names (*absinthium*, vermouth, *oxyporum*, digestive, *hypotrimma*, a sauce) and uses culinary terms borrowed from Greek (*plasso*, "form into shapes").

Greek food names began to enter Latin very early: *apua*, anchovy, *asparagus*, *garum*, fish sauce, *malum*, apple, *murta*, myrtleberry, *oleum*, olive oil, *pisum*, pea. Borrowings continued throughout the classical period: *carota*, carrot, *persica*, peach, *polypus*, octopus, *sinapi*, mustard. All these are foods Romans learned to grow, make, or enjoy under Greek influence; names of spices are also borrowed from Greek: *cuminum*, cumin, *piper*, pepper, *zingiber*, ginger. Romans liked dried plums from Damascus and used a Greek name for them, *damascenum*: this has become a variety name — English *damson*, Italian *amoscino*. *Mensae primae*, main course, and *mensae secundae*, dessert, are loan-translations: the parent Greek terms also mean first/second tables, implying that the idea of serving desserts and the habit of changing tables between courses were learned from Greece.

Initially the influence was all one way. In the late empire, Greek borrowed increasingly from Latin, and Greeks, no longer culturally dominant, imitated Romans: modern Greek thus contains many Latin loanwords, from *fava*, bean, to *taverna*. But some ancient culinary words, such as *lucanica*, Lucanian sausage, and *depsticius*, kneaded bread, seem to be a mixture of Latin and Greek. The coalescence—if such it was—was never completed: the 4th-century division between the Greek-speaking East and Latin West became a cultural frontier.

(AKD)

GREMOLATA is a mixture of finely chopped parsley, lemon zest, and garlic, added as a final seasoning to many dishes, best known as garnish to OSSOBUCO ALLA MILANESE. It is a version of the many lively sauces and relishes made by pounding herbs and other strong flavoured things, like anchovies, capers, olives and garlic together. *See also* SALSA VERDE.

GREY MULLET, *cefalo, muggino,* belongs to the Mugilidae family, and five kinds are known in Italy (*Cefalo dorato, verzelata, calamita, volpina, bosega*). Classical Romans were familiar with fresh grey mullet from Italian estuaries and the mouths of the Rhone—the species was being experimentally farmed in the first century AD—and also with salted mullet from Egypt, much prized and apparently widely marketed throughout the Empire.

They are greyish in colour, varying from brown to vaguely golden, with darker horizontal stripes, and at their best in spring and autumn, those from the sea being preferred to freshwater ones. Sweet-natured and vegetarian, grey mullet are as good as what they feed on, and best when from clear rather than muddy water. *Volpina* is said to be the best; its eggs are used, salted and cured, for *bottarga (see* BOTARGO), which is enjoyed on its own, thinly sliced, or as an ingredient in various sauces. A Sardinian recipe marinates grey mullet in oil, bay leaves, myrtle berries, crushed peppercorns, wild fennel, thyme, and chopped shallots, for several hours in a cool place, before baking in a moderate oven, and serving with a sauce of anchovies and capers, mashed up with the cooked livers of the fish. Corrado in Naples recommended simmering them in water, with salt, butter, and herbs, and serving with a sorrel sauce.

GRISSINI are breadsticks—very thin, elongated, crisp strips of bread dough enriched with lard or olive oil. After kneading and proving, the elastic dough is pulled and stretched, not rolled, by hand, to the length of your baking sheet. Artisan *grissini* are by their nature nobbly and irregular, different in texture, flavour, and appearance from the industrial products that are now available everywhere in their sterile paper wrappings. The olive oil gives them crispness, and the flavour and texture can be enhanced with sesame or poppy seeds and onion, and in recent innovative versions, the addition of chopped fresh sage, spinach, gorgonzola, or pancetta.

If crust is held to be healthier than crumb, one can understand the touching little myth about the "invention" of *grissini* in 1668 by a cook called Brunero to nourish an ailing princeling of the house of Savoy, Vittorio Amadeo II. But Costanzo Felici was writing back in the 1560s of the different variety of breads and referred to something *"intrisa in pasta morbida poi tirato, como è fermentato, in forma longa; vi entra dentro sale, anisi e finocchio"* (made of soft dough which when fermented is drawn out into long shapes, with salt, anise, and fennel in them; Felici, 1986, p. 114). So maybe the kind cook was making a special version of a known bread for his ailing master.

GROUPER, *cernia,* from the same family as SEA BASS, is a big fish, often over a metre long, of which there are several kinds. Slices can be grilled, fried, or roasted, but they have a reputation for excellence when simmered and served with a green sauce. A recipe from Genoa cooks a whole fish, or thick slices, in a mixture of chopped onion, celery, carrot, parsley, and garlic, softened in olive oil, with soaked *funghi porcini (see* MUSHROOMS), anchovies dissolved in oil, capers, and pine nuts. A version of this from Vincenzo Corrado in Naples cooked the pieces of grouper in oil with spring onions and spices, bathing it in wine and fish broth, and served them in a sauce made of mushrooms

Grouper are large fish, which often grow to over a metre long. (Shutterstock)

and crumbled *bottarga* (*see* BOTARGO). A more delicate recipe of his cooked the pieces of grouper lightly in fish broth in which he had simmered peas, lettuce, onions, mushrooms, truffles, and aromatic herbs.

GUANCIALE is cured pig's cheek or jowl, a softer, richer product than bacon, pancetta. It is used, cubed or finely sliced, in some PASTA SAUCES, like *spaghetti all'amatriciana*, or *alla carbonara* or its close relative *alla gricia*. A particularly succulent cured and smoked *guanciale* is made in Ploaghe in Sardinia from animals crossed between wild boars and local wild pigs.

GUBANA is a speciality of Friuli, made from a rich eggy buttery dough which, when well worked and risen, is rolled into a very thin rectangle and covered with a filling of various nuts, raisins, candied peel, and spices, all mixed together with some cake crumbs and grappa, flavoured with amaretto, maraschino, marsala, and rum. This is rolled up to make a serpent shape, which is then wound round itself in a spiral like a snail shell, left to rise, and baked in the oven. The texture is more dense and crunchy than panettone, and the impact of all the liqueurs makes it an ideal dessert, washed down with one of the many designer grappas now available. The ubiquitous and undocumented

Lombards are said to have brought it with them in the 6th century, but it is more likely to be from cultural connections with nearby Slav countries.

A recipe from Scappi's *Opera* of 1570 for a *tortiglione ripieno* has an almost identical dough covered with spices and dried fruit, or nuts, rolled up *di modo che venga a foggia di scorza di lumaca*, so that it ends up shaped like snail shell, and baked, sometimes on a puff pastry base. Rosewater rather than grappa was the usual flavouring then. In 1557, Cristofaro Messisbugo gave a recipe *A fare Ritortoli per quaresima o per gran vigilia*, with a strange filling of a paste of stewed eel (traditional on Christmas Eve), ground almonds, dried fruit, sugar, cinnamon, and a little pepper, spread over a rectangle of pastry, rolled up, and curled round in a dish, baked strewn with sugar and served sprinkled with rosewater; a lean or Lenten dish, but as rich as possible without being able to use butter and eggs.

GUERRINI, OLINDO (1845–1916), a writer and poet who published mildly obscene verse under the pseudonym Lorenzo Stecchetti, was a contemporary of Artusi; both were from Forlì near Bologna. His interest in food began with a random purchase from an importunate bookseller during a cycling holiday in his youth; from then on he collected contemporary and historic cookery texts with avidity. Guerrini's distinguished career as university librarian in Bologna gave him the opportunity to edit and publish historic cookery manuscripts in its collection. We owe to him and his contemporaries—Ludovico Frati, Salmone Morpurgo, and Francesco Zambrini—an important clutch of manuscripts that might otherwise have sunk without trace, including the 14th-century *Libro della cucina*, Anonimo Toscano, Cod. 158, in the University Library, Bologna, and the *Libro per cuoco* by Anonimo Veneziano, Cod. n. 225, in the Casanatense Library in Rome. These and other contemporary manuscripts

have been discussed by Laurioux (1997, p. 210) and Benporat (1996), setting them in a more accurate context than was possible for Guerrini and his fellow enthusiasts. These texts interested them as early examples of a nonliterary vernacular Italian, and as information about Italy's gastronomic traditions. That cycling holiday was symptomatic of the opening up of until then remote areas, whose food and cooking was untinged by French ingredients and nomenclature, to middle-class holiday-makers using revolutionary new means of transport—trains, bicycles, and motor cars. Guerrini and his colleagues' concern with language was both practical and patriotic, reflecting the need for a common language in the newly unified country and for a tool for forging understanding and solidarity. We have seen how in 1891 Artusi created a new, thoroughly Italian, gastronomic language in his *La scienza in cucina e l'arte di mangiar bene*. His erudite friends, from the 1870s onwards, used to give privately printed texts of cookery manuscripts, accounts of banquets, and historic menus as wedding presents for their friends, reflecting this interest in the language and food of the past.

Guerrini, encouraged by Artusi, published late in life, in 1916, *L'arte di utilizzare gli avanzi della mensa* (The art of using up leftovers), written in the same spirit of bourgeois frugality as *La scienza*. He collected recipes for many years and started to put them together after his retirement from Bologna University, which was interrupted by the war, when he was called to take over the University Library in Genoa, and enjoyed a bracing time up and down 300 steps twice a day, not counting trips to the market on the waterfront. Gradually his collection took shape, and although its cautious use of seasonings may be a dumbing down of the regional specialities he must have enjoyed on cycling tours (like the *minestra* of rice and peas, cooked in the broth from a stewed chicken, with chunks of the remaining bird in it he had when hungry in Pisa), there are

delicate little croquettes of chopped or puréed meat or fowl, seasoned with herbs or chopped onions softened in butter, bound with egg and *besciamella*, dipped in egg and breadcrumbs and fried. A "Sandwick" of thin slices of cold roast veal, buttered, enclosing slices of Parma ham, placed on a dish and decorated with chopped hard-boiled egg, parsley, dabs of anchovy butter, and olives, makes a nice antipasto. Left-over vegetables, puréed, with a *besciamella* and plenty of parmesan, make a familiar SFORMATO, and green beans, turned in a sauce of garlic, olive oil, and anchovies, do not even have to be leftovers. Roman broccoli is divided into little florets, lightly cooked, then added to a pot in which chopped garlic has been cooked in good lard with some finely chopped anchovies, turned so that they have time to absorb all this, and well seasoned with pepper. Modern versions abandon the lard and use oil instead, and some add hot red *peperoncino* (*see* CHILLI). Guerrini's version of *vitello tonnato* is pungent with anchovies and capers; the cold roast veal is marinated in a sauce made of pounded tinned tunny and anchovies, thinned with oil and lemon juice.

GUINEA FOWL, *faraona*, Numidia meleagris, was known to the ancient Romans, and its Italian name reflects its existence in ancient Egypt. We find its decorative spotted plumage in mosaic pavements, but it is probable that they disappeared during the Dark Ages (while the more amenable chicken survived) and were rediscovered some time in the 16th century in North Africa, their country of origin, and brought to Europe by the Portuguese. They appear in 16th-century cookery texts as *galline* or *pollanche d'India*, and can be confused with TURKEY, which was brought to Europe from the New World about the same time, and sometimes called *pavoni d'India*. Linnaeus used the confusing name *Meleagris*, from the Latin for guinea

fowl, for the genus to which turkeys belong. It is difficult to imagine a cook confusing fowl with plumage so dissimilar, but when plucked they might have been similar, at a time when turkeys were neither bred nor fed to today's gross dimensions.

In spite of the development of intensive rearing of guinea fowl, they still have a slightly gamy taste and darker flesh than chicken. There are delicious regional recipes. A fussy one, *faraona alla creta*, is based on the primitive method of encasing a bird in clay and baking it over, and covered by, hot coals. A tidier version involves anointing the bird with an aromatic *battuta* and wrapping it in baking parchment before covering it with clay, which allows for the drama of breaking the thing apart at table. A Tuscan version, *faraona al cartoccio*, wraps the seasoned bird in very thin pancetta, then a covering of CAUL FAT, and finally a layer of paper, cooking it in a low oven. There are also many ways of cooking guinea fowl joints.

GUINEA PIG, *cavia,* or *porcellino d'India* (*coniglio d'India* to Scappi), from the New World, joined rabbits and dormice as barnyard creatures fattened at low cost for the table. They appear in genre paintings (*see*

RABBIT and DORMOUSE). Scappi recommended stuffing them with a mixture of chopped ham and bacon, prunes and dried cherries, spices and soft cheese, bound with egg. Boned QUAIL would be a possible substitute, when re-creating a Roman banquet.

GURNARD, *cappone* or *capone,* belongs to the Triglidae family, which includes several fish with a perplexing profusion of regional names, the piper, *capone lira,* red gurnard, *capone coccio,* tub gurnard, *capone gallinella,* grey gurnard, *capone gurno,* streaked gurnard, *capone ubriaco.* They are not the same as the various kinds of rascasse or scorpion fish, but can be distinguished by their big heads with steep brows, and of course the lack of dragon-like dorsal spines. All these gurnards are good in fish soup, where the big head and trimmings contribute flavour while the white flesh can be cooked separately in the resulting broth. Piper and red gurnard are excellent and can be baked or stewed, stuffed with a mixture of chopped fresh herbs and garlic, covered with breadcrumbs and a sprinkling of white wine and olive oil. Painters of genre scenes and still lifes exploit the bright red of red gurnard and the pinks of the others.

h

HAKE, *nasello,* sometimes called *merluzzo,* which is confusing, since that is also the name for fresh COD. Hake has a delicious but rather fragile flesh, which needs careful cooking; a recipe from the Marche puts slices or steaks of hake into a marinade of olive oil and chopped spring onion, then removes them, brushes off the onion, dips them all oily in breadcrumbs, and grills them briefly, to be served with an anchovy sauce.

HAM, *prosciutto,* cooked or cured, is made in many regions of Italy, well over 20, not including PARMA HAM. Many of the regional hams are already well known from their industrial versions, typically those of San Daniele, Modena, Norcia, and Tuscany. Small producers throughout the length and breadth of the Apennines offer a huge range of mountain hams with different cures and seasonings, from chilli to juniper, only a few of which can be mentioned here. The INSOR publication *Atlante dei prodotti tipici, salumi,* lists more than 20 worthy of special attention.

Norcia produces hams using artisan and industrial methods; the *prosciutto antico,* from local Umbrian pigs, are given a period in dry salt and then dried in a slightly smoky atmosphere, seasoned with pepper and garlic, and left to mature for up to two years in a cold damp place, a longer process. The expertise of local craftsmen in the art of handling pig products, *norcineria,* has given its name to the profession, and *norcini* from Umbria and the Marche are still renowned for their skills.

Montefeltro, in the province of Pesaro, has a *prosciutto aromatizzato* which, in the hands of local experts, is processed as Cato described in *De agricultura:* dry salted, massaged with pepper, seasoned with garlic, sugar, wine, rosemary and bay leaves. The cure benefits from the mountain climate, and the pigs enjoy a traditional diet of chestnuts, acorns, cereals, and domestic and agricultural waste (with not a sight of the dreaded milk byproducts). The reintroduction of a traditional breed of pig, the *mora romagnola,* promises a resurgence of interest from both producers and their clients.

Carpegna, also in the province of Pesaro, produces a fine ham; Italian pigs fed on traditional local materials, fattened on grain, cereals, and milk products, and cured slowly after a long period of salting and drying. One version is seasoned with juniper berries.

San Daniele has a long history, probably going back to the 11th century, and these well-salted, pressed, and carefully dried hams have been the subject of poets and predators, from the Council of Trent in 1563, when an armed guard escorted a supply for the bevy of convened bishops, to the fall of the Venetian Republic in 1797, with the greedy sequestration by Napoleon's General Massena of a huge quantity of hams. The poet Antonio Frizzi in 1772 sang its praises, quoted by Barberis in the INSOR *Atlante* (2000, p. 329).

*Nel sale ancor le intere cosce asconde
per far prosciutto da mangiar la state
diviso in fette fiammeggianti e monde
del nervoso suo grasso attorno orlate.
Voi che a irrigar le fauci sitibonde,
servi di Bacco ognor lo ricercate
fate almen che il gran merto non si cele
del prosciutto gentil di San Daniele.*

The whole ham is hidden away in salt
to make prosciutto to eat in summer,
cleanly sliced in flaming swathes
haloed with sinewed fat.
You, desiring to slake parched
    throats,
servants of Bacchus, seek it
    everywhere,
at least should never deny the great
    virtue
of the sweet ham of San Daniele.

The halo of fat around this delicacy is critical to the flavour and texture, as is the climate of the region, precisely defined as being equidistant from sea and mountain, in the area around San Daniele on the river Tagliamento in the centre of Friuli. Pietraroia, in the province of Benevento in Campania produces hams from pigs reared locally, salted, smoked, and pressed over a period of several months, and matured for two years in cool cellars.

Fine cured ham is usually enjoyed as a luxury, on its own, but it can be used in cooking, as in SALTIMBOCCA ALLA ROMANA, where it presses a fragrant sage leaf into a thin slice of veal; or can be wrapped round sea bass, to bake in the oven, sprinkled with grappa.

HARE, *lepre,* are plentiful in Italy, providing a fine meat which varies according to the age of the animal—*leprotto* is a young creature of three to four months, *lepre dell'anno,* a year old, and *lepre* when older, becoming *leprone* when more mature. How you cook it depends more on age than which race of hare it is. Such is the demand that some meat is now imported, fresh or frozen. Whether the fresh meat should be hung, and for how long, depends on the age of the creature; a young one can be cooked straightaway or roasted after hanging, but with older ones it depends on the recipe. A long marinade will usually tenderise the meat sufficiently, and is better than hanging for too long, which makes the flesh rank and unpleasant.

The hunting of the hare, and feasting on it, has been enthusiastically pursued in Italy since Etruscan times. Romans loved both the chase and the meat it yielded, as well as deer and wild boar, which were in higher esteem, and they also reared hares in captivity. Dalby and Grainger (1996, p. 75) give a recipe from Apicius for roast saddle of hare, whose sauce, of pepper, bitter herbs both fresh and dry, onion, celery seed, asafoetida, fish sauce, and red wine, is used to baste the meat as it cooks, commenting that Archestratus had preferred plain spit roasted hare, eaten hot and rare, seasoned just with salt, not messing around with over-the-top recipes "as if you were cooking a cat." Anthimus in 6th-century Ravenna approved of a sweet sauce for hare, flavoured with pepper, cloves, and the pungent roots of ginger and spikenard.

Representations in art of the 16th and 17th centuries seem mainly to be of dead hares (unlike domesticated rabbits, who are shown alive and munching fruit or lettuce). The hare, as victim of the hunter, is shown inert, speed and vitality all gone, gutted (to prevent contamination of the meat), and with the rib cage held open with a wooden skewer. A similar representation is shown in a mural of a kitchen scene in Herculaneum.

HAZELNUT, cob nut, filbert, *nocciola, avellana, Corylus avellana, orylus maxima,* is found wild in Italy, but over 10 varieties are now cultivated, mainly in Campania, Liguria, Piedmont, and Sicily. These nuts can be used, along with almonds and walnuts, in

Hazelnuts, *nocciole*, also known as cob nuts, or filberts, grow wild in Italy. (Shutterstock)

many sweet things—biscuits, *torrone*, *gianduia*, and ice cream (it makes one of the most delicious nut-based ices). The word *nocciola* is used to describe browned butter, the colour of the nuts when roasted, and is also an empirical term for a small quantity of an ingredient, about a teaspoonful. *Gianduia* is a speciality of Piedmont, the name is a contraction of *Gioan d'la duja*, *Giovanni del boccale*, John of the Flagon, a mask representing a character from the Commedia del'Arte and popular in Carnevale celebrations in Turin, with a round red face and reddish-brown tricorne hat, kind-natured, quick-witted, but all for an easy life of sensual pleasures, a cheerful connection with this deep brown chocolate fondant, *gianduiotto*, a mixture of ground hazelnuts and chocolate, flavoured with vanilla. The delicacy probably existed for some time before an enterprising commercial firm bestowed this name upon it in 1865; the quality depends on the fine hazelnuts of the Langhe, with a subtlety superior to the universally popular commercial spread Nutella. A dessert with the name *torta gianduia* is an egg sponge enriched with a buttery cream of hazelnuts and chocolate, cooked, divided into two layers, the bottom one sprinkled with a liqueur like maraschino, and filled with a whipped chocolate cream, plastered with an apricot glaze, which is then coated with chocolate. Artusi has a simpler cake or pudding: shelled and peeled hazelnuts pounded with sugar in a mortar and mixed with Savoy biscuits soaked in warm milk and melted butter, then cooled and added to egg yolks and the beaten whites

and baked in a mould in the oven (Artusi, p.489). The ancient Romans ate hazelnuts for dessert with wine, and they were one of the nuts in the "upside-down patina." They are the main ingredient in an Apician recipe adapted by Sally Grainger (Dalby and Grainger, 1996, p. 133) where a fowl is roasted, covered, and then frequently basted with a sauce of pounded hazelnuts mixed with herbs, pepper, saffron, fish sauce, red wine, wine vinegar, honey, and olive oil; this forms a savoury crust over the tender bird, with the liquid juices mingling with those in the bottom of the pan.

HEAD, usually a PIG'S HEAD, *testa di maiale*, can be cooked whole, split open, boned, sometimes without parts like brain, tongue, snout, and ears which are removed for use in other dishes. After long slow cooking with plenty of seasonings, the meat can be taken off the bones and assembled with the by now stiff jelly (from the skin and connective tissues) and put into a mould or a cloth container. This *coppa di testa* will keep well, and is now usually bought ready made in a commercial version, which is not always as tasty as the homemade one. *Coppa di testa di maiale alla romana* is made as above, with the addition of pine and pistachio nuts and orange or lemon peel. *Coppa in cassetta* is a speciality of Liguria which includes the tongue, and some marsala. This is also found in northern Sardinia. There is a different version, also from Sardinia, in which parts of the head and raw meat cut off the bone are marinated with spices and flavourings, a local wine, and a little marsala, then cooked in containers, and left to cool under a weight. The heads of other animals get similar treatment.

Testina is the head of a young animal, kid, lamb, or calf, plainly grilled or roasted. In the north of Italy, a calf's head is often boned and put together again, simmered in broth, and served as part of the BOLLITO MISTO, with a variety of sauces. It was banquet fare in the past, skinned, boned, and decorated with flowers, or anointed with a sauce, and presented as a decorative dish.

The head of a WILD BOAR was even more festive, a survival from ancient hunting parties, a symbol of kingly festivities, and often served gilded and adorned with a wreath of bay or flowers.

HEARTS. *See* OFFAL.

HEMP, cannabis, *canapa*, *Cannabis sativa*, was used extensively in some regions of Italy, especially Romagna, where conditions were suitable for growing and treating this plant, an important source of seeds for oil, and fibre for clothing, coarse cloth, bags, sacks, sails, and, more important, ropes and cords for maritime and construction use. It is hard to imagine a crop, and all the activities connected with it, disappearing without trace, except for unexplained pits in the flat farmland. The long progression from tall green plants over a metre high to soft embroidered household linen involved long and wearisome tasks. The tall stems were harvested, dried, and the leaves discarded, then the stems were tied in bundles and piled up to dry before macerating them in large rectangular brick-lined tanks, where they rotted and fermented until time for the unpleasant task of hauling the odoriferous bundles out and leaving them to dry; then came the beating and bashing to loosen and separate the fibres, and the skilled work of combing them into different grades, later to be spun into threads and then woven. Some of these labours were done by specialised *canapini* who travelled the area, with a reputation for constant cheerfulness in spite of the harsh work. They were well treated, for upon their skills depended the quality of thread later to be worked by the women of the households, and the strength and reliability of cables and

ropes. The twisting of ropes and cords was done by these men—a rough, skin-scraping task. Even the poorest families provided a late morning meal of roast chicken, a luxury, and an evening pot of vegetables and beans, and the various communal tasks were a pretext for feasting and sociability. The profession died out in the 1950s, and with it the traditions and equipment associated with the crop, and even the big irrigated tanks are no longer a feature of the landscape. Recently this ecologically worthy crop has been revived to make organic textiles, using modern methods of harvesting and treatment. In the past, the seeds produced an oil which was used for cooking and lighting, and the dried leaves had medicinal purposes. They made poultices and potions to get rid of worms. The seeds were ground up with almonds, then diluted with broth, according to Martino, to make a spicy sort of soup, flavoured with ginger and saffron, which, taken at the end of a meal, medical writers claimed, would ward off drunkenness and damp down lust. But according to Camporesi, they were put to less benign use, as part of the hallucinogenic additives that infested the food of the poor, a cocktail of poisons and adulterants that, added to deficiency diseases and malnutrition, led to the creation of a literally revolting subclass. A depressing contrast to the ever cheerful, strong-armed *canapini*.

HERBAL INFUSIONS. *See* HERBS, TEA.

HERBS, *erbe aromatiche*. The word *erbe* means grass or plants; what we call "herbs" are *erbe aromatiche* or *piante aromatiche*. The principal herbs used in the Italian kitchen today are the same as those listed by Christofaro Messisbugo in 1557: BASIL (*basilico*), BAY LEAVES (*alloro, lauro*), FENNEL (*finocchio*), MARJORAM (*maggiorano*), MINT (*menta*), PARSLEY (*prezzemolo*), ROSEMARY (*ros-*

marino), SAGE (*salvia*), THYME (*timo*), together with other "various fragrant and bitter herbs," to which we can add LOVAGE (*levistico*), OREGANO (*origano*), a variety of marjoram, members of the mint family (*mentuccia, menta romana*), summer and winter SAVOURY (*santoreggia*), a similar herb, *micromeria*, of which there are many varieties, TARRAGON (*dragoncello, targone*) ... not to mention the bitter herbs which have retired gracefully from the kitchen but continue to do us all good in the many APERITIVI and DIGESTIVI which are a survival of ancient herbal brews and distillations designed to help appetite and digestion. These include HYSSOP (*issopo*), mugwort (*marrobio*), RUE (*ruta*), and wormwood (*assenzio*) (*see* SOUTHERNWOOD); and there are many more, often shrouded in unnecessary mystery, whose presence adds perfume and flavour to these allegedly healthy brews.

Giacomo CASTELVETRO defined *erbe buone* in his *Brieve Racconto*: "Before going any further I should say what I mean by 'sweet herbs' since I shall use this expression quite often. It is the name our housewives give to a special mixture of parsley, spinach beets, mint, borage, marjoram, basil and thyme (but with more of the first two since the others are so strongly flavoured), which they wash and then chop very fine. We use this mixture to season many dishes, especially fresh broad beans"(Castelvetro, p. 59). BORAGE and SPINACH here are *erbe*, well-flavoured vegetables, giving colour and body to a mass of more pungent chopped pot herbs.

Artusi defines *odori o mazzetto guarnito* as "Fragrant greenstuff, like carrots, celery, parsley, basil, etc., tied with a thread, a version of the French *bouquet garni*" (p. 35). The same ingredients, together with onion and garlic form the basis of many recipes, lightly browned at the beginning of cooking.

The *preboggiòn* of LIGURIA consists of a mass of mainly wild herbs, including, depending on the season, parsley, SALAD BUR-NET, borage, *gaggia*, a kind of wild cabbage, CHERVIL, wild beets, wild ROCKET, used as a flavouring for FRITTATAS and stews and as a filling for *pansoti*, the stuffed ravioli recognisable as little triangular parcels also stuffed with herbs and greens, ricotta, parmesan, and egg. *Preboggiòn* itself is described as "*mescolanza di almeno sette erbe selvatiche: tra cicerbita, talegua, pimpinella, dente di cane, cavolo primaticcio o bieta selvatica, prezzemolo, raperonzolo, ortica, pissarella e boragine*" (a mixture of at least seven wild greens and herbs, including sow thistle [*sonchus oleraceus*], common brighteyes [*Reichardia picroides*, also included as *pissarella*], salad burnet, dandelion, wild cabbage and beets, parsley, rampions, nettles and borage; Molinari Pradelli, 1997, p. 25).

Fresh is not necessarily best; some herbs—oregano, marjoram, thyme—have a pungency when dried which lends itself to long slow cooking; fresh young herbs would have little impact if put in at the start, and are best added at the end, as in GREMOLATA, a mixture of chopped fresh parsley, lemon peel, and garlic, a characteristic garnish to *ossobuco alla milanese*.

The use of herbs and spices varies from one region to another; the rich cuisine of Emilia-Romagna needs few aromatics, while in nearby Liguria the wide variety of local herbs is used in many imaginative ways. The basic range mentioned earlier is available in markets and commercial outlets, and is sanctioned by polite middle-class usage, but a more ancient medicinal and gastronomic use of herbs can be detected in many traditional recipes. The refined dumbing down of earthy popular cuisine already apparent in Artusi is perpetuated today in minatory references by many distinguished Italian food writers to the *uso e abuso* of herbs and spices, as a way of asserting a sort of refined moral superiority over an uncouth rustic past and a vulgar present. Patience Gray redresses the balance in *Honey from a Weed*, where she tells the story of her own experiences searching for and preparing the plants and herbs which taste good and do us good, a knowledge which is instinctive in animals, and at one time handed down from mother to daughter, and which she now hands down to us with enthusiasm and expertise.

A fascinating book on the local cookery of a small village in Umbria, *I Picchiarelli della Malanotte* (Cardillo Violati, Majnardi, 1990, p. 80), has a lyrical but hard-to-translate passage on the use of herbs:

> Wild plants and vegetables cost nothing and flourish in abundance in Umbria, which is one reason why they are so widely used in our regional cuisine. Apart from wild rocket, now part of international cuisine, there are *crispignia*, a plant with lanceolate, crinkly leaves, in roseate formation; *Sonchus oleraceus*, one of the Compositae; hog thistle, also known as *rapacciole* (*raperonzolo*, *ravanello selvatico*, *Raphanus raphanistrum*, wild turnip), a herbaceous plant a bit like turnip tops; *striguli*, which grow at the foot of olive trees, with shoots similar to wild asparagus; *dabbie*, the common wild clematis whose shoots are eaten, hence *scimedabbie*; *pàpaine*, tiny poppy plants, cut before flowering (exquisite in *frittatas*). And then there are the aromatic herbs, invaluable in mixed salads, sauces, stews, and roasts: *saprosella*, *rucoletta*, *serpollo*, wild fennel, marjoram, mint.

And here is Giorgio Cretì (p. 106) to give some idea of the baffling confusion of regional names for one of the many almost forgotten edible plants:

> *Grespino comune, sonchus oleraceaus, allatalepre, cicerbita, sonco liscio, crespigna, scixerboa, lacciussa, quarlatti, strugium, cardéla, lacciansòn, seserbde, laciusa, laitiùn, scarsonet, cuje, latasin, garzec de rìe, lattusciòne, crespin, zonco, lettisiòi, ingrassamuli, negromòro, laticiùl, lataséin, craspéin, zizercia salbedga, cascigno,*

> *straccia-cannarone, secone, trunzo, sevone, galazzo, zangùne, zugu, cardedda d'invernu, gardu minzone, carmingioni.*

Names for fish are perplexing enough, but herbs are worse. The best way is to ask in shops, or markets, or in the countryside, about how to prepare and serve them, try to remember the taste rather than the name.

Struggling to emerge from this maze of names and meanings, it is a comfort to know that Theseus, according to Pliny, before tackling the Minotaur in its labyrinth, fortified himself with a dish of *crispigni*, probably lightly boiled and seasoned with olive oil and salt. The calming and strengthening effect of this benign weed must have helped him a lot. Rabbits and hares love it, too. Mattioli tells us that the roots and fronds of this plant, known in Tuscany as *cicerbita*, were used raw in salads in winter, when the emerging plant and its root have a delicate sweetness.

A typical recipe from *I Picchiarelli* is for a sauce to go with *tagliatelle*, made of finely chopped herbs—the young fronds of wild fennel, garlic, sage, mint, bay, basil, rosemary, thyme, parsley, marjoram, chervil, and some wild asparagus tips, stirred into some butter and olive oil in which a salted anchovy has been dissolved, then mixed with the cooked and drained *tagliatelle*.

Frittata Pasqualina from the same book is made with the meat of a pork sausage and some chopped bacon, cooked and added to finely sliced artichoke and chopped wild asparagus, together with pennyroyal, mint, marjoram, sage, rosemary, finely chopped onion and garlic, all softened in olive oil, with the addition of eggs. This is cooked quickly so that the outside of the *frittata* is golden and the inside still moist, and eaten tepid or cold.

Innovative young chefs are now replacing the grannies who used to gather herbs and plants from meadows and roadsides, and a revived interest in regional cooking ensures a continuity in the use of a bigger range of herbs and wild plants than are commercially available, many of which are listed here under their English or Italian names. But there is a tension between those who seek authentic regional recipes, listing rare and out-of-the-way ingredients, and the exigencies of commercial publishing, which impose a uniformity of ingredients and recipe writing which results, for British and North American readers, in a depressing conformity rather than an expansion of perceptions and desires. Outside the range of herbs commercially available, and their uses specified by respected writers, lurks a multitude of plants, and things to do with them, crying out to be explored and described. In the distant past, wild herbs, their seeds, and aromatic roots were part of an unwritten lore of culinary and curative preparations, on a different social level from the traditions of academic medicine, and it is worth remembering that the black-garbed grannies are a living survival of women who cared for and fed families with skills as good as and probably less lethal than those of male physicians.

Whether to chop, tear, or pound herbs is discussed under BASIL, but it is as well to avoid dogmatism here, and do what seems appropriate for the dish in question, remembering that food processors or liquidizers, if insensitively used, can sometimes reduce a sauce or purée to an undesirable frothy mush. Pounding herbs or spices with a stone pestle and mortar is simple, quick, and satisfying, while cleaning up afterwards is much simpler. Pounding is said to release the essential oils in herbs and spices more effectively than the slicing, cutting effect of a mechanical food processor. Herbs finely or coarsely chopped with a knife or *mezzaluna*, however, make a decorative garnish and provide individual pinpoints of flavour rather than an amalgam.

HERRING, *aringa,* is one of the Clupeid family, to which the SARDINE belongs, and is known in its dried form rather than as a fresh fish—more popular in the past, when it figured on Michelangelo's list of simple, but good, things to eat, possibly in Lent.

HOME COOKING. *See* MEALS AND PATTERNS OF EATING.

HONEY, *miele,* has been gathered for its sweetness since prehistoric times. The mixture of fruit sugars (fructose and dextrose) is a vehicle for flavours derived from the flowers from which bees extract the nectar. As well as the sugars, honey contains traces of pollen, wax, enzymes, proteins, vitamins, and minerals, many of which still have to be analysed. They might have nutritional value beyond the energy we get from the various sugars, and the knowledge that they feed and sustain the queen and the young worker bees in a complex system of gathering, processing, and storing the nectar inspires a possibly undeserved reverence for honey by-products, which are good for bees but might not do much for humans. Platina was not slow to appreciate the political implications of the organisation of a hive, and his run-in with the Pope may have been inspired by Virgil's remarks about how bees would ditch a decrepit leader, move on, and elect a better one. In Italy, honey has been used as sweetener and preservative for centuries. It was held to be bad for those of a choleric temperament, but good for the old and sick, and recommended by Baldassare Pisanelli for congested heads and lungs, as we use it today, taking honey, lemon, and ginger in hot water for a cold. When SUGAR was an expensive medicine, honey was the principal sweetener, and although sugar was used in lavish aristocratic cooking, it did not oust honey until the professional arts of confectionery and sugar work became fashionable in the 17th century, and supplies of cheaper sugar became available. By the 18th century, Vincenzo Corrado specifies honey only once, in a convent recipe for *sosamelli,* old-fashioned spiced biscuits, with chopped roasted almonds, candied orange peel, cinnamon, pepper, and zest of fresh orange. But before then, honey was used in plentiful amounts, as in the 14th-century cookery manuscript in which orange peel is soaked and precooked till soft, then finished by boiling in honey, repeating for three days (as the peel accumulates layers of sweet crystals), and finally put into a fresh batch of honey and finished off with spices. In another recipe in the same manuscript, grated apples or quinces are cooked slowly in honey, to make a fruit paste perfumed with spices, which is cut up into morsels and stored in airtight boxes in layers, with bay leaves and spices.

Castelvetro tells of a little errand boy in Modena who was accused of nicking a melon he was supposed to have deposited for a customer in a grocer's shop in the piazza outside the Ghirlandina, the cathedral of Modena. He was completely exonerated a year later when the melon was found, in perfect condition, having rolled into a barrel of honey. The use of honey as a preservative goes back a long way, but when sugar was readily available, this proved to be more effective as well as cheaper, since when heated beyond a certain point honey caramelises, and the brown colour and change in flavour is not agreeable in the preparation of delicate fruit or sweetmeats. However, there are still many pastries and cookies which are enhanced by honey—it keeps them moist and helps them keep as well as being delicious. PANFORTE, a dense mixture of dried fruit, nuts, and spices, is made with honey. *Cavallucci*, traditional cookies from Siena, are made with honey and walnuts, flavoured with candied orange and lemon peel, coriander and anise seed; a *crostata* of rich pastry enclosing a paste of walnuts and honey, flavoured with lemon zest, is another traditional speciality. The *spongata* of Emilia is a filling of walnuts and pine nuts mixed with breadcrumbs, honey, dried and candied fruit, and cinnamon, baked in a rich pastry crust

flavoured with lemon zest. The *cuddureddi* of Sicily are Christmas cookies in which a similar filling of nuts, dried fruit, and spices is bound with honey, though here dried figs are the main ingredient, and enclosed in a rich pastry. A similar walnut and honey filling goes into the *nucatoli* of Modica (Simeti, 1989, p. 54). A version called *luna di Maometta* is a rich filled pastry made in a crescent shape, a reminder of the sweetmeat's Arab origins. The *struffoli* of Naples have a long and complex pedigree; similar to many of today's Middle Eastern confectionery, they are perhaps a legacy of Arab civilisation, later integrated into medieval convent life, and now a Christmas speciality. A mixture of flour and eggs, slightly sweetened, and flavoured with an anise seed liqueur, is made into small morsels and deep fried in oil; then the golden gobbets are dunked in warm melted honey and chopped candied orange and lemon peel, and served all hot and sticky, sprinkled with sugared comfits. Sicily has its *sfinci ammilati*, a rich eggy choux pastry deep fried in oil to make little golden puffs which are then soaked in hot honey and served at once, or a version called *teste di turco*, in which the puffs are flavoured with zest of orange and dusted with cinnamon after the baptism of honey. In classical times, honey from the Hyblaean mountains behind Syracuse was held to be as good as that from Mount Hymettus, and Heracleides of Syracuse wrote of liturgical offerings to Demeter and Persephone: "cakes of sesame and honey were moulded in the shape of the female pudenda and called throughout the whole of Sicily *mylloi* and carried about in honour of the goddess" (Simeti, 1989, p. 48). *Crispelle di riso*, deep-fried fritters of rice cooked till soft in milk, mixed with ricotta, flavoured with orange peel, and served doused in hot honey and sprinkled with cinnamon were the product of a wealthy Benedictine monastery of San Nicola in Catania. Biscuits with a strong reminder of medieval spice cookery are the *piparelli* of Sicily, made with flour, lard or pork fat, sugar, honey, almonds, black pepper, and zest of orange.

Savoury dishes include a sauce from Piedmont served with *bollito*, made of pounded skinned walnuts, diluted with some of the broth and flavoured with honey and mustard. Onions in *agro-dolce* are browned in butter or oil, then cooked until soft in a mixture of vinegar and honey. As with sugar, honey can be a condiment or catalyst for other flavours rather than a sweetener, so its use in many savoury dishes might seem outlandish, but this is not so. Sicily in 400 BC may have been the setting for a banquet described by the poet Philoxenus which included a dish of honey-glazed shrimp, which Sally Grainger (Dalby and Grainger, 2000, p. 48) recreated from her knowledge of classical cuisine: cooked and shelled shrimp are immersed in a hot mixture of fish sauce (Thai *nam pla* is the ideal substitute), olive oil, and honey; after marinating in this for a while, they are served seasoned with freshly ground black pepper and oregano. Another Grainger interpretation is a simple dish of honeyed mushrooms from Apicius in which sliced mushrooms are cooked briskly in a mixture of olive oil, fish sauce, honey, pepper, and fresh lovage until the liquids have evaporated and the mushrooms are coated in a rich glaze. Most of the sauces in Apicius need honey, often in quite small quantities, usually with vinegar and sometimes sweet wine as well, along with the usual lovage seeds, pepper, and various herbs like rue, rosemary, and parsley; seeds like cumin, fennel, and caraway; and possibly dried fruit or fresh plums, together with the usual oil, fish sauce, and cooking liquid where appropriate. Seen in this context, honey adds small touches of sweetness and aroma to an already complex brew.

Honey is produced on a commercial scale in Italy and also by small producers whose bees gather nectar from local flowers and supply a carefully nurtured product, *vergine*

integrale, virgin organic, with appropriate labelling. Acacia honey, especially that from the Veneto, has a delicate amber colour and a runny consistency and is good in cooking. From Calabria and Sicily comes a fragrant orange blossom honey, used in tisanes and confectionery. Sicily produces a fine thyme honey, one from lemon blossoms, and one of thyme and mint from Trapani; from Tuscany and central Italy comes lime flower honey; the lavender honey of Liguria is renowned, from Piedmont, a honey perfumed with oregano is particularly useful in cooking, and chestnut honey is produced throughout the peninsula, as are almond, rosemary, dandelion, lily, eucalyptus, clover, sunflower, and many more.

HOPS, WILD, *luppoli, lovertisi, bruscandoli, Humulus lupulus,* flourish in a temperate or cold climate. Wild hops are a springtime delicacy in northern and central Italy. The young shoots have a bitterness reminiscent of wild ASPARAGUS, and they are often confused. They can be served lightly boiled in salt water to remove some of the bitterness, then dressed with oil and salt and pepper, or with plenty of melted butter and parmesan. They can also be used in *frittate* and risottos, and can be floured or dipped in batter and fried. In areas where hops are cultivated for use in making beer, it is possible to harvest the young shoots when the plants are pruned in the early spring (the shoots we eat are those that spring from the ends of the growing stems, not direct from the ground like asparagus) and so produce a cash crop. Messisbugo, writing in 1557, has a rich recipe for hop shoots or wild asparagus, in which they are given a boil in water, drained, then finished in broth with saffron, pepper, and cinnamon, and served on sippets of fried bread.

However, as so often happens, nomenclature can be misleading, for *bruscandoli* is also the name given to various other edible shoots which can be prepared and eaten the same way. The 16th-century doctor and naturalist Costanzo Felici, in his manuscript work on salad plants (Felici, 1986, p. 51), lists, after wild and cultivated asparagus, 12 other edible shoots, including *lupolo*, hops; *daphani*; *clematide (vitalba)*, clematis, whose shoots look very like those of hops, but unless picked very young can be poisonous; *cyclamino secondo*; *brionia*, bryony—of which there are three varieties, two white and one black (Grieve, p. 131), whose poisonous root is the somewhat scary humanoid mandrake, and whose very young shoots, although enjoyed by Apicius, have harmful qualities and are best avoided; *rovo*, bramble; *rusco*, *brusco*, or *pungitopo (Ruscus aculeatus)*, butcher's broom, or knee holly, a prickly evergreen plant of the Liliaceae family, whose tender tips are also known as *bruscandoli*, and are used in risottos in Verona (Mattioli tells us that they got the name *pungitopo* because the sharp, prickly leaves were festooned around dried meats and salami hanging in the rafters, to keep mice away). Branches of this plant were said to have been used by butchers to sweep and scrub their blocks, and discourage insects, they were sometimes included among the fronds used in the Jewish rituals of the Feast of the Tabernacles, and in English wedding processions; *bonifacia* or *hippoglosso*, *orobanche*, and even the leaf tips of *helianthos* (*girasole*, the newly introduced sunflower plant, which was not then recognised as a source of oil). With the exception of *rosco*, few of these shoots are now eaten, but Felici's list is a reminder of the old tradition of gathering wild leaves and shoots in the countryside and on any patch of land, a pursuit based on hunger rather than gastronomy, and needing an expert knowledge of edible plants.

HOREHOUND, *marrubio, marrobio, Marrubium vulgare*, was used in the kitchen and medicinally; its bitter leaves are aromatic and can be chopped and added sparingly to marinades and stews. The Romans used it in food, and Mattioli included it in potions to alleviate liver and bile conditions.

HORSE, *cavallo*, is not protected in Italy by the aura of sentimental attachment found in Great Britain and North America. Its other uses, however, make it less common in cooking. The tale that after a bloody battle in Verona between Odoric and Theodoric in the 5th century AD, the resourceful Veronese found gastronomic uses for the multitude of dead horses, and have ever since enjoyed fresh and cured horse meat, must have some bearing on reality. Cut down in their prime, the animals must have been tender and tasty. Uccello's *Battle of San Romano*, painted in the 1450s, glorifies the huge war horses, but it is not hard to imagine the peasants in the background, those who escaped the murderous attacks of Niccolò da Tolentino's troops, recycling the great beasts who had trampled their crops and orange groves underfoot. But usually the horse's value as a means of transport kept it from the pot until it was too old to work, by which time the flesh was tough and insipid.

Another theory about the consumption of horsemeat in the Veneto is that the arduous caravan routes between Genoa and Venice left those animals too unfit to return to work, doomed to be killed and eaten. Over 70 excellent products are still made in the area around Saonara, where the caravans would once have ground to a halt on the edge of the lagoon. The taste for BRE-SAOLA and SALUMI certainly persists, and although horse meat no longer derives from battlefield or trade routes, it is now imported from eastern Europe and even greater distances, as well as being reared locally. Piedmont has its cured horse meat products: one such example is a fine salame made with prime cuts ground with fat pork

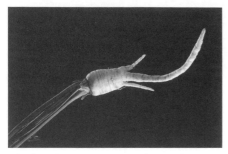

The fierce horseradish root is often subdued with cream and sugar in Italian cuisine. (Shutterstock)

belly and salt, pepper, nutmeg, garlic, and wine. The fresh meat is not as complex and rich in flavour as good beef—it has a slight sweetness; but recipes for beef will all work well with horsemeat.

HORSERADISH, *cren, rafano, barbaforte, Armoracia rusticana,* one of the Cruciferae, though not in fact a RADISH, is more common in the north of Italy, with its associations with northeastern Europe. Its pungent root, when grated, has a fierce mustard flavour, due to the presence of sinigrin, which releases an aromatic oil; this disperses rapidly, and is diminished by heat, so a freshly made sauce, diluted with sour cream, breadcrumbs, perhaps sugar, and vinegar, is a delicious, ephemeral alternative to mustard. In Venezia Giulia, it goes with boiled meats and is sometimes seen with the BOLLITO MISTO of Emilia-Romagna.

HYSSOP, *Issopo, Hyssopus officinalis,* is a plant of the Labiatae, with a strong flavour, used in small quantities in stuffings and *frittatas,* and in tisanes, cordials, and liqueurs in which its carminative and expectorant qualities help to clear up catarrh and bronchial complaints and purge the system of many unhealthy things by relaxing blood vessels and promoting sweating, so much so that it was revered in the ancient world as a cleansing and so holy herb (but we cannot be sure if the plant of that name, mentioned but regrettably not described by Dioscorides, is the hyssop we know today). Mattioli made much of the success of his pills and potions using both wild and domestic hyssop, and their use in clearing up congested minds and bodies, so its use today with rich or gamy food comes as no surprise. Small amounts go surprisingly well with fruit.

i

ICE CREAM, *gelato*, has a confusing history, which has something in common with the invention of printing from moveable type. Most of the technology was already in place—in the case of printing, engraved punches, striking matrices or moulds from them, and the art of casting molten metal in them, a screw press operated by a lever on which to print the assembled types, paper and ink, and a steady demand for the product. Gutenberg had the genius to make an imaginative leap and bring them all together. The "invention" of ice cream as we know it probably involved a similar imaginative leap, made in 17th-century Italy, but in this case it might have been carelessness rather than genius that left a beaker of flavoured water or milk in the ice bucket for far too long, ending up with something which was not frozen, but a sort of semi-solid mush, very pleasant to eat rather than drink. The main freezing elements, crushed ice or compacted snow, salt or saltpetre, had been around since antiquity; food of many kinds had been set in moulds: sweet or savoury jellies, fruit pastes, delicate mixtures of sweetened creams and fruit juices. The great breakthrough came when the two were put together and right amount of salt was added to crushed ice, and the mixture to be frozen in it had the right balance between fat and sugar, and between total solids and water (like the critical mixture of metals—lead, tin, and antimony, that goes into printing type); all being well, it would set very quickly, and the techniques of stirring to break up the ice crystals and give a smooth cream were soon learnt. So putting a container of sweetened fruit juice or cream or custard into a larger vessel, surrounded by crushed ice and salt, stirring the contents, scraping the mixture off the sides of the pot as it froze, or putting small moulds filled with the sweetened mixture to set solid, as *pezzi duri*, was not hugely innovative; what was really remarkable was the way developments in Naples, and Medicean Florence and also in France, gained momentum, and ice cream–making became a professional activity. Just when that happened is difficult to find out; later we hear of scientific experiments with freezing, quite detached from mundane activities in kitchens and pantries. Medical opinion was divided on the dangers or benefits of chilled drinks and sorbets, but while 17th-century physicians argued in an atmosphere of violent polemic, and scientists carried out abstract experiments with techniques of freezing, refreshments of chilled and frozen delicacies went on being offered during and after banquets to the rich and powerful, who enjoyed the delicious reality, heedless of theory.

Ice and compacted snow had been collected and stored in specially constructed ice-houses since Roman times, and classical writers refer to "snow" and its uses to chill food. Some recipes ask for it to be strewn over dishes, like the *sala caccabia* of Apicius, in which a decorative arrangement of cooked meats and vegetables, seasoned with herbs, spices, honey, and vinegar, are set in a meat

Hungry boys surround an Italian gelato vendor, 1877. Photograph by John Thomson, Hanz Swartz Collection. (Mary Evans Picture Library/Chris Ware)

jelly, cooled, and served sprinkled with snow (*insuper nivem*). Impacted snow or shavings of ice were added to wine or water, or wine was strained over ice in a colander into cups—welcome if the snow survived the gathering, transport, and storage in a reasonably hygienic condition, otherwise something of a health hazard. The emperor Nero had the sound idea of boiling water to sterilise it, then chilling it in ice. It is not clear if or how this practice survived the Dark Ages, but we do know of the provision of quantities of ice for cooling drinks and food in 16th-century Florence, and the great ice-houses of Medici rulers still survive, two in the Boboli Gardens, built in 1612 by the architect Bernardo Buontalenti, and also in the gardens of the villas at Poggio a Caiano and Castello. But ice is not mentioned in early writings on food and medicine. Platina has nothing to say about its gastronomic or medicinal uses, although contemporary health handbooks show scenes of ice being gathered from frozen mountain lakes and transported,

wrapped in bundles of faggots, on the back of a long-suffering mule (*Cerruti Tacuina Sanitatis*, Vienna). There is a touching tribute to one of these patient creatures in Florence, a bas-relief in the courtyard of the Palazzo Pitti. The plates illustrating Scappi's great work, *Opera*, of 1570, have no positive indications of the use of ice, not even in the cool room set aside for handling milk products. He mentions putting things to cool, but his notes on the organisation of supplies and the setting up of banquets are silent about snow and ice. Its use does not seem to have been revived enthusiastically until the following century.

Buontalenti obtained a monopoly to supply ice for sale commercially in Florence which expired in 1608. This must have mitigated the heavy summer heat in the city. There are records of a banquet masterminded by him in 1595 during which *sorbetti* in fantastic shapes were presented, prefiguring the voluptuous baroque ice sculpture of a century later, or the pyramids of fruit encased in ice which made cooling and decorative table centres. In 1685, the poet, scientist, medical doctor, and linguist Francesco Redi (quoted by Giovanna Giusti, 2001, p. 45) celebrated the delights of what we would now call a GRANITA in his poem *Arianna inferma*, sequel to his *Bacco in Toscana*, where Bacchus's consort Arianna suffers the inevitable horrors of a serious hangover:

Fanciulletto
vezzosetto, sugli ardori del mio petto
almen tu fa che vi cada
la rugiada
congelata di sorbetto:
o come scricchiola tra i denti, e sgretola
quindi dall'ugulo, giù per l'esofago,
fraschetta sdrucciola fin nel stomaco.

Wanton youth,
at least you can shower
upon my ardent breast,
the frozen dews of a sorbet:
oh how it scrunches under the teeth,

and from thence crackles through the
    gullet,
then down the oesophagus
and slithers skittishly to the depths
    of the stomach.

Redi's lyrical/medical muse understood both the scientific composition and therapeutic functions of the sorbet. He had after all taken part in the experiments of the members of the ACCADEMIA DEL CIMENTO, who produced freezing vapours in elegant glass goblets, looking, in the manuscript depiction of their work, like pink ice cream, which, sadly, it was not. In *Bacco,* he praises the ranks of

cantinette, e cantimplore
stieno in pronto a tutte l'ore
con forbite bombolette,
chiuse, e strette tra le brine
delle nevi crystalline.

cooling vessels and flasks
standing ready at all times,
with refreshing little drinks,
stoppered, and tightly packed
in the rime of crystalline snows.

An early 17th-century painting in the Galleria Palarina in Florence shows a big oval ice container with the metal wine jars and round bulbous glass flasks exactly as described in Redi's sprightly verses, packed around a huge cumulus cloud of compacted snow. Cristoforo Munari, the still life painter from Emilia-Romagna, executed many works for the Medici dukes, and some of them show *ghiacciaie* of various kinds. A simple wooden pale or bucket, sometimes with a pierced lid for the neck of the bottles within, contained ice for cooling wine—a humble domestic utensil—but for grander occasions, we see large round or oval vessels of precious metals, with several bottles and flasks embedded in lumps of ice, part of an assembly of luxury fruit and snacks, musical instruments, and lush furnishings; in one painting, a pile of dark green watermelons are nestling on lumps of ice in a copper bowl while a long-necked bottle of wine sits in a wooden pail with a cloth ready to wipe off the moisture.

The terminology in the past can be confusing; *gelare* can mean to set rather than to freeze, and a *sorbetto* could be a cool drink that was sipped rather than the almost solid mush we know today. The name might have links with the Turkish sherbet and Arabic *sharbât*—cool drinks, not ices. When Martino put a reduced broth of calves' feet to set it was a *gelo*, put to set in a cool place, and Messisbugo in 1557 wrote about a *gelatia* of calves' feet or pigs' trotters, cooked with sweet wine, spices, and vinegar, pale yellow with saffron, strained over chicken or pheasant flesh, with morsels of cooked pig's head and bay leaves, carefully arranged on white plates. (New techniques made brilliant white ceramic glazes possible, a fashionable move away from earthenware, gold, or silver, and ideal for displaying translucent arrangements of delicate morsels set in spiced and coloured jelly.) So names for the different kinds of ice cream or set jellies of the past do not correspond neatly to those of today. In 18th-century France, a kind of custard ice was called a *fromage*, not because it had cheese in it, but because it was made in a mould or *forme*, a link with one of the Italian words for cheese, *formaggio*, another milk product set in a mould. But this verbal link cannot really be used to validate the myth that Caterina de' Medici brought ice cream and secret recipes with her when she arrived in France in 1533 to marry the future Henri II. The international rich were constantly exchanging luxury treats as well as cultural enthusiasm, and from where but Italy were they likely to come? Not from the dowry of a young princess, a victim of diplomatic matrimonial manoeuvres, but from accounts of the frivolities of entertainments offered to visiting heads of state.

Elizabeth David followed up such clues with great perspicacity, and her book *The*

Harvest of the Cold Months lays out a bewildering amount of detail. One conclusion seems to be that by the late 17th century, professionals were making ice cream for a wider range of customers than earlier aristocratic clients, a trickle-down of *gelati* from the courts of the Medici dukes in Florence, the Sun King in Paris, and the Spanish rulers of the Two Kingdoms (Naples and Sicily) to the back streets of Naples and the popular quarters of Florence. A battered little booklet from this period, printed in Naples (Ignoto napoletano), of which only one copy survives, in the BING collection, is interesting not just for the variety of amazingly delicious recipes, but for the fact that there did not seem to be any need, by then, of any explanation of how to make them—ice cream had become a street trade, the techniques were known, and we shall see how Latini had to take this on board. The recipes are delicious; some include pine kernels, some are flavoured with musk and ambergris, some thickened with candied pumpkin, others made of fresh or candied oranges and lemons, reinforced with orange flower or lemon blossom waters.

These popular ices are a long way from the expensive collation offered at Castelnuovo in 1668 to Queen Christina of Sweden on her ceremonial journey to Rome. Christina had little interest in food, but loved being the centre of attention, with glittering protocol, pageantry, and symbolism lavished upon her. A contemporary account of the festivities hit the right note:

> *Viddi di giaccio, con colori, e succhi naturali composte più sorte di frutte; onde si beveva il cibo, si mangiava la bevanda, era comestibile l'acqua gelata, era potabile il piatto aggiacciato: le fruttiere campeggiavano di fiori di zuccaro, alterate de suoi proprij odori, e colori nativi.*

I saw all kinds of fruit made up of frozen juices and natural colouring, so that one appeared to be eating liquids and drinking solid food; liquid water was frozen to pass as food, while chilled dishes became drinks. Bowls of fruit were invaded by sugar flowers, usurping their perfume and native colours. (Di Schino, 2000, p. 45)

Such visual and gustatory conceits must have appealed to the volatile Christina, in spite of her preference for buttermilk and plain water. Ambiguity and paradox were her native elements, and the sensory and intellectual teasing of the food and decorations were such that she treasured all her life Sévin's visual record of the BANQUETS inspired by her visit to Rome.

A pause for rest the next day, seven miles from Rome, included *"un nobil rinfresco d'acque gelate, vini e confetture"* (noble refreshments of frozen water, wines and sweetmeats).

Some decades later, Antonio Latini, writing in Naples in 1694, while describing in detail what every competent steward and major-domo should know about everything to do with food and banqueting, tiptoed warily around the subject of sorbets: *"non hò inteso di pregiudicare alcuno de'Professori, de'Credenzieri, ò Ripostieri . . . perche qui in Napoli pare ch'ognuno nasca, col genio, e con l'istinto di fabricar Sorbette"* (I have no intention of rubbing the professionals, pastry cooks and confectioners up the wrong way . . . because here in Naples it seems everyone is born with the instinctive gift of making *sorbetti*).

Yes, and they must have given out clear signals to keep off their various patches. Latini prudently gave a few sketchy recipes and moved quickly on to flavoured waters.

A century later, Vincenzo Corrado had no such inhibitions; he summarised the method in his first recipe, for *sorbetto di cedrato*, then went on to suggest 32 more, including jasmine, melon, pomegranate; an "English" custard ice rich with milk, cream, and butter, perfumed with essence of cinnamon; *torrone* made from an egg custard with toasted and ground almonds, flavoured with coriander and cinnamon, or a water ice made with fresh fennel seeds and lemon juice; followed by three *spume*, using the froth from whipped mixtures of chocolate, milk or flavoured milk, or fruit mixtures. The accepted name for both custard and water ices was still *sorbetto*, with a passing mention of *spume*, and *stracchini* and *pezzi*, fruit mixtures frozen solid in moulds. By the 1840s, Ippolito Cavalcanti is using the name *sorbetto* for all ices, sometimes referring to *pezzi di gelati*, meaning solid ones made in little moulds, *gelati* meaning things frozen. By the time we come to Artusi, whose *La scienza in cucina* was first published in 1891, *gelato* is the accepted word for ice cream, made in a newfangled *sorbettiera*. His recipes are traditional, except for a disturbing one made with strong tea brewed for 40 minutes, and a recent innovation, *ponce alla romana*, in which lemon and orange juice are frozen with the usual sugar syrup, beaten up just before serving with a vanilla-flavoured mixture of syrup and beaten whites of egg flavoured with rum. Ada Boni, in *Il talismano della felicità*, divides homemade ices into two main categories, *gelati di crema o di frutta* and *gelati leggeri*, made in small or large moulds, with a third category, *sorbetti*, which come as *granite*, spooms, or punches. She writes with enthusiasm of the new hand-cranked ice cream machine, cheap and easy to use. Mass-produced industrial ices were developed in the United States about this time, but in Italy homemade traditions persisted. Currently, *gelato* is the name used for ice cream by discriminating consumers in the United States, possibly because of its association with high-quality artisan products.

The craze for ice cream, from an aristocratic delicacy to a popular treat, spread all over Europe, and it was mostly Italians who achieved this with their skills and entrepreneurism. Francesco Procopio dei Coltelli, known as Procope, set up an elegant and luxurious establishment in Paris in 1686, where eating ice cream became a fashionable pastime. Until industrial production spread, there was an Italian ice cream-maker in most towns in England and Scotland. Mary Contini described with affectionate nostalgia (2002, p. 347), her father's ice cream business in Cockenzie in East Lothian in the 1930s. Ice, salt, a fine vanilla-flavoured custard, and Mrs. Marshall's patent machine to make it in was all you needed, and a high profit margin could be yours. Latini was right; an inherent skill seemed to make Italians the ideal makers and purveyors of ice cream.

Today the ice cream scene appears to be one of the glories of Italian life. Most towns have at least one *gelateria* offering "homemade" ices (*artigianali*, *propria produzione*) and most people have time to enjoy them, not just as a dessert course at the end of a meal but as a pleasant thing to eat any time of day or night, a social indulgence, along with friends, in noisy groups, thronging pavements around the *gelateria* day and night. There is a difference between homemade ice cream, that produced in small quantities to sell quickly on the spot, and industrially manufactured ices made to retain their quality during transport and storage. Today there is a big range to choose from—the taste for lightness in food extends to ice cream, and the rich cream and egg custard ices are being replaced with *sorbetti*, water ices, *granite*, frozen mixtures of strong coffee, or lemon juice with a more crystalline texture, *semi freddi*, whipped ices light with air, ices made with yoghurt, milk products with a low fat content, even light cheeses, sometimes mixed with fruit, and *cassate*, inspired by the ricotta-filled CASSATA of Sicily.

Current technical handbooks give a chilling insight into today's small-scale ice cream production, adding a new dimension to the word *artigianale*; the permitted use of prepre-pared milk or fruit mixtures, stabilisers, flavouring, and colouring, together with the addition of up to 50 percent air and 25 percent water, all in the context of "homemade," makes one appreciative of the bureaucratic interference which controls the free use of these possibilities. The "overrun," the term used for increasing weight with water, and introducing a huge amount of air to increase volume, is more strictly regulated in Europe than in Great Britain and the United States, and Italy has nothing like the horrors of some of our commercial "whipped" concoctions. But note that a basic industrial "mix" can be bought in and adjusted for flavour with extra additions by the inventive small producer, and transferred from the manufacturer's plastic containers to the same sized stainless steel trays which are the hallmark of home production, and sold as "artisan." This is as good an argument as any for investment in one of the many quick and efficient domestic ice cream machines, and a book of accurate recipes.

Claims that the ice cream cone was "invented" in the United States in 1904 are flying in the face of history, for rolled or cone-shaped cookies, and wafers, *cialde*, made between hinged, heated plates, often decorated, have been around for longer than ice cream, as containers for rich creams, like the celebrated CANNOLI of Sicily, rich pastry ovals wrapped round cylinders of wood, deep fried, and served filled with *crema di ricotta*. The application of these containers to industrial production makes good sense, and in fact the earliest image of an unambiguous ice cream cone is from 18th-century Paris. Before that, though, there was the still life by Lubin Baugin showing a silver dish of rolled wafers sitting precariously on the edge of a table, with a flask of wine and an ornate Venetian glass. This reference to fleeting ephemeral pleasures is also a beautiful documentation of the kind of wafers that would have been easily adapted to eating with ice cream. We also find evidence in paintings of rolled paper cornets to hold sugar, dried fruit, or spices (an opportunity for the artist to tantalise with snatches of print or handwriting which may or may not have had con-

cealed meanings), an idea which could be adapted by rolling a wafer into a cone for holding ice cream.

IMPATIENS. *See* FLOWERS.

INTESTINES. *See* OFFAL.

ITALIAN FOOD ABROAD

seems to fall into several categories: cheap and cheerful pasta and pizza for anyone but Italians, anywhere in the Old and New Worlds; a secret network of suppliers of provisions for Italians living and working outside Italy; a world of prestigious and expensive delis offering products from all over Italy to the new breed of gastro-tourists anxious to acquire the good things they have discovered on their travels; and some exclu-

An Italian pasta chef makes spaghetti at his specialty shop in Soho, London. (Getty Images/ Felix Man)

sive sophisticated restaurants with Italian-inspired food that varies from honest CUCINA POVERA to pretentious, overelaborate offerings on very large white plates. All these manifestations of Italy abroad have their merits and low points. A hugely successful chain offering dishes that would be taken for granted in Italy has brought decent food to parts of Great Britain that have never before had anything so good; a restaurant in south London gained a long-lasting reputation for serving "North Italian Food," a concept unknown in Italy, but a brilliant venture which opened our eyes to the best in Italian cooking; a maverick chef who brought the Welsh and Italian Marches together in a small hamlet on a winding, inaccessible B road in Wales, with unsurpassable cooking and imaginative use of local materials, never equalled before or since; establishments in London and New York run by fiery temperaments which have, in spite of all the hype and high prices, extended the reputation of fine Italian cooking.

Everywhere Italians go, they take something of their food culture, enjoyed behind closed doors, or displayed for public consumption, often modified to suit barbarian tastes. Today over 25 million Americans claim Italian descent, and Italian Americans are the fifth largest ethnic group in the nation. In Great Britain, too, we are a melting pot, citizens of a nation, relaxed about our origins. But Italians somehow manage to be both; not just from a particular region, they identify with a city or hamlet. A native of San Donato Val Comino, in Abruzzo, who lived and worked all his adult life in Rome did not see himself as Roman but as Sandonatese. There is said to be a street in Brooklyn with more people from that village than remain at home. Italian communities in the United States kept their sense of identity while becoming part of a new nation, some deliberately letting the old language take second place. A new generation now actively returns to its roots, learning the language and looking up ancient relatives in far-flung spots,

proud to add the old culture to the new. (I am from Yorkshire, from a family who lived for generations in a small village near Halifax, in Brontë country, but London is where I live and work, my city, my identity. Happy to escape.)

Generations of Italians came to England and Scotland in search of work, bringing their hard labour and perfectionism to ice cream and fish and chips, shop-keeping, and the arts and entertainment with a genius for integrating into the host society while keeping their own identity. These Italian communities abroad keep links with their families and a patch of earth or a village. This loyalty is movingly chronicled by Mary Contini in *Dear Francesca*, describing her forebears' slow escape from grinding poverty in the Abruzzi mountains to the gastronomic splendours of Vivona and Crolla in Edinburgh. But a corrective to this ancestor worship is a bleak short story by Leonardo Sciascia, "*I zii di Sicilia*," in which mutual incomprehension overshadows the return of American immigrants on a visit to Sicily soon after World War II. On arrival, the members of the family gather together for a meal in the best hotel in town; the worldly and sophisticated visitors, refreshed and relaxed after a peaceful sea voyage, dine sparingly on salad and lean meat washed down with Coke, while the Sicilian relatives, dishevelled and exhausted after a wearisome journey by train, devour plates of pasta and the local wine. The *zii* and their terrible wives have moved on. But one cannot criticise earlier arrivals in the United States who rejoiced in the cheap and plentiful meat, and the chance to drown their pasta in floods of red sauce and copious quantities of meatballs.

Garibaldi was a different kind of Italian abroad; he was a mariner, trader, and buccaneer, living by his wits in South America, as well as a revolutionary leader. He first saw his companion, Anita, half Italian herself, across a valley in Brazil, and his red shirts began as the functional clothing of his fellow workers in the stockyards of Buenos Aires.

He and other politicians found refuge from time to time in England, where a boring biscuit was named for him: dried fruit and raisins between two dry crisp layers is hardly an innovation, certainly not a British or Scottish invention, but similar to the hard tack he must have known in his youth in Genoa. Long before this, there was a flourishing Italian commercial community in London—merchants, refugees from religious persecution, men of letters—with a tightly knit community in Clerkenwell. One of these, John Florio, was the author of a successful English–Italian dictionary, a man of letters, and possibly a friend of Shakespeare. He was also a friend of another ex-pat, Giacomo Castelvetro, whose career had led him from religious persecution in Modena to studies in Protestant Switzerland, cultural and diplomatic activities (spying) in Sweden and elsewhere, editorial work in Venice, and language teaching in England. He and Florio represent a different kind of immigrant, whose cultural superiority impressed the host nation: they brought modernism in music, poetry, the arts; their elegant "Italian" calligraphy was beautiful and legible, and marked a move away from the crabbed handwriting of commerce and the law; and the Italian banquet became the benchmark for sophisticated gastronomy, as it has become again today, in New York and London.

The Italian diaspora was swelled during World War II by the movement of prisoners of war all over the world, and many appreciated the benign conditions in Australia and stayed on, appreciated as hard-working citizens, swelling the population of settlers who had already come seeking work. By now the contribution of millions of Italians to Australian gastronomy is well known.

Italians writing in English about their own cuisine range from Marcella Hazan and Anna del Conte, who have written monumental reference works, and authors with Italian roots, to others with boundless enthusiasm and capacity for research who have made deep and perceptive studies of the cuisines of Italy: Carol Field, Lynne Rossetto Kasper, Mary Taylor Simeti, Fred Plotkin, and Burton Anderson are some of those who readily come to mind. They are affirmative, when other British or American writers are questing, exploring, and quite often rejoicing in the obvious. We need both approaches. Elizabeth David pioneered serious writing about Italian food, as part of her onslaught on the awfulness of postwar British food. Norman Douglas, Sybil Bedford, and Patience Gray made us think and search. This prepared the ground for Italian cooks and writers who now add to our enthusiasm and delight in Italian food. Giorgio Locatelli's monumental tome, weighing in at half a stone, offers recipes, knowledge, and autobiography with elegant restraint. Mario Batali is winning hearts and minds all over the United States with his flamboyant but deeply serious Italian cooking; he is one of many cooks and writers in the United States drawing on inherited wisdom and a dedicated return to their gastronomic heritage.

ITALIAN FOOD LITERATURE. *See* LITERATURE AND FOOD.

JAM, *confettura*, was at one time also called *marmellata*, but the official definition now confines this name to citrus fruits only, although the old usage still persists. The origin of the name *marmellata* is the Portuguese word for quince, *marmelo*. Apart from the usual fruit, cherries, peaches, plums, apricots, raspberries, and strawberries, jams are made from quinces, tomatoes, marrows, pumpkins, and melons. Conserve, our more pretentious name for jam, should not be confused with *conserva*, which means any kind of preserved food, but is also the name for a paste made in the south of Italy of tomatoes salted, dried, and passed through a food mill to get a paste, which is dried in the hot August sun until a dark, dense mixture is formed, which can be kept and used for flavouring pasta sauces or in dishes like the Neapolitan *ragù*. Another kind of reduced, concentrated preserve is SAPA, or MUST, which is made from boiled-down grape must, and can be used instead of jam.

JASMINE, *gelsomino. See* FLOWERS.

JELLY, *gelatina*, as a preserve or a dessert, has a long and ancient history. Extracted from the gelatinous parts of fish or animals, jelly was used as vehicle for sweet and savoury things. Exquisite morsels of pre-cooked fish or meat could be arranged on a white dish and flooded with a coloured jelly, decorated with herbs and flowers, to be part of a banquet glowing with colour like a late Gothic stained-glass window. Martino explained how, with ingenuity, it was possible to construct a jelly with separate compartments of different colours, red with cornelian berries, yellow with saffron, green with parsley and wheat leaves, and peacock blue from purple carrots. The basic clear jelly had been made from calves' feet, scrupulously washed, cooked in a mixture of water and vinegar and white wine, perfumed with crushed spices, skimmed with care while cooking, and clarified with beaten egg whites. The jellies could be poured into moulds to set, *gelare*, in a cold place. Such confusion here, for *gelare* can also mean to cool or freeze, and so here we find some of the technology and nomenclature which would later be applied to ICE CREAM, both the moulds and the name. (*Gelato* as a word for ice cream came into use much later than the earlier word *sorbetto*.) Small decorative jellies made from fresh fruit are available in Italy today, but they are far superior to the industrial synthetic jellies of Great Britain and the United States, which only need boiling water. Jams, jellies, and fruit pastes have always been a way of preserving fruit, often made up into sweetmeats, coated in sugar.

JERUSALEM ARTICHOKE, *topinambur, Helianthus tuberosus*, arrived in Europe from the New World, and the name, if not the plant, came to Italy from France, named for the tribe, Topinambourus, from

Jerusalem artichokes were brought to Italy by way of Brazil. (Shutterstock)

Brazil. In 1613 six Brazilian Indians were welcomed in France, bringing some of their knobbly tubers with them. These are not related to artichokes, and do not taste much like them, and have no connection with *girasole*, sunflower, from which we maybe got the name Jerusalem. In Italian cookery, they are treated imaginatively, either raw in a BAGNA CAUDA, or precooked and finished with butter and parmesan, or sautéed in oil with herbs and anchovies, or cooked and eaten cold with a SALSA VERDE.

JEWISH GASTRONOMY

arrived in Italy with waves of Jewish settlers at different periods of time. In ancient Rome, Jews were at first tolerated, and there was a large widespread community in Rome and in cities in the north and south; they were later persecuted along with Christians, and when the papacy became more powerful after the decline of the empire, the tolerance of Jews varied over the centuries, sometimes allowing Jewish intellectuals and physicians to gain prestige throughout Europe. Many cities had flourishing communities where rich commercial and banking families, and also many poor Jews, all followed their religious laws concerning diet and hygiene. When Ashkenazi Jews were arriving in Friuli, Emilia-Romagna, Piedmont, and Lombardy from northern Europe in the 14th century,

during the Black Death, and later when Sephardic Jewish communities fled Spain and Portugal during the Reconquista in the 15th century, and later had to leave the Spanish-dominated areas of southern Italy, their expertise in banking and commerce made them welcome. Many Italian rulers welcomed the skills of Jewish immigrants—especially the Medici dukes of Tuscany, where the new free port of Livorno needed their financial and mercantile expertise; and wealthy Jewish families were prominent members of the thriving community.

Jewish dietary laws and traditional recipes were applied to local produce and cooking and inspired dishes which eventually became part of the Italian as well as the Jewish heritage. It is thus difficult to plot possible exchanges of gastronomic influence, when there would have been so much give and take. Claudia Roden points out (1997, p. 409) how Jews coming to Italy from the Arab world of North Africa and the Middle East and the south of Italy brought familiarity with eggplants, still regarded with suspicion in the rest of Italy, and a taste for artichokes, asparagus, and other products, although there is no documentary evidence of their introduction by Jews or Arabs. Italians enjoyed recipes—and characteristic mixtures of sweet and savoury, sweet and sour, using dried fruit, nuts (especially pine nuts) sugar, spices and citrus fruits—that in the 15th century were part of a common culture. It is of course difficult to document the ebb and flow of all these influences, from the earlier Arab presence in Sicily and the south of Italy to the later arrival of Jews from all over Europe—and the political persecution of Spain—in Sicily and the south, and therefore hard to arrive at firm conclusions about who first brought or cooked what. Roden reminds us that today the *cucina povera* of the Ghetto in Rome is now the source of luxury items on non-Jewish menus, for example, the *fritto misto*, with its expensive sweetbreads and asparagus, once the cheap food of street *friggitori* or the *carciofi alla giudea* (or *giudia*); deep-fried artichokes; even the popular *baccalà fritta*.

The skills of deep frying in oil, from Spain and the Levant, using permitted animal fats (fish and chips are fried in beef dripping in the north of England), is a link with northern Jewish food traditions, where chicken and goose fat were a substitute for the forbidden fat, lard and bacon from pigs, and the unattainable olive oil. Claudia Roden observed that Jewish cooking has always been an adaptation of the cooking of many countries to their dietary laws, and certainly Italian recipes were adapted to Jewish requirements.

GEESE were already part of Italians' diet, but Jews settling in the north may have brought flocks with them; they certainly knew how to use every part of the bird to make preserved salami and hams in the Italian tradition; skills which have recently been revived in Mortara in Lomellina. Scappi has several recipes for extracting the fat from geese, ducks, or chickens, some of which involved stuffing a whole goose with sausages (*cervellate*), but gives an alternative stuffing of pieces of flesh from another goose, presumably to avoid using prohibited pork sausages. But he gives no hint of a Jewish origin for this useful fat, only saying that it can be used instead of butter for making pastry. Pisanelli held that geese were rank and indigestible, engendering melancholy and unhealthy humours, adding unkindly that for this reason Jews, who eat them a lot, have sad and sallow complexions. Scappi wrote of fish-balls, which remind us of gefilte fish, made from the finely chopped raw flesh of sturgeon mixed with some salted belly of tunny, herbs and spices, some raisins, and sugar, formed into balls and fried in oil or butter; and of a similar composition made from the cooked flesh of sturgeon pounded up with ground almonds, marzipan, sugar, and raw egg yolks, flavoured with cinnamon and pepper, to which is added raisins, chopped marjoram,

mint, and parsley, and which is then formed into ravioli, floured, and simmered in meat or fish broth. The same mixture can be cooked in a large loaf or pudding, to be served sliced or whole with a sauce of bitter orange juice, verjuice, sugar, butter, or oil. His pike sausage is made from the raw boneless flesh of pike, chopped up with ground almonds, thyme, fennel seeds, and pepper, mixed with little cubes of cooked carrots and belly of tunny, and cooked in a sausage-shaped linen bag. Fruitless here to argue whether this is a version of gefilte fish or whether the concept of flavoured and sometimes sweetened fish balls was common to many countries, from Lithuania to Lazio. A common heritage seems more likely than borrowing, but it is interesting to see these recipes used by a cook to popes and cardinals.

It is probable that the Jewish communities in Italy cooked and ate the same things as other Italians, and that the main differences were in the rituals of holiness and cleanliness attached to food preparation and dining, and the tenacity with which recipes were handed down, incorporating the many cultures to which an extended Jewish family belonged.

JOHN DORY, *pesce San Pietro,* is a flat fish with a big head and a large black circle on each side just beyond the gills, thought to be the fingermarks of Saint Peter. The delicious white fillets are a small part of the whole, but very good grilled or baked.

JUNIPER, *ginepro, Juniperus communis,* is a wild plant which occurs in many varieties all over Italy, whose ripe black berries are used, crushed in marinades, stews, and sauces, and to flavour drinks and liqueurs. Juniper goes particularly well with game, as a stuffing, crushed with salt and butter, or inserted under the skin of birds which are not fatty. Crushed and mixed with cream and stirred into the

Wild juniper berries can be crushed, then added to marinades, stews, and liquors. (Shutterstock)

juices of roast pork or veal, juniper berries make an aromatic sauce. Artusi used them only with thrushes, for which they were held to have an affinity (p. 274). Castor Durante held that the best thrushes were caught in winter, tender and well-flavoured by the juniper and myrtle berries on which they had fed.

Juniper berries are also used to flavour a cow's cheese from the Valle d'Aosta, *salignön*, made from ricotta, salt, garlic, olive oil, cumin, fennel, and juniper.

JUNKET, *giuncata, raveggiolo*, is made by getting warmed milk to coagulate, usually with rennet, and putting it to drain in little perforated containers, or reed baskets, from which junket got its name. This is a way of dealing with a superfluity of fresh milk, which would otherwise be wasted, for once made junkets will keep for five or six days. In the past they were eaten at the beginning of the meal. Baldassare Pisanelli, a medical doctor writing in Bologna in 1611 on the properties of foods, says that they are thirst quenching and refreshing for those of a choleric temperament, but hard to digest, and advises his readers to eat them rarely, better still never. Advice ignored by Scappi, who served them up regularly when in season, with sugar, and decorated with flowers, where, pale and trembling on fresh green ferns or fig leaves, they would have made a welcome contrast with the rich, colourful dishes in his banquet menus. Pinelli produced several engravings of the typical shepherd, coming down into Rome from the hills to sell his little pots of junket to the women and children of Trastevere, a proletarian pleasure as well as an aristocratic luxury.

k

KID. *See* GOAT.

KIDNEYS. *See* OFFAL.

KITCHEN EQUIPMENT, *batteria di cucina*, has changed with the times, and now most kitchens have mechanical aids, gadgets, electronic gear, and the assistance of microwave ovens, slow-cooking equipment, freezers and refrigerators, washing-up machines, and things that will chop, peel, mix, grate, grind, and do just about everything for us. Scappi's monumental kitchens no longer exist, with the enormous range of pots and pans, dishes, bowls, and flagons big and small, each with its own function, and the 28 pages of engravings that he included in his great book are for us a dream world of beautifully designed objects, with a fitness for purpose and an aesthetic all of their own, that we recognise in the still life and genre scenes painted by his contemporaries.

But when all the labour-saving devices of the modern kitchen have been enumerated, there remains a nucleus of things for which there is no substitute: a grater, *gratugia*, for parmesan cheese—either elegant objects to use on the table or stout functional kitchen tools, heavy and solid, like the ones wielded by stout, strong young women in the paintings of Vincenzo Campi. The curved surface, with its sticking out "teeth" have another use—soft dumplings, gnocchi, or lumps or lengths of hand-made pasta can be pressed against the surface to make indentations that will subsequently hold the sauce. Smaller graters for lemon and nutmeg have always been essential tools.

It is now possible to make PASTA in a mixer, and put lumps of it through a machine that flattens and cuts it into the desired strips. But a board on which to make pasta, and the long thin pin to roll it out, *matterello*, can still be found in many kitchens, for a hand-rolled egg pasta has an elasticity, a chewier texture, which machines cannot produce; they squash rather than stretch.

When it comes to cooking pasta, the essentials are a selection of tall, deep pans, the size depending on the amount to be cooked. These are rarely found in British or American kitchens but are essential, for a tall pan exposes less water, and so there is less evaporation as the pasta cooks, uncovered, at a rapid boil. Some sturdy strainers for draining large amounts of pasta are necessary, and slotted or perforated spoons for fishing out gnocchi and ravioli.

An indispensable tool is the mortar, which with its pestle, wooden or stone, does the job of grinding spices or crushing herbs better than any other invention. It can also be used to pound cured fat and flavourings to a cream, smash garlic cloves to make peeling them easier, and concoct a whole range of sauces. PESTO is the best known of these, and although commercial versions made on an industrial scale use mechanical equipment, promotional information always shows them being made according to time-honoured rituals, with a pestle and mortar. The rotary, crushing movement of the pestle around the sides of the mortar releases flavour and aroma better than the cutting action of the blades of a processor, which can often reduce ingredients to a frothy mush. And it does it a lot faster, while being much easier to clean. Walnuts can be ground to a paste with garlic for *agliata*, taking care to moisten the mixture to prevent it getting oily. When historic recipes call for a half or quarter of a nutmeg, you can bash one in a mortar to get the amount needed.

Another tool that will never go away is the *mezzaluna*, a two-handled curved blade which chops with a rocking motion anything from herbs for garnishing, to fat, meat or fish, for stuffings and fillings, and vegetables and meat.

Apart from pans for pasta, there is a special one for cooking POLENTA, the *paiolo*, a round-bottomed, unlined, copper cauldron, traditionally suspended over the fire, and in many areas in daily use for cooking polenta. An electrical version is available which does away with the misery of constantly stirring the mixture over a high heat. Long before polenta had become an almost universal staple, Giovan Francesco Rustici founded in Florence an exclusive dining society, *La Compagnia del Paiuolo,* which he inaugurated with a meal held inside a huge wooden barrel, disguised, with the help of painted canvases, as a giant cauldron. These giant cauldrons were in frequent use, and Scappi has a lively illustration of how to handle these massive and potentially lethal vats of boiling food, in which a stout pole with a hook on one end pivots on a framed structure on wheels, which can lift the vat from the flames and pull it to one side, with four men heaving and straining on the lever.

A special deep pan that conducts the heat well over sides and bottom is needed for cooking a RISOTTO, so that the grains of rice can collide with the sides during the *tostatura*, and the subsequent vigorous stirring will distribute starch into the creamy fusion of rice and liquid. Most households will have a suitable pan. A *batticarne*, a flat or slightly convex circle of metal, is used to bash slices of meat to flatten and tenderise them. (If it were completely flat, the edges would tear the meat.)

An implement for prizing lumps off a hard cheese like parmesan, which cannot be cut easily with a knife, comes in various sizes, and can often be seen in kitchen scenes. It is a thin, leaf-shaped blade with a pointed end and a rounded wooden handle, strong enough to be driven into the block of cheese, then used as a lever to detach a piece. Michelangelo applied this technique to blocks of marble.

Whisks or beaters can be electric or hand-manipulated instruments. They are used to lighten a mixture by getting air into it, and the hand tools usually give a lighter but less frothy result. ZABAGLIONE, *panna montata* (whipped cream), and beaten egg yolks can be done with electric or manual tools. A *frullino a mano* is a hand beater or whisk; a *frullino elettrico* is the electric version. A *frusta* is a balloon whisk, which can be metal or made of wood or reeds. You can see it in action in one of Scappi's engravings, in the cool room, where milk products are dealt with. A man standing upright at the work table twists and twirls a big whisk between his hands in a potbellied pot, from which he scoops the froth he is raising from fresh milk to make the light dessert known as "snow," the *neve di latte* that figures in many of Scappi's banquet menus, with a light sprinkling of sugar.

LAMB. *See* SHEEP.

LAMB'S LETTUCE, corn salad, *valeriana, Valerianella locusta, V. eriocarpa,* is a low-lying plant with rosettes of tender leaves which appear at the end of winter and are welcome in SALADS. It is now cultivated and available all the year round, becoming increasingly popular for its tender, bland contribution to mixed salads. It shares a name but not an identity with *Valeriana officinalis,* whose roots are said to be good for anxiety and which has other medicinal uses, but not in salads.

LAMB'S QUARTERS, fat hen, good king Henry, orach, *farinello comune, atriplice, Chenopodium album,* is a close relative of quinoa; its tender young leaves can be cooked and served like spinach. Mattioli wrote of it with affection, of how it is cultivated in Lombardy as a fast-growing crop in the spring, and used instead of spinach in *torta alla lombarda,* with cheese, eggs and butter. It was known and used as a pot herb and poultice in the Ancient World, whereas spinach was brought to Europe much later by the Arabs.

LAMPASCIONE, grape hyacinth, *cipollaccio, Leopoldia comosa,* is the edible bulb of an onion-like plant, with blue flowers, which grows wild in the south of Italy, in Puglia, Basilicata and Abruzzo, and is now becoming increasingly popular all over Italy. *Lampascioni* can be eaten parboiled or raw, in salads, or pickled; or cooked in oil, then scrambled with eggs and pecorino. Their bitterness can be removed by parboiling or prolonged soaking, but it is inadvisable to eliminate too much of this characteristic flavour. They were prized in classical times for their aphrodisiac properties, and often, according to Dalby, served as a soup with lentils in brothels. Apicius has some recipes in which after the preliminary boil these bulbs can be simmered in oil, vinegar, honey, fish sauce, and thyme and oregano, a sort of *agrodolce.* Onions are no substitute for *lampascioni,* which are now available in many markets.

LAMPEDUSA, GIUSEPPE DI. *See* PASTA, BAKED; PASTA SHAPES.

LAMPREY, *lampreda, Petromyzon marinus,* a primitive parasitic creature, is found in rivers and estuaries as well as the sea (*Lampetra fluviatilis*) and was once much esteemed, though the more one learns about its lifestyle the less one is likely to go for a surfeit. References to lampreys in Roman times should be treated with suspicion, as most of them result from mistranslations: it was the fierce MORAY EEL, not the lamprey, that doting owners kept in fishponds and (on one occasion at least) fed to slaves. Lampreys were, however, known to the Romans under various names, including "river moray." The earliest use of a form of their modern name is by Anthimus, writing in Gaul around AD 510 in medieval Latin: his word for the creature is *lamprida* or *nauprida*, depending on which manuscript you choose.

Early writers describe the beast in detail, with its single nostril on top of the head, its seven gills fanning out below each eye, and a suction disk below, equipped with teeth, with which it adheres to its victim and can then comfortably suck its blood. This high-protein diet produces a firm white flesh, even richer and more delicious than than of eels, and can be prepared in the same way. The lamprey has a sort of cartilaginous spine but no scales or bones, which is a bonus, and can be cooked whole, once its long gut has been removed. Martino (p. 105) and Scappi (bk. 3, pp. 122, 123) give thoughtful descriptions of how to handle them. A live lamprey was often drowned in a butt of malmsey, then washed, and its blood, particularly valued to thicken the cooking liquids, squeezed out of the gills before or during cooking and added to some of the wine and salt. Coiled up in a round metal or earthenware dish, a clove in each gill slit, and a nutmeg in the nostril, covered with oil, verjuice, good-quality white wine, cooked slowly and when done, the cooking juices thickened with the blood and wine, ground burnt almonds, breadcrumbs, and spices, lamprey makes a rich dish. They could be skinned and cut into pieces, marinated in verjuice, oil, fennel, and salt, the pieces put on spits interleaved with bay leaves or sage, and cooked slowly, then towards the end sprinkled with breadcrumbs, flour, sugar, and cinnamon to give a crisp covering, and served with the same sauce. Platina (p. 453) remarked on the size of those found in the Tiber, and ranted away about the insane prices paid for the biggest lamprey by those with more money than sense, a palpable hit at the extravagance of the papal court.

LANDI, GIULIO. *See* GRANA PADANO.

LANGOUSTINE. *See* LOBSTER.

LARD, *strutto*, is not the same as LARDO, which is cured, hard pork fat, usually from the back or back of the neck. Lard is made from rendered-down pork fat; the fat, *sugna*, is cut into pieces and melted down in a slow oven, or boiled with water, which draws impurities from the fat, until the water has evaporated and the fat runs clear. It is cooled slightly, to allow any sediment to fall to the bottom of the pan, and the by now purified fat is carefully filtered into clean containers where it can be stored, if airtight, for up to a year. The crunchy, sometimes meaty, bits left after the prolonged cooking, *ciccioli, cicoli, sfrizzoli*, are a delicacy, eaten salted as an *aperitivo* in Emilia, and often incorporated into bread (*gnocco emiliano*) or tart fillings. They have a rich flavour and—to those with a healthy tolerance of fat—are a delight, eaten with unsalted bread and a glass of lambrusco.

Lard itself has been in the past the preferred cooking medium of various regions, not just in the north, as is often maintained, but also the centre and south, and although the *terrorismo sanitario* of officialdom has engendered irrational fears about its use, there is really no substitute for lard in many traditional dishes. The *gnocco fritto* of Emilia is best when fried in lard: a light dough, made with flour, lard, and bicarbonate of soda, or yeast, rolled out thin and cut into lozenges, and deep fried to a golden, puffed-up, crisp, delightful morsel, traditionally eaten with salami and parmesan cheese. This substantial snack, washed down with a light, sharp lambrusco, used to make a restorative breakfast for workmen in Emilia, around eight in the morning, after several hours of hard manual labour.

The value of lard, and a succinct account of its production, is clearly presented in Martino's work (p. 59); he felt it important to spell out the method, on an industrial scale ("for every 100 pounds of fat take . . ."). He pounded his selected fat, *assogna*, with salt, and let it mature for a day—might this slight cure have initiated the process of conversion from saturated to polyunsaturated fats? But aside from health considerations, a good, homemade lard is above all tasty, adding flavour to anything it is used with.

Most cooks in Rome today prefer to avoid lard, and recoil in horror when reminded of Gioachino BELLI's sonnet in its praise, or Ada Boni's use of it in traditional recipes, along with PANCETTA and GUANCIALE. Her robust *pollo in padella alla romana* has chicken pieces fried in lard with some cut-up (raw) ham, seasoned with garlic and marjoram, and some white wine, and is finished, on a high heat, with chopped fresh tomatoes, which reduce to a rich, dense sauce. Compare this with her *pollo alla cacciatora*, a lighter treatment, with the chicken fried in oil and butter, seasoned only with salt, pepper, chopped ham, and sage leaves, and some white wine, which is allowed to evaporate, then cooked, covered, until the chicken is tender. This discrimination is apparent, too, in Belli, who, while celebrating the virtues of lard, insists that fish meet their natural fate fried in olive oil, not lard.

LARDO, cured back fat, is not to be confused with LARD, *strutto*, and is not the same as bacon, PANCETTA, though in some recipes the two are interchangeable. *Lardo* is cured pig's fat, usually hard fat from the back, or the back of the neck, with little trace of meat, which is salted and cured in various ways.

Lardo battuto is cured pork fat pounded to a cream, often with seasonings like herbs and garlic, to use in stuffings or to add to broths or stews at the start or end of cooking. *Lardo*

bono is a good-quality bacon or pork fat, which you use in larding an expensive cut of meat.

Lardo di Colonnata is one of several that are eaten thinly sliced as an antipasto. But to Martino, the word lardo meant several other things as well—streaky bacon (cured pork belly or pancetta), lard (rendered pork fat), or cured or uncured pork fat pounded to a cream, often with aromatic herbs and garlic.

Lardo di Colonnata became, in the 1990s, a symbol of resistance to the tyranny of the EEC's *terrorismo sanitario*, which would have suppressed, on hygienic grounds, the production of this delicacy in the small community of Colonata, near Carrara, source of a fine white marble used by Michelangelo for his monument to Pope Julius II. The name Colonata might derive from the white columns made from the quarried marble, or from the possible survival from Roman times of a colony of slaves. The pork back fat is used immediately after the pig is slaughtered, without chilling, and layered in white marble troughs or coffins, *conche*, with salt and a mixture of seasonings, including salt, black pepper, fresh rosemary, garlic, cinnamon, cloves, coriander, nutmeg, sage, star anise, and oregano. It is ready to eat after six months, the quality being monitored during the maturation period. Thanks to the porous nature of the marble and the microclimate of the caves in which the coffins are kept, the fat emerges from its entombment in perfect condition, without the intervention of stainless steel or preservatives—hence the universal outrage at the threat from Brussels. From columns to coffins, bureaucrats to boffins, this product has come a long way. Annual production has just about doubled, and now an increased demand from an appreciative public risks creating another hazard, that of inferior imitations. Since the pig fat can be sourced outside the region of production, it does not merit a DOC (its IGP [*see* DOC] does not give the same protection), so the possibility exists that the name can be fraudulently misused. The unique quality of this *lardo* depends on local factors that are subtle and hard to define, but whose absence certainly affects the finished product. However, pig fat can be cured in many ways and in many areas, as one might expect, considering that fat in its various forms was until recently the most precious part of the pig.

Lardo di Arnad is made in Arnad, in the VALLE D'AOSTA, using fat from local pigs traditionally fed on chestnuts, cereals, and vegetables. Now animals from elsewhere are allowed, but the product retains its DOP. The fat is cured in glass or ceramic containers layered with salt and a brine of water boiled with salt and various aromatics—pepper, bay leaves, sage, rosemary, cloves, cinnamon, juniper berries, nutmeg, and the alpine herb achillea. It can age from a few months to a year; a longer cure uses white wine as well. It used to be left to finish maturing in containers of chestnut wood, *doils*, until they were banished recently by health regulations. The "historic" Sagra del Lardo, dating back to 1970, encourages enthusiasm for this and other local products.

Lardo di Montefeltro is made in the area around Montefeltro in the Marche, a local product for domestic rather than commercial use, in which carefully trimmed fat from the hindquarters of the pig is layered with salt, left to mature under a weighted board for a few weeks, then hung to dry for three to four months, after which it used to be cut into pieces and stored in a *salamoia*—all these procedures a most effective way of making sure this most precious part of the pig was safe from rancidity and spoilage. In some areas, the pieces (small enough to use quickly before deteriorating) were kept in glazed earthenware pots made from local clay, or containers made from local stone, yet another example of using local resources to preserve a universal and desirable necessity. Another way was to wrap the large lumps of *lardo* in hay and store them in wooden chests in well-ventilated places. Fat-lovers fighting back

and gastro-tourists eager for strange thrills are helping to keep alive these wise and frugal delicacies, in the past by no means confined to only one or two places.

Lardo di rosmarino is back fat first dry cured with salt and herbs, principally rosemary, then kept in a cool place, massaged every few days, for three months, then vacuum packed. This is made all over Piedmont. Similar flavoured cured fat is also produced in Liguria.

LASAGNE. *See* PASTA, BAKED; PASTA SHAPES.

LATINI, ANTONIO, was born in Collamato near Fabriano in the province of Ancona in the Marche in 1641 and died in Naples in 1696. His work *Lo scalco alla moderna* was published in Naples in two volumes in 1692 and 1694. Latini was of humble origins and worked his way up from an apprenticeship in the household of Cardinal Antonio Barberini in Rome to a position of the highest rank in Naples under the Spanish regent and prime minister Don Stefano Carillo y Salcedo, who rewarded him in 1693 with the title "Cavaliere Aureato e Conte Palatino." Thanks to the diligence of furio Luccichenti, we now have access to unexpected details of his life from a 17th-century manuscript in the Biblioteca Communale in Fabriano, *Storia di Coll'Amato*, compiled by Fra Francesco Maria Nicolini, and based on autobiographical notes compiled by Latini towards the end of his life (Latini, 1992). This must be one of the most frustrating documents in food history, reminiscences strained through a prudent mesh of self-censorship and the cautious *campanalismo* of the worthy friar, leaving us bereft of both personal details and so many of the things we would have liked to know about the food preferences of his patrons and employers. It does, however, give us an idea of

the peripatetic life of an official in a noble household of the time, moving from one patron and position to another as situations changed. Furio Luccichenti and June di Schino have found archival evidence elsewhere for a large floating population of cooks and stewards doing the same, which provides a useful background for interpreting manuscripts and printed sources, and a reminder that the cooks who wrote books were just the tip of a large mountain of talent (Di Schino, 2005).

The aristocratic face on the engraved frontispiece of Latini's book indicates a refined sensibility, enhanced by a voluminous full-bottomed wig and narrow fingers elegantly holding open a book. In fact, Latini was from a modest background; orphaned at the age of five, he lived from hand to mouth. After the first shock of grief at the loss of his parents, young Antonio became a streetwise urchin, and where most lost children would have settled for a crust and a roof over their heads, he used his considerable wits and exploitative charm to move from various situations, some kind and some less so, until he found a place in the household of the Razzanti family in Matelica, where he was taught to cook as well as to read and write. Restless and ambitious, in 1658 he left them after two years to seek his fortune in Rome. There the precocious 16-year-old found employers and patrons, learnt new skills (carving, fencing), squandered what he earned, and—still volatile and wayward—charmed his way in and out of jobs in ecclesiastical and noble households, where, in the full tide of baroque extravagance and splendour, he enjoyed the best and, we suspect, the worst of Roman life. Self-discipline and prudence did not come easy, but after 10 years, Latini sobered up and determined to settle in Macerata, away from the temptations of Rome. After a year there, he left with his employer for a three-year stint in Mirandola in Emilia, then he was in Tuscany with a different employer, then back

to Macerata, and eventually, after 12 years' absence, was back in Rome, where he served various patrons as *scalco* or chief steward, organising every detail of domestic life, including banquets, with periods of work in Sora and Bologna, before settling in Naples for good. There, towards the end of his life, Latini wrote his work *Lo scalco alla moderna* (the first volume was published in 1692), covering food, recipes, and festivities for meat days, followed in 1694 by the second volume, with fish and lean dishes and descriptions of banquets. Written at the peak of baroque gastronomy, before the creeping undertow of French fashion sapped its strength, this work is a joy to read, a wonderful synthesis of aristocratic Italian cuisine, incorporating regional variations in a strong Neapolitan accent, with Spanish customs and ingredients lurking in the bubbling pots and sumptuous pies. CHILLIES and TOMATOES are seen for the first time in printed recipes, not as house plants of dubious reputation (compare Felici's *"piu presto bello che buono"*) but as ingredients associated for the most part with dishes from Spain, or local Neapolitan dishes. There are not many of them, but they are revealing—a raw *salsa* (vol. 1, p. 444; vol. 2, p. 162) seems to come directly from the New World: peeled and chopped tomatoes are mixed with finely chopped onion and chilli, a little thyme or mint, oil, vinegar, and salt, *"molto gustoso."* A *cassuola alla Spagnola* (vol. 1, p. 390) is a stew of pigeon joints, pieces of breast of veal, stuffed chicken necks, with cocks' combs and testicles, seasoned with the usual herbs and spices, and enhanced at the last minute with tomatoes, singed to remove the skins, but not overcooked, for *"queste vogliono poco cottura"* (they need little cooking), a lesson we still need to take on board. Olives are marinated in a sauce made of fresh chillies, oregano, two kinds of mint, fennel seeds, garlic, sugar, salt, oil, and vinegar pounded in a mortar (vol. 2, p. 162). When guests, even the most high-ranking, are Spanish, they are usually offered one or two dishes redolent with garlic, chillies, and sometimes tomatoes. The Italian nobility were given more conventional banquet fare. Chillies figure in dishes presented at a wedding banquet for the daughter of a high Spanish official; parboiled chicken joints are marinated in a mixture of chilli, garlic, oregano, and vinegar, then floured and fried and served with a sweet-sour sauce of pine nuts, olives, capers, candied fruit, spices, and vinegar (p. 575.). The homely touch of garlic and chilli in this elaborate preparation might have cheered a homesick young bride. Roast grey partridges were served up in a sauce of grilled chicken livers, pounded in a mortar with garlic, chilli, white wine, orange juice, and olive oil; this robust dish was of considerable visual sophistication, decorated with arabesques of deep-fried pastry and serrated lemon slices (p. 575). The pleasurable shock of garlic and chilli amongst this ornate finery could have been a deliberate reference to Spanish home cooking. "Here in Naples we have a way with fillet of beef," Latini said (p. 135), in the section on meat cookery, which is to marinate it in smashed garlic cloves, oregano, finely chopped chilli, salt, and a light aromatic vinegar, then poach or roast it lightly, and serve thinly sliced. In volume 2, on vegetable cookery, we find a recipe for *molignane*, EGGPLANTS (vol. 2, p. 55), chopped, and fried in oil, along with finely chopped onion, courgettes, and tomatoes, with the usual herbs and spices; "*che riuscira una minestra alla Spagnola assai bona*" which (will turn out a really nice dish in the Spanish manner).

Latini was not being innovative or adventurous in his use of chillies and tomatoes; he was giving his patron what was appropriate, with tact and imagination, but little originality. His whole career had been based on giving clients what they wanted, food responsive to their personal tastes, based on regional and national cuisines and local produce. This is what makes these early sightings of these two New World plants so exciting, in-

dicating an early acceptance of these ingredients before they caught on in the rest of Italy; since they flourish easily in the soil and climate of CAMPANIA, these by then cheap and easy-to-grow condiments might well have been used in popular cooking before infiltrating aristocratic kitchens. It is far from clear if they came direct from Spain. There is hardly any mention of them as ingredients in Francisco Martìnez Montiño's *Arte de cocina* of 1678 or Juan de la Mata's *Arte de reposteria* of 1747. In fact, de la Mata's recipes for tomato sauce are similar to Latini's, published 50 years earlier. But Velasquez showed chillies and garlic waiting to be pounded in a mortar in one of his early *bodegones*, painted in Seville as early as 1618, and de la Mata's contemporary Luis Meléndez includes tomatoes in some of his down-market still lifes of the 1770s.

Latini uses RICE in ways which reflect different tastes—one recipe, *minestra di riso alla Spagnola* (bk. 1, p. 282), seems familiar to lovers of *paella*; the rice is cleaned, dried, cooked first in finely chopped or pounded pancetta, to which broth is added, with two heads of garlic, spices, and saffron, and when the liquid is all absorbed, the rice is mixed with small roasted game birds, finished off in the oven, and served as a dry dish. Another, *altra minestra di riso* (vol. 1, p. 282), has a sloppier texture; the cooking method is not spelled out for cooks who presumably knew what to do, but it is not light-years away from a RISOTTO, with the cleaned and dried rice cooked in broth with parmesan, and when cooked, served in bowls with more of the cheese. Chickpeas appear in recipes with a Spanish influence, but do not usually figure in Italian banquet food elsewhere. A late 17th-century recipe from Francisco Martínez Montiño, *olla de liebre*, cooks joints of hare, fried with chopped bacon, in a pot with chickpeas and water, seasoned with spices and cumin, to which *todos verduras*, all kinds of green vegetables, several onions, and a whole head of garlic are added towards the end of cooking (p. 80). We find in Latini an *oglia alla Spagnola* (vol. 1, p. 506) reminiscent of today's *cocido madrileño*, in which chickens, joints of fresh beef and mutton, cuts of salted meats and bacon, ham, and cured sausages are cooked with chickpeas in a pot, seasoned with herbs and spices, saffron, and a whole head of garlic, and finished with various vegetables like cabbages of different kinds, and turnip tops, presented in an ornate pastry case, decorated with arabesques and coats of arms, glazed with sugar and gold leaf. This was served at a political banquet given by the regent, Don Stefano Carrillo y Salcedo, at his country villa in Torre del Greco, where a relaxed rustic setting would facilitate diplomacy, and for which was provided an improvised rural structure under a flowering mulberry tree, complete with shrubs and bushes, with tinkling fountains and artfully placed bunches of every kind of fruit. The culture shock of meeting this homely dish in court costume must have been a delight to the visiting grandees. Latini gives several recipes for a *minestra di foglia* in the Spanish or Neapolitan style (vol. 1, pp. 280, 281), in which fresh green vegetables, usually cabbage, are added to a casserole of mixed meats, together with fresh herbs and spices and saffron. A more refined *cassoliglia* (vol. 2, p. 233) was on the menu for a group of noble personages on a trip to Pietra Bianca to watch Vesuvius in unusually active mode on 17 April 1694: a delectable mixture of fresh young peas and broad beans, artichokes, asparagus tips, mushrooms and sprigs of cauliflower cooked with fish fillets, shellfish, fish *polpette*, in a lobster sauce thickened with milk of pine nuts. Latini mentions with pride an occasion when a group of noblemen, on a trip to Posilippo, were so impressed by the *oglia alla Napolitana* (vol. 1, p. 384) that they left untouched the other 11 dishes on offer, "*con gran applauso del Cuoco, e di chi l'ordinò*" (with great praise for the cook and the person in charge). Here Latini spells out the VERDURA and root vegetables, and

we notice the subtlety of this combination of delicate flavours and textures, enhanced with truffles, parmesan, shellfish, and fresh herbs. The Spanish version has chickpeas and two whole heads of garlic as well (vol. 1, p. 50). Another variation adds skinned and quartered tomatoes instead of the greenery. A more sophisticated *cassuola*, which is more characteristic of courtly cuisine, is made with veal, pigeons, ham, sweetbreads, lambs' testicles, mild fresh sausage, peas, artichokes, various shellfish, and truffles, served under a lattice-work of gilded pastry (vol. 1, p. 527). An *oglia in piatti reali* is a sumptuous version made with turkey, partridges, and woodcock, first roasted, then finished in a pot with delicate sausages and unctuous pigs' snouts and ears, to which are added chickpeas, chestnuts, whole truffles, peas, cardoons, young fennel, turnips cut in fine strips, pieces of ham and pine nuts, breadcrumbs, the "usual spices" (discussed later) and "altri nobili ingredienti," all arranged on a serving dish with, in the centre, a whole cabbage stuffed with sausage meat, chopped veal, egg yolks, and cheese. These *piatti composti*, mixtures of meat, fowl, vegetables, and lighter seasonings, are not just a posh adaptation of the food of the lower orders, the *cocidos* and *ollas* or *oglios* of urban Madrid and Naples, but a portent of the lighter, fresher cuisine that was to become fashionable. French manners and ways of doing things would come to predominate, but these intimations of lightness and clarity were already there, as indeed they had been found in English country house cooking a generation earlier. A recipe with the somewhat tentative name *Altro piatto, di mezza bisca* (another dish, a sort of bisque) involves tender young pigeons, partly cooked on the spit, finished off in a dish with slices of veal, sweetbreads, meatballs, and smaller birds, with fried artichokes, pieces of cardoon, and "other noble ingredients" each cooked separately and added later, with their own cooking juices, carefully arranged over a *zupetta* of slices of toasted white bread, the dish decorated with tiny tartlets of minced veal, and the whole adorned with shelled and skinned pistachios. A hundred years later, Vincenzo Corrado would revel in exquisite little vegetable dishes, but already Latini was achieving the delicate balance between familiar aristocratic dishes in the old style and newer recipes that took advantage of the fruit and vegetables of Campania, particularly asparagus, artichokes, cardoons, and young green peas, and also the fresh young leaves of the different kinds of cabbage, lettuce, and endive. In his second volume of *Lo scalco alla moderna*, devoted to lean or Lenten dishes, as well as a big section on fish, we find a few salads: the *insalata alla reale* (vol. 2, p. 50) is a sumptuous pile-up of ingredients on a base of dry biscuits or *taralli* soaked in salt water and vinegar, then covered with plenty of chopped green endive and other raw leaves, interspersed with various radishes, which act as a foundation for a decorative arrangement of pine nuts, stoned olives, capers, pomegranate seeds, black and white grapes, salt anchovies, salt tunny, various cured fish roes, hard-boiled eggs, preserved citron and pumpkin, raisins, shelled pistachios, and sugared comfits, dressed just before serving with salt, oil, and vinegar. This is close to the salad in the painting of a hunt picnic by Carlo Cane, and also to a description of the *capon magro* (Lenten capon) of Liguria. This use of soaked bread as a basis for other things, fish, fowl, and vegetables, is a link with Spanish gazpacho, where breadcrumbs or toasted bread give body to chopped vegetables and other things. It was described in 1747 by Juan de la Mata—"*El gazpacho mas comun es el llamado Capon de Galera*" (the most common gazpacho is called fisherman's capon)—and he tells how it is made, with toasted crusts of stale bread soaked in water and a sauce of pounded garlic, anchovies, sugar, salt, oil and vinegar, upon which an assortment of chopped salad things can be arranged, apple, celery, onion and mint, which is then gar-

nished with capers, stoned olives, anchovies, hard-boiled eggs, pine nuts, pomegranate seeds, wedges of green lemons and slices of citron (p. 164).

Latini's second volume also has a very significant section "*In cui s'insegna il modo di cucinare e condire vivande senza Spezierie*" (In which we learn how to cook and season dishes without spices) (vol. 2, p. 153). Instead of spices he recommends using herbs—parsley, thyme, peppermint, basil, marjoram, pennyroyal, catmint, and chilli, saffron, and ginger. They should be picked in late May or early June, dried in the shade, each one pounded to a powder separately in a mortar and kept in a dry place, for use throughout the year, as a substitute for spices (not for green herbs, which are used fresh all the year round). They are "*gustosi al palato, giovevoli allo stomacho, e alla borsa*" (delicious to the palate, and a delight to the stomach and to the purse). So much cheaper than spices, and a real saving on pepper, he says. The inclusion of chilli as a substitute, without comment, implies that it was readily available. Latini then goes on to give a by then old-fashioned spice mixture that he uses in "*addobbi alla Spagnuola, e pignatte alla Napoletana*" (Spanish and Neapolitan dishes), which includes cinnamon, coriander, nutmeg, mace, and cloves, with pepper as an optional addition. This was long after La Varenne had banished most of these spices from his plain, delicate sauces, and it is perhaps significant that the Kingdom of Naples followed Spain in an unwillingness to relinquish such pleasurable ingredients. But the shape of things to come is there in recipes for vinegars and perfumes using MUSK and AMBERGRIS rather than the conventional spices, a fashion found in England and the Low Countries as well as France. Latini was perceptive enough to follow fashion as and when it pleased his patrons, thus giving us a unique insight into the splendours of baroque banqueting and yet pointing the way to later refinements.

LATTERINI. *See* SAND SMELT.

LATTONZOLO.
See SUCKING PIG.

LAVENDER, *lavanda, Lavandula angustifolia,* and many other varieties, was not traditionally used in the kitchen, but today, with the revived interest in edible FLOWERS, the blossoms and essential oil are used to perfume both sweet and savoury dishes. Lavender seems to have an affinity with rabbit, and there are recipes which include it with other herbs in cooking and garnishing rabbit. The flowers, candied, can be used as decoration, and ices, sorbets, and fruit jellies all benefit from the fragrance.

The therapeutic value of lavender has been prized for centuries, to assuage exhaustion, relieve faintness, clear away misery and depression, and repel insects. An infusion helps provoke urine, thus earning it the name *gorgolestro* (a gurgling torrent) in Tuscany, reported by Mattioli and repeated with glee by Felici.

LAZIO stretches from the Apennines westwards to the extensive Tyrrhenian coast of the Mediterranean, with the products of the Maremma and riverside pastures down on the now drained Pontine Marshes; a mountainous area abutting on ABRUZZO to the east; fertile volcanic soil on the Campagna below; the rolling hills and precipitous valleys of ancient Etruria, Tuscia, to the north, with its lakes and streams, and relics of ancient Etruria; to the south, up the Via Appia, the Castelli Romani; and beyond the wild and fertile hills and meadows of the Ciociaria, stretching towards CAMPANIA and NAPLES. Then there is Rome, with the pope and Cinecittà and a football team, and its complex relationship with its classical past, austere republican virtues and decadent imperial luxuries, its urban baroque heyday, quiet provincial stagnation, and sprawling modern cacophony. Impossible now to be sentimental about the old symbiosis of town and country, of *rus in urbe,* when rising tides of concrete and congested motorways force their way into the silences of the Campagna and up through the neglected olive groves as far as Tivoli. The Rome of Fellini and Antonioni, noisy decadence and solitary alienation, has its gastronomic equivalents (think of McDonald's in the Piazza di Spagna, and the Irish pubs) but against all the odds a characteristically Roman cuisine survives (for more detail, *see* ROME). That of Lazio needs to be considered in its own right, giving perhaps rather more than it takes from the city. Both rural poverty and urban deprivation created dishes using offal and extremities, pasta sauces made with the simplest ingredients, vegetable dishes using the superb local produce, and in contrast, lavish dishes like *garofanato,* using a cheap cut, shin of beef, or chicken dishes, of which *pollo alla romana,* with tomatoes and sweet peppers, is one of the most characteristic; and chicken cooked in *porchetta,* using the strongly fennel-flavoured seasoning used for whole roast pig; also *coda alla vaccinara,* an oxtail stew, perhaps referring to the perks of the *vaccinari,* workers in the slaughterhouse, the tail and cheeks of cattle. People and produce flowed in and out of Rome; the contrasting areas of Lazio provided preserved meats; shepherds in their sheepskin jerkins brought cured and fresh cheeses and ricotta, kids for fattening or the pot; herdsman drove in fierce, resentful bulls for slaughter; market gardeners came with carts of seasonal vegetables; fish from coast and mountain lake were brought in; butchers' boys worked the streets with trays of heads and trotters; the tripe-seller had a following of cats and dogs. Pinelli engraved vignettes of these idealised peasants amid picturesque ruins, with classical profiles but displaying the gestures and facial expressions of the raucous proletariat whose voices were caught by Belli in his sonnets.

Porchetta (that of Ariccia and the Castelli Romani being particularly renowned) was a festive country preparation, now widely sold, and best eaten warm or tepid, carved from the boned and stuffed pig, straight out of the oven and onto the street, something the health police would deny us, for refrigeration hardens the fat and dries out the glutinous juices. Lazio has some fine salumi, for example, *mortadella romana schiacciata*, a flattened squashed salame flavoured with pepper and garlic. The climate in Val Comino is ideal for curing salame, and the *salsiccia della Val Comino* is made of the offal and fat of pigs fed on chestnuts and acorns, seasoned with chilli, pepper, orange peel, and garlic, and includes diced apples; a version of this is made in Monte San Biagio, including pine nuts, raisins, coriander, and bay leaves, as well as the orange and chilli; also from Monte San Biagio and Fondi in the plain below, where in the film Sophia Loren got off the train, kicked off her shoes, put her luggage on her head, and walked off into the Ciociaria for a very bad war (Moravia, 1957), comes a salame made of coarsely chopped pork, seasoned with chilli and roasted coriander seeds, redolent of the oak and cork groves grazed by semiwild pigs of the locality, and the time spent maturing in the smoky *pagliai*. From Viterbo comes the *susianello di Viterbo*, a mixture of offal and cheap cuts, flavoured with pepper, chilli, garlic, and wild fennel, a soft, uncured spreading sausage to be eaten fresh. Fresh cheeses of various kinds, from the milk of sheep, goat, cow, or buffalo, are characteristic of the various provinces of Lazio. *Ricotta genuina romana*, from their whey, is eaten fresh, an ephemeral local produce, not as well protected as it might be from inferior imitations. This delicacy is best bought fresh every day; it does not keep, and the packaged kinds made for a long journey abroad in refrigerated container lorries, well wrapped up for a long shelf life, are a travesty, inedible once you have tasted the real thing. A dried and salted version is appreciated for cooking and

eating. The same can be said of the increasingly popular *mozzarella di bufala*, now almost a cult item, with special boutique outlets, in Rome and elsewhere.

Fish from the lakes in the north—Bracciano, Vico, and Bolsena—include *corregone* (whitefish, which has the added virtue of devouring mosquito larvae), perch, pike, and tench, the tiny *latterini* (*see* SAND SMELT), smaller than whitebait, freshwater sardines, and eels, large and small, cooked in various ways, the glory of lakeside restaurants. The huge female eel, *capitone*, is a delicacy served on Christmas Eve; the small one, *ciriola*, a Roman speciality, can still be fished in the Tiber and is good grilled or spit roasted. At Marta, where the river of the same name flows out of Lake Bolseno, fish have been farmed and gathered for centuries, with consignments sent far afield to other papal possessions—1,120 eels to the Papal Court at Avignon in 1363. Restaurants still offer a wonderful range of eel dishes. On the shores of Lake Bracciano, the little fortified town of Anguillara Sabbazia was also famed for its eels, and *corregone* there is much tastier than the whitefish found in the lakes of northern Europe. A local recipe involves stuffing the gutted fish with a mixture of chopped parsley, garlic, and lemon, and cooking it in the oven on a bed of thin lemon slices.

LEFTOVERS. *See* GUERRINI, OLINDO.

LEMON. *See* CITRUS FRUITS.

LEMON BALM, *melissa, cedronella, Melissa officinalis,* a plant of the Labiatae family, has leaves with a delicate lemon flavour, and—apart from the well-known infusion with its calming and digestive properties, driving away both melancholy and colic (according to Mattioli, it "gets rid of palpitations, false worries, and the fantasies and imaginings that generate melancholy")—has many uses in the kitchen. It goes into mixtures of chopped herbs for stuffings and marinades, *frittatas* and salads, and flavours jams and jellies, and is one of the components of many herbal liqueurs, as well as eau de Cologne.

LEMON VERBENA, *limoncina, erba Luigia, cedrina, Lippia citriodora, Lippia triphylla*, is one of the many Verbenaceae, brought to Europe from South America, and perhaps best known for its fragrant leaves, with their powerful lemony scent. These can be used fresh or dry as a tisane, or to impart lemony-ness without acidity to both sweet and savoury dishes. They have sedative and curative powers similar to lemon balm.

LENTIL, *lenticchia*, is an ancient pulse or legume, known to the ancient Greeks and Romans. The high protein level and the amounts of iron and phosphorous, together with a nice amount of fibre, make them a valuable staple. The little lens-shaped seeds of this legume have been cultivated since 6000 BC. They are one of the pulses that do not need soaking and, if not too old, will cook in about 45–60 minutes. They have an individual nutty flavour and almost floury texture which takes up whatever seasonings are put with it. Apicius had a recipe, interpreted by Grainger (2006, p. 92), which is

Lentils have been cultivated for more than 8,000 years. (Shutterstock)

vibrant with the sweet-sour, fishy, fruity, and bitter combination of honey, vinegar, raisins, *nam pla*, leeks, coriander, dried and fresh, and rue. In Italy today, there are simple soups, thicker dishes to serve as *contorno*, or versions to accompany, or be cooked with, *cotechino*, where the lentils make a wonderful contrast to the rich, glutinous sausage. The quality of lentils depends on where they are cultivated, and certain Italian varieties have international renown. The dry uplands of Umbria, around Castelluccio in Norcia, produce a small fragrant lentil, about two millimetres across, that does not need soaking, but is best eaten within a year of its harvesting in August. Cultivation has always been "organic," using a system of crop rotation which eliminates the need for fertilizers, and the work of harvesting, drying, and sorting is done by hand, which makes for an expensive product, protected by its IGP.

LESSO, *a lesso*, is something cooked gently in abundant liquid, seasoned water or light broth, and means more or less the same as BOLLITO. "Boiled" is an unhappy translation, for the meat or fish simmers slowly, often with onion, carrot, and celery, and can be eaten with vegetables and piquant sauces. The noun *lesso* is usually applied to a single piece of beef, a more austere dish than the than the rich BOLLITO MISTO of Lombardy, the Veneto, and Emilia.

LETTUCE, *lattuga, lattuca*, is one of the huge Compositae family, which includes chicory and endive, and has been enjoyed wild and cultivated since prehistoric times. In the past, the narcotic milky substance in the robust stems was employed medicinally as a sedative, and for this reason lettuce was taken in salads at the end of a meal, to promote postprandial drowsiness and contentment, though there is little in today's lettuces to do this, so a salad can start a meal without

fear of a Flopsy Bunnies situation. Lettuce was held to stimulate digestion, act as a tonic to the system, and be highly nutritious; after it cured the Emperor Augustus of a mortal illness, he is said to have erected a statue in its honour, which must have been a curious sight. Castelvetro was succinct and accurate in his description of the different kinds of lettuce and how to prepare them. The hearted or *capucina* is available today in many varieties; typical is the *Regina di Maggio*, and the smooth-leaved kinds like *romana*, of which *verde d'inverno* is a winter variety, while the small-leaved lettuces are now widely available. Castelvetro praises hearted lettuce grilled or roasted over charcoal, eaten with olive oil and bitter orange juice, and admired the crispness of cos lettuce, when the leaves are tied tightly round a cane and blanched. For his views on salads, *see* SALAD.

LIBERATI, FRANCESCO,

published *Il perfetto maestro di casa* in Rome in 1658 and a revised version in 1668. Its three sections contain all the information one could possibly need to run the large Roman household of a prince or cardinal, outlining the duties of the various officials, the etiquette and protocol, provisioning, costing, the transfer of the household to a country villa in the summer, as well as the conduct of a less imposing private establishment, and finally the complex organisation of the election of a new cardinal and the funeral of a deceased one. After 35 years of experience in various noble households in Rome, Liberati retired to his villa on Monte Mario to reflect on his long and distinguished career, emerging briefly to resume duties with Cardinal Alessandro Bichi, until his death in 1657, before being spurred to set his thoughts down on paper after reading an inferior work on household management which provoked such indignation at the passage on how to skimp on materials for the construction of a cardi-

nal's coach that Liberati felt he had to set the record straight. Unlike some of the many works on the duties of chief steward or *maestro di casa*, this does not include recipes and menus, and so does not figure in histories of banqueting, but the insights into the daily life in a grand household and Liberati's realistic tone of voice make this a good read. Liberati makes no pretence to fine writing, or pompous eulogies; his style, he says, is *"inculto, e privo di ornamenti, e così puro, come io soglio parlare per essere inteso: nel che hò procurato d'imitare que' Pittori, che adoperando il carbone rozzamente, fanno i ritratti simiglianti, e al naturale"* (uncouth and unadorned, as simple as the way I speak to make myself understood; like those painters who make natural and life-like portraits with a crude stick of charcoal). Down to earth and practical, one can almost hear this warm, good-humoured Roman voice telling it the way it is, with a natural authority, beginning with a timely warning to the master to get his priorities straight, and not listen to complaints about the *maestro di casa* from the *cuoco, spenditore, credenziero, dispensiero, canevaro, bottigliere*, all fine fellows, who if left to themselves would rip him off unmercifully. *"La buona opinione mal fondata d'un servitore porta disconcerto alla casa"* (Your undeserved good opinion of a servant brings disharmony to the household). Having sorted the boss, Liberati goes on to advise discretion on the part of the *maestro di casa* in his dealings with both his master and his subordinates.

Much detail follows about the performance of household staff during various functions of the papal court; how much to pay or tip, in money or gifts, the various officials; and a surprising section on the metal kitchen pots needed for these occasions, and their relative prices, with a special reminder that the retinned copper pans should not contain lead.

A section on how to site and construct a villa for a nobleman wishing to escape the heat and noise of Rome is full of practical advice, echoing much written by Palladio over a century earlier, but disdaining the frequently incomprehensible references to ancient literature. The qualities of the soil and the location (for fresh breezes and a handy water supply) are discussed with a warning about the awfulness of bad neighbours and a sullen peasantry. Although contemporary maps show that many princely households had vineyards and orchards in the centre of Rome, patches of green and shade among the intensive urban renewal, there was a need to get away; away, but not too far, Liberati suggests, for like the proverb "*L'occhio del padrone ingrassa il cavallo*" (It is the eye of its master that fattens the horse), the best possible fertiliser for the land is the frequent unexpected appearance of its owner, a real incentive to productivity. It is in the master's interests to know the daily tasks of each month of the year—the planting, sowing, pruning of vines and vegetables and pulses in the fields and herbs and plants in the kitchen gardens. (This gives an insight into the amount of fresh produce the villa would provide for the household, from peas, spinach, fennel, lettuce, cabbage, to fruit of all kinds, melons, cucumbers, and gourds.) And with all this there is the need to build a good relationship with the workforce, avoiding the *malizia dei villani* and seeing that the *buoni contadini* get a fair deal, with fairness, affection, and vigilance, always remembering that the best worker in the vineyard should be the master himself. Indeed Liberati writes with such enthusiasm and affection that one suspects that the labours of managing a villa were a refreshing compensation for the cares of a teeming and contentious urban household. His knowledge of local wines and wine-making was wide and is here simply explained. His account of the various court functionaries includes the *coppiere*, who watches over the choice and presentation of everything his lord and master drinks, and the *scalco*, who has his master's life in his hands—responsible for seeing that his food

is ready when needed—and has as little contact as possible with anyone else. He has to work closely with the cook, and be knowledgeable enough to be able to prepare food himself—"*mettere le mani in pasta*," as Liberati puts it—and responsive to the desires and state of health of the great man, assisted by the *medico* and the *infermiere*, both concerned with the health of the household and the prescription not just of medicines but spices appropriate to his needs. The *cuoco segreto* was the private cook, preparing food for the master and his close associates, obedient to the orders of the *scalco* and clean in his person and behaviour, settled in his ways, strong and hard-working, not given to drink, and intensely jealous of the quality and exclusiveness of his work. This paragon of all the virtues is defined by Liberati by what he is not, and this gives perhaps a more realistic idea of the average cook. Watched like a hawk by the *scalco*, he makes good use of everything that comes into the kitchen, not rustling up little delicacies for his friends on the side, for you might otherwise think that meat and fowl came into the world without necks, wings, heart, or liver. The *trinciante* or carver had to be young, robust, of pleasing appearance, and modest in his performance, no longer the acrobatic show-off of half a century earlier. The *tinello* or staff dining room is discussed at length; this could be a horrible affair, a noisy, crowded scramble for the leftovers from the master's table, or a disciplined series of several sittings, first the noblemen, then the lesser servants, with a menu carefully set out and checked by the *maestro di casa*. Here Liberati describes the everyday fare of the gentlemen: about a pound of meat per head, roasted and stewed, preceded by an antipasto of salami or ham, followed by a *minestra*, the meal ending with cheese and fruit and some fresh or preserved fennel; and on top of this, any choice morsels left from the master's table, with adjustments to the set menu by the watchful *scalco* to make savings on the overheads. Snacking and nibbling as the service unfolded was forbidden, otherwise the *tinello* would degenerate into an *osteria*, but an exception was made for the cleaners, the *scoppatori*, who were continuously at work clearing away the mess and needed some comforts. One begins to understand the charms of Liberati's vineyard on Monte Mario, away from the treacheries and complexities of court life.

LIBER DE COQUINA is the title of an early 14th-century cookery manuscript, of which many versions survive. The pursuit of these early cookery manuscripts, and their often complex relationship to each other, involves a sort of scholarly detective work that is of more than academic interest, for apart from the thrill of the chase, we have an increased understanding of the regional traditions of Italy and the significance if Italian gastronomy to the rest of Europe, as well as the delight of exploring familiar and unusual recipes. Seven known manuscripts of *Liber de coquina* survive, and it has been argued that the style of cooking it represents may be that of the Angevin court of Naples. Whatever its origins, this manuscript was copied, modified, and circulated all over Italy and was known in France and Germany as well, a courtly aristocratic cuisine, written in Latin for an elite whose cooks would have had the necessary skills, and did not need recipes spelled out. It is dangerous to generalise from the known copies and their provenance, exhaustively researched and listed by Bruno Laurioux, but *Liber de coquina* seems to indicate the popularity of a style of gastronomy which can be described as "Italian," regardless of the political complexities of the peninsular during the 15th century. Versions in the vernacular were also in circulation during the 14th and 15th centuries. One of them, *Libro della cocina*, attributed to an Anonimo Toscano, was one of several surviving cookery manuscripts reprinted in the 19th century as curiosities by Italian antiquarians (Olindo Guerrini, Ludovico Frati, Zambrini), diverted by the mixture of the curious and the familiar in the recipes. They would not be mentioned here if the recipes were irrelevant, but a great many of them are either familiar or delicious in their own right. From *Liber de coquina* comes recipes for *limonia* (a recipe derived from medieval Arab gastronomy), in which chickens or capons are parboiled, jointed, and fried in lard, then finished in a sauce made from ground almonds, some chicken broth, coloured with saffron, flavoured with spices and lemon juice tempered with sugar, and served with a dusting of cinnamon. The sourness could be got from bitter oranges or verjuice. This presupposes the availability of good broth, expensive almonds and citrus fruit, and the even more costly cinnamon, saffron, and sugar, all to be found in the kitchens of the rich. No wonder Platina, over a century and a half later, made so much of Martino's exquisite chicken with verjuice flavoured simply with native seasonings of mint and parsley, some cinnamon, and the juice of fresh unripe grapes, an elegant example of the Nuova Cucina (offspring of the New Learning of the Renaissance). (Laurioux, 2006)

Another tradition of vernacular cookery manuscripts is attributed to the "12 gluttons," linked by some commentators on Dante's *Inferno* to the *Brigata spendereccia* in SIENA, 12 self-indulgent young men of good family the poet castigated unfairly for their gastronomic excesses. Laurioux notes that in the eight surviving manuscripts derived from it, the recipes are for 12 people, and have a sense of proportion and precision not found in other cookery manuscripts. Capatti and Montanari see this as an indication of an urban gentry or merchant class wanting a more practical vernacular handbook than the contemporary *Liber de coquina*. If the stories about the 12 gluttons have any basis in reality, they might well have been self-catering. In their retreat from plague-stricken Siena, with so slight a chance of survival, it would not be unreasonable to spend every last penny of one's resources on cheerful hedonism—more deserving of a slot in Paradise, I would have thought, than ending up in Dante's *Inferno*. A book that was a practical instruction manual would have met their needs and those of many of their contemporaries. A version of this in a recognisably Venetian vernacular was published by Frati in 1899, *Libro di cucina del secolo XIV*, and more recently in the Einaudi paperback edition of Faccioli's *Arte della cucina*. Recipes include the universal favourite, *brodetto camelino a caponi*, in which stewed chickens are jointed and served in a sauce made by thickening their cooking liquid with almonds pounded in their skins, to give that "camel" colour, further enhanced with *specie fine*, and long pepper and nutmeg, and sharpened with verjuice and a little dry wine. The recipe insists that the chicken joints are not cooked in the sauce, but smothered with it just before serving, with a final powdering of "the best spices you have." Another recipe for a civet of wild boar, *civiro overo savore negro a cengiuro*, is a really dark mixture of bread toasted to blackness, soaked in vinegar, and pounded with some of the cooked meat, and a spice mixture of long pepper, meleguetta pepper, and ginger, "ground really well by the druggist," and cooked together in a separate pot with vinegar and some of the degreased cooking liquid. This is served as a sauce over the meat, and the recipe ends with a precise definition: "This sauce needs to be black, strongly spiced, and sharp with vinegar." The contrast between the pale boiled meat and the dark harsh sauce must have been a visual and gastronomic pleasure. This is typical of these entrancing recipes: very clear about what the finished dish should taste like, and with sensible instructions about how to get there. A *"bon savore da polastri"* (a good sauce for fowl) is made by squeezing pomegranates in the hand (this will gently release the juice without bruising the fibres and seeds and releas-

ing the harsh tannin) and flavouring it with *specie dolce*, sweet spices (cloves, ginger, cinnamon, nutmeg, in specified proportions), but adding some pounded anise or rosewater if it seems too strong. A sharp-tasting pomegranate would need the juice of sweet grapes to balance it. This sauce *"non vole star fatto che se guasta"* (should not sit around once made or it will spoil). The Neapolitan court cooks would have known this, but a Siennese domestic servant might have needed telling. Many of these recipes imply recipes based on plainly boiled or roast meat or fowl, unlike the more elaborate composite dishes of *Liber de coquina*, so the prodigal use of spices that Dante disliked was seen as an aristocratic luxury.

Today we are better informed about the role of spices in Italian gastronomy, and so find these surviving recipes enjoyable and accessible.

LIGOZZI, JACOPO (1547–1632),

left his native Verona in 1577 to work at the court of the Medici dukes of Florence and stayed there until his death, first producing a series of accomplished botanical studies, then going on to organise the workshops of applied arts, and to design interior decoration, works in *pietre dure* (mosaics in semi-precious stone), embroidery, jewellery, and costumes. In all these areas, we can follow the contemporary interest in accurate representation of nature, though the plant studies are what concern us here, especially the angelica, where the plant is so alive that its leaves seem to be moving in a slight breeze, or the branch of figs shown in different stages of ripeness with three exotic birds poised among the curving, writhing leaves, ready to attack the vulnerable fruit. The great botanist Ulisse Aldrovandi was so impressed, on a visit to Florence, with Ligozzi's work that he persuaded the duke to send him spares and duplicates of Ligozzi's studies, and also commissioned work from him,

Bream, by Jacopo Ligozzi (1547–1632). (Scala/Art Resource, NY)

many of which are still to be seen in the University Library at Bologna.

LIGURIA has a coastline that stretches from the French Riviera in the west down to the Tuscan coast, and inland it abuts on PIEDMONT, EMILIA-ROMAGNA, and TUSCANY. In many places the land rises precipitately from the coast, with tiny bays and little ports which until recently were only accessible by sea. Terraces reached by steep steps are cultivated in defiance of gravity and the tenuous hold of soil on rock, for the long hours of sunlight and the benign sea breezes give concentrated flavours and aromas to vines, herbs, and vegetables which repay the enormous effort. Inland, the rolling hills and wooded slopes produce crops of fruit and vegetables, vines, and olives. The Ligurian Riviera—Ponente to the west of Genoa, and Levante to the south—has year-round sun and winter warmth, and is fragrant with aromatic herbs and plants, sharing with the French Riviera a warm southern cuisine, fish

soups, *FOCCACIA*, preserved fruits, perfumed flowers, and a lucrative tourist industry. Genoa, in the middle of this boomerang-shaped coast, is today the largest port in Italy, and in the past, rivalling Venice, was the hub of trade with the East, bringing luxury commodities and spices to Europe, although little of these trickled down to the kitchens of the frugal, hardworking Ligurians. The main influences on their cuisine are the fragrant local herbs and vegetables, the subtle olive oil, and products devised to survive and sustain people during long sea voyages. Things that will keep well—dried salt cod, salted anchovies, preserved sauces and relishes, dried pasta, ship's biscuits, and food that will cook easily, like some of the fish soups made with the less prized fish of the catch, have permeated the regional cuisine, producing incomparable recipes. Although meat and dairy produce can be had from the hinterland, they are not of first importance in a diet that for many was almost completely vegetarian. The quality of vegetables and herbs is so high, the variety of bread and pasta so varied, that satisfying dishes and snacks that are both sophisticated and frugal can be enjoyed as street food or family meals. Fred Plotkin's devoted account of Ligurian food, *Recipes from Paradise*, has many insights. He remarks that meals do not follow the usual pattern of the rest of Italy, with the family assembled maybe twice daily round a conventionally structured meal; rather, in a society where mariners or merchants are often away, a more relaxed pattern of snacks and simple food became the habit. Women in this social structure had to keep homes and businesses going, and save as much as they could while preserving and putting by all the produce of the land and sea for future use. The many sauces, fresh and preserved, of Liguria are part of this tradition, where quickly cooked pasta or a pancake or fritter, or some *focaccia* from the baker, could be seasoned with salt, olive oil, and a relish, and so, with cheese, fruit, and some wine, a good meal is at once to hand, often at short notice. At present, a normal working day is more likely to be punctuated with something similar from the many bakeries and food shops, reminding us that ancient Ligurian traditions of fast food are more relevant, and certainly healthier, than modern versions.

Ligurian Bread

Focaccia is perhaps the best known of the breads of Liguria, good on its own or as a vehicle for the many sauces and spreads. These flattened rectangles or circles of bread dough, anointed with olive oil and salt crystals, often with onions, rosemary, sage, cheese, or sausage, are street food, baked several times during the day and meant to be eaten hot and straight out of the oven. The *fougasse* of the French Riviera is similar, using dried rather than fresh herbs. You could think of *focaccia* as PIZZA without the *pomodoro*, or alternatively see pizza as a later southern version of the ancient northern flattened bread. *Piscialandrea* is a *focaccia* which does use

tomatoes, along with anchovies or sardines, onions, olives, and herbs, rather like the *pissaladière* of Nice, named for Andrea Doria, the great Genoese admiral. *Sardenaira* from San Remo has a topping of tomato and anchovy sauce, capers, olives, basil, oregano, and olive oil. A *focaccia* with cheese is made in Recco using a light fresh young cheese, *crecenza*, or *invernizzina*, confusingly now often obtained from Lombardy.

An even more ephemeral street food is *fainâ*, *farinata*, a thin layer of batter made from chickpea flour and water enriched with olive oil and often flavoured with onion or rosemary, cooked in a special copper receptacle, and unappealing unless eaten scalding hot from the oven, described with consummate tact by Anna del Conte as "the sort of food that can only be appreciated in its native habitat" (like a waterfront bar with a glass of dry white wine, or on the sundrenched pavement outside the baker's). However it can work surprisingly well in a domestic kitchen in midwinter, using a good olive oil and baked nicely crisp and golden, with an addictive nuttiness. Then there is *paniccia*, called a bread, which is really a POLENTA made of chickpea flour, and good served hot in slices with olive oil and condiments. A similar version is made with broad bean flour. Made with skill, and eaten with one of Liguria's many sauces or relishes, these ingredients of CUCINA POVERA become delicacies. The rustic bread of Triora is made of rye and wheat flour, and Chiavari has a bread rich with olive pulp and oil.

Versions of hard twice-cooked breads and biscuits are to be expected in a seafaring region, but the truth about the Garibaldi biscuit, many currants squashed between two layers of pastry, is that its commercial form might have originated in Scotland, and later been manufactured by John Carr for Peak Freen in Bermondsey to celebrate a visit to London in 1861 of Italy's revolutionary hero. Garibaldi belonged to Liguria, for he was born in Nice when it was part of the Republic of

Genoa, and it was from near Genoa that he set out with his Thousand to unite Italy, although not in the republican form that Giuseppe Mazzini, born in Genoa in 1805, had striven for. History gave both of them a distrust of monarchy and papacy, and Italy's eventual unification under the House of Savoy seemed to many a tragic betrayal of their republican ideals.

Génoise, a boring sponge, is a British travesty of a Ligurian speciality, *pandolce*, a rich yeasted cake full of not only dried fruits and candied peel, especially citron and lemon, but also the bland pumpkin or marrow, which acts as a sort of catalyst to the other flavours—pine nuts and pistachios, delicately spiced, with fennel predominating—and perfumed with lemon or orange flower water and marsala, baked ready for Christmas but potentially lasting until Epiphany in early January. This is a more solid kind of fruit cake than the lighter, fluffier PANETTONE of Milan, different from the fruitcake we call Genoa cake. There are many different recipes, with variations on the basic ingredients and method, for this is a cake usually made at home, and every household had its own version.

The Herbs of Liguria

A characteristic use of wild herbs and plants is the *preboggiòn*, or *praebuggiùn*, a bundle of at least seven, or even more, fresh herbs and fragrant green plants, which might include all or some of these: *cicerbita*, smooth sowthistle, *pimpinella*, salad burnet, *dente di cane* or *talegua*, dandelion, *cavolo primaticcio* or *gaggia*, wild spring cabbage, *bieta selvatica*, wild beets, *prezzemolo*, parsley, *raperonzolo*, rampions, *ortica*, nettles, *pissarella*, dandelion, *borragine*, borage, *cerfoglio*, chervil. This mixture of edible wild plants, unique to Liguria, varies from place to place and is put to varied uses: they can be washed, softened in their own juices, turned in olive oil with garlic and anchovies, and then chopped and cooked with rice; included in a vegetable stew or minestrone (*see* SOUP); used in stuffings for pasta (the characteristic *pansôti*), or with fish, fowl or meat, or in a FRITTATA; mixed with cheese, pine nuts, and ricotta and put in pies and tarts; stirred into mashed potatoes; or eaten cooked or raw as a salad. These are the herbs that straight-backed, barefoot old ladies used to carry in baskets on their heads as they came down from the steep terraces of the Cinque Terre to the markets below.

This wealth of herbs is now overshadowed by the commercial production of *pesto alla genovese* (*see* PESTO) on a commercial scale, so that what was until quite recently one sauce among many has become an internationally revered icon, an industrial product, however exquisite, whose long shelf life belies its main virtue as a freshly made, local, ephemeral sauce. The fresh aromas of crushed BASIL fade rapidly, and any version which tries to disguise this with the addition of pecorino, garlic, pine nuts, and whatever is flying in the face of nature. The *Cuciniera genovese* of the 1850s has a *Battuto alla genovese* with the name *pesto* as an afterthought in brackets, but by the 1990s, when Fred Plotkin wrote his *Recipes from Paradise*, he described the different versions of pesto throughout the region, and the passionate views held by every Ligurian about how to make it. He reminds us that they have the advantage over us of a supply of superlative perfumed small-leafed basil, and then gives 16 different versions of the sauce.

Pounding up herbs with nuts, sometimes breadcrumbs, garlic, salt, and olive oil is an ancient and universal way of making a sauce, and this is how we can best understand, make, and enjoy pesto, or any of the other sauces, unimpeded by dogma.

Sauces

There are many superb sauces which are true to their ancient origins, unpolluted by the ubiquitous tomato. Pale, creamy sauces based on nuts, light fresh cheeses, pale herbs, or tawny mushrooms go very well with the delicately flavoured and sometimes coloured pasta of Liguria.

A recipe for *tagliarini alle erbe fresche* dresses fresh egg pasta with a mixture of fresh herbs—basil, marjoram, rosemary, sage, and mint—crushed lightly but not pounded in a mortar, and heated gently in some cream, into which the just-cooked pasta is stirred just before serving. Plotkin's sensitive version eschews parmesan, but a little can enhance rather than overwhelm the flavours.

Tocco di noce, a sauce made to have with *pansôti* (fat ravioli with a filling of greens, especially *preboggiòn*), is a mixture of pounded skinned WALNUTS, breadcrumbs, garlic, and parmesan, flavoured with marjoram and diluted with *prescinseua*, a Ligurian milk product which is more like acidulated clotted full cream milk than cheese. It gives body and a creamy acidity to sauces and stews and vegetable preparations. *Prescinsoeua* can be made by clotting rich milk with rennet or adding lemon juice to warmed milk and straining the resultant curds.

Garlic and walnuts also made a traditional *agliata* (*see* GARLIC), one of the most popular sauces of the past; a subtle variation, *pesto bianco*, is made with shelled and peeled walnuts, ground to a paste in a mortar with garlic, stirred with light Ligurian olive oil, and then some fresh ricotta beaten in to make a creamy sauce, to go with fresh pasta. The ephemeral *crema ai pinoli* is made by pounding pine nuts with garlic, fresh marjoram, and butter, loosened if necessary with a little milk, with some whole pine nuts stirred in. This is served in Genoa with *corzetti* or *fettucine*.

Marò or *pestùn di fave* is made from very tender young fresh raw broad beans, shelled, their outer skins removed, pounded with garlic, *pecorino sardo*, and mint in a mortar, diluted with a little olive oil, and seasoned with salt and pepper. Another fresh sauce, ideal with gnocchi, is made by mixing finely minced sweet onions or the more assertive chives into fresh ricotta with salt and Ligurian olive oil.

Some sauces are for keeping and can be put up in jars and bought out to have on BRUSCHETTA or pasta or with vegetables. One made from young artichokes, trimmed and finely sliced, softened in oil and butter with chopped onion and garlic, then cooked with dry white wine, chopped parsley added at the end, can be used as it is or creamed in a mortar. Sun-dried tomatoes and preserved baby artichokes (but not on any account those pickled in vinegar) are combined with basil, walnuts, olive paste, oil, and a little chilli pounded to a paste.

Tocco di funghi is ideally made from fresh *funghi porcini*, which are abundant and very good in Liguria, but dried ones, soaked and strained, can be combined with ordinary field mushrooms for this sauce, in which the sliced mushrooms are cooked in a mixture of pounded garlic, rosemary, pine nuts, butter, and oil, cooked until fragrant in a little dry white wine, and served with salt, pepper, and parsley. This is good with pasta or risotto, with or without parmesan.

Cheese and Salame

Local cheeses are made in the alpine regions of Liguria, like *bruzzu*, a fermented sheep's ricotta, or a matured goat's cheese used in making pesto. Trading connections with Emilia along an ancient road snaking through the hills, have been a traditional source of parmesan, and pork products from elsewhere. There are also some renowned local products—*zeraria* is made in winter from the meat of a pig's head, including tongue and throat, cooked with aromatics that vary but are usually salt, pepper, lemon, bay leaves, and sometimes saffron, the meats taken off the bone, chopped, and put to set in the cooking liquid, and eaten cold, sliced. *Testa in cassetta* is a similar product, cooked with seasonings and marsala, then set in a casing. From Sant'Olcese in the province of Genoa comes a salame made from mixed beef and pork meat, lightly smoked, and a by-product of this is *mostaradella*, made with the trimmings, cubes of LARDO, and plenty of garlic; this is then cured and can be eaten as it is or fried with eggs.

Fish

The fish from the Ligurian coastline of the Tyrrhenian Sea are not as rich and varied as in other areas, but good use is made of them. This said, it is worth looking at the list of fishes available in the market at Genoa in the 1850s, an appendix to *Cuciniera Genovese*: there are 72, including crustaceans, with scope for some sophisticated fish cookery, not just fry-ups. The two main soups or stews of Liguria are BURIDDA, in which a variety of prepared fish are cut up and either stewed in a SOFFRITTO or a mixture of chopped garlic, onion, celery, and carrot softened in olive oil, cooked down to make a pleasant sauce, in which the fish are simmered until done; or sometimes layered with the vegetables in a terra cotta pot and cooked for several hours, often with the addition of salted anchovies, dried mushrooms, pine nuts, and capers, and usually some tomatoes as well, maybe with white wine instead of water. All this could take hours, ending up with mature squid and octopus nice and tender and the other fish disintegrated; or the fish could be added in sequence according to their cooking time. These might include angler fish, rascasse, gurnard, weevers or stargazers, dogfish, octopus and squid, mussels, shrimp, and razor clams. (The name *buridda* is similar to the provençale *bourride*, but the method is not—a *bourride* is cooked quickly with the raw sauce ingredients and thickened to a velvety softness with aïoli and egg yolks.)

The other fish stew or soup, *ciuppin*, humble ancestor of the sumptuous *cioppino* of San Francisco, California, is said to have originated in the ways mariners or fish-sellers had of using up lesser or damaged fish, fresh but not commercially viable. At its simplest,

they were all boiled up together with their heads and bones and whatever aromatics came to hand and poured over slices of stale bread; in restaurants, the mixture is cooked in a carefully prepared *soffritto* and then forced through a sieve to get rid of the skin and bones, resulting in a thick fragrant soup, in which select pieces of fish are sometimes cooked briefly. Both these recipes, and the many variations on them, can involve long slow cooking, anything from 20 minutes to two hours, first of the sauce, and then of the pieces of fish, unlike the fierce rapid boiling of the *bouillabaisse* of the French Riviera. (The CACCIUCCO of Livorno is an altogether wackier dish, made and drunk with red wine, fiery with red CHILLI PEPPER, and the mopping-up bread pungent with garlic, using the more assertive fish of the Tuscan coast). The migrant fishermen from Sestri Levante who settled in San Francisco in the 19th century brought the recipe, or rather method, of making *cioppino* with them, and many imaginative versions are made today, exploiting the rich harvest of the bay, in many ways more luxurious than the original versions, were it not for the tendency to overdo the tomatoes.

Other recipes have an imaginative combination of fish and vegetables, prepared pieces of squid, octopus, or cuttlefish started off in olive oil and garlic, then stewed with tomatoes, white wine, and desalted capers, and finished, when almost tender, with fresh green peas; there is a version of this beginning with the usual chopped onion, celery, and garlic, and completing cooking with parboiled spinach and chopped reconstituted dried mushrooms. The sweetness of cuttlefish or squid goes well with the slight bitterness of artichokes in a recipe which starts the strips of squid in chopped mild red onion, garlic, and parsley simmered in olive oil, then cooked in white wine with trimmed and sliced artichokes, and finally stewed until soft in a little fish broth. Plotkin describes very tender baby artichokes, trimmed and chopped, cooked quickly with monkfish fillets which have been dusted with flour and lightly fried, and finished with parsley in white wine which is allowed to evaporate. He also adapts a more complex restaurant recipe for asparagus and sea bass fillets: these are marinated in delicate Ligurian olive oil and lemon juice, then cooked in a mixture of white wine, garlic and shallots, and some of the asparagus cooking water, and served with a creamy asparagus sauce, and the delicate tips. Cuttlefish in greens is another lovely recipe, sometimes served with chickpeas as well, and often embellished with toasted pine nuts and raisins.

Food from the Hinterland

Perhaps the most vivid evocation of the inland landscape of Liguria is found in Italo Calvino's *Il barone rampante*, in which the young Cosimo Piovasco di Rondò lives his life in the treetops of the mythical Val d'Ombrosa. The nuts, chestnuts, olives, fruit, mushrooms, and game of the region are exploited by the ingenious Cosimo, but it is the snails that precipitate his leap for freedom, and Calvino's description of their captivity and escape, and final gruesome fate in the kitchen of the sinister little sister Battista, sets the tone of the narrative, both as a metaphor for freedom and revolt (and revulsion) and an insight into domestic tyranny and a child's instinctive dislike of unpleasant food. A recipe from Finale has something of the laboriousness of Battista's efforts without the horror. After a lengthy purging, the snails are cooked in acidulated water and then finished slowly in a *battuta* of onions, celery, basil, parsley and marjoram, tomatoes, and white wine, and served with a sauce of pounded walnuts, hazelnuts, capers, and pecorino.

Mushrooms, dried and fresh, are another of the glories of the hinterland, and like the herbs and vegetables, they appear in unexpected combinations with fish, as in the recipe for angler fish (*coda di rospo*, also called *pescatrice* in Liguria) or angel fish, also con-fusingly known as monkfish but actually one of the shark family, *squadro*. Here sliced *funghi porcini* are added to fillets of monkfish that have been floured and fried in oil, together with finely sliced onion and garlic, and cooked with a slug of brandy or grappa and fish or vegetable broth. Dried porcini go into a dish of red mullet *alla genovese*, which are baked, covered with breadcrumbs, in a sauce made of capers, anchovies, chopped onions, fennel seeds, and tomato paste, reduced to an aromatic density with some white wine and fish broth. Soaked pieces of salt cod (*see* BACCALÀ) are cooked with softened dried porcini, chopped with garlic and rosemary, cooked golden in oil, and finished in a sauce of tomato concentrate diluted with a little vinegar, and pine nuts, raisins, and sugar. A soup of puréed chickpeas is served with porcini sautéed in oil and garlic.

Artichokes from Albenga, the *carciofi violetti*, are used in sauces, egg dishes, pies, and *frittate*, cooked with other vegetables, and enjoyed raw when young. They have the advantage of being both tender and slightly crunchy.

Rabbit used to be eaten more than butcher's meat, cooked with the usual mixture of celery, onion, and herbs, together with pine nuts, walnuts, and olives, moistened with red wine and broth made from the head and liver. *Cima all genovese* is a dish made from a cheap cut of veal, the breast, boned and with a pocket made to take the stuffing, which is made from innards and entrails, including udder, testicles, brains, sweetbreads, and bone marrow, simmered, then chopped, and mixed with artichokes, green peas, breadcrumbs, parmesan, and eggs, and seasoned with marjoram and spices. This is sewn carefully into the pouch and simmered for several hours; the dish is usually eaten cold or tepid. Plotkin was told a more refined version, with cooked vegetables, including green beets, zucchini, and red peppers, dried *funghi porcini*, and pistachios, with strips of cooked ham and hard-boiled eggs instead of the weird body parts, cooked in water with celery, carrot, and onion. There is a simpler 15th-century version in Martino, using pepper, saffron, raisins, mint, parsley, marjoram, and grated hard cheese.

Apart from the mainly wild herbs and greens in *preboggion*, there are the vast commercial hothouses for keeping up with the demand for basil. Cardoons, artichokes, spinach, beets, cabbages, cauliflowers, tomatoes, and eggplants are grown and are the basis of the healthy Ligurian diet. The *torta pasqualina* was once an Easter dish, but is now enjoyed all the year round. Green chard is cooked, chopped, and mixed with parmesan and ricotta, flavoured with herbs, and placed on multiple layers of very fine rich pastry; indentations in the filling contain raw eggs and butter, and the pie is covered with more layers of pastry (33 in all, one for each year of Christ's life) and baked; when sliced, the eggs glow among the pale greens of the filling and the crisp golden pastry.

Violet honey flavours chestnuts, and rose petals pounded with lemon juice perfume a sugar syrup, for use in confectionery. In the past, cordial waters and syrups flavoured with fruit and blossoms found their way into sorbets and creams. *Paciugo* or *pacciugo*, the celebrated ICE CREAM made around Portofino, is a concoction of whipped cream, bitter chocolate ice cream, fresh fruit, bitter cherries in syrup, and a raspberry or strawberry coulis. Baldly expressed, it sounds like just another sundae, but when the balance of fresh fruit, bitterness, and sweetness is right, it has the complexity and harmony of the *cappon magro*. An improbable legend tells of a couple living in similar close harmony, Pacciugo and Pacciuga; he was a mariner, taken captive by pirates, and in his absence his devoted wife went every Saturday to a nearby shrine to pray for his return; when he came back 15 years later, Pacciugo became irrationally jealous of stories of her absence on Saturdays, took her out to sea on his boat, killed her, and tossed the body overboard. Then, filled with remorse, he slunk off to the shrine to beg forgiveness, and there Pacciuga was, safe and sound, restored to life by the Virgin Mary. The ice cream was created as a tourist attraction in the 1930s, perhaps influenced by the legends collected by the local historian Michelangelo Dolcino. *Pacciugo* means *imbroglio* or *pasticcio*, a right mix-up, which could apply to both the mariner and the ice cream.

Cappon magro, or Lenten capon, is a dish that unites the fruits of sea and land, a sort of synthesis of the delights of Liguria, perhaps at one time a celebratory meal for returning mariners. It has a solid, unremarkable base of ship's biscuits soaked in oil and salt water, interspersed with pieces of salt tunny, a reminder of hard tack and hard times on the high seas, and is then covered in an extravagant elaborate towering symmetrical arrangement of cooked vegetables, piled high (long before this became a show-off thing to do), each layer dressed with a rich and complex sauce combining anchovies, capers, olives, hard-boiled egg yolks, oil, and vinegar, and the imposing structure embellished with a lush assortment of fish and shellfish, lobster, oysters, prawns, and dark olives, with glowing quarters of hard-boiled eggs round the rim. With all the prime products of the region at their freshest and best, this meat-free pile-up of luxuries is a flamboyant way of demolishing the tired old cliché of Ligurian parsimony. The name might be an ironical reference to the "lean" diet of fast days and Fridays, intended to promote abstinence but circumvented by the wealthy to produce meals as gluttonous as "meat" days. The vagaries of spelling, reformed or unreformed, are confusing; *cappon* (with two *p*s or one) could refer to capon, the fat neutered cockerel forbidden in Lent, or any of the several fine fish, used during 'fast' days, of the Scorpaenidae and gurnard families (whose appearance and many regional names can reduce one to despair), including the decorative bright red scorpion fish, called *cappone* or *cappoun*, or perhaps rascasse or gurnard, all of them pink and tasty. The *cappon magro* is a link with the "Great Salad" of 17th-century banquets, with the concentric rings of decorative things arranged on a huge serving dish, slices of lemon and bitter orange, oysters, and shiny olives, very like the huge salad platter in a 17th-century painting attributed to Carlo Cane, now in Milan, which shows a hunt "picnic" out of doors, with cold food arranged on a table and the ornate dish presided over by a formidable matriarch, knife in hand, subservient family grouped in respectful attendance. If hers were the hands that arranged the salad, the painting might be an implied tribute to female powers of organisation, for although the men in the party all carry emblems or instruments of hunting, they seem somewhat cowed, and the food must have been carefully preprepared in the domestic kitchen: a huge ornate pie, a dish of cold cuts with slices of lemon—not the usual spit roasted fruits of the chase, an impromptu meal at the end of a long day's hunt, wolfed down by tired men and dogs. This recipe reminds us of the grand salads of 17th-century Naples described by LATINI, and also an 18th-century description by Juan de la Mata of his gazpacho, which he says is also called *Capon de Galera*.

A little vignette of Genoese life comes from Olindo GUERRINI, man of letters and contemporary of Artusi, who spent an idyllic time towards the end of his life as university librarian in Genoa, helping out during the First World War. Twice a day he went up and down the 300 steps between his flat and the library, invigorated by the fresh air and sunshine, and it was a local saying "*Un bon pasto o dûa trei giorni*" (A good meal should last three days)—which, as his granddaughter reminded him, implies an imaginative use of leftovers—that inspired Guerrini to get on with the project he had earlier discussed in Bologna with Artusi, *L'arte di utilizzare gli avanzi della mensa* (The art of using left-over food), which became a best-seller. A profu-

sion of good things, combined with the native frugality of Genoa, had an immediate appeal to this elderly Bolognese. His recipe for a *minestrone alla ligure* adds left-over vegetables—green beans, fresh haricot beans, mushrooms, cabbage, eggplants, courgettes, and potatoes to a broth flavoured with basil and parsley pounded with garlic and parmesan, in which some vermicelli have been cooked. He describes another Ligurian way of preparing *scorzanera* which would work equally well with the freshly cooked vegetable, turned in hot butter, then seasoned with a mixture of chopped basil, parsley, anchovies, and mushrooms, and finished in white wine and broth; such vegetables are of a quality that they make a meal in themselves, not just a *contorno*.

Pasta in Liguria

Ways of treating flour so that it lasts and does not get rancid or mouldy were probably behind the "invention" of pasta. The dry sunny climate of Liguria, and the availability of wheat, either grown locally or imported, might have made it a good place for this to happen, but there is no written evidence that it ever did. Sabban and Serventi have cautiously concluded that the mention of a barrel of *maccheroni* in the will of a Genoese merchant implies an imported pasta, probably from Sicily, or nearby Sardinia, once a major producer. Since dried pasta was good to take on long sea voyages, it would travel along with the twice-cooked BISCOTTI or ship's biscuits, but the ingredients for fresh pasta were also carried on board, perhaps to save inroads into the dried version, which was also a trading commodity.

Some dried *ravioli*, stuffed with a hard cheese, were taken on long journeys. *Pansôti* are plump, pot-bellied ravioli filled with a mixture of greens, ideally *preboggiòn*. Stuffed pasta, *ravioli*, are said to have been invented in the town of Novi Ligure in Liguria, although why the Italian genius for inventive pasta should be focussed on one spot is never made clear. Ortensio Landi claimed in 1548 that ravioli were invented in Lombardy by Libista, a peasant woman from Cernuschio, using simple local herbs and greens, in contrast to the luxurious cooking of the rich. The best known brand of pasta in Liguria today is made by Agnesi, who created the Museo Nazionale delle paste alimentari in Rome and produces industrial versions of domestic types of pasta. *Trenette*, with their flat rectangular section, almost as thin as linguine, are associated with pesto, and in the recipe *trenette avvantaggiate* are cooked with diced potatoes and green beans, in the same water, timed so that all ingredients are cooked to perfection at the same time, then strained of most but not all of the cooking liquid, and served with pesto.

Fresh pasta can be made with or without eggs, sometimes with the addition of white wine or olive oil, to give a lighter version than the egg-rich pasta of Emilia-Romagna. Sometimes this is coloured and flavoured with a green vegetable, preferably borage, although spinach can be used. Marjoram is often used to flavour sheets of pasta, pounded and mixed with the eggs, and this goes beautifully with some of the cheese, mushroom, or nut sauces. Chestnut flour, once a cheap substitute for wheat flour but now almost a luxury, can be used. *Trofie* or *troffie* are little twisted fragments of pasta, said to have originated in or near Recco, usually served with pesto; a flour-and-water dough is rolled between the palms of the hand or fingers, a small olive-sized lump at a time, to produce irregular worm-like shapes which cook in a few seconds, and are the only pasta that seems to need a drop of oil in the cooking water—said to be the product of a frugal Ligurian housewife rubbing sticky dough from her hands, a "blissful accident of creation," as Plotkin puts it. *Corzetti* are made from rolled-out pasta pressed by a round wooden stamp into a pattern resembling a coin. They are to be found in Recco, Genoa, and Chiavari. An undecorated version, made in the *entroterra* in Val Polcevara, pieces of pasta pulled out to make figure-of-eight shapes, are also called *corzetti*, being another coin shape.

LIME. *See* CITRUS FRUITS.

LIMONCELLO.
See CITRUS FRUITS, DIGESTIVI.

LINGUATTOLA is a sinistral flat
fish of the same family as brill, but smaller. When very young this little fish, *zanchetta*, is almost transparent and can be dipped in flour and fried crisp in olive oil, a delicacy much appreciated in the Marche.

LIQUORICE, *Glycyrriza glabra, liquirizia, regolizia*, is much loved for its sweet,
pungent roots, enjoyed in the most primitive form by children who chew them, dried, to enjoy the flavour. Some of the best liquorice is produced in Rossano in CALABRIA, where the terrain is ideal, arid, hot, and sandy, with room for the deep roots of the plant to grow protected from extremes of temperature. In the past, these were cut, dried, and soaked in vats of water, which was then boiled down in great copper vats over fires of olive wood, to get a dense aromatic liquid, which would be flavoured in various ways and processed into tiny hard pastilles to suck, sweetmeats to chew, liqueurs, and medicinal products. Today the process is more high-tech, but the sweets have the same strong, primitive pungency. It was used medicinally in the ancient World, and MATTIOLI knew its virtues as cough medicine and for stomach troubles, and for sweetening bitter medicines. He sneered in a pedantic way at the terminology of mere druggists and quack doctors, who called it *liquirita*, but history was on their side.

LITERATURE AND FOOD.

Italian food has been written about by native writers and historians, by foreign travellers, and by cooks and enthusiasts from all over the world. Italians have in-built knowledge and experience, they know and understand things we can never know, while outsiders have insights and points of view that contribute to a wider critical view of things. Generations of foreign writers have travelled and written about Italy, sometimes in attempts to escape from, or find, themselves, like Goethe or Stendhal, some in pursuit of culture or aspects of history, who stumble upon food and become obsessed by it. Some are already celebrities, like Loyd Grossman and later Jamie Oliver, who find the moment ripe for their own special take on Italy, and combine book, television programme, and retail outlets with consummate skill. A young and charismatic chef (with a huge unseen backup support team) goes to chat with grannies and fishermen, and takes rebuffs, success, and confusion in his stride, little knowing that his beat-up white van and its decrepitude might be endearing to us, but a brand new Maserati would have won over the grannies sooner. But he gets through to a public that will now go out and eat, and cook, genuine Italian food for possibly the first but certainly not the last time. The accomplished broadcaster Lloyd Grossman added to his television successes with a smooth run through all the regions of Italy, giving the viewers of Granada Television the take on Italian food that was just right for the 1990s. Delia Smith's fifth publication was on Italian food, and even though she confused risotto with *riso al forno*, she gave her fans the recipes they wanted in a form that never ever fails, thus extending understanding of Italian food across the length and breadth of the British Isles. Her timing is always impeccable, and it was at precisely the moment that Middle England was ready for sun-dried tomatoes and ersatz balsamic vinegar that Delia produced workable versions of familiar and more challenging Italian favourites.

Experts in their own particular fields, like Claudia Roden, with her definitive works on Middle Eastern and Jewish food, have written with great perception on Italian cooking, bringing insights and understanding of the cultural context not easily observable from within. In addition, some helpful translations of Italian culinary classics have become invaluable: Artusi, *The Silver Spoon*, Ada Boni's *Talismano*, and at last the immensely helpful *Reader's Digest Illustrated Encyclopedia*. A translation of Scappi is in preparation; Martino has been translated in book form and as a CD; and Platina is available in a translation with a learned commentary. *The Futurist Cookbook* is now available in English. Meanwhile, bilingual Italians with reputations as restaurateurs or cookery teachers are writing in English for British and American readers. Marcella Hazan combined cookery classes with some definitive books on Italian food; our own Anna del Conte teaches and is producing a wide range of cookery and reference books; Antonio Carluccio has brought accessible Italian food to a delighted mass market in his delis, television programmes, and books, as have others in the United States like Lidia Bastianich, host of several shows and author of six cookery books, or even more recently, Giada De Laurentiis; up-market restaurateurs, such as Giorgio Locatelli and Mario Batali, are offering elegant versions of both rustic and refined classic dishes, with innovative gestures that bring Italian food into the sphere of international cuisine (*see also* COOKBOOKS).

LIVER, *fegato,* is one of the more prized items of OFFAL, and enjoyed today when other organs are despised and rejected. The name is possibly derived from the Latin *ficatum*, which means stuffed with figs, and refers to pigs who were overindulged with dried figs to enlarge and flavour their livers.

A recipe from Abruzzo today depends on the forage of the local pigs to give the liver its characteristic flavour: *fegatazzo d'Ortona* is made from liver, lungs, spleen, jowls, and belly of pork, flavoured with orange peel, chilli, salt, and garlic, and stored, when matured, in lard or oil. Another product from Abruzzo is the *fegato dolce*, seasoned with honey, and sometimes candied citron and orange peel, pistachio, and pine nuts, in which the free-range lifestyle and food of the pigs is essential for flavour and keeping qualities. Liver has a high vitamin content and can be tender when properly cooked. That of calves is the most delicate, tender, and expensive; that from beef depends on the age of the animal, but is full of flavour; lambs' liver is fine cooked quickly and in slow-cooked dishes; while that of the pig has a coarser texture, but lends itself to the various dishes like FEGATELLI. In the past, liver was added to mixtures for meatballs and fresh sausages. Often a whole liver would first be parboiled, then grated on a coarse cheese grater, as in Scappi's recipe for *cervellati*, where veal liver is mixed with pounded veal and veal fat, spices and herbs, yellow with saffron and egg yolks, flecked with chopped mint and marjoram, wrapped in caul fat, and roasted or grilled. Brains, *cervello*, cannot be found in any recipes for this sausage, however far back one goes, so perhaps they never contained brains, but have some kind of link with the *cervelas* of France, a neat little reminder that gastronomic influences moved around in an international circuit of cooks and nobility, rather than in the baggage of princesses (*see* MEDICI, CATERINA DE'). Martino's recipe was similar, a boiling sausage, for immediate consumption. Scappi's *tommacelle* were made from grated pigs' liver, mixed with beef marrow, raisins, diced pork fat, parmesan, sugar, cinnamon, nutmeg, cloves, saffron, and egg yolks, all cased in caul, left to mature for a day, then fried or grilled. Liver was traditionally included in many preserved sausages and salami, and in cooked dishes of mixed offal,

CORATELLA. Many of these come from the need to make use of perishable parts as quickly as possible. The great "fry-ups" of pig-killing time were both a treat and a necessity, but often the liver was preserved, as in Tuscany: cut up, seasoned with fennel and bay leaves, cooked inside a casing, then put in a crock and covered with melted lard, to keep in a cold place for as long as a year. Probably the best known liver recipe is *fegato all veneziana*, which is not a uniquely Venetian dish, being made in different versions all over Italy. Finely sliced onions are cooked in oil, and when they are almost browned, thinly sliced liver is added and cooked on a raised heat very quickly so that it is brown on the outside and still a pale pink within. *Verde* was the term Scappi used for meltingly underdone liver and game. Chicken livers, FEGATINI, are a delicacy deployed in many different ways—often on *crostini* (*see* BRUSCHETTA).

LOBSTER, *astice, aragosta,* is the biggest of the lobsters, also called in Veneto *langusta, agosta,* and in central Italy *aligusta,* and *alaustra* in Sicily; there are also langouste (crawfish) and *scampo,* Dublin Bay prawn, also called langoustine, or scampi; there is cicada, a flat lobster, or aragosta. The two names *astute* and *elefante di mare* go back to classical times (Latin *astacus* [from Greek] and *elephantus*), and the lobster was familiar to gourmets from the 5th century BC onwards, beginning with Epicharmus, from Greek-speaking Sicily. Archestratus, a century later, claimed that the volcanic island of Lipara produced the best lobsters. Lazy gourmets, tired of the complexities of eating lobster, impelled the invention of cakes made of minced lobster (for which Apicius provides a recipe; *Apicius* 2.1.1); thus the cook could do all the work, at least until digestion set in. Corrado had a version of this recipe, in which the lobster flesh is seasoned with *bottarga,* anchovies, and herbs and mixed with egg and breadcrumbs, a bit of a waste of a

delicate luxury; his recipe for simply grilling his *ragosta*, topped with butter, breadcrumbs, garlic, and parsley, is more congenial; or serving it warm, with butter, herbs, and spices, with that novelty, a tomato sauce. (AKD)

LOMBARDY is a huge region in the north of Italy, with EMILIA-ROMAGNA to the south, PIEDMONT to the west, and TRENTINO ALTO ADIGE and VENETO to the east. The great river Po forms a natural boundary in the south, the Alps to the north, with Lakes Garda on the right and Maggiore and Como on the left forming part of the eastern and western limits, with waterways connecting all parts of the region, linked by canals, which in the past were more reliable routes than roads, and later motorways and a rail network, which go under rather than over the bleak mountain passes. Lombardy enjoys the plentiful variety of produce from fertile plains, hills, and mountains, and although it lacks a coastline, its lakes provide freshwater fish and aquatic traditions.

The direct link with Rome, down the Via Emilia from Milan to Rimini, then south along the Via Flaminia, was for the rapid transit of armies and messengers; trade followed the waterways and meandering local roads. But long before the Romans exploited the advantages of the region that is now Lombardy, waves of Celtic migration had founded cities: Milan, Brescia, and Bergamo. The Romans exploited and left their mark on the whole of the Po Valley and Padania, and after the collapse of Roman rule and the incursions of Ostrogoths, the Lombards arrived, with a different way of life (with gastronomic implications that have passed into legend), which predominated for two centuries, with Pavia as the capital, until incursions by the Franks brought Lombardy into the hegemony of Charlemagne's Roman Empire, and later into conflict with his heirs, resulting in the anti-imperial Lombard League,

which successfully sent off Frederic Barbarossa, and became by the 11th century a grouping of strong, prosperous independent cities. The Visconti of Milan made their mark in the 13th century, and inaugurated a period of cultural and political splendour, carried on by the Sforza family, who succeeded them. When the last heir died, the Spaniards, who vied with the French for influence and possessions in Italy, got hold of Milan, and a period of neglect and decline followed. In the 18th century, Austrian links with Spain left Milan under the benign rule of Maria Theresa, with the eastern parts of the region under the control of Savoy, and the whole area became prosperous again, but Napoleon's ambitions, their collapse, and the subsequent reimposition of Austrian domination did little for morale, although the area remained prosperous. Stendhal noticed this, but was a disappointment from our point of view, too concerned with music and the arts to write about gastronomy. Austrian rule was intellectually and politically repressive, and all classes of society clung to the "Italianness" of their culture, in the teeth of French, Swiss, and Austrian influences, and, in spite of the disappointments of unsuccessful revolts in 1848 and 1859, were reconciled to becoming part of the new Kingdom of Italy under the House of Savoy in 1861. Agricultural and commercial prosperity grew, helped by the rail links with Europe after the construction of the San Gothard tunnel in 1882. An enthusiasm for local customs, dialects, and food was a way of affirming Italian identity, and many writers did this both openly and surreptitiously. Manzoni's historical novel *I promesi sposi*, published in the 19th century, was in its theme and language a patriotic statement. Giovanni RAJBERTI (1805–1861), an obscure doctor, combined a love of food and literature with a modest career in medicine, and wrote with good humour and avuncular jollity that concealed subversive and radical approaches to both gastronomy and politics. "*Se mi dimandeste dove si potreb-*

bero scrivere senza impostura le parole libertà, eguaglianza, fraternità, risponderei: sulle pareti d'una sala da pranzo" (If you were to ask me where one might write with impunity the words liberty, equality and fraternity, I would reply: on the walls of a dining room). To Rajberti, preparing and eating *polpette* (we know them as *involtini*) was both an innocent domestic pleasure and a way of asserting Milanese identity, and the local dialect was a vehicle for this, an instinctive response to a resented foreign presence. Calling a respectable vegetable stew or *minestra* by the popular name of *galba* was another way of making the point.

Today, having assimilated influences from its complex past and adjoining regions, Lombardy is one of the most prosperous and dynamic regions of Italy, with a flourishing industrial sector and small producers on the plain, in the foothills, and in the mountains making artisan cheeses and salame, and growing organic grain and vegetables, alongside successful commercial enterprises. Communications with the rest of Europe provide a wider market for these products. The resuscitation of ancient orchards and old breeds of fruit has created a market for "rare-breed" apples, grown from ancient stock. Lombardy's well-watered plains have been fertile throughout its history, in spite of the skirmishes of armies and the fluctuations of politics. Bonvesin de la Riva was boasting in the 13th century of the cartloads of supplies coming into Milan daily from the countryside, tilled, if we are to believe him, by 30,000 pairs of oxen. To the sweet and sour cherries, the early and late apples, the pears, quinces, strawberries, vegetables like cabbage, spinach, turnips, lettuce, and celery were added artichokes, asparagus, and later tomatoes, aubergines, and exotic fruit in the 15th century.

The numerous lakes (almost half of the lakes in Italy are to be found in Lombardy) and rivers more than made up for the lack of salt water fish. Bonvesin reels them off with

confidence, while two centuries later Martino would have served up the same noble freshwater fish to his employer in Milan. Scappi would later remember the fishes of his native Lombardy, and the freshwater sardines of Lake Garda, where he was born some time in the late 15th or early 16th century, in Dumenza, 5 kilometres from Luino in the province of Varese.

Lake Garda, then known as Benaco, has been since classical times a resort for pleasure seekers. Ovid and Virgil came here for the benign climate and scenery, and visitors like Ezra Pound have since enjoyed the nostalgia of following in their footsteps. *Jubilatio*, an account by Felice Feliciano of a trip with Andrea Mantegna and his friends Samuele da Tradate and Giovanni Antenoreo on a bright autumn day in 1464, is full of the delight these wild young men took in their search for classical inscriptions, not just as antiquarians, but in the very specific pursuit of the beautiful inscriptional letters used in imperial Rome. They must have made rubbings and accurate drawings, for Felice Feliciano published an alphabet in the 1460s showing how to construct them; calligraphers and epigraphers used these letters in works connected with the New Learning of the Renaissance. Mantegna's version of them can be seen on the banners in the recently restored series of paintings, *The Triumphs of Caesar*, at Hampton Court, and in many of his religious paintings. (Matthew Carter made a font of titling caps based on them called Mantinia, the Latin version of the artist's name.) They combine well with Mantegna's almost sculptural figures and cool classical architectural backgrounds. The scribe Bartolomeo Sanvito wrote perfect examples of these, and the title page of a work on statesmanship by Platina, dedicated to Federico Gonzaga, Mantegna's patron, is a wonderful example of these flowing capital letters; he also wrote out the title page of the presentation copy of Martino's cookery book with the same virtuosic nervous energy, which indicates that the new cuisine of the Renaissance was being taken as seriously as the New Learning. Isabella d'Este later wrote with some irritation to her brother Alfonso, duke of Ferrara, of the difficulty of finding a good cook, asking him to have a promising apprentice, Agreste, trained by the head cook at Ferrara. Enjoyment of food was part of the culture. Isabella also wrote from Mantua to her brother, about some carp and trout that she had had pickled in vinegar, so good that she felt he ought to have some, advising that the carp are best eaten cold, but the trout benefits from being heated up. A recipe in Messisbugo's book of 1549 has a nice pickle for freshwater fish which includes pepper, cinnamon, ginger, cloves, and saffron; the cleaned and salted fish are dusted with flour and fried in oil, drained, and plunged still hot into the vinegar and spices, left for a while (the length of a *miserere*), taken out, dried, and packed away in bay leaves, and so handled will keep for up to 10 days in all weathers.

Mantua was surrounded on several sides by open water, lakes, ponds, and the mighty river Po. The background to Mantegna's *Death of the Virgin* of the 1460s shows the Ponte San Giorgio crossing the lake, and gives some idea of the openness and beauty of the setting—and we can imagine the edible resources, frogs, fish, and eels that abounded. Vittorio Carpaccio painted an evocative scene of wildfowl hunting and fishing on the Venetian lagoon which gives some idea of the small craft likely to have been used by the young antiquaries, although fishing with tame cormorants, trained to catch and obediently hand over fish (Knauer, 2003) is hardly likely to have appealed to them, as it did to Carpaccio's hunters.

The catching and preservation of freshwater fish was a preoccupation of rich and poor. Lake Iseo, in the centre of Lombardy, has kept many of these ancient traditions, with a culture still based on boat building, the making of nets, and the salting and dry-ing of fish, even though refrigerated transport and outboard motors, not to mention changes in the fish population due to pollution and the unwise introduction of alien species, have transformed the life of towns along the shore and the great mountainous island, Montisola, in the middle of the lake. There traditional skills and materials have been adapted to the market for luxury craft, mainly in North America, and the making of nets, once an everyday domestic occupation, still competes successfully with cheaper products from the Far East, nets for sport and leisure activities made from synthetics, and genuine traditional nets for discriminating anglers.

The freshwater fish sardines, chub, perch, *coregone* (whitefish), and tench appear on local menus, preserved and fresh, but the use of pungent salted and dried fishes as a condiment for subsistence food is now less common; lately polenta has overtaken the vegetable and pulse porridges of the past, as a good base for preserved fish, and the strong-tasting dried chub has been used sparingly as a surprise garnish to a celebrity chef's scrambled eggs.

The lakes Maggiore and Como were famous in the past for their TROUT. Scappi wrote of big ones weighing over 40 Milanese pounds (28 ounces to a pound). In Milan they cooked them, he says, by scaling, gutting, and cutting them up into steaks, laying them closely side by side in a capacious pot, covering them with white wine and salt, and cooking slowly until done. They will then keep for about three days, and can be eaten cold with parsley or various relishes. The shad or river herring, *carpioni*, of Lake Garda are the best in Italy, according to Scappi—"tanto delicato e raro"—and can be kept for several days after deep-frying in olive oil, then plunging into hot white wine vinegar for 15 minutes, cooling and drying, and packing into boxes with bay leaves and myrtle berries. The grayling, *pesce temere*, Bonvesin's *timulus*, is found in Lombardy in the rivers Ada and Ambro, and can be prepared the same way. Lake Como has another kind of shad, *agoni*, enjoyed and preserved in the same way. Perch, *pesce persica*, are found all over Lombardy, especially in Lake Maggiore and the river Ticino; very white and small ones were good for invalids, according to the physicians of Milan. Chub, *cavedano*, is another small freshwater fish found in Lombardy, and Scappi takes the trouble to give its local names elsewhere, not a bit fazed by the complexity. CARP, known as *carpina* or *carpa* or *reina*, the queen of fishes, is plentiful in the waters around Mantua and in Ferrara, while similar fish, *scardue*, are brought to the markets of Milan. Of the many recipes given by Scappi, there is a delicious one in which the carp is gutted and cut into pieces, not too large, and marinated for two hours in vinegar, salt, pepper, garlic, and fennel seeds all pounded together, then simmered in wine, salt, and pepper, and served hot or cold, the skin removed, seasoned with cinnamon, sugar, and chopped fresh herbs. Tench, *tinca*, are best from the Tiber or the Po, but very large ones are brought to Milan from Lakes Como and Maggiore. They can be added to a pot of fresh young peas, cooked in oil, wine, salt, spices, and some chopped spring onions, and served with chopped fresh herbs. PIKE, *luccio*, can be enormous in Lakes Como and Maggiore, but those from the Po are smaller and much liked in Mantua and Ferrara. Scappi gives recipes for EELS of all sizes which were available in abundance. Recipes today include one said to have been enjoyed by Pope Martin IV in the 13th century, which earned him a place in Dante's *Purgatorio* for being a genial glutton but a bad pope. He liked to drown his eels in *vernaccia* and have them cooked in a sauce of chopped celery, carrot, and onion, with garlic and anchovies, herbs and spices, and more of the wine in which they met their fate. Modern versions include tomato and chilli, which seems unnecessary.

Meat is plentiful today as in the past:

beef from working cattle (hence recipes for long slow cooking) on the plains, with BRESAOLA, salted and dried but meltingly tender lean beef; and in the prealpine and mountainous areas sheep, goats, and game, pigs and pork products, salted and dried, converted into an impressive range of SALAMI and cured meats. This huge range of *salumi* includes the various *bresaole* and sheep and goat products in the north and the rich fatty, garlicky pork products of Cremona and Mantua in the south, cooked salami, some cured and intended to be heated up or boiled before eating, salami made with liver and offal and head meat, sophisticated ones made from prime cuts, the *soppressata* of Brescia, the *salame d'la duja*, along with the various salami and products from the now flourishing goose population.

Many of the traditional dishes of Lombardy use prime cuts of meat where other regions used inferior ones, but the *lesso* of Milan simmers together noble portions of beef, chicken, a calf's head, and other meats, sometimes including a COTECHINO *di Modena*, using the small amount of concentrated rich broth as a dressing for the meats, eaten as separate dish with pickles and *mostarda*, or diluted for the *risotto alla milanese*. Breaded veal chops, *costolette alla milanese*, which can be so disappointing elsewhere, are superb when made with grass-fed veal, dipped in the freshest egg and good-quality breadcrumbs, and fried carefully in butter. But offal and extremities are used in characteristic dishes; the *busecca* or tripe stew or soup, enriched with pork rinds, is good enough to be noted in the illuminations of a 15th-century *Tacuina sanitatis*. Then there is a salad of NERVETTI: not really nerves (though they do come into it), but a dish made from the glutinous edible portions of long-stewed calves' feet and pancetta with *girelli di vitello*, cuts which include tendons and connective tissues which cook down to chewy tasty morsels, not, it must be confessed, to everyone's taste. The *cazzoeula* is made from a pig's trotter and an ear cooked with pork rind until soft, to which are added pork spare ribs, chopped celery, carrot and onion, white wine, and eventually a fine coarsely chopped fresh cabbage (sweetened and crisped by the winter frosts) and a cooking sausage, often *luganega,* and some slices of *salamitt di verz,* the whole simmered gently to produce a dense, lipsticking broth, often described as *collosa,* best enjoyed with plenty of polenta. Variations on this method are many, and sometimes include chicken wings and giblets. Discussion on the origins and spelling of this dish can become unnecessarily heated; the summary in the *Grande Enciclopedia* puts things in perspective (2000, p. 214). Using what comes to hand in the many areas where pigs and cabbages abound has always been just good Celtic housekeeping.

Another cheap cut, slices of shin of veal from the hind leg cut across the bone, complete with its rich marrow, is *ossobuco alla milanese,* which in its purest version is simply floured and fried in butter and cooked with chopped onions previously browned in butter, moistened from time to time with dry white wine and good meat broth, and garnished with a *gremolata* of chopped garlic, parsley, and lemon rind, usually eaten with a plain risotto, or the saffron-flavoured *risotto alla milanese,* but which some consider too strongly flavoured for this dish. Many add tomato, a latecomer on the scene, and not really necessary.

RICE has been a traditional crop in Lombardy since the 15th century, and there are many rice dishes besides the familiar *risotto alla milanese,* some of them runny enough, *a l'onda,* to be eaten with a spoon, in which each grain of rice still has a substantial bite to it, while swimming in a rich amalgam of rice starch (loosened by the vigorous stirring of the rice), butter, cream, and parmesan. More liquid versions are like substantial stews, a few handfuls of rice thrown into a broth made perhaps from frogs, offal, shellfish, or vegetables. Rice can be cooked in

a broth made by simmering chicken hearts and gizzards, to which the chopped livers are added just before the rice is done, along with chopped parsley and sage and abundant parmesan. *Risotto alla certosina* is said to derive from the nourishing but strictly vegetarian diet of the severe Cistercian order, which drained and cultivated unpromising land around Pavia. Frogs were permitted, but butter was not, so oil was used instead. Rice is cooked following the risotto method in a broth made from the bodies of frogs and the shells and limbs of freshwater prawns, and the bones of any other freshwater fish available (the delectable fleshy frogs' legs and the tails of the prawns are kept on one side). A base of chopped onion, celery, and carrot is fried in oil and moistened with dry white wine before adding the rice, to which peas and the frogs' legs and prawns' tails are later added, depending on the time they need to cook. *Risotto alla pilota* is not really a risotto but a hearty rice dish, less time-consuming than the stirred version, said to have been made by workmen who wielded (*pilare*) the pestle in a heavy mortar to bash the outer husk from grains of rice. Rice is poured so as to land in a conical shape into a heavy pot of boiling water and cooked quickly for 12 minutes, still in its conical pile, then covered and hermetically sealed and left to itself, while the hungry workmen carry on with their shift. When the rice is done, a lean cured sausage, *salmonetta,* is crumbled and quickly fried in butter, and stirred into the rice—a carbohydrate rush invaluable to the physically exhausted but to be treated with caution by the rest of us.

The cultivation of MAIZE came later, and it now equals rice in popularity. The main use is in the various kinds of POLENTA made from fine or coarse maize flour, which is such a versatile accompaniment to so many different dishes that to addicts it is unmatched by anything else. A stiff, plain polenta can soak up the sticky juices of a *cazzoeula,* a sloppy one can envelop one of the rich recipes for salt cod, its gentle mildness a foil to the pungent fish. A slab of cooled thick polenta can be grilled or fried and served with rich stews or simply grilled and roast meat or fish.

As for PASTA dishes, *pasta rostida* was traditionally made in the *navigli* of Milan by the watermen, who cooked up sustaining dishes as they worked: a basic flour-and-water pasta was cooked quickly, then finished off in a frying pan in which onions and bacon had been cooked to a turn. *Pizzoccheri*, which seems to have originated in Teglio in Valtellina, is an unbelievable dish made from a basic pasta cooked together with cabbage and lots of butter, welded together with local cheese, and served piping hot, seasoned with sage and garlic.

MILK flowed from the plains and upland pastures, a highly perishable food, transformed, with care and time, into cheeses that mature and keep, with by-products from these labours—cream, MASCARPONE, RICOTTA, soured milk, wobbly junkets, and butter—which are valued for their ephemeral qualities and figure in the cuisines of rich and poor.

Many of the cheeses of Lombardy are protected with a DOP, and are described in detail in the publications of INSOR (INSOR, 2000) and SLOW FOOD. The ones eaten young and fresh include *mascarpone*, a soured cream so ephemeral that it can only be enjoyed on the spot (pasteurized versions with a longer shelf life have a horrid "cooked" taste and texture). The little *agrì di Valtorta*, made in a remote valley in Val Brembana in Bergamo, with a slight acidity and milky flavour, are best eaten fresh. *Bernardo* is an alpine cheese made in summer and eaten after a few weeks. *Crescenza* is cured with salt and heat, eaten fresh, and often used in cooking; produced industrially, it is in demand in other regions, particularly in Liguria, where it is important in the cheese *focaccia*, and the little fried *focacette*. *Torta* is another creamy fresh cheese. Various kinds of *formaggella*

made from goats or mixed milk are typical of the fresh young cheeses made up in the Alpine pastures in summer. *Quartirolo lombardo* when unripened, has a gentle, creamy flavour, and *stracchino* is made in a similar process, and also eaten fresh or after a few weeks' ripening. *Cingherlino* or *zincarlin* is a fresh cheese, lightly salted, and often eaten with pepper and olive oil. *Robiola* is another light cheese eaten young. This profusion of rich creamy little cheeses led Ugo Foscolo to call Milan *Paneropoli*, the metropolis of cream. Many of the few mentioned above are best bought and eaten on the spot; displayed with artistry in a famous food emporium in the city, they rival the glories of the Breda.

Of the mature cheeses, the most widely used is GRANA PADANO, made in Lombardy, Piedmont, Veneto, and Emilia-Romagna, with a protective legal definition and designated geographical areas, distinct from, although in some ways similar to, PARMESAN, *parmigiano*, and not to be confused with the revived production, mainly in Lodi, of *granone lodigiano*, which was to a staunch patriot like Rajberti infinitely superior to any other *grana*. He called it the Jove of cheeses, towering above all the lesser gods, and the best and only cheese to have at the end of a superb meal. However, the mature and hard cheeses of Lombardy are as fine in their own way. Some are associated with a particular dish, like the *bitto* of Valtellina in *pizzoccheri*, or in *polenta taragna*. Many versions of *bitto* are made in the mountain valleys of the river Bitto in Sondrio which are both renowned and expensive and protected with a DOC. Some authorities note that this can handicap the producers of similar versions in the rest of Valtellina, where the system of pasture and methods of cheese-making and ripening are preserving a vulnerable alpine environment. *Bagòss di Bagolino* in Brescia is a hard cheese for cooking or eating, using the milk of brown alpine cows, fed on mountain pasture or local hay, and made using ancient implements and procedures, with flavours that develop and intensify with age, attributed by some to inadvertent contact with the inevitable farmyard detritus, as well as the permitted saffron for colouring. There may or may not have been health hazards in the use of dried cows' dung to cover the cheese while maturing, or to disguise it from marauding invaders. *Formai de mut*, from the Alta Val Brembana in Bergamo, is another fine alpine cheese with its DOC; a version of this, *branzi*, can be eaten fresh, when it is soft and delicate and delicious in cooking.

LONG PEPPER, *Piper longum*, and *Piper retrofractum*, *pepe lungo*, is produced in southern India and Malaysia. It was used far more in the past than it is now, and was specified often in spice mixtures during the Middle Ages and the Renaissance. The flavour is peppery, hotter, and more complex than the peppercorns we still use, perhaps a bit musty, not as fragrant or biting as the CHILLI pepper (a different family), which became cheaper and whose popularity, according to Philip and Mary Hyman, was the cause of the long pepper's disappearance. The decrease in its medicinal use might also have accounted for a lack of demand.

LOVAGE, *Levisticum officinale*, *levistico*, *sedano di montagna*, is another umbelliferae, like CELERY, and sadly superseded by this milder plant. It grows astonishingly tall, a giant in the herb garden, but its leaves, when young and tender, have a distinctive flavour and in the past were used in salads and stews. The unfortunate association with its overuse in a commercial brand of stock cube may have put some people off, though long before that it seems to have fallen out of use. It does not get a mention in the 15th-century *Taccuina Sanitatis* and does not appear to have been revived by Renaissance enthusiasts for the cooking of ancient Rome.

Dioscorides said that lovage originated in Liguria—hence the name—where it grew everywhere, and described the seeds as like those of fennel, but black, longer, with a peppery taste. This is not quite the same as the tender leaves, which have more bitterness. The seeds, stems, and roots, as well as the leaves, were used a lot by the Romans, and Apicius specifies *ligustico*, lovage (if that is what it was . . .), in over 50 of his recipes. It is not always clear from the context whether he means the seeds or the leaves. For example his *mortaria*, an all-purpose green sauce, consists of fresh green mint, rue, coriander, and fennel leaves, pounded in the mortar with crushed peppercorns, lovage seeds, and honey, diluted with vinegar and broth. A dish of mange-tout peas is dressed with chopped leek, coriander leaves, lovage, oregano, and crushed peppercorns pounded together with oil and a little wine.

There is some discussion about *ligustico*, defined as a wild version of lovage, not as tall, with thinner leaves, and not much used today. Mattioli was convinced that they were two different plants, and a somewhat laconic entry in the *Grande Enciclopedia* agrees.

LUCANICA, *luganiga*, *lucanica*, are well-spiced and strong-flavoured sausages. They were named for Lucania, in BASILICATA, the region where they originated, but are now known nationwide as a variety made on an industrial scale. They have a long history and were probably known throughout the Ancient World. There is a legend that predatory Venetian mariners grabbed both the sausage and the recipe when rampaging up and down the Adriatic, though, as Dalby points out, there is a Greek version, *loukánika*, which is used "from end to end of the Mediterranean and beyond." The recipe for *lucanicae* in Apicius is worth noting (Grocock and Grainger, 2006, p. 153): well-pounded pork meat is seasoned with a mixture of

spices and herbs ground in a mortar and moistened to a paste with liquamen, then chopped pork fat, whole pepper, pine nuts and more liquamen are added, and the mixture is put into thin natural casings, which are then smoked. This recipe is more a narrative method than a specification of quantities, but the spices are all named: pepper, cumin, the roasted seeds from bayberries, rue, savoury, and parsley, which all contribute to flavour and keeping qualities; the necessary salt is in the liquamen.

Luganiche or *lucaniche* or *luganeghe* are made today mainly in the north of Italy, and no longer have a direct connection with Lucania in the south. Those from Milan and Lombardy are delicate fresh sausages, made from pork meat and fat and a little beef, sold "by the yard" in long coils to be grilled or fried. A *lucanica* from Trentino, eaten fresh or mature, is made mainly for local consumption, with ground pepper, garlic, and white wine, with variations in every little valley, sometimes more spices, sometimes smoked, sometimes different animal meats, all used in local cooking in imaginative ways. The Veneto has one among many versions, from the province of Treviso, seasoned with pepper, two kinds of cinnamon, nutmeg, mace, and coriander, eaten grilled or fried. Many of these are traditionally served with rice.

LUMACHE. *See* SNAILS.

LUNGS. *See* OFFAL.

LUPIN, *lupino, Lupinus albus* or *sativus*, is a plant of the PEA family, and its hard bitter seeds have been used as food for centuries. They were known in the Middle East before Roman times, and seem always to have had a reputation as coarse, common food. In fact, after prolonged soaking, cooking in frequent changes of salt water, and sometimes treatment with lye, they have a pleasant nutty flavour and chewy texture which make them addictive street food, in Italy as well as their land of origin. Lupins can now be bought vacuum packed, or from street vendors, a civilised snack, and a pleasure to eat between meals, at the cinema, during a *passegiata*, summer and winter. Castelvetro dismissed lupins as appealing to pregnant women and silly children, while Costanzo Felici said that people ate them as *trastullo o passatempo*. However, their high protein and considerable fat content would have made them more than just a whimsical snack. The fresh plants, before the toxic alkaloid content develops, are used as animal fodder and ploughed back into the land to enrich it between crops.

m

MACCHERONI (macaroni). *See* PASTA, BAKED; PASTA, FRESH; PASTA, HISTORY; PASTA SHAPES.

MACCO. *See* BEANS, BROAD BEANS.

MACE *Myristica fragrans, macis,* is the outer covering, aril, of the NUTMEG, with a similar aroma, perhaps less pungent, more subtle, and is best used in its dried form, in blades rather than powdered. The sometimes prolix Mattioli is vividly direct in his description: "*sottile, fervente, acuto, odorato & quasi insensibilmente amaretto*" (subtle, burning, acute, and with a slight almost imperceptible bitterness). It was known in the Ancient World and China but does not seem to have been used in ancient Rome, and came to Europe by the 6th century. By the 14th century, it was used in the milder spice mixtures—*specie dolce* (*see* SPICES). Mace is used to flavour some cured meats such as MORTADELLA, and in confectionery. The essential oil is used in liqueurs, especially ALCHERMES.

MACEDONIA DI FRUTTA. *See* PUDDING.

MACKEREL, *sgombro,* is one of the blue fish that needs to be cooked as soon as possible, for when its fatty oils are stale, the fish smells and tastes unpleasant. Really fresh, it is grilled or baked, and a modern recipe suggests cooking boned mackerel fillets with young peas.

MAESTRO DI HARTFORD (active in Rome in the 17th century) was a phantom painter we know nothing about, named for the location—the Wadsworth Atheneum in Hartford, Connecticut—of his most famous work. Problems of attribution are considerable, and some authorities associate this, and other works, with the activities of Caravaggio in his early years in Rome, in the first decade of the 17th century. The importance for us is that these paintings show how fruit, flowers, and vegetables might have been displayed on a table, sideboard, or larder at that time. In the Hartford painting, a white surface (perhaps the last clean tablecloth of the last service of a banquet) is covered with fruit—a quince, figs, grapes, apples, pears, nuts, a peach, a melon bursting

Four mackerel (Shutterstock)

open with ripeness, and a basket of fruit with some broad beans and peas. The motif of the basket of fruit is surely more an indication of common usage than the hallmark of a particular painter, as are the round carafes of flowers, and characteristic of the delight both painter and client appear to have taken in this everyday display of produce.

A work by the same painter in the Borghese Gallery in Rome depicts a pantry or larder, with fruit ready to be served, and other things ready for use. There are cabbage, root vegetables, celery, cardoon, gourd and marrow, with wild strawberries, various kinds of grapes, many citrus fruits, apples, plums, pears, possibly some of the beans from the New World that would eventually compete with the local products, and in the bottom right-hand corner, very early sightings of the two exotic plants that would change the face of Italian cuisine forever—a TOMATO and two CHILLIES, described by Costanzo Felici in the 1560s as novelties rather than serious food, but here included, even though to one side, in this round-up of comestibles.

A companion to this "larder" piece is an array of dead birds, most of them edible, many of them suspended against a dark background, others on and below a deep shelf. They are not the triumphant display of a hunter's spoils, but a prosaic line-up of routine slaughter for the table, suspended until they have hung enough to become tender and tasty enough to eat, presided over by a baleful live owl, symbol of many things—wisdom, sleep, but mainly death. In a dish placed on top of a wicker basket, almost a parody of the beans and pink roses of Campi's northern fruit-seller, is a collection of small birds, plucked and ready to be put on the spit.

Another painting by the same artist, or one from the same circle, shows the presentation of a "bunch" of strawberries on their stalks, tied together with string and displayed, stalks upwards, in a decorative mass of fruit and flowers.

MAIALE, *maialino. See* PIG.

MAIZE, *mais, Zea mays, granoturco,* is a cereal crop which arrived in the 16th century from the Americas. Maize flour (corn meal) is used in bread, cakes, and biscuits, especially in the north. The *pane di mais* of Lombardy and the Veneto is usually made with a mixture of maize and wheat flour, and even when mass-produced white bread is now freely available, nostalgia and affection account for this bread's continuing popularity. In the Marche, a bread made with maize flour only is widespread, a link with the past, when broad beans and other legumes went into bread, in many ways a healthier option. The Abruzzo has a maize bread, usually made during the winter months, which is increasingly popular. *See also* POLENTA.

MALLOW, *malva,* is a plant of which there are many edible varieties, from the tender shoots of the young plant, eaten in spring like hop shoots, to the leaves of the mature plant, which are used raw in salads or cooked in various ways. The *melokhia* of Egypt is of the same family, the Malvaceae; its mucilaginous leaves thicken the national soup, which is a reminder of the value of this plant throughout the Mediterranean area, where it is found both wild and cultivated. Its many health-giving properties were valued in the Ancient World. Mattioli listed its uses—as medicine, as poultices for wounds and insect bites, as a healthy spring vegetable, and as a comforting soup for women in childbirth; while Castelvetro wrote that the mucilaginous leaves help relieve constipation and urinary problems.

MANDORLE. *See* ALMOND.

MANNA. *See* CALABRIA.

MANTEGNA, ANDREA (active 1441/5–1506), does not usually come to mind in connection with food, but he deserves mention here for the depiction of CITRUS FRUITS in many of his devotional and mythological paintings. Influenced perhaps by his master Squarcione, who took the classical theme of swags of fruit and foliage and worked it into architectural backgrounds, Mantegna delights us with accurate representations of the many varieties of oranges, lemons, citrons, and limes available at the time. His *Madonna della Vittoria* of 1496, now in the Louvre in Paris, shows the Madonna sitting with the Infant Christ in a bower resplendent with citrus fruit, glowing amongst their dark glossy leaves and fragrant blossoms. The symbolic meanings of fruit in religious works must always account for their presence, but could have been only one aspect of this celebration of a cash crop of great beauty and value. The lemon, producing flowers and fruit at the same time, was symbolic of both the purity and fecundity of the Virgin; lemons were used to assuage the pains of childbirth, and citrons (*etrog*) had an important part in the ancient Jewish fertility ritual, the Feast of the Tabernacles. Local agribusiness, depending on a big capital outlay to fund the complex system of terraces, hydraulics, and frost protection needed for the cultivation of citrus fruits, supplied an expanding market, and recipes show their use in many ways, not just squeezed over rich food, but sliced to decorate the rims of dishes, and chopped or sliced, dressed with sugar, salt, and cinnamon, as salads.

Mantegna had firsthand experience of citrus cultivation when he went on a day trip to Lake Garda (Benaco of classical times) in search of classical Roman inscriptions. He set off in the company of his disreputable friend the antiquarian Felice Feliciano and a few others, on a bright autumn morning in 1464, and they filled notebooks with the texts of inscriptions and possibly rubbings of the letterforms. Later Feliciano produced a manuscript of his geometric reconstruction of the ideal Roman alphabet, with instructions on how to draw it, which was later published as a handbook for architects and epigraphers. These beautifully proportioned Roman letters were used by Mantegna in his paintings, by his contemporary Bartolomeo Sanvito in his calligraphy, and by Platina in his work as epigrapher to Pope Sixtus IV; Alberti used a version of them on many of his buildings; Poggio Bracciolini was jotting down notes about inscriptions on excursions to Tivoli, where he ogled the local girls and enjoyed the *vino de Castelli*; the Gonzagas, key figures in this revival of Roman culture, for Virgil was a native of their city, Mantua, promoted and encouraged this exploration of classical culture, and it was the warrior Francesco Gonzaga who commissioned the *Madonna della Vittoria*.

The clear light and idyllic surroundings of that autumn morning in 1464 were to Mantegna and his companions as intoxicating as the rich haul of classical inscriptions; crowned with wreathes of bay and ivy, they went roistering among the lemon groves of the shores of Benaco, loud with birdsong and perfumed with lemon and orange blossom, celebrating their success at lakeside taverns, and gliding across the lake in a boat decked with oriental carpets and every comfort, to the sounds of Samuele's lute. It is not too fanciful to imagine Mantegna and his friends feasting in lakeside taverns on the freshwater SARDINES and TROUT for which Benaco was famous, perhaps fried and eaten with a squeeze of bitter orange juice, or, according to Martino's recipe, gutted and cut into pieces lengthways, then put in one layer in a capacious shallow pot, skin side down, salted, and then carefully covered with water and vinegar so as not to flood away the salt, simmered, skimming the while, very slowly until done, then taken out, drained, dusted with sweet spices, and served with a white sauce made by pounding skinned almonds with the crumb of white bread soaked in verjuice, diluted with lemon or bitter orange juice and flavoured with ginger.

Felice does not say. Mantegna, revered in his lifetime as the austere "man of rock," was perhaps not unmoved by this joyful expedition, but when citrus fruits figure with such brilliance in Mantegna's paintings, from the triumphant painting in the Louvre to the tender domestic portrait of the Holy Family in the National Gallery, London, where oranges loom "like golden lamps in a green night" in the background, it is not entirely unreasonable to think of this idyllic outing as a formative influence.

MARASCHINO. *See* CHERRY.

MARCHE, THE, *Le Marche, territorio dei piccolo incanti* (land of little enchantments), one of Italy's most beautiful regions and as yet little known, is situated on the central east coast; it forms a long rectangle between the Apennines and the Adriatic Sea, bordered by ABRUZZO, ROMAGNA, TUSCANY, and UMBRIA. It is an unspoilt area of mysterious, rugged, almost savage mountains, the Sibillini, where folklore abounds, situated in the south, with hills occasionally broken by short stretches of lush flat farmland stretching down to the sea; the coastal area is about 180 kilometres long, stretching from Rossini's birthplace, Pesaro, to San Benedetto del Tronto, an important fishing port but also a holiday resort with miles of sandy beach and dramatic palm trees. In his writings the poet and writer Gabriele d'Annunzio called the Adriatic Amarissimo, because it is saltier and more fertile than the other seas. Breathtaking vistas take in medieval and Renaissance towns and villages perched on top of rolling hills, fields of changing colours, different shades of green, yellow turning to gold, brown to rust in geometric forms, like a huge mosaic. Here are dramatic forests, woods, hectares of vineyards in serried rows, and olive groves, leaves shimmering green and silver. Farmhouses are dotted here and there, some whitewashed, some warm with the colour of brick, always with a clump of pine trees standing sentinel nearby; distinctive white roads wind their way through this scene.

Artists such as Crivelli, Raphael, and Lotto drew inspiration from this countryside and their works are to be found not only in grand places but, as in the case of Carlo Crivelli, in tiny churches up in the mountains—to open the door to some remote church and discover such treasures is awe-inspiring.

The gastronomy of the Marche is simple, only using the best of ingredients furnished by its own fields and the sea. The flavours are strong; herbs such as rosemary and wild fennel flavour the dishes. The smell of food being cooked *in* POTACCHIO pervades the streets and alley ways. It is a method of cooking peculiar to the Marche; white wine, garlic, tomato, and rosemary are the basic ingredients, used with fish, poultry, and rabbit. The word *potacchio* derives from the French word *potage*. The Marche is a region where north and south meet, and the gastronomy of the area has much in common with its border regions. It is a gastronomy that is scrupulously made with love and care, an ancient craft. Cooking comes naturally to the Marchigiani; they are proud of their heritage.

Towns, villages, and hamlets, to this day, jealously defend their gastronomic inheritance. To this end, *sagre* (festivals) are held to celebrate specialities, such as *porchetta,* whole roast pigs stuffed with herbs and garlic. In Cartoceto, a small village not far from Pesaro, they hold a *sagra* for *vincisgrassi,* the local lasagne-type pasta, made from sheets of pasta rich with eggs and layered either with a meat and chicken liver *ragu* or porcini mushrooms, rich béchamel, *prosciutto,* and truffles. This speciality has a long history; the story goes that it was named after an Austrian general, Windish Graetz, who was with his troops in Ancona in 1799 during the Napoleonic War. Actually, Antonio Nebbia, who earlier wrote a gastronomic manual in 1784, mentioned in it a similar dish called *princisgras.*

PASTA is one of the great glories of Le Marche gastronomy. It is still made by hand, and when it is industrially made, the machines are designed to give the nearest possible approximation to the handmade variety. Campofilone, a medieval village in the south of the region, is entirely dedicated to the making of the pasta of the same name, which is smooth like silk and rich with deep yellow eggs. There are also *sagre* for *formaggio di fossa,* cheese matured in ancient limestone caves, *sughitti,* a sweet made from *mosto,* the first pressing of the grape, the *sagra* of the SNAIL, snails cooked in every way imaginable, and on the coast, BRODETTO, a fish stew made from 13 different types of fish and shellfish, corresponding to the number of people who were present at Our Lord's last supper—fewer can be used but never 12, as this is considered to be an unlucky number, reminding us of the traitor Judas. Every coastal town has its own version of this dish, which was originally only eaten by the fishermen to use up the catch not sold. *Sagre* for wine are also held; the white intense Verdicchio dei Castelli di Iesi, so perfect with the local fish dishes, is without a doubt the jewel of the region, produced there for over 600 years. Rosso Conero is the red wine made from grapes grown on the foothills of the mountain of the same name, just south of Ancona, a wine which was particularly appreciated by the ancient Romans. Then there is the unusual sparkling ruby red dessert wine, Vernaccia from Serrapetrona, and many more varieties.

There is a whole range of specialities to be discovered in the region, some common, including *sapa, mosto* or MUST, cooked down to be used for sweetening dishes or making into sorbet. There is even a *sagra* for *mosto*—people arrive with their bottles to be filled, rushing home, before the *mosto* ferments, to make *biscotti di mosto* and *pane nociato,* a bread made with *mosto,* walnuts, candied peel, and pecorino. The biscuits and bread can only be made during the autumn, when the air everywhere is perfumed with the smell of baking. *Agresto* is made from the immature grapes known as *agresti,* found at the top of the vine, which are gathered during the *vendemmia,* grape harvest; they are pressed and the juice boiled down to make a thick type of vinegar (*see* VERJUICE). Agresto is known locally as "Jewish vinegar." The Marche had at one time a thriving Jewish community, and their influence is still found in many local recipes.

Carpegna is famous for its *prosciutto,* salami from Fabriano, and the unusual spreading salami called *ciauscolo* from Visso. Truffles from Acqualagna and Sant' Angelo in Vado. From Ascoli Piceno come the *olive ascolane,* large green olives stuffed with minced meats and herbs, dipped in egg and breadcrumbs, and deep fried until crisp, dry on the outside, moist within. Iesi, the birthplace of the composer Pergolesi, offers us *crescia di formaggio,* a cheese bread to be eaten with *prosciutto* or salami at Easter time. Around Macerata, figs are dried and made into sweet "salami" with walnuts, almonds, and chocolate all minced together with MISTRA, a local anise seed–flavoured liqueur, brandy, and spices. Sliced, it is eaten with fresh pecorino cheese, made from sheep's milk. Shepherds still sell their own products. Fresh, warm sheep's milk ricotta is eaten with wild strawberries sold in the local markets, picked freshly in the morning before the sun comes up. *Ambra,* a pungent sheep's milk cheese, otherwise known as *formaggio di fossa,* aged in caves, or airtight pits cut out of the volcanic rock beneath the cellars of old houses, comes from Sant' Agata Feltria and Talamello.

Giacomo Leopardi, the poet and philosopher, one of the greatest writers of the 19th century, who was born in Recanati, missed his local food so much when he moved first to Florence, then to Naples, that he wrote that nothing gave him more pleasure than a parcel from home containing figs and cheese. It is still the custom for people to bring in their surplus produce to the daily markets, baskets laden with *misticanza*, a mixture of young wild salad leaves and herbs to make the most fragrant of salads (*see* SALAD). There are warm peaches, straight from the tree; among the many varieties there is one called *Saturnia*, a small flattened peach with a tiny stone, and the highly perfumed *Sangue di Dragone*, a very red peach/plum. Freshly picked figs, the dew still on them, are lovingly laid out on fig leaves, the fruits slightly splitting, showing their deep red interiors. Giovanna Garzoni was from the Marche, and her life-sized paintings of figs celebrate this exuberance.

Food is taken seriously in the Marche; they do not play at eating and cooking. Real food still reigns here, following the seasonal offerings. Eating is still a ritual to be respected. Walk around any town in the Marche and listen to snippets of conversation: food is invariably the topic, what they are going to eat that day or what they have eaten. A friendly fisherman will take time to tell you how best to cook his catch. The man selling fish in a fish shop will ask, would you like your fish prepared for such and such a dish; everyone, the butcher, the grocer, and the greengrocer, has time to discuss the best way of cooking or preparing the products they so lovingly sell.
(A and FT)

MARINETTI, FILIPPO TOMMASO

(1876–1944), was one of the founder members of the Italian Futurist movement in 1909. The interests of the group covered every aspect of human endeavour—poetry, music, the fine arts, and the brave new world of rapid travel, high-tech industry, and global warfare. Inevitably, gastronomy mattered, both as a vehicle for their revolutionary talents and, more practically, as fodder for the superior race of born-again Italians, creative, fecund, and aggressive, they thought were destined to implement the Fascist aspirations Marinetti so admired.

The Futurist cuisine was inaugurated at a banquet in the Penna d'Oca in Milan in 1930, and their manifesto, *La cucina futurista*, published in 1932, was, as Lesley Chamberlain points out, a "serious joke," sending up and rending asunder the pretensions and norms of bourgeois gastronomy, but with a serious agenda: the nurturing of the creative and virile faculties of a master race, and the exploration of new forms of artistic endeavour in food preparation and presentation. Just as new art forms based on machines, speed, and violence could reshape the world, so new forms of food could reshape the Italian people. Abandoning pasta seemed to be a step in the right direction, and Marinetti wheeled on pseudoscientific statements from leading authorities to support his claim that pasta made people inert, stodgy, and lacking in ambition. (We now feed pasta with all its slow-release energies to athletes to stimulate in them the competitive vigour of the futurist ideal.) Less daft was Marinetti's insistence, amidst all the bombast and rhetoric, on exploring the chemical properties of food, on the nutritional content of vegetables, of the importance of rice (a patriotic, home-grown food, unlike pasta, which depended on imported grain), on the desirability of the pleasure principle in cooking and eating, of gastronomy as a performance art. Some aspects of his manifesto were prophetic—laboratory procedures applied in the kitchen, to conjure up a rapid succession of minuscule portions of items designed to stimulate by using innovative contrasts of flavour and texture, colour, and aroma (sound familiar?), and the idea of isolating the essential ingredients of a recipe, and re-assembling them in shocking and pleasurable combinations.

Some of Marinetti's recipes disappoint, and some are welcome. *Carneplastico*, the contribution of his co-author, Luigi Colombo, known as Fillìa, symbolising the flocks and herds, the gardens and orchards of Italy, consists of a cylindrical veal meatball, enclosing a mixture of 11 cooked vegetables, roasted in the oven, and erected on a plinth of a thick slices of salame, resting on three balls of deep-fried chicken, the whole topped with a crust of solid honey, seems agreeable if unremarkable. The risotto, *Golfo di Trieste*, contributed by the poet/aeronaut Bruno Sanzin, has shelled cockles cooked with rice in a sauce of garlic and onion, served with an unsweetened vanilla custard. The poet Giuseppe Steiner offered an ice, *Gelato simultaneo*, made of cream and cubes of raw onion, while the aeronaut/painter Diulgheroff's *Pollo d'acciaio (Pollo Fiat)* is a roast chicken, cooled, cut open down the back, and filled with red zabaglione dotted with round silver comfits and decorated with cooked cockscombs. (This could have come straight out of Scappi— a sweetish sauce, in this case coloured red, probably with *alchermes*, and the traditional decoration of jagged cockscombs, arranged round the pierced interior, but here to make a sort of visual pun on the car mechanic's equipment. It's worth remembering that Petronilla's conventional mother-in-law was tarting up poached eggs on toast with decorative edges cut like cockscombs.) Pascà d'Angelo's *Bombardamento di Adrianopoli* are larger than usual ARANCINI, or SUPPLÌ, balls of rice cooked in milk and butter, bound with beaten egg, but with a more enterprising filling— mozzarella, capers, anchovy, stoned olives— dipped in egg, rolled in breadcrumbs, and deep fried. (Conventional *supplì* are balls of rice or risotto with a savoury filling, meat or

cheese, rolled in egg and breadcrumbs and deep fried, enjoyed as a bar snack). The golden orange colour accounts for the name *arancini* given to the meaty ones; the other filling, usually a mozzarella type of cheese, becomes stringy when bitten into and so was named *supplì al telefono*, a reference to that modern invention the telephone, which is perhaps why Marinetti's friend the futurist poet Mazza also contributed a recipe. To end this selection comes Fillìa's *Aerovivanda*, not "airline food" but a series of tactile and organoleptic sensations structured like this: by the diner's left hand are a square of sandpaper, one of red silk, and one of black velvet; he is served from the right with a dish of black olives, raw hearts of fennel, and some kumquats, and is required to eat them, right-handed, with his fingers, whilst lightly caressing the different surfaces with his left, sprayed on the nape of the neck with carnation perfume, to the sound of violent airplane engine noises and some *dismusica* by Bach (perhaps one of the composer's more frighteningly cerebral works).

Conventional attitudes towards haute cuisine, which for centuries had been dependent on French recipes and vocabulary, had already been rejected by Artusi, and a new generation was now discarding his staid middle-class certainties. Ada Boni's *Talismano della felicità* propped them up, with her and their aristocratic aspirations, but at the same time, the Roman intellectual elite (among them Ada's husband) were exploring the trattorias of Trastevere (Ada's book on Roman cooking came out the same time as the *Cucina Futurista*), the Touring Club Italiano was gathering and publishing information about regional food; slow changes in attitude were in the air, but gentler than the Futurists' rhetoric.

MARJORAM, *Origanum majorana, maggiorana*, exists in a bewildering variety and is often confused with OREGANO. Davidson

Fresh marjoram. (Shutterstock)

and others explain how the *flavour* of oregano can be found in herbs of different genera, which is some help, but not a lot. He lists four versions. In addition to the above there are: *O. vulgare*, sweet marjoram, wild marjoram or common oregano, of which there are many different kinds of cultivated varieties, with different coloured leaves and fragrances; then *O. onites*, pot marjoram, which can be confused with Cretan DITTANY, less sweet and more pungent; and *O. heracleoticum*, winter marjoram, which can be cherished all year round, and was already well known in 16th-century Italy when Mattioli noted that women loved to have this perfumed plant in window boxes and on terraces. (He mellows considerably when writing of the domestic uses of plants, saving his spite and venom for men of his own profession.)

Generally speaking, the hotter the climate, the greater the presence of the essential oils, which include thymol and carvacrol, and the more pungent the aroma. So the mild, gentle flavour of any of these kinds of marjoram grown in a temperate climate will be very different from those found in hotter parts. Dried wild marjoram and the mild fresh kind are both used in Italy, and it is up to the user to decide which kind is appropriate in a particular recipe.

Ada Boni used a pinch of fresh marjoram, *persa* in Roman dialect, as the finishing touch, together with parmesan, to her *brodetto*

pasquale, a rich broth of beef and lamb, thickened with egg yolks flavoured with lemon.

MARRONE. *See* CHESTNUT.

MARROW, *zucca*, is one of the huge family of *cucurbitaceae*, which also includes squash, gourd, and PUMPKIN, all of which are conveniently but confusingly known as *zucca*. Larger marrows can be roasted, boiled, fried, kept in a dry place for the winter, dehydrated, and preserved in sugar, as Mattioli advised, to mitigate their insipid wateriness. But their seeds contain delicious kernels which are good to eat and when pounded in a mortar make a paste which in the past was diluted to make a liquid, a substitute for milk on fast days. *See also* ZUCCHINI.

MARSALA. *See* SICILY.

MARTINO DE ROSSI (active 1460s), or Martino of Como, as PLATINA called him (p. 293), also known as Maestro Martino, was a great cook, and the surviving manuscripts of his *Libro de arte coquinaria* are our main source of information about gastronomy in Renaissance Italy. The best short appraisal of his life and influence is by Bruno Laurioux (*Et coquatur ponendo*, 1996, and Laurioux, 1996). Little was known about Martino's origins until the discovery in 1993 (the complete text is in Benporat, 1996) of a manuscript in the civic library of Riva del Garda, which begins: "*Libro de cusina composto et ordinato per lo egregio homo Martino de Rossi dela valle de Bregna, mediolanensis diocesis descenduto de la ville de Turre, nato de la casa de Sancto Martino Vidualis coquo del Illustre signore Jo.Jacopo Tribultio,*" enabling us to locate his birthplace in a little valley in the canton of Ticino. We know that he worked in his youth at

the court of Milan, then for a time in the service of Francesco Sforza (as did Platina), followed in the early 1460s by employment with the patriarch of Aquileia, Ludovico Trevisan, a warrior-priest who kept a renowned table, after whose death in 1465 he worked for the famous condottiere Gian Giacomo Trivulzio. It was while working in Rome in 1463 as cook to Trevisan that Martino probably met the humanist scholar Bartolomeo Platina. Their friendship produced a best-seller, Platina's work *De honesta voluptate et valitudine* (Of virtuous pleasure and good health), written in the 1460s and circulated in manuscript before the appearance of many printed editions, the first of which was in 1470. In it he combined Martino's recipes with information about the nutritional and medicinal qualities of food, written in an elegant Latin, the international language of scholarship, while Martino's text, *Libro de arte coquinaria*, was in an articulate, hands-on vernacular, the everyday Italian of kitchen and marketplace. The presentation copy of Martino's work was produced by Platina's colleague Bartolomeo Sanvito, the finest calligrapher of the time, and is carefully preserved in a private collection.

What little we know about Martino's personality comes from references to him in Platina's text. The love of food and conviviality that brought them together made them ideal collaborators; it was certainly not a matter of Platina the intellectual plundering the cookery notebooks of an illiterate chef. He speaks affectionately of Martino in his recipe for BIANCOMANGIARE (a by then familiar dish of chicken breasts pounded with ground almonds, flavoured with cinnamon, sugar, and rosewater, its unearthly whiteness sometimes embellished with the red globules of pomegranate seeds, eaten as a dish on its own or an accompaniment to other things).

I have always rated this above Apician condiments, and in fact there is no reason why the tastes of our forebears should be preferred to our own, even though we are surpassed by them in just about all of the disciplines, in gastronomy we are invincible. In fact there is no delicacy in the whole wide world that has not been served up in our taverns, those grammar schools of gastronomy, where every aspect of cooking is fiercely discussed. What cook, oh you immortal gods, can be compared to my Martino of Como, from whom I got most of what I write. You would take him for another Carneades if you could hear him improvising [holding forth] on these matters.

Not much has changed in Roman eating places, and Martino's eloquence and expertise must have been equal to Platina's erudition when it came to food, the great levelling force in Italian society. Platina was of humble origin and much given to roistering, and while a witty and erudite guest at the tables of the rich, he had plenty of experience of the simple living he extolled, and also of the rowdier kind of enjoyments on offer in the taverns of Trastevere and the backstreets of Rome. Martino must have been a congenial dining companion as well as the source of Platina's recipes, and the collaboration, according to Laurioux, was a four-handed exercise, resulting in a technical manual and a theoretical treatise, compiled with a mutual respect for one another's skills.

Martino was not unaware of the indissoluble link between medical theory and culinary practise, where the choice of ingredients and seasonings was governed by the humoral theory. When he says "or to suit the taste of your patron" in describing a finished dish, he is encapsulating what everyone knew, that ingredients were chosen to get a balance between the four qualities (hot, cold, dry, wet) of foods, and the four temperaments (choleric, sanguine, phlegmatic, melancholic) of human beings (so sorrel purée counterbalances a rich salmon, or a pinch of sugar softens a sharp sauce) and also to accommodate not just the personal preferences but the digestive system and physiology of the head of the household. But this was a practical handbook, with no need to spell out the underlying theories, while Platina, in his work, enjoyed linking recipes to the tastes and temperaments of his close friends, with some shameless name-dropping, as well as describing the medicinal properties of different foodstuffs and their effects on both mental and physical health.

Martino and Platina were also writing about attitudes to the pleasures of the table and a style of cooking that was to become known as the new cuisine (offspring of the New Learning of the Renaissance), very different from the gross profusion and coarse ostentation of the traditional banqueting style of the rich and powerful. Both writers included some of the classics that would never go away—the strutting peacock in its plumage, for example—but there are also delicate dishes, like chicken with verjuice, which Platina boasts of having eaten in the Poggio household in Florence; veal *involtini* with a light flavouring of fennel seeds and herbs; the open tarts with a filling of cheese and spinach; fish cooked simply with herbs and wine. This was part of a movement towards lightness and refinement that culminated a century later in the monumental work of Bartolomeo Scappi, whose recipes and menus give a complete picture of this high point in Italian gastronomy. This delicacy and clarity is part of the humanist culture Martino and Platina were familiar with; their pioneering gastronomy was as important as the innovative developments in painting and sculpture.

About the mysterious presentation copy we know nothing except for the title page reproduced in a bookseller's catalogue. The manuscript in the Vatican Library (Urb. lat. 1203) is more coherent than that in the Library

of Congress (Rare Books MS 153). The Garda manuscript, which comes from later in the 1460s, contains changes Martino must have made when revising his earlier version. There are also quite a number of manuscripts by named or unknown cooks of the period incorporating much of Martino's material. Laurioux (1997, 2006) and Benporat (1996) discuss this in detail.

The Vatican manuscript starts with a list of the contents of each chapter. The first contains 39 recipes for meat and fowl, including delicate veal escallops, a simple roast chicken seasoned with sugar, cinnamon, and rosewater, and some delicious sausages. The second has 63 recipes for broths, soups, stews, pasta, and vegetable dishes, including peas with bacon, pasta prepared and seasoned in various regional styles, a green soup of cooked spinach beets and fresh herbs in meat broth. The third consists of 24 recipes for sauces and relishes: red, green, and black sauces, garlic sauce, several kinds of mustard, and the old-fashioned "camelline" sauce, tawny and rich with cinnamon and cloves. The fourth has 39 tarts, pies, and turnovers, a lovely white cheesecake, followed by a brilliant green tart coloured with spinach and chopped herbs. The fifth has 21 fritters and 15 egg dishes, elderflower fritters, fish-cakes perfumed with sugar and rosewater, a lightly-cooked herb *frittata*. The sixth and final chapter has 69 recipes for salt, dried, fresh-water, and sea fish, shellfish, including sensitive instructions for grilling, roasting or simmering, with appropriate marinades and sauces, and a couple of rice recipes tagged on at the end, followed by the inevitable old party-piece— live birds concealed inside a pie.

MARZIPAN, *marzapane*, or almond paste, *pasta di mandorla*, *pasta reale*, is made of ground almonds, sugar, and egg, and used both as it is and cooked, in cookies or made into various confections, like the *frutta di Martorana*, so called because they are said to

have been made by the nuns of the convent of the Martorana in Palermo to impress the archbishop when he visited on 1 November, the Day of the Dead, or All Souls, and was delighted to see these fruits suspended from the trees in the cloister. They are now made all the year round, but still given to children as treats in memory of the dead on All Souls' night. Beautiful marzipan fruits can be made in moulds or shaped by hand, and then painted in glowing colours. The paste can be flavoured with lemon zest or cinnamon. Corrado had an elegant pure white version, using lemon juice, colourless cinnamon water, and pounded peeled almonds, cooked in a sugar syrup, then spread over wafers and cooled, then covered with a white icing. *See also* ALMOND.

MARZOLINO,

MARZOLINO, a cheese made in the month of March, when pastures are rich and fragrant, was described by Platina as one of the two foremost cheeses of Italy, along with parmesan; but today this traditional version of CACIOTTA is almost extinct. This fresh, uncooked, rich sheep's milk cheese is made from the warm morning's milk added to that of the night before, coagulated with wild artichokes, shaped and pressed by hand, and hung to dry in cloths. The version made in Chianti, between Florence and Siena, is probably as near as one can get to that enjoyed by Michelangelo, who insisted on consignments being sent from his Tuscan properties to Rome; on 7 January 1559 he wrote thanking his nephew Lionardo in Florence for the "fifteen *marzolini* and fourteen pounds of sausages, I am very glad of them, particularly the *marzolini*, because there is a shortage of such things." It was described by the physician and cheese enthusiast Pantaleone da Confienza (p. 57) in 1477:

> Marzolino cheese is commonly called Florentine cheese because it is made in Florentine territory, in Tuscany and

Romagna. They are round, fairly big cheeses, very clean and brilliant, and when mature a lemony wax colour. They are made for the most part with sheep's milk, although some add some cow's milk as well. They are fairly compact in consistency and consequently without holes. They have a good flavour when hardened with time and last well, depending on their size. I think this is partly due to skill in handling them, and to the dry fodder of the animals who give the milk. And the way they are stored has no small influence. They are esteemed cheese and are exported all over—I have even eaten them in France. They are offered as much sought-after gifts.

MASCARPONE

MASCARPONE, in its pasteurised or UHT (ultra heat treated or long life cream) state, is popular abroad, and used in many recipes, like TIRAMISÙ, being considered less rich than fresh cream, though it is not. Being unsalted, it is highly perishable, and, sadly, its subtle flavour and texture are lost in the process of being sterilised for mass marketing. The real thing is made all over Lombardy, especially in Abbiategrasso, Lodi, Cremona, and Mantova. Fresh cow's milk cream is heated in a double boiler and then mixed with an acidic coagulant, left in a refrigerator for 12 hours, strained, then chilled some more in wooden containers, strained again, and is ready for immediate consumption. The artisan product, uninhibited by hygienic regulations, has a sharper, fresher taste and is somewhere between butter and cream in texture. The origins of the name are uncertain. A fatuous remark, variously attributed to the emperor Charles V or anonymous dignitaries of the Church, who, when offered some at a banquet, said *"Mas que bueno!"* (Better than good!) seems highly improbable, even allowing for a Spanish presence in northern Italy. *Mascarpa*, the dialect word for ricotta, which looks a bit like *mascarpone*, seems more plausible.

Milanese cuisine uses *mascarpone* in both sweet and savoury recipes, versions of what we call trifle (sponge biscuits soaked in various flavourings, layered with a *mascarpone* cream); and mixed with egg yolk, seasoned with pepper and parmesan, as a sauce for *tagliatelle*. It goes into *malfatti di spinaci*, spinach gnocchi. A traditional recipe from Lombardy is for a pot-roasted pheasant stuffed with *mascarpone* mixed with slices or peelings of white truffles, and served, carved, with the resulting sauce and some more freshly sliced truffles. But *mascarpone* is also enjoyed simply spread on bread, or with cheese at the end of a meal. When made with cream from buffalo milk, like the *mascarpone di Battipaglia* in Campania, the result is more pungent, with a musky perfume, best in spring when the animals graze on fresh grass and herbs. As well as being a regional speciality, though, *mascarpone* is a traditional by-product of any surplus of cream, and probably the only milk product in Italy that one could make with success at home.

MASSONIO, SALVATORE

(1554–1629), was born in Aquila, where he studied letters and philosophy. He subsequently moved to Rome, where he studied medical sciences with the notable papal physician and author Andrea Bacci (*De Naturali Vinorum Historiae de Vinis Italiae*) and Alessandro Traiano Petronio philosopher and physician (*De Victu Romanorum*). When he returned to Aquila, in 1581, Massonio revived the ancient Accademia dei Velati and devoted himself to the study of archive material relating to his native town. Massonio was a humanist, man of letters, physician and botanist and has been defined as a "most diligent preserver of ancient memories." He was the prolific author of 18 unpublished volumes, including a comedy, some sacred plays, an ironic

An edible pink impatiens. (Shutterstock)

dialogue between "Salvatore" and "Massonio" on the origins of the city of Aquila, and 12 unpublished papers, including several sonnets, some other poems, and a study of the herbs that grow in the province of Aquila.

Archidipno overo Dell'insalata (known as the *Archidipno*), concerning salad and its usage, is the most outstanding of all his works. The first printed book in the history of gastronomic literature dedicated exclusively to salad, it is a typical example of 17th-century never-ending erudition, remarkable for the extraordinary abundance of information about *herba saloacetari*, as Massonio calls it. The first edition was printed in Venice by Marcantonio Brogiollo in 1627, with a foreword by Alessandro Magonza. This original treatise consisted of 68 chapters covering everything that could possibly be said about salads. It examines salads at the beginning and the end of the meal and as the main course, where he refers to a sumptuous salad of all sorts of herbs: watercress, chicory, and capers served with cold pheasant, capon, and peacock, *pasticci di selvatico*, salted meat, and tongue. He describes its composition and dedicates several chapters to the qualities of the different seasonings—salt, vinegar, oil, pepper, lemon, and orange juice, as well as all the positive and negative effects of every single plant, legume, shoot, and flower. The properties of all types of salad are classified as: *irritante* (stimulating), *nutrimento* (nourishing), or *medicamento* (therapeutic). The good reasons for eating salad are discussed, together with further connected topics such as the growing of plants and the selection of the wild varieties, salad in history, and so on. Massonio recounts all these aspects often with personal anecdotes and a degree of humour: "I consider radish salad should be enjoyed not simply for its taste but for the pleasure of crunching tender white roots with your teeth." He describes numerous original and appetizing ways of serving salads and combines, for example, finely cut lettuce, lemon wedges, anchovies, and raisins with tuna, topped with parsley. Among the myriad varieties of salad enjoyed in the 17th century we find a complete chapter on rocket (both the domestic and the wild kind), an antidote for scorpion bites also known for its aphrodisiac qualities.

This unique work is crammed with an enormous amount of learned quotations—over a hundred references to renowned authors—Arab writers, Greek and Latin classical authors, medieval to 16th-century literati, and the Scuola Salernitana. Despite the fact that sometimes the overabundance of quotations seems to overwhelm the text itself, Massonio very skilfully manages to maintain an equilibrium in this complex scientific, literary, linguistic, and bibliographic *misticanza*. Probably Massonio was not acquainted with the long and colourful *Lettera sull'Insalata* (1569) by Costanzo FELICI, and it is unlikely that he knew *Brieve racconto di tutte le erbe*, the nostalgic gastro-sentimental recollection written by Giacomo CASTELVETRO in London in 1614. (JdS)

MASTIC, *Pistacia lentiscus, lentisco, mastice*, is an aromatic, somewhat camphorous resin which exudes from shrubs of the pistachio family when wounded. The best known, and most fragrant, is from the Greek island of Chios, but many other aromatic gums from plants of this family were used in Italy in the past to flavour food, drinks, and medicines, and Mattioli stresses how common this plant is all over Italy. The gum was mixed with wax and chewed both for its flavour and to purify the breath and alleviate toothache. Like camphor, another pungent resin, it was used in poultices. In Sardinia, an oil is made from the fruit of the plant. It is used in sweet and savoury dishes in Middle Eastern cooking.

MATTIOLI, PIER ANDREA

(Siena, 1501–Trento, 1577) was a medical doctor and botanist, who practised in Siena, Rome, Trento, and Gorizia in Bohemia, becoming physician to the Austrian emperors Ferdinand and Maximilian II. He was renowned for his commentaries on the ancient Greek herbal by Dioscorides, surviving in several later versions, some with illustrations copied from copies of long-lost originals. Mattioli produced a translation of the text into Italian, with his own notes and comments, and clear and accurate woodcut illustrations of the plants described. His versions of remedies, his interpretations of what Dioscorides might have meant, and his fulminations against everyone who had the temerity to disagree with him, or criticise Dioscorides, make for prickly reading. His prose crackles with indignation and irritation, some of it even directed at his hero. Several of his more bitter quarrels damaged the careers of contemporaries, but writers like Aldrovandi tiptoed round the controversies with good-humoured tolerance, recognising how much Mattioli had achieved in this pioneering work, though the botanist Michiel, in a letter to Aldrovandi about the problems of trying to grow rare and unknown plants from seed, mentioned that seeds from Mattioli were often old and failed to germinate.

Mattioli is of interest to us more for his notes on contemporary uses of plants than for his concordance of references to them in

ancient authors. We sense in him exaspera-
tion with modern superstition and old
wives' tales and frustration at the lack of
clear information. The pointless tedium of
squabbling about whether Pliny might or
might not have believed that a handful of
basil leaves inside a plant pot would generate scorpions, or that no one, having eaten
basil, could ever be cured of their bites,
made him cross, and we cannot help sym-
pathising. But he does say that every house
in Italy has a pot of basil on the windowsill or
the terrace or in the garden, and describes the
three main kinds—a welcome glimpse of
everyday life, like the pot of basil in Crivelli's
Annunciation with Saint Egidio.

We now know that watermelon, *Citrullus
lanatus,* does not belong to the *Cucurbitaceae,*
as do melon, *Cucumis melo,* and cucumber,
Cucumis sativus, but what with the tendency
they all have to hybridise, and with the profusion of regional names, it is slightly unreasonable of Mattioli to berate Fuchs for
getting Tuscan usage back to front: "just because we [Tuscans] call watermelons cucumbers does not mean that we call cucumbers
watermelons," he grumbled.

Lettuce brings out a touching glimpse of
Mattioli in old age, when a friend suggested
that he ate the tough stalks of lettuce
cooked, with oil and vinegar, to spare his
sensitive teeth. He mentions how in his
youth he found lettuce eased his "choleric"
stomach, and in old age, eaten at the end of a
meal, helped him get to sleep.

Two hundred years before Linnaeus, he
was feeling his way towards a rational system
of classification; it was Mattioli's passionate enthusiasm for the accurate descriptions
of plants that inspired generations of collectors and describers, and so made this
possible.

MEAGRE, *ombrina boccadoro,* is similar
to OMBRINE, *ombrina,* and can be cooked
the same way as SEA BASS.

MEALS AND PATTERNS OF EATING

are more relaxed than
they used to be, with a less rigid pattern,
both at home and when eating out. Printed
menus show the conventional sequence of a
formal meal, and this would be followed in
the home on special occasions. *Menu* is a
French word for the scope and contents of a
meal, not entirely at home in Italy, where
many prefer to ask for *la lista (delle vivande)*
rather than *il menu.* This comes in spoken
and printed versions, often with translations
for the benefit of foreign visitors. The spoken *lista* is what most regulars prefer, when
the waiter will say what is special that day,
and often recommend something to the taste
of the client, and is still the best way of finding out about specialities and dishes that
may not be of general appeal. Reciting the
menu in a singsong voice is the vice of pretentious foreign establishments aping Italian
usage and can be irritating, but in Italy it is a
low-key form of communication, and a
helpful waiter can help create a memorable
meal this way. In a small country restaurant
with clients from the clothing and white
goods trade around Carpi in Emilia, a waiter
once unobtrusively served a young foreign
businesswoman, not too happy about eating
alone, with what she said later was the perfect meal—no chatting up, just a tactful
presence bringing the right food and wine
harmoniously together.

Menus in both home and restaurant usually follow a pattern of hors d'oeuvres, antipasti; first course, *i primi*; second or main
course, *i secondi*; accompanying vegetables,
contorni; then cheese, *i formaggi*, or dessert,
dolci. Wines are listed, but it is a good idea to
ask about the house wines, which are usually
selected to do justice to the food. Until recently one ate one's way happily through the
complete menu, a matter of both form and
pleasure, but now many Italians, preoccupied with healthy eating, sometimes omit a
course or two. Those who really only need a
light meal can find a wide choice of alterna-

tives (*see* EATING OUT).These can be sought out by the hungry traveller: the various flatbreads and stuffed breads in local bakeries; *porchetta* from street stalls, or the nuts, roasted seeds, olives, and *lupini*; and chestnuts in season, sold in most public places.

The historic menus that have come down to us in printed cookery books or manuscript sources provide insight more into the splendours of the Italian BANQUET than everyday food. Scappi, Messisbugo, Stefani, and many others gave descriptions of special feasts, pageants, music, and dancing, where a banquet or refreshments were part of courtly or diplomatic events, designed to impress visiting notables and the curious rabble. Writers like Corrado gave specimen menus through the seasons, rather than describing particular meals like Scappi, with dishes using available produce. By the late 19th century, Artusi offered modest bourgeois menus, to give his readers possibilities and combinations that might inspire them. These modest meals would begin with a *minestra*, then something unsubstantial like *principii* (*crostini* or cured ham and figs) followed by a *lesso*, boiled meat, chicken, or fish; then *umido*, which was not a stew but something delicate like a veal chop, or a *sformato* or stuffed chicken breasts; followed perhaps by a *tramesso*, little pasties or a *vol au vent*, or a soufflé; next a serious *arrosto* of meat, fowl, or fish; and finally *dolci*, *frutta*, and *formaggio*. There would also have been *erbaggi*, cooked vegetables, and maybe a salad. In some ways, this modest meal was more of an endurance test than picking one's way through a Scappi banquet, where at least one could select from the massive succession of dishes.

MEAT, *carne,* has a modest role in Italian gastronomy. Perhaps the sanest view of meat is that of Giacomo Castelvetro, who wrote extolling the virtues of fruit and vegetables. No vegetarian, his frequent use of meat

broth, fat, and the by-products of a meat diet in vegetable cookery are typical of the Italian attitude to meat—something that is often the least substantial part of a meal, small in quantity, beautifully cooked and presented and eaten on its own, with a bit of bread and maybe a vegetable on the side, a vegetable to which as much care and attention has been given. Meat broth, bacon, fat, and various preserved meats are still used to enhance vegetable recipes, and although there are few rigid vegetarians in Italy, meat is usually eaten with discretion.

MEATBALLS, *polpette,* have a particular resonance for early Italian settlers in the United States, mainly from Naples, who came in search of work and a better life; to them, the abundance of inexpensive meat was proof on the plate that this was possible. Meatballs with pasta in a rich tomato sauce is alien to the Old Country, but now part of America's gastronomic heritage. The Neapolitan meatball traditionally had sultanas and pine nuts in the mix of ground meat (veal, pork, or beef), breadcrumbs, parmesan, egg, and parsley; it was fried briefly, then finished in a tomato sauce flavoured with basil and garlic, and eaten on its own. There are many different meatballs, some made from raw ingredients, some as a way of using cooked leftovers. *Polpette* can also be made of fish or vegetables. Martino had a different name for meatballs—he called them *tomacelli*, a name which survives in a recipe from Liguria (*see* POLPETTE).

Carnacina and Veronelli (1977, bk. 3, p. 22) have a recipe for *maccheroncelli con polpettine di carne alla partenopea* in which tiny meatballs the size of a hazelnut are made from the cooked meat of a *spezatino* or *genovese*, minced, bound with egg and bone marrow, seasoned with parsley, zest of lemon, salt, and pepper, lightly simmered in water, and added to small short *maccheroni*, which have been dressed with butter, parmesan, and some of the dense cooking liquid. Tomato is part of the meat juices, a subdued presence.

The addition of small aromatic meatballs to stews of meat or fowl was part of the Arab gastronomic legacy, but there is no written evidence of direct influence here, although many writers have explained the beneficial legacy of the Arab presence in Campania.

MEDICI, CATERINA DE',

1519–1589, is obscured by myths. As a historical figure, she emerges as a ruthless and unscrupulous politician who ruled France after the death of her husband Henri II in 1559, in the interests of her unpleasant and inadequate children. Caterina, whose parents died shortly after her birth in Florence in 1519, was brought up by her uncle, Pope Clement VII, who was well aware of her importance in the web of dynastic marriages and alliances of European politics, and so gave her an education to fit her for whatever role she might be obliged to assume. By the time of her marriage, at 14 years of age, to Henri, son of François I, she was an intelligent and spirited young woman, and although her pop-eyed, jowly Medici looks were no match for the charismatic Diane de Poitiers, her husband's mistress, she got on well with her father-in-law, François I, and bided her time, to become the mother-in-law from hell to many of the nobility and crowned heads of Europe. The myth that Caterina brought the appurtenances of civilised living to the barbarous French is ridiculous but still widely held, in spite of the crisp demolition job by Alberto Capatti and Massimo Montanari (Capati and Montanari, 1999, pp. 126–131). She could never have crossed the Alps with luggage burdened with all the things she is alleged to have crammed into her bags— corsets, side saddles, high-heeled shoes, forks, artichokes, green peas, asparagus, broccoli, truffles, melons, sorbets, puff pastry, cheese tarts, and numerous recipes, most of which had been enjoyed by the French for centuries

before she arrived. *Caneton à l'orange* is held by many who should know better to be Caterina's gift to France, without a shred of documentary evidence. The bitter orange, *bigarade*, was being used in France as early as the 14th century as a sauce for fowl. Nobles and royalty travelled with a retinue of servants, including cooks, and Caterina was no exception, though her chefs were not breaking new ground, but joining a floating population of professionals cooking in the modern European style. Her wedding feast in Marseilles in 1533 would have been one of those international banquets that celebrated such political manoeuvres, and Caterina's most dramatic contribution was her jewel-encrusted garments of brocade and silk, and her insistence on expensive luxuries and all the visible trappings of power. Her greed, which became more apparent in later life, was that of an active, grasping woman who always ended up getting what she wanted, and her habitual indigestion was a direct result of this rather than her alleged interest in poisons. Some sources mention Caterina's overindulgence in CIBREO, a dish she is said to have brought with her from Florence. In fact, this was already known in France and Italy—a delectable concoction of the livers, feet, testicles, and combs of cockerels, often served in a sauce enriched with egg yolks and flavoured with herbs, only later to become associated with the popular food served around the Sant' Ambrogio market in Florence. Capatti and Montanari show that 18th-century writers in Italy, reacting to the predominance of French cuisine throughout Europe, might have created the myth to redress the balance, also quoting Montaigne's conversation with an Italian cook, which he gave as a misuse of language but has since been cited as an example of Italian gastronomic superiority. They point out that however sophisticated Italian food was, it could be matched by the gastronomy of many other European nations.

To redress the balance, we might note

that when Renée of France married Ercole II Este and came to live in Ferrara in 1529, she brought French cooks and French manners to an already sophisticated court, and Messisbugo had the wit to provide "fusion" food at the celebratory banquet offered by his employer, Ippolito, Ercole's brother, to welcome her. Ippolito had spent some years in France, returned to Ferrara, and then gone on to Rome, with a French chef and pastry cook on his staff. In the world of international negotiations, fashions in food were deployed as elements in diplomacy, as we can detect in Scappi's menus, and French, Spanish, and even British ways of cooking played their part. Caterina can now be seen in a more sinister perspective, making more of an impact on politics, possibly even as poisoner, than on gastronomy. High time this myth bit the dust.

MEDITERRANEAN DIET

has become a peg on which writers and journalists have hung many a Pied Piper's garment, beguiling a host of happy children and grownups into following a pattern of eating and drinking which has a potential to improve the health and economies of individuals and nations on a global scale. This admirable concept is best understood in the diagram conceived by the Oldways Preservation and Exchange Trust, founded in Boston in 1988 by Dun Gifford, inspired by the work of Ancel Keys in southern Italy in the 1950s. This pyramid of healthy eating is a brilliant visual exposition of a practical way to a healthy diet.

The foundation plinth is an active lifestyle, with plenty of daily exercise. Upon that is built a solid base of bread, pasta, rice, couscous, polenta, and whole grains. Above this is a deep layer of blocks of fresh fruit, vegetables, beans, pulses and nuts, raw or lightly cooked, followed by olive oil (replacing butter and other fats); above it smaller quantities of cheese and yoghurt; followed by fish, ideal source of protein and omega-3

oils, taking precedence over poultry and eggs; sweet things in the penultimate layer, and a very little meat, not totally despised and rejected, right at the apex. The quantities and quality of the items, locally grown, if possible organic, can be worked out by individuals to suit their own needs.

The diet of many Italians in historic times could have been described as Mediterranean, with meat a mere luxury, but since the required balance of nutrients was not likely to be achieved by a rural population sunk in poverty and deprivation, the healthiness is something of a figment of our own overfed imaginations. An example of the Mediterranean diet at its best could be found when Liguria was dependent on the sea for communication with the rest of the world. Before roads and railways came about, people were up and down the almost vertical terraces, tending vines, olive trees, and vegetable patches, strong and hearty on a diet of bread, oil, fish, herbs, and vegetables, with the addition of small amounts of cheese and salami (for more detail on the realities and aspirations behind the promotion of the Mediterranean diet, see CUCINA POVERA).

It is likely that the 16 countries bordering on the Mediterranean, with such a range of different races, climates, and produce, can enjoy as much unhealthy food as the rest of the world, and the myth of a universal, simple, beneficial diet universally enjoyed by a legendary race of sprightly elderly peasants is a salutary ideal rather than a reality. "Mediterranean" has become a mantra for the obese and unwell, a magic land where the sky is always blue and the sea warm and clear, and we are forever happy, slim, and well. But the concept itself is admirable, and has been road-tested by scientific and medical organisations and shown to be a force for the good. As a tool for weaning the developed world off processed food and a diet with too much saturated fat, salt, and sugar, it is a winner. The popularisation of the pyramid has developed alongside this academic research, and both promote awareness of healthy eating; meanwhile, the Mediterranean goes its own way, with polluted beaches, fast food outlets, neglected olive groves, and depleted fish stocks. Perhaps the concern for our health will in itself promote more awareness of the delicate balance of the state of health of the Mediterranean itself.

MEDLAR, *Mespilus germanica, nespola comune,* is one of the Rosaceae, like hawthorn and azarole, with similar fruit, or drupes, with a pulpy flesh surrounding a few seeds or pips—in the case of the medlar, five—clustered together in the eye of the fruit. These brown, shiny fruit are astringent when fresh, but when left to rot, or bletted, they develop a sweet soft flesh and are eaten as a dessert fruit. Pisanelli claimed that they helped prevent drunkenness and indigestion, which might explain their appropriateness in this context—the chosen fruit to eat when sampling the year's new wine on the feast of San Martino, the night of 10 November. Castelvetro remembered how on that night children were allowed to stay up late, to join the grownups in the game of *ventura,* in which each person selected a medlar from a basket, and the lucky one could keep the coin concealed within the fruit's aperture. "I well remember the indescribable joy I once felt on finding the money in a fruit. When the cheerful commotion has died down, the medlars are eaten and the wines sampled. There are so many wines to taste, that even though everyone takes only a sip, some of the party have been known to go up to bed somewhat merrier than usual, much to the delight of the rest of the family."

MELON, *melone, popone, Cucumis melo,* probably arrived in Italy during the Roman period, but the evidence is anecdotal—for example, the story of the emperor Claudius Decimus Albinus, who fought against Septi-mius Severus in 197 but was more famous for eating at one sitting 100 peaches from Campania and 10 of the melons of Ostia, recalled by Platina when the melons of Ostia were probably much more delicious than the elongated ones, chat melons, of Roman times. There is some confusion about what the ancient Greeks and Romans grew, what they called them, and what they were like. Whatever they were, they fell out of use during the Dark Ages, and we have the Arabs to thank for introducing melons cultivated by them in the Mediterranean area to Spain and Italy. By the 16th century, Mattioli preferred to use the evidence of his eyes and describe the differences among the *cocomeri,* cucumbers, *meloni* or *poponi,* melons, and *angurie,* watermelons, known, grown, and enjoyed by his contemporaries, instead of trying to sort out the futile linguistic squabbles of the theorists, confused by the profusion of regional names and obscure classical references. (Lombardy, Tuscany, and Venice all used *anguria* and *cocomero* to mean different things).

Medical theory of the time was against eating melons at the end of a meal, when they would impede digestion; their place was at the start, refreshing on an empty stomach. At the time Platina was writing his *De honesta voluptate et valitudine* in the 1460s, he could not have known how grateful he would later be for the dubious charms of melons; it was a surfeit of them, one hot summer night in 1471, that caused his enemy Pope Paul II to expire of apoplexy, something any sound physician could have warned him of. Castelvetro loved melons, their wonderful perfume and delicious flavour, and his recollection of a missing melon found months later in a vat of honey is a nostalgic memory if his youth in Modena. This might be an early food myth, for preserving food in honey was hardly a 16th-century invention, but it is a reminder of the way Italian men have always cared about the quality of their food.

Melons today are either winter melons, with smooth skin and pale green or whitish flesh, which ripen late and are suitable for export; or musk or netted melons, with sometimes a grooved surface, and aromatic flesh, which can perfume the air as they sit piled up on market stalls, and cantaloupe melons with a knobbly skin and orange flesh. One of the glories of Italian eating today is the combination of ham and melon at the start of a meal, where the sweetness and perfume of each acts as a foil to the other, with the saltiness balancing the sugar, and the contrasts in texture enhancing the pleasure.

The beauty of melons has been exploited by still life painters who have relished the contrast between the rough knobbly skin and the glowing flesh within, sometimes bursting exuberantly out of its carapace, or helped along by being thrown from a great height to achieve the same effect.

MENTUCCIA. *See* PENNYROYAL.

MESSISBUGO, CRISTOFARO, was born in Ferrara some time in the late 15th century and died there in 1548, a year before the publication of his book *Banchetti, composizioni di vivande et apparecchio generale* in 1549. This was reprinted 17 times, some versions with the title *Libro novo nel qual s'insegna a' far d'ogni sorte di vivanda.*

Messisbugo was from a well-connected family in the city, with the social standing appropriate to his function as steward and court official to the Este family. He married into the local nobility, and in his book are descriptions of two banquets held in his home, where his patron, Duke Ercole II d'Este was entertained in lavish style. Ennobled by the emperor Charles V, Messisbugo enjoyed the title of count palatine, an appropriate reward for his organizational skills, which must have been formidable. Unlike Martino in the previous century, who was renowned for his cooking, Messisbugo's role was to devise, plan, and execute events,

which included theatrical performances and musical offerings of many kinds as well as banquets. The book must have been intended for officials in his position rather than cooks, so the recipes are sometimes sketchy, often giving more detail for new ones, or those with foreign origins, than for well-known dishes. What are possibly draft versions of the published work indicate that Messisbugo travelled extensively with his master, Duke Ercole, organising every aspect of his life, with the expensive pomp considered necessary for someone of his standing.

His origins, said by some to be German or Dutch, and the bizarre variations in the casual spelling of his name—Sbugo, di Messi, di Messi Sbugo—created some confusion, but thanks to Claudio Benporat, we now know that the name on his tomb, in the church of Sant' Antonio in Polesine in Ferrara, is Messi Sbugo, and that his family had been well established in Ferrara for generations. A manuscript presentation copy of his work, now in the Biblioteca Estense in Modena, can be dated by its dedication to the ambitious and profligate Ippolito II d'Este, brother of Duke Ercole II, on his appointment as cardinal in 1538.

The work starts with a fulsome dedication to Cardinal Ippolito in which a banquet that never happened (the funds went missing, possibly due to fraternal jealousy) is described as "*tutto ombra, sogno, chimera, fittione, mettafora, e allegoria*" (all a shadow, dream, chimera, metaphor, allegory, and a figment of the imagination), a premonition of descriptions of baroque banquets that were to come. Messisbugo then gives some detailed accounts of banquets that did happen, and includes short descriptions of the musical entertainments presented between courses, as well as listing all the different dishes. Research in the d'Este archives in Modena by Mary Hollingsworth (Hollingsworth, 2004) reveal details of the cost of Ippolito's expensive and ruthless rise to ecclesiastical power.

This is the context of Messisbugo's banquets and recipes, devised for a court with an international reputation for wealth and culture; where Ariosto had served an earlier Cardinal Ippolito (the younger Ippolito's uncle) his bedtime posset, and Messisbugo, count palatine, checked (and possibly fiddled) Ercole's laundry lists and household accounts. The dedication to Ippolito was an astute gesture, for by then the cardinal was a close ally of François I, and his household accounts reveal the story of the earlier journeys of this charismatic young man to the French court, his bonding with the wily king, and the relentless networking and present-giving that were eventually rewarded with a cardinal's hat. Ippolito made it in the end, with the wary connivance of his brother Ercole, who had at the same time to manipulate his own relationships with the pope, from whom the Este had prized Modena and Reggio after the sack of Rome, and with the Emperor Charles V, who was nibbling away at parts of northern Italy and eastern France, and with local cities like Milan (Ippolito had been made its bishop at the age of nine) and Mantua, where the Gonzagas could tip the balance any which way. Having a cardinal in the family would be advantageous to the Este dynasty, but at a cost, and the prodigious flow of money in and out of their coffers gives some idea of the scale of these ambitions. Every detail of these incomings and outgoings was recorded by stewards and bookkeepers who noted the various sources of income and how it was spent. These documents have been interpreted by Hollingsworth, whose diligence and enthusiasm have brought to life not just the confusing politics but the details of the everyday life that sustained them. Every pea in every pod, every egg, twig, and wisp of hay was noted by bailiffs and accounted for by factors; grain, greens, cattle, poultry, wood, wine, and cheese were listed, priced, extorted, and consumed with ruthless efficiency. The country folk who toiled to produce all this got in return protection, seed for the next harvest, repairs, and help, sometimes, when times were hard. The balance between plenty and dearth was delicate, for the price of produce accounted for a large percentage of the ducal revenue, and this depended on weather, war, the vagaries of the harvest, and the pressures of demand. And a lot of these pressures seem to have been for an extraordinary quantity of provisions, not just for a banquet for a group of notables but for the feeding of a huge retinue of staff and servants.

Hollingsworth tells us of Ippolito's cook Andrea and his assistants, the supplies provided for them by Zoanne da Cremona (the purveyor), the kitchen equipment, the preparations for banquets, and the money spent on every item in the menus, on all the elaborate décor and table furnishings, and the musicians and their performances. These accounts flesh out Messisbugo's descriptions of the banquets he masterminded for Ippolito's brother Ercole, and the choice of dishes on his menus. It is not known if his own accounts survive in the massive d'Este archive, for Hollingsworth concentrated on the saga of the younger brother's ambitions, but we learn from Ippolito's calculated extravagances something of what Messisbugo must have been providing.

Music and theatrical entertainments were important in the structure of these festivities, and Messisbugo names the musicians and their instruments with an enthusiasm he never expresses for the cooks and their performances. Sometimes the music was a serious instrumental concert, a welcome break between eating and talking, a period of repose and contemplation; sometimes it was light relief, with singers and dancers and comic turns, a time of détente when diners might get up and stretch, wander around, and chat among themselves. Messisbugo's brief summaries of interludes between or during courses tell us much about the sophisticated tastes of the court. "*E subito che fu posta in Tavola questa vivanda fu fatta con somma harmonia, & somma piacere de gli ascoltanti una Musica di Tre Tromboni, & Tre Cornetti, I quali parevano veramente all'gora venuti dal sommo choro, & continuarono fino a tanto che fu portata la seconda vivanda"* (And as soon as these dishes were served up music was played by three trombones and three cornets, with the utmost harmony and to the great delight of the listeners, which seemed to come from the celestial spheres and continued until the arrival of the next course; p. 10r).

Some of the entertainments were light-hearted burlesques, with singers and dancers dressed as peasants, rendering vulgar popular songs in dulcet tones, or bringing rough street sounds into the perfumed bowers of the dining room. Some of these are echoed in the menus, where the trend in posh circles for "peasant food" introduced raw salads and dishes of pulses and root vegetables into the company of noble joints of meat and fish.

Poggio Bracciolini, the great Florentine humanist, wrote a book of jokes which disappoint today with their schoolboy smut, and a century later things had not changed much. Performers of these songs, with their profusion of coarse double meanings and obscene puns, today achieve a balance between refinement and rudeness which is closer to the age than earlier high-minded concepts of Renaissance art.

The ordered sequence of events described by Messisbugo can seem rather intimidating; the regular progression of exquisite dishes from kitchen to *credenza* (sideboard) or table and their ceremonial presentation to the guests sounds almost too good to be true. The bustle and to-ing and fro-ing in the huge banquet scenes of Veronese (*see* VERONESE) give a better idea of the realities of animation and near confusion of a big banquet.

Messisbugo's cuisine was both international (not a helpful word, as Laurioux points out, for although the names might

have been the same, the ingredients varied from country to country) and local, with dishes from the Italian regions, specialities of Emilia and Lombardy, and Italian variations on the luxury foods of France, the Low Countries, and England. Some notice a move away from the new cuisine (offspring of the New Learning of the Renaissance) of Martino and Platina of the previous century towards what was to become yet another new gastronomy, culminating in the riotous splendour of baroque feasting in the years to come. But, as always, the Italian virtues of simplicity and respect for quality are there in even the elaborate menus. Lenten, meatless menus relied on fish, dried and salted, but also on a range of root and fresh vegetables, and fresh herbs. There were sophisticated recipes using luxury vegetables, fresh young garden peas, asparagus, and artichokes, or even the humbler pulses and field crops, broad beans, field beans, lentils, chickpeas. The rustic tastes in food that some historians claim was an aristocratic fad (Grieco, *Et Coquatur*, p. 147) could have been simply a delight in salads and simple vegetable dishes, a necessity for the poor, but for the rich a seasonal pleasure as well as an amusing whim. In Ippolito's household accounts, a serious liking shows up for salads, often procured for refreshment on his long, tiring journeys to France, when in spite of the large amounts of meat, usually veal, bought by Zoanne da Cremona, his purveyor, there would be vegetables and salads. Peas are noted, and cabbage for *aqua cotta*, a simple vegetable soup.

Messisbugo has some extraordinary recipes for *Mollegnane overo Pome disdegno*, EGGPLANT; the name implies that it is something of a rarity, a bit of a weirdo (*melanzana* is said to derive from *mela insana*, crazy apple, and *pome disdegno* implies an inferior sort of apple). The dishes are inventive, and the laconic author even describes one of them as a *minestra divina*: eggplants are peeled and cut in pieces, which are first blanched, then finished cooking with cheese, spices, eggs, and fragrant herbs; another suggestion is to bake slices layered with cheese, a little finely chopped ham, and basil, *"il suo vero condimento"* (its true seasoning).

Painters in northern Italy were providing patrons with images of fresh seasonal fruit and vegetables, not so much rarities as prime local produce, and the still lifes and market scenes hung on the walls of the rich and powerful did not look much like slumming, more a flaunting of the results of good husbandry and selective plant breeding. Vincenzo Campi from Cremona painted market and kitchen scenes; his buxom fruit-seller in the Brera Gallery in Milan presides over piles of fruit and vegetables in bowls and baskets, grouped like the dishes and platters on a banqueting table. Artichokes and asparagus are together, special and seasonal, and they figure in one of Messisbugo's banquets on 28 May 1530: asparagus and strawberries at the beginning of the meal, stewed peas with *marzolino* cheese in the middle, and at the end raw baby artichokes with salt and pepper, with bowls of cherries and stewed muscat pears, junkets, and maraschino cherries dusted with sugar and piled on vine leaves. Among the recipes for meat, fowl, and fish are some good vegetable dishes, lentils enlivened with a sauce of stoned raisins pounded with bread soaked in wine and vinegar, sweetened with honey to get a balance of sweet and sour, and seasoned with pepper and cinnamon. Hop or asparagus tips are first given a boil (to get rid of the bitterness) and finished off in good broth with a piece of ham, cinnamon, saffron, and pepper, and served with their broth, when just tender, on slices of fried bread. Chickpeas, washed in water from the Po, are cooked first in this water, and finished in rich broth seasoned with pepper and ginger, to which is added some cured bacon fat pounded with chopped fresh herbs, with a preponderance of mint, and some *codeghe*, pork rind, previously cooked and cut into little squares. The

rich unctuousness of the slowly simmered rind, and the savoury fat and herbs, make a perfect foil for the mealy chickpeas. A *minestra d'herbicine alla Francese*—perhaps to please Renée, Ercole's demanding French wife—is a mixture of aromatic greenery (Messisbugo does not specify which) blanched, drained, chopped, and fried in cured pork fat, then finished in good broth, not too liquid, seasoned with salt and pepper only, and served over slices of toast, garnished with slices of fried bacon. A recipe for *crema alla francese* is a *crème patissière* made with milk, eggs, sugar, flour, and rosewater, for filling pastries, an innovation perhaps also brought by Renée (Messisbugo, p. 79v.). Correspondence between the Estes and the nearby Gonzagas in Mantua shows a shared interest in food and provisions, and down-to-earth tastes that help to put the interminable banquets in perspective. Isabella d'Este wrote from Mantua to a friend on 9 May 1501, thanking him for the *zambudelli* (a kind of sausage) which arrived just in time to eat with a crop of fresh peas, and sent in return a *formazo duro* (possibly parmesan) to have with the new broad beans. Later, in 1537, Ercole's wife, Laura Dianti, his former mistress of humble origins, whom he married after the death of Lucrezia Borgia in childbirth, was in charge of the curing of salami and hams from over 30 pigs sent from his estates in December. It took her and a team of women a month to process all the salami, sausages, and hams, a delicate task entrusted only to the highly skilled. These specialities of Ferrara made special gifts for visiting ambassadors and heads of state.

Messisbugo did not give recipes for salads, but mentions them in his banquet menus. Often the salad items, which, as the name implies, were salami or salted fish as well as vegetables, were a cold collation displayed on the ornately decorated table, for guests to sample before embarking on the serious succession of courses. For a meal on 24 January 1529, not an ideal time for salads, he provided a mixture of the shoots of chicory, endivia, and *ramponzoli*, which could be either roots or shoots, and a salad of turnip roots carved in decorative animal shapes. Halfway through the meat and fish dishes came a course of cold meats in jelly, pickled fennel, olives, fresh fruit, and crunchy raw cardoons with salt and pepper, accompanied by suitably rustic music, with singers in modern peasant costume prattling in the local dialect of *cose contadinesche*—a prelude to 1,000 oysters with bitter orange and pepper (10 per head, which seems like gastronomic suicide at this stage in the meal). More serious music accompanied the final course of candied fruits and nuts, citrons, lettuce stalks, and cucumbers in syrup, an ensemble of voices, strings, and woodwind.

Messisbugo did not have the magisterial authority and metropolitan experience of Scappi, later in the century; his writing is less assured, but he does contribute to our understanding of the atmosphere of a small but powerful ducal court in the mid–16th century.

MEZZALUNA. *See* KITCHEN EQUIPMENT.

MICHELANGELO BUONARROTI (1475–1564), was

not displeased with the image his biographers Vasari and Condivi crafted of him as a towering genius with a mind above the niceties of fine linen and good living. It was the way he wanted posterity to see him. But his friends and relatives knew a different side of the man who intimidated the redoubtable Pope Julius II and berated his nephew Lionardo for sending him a batch of unsatisfactory wine. Michelangelo put much of his money and effort into the administration of his family's estates in Tuscany, but chose to live in Rome, away from their bickering and cupidity. So there was a constant traffic of produce, of chickpeas, beans, marzolini cheeses, Trebbiano wine, oil, hams and

Michelangelo's *Moses* in the Church of San Pietro in Vincoli, Rome. (Scala/Art Resource, NY)

sausages on the arduous journey from Florence to Rome. Most of this is recorded in the five volumes of Michelangelo's correspondence, and in documents connected with his estates. One of these is a helpful indication of Michelangelo's food preferences—a list of menus, with little thumbnail sketches to illustrate them, on the back of a letter dated 18 March 1518. Michelangelo was at the time in Pietrasanta, arranging for the purchase and transport of marble from the quarries there, a less exasperating environment than the quarries of Carrara, where he battled with obdurate blocks, a sullen workforce, and a harsh climate. Commentators use this list as an illustration of Michelangelo's austere tastes, but a close perusal shows that at even this early stage in his career he had an appreciation of the pleasures of good food: simple ingredients, carefully prepared and elegantly presented. Here is the list:

pani dua, two bread rolls
un bochal di vino, a jug of wine
una aringa, a herring

tortegli, tortelli

una insalata, a salad

quatro pani, four bread rolls

un bochal di tondo, a jug of full-
bodied wine

un quartuccio di bruscho, a quarter of
dry wine

un piatello di spinaci, a dish of spinach

quatro alice, four anchovies

tortelli, tortelli

sei pani, six bread rolls

dua minestre di finochio, two dishes of
fennel

una aringa, a herring

un bochal di tondo, a jug of full-bodied
wine

Each of these items is presented in an appropriately shaped pot: the salad in a wide,
shallow dish with a neat, tiny plinth, the
spinach piled in a smaller bowl, the four anchovies draped elegantly over the curved
mouldings of their basin, the stewed fennel
in round, rimmed bowls; only the herring
swims in midair, while the mysterious *tortelli*
have no container to convey some sense of
scale to their writhing *contraposto*.

This is typical Lenten, or lean, fare, but
far from austere, so perhaps Michelangelo
was trying to show how good a simple vegetarian diet could be, not CUCINA POVERA,
but good-quality ingredients carefully handled. Settled in Rome, he was the dining
companion of popes and nobility, and
would have been familiar with the banquet
menus in Scappi's *Opera*, and the many vegetarian dishes he cooked for lean days, like the
dish of stewedfennel, simmered in oil and
salted water, then seasoned with saffron,
pepper, and cinnamon, thickened with
breadcrumbs soaked in the cooking liquids.
(On "meat" days he could have used butter
instead of oil, and parmesan crusts to give
added richness.) Scappi also gives a recipe
for young spinach leaves, washed and dried,

cooked gently in oil and a little salt, then
chopped and seasoned with bitter orange
juice, cooked grape must, raisins, pepper,
and cinnamon.

Michelangelo made his home in Rome,
where his heart was. The affection and support of friends like Vittoria Colonna and his
close friendship with Tommaso de' Cavalieri
were a welcome antidote to the tiresome behaviour of his father and brothers, who
appear to have been both grasping and incompetent. Working on commissions in Florence in 1533, Michelangelo missed the calm
and comfort of his Roman home, with its
airy *loggia*, terrace, and gardens. His friend
Bartolomeo Angelini wrote reassuring letters: "Your house is watched over all the
time. I go there often during the day—the
hens and their master the cock are flourishing, and the cats miss you dreadfully, though
not enough to put them off their food."

In another letter, Bartolomeo says he has
sold off all the inferior wine, and will buy
some of better quality for when Michelangelo returns. In July, "the heat is intense, but
we survive and the figs are doing well." In
August, "the house and garden and animals
are well, but we all miss you. The muscat
grapes are ripening and Tomaso will have his
share if they survive the magpies." A fortnight later, they are still not quite ripe, but
the figs in the courtyard are fine, the little animals are all well, and there has been a bit of
rain, so the garden has had a drop to drink.
Michelangelo's replies have not survived, but
the kind, soothing letters continue throughout the summer. By early October, the
peaches and pomegranates are ripe; a basket-
ful goes to "Messer Tomaso" and one to a
friend's little boy. "They have been really
beautiful this year."

During the 1550s, presents arrived from
Cornelia, the widow of Michelangelo's
friend and assistant, Francesco Amatori,
known as Urbino. His death in 1556 was a
tragedy for Michelangelo, who had come to
depend on the younger man, who had

worked for 25 years as his housekeeper, works overseer, studio manager, and companion. "I made him rich, he was to support and cherish me in my old age," Michelangelo wrote bleakly. Instead he found himself responsible for Urbino's young wife and two small children, administering their inheritance and dealing with almost saintly patience with the attempts of her grasping family to get their hands on the money, prudently stashed away in a bank in Rome. Cornelia wrote from Casteldurante long gushing letters, affectionate, egregious, naïve, and demanding, prudently backed up with gifts of local *prosciutto*, cheeses, and sausages: "Friday 1 January, 1557 . . . since today is New Year's Day, when it is our custom to greet our masters, I am sending your honour a little present of *guaimo* cheese, eight pounds in weight," and in April 1558, "I am sending you two hams and two pairs of *guaime*, which we would like you to enjoy for our sakes." Unwell and overwhelmed with commissions, Michelangelo still found time to return their kindnesses; in January the following year, Cornelia writes from Casteldurante: "*Magnifico e come padre amantissimo*, I received your letter together with some bitter oranges and lemons, for which I thank you as much as I know how."

As well as mitigating the master's *terribilità*, these small insights into the gastronomic Michelangelo are a helpful indication of attitudes to food in his time. Generous and frugal, Michelangelo was following the precepts of Alberti, whose short essay, *Villa*, makes it clear that to spend good money in the city shops on something you could get from your country estate was bad housekeeping. The difficult transport of provisions from Florence to Rome makes sense in this context. Michelangelo's irascibility about money is understandable—haggling over contracts with the pope, and the price of lentils with his nephew, while penning soulful sonnets to Vittoria Colonna, was multitasking on a titanic scale.

MICHETTA, or ROSETTA, is a small BREAD ROLL, like a rose with five petals, with a crisp outer crust and an almost hollow interior. It originated in northern Italy. Piedmont has a good claim—artisan versions are still made there and in Lombardy—and it is much loved in Milan, though now available all over Italy. It is lighter than some other bread rolls, and the hollow inside lends itself to voluptuous fillings. The name is a diminutive of *micca*, the large round loaf of Milan. Versions of *michetta* are sometimes called BIGNÈ.

MICROMERIA, *micromeria*, a plant of the Labiatae, comes in several varieties, two of which resemble hyssop. It has a more delicate flavour than hyssop, and goes well in stuffings, stews, and any dish enhanced by the addition of green herbs. It is one of the many aromatic plants that are not cultivated and sold on a commercial scale, and so are not found in conventional recipes, but are used in traditional cooking by enthusiasts who grow and use the less common ones.

MIGLIACCIO is the name given to various different preparations with nothing in common except that they once were made with millet or millet flour. In Emilia-Romagna there is a sweet dish made with fresh PIG'S BLOOD, mixed with milk, ground almonds, chopped candied citron, spices, bitter chocolate, and acacia honey, baked on a base of short pastry. In the past, millet would have been used to thicken the mixture, as pearl barley or oatmeal serves the same purpose in England's North Country "black pudding." In Tuscany, it is made with coarse maize flour and raisins, baked with rosemary in a shallow tin greased with lard. If made with chestnut flour, it is called *castagnaccio*. A version from Naples bakes a polenta mixture made with coarse maize flour with *ciccioli* and cooked sausage, parmesan and pecorino, and a handful of chopped parsley in a tin lined with LARD and bread-crumbs. The more usual name for dishes using pig's blood is *sanguinaccio.*

In the past, millet was used as a filling for tarts, but as early as the 1460s Martino was using the term *migliaccio* for a luxurious dish of fresh young cheese pounded with egg whites, thickened with flour and sweetened with sugar, cooked like a crèpe in plentiful hot lard, and served sprinkled with sugar and rosewater—no millet involved. His *torta di miglio* was made with husked millet cooked until soft in goat's milk, the liquid thickened with flour and egg whites, sweetened with sugar, spread out on a board to cool then cut into wedges, and fried until golden in lard, served with the inevitable sugar and rosewater; on lean days it would be made with almond milk and fried in olive oil. A tart filling, but cooked like fritters.

MILK, *latte alimentare,* is defined as a product obtained by regular milking from the udders of animals in sound health and with good nutrition. *Latte* is milk from cows; that from other animals is *latte di capra,* goat's milk, *latte di pecora,* sheep's milk, and so forth. The purity of newly expressed milk is equalled only by its perishability; once exposed to the atmosphere, and milking and handling, it is invaded by bacteria, which contribute to its transformation into the products we appreciate, aided and abetted by sterilisation and pasteurisation, temperature control, and a variety of ways of maturing, storing, and distributing this complex substance, all aimed at nurturing the "good" bacteria and zapping the "bad."

Yoghurt, *yogurt,* is one of the many kinds of coagulated milk, in which the appropriate bacteria, added at the right temperature, cause the milk to solidify while producing lactic acid. This process is not of great importance in Italian gastronomy, as it is in many Mediterranean and Near Eastern

countries, and although yoghurt is now made industrially in a variety of flavours, it is rarely used in cooking, though it can be added to rice dishes, sometimes along with tomato sauce. The 15th-century health handbooks, *Tacuina sanitatis,* have among the milk products illustrated *lac acetosum,* soured milk, *lac coagulatum,* coagulated milk (possibly junket), ricotta, which is made from whey and not milk, but has something of the immediate freshness of yoghurt. Pinelli engraved a *gioncataro* coming down from the hills with a basket of fresh junkets on his back, and in another image he is seen selling them to a group of women and small children gobbling them from earthenware pots, as they would yoghurt today. Perhaps the creamy acidity of yoghurt in the food of Bulgaria or Turkey was obtained in Italy from verjuice and animal fat or butter.

Milk, raw or treated, is not used a great deal in cooking, but it has its uses in the kitchen. Some salt fish, like anchovies and herrings, benefit from soaking in milk. *Prescinsoeua,* slightly soured milk clotted with rennet, remains popular in Liguria, where it forms part of a delicious walnut sauce called *tocco de noxe.* A number of recipes for salt cod (*see* BACCALÀ) and STOCKFISH use milk as a gentle cooking medium, which preserves the whiteness essential to many baccalà dishes. From Piedmont and Lombardy come savoury rice dishes cooked in milk, and there are sweet versions. There are recipes for pork cooked in milk, where the milk condenses into a granular sauce over prolonged cooking, often flavoured with fennel, garlic, bay leaves, sage, or rosemary. CUSTARDS and CREAMS made with milk are used in desserts and *pasticceria. See also* CHEESE.

MILLET, *Panicum miliaceum, miglio,* common millet, and *Setaria italica, panico,* foxtail millet, have both been eaten, as a grain in soups and porridge and as flour in bread, since Roman times. The name survives still, MIGLIACCIO, in various recipes in which it was once used but is now no longer an ingredient. It gave its name to a bread, *pan de mei*, or *pan meino*, which used to be made in Lombardy using millet flour, which gave it a pleasant sweetness when eaten hot from the oven. Crusty old Mattioli wrote with warmth about the bread made in Lombardy with millet flour:

> Bread made from millet flour, when made with a certain skill (as the bakers in Lombardy, particularly Verona, possess) is eaten hot, as it comes from the oven, and has a particular sweetness on the palate, so that many, many people buy it and eat it with delight; and there is no shortage of vendors crying it through the city, shouting "millet bread, hot and hot." But when it cools it hardens and loses all its flavour.

Millet flour has the advantage of rising well, and is still sometimes used in starter dough. It goes into a *pagnotta di miglio* from Bolzano, made with wheat flour, wheat bran, and millet, enriched with egg, sugar, and butter.

MINESTRA. *See* SOUP, ZUPPA.

MINESTRONE. *See* SOUP.

MINT, *Mentha* (in its many varieties), belongs to the Labiatae family. Peppermint, *Mentha piperita*, and *Mentha romana*, or *gentile*, a short-leaved, milder mint, a garnish to *trippa alla romana*, together with *mentuccia* or *Mentha pulegium* (pennyroyal), supposed to repel bugs and renowned for its use in *carciofi alla romana* (*see* ARTICHOKE), are the main kinds available commercially, but there are many different kinds with different aromas, including *Mentha spicata* (spearmint), *Mentha*

aquatica (watermint), and *Mentha requieni* (Corsican mint), a tiny-leaved mint found in Corsica and Sardinia, often used in fruit salads and in ICE CREAM and sorbets. Catmint, *nepeta cataria*, *erba dei gatti*, is another one of the Labiatae, but without the freshness of most mints; it has a dry pungency loved by cats, and a rather harsh flavour, rarely used in cooking—not to be confused with *nepitella*, *mentuccia*, *calaminta* (*Calamintha nepeta*), another of the Labiates, also called *Satureia calaminta*. Early herbalists stressed the digestive powers of mint, how it balanced the "coldness" of some salad plants, like lettuce, and stimulated the appetite, but also acted as an antiaphrodisiac. The nymph Minthe, loved too well by the god Pluto, was turned by his enraged spouse into an attractive plant with precisely this effect. An apt revenge.

Corrado is both original and discreet in his use of mint, for example in a sauce made with lemon juice, to eat with a cold chicken which has been cooked in water with salt, pepper, bay leaves, and the peel of a green lemon. The acidity of the lemon, the fresh pungency of the mint, and the underlying aromas of bay and green lemon make a lovely foil to the delicate fowl. A more robust recipe from Corrado is for pigeons larded with ham and pork fat, stuffed with the birds' liver chopped with ham and mint, spit roasted, and served with a pomegranate sauce. He cooked partridges stuffed with ham, truffles, veal fat, spring onions, and mint, stewed them in Burgundy with garlic and sage, then baked them in pie with more aromatics.

A modern recipe using mint with fish instead of the usual parsley is for fresh anchovies dusted with flour, fried in oil, and marinated in a sauce of fried garlic, red wine vinegar, and chopped fresh mint leaves. Mint is often used along with parsley and basil to flavour salads and cooked vegetables, as in a dish of grilled or roasted peppers, peeled and torn into strips, and marinated in garlic, olive oil, and the chopped herbs.

The essential oils found in the leaves and flowers of mint are used commercially to flavour liqueurs and confectionery; Fernet Menta is a version of Fernet Branca (see APERITIVI and DIGESTIVI) in which mint predominates over the many other herbal flavours—a useful digestive, and also good dribbled over ice cream or sorbets.

MISCHIANZA. *See* SALAD.

MISTRÀ is an anise-flavoured liqueur, similar to ouzo and the various kinds of *pastis.* It is said to have become fashionable in Venice through the republic's eastern contacts and conquests, and to be named for the city of Mistra in Sparta. It is also associated with Marseilles, where it is thought to have been named after the *mistral.* It is today a speciality of the Marche, both as a commercial product and a favourite homemade liqueur. The anise flavour can also come from star anise.

MITELLI, GIUSEPPE MARIA (1634–1718), is known for his tarot cards, but is interesting to us for his other engraved board games, many of which show trades, inn signs, and professions of his native Bologna. Unlike Pinelli in Rome a century later, his engravings are not very topographical, but are full of details of trades connected with food, with little vignettes of a baker at work, a seller of aquavit, a printmaker, an innkeeper, and a butcher. A series of figure studies of the street life of the city, based on drawings, now lost, by Annibale Caracci, depict types rather than individuals, but show some popular food: the tripe-seller, with two huge pots suspended from a yoke, providing a tasty dish for those without the resources of time and fuel for the arduous preparation and slow cooking needed; the

anisaro e solfarolo, who sold slugs of crude spirits and bundles of sticks of cinnamon; a youth with a shallow tray of chickens' heads, gizzards, and livers, potential delicacies; the *ciambellaro,* with bread rings strung on poles and piled in a basket; the *ortolana,* with a mass of vegetables in a shallow wicker basket balanced on her head; and the butcher's boy, with a dish of off-cuts and bits and pieces for the cats who flock around in answer to his low, whistled cry. (Cats really earned their keep, not as pets but as exterminators of vermin.) A long engraved frieze of a civic procession shows all the items in a gargantuan communal feast being paraded through the streets—sausages, great hams, pies, cheeses, baskets of salad leaves, barrels of wine, and mysterious banners proclaiming "liberty," thus celebrating Bologna's famous rich cuisine and civic pride.

MOLISE is south of LAZIO and ABRUZZO, with CAMPANIA to the southwest and PUGLIA stretching to the southeast. It shares a common history and geography with the mountains and national parks of Abruzzo, and only acquired an independent name in the 1960s. The ancient feudal principality which gave Molise its name emerged from waves of invasion by Byzantines, Lombards, and Saracens, but had disintegrated by the 14th century, and so the region never had the gastronomic culture of princely courts; instead it was a society of herdsmen and peasant dwellers on the wooded Apennines, and its small fragment of coastline on the Adriatic. The cuisine, similar to that of Abruzzo, of which Molise was once a part, is based on local natural resources, meat, salame from local pigs, cheeses from the herds of sheep and goats, and vegetables and herbs from fertile gardens and orchards— sweet peppers, small and flavoursome *cannelini* beans, broccoli, celery and fennel, onions, small black figs, peaches, apricots,

and apples. Polenta is eaten in Molise more than in other southern regions, often combined imaginatively with vegetables, as in *polenta a tordiglioni*, green vegetables turned in oil or lard and seasoned with chilli and garlic, or cooked to a solid consistency and then sliced and grilled with meat or sausages, or baked in the oven with pancetta and sausages, or covered in a pork *ragù*. Pasta dishes often combine inventive shapes with vegetables and pulses, usually highly seasoned with herbs and chilli. Of the many pasta shapes *crejoli* are like the *maccheroni alla chitarra* of Abruzzo; there are *ciufeli e tanne de rape*, pasta shapes with well-seasoned turnip tops, *taccozzelle con i fagioli* are similar to many bean and short pasta dishes. Meat is a luxury, often spit roasted with herbs, and much use is made of offal, especially tripe and intestines stuffed in various ways. The climate of Molise is not one for curing the noble parts of the pig, so the meat which would elsewhere become ham is put into very fine salami like the *saggicciotto*, or the *ventricina* of Campobasso, large pieces of prime leg meat seasoned with paprika, chilli, fennel, and salt, packed into the bladder, while the lesser parts and organs go into the *salsicce di fegato di Rionero*, where generous amounts of chilli and garlic help preserve the lungs, livers, hearts, and soft fat that they contain. Blood pudding, *sfarricciato*, gets its name from the use of cooked *sfarro*, emmer wheat, added to the mix of fresh pigs' blood, sugar, pine nuts, raisins, orange peel, cocoa, and hard back fat. Local pigs reared in semiwild conditions—eating the woodland nuts, roots, and tubers, wallowing in the mud of streams and ponds in the summertime—account for the special qualities of these products. Pecorino cheeses are as excellent as the meat from the sheep grazing on the fragrant vegetation, and refrigeration now makes some of the delicate fresh young cheeses, like the cow's milk *stracciata di Agnone*, more widely available. The *cacciocav-*

allo and *burino* are renowned, as are the fresh *mozzarella di bufala* and the *fior di latte* of cow's milk, paler and more delicate, to be eaten as fresh as possible.

MONKFISH is the name we give to two different fish: angel shark (sometimes called angel fish), *squadro*, *Squatina angelus*, a flat shark with a floppy body that looks vaguely ecclesiastical, and angler fish (also known as goosefish), *rana pescatrice, coda di rospo, budegasso, diavolo di mare* (*Lophius budegassa, Lophis piscatorius* or *Lophius americanus*). This is a rapacious, ugly fish which attracts its prey by waving the various excrescences on top of its huge head, then when they come to investigate gobbles them up into its wide mouth and vast stomach, making possible a varied diet which has been known to include several wild ducks, a mature otter, large cod, and many a crab and lobster. The small compact tail is something of an anticlimax, but has the advantage of a cartilaginous central spine without bones, and firm white flesh which is often said to ressemble lobster, and once the successive layers of protective membrane have been peeled off, makes a prime cut of firm tasty white flesh for roasting or grilling, after a marinade in oil, lemon, and parsley. Anyone who can confuse this with lobster deserves to be fobbed off with it, for it lacks the juicy sweetness and delicate texture, and when overcooked exudes moisture and becomes tough. The challenge is to cook it in a way that seals in the juices or in a coating that absorbs them. Many innovative chefs have risen successfully to this challenge, and monkfish have in recent years progressed from a despised to an endangered species. A recipe from Romagna briefly fries slices of monkfish in olive oil, then finishes them in a hot oven covered with a mixture of breadcrumbs, chopped hard-boiled eggs, garlic, and herbs. *Coda de rospo fumegada* is a traditional

Venetian recipe in which a whole tail of monkfish is skinned and then marinated overnight in a lot of crushed black pepper; this is then brushed off and the fish wrapped in slices of smoked pancetta and roasted or grilled, turning it from time to time until done, then served, the pancetta removed, with potatoes drenched in melted butter.

MONTASIO is a cooked cow's milk cheese which gets its name from the Alpine area in Friuli where it was made for centuries; some idea of its prestige is a decree issued in Udine in 1773 which values the "genuine" *montasio* highest of all the local cheeses (19 *soldi* a pound, compared with only 4 for lesser ones). Already the need for identification and protection of the real thing was recognised, and by the 19th century, cooperatives were being set up to organise and regulate production, which today covers a much wider area, plains and low hills as well as the mountains, now with a DOP and a rigorous definition (Friuli, the provinces of Belluno and Treviso in the Veneto, and parts of those of Padua and Venice) along with procedures and quality control. The milk is of primary importance, from the local red-spotted breed, with some Brown Alpine and Frisian; what they eat is important, and meticulously specified. To achieve a uniform cheese when it is made in so many different places, the use of lactic culture is required, to encourage the fermentation that creates its own special microflora; after coagulation with liquid calf's RENNET, the curds are cooked, and the process of draining, pressing, and salting is underway, followed by a short maturing period for young *montasio*, which is enjoyed as a table cheese, then an intermediate stage, and a longer one for the harder grating cheese.

MONTE VERONESE has been made with different names for centuries in the area known as Lessinia, and the heights around Monte Baldo. It is now accorded a DOP definition of its two modern versions, one a rich full-fat cheese, matured for only a few months, with a delicate fragrant aroma, and one from skimmed milk, matured for months and even years, with a more pronounced flavour. The hills and upland pasture of the geographical area provide good grazing almost all the year round, and the combination of soil and sunshine encourages a variety of aromatic plants which account for the fragrance of the milk. The cheese is made by small producers.

MORAY EEL, *murena,* is a carnivorous big bully of a creature, though it is highly unlikely to have devoured a slave, even when dismembered. It might still be true, as reported, that the Roman landowner Vedius Pollio punished a slave by throwing him to the morays in his fish pond, and that the slave died, for the moray has a dangerous bite, owing to poison glands among its sharp teeth. The rich politician Crassus wept as bitterly for a pet moray as Domitian wept for his three wives, in a story told by Plutarch. Classical Roman gourmets kept their captive morays separate from other fish, which they were fierce enough to kill. Romans also knew that morays were well worth hunting off Rhegium at the southern extremity of Italy, where they grew to great size, basked on the sea surface, and were called *plotai,* "floaters," in Greek and *flutae* in Latin. The flesh is said to be as subtle and delicious as EEL, but as well as having toxic blood, when raw, the moray eel has a nasty bite, from the poison glands among its teeth. But once the hazards of preparing it are surmounted, it can be very good to eat, using any of the recipes for eel. It lives in the sea, not fresh waters.

Their usual Latin name, *muraena,* was also used (like English "shark") as a term of abuse. Having served as the nickname of a villain plutocrat, it became the proudly borne surname of his descendants, the noble Roman family of Licinii Murenae. (AKD)

MORTADELLA is a product known and liked the world over, and probably made the world over as well—at its worst a mild, bland, soft pink, cooked SALAME studded with fat, peppercorns, and pistachios, with the sort of rubbery, cloying texture reminiscent of the wartime Spam that kept some of us alive but is ungratefully remembered by its survivors. One version, *mortadella Bologna*, with its IGP (*see* DOP), is made not only in Bologna but in an area wide enough to include Piedmont, Trentino, and Lazio, Tuscany and the Marche. Inferior versions make an unremembered filling for a cheap *panino*, a mixture of lean pork meat and fat, with permitted additions which might include pig's stomach, water, processed fat, egg white, dried milk, natural permitted aromas, sugar, and MSG (and that's the permitted version). This mixture is then ground to a fine paste, put into large casings, cooked slowly, cooled quickly, and is ready for use. Superior versions, with subtle flavourings and real fat (not the white meat which is sometimes substituted) are still made by small local producers and best eaten not sliced but cut into half-inch cubes, a better way of enjoying texture and flavour, as an agreeable aperitif. The name might come from the mortar in which the meat was pounded or the myrtle berries used to flavour it. Mortadella was excellent enough to add lustre to the reputation of *Bologna la grassa e dotta*, already a centre for fine salumi, but the many historic recipes are so varied that it is hard to find a direct ancestry for today's renowned mortadella from Bologna.. Scappi's *mortadelle* are a mixture of lean and fat pork from the buttocks, chopped very fine with two knives to make a paste that can be worked in the hands, well salted, moistened with a little water, flavoured with spices and herbs, put into casings, left to mature for

a day or two, then fried or grilled—a raw fresh sausage for cooking, not a cooked one. His final words are *"Delle mortatelle et altri salami che si fanno della detta carne, non ne parlo, percioche non è mai stata mia professione"* (I cannot speak of the mortadelle and salami made with this meat, for I have no professional experience of them; Scappi, bk. 2, p. 46v). This seems to imply that the specialist production of *mortadella* and salami away from the domestic kitchen was already established by the late 16th century. Cristofaro di Messisbugo, working in Ferrara in the 1560s, has a recipe for *mortadella* which needs to be read alongside descriptions of today's SALAMA DA SUGO (he is nowhere near as articulate as Scappi, so what follows is my interpretation of what he wrote): fat and lean pork meat pounded to a fine paste, then the addition of hearts, spleen, and liver, chopped very fine, well kneaded together with a some heavy red wine, put into carefully prepared and salted casings, and then left to mature for a few days, presumably before drying for some time. This is one of a clutch of recipes for cured, not freshly cooked, pork products, far from his section on cooked sausages, so perhaps it is one of the jigsaw pieces linking Ferrara with Bologna on the salami map.

MOSCARDINI were pastilles or lozenges of pressed candied sugar flavoured with MUSK, a rare and expensive commodity, deployed as perfume, flavouring, medicine, and aphrodisiac. These *moscardini* sweets were sometimes used to flavour other confections, for the aroma of musk is penetrating, and even a subliminal dose will enhance food. A squid-like creature of the same name has a similar flavour.

MOSTACCIOLO is a cookie whose name derives from the Latin *mustaceus*, and more directly from the Italian *mosto*, grape MUST, which, when cooked down to a thick

A market stall in Padua, Italy, displays fresh mortadella and other specialty meat products.
(Shutterstock)

syrup, was a traditional sweetening, cheaper than honey or sugar. These biscuits are some of the most ancient of Italian confectionery and the different regional variations still have much of the character of the hard, sweet, heavily spiced morsels that graced the first courses of medieval and Renaissance banquets. Scappi almost invariably served them from the *credenza* or sideboard, along with other biscuits, marzipan, little pots of clotted cream, olives, sometimes a salad of borage flowers, along with wines chosen to stimulate the appetite and get the digestive juices flowing for the challenges ahead. He mentions *mostaccioli Napoletani* and *Romaneschi*, also referring to them as *morselletti*, and gives a recipe for the Milanese kind—an aristocratic version using sugar, eggs, and flour whipped for a long time to make a foamy batter, flavoured with powdered anise seeds or coriander, and musk, cooked until puffy in flat tart tins, cooled, cut into shapes, and cooked again to dry them out. He gives another kind made with pulverised white breadcrumbs and flavoured with rich dessert wine and musk, a fashionable aroma in 16th- and 17th-century Europe, a conscious move away from the heavy spicing of earlier times. Half a century later, the convent kitchens in Perugia were still making a more ancient version, heavy with honey and must, spiced with pepper, cinnamon, cloves, and musk-flavoured comfits (*moscardini*), made to keep, and prepared specially for 15 December, the feast of San Tommaso. Scappi may have given the recipes because they were innovative and different from the much spicier traditional ones bought from the *speziarie* or imported from the towns of origin. He intended his more refined *moscardini* to accompany fine wines in the winter time, a similar custom to dipping CANTUCCI in *vin santo*, enjoyed in Tuscany today, but at the end of the meal, not the beginning. In 18th-century Naples Corrado was using three recipes for *mostaccioletti*, which involved making a paste of flour, sugar, cinnamon, cloves, and nutmeg mixed with water, which was then left to ferment for two days, kneaded briefly, and made into "whatever shapes you please" about the size of half a finger, cooked until done, spread with cinnamon icing, and put to dry in a warming oven, *stufa*. A variation uses pepper instead of nutmeg, and includes chopped candied citron and chopped burnt almonds, finished with a chocolate icing. His *sosamelli alla monaca* are similar to convent recipes, still using honey, and are very like those of Maria Vittoria della Verde, heavily spiced, with candied citron and orange, but with the addition of chopped burnt almonds and fresh orange zest, finished with an orange icing.

In Sicily today, these hard cookies, best when dunked in dessert wine, are made in a plain version using cloves, cinnamon, and ground almonds, and as a festival speciality for All Souls' using oranges, pepper, and honey or cooked grape must, rolled in sesame seeds before baking (Simeti and Grammatico, 1994). *Mostaccioli* is a name recently given to a pasta shape, ribbed things looking like a moustache, which is both misleading and inaccurate.

MOSTARDA DI FRUTTA,

preserved fruits in a spiced syrup, is today associated with Cremona, in Emilia, where this delightful relish is produced commercially, and served with the BOLLITO MISTO of that region. Mostarda has been around for a long time, made in many different areas of Italy, using in a pragmatic way the preservative powers of boiled-up grape MUST and various spices, of which MUSTARD seeds are the most important. Since the biting quality of mustard is released when the ground grains are in contact with water, but destroyed when salt and vinegar are added too soon, it has been observed that commercial *mostarda di frutta* can eventually lose its pungency.

Mostarda veneta is a version made with quinces, apples, and pears, cooked to a thick, reduced paste, and flavoured with sugar and mustard.

MOSTO COTTO, *saba*, or *sapa*, is

the juice of ripe grapes boiled until considerably reduced, usually to one-third of the original amount, to give a dense fruity syrup, which in the past was used as a substitute for the more expensive honey or sugar. It is still used in Emilia and the Marche as a flavouring and ingredient in tarts and cookies, and of course in the MOSTARDA DI FRUTTA of Cremona, in which fruits are cooked in must and spices, including *senapa*, mustard, which gets its name from the must and not the other way round. In Martino's recipes for *mostarda*, he uses pounded raisins or verjuice along with soaked mustard seeds and many spices. Artusi remembered how small children would mix *sapa* with fresh snow to make improvised ice cream.

MOZZARELLA DI BUFALA

is a very fresh pulled cheese made from full-fat WATER BUFFALO's milk; that made from the milk of cows or other animals is, strictly speaking, *fior di latte*, but is confusingly also referred to as mozzarella. Mozzarella, when made on an industrial scale for export and widespread distribution, is packaged to sustain long journeys in refrigerated transport and give a long shelf life; this is what most of us outside Italy have to put up with. But the enclosure of the mozzarella, in its watery bath of whey, in a plastic bag or rigid container cuts it off from the reaction with the air in its immediate surroundings, and all the subtle developments that happen with hours—no substitute for that ephemeral product made locally and eaten the same day, sold naked from a bowl to connoisseurs who avidly distinguish mozzarella made from the morning's milking from that of the evening. Genuine *mozzarella di bufala* has become a luxury product, with its own boutiques and cult usage, which can lead to blunders by those enthusiasts who insist on using nothing but the best when making the perfect PIZZA, and drown the dough in the fluids from an evanescent buffalo mozzarella, which should really be eaten fresh, on its own, in order to savour the mossy, milky aromas to the full. Even the classic *insalata caprese*, made with mozzarella, tomatoes, basil, and a delicate extra virgin olive oil, is almost too much of a good thing, compared with eating a genuine *mozzarella di bufala* on its own. The sort one can buy easily abroad is ideal for salads and cooking, bearing in mind that the proliferation of contradictory legislation allows for some strange mixtures of cow and buffalo milk, and as much as 65 percent water. Here

imprecision is the mother of fraud, and the word *bufala* on a label is no guarantee that the cheese is made from anything more than a small percentage of buffalo milk.

In the past, mozzarella was made from the milk of semiwild creatures who grazed and wallowed comfortably in the unhealthy swampy regions near rivers and lagoons, mainly in central and southern Italy, herded together for milking morning and evening, a pleasant enough life for the buffaloes but miserable for the unfortunate countrymen, who suffered from malaria and the attrition of long hard work in unhealthy surroundings. The milk is treated with heat and a starter serum, then coagulated, heated again in its whey, and eventually pulled in very hot water (some of which it reabsorbs), put to cool in cold water, made up into pieces, left for a varying time in salt water, and sold without wrappings, enclosed in its less than millimetre-thin skin, in its own liquid. It is paradoxical that the product of a once depressed and underprivileged rural class is now a rare and expensive gourmet delicacy.

The milk from animals grazing on natural palludial vegetation has a quality quite unlike that produced by the farmed buffaloes, often fed on unsuitable agricultural by-products, from which the greater part of today's commercial mozzarella is made. Properly farmed buffaloes today are grazed and fed with hay or feed produced locally, not housed in fetid swamps, but with en suite pools and showers to supply the necessary relief (they have no sweat glands so need exterior sources of water). As already noted, at its best, mozzarella is eaten on its own; for cooking, the commercial brands usually work fine, or indeed any soft, fresh melting cheese like *provatura* or *fontina*. There are "mozzarella type" cheeses, many made in other European countries like Great Britain or Denmark, which are not bad on pizzas. Perhaps the best known dish in which it figures is the classic *parmigiana di melanzane*, in which fried slices of eggplant are layered with tomato sauce, sliced mozzarella, and plenty of grated parmesan, where the umami effect of the parmesan seems to bring out the separate flavours of all the ingredients (*see* UMAMI) and the preliminary frying in good olive oil is a pleasure the health police should not be allowed to deprive us of.

MULBERRY, *mora di gelso, Morus nigra, Morus alba,* was a common fruit when the silk industry flourished in Italy, and silkworms ate the leaves of the mulberry tree, while humans enjoyed the dark, rich-tasting fruit, and chickens were fattened on the white (in fact a pale grey) and less interesting fruit. Early writers tended to confuse them with blackberries, while advising us to eat both fruit on an empty stomach at the start of a meal, to help digestion. They were made into preserves and syrups. A bowl of mulberries can be seen in Vincenzo Campi's painting of a fruit seller.

MULE, *mulo,* was eaten in similar ways to the flesh of HORSE and DONKEY. *Mula* is a salame of pork head meat and tongue, made in Piedmont, which is cured in a horse's intestines, and tied up with string, looking like a segmented melon.

MUNARI, CRISTOFORO

(1667–1720), was born in Reggio Emilia and worked in Rome and later Florence. His still life paintings are virtuoso displays of luxury goods, musical instruments, Chinese porcelain, ornate glassware, and more rustic kitchen matters, fried eggs, slices of fatty bacon, cabbages, and the pots and pans of humble domestic kitchens. These paintings reflect the taste of his patrons rather than the state of gastronomy in his native province,

although a recent exhibition at Reggio Emilia seemed full of local references, a towering golden slab of *grana* cheese dominating a composition of salame and fried eggs, or a chunk of cured ham athwart some cardoons, bread, and salame. Munari and many other artists were in demand at a time when ostentatious dining had never been more lavish, or refined, and it is revealing that alongside paintings of exquisite pastries and sugared comfits and fine wines in elaborate and fragile glasses, the simple basic things that are the glory of Italian gastronomy were hanging on the walls of some of the county's most sybaritic rulers. The Grand Duke Ferdinando de' Medici and his brother Leopoldo saw patronage of the arts and sciences as a means of enhancing their prestige—the glasses highlighted in Munari's virtuoso technique were in the Venetian style, but probably manufactured in Florence at Ferdinand's instigation, and designed by the same artists who specified the instruments used by the Accademia del Cimento in their experiments to explore and record the natural world. Munari was a colleague of the great Bartolomeo Bimbi, who was also recording the natural world for the Medici, in massive canvases depicting every known version of fruit grown in their dukedom; and two paintings of pears by Munari, showing all those ready in July and August, might have been a homage to the other painter.

Two paintings sent to Ferdinand from Rome, probably in 1703, and now in the Palazzo Pitti, might well show stylistic influences from northern Europe, but Munari is surely celebrating the immediacy of simple "fast food" and a meal combining the luxury of a nicely cooked *faraona* (GUINEA FOWL) with *uove al tegamino*, and some decent wine in a delicate glass, such as one might hope to get in a superior hostelry or modest family home. The *faraona* deserves a second look, alongside a similar fowl in Caravaggio's *Supper at Emmaus* from a century earlier. We can find out about how it might have been cooked from contemporary recipes—in Munari's painting we see the head tucked under the wing of our guinea fowl, and the liver, heart and gizzard peeping from inside the thigh and wing—a way of dealing with innards that is seen frequently in still life paintings in the Netherlands. A lean or mature bird would have been larded with fine strips of fat, but this one looks as if it was basted as it turned on the spit, and then just before serving sprinkled with sugar and salt, visible as tiny specks like hoar frost, and seasoned with the cut bitter orange shown in the foreground.

MURAZZANO is a soft, fresh, uncooked cheese from the mountain communities of Alta Langa Montana in the province of Cuneo in Piedmont. It is one of the many ROBIOLA cheeses, but distinguished by the addition of a minimum 60 percent of sheep's milk to the usual cow's milk. It is made by coagulating the heated milk, letting it sit a while, then draining it into small cylindrical moulds, and salting; after 4 to 10 days, it will be ready to eat. When matured for longer, it acquires a stronger taste. Pliny the Elder wrote of this ancient cheese, *cebanum*, with the characteristic addition of sheep's milk, named perhaps for Ceva, a village in the Alta Valle del Tanaro which now produces a different kind of *robiola*. The exquisite flavour of *murazzano* is best appreciated eaten on its own, *"in assoluta solitudine"* (in complete solitude), not as part of a cheese board. Once the fresh bloom of youth has gone, the strong taste of the mature version is sometimes enhanced by turning it into *bross*, a harsh pungent cream created by a secondary fermentation. Pantaleone di Confienza observed, writing of other mountain cheeses, that when mature and excessively pungent, they can only be eaten in small amounts, a useful condiment for the rough food of the poor, and the harshness a corrective to overeating.

MUSHROOMS, *funghi,* are the fruiting body of fungi of the Agaricales order, or of the Boletales. Unlike the timid and ill-informed British, Italians have a love for mushrooms of all kinds, supported by considerable knowledge, and backed up by specially trained officials who can help identify, and if necessary discard, those gathered in the wild. In the autumn, regional markets display hundreds of varieties, while free-lance gatherers throng woods and fields, in a competitive and acquisitive spirit, picking with skill and care, mindful of future harvests. Even so, the incidence of mushroom poisoning in Italy is the highest in Europe, perhaps because the consumption is also so very high. Costanzo Felici, who knew a thing or two about mushrooms, called them *"cibo molto stravagante e pericoloso e più presto da lasciarlo fuora della tavola che nella tavola porlo"* (a very eccentric and dangerous food, better kept away from the table than dished up on it; Felici, p. 136). Castelvetro reproached the British for their wilful ignorance of the different kinds of mushroom, and replied with mock impudence to his hostess, Lady Newton, who had spurned with horror his offer to cook a particularly fine specimen growing in her park at Eltham, "No problem, my Lady, all the more for me." Mushrooms were found in a cooking pot in a Bronze Age house at Nola, and later might have been a handy vehicle for the poison that killed the Emperor Claudius. Apicius has some good mushroom recipes; one interpreted by Sally Grainger (2006, p. 105) simmers thickly sliced mushrooms in a little fruity dessert wine (Turkish *pekmez* works well) with pepper and coriander stalks, seasoned at the end with some fish sauce, *nuoc nam,* and the chopped coriander leaves. One of the best loved modern Italian recipes is *funghi trifolati,* sliced mushrooms, whatever the kind, cooked in olive oil (in the south) or butter (in Lombardy) with garlic and parsley, served perhaps with a squeeze of lemon. This method, when applied to other vegetables, is sometimes called *al funghetto*, and works beautifully with sliced or cubed eggplants. Mushrooms can be stuffed and baked, grilled, fried whole, added to soups and stews, and used as a sauce for pasta.

The varieties available include four kinds of *funghi porcini* or ceps (and one poisonous), of the *boleti* group, of which there are 10 different kinds, all of them good. There are *cantarelli*, orange-coloured and fragrant; *chiodinii* of various kinds; *prataioli*, field mushrooms; *pioparello*; *gelone*, oyster mushrooms; *volvarie*, *porcinelli*, brownish and rosy pink; a group of *amanitas*, four of which are edible, including *ovoli*, and three deadly poison, which are not all that dissimilar in appearance to the benign ones.

Cultivated mushrooms are also on sale in Italy, and many kinds we knew first as wild can now be grown, either in artificial conditions or in their chosen habitat, certain trees, decomposing matter, or in symbiosis with other plants. Mattioli quotes how in his time in Rome it was fashionable to grow mushrooms in earth placed over certain stones, presumably imbued with spores, from which mushrooms would spring; Castelvetro (he was Protestant) gently mocked the idea of princes of the Church tenderly picking these delicate morsels with their own fair hands. The illustrations in Mattioli's work are accurate as well as beautiful, but his mushrooms, while less than detailed, have a surreal quality; a strange perspective sends them soaring upwards in a trance-like state.

Dried mushrooms, especially *porcini* and *boleti*, are available all the year round, and are a wonderful way of getting a concentrated mushroom flavour into a stew or risotto, and often boost the flavour of fresh ones. They can be reconstituted and chopped to make a filling for pasta, or added to a sauce. They can be bought loose in local markets, or packaged, and are essential in the store cupboard. Pickled, salted, or preserved in oil, mushrooms can be served as antipasto or in SALADS.

MUSK, *muschio*, is a secretion from glands of the male musk DEER, a native of the Himalayas. It has a very powerful aroma, used in perfumes and confectionery. Small amounts, combined with AMBERGRIS and rosewater (*see* ROSE), were used in the Middle Ages and Renaissance to flavour food, and must have added a sensuous dimension to the heady mixture of scents and flavours in princely banquets, where the aromas of the food vied with those of flowers, sweet-smelling herbs, scented waters, and incense. Musk became fashionable in the 17th century, and was one of the perfumes used in making expensive soft gloves, as was civet, extracted from glands of a wild cat (understandable to those who caress the top of the head of a healthy male cat—a perfumed smell that has nothing to do with the more familiar tomcat odour). Corrado used civet and musk in one of his perfumed waters, *acqua alla reale*: storace, benzoin, aloes, sandalwood, cinnamon, and cloves were boiled in water, then civet and musk were added and the mixture allowed to steep in the sun, then filtered.

This does not seem to connect with the dish named civet, *civé*, a type of stew which survives in the French *civet*, now associated with a dish of hare thickened with the blood of the animal. *Civero*, or *civiero*, a term used by Martino for a game stew, using softened chopped onions pounded up to thicken the sauce, was Latinised by Platina as *cibarium*, of which he says *civerium*, or *civero*, is a corruption. The Hymans suggest more plausibly that *civet* might derive from *cive*, a French term for the onion family, and so refer to the thickening element, which might well include blood and the liver of the beast and breadcrumbs as well. You do not have to be French to put onions in a stew. Perhaps the civet was an international dish, but the puzzle around the name remains—in the 14th-century *Libro di cucina*, a *civiro overo savore negro a cengiaro* (civet or black sauce for wild boar) is made of burnt toast soaked in vinegar, pounded up with some of the stewed meat and mixed with ground spices—long pepper, grains of paradise, and ginger—then diluted with some of the broth and vinegar and cooked for a while. No onions. By 1558, Messisbugo had three similar black sauces for meat or game which included dark dried fruit, one of which has chopped onions softened in lard added towards the end, but he did not use the name *civet*. Scappi wrote of spit roasted hares covered with a civet and comfits of coriander; then the name vanished almost forever, except for a solitary appearance in Corrado's *Cuoco galante* as a sauce for venison, *in Sivè*, in which the broth from venison cooked in white wine and water with bay leaves, spices, and green lemons is thickened with *mostaccioli* and flavoured with vinegar, sugar, and green lemons, and served decorated with split pistachio nuts; a pale, gentle sauce a long way from the sombre, heavy dish of 200 years earlier.

MUSSEL, *cozza, muscolo, peocio,* is named for the little mouse which it is supposed to resemble, and as Alan Davidson pointed out, a beady eye, a whisker or two, and a little tail, and it's getting there.

MUST, *mosto,* is the juice of ripe grapes, produced at the start of wine-making, but with other uses; it is condensed as a sweetener, MOSTO COTTO, *sapa, saba,* and that from certain varieties of grape is used to make the genuine BALSAMIC VINEGAR.

MUSTARD, *senape, senape nera, Brassica nigra; senape indiana, Brassica juncea; senape bianca, Sinapis alba,* are seeds from three plants of the CABBAGE family, and all go into making the familiar condiment we call "mustard," not to be confused with MOSTARDA DI FRUTTA, which consists of various fruits preserved in a strongly flavoured

sweet syrup, eaten as a seasoning with boiled meats. Being a good preservative, mustard was a useful addition to the spices added to this concoction. Our name for the both the condiment and the plant derives from *mosto,* or grape MUST, from which the syrup used to be made. I cannot see why the ancient Roman *mustum* or the French *moutarde* can claim to be the origin of this relish; usage and language might indicate that this was around in Italy long enough for it to belong there, without any need for having to borrow either the product or the name from another source. The 14th-century *Libro di cucina* has a *mostarda* made from ground mustard seeds soaked in water, and heated up with *sapa,* reduced grape must, and juices from a roast. A century later, Martino describes a *mostarda* made from soaked mustard seeds, ground almonds, and breadcrumbs diluted with verjuice, *agresto.* He also has a handy recipe for a portable mustard for travellers—soaked mustard seeds are ground up with raisins, cinnamon, and cloves, made up into bullet-sized balls, and dried. They can be reconstituted with *agresto* or *sapa* when required. Mostarda made with mustard seeds was well known when Mattioli was writing in the 16th century, and he also mentions the export of sweet grape must with mustard seeds from Trentino to Germany. But in 18th-century Naples, mustard is mentioned but once by Vicenzo Corrado in his dazzling array of over 60 sauces and 40 relishes, where it figures mixed with candied fruit, orange flower water, musk, cinnamon, and cloves in his version of *Alla moda,* as if the crudity of mere mustard as we know it had no place in his sophisticated repertoire.

MUTTON. *See* SHEEP.

MYRTLE, *Myrtus communis, mirto, mortella,* is an aromatic plant growing in mountainous and hilly regions where the leaves and black berries are used in local cooking. Roast and grilled meats can be flavoured by wrapping them in the leaves to draw out the scent, and the berries, fresh or dried, can be used like pepper or juniper berries, or to make infusions. Myrtle flourishes in Sardinia and is widely used, the leaves sometimes burnt on the fire to perfume spit roasts. Myrtle is one of the "hidden" condiments that went on being used by the rural poor long after it had disappeared from the kitchens of the rich. The leaves and fruit are still used in perfumery and in the production of liqueurs. The ancient Romans used myrtle, emblem of Venus, whose fronds graced the brows of heroes and artists, in the kitchen in many sauces, for example, pounded up with lovage, oregano, mint, coriander, grape must, and broth to dress mullet or stewed eels. Corrado made a relish of myrtle berries soaked in wine, cooked in *malvasia*, sieved, and cooked again with sugar, jasmine water, candied apple, and spices.

Mantegna's successful pursuit of classical inscriptions on the shores of Lake Garda left him flushed with success and crowned with myrtle, and the foliage and flowers of this fragrant plant can be seen in the work of artists of the period.

MYTHS about food and recipes are part of Italian culture, a way of fondly expressing pride in a rich gastronomic heritage. A fertile crop has arisen of stories and legends which are constantly repeated with pleasure to strangers and those already familiar with them. But myths can also be an endearing aspect of Italian life, a vivid way of showing one cares about cooking and ingredients, with anecdotes and real or imaginary personalities bringing a human touch to the plain facts.

History sometimes merges sloppily with barefaced invention, and this can be irritating, as when a well-known Italian restaurateur in London recently said that Caterina de' Medici brought *caneton à l'orange* to France, a land where ducks and oranges had been reared and used with considerable sophistication long before the Medici princess arrived in 1533. There are 14th-century recipes for orange sauce with duck, and bitter oranges were grown in Provence by the end of the 15th century.

There is a myth that when in 1525 the Emperor Charles V drove François I from Milan, the defeated French monarch took refuge in a hovel, La Repentita, after the battle of Pavia, where a peasant woman succoured him with this light but sustaining soup, the recipe for which, of course, he took back with him to France to impress his subjects. *Zuppa alla pavese* is a delicate soup where chicken broth is poured over a fresh raw egg sitting on a slice of bread fried in butter, the whole sprinkled with grated cheese.

A myth about coffee tells how the pragmatic Pope Clement VIII, when urged to condemn it as an infidel drink, accepted the reality of the situation and baptised it instead—an anecdote given different dates, but with the ring of truth.

Myths about the invention of PASTA used to include the assertion that it was "discovered" and brought to Europe by Marco Polo, who claimed to have travelled all over China, and came back to astonish Europe with all the secrets of the complex technology. Françoise Saban and Silvano Serventi have dealt with this assertion with elegance and erudition in *La Pasta, storia e cultura di un cibo universale.* Pasta was being made and enjoyed in Europe long before the intrepid Marco was born, while a parallel development in China was going on independently.

Myths about regional pasta dishes include the story of the *capelletti* of Ferrara—more like the typical three-cornered bonnets than Venus's navel, although much is made of this possible resemblance, as Alessandro Tassoni said in "*Secchia rapita,*" a comic poem alluding to the ancient rivalries between Bologna and Modena:

L'oste che era guercio e bolognese
Imitando di Venere il bellico
l'arte di fare I tortellin apprese.

The cross-eyed innkeeper from
    Bologna
who by imitating Venus's naval
learned how to make tortellini.

This innkeeper, working at that time in Castelfranco in Emilia, happened to have Mars, Venus, and Bacchus as guests, and a chance glimpse of the goddess's naked beauty sent him reeling into the kitchen to deploy his skills in celebration of her charms. Another version suggests that a besotted cook was inspired by a restricted glimpse through a keyhole of a local beauty's navel. We do know that Messisbugo was deploying these delicacies in Ferrara, while similar versions were enjoyed in Bologna and Modena.

Capatti and Montanari dedicate their *Cucina Italiana* to "*Libista, contadina lombarda da Cernuschio, inventrice di far ravioli avviluppati nella pasta*" (Libista, a peasant woman from Cernuschio in Lombardy, the inventor of stuffed ravioli). Ortensio Lando had immortalised her in 1553 in his *Catalogo de gli inventori delle cose che si mangiano e bevano* and also praised a certain Meluzza Comasca, to whose fertile invention he claimed we owe lasagne and related flat pasta. This vivid recognition of the unacknowledged skills of generations of forgotten women, giving a place and name to an imagined representative of all these loving skills, is the best of all Italian food myths.

Another modish pasta dish, *spaghetti alla carbonara*, has accrued some conflicting myths about the recipe. This doubtful combination of bacon and egg, sometimes with the dire addition of cream, butter, and parmesan, as a pasta sauce, has been described as an attempt to tame the unfamiliar spaghetti with the bacon and egg longed for by homesick American soldiers in Italy during World War II. The absurdity of this at a time of hardship and intolerable shortages calls for no comment. It is equally strange that the wild and lawless *carbonari*, the charcoal-burners of Abruzzo, might have invented this rich dish. Dried pasta seasoned with bits of fried *guanciale*, and the accompanying *pecorino romano*, would have been familiar to itinerant workers in Lazio, but the eggs might not have been easily to hand. But all these ingredients would have been within reach of any urban housewife, so the recipe might be part of the recent enthusiasm for popular Roman food, an oral rather than a written legacy.

Sabban and Serventi recount with the necessary scepticism a legend about the invention of *zuppa inglese* in Siena in 1552 to beguile Cosimo de' Medici into diplomatic intervention on the city's behalf, who then took the recipe back to Florence, where visiting Brits took to it, hence the name. Many more local specialities have touching, or improbable, stories attached, which should be enjoyed in the spirit in which they are meant.

n

NASTURTIUM. *See* FLOWERS.

NEBBIA, ANTONIO, wrote *Il cuoco maceratese* in 1779, with an amplified edition in 1784, and although he is uneasily attempting to incorporate material from *Il cuoco piemontese perfezionato a Parigi*, based on Menon's *La cuisinière bourgeoise*, repository of French recipes and styles of cooking, he joyfully rejects the tyranny of French taste without actually spelling out his subversive intentions, for by the late 18th century, Italians, particularly the middle and lower ranks of society, were glad to celebrate local products and cuisines, and the cooking that most people preferred to the elaborate and in many ways alien French manner. So here we have, in its best bits, a regional cookery book, celebrating the products and gastronomy of the MARCHE, with pasta dishes, simpler than the renowned *vincisgrassi*, like his *lasagne con salsa di alice*, with a sauce of fried fresh anchovies and sardines, chopped with herbs and garlic, and seasoned with the *spezieria dolce* that were old favourites in Martino's time. He has a simple dish of rice cooked in broth and seasoned with a rich tomato sauce, and the fish, vegetables, and fruit of the region are deployed with simplicity and economy. It is a pleasure to navigate through his somewhat chaotic presentation, unlike the more structured works of his contemporary in Naples, Vincenzo Corrado, to discover the innate Italian delight in local products and ways of cooking them.

NEPITELLA. *See* CALAMINT.

NERVETTI are the sinews, ligaments, and cartilaginous stuff connecting muscle and tissue that are most tender from veal, and look like whitish rags and stringy bits and pieces. Cooked and seasoned with care, served cold and sliced, they make a nice snack with a sort of chewy bite to them. They are also part of the BOLLITO MISTO of Emilia, gaining from being cooked in, and adding body to, the rich broth in which various meats are simmered slowly. Traditional butchers sell them in local markets, and they can also be bought already cooked and pressed.

NETTLES. *See* WILD GREENS.

NOCINO is a dark brown, potent liqueur made from green unripe WALNUTS, complete with their *mallo*, drupe or outer covering. They are steeped in spirits or wine with spices and herbs to add to the pungent flavour, sweetened with sugar or syrup, and matured for any length of time. Traditionally the walnuts are picked by barefoot, bareheaded maidens on the eve of the feast of San Giovanni Battista, the night of 23 June, which coincides with the summer solstice. Thanks to global warning, walnuts are now picked earlier in the month. The important thing is to get them when the outer covering is still soft and green, and the contents rich in flavour. Nocino has digestive and medicinal properties, and in the past was one of the many household preparations used to calm coughs and asthma, relieve intestinal problems, clear the head (taken sparingly), and comfort the weak. It was made wherever walnut trees grew, so inevitably many regions of Italy now lay claim to its origins; CAMPANIA and EMILIA-ROMAGNA both have legends about its invention.

Every household had its own "secret" recipe, and today commercial and domestic versions differ. Some expose the walnuts steeping in alcohol to sunlight, adding the sugar as a syrup before straining and maturing for several months; others vary the spices used, and some include herbs, while other versions keep the liquid in a cool dark place.

NUOVA CUCINA is Italy's version of *Nouvelle Cuisine*, a response by young chefs to what they see as a regrettably slavish return to the past in the revival of regional and "granny" food. They practise a lighter, vegetable-based style of cooking, influenced by Japanese and oriental cuisines, and enjoy the presentation styles now fashionable: stuff piled up in towering ziggurats with pretty trimmings and dribbles of coloured sauces, which on one level are a return to decorative historic *imbandigione* but are a negation of the simplicity that forms the essence of many traditional dishes.

The new cuisine practised by Martin and extolled by Platina in the 1460s was also a movement towards lightness and simplicity (Laurioux, 2006).

NUT is to us a generic term, applied to different kinds of nuts. Italian is clearer and more specific, with a name for each nut—*noce*, WALNUT, *nocciòla*, *avellana*, HAZELNUT or filbert, *pinolo*, PINE NUT, *mandorla*, ALMOND, *pistaccchio*, PISTACHIO; but *noce* is

used when naming other kinds of nut, usually of foreign origin: *nocciola americana* *arachide*, PEANUT, *noce di cocco*, COCONUT, *noce del Brasile*, Brazil nut, *noce pecan*, pecan. NUTMEG is called *noce moscato* because it looks a bit like a walnut. When a recipe tells you to add a lump of butter the size of *un noce* it means a walnut, also a useful way of describing the size of meatballs. Nuts as a thickening agent in sauces and desserts are making a comeback now that the tyranny of the French tradition of flour-based sauces is on the wane, for they provide texture, smooth or crunchy as desired, and flavour. PESTO *genovese* is an example of a nut-thickened sauce, a survival of a wide variety of the green, red, white, or yellow sauces or relishes of the Middle Ages, using whatever nut was appropriate or available (a reminder not to be too pedantic about which nut to use when making pesto at home). Among nut-based confectionery, Scappi offered *pignoccati romaneschi*, *mostaccioli napoletani*, and *caliccioni di marzapane alla veneziana* at a collation at the end of July, where the new season's almonds were served shelled, on vine leaves, along with fresh walnuts, shelled and peeled and soaked in red wine. Nuts, walnuts, almonds, and sometimes pistachios go into the filling of *cuddureddi*, Sicilian pastries stuffed with dried fruit, nuts, and spices. A festive, ring-shaped version of this, *buccellato*, is decorated with chopped pistachios.

NUTMEG, *Myristica fragrans*, *noce moscata*, is the fruit of a plant grown in the tropics, the Philippines, and Indonesia, as well as in the West Indies. It bursts eventually from its soft outer layer enclosed in a shell, which covers a brilliant red sheath or aril, which when flattened and dried becomes MACE, *macis*, which has a similar flavour. In the past, nutmeg was prized because it sweetened the breath, settled a windy stomach, and helped the eyesight, according to Mattioli, who must have read it in the *Tacuinum Sanitatis* of Ibn Botlân (an illustrated health handbook from 15th-century northern Italy), but Platina had stressed that it was also particularly good with food. Although it was, and is, common in its dried state, nutmeg did come into Europe candied in syrup when the nut was still soft, and was sometimes served at the start of banquets.

Nutmeg is one of the spices still much loved in the Italian kitchen today, used in many dishes, especially those with spinach, with which it has a particular affinity. It is always best freshly grated into food at the last minute, since its evanescent aromas vanish quickly. Nutmeg is also used in cured meats and sausages, a familiar element in the tasty COTECCHINO and ZAMPONE MODENA.

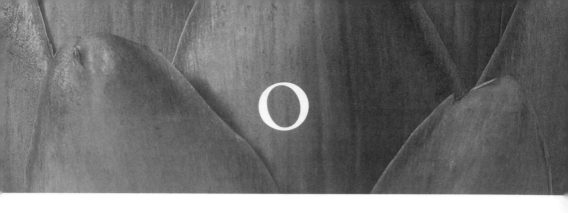

O

OATS, *avena, Avena sativa,* were not much thought of in the Ancient World, and have been used mainly as animal food. With a higher fat, mineral, and protein content than most grains, but no gluten, oats have a high nutritional value, and yet are not suitable for bread-making. Flour or flakes are used in biscuits, fritters, and a sweet pudding, *budin di avena,* lightened with beaten egg whites and flavoured with zest of lemon and orange. A bread of mixed flours, including rye, wheat, and oat flakes and crushed grains is made in Trentino Alto Adige, where the flavour and nutritional qualities are enjoying a revival. In Bolzano, there has always been a tradition of mixed flours, and the *pagnotta ai quatro tritelli,* made with oats, barley, rye, and wheat, is typical of the region.

OCTOPUS, *polpo,* is a cephalopod, of which there are two other kinds, *polpessa* and *moscardino,* which are smaller. They are tough and need long cooking, but the time depends on the size of the creature. The biggest is the best, but large ones need to be bashed against a rock or pounded with a meat tenderiser. They can then be stewed in various ways, but since they give up liquid as they cook, they need only oil, chopped tomatoes, and the chosen seasoning. Sometimes red wine is added. Their dramatic appearance when alive made octopus a good subject for decorative mosaic pavements in the ancient world, including a famous example at Palestrina. Italian *polpo* comes via Latin *polypus* from

ancient Greek *poulypous,* many-feet, so perhaps it was the Greeks who taught the Romans to appreciate this marine delicacy; but although the Greeks really thought of their tentacles as feet, in Latin they are always described as *crines,* hair.
(AKD)

The bigger the octopus, the better the flavor, but as their toughness increases with their size, the best ones need to be bashed or pounded before cooking. (Shutterstock)

OFFAL, organ meat, variety meats, *frattaglie,* are enjoyed in Italy, where there are few if any prejudices about eating what in Britain and North America are sometimes considered inferior or repulsive parts of animals. *Rigaglie* are the offal and bits and pieces of chicken and other fowl. Not just organs like brains, heart, kidneys, liver, spleen, sweetbreads (both pancreas glands), and testicles but also intestines, stomach, womb, udders, lungs, sinews, and extremities like heads, feet,

Pig ears, intestines, and trotters for sale at an outdoor market. (Hugh Threfall/Alamy)

trotters, tails, ears, snouts, tongues, throat, cheek, and skin are all enjoyed, cooked in ways that enhance their qualities, exploiting gelatinous connective tissue, crunchy cartilage, chewy sinews, and the melting softness of brains and blood. Muscle meats can be cured, allowed to hang, or eaten fresh, but offal needs to be eaten soon after slaughter, and became the excuse for great meals in which a profusion of perishable food was enjoyed as part of the ritual sequences of feast and fast connected with pig killing and the culling of surplus stock, glorious arguments against the tyranny of the "balanced diet." It used to be said that in cities like Rome, where there is still a lively tradition of enjoying offal, it was a trickle-down from the lavish tables of noble families and the households of wealthy churchmen, when the poor got the lesser cuts. This might have been the case in the bourgeois circles of Ada BONI, and the restaurants clustered round the *mattatoio* at Testaccio, in expanding 19th-century Rome, but long before that SCAPPI's 16th-century banquet menus showed offal served forth alongside prime cuts of meat, sows' udders decorated with borage flowers, dishes of tripe, brightened with costly saffron, the substance of calves' feet served as a salad, cold tongue, a sort of brawn of pork trotters, snouts and ears in a jelly, a boned kid's head smothered in garlic sauce, and many more. *See also* PIG'S EXTREMITIES, PIG'S OFFAL.

OLIVE, *oliva* (or *uliva*), is the fruit of *Olea europaea sativa*, a tree which is a potent part of our collective images of the Mediterranean, where its cultivation shaped landscapes and is reflected in countless backgrounds to early Italian paintings, where the timeless shapes and contours give a sense of place and continuity to the biblical and everyday scenes enacted in the foreground. When the Florentine merchant Francesco Datini got wealthy enough to invest in land, he took olive oil from his farm to use, and sell, during a stint in Bologna. They can be seen in the frescoes of Ambrogio Lorenzetti in Siena, where the neighbouring hills have their olive trees neatly spaced out, examples of good husbandry. These images of labour-intensive cultivation of a basic staple crop give a false picture of serenity, for the terracing, pruning, weeding, and eventual harvesting, and processing of the berries involved hard work and considerable skills. The results of all this effort, the fruit and the oil, are the bedrock of Mediterranean cuisine, together with bread and wine. The olive tree came to Italy during classical times, growing wherever it is warm enough, and the oil was essential to Roman life and gastronomy, as well as being used for lamps, perfumery, and dressing leather and cloth. Perhaps the most poignant evocation of the olive tree comes not from the classical poets but from the thriller writer Andrea Camilleri, who described a centuries-old tree, up a winding dirt track in a remote part of Sicily, whose tortured twisting and interlacing branches seem to Salvo Montalbano, the intransigent and independent-minded *commisario*, to express the wilful complexity of both his current preoccupations and the tragic history of the island; the tree, by the end of the story, is cut down by a developer (*La Gita a Tindari*, p. 97). Several varieties of olive were known, and today in Italy there are many, some used for oil and some for eating and cooking. The type of fruit, the land it grows on, the climate, the harvesting and processing all contribute to the huge variety of flavours and textures. Olives can be picked unripe, green, in late summer, or during the winter, when they are ripe, black, and more oily. Of the many kinds, those of special note are *Ascolana, Cerignola, Maiatica, Nocellara, Sant' Agostino, Santa Catarina.* Some used mainly for oil can be delicious as table olives, like *Taggiasca.* The challenge is to convert the hard, bitter fruit into something edible that will keep, so a process of curing evolved which includes soaking in fresh water, fermentation, and salting, then keeping in oil or various kinds of pickle, whole, stoned, or stuffed. Different techniques for different olives include the simple soaking and mild salting found in Calabria; the treatment with lime and caustic soda, yielding a large sweet bright green olive, like those from Ascoli Piceno in the Marche and Puglia; then the same treatment followed by preservation in a salt solution; some after salting are lightly fermented, *conciate,* with aromatics—garlic, herbs, chillies. Black olives get a mixture of these treatments, some cured in dry salt, emerging wrinkled and chewy; some like those called *di Gaeta* are soaked in water, then salted, then soaked some more; with a lovely deep purplish tint and a slightly acidic bite, they are good for eating and cooking. After the initial treatment, many olives can be *aromatizzate,* with onion, garlic, herbs, slices of lemon or orange, and dressed with oil—something often done at home. Olives are treated commercially on an industrial scale and also in small qualities by artisan producers. Cooking with olives gives a rich, salty meatiness to many dishes, and can provide visual excitement, as when black olives sit among the bright tomatoes and pallid cheese on a pizza, or green olives bob among the meat and juices of a rabbit casserole. *Olive ascolane* are the big green olives of Ascoli Piceno in the Marche stuffed with an aromatic mixture of chicken, pork and veal, flavoured with cinnamon, nutmeg, and lemon zest, rolled in flour, dipped in egg and covered

with breadcrumbs, then deep fried. Traditional stuffings for preserved olives are anchovies, chillies, sweet peppers and garlic. When olives were served during Scappi's banquets, he specified what kind—*Di monte Rotondo, di Spagna, Napoletane, di Bologna, di Tivoli, di Tortona, di Cicilia*; a roast loin of veal was served with stoned olives. Pisanelli wrote of the different kinds and said that although the ones from Spain are bigger than Italian olives, they taste of leather and look unpleasant, whereas Italian olives are fresh and green as if straight from the tree, especially those from Bologna.

OLIVE OIL, *olio di oliva,* is traditionally made by crushing the ripe or nearly ripe undamaged berries under pressure, using stone or wooden equipment, a subtle process that has to be done without breaking the stones. The resultant mash is then treated to

Romans pour scarce olive oil into bottles to sell on the black market in 1947. Photo by Alfred Eisenstaedt-Stringer. (Time & Life Pictures/Getty Images)

get rid of the bitter watery residue and extract the pure oil. What is left of the mash can then be treated to get an inferior oil which can be used, with the addition of other less precious oil, to make the many reliable but dull commercial brands with familiar household names. Centrifugal and heat treatment get more from the mash, but the quality is different. Cold-pressed oil has a low acidity and an astonishing range of flavours, which range from mellow, fruity, flowery aromas to pungent peppery tastes that linger on the palate. The wholesale manufacture and marketing of olive oil is regulated by the International Olive Oil Council, an organisation based in Madrid, exercising quality control and defining the production and nomenclature of the different kinds of oil. Extra virgin olive oil has to conform to a strict definition and be passed by a team of qualified tasters; it has a low acidity and considerable variations in colour, flavour, and texture, depending on the kind of olive and where it is grown; the oil must be extracted "under thermal conditions that do not lead to alterations in the oil." Virgin olive oil is of a lower quality and has more acidity. Ordinary virgin olive oil has more defects and higher acidity, and cannot be bottled under EU laws but has to be sent for refining. Oil with severe defects (*lampante*) and refined oil can be unfit for human consumption, and must be put to other uses. Olive oil is the name of the category into which the bulk of oil sold on the world market belongs, a blend of refined and unrefined virgin olive oils. For this purpose, the oil is refined by complex processes that get rid of bad flavours and harmful elements, and produce a benign but tasteless result, which then has to be mixed with a pleasant-tasting one. Quality control is indeed desirable when mass movements of oil produced on an industrial scale in many EEC and non-EEC countries can legally be sent to Italy, blended with a proportion of local oil, and sold as a local product, labelled with old-fashioned and reassuring artwork,

including the ambiguous words "produced in Italy." These oils have their uses, and the virtue of consistency, but enthusiasts are now able to seek out local oils made with traditional equipment by small organic producers, and select something that appeals to their taste. Many Italians bring jars or tins of oil back home from visits to the countryside where small-scale production for domestic use at local cooperatives, not intended for the open market, is available to friends and relatives. There are also special qualities of olive oil that have the protection and definition of DOC and DOP. That from Brisighella in Emilia Romagna comes from a small area with its own microclimate and a unique olive tree. Produced in a cooperative using cold pressing methods that get the same results as ancient procedures, the oil is a greenish gold, with overtones of artichokes and olives and a peppery, slightly bitter aftertaste. Oils from the regions of Italy have their characteristic oils—light and delicate in Liguria, heavier and more pungent in Calabria, and robust and well-flavoured in Tuscany; all go well with local dishes. This labour-intensive product was never cheap, and was used with respect, as it was known that animal fats, lard, and dripping were less expensive and more plentiful. Seed and nut oils were also used, medicinally and for lighting.

Olive oil today is used mainly as cooking medium or condiment. Cheaper brands of oil are good for frying, and as the characteristic cooking smells pervade the air, create an evocative experience if the oil is fresh and pure. But frying with an oil of quality is a wanton waste of a precious commodity, like freshening the kitchen sink with Chanel No. 5. A combination of snobbery and gullibility encourages us to spend vast sums on "designer oil" in an understandable wish to avoid some of the boring mass-produced olive oil on the market, but when it comes to cooking, it is a good idea to choose an oil which will survive and enhance the chosen process. Starting a slow-cooked stew or braise with olive oil, butter or cured pork fat will give different results; intelligent choices and combinations can be made, so that the flavours from different fats will add to the complexity of the whole. Seasoning a cold dish with a specially chosen olive oil is a wonderful way of enjoying an expensive luxury. Cold or lukewarm asparagus, artichokes, and fresh young peas and beans need only a modest amount of oil and a little salt and pepper. Salads of all kinds benefit from a very good oil, and very little vinegar or none at all, as many proverbs and sayings tell us. Olive oil added just before serving gives a hot dish, perhaps a vegetable stew or soup, a last-minute charge of flavour as the heat releases the aromas in the oil. An expensive oil used this way is at its best, and a small amount goes a long way. (This restrained pouring or sprinkling of oil cannot honestly be described as DRIZZLE, a sloppy word incompatible with the dense viscosity of oil.) Another use for oil is in baking, both sweet and savoury, and it gives a characteristic flavour to biscuits and cakes, and of course to many versions of FOCCACIA and FLAT-BREAD. Toasted country bread rubbed with garlic and anointed with olive oil is the most basic form of CROSTINI and BRUSCHETTA. These also make a pungent base for fish and vegetable stews. Italians do not have oil in little dishes sitting getting stale on restaurant tables; this strange foreign aberration is a tribute perhaps to the enthusiasm of foreigners for the good regional oils now becoming available, a misguided way of enjoying them. Oil does not keep, so even luxury products have to be used within a year of production. It deteriorates on exposure to light and air, and needs to be kept somewhere dark and cool.

OMBRINE, *ombrina*, a fish of the Perciformes, is as good as SEA BASS or MEAGRE, and can be cooked in the same way, although its flesh lends itself better to gentle simmering, along with its head, according to Scappi, in salt water or a mixture of oil, verjuice (or gooseberries), pepper, saffron, cinnamon, and a handful of chopped fresh herbs. He also describes a *pottaggio alla Venetiana*, in which scaled and cleaned *ombrine* are simmered gently for a short time in white wine, water, verjuice, oil, sugar, and spices, with dried fruit, and served hot over slices of toast.

ONION, *Allium cepa, cipolla,* belongs to the lily family, and has been domesticated for so long that sorting out its origins is not particularly necessary for the cook, though there are many different varieties produced today, and choices can be made between white or red varieties with many different shapes and flavours. The sharp pungency of raw onion is a complete contrast to its mild, smooth sweetness when cooked, and these qualities are exploited in Italian cuisine. A bunch of fresh small onions, *cipollotti,* eaten with unsalted bread and some coarse local salame, makes a fine meal or snack, while chopped onions, softened in oil or lard, can melt imperceptibly into a slow-cooked stew or, softened in butter and water, be spread over the surface of a flattened ring of bread dough to make the *fitascetta* of Como. Onions chopped and softened in oil or pork fat along with celery and carrots form the SOFFRITTO, or starting point of many dishes and sauces, and are also served stuffed, and baked in various ways; and the small *cipolline* are pickled and cooked in a sweet/sour sauce with good vinegar and sugar. (It is inadvisable to use genuine *aceto balsamico tradizionale di Modena* for this, as a good-quality wine vinegar aromatised with cinnamon, pepper, cloves, bay leaves, and garlic will be as effective at a fraction of the cost.)

Annibale Carracci's *Bean Eater* shows a bunch of well-washed spring onions alongside a bowl of stewed beans, some bread rolls, a spinach pie, and a majolica jug of wine. This puzzling painting seems to be a celebration of good basic vegetarian food, plentiful and nicely served, on a clean white tablecloth, with clear red wine in an elegant goblet, rather than coarse rustic fare, and although his table manners leave something to be desired, the bean eater is clean shaven and wearing a nice white shirt under his rough jerkin. Certainly not the diet of the cardinals and princes Carracci was later to work for in Rome, but the everyday food of many, where onions were the chosen seasoning, seen in the context of a visibly hungry man enjoying a good and by no means primitive meal.

The bite of raw onion which makes us weep when peeling and chopping them is a defence mechanism in which an enzymic reaction produces compounds (including sulphuric acid) which sting and burn. Combining this with the pleasant crispness of raw onion is a useful gastronomic tool: raw onions, chopped or sliced, make an agreeable contrast to the blandness of tinned tuna, boiled beans, or cooked potatoes. Cooking drives off these violent elements and produces a sweetness which can mitigate the strong flavours of game, as in the sauces discussed under CIVET, or become a deep caramelised finish, as in the various baked onion recipes, or the use of cooked or raw onions as a pizza topping.

Many regions have their versions of onion soup, of which the *cipollata* of Siena is typical—peeled and sliced onions (the large *ramata* if possible) are softened until a pale gold in olive oil and *rigatino* (pancetta) and then cooked very slowly in broth made traditionally from the bone from a raw ham, though fresh pork on the bone can also be used, to produce a dense, creamy soup, to which the bits of meat off the bone are added, along with freshly ground pepper, served over slices of toast rubbed with garlic. Scappi had a more delicate onion soup, in which onions and the white parts of leeks are parboiled, drained, then softened in olive oil, and simmered in water coloured with saffron and thickened with almond milk (or ground almonds), seasoned with verjuice, chopped herbs, and grated cheese, and served sprinkled with spices.

ORANGE, *Citrus sinensis, arancia,* is dealt with under CITRUS FRUITS, but its uses as flavouring and condiment are mentioned here. Evidence seems to indicate that in the past, bitter oranges (*Citrus aurantia*) were more common than sweet ones, but both kinds were available and may have been introduced into Europe by the Arabs, or hung around after being known to the Romans. By the 1460s, Platina was adding to Martino's recipes a section on the properties of various foods, in which he mentions oranges, both sweet and bitter, among the many varieties of citrus fruit grown in Italy. The sweet ones were a healthy thing to eat at the beginning of a meal, and both sweet and sour fruit made a delicious salad, thinly sliced (peel and all), and dressed with sugar, salt, oil, and vinegar. A similar salad is made today in Sicily with peeled sweet oranges dressed with olive oil, salt, pepper, a little lemon juice, and stoned black olives. Their use with grilled and roast meat and fish appears in many historic texts, either sliced, unpeeled, and arranged round the rim of a serving dish, the edges crimped to make a decorative frill, or laid over a joint of fish or fowl, or, most agreeable of all, as a final dressing of a squeeze of bitter orange juice, with a sprinkling of sugar and cinnamon, on plain fried or roast chicken. Scappi served spit-roasted guinea fowl with sliced bitter oranges; with sugar, they seasoned a fat, stuffed, roast capon; he used the juice on caviar and *bottarga*; ham cooked in wine was thinly sliced and seasoned with it and sugar; stewed truffles were seasoned with olive oil, bitter orange juice, and pepper. He used this aromatic bitter juice in vegetable cookery, over fried eggplants, and as a dressing for lightly cooked sprouting broccoli, finished in hot olive oil, flavoured with a smashed garlic clove, and seasoned with plenty of pepper.

Corrado used sweet oranges, *aranci di Portogallo*, to make a rosolio by steeping the grated peel of two oranges with cinnamon in spirits of wine, filtering it after a day, and sweetening with syrup. His *acqua di perfetto amore* used orange, citron, lemon, cinnamon, and cloves coloured with cochineal. Orange blossoms were distilled to make orange flower water, used to perfume creams, ices and jellies. It served the same purpose as rosewater (*see* ROSE) during the medieval and Renaissance banquet: to perfume food by sprinkling on before serving, and to refresh the sticky fingers of guests. The flowers could also be candied and used to decorate desserts.

The peel was candied and preserved in syrup, for flavouring confectionery and sometimes savoury dishes. It still is, but we do not always realise the extent to which the ancient mixtures of fruit and spice get into modern artisanal products. Some regional pork products, like the *salsiccia di Monte S. Biagio* in Lazio, include orange peel in the ingredients of a sausage made from offal and innards flavoured with salt, hot red chilli, bay leaves, pine nuts, raisins, and coriander. Orange peel also goes into the *ventricina di Guilmi* in Abruzzo, in which instead of offal, prime cuts of pork are sliced into strips and cured, flavoured with salt, hot and mild red chilli, and fennel seeds, in a bladder aromatised with orange peel. A blood sausage, or black pudding, from Molise, *sfarricciato*, is made with fresh pig's blood mixed with precooked emmer, crushed walnuts, pine nuts, raisins, sugar, cocoa, orange peel, and chopped back fat, cooked in natural casing. One of Corrado's more outrageous recipes is for a pie made with ham cooked in champagne with tarragon vinegar, bay leaves, coriander, cinnamon, cloves, crushed long pepper, and lemon peel, sliced and layered in its crust with a sauce of vinegar, lemon juice, candied orange and citron, sugar, and spices. A simpler use of sweet oranges is to pound them (presumably with their peel) and dilute with lemon juice, as a sauce for squabs cooked in white wine and verjuice, bay leaves, and whole spices, and eaten cold. His version of *sauce à la mode* is made with pounded candied orange and citron cooked with sugar, orange flower water, cinnamon, musk, cloves, ground mustard, and *malvasia* vinegar.

Orange peel, fresh and preserved, is used in confectionery, to flavour ice cream and sorbets, and in many liqueurs and aperitifs. The essential oils are prepared commercially and widely used in food manufacture.

Production today is concentrated in Sicily, Campania, Calabria, Basilicata, and Sardinia. The main varieties have red or pale flesh; the red, or "blood," oranges are enjoyed eaten fresh, with *moro* available early, in November, followed by *tarocco* and *sanguinello*; the *ovale* or *calabrese* are the main "pale" oranges.

When bitter oranges come onto the market for the annual ritual of marmalade making in Great Britain, it is always a good idea to keep some back for flavouring marinades and sauces. In Italy it is much easier, for many of the decorative orange trees in parks and public gardens are the bitter variety, an almost forgotten resource, and can be picked up off the ground.

ORANGE FLOWER WATER. *See* ORANGE.

OREGANO, *origano, Origanum vulgare*, can easily be confused with the many different kinds of MARJORAM, so what must count for us in the kitchen is the flavour shared by all these herbs due to the presence of carvacrol and thymol. (This is one of the herbs that retain their flavour when dried, and bunches of dried oregano are essential in the Italian kitchen.) It is used to flavour cured PORK products, especially those of

Sicily, where the antioxidant and anti-microbial properties of the thymol are appreciated as much as the flavour. *U suppessato*, made from prime cuts of the meat from happy black pigs, grazing freely on the aromatic slopes of Monte Nebrodi, then fattened on grains, roots, and chestnuts, is first marinated in a mixture of garlic, oregano, wild fennel, salt, vinegar, pepper, and chilli, dried, and then matured and cured in an equally pungent coating of chilli, pepper, oregano, and garlic. *Budello origanato*, also from Sicily, is a delicacy derived from subsistence agriculture, in which even the intestines of the pig are salted and dried, with oregano acting as preservative as well as flavouring, although the quality traditionally depended also on young pigs fed on the vegetables and roots of their native woods. It can be cooked with broad beans in the spring, or grilled and eaten in a bun as festive food.

The powerful whiff of dried oregano coming off a PIZZA *napoletana* is a perfect match for the strong flavours of tomatoes, anchovy, and salty olives, but would overwhelm a delicate chicken broth green with fresh young herbs. The gentle fragrance of fresh oregano, combined with garlic, parsley, thyme, and a little chilli, appears in a sauce for fried swordfish. Dried oregano, with garlic, parsley, and lemon juice, is beaten up with olive oil and a little water to make a more pungent dressing for grilled slices of the same fish.

served with a *gremolata* of chopped parsley, lemon peel, and garlic, one of the few dishes that is not eaten on its own but accompanied by a *risotto alla milanese*, a plain risotto delicately coloured and flavoured with saffron.

OSTERIE. *See* EATING OUT.

OSTRICA. *See* OYSTER.

OXTAIL. *See* CODA ALLA VACCINARA.

OYSTER, *ostrica*: wisely described in the 5th century BC by Epicharmus, Sicily's earliest known gastronome, as "hard to open but easy to eat." They still are. By the Roman period, an empire-wide geography of oyster gastronomy existed. Reputed among the best were those of the Hellespont or Dardanelles, where the poet Catullus served in the provincial administration: he characterized these straits as "*ceteris ostriosior oris*" (more oysterous than other shores). But there was also a fine supply from the territory of the Cantuarii (Kent), doubtless the same oyster beds now associated with Whitstable but at that time with the nearby Roman naval base Rutupiae. Gaul produced oysters on its

ORZATA. *See* BARLEY.

OSSI DA MORTA. *See* BROAD BEAN.

OSSOBUCO ALLA MILANESE is made from slices of leg of VEAL cut through the bone, marrow and all, braised with white wine, butter, and aromatics, and

Oysters were described in the 5th century BC by Epicharmus, Sicily's earliest known gastronome, as "hard to open but easy to eat." (Shutterstock)

Mediterranean coast, near Narbonne, and its Atlantic coast, where the best were gathered by the Meduli (whose name survives in Médoc) and in Brittany. Closer to Rome, the oysters of Brindisi, Taranto, Lucca, and the coast of Istria all had an excellent reputation; best of all, Pliny assures us, were Brindisi oysters transported alive in their youth across the Apennines on ox-carts, at truly enormous cost, to be fattened in Lucrine Lake, Lago di Lucrino, near the fashionable Campanian seaside resort of Baiae. Farmed Lucrine oysters were first popularized, it was said, in the late 2nd century BC by the fashionable gourmet Sergius Orata; his cognomen means "Gilthead," so perhaps he liked those too.

The philosopher Seneca, Nero's tutor, gave up oysters (and mushrooms) as symbols of luxury, and as sacrifices to the vegetarianism and asceticism he toyed with. Others continued to enjoy them. The emperor Trajan, while campaigning in Mesopotamia in AD 115 to extend the Roman Empire to its furthest east, demanded and got fresh Mediterranean oysters for his table, thanks to the ingenuity of his cook, one of several Roman foodies named Apicius. A method for keeping oysters (fairly) fresh is actually described in the Roman cookbook *Apicius*. Romans sometimes ate oysters raw; several recipes in *Apicius* offer dressings for oysters, raw or grilled. Among the more costly recipes is an ancient seafood platter, *Embractum Baianum*, evidently a speciality of Baiae, which requires oysters, mussels, and sea anemones to be pan-fried with flavourings including pine nuts, rue, celery, pepper, coriander, cumin, honeyed wine, fish sauce, dried dates, and olive oil.

Platina, in *De honesta voluptate et valetudine*, observes that oysters were popular with devotees of luxury, and had been so ever since classical times, owing to their aphrodisiac effect. Antonio Carluccio (1997, p.22) discreetly claims to have experienced some such effect after consuming a total of 126 oysters. A less expensive use for oysters in the pursuit of sensual pleasure is described by Casanova (*Memoirs*, vol. 12, chaps. 2–4). In 1770, in Rome, he persuaded the young Armelline to share a mere 100 oysters with him, probably forgetting to mention that he had previously tested the method in other company: each oyster is sucked from its shell by one of the pair and transferred to the mouth of the other with a kiss. There is no better sauce for oysters, Casanova claims, than a lover's saliva. Armelline's confessor disapproved.

There is no sign in early sources of the species difference between the European or round or flat oyster or belon (*Ostrea edulis*) and the rougher-shelled Portuguese oyster (*Crassostrea angulata*), apparently unknown in the classical world, which has in recent times become the most popular in France. In modern Italy, the belon remains the most popular. It is still farmed, just as it was 2,000 years ago, along the Adriatic coast of Puglia and at Taranto. It is typically eaten raw, with a little lemon juice; but a recipe for oysters *alla Veneziana*, given by Cavanna in *Doni di Nettuno* (1913), calls for the oysters in their half-shells to be covered with a mixture of chopped parsley, celery, other herbs, garlic, breadcrumbs and a little olive oil before being grilled over a wood fire. Again, they are sprinkled with lemon juice before serving. (AKD)

P

PAGLIERINA DI RIFREDDO

PAGLIERINA DI RIFREDDO is a young cheese made of unskimmed cow's milk, pasteurised for the most part, and ready to eat after maturing for a few weeks, with a melting, yellowish texture. It has a characteristic surface pattern and pungency from the straw mats on which it is put to mature. This particular version of *paglierina* is made in the province of Cuneo, mainly in cheese factories, in the past from a mixture of sheep's and goats' milk but now from the Piedmontese breed, with some Frisian.

PAJATA, *pagliata,* is a Roman speciality. The intestines of milk fed calves, cleaned, but not too thoroughly, so as to retain the milky deposit, chyme, the partly digested milk that has moved from the stomach to the intestine, are seasoned well, cut into lengths, which are then secured to retain this residual matter. They can be stewed or grilled, but are not at their best drowned in a harsh tomato sauce and served with *bucatini,* which is what many Roman trattorias do today. There are recipes in Ada Boni (*La cucina romana*, pp. 150, 152). The intestines of other milk-fed animals can also be used. The chitterlings of traditional British fare, and the North American rural south, are made from pigs' intestines.

PALOURDE, or carpet-shell, *vongola verace*, is known to lovers of *spaghetti alle vongole*, where firm spaghetti is served with the bivalves cooked quickly in hot olive oil in which plenty of whole cloves of garlic and a few *peperoncini* (chillies) have been lightly browned, with maybe a splash of white wine and a sprinkling of chopped parsley. The shells are beautiful, pale cream tinged with golden brown, and the pleasure of sucking, or more politely extracting the little tasty morsel from them with a fork, is equalled by the visual delights of this dish. Palourde is known as *arsella* in Tuscany and Liguria, a name also given to the *tellina* or wedge shell clam.

PANADA, *panatella,* are just two names for the many dishes based on breadcrumbs, like the *panada di Milano*, in which boiling beef broth is stirred into a tureen containing a mixture of eggs, parmesan, and breadcrumbs and garnished with softened breadcrumbs cooked golden in butter; the eggy mixture forms swirls and straggly bits which float in the clear broth. There is *panada reggiana*, a simpler dish in which stale bread is torn into bits and cooked in lightly salted water until it forms a pap, which is eaten generously anointed with butter and parmesan. Artusi (p. 53) has a *panata* in which grated firm breadcrumbs are mixed with parmesan and eggs, flavoured with nutmeg, over which hot broth is poured and brought to the boil, stirring, so that the mixture forms little lumps surrounded by clear liquid, to which cooked peas and other vegetables can be added. The swirling contents of the broth preclude rigid definitions, so it is hardly surprising that variations on these lovely soups are known by many names—from the *stracciatelle* of Rome, to the *zanzarèle* of the Veneto (recalling the *zanzarelle* of Martino in the 1460s), the *sansarelis* or *cianciarelis* of Friuli (perhaps all linked to the words for rags, *cenci* or *stracce*), and the *grattinato* of Pisa (from *grattare* to grate, nothing to do with a *gratin*).

PANCETTA, dry salted or salted and smoked, sometimes rolled, sometimes in a flat, pressed piece, is the nearest we can get to an Italian version of bacon (*see* LARDO). It is from the belly and part of the rib of a pig, boned, salted, and cured in various ways in different regions. The *pancetta piacentina* is a speciality of Piacenza and its particular microclimate; the piece of belly is boned, and salt and seasonings (black pepper and cloves) massaged in by hand; the meat is left to dry, then trimmed and wiped and rolled up, dried out some more, and then hung for up to two months, exposed to the local atmosphere. A *pancetta stagionata* from Ferrara is seasoned with salt, pepper, garlic, and rosemary and cured for at least six months. From Trentino comes a smoked pancetta, begun in a salt solution seasoned with pepper, garlic, lemon, white wine, cinnamon, cloves, and juniper berries for three weeks, rolled, then smoked over juniper wood, and finished in a cold dry place for just over a month. As far south as possible, where conditions are less favourable to a long, cold cure, comes the *pancetta arrotolata dei monti Nebrodi* in Sicily, in which the belly, the cut used for streaky bacon, of a semiwild pig, which has rootled for the good things abounding in oak and beech woods, is steeped in salt, pepper, vinegar, garlic, chilli, wild fennel, and oregano, then thoroughly dried and rolled and cured during the cold months, the preservative effect of the seasonings being vital to its survival.

Unlike the bacon of Europe and North America, pancetta is not usually fried as rashers and eaten with eggs, though we have seen hints of it accompanying them in some still life paintings. Some kinds of pancetta are sliced thin and eaten raw, especially the rolled varieties, and there is even a pancetta linea, perish the thought—a "slimmers' version," with less of the delicious fat. Sometimes the fatty belly is wrapped round a leaner cut, like COPPA, to get an interesting balance of fat and lean. A good pancetta can have the same distinction as lardo, the fine cured back fat which is eaten raw and wafer thin as a delicacy. But apart from its appearance in a selection of cold cuts, the main use of pancetta is chopped and cooked, usually with chopped onion, carrot, and celery, in the SOFFRITTO or BATTUTO at the start of a slow-cooked dish. It can also be chopped or pounded with garlic and herbs to a creamy consistency and used in the preliminary browning of ingredients, or to flavour soups and stews.

PANCOTTA(O) is a basic bread soup found as far apart as Lombardy and Calabria. Stale bread of the region is cooked in water or broth with vegetables, seasoned with herbs, garlic, and *peperoncino* (chilli), and enriched with olive oil and cheese, parmesan or pecorino, at the time of serving. Some recipes cook everything together, some add the bread towards the end of cooking, some fry the herbs and vegetables at the beginning and put the bread in halfway through.

PANDORA, *fragolino*, is one of the bream family, of a pinkish hue. Scappi describes them in detail, and liked the firm, not slimy, white flesh, which was good for invalids. They could be grilled, or scaled, and floured and fried. They were good in a *pottaggio* simmered with oil, wine, vinegar, verjuice, cinnamon and saffron, spring onions, and gooseberries, with chopped herbs added just before serving, and thickened with ground almonds if necessary. The lucky invalids could be tempted with fish balls made with the carefully trimmed flesh of lightly poached *fragolino*, chopped up with egg, marjoram, mint, salad burnet, and other herbs, a little sugar and raisins, and some fresh verjuice, simmered in broth with butter and salt.

PANDORO. *See* PANETTONE.

PANE DI GENZANO.
See BREADS, RUSTIC.

PANE DI RAMERINO, bread
with ROSEMARY, is a speciality of Tuscany, where in the past it was made in quantities for the Thursday and Friday of Holy Week, as an accompaniment to the ritual devotions of country folk. The rosemary leaves, lightly cooked in olive oil, together with some soaked and dried raisins, are kneaded into the dough after its first rising, which is then formed into little flattened bread rolls, cut with a cross, and brushed with egg yolk before baking. The *schiacciata* of Tuscany is a version of FOCACCIA with a topping of olive oil, salt, and rosemary.

A modern bread, *panmarino*, was discovered by Carol Field in Ferrara, where an inventive local baker has reconstructed a bread once served at banquets for the self-indulgent Este family—a delicate white loaf perfumed with finely chopped rosemary and glistening on top with diamond-like salt crystals.

PANE E COPERTO is the "cover
charge" in most restaurants, which gets you unlimited bread, the basket replenished on request, usually locally made and very good.

PANETTONE, or "great big bread
loaf," is a large domed yeasted dough, with

A slice of *panettone*, typical Italian Christmas cake. (Shutterstock)

a density of aroma that belies its light but firm texture, with a golden yellow interior and a brown outer surface, the top sprinkled with candied sugar, and the inside studded with dried fruit and candied peels. The mixture is rich with sugar, honey, butter, and eggs, perfumed with vanilla and sometimes liqueurs, and has a softness and lightness that makes it an ideal cake to have around at Christmas time. It keeps well, so in many Milanese households a quarter of this festive bread would be hidden away until 3 February, the feast of San Biagio, a saint who intercedes for those with earache and sore throats, when as a potent relic of the Christmas rites it would be eaten for breakfast to ward off winter colds, delicious and still moist, though sometimes with a whiff of mothballs from the wardrobe where it had lurked. This survival from ancient Christmas rites was once connected with the family rituals around the *ceppo*, a tree trunk or log, decked with evergreen fronds, upon which gifts for the household and family were placed, and which, after their distribution, was ceremoniously burnt on the fire, libated with wine by each participant, and poked to send up glittering sparks to delight the children. The ashes were carefully preserved to protect crops from hailstorms. Stale cake as cold cure seems a doddle after this. The name *ceppo* came to be applied to Christmas gifts and gratuities.

The industrial production of *panettone* originated in Milan in the 1920s, when Angelo Motta and Giacchino Allemagna started producing them, and now they are made all over Italy. But before then, Artusi had annoyed some of his readers by printing a version perfected by his cook Marietta Sabatini using bicarbonate of soda and cream of tartar (baking powder) instead of fresh yeast, so one can deduce that the Milanese version was already known, loved, and passionately defended in the early years of the 20th century. Making *panettone* at home is tricky, needing several lengthy risings in secure conditions, and a false step taking it out of the tall mould can produce a collapsed ruin.

There are other fine yeasted cakes. The *pandoro* of Verona, golden with eggs and butter, fragrant with citron, lemon, and vanilla, is so complex that production today is almost entirely industrial. The *colomba pasquale*, special at one time to Milan and Pavia, celebrating the intervention of the Holy Ghost in patriotic battles against barbarians (Alboino, a horrible Lombard, and Frederick Barbarossa, who both suffered ignominious defeat by two white doves), bringing peace and security for a time, is enjoyed all over Italy today for the celebratory Easter meal; it is a flat, aromatic yeasted cake, made of two elongated parts crossed over each other, vaguely like a dove, with a recipe similar to *panettone* but without the raisins and with a more pronounced orange flavour. It is highly unlikely that the Lombards in the 6th or 12th centuries would have enjoyed candied citrus fruits, and certainly not today's all-pervasive vanilla; indeed, both legends have the whiff of 19th-century antiquarianism about them.

The *pizza Civitavecchia* is an Easter bread from the port of Rome, with a very different spectrum of flavours, anise, cinnamon,, lemon zest, and rum or port, with ricotta and almonds giving a different texture. The well-risen dome has a characteristic slanting top. Ada Boni has a less sophisticated version, a *pizza ricresciuta di Pasqua*, without the anise and rum.

PANFORTE is a flat, solid, heavily spiced cake, stiff with nuts and candied fruit, and although now associated with Sienna, it is unlikely that it was invented there. Originally made with honey for sweetening and breadcrumbs to bind the mixture, it is now made with sugar as well and perfumed with vanilla, alongside the traditional spices—cinnamon, coriander, nutmeg, cloves, and some peppercorns, to which might be added cardamom and anise or fennel. The honey and sugar are melted, and the toasted and chopped nuts, almonds, hazelnuts, and walnuts, and diced candied peel of citron and orange, lemon zest, and spices, are stirred in with a little butter or oil. If the whole spices are whizzed up in a coffee grinder, it is a good idea to include a short length of a vanilla pod, for although anachronistic, it enhances the aromas; a pinch of salt helps, and there is no call to go easy on the pepper. The mixture is poured into a shallow tin lined with wafers or rice paper and cooked slowly in a low oven. There are many published recipes, and unlike some of the ethereal yeasted jobs, *panforte* is so easy to make that success comes to all who attempt it.

Spiced cakes or bread were described by Costanzo Felici in the 1560s. There were a great many of them, with a multitude of shapes and names, mostly heavily spiced and containing dried fruit, figs, and nuts, sweetened with honey or *sapa*, hence the name *pan melato* or PANPEPATO; this concentration of strengthening sweetness and stimulating spiciness was the ideal gift for women after childbirth, when expensive ritual foods were brought in procession by friends and family, in majolica vessels specialy designed and decorated for the purpose. For the feasts of All Saints, pastries with a filling of spiced and sweetened breadcrumbs were made for family gatherings, and for San Martino, when the new wines were sampled, a custom in Rimini where Felici lived much of the time. He writes of salted breads flavoured and coloured with saffron and spices, containing walnuts, cheese, and sometimes raisins, similar to traditional breads of the Marche today. A spiced filling for *cascioncelli*, small festive pastries, enjoyed at peasant weddings, was made of honey, breadcrumbs, and spices, and shaped in decorative moulds. Felici's cheerfully inquiring mind and delight in listing the names and varieties of things, combined with a practical understanding of how these breads were made, has left us a few pages of brilliant summary of the breads and pasta of his time.

Maria Vittoria della Verde in the late 16th century set out several versions of a *panmelato* in her convent cookery notebooks, where breadcrumbs soaked in sweet wine are boiled in *sapa*, with shelled and skinned walnuts, candied orange peel, and plenty of pepper, then mixed with honey, cloves, and cinnamon; the final cakes, presumably finished in the oven, are packed with bay leaves. The industrial quantities specified for the *panmelato della priora*, the prioress's spice bread, indicate that it was a nice little earner for the convent. A similar recipe is to be found in a 17th-century manuscript in Bologna.

PANINO, PANINI is the name for all kinds of little BREAD ROLLS with a filling, sold in most bars and on the way to becoming the classic fast lunch, a meal in a bun, but what a bun, and what a filling. The simplicity of a few slices of cured raw ham or mortadella, contrasting with inventive combinations of mayonnaise, asparagus, artichoke hearts, and tunny, and always freshly prepared. A similar inventiveness is applied to sandwiches, *tramezzini*. This is a new development, reflecting changed patterns of working and eating, a different work ethic, discouraging the traditional long lunch hour, but expecting high quality and concessions to recent dietary preoccupations.

A less than enthusiastic reaction to *panini imbottiti* is that of Salvo Montalbano, Andrea Camilleri's fictional detective, on a reluctant trip to an idyllic Sicilian beach with his implacable Genoese girlfriend, Livia. A long distance to row, with the dismal prospect on arrival of a "*pinnichich*," brings back memories of the *pane, cacio e formicole* (bread and cheese and ants) of his youth. A heaven-sent squall blows away plastic cups and paper napkins and, to his delight, sends the *pannini* rolling, covering the *frittatina, formaggio e prosciutto* with a light coating of sand (Camilleri, 1998, p. 304).

PANISSA (OR PANICCIA). *See* CHICKPEAS.

PANMELATO. *See* PANFORTE.

PANNA. *See* CREAM.

PANNA COTTA is a dessert from Piedmont; it is not cooked, as its name implies, but rather is a delicate CREAM, usually flavoured with vanilla and peach brandy. Gelatine is dissolved in warm milk and stirred into cream which has been heated but not boiled, then put to set in small pots, from which it is unmoulded before serving, often with fruit or genuine balsamic vinegar. It is softer and lighter than cooked custard, and is increasingly popular with enthusiasts of the lighter side of Italian food. PANCOTTA is a different thing, a soup or stew whose basis is bread.

PANPEPATO is a version of PAN-FORTE; a modern recipe mixes dried fruit, nuts, pine nuts, almonds,and walnuts, and spices, including cinnamon, nutmeg, and coriander, and ground black pepper, with flour (rather than breadcrumbs) and honey and a sufficient amount of dark chocolate to make a dark, dense mass, which is cooked in a low oven, and often finished with chocolate icing. When Anna Maria Luisa de' Medici married the elector of Palatine in 1691, she took her tastes for finery and her interest in the arts to his court at Düsseldorf, and it was probably there that paintings of the couple in festive attire were executed by Jan Frans van Douven around 1700. Giovanna Giusti Galardi, in her brilliant investigations into sweetmeats in the Medici court, links the extravagant background, showing a table loaded with *trionfi* (decorative sugar sculpture) and festive food, to archive material describing some of the dishes. Early in her marriage, Anna Maria had written to her uncle, looking forward to a promised *panpepato*, hoping it would not dry up during the journey, and saying how it would be appreciated, "for spicy things are much liked in this country." Well it might, for the universal gingerbread of eastern Europe was part of this tradition of sweet spiced breads. Giusti quotes a contemporary manuscript recipe in the National Library in Florence which bears this out: a mixture of candied pumpkin and oranges boiled in honey, spiced with pepper, ginger, sandalwood, and nutmeg, thickened with flour and walnuts, and baked as flat cakes decorated with heraldic pastry shapes, similar to the ones illustrated in the cookery book of Robert May, an English cook in the international courtly tradition. The scholar-courtier Francesco Redi defined *panpetato* as coming in three versions: the *sopraffina*, made with refined sugar, decorated with marzipan shapes and coloured icing; a medium quality made with honey and ordinary ingredients; and the inferior sort, which to us sounds rather good, made with wholemeal flour and bran, pepper, dried figs, walnuts, and honey.

PANTALEONE DA CONFIENZA. *See* CHEESE; FONTINA.

PANZANELLA

PANZANELLA is one of the simplest ways of using up dark Tuscan country bread. Slices are first soaked in water, then squeezed dry, torn into bits, and mixed with sliced tomatoes, onions, maybe other chopped vegetables and herbs, and seasoned with a little vinegar and peppery olive oil. This is the Tuscan tradition, but further south anchovies, garlic, and hard-cooked eggs are added. The chemistry of the amalgamated flavours is something like the Spanish gazpacho. This is best eaten cool or at room temperature but not chilled. It depends on superb-quality ingredients, everything fresh and full of flavour except for the matured rustic bread. A lyrical description of one way of making this simple, satisfying dish comes from a book written in the 1980s, before Italian regional food had become as widely sought after as it is now, in which Elizabeth Romer described the home cooking on a farm in a remote Tuscan valley (Romer, 1984, p. 108).

PAPPA AL POMODORO

PAPPA AL POMODORO is another Tuscan soup, in which garlic is cooked to pale gold in olive oil, then added with tomatoes and basil to a light chicken broth, then cooked for a short time with stale *pane toscano rustico* to yield a light and refreshing mass, which is covered and left to mature for half an hour or so and can then be eaten cold, hot, or at room temperature. What makes this so special is the reaction of the bread as it soaks up the liquid, rather like the traditional "bread sauce" of English cookery, in which, as bread cooks slowly in broth with the usual onion stuck with cloves, a magical transformation in texture and flavour occurs as the starch molecules expand and change character.

PARMA HAM, *prosciutto crudo di Parma,* is not only one of the greatest glories of the region, but a redeeming feature of our gastronomically degenerate times, for in the form that we know it Parma ham is a relative newcomer, with a massive increase in production over the past half century. Hams in the past were prepared and used for various purposes, but their chewy and fibrous flesh was valued less than cured fat and bacon and mainly used in cooking or as part of a snack, along with other SALUMI, rather than as a luxury product. Still life paintings of the 17th and 18th centuries bear this out, with cured shoulder or chunks of ham portrayed with fried eggs and lumps of cheese as a rustic snack. A century ago, Parma ham as we know it did not exist. Then Anglo-Saxon breeds of pig, Landrace or Large White, fattened on by-products from the PARMESAN cheese industry, more suitable for producing the ample hind legs that are needed for Parma ham, ousted the smaller black autochthonous pigs, with smaller hams and a tastier but less tender flesh, which had for centuries grubbed and snuffled in forests and backyards. Refrigeration made storage and transport easier, and the invention by a local genius in 1873 of a slicing machine completed the revolution, together with demographic changes that led to a demand for "store-bought" products like fine slices of a luxury meat—a sign of upward social mobility—available to customers with a higher income, and a preoccupation with dietary fat (Parma ham has less fat, and is better cured and rich in unsaturated fatty acids). The ethereal transparent wisps of tender pink ham that melt in the mouth are the product of an industrialised process, with "technological" pigs housed and fed in hygienic, temperature-controlled automated surroundings, their hams processed in a similarly high-tech manner. What is unique is the microclimate of the area; a strict legal definition of the protected DOP product specifies: "south of the Via Emilia at a distance no less than 5 kilometres, up to a height of no more than 9,000 metres, defined in the east by the river Enza and in the west by the torrent of the Stirone." Here is to be found the ideal balance of humidity, dryness, and temperature, along with the microorganisms needed to process and mature the hams. First the hams are trimmed; in the first salting, the skin is treated with damp salt and the flesh with dry salt and left in a refrigerated chamber for six or seven days; it is then wiped clean and salted again; this second salting goes on for over a fortnight, depending on weight, then the ham is wiped again and left for up to three months resting in a controlled temperature, breathing gently without drying out, then washed, dried, and put to mature for two more phases in a carefully monitored natural atmosphere, in chambers with windows that can be opened or shut to ensure a prolonged and even drying and maturation, the whole process taking up to a year from start to finish. Recent agitation has rescued the surrounding "halo" and marbling of fat from the *terrorismo sanitario,* and its contribution to the flavour of the ham is now widely respected, particularly now that rancidity can be avoided by getting the right vitamins into the pigs' diet.

PARMESAN is known worldwide in two versions—*parmigiano reggiano* and *GRANA PADANA,* both referred to as *grana.* It is a hard, aged, grainy grating cheese, which enhances everything it is used in; its concentrated flavour is sweet, salty, mild yet distinctive, gentle and powerful at the same time, with a fresh milkiness that reminds us of the

An artisanal cheese maker in Castel d'Aiano, a small town in Emilia-Romagna, with an open wheel of parmesan. Photo by Massimo Borchi, 2005. (Atlantic Phototravel/Corbis)

lush green pastures and fragrant hay which nourished the cows themselves. The graininess is enhanced by crystalline elements, defined by some as pure UMAMI, and this is what makes even a small amount of freshly grated parmesan the perfect flavour enhancer, on PASTA, in soups or RISOTTOS, mixed with stuffings and in sauces, even in some sweet dishes. To use it indiscriminately as a "cooking cheese" is to deny its almost magical powers. It is always freshly grated at point of use, never ever tipped from a package, for the complex elements in parmesan are so ephemeral that once grated, the aromas dissipate at once, lost forever. One disdains the phallic peppermill, but must always appreciate the attentive grating, at the table, of parmesan over pasta or soup, as magical in its way as shavings of truffles.

The nutritional properties of this cheese are amazing; it is ideal for athletes, giving a stimulus to the way proteins and 17 amino acids get into the system and help to spur the muscles into dazzling form. Paediatricians recommend it for weaning infants; added to vegetable soups and paps, it gives minerals and vitamins no other food can supply. It also helps prevent enteritis in the very young. We are getting calcium, phosphorus, sodium, potassium, magnesium, zinc, iron, copper, manganese, selenium, and cobalt, added to a galaxy of vitamins, including A, B-carotene, E, B1, B2, B6, B13, PP, pantothenic acid, biotin, and choline. Higher in protein than most meats, high in calcium, low in cholesterol, low in sodium, and with less fat than many cheeses, with amino acids that complement and increase the protein content of vegetables, and proteolytic processes that to some extent predigest proteins, parmesan is an ideal food, as well as a flavour enhancer. The amount grated over a dish of pasta, about 10–15 grams, has more protein than a serving of chicken.

Parmesan is an incomparable cheese to savour at the end of a meal, hewn into chunks, and in its homeland is sometimes doused with a *battesimo*, a baptismal sprinkling, of *aceto balsamico tradizionale di Modena*. Eaten this way, the texture and flavour, as it crumbles on the tongue, is extraordinary. Many restaurants in the area of production offer only parmesan at the end of a meal; nothing else can compete. Scappi produced these chunks regularly in his 16th-century banquet menus.

Parmigiano reggiano is made in the provinces of Parma, Reggio Emilia, Modena, Bologna (on the left bank of the Reno) and Mantua (south of the Po). The contents and production methods are strictly regulated by the DOC and DOP, and the care of the product, the maintenance and safeguarding of standards, the promotion, and vigilant protection from fraudulent imitations is in the care of the Consorzio del Parmigiano Reggiano. A subdivision of *parmigiano reggiano* is a version made from the milk of an ancient breed of cow, the *razza reggiana*, or *vacche rosse*, the red cows of the region, a species in danger of extinction, giving a lower yield of milk, of a high quality that compares favourably with that from the high-yield Frisians that are reared to meet the increasing worldwide demand. This is a paradox at the heart's the success of parmesan cheese, when increased output is needed to meet ever greater demands, while at the same time consumers are demanding parmesan made with artisan methods from the milk of rare-breed cattle.

Production of *parmigiano reggiano*, whether by small cooperatives or large units, still follows traditional methods. The milk comes from morning and evening milkings, partly skimmed of cream. It is treated with natural whey ferments, and heated; the curds are obtained with a coagulant, and are then heated in their whey until the consistency and temperature is judged to be correct. They sink in a mass to the bottom of the vat and are then manipulated into a large cloth for draining, lifted from the whey, drained in moulds, then shaped under pressure, drained some more, and put to salt in vats of brine, before start-

ing the long journey of being dried, turned, lovingly scraped, polished, and brushed towards perfection some three years later. Even with stainless steel vats, state-of-the-art temperature control, and high-tech measuring instruments, the process depends at every stage on the expertise of the cheese-maker; the size and texture of the curds, the "feel" and smell of the grainy mass, are tested as often as not by a wizened elderly man who dips a crooked finger into the mass and nods a considered approval. Heaving the huge cloths, heavy with curds, out of the vats of whey is like a solemn birth ritual—one false step, and the fragile though ponderous mass is lost, and with it the large capital outlay in milk. Passing into the tall chambers where maturing forms of cheese are piled up in great high columns is like entering a temple, with white-robed priests going about their continuing tasks of shifting, turning, tapping, and brushing the huge forms. Only after passing the Consorzio's stringent quality control can the cheeses be branded with name and logo and then go on sale. They are indelibly marked on the outside in such a way that the customer at point of sale can check the genuineness of even a small chunk of the cheese.

What makes *parmigiano reggiano* and *grana padana* unique are the quality of the milk, depending on the breed of cow and what it has fed on, the method of making and maturing the cheese, and the microclimate of the designated areas where it is produced. As in the case of Parma ham, *culatello*, and the *aceto balsamico tradizionale di Modena*, the environmental conditions and sometimes horrible weather are unique and not found anywhere else in the world. This does not prevent imitations of this unique product, but their inferiority and the vigilance of the Consorzio continue to protect *parmigiano reggiano* from worldwide fraudulent imitations. There's a lot in a name; the *petit morceau de parmesan* that Molière demanded on his deathbed was *parmigiano reggiano*, whose double name dates back to Charlemagne, when he "twinned" the diocese of Parma with the ducal city of Reggio, thus inaugurating a thousand years of linguistic and administrative confusion, linking territories which included the *Prati del Duca*, lush green pastures of the Duchy of Parma irrigated with the copious waters of the river flowing through the city, which gave abundant summer grazing and fragrant winter forage. The use of the word *parmesan* today is somewhat loose, and with a world market clamouring for the product, or something like it, the Consorzio is actively protecting the name and the *marchio*, or trademark, from unauthorised initiatives from Malmo to Melbourne, hoping to cash in on the name with a vastly inferior grating cheese. This is not *campanalismo*, it is a legitimate battle to protect the lustre of the name, and the high standards that won the cheese its DOP in 1996. Both the Italian government and the EEC, not always seen as fairy godmothers, are actively supportive of this initiative.

Lustre is what Molière's contemporary Cristoforo Munari (1667–1720), the still life painter in Reggio Emilia, saw in the great golden wedges of parmesan in many of his kitchen scenes. As far as possible from the complexities of symbolism in the Netherlands, he showed the region's products, cured ham, salami, cheese, and eggs, in the context of a hearty unsophisticated meal—a deliberate contrast to the assemblies of luxury goods, Venetian glass, hothouse fruit, and musical instruments he also executed for his patrons. A composition of a flask of wine, figs on a vine leaf, a bread roll, and some slices of salami is dominated by a huge wedge of parmesan, glowing in sunlight streaming in from the left, leaving the rest of the ingredients in shadow. Another work has an earthenware pot, a wooden wine cooler, and a hunk of bread deep in shadow, while a terra cotta pan of fried eggs and a huge inclined plane of parmesan are golden in a beam of light. Another northern painter,

Vincenzo Campi (1530–1591) from Cremona, showed hunks of parmesan in kitchen and market scenes, one in which the central figure is a majestic cook, a woman with the robust physique of one who manipulates pasta and wields the heavy iron grater shown in another kitchen scene, where the lump of golden cheese reflects her glow of health. He also painted parmesan in the context of a robust rustic snack enjoyed by the vendors in three different versions of a fishmonger's stall. A cheerful woman with a stout wriggling infant on her lap seems to be feeding it, her husband, and herself with stewed beans, and presumably grated cheese (see earlier for its value as baby food), with ribald references to the inevitable consequences. In Florence, the voracious Jacopo Chimenti da Empoli (1551–1640) has a piece of parmesan at the centre of a composition of a kitchen scene, with fowl, cooked and cured meat, garlic, sausages, and vegetables, said by his detractors to have been composed with their subsequent consumption in mind. Giovanna Garzoni put a lump of parmesan in her strangely surrealist collection of products, possibly from one of the Medici estates—luminous objects in a grouping of separate still lifes all out of scale, with a large soppy dog looming in from the left, as big as the peasant with couple of hens appearing from a heap of rocks on the right. As far south as Naples, there is a glimpse of a wedge of parmesan and some *maccheroni* side by side on a shelf in a paining by Giovan Battista Recco, an inevitable association after Boccacio's mention of the *maccheroni* eaters hard at work on a mountain of parmesan in the fabled land of Benegodi. A remarkable work painted in Rome or Naples in the 1650s shows a kitchen table piled with fresh vegetables and cheeses, a cured ham, and some salami. The centre of the composition is a golden wedge of parmesan, allowed to join the trio of local delicacies—a pulled cheese, possibly mozzarella, swirled in a spiral on a dish, glistening with freshness, a pair of *ca-*

ciocavallo or provolone cheeses, linked with their double string, and half a round, pale cheese which might be a fresh goat's cheese. At the same time, Paolo Antonio Barbieri in Emilia-Romagna was putting golden wedges of parmesan in his compositions, the texture and colour vying with red meat, rosy apples, and green cabbage. Working in Udine in the late 17th century, Paolo Paoletti executed two decorative panels of food and vegetables, heroic in scale and composition, in which a mountain ham and a wedge of parmesan dominate the composition, placed at dramatic angles to one another against a wooded mountain backdrop.

These sightings of cheese in works of art confirm the impression that parmesan was appreciated all over Italy from early times. It had an important role as a cooking cheese and a luxury snack; its beauty and value gave it special significance in the context of good living; but parmesan was not flaunted, as cheeses were in the Low Countries, in displays of wealth. The great cheese stacks of Dutch still lifes represented an enormous amount of capital, as large as that invested in the Turkey carpets and lace-trimmed damask cloths on which they sat, but a whole form of parmesan is never seen in Italian art; the modest sized golden wedges are everyday fare, not conspicuous consumption.

PARMIGIANA is the name of a dish, *parmigiana di melanzane*, associated with the southern regions of Italy, usually made with eggplants, sometimes zucchini, fried in oil and layered with tomato sauce, slices of a melting cheese such as mozzarella, with a plentiful seasoning of freshly grated parmesan, then baked in the oven long enough for the flavours to amalgamate. Some versions include hard-boiled eggs, onions, basil, and fennel-flavoured sausage. It is best eaten warm or tepid. *Alla parmigiana* means "in the manner of Parma," so there is some ambiguity here when the recipes have little to do

with this northern city, and a more appropriate name might be *al parmigiano* for dishes in which the star ingredient is *grana padano* or *parmigiano reggiano.*

PARSLEY, *prezzemolo, petrosello, Petroselinum hortense, Petroselinum,* is one of the best-loved HERBS in Italian cooking. Pliny said it was so popular that its fronds were floating in every pot, though what he meant by the name he used, *apium,* is still unclear. (Parsley, celery, and lovage have pungent leaves and aromatic seeds, all of which were used in classical times, and there is a pardonable confusion about what Apicius and earlier cooks might have been using, hence a difficulty in trying to translate them.) The broad-leaved variety of parsley, *gigante d'Italia,* one with even bigger leaves, is used at the start of long-cooked dishes in the preliminary BATTUTA, or raw, chopped, as a final garnish. Almost every herb mixture for stuffings or seasonings will include parsley; Baldassare Pisanelli in his *Trattato della natura de'cibi* of 1611 said: "*Quanto ch'entra nelle salse, nelle minestre, ne guazzetti, ne gli intingoli, & in tutti gli altri condimenti, di maniera che pare che non si possa far cucina senza il Petroscello*" (For it appears in sauces, broths, pottages and stews, and every condiment, to such an extent that it seems that one cannot cook without parsley; p. 52). Diuretic and emmenagogue, parsley can relieve kidney stones and settle the stomach, and used to be thought an antidote to poison. Its flavour not only combines well with other strong aromas but also mitigates them, as in *gremolata,* finely chopped garlic, parsley, and grated lemon peel, the traditional garnish of OSSOBUCO *alla Milanese,* stirred just before serving into slices of leg of veal, complete with marrow bone, cooked slowly in white wine and broth, with previously fried onion, celery, carrot, and some sage leaves. Vincenzo Corrado has a sauce called *ramolata,* perhaps a Neapolitan version of *sauce* *rémoulade*—salted anchovies, parsley, chives, capers, mint, a touch of garlic, all pounded together with oil, vinegar, lemon juice, and spices, then passed through a sieve. Sometimes it is the simple final touch to a plainly grilled or fried fish, or tossed at the last minute into a dish of *spaghetti alle vongole*, in which the heat releases the aroma of the parsley in great wafts of flavour.

PARSNIP, *pastinaca, Pastinaca sativa*, with its peculiar mealy sweetness, agreeable to some, disliked by others, was a common vegetable in the past, but was superseded by the more acceptable potato, and by the 18th century became relegated to animal food, despised as such, and eventually vanished from the Italian kitchen. A phone call some years ago from a chef near Modena—asking what on earth a *pastinaca* was, got the reply "Like a carrot, only white and somewhat sweeter." "Could I grow it here?" Packets of seed came in the post from England, and soon the claggy soil and cold damp winters of Emilia produced a bumper crop, with tourists arriving in busloads to enjoy a soup made from this rare and exotic vegetable, using broth from the BOLLITO MISTO and crusts of parmesan.

The emperor Tiberius had a great fondness for a variety specially imported from Germany. In the past, parsnips were cooked as sweet fritters, with dried fruit and spices, served with honey and sugar, or parboiled, the woody core removed, dipped in batter, and fried, as a cheap substitute for fish. Martino cut away the woody centre and deep fried the parboiled slices in a batter made of white flour, sugar, cinnamon, saffron, and rosewater.

Vincenzo Corrado has a recipe for little parsnip soufflés in which the peeled and chopped parsnips are sweated in butter and spices, then mixed with pounded chicken breasts, egg yolks, cream, and beaten egg whites, and baked in the oven in buttered ramekins. Cooked in an ovenproof dish in a baking tin of water, this makes a fine *sformato*.

Pastinaca is also the name of a fish, one of the stingray family; perhaps the slightly boring flesh resembled the blandness of fried parsnips.

PARTRIDGE, *pernice*, is one of the vast pheasant family, and there are several kinds, sometimes confused with each other. The grey partridge, *coturnice*, is more like a large quail, and is tastier than most others. Recipes for all these small birds are interchangeable; roasting, pot roasting, or cooking on the spit. Sage is a characteristic seasoning; *all'uccelletto* is the name for a Tuscan way of cooking dried *cannellini* beans, flavoured with sage, garlic, olive oil, and sometimes tomato.

PASSATELLI are "special fat little noodles of bread, eggs and cheese," a speciality of Romagna. In Emilia-Romagna and the northern Marche (Field, 1985, p. 194), the stiff breadcrumb mixture is forced through a special perforated disk to get these dumplings which look like short pasta— mentioned also by Artusi, who thought that adding some beef marrow made them more tender. The Taruschios made a version from Pesaro, in which the cooked *passatelli* are served on a puddle of rich sauce with slivers of deep-fried baby artichokes (Taruschio, 1995, p. 108).

PASTA. *See* the entries that follow: PASTA ALIMENTARE, PASTA AROMATIZZATA; PASTA, BAKED; PASTA, COOKING IT; PASTA, DRIED; PASTA, ARTISAN; PASTA, FRESH; PASTA, HISTORY OF; PASTA SAUCES; PASTA SHAPES; PASTA, STUFFED.

PASTA ALIMENTARE is the generic name for all kinds of spaghetti and similar products, to distinguish them from the other things covered by the word *pasta*—different kinds of pastry or dough. The main groups are fresh and dry. But within each of them are further distinctions. The content and conditions of the production of commercial pasta are strictly controlled by law (Legge, 1967, n. 580 in Giarmoleo, 1998, p. 25) specifying the type of flour (*farina* or *semola*) obtained from the milling of grain from hard wheat, its moisture content, and the required amounts of cellulose and gluten.

In Italy today, pasta is never served as an accompaniment to other things, as in some food cultures, not even with meatballs, whatever the song says. It is usually served after the ANTIPASTO as a first course (*primo*), and before the second (*secondo*). But in the past, some kinds of pasta were served over other dishes, for example, Scappi's *Capponi grossi alessati, coperti di maccaroni serviti con cascio, zuccaro, & canella*, stewed fat capons, covered with *maccheroni*, and seasoned with cheese, sugar, and cinnamon; another dish of stewed chicken was served covered with *annoletti*, perhaps today's *agnolini*, small filled triangles of pasta with the pointed ends folded firmly together to make "little rings." These would have made an interesting contrast in flavour and texture to the boiled chicken. We are not told if the *annoletti* were floating with the chicken in its broth, like *tortellini in brodo* today; they were probably heaped on top.

Some of the tiny, delicate, and often visually charming little pasta shapes can be cooked and served in a clear broth, and again, the odds and ends left over from cutting fresh pasta, *maltagliati*, or even chunkier shapes, are added to vegetable stews, or stirred into hefty dishes of beans (*pasta e fagioli*), and the substantial dish MINESTRONE, the "great big *minestra*" or soup, will include pasta in some form or other. But however substantial the sauce, it is essentially a garnish, providing contrasts of flavour and texture to the main ingredient.

PASTA AROMATIZZATA,

flavoured and coloured pasta, might be frowned on by purists, but some kinds have an honourable history, like the noodles coloured with spinach in Emilia or borage in Liguria, recorded as far back as the 15th century. It is debatable whether the flavour of sun-dried tomatoes, nettles, dried mushrooms, beetroot, and so forth are better enjoyed this way or added later in a sauce. The visual pleasure of *paglia e fieno* (hay and straw) with its strands of pale green and yellow pasta dressed with a simple sauce of chopped fresh herbs, butter, and parmesan, is undeniable. Black as sin, *tagliolini* coloured with squid ink, a recent innovation, provide a pleasurable frisson on the very big white plates of fashionable restaurants.

PASTA, BAKED, is a different thing,

almost a contradiction of the conventional cooking method, with its exhortations to serve and eat immediately, for here stuffed or short pasta are enveloped in a rich meat sauce, layered with a béchamel, and enriched with a variety of things like chicken livers and mushrooms, sometimes inside an ovenproof container or pastry crust, and baked in the oven.

Various kinds of cooked pasta, from *tagliatelle* to sheets of lasagne, are finished in the oven with a variety of other things, where the pasta acts as a foil and sometimes container to different textures and flavours. Perhaps the most spectacular are the ones where short pasta, usually *maccheroni*, is presented inside a sweet short or flaky pastry pie crust with a great many other delicious things, from truffles to meatballs, wallowing in a rich fragrant sauce, described in Lampedusa's

Gattopardo (p. 98). Being essentially an aristocratic dish, it comes as no surprise to find it as the star turn of the dinner celebrating Don Fabrizio's arrival at the family's country estate, Donnafugata, after the long exhausting drive from Palermo. But by 1860 it was also old-fashioned, chosen to reassure the small-town bigwigs who were dreading having to eat some alien *brodaglia.* They need not have worried:

> Three powdered servants in green and gold livery came in, each carrying an enormous silver dish containing a towering *timballo* of *maccheroni*. . . . The golden brown of the pastry, the aromas of sugar and cinnamon that wafted from it, were but the prelude to the delightful effects released from within when the knife pierced the crust: steam burst forth heavy with fragrance, then chicken livers, hard-boiled eggs, strips of ham, gobbets of chicken and truffles could be discerned within the unctuous, piping-hot mass of short *maccheroni*, bathed in the precious glow of a meaty essence smooth as suede.

Anna del Conte and Mary Simeti have given us versions of this dish, and it is often on the menu in restaurants in Emilia.

Other baked pasta dishes include *lasagne al forno*, flat sheets of cooked pasta layered with a rich meaty sauce and a rich cheesy béchamel, and sprinklings of parmesan; the many versions of *cannelloni*, large hollow short pasta with a filling, baked in a sauce; *timballi*, originally named for the beaker-shaped tin or container in which it was cooked, from the French *timballe*, pasta finished in a sauce and baked in individual molds; *maccheroni* baked in a shallow dish in the oven, simply, with cheese or a tomato and cheese sauce or with considerable complexity, as in the *pasta infornata* of Puglia, where the lightly cooked pasta *mezzani, penne,* or *ziti* is layered in a sauce of sausage, wine,

tomato, and little dumplings containing horse meat, slices of mozzarella, and grated pecorino, and baked in the oven. Stuffed pasta baked in a pastry crust can be equally elaborate; the *pasticcio di cappelletti alla Reggiana* is a pie made of *pasta frolla* containing *cappelletti*, with a filling made of fresh meat and pork cooked slowly in red wine with cloves and pepper, then ground with *mortadella* and *prosciutto crudo*, seasoned with mace, and mixed with parmesan and egg; to these rich morsels are added bone marrow and chicken livers and gizzards cooked in some of the *sugo* from the meat, flavoured with marsala, bound with a rich milk and butter béchamel, moistened with more of the *sugo*, and bedded down in the pie with handfuls of parmesan. This magnificent overkill is typical of the rich cuisine of Emilia-Romagna, but we have seen how as an element in aristocratic cuisine, it was found as far south as Sicily.

Another kind of pasta is a phantom category, where the filling is cooked and served without the enveloping pasta, *ravioli nudi*, of which the best known are the Florentine spinach gnocchi, made with well-drained, chopped, cooked spinach bound with ricotta, egg, and parmesan, seasoned with salt, pepper, and nutmeg, lightly rolled in the thinnest possible covering of flour, and gently poached in simmering water until they rise to the surface, then served with plenty of melted butter and parmesan (*see* Gnocchi). We find these "naked" gnocchi mentioned in Scappi's menus, and *ravioli sensa sfoglia*, interesting because they refer back to a pasta product rather than a meatball or dumpling mixture.

PASTA, COOKING IT. The current preference is for pasta cooked al dente, with some bite to it, but the degree of doneness is a matter of taste, and although discussions around this subject are entertaining and instructive, it is eventually a personal

choice. One could do worse than follow the manufacturer's instructions, adjusting them to suit your preferences, but constant sampling is best, testing until just before the state you want the pasta to be.

Start with a very capacious cooking pot, about half full of well-salted water, allowing 1 litre to every 100 grammes of pasta. Allow 100 grammes per person for an average helping, more if for a main course. The salt is the first condiment of the pasta; it brings out the flavour, and is added to the pot just before the pasta. Putting some oil into the pot to prevent it boiling over is pointless; what you need to do is ensure that the pot is plenty big enough and not too full. In countries where kettles are always being boiled for tea or coffee, it makes sense to boil the water first in a kettle, which is much quicker. Italian friends prefer to bring a huge pot of cold water slowly to the boil, saying they need all that time to prepare the sauce.

What happens when you put the pasta into the boiling water is this: the starch molecules absorb water and are affected by the heat; a chemical transformation causes them as they do this to become "gelatinous," wriggling loose from their containing protein web of gluten, causing the pasta to swell. If this goes on too long, it loses its elasticity

---

To quote Andrea Camilleri again, to show the importance of cooking pasta just right: when Montalbano (his fictional detective) needs to consult a sympathetic journalist, Zito, at a highly inconvenient moment, over a nasty, politically motivated murder, he bullies him into coming over late one evening, offering food as an incentive:

As soon as the doorbell rang he put the pasta on and let him in.
    "What are we eating?" asked Zito as he arrived.
    "Pasta all'aglio e oglio; then shrimp with lemon and olive oil."
    "Great."
    "Come into the kitchen and give me a hand; meanwhile here's the first question: can you pronounce improcrastinabilità?"
    "Bloody hell, I break my neck getting all the way from Montelusa to Vigàta just to be asked to pronounce some easy word."
    After three or four attempts, obstinately getting more and more tongue-tied, he gave up.
    "You have to be very clever to manage it," said Montalbano, thinking of the devillish cunning of Rizzo, the villanous lawyer from whose smooth tongue the word had flowed so easily.
    They ate talking, as always, of food. Zito, after remembering a dreamlike dish of shrimp ten years ago in Fiacca, criticised the length of time Montalbano's had been cooked and expressed his reservations about the absence of just a suspicion of parsley . . .
    It was only as they were finishing off the wine—a little beauty of a white wine his father found near Randazzo that they got down to business. The careful timing of the pasta, the well-informed critical comments on the shrimp, the very special local wine, all took precedence over the sinister Rizzo and his machinations.

and becomes slippery and soggy. Aim to stop cooking a minute or so before the core of un-cooked starch in the centre of the pasta disappears; tongue and teeth and the naked eye are the best measuring instruments for assessing this. The pasta will go on cooking for a bit longer in its own heat. Drain and serve on warmed plates with its sauce.

Sometimes a little of the cooking water is kept back to loosen a thick sauce, or add to a simple dressing like *oglio, aglio, peperoncino* (oil, garlic, and chilli). A correctly made pasta will absorb the sauce as it is manipulated on the plate, changing the nature of the experience as you eat, and leaving barely a puddle of sauce behind.

Pasta cannot be prepared in advance and kept warm or microwaved, for it will get soft and slimy. It has to be cooked just the right amount and served and eaten at once. *"Ragazzi, a tavola!"* is a cry no right-thinking Italian will ignore. Likewise, in a good restaurant, everyone is prepared to wait for the time it takes to make a pasta dish from scratch.

PASTA, DRIED, *pasta secca,* is made

commercially on a huge scale, with strong flour (the kind we use for bread because of its high gluten content), *Triticum (turgidum) L. durum,* the *silicum* of the Romans, today's *semola.* It is also made using artisanal techniques, or with simpler machinery; the "handmade," though different, is not necessarily superior. The components of *pasta secca* are controlled by law, but within these parameters there is scope for differences— grain, flour, water, climate, processes are all variables, and brand loyalties are fierce and passionately held.

To simplify what is in fact a complex situation: carbohydrates and protein are the principal elements in a grain of wheat. The carbohydrates are composed mainly of starch, whose structure in hard wheat, which produces strong flour, causes its expansion when exposed to water and heat during man-

ufacture and cooking. The proteins unite during the process of manufacture to form gluten, which gives the cooked pasta the desired bite and elasticity.

The selected grain is stored in controlled conditions, the humidity is adjusted, then the grain is cleaned and conditioned, passed through several milling and sieving processes, and seven other purifying procedures, all of which aim to eliminate chaff and other by-products with uncanny accuracy. By this time the flour is ready for storage and selection.

The next step in making pasta is mixing the flour and water in great centrifugal vats, with the dosage of water and humidity and the temperature carefully controlled (no salt at this stage; it gets added when cooking). Microorganisms and foreign bodies that might cause rancidity are got rid of at this stage, and the still far from smooth mass is put under a vacuum to eliminate bubbles of air. Meanwhile, the water has been reacting with the starch and proteins, which will all go to help the texture of the cooked pasta. Some more of this happens during the *impastamento,* the working of the flour and water under intense pressure and the business of extruding it into its final form through perforated metal discs. This is when the grains of starch get a coating of gluten, which, as we shall see, is important to the final texture of what you get on your plate. The temperature of the machinery is controlled so that the heat generated by the process does not upset that delicate balance of gluten and proteins.

Yet more to come: perhaps the trickiest part—when the finished pasta is gradually dried out, in four different processes: *pre-incartamento, incartamento, essiccamento, stabiliz-zazione,* to achieve the legal level of humidity, 12.5 percent, taking care not to crack, damage, or overheat the product, and, while zapping undesirable enzymes and microbes, always solicitous of those gluten protein chains. It is then ready to be stored, packaged, and eaten.

The final hurdle is cooking the pasta, where similar pains are taken. The *incarta-*

mento in the first stage of drying has enclosed the pasta in a paper-like outer covering, which—if the right thickness, and if the inner part has been dried at the right speed and at the right temperature—will protect the pasta from softening and falling apart as it boils.

PASTA, DRIED, ARTISAN,

is produced by small producers who grow their own wheat and so are able to select varieties for flavour and suitability to the terrain, and can thus offer dried pasta with a choice of taste and texture much appreciated by enthusiasts who prefer this to the uniform predictability of the industrial product. Artisan production, as well as being organic and often linked to environmentally sound projects, offers a different kind of pasta. Apart from ingredients, the texture is different because the old semimechanised ways of extruding pasta produce a less smooth finish, a rougher surface, to which the sauce clings in a different way. The irregularities that occur in the shaping, and drying in totally different circumstances, give a much more interesting texture to the cooked pasta, and although its keeping qualities are less, the retention of flavour gained by drying in a natural environment (and the survival of some of the elements that have to be eliminated for commercial reasons) is said to make for a tastier product.

PASTA, FRESH, *pasta fresca*, is not

necessarily better than dried: it is different; there is no moral virtue in it. Poor-quality commercial fresh pasta can be quite unpleasant; a good brand of dried pasta might be cheaper and nicer.

Fresh egg-and-flour pasta is handmade by many families and restaurants, particularly in Emilia, though other regions have versions of fresh pasta, not always with egg. It is made with soft flour, *Triticum aestivum* L.

aestivum, known as *farina*, the *siligo* of the Romans. The eggs and flour, in varying proportions, depending on the area, are kneaded vigorously together and left to rest. The mass is then rolled out with a long thin wooden roller on a huge wooden table until it is so thin that you can see the grain of the wood through it. A lump the size of a big fist will make a *sfoglia*, sheet, as large as a square metre. Rolling it out takes a long time and much effort, a skill acquired with practise, and has usually been a communal activity, both now and in the past: a group of women are gathered round the table, taking turns with the different operations, gossiping, spreading news, making and breaking reputations—a form of social cohesion in a world of small towns and villages. It is now possible to buy small domestic machines that will roll and cut the egg pasta for you. The flavour of good eggs and flour will be agreeable, but the texture is not the same as the tender but firm hand-rolled pasta, probably obtained by the exclusion of air and the manipulation of the gluten, with a less even surface, more receptive to a sauce than the smooth machine made version.

Once rolled out, and kept moist under a cloth, the sheet of pasta is cut up with a serrated cutter, and either stuffed or twisted into various shapes like *farfalle* (butterflies). The sheet of pasta can be folded or rolled up and cut into strips of varying widths, *tagliatelle* or *tagliolini*, which are then deftly unrolled and coiled into portion-sized nests, or spread out in straight lengths. Any bits left over, *maltagliati*, can be used in soups, or with beans and vegetables, or cut up very fine to make *pastini* for broth. Various implements survive (*see* PASTA, HISTORY OF) which make different kinds of ribbon or textured pasta, for example, a thing called a *chitarra*, with rows of metal strings over which a sheet of pasta is pushed, producing strips with a square or rectangular section, or a ridged wooden board over which it is pressed with a small wooden rod to produce squares of serrated pasta, which can then be rolled to make *maccheroni*-like shapes.

Fresh flour-and-water pasta, without eggs, is less flexible, but is often torn, pinched, or twisted into shapes like *strozza preti*, priest stranglers (a name for either this pulled pasta, or gnocchi made with potatoes, like the *srangolapreti* of NAPLES, an unkind way of hinting at the effects of a somewhat coarse pasta on a gluttonous priest) or the *cavatiddi* of SICILY and the south, in which lengths of rolled strips of a salted flour-and-water pasta are roughly scrunched with finger or thumb, or pushed against the perforations of a sieve, to get a curved, concave shape, similar to the *malloredus* of SARDINIA or the *cecatelli* of PUGLIA. Umbrian *picchiarelli* are made by rubbing lumps of a mixture of flour, salt, and water in the palms of the hands to form irregular strips like malevolent serpents, served with a rich sauce of veal, pork, and wild mushrooms. *Picchiarelli della Malanotte* is the intriguing name of an Umbrian cookery book, which, loosely translated, could mean "fisticuffs and a bad night out" at the Malanotte *taverna* in Sangemini in the centre of UMBRIA, where many local specialities have been revived.

Stringozzi are made with a flour, egg white, and salt dough, rolled out thick and sliced into strips like shoelaces, hence the name. Genoa has its *corzetti*, small lumps of an egg-and-flour pasta rolled in the hand to little strips, which are then joined to make a ring, which is twisted round itself to form a figure of eight, cooked, and served with a sauce of pine nuts, butter, and fresh marjoram.

Many of these handmade shapes are now produced commercially, using semiindustrial processes. Some versions of these hand-shaped things, often including breadcrumbs or potato, are getting pretty close to dumplings and the whole range of similar delicacies, for example, *strappatelle*, lumps of leavened dough pinched between thumb and forefinger, or the *ravioli nudi* of Florence, a spinach, ricotta, and parmesan mixture

lightly dusted with flour instead of being enclosed in the usual layer of pasta. Couscous is another close relative, being not a grain, but durum flour moistened and worked in the hands to form minute clumps, which are then steamed over the accompanying sauce or stew. (This may be part of the Arab legacy, for it is found mainly in Sicily and the south of Italy.)

PASTA, HISTORY OF.

Pasta as a cheap, easily available food, quickly cooked and capable of an infinite variety of manifestations, did not become the national food of Italy until after World War II, and subsequently took the world by storm as a symbol of a country and its culture. The story of how this came about is fascinating.

Documentary evidence explodes the myth that pasta was brought to Europe from China in the 12th century by Marco Polo. It was known in Europe long before he was born. Pasta has been made in the Far East for centuries, with a parallel history in Europe,

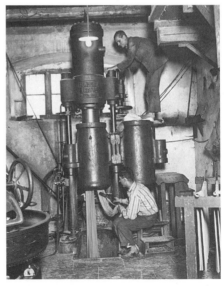

Two men operate a macaroni machine in Naples. The man at the bottom is cutting off lengths of pasta. (Hulton Archive/Getty Images)

but no traceable connections between the two. This story is told in detail by Silvano Serventi and Françoise Sabban, and what follows is a summary of their complex and interesting account. They delight in the irony of how the maccheroni of Pulcinella (Mr. Punch, hero of the *Commedia del'arte*), the subsistence-level food of the Neapolitan rabble, became the Mezzogiorno's revenge for its subjugation by the alien House of Savoy, imposing itself irrevocably from the top to the toe of the Peninsula, after World War II (2000, pp. 289–90), becoming a unifying force stronger than any political form of persuasion.

From the time wheat was milled and turned into flour, there existed the possibility of making pasta, both dried and fresh, but lack of evidence and a certain confusion regarding the terminology coming down from the ancient World leaves us in doubt as to whether the Romans made and ate pasta as we know it. The Latin *laganum* and the Greek *itrion* or *tria*, itself reflected in the Arabic *itriyya* (possibly derived from Syriac), might correspond to present-day lasagne, or ribbon or extruded pasta, but surviving descriptions and references are to products made and cooked very differently. Written evidence adds to our bewilderment—for medical and literary writers were somewhat divorced from the hands-on world of cooks and kitchens, and used different names for things. The early Christian Fathers called a flat, rolled-out sheet of unleavened dough *laganum*, but this was baked, grilled, or cooked in or on an oven, as it had been in classical times. By the 7th century, Isidore of Seville was describing something much nearer to our lasagna when he wrote of a flat sheet cooked in water and then dressed or cooked in the oven, *lasagne al forno* at last. As for dried lengths of pasta, there is a mention of *tri*, the learned term for an Arab product, in the translation by Gerardo di Cremona of the 11th-century health handbooks of the Persian physician Avicenna (Ibn Sina) at the

end of the 12th century, and by the physician Simone of Genova at the end of the 13th century, just at the time when European cookery manuscripts were calling it *vermicelli* (little worms), an unpretentious vernacular word. In the 15th century, translations of Avicenna circulated in manuscript in the north of Italy, beautifully illustrated with decorative pictures of the foods described in the text— contemporary Italian everyday life alongside earlier, but still relevant, medical and gastronomic advice. *Trii*, the learned word for pasta, is being made by two elegant young women in low-cut dresses and clean white aprons, with their hair neatly tied back in caps; one kneads and rolls the pasta, and the other carefully drapes the finished ribbons to dry over a wide, ladder-like contraption. The text recommends sugar as an antidote to its possibly harmful qualities, so the ritual sprinkling of sugar and cinnamon before serving was therapeutic as well as delicious.

Sabban and Serventi argue that religious connotations might have made the diffusion of pasta as everyday fare more difficult. Both the early Christian Fathers and Talmudic commentators were preoccupied with definitions of the liturgical use of bread or wafer, unleavened or made with yeast, and how it was cooked. Symbolism and ritual muddied the waters for food historians, seeking references to everyday life rather than abstract theological debate. But indications emerge of sheets of pasta boiled in water, as well as cooked with a dry heat, as early as the 3rd century AD, long before the diffusion of pasta during the spread of Arab civilisation from the 6th century onwards.

The "common sense" approach can be misleading—the theory that nomadic Arabs might have found dried pasta a quick and easy convenience food begs the question of how they could have access to the sedentary processes and resources that pasta-making required.

However, once the Arabs were settled in southern Italy and Spain, among the many civilised practices they introduced was the manufacture of *pasta secca*, already well known by the 10th century, often by the name *itriyyah*; while Avicenna called it *rishta* or *reshta*, the name used in his native country. This has been documented by Bruno Laurioux and others, and is summarised by Serventi and Sabban. Serious wholesale manufacture for export, using strong flour, has been recorded in wheat-producing areas— Sicily, Sardinia, and probably Liguria—from the early Middle Ages. Meanwhile, fresh pasta, using soft flour, was being made on a domestic scale in urban areas all over Italy. Legends about intelligent and inventive women in medieval Lombardy feed our need for personality-based myths, and though reluctant to disinvest Libista of her ravioli, or Meluzza Comasca of her lasagna, we have to acknowledge a more prosaic situation, where records of price regulation and trading statistics indicate a widespread consumption of both dried and fresh pasta, made in homes and small workshops. Cookery texts do not always reflect this situation; it has been suggested that eating pasta was so widespread that recipes needed no explanation, or that, being easily available, cooks in aristocratic and princely households would disdain it as common food, and only offer luxurious "in-house" versions of pasta, made in their own kitchens, as did Martino and Scappi. Laurioux has found records of Martino in charge of the pasta station at a papal banquet in 1466.

There is early evidence for both domestic and semi-industrial manufacture of pasta and by the end of the 17th century, pasta manufacture was organised and regulated and benefiting from the use of mechanical devices: a *stanga*, a lever-operated lump of wood which is brought repeatedly down on a mass of dough or pasta to speed the kneading process; and a press, on the same principle as a wine press—a screw operated by a handle forces the dough under great pressure through a perforated metal disk to produce the desired shape of pasta. An early image

can be seen on one of the *pale*, the ceremonial shovels of the Accademia della Crusca in Florence, and the Museo Nazionale delle paste alimentari (National Pasta Museum) in Rome has surviving examples, models, and illustrations of early pasta-making equipment, including a model of a horse-operated wooden machine, with its interlocking wheels and levers powering the massive *stanga*, and a metal screw press for extruding it into lengths and shapes.

Drying the prepared pasta was complicated, depending on dry heat from the sun to give the pasta a preliminary quick outer coating, paper thin and of the right consistency to resist the rest of the treatment and subsequent cooking; then a stay in cool areas for continued drying; and a final finishing process—all dependent on the vagaries of climate and weather. A pasta-maker needed to be something of an astrologer and meteorologist, as well as skilled in the techniques of his trade. Naples, in particular Torre Annunziata and Gragnano, had the benefit of a good drying climate, as did the Ligurian coast. The poor hygienic conditions of hanging pasta to dry above streets and in courtyards caused no concern whatsoever.

From early mechanical devices in the 17th and 18th centuries it was but a short step to today's mass production in all its complexity, with machines at last taking on the arduous work once done by men and women, culminating in a computer-controlled continuous operation. It was some time, though, before the rice and polenta of the north were overtaken by the *pasta secca* of the south, but by the middle of the 20th century pasta was Italy's national dish, and was triumphantly taking over the world.

PASTA SAUCES are listed here in a selection from the many pasta recipes in current use. Sometimes a sauce is associated with a particular shape of pasta, *bucattini all'-Amatriciana*, or with spaghetti *aglio e olio*, while other sauces, like the RAGÙ of Bologna, or the PESTO of Genoa, can be served with different kinds of pasta. But however substantial the sauce, it is essentially a garnish, providing contrasts of flavour and texture to the main ingredient, the pasta itself.

Sauces based on the combination of cream, butter, and herbs contrast with those based on a slow-cooked rich meat and tomato mixture, and with a light tomato-based sauce, quickly cooked and often vegetarian.

We have historical examples of complex sauces for which pasta is merely the vehicle. There are many. And there are reticent sauces which are used solely to enhance the flavour and texture of the pasta, whether fresh or dried. Connoisseurs of pasta love both kinds, and there are many books of the "hundred best," even attempts to list them all. Traditional sauces, like the *alla puttanesca* of Rome, can be found listed alongside in novative and inventive concoctions, like Gualtieri's delicate helpings of *orecchiette* served with turnip tops and *foie gras*. To combine these with the huge variety of pasta shapes available, each appropriate to a particular sauce, it would be necessary to eat at least three or four versions a day for a lifetime to sample just a selection from the whole spectrum.

Freshly made egg pasta has a delicate flavour and needs little more than a few chopped herbs and a nob of butter, nothing else, not even parmesan. Some varieties of short dried pasta are often eaten as *cacio e pepe*, with just a grated hard cheese, often pecorino, and much freshly ground black pepper, moistened with a bit of the cooking water. A simple sauce of peeled and chopped raw tomatoes, seasoned with chopped basil, garlic, salt, pepper, and olive oil puts many of the commercial sauces to shame. In fact, why spend money on something that, however pleasant, will always taste "industrial," when in the time it takes to boil the pasta you can throw together a sauce from whatever fresh ingredients are to hand? The chopped tomatoes can be enlivened with salted anchovies, rinsed, boned and trimmed, finely chopped shallots, and olive oil.

Spaghetti *aglio olio peperoncino* is seasoned by cooking as much garlic as you choose in olive oil, adding hot dried chillies to taste, and stirring this, and sometimes chopped parsley as well, into freshly cooked pasta, moistened with a bit of the cooking water.

The standard commercial *pesto* can be a harsh sauce for a delicate pasta, with pecorino and pine nuts overwhelming the basil, but a handful of basil leaves pounded in a mortar with some salt and garlic, diluted with olive oil, and stirred into not too well drained pasta, with freshly grated parmesan served separately, is a more subtle thing.

Delicate, though, is hardly the word for *pasta alla Norma*, from SICILY, named for Bellini's *Norma* (*see* BASIL), in the sense that it presents a gastronomic triumph comparable with the success of the opera. After eating this heavy sauce of fried eggplants, tomatoes cooked in oil and garlic, grated salt ricotta, and torn basil leaves and parmesan, served with spaghetti or penne, the fat lady might never sing again.

Spaghetti alla carbonara hovers on the edges of myth, which has it that the itinerant charcoal-burners of LAZIO and ABRUZZO fell upon this as a last resort when living and working away from home comforts. Diced GUANCIALE (cured pig's cheek, a softer cut with a gentler cure than pancetta) cooked with garlic in oil or lard, stirred into pasta seasoned with beaten eggs and parmesan or pecorino, can be made by anyone with eggs and bacon to hand; you do not have to be a charcoal-burner. This dish is said to have been much appreciated by the Allied forces at the end of World War II, homesick for their bacon and eggs.

A typically Roman sauce, *all' Amatriciana*, sometimes spelt differently, *alla Matriciana*, to annoy the purists, who rightly point out that it comes from Amatrice, in the Abruzzi, uses diced *guanciale*, cooked with chopped onion in lard or oil, with tomatoes added, just enough to colour it, and some hot red chilli, and pecorino rather than parmesan. A more complicated version uses a denser tomato sauce enriched with the rinds of cured ham, and lively with chilli. The preferred pasta shape is *bucatini* or *perciatelli* (both different grades of hollow spaghetti).

PUGLIA contributes the classic *orecchiette con i broccoli*, in which the pasta shapes, like little ears, or bowls, are cooked in the water in which tufts of broccoli have been boiled until almost tender, and eaten with the broccoli, finished in olive oil, garlic, and chilli, served with abundant pecorino. The chewy *orecchiette* make a pleasant contrast to the softer broccoli.

The dense, rich *ragù* of Bologna, made from coarsely chopped beef, pork, and pancetta, is cooked for a long time with the usual carrot, celery, and onion, absorbing frequent libations of wine, good meat broth, milk, and tomato to get a thick aromatic sauce to go with the handmade egg *tagliatelle* of the region. Marcella Hazan's affectionate version of this is clear and practical (1981, p. 109).

The *fettucine* of Rome hardly need Alfredo's gross sauce of butter, cream, and cheese, *al triplo burro*; the golden spoon and fork with which he served them in his restaurant during the 1940s and 1950s (a present from Douglas Fairbanks and Mary Pickford on their honeymoon) sound like the best part of this recipe. *Fettucine* are usually served with a light tomato or meat and tomato sauce.

Whether the sauce is assertive or self-effacing, the amount served should be just enough to flavour the pasta but not overcome it, and it should never be too liquid. Sometimes a dollop of sauce is put on top of a serving of spaghetti and parmesan offered separately, and the diners can adjust things as they eat. Other sauces are stirred in by the cook before serving, but whatever way, restraint is the best policy.

PASTA SHAPES are difficult to categorise. A browse in any well-supplied Italian produce store will tell you more than any alphabetical listing could do, and most Italian shopkeepers will gladly, if they have the time, suggest sauces and ways of serving them.

Industrial pasta spans national tastes, though there may be regional preferences, which manufacturers and distributors take into account. Artisan products, or handmade specialities, are more likely to be special to a region, but often it is the accompanying sauces which give a local character. Names change from one region to another; the *tagliatelle* of Bologna become the *fettucine* of Rome, and the spelling of *maccheroni* has only recently become standardized. Both the shapes and their names are evidence of Italian gastronomic inventiveness and fantasy, transforming basic materials into things of beauty, delicious and worthy of respect. Boiled vegetables and a hunk of bread are basic sustenance, but the same flour and water, made with hard work and ingenuity into beautiful shapes that please the eye and charm the palate, join with carefully treated wild or cultivated greens to make a meal of considerable sophistication. The mythical Libista of Cernuschio, said to be the inventor of stuffed pasta, is the embodiment of every woman in Italy who, throughout the centuries, toiled away, exhausted and anonymous, to perfect the making of pasta.

Pasta lunga, extruded long pasta, are long strands of circular, hollow, or ribboned strips, of different diameters, with a round section of varying sizes, such as *capellini*, *spaghetti*, *spaghettini*, *vermicelli*, all in numbered grades, or with a hollow section, like *ziti*, *bavette*, *perciatelli*, *reginette*, *fusilli lunghi*, or *bucatini*; or ribbons, like *linguine*, *bavette*, *fettucine*, or *tagliatelle*, some plain, or with frilly edges like *reginette* or *pappardelle* to take up the dense sauces of slow-cooked game or beef.

Pasta corta are extruded short pasta. Some are cylinders, smooth or ridged, like *mac-*

cheroni, penne, rigatoni, mezze maniche, ditali, ca-
vatappi, bucatini, gomiti, sedani, lumache, eliche,
fusilli, pipe, malloreddus, rigatoni, tortiglioni, tu-
bettini (sometimes called avemarie or paternos-
ter). Curved variations of these straight short
cylinders are cannolicchi (denti di pecora),
margherita messinese lunga (curved short
strands, hollow but open along one edge).
There are many other free shapes, including
fusilli, or elicche, dischi volanti (imitating the
stuffed pasta cappelletti, a more terrestrial interpretation), cappello napoletano (like a brig-
and's bonnet), variations on corkscrew
shapes of different sizes, and radiatori. There
are shapes of all sizes based on sea shells and
snail shells—cociolette, conchigliette, conchiglion;
twisted cornetti di bue (rolled pasta a bit like
ox horns, also known as gigli, lilies); luma-
chine; and pierced shapes with the effect of
openwork patterns, like rotelle, wheels, and
merletti, like baroque lace patterns.

Pastina are tiny little shapes and specks to
cook in soup. Some are like grains of rice, or
wheat, or melon seeds. They include puntine,
puntette, stelline or fiori di sambuco (looking
like tiny white elderflowers), semi di mela,
anellini, farfalline, ditalini, tripolini, tempestina,
quadruci, occhi di passero (tiny pierced disks
looking more like occhi di trota, trout's eyes,
weird to find in one's soup), and so on.

Pasta stampata tipo Bologna are Bologna-
style pressed shapes, and twisted shapes.
They include farfalle, a square shape nipped
in the middle to look like a butterfly or bow
tie, farfalle tonde, the same made from a circle;
cravattine, funghetti, sometimes rolled over
themselves, knotted, almost knitted and
contorted to resemble the shapes like strozzapreti that in the past came more easily to
nimble fingers than machines; Ballerine, flat
frilly-edged pieces twisted into pretty cones,
and so on.

Pasta a nido are ribbons of thin thread-
like pasta, for example, paglia e fieno, or tagliolini, capelli d'angelo, capellini a matassa, or
thicker ribbons, in little curled-up nests
which unwind as they cook. There are sheets,

square, rectangular, or in very wide strips, for
making baked lasagne. Some shapes are still
made by hand from rolled-out sheets of
pasta—for example, the garganelli of
Bologna, small squares of egg pasta rolled
round a little cylindrical pin, which is then
rolled over a ridged piece of wood to make
little cylindrical, ridged pieces of pasta. The
off-cuts from sheets of egg pasta can be cut
into uneven shapes more or less the same,
and these maltagliati, or more symmetrical
lozenge shapes, are then simmered in the liquid in which borlotti beans have been cooked,
along with pork rinds and aromatics, to
which the beans, some of them puréed, are
added just before serving, in that hefty dish
pasta e fagioli. Also from Emilia are passatelli,
short worm-like shapes made by pushing an
instrument down from above onto a savoury
mixture of seasoned breadcrumbs, parmesan, and egg, sometimes enriched with meat
and bone marrow; then to be lightly poached
on broth. Some pasta shapes are made from
unrolled dough, which is torn off a big lump
and rolled, flattened, or twisted in the hand
to make shapes like the pointy picchiarelli of
Umbria, or the round, hollow orecchiette of
Puglia and Basilicata. The corzetti of Liguria
are made by rolling a lump of egg pasta the
size of a chickpea into a strip, which is
twisted into a little figure of eight and eaten
with a sauce of pine nuts cooked golden in
butter with a sprinkling of fresh marjoram.
further south, a whole range of vegetables go
with the hand-made shapes of water paste,
orecchiette and turnip tops. The malloreddus of
Sardinia are little irregular-shaped gnocchi
sometimes coloured with saffron, formed by
hand, dried, and eaten with a sauce of
tomato and basil.

Since many families eat pasta at least
once a day, every day of the week, the need
for variety is obvious, and leaving aside the
sillier shapes, like radiators or flying saucers,
it makes sense to vary the pasta and sauces to
avoid monotony. The appropriate sauce for
the right shape is a matter of more than mere

functional utility. Those that will adhere to short pasta, smooth or grooved, are different from sauces for long strands of ribbon or tube pasta. Flat sheets of pasta ask for different treatments. Some kinds of pasta will stand up to baking in various ways, while others have an ephemeral texture that is destroyed by overcooking. The fine egg *tagliolini* of Emilia-Romagna cooks in a few minutes, and melted butter and a dusting of herbs are all they need. But they can also be drenched with *mosto cotto* and possibly *alchermes* and baked, uncooked, in a tart. The TIMBALLO immortalised by Lampedusa needs robust short pasta to hold its own against the lush tide of rich sauces and sweetbreads, truffles, meatballs, and chicken livers. A *spaghettata* dressed with only olive oil perfumed with garlic and chilli needs neither parsley nor tomato to confuse the robust simplicity of this most comforting dish—*oglio, aglio, e peperoncino*. *Fusilli*, twisted spirals of short pasta, will hold a loose sauce of skinned and chopped raw tomatoes, cleaned and coarsely cut salt anchovies, and capers. The slow-cooked, densely rich *ragù* of Bologna is used sparingly on the region's fresh egg pasta.

Appearance, texture, and aroma affect the way pasta is enjoyed in a series of gustatory, emotional, and tactile sensations, such as anticipation, perfume, mastication, and flavour, all five senses working to achieve a perfect harmony of satisfaction and well-being.

PASTA, STUFFED, *pasta ripiena.*
Pockets, parcels, or tiny twists of fresh pasta with a variety of fillings are made by hand in characteristic shapes in many regions of Italy, and also commercially using machines. Large ones, filled with a cheese, ricotta, and herb mixture, or with mashed pumpkin very discreetly flavoured with AMARETTI, or a mixture of fresh and cured meats vary in design and name according to the region, but the principle is the same: they are cooked in

simmering water or broth (a roaring boil might make them burst) until the filling is cooked through and the enclosing pasta is just done. The parts of the package where edges are compressed together to seal in the stuffing will be twice the thickness of the rest, so in the mouth there will be a range of textures, from soft to chewy, with the contrasting filling, and the dressing of melted butter and parmesan, adding to the sensory complexity.

The main kinds are: ravioli, square cushions with serrated edges; *tortelloni*, square shapes with the filling placed on one side of a square, then folded over to make a triangular shape which is sealed with gentle pressure round the edges, and the two pointed ends of the triangle brought up and joined firmly together; *tortellini*, smaller versions of this, usually with a meaty filling (often made with a mixture of finely chopped *prosciutto crudo*, *mortadella*, cooked pork, perhaps chicken, parmesan, and salt and pepper, possibly a little nutmeg, to get a densely flavoured filling which has to make its impact in very small quantities); *capelletti*, a similar process but a slightly different shape; *agnolini*, even smaller, shaped to contain its filling by twisting round the tip of the forefinger. There are many regional variations on these main shapes, many different fillings, and a wide variety of names.

Sometimes the filling, rather than the shape, defines the product. *Anolini*, a speciality of Parma, are circles of pasta folded over a filling, to make semicircles. Their filling is traditionally made with a lump of beef, larded and seasoned with cloves, cinnamon, chopped onion, green celery, and carrot, topped up with broth and cooked at a barely perceptible simmer for 16 to 24 hours, until the meat is virtually dissolved in the sauce. This is then used, strained or mashed up, to moisten some toasted breadcrumbs, which together with parmesan and eggs, seasoned with nutmeg, make the filling. Here a *brodo ristretto* is the powerful flavouring element in a dense, concentrated mixture. A version from Piacenza used a less reduced meat mixture (cooked for only 8 to 10 hours, pounded up to give a more fibrous texture). But laborious and overcomplicated as they may seem, these fillings are a way of feeding and giving pleasure to many more than a stew or roast would have done—festive food with all the frugality of a canny Emilian housewife, making an expensive commodity, a lump of meat, go a very long way on special occasions. These are a complete contrast to the quickly prepared mixtures of fresh spinach, cheese, and herbs, or the stuffing of ricotta and herbs, which are also used as fillings around Parma and Modena, light and fragrant, made richer by the copious amounts of melted butter and parmesan in which they are served. In Liguria and Umbria, we find a varying mixture of fresh and wild herbs, precooked and mixed with whatever is appropriate, used to stuff pasta and breads.

Capelletti are stuffed pasta named perhaps for a medieval bonnet, but also existing in their own right as an ergonomic use of thin pasta and fillings, a functional shape that can be twisted competently in the fingers of women devoting time and energy into making small quantities of ingredients go a long way, transforming them into a festive luxury. After the energetic and exhausting business of rolling out the pasta stuffing, it is a satisfactory thing to do sitting down, a good example of division of labour in an efficient domestic production line. The dimensions of these functional and beautiful filled and twisted pockets derive from the potential and limitations of the way fingers can work.

The evidence we have from the Middle Ages and Renaissance suggests, according to Serventi and Sabban, that stuffed pasta was an aristocratic luxury, which, when Italian gastronomy was being overtaken in some circles by French fashions, trickled down from princely courts to lesser levels, and became by Artusi's time popular middle-class fare. In rural areas, filled pasta was made and enjoyed

Pasta: Nutritional Notes

Long before athletes and footballers came to value it as a useful source of slow-release energy, Sophia Loren always travelled with a plentiful supply of pasta in her luggage—comfort food after a hungry childhood, memories of the hardships and warmth of her native Pozzuoli. At that time, pasta was considered "fattening," so from time to time the diva would run up and down stairs instead of taking the elevator.

We now know that pasta—in the right amount, with appropriate accompaniments or sauces—can supply most of the nutritional needs of a moderately active person. A helping of pasta contains carbohydrates, lipids, protein, and various minerals. If cooked al dente and eaten with olive oil, beans, and cheese, the balance of nutritional requirements is just about perfect. This mix also has the advantage of being easy to digest, providing energy slowly over a period of hours, absorbing enough liquid to benefit the alimentary tract, and tasting good.

by even the humblest folk, who scraped and saved to make festive foods perhaps only two or three times a year.

Overrefinement and a mania for novelty in stuffed pastas can produce horror and disillusionment, as when fashionable Italian restaurants abroad serve up a modest helping of what they quaintly term "plump cushions" of outsize ravioli, one pink, one green, one yellow, with a dribbled pattern of brightly coloured sauce and inappropriately scattered plant life. A normal plain-thinking, plain-living Italian would gulp them down in one and remind us how her granny used to serve up 12 of each in every portion. "At the end of a meal we like to feel we have eaten," muttered a London-based victim of this trend. This ambivalent situation highlights a paradox in the production and consumption of stuffed pasta—in the past, these delicacies were festive food to celebrate saints' days or family events, using ingredients hoarded over months, and time-consuming methods of preparation; now, one can choose them at random from a restaurant menu.

So in a way the poncy restaurant was on the right lines by treating them as something special, but a little misguided in overlooking the abundance with which such food was traditionally offered. A feast for a wedding, christening, or *cresima* is deliberately gross, a time of indulgence mitigating perhaps months of shortages and plain fare—which is what so much good Italian food is all about: the alternation of austerity and abundance.

PASTELLA is batter, a liquid coating for ingredients that are to be shallow or deep fried. This will vary according to the recipe, sometimes simply flour and water, sometimes with the addition of olive oil and beaten egg whites, or yeast to give a more spongy texture.

PASTICCERIA, confectionery, is a term that covers a large range of *dolci*, which can be buns, pastries, or yeasted cakes (*panettone, pandoro, colomba*), but excludes biscuits (*biscotti*), ice cream (*gelati*), sugared sweets (*confetti*), and preserved fruits (*canditi*). The different pastries—*pasta frolla, pasta sfoglia,* and the different kinds of cake, *torta,* are all deployed in an assortment of light, delicious creations which vary from one region to an-

other. A variety of light, elegant pastries are prepared every day for breakfast, to be eaten in bars or brought back home. Names vary: *cornetto* is more usual than *croissant* for the sweet or salty twisted crescent-shaped pastry, but *brioche* is also used. We can forget the legends about these being invented in Austria to celebrate victory over the Turks, for this shape is universal.

PASTICCIO (for more detail, *see* PASTA, BAKED) can mean PIE, usually a covered or enclosed pastry crust within which a sweet or savoury filling is cooked. The kind of pastry can vary, as can the filling. The name has come to be applied today to short or stuffed pasta, along with many other good things, baked in a crust, sometimes also called *timballo. Pasticcio* is also a colloquial word for an untidy mess, applied to a job, a general behaviour, or the more abstract concept of a situation in which people and things are falling apart. "*Quer pasticciaccio della via Merulana,*" the title of a sombre novel by Emilio Gadda, is about a domestic situation in which Roman dialect words are artfully deployed to add to the tortured atmosphere. *See also* ROME.

PASTRY is confusingly known as *pasta,* usually with a descriptive adjective, *pasta frolla,* short crust pastry, *pasta sfoglia,* flaky or puff pastry; *pasta reale* is marzipan, *pasta da pane* is a yeasted bread dough, and there are many more. The heavy wholemeal flour-and-water pastry used by Scappi to enclose a partly cooked tongue, seasoned with spices and covered with slices of bacon or cured pork fat, before baking in a hot oven, was a protective carapace, not intended to be eaten (*see* PIE). Scappi did the same with fillet of beef, Wellington avant la lettre, larded with fat, encased in a craggy crust, as one can see in a still life by Sébastien Stosskopf, showing the tempting contents of a rather ordinary pasty-shaped pie. Scappi used an edible alternative made with finer flour, salt, water, and a little lard, to make a *cassa*, a stand pie, for the same spiced tongue to be served hot, this time not hermetically sealed but with a hole in the top to let out the steam and so prevent the crust from fracturing, into which some of the meat's marinade was poured before the end of cooking.

PEA, *pisello, Pisum sativum*, one of the Papilonaceae family, has been cultivated all over Europe and the Middle East since time immemorial, but it is likely that in early days was used dried, a coarse pulse like LENTILS or BROAD BEANS, not the tender seasonal luxury we know today. The ancient Romans made these coarse field peas into *conchicla* (from the Greek *khonkos*; Dalby, 2003, p. 252), a sort of mushy pea soup, seasoned with oil, herbs, and spices, or a stiffer mash, which could be layered with cooked sausage, pork, fowl of various kinds, herbs, and pine nuts in a dish lined with caul fat, and then baked—something very like *pease pudding*, once much loved in Britain, but not invented there. Other pea dishes noted in Apicius also sound like dried pulse dishes, and some evoke happy memories of *erwtensoep*, Dutch green pea soup, made with a selection of winter vegetables, ham hock, bacon, smoked sausage, and herbs and spices. *Conciclam Apicianam* cooks the peas with LUCANICA, pork forcemeat balls, and some pork shoulder, seasoned with lovage, green coriander, dill, oregano, onion, and some fish sauce. Later, during the Middle Ages, the water in which dried peas were cooked made a broth to use on nonmeat days—an important liquid item in the Lenten kitchen, which went on being used even when the new tender fresh peas were in fashion. It is hard to pinpoint the moment when coarse field peas, animal and peasant food, became upwardly mobile inhabitants of the kitchen garden, a rare luxury for the rich, but Martino in the 1460s used

both kinds, young peas in their pods, parboiled and finished with strips of bacon, and dried peas pounded with bread soaked in pea broth and ground almonds, to make a meatless BIANCOMANGIARE. Isabella d'Este wrote from Mantua to a friend on 9 May 1501 thanking him for the *zambudelli* (a kind of sausage) which arrived just in time to eat with crop of fresh peas, and sent in return a *formazo duro* (possibly PARMESAN) to have with the new broad beans. On 26 February 1519, she sent some "novelties" (*"qualche stranieze"*) to her brother in Ferrara to refresh his jaded appetite after a long and exhausting journey—a little basket of fresh young peas was among them; and by 1580, the painter Vincenzo Campi included a bowl of shelled peas in the display of his buxom market vegetable seller. Costanzo Felici liked tender sugar snap peas in salads, and enjoyed them stewed in stews. Scappi at the same time was serving *scasi teneri con le scorze*, tender young peas in their pods, mange-tout or sugar snap, and also a Lenten dish, *minestra di piselli*, in which the fresh peas are simmered a little while in olive oil, then finished cooking in water and saffron, thickened by some of them pounded in a mortar, and seasoned with herbs. His recipes make it clear that by then dried, shelled and mange-tout peas were all available, and being given sophisticated treatment. They were on sale in Rome from the end of March to June, he said, and gave a recipe very similar to a dish served in Rome today, in which the plump, tender young peas are cooked with GUANCIALE and seasoned with herbs. These Roman peas were also cooked with young pigeons or ducklings. "*Piselli teneri alessati con la scorza, serviti con aceto, sale e pepe*" made a cold salad on 15 May. Castelvetro, a generation later, described peas as "the noblest of vegetables," cooked with broth, seasoned with herbs and creamed bacon fat. Corrado has elaborate recipes, of which *piselli piccionati* is typical: the pigeons are subordinate to the peas, which are cooked with butter, chives, parsley, and ham, and served with the roasting juices and the hashed pigeon meat as a garnish. He cooked peas in butter with herbs, let them settle in cream, and served them in hollowed-out bread rolls fried in butter. And today, there are a variety of ways of cooking with peas, from the VIGNAROLA of the Roman spring to the *risi e bisi* of Veneto, the rice and peas of Lombardy, where they are also cooked with tench—and in Tuscany with eels, with pasta in many regions, and simmered with squid or octopus. The arrival of peas and other delicacies in France might well have been the sort of exchange we saw going on in the d'Este family—rich people sending each other little luxuries—and it would have been reciprocal at a time when rare and delicate vegetables were being exchanged by horticulturalists and gluttons. No need to travel in the Medici baggage, or assume the French were backward in these things.

PEACH, *pesca, Prunus persica vulgaris,* is another oriental drupe said to have been brought to Europe by Alexander the Great. The Romans were cultivating peaches by the 1st century AD, already improving quality and yield by grafting. Peaches can be seen in Roman paintings and mosaics. A wall painting from Herculaneum shows a branch of hard green peaches on a ledge, one of them with a bite taken out, perhaps rashly, for the tooth marks indicate a hard unyielding fruit, more suitable for a cooked dish like *mishmishiya*, where the fragrant acidity would balance a richly spiced meat stew. A large variety of dessert peaches are grown in Italy today, and are enjoyed fresh or in desserts, candied or as preserves. The saying quoted by Castelvetro, *"A l'amico monda il fico / e il persico al nemico"* (Peel a fig for a friend, and a peach for an enemy), might be taken to mean that peeling a peach, which needs only wiping with a clean cloth, is an expression of insincere concern, or just that figs are a healthier fruit. Safer by far to enjoy

a *Bellini,* invented in Harry's Bar in Venice in the 1940s, a sweetly pretty companion to the CARPACCIO, white peach juice and champagne, which is only a posh version of the old custom of dunking peaches in wine at the end of a meal, enhancing the flavour of both. Peaches served the fine arts well; Giovanna Garzoni painted a branch of ripe fruit on a worn majolica dish, and later Bartolomeo Bimbi did a group portrait of the many varieties sought after by his Medici patron, Cosimo III. Their apotheosis is perhaps in Christian Berentz's celebration of summer fruit in Rome, in which a rosy-cheeked country girl balances on her head a basket of fruit, her cheeks glowing like the sun-kissed peaches, in this late baroque pile-up of fruit and flowers.

PEACOCK, *pavone,* has always been prized for its splendid plumage, and although the flesh is acknowledged to be tough and uninteresting, it went on being presented as the triumphant focus of banquets throughout the Middle Ages and the Renaissance. The bird was skinned, with the feathers intact, not plucked, and then spit roasted and put back into its plumage (the skin had been carefully dusted with spices to prevent decay while the bird was cooking). A skilful cook, as instructed by Martino (Ballerini and Parzen, 2005, p. 54), would then insert iron rods to support the otherwise floppy creature, which could, with the help of a clockwork mechanism, strut along the table, spouting fire from its beak, to the delight of the assembled company, who would have seen this over and over again. The futility of this conspicuous consumption enraged Platina, who poured out his scorn in a thinly disguised attack on Pope Paul II: "This is a dish for those who have risen from base hovels and taverns, not to wealth, which is forgivable, but to the highest rank, not through honest toil, but by mere luck and the exploitation of human credulity."

Introduced by the Romans, the peacock became a symbol of Christianity because its flesh was alleged to be incorruptible; this and its visual association with imperial splendour is another reason for its popularity, which had nevertheless declined by the 17th century. For this reason, there are many images of peacocks in all their splendour, from Roman and Byzantine mosaics to manuscript illuminations of mythical or actual feasts, an aspect of international gothic cuisine which Phyllis Pray Bober reminds us echoes the glowing colours of medieval stained glass, as well as the gaudy appearance of the food (1999, p. 258).

Renaissance health handbooks describe peacocks as tough and indigestible, needing to be hung and cooked with plenty of spices. Corrado seems to have had the last word on peacocks—they live to such a ripe old age that a cook can be lumbered with a very tough old bird indeed, so the thing to go for is a young pea hen; his own audacious recipe is to spit roast it, wrapped in buttered paper, with a stuffing of slices of swordfish, veal fat, ham, anchovies, capers, lemon juice, and spices.

PEANUT, groundnut, monkeynut, *arachide, Arachis hypogaea*, is best known in Italy as a snack, roasted, skinned, and salted. The refined oil is also used in cooking when a mild or neutral flavour is desired. Its high smoke point makes it good for deep frying.

PEAR, *Pyrus communis, pera*, of the Rosaceae family, was known in ancient Rome; Apicius had some nice recipes, and Pliny wrote of 44 varieties, eaten both raw and cooked. Traditional kinds today are *pere butirre, bergamotte, verdi lunghe, caravelle, campane, rossette, moscato*, and a whole range of cooking pears, with many different kinds in each subdivision. Commercially, the list is more restrained, with over recent years De-

cana, Max Red Bartlett, and Abate Fetel increasing production and catching up with the favourites Conference and William—a very different scene from Tuscany in 1699, when Bartolomeo Bimbi painted for Grand Duke Cosimo III a huge canvas showing every kind of pear produced in his domains, 115 of them, divided into sections according to their times of ripening, and arranged in baskets and on platters, each fruit numbered and named in a cartouche below: *branchetta, brutta e buona, grossa bianchetta, buoncristiana muschiata*, and many more. These fruit portraits were a scientific record of production, as well as a glorious composition in a setting of classical columns and statuary, and every fruit was an exact record of its size and colour, with characteristic markings and blemishes, which would have got them banned from today's supermarkets. Costanzo Felici wrote of over 30 varieties and many more whose names he could not remember; he recalled that in some areas the poor would dry pears for winter use, and grind them up to use when making bread.

Depending on the quality of the fruit—astringent, juicy, sweet, sharp—pears were eaten at the beginning of a meal to sharpen the appetite, or at the end to help settle things. But between the end and the beginning, pears appeared in a wide range of dishes, savoury and sweet, with considerably more invention than our limited offerings of pears with cheese, and the usual pies and tarts—although recently a family restaurant near Modena devised a starter of sliced pears dressed with crushed raspberries, *aceto balsamico tradizionale di Modena*, and dandelion leaves, which has echoes of the sweet/savoury mixtures of the past. Sally Grainger recreated a savoury custard from Apicius, in which pears cooked in honey and wine were puréed and mixed with eggs, cumin, and Thai fish sauce (*nam pla*), baked and served with freshly ground black pepper (Dalby and Grainger, 1996, p. 125). Martino put a similar mixture into an open tart: pears, quinces, or turnips, or a mixture of all three, were first baked, then skinned and cooked in meat or chicken broth, puréed and mixed with soft and hard cheese (possibly ricotta and parmesan), chopped cooked pork belly, eggs, sugar, cinnamon, and ginger, and cooked in the oven, the top covered to prevent it burning, and served sprinkled with sugar and rosewater. Maria Vittoria della Verde had a recipe for huge tarts for the *frati*, with a filling of apples or pears, cheese, pounded walnuts, candied fruit, and eggs, sweetened with honey and perfumed with rosewater, served with a sprinkling of cinnamon and sugar. A century later, Corrado described the versatility of muscat pears, and how, as well as in tarts and fritters, they were good as a soup, simmered in meat broth, or stuffed and cooked in a ham *coulis*.

PEARÀ is a sauce from Verona quite different in character from the more formidable *pevarada*. It is a creamy sauce, reminiscent of our bread sauce, but without the onion, made by beating to a cream bread or breadcrumbs soaked in broth, with butter, bone marrow, grated parmesan, salt, and abundant pepper. It is served with *bollito misto*.

PECORINO is a cheese made from sheep's milk (sometimes cooked or pasteurised), drained, pressed, and put into moulds. There are many kinds, which vary depending on the region, the type of sheep, what they eat, and the method used. Some of the main categories are described here, but the varieties are many, and confusing. The *Atlante* (INSOR, 2001) lists over 40, each with its own identity. Sheep provide over 40 percent of the cheese made in Italy today, not counting mixtures of sheep's and goat's or cow's milk. The ideal sheep's milk cheese is made by exploiting the warmth of the freshly milked product, and using a vegetable REN-

NET (milder though with a lower yield) without any subsequent heating of the curds. Around this ideal, not always easy to achieve, of primitive artisan prrocedures, the worlds of producer and consumer, caught up in the opposing pull of a nostalgic collective imagination and the dark forces of industrialisation, seethe, in the words of Corrado Berberis, like milk in tumultuous fermentation.

PECORINO ROMANO is a much-loved cheese made in huge quantities, and not just in the region around Rome, the Agro romano. It is manufactured in Lazio, the province of Grosseto in Tuscany, and Sardinia, where in the 19th century cheesemakers from Rome and Naples realised they could meet the massive demand from Italian immigrants abroad, and where today the Consorzio has its seat, overseeing Sardinia's 90 percent of the total production of *pecorino romano*. The procedure is the same, and as a DOP (*see* DOC) product is subject to rigorous definition and control. The milk, from Sicilian, Sardinian, and Comisana sheep grazing naturally, is collected daily and either processed on the spot or sent to centres where the procedure follows traditional practise, first heating the milk to a high temperature, then adding a lactic culture to start fermentation, before putting in the coagulant, usually kid's or lamb's rennet (following local traditions and the personal judgment of the cheese-maker). The curd is broken into small grains, the size of rice or wheat, heated some more, drained, pressed, and put into moulds, then dry-salted for up to two months before ripening for eight months to a year. The rind is indelibly marked with the Consorzio's trademark, the individual mark of the maker, and the place and date of manufacture.

Pecorino is traditionally the grating cheese to have with pasta and many other dishes in Rome and the surrounding area, where its strong flavour and piquancy go well with the robust local cuisine, in dishes like *buccatini al'Amatriciana, spaghetti alla carbonara,* or the aromatic *trippa alla romana.* When young and fresh, it is less pungent and makes a good table cheese, often eaten with the first tender broad beans of the spring, which used for Romans to be part of the ritual trip to the countryside, after winter, to buy fava beans from local growers and eat them with bread and cheese and the white wine of the Castelli.

PECORINO SARDO is working its way up the charts (DOP in 1996; *see* DOC), and possibly misguided aspirations towards DOP status have led to the amalgamation of two highly characteristic but different cheeses, *caciotta* and *semicotto,* under the names *pecorino sardo dolce* and *pecorino sardo maturo* (*see* CACIOTTA).

PECORINO TOSCANO is less assertive than *pecorino romano,* mild when young, with more pungency when matured, sometimes made in a gentler version using artichoke or other vegetable coagulant. The version, made throughout the entire region and also parts of UMBRIA and Lazio, is a uniform product, though respecting traditional practices, and got its DOP in 1986 (*see* DOC). But there are many other kinds of pecorino in Tuscany, a source of pride and pleasure, not to be eclipsed by the growing popularity and export potential of cheaper "regional" cheeses made on an industrial scale, although threatened by the danger of being constrained in the straitjacket of the DOP definition. The wide differences in terrain, pasture, methods of cheese-making, local tastes, customs, and surviving skills account for an increasing public enthusiasm for all these different varieties. One of them, the *cacio pecorino delle crete senesi,* is a remarkable cheese made from the milk of sheep grazing on a unique geological

formation, Pliocene clay unevenly covered with patches of sand, an arid area extending over 80,000 hectares (about 200 acres) to the southeast of Siena, always hard to cultivate, and suffering from erosion since its depopulation during the Middle Ages, but home to a wide range of fragrant and pungent herbs and shrubs (*assensio, plantago maritima o serpentina,* juniper, *santorregio, salvastrella, finichiella,* and *pepolino,* to name just a few), which give the cheese its unique flavour. The breeds of sheep that graze there today are not the same as those that produced the cheese that captivated Pope Pius II and Lorenzo de' Medici, for sheep and shepherds from Sardinia came over in the 19th century, and mingled with local breeds, but their yield is higher, and milk production goes on for more months of the year. The quality of the milk and the methods used are unique, not to be confused with other versions of pecorino in Tuscany. These include *pecorino della Versilia,* an artisan cheese made in small family units from the milk of the Massese breed of sheep, coagulated with a homemade rennet, and worked with traditional rustic techniques (a fingertip appraisal of the heat of the curds is the typical "organic thermometer"), being a soft, fragrant, mild cheese, with in the spring aromas of grassy pastures; *pecorino della garfagnana* is made in the province of Lucca from milk from the same breed of sheep, mild or piquant depending on the type of rennet used; *pecorino baccellone* is a fresh, pasteurised, young cheese made in the whole of Tuscany from March to June, named for the custom of eating it on springtime outings with the first tender young broad beans, *baccelli; pecorino toscano da serbo* is a matured sheep's cheese made in the Maremma and the hills between Siena, Pisa, and Grosseto; the *pecorino stagionato da Pienza* is a mature pecorino, with an almost chalky texture and a more pronounced flavour, sometimes preserved in jars with bay leaves; *pecorino fresco di Pienza* is made in the province of Siena, differing from that of the *creti senesi* in the influence of semi-industrial techniques, to meet the increasing demands of gastro-tourism; *pecorino senese*, made around Siena, is another version with its own character; a mountain pecorino, *tipo Amiata-Seggiano*, is characteristically acidic and crumbly, very different from the standard *pecorino toscano*. Visitors to the Botanical Garden of the Botanical Museum, University of Florence can see beds of aromatic edible plants and herbs from the three main geographical areas of Tuscany, which neatly inform us of their different aromas and flavourings, and of their impact on cooking and preserving local food.

Other regions have their versions of pecorino; in BASILICATA are *pecorino di Moliterno* and *pecorino di Filiano*, with its pronounced and highly individual flavour (*particolarissimo*, as the *Atlante* [INSOR, 2001] puts it)—a cheese once despised as the coarse fare of the underprivileged and now a sought-after gourmet speciality; commentators have remarked that its DOP (*see* DOC) and subsequent overproduction might modify the impact of its visceral appeal to the collective subconscious. In Umbria, the *pecorino di Norcia has* two versions, one made by artisan shepherd cheese-makers in a restricted area, using a lamb's rennet made by each individual, dried in woodsmoke, which gives a particular flavour to the cheese, which, unlike the industrial version, is scalded in boiling whey, after a preliminary draining, to firm up the crust. *Pecorino Marchigiano* is strong-flavoured and aromatic; the dried and salted cheeses is also scalded in whey. A version from the Monti Sibillini, traditionally prepared by women cheese-makers, uses a mysterious herbal coagulant made from thyme, marjoram, basil, blackberry shoots, cloves, nutmeg, grated pecorino, pepper, oil, and egg yolk which gives the finished cheeses quite a kick. In Friuli–Venezia Giulia, two artisan operators, still using ancient techniques, make *pecorino dei Pian di Vas* and *pecorino Monye Re* (with origins in Yugoslavia). An artisan pecorino is made in Lazio, and pecorino is made all over Abruzzo; that from Farindola is coagulated with rennet made from pig's stomach, with an intense aroma and a powerful flavour, redolent of mountain herbs and wild hedgerow flowers. From Capricotta in MOLISE comes a fragrant pecorino, excellent, like the meat of the sheep, because of the quality of the pasture. CAMPANIA produces many fine versions, especially a pungent one from Fortore. In PUGLIA, there is a pungent one from Brindisi and a milder version from Lecce. CALABRIA's various pecorini are redolent of wild herbs and often aromatised with peppercorns or chilli, adding to the pungency of the cheese.

PENNYROYAL, *mentuccia, pulegio, nepetella, Mentha pulegium,* is a plant of the Labiatae family, but sorting out these various kinds of MINT, which cross and hybridise easily, is a bit complicated, and on top of that, the Italian names vary from place to place. *Mentuccia* is essential for preparing *carciofi alla romana*, and a bunch of it is given away in Roman markets when you purchase your artichokes. It has a pungent, almost acrid mintiness which mitigates the bitterness of artichokes; when mixed with garlic, salt, and pepper and stuffed into the prepared artichokes, then cooked slowly in olive oil and water, all the flavours mellow and come together in an unforgettable combination. In TUSCANY, it is called *erba da funghi* and is used in cooking mushrooms, especially boletus. *Mentuccia*, however is not the same as *menta romana*, used in Rome for tripe dishes, which is yet another member of the mint family. (*See also* DITTANY.)

PEPERATA. *See* PEVERADA.

PEPOSO is a humble Tuscan stew made of cheap cuts of beef or pork (*see* PIG), usually *muscolo* (shin), cooked very slowly in an earthenware pot with a variety of additions, the important ones being red wine and a great deal of crushed black peppercorns; these provide a pungency and aroma without the searing bite of chillies, which would not have been known in Renaissance Florence. It was traditionally left for hours in a cooling bread oven or in the kiln in which terra cotta tiles and ceramics were made. The recipe sometimes includes a calf's foot or pig's trotter to add unctuousness, and often has the usual mixture of chopped onion, celery, carrot, much garlic, fresh herbs, and maybe some tomato in some form or other. It has been revived in restaurants around Impruneta, and when made with cuts of beef of the region, and local wine it is incomparable, served on slices of toasted Tuscan bread to mop up the rich concentrated juices. Eaten from traditional ceramic dishes, in the same ambience in Impruneta where Brunelleschi worked with perfectionist zeal to oversee the production of the tiles used for the great dome of Santa Maria del Fiore in Florence, it is hard to reject the legend that alongside the tiles bubbled a pot of *peposo* cooked to the master's own specification. Even made with cheap cuts, though, it is unlikely that Renaissance artisans, however skilled, would have been able to afford this meaty stew, and the expensive spice pepper would have been way beyond their reach, not to mention the still unknown tomato; but we can still allow Brunelleschi and ourselves this indulgence, whichever recipe we follow.

PEPPER, *Piper, pepe*, is the one spice from the rich mixtures of the past that survives in everyday cooking and in preserved meat products, often imperceptible, but always an aromatic presence. When attempting to illustrate the pepper plant, Mattioli had to rely on a sketch made for him by a Portuguese mariner who had seen the fresh pepper vine in India, and it was not until then, 1568, that users of this, perhaps the most popular spice, both now and in the past, had any idea of how it grew. Black pepper seems to be the most popular, while the ripened and decorticated whole pepper gives pungency to a white sauce or stew without sullying the appearance. It was bought, at vast expense, by the ancient Romans, draining the treasury of gold and silver coins, and used by them a great deal. Apicius used crushed or ground pepper in just about all of his sauces—a typical sauce for braised meats has peppercorns pounded with cumin, celery or lovage seed, rosemary, thyme, and oregano, mixed with stoned fresh damsons, white wine, vinegar, honey, and some of the cooking juices, a pleasing, sweet/sour mixture in which the meat finishes cooking. Pepper is the only expensive ingredient here, adding a touch of luxury to less costly seeds and herbs.

Pepper figures as just one of many spices in the cooking of the Middle Ages, and in most of the spice mixtures, but is not universally used. It does, however, give its name to a sauce, *peverata*, even though by the 14th century it is not always listed in the ingredients, as in the *Peverada scl.eda per zoè schutelini* (smooth pepper sauce for two serving dishes)... in which the cooking juices of meat or fish are thickened with a mixture of white flour, vinegar, and honey, flavoured with spices and coloured with saffron (perhaps an early sighting of a flour-based sauce). Martino has a different version, a *peperata de salvaticina* (a peppery game dish), in which game cooked in red wine and water is served in a sweet/sour sauce made of stoned raisins, burnt toast soaked in vinegar, cooked grape must, all pounded together and diluted with some of the vinegar and juices from the meat, some of its blood if available, passed through a sieve, and flavoured with spices, pepper, cloves, and cinnamon or cassia; "the blacker the better," he commented. The modern *peverada* or *peará* of Venice and the surrounding region is a survival of this. The Venetian version for game consists of the pounded liver of the animal cooked briefly in olive oil and diluted with vinegar and lemon juice, as well as juices from the roast, and seasoned with freshly ground black pepper. From Padua comes a more complex mixture with anchovies, chicken livers, a pickled chilli, parsley, grated cheese, lemon zest, and breadcrumbs, with plentiful black pepper, finished with lemon juice and vinegar. Other versions have pine nuts, sultanas, butter, sugar, and onion. Vicenza uses bone marrow and breadcrumbs cooked to a creamy sauce with chicken or meat broth. A very peppery dish from TUSCANY, PEPOSO, is meat stew unctuous with pigs' trotters, red with tomatoes, the usual SOFFRITO of garlic, celery, carrot, and a horrendous amount of freshly crushed black pepper cooked slowly in red wine.

By the early 16th century, Castelvetro, writing of everyday fare, not the food of the rich, mentions pepper more than any other spice, usually as a condiment, with salt and oil, for plainly cooked vegetables, added freshly ground just before serving. The much-mocked outsize phallic pepper-grinder of Italian trattorias abroad is only making the point that powdered or ready-ground pepper is really no good at all, having lost its aroma long ago—freshly ground at the point of serving is the only way, with simply cooked grills and roasts, or complex stews and sauces. (*See also* LONG PEPPER.

Pepper has preservative properties which make it valuable in cured meats and as a coating for hams and pancetta.

PEPPERS (CAPSICUMS). *See* SWEET PEPPERS.

PERCH, *pesce persico*, a freshwater fish, is not to be confused with *perchia*, which is one

of the groupers. It has a fine firm flesh, and is often sold as fillets, which are traditionally coated with egg and breadcrumbs, fried in butter, and served on a RISOTTO made with a good fish stock. It can be simmered in water and a little vinegar, and then skinned and taken off the bone and served with a garlic sauce, according to Martino.

PERSIMMON is the name of the American persimmon, *Dyospiris virginiana*, of the same family as *cachi, kaki, Dyospiros kaki* which eventually superseded it after arriving in Europe from the Far East in the mid-19th century. Its attractive pinkish red fruit are harsh with tannins when unripe, but become sweet and fragrant. Kaki is cultivated commercially in Romagna and Campania, and can be eaten as a dessert fruit, in ice cream, or as a preserve.

PESCE PERSICO. *See* PERCH.

PESCE SAN PIETRO. *See* JOHN DORY.

PESCE SPADA. *See* SWORDFISH.

PESTLE AND MORTAR. *See* KITCHEN EQUIPMENT.

PESTO was not in the past unique to LIGURIA, being simply a mass of aromatic herbs pounded in a pestle and mortar with salt, garlic, olive oils, cheese, and perhaps nuts, which could then be diluted with vinegar or verjuice or broth and used as a sauce or relish with all kinds of things. The recipe has now become fossilised, in areas outside Italy, into an industrial product eaten almost exclusively with PASTA, where in fact a more imaginative use is made of this BASIL-based

sauce at home. It is so easy to make oneself that the fragrance (and cheapness) of a freshly prepared version is preferable, and can be modified by adjusting the flavourings to the dish you are eating; often a gentler version without the PECORINO and PINE NUTS is preferable, and a pasta sauce can equally well be made with chopped basil, and oil or butter alone, stirred into the drained pasta. One version, *pesto avvantaggiato*, is made by cooking homemade *trenette*, the Ligurian term for a long, thin, flat, dried pasta similar to vermicelli, in water in which some sliced potatoes and little green beans have been simmered until almost tender, using *pesto* and some of the cooking water as a sauce.

PETRONILLA

was the pseudonym of the distinguished medical doctor Amalia Moretti Foggia, born in 1872 in Mantua, who after completing her medical studies lived and worked in Milan until her death in 1947. A concern for the health and lives of the poor and underpriviledged was behind a series of what we would now call lifestyle columns in the popular Milanese weekly *Domenica del Corriere*, and this led to a successful series of recipes. Her chatty, almost fluffy, reassuring tones created a demand for the recipes in book form—*Ricette di Petronilla* and *Altre ricette* (Milan, 1937)—that were best-sellers at exactly the moment Marinetti was mocking and rubbishing this abhorred lower-middle-class style of cooking. The cover of *Altre ricette* shows a happy young woman in white apron rolling out egg pasta in a modern, but not luxurious, kitchen. Petronilla was writing for a host of *amichette*, little girlfriends, who stayed at home and tended their families, struggling along on a narrow budget, or who worked late at the office but still needed to produce a nourishing and not too costly meal every evening. Petronilla encouraged inventiveness—"you don't have to keep on cooking the same

things"; "try something new for a change" (she cannot have been unaware of Marinetti)—and pointed out that you could overspend a bit in the interests of domestic harmony, a way of delighting husband and children, that made that little extra expense well worth while. (A lavish amount of parmesan in her artichoke risotto made a big hole in the budget.) The breathless tone (so many ellipses and unfinished sentences), combined with an endearing mixture of snobbery and parsimony, make Petronilla a strangely touching read today. A website offers a selection from her books, and gives a good idea of the chatty tone of voice and the reassuring combination of cautious novelty and conventional wisdom. "*Escabeche*," her version of a Peruvian dish (fried fish marinated in a sauce of cooked onions, red peppers, garlic, tomato, and vinegar) went down so well that she felt she could offer it to her readers: "My husband, seeing this apparently extravagant dish, then tasting it, asked me what 'this stuff' was, and having replied that it was actually American, well Peruvian . . . and then kids and husband having all said 'but it's really lovely . . .' I felt I could safely let you have the recipe."

Most of Petronilla's recipes are "*squisitissima*," "*lesta a fare*," and "*di poco spesa*"—utterly exquisite, quick to do, and not expensive. But they now seem to us a bit fussy, and while attracting applause from the ever appreciative husband and children, seem to lack the essential simplicities that we look for in Italian cooking. A recipe for eggs scrambled with chopped cooked spinach and parmesan provoked a visit from the mother-in-law, who bounded into the apartment "like an asteroid" with a fancier version involving a mound of buttery spinach surrounded by poached eggs on slices of bread, edges cut in a zigzag pattern resembling cockscombs, fried in butter. Her *Cavolfiore alla besciamella*, cauliflower cheese, is utterly bland and boring. And this was the time when the Touring Club Italiano was directing readers of its *Guida gastronomica d'Italia* to far-flung places with pungent regional food, initiating a spate of regional cookbooks and guides.

Petronilla's dinner party menus are an agony to read; a merry supper with a few friends is work enough, but a posh dinner is overwhelming, even with a host of servants; the succession of dishes and then the business of clearing up afterwards, as set forth, is mind-boggling—but with only one *servetta* (skivvy), you leave the dishes until tomorrow, after all, it's your kitchen, you can do them yourself in an *oretta* (less than an hour...) the next morning.

But the prevailing commonsense and humanity of Petronilla are an antidote to the bombast of Marinetti and the avuncular gentility of Artusi.

PEVARADA

PEVARADA or *peperata* is a sauce which survives in Venetian gastronomy today, and goes back a long way, to the earliest cookery manuscript, in which, even then, the mixture of spices might or might not include pepper. It was pungent with spices, sharp with vinegar, sometimes sweet with honey or dried fruit, and may have been darkened with burnt toast and the livers of the fowl it was to accompany. Martino's *peperata* was a dish of game stewed in wine and water, served with a sauce made from dark toast soaked in vinegar, raisins, spices, the liver and blood of the creature, pounded up together, put through a sieve and cooked with some of the vinegar the bread was soaked in, some sweet or fortified wine, and the cooking liquid, "the blacker the better," he said. The various versions of this dark, sweet/sour, heavily spiced sauce may have survived in Venice because of its historic links with the spice trade. Nowadays, pepper seems to be the main spice, used in abundance with the pounded liver of the game bird or animal, with vinegar and lemon juice added just before serving. Some versions, like one from

Padua, are more complex, containing anchovies, lemon zest, a small pickled chilli, chopped onion, parsley, and breadcrumbs as well as the liver vinegar, and other spices as well as pepper. Every family had its own recipe, but the dark peppery, sweet/sour character is common to all of them. *Peperata* is a heavily spiced sweet/sour dish, lumps of venison stewed in red wine and water, then fried briefly in lard, and served in a sauce made from dried fruit, toasted bread soaked in vinegar, sweet grape must, spices, all pounded together with the cooking liquid and the blood of the beast. Similar recipes are followed in the Val d'Aosta today.

PHEASANT

PHEASANT, *fagiano,* is well known for the beauty of the male plumage, and the tastiness of its well hung flesh, though it is not usual to hang them as long in Italy as in Great Britain. Like the peacock, the male was often served at banquets cooked and stitched back into its feathers. It is not certain when the pheasant arrived in Europe from the Caucasus where it originated; pheasants were reared and hunted in Greece and Rome in classical times and can be seen in mosaics, while recipes survive from the early Middle Ages. Platina got a sardonic satisfaction from the legend that Itys, the son of the king of Thrace, was turned into a pheasant, so its ostentatious appearance on the tables of the great was a gruesome reminder of its origins, not for the likes of his friend Pomponio Leto, who fed his guests on onions, shallots, and garlic.

PIADA, PIADINA. See FLAT-BREADS.

PIE

PIE or tart (*see also* PASTICCIO), can be *torta, tortino,* usually with a savoury filling, often vegetables, open or covered. The word *torta* can also mean a layered dish, baked in the oven, but quite without an upper or lower layer of pastry. *Crostata* is a sweet open tart, of ricotta, jam, or marzipan, with many variations. The pie in all its glories typifies the polarities of Italian cuisine—on the one hand a simple way of enclosing a filling in dough or pastry and cooking it in various ways, on a hot surface, under a lid covered with coals, or in an oven—on the other hand a complicated construction with an equally complex filling, reminding us of Carême's dictum that architecture was a branch of *patisserie.* A delicacy for immediate consumption or a way of preparing food to prolong its keeping powers, pies evolved from a hard protective crust that was not meant to be eaten but intended as a method of sending a present of game to a distant friend.

Sometimes claimed as an Italian invention, a complex version of the pie, the *torta parmesana*, might have been a medieval attempt to emulate the creations of classical Rome, passed down through the Arab world, with distant relatives in ancient Mesopotamia, and a strong presence to this day in the cuisines of the Middle East, where *bstilla*, a chicken or pigeon pie enclosed in a sweet pastry crust, spiced with cinnamon, is a reminder of the spicy, sweet meat and chicken dishes of Renaissance Italy. The "four and twenty blackbirds baked in a pie" of the nursery rhyme was one of the party pieces of a Renaissance banquet, when a huge ornate pie would be produced and ceremoniously cut open to release birds, rabbits, or other live creatures to delight and surprise the guests. As the birds, often tethered with string to enable them to be recycled, or rabbits cavorted over the tablecloth, the pages would produce a smaller pie from within the towering edifice, to cut up and hand round. From a courtly artefact, elaborated during the Middle Ages, to a practical edible container, to hand-held street food, the *pasticcio* could be a performance art or a basic necessity. It was also a hygienic and convenient way of taking perishable food on long journeys, for the stout outer covering preserved the contents, if properly cooked, from exposure to air. Scappi was at pains to point out how long his different kinds of pie were expected to keep, in hot and cold weather. He made a pie with boned chicken or squab, ground almonds, seasoned with cinnamon and other spices, perfumed with rosewater, and with an enigmatic touch of sugar within and a sprinkling of sugar and cinnamon without, similar to the familiar *bstilla* of Moroccan cuisine. BOCCA DI DAMA evolved a century later into a layer of rich, spiced marzipan between two layers of puff or flaky pastry, described by the Bolognese Bartolomeo Stefani, who also had a *bstilla* recipe he called *torta reale di piccion*, the name *pizza* having evaporated, not used in 17th-century Bologna. Eventually *bocca di dama* relinquished its pastry covering and is now a rich baked marzipan. Moralists in the Low Countries made much of this, and still life paintings show pies cut open to reveal the rich contents of meat, dried fruit, and spices exposed to the corruption of the world, while Italian painters were content to depict the beauties of complete pies ornamented with baroque pastry decorations and lattice work, which are hardly ever described in recipe books, and so a great help to hands-on food historians.

PIEDMONT lies north of LIGURIA, just touching on EMILIA-ROMAGNA to the east, with VALLE D'AOSTA and Switzerland to its north, and in the west a border with France. The region has alpine mountains, the rolling dimpled hills of Langhe and Monferrato, and fertile valleys and large areas of the *pianura padana*, the Padanian plain, with the vast irrigated rice fields round Vercelli and the Canadese, Vercellese, Novarese, and Lomellina, and Cuneo in the south. Wheat and maize are grown as well as rice, together with oats and forage plants. Lake Maggiore lies to the northeast, providing freshwater fish, which is also to be had from irrigation channels, although until recently there was no easy access to saltwater fish. There are many eel and frog recipes. Piedmont has forests, many nature reserves, a strong industrial presence, and at the same time production of beef, pork (*see* PIG) products, and cheeses based firmly on artisanal methods. The beef cattle, mainly the creamy white *razza piemontese*, flourish on the plains with rich winter forage, and summer nourishment on the high pastures, producing a meat that is renowned worldwide for flavour and tenderness. Abundant vineyards create superb vintages, and a range of everyday wine. Nuts, in particular HAZELNUTS, abound. The variety of terrain and climate and the many influences from neighbouring and foreign regions have formed a rich and very diverse gastronomic tradition.

Recent history has to some extent overshadowed the layers of influence from prehistoric times, with Celts and Ligurians leaving their mark before the Roman presence produced settled towns, agriculture, and efficient communications, only to dissolve as barbarian invasions wiped just about everything out, to be gradually replaced by independent *marche* or dukedoms. By the 10th century, the land reclamation work of the huge monastic corporations, and these increasingly powerful independent dukedoms, were all eventually clustered under the dominion of the House of Savoy (a dynasty as well as a region, as was the case with Burgundy). By the 13th century, the name was applied to a huge territory; Spain and Austria made incursions, and the area was rent by predatory dynasties, not to mention French incursions, until by a complex combinations of politics and wheeling and dealing the unification of Italy in 1861 came about under the Piedmontese of the House of Savoy, by now linked with the Kingdom of Sardinia, with its capital in the city of Turin, a mixed blessing for southern patriots,

who resented the rule of these northern aliens, even more so when the seat of government moved to Rome.

The diversity of terrain produces a wide range of good things—cheeses, cured meats, fruit, and vegetables. The artisanal treatment of fresh and cured meats depends on rare human skills and local microclimates, and the results vary, unlike the standard industrial production using prepared spice mixtures and uniform procedures. The region of Piedmont has an official listing of over 100 different types of salumi, both industrial and artisan.

The *Atlante* (INSOR, 2002) describes 45 of them, aiming to make known those with exceptional qualities—including the large- and small-scale production of salami and cured meats from various animals, not just pig but beef cattle, donkey, sheep, goat, horse, deer, and wild goat. The violin-shaped cured legs of goat or chamois lend themselves to touristic poses, but have agreeable flavour and texture, cured in herbs and spices and air dried for some months. As well as prime cuts of meat and fat, there are cooked and raw concoctions using lesser cuts, and less appealing organs, transforming them into delicacies, like the *frisse* of Langhe in the province of Cuneo or the *galantina* of pig's head, tongue, throat, and shoulder, flavoured with bay leaves, white rum, anise, nutmeg, cloves, cinnamon, coriander, mace, pistachio, and pine nuts. *Frisse* and *griva* are made from pork liver, fat, and juniper berries, and the latter with sultanas—a fresh product to be consumed at once. *Bisecon* is made for home consumption or in restaurants, and is one of those basic "brawn" mixtures which can be gruesome or delightful, depending on the care and imagination that transforms them; carrots give points of colour rather than flavour, garlic and cinnamon help, and a long marinade in red wine prepares the ingredients for long slow cooking, after which the mixture is cooled in a pig's stomach and served cold, sliced. *Testa in cassetta di Gavi* is made from pig's head boned and cut up and cooked with lesser bits of veal, flavoured with salt, chilli, wild fennel, thyme, and other herbs, some pine nuts, and rum, put into casings, cooked, and eaten sliced. Another once-prized ingredient is blood, and when mixed with milk, pork fat, fried onions, and unloved organs like the pancreas, flavoured with cinnamon and fennel, put into casings, and cooked slowly can be eaten hot or cold, like the *brod* of Santo Stefano Belbo, which is also made commercially in Liguria. This genius of the Piedmontese for delicacy in the treatment of strange bits extends to nobler cuts, the different kinds of BRESAOLA, cured hams, and salami. *Filetto baciato* is a speciality of Ponzone in Alexandria: a fillet of pork, partly cured with aromatics, is rolled up in a mixture of chopped lean pork and fat flavoured with salt, pepper, nutmeg, garlic, and red wine, and cured for up to six months, then sliced very thin. There is a part of the province of Cuneo where sea and mountain breezes collide to produce the perfect atmosphere in which to cure *lonzardo*, loin of pork seasoned with sea salt, spices, and local herbs, which can be eaten raw or cooked. Fresh sausages are made throughout Piedmont, usually of mixtures of pork and veal, pork fat, garlic, and a variety of spices. Those from Bra are made of veal meat only, with a proportion of pork and veal fat and a selection of spices that might include cinnamon, nutmeg, pepper, fennel, and mace, enhanced by local wine and cheeses; when the meat is from the gentle white animals of the *razza piemontese*, reared traditionally, the quality of the product is as healthy as it is delicious, with a *tutela* which guarantees quality and monitors production. These delicacies can be eaten raw as well as cooked. Throughout the region, pork fat is cured in salt and rosemary and other herbs, eaten on its own or used as a condiment.

Tender cuts of beef can be sliced very thinly, or minced with a sharp knife, and eaten raw, *all'albese*, dressed with olive oil and garlic, and often white truffles.

Cooked dishes, using local wine and meats, include the BOLLITO MISTO, which in its most grandiose manifestation conforms to *la regola del sette* ("the rule of seven") and becomes the *gran bollito*. Rigidly following this definition, one would have to include seven cuts of beef (say), seven *ornamenti* or accompanying meat objects (a whole calf's head, a beef or veal tongue, a tail, a foot, cooked together, a chicken, a *cotechino*, each cooked separately, and finally a rolled breast of veal, roasted with herbs). The seven sauces must include red, green, horseradish, and mustard, and the seven *contorni* of assorted vegetables must include plain boiled potatoes, buttered spinach, and a salad of red onions in vinegar. Plain country bread, coarse rock salt, and a robust Barbera complete the experience. Thus does a simple method (simmering various kinds of meat slowly, apart and together, for appropriate times to bring out the different qualities of each, with a useful broth as a by-product) become encased in the straitjacket of dogma, and a frugal way of making the most of the less noble parts of various animals too old to work becomes a luxury performance, the preferred dish of Vittorio Emanuale II and the glory of grand restaurants. The sauces, or *bagnèt*, include a green one made from finely chopped parsley pounded in a mortar with deboned and rinsed salt anchovies, garlic, breadcrumbs soaked in mild vinegar and squeezed dry, and sometimes capers, to which olive oil is added slowly to produce an unctuous green mass. The red version is made from tomatoes, chopped and simmered with garlic, onions, celery, a little chilli, salt, and sugar, with olive oil and red wine vinegar to taste.

Cassöla is similar to the *cassoeûla* of Milan, a rich mixture of cuts and extremities of pork, fresh and cured, cabbage being the principal vegetable, and in the case of *cassöla*, goose fat and meat as well as or instead of the pork.

BRASATO *al Barolo* is another Piedmontese speciality. A large piece of beef is well larded and browned in lard, butter, or oil; then the usual celery, onion, carrot, and garlic are softened in the same fat, and the meat is turned with them, then allowed to absorb glass after glass of a bottle of good robust Barolo. The pot is then sealed, and the beef finishes cooking for three or four hours in a very low oven. Some versions marinate the meat in the wine and aromatics for a day or so before doing all this. The meat is served sliced across the grain with the by now reduced cooking liquid. Everything depends on the quality of the local beef and wine.

POLENTA is an accompaniment to many of the region's rich meat dishes and is also the basis of recipes like *puccia*, in which a lean cut of pork is cooked with the usual aromatic vegetables, then cut into small pieces and mixed, along with some lightly cooked cabbage leaves, with a light polenta, into which butter and parmesan are stirred just before serving. The mixture can be cooled, sliced, and fried.

Piedmont produces some of the finest rice to be had. The cultivation of rice was established as early as the 15th century, and by now the area around Vercelli is the most productive in Europe; when the rice fields are flooded in early spring, they are visible from outer space, while to those in their midst there is the fascination of a changing landscape, from the first brilliant covering of young plants in May to the warm autumnal colours before harvest.

The main varieties produced today are *vialone nano, carnaroli, arborio, baldo, roma, balilla,* and *sant'Andrea.* The first three are best for risottos, with *baldo,* a relative newcomer, suitable as well. The others are appropriate for desserts, stews and soups, and baked or moulded dishes. The techniques of cooking a RISOTTO are one of Italy's great gifts to

gastronomy, turning a staple cereal into an economical meal, with methods and ingredients different from all the other great rice cuisines. Grains of rice that, without disintegrating, allow starch to add a creamy density to the cooking liquid, while retaining a firm interior, are the basis of many recipes. The delicate *risotto piemontese* or *in bianco* is a way of appreciating the flavour and texture of good-quality rice without interference from intrusive elements. The rice is cooked in a simple, pale, meat or chicken broth, with the addition of butter and cheese towards the end of cooking; sometimes white wine is included in the cooking liquid, and when served with a shaving of truffles, this becomes a rare delicacy. The *panissa* of Vercelli is, on the other hand, a robust mixture of fresh *borlotti* beans cooked with pork rind, whose cooking liquid is used, together with some red wine, to make the risotto, which is started off in a BATTUTO of chopped onions and cured pork fat. The *paniscia* of the Novarese is made with the liquid of the *borlotti* beans cooked along with chopped celery, cabbage, carrots, and tomatoes, and started off in the *battuto* made with *salamino d'la duja* (*see* SALAM D'LA DUJA) and onions, with red wine to begin with. The rice fields and irrigation channels provide an abundance of frogs, which can be served in a risotto *alla novarese*, made from the carcasses cooked to make a broth, served with the reserved legs cooked in butter and garlic and finished in wine. Plain boiled rice has the odd name *riso in cagnone* when it is finished with diced FONTINA and melted butter. CARDOONS and ARTICHOKES are used in risottos, with meat or vegetable broth.

Cardoons, asparagus, artichokes, fleshy red peppers, cabbages, and celery are among the abundant vegetables of Piedmont. A delicious vehicle for these is a BAGNA CÀUDA or *càôda,* a hot sauce into which the raw vegetables are dipped, and eaten with rough bread and a fresh young wine. Butter and olive oil are melted in a terra cotta pot into which finely chopped garlic and salt anchovies, deboned and well rinsed, are stirred over a low heat until they have dissolved into a pungent creamy sauce. Plain boiled asparagus can be served with an unsweetened *zabaione* made with dry white wine, egg yolks, and butter.

There is a rich supply of dairy products and cheese from the plains and the hills and alpine areas. Butter is widely used as cooking medium, without excluding the delicate oils of nearby Liguria (reminding us that the so-called oil/butter divide is an unreal journalistic concept). SLOW FOOD lists 48 special cheeses for Piedmont, and INSOR has 30; both compilations aim to give status and protection to products worthy of merit or threatened with extinction. When pasteurisation is an integral part of the process, it is described, but where it is imposed by the health police, a good case is made in both publications for hanging on to cheese-making that works better without it. CASTELMAGNO, ROBIOLA, RASCHERA, BRA, and TOMA are some of the best known. *Toma piemontese* is one of the huge family of *tome* found all over northern Italy and adjoining countries, a cheese which is made following different methods, shapes, and sizes and varies from hard to soft. The DOC and DOP protecting the *toma piemontese* does not extend to the many versions of this cheese which are emerging and flourishing as small-scale production arouses more and more interest. The alpine *toma di Balme,* made from milk from the Valdostana race of cattle, fed on local pasture and hay, has unique procedures, poetically named implements (*bourcet, reirola,* and *iloira*), and special qualities. *Toma di Lanzo* is a valley cheese, from the Valle di Lanzo and its branches, pressed as well as drained, dry salted, and with a firmer texture. *Testun* is another alpine *toma* made from mainly sheep's milk in the province of Cuneo; there are many more. *Bra,* both hard and

soft, used to be the name for cheeses made all over the province of Cuneo and the commune of Villafranca, and brought down from the high mountain pastures to mature and later be distributed from the town of Bra; now a more rigorously defined cheese has its DOC and DOP, while a generic *bra* is also made on the plains. The hard version makes its way across to nearby Liguria for use in *pesto,* a reasonable substitute for pecorino. RICOTTA is widely made throughout the region, both ephemeral and keeping; a version called *seirass* has a characteristic shape from the conical fabric bag in which it drains; we can see this clearly in a still life of 1652 from Rome or Naples. *Castelmagno* is made in the province of Cuneo, and that from the commune of Castelmagno is particularly renowned. After heating, coagulating, draining, pressing, mixing, and more draining and pressing, it matures for some months in cool damp conditions, where in the fullness of time, blue-green veins occur, although this cheese is often eaten fresh and soft, before the *erborinatura* becomes apparent (a name derived from the regional word for parsley). *Robiola* is a soft fresh young cheese made in many areas of Piedmont; in the past it was dismissed as "women's work," but today is known and appreciated in many versions— robiola *Alta Langa,* robiola *d'Alba, di Ceva, di Cocconato, Robiola di Roccaverano*; in its classic form it is made from goats' milk, and is the only Italian goats' cheese to have its DOC, putting it up there with the best of the *chèvres,* depending on the race of animal, its perfumed, herby pasture, and the once despised domestic skills of the makers. The version of *robiola di Roccaverano* that has the disciplines and protection of a DOP can be made with a percentage of cow's milk, although many prefer to seek out those made from pure goat's milk. *Raschera* is made on lowlands and alpine areas in certain parts of the province of Cuneo, from a permitted mixture of the milk of cows, goats, and sheep, and is matured from three weeks to three months. The quality of the milk and the skills of the *margari*, artisan cheese-makers, have been enshrined in a DOP since 1996. *Bruss* or *brozz* was once a frugal way of using left-over bits of cheese, trimmed, cut up, mixed with fresh milk to induce fermentation, and left to become pungent and creamy, the process arrested by a slug of grappa when the pungency gets excessive.

PIG, *suino,* is the animal, and *maiale* is the word for both the animal and its meat, pork. The name *maiale,* from the Latin *maialis,* is said to derive from the goddess Maia, or Ceres, the great earth mother, symbol of life and fecundity, to whom a castrated boar was sacrificed. The dual nature of the pig is reflected in its other name, *porco,* hinting at its love of scavenging and wallowing in muck and its origins in dark dangerous forests, haunt of evil spirits and unknown terrors. Thus the word *porco,* close to *sporco,* dirty, can be used for the creature but has pejorative connotations, as in the expression *porca miseria,* and others too blasphemous to quote. Just as we use "swine" as an insult, so *porco* can be a derogatory expression, while *maiale* is classical, squeaky-clean, and respectable. Anthropologists and sociologists remind us of the transformation by ritual slaughter of the unclean swine into to the pure and edible meat, pork. Killed by cutting its throat, drained of the contaminating blood, scalded, scraped of its coarse hairy covering, gutted, washed, salted, spiced up, dried, and fermented, an almost sacramental transformation, the foul animal becomes benign meat. Perhaps. Written evidence for the semantic corroboration of all this is sparse. Platina was content with *suilla* and *porcus, porcellus*; the pagan connection with Maia would have been to his taste, but he did not make it. His contemporary Martino used *porco* and *porchetta.* By 1612, the ACCADEMIA DELLA CRUSCA had published its vocabulary, which

embodied their earnest endeavours to purify the Italian language, based on the Florentine dialect, and their definition of *maiale* as a male pig, *verro,* castrated between the age of six and ten months, came to be applied much later to all pigs. (The vocabulary used *porco* when talking of pigs in general.) An early sighting of *maiale* is in Antonio Nebbia's *Il cuoco maceratese,* Venice 1783; his contemporary the sybaritic, well-connected Corrado in Naples remained content with *porco* in 1778, while Francesco Leonardi's *Apicio moderno* of 1797 used *maiale*; a Roman, Leonardi was a cook of wide experience, having worked in Russia and Europe, with an interest in food history. Giovan Felice Luraschi, another much-travelled pragmatist, used the term *maiale* in his *Nuovo cuoco milanese* of 1829, and the Tuscan Giacinto Carena, whose *Vocabulario metodico della lingua italiana* of 1846 is based on pure Tuscan speech with a decided preference for that spoken in Florence, used *maiale* consistently. Vincenzo Agnoletti in Pesaro in the Marche wrote of *maiali,* while his contemporary Ippolito Cavalcanti, in broad Neapolitan, cooked *puorco.* Giovanni Vialardi, Piedmontese, has a chapter devoted to the pig, *maiale,* in his *Trattato di cucina* of 1854. But pigs were *porci* to Vincenzo Padula, who wrote with bitter realism of the conditions of the poor in Calabria in the 1860s in his periodical *Il Bruzio, "Il calabrese nasce tra i porci e le porcelle"* (the Calabresi are born between pigs and sows; Faccioli, 1962, p. 137). Pigs with wings are a common fantasy. *"Se il porco avesse l'ali, sarebbe simile all'angelo Gabriele,"* a Calabrian monk said (if the pig had wings it would be like the angel Gabriel), and the pigs who shared the miserable lives of the poor in Calabria remained unmolested, in spite of attempts by the municipalities to stop them wandering freely, scavenging, and tidying up as they went. In Abruzzo at the same time, pigs were members of the family, as Antonio De Nino described: *"Il signor porco"* was what the peasants called the *maiale*; sick baby pigs were bathed in the hot water the pasta was cooked in, dosed when unwell, and cherished as members of the family. On 17 January, the feast of Sant'Antonio Abate, a piglet, dedicated to that benign saint, protector of animals, which had been the cherished pet of the whole community for months, running freely from house to house, fed on demand, growing from *porco* to *porcone* and finally *porcaglione*, was raffled off, and the winner would later regale neighbours with a feast. The author uses the word *maialino*, but the Abruzzesi he describes used *porchetto*, and we can see the class distinction in the two words, the voyeurism of sociologist and man of letters, at a comfortable remove from the humble southern squalor he is describing.

Sant'Antonio Abate was not well served by his iconography—he took himself off into the desert, renouncing the unclean pleasures of the flesh, and early images of him show him trampling their symbol, a pig, underfoot; but later versions falsify the relationship with this fond creature, who appears to be enjoying his company and he eventually became transmogrified to patron saint of animals, whilst still renouncing greed and lust. And the pig could be comfortably seen not just as a useful and much-loved animal, but representing both filth and purity.

The Pig in Domestic Economy

The pig's value in the domestic economy of the poor is made clear in a saying from Calabria: *"Cu' ammazza lu porcu sta cuntentu'nu annu, cu'si marita sta cuntentu 'nu jornu"* (He who kills a pig is happy for a year, he who marries is happy for a day).

Or equally poignant: *"Allu riccu le mora la mugliere, Allu poveru le mora lu puorcu"* (The rich man mourns his wife, the poor man his pig; a loose translation).

In peasant society, being unable to afford to rear a pig was the ultimate stigma of poverty, and the distribution of cuts of meat at pig-killing time was a ritual of obligation, not only to helpers but to those less fortunate.

Breeds of Pig

Several breeds of pig are farmed in Italy today. It is unlikely that any of the ancient indigenous Mediterranean ones survive, having been overtaken in the course of the last two centuries by breeds from Europe and England bred for their rapid growth and admirable fecundity—the Large White from Yorkshire, and the prolific Landrace, crossed with other varieties, all of which have the advantage of growing fast and yielding plenty of flesh with not too much fat on it, a doubtful virtue but one pursued by the health police and the food industry to our gastronomic disadvantage. Changes in taste have created a demand for soft lean cured products like Parma ham, from lean creatures with large backsides, and for lean cuts of meat for rapid, low-fat cooking, but a recent awareness of the potential qualities of rare and ancient breeds and a renewed interest in traditional ways of rearing, feeding, and processing them, not to mention a better-informed attitude to animal fats, has opened up new markets, nourished by rampant gastro-tourism, a plethora of cookery schools, and a growing interest in rural culture. The *Razza Napoletana*, the *Nera Parmigiana*, the *Borghigiana*, and the *Mora Romagnola*, together with a breed derived from Chinese stock, are now replacing in some areas the ubiquitous Landrace and animals crossed with it. The *Cinta senese, Mora romagnola, Nero siciliano, Casertana*, and *Calabrese* are just some of the groups from which local breeds are being identified and snatched from the jaws of oblivion. Research institutes and a genetic bank are at work on this. Small farmers have been able to feed their rare-breed animals on something approximating the natural diet of snuffling scavengers, including acorns, chestnuts, nuts, and tubers, often in semiwild conditions. The *Cinta* race of semiwild pig, the *Brado delle terre del Montefeltro*, have a free-range diet supplemented with locally grown organic food. This produces a flesh and fat with an altogether different texture and flavour from the industrial pigs fed on a carefully controlled diet which includes maize, soya beans and their derivatives, and the whey and milk which is a by-product of the parmesan cheese production, and contributes to the smooth softness of Parma ham. This symbiotic relationship between cow and pig is not necessarily a good thing, and the combination of industrially reared animals crowded together in a small intensively cultivated agricultural area is seen by some as a potential environmental disaster, with the long-suffering terrain battered by pesticides and fertilizers and the waste products of the animals seeping into the earth and affecting the water table and the atmosphere. Many pigs are imported for fattening on an industrial scale in almost completely automated environments, where they are fed, watered, ventilated, medicated, and kept clean in conditions of clinical purity. The wild bands of pigs of the past may not have been healthy, well fed, or happy, but at least for better or for worse they were following their instincts. It is well known that pigs penned and confined for generations can revert in a twinkling to riotous, gregarious behaviour when accidentally let loose, but if one has seen a world-class Tuscan vineyard the morning after a going-over from a herd of wild pigs, one cannot get too sentimental about this tendency.

Market forces seem to be working in two directions—the growing worldwide demand for Italy's industrially produced salumi means that industrial production will increase, along with developments in animal husbandry, disposal of waste matter, refinement of the products, and more sophisticated marketing; at the same time, a growing awareness of the salumi made by small producers from rare-breed pigs fed and reared in ecologically harmonious conditions means that there is also a sophisticated market for these products, with appreciative and knowledgeable consumers

happy to pay the inevitably high prices. Homemade *insaccati* by private families do not always meet regional and European requirements for commercial distribution, but they circulate among discerning friends and relatives, and commercial products are judged against this discriminating benchmark. But the situation need not be seen in terms of black and white—when it comes to cheeses and salumi, Italy can offer superb examples from both the industrial and artisanal sectors.

Fresh Pork Meat

Fresh pork used to be considered a coarse and overrich meat, when the animals were bred and fed for a high yield of fat, but nutritionists today see it in a more benign light, as being as digestible as beef, and in many breeds just as lean—as lean as lamb and veal—and with fewer saturated fats. Rare-breed pigs have a different disposition of lean and fat and are appreciated all the more since we have come to an appreciation of the desirability of fat for both its flavour and texture. In the last few years, there has been a positive boom in cured pork fat like LARDO DI COLONNATO, and quite a lot of delicious copycat versions are now on the market. Cooking with lard was once renounced as seriously unhealthy but is now understood and tolerated by enthusiasts of regional cooking, even if it is hardly likely to replace the boring and often suspect "healthy" oils that are used instead. Well-soaked salt cod fillets, coated in batter and fried in lard are incomparable, and the *gnocco fritto* of Emila Romagna, once eaten with salami and washed down with sharp light local Lambrusco as a midmorning snack for manual labourers, are at their best when cooked in lard. Good to know that the higher burning point of pork lard produces fewer harmful oxidants. But health handbooks through the centuries have warned that pork is not for the sedentary, obese, or phlegmatic. Today, lean cuts are mainly roasted or grilled, and we rarely make the stews of medieval and Renaissance Italy—fat cuts cooked in rich broth with chunks of bacon.

The *arista* of Florence is a lean cut of loin with the rib bones sticking out (perhaps the name derives from *arìsta*, stalks of chaff or ears of corn?) larded with garlic, salt, fennel seeds, and rosemary, and roasted, preferably on a spit, and best eaten cold. Artusi thought the name *àrista* was a Greek word of praise uttered when the Council of Trent was deliberating in Florence in 1430, beguiled by this local delicacy, but Franco Sacchetti writes in one of his stories of *"avendo mandato un tegame, con un lombo, e con arista al forno"* (having sent to the [public] oven a dish with a loin [of pork] with its bones) a century before the Council of Trent. The Accademia della Crusca sat on the fence in 1612, endorsing both possibilities.

Another good way with a joint of pork is to cook it in milk; the milk tenderises the meat and gives it a rich buttery flavour; as it heats up and condenses during cooking, it coagulates and becomes grainy, and can be boiled down at the end of cooking to make a rich sauce. There are versions from many regions. From Reggio Emilia comes one in which a loin of pork is marinated in a cool place for up to 24 hours in a mixture of vinegar, olive oil, rosemary, garlic, and juniper berries. It is then cooked slowly in milk in a covered casserole for an hour or more, then uncovered and finished over a high heat to reduce the by now grainy sauce and colour the meat. Another version uses white wine for the marinade, and seasons the milk with sage, rosemary, and nutmeg.

A recipe from Anna del Conte for pork shin or shank, with its rind and connective tissues, braised slowly with garlic, onions, tomatoes, wine, and fresh herbs, shows how a cheap cut can make a rich and comforting dish. This particular joint, *stinco*, is now a by-product of the salumi industry, and can be bought precooked in vacuum packs to a different recipe.

Even richer is the outrageous recipe from Vittorio Metz, inspired by an anticlerical sonnet *"Er cardinale"* by Gioachino Belli; in this a boned loin of pork is sliced vertically, but not all the way down, so that the slices open like the pages of a book, and in between these is put a stuffing made from veal, fatty *prosciutto crudo*, *mortadella*, parmesan, bone marrow, egg yolk, and nutmeg all pounded together. The pages are closed, the joint wrapped in CAUL and cooked slowly in a casserole for several hours. Belli's cardinal ate a kilo and a half of this before going on the procession round the seven basilicas, the *sette chiese*, sitting comfortably in a coach, unlike the pilgrims who follow this penitential route on foot, and was not unsurprisingly overtaken by an attack of apoplexy in the middle of the night.

Pork in the Past

The ancient Romans enjoyed pig products, although some historians suggest that these were not of the highest quality. The Etruscans had wild pigs, and there have been speculations that they were interbred with domesticated animals introduced by the Romans, possibly the ancient *suino iberico*, the original Mediterranean pig, which in turn were said to have been supplanted by a wild breed brought by the Visigoths from their gloomy northern forests as the Dark Ages closed in on the once tranquil civilisation of Rome, symbolised perhaps by the wild hairy scavengers rooting where once stood villas with underfloor central heating; while now, in their turn, come the indolent northern barbarian Landrace, Euro-barbarians ousting earlier breeds (*see* SALUMI). These earlier semiwild pigs flourished in wood and scrub land in the past, but by the 18th century, methods of breeding and fattening were being introduced from England, where progressive stock breeding by wealthy landowners created pigs with big fatty carcasses. Later genetic manipulation has produced large lean animals, having tender flesh without much fat on it.

Vincenzo Corrado (1778, p. 30) wrote of pigs when they were still called *porco*:

Although the pig is a filthy creature it has the most tasty flesh and is the most delicious af all meat, and indeed without it all others seem insipid. For this reason it is widely used, not just in the kitchens of the great, but in those of humbler folk, and when it is lacking our palates are deprived of that essential spark. Since pork meat has innumerable flavours, it can be cooked and seasoned in an infinity of ways.

Corrado was referring to cured pork products as well as fresh meat, and this tradition of adding bacon, cured fat, and various other parts like cheek, belly, or udders, to other dishes persists and, as he said, gives many dishes that essential spark.

Scappi wrote of many cuts of pork as interchangeable with veal, and of the use of pork meat cut up or ground in sausages and meatballs as well as cured products. He gives a simple recipe for pork chops *alla Veneziana* which involves covering them with salt, crushed pepper, and ground coriander and leaving them under a weight for several hours before grilling slowly over a low heat. Martino has a recipe, *coppiette al modo romano*, for spit roasting pork or veal; the meat is cut into cubes more or less the volume of an egg, but the pieces ar not completely severed. They are seasoned with salt and ground coriander or fennel seeds, interleaved with thin slivers of bacon, and then threaded onto a skewer.

PIG'S BLOOD was not wasted in the past; during the slaughter of the animal, it was collected and made into many savoury and sweet dishes. After the ritual purification of the unclean swine, transforming it into the pale flesh and white fat of pork, purged of blood, scalded, and scraped, its blood had to be eaten quickly, so the first dish at pig-killing time was its blood—coagulated, seasoned, and fried in lard, or cooked in a pot.

The uncoagulated blood can be made into a variety of tasty dishes. We are used to the idea of blood sausages, or *boudin noir*, and not unsurprised by blood as a thickening for stews and soups, but intrigued by the traditional *sanguinaccio* of the south and the *migliaccio* of Emilia-Romagna and other areas, which in its many versions is a mixture of coagulated blood, with sugar, dried fruit, pine nuts, candied peel, herbs, and spices, and sometimes chocolate, either cooked in casings and then fried or grilled, or baked on a pastry base. This is a legacy from the past, when sugar was as much a catalyst as a sweetener and was used to enhance other flavours. Scappi made his *sanguinacci* in the shape of French *boudin noir*, using strained fresh blood before it coagulated, seasoned with spices (cinnamon, cloves, nutmeg, pepper, anise seeds, all ground), salt, sugar, diced pork fat, dried fruit, and cooked chopped onions, cooked carefully in water, then grilled or fried and eaten with mustard and other relishes. His *migliaccio* is a mixture as already mentioned but with the addition of some ginger, chopped fresh herbs, soft cheese, grated dry cheese, milk, and egg yolks; this is baked in a pastry crust, or on its own, or can be made into sausages.

It is not made industrially in this form, but small producers have an increasing following of enthusiasts, and output is increasing. Commercial products made with dried blood, a by-product of industrially reared pigs, is to be avoided. The blood of rare-breed animals fed traditionally, cooked at once, and eaten straight away is quite different. Quite often cooked grains like millet, rice, spelt, or emmer wheat, even pasta, are included along with other ingredients to give body without richness, and sometimes the product gets called after the grain—*migliaccio, sfarriciato.*

There are strict regulations about the consumption of perishable fresh pigs' blood, so most of it is treated industrially and used in animal fodder, and also goes into commercial salumi and cooked meats—part of the food chain we do not hear much about.

PIG'S EXTREMITIES, ears, snout, tail (*codino*), and trotters, were in the past essential for the making of jelly and gelatine, sweet and savoury. Both the medieval and the Renaissance table delighted in brightly coloured jellies and things set in jelly, shapes of jelly made in little moulds and used to decorate big setpieces, multicoloured and layered jellies, and all kinds of meat, fish, and fowl set in what we now call aspic. But some of these extremities were enjoyed in their own right, or went into stews and dishes which still survive in rich, hearty dishes like *casoeûla*, a dish associated with Milan, though versions of it are known all over areas once lived in by Celts—a rather vague theory, as any culture based on pig farming will have a copious supply of cheap cuts to make this dish from. Pigs' tails, ears, and trotters and rind are cut up and cooked with cheaper cuts of fresh pork like spare ribs and belly, and various cured sausages and bacon, with chopped onion, celery, carrot, white wine, and a generous amount of cabbage, softened perhaps by winter frosts or wilted in its own liquid, all in a dense glutinous broth. Seasonings are according to taste, as is the much-discussed inclusion of tomato paste, what kinds of sausage, whether the cabbage should be crisp or soggy, all happy topics to chew over whilst enjoying this with polenta and plenty of good red wine.

Trotters make fine ZAMPONE, and can also go into the BOLLITO MISTO of Emilia, which also includes NERVETTI. These boiled dishes (in fact simmered slowly) depend on a method of slow cooking in which the different cheap cuts enhance each other's flavour and provide contrasts of texture. At present, most of these bits and pieces go into processed animal food or the cheaper industrial meat products.

PIG'S FAT can be used in a number ways—fresh, cured, or treated to make lard. Confusion arises when we translate LARDO, which is cured back fat, salted and sometimes smoked, as "lard," which it is not. *Strutto* is the name for LARD: fat from all parts of the carcass, internal and external, rendered down—the delicious crispy bits left over are called *ciccioli*. *Sugna* is fresh pork fat, often used cubed in the SALAMI and fresh SAUSAGES made at pig-killing time. Fresh or cured hard fat from the back or the back of the neck can be cut into lardoons or strips for larding meat. PANCETTA is the fatty part of a pig's belly cured in salt, sometimes with herbs and spices, and occasionally smoked as well, sold flat or boned and rolled; both can be eaten raw in the same way as hams and salami. Bacon is what one might call it, but to use the watery, flabby bacon commercially produced in the British Isles in a recipe specifying pancetta would be disastrous, so it is best to seek out a slow, dry-cured bacon or Italian pancetta for Italian recipes using bacon. Pig fat is a delicious and indispensable cooking medium, and cooks are now emerging from the tyranny of the health police and using it in moderation for flavour and texture.

PIG'S HEAD, *testa di maiale*, can be cooked whole, split open, and boned, sometimes without parts like brain, tongue, snout, and ears, which are removed for use in other dishes. After long slow cooking with plenty of seasonings, the meat can be taken off the bones and assembled with the by now stiff jelly (from the skin and connective tissues)

and put into a mould or a cloth container. This will keep well, and is now usually bought ready-made in a commercial version, which is not always as tasty as the homemade one. *Coppa di testa* or *coppa di testa di maiale alla romana* is made as above, with the addition of pine and pistachio nuts and orange or lemon peel. *Coppa in cassetta* is a speciality of Liguria, which includes the tongue and some marsala. This is also found in northern Sardinia. There is a different version, also from Sardinia, in which parts of the head and raw meat cut off the bone are marinated with spices and flavourings, a local wine, and a little marsala, then cooked in containers, and left to cool under a weight.

PIG'S OFFAL, *frattaglie*, are variety meats—liver, lungs, spleen, kidneys, heart, brains, tongue, head, pancreas, sweetbreads, and testicles. They are either eaten, with much enjoyment, on their own, or go into various combinations of body parts, similar to the brawn and faggots and haslett of traditional British cooking. In Italy, regional versions of these are made and consumed locally but are not produced for the international market. Sausage from Molise, the *salsicce di fegato di Rionero*, is made from fresh pork meat, chopped up with soft fat, lungs, liver, and heart, well seasoned with salt, pepper, garlic, and chilli, matured for a few days, and hung for a week or so. Usually this sort of mixture needs to be eaten immediately. *See also* OFFAL.

PIGEON, *piccione*, has always been around in Italy, sometimes wild, sometimes in the barnyard or raised in coops, many in dove cotes, some fat and lazy from a nourishing agricultural habitat, some the scrawny urban *colombo di piazza*. *Piccione* is today the name for domestic birds; *colombo*, or *colombaccio* or *palombaccio*, are wild ones. Today's intensively reared domestic pigeons, squabs, are different from the leaner, more gamy wild birds, so recipes must be chosen with care. In the past, these various kinds of pigeon were held to be warming and invigorating, suitable for cold and frigid temperaments, and so needing to be cooked with fresh acidic fruit or herbs to mitigate their richness. Scappi recommended VERJUICE or unripe grapes in early summer, and quince or bitter orange at other times, and often stuffed pigeons and small fowl of all kinds, roast or stewed, with its liver chopped with *lardo*, wild fennel and spices, bound with raw egg. Corrado, inventive as ever, often flavoured pigeon dishes with basil (for some of his recipes, *see* BASIL). Artusi said that the happiest fate for pigeons was to be served up with peas, and gave a recipe in which they are browned with chopped onion and ham in butter and oil, then finished cooking in broth, which is then strained and the fat removed, and used to cook the peas, which are dished up around the pigeons. In another version, the pigeons are browned in butter with whole sage leaves and ham, finished in broth, and served with a squeeze of lemon or some verjuice. He quoted the saying *"Quando Sol est in leone / Bonum vinum cum popone / Et agrestum cum pipione"* (At the height of summer / take wine with melons / and verjuice with pigeons). Sound gastronomic and medical advice. The same use of an acidic counterbalance is in a recipe for *palombacci* from Ada Boni's *La cucina romana*, in which she cooks wild pigeons, jointed, slowly in a mixture of wine and vinegar, after browning them in chopped onion, celery, and carrot, with herbs (sage, rosemary, marjoram, thyme, and bay leaves).

A painting by CRIVELLI, *The Annunciation with Saint Emidius*, celebrating the granting of civic independence to the little city of Ascoli Piceno in the Marche, depicts some of the different kinds of dove or pigeon: the supernatural one, symbol of the Holy Ghost, appearing to the Virgin; those destined for the pot fluttering around their airy pigeon lofts; and the intrepid carrier pigeons, who brought the news of independence faster than human messengers.

PIKE, *luccio d'acqua dolce,* is a carnivorous ("*carnivoro atroce e crudele,*" said the physician Baldassare Pisanelli in the early 17th century) freshwater fish which can grow very big, well over a metre long, but is best to eat when of medium size, preferably from clear waters. Its wild and savage nature makes it unsuitable for farming. The flesh is compact, white, and delicious ("*tenere quanto è il latte,*" tender as milk, according to Pisanelli) but the bones can be a nuisance. It is usually cooked in a *court bouillon,* and then carefully skinned, filleted, and boned, and either marinated in a sauce of anchovies, capers, garlic, and onion or breaded and fried, as they do in Lombardy. Scappi quotes an old-fashioned French recipe in which pieces of the prepared fish are cooked fast in a mixture of white wine, vinegar, and sugar, then fresh butter is added, along with spices, and sometimes dried fruit or slices of quince or apple, a retro glimpse of the sweet/sour spicy food of the Middle Ages. He also explains a way of making *salcicconi* of skinned and boned pike flesh, chopped up with a little salt tunny, with whole fennel seeds, crushed pepper, and thyme, mixed with diced firm belly of tunny, diced cooked carrots, and slivered almonds. This "sausage" mixture is packed into a long thin linen container, boiled in red wine, smoked for a few hours, then taken out of its bag and grilled, basted with oil.

Maria Vittoria della Verde, a nun in 17th-century Perugia, stuffed her pike with rosemary, orange peel, garlic, and slivered almonds, wrapped it in branches of bay, and roasted it on a grid, over coals, basting it towards the end of cooking with a mixture of oil, must, or *agresto*; when done, the fillets were put in a pot with the drippings from the basting sauce and finished off with saffron, pepper, and cinnamon.

PINELLI, BARTOLOMEO

(1781–1835), was born in Rome, in Trastevere, but moved with his parents to Bologna, where he studied painting and sculpture, then after a bit of trouble with an actress, hurried back to Rome, where he spent the rest of his life. A revolutionary skirmish in his youth led to his flight into the mountains, where he took refuge with shepherds and bandits; his subsequent series of prints of bandit life, based perhaps on personal experience, show them eating and drinking as well as harrying distraught travellers, and might account for the desirable company of two very large mastiffs which figure in many of his self-portraits, draped in elegant attitudes in the studio, and suitably alert on expeditions to the wild surrounding countryside, where he made studies of picturesque local costumes and country folk, to sell later as engraved prints, the tourist postcards of the time. These, and Pinelli's studies of popular Roman street life, have more appeal than his subjects from Roman history and mythology, inspired by contemporary painters, which now seem stilted and sometimes mildly ridiculous. His pure neoclassical line and exquisite draughtsmanship are an ironic contrast to the raucous scenes he depicted with such skill and affection. The elegant profile of a market woman or vendor of pigs' heads does not belie the open-throated, very loud sounds of Roman street life bouncing off the close walls of narrow alleyways or echoing among the ruins and baroque monuments where stall-holders and food-sellers roared and wrangled with both dignity and abandon. This rich mix of classical antiquity and everyday life was, and is, what makes Rome so unique and wonderful. But Pinelli sensed that things were changing and that the people and places he knew and cared about would not survive the political and demographic changes of the time. He took his sketchbook and faithful mastiffs everywhere, drawing, recording, and carousing; perhaps the sense of impending change exacerbated the alcoholism which hastened his death. "Tutto finisce" is the melancholy motto on the studio wall in a pensive self-portrait. Pinelli's wife and family are shadowy presences, but his many scenes of women and children, for the most part confined to the house or courtyard, show understanding and affection. Toddlers were breast fed until they went to infant school, cherished, adored, strictly disciplined, and ended up as right tearaways—a constant theme in Roman life and art up to this day.

Pinelli's sense of place and character allow us many insights into street life and food. A *friggitore* fries fish, fresh and cool on a mass of decorative leaves, in a broad shallow pan over a wood-fired stove. His wife sells them from a neat table; there is an antique bas-relief in a crumbling wall in the background, while through an arch on the right are vistas of vineyards and ruins. Perhaps this was the feast of San Giuseppe on 19 March, superimposed on a pagan spring festival, and celebrated on the streets with fried fish and fritters. The *carnacciaro*, with his steelyard and his unappealing wares (scraps from the slaughterhouse) suspended gracefully from a yoke, strikes the attitude of an antique hero, watched by a pensive housewife, several importunate cats, and one of the artist's mastiffs in a setting of ancient arches and modern decrepitude. A wild and noisy scene of herdsmen driving fierce longhorned cattle, no longer able to pull heavy carts or ploughs, to the slaughterhouse, gives an insight into the length of time needed to tenderise the flesh of these long-suffering beasts in a *stufatino*—two hours at least, after a preliminary cooking in wine and aromatics. The carcasses hang in heroic profusion in the *macellaio*, a contrast to the pile of artichokes on the right, whose decorative fronds are curved and contorted like the curlicues on a baroque fountain. The familiar mastiff meanwhile quietly steals the purchase of a gossiping woman.

An outdoor meal in Testaccio, with the *fontanone* (Aqua Paola) in the distance and the dome of St. Peter's glimpsed beyond the wooded slopes, takes us back to Platina's praise of Martino "holding forth on gastronomic themes" in the taverns of Rome. The speaker is improvising verse, but he could easily have been holding forth about one of Martino's sauces, with gestures possibly anticlerical, like a ribald sonnet by Belli, Pinelli's contemporary, who mourned Pinelli's premature death in 1835, probably from alcoholism, with a sonnet, "*La morte der zor Meo.*"

The *cocomeraro* cries his wares, "*Taja ch'è rosso!*" (See that lovely red!) in front of a stepped display of slices of bright red watermelons, kept cool on fig leaves over a bed of ice, with St. Peter's in the background and the crowd enjoying his patter: "*Venite da Riccetto, che ve rinfresca er petto, cocomeri sotto er ghiaccio, una fetta un bajoccaccio*" (Come to Riccetto's to refresh the heart with chilled watermelon, a slice for a *baiocco*). The *gioncataro*, dressed in the shepherd's traditional sheepskin jerkin, sells little pots of junket freshly made that morning, a wholesome way of treating perishable milk to make a popular delicacy. (Freshly made ricotta, made from whey, not milk, is still prized today in Rome.)

PINE NUTS, *pinoli* (*pignoli*, *pinocchi*), are the seeds of *Pinus pinea*, the Mediterranean stone pine, indigenous to central and southern Italy, and enjoyed since prehistoric times. Where pine trees are plentiful and the cones can be gathered and dried, and the little nuts removed from their outer casings, they are used in abundance, but elsewhere they are expensive, and their ephemeral aroma can quickly turn to rancidity. Nuts with a dark patch at the narrow end are to be avoided, and a counsel of perfection is to taste before buying, if they are sold loose. The flavour is brought out by toasting or lightly colouring them in oil or butter; and when baked in biscuits or cakes, they add a fine texture and flavour. The Romans used them in sauces, soaked and pounded with pepper, cumin, celery seed, lovage, thyme, honey, vinegar, meat stock, and olive oil as a relish to have with cold meats—or as a final thickening for braised meats, pounded with peppercorns, lovage, or celery seed, cumin, thyme, honey, vinegar, and olive oil or butter, added to the dish half an hour before serving, and simmered gently.

The gentle slightly resinous flavour goes well in both sweet and savoury recipes. In *pinoccata*, once common all over Italy, now associated with Perugia in Umbria, pine nuts are stirred with chopped candied peel into a sugar boiled to the thread state, and then creamed, and spread to dry on wafers. A version of this is *torcolo*, a large circular *ciambella* made with pine nuts and raisins, flavoured with anise. Latini was using pine nuts in ice cream in 17th-century Naples, and this agreeable taste and texture has recently been revived by artisan ice cream–makers. In *confetti*, made the same way as sugared almonds (layer upon layer of sugar applied by swirling the nuts in sugar over a low heat), pine nuts met all the requirements for a healthy item in the final dessert course of a baroque banquet: combined with sugar they were digestive, aperient, and tonic, helpful for headaches, and aphrodisiac. Mattioli had earlier stressed these healthy qualities, if the pine nuts are soaked before use, and taken with sugar or honey—good for aches and pains, beneficial to the stupid or paralytic, clearing up ulcers, and coughs, and of considerable nourishment.

Umbrella pines embellish the landscape of Liguria, and their kernels enhance the cooking—in *pesto genovese*, they add richness and flavour to the basil, but in many other sauces and dishes, pine nuts add body and a delicate fragrance; pounded with marjoram, garlic, butter, and salt to make a creamy sauce to have with pasta; pounded in a mortar with garlic, anchovies, capers, and parsley, which is mixed with hard-boiled egg yolks, then slowly worked with olive oil to make a sauce for fish; these are just a few of the uses of pine nuts chronicled by the indefatigable Fred Plotkin, who perhaps more than any other writer conveys the impact of the aromas and visual delights of Liguria. His version of a dish of *funghi porcini*, boletus mushrooms, has them sliced and sautéed in butter and Ligurian olive oil, then finished with a little finely chopped onion, plenty of pine nuts, and some chopped parsley. A sauce for short pasta is made of baked ricotta (substitute for the local *bruss*, or for a fresh goat's cheese), mixed with pine nuts and rosemary heated in butter to bring out their aromas.

PINZIMONIO, AL. *See* ARTICHOKE.

PIRCIATI, *perciatelli*, a long, hollow PASTA, similar to *bucatini*, are bigger and so a good vehicle for sauces like the one described in the following excerpt from one of Andrea Camilleri's detective novels. *Pirciati ch'abbruscianu* are an example of a robust pasta intended to hold its own against a fiery sauce. They are inflicted upon Commissario Salvo Montalbano by the taciturn owner of a small trattoria, *Giugiù 'u carritteri*, 10 kilometres outside Montelusa. This badly lit, unprepossessing spot, down an almost impassable dirt track, seems unpromising, and Montalbano almost turns and leaves.

Then there arrived, gently, gently on the evening breeze, an aroma that dilated his nostrils: an aroma of genuine tasty food, the aroma of dishes cooked as the Lord intended. He hesitated no longer, but opened the door and walked straight in. There were eight tables, only one of them occupied, by a middle-aged couple. He sat at the first table he came to.

"Pardon me, but this is reserved," said the owner/waiter, a tall, potbellied chap in his sixties, clean-shaven but with a handle-bar moustache.

The Commissario obediently got up. He had his hands on the back of a chair at the next table when Handle-Bars spoke again.

"So's that."

Montalbano began to feel himself getting into a rage. Was he being wound up? Were they spoiling for a fight? Was this deliberate provocation?

"They're all occupied. You can sit there if you like," said the owner /waiter, well aware of the glint in his client's eyes.

He indicated a little side table, cluttered with cutlery, glasses, and plates, right next to the kitchen, source of those aromas that filled one up before even starting to eat.

"Fine," said the Commissario.

This was like solitary confinement, his face right up against the opposite wall, no way of seeing the rest of the room without turning right round in his seat. Why the hell should he want to anyway?

"If you really meant it [*Se se la sente:* an untranslatable use of *sentire*, which can mean "smell" or "understand"] you could have some *pirciati ch'abbruscianu,*" said Handle-Bars.

He knew what *pirciati* were, a special kind of pasta, but what could "burnt" mean? He didn't want to give the other the satisfaction of explaining how they were cooked, these *pirciati.* He just asked: "What do you mean by 'if you really meant it'?"

"Just what I said, if you really meant it," was the reply.

"I really meant it, don't worry, I really do."

The other shrugged and disappeared into the kitchen, came back after a while and stood staring at the Commissario. He was called away by the couple who wanted their bill. Handle-Bars gave it them, they paid, and left without saying goodbye.

"Greetings aren't exactly the house style," thought Montalbano, but remembered that he too had arrived without bothering to greet anyone.

Handle-Bars came back from the kitchen and assumed the same pontifical position.

"Ready in five minutes," he said. "Would you like the television on while you wait?'

"No."

Eventually a woman's voice from the kitchen: "Giugiù!"

The *pirciati* arrived. They smelled of heaven on earth. Handle-Bars propped himself up in the doorway and settled down to enjoy the floor show.

Montalbano decided to inhale the aroma and fill his lungs with it.

While he breathed in deeply the other said: "Would you like a bottle of wine by you before starting to eat?"

The Commissario nodded his head, reluctant to speak. A flask of wine appeared in front of him, a good litre of seriously heavy red wine. Montalbano poured himself a glass and then put the first forkful in his mouth. He choked, he coughed, tears came to his eyes. He had the clear sensation of all his taste buds on fire. He gulped down the glass of wine in one go, not exactly lacking in strength itself.

"Steady now, easy does it," advised the waiter/owner.

"But what's in it?" asked Montalbano, still half choking.

"*Oglio, mezza cipuddra, dù spicchi d'agliu, dù angiovi salati, un cucchiarina di chiapparina, aulive nivure, pummadoro, vasalicò, mezzo pipiruncinu piccanti, sali, caciu picurinu e pipi nìvuru"* [Olive oil, half an onion, two cloves of garlic, two salted anchovies, a spoonful of capers, black olives, tomato, basil, half a hot chilli, salt, peccorino, and black pepper]," recited Handle-Bars in a sadistic tone of voice.

"Christ," said Montalbano. "Who have you got in the kitchen?"

"My wife," replied Handle-Bars, going off to attend to three new customers.

Alternating forks of food with gulps of wine, groans of extreme agony and unbearable bliss ("could a dish really exist with the intensity of intense sex?" he asked himself at one point), Montalbano even had the courage to mop up the remaining sauce with a piece of bread, wiping his brow from time to time.

"What would you like next, *signore?"*

The Commissario recognised *"signore"* as a tribute to his prowess.

"Nothing."

"Quite right. The worst of *pirciati ch'abbruscanu* is that you lose all sense of taste till next day." (Camilleri, 1994)

PISANELLI, BALDASSARE,

active late 16th century, was a medical doctor in Bologna. Although he wrote philosophical works, a treatise on the plague, and a work on scorpions, he is best known to us for his *Trattato della natura de' cibi e del bere*, first published in Rome in 1583, with many editions in print throughout the 17th century. He described all known foodstuffs and beverages, with a summary of their virtues, *giovamenti*, and vices, *nocumenti*, and how to exploit the former and remedy the latter, with reference to Galen's theory of the four humours. This is complicated to explain, as each one of us is made up of our own individual mixture of these humours, and so must choose and season our food accordingly; nothing as simple as "We are what we eat"; more like "We should eat according to what we are," and so a good doctor had to get his head round the nature of all ingredients, how they are grown and prepared, and how they can be used to promote good health and cure bad health in a lot of different individuals. Pisanelli goes about this with more humour and clarity than one would have thought possible, with none of the tedious mystification of much medical literature, for he was writing for a comfortably off public with no medical knowledge, who needed simple advice and instructions. He organises the work in groups of different foodstuffs with an alphabetical index at the end, and each entry has a short section on the ingredient in question, when to get and cook it, its virtues, then its vices and how to mitigate them, where it comes in the different grades of humours, and what humoral temperament it is best suited to, followed by a paragraph of general information, with snippets of history, anecdotes, and gastronomical advice.

Some of the agreeable and tasty ways of cooking today still follow these ancient preventive or remedial precepts—cooking pulses, which *"fanno venire sospiri & inducono strane meditazioni"* (bring forth sighs and strange meditations) with something salty and fatty, plenty of pepper, and sour fruit juice, as in *piselli*, or broad beans, which *"genera molta ventosità, fa stupidi i sensi, e fa venire sogni pieni di travaglio e di perturbatione"* (generate much windiness, dull the senses, and call up dreams full of travail and perturbations) and so need to be cooked with salt and oregano, or, if dried, with plenty of pepper and cinnamon. Chickpeas, which are good for most of us—clearing the lungs, breaking up kidney stones—can be cooked with poppy seeds to lessen any bloating they might cause (as in hummus, which uses sesame seeds), or seasoned with pennyroyal and cinnamon. Onions, which are hot and dry, counterbalance cold and wet things, like cucumbers, so a salad of cucumber, dressed with onion, mint, tarragon, and rocket, all hot substances, and seasoned with pepper, is a good balance of humours. But onions change their nature when cooked and are mild and beneficial, especially when served with parsley. Pisanelli discards theories in his enthusiasm for the large sweet onions of Gaeta, which are sold on the markets in Rome, and when sliced and soaked in cold water become wonderfully sweet like pears. Garlic, which is hot and dry, is what you need with salads which are cold and wet; its harshness can be overcome by cooking, when it is good with other foods, or with oil and vinegar. Recommended for mariners, garlic mitigates the qualities of their often unpleasant provisions, helps ward off seasickness, and gives the rowers strength for their task. It purges the system of catarrh and inflammation of chest and throat, but taken in excess can trouble the sight and brain. Carrots and parsnips are hot and wet, and need to be well cooked and served with aromatic spices, oil, and vinegar, as a salad, or cooked in meat stews, where they are a pleasant addition. Lettuce is cold and wet, best eaten unwashed, that is, dry, as damp lettuce is indeed unpleasant, with its beneficial properties seeping away into the water and leaving the consumer prone to flatulence, weakened eyesight, and debility, whereas the crisp young leaves in the centre will ward off sunstroke, frenzy, and erysipelas, and when eaten at the end of a meal, as in the ancient World, will clear the head of alcoholic fumes and induce refreshing sleep.

It is a relief to come to capons, young, plump, and free-range, which have many virtues and no defects, and so are ideal food for old and young, sick and well, except for the fat and idle, who are crisply advised to eat smaller helpings and get more exercise. Ducks, on the other hand, are hot and wet and very rich, fine for the busy and active,

with a *stomaco di fuoco* (what we would call a cast-iron stomach), and best cooked with a stuffing of spices and aromatic herbs. His remarks on venison coincide with modern usage to a remarkable degree: the meat is best when young, preferably from a milk-fed or castrated animal, and best cooked well larded or with fatty meats, as in venison pasties and pies. His remarks confirm what we know of deer parks in the past, where deer were "farmed" and tended as a resource for pleasure and provender. The delicious tender meat from young animals in controlled semiwild conditions in various regions of Italy is today much sought after.

Pisanelli's dismissal of mushrooms as *"mai buoni in nessun tempo, a nessun età, & per nessuna complessione, perche fanno più danno che utile"* (never good, whatever the season, or for any age or temperament, because they are more harmful than useful) must have come from his professional experience of fatalities from poisonous varieties or apoplexy brought on by sheer greed. He grudgingly admits that field mushrooms and porcini can be good, and adds a tantalising mention of the practice in Rome and Naples of growing mushrooms on a special stone warmed with tepid water (*see* MUSHROOMS). Cooking them with unripe pears, basil, garlic, breadcrumbs, and *calamari*, seasoned with salt, pepper, and oil, mitigates their defects.

A final section on condiments has an entry on sauces, with a basic recipe using many aromatic herbs, including thyme, mint, and basil mixed with cloves, vinegar, toasted bread, and garlic, for those it pleases. This stimulates the appetite, helps digestion, and refreshes the stomach, and for those who find this an irritant, the juice of bitter oranges or verjuice will provide an antidote.

Today, Pisanelli is enjoyed more for his vivid little glimpses of everyday life than for his medical information, and the insights these give into aspects of 16th-century gastronomy that are not described in cookery books.

PISTACHIO, *pistacchio*, is the nut of the tree *Pistacia vera*, said to have been brought to Italy by the emperor Tiberius, and now grown in southern Italy and Sicily. As well as being an attractive green colour, when removed from their shell and skin, pistachios have a pleasant, distinct flavour, which makes them an ideal nut for nibbling, or using in stuffings and cured meat, like some versions of *mortadella*, or in ice cream. If made at home, starting from good quality pistachios, shelled, skinned (a horrid task), and pounded in a mortar, this ice cream will be a revelation, very different from the commercial varieties, often made with an industrial preprepared nut paste and synthetic flavouring and dyed a lurid shade of green—the quality reflected in the price. Vincenzo Corrado described a *sorbetto* made with pounded pistachios and a sugar syrup flavoured with zest of citron, but no milk or cream. He also used the nuts in *confortini*, fondant sugar sweets, the sugar solution beaten to a soft whiteness with ground pistachios; and in comfits, where the nuts are painstakingly covered with layer upon layer of a hard sugar coating. For a tart or pie filling, he mixed blanched and ground pistachios with egg yolks, beaten whites, sugar, butter, and cream, flavoured with candied green lemons and citron. A light cake was made by pounding peeled pistachios with butter and some candied citron peel, mixing with egg yolks and sugar, folding in beaten egg whites, and baking in a buttered tin lined with breadcrumbs, served with an icing coloured bright green with spinach juice. A sharp relish was made with pistachios pounded with leaves of spinach beets (perhaps blanched), candied citron peel, sugar, cinnamon, and verjuice. Pistachios reinforced the colour of a green herb relish, where pounded basil, marjoram, and thyme were mixed with breadcrumbs soaked in orange flower water, flavoured with sugar and spices. A boned turkey is stuffed with a forcemeat of minced veal, strips of Parma ham, capers, olives, anchovies, *bottarga*, pistachios, tarragon, and *malvasia*, simmered gently for five hours, then lapped in pancetta and ham, covered in pastry, and baked, to be served cold as a pie. The visual effect must have been beautiful, with the pale veal a foil to the pink ham, black and green olives, pale green nuts, the murky roes, and flecks of tarragon. Boned pigeons got a similar treatment, with a delectable stuffing of basil (Corrado's favourite herb for pigeons), pistachios, veal forcemeat, and bone marrow; after browning in butter and spices, the little birds were laid on a bed of minced veal, covered with a *salpicon* of sweetbreads, encased in pastry, cooked in the oven, and served warm as an entrée. A similarly delicate stuffing for boned pigeons is of egg yolks, cream, butter, parmesan, raisins, and chopped pistachios; fried in butter and finished in a clear broth, the birds are then covered in breadcrumbs and fried, and served with *crema di pasticchio*, a custard sauce made with egg yolks, milk, flour, and peeled pistachios pounded with candied citron peel; a pale green delicate effect on the tender young squabs. A stuffing for sole is made of cooked flesh from another fish, pounded with capers, anchovies, herbs, and pistachios; this is placed on one fillet, is covered with the other, the whole coated in butter and breadcrumbs and baked in the oven.

A Sicilian concoction with the name *fedde del cancelliere* (chancellor's buttocks), a sort of visual pun (Simeti, 1989, p. 232), contains roasted and chopped pistachios, embedded in a cooked semolina mixture, made into a sort of rounded patty, deep fried, split open, and filled with slices of a sweet corn-flour cream. A more subtle way of adding colour and flavour is described in Simeti's account of a dessert called "triumph of gluttony," a speciality of Sicilian convents:

If its outward appearance was touchingly naïve, within the golden stripes of *pan di spagna* framed bright green chips of pistachio and greeny-gold cubes of glistening *zuccata*, which floated in the pale *biancomangiare* like so many tesserae from the mosaic wall of an Arab-Norman chapel. This harmony of colour was echoed by equal sophistication in the balance of the flavours: the *zuccata* was a miracle of delicacy; the pistachio was present yet not obtrusive; the faint suggestion of jasmine gave context to an affirmation of stick cinnamon, crushed in a mortar and sprinkled over every layer. (Simeti, 1989, p. 251)

PIZZA is a flattened lump of bread dough, usually round, flavoured with whatever comes to hand—oil, cheese, herbs, or onion—and cooked in a hot wood-fired oven. Its ancestors, with a confusing variety of names, were made in ancient Greece, were enjoyed by the Etruscans, were part of daily life in ancient Rome, and have been available up and down the peninsula throughout history. The name we use today is the Neapolitan one. The pizzas of Naples, Rome, and Sicily, and the *focaccia* of Liguria and *schiacciata* of Tuscany, have an inspiring heritage: "a platter of bread topped with the provender of the countryside and mixed with real passion and imagination," described in unpedantic detail by Carol Field, who inspires us to cook as well as eat them (1985, p. 272). The name *pizza* is of uncertain origin. When Scappi used it in a recipe *Per fare torta reale di polpa di piccioni, da Napoletani detta pizza di bocca di Dame*, he is describing a pie or tart very like today's Moroccan *bstilla*, not a pizza as we know it. When Scappi wrote about *pizza*, he described it as the Neapolitan word for what we would call an open tart, a border of rolled puff pastry surrounding a flat pastry base, with all kinds of toppings. He

also described a *pizza sfogliata*, which was made from a rich eggy pastry, rolled thin and anointed with liquefied butter or lard, sprinkled with dried fruit, sugar, and spices, rolled up, and then wound round itself in a spiral like a snail shell or a "labyrinth," perhaps similar to the *gubana* of Friuli, which is based on a bread dough, not a pastry, and laced with grappa.

The *pizza napoletana* as we know it began as fast food in the 19th century and has now taken over the world—floods of red gloop and synthetic cheese over preformed industrial pap masquerading as the original street food of Naples. This is, however, a relatively recent phenomenon, and Neapolitans have every reason to defend with pride their authentic version; they will take you by the hand to the very spot where the one and only genuine Neapolitan pizza is resplendent in its uniqueness, and then round the corner to an equally impressive establishment with similar claims. The nature of the dough and the way it is cooked, soft with a raised *cornicione* round the edge to contain the melting topping, the toppings themselves, and the seasonings all show a great restraint. The simplest of all, the *pizza alla Napoletana*, has a topping of fresh or tinned Marzano tomatoes (chopped, or made into a sauce), with finely sliced garlic, dried oregano or fresh basil, salt, and olive oil. The addition of anchovies makes it *alla marinara* (according to some). The *Margherita*, named for Queen Margherita, who in 1889 came with King Umberto I from the bleak northern wastes of Savoy to visit the dazzling southern regions of their new united Kingdom of Italy, and was said to be enchanted by the invention of Don Raffaele Esposito, who tactfully constructed a pizza resplendent with the national colours—red tomatoes, white mozzarella, and green basil leaves, a good move for both parties: free publicity for one and a great gesture of national unity.

In Rome, the dough is thin and crisp, baked in a six-foot-long strip, with the simplest seasoning of olive oil and salt, or perhaps some tomato and mozzarella, brushed with oil, and sold in cut-up portions. Although the argument that it should really be cooked by professionals in a wood-fired oven is convincing, pizza is so easy and cheap to make at home that sending out for a far from cheap imitation of the real thing is something to think twice about.

PLATINA, BARTOLOMEO SACCHI (1421–1481), was known by the Latinised version of the name of his birthplace, Piádena, a small town near Cremona in Emilia. He was one of the most charismatic and catastrophic personalities of the Italian Renaissance, with a lively wit and gift for friendship, combined with a wild, tempestuous temper, prone to jealous rages and outbursts of violence. It says a lot for his nice side that Platina's many devoted friends rallied round him in times of trouble. He was from a poor family about whom we know nothing, although we learn that he had siblings who benefited from the connection later on. After some years as a freelance soldier of fortune—for hire by the many warring condottieri of the time, one of them Francesco Sforza, later Duke of Milan and employer of the cook Martino—in his twenties, he found a humble position at the court of the Gonzagas in Mantua, while studying with Ognibene da Lonigo, tutor to the children of Duke Ludovico and his wife Barbara of Brandenburg. He later took over the post, staying in Mantua for the next seven years. His patrons encouraged Platina to go off and study Greek in Florence, where he made friends with the leading humanists there, and perhaps met the distinguished humanist Poggio Bracciolini, elderly by then, in whose house, or that of his son, Platina enjoyed one of those simple but exquisite dishes of the new cuisine (offspring of the New Learning of the Renaissance), chicken with verjuice (Platina 1998, pp. 276-27). He

drops the distinguished name Poggio into his version of Martino's recipe—chicken pieces fried in oil with bits of bacon, when golden smothered with some pitted unripe grapes, with a little white wine, and served, when done, with a scattering of fresh herbs. I mention this at length because it is not by chance that this dish was served in the house of the pioneer of a similar simplicity and elegance in handwriting, the humanist script, described as *nitida et clara*, neat and clear, in the same spirit as the *puro e senza ornato*, pure and without ornament, in Cristoforo Landino's description of the fashionable style of painting associated with Masaccio and, in architecture, with Alberti. Thus we have quite literally on a plate the essence of Florentine humanism, tasted and later recreated by the eager, pushy young scholar—simplicity, purity, and balance, a long way from the complex architecture, calligraphy, and gastronomy of the international gothic style. Platina lapped up this intoxicating mixture of erudition and hedonism in the company of like-minded enthusiasts, and would go on to similar combinations of food, friendship, and erudition in Rome.

He moved there in 1462, probably to join his old pupil Francesco Gonzaga, who had just been made a cardinal at the tender age of 16. Topographically, Rome was a sprawling and beautiful mixture of ruins, villas, and palaces, interspersed with orchards and vineyards, with intellectual life focussed on the political and cultural activities of the papal court; very different from the neat, compact, modern city of Florence, with its network of narrow streets and public spaces, and its arguably more open system of government.

Two centuries later, another tempestuous, ambitious northerner, CARAVAGGIO, came to Rome and enjoyed a similar lifestyle, veering from the elegant company of sophisticated worldly prelates to the rough trade and violent brawls of the street life.

Platina found work in the College of Abbreviators, compilers of papal briefs, and soon made friends with congenial colleagues who shared his enthusiasm for classical antiquity, especially Pomponio Leto, whose associates become known as the Roman Academy, notorious for their interest in aspects of life in ancient Rome, and of interest to us because of their enthusiasm for ancient gastronomy. (They knew the work of Apicius, and collected references to food in Latin and Greek literature.) It was not difficult for their detractors later to turn innocent excursions to the catacombs into subversive plots against the authority of the pope.

It would be hard to imagine a less congenial venue for an orgy than the catacombs, but Platina certainly found plenty of opportunities for roistering in the taverns and eating-houses of Rome, joined by his friend Martino, cook to the patriarch of Aquileia, the hedonistic warrior-priest and friend of the young cardinal, Francesco Gonzaga. As a guest at Cardinal Gonzaga's villa at Marino in the Castelli Romani, the hills outside Rome, Platina would have had the leisure to discuss Martino's skills in a more refined atmosphere than the raucous Roman taverns. Martino had already been compiling a recipe notebook, setting out the elements of his new cuisine, and it was around 1462 that the two friends must have decided to collaborate on a joint venture, with Platina providing the theoretical approach and Martino the hands-on version. Bartolomeo Sanvito, the Paduan friend and colleague of Platina, the greatest calligrapher of the time, wrote out the presentation copy of Martino's manuscript, dedicated to Trevisan, in a script whose clarity and beauty are worthy of the contents. Meanwhile, Platina started work on his version, *De honesta voluptate et valetudine*, a title almost impossible to translate, but for which I venture to suggest "Of virtuous pleasure and good health"—gastronomy in the context of a healthy and virtuous lifestyle, a concept that must have raised a few eyebrows among his louche companions. But what began as a *jeux d'esprit* became therapy,

when a year later Platina was arrested and thrown into the dungeons of Castel Sant' Angelo, to be rescued by Cardinal Gonzaga and whisked off to his villa in Marino to recover, and be kept out of further mischief.

The sequence of events is set out lucidly in Mary Ella Milham's account of Platina's life and work in the introduction to her translation of his text (Platina, 1998) and more recently by Bruno Laurioux in his investigation of the intellectual and gastronomic background to *De honesta voluptate*. It seems that after the death of Pope Pius II, a friend of humanism, the new pontiff, Paul II, an intolerant bigot, reorganised his secretariat to get rid of the stroppy *abbreviatori*, who raised an intemperate protest, headed by Platina, whose rage and vituperation led to his imprisonment. Some of that rage smoulders in his text: the introduction to the section on poultry pours scorn on the PEA-COCK, symbol of wealth and power, and has a blistering attack on those who rise to power by dubious means (a reference to the murky procedures which got Pietro Barbo elected to the papacy as Paul II) and the vulgar tastes of his hangers-on, for whom the gaudy, and inedible, peacock and pheasant might have been invented. Platina and Pomponio had often dined on onions and garlic, simple vegetarian fare, together with their (named) companions in obscurity and poverty. (This unwise name-dropping had to be rectified by erasing the names of some of them from later versions of the text.) The section on tarts and pies has an equally rebarbative reference to the extravagant tastes of the undeserving rich, pointing out, quite rightly, that the mainly cheese and vegetable fillings of open tarts is a long way from the fancy work with meat and expensive ingredients favoured by sycophants and social climbers.

Platina, deprived of job and income, totally dependent on his Gonzaga patron, concentrated on writing and scholarship, but Paul had not finished with the Roman Academy, and in 1468 he arrested most of them for reasons not entirely clear—his suspicions of their pagan frolics and subversive behaviour combined with rumours of a plot against his life were enough to provoke imprisonment and torture. After his release and recuperation, with the generous support of the Gonzagas, Platina resigned himself to a bleak future, with no hope of resuming his career in the papal court. He wrote a lot—a genealogical history of the house of Gonzaga and preparatory work for his *Life of the Popes*—and his *De honesta voluptate* had its first appearance in print some time in 1470. A passage from it now seems prophetic—Platina warned of the dire consequences of eating melons on a full stomach, of how they are best eaten at the start of a meal, with perhaps a glass of decent wine, and relates with awe the prowess of the emperor Albinus, who in one sitting consumed 100 Campanian peaches and 10 melons from Ostia. It should have come as no surprise when, late one sultry August night in 1471, Pope Paul retired to the Vatican gardens, intemperately quenched his thirst on too many melons, and expired at once of apoplexy.

The new pope, Sixtus IV, treated Platina well, eventually making him librarian of the new Vatican Library in 1475, where his gifts made him an outstanding administrator, and his escape from financial constraints left him free to enjoy the luxury of a house on the Quirinal.

The fact that *De honesta voluptate* became a massive best-seller bewilders academic historians, concerned with other aspects of Platina's output, but gives much joy to food-lovers, who appreciate not only the elegant vehicle for Martino's recipes but the intellectual respectability this confers on what had been regarded as a low occupation. The work circulated in manuscript from 1468 onwards; eight copies are known, and the first printed edition was in 1470, followed by nine in Italian before the first French edition in 1505. His friend Martino's cookery book was also circulated in printed editions for almost a

century. Laurioux thinks heads of households and stewards, as well as men of letters, would have referred to it for guidance in planning menus, banquets, and domestic or festive meals, but not cooks, who learned their trade on the shop floor and knew what to do without having it spelt out. We sometimes wish that Martino and Platina had told us rather more in the way of quantities, timing, and so forth, but once the style is grasped, it is a pleasure to follow their narrative style of recipe, a succinct summary of ingredients and methods, leaving a clear impression of how the dish ought to look and taste. We cannot share the puzzlement of academics, for Platina is one of us, his tastes and temperament familiar—we identify with the combination of intelligence, arrogance, foul-mouthed bad temper, and voluptuous enjoyment of the pleasures of the table. He and Martino were first in a long line of scholarly, combative, eloquent, and accomplished cooks. Martino's easy good humour and Platina's prickly egocentricity made the perfect vehicle for the new cuisine, and their work, as fresh today as it was then, is as enjoyable for the food they write about as for its historic importance.

Milham's comments on Platina's rather clumsy style in *De honesta voluptate* are understandable. His language lacks the eloquence of later work; perhaps the colloquial style of Martino, and his "shorthand" versions of recipes, was hard to render into Latin, but the editorial decision to make a literal, word-by-word translation of this does him no favours. It makes for a stilted read. Perhaps someday a more adventurous rendering will convey something of the assurance of Martino's original, while a closer attention to contemporary culinary practise might clarify some of the terms.

PLUM, *susina, prugna, Prunus domestica,* is a drupe, and there are many of them, a huge family of widely different fruit, including cherries, peaches, and apricots, most of which are eaten fresh as a dessert, or poached with wine and spices. Some varieties originated in Asia and Europe, and along with those from China and Japan, *Prunus simonii*, adapt themselves well to conditions in Italy, grown commercially in Campania and Emilia-Romagna. Wild drupes were used in the past to flavour syrups and liqueurs, and all plums were used medicinally in the past, to cure fevers and dysentery. The sharp sloe and the bigger bullace, too acidic to eat raw, are macerated in alcohol, familiar to us as sloe gin. A distilled version, *slivovice*, with its woody bitter almond notes, is found in the north, where Friuli partakes of cultural influences from Austria and the Balkans.

Plums can be dried (prunes), *prugne secche*, and eaten soaked then simmered in wine, or used in tarts and desserts. Scappi has a version of what we know as summer pudding, made with sweet and sour cherries or other drupes, plums of various kinds, hard peaches, simmered with sugar and spices and enough wine to draw out the juices, then poured over slices of toast or bread fried in butter. A similar *suppa* is made with dried fruit, prunes, or raisins. There were numerous sauces at that time using the bulk and flavour of dried fruit, now only a memory, although *mostarda di frutta*, dried fruit, cherries, and prunes, went into a stuffing for stewed gosling.

POLENTA was originally the name given to any pulse or grain boiled to a mush or porridge and seasoned with herbs, cheese, bacon, or whatever was available. These dishes still survive, but today polenta is made from maize flour of different grades, some prepared in the form of "instant polenta," which cooks in 5 or 10 minutes but is not as good as the normal kind, which needs to cook for 45 minutes to an hour, stirred all the time. This is not too arduous when one is doing other things at the stove, but a version

from Anna del Conte explains how the mixture is cooked for 15 minutes, then covered with foil and baked in the oven for 45 minutes more. Devotees of really long cooking allow the process to go on for hours on a heat low enough to avoid sticking and burning, thus avoiding the chore of continuous stirring, with delicious results. Polenta can be firm, so that when poured out onto a board, in the traditional manner, it will set so that it can be cut into slices or wedges and grilled or fried, as accompaniment to rich dishes of salt cod, and game stews. A looser version can be served as a purée, sometimes enriched with butter or parmesan. Baked polenta, layered with melting cheese such as *fontina* or *toma*, or with butter and parmesan, perhaps bits of cooked sausage, or mushrooms fried with garlic—the possibilities are endless—is a wonderful dish and makes a meal in itself with a green salad.

This is comfort food of a high order, and one can understand how it came to do the damage it did. Cheap to grow and easy to keep and cook, maize, *gran turco* ("foreign grain," when Turkish meant exotic, from far away) originated in the New World (although there is the possibility that maize found its way to other parts of the world before Columbus set out), was being cultivated in the north of Italy from the 16th century onwards, and was well established by the 18th century. It became the staple food of the poor in many areas, and with it came the deficiency disease pellagra (from the Italian *pelle agra*, chapped skin). What did not come from its original home in Mexico was the technique of nixtamalisation, which must have been empirically developed over centuries. The grains were boiled with lime or wood ash, softening the outer skin, which could then be removed. After rinsing the cooked grains well and then grinding them on a stone *metate*, a nutritious mash, drained to form a dough, *masa*, was made into tortillas, baked on a *comal*, and eaten with an almost nutritionally perfect range of things—

beans, squash, chillies, and tomatoes, to get a complementary balance of vitamins, protein, and other nutrients, which the starving peasants of northern Italy never achieved on their diet of untreated corn and very little else. The alkaline lime or ash released niacin, an amino acid in the grain which enhanced the protein content. Together with the nutritional contents of beans (niacin, tryptophan, and lysine) and the vitamin C in chillies, the traces of calcium in the lime, and whatever minerals get rubbed into the *masa* as it is ground, the Maya and Aztec rural poor were in better shape than the sharecroppers in 19th-century Lunigiana quoted by Camporesi: "*Polenta di formenton, acqua di fosso, / Lavora tu, padron, che io non posso*") (Ditchwater and polenta, it is true, / Leaves me less fit to work, my lord, than you).

Regional recipes today go some way to correct the balance: a seasoning of cured back fat, LARDO, pounded to a cream with garlic, parsley, and pepper, from Lombardy; from the Appenines above Reggio Emilia, a rich sauce of cooked *borlotti* beans, diced pancetta, tomatoes, and onions softened in the bacon fat is stirred into the cooked polenta before serving. Now that polenta is no longer a malign subsistence food, it is enjoyed by connoisseurs who eat it with things that give a good nutritional balance, and cultivate the rituals of making and serving, the different implements deployed and the slow clockwise stirring, which is alleged to enhance flavour and texture as the mixture makes contact with the hot sides and base of the traditional iron pot, as the meal softens, and the golden mixture thickens, the aroma perfuming the air. The subsequent grilling or toasting with intense heat intensifies the flavour, and the almost charred bits contrast with the soft creamy interior. As a catalyst, bringing out the taste of other foods, polenta is a delight, with either a firm texture or a melting sloppiness, depending on local tastes or the dish it accompanies—firm for mopping up the rich sauce of the *baccalà* of

northern regions; runny for the rich meat stews of central and southern Italy. Artusi mentioned the tricky way of cooking little stewed game birds in a mould lined with stiff polenta, while the more traditional treatment is to surround a steaming mass of polenta with small birds spit roasted with bacon and sage leaves. Layering lozenges of firm polenta in a dish, with a melting cheese like *fontina* and generous lumps of butter, or with fried or roasted sausages, skinned and mixed with a rich tomato sauce, makes a substantial family meal. The *bordatino* of Pisa is a version of the many dishes evolved by mariners, using stocks of dried beans and polenta, with the addition of anything else that came to hand—dried or fresh fish, and once back home on land, vegetables, especially *cavolo nero*, and a good rich stock. The polenta is cooked in the liquid from the stewed dried beans, which are puréed and added to the mixture. The *infarinata* of Garfagnana in Tuscany is similar, sometimes using the broth in which a nice rich *cotecchino* has been cooked, an assortment of vegetables softened in *lardo*, the dried or fresh beans, and finally the maize flour.

POLPETTE

POLPETTE can mean MEATBALLS, or balls of pounded fish flesh, or vegetables, fried or poached, sometimes finished in a sauce. The name derives from *polpa*, which can mean the lean flesh of meat, or pulp of fruit. In the past, *polpette*, as described by Martino, were not meatballs but were made from strips of lean meat, trimmed of fat, seasoned with spices and herbs pounded up with cured pork fat, rolled up, and cooked on a spit, similar to today's *involtini*. Martino's version of today's *polpette* were called *tomacelli*, made from liver, parboiled, and then grated and pounded with chopped pork belly, herbs, cheese, and eggs, made into little balls and wrapped in caul fat; Platina called them *omentata*, which he got from *omentum*, caul, in his Latin version of his friend's recipes, which he felt was more suitable than the colloquial *tomacella*. He would have known from his reading of *Apicius* that *omentata* were meatballs, served with a relish of fish sauce, wine, lovage, oregano, and pepper (Apicius, 2006, p. 147). There is a modern version from Liguria, *tomaxelle*, a sophisticated mixture which includes veal sweetbreads, minced veal, dried porcini mushrooms, marjoram, spices, cheese, eggs, breadcrumbs, and garlic, mixed to a smooth paste and spread over slices of thin veal, which are then rolled up and fried in butter.

In the 19th century, Milan was renowned for its *polpette*; RAJBERTI quoted a local notable who said if all the *polpette* he had eaten in his life were assembled together, they would pave the streets of Milan from the Piazza del Duomo to the Porta Orientale. But, confusingly, these *polpette* were not meatballs, but the many versions of a savoury stuffing enclosed in strips of meat or vegetables. The renowned meatballs of Milan were called *mondeghilj*, and although the name derives from *albondigas*, Spanish for meatballs and a reminder of alien rulers and past hardship, 19th-century writers on the cuisine of Milan hasten to inform us that these are not the same as the *polpett de la serva* or the *polpett de verz*, a stuffing enclosed or rolled up in something, meat or vegetable, or the *involtini* of the rest of Italy, or the *crochette* of the French. Rajberti was using *polpette* as an insidious form of resistance to the Austrian occupation of Milan, for by serving this humble domestic dish at posh dinner parties, the host and guests could wordlessly and with impunity thumb their noses at the hated foreigners. It was customary to claim that the *polpett de la serva* were so good that the most foul-mouthed unreliable slattern would always remain a treasured member of the household because of her *polpette*.

POMEGRANATE, *Punica granatum, melagranata, melagrana*, is spectacularly

beautiful; its outer skin is tough and leathery and varies from shades of red, pink, and gold to dull yellow, and the opened fruit is bursting with seeds with a bright red or pink covering of sour/sweet juice—a gift for still life painters, who enjoy the voluptuous appearance, and for cooks, who relish both the decorative qualities and the fruity astringency of the seeds. Eating pomegranates from scratch, as it were, can be a messy business, extracting the seeds from the bitter membranes that contain them, coping with the abundant juice, and wondering what to do with the pips. A Renaissance kitchen had the manpower to extract the seeds (offered sprinkled with sugar towards the end of a meal) and express the juice, saving guests a chore, and used the bright juice in sauces and relishes, and the red globules to decorate pale food like BIANCOMANGIARE and boiled fowl. Scappi served a dish of stewed and boned goats' heads, covered in *biancomangiare*, decorated this way. The use of the juice to give a fruity astringency to sauces in the past survives in recipes from Venice and Vicenza for *paeta*, roast turkey with pomegranate sauce. The juice can be boiled and reduced to a thick syrup (as in many Middle Eastern cuisines) or taken as a refreshing drink. Pomegranates are sweet, sour, or a mixture of the two, and the fruit needs to be selected to suit the use you intend; the sweet/sour kind would be best for a sorbet made with pomegranate juice, sugar, and lemon juice.

Pomegranate was revered for its youth-preserving qualities long before the word "antioxidant" even existed. (Shutterstock)

Most early writers tell of the large amounts of juice pressed, filtered, and stored in bottles for everyday use, and Mattioli dwells on the beauty of the flowers, sometimes brought from abroad, to delight the citizens of Venice. He mentions the close affinity pomegranate bushes have with myrtle, and how they bring out the best in each other, often planted together for their decorative effect.

The high tannin content of the dried and ground outer skin was useful in curing leather, but mainly used in medicine.

The rich red juicy seeds bursting from a ripe fruit made the pomegranate an ideal symbol of fecundity, as seen in Renaissance religious art. But by the mid-17th century, Giovanna Garzoni produced for the Grand Duke Cosimo an astonishing, almost surreal, portrait of a larger-than-life pomegranate on a white ceramic dish, looming out of a rocky background, in which all notions of space and distance seem to dissolve, and a dragonfly, two chestnuts, and snail merely emphasise the uncanny aura of the fruit, without straining to impart symbolic messages.

From closely observed fruit portraits in 17th-century Florence to a cacophony of ripeness and abundance in baroque Rome, where Christian Berentz, in his works for the count Pallavicini, depicted pomegranates overflowing with rosy seeds alongside peaches, apples, grapes, melons cut open to reveal their juicy orange interiors, and watermelons hacked up into black-studded blood red chunks. In the foreground of an exuberant larger-than-life painting of a young woman in the garden of a Roman villa, balancing an overflowing basket of fruit on her head, he places whole and bursting pomegranates in contrast to dark grapes, glowing peaches, pink as the maiden's cheeks, figs, roses, towering hollyhocks, and a white rabbit nibbling at the display—here everyday fruit are celebrated among luxury goods spread nonchalantly over a stone balustrade, white linen crumpled on an oriental carpet, pastries and a peeled orange on a silver dish close to a tray of Venetian glasses, teetering far too close to the reaching girl, with the pomegranate a pivotal point of the composition. (This is now in the Capodimonte Gallery in Naples.)

PONTORMO, JACOPO CARUCCI, IL (1494–1556), kept a diary during the last years of his life, on a few folded sheets of paper. In it he records work done on a massive commission to decorate the choir of the church of San Lorenzo in Florence with frescos, an arduous task, physically and emotionally, and his laconic notes and sketches record what he did in the space of a day (the paint had to be applied while the surface was wet, *fresco* or fresh, and so the progress of the work was as much a matter of rational calculation as mood or inspiration). Pontormo also jotted down what he had to eat most days, and a bit about his state of health. This is helpful information about the everyday diet of an elderly and frail but determined painter, with comfortable means, and of a solitary disposition, preoccupied by the effect of the moon and weather on his health and states of mind. How on earth it got to be described as "obsessive and deeply neurotic" by art historians who should know better is beyond me. Pontormo shunned the distractions of social life, which seems reasonable, considering his workload, but enjoyed days off in the company of good friends in the circle of BRONZINO, once his pupil and now a close and caring friend. They ate well—the first entry, 11 March 1554, mentions both chicken and veal—sometimes too well. Sunday lunches were followed by a light supper, so that on some occasions nothing more than a rolled omelette, *uova pesce*, a salad, and a lump of bread was needed to redress the balance. A frugal diet, but sufficient to keep him going, with plenty of good Tuscan bread and wine and seasonal vegetables and

salads, broad beans (raw with cheese perhaps), in March, a few days later some stewed peas, salad, and another rolled omelette, eggs and asparagus in April (the sun shone, "a nice day"), but two weeks later it was too cold to work, so he stayed at home and had the best possible joint of baby lamb. In mid-May, a delicious meal with Piero of "fish from the Arno, lots of ricotta, eggs and artichokes, then the next day a lavish Sunday lunch with Bronzino, and nothing at all in the evening—"just my bad luck to have eaten too much." Sometimes he contributed to these meals, paying for mutton, or some nice fish. One Sunday morning: "I bumped into Bronzino in Santa Maria del Fiore, who asked me to lunch.... I stayed on to supper, and went to Piero's for some wine, and there was Alessandra so we came back together. The meal really disagreed with me, and I fasted until Wednesday night, when I had some of the Trebbiano and a couple of eggs."

Christmas was a time of good food, at Bronzino's and in the house of Daniello, husband of the lively Alessandra, sister of the painter Allori, part of Bronzino's complicated case-load.

The contemporary painter and historian Vasari made much of Pontormo's solitary disposition, but with his own secret agenda of jealousy and snobbery, which led him to disparage a painter who chose to live in a quarter of Florence inhabited by artisans and minor painters, and built himself a modest house, with none of the pomp and display of worldly goods that he, Vasari, aspired to. He deliberately misleads us with his spiteful account of how Pontormo would hide from his friends, up a retractable wooden ladder that led to second-floor room where he sometimes lived and worked, overlooking the quiet gardens at the back; and post-Freudian gobbledegook wilfully makes of this a sign of deep neurosis and a sadly deranged mind. Elizabeth Pilliod redressed the balance with careful investigation of

Pontormo's house and his way of life, and a more wholesome personality emerges. The notorious ladder was the normal way of access to the upper floor of a town house in the *borgo* where Pontormo lived, and the need to escape the solicitous concerns of the young is a feeling common to many independent and touchy old people. Our suspicion that his diet was equally free of psychological complication is confirmed by this sensible clarification, and we can now see it as a reasonable, and enjoyable, way of eating. Elizabeth David's preference for "an omelette and a glass of wine" is typical of this frugal hedonism, and she, too, might well have used a retractable ladder to escape importunate friends and relatives. Pasta is not mentioned in the diary, except towards the end of his life, when Pontormo twice mentions vermicelli offered him by Bronzino, perhaps as soothing food for a by now very frail old man.

POPPY, *Papaver somniferum, papavero,* is not narcotic in the form in which the ripe seeds are used in cooking, and their harmless presence in confectionery gives a pleasant nutty texture and flavour. Widely used in northern Europe, poppy seeds figure also in the cooking of the Alto Adige, with its slightly sweet *pane al papavero,* brushed with egg and coated with poppy seeds; in Venezia Giulia; and in the *mohnnudeln* of Trieste, a sort of noodle made with flour and potato, rich with egg and butter, which when cooked is rolled in poppy seeds and powdered sugar. Poppy seeds have been sprinkled over, or worked into, bread since time immemorial, and Petronius left us a somewhat skewed but unforgettable sketch of a pretentious but second-rate Roman meal in Trimalchio's feast, with its arrangement of *amuse-gueules,* which included dormice glazed in honey and rolled in poppy seeds. Unfair on poppy seeds, which must have made a pleasing caramelised crust in contrast to the tender flesh within, and did not deserve to be the subject of mockery.

PORCHETTA

PORCHETTA is the name of a whole boned and roast young pig, of about 50 kilos (not a SUCKING PIG, which is *maialino, porcetto, porcello, porcellino di latte*, or *lattonzolo*), a speciality of central Italy, and much loved in Umbria and Lazio, where it is sold from stalls at fairs and festivals. The skin is singed, scalded, and shaved, and the pig boned, the carcass seasoned with salt, pepper, garlic, and wild fennel, then stuffed with its prepared entrails, sewn up, roasted slowly in a wood-fired bread oven, and usually eaten cold. The expression *in porchetta* can mean "cooked and seasoned like a whole roast pig," usually with fennel, the characteristic seasoning, but can be applied to other meats, or to fowl, as in *pollo in porchetta*.

PORCINI. *See* MUSHROOMS.

PORK PRODUCTS. *See* SALUMI, PIG.

POTACCHIO (*potaggio*). *See* FISH SOUP.

POTATO, *patata, Solanum tuberosum*, is one of the Solanaceae from South America which took a long time to become known as edible rather than just a plant with pretty flowers. Its tubers never invaded the Italian kitchen the way they did other European countries, as a bland and universal accompaniment to other things, and so benefited from a more sophisticated treatment, as an ingredient in its own right. Cooked in the oven with the roast baby lamb of LAZIO, potatoes take on the flavours of the meat and its seasoning of rosemary and garlic. In

BASILICATA, they are matched with BACCALÀ. There are potato GNOCCHI in PIEDMONT; in PUGLIA they go into *focaccie* and pizzas; LIGURIA has *trenette al pesto*, little green beans and cubes of potato cooked together with thin strands of pasta, timed for each ingredient to be done to perfection, served with a basil *pesto*. Also from Liguria is a dish of ARTICHOKES and potatoes, cooked after trimming the artichokes of the outer leaves and chokes, in garlic coloured in oil with a little broth, and finished with parsley, thyme, and oregano.

In the late 18th century, Corrado championed the potato—cheap, easy to grow, harvest, and keep—as a useful food for everyone, in a countryside where they could be combined with other nutritious products, and particularly suitable for literati, who needed mild food for their sedentary lives. Among the mashed and fried potatoes familiar to Artusi is a recipe for thinly sliced parboiled potatoes layered with shavings of truffle, butter, and parmesan, moistened with a bit of good gravy, cooked in the oven, and served hot with a squeeze of lemon. With nothing to recommend them visually, potatoes do not figure in art very much, and Italy never had the equivalent of Van Gogh's *Potato Eaters*. As a mild-flavoured tuber with associations with refined French cooking, potatoes might have ousted the more distinctive parsnip, which was relegated to animal food before finally fading away. Potato flour is occasionally used in bread and confectionery.

POULTRY, *pollame*, are farmyard birds: CHICKEN, GUINEA FOWL, TURKEY; as well as web-footed birds: DUCK and GOOSE. Italy is better placed than many other countries to compete with all the cheap, tasteless industrial versions of these fowl, with a wide range of small suppliers and local markets providing tasty birds. Farmed QUAIL, PHEASANTS, and PARTRIDGES are also available.

PREBOGGIÒN is a Ligurian mixture of mainly wild herbs and plants, often sold in prepared bunches, and could include all or most of the following: spinach beets, spring cabbage (*gaggia*), chicory, parsley, borage, salad burnet, dandelion (*dente di cane*), watercress, rocket, and fennel (Molinari Pradelli, 1997, p. 25). The mixture will depend on the season and the availability of plants, but the essence of *preboggiòn* is a balance between tasty and aromatic things unique to the climate and terrain of Liguria. They are used in *frittatas* and *pansôti*, a special kind of triangular-shaped stuffed pasta, the thin, light pasta made with less egg than other kinds, plus a little oil or wine, and with a generous filling of *preboggiòn*, the greens steamed and chopped, the herbs finely chopped but uncooked, mixed with sheep's ricotta, egg, salt, and nutmeg.

A dish of cooked, chopped chicory seasoned with a sauce of garlic pounded with salt, softened in olive oil with sage and rosemary, cooked a little with red wine, mixed together and served cold is also called *preboggiòn*.

The same mixture of greenery and herbs can be thinly sliced, simmered in salted water, to which rice is then added, to produce a looser result than risotto, and finished with *pesto genovese*, olive oil, and parmesan.

PRECEPTS AND PROHIBITIONS

are inevitable in a nation with a pride in its culinary traditions. The right and wrong way to do things is discussed and argued about and can become dogma. It is not so much the mother-in-law's petty tyranny as the absolutism of the expert. These *dos* and *don't*s are, however, instructive and comforting, and when they are questioned can lead to greater understanding of ingredients and what to do with them.

BASIL, we are told, should never be cut with a knife. The blade damages the cell walls in a way that spoils the flavour. Basil leaves should always be torn, not sliced. Harold McGee, writing of the browning caused to tender leaves by rough treatment, said "as long as your knife is sharp it doesn't matter whether you cut or tear the leaves" (1992, p. 72). Fred Plotkin is adamant that "herbs and greens do not take well to metal blades, and the act of cutting robs herbs of some of their properties." A lot must depend on how the basil is being used—in a salad, or sauce, or incorporated with other herbs during cooking (Plotkin, 1997, p. 62). Some recipes ask for herbs to be chopped, some pounded in a mortar, some dealt with in a food processor. If chopping basil with a knife is wrong, why is it permissible to chop parsley finely with a knife or a *mezzaluna*? The fictional paragon of domestic virtue, Paula, the wife of Commissario Brunetti, is allowed by her creator, Donna Leon, to chop basil before sprinkling it over an *insalata caprese*. Is this a sign of Paula's waywardness, or evidence of modern Venetian usage? The "official" recipe for making the genuine DOC version of *pesto*, not to be confused with *pesto alla genovese*, in the manner of Genoa, which could be (and is) made on an industrial scale anywhere, explains that the basil leaves should be gently crushed, not pounded, in a circular motion, with a wooden pestle in a marble mortar, to release the essential oils present in the "veins of the leaves." McGee goes into welcome detail about plant cells, going deeper than the veins of the leaves to the *vacuole* in the middle of each cell, which is where the flavour is, in pre-formed phenolic compounds that seem to be at their best in a coarse *pesto* (2004, p. 622). Mechanical processing involves attacking the basil leaves with blades, a less effective way of getting a dense flavour and texture.

POLENTA is said to need continuous stirring, for 45 minutes to an hour. But you can alternate stirring with doing other things if you use a nonstick pan. The stirring is to get the mixture into uniform contact with the hottest part of the pan, the base, and sides, so that it cooks evenly. But Anna del Conte points out that this even distribution of heat can be got by cooking the polenta, after the first 20 minutes, in a shallow baking dish covered with foil in a medium oven. As to whether polenta and other dishes should be stirred clockwise, Bill Buford has the last word on this. He knows his molecules, but has had an empirical understanding knocked into him as well, and his account of four-hour polenta, casually stirred or whisked occasionally in a copper pan on very low heat, puts received wisdom in perspective (Buford, 2006, p. 152).

The pith of LEMONS, the albedo, is usually said to be so bitter that it can ruin a dish. One is constantly told to pare a lemon carefully to avoid any pith. A scrutiny of recipes from the past indicates that this was not always the case. It has to depend on the citrus fruit; the citron, for example has a thick layer of aromatic pith which is pleasant and aromatic both raw and preserved. Scappi lists salads and relishes of thinly sliced citrus fruit, dressed with sugar, salt, rosewater, or vinegar, and uses sliced lemons and bitter oranges as a garnish on rich or dull-looking dishes. Inspired by this, it is possible to concoct a lovely sweet/sour sauce or relish by chopping a lemon or bitter orange finely and seasoning it with salt, sugar, and rosewater, to use with fish or rich roast meat. Chopped lemon, parsley, and garlic make a fine stuffing for baked fish. Whole lemons or oranges can be popped into the cavity of a bird that is to be roasted. So choices can be made, combining the aromatic oils of the peel, the acid juice, and the gentle bitterness of the pith, depending on the recipe and one's own taste. There is no sense in any dogmatic prohibition.

PRESCINSOEUA. *See* LIGURIA.

PRESSATO is a low-fat cow's milk
cheese which has been made for centuries in an area including the provinces of Vicenza and Belluno, as well as Treviso, Venice, and Padua. Its name, however, has come to be applied to so many versions using the traditional method but of sometimes inferior quality that the product has been overtaken, some say swallowed up in, *asiago pressato*, a milder, younger version of *asiago*, whose blandness appeals to modern tastes.

PRETZEL is a much-loved version of
the braided breads that are found all over Europe, and it is perhaps confusing to link them all too closely with the crisp salty ones enjoyed in New York, with their Germanic origins. (For more detail, *see* BREADS, BRAIDED.)

PRICKLY PEAR, *fico d'India, Opuntia ficus-indica,* was brought to Europe from
the New World and has become part of the landscape in Sicily and southern Italy. The fruit, when free of the treacherous little spines, is pleasant raw or made into sweet pastes or preserves.

PRIMIZIE are fresh young vegetables
which can be had out of season, or prematurely, some produced by forcing, some imported from countries where conditions make them available before normal crops. Gastro-tourists prize the seasonality of Italian produce, which is what we look for in markets and shops, expecting it always to be fresh and locally grown, not wanting to know that the plastic-wrapped, tasteless babies we spurn at home can be had in Italian supermarkets, too. Produce grown under modern high-tech conditions can legitimately bring tomatoes, broccoli, asparagus, and peas from the south to brighten the markets of the north, but there is still a discriminating market for the first local delicacies, in defiance of the international food industry,

and the walnut-sized baby artichokes that appear in Tuscan markets before the first signs of spring or, later on, the fat tender buttery peas of Rome cannot be replaced or replicated while customers demand them. Now that market produce has to be accurately labelled with the area of origin, it is possible to make intelligent surmises about the provenance and quality of what we buy.

PROSCIUTTO, cured, cooked. *See* HAM, PARMA HAM.

PROVATURA is a pulled cheese made from buffalo milk, similar to mozzarella, sometimes smoked.

PROVOLA is a pulled cheese made usually from buffalo milk, salted, then ripened, sometimes smoked as well. The milk can be from cow or buffalo, or a mixture of both. The *provola affumicata* of CAMPANIA can be variations of this procedure, and was preferred in the past to fresh mozzarella, and figures in many 18th-century *presepi* (Christmas cribs with local products). *Provula di Floresta* or *di Casale* is from the highest commune in Sicily, a local product best enjoyed on the spot, made in a complex version of the pulled-cheese method: cow's milk coagulated and drained, then heated in whey, cooled, pressed, cut into strips and dried, then heated again in whey, and finally pulled and given its characteristic pear shape, then salted and dried, to be enjoyed after a few days, or ripened for some months. There are many versions—*provolone affinata* is ripened in pungent local herbs and vine leaves. Sardinia has several kinds: *peretta*, enjoyed fresh, is also used in *sebadas*, cheese-filled ravioli flavoured with orange and lemon peel, fried, and soaked in an aromatic bitter honey.

PROVOLONE originated in the south of Italy—the name is from the Neapolitan word *prova*, meaning sample or tasting—but *provolone* has also been made in the north for some time, possibly since the Austrian presence in the 18th and 19th centuries, which encouraged cheese-makers from the south to move north and use the plentiful milk available at less cost. Cheese-makers from Naples have for generations been taking advantage of the superior quality of milk in the north to make this drawn curd cheese and send it for distribution in the south, with the quality assured by its DOC definition. This seems quite old-fashioned compared with the vast refrigerated trucks conveying pasteurised milk all over Europe, to be made into who knows what. The DOP of 1996 is consequently a necessary protection for all the varieties of *provolone* made in Italy today, of which there are many kinds. *Provolone Valpadana* is a northern cheese made in the area radiating out from Cremona in Lombardy, Veneto, and Trento, defined and protected by its DOP (*see* DOC). It follows the usual procedure for pulled cheeses, using kid's or lamb's rennet for the strong version, and calves' rennet for a milder cheese, depending on the desired piquancy, pasteurised milk rectified with a lactic ferment, coagulated, the curds broken and cooked, then fermented and pulled, and given the required shape before drying and hanging up to mature for about 20 days, then ripened for months or a year. *Provolone sardo* and *peretta* are made in Sardinia; the latter is a fresh creamy cow's milk cheese, pulled and ready to eat in a few days; the former is ripened for several months and has a stronger flavour.

PROVOLONE DEL MONACO is perhaps the only surviving genuine provolone in the south, made from the milk of local cows, the *razza agerolese*, a breed specially suited to the benign conditions of the Monti Latteri, the "milky mountains" of

Campania. This is not an ancient race like the *podolica* but owes its existence to an entrepreneurial general Paolo Avitabile, who retired to his native province in 1845 to improve the local breeds, *podolica* and *bruna*, by crossing them with some nice Jersey cows and a bull presented to him by a grateful nation (he fought for the British in India). The experiment worked, and the milk, though of low yield, makes cheese with an exceptional flavour.

PROVULA DI FLORESTA,

Casafloresta, is a pulled cheese made from the milk of cows grazing in Catania on the pastures of the highest commune in Sicily. The procedure is more or the same as for *caciocavallo*, but the drained and compressed curds, after cooking in their whey, are pressed, dried, cut up, and cooked some more, using traditional techniques and implements, so that both the method and the wooden tools and reed baskets, the local microclimate, all contribute to its excellence. Sometimes a small green lemon is inserted into the heart of the pear-shaped cheese as it is being shaped, adding its perfume to the existing aroma.

PRUNE. *See* PLUM.

PUDDING, *budin, budino*, may be derived from the French word *boudin*: something cooked in a casing, often of animal origin, a way of cooking found all over Europe—so maybe the British claim to have invented the pudding is as chauvinistic as similar territorial attitudes to trifle. These things evolve from usage rather than invention, and since putting food, to be cured or cooked, in the stomach or intestines of an animal, or wrapped in a cloth, has been around for centuries, it is more reasonable to say that such methods seem to have been

more popular in England than in Europe, from the 17th century onwards. A nice, hot, substantial, filling, nourishing pudding in the English style is quite alien to the Italian way of eating; these qualities are to be found in the first course of a meal, as pasta, rice, polenta, or a thick soup, and at the end, a dessert would most likely be fruit, cheese, or something light. The often somewhat robust *zuppa inglese* is, as its name implies, a foreign concept, if not a foreign invention. Light creams of ricotta, small biscuits, perhaps a delicate *torta*, fresh fruit from the fruit bowl or presented as a *Macedonia di frutta* or fruit salad (prepared, cut into cubes, and left to macerate in sugar and orange or lemon juice, served without cream) are more characteristic of the Italian dessert.

PUGLIA is separated from the rest of Italy by the Apennines—with CAMPANIA and BASILICATA to the west and surrounded on the east and the south by the Adriatic and Ionian seas—and has preserved a separate identity and links with Greece, which distinguish it from the rest of the peninsula. Fertile soil and a benign climate, with mild winters and long hot summers, produce fruit, vegetables, wheat, olives, wine, and cheese in profusion, making it "the garden of Italy," and inspiring a distinctive cuisine. This present-day idyll is recent, thanks to improved irrigation and a degree of political emancipation, which make up for centuries of exploitation and hardship. Horace wrote of the dry plains of these empty spaces, and its wily inhabitants. He was glad to get through this land of grazing and drove roads to the fishy delights of Bari and Brindisi, where Greece begins (Dalby, 2000, p. 64). The Romans had seen off the Greeks, and brought peace, and rapid communication with Rome along the Via Appia as far as Brindisi, but Puglia was subsequently submerged by waves of invaders—Lombards, Byzantines, Franks, Angevins, Venetians, Saracens, and so on. In the 12th

century, the Hohenstaufen emperor Frederick II made Puglia his home, as the cathedrals and fortresses testify, for he was born and bred in the Kingdom of Sicily, of which Puglia was then a part. With a pragmatic view of world events and a sense of tolerance that was at variance with the rigid ideology of Pope Innocent III, he shrugged off several excommunications and achieved bloodless crusades and domestic reforms, unique at the time. His concern for public health led to laws severing the corrupt links between physicians and apothecaries. But over the centuries, political mayhem and poor administration did little to improve the lot of the masses, and the Spanish and Angevins did a nice job of stifling both agriculture and trade, until the Bourbons brought a semblance of prosperity, but with it a hatred of foreign dominion which engendered revolts and rebellions, brutally suppressed, culminating in support for Garibaldi and the concept of a united Italy, which, when it came, brought a redistribution of land which made agricultural progress slow and difficult.

In the past, wheat and herds of sheep and goats flourished on the arid plains, and a diet of pasta, wild and cultivated vegetables, cheese, and game, alongside the ubiquitous pig, sustained rich and poor. Fish from the coasts were cooked in a variety of original ways, and wine, olive oil, and nuts were in abundance. Horace wrote of the agile Apulians, sunburnt herdsmen and stock-breeders, the export trade in wine and wheat, and the rolling plains and good grazing on the Apennine foothills (p. 64). Wool of superb quality was exported all over the Roman Empire, and today flocks of sheep are still led to graze on the Apennine foothills and then back down to winter on the rolling acres of the plains.

Now that improved agriculture and tourism have brought a smile to the face of the region, Puglia can offer an abundance of good things, alongside recipes and styles of cooking that depend more on local produce than on its confused history. The once dry and arid countryside is now irrigated with water brought by aqueducts from neighbouring regions, and power pumps that draw water up from the hidden underground reserves beneath the porous limestone, where rainwater sinks without a trace, so that no rivers can form. The delicate balance between lavish use of a dwindling natural resource and wider factors like global warming has generated water conservation schemes of considerable complexity, and brought a hidden frown to the smiling face of Puglia, where the depletion of wells near the coast draws saltwater into the water tables.

Wheat has been grown in Puglia since Roman times—a big export crop—and pasta, made today from hard durum wheat flour, comes in many shapes and sizes, with a huge variety of sauces, including fish, cheese, meat, vegetables, and herbs. At one time it was made at home, and the entrancing range of affectionate names—*orecchiette* (*recchietelle*), *lagane*, *laganelle*, *fusilli*, *strascinati*, *chianchiarelle*, *mignuicche*, *pociacche*, *fenescecche*—indicate the inventiveness of the domestic cook. The diverse shapes adapt themselves to different sauces, many of which are made from combinations of vegetables, wild and cultivated, herbs, and much onion and garlic. *Orecchiette*—small lumps or disks of pasta dough shaped by thrusting them round a thumb into little cup-like shapes resembling an ear or a shell—are seasoned with cooked turnip tops mixed with garlic and anchovies melted in olive oil. They are a good shape to hold many other rich sauces, meaty or fishy, like *ciambotto*, made from a range of fish. *Cavatelli* or *cavatieddi* are made from an eggless flour-and-water pasta, twisted and rolled into various shell shapes, depending on the region, and served with variations of a sauce made from garlic, onion, and tomato, with the possible addition of anchovies and chilli. The pasta can be cooked on its own and finished with a bunch of coarsely chopped rocket, or the bitter greens can be cooked together with the pasta, then drained and dressed with the pungent sauce. *Stracinati* are made by dragging pieces of rolled-out pasta over an implement which leaves one surface rough, ideal for a clingy sauce. *Troccoli* are like the *maccheroni alla chitarra* of Abruzzo. Perhaps the finest pasta sauces or accompaniments are the herbs and vegetables, from cabbage greens to aubergines, broccoli, and courgette flowers, enriched with different cheeses or rich combinations of garlic, onion, and tomato, and the flavoursome local olive oil.

Lagane or *laganelle* are egg *fettucine* made in broad or thin strips, and served with a variety of sauces; perhaps the most characteristic is one with cabbage greens and turnip tops, partly cooked, then finished together with the pasta in their cooking water, dressed with garlic and chopped pancetta or cured pork fat fried in oil, and seasoned with deboned and pounded salt anchovies. The same pasta is served with a rich sauce of tomato, onion, and garlic and chunks of eel, fried crisp and golden.

Pulses and their uses might reflect contacts with Greece; chickpeas, cooked with garlic and rosemary and seasoned with fried onions, are served, half of them puréed, with strips of fresh homemade pasta, which are cooked in the chickpea cooking water, and garnished with some of the same pasta fried crisp.

Broad beans are prepared in many ways, young and fresh, stewed with tender young artichokes, or with bitter chicory, 'ncapriata, as a purée with greens, turnip tops, or *lampascioni* (the bulbs of a wild hyacinth of the Liliaceae family), or grilled red peppers. When dried, they have many uses, and like other pulses are often combined with pasta. Those from Carpino in the province of Foggia are grown on the limestone and clay soil, without fertilizers or insecticides, harvested while still green, and dried on the plant, then trampled and tossed to get rid of the pods and stems. They are cooked to a melting tenderness in a terra cotta pot over a slow heat, and are good on their own with olive oil, or with pork or wild greens.

Some vegetables are unfamiliar: *caccialepre*, a plant of the Compositae family; various kinds of chicory or endive; wild fennel; *crispigni* or *grespigni*, another of the Compositae, *Sonchus oleraceus*, with a sweeter flavour than the wild chicories, which it complements, cooked or raw; wild *lampascioni*, or *lampasciuni*, eaten raw in salads or cooked; and *marasciuli*, a sort of wild rocket.

Tiella or *teglia* is a layered dish that can be made up of everything from fish and potatoes to combinations of rice, vegetables (spinach, zucchini, tomatoes), cheese, and shellfish, baked in the oven with enough liquid to prevent drying up, much fragrant local olive oil, plentiful herbs, and garlic. It was originally a way of cooking a fairly fast dish on getting back home from work in the fields, using everyday ingredients, simmered or baked in a terra cotta pot. Linking this delicious dish with Spanish *paella* is not doing it any favours, for the ritual around any of the traditional *paella* recipes creates a very different thing. A *tiella* allows for a more pragmatic and easy-going approach, with rice as only one among many other ingredients. Carnacina and Veronelli (1974, vol. 3, p. 110) have a version in which the precooked mussels and their strained liquid are added towards the end of cooking the other ingredients.

TIELLA GAETANA is a sort of pie made from bread dough within which can be baked a multitude of things, usually fish or shellfish, well seasoned with herbs, garlic, tomatoes, and plentiful olive oil. It is said to have been handy portable food for mariners, with the crisp, well-baked crust of dough keeping the filling moist without itself going soggy, and emitting a stream of aromatic olive oil trickling from wrist to elbow as the hungry eater bites.

The best-loved salami and pork products of the region are made following traditional practices, usually from the ubiquitous Landrace or Large White, but sometimes from "rare-breed" pigs reared in a semiwild state and carefully fed on forage and foodstuffs that encourage slow growth of the carcass and the development of tasty meat. The custom of keeping a pig for personal use dies hard, and even townsfolk manage to arrange to have a pig reared and processed by local small producers. The region round Martina Franca has—as well as fascinating *trulli* and glorious baroque buildings—the benefit of breezes from the Adriatic mingling with those from the Ionian seas, and thus a unique microclimate for the maturing of the fine *capocollo martinese* and the *soppressata di Martina Franca*. The *capocollo* is a kind of *coppa*, salted, doused with *vino cotto*, dried, and then smoked, before months of maturing in an airy location. The seasoning is whole peppercorns, specially selected to give a uniform flavour. More vibrant flavours go into the *salsiccia di Ginosa*, where salt, pepper, chilli, wild fennel, and saffron season this mixture of prime cuts of pork and some fat cut finely with a knife. A spicy sausage from the province of Lecce is flavoured with salt, pepper, white wine, lemon peel, cloves, and cinnamon.

Cheeses from the grazing herds of sheep and cows are noteworthy; their excellence depends on the race of animal and its pasture on the arid alpine terrain of Gargano in the province of Foggia, which produces *caciocavallo podolico del Gargano* with fragrant grasses and herbs which help preserve it. The survival of this rare and wonderful cheese is threatened by the mechanisms for its protection: its inclusion in the DOC and DOP awarded to the *caciocavallo silano* of Calabria and other regions of the south, and the restrictions of European Economic Community (EEC) milk quotas. The establishment of a SLOW FOOD presidium is a helpful step in the right direction.

Other cheeses include *burrata*, a creamy cow's milk cheese; *cacioricotta leccese*, a light young cheese which is eaten fresh or used as a condiment with chopped fresh tomatoes to make a creamy, refreshing sauce for pasta, as does the more piquant *ricotta forte*, this time a real ricotta, acidified and fermented for several weeks; *canestro pugliese*, a stronger matured cheese, used for grating in many local dishes; various fresh cream cheeses, *cacciofiore* and *cacciogargana*; *scamorza*, a fresh sheep's milk cheese used in *quagghiaridde* (a dish with more refinement than our haggis: a sheep's stomach, stuffed with the chopped up innards of lesser esteem, eggs, *scamorza*, and salami, is boiled or baked in the oven and served with cooked bitter chicory and its own gravy).

Another preparation, *gnemeridde* or *gnummerieddi*, are sheep's offal cut into strips which are rolled up and wrapped in caul like faggots, seasoned with pecorino, bacon, lemon, and herbs, and baked or grilled—a dish known in ancient Greece and still enjoyed today.

The local flour is used to make the renowned bread of Altamura, and other specialities—*taralli, friselle, puddica, parruozze, pan rozzo, pettole*. The precise specification of the *presidio* which controls the production of this bread demands strong flour grown in five communes northwest of Alta Murgia, fermented with a natural sourdough, and after long risings, baked in stone-built ovens fired with oak wood. Sometimes the round loaves are shaped with a circular cut which gives them the look of a floppy broad-brimmed hat. They can be large or gigantic, for their keeping qualities encourage big loaves made to last. Various twice-cooked breads, twists of dough like *taralli*, or *friselle* are part of the inheritance of seafaring and peasant survival food. More ephemeral uses of bread dough are the flatbreads, often with fillings or toppings of mixtures of pre-cooked vegetables and other ingredients, baked or deep fried to make *calzoni* or pizzas. *Panzarotti* are made from a rich eggy pasta rolled out and cut into circles, filled with various mixtures (mozzarella and anchovy, ricotta, soft cheese and egg) folded into a half-moon shape and deep fried; *pizzelle* are circles of pasta dough incorporating cooked potatoes, fried golden in oil, and finished with tomatoes, basil, and cheese.

The fish from the Adriatic and the Ionian seas are of a quality and freshness that make them ideal for eating raw—baby squid from Bari, *polipetti*, swirled in a basket to make them curl up, anchovies, plump mussels from Taranto, baked with garlic herbs and bread-crumbs, oysters also from Taranto, reared fat and plump on tamarisk poles in underwater "gardens," blessed with mysterious hidden currents of fresh water. There are noble fish like the *triglie di scoglio* of Polignano, or the lesser creatures which go into soups along with herbs and vegetables, like the stews and sauces for pasta. A fish stew of grouper or mérou, *zuppa di cernia*, is made with the characteristic use of potatoes, garlic, and onions, which are cooked together with thyme, parsley, celery, chopped tomatoes, and white wine, in which the slices of fish are briefly simmered and served over slices of toasted bread rubbed with garlic to soak up the rich juices.

PUMPKIN, *zucca*, is one of the Cucurbitaceae family, and includes MELON, MARROW, WATERMELON, and ZUCCHINI, but the name *zucca* is also applied to the genus *Cucurbita*, part of this confusingly extended family. *C. pepo* includes squash (winter and summer), pumpkin, gourd, zucchino. Sorting out their different names is less important than finding out how some of these are cooked in Italy. Pumpkins are less watery than marrows, with a harder outside skin and firmer flesh that needs longer cooking. The main kinds grown in Italy are the big orange and knobbly dark green ones of the north, of which *marina di Chioggia* is one of the best, and *cocuzze*, the smooth long green ones of the south; *D'Albenga* is one of these. The quality depends so much on the terrain and climate, and even then, pumpkins from the same plant can vary, depending on ripeness. Recipes and seasonings need to adapt. The pumpkin filling for the *tortelli* of Mantua is made with a discreet amount of *amaretti* to enhance the nutty sweetness; anything beyond discretion ruins the effect, especially if the biscuits are made with synthetic flavouring. A pumpkin risotto, sometimes served in the hollowed-out shell, needs a well-flavoured broth, and a cooking time adapted to the firmness of the pumpkin, which can be cubed and precooked in broth before adding to the risotto towards the end of cooking. Plentiful parmesan is a good seasoning. A Venetian recipe marinates fried slices of pumpkin with garlicky vinegar and basil, sometimes with sultanas as well, to be eaten cold after a day or so. Cubed pumpkin fried gently with chopped *lardo* and onion, with garlic and some chilli, finishes cooking in water into which some short pasta is thrown, and the soupy result is enjoyed with parmesan. Ripeness is critical, and was almost disastrous for Bartolomeo Bimbi when he was ordered to paint the life-sized portrait of a giant squash brought by donkey cart from Pisa for his patron Cosimo III Medici 1711, who liked to display, in his Villa alla Topaia, life-sized images of huge freak vegetables and fruit. This one was deliquescing as the painter worked against time, but is now immortalised by his skills, against a lowering evening sky and the Duomo and Leaning Tower of Pisa, dwarfed in the distance, while the burly monster poses propped against a small oak tree, along with a slice hacked from its backside.

PUNTARELLE. *See* ENDIVE.

PURSLANE, *porcellana, portulaca, Portulaca oleracea*, is a salad plant with fleshy leaves, growing wild all over, and also cultivated for use in mixed salads, or eaten on its own with chopped onion and pungent herbs like rocket, mint, and basil, to counteract the refreshing watery mildness—"insipid" was Mattioli's word for it. He and his contemporaries found this "coldness" helpful in treating inflammation in the mouth or the digestive tract. The leaves can be preserved in salt or pickled

QUAIL, *quaglia*, is now mostly farmed, and since it does not sing, is acceptable to those who have reservations about eating wild birds. Wild quail are slightly bigger and more tasty. Quail are good roasted, grilled, or pan fried; in addition, they can be cooked in a casserole with butter, herbs, and Marsala and served with their juices with a simple risotto or a *risotto alla milanese*. Platina lumped them with the Phasianidae family, and describes, long before Patrick O'Brian, the confusion migrating quails can create on board ship. His contemporaries thought that quail ate hellebore and poisoned seeds and so could be a health hazard, and he recommends eating them in the autumn, when their feeding must have been good. A contemporary health handbook warns against indigestion, and suggests tempering the richness of the quail with pomegranates, nuts, and cinnamon.

Most quail consumed in Italy today are farmed, though wild quail remain superior in flavor and texture. (Shutterstock)

QUARTIROLO LOMBARDO is today made all over Lombardy, mostly on an industrial scale, producing a good table cheese of uniform quality. Lactic ferments are added as well as the coagulant, and the curds are heated for a varying period of time in their whey before salting and then storing the cheese in humid conditions at a low temperature. This soft aromatic cheese can then be eaten fresh or matured for a month. The name comes from the autumn grazing on the fourth crop of grass in the lowland meadows, to which the cows returned after their summer in the mountains—a last taste of fresh greenery, redolent of the fresh growth of plants and flowers enriched by the long summer, before their winter diet of hay. Now, apart from some artisan versions made in Valsassina, Val Varrone, and Val Taleggio, the DOP specification sanctions a scrupulous replication of the natural lactic ferments of the past, and the dank caves once used for ripening can be recreated in refrigerated chambers. *Quartirolo* is one of the *stracchino* family of cheeses produced in Lombardy, where their names, and official descriptions, are relatively recent, although their history goes back a long way.

QUINCE, *Cydonia oblonga*, *cotogna*, might have been the Golden Apple of the Hesperides, which was awarded to Aphrodite by Paris, the most wonderful of fruits for the

The involved preparation methods necessary to transform raw quince into a palatable jelly have largely fallen out of practice. (Shutterstock)

most beautiful of the deities (although it might have been an orange or even an apple, all three of which originated in the Caucasus). The quince is declining in favour in the modern world, for the exquisite aroma is offset by the hard astringent flesh of this ancient fruit, which is inedible raw and needs much work to convert the flavour and texture into the many delicious products enjoyed in the past—marmalades (our orange preserve gets its name from the Portuguese *marmelada*, a quince preserve), relishes, thick pastes, and clear jellies. It has a long shelf-life, and many uses, but is quite eclipsed by the user-friendly but dreary apples and pears of international fruit commerce.

Costanzo Felici (1986, p. 94) has a succinct description of the quince: "so esteemed in cooking for its fine aroma, taste, and [medicinal] virtues, it is eaten raw, or cooked in the coals, in water, in wine, in must, in reduced must, in honey and in sugar; it is made into quince paste, jellies, and delicate relishes and goes into roasts, stews and many other dishes to whet the appetite."

The northern Italian *Tacuinum Sanitatem* (a 15th-century illustrated health handbook) shows a group of fashionably dressed people decoratively grouped round a quince tree, each holding and sniffing at a fragrant fruit. A few quinces in a bowl perfume the room, comfort "the passions of the heart," and can mitigate drunkenness, according to Pisanelli and Mattioli, who listed their many uses

with enthusiasm, while Platina explained how, eaten at the end of a meal, quince sweetmeats could help digestion. Quince paste, *cotognata*, with cheese is still a popular dessert, and versions of this, inaccurately known in English as "cheese," are made all over Italy, from Sicily to Genoa, often in decorative moulds. (This use of the name *cheese* is similar to that of the French word *fromage*, when applied, in 18th-century handbooks, to ice cream made in moulds, derived from *forme*, the word for mould, and familiar in Italian *sformato*, or "unmoulded" vegetable pudding.) Quinces were known in ancient Rome, and the name for a sweet variety, *melimelum, marmelo*, lives on in Spain and Portugal. But another use of quinces, familiar to lovers of Middle Eastern food, is in savoury dishes, common in medieval and Renaissance cookery in Italy. Here a glorious aspect of the fruit is revealed—the astringency, instead of having to be mitigated, is ideal with rich fatty meat like lamb or pork, and its perfume mingles with the spices, rosewater, and honey which are added during cooking. Our use of apple sauce with pork is a survival of this. Apicius cooked quinces and leeks together in broth, enriched them with olive oil and some dessert wine, and sweetened them with honey. (*Vin santo* would work well here.)

Scappi served stuffed roast duck with peeled, cored, and chopped quinces cooked in wine and sugar, sprinkled with anise seed comfits (p. 285). He made a clear sauce of the juice of grated quinces boiled with sugar, vinegar, and wine, flavoured with cinnamon, nutmeg, and cloves. A savoury stew, *minestra*, was made with peeled and cored quinces cooked in broth, with cinnamon and nutmeg, and thickened with cheese and egg, which must have gone well with roast meat and fowl. A strongly flavoured savoury jelly made from sheep's feet, clarified and boiled up with dry white wine, apples, verjuice, and vinegar, spiced with cinnamon, nutmeg, ginger, cloves, and pepper, was put to set with quinces cooked in wine, pine nuts, and blanched almonds, then served up as a relish. Best of all was a wonderful sauce made of quinces, peeled and cored and boiled with sugar and a little water to make a syrup, which is then boiled up with bitter orange juice and pepper, cloves, cinnamon, and nutmeg. (For us, this is an ideal thing to make in early winter when late quinces and marmalade oranges are to hand.)

Maria Vittoria della Verde, a nun in a convent kitchen in 17th-century Perugia, made a quince relish by cooking peeled and cored quinces in grape must, passing the mixture through a sieve, thickening it with pounded walnuts, and flavouring it with salt, pepper, cloves, and vinegar, with cinnamon sprinkled over it just before serving (Casagrande, 1989, p. 310). Corrado cooked them in wine to make a sauce with reduced veal juices, in addition to using them in jams, jellies, and *cotognata*. Scappi has a wonderful recipe for peeled and cored quinces, cooked with cloves and cinnamon in their weight in sugar, creating a thick syrup, to which is added bitter orange juice, to make a relish that will keep for over a year.

r

RABBIT, *coniglio*, is consumed in both its wild and domesticated states. Tame rabbit was always an important part of the domestic economy of rural households, more as a cash crop than food for the family, along with hens and their eggs—a source of money to pay for salt, sugar, and clothing. It was and is reliable meat when its food and health are monitored, being tender and with a lower fat and cholesterol content than beef or other meats, more reliable in fact than meat of wild rabbit, where age and health are less predictable, and the flavour can be affected for better or for worse by what it has been eating. A recipe from the Marche for wild rabbit includes the aromatic herbs it might have browsed among, thyme, wild fennel, and garlic, along with other good things from the terrain—olives, mushrooms, and pine nuts; the joints are browned in olive oil with bits of bacon, and bathed in a generous slug of the local white wine, which evaporates, leaving the joints and the chopped liver and heart to cook very slowly, covered, for several hours. A recipe from Umbria marinates pieces of rabbit in olive oil, rosemary, garlic, and pepper, then fries them lightly in oil, adding desalted capers and anchovies, diluted tomato purée, and lemon juice, and cooks them slowly until tender.

A rather sinister diagram in a standard work of reference shows how to tell the difference between the bones of cat and rabbit, a precaution which speaks for itself.

A painting noted in an inventory of 1618 of works owned by Grand Duke Cosimo II of Florence shows an idealised farmyard in a classical landscape, full of rabbits and very plump guinea pigs as well as a hedgehog and a porcupine, all of them reared for the table. Influenced by painters from the Low Countries, where exotic fowl were prized like the variegated tulips they surpassed in splendour, many Italian genre painters provided animal portraits for patrons with similar interests, and alongside the scientific illustrations of the natural world there developed decorative representations of animals, often associated with kitchens and market places. While works showing the spoils of the chase depict dead animals, proof of the hunter's prowess, these barnyard scenes are bustling with life, a tribute to the skills of the housewife or stock-breeder. Plump little conies and cavies, chickens, hens and fierce cockerels, amorous doves, and watchful cats and dogs adorned the walls of salon and dining room, while their fate was spelled out in kitchen scenes from which we can learn much about their quality and preparation. A late 17th-century group, maybe a send-up of aristocratic family portraits, of three adult rabbits and a little one, by Giovanni Agostino Cassana, gives us some idea of the breeds known then, and another by him places guinea pigs, pigeons, and a little kid in a landscape with roses and a butterfly among the kitchen pots and pans that foreshadow their doom.

The theme of rabbits or fowl eating fruit was common in the murals of villas in Pompeii and Herculaneum, where the sometimes rather trivial interior decoration of moneyed upstarts informs us of much more than their rather banal tastes, with *trompe l'oeil* renderings of votive offerings, or presents of food for guests, or the things you might see in kitchen or pantry, rendered in quick brushstrokes by local painters and decorators. The creatures will be punished for stealing by being sacrificed to the gods and eaten in their turn, a theme also explored in epigrammatic literature. A rabbit eating figs on a mural in Pompeii can be read as a moral message, or as a gourmet's strategy for fattening and flavouring a wholly innocent creature.

RADICCHIO is the name for several varieties of the ENDIVE or CHICORY family, *Cichorium intybus*. Confusion over names, endive or chicory, need not deter enjoyment of the many different kinds. Of the three main groups of endive, the red or variegated radicchio is available in different varieties. Those from Chiogga and Verona are usually enjoyed in salads, while those from Treviso and Castelfranco Veneto can also be cooked, grilled, or roasted with olive oil; they make a fine *contorno* or part of a main course of roasted vegetables.

RADISH, *ravanello, rapanello, Raphanus sativus*, is available in many varieties, which need to be eaten when the crisp, peppery

Radicchio is the name for several varieties of endive, also known as chicory. (Shutterstock)

root is not quite mature and still full of flavour. Taken with salt, or salt, pepper, and olive oil, radishes are a refreshing contrast to rich food, and were often served at the start of banquets. They are also included in mixed salads. Wild radishes gave a kick to rustic food, and were a substitute in the past for expensive seasonings.

RAGÙ can be the dense concentrated meaty sauce made in Bologna to accompany the egg TAGLIATELLE of the region, or a dish of slow-cooked beef or pork from Naples, whose thick dark cooking juices season ridged short pasta, the meat making a delicious second course. This Neapolitan recipe used to be made by the *portinai*, or doormen, who sat watchfully observing both the comings and goings of tenants and the murmurings of the barely simmering pot. Both recipes have nothing in common with that Anglo-Saxon abomination Spag Bol, *spaghetti bolognese*, a recipe loved the world over but quite unknown in Italy. It is worth remembering that Bologna, *la dotta e la grassa*, had a name for intellectual rigor and good living long before the tomato came along to muddy the waters and add what is not necessarily a helpful dimension to a rich meat sauce. Also we should note that a sauce that clings to long ribbons of egg noodles will just slither off the smooth spaghetti of the south, so all in all, it is best to stick to these two regional recipes with the appropriate pasta, remembering as always that the flavour of good pasta should never be swamped by a sauce, however delicious. A good *ragù* is best made with a tasty cut of beef suitable for slow cooking, and some pork, cut up coarsely rather than minced, together with the usual *battuto* of onion, celery, carrot, cured pork or bacon, and herbs, and garlic, liked by some, as well as a discreet amount of tomato in some shape or form. Cooked for a long time, with amounts of wine and broth fed in from time to time and allowed to evaporate slowly, along with tomato in some form or other, sometimes milk or cream, this could make a sauce that can be dry or unctuous, to be spooned over drained pasta on the plate, or mixed into it before serving. The efforts of one of our scientifically minded chefs (Blumenthal, 2007) to isolate what's going on in all this, and come up with a supercharged version (mercifully not a deconstruction), is in the best traditions of medieval and Renaissance Italy, using spices (in this case star anise, coriander, cloves), and some not-so-outlandish flavouring elements like Thai fish sauce, Worcestershire sauce, and a drop or two of Tabasco, to add extra pinpoints of sensation, just as any inspired cook of the past might have done.

RAGUSANO is a type of CACIOCAVALLO made in the province of Ragusa in the centre of Sicily, on the high uplands of Ibla. In a country where pasture was often sacrificed to large-scale grain production, some enlightened 18th-century landlords allowed a small degree of independence to tenants, who in other areas were so oppressed that they had no incentive to make decent cheese when it was exacted from them in dues, and this is said to be how a tradition of fine cow's milk cheese evolved. Today cows of the Modican breed graze on the fragrant vegetation, with the honey-coloured dry stone walls echoing the golden baroque cities below, Noto, Modica, Ragusa Ibla, rebuilt after the earthquake of 1693. Ragusa Ibla is the setting for film versions of Andrea Camilleri's crime stories, and fans of his fictional Commissario Salvo Montalbano will be familiar with this romantic vision of the fictional Vigata, not quite the same as Camilleri's gritty sense of place, with its *speculazione edilizia* and fly-blown shanty-towns. The mafia boss is housed in the crumbling palace of *Donna fugata* (the name, not the location, borrowed by Lampedusa for the country seat of a more benign tyrant). It was a local *caciocavallo* that Montalbano had for lunch when his cleaning lady, Adelina, was preoccupied with her delinquent sons, sent down by the Commissario for petty theft: "*S'accattù aulevi virdi, passaluna, caciocavallo, pani fresco con la giuggiulena supro e un barattolo di pesto trapanisi.*" (He got some green and black olives, *caciocavallo*, fresh bread covered with sesame seeds, and a tin of *pesto* from Trapani.) The same cheese went into Adelina's *arancini*, in a real cliff-hanger of a short story, in which Montalbano had to divert the course of justice in order to enjoy these special *arancini* made to celebrate the all too infrequent periods of liberty of her bad lads. The *ragusano caciocavallo* is made in a complex traditional way, similar to the procedure for *caciocavallo*, but formed into large rectangular shapes like huge golden stone steps, *scaluni*, which show traces of the ropes from which they are suspended while maturing. One reason given for this difference from the traditional pear shape is that the cheeses were made in large quantities in this economical and long-keeping form for export to Sicilian immigrants all over the world.

RAJBERTI, GIOVANNI, was born in Milan in 1805, and although his contradictory aspirations as doctor and writer did nothing to enhance his career, their mutual incompatibility did not dent his affable good humour and humanity. He died in 1861, two years after a debilitating stroke. Rajberti described his appearance as being his worst enemy: "*una cera disperata di ogni celebrità, grassa, rubiconda, gioviale: sarebbe buona per un ingegnere*" (an appearance devoid of all celebrity, plump, rosy and cheerful, which would have done nicely for a civil engineer). Much of his poetry and prose was written in Milanese dialect, and Rajberti was scornful of academic attempts to reform the language and by implication the "manners" of his fellow citizens. He was living through times of struggle for political and intellectual independence, and was uncomfortable with the repressive censorship of Austrian rule. His use of popular language in his work *Medico-Poeta*, and indiscreet *brindisi*, or verses in praise of Rossini (whose operas had subversive plots that the authorities hated but could not change), caused him to be put under surveillance. (He said that Rossini's operas *"mise in orgasmo le spie e fece lattrare i cagnotti"*; sent the spies into orgasm and set their servile dogs barking.) His hard and conscientious work as a doctor was equally an impediment to his literary career.

In his work *L'arte di convitare* (The art of hospitality) of 1850, Rajberti wrote with apparent light-heartedness about the food and eating habits of middle- to lower-middle-class citizens, being careful not to endanger his standing with higher levels of society, where he was also well received. He distinguishes between the robust food of the middling and lower orders and the vapid concoctions of French chefs. Writing of the Milanese *minestra* or *galba* (*see* SOUP) he describes this dish as *"nobile o del cuoco"* or *"minestra plebea o della serva"*: the more robust and tasty version being that of the servant girl, the posh one a piddling little cup of a clear watery soup (oh dear). The real thing is *"una minestra di risi, cavoli e fagiuolo, con un pochettino di sedano e carote, brodo superbo di manzo e di cappone, una buona pestata di lardo, e quattro fettine di cotica di majale,"* a dish of rice, cabbage, and beans, with just a little celery and carrot, really fine beef or chicken broth, some pounded *lardo*, and four slices of pork rind. In some versions, chopped garlic and parsley are included, and the rice and cabbage added towards the end of the long slow cooking.

Calling a respectable vegetable stew or *minestra* by the popular name of *galba* was a way to express solidarity and defiance of Austrian rule, without being identifiably subversive—much more than a regional accent, an instinctive response to a resented foreign presence.

To Rajberti, preparing and eating *polpette* was both an innocent domestic pleasure and an affirmation of Milanese identity. *Polpette*, or *involtini* as we know them, were thin slices of meat, or cabbage leaves, stuffed or rolled up around a mixture of chopped meats and seasonings, and were claimed as being unique to Milan (which of course they are not). There are many recipes; one from 1809 must have been known to Rajberti: flattened slices of veal or pork are rolled round a filling of chopped onion, garlic, herbs, spices, sausage, cured pork fat, breadcrumbs soaked in meat broth, grated cheese, and egg. They are then browned in fat or butter and finished in a little broth, some chopped celery, carrot, ham or *lardo*, and an onion stuck with spices. A similar filling using left-over meat and salame is enclosed in parboiled cabbage leaves, which are browned in butter, then finished slowly in white wine until the juices have been absorbed. A large meat roll is a *polpettone*, and there are many delicious variations on this, including one where a large flattened piece of tender meat is covered with a layer of *prosciutto crudo*, then a thin spinach *frittata*, rolled up and roasted slowly in butter with sage and rosemary. Meatballs were also called *mondeghili* (a word derived from the Spanish *albondigas* of an earlier period of foreign domination), and there were many versions of them. Of course they should appear on grand menus—*"non difenderemo fino al'ultimo respiro la nazionalità e l'indipendenza . . . almeno nelle polpette?"* An audacious rhetorical question.

Rajberti became enraged when good local *grana* was referred to as parmesan; he could not see why Parma should intrude on a fine local cheese, *lodigiano*.

Rajberti wrote *L'arte di convitare* at a dark time in the history of Milan, when its citizens were still reeling from the defeat of their hopes in 1848, a year when much of Europe was in a ferment of revolutionary activity.

Milanese of every social class revolted together against the hated Austrian rulers and expelled them during the *cinque giornate*; then confusion and disunity set in and the Austrians stormed back, even more repressive and unlovable than before. Rajberti's good-humoured loquacity has to be read against this background, and turns out to be deeply subversive. He handles his *polpette* and *galba* with a lightness that conceals their power. "*Se mi dimandeste dove si potrebbero scrivere senza impostura le parole libertà, eguaglianza, fraternità, risponderei: sulle pareti d'una sala da pranzo*" (If you were to ask me where one might write with impunity the words liberty, equality and fraternity, I would reply: on the walls of a dining room).

When it comes to wine, he seems to be merely gently mocking foreign taste, and pours scorn on the pretentiousness of costly bottled wines from abroad when good local draught wine from the wood is cheap, light, and healthy. At a posh dinner party, he warned guests at his end of the table that if their host brought out his horrible dark bottled stuff they might feel obliged to call for the police: "*Se costui seguita a darci questo infame d'un vino brusco, bisognerà risolverci a farlo chiamare alla Polizia.*" The roars of horrified laughter had to be explained away with a harmless joke, for this was skating on very thin ice indeed. A visit from the *Ufficio del ordine publico, o di publica sicurezza* was no laughing matter, but as a way of putting down a pretentious wine buff and cocking a snook at the powers that be, the idea went down well. Friends for some time after used to stop him in the street and ask if he'd informed on his host yet. "*Legitimo e onesto*" are loaded words to describe the wines of Lombardy in this context, and *pasteggiabilità*, meaning something on the lines of "easy drinking" but without any pejorative implications, reinforces Rajberti's theme that in an oppressive society, an atmosphere of good will and decency at table, loaded with patriotic local food and wine, is a powerful way of expressing solidarity. His spirit consoled and inspired his fellow-citizens during a painful time, and his kindness and common sense inspire us still.

RAMPION, *raponzolo, raperonzolo, Campanula rapunculus,* is a root vegetable with a pleasant mild flavour, a salad ingredient in winter and spring, which can also be cooked in broth and eaten hot with cheese and pepper, according to Castelvetro. Corrado is both eloquent and appreciative of these now almost forgotten little roots, calling them *figli veraci della terra*, true sons of the earth, growing wild without any help, especially around Rome and in Tuscany, where they are eaten raw and cooked, seasoned with oil, vinegar, and anchovies, or parboiled and then fried in oil with garlic and parsley and served with anchovies, raisins, and pine nuts.

RANA. *See* FROG.

RASCHERA is an alpine cheese made in various localities in the Valli Monregalesi in the province of Cuneo in PIEDMONT from the milk of Piedmontese cows fed on pastures rich in grasses, sometimes with the addition of a little sheep's or goat's cheese. The long, rather complicated procedure involves heating freshly milked, full cream milk, adding coagulant, and covering with a blanket to set, then breaking up the curds, which are drained, broken up again and put into moulds, drained and pressed, salted and turned for several days, then matured for a month or more, in a cool even temperature, traditionally, when made on the alpine uplands, in caves or underground pits. The cheese is made today on the high grasslands and in the valleys, each type clearly labelled. The shape can be either square or round.

RASPBERRY, *lampone, Rubus idaeus,* is a cultivated version of a kind of BLACKBERRY that in ancient times grew wild on Mount Ida in Crete, and still does. Mattioli mentions raspberries, but as wild fruit. They became domesticated around the 16th century, and their astringent, acidic properties, as well as delicious flavour and vitamin content, make them popular in the north of Italy, where they are mostly grown, but since they freeze well, their use in confectionery and ice cream is widespread.

RATAFIA. *See* APERITIVI.

RAVIOLI. *See* PASTA, STUFFED.

RAY or skate belong to the same family, but the ones that are more agreeable to eat we tend to call skate and the ones to be avoided, ray; in Italy they are called *razza,* with the exception of *pesce chitarra* or *violino,* guitar fish. *Razza chiodata* or *commune* is thornback ray, the best to eat; *razza quattrocchi* is another ray with four spots on it; *razza bianca* is white skate.

Artists have not been slow to exploit the uncanny resemblance of its underside to a human face, with its thick-lipped mouth and little piggy eyes (not eyes at all, but what might be called the corners of its mouth; the ray's eyes are on the other side). Languishing on the beach or fishmonger's slab, a large pinkish ray can excite both pity and recognition. A life-sized skate in an imposing ornamental frame painted by Gianbattista Ruoppolo in the 1670s might be the mug shot of one of the less appealing rulers of Naples.

Ray needs to be a day or two old to be enjoyed at its best, but after that it has a nasty ammonia-like smell, due to the deterioration of its cartilaginous structure. The absence of bones, however, makes it a user-friendly fish, but is not widely appreciated in

Italy, probably because other fish are more highly esteemed. A traditional Roman recipe, *pasta e broccoli nel brodo d'arzilla,* cooks pasta and broccoli in a rich broth made from skate and its trimmings, cooked for a long time with garlic to extract the flavour and unctuousness. The broccoli florets are started off in a lightly cooked mixture of garlic, chilli, tomatoes, salted anchovies, and white wine, then topped up with the fish broth and finished cooking with *strozza prete* or any short pasta.

Stingrays and electric rays are now seldom regarded as gourmet food. In the ancient world they had a higher reputation. The electric ray (Latin *torpedo*) is mentioned by the early Sicilian food poet Archestratos, who recommends that it be stewed in olive oil and wine with fragrant fresh herbs and a grating of cheese. Socrates is irreverently compared to an electric ray in Plato's *Meno:* "Not only in outward appearance but in other respects as well you are exactly like the flat electric ray that one meets in the sea. Whenever anyone comes into contact with it, it numbs him, and that is what you seem to be doing to me now."

RAZZA COMMUNE. *See* RAY.

RED MULLET, *triglia,* is of two kinds, the *triglia di scoglio (Mullus surmuletus),* mullet of the rocks, who live off smaller fish and crustaceans in clear deep water, and the *triglia di fango (Mullus barbartus),* mullet of the mud, who live in sandy or muddy waters and eat all kinds of things. The first is the most highly esteemed; it is usually eaten without being gutted, and the liver gives it a gamy overtone which many appreciate. The bones are a nuisance, but the tender white flesh is exquisite—the *triglia di fango* somewhat less so, depending on what it might have eaten in its muddy habitat. To tell them apart look, in the *triglia di scoglio* for stripes on the first dorsal fin, and when fresh, three or four yellow horizontal streaks along the sides, a brighter pinkish red colour, and a less abrupt profile; and in the muddy version, a paler colour and a snub-nosed profile. The bright, almost luminous red colour appealed to painters, who used red mullet and scorpion fish to add a sumptuous note to arrangements of fish, as we have seen, in the same way Dutch still lifes flaunt huge boiled lobsters for their beauty rather than their immediate gastronomic use.

Ancient Romans kept red mullet in pools, learned to fatten them artificially, and paid extremely high prices for them. A reported price of 30,000 *sestertii* paid for three red mullet impelled the emperor Tiberius to legislate against luxury. Not long afterwards, a fisherman who startled the reclusive Tiberius in his retreat on Capri, intending merely to present a fine red mullet, was taken for an assassin and killed by the guards. The gourmet Apicius ruled (according to Pliny) that red mullet were best to eat if drowned in *garum sociorum*, the finest Spanish fish sauce. They were sometimes considered aphrodisiac; Pliny, again, adds (credibly enough) that drinking wine in which a red mullet has died and been left to decompose will put you off wine.

Although it is very good simply grilled or fried, there are many recipes which bring out the flavour of red mullet. Corrado in 18th-century Naples cooked them in a hot oven (*con fuoco sotto e sopra*), scaled, laid neatly in a dish, and covered with his version of *sauce remoulade*, *alla ramolata*, a mixture of chopped onion, garlic, parsley, marjoram, salt anchovies, and capers, seasoned with salt, pepper, oil, and lemon juice. The fictional detective Salvo Montalbano was endowed by his creator Andrea Camilleri with an insatiable appetite for red mullet, fresh from the rocks and fried or grilled by Don Calogero to be eaten piping hot, or prepared by his cleaning lady, Adelina, lightly simmered, then bathed in oil and lemon juice, improving as they awaited in the refrigerator his uncertain arrival. Martino grilled or roasted them, basted with a mixture of salt, oil, and vinegar, applied with a sprig of rosemary or a branch of bay, in which they could be kept, once cooked, for several days. Ada Boni assembled a clutch of delicious recipes; the simplest is *alla Calabrese*, prepared red mullet aligned in a well-oiled, oven-proof dish, seasoned with salt, pepper, and lemon juice, sprinkled with abundant fresh oregano and more oil, and cooked for 10 minutes in a very hot oven, from which they emerge swimming in their own juices.

RENNET, *caglio*, is the coagulant used to make milk divide into curds and whey. When rennet is in contact with warmed milk in a particular state of acidity, due to the action of lactic acid bacteria, the proteins become semisolid, and can then be broken up into particles of a size appropriate to the cheese being made. Rennet is usually taken from the principal stomach of calf, lamb, or kid; it can be bought ready for use, liquid, dried, or as a paste. In the abomasum, or fourth stomach of a milk-fed calf, there is an enzyme, chymosin, which gets to work on the casein molecules, making them coagulate. Small artisan producers often make their own rennet from their own animals. Harold McGee describes this as "humankind's first venture in bio-technology" (2004, p. 56), and although industrial cheese production today relies on a genetically modified vegetable rennet, Italian cheeses are usually made with one or other of these animal rennets, or from *presura*, made from figs, cardoons, or plants of the thistle family. These all have the capacity to give the cheese in question a characteristic flavour, gentle in the case of veal rennet, used for young, mild cheeses, or strong when kid or lamb rennet are used for more mature cheeses. There is one instance of pig's rennet being used for a sheep's milk cheese, *pecorino di Farindola*, a pungent cheese made in Lazio. The *pecorino di Norcia del pastore* has a distinctive slightly smoky flavour from the rennet the shepherds make themselves, by hanging the lambs' stomachs to dry in the chimneys of their wood-burning hearths. Vegetable rennet gives a milder flavour and a lower yield but is preferred by vegetarians and those with certain food intolerances.

The kind of rennet used, the amount, and the way it behaves is a matter of judgment by the cheese-maker, and although procedures that have legal protection and definition specify measurements for the different temperatures to which the milk or whey is brought, or that of the atmosphere in which the cheeses are matured and later ripened, when it comes to the size of the curds, there is no measuring instrument that can equal the verbal description of what the eye can see—lumps as big as a walnut, a hazelnut, a chestnut, a pea, a corn kernel, a grain of wheat, a grain of millet, a grain of rice.

RHUBARB, *rabarbaro*, is one of many

varieties of *Rheum rhabarbarum* which were known to Dioscorides, and to later writers, for the medicinal properties of the root, an effective tonic and purgative, as we gather from Castelvetro (p. 86), who was cured of chronic constipation with a mixture of raisins and rhubarb. The roots of various varieties of this plant were known in China, India, and Turkey and were found on the shores of the Bosphorus, widely used in Arab medicine. Mattioli quoted a medieval Arab physician who said it was *"medecina benedetta, eccellente e solenne"* (a blessèd medicine, excellent and serious), and indeed the root, fresh or dried, along with a pleasant-flavoured wine to mitigate the bitterness, was an effective cure for gastric disorders, kidney stones, liver trouble, dysentery, and constipation, loss of appetite, and, as usual, the bites of scorpions and mad dogs. It had no ill effects and could safely be given to

Rhubarb was used as a remedy for gastric disorders, kidney stones, liver trouble, and dysentery. (Shutterstock)

pregnant women and young children, unlike the pink stems we eat today, which need to be taken in moderation. These only became known and used in the 18th century. A tonic and restorative liqueur, *rabarbaro*, was made in the 19th century using rhubarb root, quinine, and other medicinal plants, which, like many Italian bitter aperitifs and liqueurs, do indeed have health-giving properties.

RIBOLLITA is a Tuscan speciality

which may have originated in using up on Saturday the left-over stewed dried beans prepared for Friday, a lean day, recooked with vegetables, and served over slices of stale bread, *pane raffermo*, toasted or hardened in the oven, and anointed with the rich peppery local olive oil (*see* SOUP). It is now one of the iconic glories of CUCINA POVERA, and figures on the menus of Tuscan restaurants with a pride in the specialities of the region. Siena and florence squabble over claims to its "invention," but it is only recently that this particular way of enjoying a bean and vegetable stew with bread has gained renown and a name, perhaps to the exclusion of other pulse and vegetable dishes. When authenticity collides with dogma, we get trapped in rigid definitions of what must always have been a fairly pragmatic use of a staple—dried beans, and a common cabbage, *cavolo nero*, and any other vegetables that came to hand. Methods vary. One version layers the toasted stale bread with the beans and vegetables, moistening it all with the cooking liquid, then heating slowly in the oven, covered with a layer of thinly sliced onions anointed with olive oil, until a nice crust is formed. Another version simmers the bread, hardened in the oven or toasted, layered in a pot with the beans, vegetables, and cabbage. Some recipes are meatless; others use bacon or bacon rinds or possibly a ham bone.

So *ribollita* needs to be enjoyed in the perspective of all those other fine vegetable-based stews and soups, often incorporating bread in some form or other, but which were not given the name *ribollita* until quite recently. Ada Boni has a huge range of hearty vegetable soups and stews; one of them, *minestrone alla toscana*, the usual mixture of cooked beans, puréed beans, and vegetables, including unspecified cabbage, is served over slices of toasted bread, and left to mature for 10 minutes. Her *minestrone alla fiorentina* is similar but made with chopped ham and ham bones, the usual cooked white beans, half of them puréed, and *cavolo nero*, with a characteristic seasoning, added towards the end, of garlic, thyme, and rosemary browned in olive oil. She adds that toasted *pane nero* can be added before serving, or cooked with the mixture for about half an hour. Here *minestrone*, a "great big hearty soup," is the accepted name, and no mention is made of heating it up. Elizabeth David's pioneering book on Italian food (David, 1954, 1987), which first opened our eyes to what real Italian food was about, gave some *minestrone* recipes which are not quite what we now recognise, a rather perfunctory Tuscan bean soup, and a lovely bean dish from Piedmont, but had not a whisper of the uses of bread or the splendours of *ribollita*. In the 1960s, Luigi Carnacina and Luigi Veronelli, in their classic survey of Italian regional food *La cucina*

rustica regionale (Carnacina and Veronelli, 1966) give a recipe for *zuppa di fagioli alla fiorentina* and explain how, when left to get cold, it can be anointed with more oil and reheated. They include diced bread toasted in the oven, almost as an afterthought.

Much later (Romer, 1984, p. 27), we find a Tuscan recipe, *zuppa di pane*, in which leftover *minestrone* is layered with stale bread and the cooking liquid, covered with the cooked beans, and heated through in the oven. When this is reheated yet again, it is called *ribollita*, and here we at last see the name for something that Elizabeth Romer, an early and sensitive resident in Tuscany, says is "served this way in many a celebrated and expensive Tuscan restaurant."

The second cooking, which once made a virtue of necessity, now deliberately exploits the enhanced flavour often found in left-over food which has matured agreeably, and in the intensified aromas of toasted stale bread allowed to expand in broth, gaining all the time in flavour. Earlier writers use different names for what must have been a common ancestor. Artusi's *zuppa di faginoli* is a way of enlivening cooked white beans with a *soffritto* of onion, celery, garlic, and parsley, adding some *cavolo nero* simmered in the beans' cooking liquid, and pouring them over toasted stale bread. His *zuppa toscana di magro alla contadina* is again based on cooked white beans, this time some bacon or ham rinds (so much for *magra*); the chosen vegetables, in this case various kinds of cabbage including *cavolo nero* and a diced potato, are started off in the usual *battuto* or *soffritto* and finished in the cooking water of the beans to which is added some whole beans, and the rest passed through a sieve. This is poured over slices of stale rustic bread and allowed to sit for 20 minutes and eaten *diaccia*, tepid. The bread in both these recipes undergoes changes which enhance the flavour and alter the texture.

Back in the 1970s, in an elegant little work on using left-over bread written from personal experience by Mariapaola Dèttore, a translator and enthusiastic cook, a careful recipe for *zuppa di cavolo nero* (Dèttore, 1979, p. 98), "a typical Tuscan soup," does not mention reheating or the name *ribollita*, but does stress the importance of using *cavolo nero*, with its unique flavour for which there is no substitute, and goes on to make clear the need for a dense texture, achieving this by pushing half the cooked beans through a sieve, and adding to the beans and vegetables as they simmer. A pinch of thyme is added towards the end, and the prepared toast is rubbed with garlic before being dressed with plentiful Tuscan olive oil, and layered with the vegetables. The dish needs to rest a while before serving, a comfort when guests are late. *See also* ZUPPA.

RICE, *riso, Oryza sativa,* was cultivated in the central Yangtze Valley 8,500 years ago. The wild plant probably originated in India and spread slowly west through Persia, adapted to varying conditions, being a plentiful and nutritious crop, a staple and also an element in many luxurious cuisines. It was known to Alexander the Great, but never made much impact on the Greek or Roman kitchen, being used mainly for medicinal purposes, for upset stomachs, as congee is used today. When Arab political power and culture spread, rice cultivation came to Sicily, and North Africa, as well as the south of Spain. It was grown there by the 10th century, but the eventual triumph of rice in Italy might have come from the north, introduced by Venetian merchants. A letter from Galeazzo Maria Sforza in Milan to the ruler of Ferrara indicates that by 1475 rice was already a serious crop in the north. By the 16th century, it was being used, like maize, to avert famine, and was regarded as food for the poor, yet went on appearing in recipes for the rich, from which the risottos of the north and the *timballi* and *sartù* of the south would evolve.

Rice dishes, often flavoured with sugar, rosewater, and saffron or cinnamon, were a continuation of the medicinal tradition, but still a luxury. Martino, writing in the 1460s, has a simple recipe for well washed and dried rice cooked in goat's and almond milk, which gives the rice more body than water, lightly salted and well sugared. A more complex dish is a leavened tart filling using pounded cooked rice, ground almonds, moistened with the rice's cooking water, crushed pine nuts, thickened with starch, baked in an open tart, protected towards the end of cooking with a thin layer of lasagne, and sprinkled with sugar and rosewater before serving.

One of the surviving Martino manuscripts has a recipe for *Riso alla Italiana* in which well-washed rice is cooked in good meat broth, stirred to prevent sticking, with eggs and grated cheese stirred in just before serving. A not so remote ancestor of RISOTTO.

A century later, Scappi is specifying rice from Lombardy or Salerno, used in sophisticated recipes reminiscent of contemporary Middle Eastern food. A butter-drenched mixture of rice cooked in a rich broth, layered with the meat, and seasoned with sugar, rosewater, and cinnamon takes us right back to the marketplace in 9th-century Baghdad, where Charles Perry has traced the fortunes and composition of *judhaba* (2001, p. 220), with rice or a mixture like Yorkshire pudding mopping up the cholesterol-laden juices of a roast. Historians have few fixed certainties around the arrival of rice cultivation in Italy, but the link between Arab Spain and the Kingdom of Naples is clear, and the political and cultural ties with the north make the diffusion of both rice and recipes likely. It is possible then that the baked rice dishes of the south, although burdened with French names, *timballi, sartù,* owe more to the past than 18th-century fashions for French food and manners.

The strange trajectory of rice, from imported luxury health food for the rich in the late Middle Ages to high-yield crop for progressive landowners during the Renaissance, to staple subsistence food for the underprivileged in the mid-19th century, and finally to its role today as quality food across the whole social spectrum, is an intriguing story. Italian culinary genius gave the world a unique way of cooking rice, the risotto, and evolved versions of the *japonica* strain that are well adapted to this method. Its popularity puts Italy at the top of European rice production, with sophisticated forms of cultivation, pest control, and harvesting which do in 50 hours per hectare the work that would have taken 1,026 hours only a short time ago. The main areas are Lombardy, Piedmont, and Veneto, with pockets of activity in Emilia-Romagna, Tuscany, and Sardinia. Of the 2,000 hectares under rice cultivation, 90 percent is grown in the triangle of Novara, Vercelli, and Pavia.

The many varieties of rice produced in Italy are classed in four categories: *comune, semifino, fino, and superfino. Comune* is the *originario*, the native strain; a version of it, *balilla* with a softer, more melting texture, is used for broths and puddings, fritters, and the delectable ARANCINI. Of the *semifini, vialone nano*, with its high amylose content, and relatively rapid cooking time (the official timing of the transformation of the starch elements is 16.52 minutes), expanding to a soft but firm grain, makes fine risottos. This, too, is good for *supplì* or *arancini*, and baked and moulded dishes. The *fino* category includes *S. Andrea, Roma,* and *Europa*, both with a shorter cooking time, and is good for risottos and plain boiled rice. Among the *superfini* are the well-known *arborio* and *carnaroli*, wonderful for risottos, with their admirable combination of firmness and stickiness, and a slightly longer cooking time. Descriptions give approximate times, but so many factors affect the process that, as with monitoring the cooking of pasta, the cook needs to taste and evaluate all the time.

Italian rice cookery is by no means confined to risottos. There are boiled, baked, fried, and stewed dishes, both sweet and savoury. Rice is used to stuff things, rice starch to thicken; cold cooked rice goes into salads; and it is much used as a simple *contorno* cooked *in bianco*, plain boiled rice with perhaps some butter and parmesan stirred in before serving. (For more detail on rice recipes, *see* PEA and VENETO for *risi e bisi*, and PIEDMONT for *riso al cagnone*.)

RICOTTA is a MILK product, often described as a cheese, using the whey left over from cheese-making. It is heated again (hence the name *ricotta*, re- or twice-cooked) sometimes with an acidic coagulant and some extra milk, and the resulting curds, made up of the remaining fats and lactic proteins, are lightly salted, drained, and ready for immediate use. It is known as *puina* in Tuscany, *seras* or *seirass* in the Valle d'Aosta and Piedmont, and *giuncà* in Piedmont. The most prized kinds of ricotta, like the *ricotta genuina romana*, made around Rome, as well as the renowned ricotta of Sicily, are made from the milk of sheep, *pecora*, but it can also be made from the milk of goats, cows, and buffaloes, or a mixture. Experts can tell if ricotta is from sheep's milk alone, but many consumers cannot, and some producers can thus enjoy the benefit of the doubt. Apart from industrial production, which for export gets the UHT (long life) treatment, which drastically alters the flavour, there are many regional variations. Ricotta needs to be eaten fresh, ideally where it is made, when its evanescent flavours are best enjoyed on their own, perhaps with bread and honey. The Sicilian *ricotta ccu sieru* of Sicily is a sort of soup of ricotta swimming in its still-warm whey, to be eaten on the spot, the ultimate in freshness. Its use in desserts and pastries is widespread, particularly in the south, where, passed through a sieve, the resultant creamy mass, flavoured with sugar, vanilla, chocolate, and candied fruit, is a filling for pastries, an ingredient in *cassata siciliana*, or the dessert made with boiled wheat grains, *cuccia*. It is also used all over Italy in many cooked dishes, both sweet and savoury, cakes, tarts, vegetable dishes, and fillings for pasta. The stuffed *tortelli* and *tortelloni* of Emilia-Romagna often have a filling of ricotta mixed with parmesan, chopped cooked spinach, and herbs, sometimes flavoured with nutmeg. Mixed with eggs and parmesan, ricotta makes a filling for a huge variety of tarts.

In the past, this by-product of cheese-making was eaten fresh on the spot, as a miniature in one of the north Italian *Tacuina Sanitatis* from the 1460s illustrates—a woman stirs the vat of heated curds, and on a table close by are the strainer and pierced ceramic pot for draining, a fresh ricotta turned out onto a dish, and a man greedily eating it, standing up, with a spoon, a jug of wine, and a lump of bread close by, while a youth sits comfortably on the ground devouring ricotta from a bowl, watched by an enormous, melancholy black and white dog. Another illustration shows a man walking away with a large unmoulded ricotta sitting in a plate on a bed of reeds or straw. Another shows a scene in a street or courtyard, with a man spooning the coagulated whey from a huge vat into a pierced bucket, while a child walks off with a small cone-shaped reed container, looking like the equivalent of today's ice cream cone. The immediacy of these scenes emphasises the freshness and ephemeral qualities of ricotta. The conical container, sometimes a fabric bag, produces a cheese which keeps its conical shape as it subsides on the plate. This can be seen in a still life by an unidentified painter in Rome or Naples of the 17th century in which the voluptuous mound of ricotta is surrounded by other good things to eat—parmesan, *caciocavallo*, cured ham, a salame studded with lumps of fat and peppercorns, with a florid cabbage, fresh young peas, artichokes, and a flask of wine, all justifying the sheet of music on which the cheeses rest, entitled *Canto del cra-*

panica (A hymn to gluttony; *La natura morta al tempo di Caravaggio*, p. 63). A genre scene of 1580 by Vincenzo Campi in the Musèe des Beaux Arts in Lyon depicts a rustic family tucking messily into a large wobbly mound of fresh ricotta. Almost a century later, one of the emblematic *pale* (ornamental shovels with the name and motto of each member) of the Florentine ACCADEMIA DELLA CRUSCA plays on the word *mantenuto*, upright, showing a beautifully rendered mound of ricotta in a ceramic bowl, with a finger of dried bread upright in the middle—a way of absorbing surplus liquid and keeping the cheese firm and fresh. This emphasis on freshness is clear in health handbooks of the period which say it is best eaten while still warm, ideally with butter and honey to counteract its indigestible qualities, best in small quantities, which seems like a sensible warning after these scenes of enthusiastic indulgence. A still life from Spain, with a bowl containing a soft white cheese, perhaps ricotta, surmounted by a honeycomb bearing a spray of roses, thus carries a health warning as well as being a symbol of freshness and purity. Scappi served ricotta in the spring, usually in the first course of a banquet, often sprinkled with rosewater and sugar, the sweetness of the sugar and the delicate perfume enhancing its gentle flavour. He also used ricotta in tarts, sometimes enriched with butter and other cheeses, or with elderflowers. A white tart, *torta reale*, made with ricotta and the juice of *mel'appie* (a kind of rustic apple) or quinces, with egg whites flavoured with ginger and crushed pine nuts (bk. 5, p. 357), is served at the end of March.

When drained, salted, and smoked, then left to mature for a month or more, ricotta becomes quite pungent. Ricotta can be sun-dried, *ricotta sicca*; salted and dried out in the oven, *ricotta infumata*; or drained, salted and smoked; in these hard states it can be exported and is worth seeking out. These hard versions of ricotta are grated and used in pasta sauces, like the *pasta alla Norma* of Catania, or *pasta con le melanzane*, described by Mary Taylor Simeti, or her version of *pasta alla carrettiera*, where fresh peeled and chopped tomatoes are seasoned with a sauce of pounded basil leaves, garlic, salt, hot red chilli, and olive oil, and the pasta, spaghetti or *bucatini*, is dressed with this and grated salted ricotta (Simeti, 1989, pp. 29, 170).

The *marzotica* (made in the spring) of Puglia, and the *schianta* or *ricotta forte*, also made in Puglia, worked, turned, and drained for up to three months, has a strong piquant flavour, used in many local dishes. A smoked ricotta from Anversa degli Abruzzi is made from the milk of semiwild sheep and goats grazing on organic pasture; it is salted lightly, then smoked in juniper and beech sawdust and left to ripen for up to a year, producing a cheese with a herby, resinous aroma. In Basilicata, there are several kinds of salted and smoked ricotta, and a fresh one, made of milk from sheep and goats lightly salted and flavoured with hot chilli, a thick, pungent, creamy paste which needs to be eaten fresh. The *seirass del Lausun* is made from milk, not whey, of cows fed on the local forage in the Pinarolo area of Piedmont, a very fresh cream cheese, drained in little cloth bags, to be eaten at once. A fresh goat's milk ricotta is made in the Alpine regions around Udine and Pordenone in Friuli–Venezia Giulia, an emerging product to meet contemporary tastes. A spin-off from the growing popularity of the buffalo mozzarella of Campania is a demand for fresh ricotta made from the whey, now drained in reed baskets, but once wrapped in hempen cloths, *ricotta in salvietta*: ricotta in a napkin. Recent initiatives in the production of goat's cheese in Lazio, from grass-fed creatures, the alpine breed Saanen, yields a soft, creamy, slightly sharp cheese sometimes seasoned with herbs, while the resultant whey produces a delicate soft ricotta. The *ricotta salata di Norcia* is made by Umbrian

shepherds, from whey left from making the incomparable *pecorino di Norcia del pastore*, with milk from sheep feeding on the lush pastures of the local hills; the ricotta gets a special richness from the custom of heating the drained and pressed forms of cheese in the whey before salting, to firm up the crust, and using wood as source of heat under the cauldrons. The last word on the frustratingly unobtainable, ephemeral, unreachable quality of immediacy and freshness sought after in so many artisan foods of Italy is a long quotation from Elio Vittorini in Mary Taylor Simeti's book on Sicilian food, where a shepherd and his son make ricotta from the pale green whey left from a newly made cheese (1989, p. 44).

RISI E BISI. *See* PEAS, VENETO.

RISO AL FORNO. *See* RISOTTO.

RISOTTO is a unique way of enjoying RICE, a dish prepared specially and served the moment it is ready, for sitting around being kept warm is the ruination of both the texture and its surrounding liquid. As with pasta, it is best not to overwhelm the texture and flavour of the rice with other ingredients. There is a sort of perversity in using a fine rice as a mere vehicle for an inventive assortment of ingredients, when a risotto of distinction will let a choice rice speak for itself.

The point of the method is to cook the rice by continuous but gentle simmering in a flavoured liquid, which will be absorbed as the rice is constantly stirred with a wooden spoon in a deep capacious pot, until at the end the grains will be tender, but with some bite in the centre, surrounded but not swamped by a creamy liquid. The evaporation of the cooking liquid will condense its flavour, so it is important to start with a very good but mild stock; a really strong meat or chicken broth can fatally subjugate the rice. When *dadi*, bouillon cubes, were first invented, they seemed to be a liberation of the cook from the chore of producing homemade stock, but close attention to the ingredients listed on the packet will surely bring a sense of caution to their use, as well as an appreciation of the values of one you make yourself.

The different stages in the making of a risotto are as follows. First is the *tostatura* of the rice in a *fondo*, usually chopped onion, softened but not allowed to colour, in butter or oil; then comes the vigorous bashing, with a wooden spoon, of the raw grains of rice in the *fondo* against the sides of the pot, which will encourage them to later exude starch; if the recipe includes wine it will be added now and stirred all the time until it evaporates. Then the hot broth will be added a ladleful at a time and stirred; the stirring is of course to stop it sticking but also to release the starch surrounding each grain of rice into the cooking liquid, which needs therefore to be neither too plentiful nor too meagre. The relationship of the rice with the sides of the pot is almost percussive, as it is swept against it by the vigorous stirring, releasing more starch and picking up additional flavour. About five minutes before the end, butter or butter and parmesan are stirred in, and just before the rice seems cooked, some more butter is added, the heat turned off, and the risotto left to rest for a while. If your timing is right, the grains of rice will have reached a state of tender but firm perfection at the moment of serving. Other ingredients can be added at different points, according to the recipe you follow.

The hugely successful British cookery writer who perfected a way of avoiding all this palaver by finishing the recipe in the oven, leaving her free to drink with her guests, was making *riso al forno*, a fine thing but not a risotto. But it must be admitted that adding the wine at the beginning provides ample opportunity for the cook to refresh herself as well as the rice. Left over risotto can be made into *arancini* or *suppli*.

Risotto is only one way of enjoying rice; it appears as *riso in brodo* in runnier dishes and soups, along with meat or different vegetables, beans, peas, root vegetables, often finished with butter and parmesan or oil and lemon, and herbs.

ROACH, *lasca,* is disappearing from many lakes and streams. Platina said that Lake Trasimene was full of them, but today there are hardly any. He ate them grilled with a green sauce or verjuice.

ROBIOLA is made in prealpine valleys in Valsassina, Piedmont, and Lombardy, and there are as many variations as there are valleys; those from Lombardy have a different character, with a rectangular shape, soft, mild, and buttery when young, pungent when mature; in Piedmont they are cylindrical, mild, and gentle, getting more pungent as they age, all with different characteristics. This ancient cheese has been made from time immemorial on small farms in small communities, usually by women (whose skills were often disparaged by 19th-century male writers) using traditional skills not replicated in the small cheese factories where much of today's versions are made, usually from pasteurised milk. *Robiola Alta Langa* from the Langhe is now made with cow's milk, coagulated at a low temperature, drained, salted lightly, and ready to eat within a week; it can also be matured to give a stronger flavour. *Robiola d'Alba* is made in Alba and parts of the province of Cuneo in Piedmont, by a different procedure, a more energetic manipulation of the curds, and applications of heat, to be enjoyed after a week. *Robiola* or *tome, di Ceva* is made in the Valle

Tanaro in Piedmont, from the milk of cows fed on local pastures. *Robbiola di Roccaverano* has a DOP (*see* DOC) and high reputation and commands high prices; production, apart from that for home consumption on farms, is limited to 60 small cheese-making establishments and small producers in the commune of Roccaverano and Acqui Terme, and although esteemed as a table cheese eaten fresh, it is also preserved in oil or a green sauce made of parsley and garlic. Unlike some *robbiole*, it can include a percentage of sheep or goat's milk, adding fragrance from the wild plants consumed by these agile animals—brambles, thyme, and other wild herbs—and when the milk is not pasteurised, microbes can get to work to further enhance the flavour. A movement is afoot to get recognition for a *robiola* made only of goat's cheese.

ROCKET, *ruchetta, rughetta, rucola, Eruca sativa,* is a brassica, with the characteristic harsh pepperiness of this family. It is best known today in two varieties, a broad-leaved, less pungent plant, and the so-called wild rocket (*Diplotaxis tenuifolia*), which is widely cultivated, with smaller, more strongly flavoured leaves. Both at one time were esteemed as aphrodisiac, and prudently mixed with lettuce, which was the opposite, but nowadays rocket is enjoyed innocently in mixed salads, to which it adds a pleasing pungency. It is also used in Puglia to make the pasta dish *cavatièddi,* in which large amounts of coarsely chopped rocket are added to pasta seasoned with a homemade reduced tomato sauce and pecorino. The current overuse of whole rocket leaves as garnish in some versions of Italian cuisine is not as satisfactory as the many unpretentious recipes in which it is added, chopped, to sauces and cooked dishes. Corrado used rocket, fried in oil with garlic, to season vegetables or pulses, or pounded with parsley and diluted with oil and vinegar, as a condiment for cold meats and fish.

ROMAN FOOD

Historical and Literary Context

Founded, according to legend, in 753 BC, Rome began as a country town and became the metropolis of a world empire. In the 3rd and 2nd centuries BC, its army fought and defeated the Carthaginians, leading eventually to domination of western Europe and North Africa. In the 2nd and 1st centuries BC, victories in Greece and Asia Minor opened the way east. As republic gave way to empire, the principate of Augustus (27 BC–AD 14) marked the beginning of a 400-year period, unique in history, during which the whole Mediterranean was governed by a single political power. Travel and trade were relatively free throughout the region, though travel was slow: it was a five-month voyage from the Pillars of Hercules (Straits of Gibraltar) to Antioch in Syria. Only foods that were dried, pickled, or salted, and only special wines, would stand up to such a journey.

New territories—notably North Africa, famed for its agriculture—provided the opportunity for new developments in food production. Romans built on what they learned from Greeks and Carthaginians. Gardeners developed multiple varieties of vegetables and fruits, notably apples, pears, and grapes. Alongside more familiar farm animals (cattle, sheep, goats, chickens) Romans took trouble with various gourmet species from geese to snails, and added new ones, including dormice, ducks, and hares. They farmed many species of fish in inland pools and marine enclosures. The parrot wrasse, a pretty fish, was fetched from Greek waters in large numbers and successfully naturalized—for a century or so—in the Tyrrhenian Sea.

Meanwhile, Romans increasingly imbibed Greek fashions, spending lavishly on imported foods and wines. Moralists such as Cato (died 149 BC) inveighed against these developments, but in vain; Cato himself,

Rome's first prose author, included Greek recipes in his farming handbook (*see* GREEK GASTRONOMY, INFLUENCE OF).

Latin texts are the major sources of information on the food of Roman Italy; they are now increasingly underpinned by archaeology. The tradition of agricultural manuals culminated in Columella's work *On Farming*, written about AD 50, which includes a long section of recipes for household preserves. In his encyclopaedic *Natural History*, Pliny the Elder (died AD 79) devotes books 12–19 to a survey of useful plants, with special attention to fruits and vegetables. A dietary manual in Greek by the Imperial physician Galen (AD 129–199), *On the Properties of Foods*, enables a doctor to prescribe diets for patients, making allowance for seasonal factors and for each individual's constitution and lifestyle, in accordance with humoral theory.

Poetry and literary prose give a different perspective from that of the technical texts. The Augustan poetry of Propertius, Horace, and Ovid is full of sidelights on food and dining among the elite, incidentally showing the growth of gastronomy (and the opportunities for seduction at dinner parties). The picaresque novel *Satyricon* by Petronius (c. AD 60) mocks the luxury and vulgarity of the newly rich. Suetonius's *Lives of the Twelve Caesars* (c. AD 115) depicts palace lifestyles, from the abstemious Augustus ("he was very sparing, almost plebeian, with a liking for brown bread, whitebait, soft, spongy hand-pressed cheese, and green figs from a twice-bearing tree") to the gourmand Vitellius, briefly emperor in AD 69 ("he would satisfy his greed while a sacrifice was in progress, with lumps of meat or cake off the altar, still sizzling from the fire; and when on the road, with smoking-hot morsels, or cold left-overs and half-eaten scraps, from wayside cook-shops").

It was a commonplace of Roman writing to despise complicated dishes designed for show rather than for taste. Yet, in practice,

rich households spent much money and slave labour on the finding of rare ingredients and the elaboration of showpiece dishes. The parrot wrasse and the dormouse fetched high prices not because of their flavour but because of the way they looked on the table. It was also a commonplace to boast of the freshness and simplicity of the farm produce offered to one's guests. A tradition of literary "invitations to dinner" helps to show changes in style as well as individual responses to food fashion. Surviving examples extend from about 50 BC (Catullus) to AD 110 (Pliny the Younger). (See Elliot [19–] for translations and Gowers [1993] for commentary.) The empire suffered frequent economic and political crises in the 3rd century. Internal instability and insecure frontiers led to the splitting of the empire into western and eastern halves divided by the Adriatic, yet there was still money, leisure, and appreciation of luxury. Spectacular silverware comes from this period, as does the Latin recipe collection *Apicius*, the only such survival from the ancient world.

Food in Society

City-dwellers in Rome, many of whom lived in apartment blocks, had little opportunity to cook: cooking required an open fire, often an unacceptable risk. Street food was, however, always available. Cakes and sweets, mulled wine, hot sausages, hot chickpea soup, and barley polenta were on sale from street stalls and at cook shops, places of sufficient importance to be regulated by the Senate. Poor country folk depended largely on the resources of their own fields and gardens, supplemented by herbs and fruits gathered from the wild. In their diet, meat and fish were uncommon. Food preparation was a shared task but the special responsibility of women.

Slaves and employees in large households were sometimes well placed in the competition for food. However, the Greek satirist Lucian (*On Salaried Posts in Great Houses*, 2nd century AD) warned a friend who had been offered a post as tutor that he would be placed at the lowest table, would be sneered at by slaves, and would taste little of the fine cuisine except the mallow leaves that garnished the serving dishes. Such houses had kitchens staffed with slaves, the skilled cook himself often being an expensive and carefully chosen acquisition. The historian Livy (died AD 17) dates Rome's decline into luxurious decadence to the first arrival of cooks and dancing-girls in the city, booty from a campaign in Asia Minor in 189 BC.

Dinner parties were among the vehicles of the patron–client relationships that pervaded Roman society in the late republic and early empire; they allowed the host to display wealth and generosity by means of costly wines, elaborate and highly spiced foods, sumptuous tableware and decorations, handsome slaves, and lavish entertainment. Baskets of food (*sportulae*) were given to clients not lucky enough to be invited to a real dinner.

By Martial's time, however, patronage was past its heyday. Roman families could no longer compete for influence as they once had, because only the emperor could win the competition. Rome's status as an overgrown city-state is signalled in one of the special privileges enjoyed by inhabitants of the city: the free bread ration. Interruptions in the wheat supply led to riots; its continuity was eventually assured by Rome's annexation of Egypt at the suicide of Cleopatra in 30 BC. Thereafter, huge grain ships left Alexandria regularly through the sailing season, bringing wheat to Ostia at the mouth of the Tiber. The emperors took close interest in its distribution, for they gradually came to act as patrons to the whole citizenry: Domitian (ruled AD 81–96) presented *sportulae* to every citizen attending the lavish Saturnalia festival over which he presided.

Meals and Menus

Romans ate little during the first part of the day. Many did not trouble to take breakfast, *ientaculum*; only the greedy wanted a heavy lunch, *prandium*. There was no better preparation for a full evening meal, *cena*, the one big meal of the day, than a couple of hours at the baths. These were fashionable meeting places, ideal locations for business discussions. One could easily spend a whole evening there: wine was sold at bars, and the satirical Martial laughs at a miser who "always ate out" and spent practically nothing, taking advantage of the snacks offered with wine at these bars. There were also restaurants serving more elaborate food.

Typical larger Roman houses of the early empire had a special dining room, the *triclinium*. Three couches arranged in a U, each large enough for three diners—thus nine in total—surrounded a central table. Later this fashion gave way to that of a semicircular or apsidal dining area for seven to twelve guests. A house with a large enough garden might also have an outdoor dining area, shaded by vines and creepers, with stone couches made comfortable with cushions and pillows. As in early Etruscan dining, but in stark contrast to Greek custom, men and women generally reclined and ate together.

At dinner parties, servants took off guests' sandals as they entered the dining room; they then reclined, on the left elbow. Their hands were washed and their fingernails trimmed and cleaned; a good idea, since those hands would reach into a common dish to take a portion of food. The emperor Otho (AD 69) ordered his guests' feet to be washed and perfumed, but this was an affectation; the fictional host Trimalchio, in the *Satyricon*, had their toenails trimmed, a *reductio ad absurdum*.

The sequence of dishes is summed up in the proverbial *ab ovo usque ad malum* (from egg to apple). It began with an optional *promulsis* or appetiser, followed by an aperitif, *mulsum* (honeyed wine) or *conditum* (spiced wine). Then came the *gustus*, a sequence of hors d'oeuvres, which might be more varied and costly than the main course, though not so bulky. We have the menu of a religious dinner, attended by Julius Caesar, at which 16 hors d'oeuvres were served, ranging from sea urchin and clams to slices of venison and wild boar.

The *mensae primae*, first tables or main course, consisted of meat dishes, variously prepared and sometimes theatrically presented; they were accompanied by bread and wine. Waiters were forever coming and going, bringing new dishes, clearing away, supplying perfumed water for finger-rinsing.

Tables were then cleared, or, if portable, new tables were brought, with desserts (*mensae secundae*, second tables) and more wine. Music and dance by hired slave performers might accompany the drinking; Augustus preferred to entertain his guests by employing actors and traditional story-tellers. A napkin which lay in front of the diners as they reclined served as a knapsack to take home uneaten delicacies and the little gifts, *apophoreta*, with which a host would regale his friends as they departed.

Some Major Foods

Roman bakers baked leavened bread, both white and wholemeal. Small-scale baking required a dome-shaped baking crock, *testum*, *clibanus*: fragments of these are often found by archaeologists. A commercial bakery, complete with fossilized loaves, has been excavated at Pompeii. The staple food of early Italy had been not wheat bread but *puls*, porridge made from emmer wheat. *Polenta*, another traditional cereal product, was made from barley.

Cows were driven through the streets of Rome to supply fresh milk. Butter was not commonly used, but sheep's, goat's and cow's milk cheeses were known in many kinds and shapes, including the smoked cheeses matured in the Velabrum district of central Rome. Flocks of sheep were grazed near the city in spring to supply the demand for spring lamb. Game included wild boar from Umbria and the Laurentian marshes. Various mushroom species were enjoyed; truffles were prized.

Always in use in the Roman kitchen were olive oil, fish sauce, and wine. All three were manufactured and distributed on a large scale. *Garum* or *liquamen* (fermented fish sauce) was the major source of dietary salt. Scarcely any *Apicius* recipes call for pure salt, though salt was used in preserving. Among sweeteners, grape syrup was commonly used in flavouring, as were honey and dates, the latter produced by the Roman provinces of Syria and Egypt.

In the recipes of *Apicius* (*see* APICIAN FLAVOUR), the flavour of the main ingredient is often enhanced with 10 or 15 spices and herbs. Recipes often begin: "Pound pepper and lovage," a reminder that both exotic spices and local herbs were appreciated (lovage, *ligusticum* in Latin, a bitter culinary herb resembling celery, was said to be native to Liguria). Other flavourings were onion, garlic, mustard, dill, fennel, rue, savoury, thyme, mint, pine kernels, cumin, and coriander, all from Mediterranean lands. Roman cooks demanded, on behalf of rich employers, exotic spices from far beyond the empire's borders: pepper, ginger, costus or putchuk, spikenard, long pepper, cloves. asafoetida (Latin *laser* or *silfi*) was imported from central Asia as a substitute for Libyan *silphium*, which was much prized in the 2nd and 1st centuries BC and was harvested to extinction. Some spices, such as sugar and cinnamon, were so costly that they were not used in food but only as medicines.

Epilogue

The western Roman Empire crumbled, disappearing in AD 476, but the Gothic king Theodoric (493–526) continued to enjoy the gastronomic wealth of empire. Danube carp, Rhine salmon, and something not unlike the Amarone of Valpolicella all found their way to his court.

Classical Roman food lacked some of the familiar landmarks of modern Italian diets.

Pasta, though known, was unimportant. Pizzas are not to be found in classical texts. The buffalo was as yet unknown. Spinach, aubergines, and oranges had still to arrive from the East. Tomatoes, maize, and sweet peppers are post-Columbian introductions. But many typically Italian foods, including bread, cheese, and olive oil, were already typically Roman. Food was already at the centre of social relationships, as it still is.
(AKD)

ROMBO. *See* TURBOT.

ROME (*see also* ROMAN FOOD) and its food is a story of despair and hope, decline and renewal, change and continuity. The noisy *osterie* whose food Ada BONI recorded with precision in the 1930s were by then on their way out, but had flourished a hundred years earlier when Giuseppe Gioacchino BELLI wrote his scurrilous sonnets about life in the papal city, and the artist Bartolomeo PINELLI engraved tavern and market scenes as tourist postcards, only a few decades before it changed from a sleepy provincial backwater with a population of 120,000 to the reluctant administrative capital of a sullenly united Italy. The close relationship between the surrounding countryside and this small pilgrim town created a cuisine based on local products brought in to the markets from nearby, or grown in the many kitchen gardens and waste lands within the city—a frugal but robust cuisine, using mainly cheap cuts and offal, and on the whole untouched by the sophisticated cuisine of the papal court and the nobility in their grand palaces. We can read of their banquets and ceremonial feasts, a world of unimaginable pomp and extravagance, in Scappi and later writers, but what is remarkable is the appearance of dishes of tripe, offal, and extremities in these lavish aristocratic meals, rather than the trickle-down of

cheap ingredients to the hungry masses that one might have imagined. One dish that did trickle down was *pasticcio di maccheroni*, which still exists in various forms, simplified and complex; originally it was a mixture of ziti, short stumpy *maccheroni*, in a rich meat sauce, layered in a sweet pastry crust along with precooked chicken livers and gizzards, not to mention their crests, mushrooms, artichokes, and truffles, all enveloped in a sauce made by diluting some fresh ricotta in some of the cooking water from the pasta, with diced *caciotta* and some grated parmesan, and the pastry topping dusted with sugar before baking for 45 minutes. When one's life or the world is in a right mess, Romans call things a *pasticcio*, and you can see why. Simpler versions have the *maccheroni* layered with fewer things and baked in the oven, a dish said to have been enjoyed by grumpy Madame Letizia, Napoleon's mother, who lived in an apartment overlooking the Piazza Venezia.

Rome has always offered street food to a huge influx of pilgrims, artisans, immigrants, and barbarian hordes, so the provision of pizza by the yard and spit roasted chicken is not an ignoble tradition. Pilgrims, the package tourists of the past, combined a search for spiritual salvation with earthly pleasures, so the Roman trattoria has always been there for those unfortunate enough not to be able to get home for lunch, with food in the local tradition for local appetites, and milder versions for the strange tastes of foreigners. Until recently, tourists would sit in the killer sunshine at tables on the pavement eating roast chicken and salad while more robust food was enjoyed in the pungent murky depths within—*trippa all romana, coda alla vaccinara, baccalà* in a rich sauce with pine nuts and raisins, or young lamb *scottadita*, plainly grilled and eaten dangerously hot in the fingers with a squeeze of lemon. The prim and proper Sidonius in faraway Gaul is quoted by Dalby (2000, p. 219) as longing to "take refuge in a dingy tavern, my eyes watering, my nostrils stopped against the smoke from the kitchen, where from aromatic saucepans the scent of sausage and thyme and juniper berries rises, and the steam of cooking pots mingles with the smoke from spitting frying pans." This is the eternal appeal of earthy Roman eating, recalled by the prim civil servant Belli writing his sonnets in scurrilous Romanesco, and later the respectable Ada Boni organising cookery classes to teach the Roman bourgeoisie all about their robust native food traditions. But then the irreversible demographic changes of the late 20th century drove the inhabitants of the historic centre out to high-rise blocks in the suburbs, the homes of humble artisans, shopkeepers and inner-city riffraff are now boutiques, studios, and apartments for media people, and the markets are supplied from a vast central organisation, the Centro Agroalimentare Roma, established in the suburbs in 2002 and distributing produce from all over Italy and Europe. Until recently, the market in the Campo dei fiori used to be bursting with fruit and vegetables brought in daily from the surrounding countryside, prepared by redoubtable market women, trimming cabbages and lettuces, peeling and cutting up vegetables for soup, dealing with artichokes (a task requiring amazing speed and skill, well worth paying for, with the tender leaf bases and soft central hearts, the choke as yet inexistent, all ready to cook). Today the market is a shadow of its former self, with half the number of stalls, and many of those awash with the cheap clothing and meretricious knickknacks that now seem common to markets all over Europe, and the vegetables and fruit no better, or worse, than those to be got cheaply in supermarkets. But the eating places of the area are changing in unexpected ways, proof that against all odds Roman food is immortal, for gastro-tourists now disdain tourist fodder, and come armed with lists of things to eat and places to eat them in, carefully compiled from guidebooks and the Web; the cheap and cheerful trattoria of the past is no

longer cheap, but has been revived by a new kind of discriminating client, and traditional recipes are cooked with care for informed visitors and discerning natives. In Belli's day, a local trattoria offered home cooking to local people who were not wealthy but knew what they wanted and how it should be. In Belli's sonnet in Roman dialect "La sabatina," a wayward youth shouting from the street to a typically possessive *mamma romana*, demanding his pipe and a *papetto* (about a euro or less), is off to wind up a Saturday night's dissipation with an unsuitable companion and a bowl of tripe. "*Giovedì gnocchi, sabato trippa,*" as the saying goes—Gnocchi on Thursday and tripe on Saturday. This shouted conversation, echoing in the narrow street, reminds us that noise is part of the Roman enjoyment of food; discreet sounds of well-bred appreciation would be swamped in most trattorias by the full-throated roar of a family weekend outing. Pinelli conveyed this in his engravings, some of which remind us of Platina's reference to the "taverns of Rome, those grammar schools of gastronomy," where he says he learnt so much from his friend Martino, who would hold forth about food like a classical orator improvising on themes. They still do.

The noisy, narrow streets still follow Roman street patterns, palimpsests of footpaths and goat tracks among the seven hills and surrounding swamps and meadows; even the great urban development of Sixtus V could not obliterate the lanes and ancient nooks and crannies, and orchards and vineyards, among the ruins where until a short time ago turkeys gobbled and cattle grazed and wild plants grew. Today *motorini* dash noisily up and down these alleys, replacing the calls of street vendors and shouted exchanges from workshops and kitchens that once so irritated the sensitive younger Seneca.

Ancient Rome (*see* ROMAN FOOD) also had a tradition of street food, supplying those who lived in tenement blocks and had

Er pranzo de le minente

Mo ssenti er pranzio mio. Ris'e ppiselli,
Allesso de vaccina e ggallinaccio,
Garofolato, trippa, stufataccio,
e un spido de sarcicce e ffeghetelli.
Poi fritto de carciofoli e ggranelli,
Certi ggnocchi da facce er peccataccio,
Na pizza aricressciuta de lo spaccio,
E un agreddorce de ciggnale e uscelli.

Ce funno peperoni sott'asceto
Salame, mortatella e casciofiore,
Vino de tuttopasto e vvin d'Orvieto.

Eppoi risorio der perfett'amore,
Caffè e cciammelle: e tt'ho lassato arreto
Certe radisce da slargatte er core.

Bbe', cche importò er trattore?
Cor vitturino che mmaggnò con noi,
Manco un quartin per omo: e cche cce vòi?

Terni, 8 ottobre 1831
Giuseppe Gioacchino Belli (1791–1863)

Lunch with the *"Minente"**

Just listen to what we had. Rice and peas,
A stew of beef and turkey cock,
Beef topside pot roast with cloves, a right old dish of tripe,
And spit roast sausages and pork liver.
Then a fry-up of artichokes and sheeps' balls,
Some sinful gnocchi to die for,
A puffed-up take-away pizza,
Sweet sour wild boar and game birds.
There were peppers in vinegar,
Salami, *mortadella*, and a fresh sheep's cheese,
House plonk, and wine from Orvieto.
Next some divine *rosolio*,
Coffee and sweet bread rings,
And radishes to gladden the heart.
So, how much did the bill come to?
Including the driver, who ate with us,
Less than a "quarter" a head, what d'you expect?

*These *minente*, short for *eminente*, were comfortably off *romanesche*, common, not posh, women of
Rome, on an *ottobrata*, an autumn outing to the Castelli Romani. One can only wonder how the
refined Ada Boni identified with them, but she certainly liked this sort of food and towards the end
of her life devoted a whole book to it.

nowhere to cook, and the hordes of visitors and workmen, not to mention the more refined personages described by Andrew Dalby (2000) in his literary and topographical excursion among the pleasures and indulgences of ancient Rome; he enjoyed everything from fried fish to sausages, boiled chickpeas, and freshly baked bread. He gives us a glimpse of the emperor Nero on the rampage in Subura (a low-lying—low in every sense of the word—area) incognito, looking for a bit of rough, wallowing in sleazy cookshops, intent on mayhem, like CARAVAGGIO centuries later. Juvenal wrote of "*candiduli divina tomacula porci*" (divine sausages of nice white pork), and Dalby reminds us how street food was a universal pleasure, even for the rich, although the *pervigiles popinae* (ever-open cook shops) were on the sleazy side.

Ancient Rome had markets where local produce and food from the countryside were on offer; Horace would stroll round them: "I go wherever I fancy and I go on my own. I ask the price of greens and flour. I stroll about the lying Circus, and the Forum as the sun sets; I hang around the fortune-tellers; then off home to a dish of leeks, chickpeas, and flatbread" (2000, p. 223)—a conscious reference to the austere vegetarian diet of the founders of Rome, shepherds, then farmers, whose sober and industrious way of life and shrewd political sense were the foundation of Rome's greatness. Today's cult of *farro*, emmer wheat, sometimes misnamed spelt, which nourished the legions on their conquering marches, is part of our own idealization of *cucina povera*, and the vegetable markets of Rome, which survive away from the tourist spots—in Testaccio, over the river in Prati, and near the Vatican—still provide, in spite of competition from elsewhere, a range of local delicacies, *nostrani*—asparagus, artichokes (trimmed and all ready for stewing with garlic and pennyroyal, *alla romana*, or deep-fried, crisp, and tawny like chrysanthemums, *alla giudea*), broccoli, large but sweet and tender fresh peas, the crisp and slightly

bitter *puntarelle* (ready prepared), and the glorious young crop of broad beans, at their best raw with some pecorino cheese, or later stewed with *guanciale* and herbs. Mounds of spinach and *cicoria*, which can be lightly cooked, drained, then turned with garlic, chilli, and olive oil, *in padella*, contrast with bunches of golden zucchini flowers, which when stuffed with mozzarella or ricotta, sometimes with anchovies and herbs as well, then deep fried, are one of the delights of the Roman kitchen, and bunches of *agretti* or *barba di frate*, to be lightly cooked and eaten with oil and lemon, and mounds of salad leaves of different kinds for the *misticanza*, traditionally a salad of wild herbs and plants, freshly gathered and with considerable exhaustion, by legendary old women in black (a custom now inadvisable because of pollution). Most of these vegetables, as well as making *contorni*, are used in pasta recipes—broccoli cooked with garlic and chilli with spaghetti or *conchiglie*; young or wild asparagus and spaghetti; *pasta e ceci*, fettucine with chickpeas, flavoured with tomato and rosemary; *pasta alla papalina*, fettucine with ham, peas, and egg; *spaghetti alla chitarra* with mushrooms, white wine, garlic, parsley, *guanciale*, and peas; pasta with broad beans, peas, and artichokes.

Faced with all, this the thought of meat becomes less and less appealing. But this is the context in which the Roman attitude to meat makes sense—a small portion on its own is all one needs; even the rich stews and offal dishes are best in small helpings, and apart from the potatoes cooked in the pan with *abbacchio al forno*, roast young lamb, meat comes on its own. Beef dishes were traditionally made from cuts from animals too old to work, and needed long slow cooking, as in *coda alla vaccinara*, oxtail stew, and *garofolato*, a piece of shin or topside stewed with cloves, while expensive luxuries like baby lamb and sucking pig would be enjoyed after filling up with plenty of pasta, and accompanied by a generous *contorno. Saltimbocca alla romana* makes the most of an expensive cut, with a sage leaf or two sandwiched between thin slices of veal and *prosciuto crudo*, fried quickly on each side, the pan juices thickened with a pinch of flour and some white wine. An exception is a dish made with the plentiful offal from a grown lamb, and artichokes, also cheap and plentiful—the *coratella*, or liver, lungs, spleen, and heart, are cut up small, each cooked the appropriate length of time with sliced onions and white wine, then finished off with the artichokes, which have been trimmed and cooked in lard or oil, the whole thickened with beaten egg stirred into the mixture, with plenty of marjoram or pennyroyal.

Rome is not without elegant and expensive restaurants, bars, and ice cream parlours, but they have never lost touch with their earthy antecedents. Even the postwar prosperity and the influx of foreigners, politicians, and film moguls, and those heaped dishes of *fettucine al triplo burro* (a fashionable aberration, invented at Alfredo's to delight Douglas Fairbanks and Mary Pickford on their honeymoon, served with golden implements in a sauce of butter, parmesan, and cream), cannot stifle the Roman love, at all levels, of this robust and characteristic cooking.

ROMOLI, DOMENICO (PANUNTO),

about whom little is known, published his *La singolar dottrina* in Venice in 1560, in which he describes the role of *scalco* or chief steward of a noble household, going on to deal in entertaining detail with the other household officials, in particular the *cuoco segreto* or private cook of the master himself, and then on to recipes and ingredients. He admits that his own experiences of the responsibilities and perils of the job, from which he nevertheless emerged with distinction, were quite terrifying. The ideal cook, he said, should be like a wise old physician, with a *"corazza copiosa di carità, di fede e diligenza"* (a heart overflowing with charity, loyalty, and diligence), with the help of younger cooks to handle the heavy work—strong, clean, well-groomed, and *"piacevoli, ubbidienti, umani, allegri, e quando possibil fosse italiani e non tramontani"* (pleasing, obedient, humane, cheerful, and where possible Italians and not foreigners). A good cook needs to be kept cheerful and willing, but not with drink. With all these qualities, he has also to be something of a clairvoyant, keeping a step ahead of the capricious tastes of his master. The section on the *bottigliere*, cellarer and wine waiter, is a really helpful summary of the wines enjoyed at that time:

> He has the responsibility of ordering up the wines needed for each meal, red, white, sweet or dry, and when to serve them. Beginning with the first course of melon and salad, there should be *vin greco* and *salerno bianco*, in winter *malvagía*, *moscatello*, or *vernacia*; with the antipasti and boiled dishes serve light white wines; full-bodied reds with the roasts, and with the fruit, *ippocrasso*, *magnaguerra* or a sweet red *salerno*. . . . Of course they should have an in depth understanding of their wines, but as *bevitori e non bomboni*, tasters not topers. (Faccioli, 1992, p. 368)

Quite apart from the details of recipes and insights into the princely households of the time, Romoli is a really entertaining read, with a wealth of colloquial expressions, a wry sense of humour, and the warmth of a lifetime's triumph of hope over experience.

ROSE,

Rosa damascena, Rosa centifolia, Rosa canina, Rosa rugosa (and many others), *rosa*, is a plant of the Rosaceae family to which belong quince, azarole, and medlar, source of a flavouring and perfume much used in the past, in the form of distilled scented water, oil, and the petals, fresh, preserved in syrup, or crystallised. The hips can be boiled to make jelly or syrup. Today we associate rose-water with perfumery and cosmetics, old-fashioned potpourri, and the cuisines of the Middle East and the Indian subcontinent, forgetting our own culinary heritage. The perfume of rosewater hovered over the splendours of the medieval banquet, in the ritual washing of hands at the beginning of a meal, the sprinkling over certain foods just before serving, or its use in some sauces, and the final cleansing of the eaters' sticky hands at the end of the meal. It went on being used during the Renaissance, in cooking and as a perfume, and often rose petals were strewn over the white tablecloth, with other fragrant flowers, to add visual and olfactory delight to the meal. Martino used rosewater lavishly, in junkets, almond dishes, and a lovely marzipan tart, in which finely pounded almonds, flavoured with sugar and rosewater, are baked in a thin layer over sweet wafers soaked in rosewater. Messisbugo used rose-water lavishly in pastries, biscuits, and soft sweet white bread rolls; it went into the basic mix for a very rich sweetened pastry to enclose spiced pigeons and ham, moistened with bitter orange juice, spiced with sugar and cinnamon, interspersed with pine nuts and baked in the oven, served sprinkled with more sugar. And Messisbugo's *brezzatelle* are familiar (*see* BREADS, RING-SHAPED)—a yeasted sweet dough, with butter, eggs, sugar, rosewater, and milk, shaped into rings, plunged into boiling water, then dried and baked in the oven. He flavours fresh fruit stewed in butter with cinnamon and rosewa-ter, and puts rosewater into a custard thick-ened with eggs and flour to be served in little tarts or pastries with sugar and cinnamon.

Although roses perfumed food and wine in classical times, and Greek colonists brought their use to southern Italy, it was the spread of Arab culture that brought the arts of cultivation and distillation of rose petals to Spain and southern Italy; and trade in spices and flavourings perpetuated some aspects of the Arab legacy long after their ori-gins were forgotten. This expensive perfume and flavouring became a European luxury, prepared by housewives as well as pharma-cists, and was only superseded by the growth of commercially produced scents and flavour-ings in the 19th century. Apart from the weight of symbolism attached to the fragrant flower with its protective thorns (roses asso-ciated with love, suffering, celebrations, and even some strident forms of nationalism), what concerns us here is the hardnosed, large-scale production of the plant whose fragrance had so many uses. It took 10,000 pounds of roses to make 1 pound of the es-sential oil, so if an acre of land, with 5,000 rose trees, yields 2,200 pounds, then one un-derstands how the fertile plains of the Guadalquivir or the valley of Kazanluk in Bulgaria wafted their perfume over an entire region. It seems that in Italy, imported rose-water from the major areas of production was used alongside homemade varieties, which were produced either by steeping the prepared rose petals (the astringent white base of each petal had to be removed) in water or spirits, or by distillation. The *Tacuinum Sani-tatis* (an illustrated health handbook from 15th-century northern Italy) has separate en-tries for rose, whose flowers, leaves, pollen, and stems all have their uses, and rosewater: "at the right moment during the summer the women of the house will have prepared rose-water, which is made from the most fragrant flowers in the rose garden, without adding water but using only their natural moisture," which implies an awful lot of roses. Mattioli insisted that a glass and not a lead alembic should be used, for it produced a more deli-cate liquid, thinking here of its medicinal uses; apart from cheering the heart, it was good as an astringent poultice; a wash to soothe a headache, calm disturbed spirits, help sore eyes; a cream for a bad skin; a cor-dial and a binding for those with gastric up-sets; but above all, an aroma to stimulate the appetite and enhance flavours. Corrado made a rose-flavoured vinegar; distilled rosewater from water in which petals had been steeped for days; and made a *rosolio* from rose petals macerated in spirits and sweetened with syrup as well as a *marmellata* of petals in hard crack sugar syrup.

ROSEMARY, *rosmarino, ramerino, Rosmarinus officinalis*, is today in common use in stews and roasts, especially, lamb, pork, and kid, the fresh evergreen leaves either finely chopped or used as whole sprigs. Dried rosemary quickly loses its essential oils and becomes unpleasant in both flavour and texture, and is best avoided. A simple sauce of finely chopped garlic and rosemary cooked gently in butter can go with meat, fish, or pasta. There are some fine fish recipes; turbot, marinated in salt, grape must, and vinegar, grilled on a bed of rosemary branches dipped in oil, and basted with the marinade, sounds modern enough, though it comes from Scappi (1570). A recipe from Liguria for octopus includes chopped onion, garlic, tomato, hot red chilli, and a branch of rosemary, cooked very slowly, with no additional liquid, in a sealed pot, for four hours, finished with potatoes cooked in the resultant fragrant liquid. A sprig of rosemary can be used to baste spit-roasted meat or fish, or placed inside a large baked fish. Finely chopped leaves sometimes flavour the Ligurian *fainà, farinata,* made with chickpea flour beaten to a runny batter with water and salt, left to mature for several hours, mixed with

olive oil and chopped rosemary, and baked in thin sheets in shallow copper trays in a very hot oven. The pretty pale blue flowers, fresh or candied, can be used as decoration for salads and cold cuts.

The camphorous aroma of the distilled oil is valued in perfumery and in liqueurs but can be overwhelming unless used with discretion. Like lavender, rosemary was used to calm digestive disturbances, relieve rheumatic pains, soothe the troubled mind, stimulate the brain, and invigorate the memory, and so became an emblem of friendship and fidelity, as well as one of the most agreeable herbs in use. The Romans are said to have used it in garlands. Mattioli, to whom the Tuscan *focaccia* must have been familiar, says that eaten with bread and salt the tender leaves and flowers of rosemary will improve weak sight, which is a reminder of how medicine and gastronomy overlapped. The Botanic Gardens in Florence list the therapeutic qualities of rosemary in a recent publication (Causer and Luzzi, 2002) and describe how in the Pistoian countryside an infusion of rosemary and sage is given to calm anxiety, and helps the mentally and physically exhausted when added to their bathwater.

ROSETTA(E). *See* BIGNE, BREAD ROLLS, MICHETTA.

ROSOLIO. *See* APERITIVI.

ROSPO, CODA DI. *See* MONK-FISH.

ROSSELLI, GIOVANNI DE', is the "phantom" author of *Epulario*, published in 1516 in Venice, one of the many plagiaries of the work of MARTINO, which went on being copied in manuscript and in

Sprigs of rosemary. (Shutterstock)

various publications until superseded in the 1550s by new works reflecting changes in taste.

ROSSETTI, GIOVANNI BATTISTA,

active 1550s, was *scalco*, chief steward, to Lucrezia d'Este, duchess of Urbino (named for her much-loved grandmother Lucrezia Borgia) who was living in Ferrara when his book *Dello scalco* was published there in 1584. He was from a noble Ferrarese family and writes of his role as one requiring the highest standards of breeding and professionalism. After 27 years' experience he had a lot to tell, and he did so with conviction and vigour. The book is in three parts; the first describes the qualities and functions of a *scalco* or chief steward and his staff; the second, the longest, lists many of the most important banquets and meals masterminded by Rossetti for his employers and their illustrious guests. The final part is a listing of all the possible ingredients and what can be done with them; this sounds dull but is in fact full of interest, and gives an insight into the ways a head of household can make the best use of provisions, and also how Rossetti drew on foreign as well as Italian ideas and recipes. His lists read like the index to the cookery book that never was. The introduction by the printer and publisher Domenico Mammarello sounds familiar—he tells ruefully of how after waiting in vain for years for the promised manuscript, he was surprised and overjoyed when, out of the blue, it arrived with an exhortation to publish urgently at popular request. Rossetti and his publisher both go out of their way to praise the cookery books of Sbugo (Messisbugo) and Scappi, pointing out that Rossetti's publication covers ground not dealt with by these authors, looking at menus and provisioning from the point of view of the organiser rather than the cook and kitchen staff. There is a hint of a second book by Rossetti, already under way, with recipes, and descriptions of seasonings, cooking methods, and sugar work, to follow the hoped-for success of this first volume. Nothing came of it, to our loss, but throughout *Dello scalco* we get tantalising glimpses of Rossetti's interest in cooking and recipes, his inventiveness and imaginative approach to ingredients, and his awareness of the need for balanced menus and appealing combinations of dishes. He writes of how a good steward will plan a week's menus in advance, control the ordering of provisions, but adjust both lunch and dinner menus to suit the mood of his employer, carefully monitoring what he eats at lunch time, and revising the second meal of the day to complement his earlier intake. He mentions how it is always a good idea to have an arrangement with the cook to rustle up some little exotic surprise, perhaps an unusual combination of leftovers, to charm and tempt the ducal appetite. This can be done at no extra cost, using existing stuff. He admits candidly that a good steward can learn a lot from an inventive cook, and the cook in turn can be stimulated by ideas from the *scalco*. These insights into everyday eating are in many ways more fascinating than the long and frankly improbable banquet menus of his contemporaries, Scappi and Messisbugo. The small dinners, with perhaps two courses and *frutta* (the name of the dessert course) give a much better idea of how Italian food was enjoyed by upper classes of the time. The requirements of lesser members of the ducal court, down to the servants and staff of visiting foreigners, are also described. Rossetti is honest about the need to balance the expense of splendidly extravagant occasions against the need for economy in others—to know when to "*caminare per la strada larga dello splendore, & liberalità, & quando per l'angusta della parsimonia, & quando, & per lo più, per quella come per più lata & laudata, della mediocrità, ove può meno errare*" (stride along the broad highway of splendour and liberality, when to take the narrow road of parsimony, or when, for the most part, to choose the more spacious and esteemed middle way, where one is least likely to go astray).

Rossetti travelled with his Este employers all over Europe; he observed the styles of preparing and serving food in Bohemia, France, and Germany, and says with some pride that their new ways of cooking and seasoning have been refined and perfected by Italian cooks. The idea of seating guests round a number of small square or round tables, with the main dish in the centre, surrounded by smaller ones, is a change from the long—sometimes very long—trestle tables in the Italian style, with an array of dishes placed according to the importance of the guests. We have seen how Messisbugo served an *oglio* in the middle of a round table, so that diners could help themselves from this "meal in a pot." Rossetti describes a domestic dinner in the German style for Duke Alfonso and a few friends, sitting round a square table, in the centre a main dish containing several large steamed fish, each with its sauce, surrounded by smaller accompanying dishes of perhaps snails in a sauce, small sturgeon pasties, puréed chickpeas, stuffed squid, stewed plums, stuffed squid in broth, all on sippets of bread. Then come the fried and roast dishes—sturgeon; smoked *miglioramenti* or eel; marinated, fried pike; and a fried salt carp—arranged in a large platter with slices of orange and lemon round its rim, and small dishes of fried trout, sardines, squid, and turbot, a lamprey in its sauce, little yellow almond tarts, and some sour cherry sauce. The final course was a big bowl of red and white grapes surrounded by red apples, and various sugared and candied fruit, ALMONDS, pistachios, pine nuts, and raisins, and the inevitable fresh and crisp cardoons to refresh the palate, along with a few truffles.

Another suggestion, which Rossetti felt was an improvement on Italian usage, was the elimination of sweet things from the first course of cold dishes from the *credenza* or sideboard. These appetizers could have the reverse effect, he said, cloying and sometimes so strongly flavoured that they desensitised the taste buds and detracted from the enjoyment of the rest of the meal. He recommends starting with salads and cold prepared food, followed by boiled dishes, then a selection of roasts or fried food, after which came the *frutta* (not just fruit but raw cardoons, fennel, artichokes, perhaps more salads, nuts), sometimes followed by a final course of *confetture*, candied or sugared fruits and nuts. This was the usual practice abroad, and he followed it in small select gatherings for Lucrezia and family, served without the pomp of court banquets. These simpler meals, *ordinari*, have a rhythm and balance; they make sense, even though the number of dishes still seems a lot to us.

One lean or meatless banquet, on a Friday in March (p. 205), was meant to be structured round a quantity of large trout which never materialised, so Rossetti decided that the meal should still happen, with no fish whatsoever, salted or fresh, and went ahead with an entrancing menu of salads and vegetables prepared in an astonishing variety of ways. The scale and apparatus were that of a banquet, not a domestic supper, with pleated table linen and floral decorations. There were five courses. The first offered salads of fresh chicory and young wild garlic shoots, lettuce and spring onions, young radishes, their leaves picked out with gold leaf, stuffed and fried artichokes served with gilt bay leaves around the dish, little tartlets of truffles, surrounded by gilt artichoke leaves, spinach ravioli decorated with sugared anise seeds, a soup of dates and sour cherries cooked in Trebbiano wine with cinnamon, and various light creams made from almond milk and butter. (This was strictly egg and dairy free, as well as without meat and fish.) A mysterious *suppa* seems like an early sighting of a *zuppa inglese*—bread soaked in cinnamon water and sweet almond oil, layered with *ricotta da monache* (this would be fake ricotta made from almond milk), and sprinkled with sugar and cinnamon. The second course had 17 dishes, including maccheroni with a walnut and garlic sauce, spinach in a spicy sauce, fresh broad bean purée garnished with fried leeks, broccoli with bitter orange, stewed fennel and mushrooms, stewed white cabbage hearts with bitter orange juice. Then came the fried things: fritters of bitter herbs garnished with sprigs of tarragon fried in batter, artichokes splayed, stuffed, and fried (sounds like *carciofi all giudea*), parsnip tarts surrounded by fried parsnip slices, mushrooms stuffed with wild garlic and leeks, wrapped in paper and cooked on the grill, long thin tartlets of cardoons and truffles. The next course, called *frutta*, was a mixture of fruit, cooked and raw vegetables (cardoons, artichokes, peas, chestnuts), little tartlets of dried fruit and nuts, little truffle pasties garnished with fried almonds, dishes of olives, pickled vegetables, almond milk junkets decorated with herbs and flowers, and finally the really sweet things —fruit pastes, candied fruit and nuts, sugared nuts and spices, all served on a fresh clean tablecloth, with toothpicks, posies of fresh flowers, and gifts of perfumed gloves.

Much of the interest in Rossetti's book is the contrast between his magisterial cool and the almost manic inventiveness of his menus and recipes. The silent imposing figure, head and shoulders above his underlings, monitoring every move before and during the meals and events he controlled with rigid discipline and a will of iron, was also genial, appreciative, and responsive to the moods of both his master and his staff, sympathetic but never familiar, detached but not unheeding, caring for visiting notables and sick servants with unfailing good humour. From his descriptions of the duties of the steward and other officials we can build up a picture of a man happy in his work, which seemed to go on from crack of dawn to late at night, but with a continuing enthusiasm for creating a pleasurable lifestyle for his employers within a controlled and carefully budgeted environment.

RUE, *ruta, Ruta graveolens*, is one of the really bitter herbs, used a lot by the Romans, but less so today. A decorative plant, with its greyish small leaves and yellow flowers, it looks well in herb gardens, and the leaves, finely chopped and used sparingly, add grace notes to any dish which involves a balance of different herbs. Rue was said to be a useful antidote to poisons and so was added to mushroom dishes. Corrado said it helps to mitigate the strong flavours of some pork recipes. Before grappa became a designer drink, it was sometimes flavoured with rue, and it still goes into many liqueurs and *aperitivi* which depend on bitterness. It is both sedative, and good for the circulation, taken in moderation.

RUOPPOLO, GIOVAN BATTISTA, AND GIUSEPPE RECCO were the

foremost of the many artists in 17th-century Naples meeting an enthusiastic demand for still life paintings of fish, vegetables, and fruit. (The former [1629–1693] is not to be confused with his nephew Giuseppe, and the latter [1634–1695] is not to be confused with his father, Giacomo, and uncle, Giovan Battista, who also painted still life and genre scenes.) With so many similar names and initials and so many unsigned works, problems of attribution, influence, and provenance worry historians a lot, but fortunately cannot obscure for us the delight so many painters and patrons seemed to take in hedonistic images of things to eat. Naples was at that time a pleasure city, in a spectacularly beautiful setting, enjoying a balmy climate and the bounteous produce of the sea and surrounding countryside. Fruit, vegetables, fish, cheese, meat, and game poured into the larders of the nobility and prosperous bourgeoisie, and were recorded in all their lush profusion so that they could be enjoyed on their walls as well as on their plates. The foremost figure painter of the time, Luca Giordano, was happy to collaborate with Giuseppe Recco in a flamboyant *Marine Still Life with Fisherman*, providing the operatic fisherman and his wicker tray, while Recco filled in with sea bass and lobster against a rocky sea shore with a lurid sunset over the Bay of Naples and a chorus line of lively red mullet, gurnard, spider crabs, squid, and a great many more, making a great deal of noise. Giacomo Paravagna, Marchese di Noja, paid 100 ducats for this in 1669. A kitchen scene by Recco displays brilliantly coloured fish on plates, tables, and ledges, against a sombre background of kitchen pots and pans and a smouldering wood fire.

A still life, sometimes attributed to Recco, sometimes to Tommaso Realfonso, reminiscent of many displays of luxury goods in paintings from the Netherlands, is of particular interest to the historian of confectionery, with its enormous platter of cakes, biscuits, tarts, *panforte*, sugared comfits, preserved fruit, and nuts, which quite eclipse the violin, embossed leather cushion, oriental rugs, and vase of rare flowers. This has nothing to do with sweetmeats as symbols of ephemeral and transitory pleasures, but a blatant display of delight in expensive indulgence—no regrets, no remorse. A dish of sweetmeats is the most interesting and lively item in a rather boring allegorical painting by Recco of the five senses, in which he conveys the contrasting textures and surfaces of sponge fingers, puff pastry, *biscotti*, diamond-shaped flat pastry shapes decorated with silver leaf, caramel-coated almonds, and a frosted waffle with a bravura use of perspective. A pair of paintings that might be by Recco are particularly interesting—*Colazione pasquale salata* and *Colazione pasquale dolce*, a salt and a sweet Easter snack or breakfast, one showing an ornate decorative wreath of bread, a bowl of hard-boiled eggs, various cheeses, and salami, strewn with pink jasmine flowers; the other showing a dish of deep-fried and sugared, knotted, pretzel-shaped doughnuts decorated with rosemary, and a plate of white almond biscuits adorned with slices of candied citron and olive branches, with two wooden barrels in the background, probably containing fruit in syrup.

In contrast, a more sombre kitchen scene by Recco shows items of offal, the pluck and neck of a turkey, a pigeon—all things that need attentive cooking to become attractive and desirable—and on a shelf alongside, a cheese grater and some lumps of parmesan, and a rare sighting of uncooked pasta: a paper-wrapped bundle of what looks like *maccheroni*—long, hollow, mud-coloured strands bent double in the form in which they must have been dried. This celebration of not very visually exciting ingredients for their own sake is an indication of the Neapolitan delight in food and cooking, and as eloquent in its own way as the more decorative fruit pieces by these artists. Another image of *maccheroni* is in a painting by Giacomo Nani of a kitchen table with presumably the contents of a shopping bag all over it—a leg of lamb, some leafy vegetables, a lump of cheese, some bread rolls, several artichokes in a jug, and a sheet of crumpled paper with a bundle of pasta, indicating that pasta by then was a commercial rather than homemade product.

Giovan Battista Ruoppolo is renowned for his voluptuous fruit paintings, in which grapes, apples, pears, medlars, plums, pomegranates, melons bursting open with ripeness, and glowing cut watermelons tumble in profusion, with an exuberant abandon. His contemporary Abraham Brueghel (Neapolitan by adoption) used to throw melons from a great height to get them to burst open, and surround them with spontaneous scatterings of fruit and vegetables, and this somewhat wild approach to composition and colour is there in Ruoppolo, but does not exclude a scrupulous accuracy in the delineation of different varieties of fruit and fish. His fish-scapes have a wild beauty and the same accuracy, and his vegetables, piled together with citrus fruits in a painting in Spoleto, include celery, cardoons, artichokes, asparagus, various fresh salad leaves, cabbage greens, blanched chicory, and white radishes, their sombre colours a contrast to the brightly lit citrons, lemons, and bitter oranges, with their fragrant white flower buds, and some bright red strawberries, still on their stems, bunched like posies of red flowers round a central stick. (We find similar bunches of strawberries and cherries in earlier works by Luca Forte.) A pale, almost monochrome composition dominated by white flowers (*boules de neige*), blanched celery and chicory, with artichokes and asparagus almost hidden in a dark background, has a "bunch" of pea pods tied together with reeds, perhaps an indication of a Neapolitan way of displaying and selling things. The apparent random profusion of a huge canvas of fruit and foliage is in fact a carefully arranged composition of things, some in natural bunches, like the five different kinds of grapes, the figs on the branch, while figs in a basket, lemons in another basket, and groups of small pears and apples seem on close examination to be carefully tied up in neat bundles, which may reflect the current practises of the marketplace as well as the exigencies of organising such a complex canvas.

More glimpses of the marketplace can be found in other painters. Tommaso Salini in Rome shows whole pine cones with the nuts emerging, dried, shelled chestnuts strung on string, and a stalk of fennel with its fresh flower heads and seeds. Another work by the same artist has the rare appearance of two fresh red chillies, along with apples, mushrooms, lemons, asparagus, and a flask of wine. An anonymous painter in the south shows alongside the familiar watermelon and fruits some small eggplants on the branch, with fresh red chillies close by. An unusual detail in another Ruoppolo is a hunk of salted tunny still in its wrapping paper, with bread rolls, fruit, and a cabbage.

RUSPANTE. *See* FREE RANGE.

RYE, *Secale cereale, segale,* has been cultivated since prehistoric times. It is especially suited to cold northern climes and was the sustenance food of many areas in northern Italy, where wheat was difficult to grow, and is still cultivated in some alpine valleys. In Teglio and Valchiavenna in the province of Sondrio in Lombardy, rye bread is made with a very low percentage of wheat flour, added after long rising, shaped into small bread rolls, which can be eaten fresh, or cooked again to harden them for long keeping. In Trentino Alto Adige, there are several breads made with mixtures of wheat and rye flour: one flavoured with cumin seeds; a *schiacciata Aldino* from the commune of Aldein near Bolzano, flavoured with fenugreek, anise, and fennel and enriched with egg; another flatbread flavoured with anise, *schiacciatina*. From the Valtellina in Lombardy come *ciambelline*, little rings of long-keeping rye bread, hung on strings in a dry kitchen, or a bigger version, *brazadei*, worn like bracelets to leave a hand free for pouring out the wine, made with rye and buckwheat flour. The *puccia di Cortina* from Cortina d'Ampezzo in the province of Belluno are little flat loaves of wheat and rye flour, flavoured with *zigoinr*, a wild oregano unique to the locality, toasted and stuffed with local products, and devoured in alpine huts (INSOR, *Pane,* p. 127). The *otto di Merano* is a figure of eight–shaped loaf, made with rye and unbleached wheat flour, with the addition of lard and caraway seeds. Rye breadcrumbs, softened in milk and water, are made into dumplings, *canederli,* in Trentino Alto Adige, mixed with chopped onion and garlic, pancetta, or speck.

The carbohydrates in rye have the capacity to absorb large amounts of water, more than other grains; hence the moistness of long-keeping rye breads. When dried, as in crispbreads and the *ciambelle* mentioned earlier, they get to work absorbing moisture in the digestive tract, giving an impression of fullness—helpful to hungry peasants and the weight-conscious.

A disadvantage of the cool climates in which rye flourished is the growth of the ergot fungus on damp and rotting grains, which, when used in flour, we now know caused epidemics of Saint Anthony's fire, a disease inflicting gangrene and horrible hallucinations on the sufferers, usually starving peasants and the rural poor—chronicled by Camporesi in anguished detail. *See also* FLOUR, BREAD.

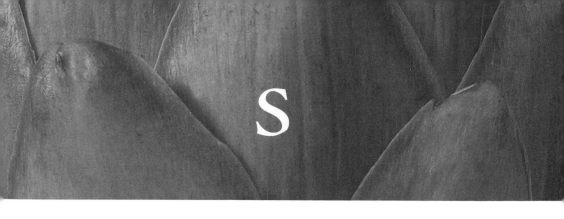

S

SABA, SAPA (grape must). *See* MOSTO COTTO, MUST.

SADDLED BREAM, *occhiata*, is one of the many breams, with big eyes and a black band where the tail joins the body (*see* BREAM). It is best eaten fresh, grilled, or fried. A Sicilian recipe adds pennyroyal and garlic to the fried fish, and douses them in vinegar.

SAFFLOWER, *Carthamus tinctorius, cartamo*, is often a possible substitute for SAFFRON, when colour is more important than flavour, but it is also used as an adulterant, which is why it is best not to buy powdered saffron. It is fine in strongly flavoured, highly spiced Middle Eastern and Indian dishes, and can make a substitute for saffron when trying out medieval Italian recipes in which your precious stock of saffron might be swamped by the stronger spices.

SAFFRON, *Crocus sativus, zafferano*, is one of the most expensive and pleasing of spices. The stigmas of the saffron crocus, three to a flower, are gathered by hand (at the right moment in the life of the plant, just as the flower opens, in the cool of an autumn morning or late afternoon), carefully removed, and carefully dried. A patient, time-consuming skill, with a small and precious

yield. Saffron is grown in Italy in Navelli near Aquila in Abruzzo, in Tuscany, Umbria, Sicily, and Sardinia, where the terrain and climate of San Gavino Monreale in the province of Cagliari yields some of the finest available today, produced organically. It takes about 200,000 stigmas to make a kilo of saffron, and so acres and acres to give us the quantities consumed worldwide. Adulteration is consequently a likelihood, and the purchaser would be advised to avoid powdered saffron and also beware of the dried petals of SAFFLOWER, *cartamo*, which are often sold as saffron. In fact, their use as a colorant in much Middle Eastern food makes sense, for the flavour of genuine saffron could be cancelled out by the other spices. It takes from 50,000 to 75,000 flowers to produce a pound of saffron. Labour intensive, and taking up much space, this is a commodity that could never be cheap; fortunately, a small pinch is enough for most

Saffron has long been the world's most expensive spice because it must be delicately harvested from the stigmas of the saffron crocus. (Shutterstock)

recipes. The colour is strong enough to tinge a dish of pale rice or bread a delicate yellow (*see* RISOTTO), and the essential oils provide a powerful aroma which would be overwhelming in large amounts. It is by no means clear exactly when saffron was first cultivated in Italy. The Romans used it as a spice and a dye, and Dalby quotes contemporary writers on the extravagance of spraying a solution of saffron in sticky sweet wine to perfume theatres and circuses, while spectators lounged under awnings dyed red, yellow, and maroon, bringing shade and a flow of rich colour (Dalby, 2000, p. 235). This lavish use of an extremely expensive spice was characteristic of ancient Rome, and the liberal use of it in Italian medieval and Renaissance cookery might also have been a way of flaunting wealth, for saffron is probably the most expensive and labour-intensive flavouring in the world. Its use during the Middle Ages with many other spices seems wilful, adding at great expense to a wide spectrum of flavours, and its inclusion in recipes may have been an example of conspicuous consumption. Dioscorides praised that from Cilicia, but also mentions Sicily as a source of saffron, and the legends around the invention of the Sicilian classic *pasta con le sarde*, pasta and sardines, as told by Mary Taylor Simeti (1989, p. 60), imply that saffron was there for the cooks of the conquering Byzantines to grasp and use in an improvised meal to feast their leader Euphemius in AD 827. They are said to have given him *bucatini* layered with cooked wild fennel fronds, fried sardines, and a sauce of onion, pine nuts, raisins, anchovy fillets, and crushed cooked sardines moistened with a little saffron-flavoured water, sprinkled with toasted breadcrumbs.

Saffron's medicinal properties were known in the Middle Ages through Arab writers; the name is Arabic, *za'faran*, and it is still much used in Middle Eastern cooking. Saffron was cultivated by the Arabs in Spain and in southern Italy, though it appears to have been a cash crop long before they arrived. The *Tacuina Sanitatis*, health handbooks produced in northern Italy in the late 15th century, show a woman in a pale blue robe carefully placing saffron flowers in a basket, a familiar sight to both the 9th-century Arab author and the Renaissance illustrator. Taken in large amounts, saffron was narcotic, but its expense and strong flavour made this unlikely; correctly handled, it could cheer the heart and do good to lungs and various organs, though while warding off drunkenness and cheering the heart it might also cloud the brain. Two anonymous manuscripts from the early 15th century (Bergström, 1985) indicate a frequent use of saffron in the south of Italy, in a *grattonata* of chicken joints fried with onion and *lardo*, the sauce thickened with verjuice and egg yolks and coloured with saffron; a *sarcamone* of lamb or mutton, boiled, then fried, and seasoned with spices, coriander, and cloves, and coloured with saffron.

Martino, also writing in the 15th century, used saffron with more subtlety, to colour a pallid *biancomangiare* a golden yellow, or in sauces where colour was important, like the *sapor fior di ginestra*, "broom blossom" sauce, made of ground almonds, egg yolks, and saffron diluted with verjuice and flavoured with ginger. His *suppa dorata*, a golden dish, was made by soaking some slices of lightly toasted bread, crusts removed, in eggs beaten up with sugar and rosewater, then frying them in butter and serving sprinkled with rosewater coloured with saffron and plenty more sugar. Here the dribble of bright liquid over the rich yellow egg and the paler white within is indeed a golden dish. As both colouring and flavouring, saffron went into a rich golden soup, *brodetto bono e bello*, in which a chicken broth was thickened with egg yolks and verjuice flavoured with sweet spices and saffron, and stirred over a very low heat, then taken off and stirred some more, for the space of two paternosters, to make sure it didn't curdle. A simple lemon sauce, *limonata*, in one of the many manuscript versions of Martino's work, was made of ground almonds diluted to make almond milk and simmered with spices and saffron, strained, and flavoured with lemon juice.

Platina stressed saffron's medicinal properties, and its uses in cooking, often to give pallid bland food a more vibrant appearance and flavour. A sauce of ground almonds and verjuice could be rather drab, but mixed with egg yolks, a little powdered ginger, and saffron, it became a lovely mixture the colour of broom blossoms that he called *ginestrata*.

Mattioli wrote in 1568 that saffron was used everywhere, and commends the quality of that from Aquila in Abruzzo, with a good word for that of his native Siena: *elettissimo*, outstanding. By then it was being grown in sufficient quantity in Italy, especially Aquila and Siena, that there was no need to import any from the Middle East, or indeed from Vienna, where the local crop was all used up by Germans and Hungarians, "who used so many spices." Spice merchants in Venice were by then selling Italian rather than imported saffron.

Costanzo Felici (1986, p. 131) wrote about the same time as Mattioli that saffron was in common use, "*tale che quasi vole entrare per tutto, contribuendo alquanto il suo sapore e odore e corregendo molti difetti d'altre vivande e poi mostrando il suo bello colore giallo*" (so much so that it seems to want to get into almost everything, contributing as much with its flavour and aroma, while correcting the defects of other ingredients, as well as displaying its beautiful yellow hue). It is interesting that both naturalist and physician stress its popularity, at a point when saffron was falling out of use in the kitchens of princely courts. What they really meant was that saffron was in demand, not for culinary use, but for so many different things: ointments, poultices, medicines, cosmetics (rouge and a spectacular hair dye), liqueurs, cordials and herbal tonics, stimulating drinks (some aphrodisiac), painters' pigments, dyes for fabrics, and probably alchemy. So it was stocked by pharmacists and easily available to old-fashioned cooks who still enjoyed using it.

Scappi, however, uses saffron sparingly in his work of 1570, to colour food that would otherwise be white or sludge-coloured, or where cinnamon and ginger would have made a sauce or stew look muddy. He uses it to colour the gelatine made from bones and cartilaginous material in which carefully prepared pieces of fish or flesh can be set in a decorative pattern, or to brighten dull dishes, like a rich egg custard, described as a tart without a crust, which was delicious with rosewater and cinnamon, raisins of Corinth cooked in wine, and much butter; when done, the top was sprinkled with sugar and cinnamon (an early sighting of *crème brulée*). Fritters and pancakes are coloured with saffron, and it gives a golden glow to tasty but monochrome dishes of grains of wheat or spelt. A stew, *pottaggetto*, of soft fish roes is made by cooking them in butter or oil, then finishing with fish broth, whole seeded sour grapes and some chopped herbs, thickened with ground almonds and some saffron "to give it colour." The same goes for various fish balls, dull in themselves, and so finished in a broth yellow with saffron. The flavour must have also counted in a lovely *pottaggetto di gongole*, in which shellfish like clams or mussels are cooked, removed from their shells, the juices saved and strained, and finished in butter or almond oil, white wine, verjuice, cinnamon, ground almonds, herbs, and saffron.

By the 18th century, saffron seems to have fallen out of fashion, with hardly any mention by Corrado in Naples, except for its inclusion in his recipe for *riso alla Milanese*, in which rice is simmered in chicken broth coloured with saffron, and served *brodoso*, nice and runny. In other dishes, Corrado seems to prefer egg yolks for colour, in spite of his listing of saffron as "excellent in the kitchen to colour and flavour jellies, broths, and potages, especially those made with rice." This probably reflects a change of taste throughout Europe, where the movement towards gentler, softer flavourings was perceptible in all cuisines during the 18th century. It is still used in the traditional cuisine of Sardinia, and in areas reflecting ancient Arab gastronomy, or, more likely, influences from north Africa. A version of couscous from Trapani uses a saffron-coloured fish broth, but Scappi got there first—his detailed and painstaking description of how to make what he called *succusu* uses saffron in both the couscous and its meat sauce. Saffron colours some Sicilian *arancini*. At Borgopace in the province of Pesaro in the Marche, a ritual Easter bread is made which includes pepper and saffron—small rolls slashed with the shape of a cross to be eaten with holy eggs on Easter Sunday. The classic use of saffron today is in *risotto alla milanese,* in which a gentle meat or chicken stock and a minimum of other flavourings (wine and a little onion) leave the saffron to speak for itself, enriched with butter, parmesan, and sometimes bone marrow. It is doubtful that this dish originated there, but its sumptuous austerity is characteristic of Milanese food today. (If it is a very dark yellow, one might question what colouring was used, for to get the balance of flavour right, the saffron needs to be understated.) Many fish stews are flavoured and coloured with saffron. The Sicilian *pasta con le sarde* is a dish of *bucatini* layered with a sauce of fried, boned, and cleaned sardines, cooked wild fennel, pine nuts, raisins, toasted almonds, chopped onion simmered in oil with anchovies, and saffron—all native products of that smiling land at the time of the arrival of Arab warriors and settlers in the late Roman period. This may or may not be an Arab dish, but Mary Taylor Simeti puts the legends plausibly in context (1989, p. 59). Sardinia has *malloreddus*, pasta shells coloured with saffron, and *pardulas*, little tarts with a filling of fresh cheese or ricotta, flavoured and coloured

with lemon and orange zest and saffron, served hot with honey as an Easter speciality; there is also a savoury version with parsley. *Zippulas* are a Sardinian version of *zeppole*, carnival treats, ring-shaped doughnuts made of an unsweetened yeasted dough and some mashed potato, coloured with saffron and flavoured with grappa and orange zest and juice, deep fried, sprinkled with sugar, and eaten hot. There are also innovative new dishes, especially pasta in sauces bright with saffron, a sauce of prawns, capers, saffron, and basil to go with linguine, or one of pancetta, ricotta, and saffron with *trofiette.* Today the pungent aroma is almost forgotten, replaced by the ubiquitous vanilla and cheap yellow dyes.

SAGE, *salvia, Salvia officinalis,* is a one of the Labiatiae and was used in Italy for medicinal purposes before becoming by the 15th century one of the best-loved herbs in the kitchen. "*Cur moriatur homo cui salvia crescit in horto?*" as the ancients said. (What man need die when he has sage in the garden?) Stimulant, astringent, tonic, and carminative, sage has traditionally been used to cure mouth and throat infections and assuage the ravages, both mental and physical, of fevers and nervous afflictions. Platina suggests rubbing the teeth with sage leaves (to clean them and strengthen the

Sage was prescribed in Italy for medicinal purposes for centuries before becoming one of the most popular herbs in the Italian kitchen. (Shutterstock)

gums) and says it is good for paralysis, and the bites of scorpions; by this we understand both insect bites and skin infections, and indeed sage is recommend in a strong infusion as a poultice for ulcers and skin abrasions.

Its oval leaves have a pungency when grown in a hot climate which is dramatically different from the flavour of the sage we are familiar with in northern countries. Its use in *saltimbocca alla romana* gives an explosion of flavour when combined with *prosciutto crudo* and parmesan to enliven a fillet of veal. It combines well with liver and onions in *fegato alla veneziana*. Sage leaves cooked in butter make an aromatic dressing for fried or grilled meat. Their use in dishes named *all'uccelletto* is said to be derived from the use of sage in recipes for wild birds, so *fagioli all'uccelletto* are *cannellini* beans cooked with garlic, sage, and oil, best without the ubiquitous tomato, a late-comer on the scene.

Platina talks of little fritters of sage leaves dipped in a batter flavoured with cinnamon, saffron, and sugar, and fried in lard or oil; and Scappi, nearly a century later, describes a sophisticated yeasted batter made with almond milk, flour, olive oil, white wine, salt, and sugar and coloured with saffron, into which chopped bitter herbs, or whole sage leaves, can be introduced before deep frying.

Corrado has a recipe for chicken cooked in milk with cinnamon sticks and sage leaves, served cold with a thick cream sauce.

A gentler use of sage as the main ingredient is in *salviata*, a sage pudding, made with fresh young sage leaves, parmesan, eggs, and cream (Del Conte, 2004, p. 5), which makes a delicious accompaniment to roasts or a vegetarian dish on its own.

SALAD, *insalata,* can consist of a single vegetable, raw or cooked, or several kinds of leaf or root, mixed together and dressed with salt, oil, and vinegar. The idea of a prepared "salad dressing" is quite alien to Italian gastronomy; these condiments are added to the salad at the last minute, or diners help themselves from oil and vinegar on the table. The rapid application, then mixing, of these is done at the last minute so that the salad will not wilt or get soggy. Green vegetables like spinach, chicory, endive, and beets can be served lightly cooked, cold, or tepid, with just oil and lemon juice. Wild and raw plants can be mixed, carefully trimmed and washed, and dressed in the same way. The use of edible FLOWERS is not new; rose petals, pansies, violas, marigolds, and many more were used in the past as decoration, adding colour and fragrance to cooked and raw dishes, not always vegetable. The term *salad* was applied to a startlingly inventive range of cold dishes, like the things one might find today as antipasti: cooked and raw baby artichokes, young peas, sugar snap peas, seasoned with pepper and vinegar.

Salads had been enjoyed in the classical world, but the Dark Ages preferred the spoils of the chase, and the produce of wandering herdsmen, with precious little green stuff— plants and roots were devoured by brute beasts and peasants, not the gentry. But by the 16th century, things were changing, as Alan Griego has explained (*Et loquatur ponendo,* 1996, p. 147), and a tide of greenery flowed inexorably from orchards and gardens to the kitchens and tables of the rich. Salads became fashionable; they appeared on aristocratic menus, writers on health and medicine extolled the value of plants eaten for pleasure, and scholars discovered the joy of salads in classical writers. The *frisson* to be got from enjoying rustic delights in privileged surroundings was also found in music and dance; the nobility, banqueting on salads and the fashionable asparagus and artichokes, were entertained by court musicians warbling peasant ditties, some of them rich with salacious double-entendre, and dancing the crude steps usually seen on the village green. The rustic salad became a necessity in courtly dining; when in the spring of 1536 the young Ippolito d'Este made the long and arduous journey from Ferrara to Lyon, his steward's shopping list most days included salad, as well as the usual huge amounts of meat.

As early as the 1460s, PLATINA had vaunted the diet of poor intellectuals, happy with their garlic and onions. He described a mixed salad, perhaps one of the earliest sightings of a *misticanza* or *mischianza*, which included lettuce, borage, mint, pennyroyal, fennel, parsley, thyme, oregano, chervil, dandelion, lambs' lettuce, huckleberry (an edible member of the nightshade family), double-entendre *scarpigno* (sow thistle, a much-loved culinary herb in Romagna). He praised the healthy properties of salads and how a few pungent herbs would mitigate their "coldness." A century later, Costanzo FELICI of Piobbico wrote *Lettera sulle insalate* (A letter on salads), which started as a literary exercise, quoting Platina's *misticanza*, and evolved into an enthusiastic overview of all Italian produce. The salad is at the heart of Giacomo CASTELVETRO's tactful attempt to get the English to appreciate fruit and vegetables, and eat less meat and sweet things. Like Felici, he quotes a well-known saying about the seasoning of salads:

"The secret of a good salad is plenty of salt, generous oil, and little vinegar, hence the text of the Sacred Law of Salads: '*Insalata ben salata, / poco aceto e ben oliata*'" (which could be roughly rendered as 'Salt the salad quite a lot, / then generous oil put in the pot, / and vinegar, but just a jot'). And whosoever transgresses this benign commandment is condemned never to enjoy a decent salad in his or her life, a fate I fear lies in store for most of the inhabitants of this kingdom."

Castelvetro described a mixture of salad leaves, *mischianza*, which has recently had a revival, and can now be bought in supermarkets all over the place. His selection is much more varied and pungent: "the young leaves of mint, those of garden cress, basil, lemon balm, the tips of salad burnet, tarragon, the flowers and tenderest leaves of borage, the flowers of swine cress, the young shoots of fennel, leaves of rocket, rosemary flowers, some sweet violets, and the tenderest leaves of the hearts of lettuce."

Felici remembered how at the first signs of spring, countrywomen had a saying: "*ogni herba verde fa nel'insalata*" (for a salad any green plant goes), as they picked the first green leaves and shoots of wild plants, some without a name. This instinctive gathering of wild plants at the end of winter is a holdover from the days when countrywomen cared for the health of families too poor to afford a physician trained in the great schools of medicine, with skills that were probably considerably more effective.

This fashionable taste was now trickling down as well as up, and the meeting in the middle took place when professional men like Felici and Castelvetro extolled the delights of salads in manuscript, circulated among naturalists and botanists, in a more conversational tone than the smug and winsome tones of John Evelyn in his *Acetaria*. Then in 1627 came Salvatore MASSONIO's massive printed text *Archidipno, overo dell'insalata*, which praised and described salads at great length, and with some verbosity, bringing together information about edible plants and their uses in salads, with references from classical literature, medical writers, and his own experience. A salad at the start of a meal could both stimulate the appetite and fill the diner up with benign, light food, thus preventing overindulgence in too much rich fare, he said: "*una buona insalata è principio di una cattiva cena*" (plenty of salad is a good beginning to a light meal). The need for care in the preparation of salads was brought home to Massonio when he once speared a long-dead scorpion on his fork, causing "*non leggiero turbamento e di rincrescevole nausia*" (not inconsiderable distress and repellent nausea).

Salads are listed in banquet menus, but recipes are rarely given in historic cookery books; we have to guess at the reality behind Scappi's *Insalate cotte, & crude di verzura di piu sorte*, or the *insalate di fiori di borragine* in early spring, and a Lenten supper starting with salads of *indivia* (cooked or raw?), asparagus, alexanders, and citrons (finely sliced) with sugar and rosewater, raw cardoons with salt and pepper, baby artichokes, cooked and raw, with salt and pepper (as we do today in *pinzimonio*). A meal during Lent had a salad of spring onions and lettuce, a salad of citron flowers, an *insalata di mescolanza* with borage flowers, and a salad of capers, raisins, and sugar, a dish of anchovies dressed with oil, vinegar and oregano, and a first sighting of asparagus served as a salad.

Paintings sometimes tell us a little, like the salad shown in *The Supper at Emmaus* by the 17th-century painter Matteo Rosselli, there for probably symbolic reasons, but showing lettuce leaves in a bowl, to be found in another version of this subject by a follower of Caravaggio. Pale cos lettuce leaves are displayed alongside shelled peas and red roses in one of Vincenzo Campi's market scenes, in which a comely *fruttivendola* is surrounded by bowls and baskets of fresh produce, including some darker-hearted lettuce lurking beneath a dish of cherries. Many still lifes and market scenes show the different salad plants of the time, like the craggy cos lettuce in Carlo Magini's still life of a jug of wine, a bottle of a liquid that could be oil or a liqueur, and the makings of a humble meal heaped on a kitchen table—lettuce, spring onions, a hunk of bread, and a handful of herbs. The large composed salad in Carlo Cane's *Hunt Picnic* is often reproduced. Meanwhile, the art of botanical illustration developed as the Medici dukes of Florence, patrons and collectors, founded botanical gardens, and built villas with gardens and orchards planned and stocked by the leading naturalists of the time. They commissioned, from artists with the skills of Jacopo Ligozzi and Bartolomeo Bimbi, visual records of the plants that were studied

and classified by naturalists like Mattioli and Aldrovandi—with Cristoforo Munari and Jacopo Chimenti da Empoli taking care of the contents of the larder. It is helpful to imagine Cosimo, Francesco, and Ferdinand chomping their way through the products of their estate kitchen gardens, enjoying the plants they so assiduously collected and cultivated.

The salad today can be exquisite or perfunctory, but at its best demonstrates the polarities of Italian gastronomy—freshness and simplicity, and complex, brilliant inventiveness, from the plainest salad of fresh young spinach leaves carefully cooked and eaten when just cool, with salt, good olive oil, and a few drops of lemon juice, to the innovative mixtures that now go into a *mischianza*.

SALAD BURNET, *pimpinella, salvastrella, Sanguisorba minor*, has delicately flavoured leaves reminiscent of cucumber, which are good chopped in salads, stuffings, and sauces, and used to flavour vinegar. A Tuscan saying, *"L'insalata non è bella, se non v'è la salvastrella,"* or Costanzo Felici's version, *"L'insalata non è né buona né bella se in essa non vi entra la pimpinella"* (A salad is no good without burnet), or Corrado's more melodious version, *"L'inslata non è buona nè bella ove non è la Pempinella,"* all confirm the agreeable qualities of this herb, perhaps best known to us as an ingredient in refreshing summer wine drinks.

SALAM D'LA DUJA, *salame sotto grasso*, is a speciality of the provinces of Novara and Vercelli in Piedmont, made of prime cuts of pork and belly fat, ground to a medium consistency, seasoned with salt, pepper, red wine, and garlic, and after maturing for three weeks in a controlled climate, put to rest in terra cotta pots called *duja*, completely covered with molten lard,

which, when set, keeps everything soft and fresh for up to a year, ready to be brought out and enjoyed by the light of the new moon in March, when the new wines are ready to be drunk. It has been observed that with climate change and industrialisation (not unrelated), this traditional technique looks to be a more consistent treatment. A similar technique to the preserved *confits* of France.

SALAMA DA SUGO is a speciality of Ferrara, and until recently was little known elsewhere. Its rise in popularity and its potential fall from grace is a microcosm of salami production in Italy today; the "industrial/bad vs. artisan/good" view does not necessarily apply here, though the pressures to get away with quantity rather than quality have been a problem in both these modes of production. The product is a mixture of pork meats—neck, belly, throat, with a small amount of liver and tongue, mixed, after salting and flavouring, with a good-quality unpasteurised red wine, preferably Barbera or Sangiovese, enclosed in a strong casing (a bladder, tougher than the usual intestines). The cure is begun in a warm place for a few days and finished in a carefully controlled, dark, well-ventilated atmosphere for six to twelve months. If this atmosphere is infiltrated by the wrong kind of microorganisms, the finished product risks being far inferior to the best of its kind. So if—after the obligatory four or five hours' gentle simmering in water, the ceremonial cutting open at table, spooning out of the soft flesh, and extraction of the by now unctuous dark purple juices—the *salama* is not very nice, time, care, and good materials have been wasted, and clients are displeased. Some industrial products are excellent, and some artisan ones are less good; in both cases the problem seems to lie in the microclimate in which they are matured and cured, and the quality

of the raw material used. When the pigs, a hybrid of Large White and Landrace, are fed with traditional vegetable and cereal-based feed, they do not suffer from dietary deficiencies, and so their flesh has the vitamin content needed to produce the necessary fermentation which creates the desired flavour. Tests conducted by the University of Bologna have made it possible to work out parameters within which a decent *salamina* can be produced, and suggest a legal *Disciplinare di produzione* and a *Consorzio* to enforce it. Quality, not quantity, seems to be what consumers want in this case, and they are prepared to pay for it. This is a good omen.

SALAME, *salami, salumi, insaccati,* with over 300 types listed in one publication, double that in another, are some of the glories of Italian gastronomy (INSOR, 2002; Ballarini, 2003). They consist of meat and fat, usually but not exclusively pork, chopped or ground, salted, seasoned, put into casings, then cured by drying or smoking or a combination of both. This maturing process, *maturazione*, involves fermentation, which develops flavour and texture; the next stage is *stagionatura*, when the salame, in its casing, dries, shrinks, mellows, and develops flavour and texture. Salami are made on an industrial scale by commercial manufacturers, in small quantities by regional artisan producers, and by private individuals for their own consumption. Many are widely available in Italy and exported all over the world; others are only enjoyed by the producers themselves and a small local market. Until recently, many families would make their own, using their own resources, and even now, when links with the countryside are in some urban areas all but severed, most families treasure salami made by an uncle or a grandparent back home in their native region. But just as wine production has undergone dramatic changes, not all for the worse, so has the craft of salami-making, with a similar panoply of stainless steel vats, temperature-controlled premises, and improved varieties of raw material. Although ingredients, methods, and marketing are no longer the same, the ethos and integrity of traditional salami continue to inspire both producers and consumers. A famous London-based Italian chef recently claimed that the complete works of Raphael tell us far less about Italian culture than a salami which has been made in the same way, in the same region, for hundreds of years. He should be so lucky. Raphael would be turning in his grave if he knew the changes in both content and style of most modern salami, artisan or otherwise (*see* SALAME MILANO). The breed of pig, how it is fed, the way it is slaughtered and butchered, the environment, the methods of manufacture are all changing, and the small local producer able to rear the fine pigs of the past and slaughter and process them as his ancestors once did is faced today with health and safety regulations and changes in lifestyle which make his task difficult if not impossible. Some persevere, however, and their products are listed in the comprehensive survey by INSOR (2002), in which 309 products, both industrial and small-scale, are described in detail. Many of these can be seen and sampled in the Salone del Gusto in Turin, organised by the SLOW FOOD movement. Meanwhile, the works of Raphael do at least provide a consistency and cultural coherence easier to grasp than this amazing kaleidoscopic overview offered to food lovers, who have somehow to navigate between the good and the mediocre in all sectors.

The breed of pig is important, and is taken into account when salami are described and evaluated. Instead of local breeds (the black pig of the Apennines, the red pig, those from Caserta, Calabria, Lucania, and others), many manufacturers rely on larger animals imported from all over Europe, usually the Large White or Landrace variety, be-

nign creatures with tender flesh, ideal to be fattened and treated for rapid growth, dosed with hormones and antibiotics, the meat topped up with preservatives and antibacterial substances, seasoned with the standard spice mix, processed in conditions of clinical purity, climate and humidity controlled with rigid care, and ending up as a uniform industrial product lacking the character and health-giving attributes of salami and hams processed in the old rustic manner. The hygienic stainless steel and plastic surfaces and containers are not a congenial home for the microorganisms which in the past contributed to the changes that went on in the product as it fermented and matured in or on stone, ceramic, and wood. The drying out near a wood-fired cooking stove or fire, the long slow sojourn in naturally ventilated attics, lofts, or sheds, and sometimes the immersion in oil or lard encouraged the development of wondrous complex flavours and textures; it also did things to the pig fat to transform its saturated fatty acids into benign polyunsaturated ones, making salami a much healthier and tastier food than it is today. But it does look now as if the recent panic terror over dietary fat is giving way to a more rational appraisal of the role of different kinds of fat in nutrition and gastronomy; that and the appreciation of quality in the products of small regional craftspeople, together with the willingness of the public, in Italy and abroad, to pay a fair (high) price for them, is turning the tide, rescuing many unknown local salami from extinction and encouraging a discriminating consumption of what is now a luxury product.

Some have observed that in the past, pig products, as subsistence food of the lower orders, were not rated very highly, being family food, not for fine eating. Corrado Barberis reminds us that the cuts we prize the most, ham, *culatello*, and *coppa*, were valued well below fat and cured fat, which were the most costly and desirable. Hams from small pigs dried out in the cure and became tough and stringy (all right to cook with cabbages and put into stews), unlike the smooth, soft, and sometimes bland hams we pay the earth for today; so the meat from the buttocks would often be cut up for cooking sausages or salami, as they still are for some of the more expensive ones. The change in fashion, from pungent, sometimes chewy salami to bland, smooth, cured *prosciutto crudo* is relatively recent. And the switch to using cured pig products as convenience food, something to whip out of the refrigerator and save oneself "the bother of cooking" has changed patterns of consumption, an occasional rustic treat becoming a daily standby. Ballarini reminds us that changing patterns of eating, whether we like them or not, are here to stay, and the Italian version of FAST FOOD, *panini* eaten on the hoof, can be a gastronomic experience when good bread and fine salami are deployed—unlike the pretentious designer sandwich of North America and Britain, where a superfluity of ill-matched things drenched in industrial mayonnaise is a logistical and gustatory nightmare. The balance between crust and crumb, lean and fat, in a good *panino* is all that is needed; adding butter, mustard, or pickles would be an insult.

In the past, the calories in fresh animal fat got burned up keeping active people busy and warm, and as such get a whole page to themselves in the *Tacuinum Sanitatis* (an illustrated health handbook from 15th-century northern Italy), in which the butcher and his assistant can be seen cutting the internal fat from a pig, and chopping beef fat into cubes for its many uses—"as nourishment it is excellent." Cured meat and fat are depicted in another shop, where bacon, hams, and shoulders hang from a rail and the shopkeeper does a roaring trade in slabs of cured fat, one customer carrying off a whole side over his shoulder. The accompanying text says "it is suitable for phlegmatic temperaments who do tiring work" but warns that it "produced

melancholic blood" and needs to be eaten with butter and eggs. So it appears in 17th-century still life paintings by Cristoforo Munari, where a shallow earthenware pan of fried eggs is often seen in proximity to a freshly sliced cut of salt shoulder, or ham, bread, and a hunk of parmesan cheese. (Fried rashers are a North European or North American delicacy; this is not the usual way of eating bacon in Italy, and the cuts here would not have needed cooking.) The bland richness of eggs makes a perfect foil for the salty, firm-textured ham or bacon. Munari was from Reggio Emilia, so he might have been celebrating local produce, but since he also worked for patrons in Rome, and executed commissions for the grand duke of Tuscany, one might cautiously assume that he was painting a fairly universal use of salt meats, as fast food, or a light snack, that found favour with the rich as well as the labouring poor. Eggs, parmesan, and bacon or ham crop up so often in his paintings that one might guess that this is a not only a common food but recognised with pleasure by his wealthy patrons, perhaps jaded victims of the baroque banquet, who delighted to have on their walls a reminder of simpler pleasures—not depicted as comic rustic fare, though, for in a work of Munari from the early 18th century we see familiar fried eggs and some ham on a shelf, alongside humble pots and pans, above a table with slices of ripe melon, some plums on expensive blue and white china, crayfish on a silver platter, and wine in a delicate glass; local produce for the discriminating, not a condescending look at low life. An earlier composition shows ripe figs carefully arranged on some vine leaves, above a huge wedge of parmesan, sitting with some freshly cut slices of salame on a sheet of wrapping paper, with a bread roll and a flask of wine to complete the meal, and a strong light from the right casting a golden glow on the cheese and the rich red interior of the salame, with its irregular lumps of fat, not from cubes of fat mixed in with the meat, but long strips running its length. Conrad Berentz, who worked with Munari in Rome, took this theme even further—his *spuntino elegante*, elegant snack, of 1717 is a reference to Dutch still lifes flaunting luxury and wealth, with whole fat hams and hothouse fruit tumbling promiscuously over Turkey carpets and expensive musical instruments, while here we have an impromptu little meal thrown together on a coarse wooden kitchen table, a fringed linen towel, not starched damask, flung in haste over one corner, and upon it a silver salver with Venetian glasses, a decanter of wine, and a bottle of *rosolio*, next to a porcelain plate with slices of beautiful ham and salame, some white bread, and a cut bitter orange—simple but exquisite, a real celebration of the basic and unsurpassable qualities of Italian food. The Roman cardinal who commissioned this was truly discriminating. This pride in ordinary food is seen in a painting by Munari in which a slice cut from a cured shoulder of pork rests athwart a prime cabbage, like the forshortened skull in Holbein's *Ambassadors*, on a battered kitchen table, with the pots and pans that will be used in a robust stew, along with the big gourd in the background. The Spanish painter Luis Meléndez was active in Italy in his youth at this time, and his own later choice of subjects that clearly spell out a meal or, as in this case, a recipe might owe something to these pioneers of cool rational realism. So cool, in fact, that the tinge of green mould on a bread roll in a "snack-scape" by the Neapolitan Tommaso Realfonzo makes one anxious about the condition of the rugged salame which dominates the composition—it is a huge beast, about 130 millimetres (over 5 inches) in diameter, with great lumps of fat irregularly disposed in unidentifiable meat ranging from reddish brown to black, studded with peppercorns. A crumbling hulk of parmesan looms above it, with a bottle of wine and some cherries to complete the meal. Giacomo Ceruti, who worked in the same spirit of realism, mainly in the north, shows a more appealing salame, some walnuts, a fresher-looking roll, a jug of wine and stout tumbler; this salame is a mixture of irregular shreds of meat and fat, unsophisticated compared with the more refined product chosen by Munari for his posh snack. Hard-cooked eggs are the centre of a painting by Realfonso depicting an Easter breakfast, piled up on a platter with cheeses and salami of various kinds, the ring of decorative patterned bread, the fragrant flowers and freshly picked lemons, all with their burden of symbolism, but a lucid picture of simple festive food, especially the salame, at its peak of perfection after five months' cure. Food historians are working on comparisons of contemporary images and recipes which might tell us much about early traditions of salumi.

SALAME DI FABRIANO is produced on the high slopes of the valle dell'Esino, in the Fabriano region of the province of Ancona (*see* MARCHE) The pigs used in the past were from a small, black native breed, who rootled around in the upland meadows and woods of the region, and whose size made them unsuitable for hams, so this prime cut of meat was used, finely ground and interspersed with strips of the best quality back fat, for these high-class salami. The same cut is used today, and the salami still merit the praise once lavished by Garibaldi on a precious gift of them from an admirer.

SALAME DI NAPOLI is made all over the Campania region on an industrial scale, from quality cuts of pork, carefully trimmed, and coarsely ground—a method that indicates clearly the nature of the contents and so the impossibility of adulteration (a fine-textured salami with worldwide popularity might have been open to possible fraudulent imitators pumping the mixture out with emulsified fat). The meat and fat are seasoned with salt and black and white pepper, and this is first briefly smoked then cured for 20 days. The draconian imposition of sanitary norms make it difficult for small producers to carry on as they did in the past.

SALAME DI VARZI is made in

Lombardy, in the region around Pavia, which was the court of the medieval rulers of Lombardy, and to its ancient renown can be added the glory of being one of the first salame to obtain a DOC (now DOP). Enriched with fat from cheek, shoulder, and the trimmings from CULATELLO, it has a coarse texture and is seasoned with garlic steeped in red wine and whole peppercorns; it matures in a warm kitchen, hangs for several months in a warm, well-ventilated spot, and is finally cured in a damp cellar, well below ground.

SALAME D'OCA is made from

goose flesh and fat encased in the delicious fatty skin of the bird, ideally the neck, sometimes with pork and pork fat as well (*see* GOOSE). It is made in a cooked version, which can be eaten hot or cold, or raw. Some goose salami are kosher, made without pork and with proper rabbinical supervision, based on recipes from the Jewish community in Venice; others are less orthodox and part of the food culture of many areas in the north of Italy. The main areas of production are Mortara, in Lomellina in Lombardy, and Palmanova, in Basso Friuli in the Veneto. Geese reared in other parts of Italy have been valued like pigs, as nice little scavengers no part of which need be wasted. Their soft feathers, tasty fat, and rich flesh have been esteemed wherever they can be reared, so the salami tradition is not exclusively Jewish.

It is one of the ironies of history that the basic food of a religious minority, itself derived from the subsistence food of areas in Italy into which dispossessed Jews moved and settled, by law, in the Middle Ages and the 16th century, should be saved from extinction by the appreciation of wealthy customers who enjoy and can afford what is now an expensive delicacy. Luciano Curiel, one of the last Jewish kosher butchers in Venice, revealed his recipe for *salame d'oca* to Antoniello Pessot and inspired him to explore and encourage almost extinct rural products. Like the geese on the Roman Capitol that scared away the barbarian Gauls, Pessot's white geese of Jolanda de Colò put to flight the pretensions of Gallic cuisine and encouraged restaurants and *salumerie* all over Italy to enjoy these local delicacies.

The cost of rearing, feeding, caring for, and subsequently processing this amiable bird is today high; maintaining quality is complicated, and it has taken the enthusiasm of entrepreneurial gourmets and local producers to ensure a consistently good and protected product. Whether the geese are hatched and reared locally, imported as tiny goslings, or bused in from eastern Europe, the regulations safeguarding the genuine salamis and hams stipulate that the creatures, of a specified breed (emden crossed with romagnola) have to be fed on natural feed, not any of the well-known fattening products like manioc, and the proportion of fat to meat in the salami, the seasonings, the added wine (a good local wine that has not been pasteurised is needed for proper fermentation), and the time for maturing and curing, are all carefully controlled. The legs of geese are made into hams, salted, and kept in fat or suspended in a dry atmosphere, while the breasts are salted and smoked. From Monti Berici in the Basso Vicentino comes *Oco in onto*, joints of goose cut up and salted for five to ten days, then preserved for several months in rendered goose fat, ready just in time for 25 April, the feast of St. Mark, at which it becomes an ingredient of a version of *risi e bisi*, along with the first tender young peas from Lumignano.

SALAME FELINO, once known

as *salame di Felino*, is a speciality of a small town and the surrounding area south of Parma in Emilia-Romagna. There is nothing feline about it. A similar product made elsewhere in Emilia must be called "tipo felino." Giovanni Ballarini suggests that the name might derive from very early times when Etruscans with the name of Felsini occupied the town, Felsina, today Bologna (Ballerini, 2002, p. 156). Already by the 18th century it was a speciality of the area round Parma, and the French administrator Du Tillot, in charge of the Bourbon city of Parma, when he was made marquis of Felino, remarked wryly that he had become lord of a land of salami. This salami is one of the more refined pork products, made with prime cuts, about 25 percent fat, carefully trimmed of connective tissue, with the addition of salt, pepper, and sometimes garlic, wine, and permitted preservatives and cultures. The meat has to be from pigs from Emilia-Romagna, Lombardy, Piedmont, Tuscany, and the Veneto. The initial drying out of the meat before grinding, the method of enclosing it in its casings, the subsequent dehydration, maturing, *maturazione,* and ripening, *stagionatura*, are required by law to be done slowly and in controlled temperatures, without any unnatural acceleration, allowing the bacteria and enzymes to get to work to achieve in their own good time a small, refined salami, with a concentrated flavour and close texture.

SALAME "GENTILE" gets its

name from the soft, fatty part of the intestine in which the mixture is encased. It is made commercially throughout Emilia-Romagna.

SALAME MILANO, *Crespone,*

with an industrial production of around 50,000 quintals (5 million kilos), is Italy's most widely consumed salami, with only about 5,000 kilos made by small traditional producers. This is a large salami, about 3–4 kilos, made of lean pork, 25 percent beef, and about 25 percent pig fat, flavoured with salt, pepper, and sometimes garlic and white wine, ground so that the lean and fat remain distinct. It is matured for three to six months.

When Milan was a small town in a predominantly rural area, it was renowned for a local speciality, *cervellato,* which in the past was enriched with cheese and saffron. Martino and Scappi have recipes, already of national renown by the 1460s, for a cooking sausage of that name. It may have developed after the barbarian Lombards infiltrated Italy during the decline and fall of the Roman empire, bringing with them a cult of the pig and its products, based on a very different environment and lifestyle, where pigs rootled in the dark mysterious undergrowth of wild Teutonic forests (as opposed to the urban and agricultural culture of the Etruscans). Their cured hams and sausages had been imported into metropolitan Rome long before the turmoil of later centuries. The plains of Lombardy (named for the invaders) were then well wooded and watered, suitable habitat for semi-wild pigs.

Ballarini has a kindly scepticism towards the myth of fine tasty hams and salumi from these happy vagabond pigs, whose diet was not invariably agreeable and whose health was often poor; he contrasts them with the healthy creatures of today, fed a carefully calculated scientific diet, often much better than that of their owners, producing a more reliable product, transformed under controlled conditions, with predictable results and virtually no wastage. Enthusiasts for artisan methods of pig rearing and curing see this corrective viewpoint as another urban myth, reminding us of the loss of flavour when the good microorganisms get zapped along with the bad, and how the exigencies of commercial production are not always compatible with the flavours and textures of salumi sought out by an increasing herd of dedicated trufflers. Industry replies by suggesting the possibility of re-creating in laboratory conditions the "good bugs" that might pep up the bland commercial products (tests show that they do), while older people in the region tell of a land poisoned by the effluents from mass-produced piggeries, with pig urine penetrating the water table, and the pesticides and antibiotics of agribusiness adding to the damage. The myth of a symbiotic relationship between salumi, cheeses, and the land, with pigs feeding contentedly on the whey from parmesan cheese, and cows grazing in the lush meadows manured by the grateful pigs, has perhaps been wrecked by a new wave of agri-barbarians, where the milk creates pale bland hulks with tasteless waterlogged meat, and the land no longer enjoys the delicate balance of agriculture and husbandry.

SALAME TOSCANO is produced on an industrial scale all over Tuscany, about 100,000 kilos annually. It is made of finely ground pork meat with fat, cut into cubes, flavoured with salt, pepper, garlic, and white wine, dried for a few days, and matured for up to six months. This is what can be bought in most delicatessens abroad, but the real glories of Tuscan salumi are still being produced on a domestic scale for private consumption, often from different breeds of pig, fed on cereals, domestic scraps, and sometimes chestnuts and acorns, allowed to graze or living in large enclosed pens close to oak trees or chestnuts. *See also* FINOCCHIONA.

SALATO MORBIDO FRIULANO is a fresh soft cheese preserved in special salting troughs, sometimes made of larch wood, in a salty solution containing milk and cream, adjusted and stirred constantly to keep it healthy. The resultant cure produces a soft pungent cheese, a bit intense to eat on its own, but good with vegetables and polenta.

SALMORIGLIO, or *sammirighiu*, is a simple sauce enjoyed in Sicily and Calabria, usually served on grilled fish, and sometimes meat. It is made by vigorously mixing together olive oil, lemon juice, garlic, salt, parsley, and oregano to form a sort of emulsion that can be used cold, or heated with the addition of a little water. A version made in Sicily with only oregano is called *salmorigano*. It also makes a good marinade for fish, which can be bathed in this a while before grilling or baking.

SALSA VERDE is a green sauce made by chopping together a mixture of fresh green herbs and leaves, along with garlic, capers, hard-cooked egg, and anchovies, and thickened with breadcrumbs soaked in lemon juice or vinegar, to which a light but fragrant olive oil is added to taste. The mixture can be made in a blender or processor, but if overmixed can get too homogenised and frothy. Chopping by hand, or pounding in a mortar, is a pleasure to do and gives a tastier result with more personality. The ingredients can be adjusted according to what the sauce accompanies. Its freshness and piquancy go well with the rich *bollito misto* of the north. Scappi's *salsa verde* included parsley, the leaves of young spinach, sorrel, salad burnet, rocket, and a little mint, all chopped very finely, then mixed with toasted breadcrumbs pounded in the mortar, seasoned with salt, sugar, and vinegar. The absence of oil would have made this a sharp, bright green sauce, a fresh contrast to rich meat or fish. Corrado's approach to sauces is a useful corrective to today's taste for defining and codifying recipes. Recipes collected on his

travels and a fertile imagination inspired 61 sauces, in six of which fresh green herbs are chopped or pounded with other things, and he gives three relishes which are similar. Some of these are his versions of French sauces; his *ramolata* is made by pounding anchovies with parsley, spring onions, capers, mint, and a hint of garlic, mixed with olive oil, vinegar, lemon juice, and spices, to serve with cold fish. A similar sauce, but without the acidic elements, is mixed with the gravy from roast mutton and served hot. A blast of flavour comes with the *salsa al tornagusto*, green chillies, oregano, peppermint, fennel fronds and seeds, garlic, and anchovies pounded together, diluted with oil and vinegar, and used as dressing for olives—a mighty appetizer. The rustic *alla campagnola* has parsley, basil, and marjoram pounded with breadcrumbs soaked in muscat wine, almonds, and spices, diluted with verjuice and apple juice. A sauce from Lombardy to serve with frogs is the nearest we get to what is now known as *pesto genovese*, with basil, fennel fronds, garlic, and pine nuts pounded together with vinegar and verjuice. The relishes are sharper; one has basil, anise, marjoram, and thyme pounded with pistachios and breadcrumbs soaked in orange blossom water, spices, and sugar, and thinned with a light vinegar and orange juice. This digression on Corrado is really to emphasize the need to use imagination and adapt herb sauces to what you are going to eat with them.

SALSICCIA is a fresh, sometimes partly cured, sausage in a casing that can be eaten raw or cooked, usually made of pork meat and fat, with salt and spices according to local taste. The dividing line is hard to draw, but raw fresh sausages are usually fried or grilled, and partially cured ones can be eaten like other *insaccati*, or the contents crumbled to add to sauces and stews, or added whole to other dishes. They can be found listed under the general heading SALUME, but there is a wide variety of both products and names for them, for most regions have their specialities, and many families make sausages for their own consumption, special mixtures, of either prime cuts of pork or oddments and trimmings that have to be used up after the creation of more refined products, and need to be eaten up quickly. In Lombardy there is a *salsiccia alla milanese "antica"* that is well spiced, to be cooked with *minestrone* or cabbage dishes. The north is now the home of an ancient sausage which originated in Lucania in the south, LUCANICA, possibly Roman in origin. Monza in Lombardy is famous for its version, delicately spiced and sometimes flavoured with wine and cheese. There are regional variations in the seasoning of sausages, with generous amounts of chilli in Lazio and the south, fennel and coriander in many areas, and strong cheese, dried fruit and pine nuts, orange peel, and apples. The *salsiccia della Val Comino* is made from the offal of pigs that have grazed on the local chestnuts, acorns, fruit, and household scraps, seasoned with salt, pepper, chilli, garlic, orange peel, and chopped apples. The *salsiccia gialla* or *fina* of Modena was in the past a fragrant composition of pork meat seasoned with sugar, salt, pepper, cinnamon, ginger, nutmeg, cloves, musk, and rosewater, yellow with saffron and parmesan, similar to today's *salsiccia passita*. In Piedmont, the *salsiccia di Bra* is unique in being made from the meat of veal and pork fat, seasoned with salt, pepper, cinnamon, nutmeg, fennel, mace, wine, and parmesan and local cheese, a legacy of the Jewish community settled near Bra. Sausages of other meats such as goose, horse, and beef were an enrichment of the Italian tradition.

SALSIFY, *scorzonera, scolymus,* are all pleasant-tasting long thin roots of the Compositae family. The dark-skinned version, *scorzonera*, is tastier and less bitter than the white salsify, *salsifica*, or *scorzobianca*, and both *Tragopogons* are sometimes confusingly called *barba di becco*, or *barba di prete*. The grass-like green leaves of *Tragopogon pratensis* and *Tragopogon porrifolius* are described under AGRETTI. *Salsifica* grows wild, is now cultivated, and has been enjoyed in Italy for centuries; *scorzonera* was first cultivated in Spain and introduced into Italy in the 16th century. The name does not mean "black skin" as one might suppose but, according to Mattioli, is from the Spanish for viper, which he says is *scurzi*. This (nonexistent) word was probably *escuerzo*, toad, then considered as poisonous as a viper, but anyway Mattioli enjoyed writing about this new plant, since it came with the reputation for curing the bites of venomous snakes and other creatures. Its medicinal use was considerable; he claimed that chewing on a root would *"caccia via la tristezza dell'anima, e fa l'uomo giocondo e allegro"* (cast forth melancholy from the soul and make a man merry and cheerful). Its insulin content made it useful for diabetics, and it was diuretic and sudiforous. Mattioli's sometimes irascible castigation of his contemporaries fades away when he writes about a new plant like this, and he acknowledges the collaboration of his contemporaries with great generosity of spirit: Giacomo Antonio Cortuso of Padua sent plants, the doctor Giovanni Odorico Melchiori of Trento, doctor to the consort of Emperor Maximilian II, sent a dried specimen, and not long after that the emperor Ferdinand had some plants brought from Spain. How this "toad buster" got to Spain is a mystery, for botanists find no mention of it in classical writers or in later Arab agronomists. So Mattioli's account of *scorzonera* being brought from Africa to Lerida in Catalonia by a Moorish slave, who used it to cure a peasant bitten by a snake when reaping corn, seems plausible.

This new but not unfamiliar root was close in flavour and appearance to the native plant salsify. It took its place among the many edible roots which were gathered in the wild, with varying degrees of bitterness and sweetness. Today they are cultivated for a milder taste, and can be eaten raw or peeled and cooked in salted water until tender, then dressed with oil and vinegar, or melted butter.

SALT, *Sodium chloride, sale,* is valued as flavour enhancer and preservative, and has been procured in Italy since prehistoric times from deposits of rock salt, and evaporated from brine in bays and estuaries. The main sources and the ancient routes which took this precious commodity to all parts of the peninsula are remembered in names like *Via Salaria.* The Eruscans were getting rock salt from Viterbo which vied with salt from the estuary of the Tiber. In ancient Rome a salty fish sauce, *garum*, or *liquamen*, was made on an industrial scale from freshly caught fish and their entrails, salted and fermented with the help of enzymes, in hot, dry conditions, not rotted or putrified, as those who have never tasted this delicacy have claimed in their ignorance (*see* APICIAN FLAVOUR). Enlightenment and understanding come to users of Vietnamese *nuoc mam* and Thai *nam pla*, which are essential when re-creating food from Apicius. This strange-smelling product adds saltiness and flavour to food, both sweet and savoury, as explained in detail by Dalby and Grainger (1996, p. 32). The nearest thing to its use in present-day Italian cooking is when anchovies preserved in salt (not those in oil) are added to recipes. Pasta sauces from Sicily use salted anchovies, carefully cleaned of their backbone, spines and guts, dissolved in garlic-flavoured oil, and added to soaked raisins, pine nuts, tomato paste, and other ingredients—or without the upstart tomato in a really archaic combination of things: cooked wild fennel (the pasta is cooked in the same water), fresh oregano, and parsley, finished with toasted breadcrumbs, as explained by Simeti (1989, p. 15). Salt flavoured with spices and herbs was used as a table condiment in ancient Rome, and occasionally a superior-quality *garum* would be made into a table sauce, as it still is in Southeast Asian cuisine.

Salt as a preservative is a treasured commodity, and in areas where it was expensive it was often recovered from the brine and other residues from curing meat, to be recycled. Where salt was in short supply, people had recourse to plants and herbs which would give food the lift that we normally get from salt. In a rich kitchen, salt was readily available, and also present in things like pancetta, ham, and other cured pork and fish products, so writers often warn against adding more salt to dishes which include ham or bacon. From being a necessity, a luxury, and a preservative it has become, unfairly, a health hazard and something to be shunned.

The *pane sensa sale* which we associate with Tuscany but is in fact widely available is not a bio-fad but a sensible accompaniment to salty cheese and meat. The overuse of salt in commercial products, from confectionery to preserved things, is quite wicked, but when you get to eat a robust Tuscan vegetable soup, with ham stock and plentiful cheese, the presence of unsalted bread (as in *ribollita*) is a positive factor, a perfect foil to the well-seasoned food which in its turn brings out the flavour of the bread.

The combination of salt and citrus fruit was exploited more in the past, when the distinction between sweet and savoury food was less rigid; sliced, unpeeled citrons, lemons, or oranges were dressed with salt and sugar, sometimes olive oil and rosewater as well, and often used as a garnish for roast or boiled food, or arranged decoratively round the rim of a serving platter. Here the saltiness enhanced the sharpness of the fruit; it was also used to preserve citrus fruit, making a pickle with their own juices, or combined with oil, something familiar to lovers of Middle Eastern food. Salt was the catalyst in one of Italy's greatest gifts to gastronomy—ICE CREAM. There is no conclusive documentary evidence to support theories about the exact moment or place (maybe 16th-century Italy) when crushed ice was combined with salt (or saltpetre) and found to freeze rather than just chill a sweetened liquid in a container surrounded by this mixture. It is likely that scientific experiments and the serendipitous behaviour of cooks went hand in hand, and that the scientists might have been joyfully investigating a beneficial phenomenon, while the ice cream makers cheerfully went on doing what they knew worked empirically. Adding salt to ice created a certain amount of molecular mayhem which lowered the freezing point, as did sugar in the mixture being frozen. So salt is the prime mover in one of Italy's best gifts to mankind.

Salt is used in curing and preserving meat and meat products. It inhibits the growth of microbes, and also draws water out of the tissues. Brine or dry salt curing, along with drying and smoking, is applied to pork meat, in the form of hams, sausages, and salumi, with herbs and spices to improve the cure and add to the flavour. A balance is obtained between salting, drying, and smoking, controlling or inhibiting the desired degrees of bacterial activity, and the behaviour of enzymes, to get different kinds of cure.

Cheese-making, too, requires salt, which is used to draw water from the curds, and slow down the ripening process; it is added directly to the curds, or whole cheeses are soaked in brine, or rubbed with dry salt, and these different procedures affect the nature of the cheese, its texture, crust, flavour, and keeping qualities.

The cost and availability of salt is no longer an important factor in preserving and cooking food, but what we have gained in convenience and economy by using cheap refined salt we have lost in flavour and nutrition, for the mineral content of refined and purified salt is low, and so lacks flavour, apart from saltiness, and many trace elements. Other techniques of preservation have influenced Italian food traditions, and "ice-box gastronomy" as well as the food industry have created a situation where salting is no longer needed to preserve food, but is now done for gastronomic reasons. Although the tyranny of the health police has engendered a fear of salt and fat that has influenced choices, an appreciation of traditional curing with salt makes it possible for small producers to continue supplying an increasing market for SALUMI.

SALT COD. *See* BACCALÀ.

SALT FISH. *See* BACCALÀ; FISH, PRESERVED; STOCKFISH.

SALTIMBOCCA ALLA ROMANA is made with thin slices of veal upon each of which a fresh sage leaf is placed, then a slice of *prosciutto crudo* secured with a toothpick; the slices are fried rapidly in butter and served at once with a quick sauce made from mixing a pinch of flour with the cooking residues and fat and adding a very little white wine. Martino had a more subtle version, in which the flattened slices of veal are sprinkled with pulverised salt and fennel seeds, then spread with a mixture of cured fat pounded with marjoram and parsley and a few spices, rolled up and spit roasted gently so that they do not dry up. This is similar to the *uccelli* or *uccellini scappati* of Emilia, where thin slices of veal or pork are covered with pancetta or *prosciutto crudo*, rolled up, secured with toothpicks, and fried in butter. A version from Lombardy alternates on a skewer cubes of veal liver, lean veal, or pork, interleaved with sage leaves and cubes of cured fat, to be fried in butter, and finished in white wine.

SALUME (pl. *salumi*) is the generic name for all salted and cured meat products, of which SALAME is one of the most important. Other things in this category are whole cuts of meat cured in various ways, ham, shoulder, *speck, culatello, coppa,* pancetta or bacon, rolled and flat, *lardo* (cured back fat), *bresaola, fiocchetto*; salami made of cut or ground meat and fat, seasoned and treated in various ways, to be eaten raw; cooked items like *cotechino, zampone, capello da prete,* to be eaten hot; and *mortadella* and others, to be eaten cold. Pork is the main meat used for salumi, but meat from a surprising range of other animals is also used—cow, veal, lamb, goat, wild animals. The skills and processes that go into making salumi are called *salumeria,* and they are made in a *salumificio.* The skilled craftsman, often peripatetic, who often takes care of the pig killing and the cutting up and processing of the carcass, is a *norcino* or *mazèn.* Salumi are sold in a *salumeria,* or *norcineria,* by a *salumiere* or *pizzicagnolo,* or in general food stores and some butchers.

PIG, *porco* or *maiale,* is the animal; *maiale, carne suino,* is pork, its meat, to which we owe the splendours of salami, and both have a much-loved part in Italian culture. No other creature offers humankind so much, is so loved and reviled (the adjective *sporco,* dirty, is derived from *porco* and figures in many oaths, most of them unprintable, which reflect this dual identity).

Pork is one of the most enjoyed and widely consumed meats today. The fresh meat is available in 11 or more cuts, and nothing is wasted; as well as the parts used in *salumeria,* there are many strange bits which rightly handled produce dishes of great delicacy—tails, ears, head meat, skin, and of course the trotters. Florence goes further—Giotto and a band of admirers were on an outing when a herd of pigs scampering down the narrow Florentine street knocked the artist over. They picked the great man up and dusted him down, and asked puzzled why he was roaring with laughter: "I had it coming to me, his bristles have earned me thousands of lire over the years and I never even gave the poor pig a bowl of soup!"

A sad anecdote about a follower of Saint Francis tells how kindly Brother Juniper, concerned for a sick friar who craved a pig's trotter, wished to cook one for him, and searching in vain, was obliged to cut the foot off a live pig. This comforted the invalid, but the reactions of little brother pig are unrecorded. This sorry tale of stupidity and sadism is sometimes quoted as the origin of *zampone*. A nasty myth.

Historians of the pig have found archaeological evidence, and writers from classical times until the present day have supplied much written information, about pigs and pork products in the past. The Etruscans were around before the Romans—they had eliminated the earlier inhabitants, the Celts, and were in turn eliminated by the Romans. All of these very different cultures had a use for the pig, and we can piece together what they did. Bologna, as we know it today, was capital of an area taken over by the Celts from the earlier Etruscans, who had called the city Felsina (the name persists in Felino, near Parma, whose fine salame is named for the locality), while to the Romans the city was Bononia, already an important settlement on the great east–west route. A funerary monument survives from this time, that of a man who earned enough from his trade to erect a fine tomb, showing on one side himself with a herd of pigs, his raw material, and on the other a great stone pestle and mortar, symbols of his profession—maker of *mortadelle*, pig meat ground fine in a mortar and seasoned, maybe with myrtle, in a cure that was his professional secret.

It does seem that, however skilled the ancient Roman butchers were, the kind of pig, its size, and the methods of preservation did not produce salumi of the quality we enjoy today. They are hardly ever mentioned in accounts in literature of posh food and grand dinners, though we know that sausages and cured hams and shoulders (*perna* and *petaso*) were eaten and enjoyed at humbler levels of society. They did not figure in Trimalchio's vulgar nouveau riche banquet, and when Horace extolled a meal of ham, cabbage, and pulses offered by a tenant farmer to his boss, he was being self-consciously rustic. Cured hams and shoulders were from lean beasts, chewy or even tough, needing to be cooked with other things rather than eaten like Parma ham today as an expensive luxury. *Luganiche* (*see* LUCANICA) were cured sausages, eaten raw, after hanging in the chimney, but not for long. Improvements that have not been documented came about during the Dark Ages, and it is likely that barbarians from dank Germanic woods, the race that gave Lombardy its name, the Longobardi, seeped into the Roman Empire, bringing with them a different way of life and a different race of pig. This semiwild black pig of the invading Longobardi, rootling and snuffling in and around the margins of vast forests, was different from the smart, red, almost urban creature of the sunlit Etruscan uplands, which scavenged and were reared in a domestic context, but both share heroic gastronomic myths that flourish, without documentary evidence, comfortably bridging the gap between between belief and knowledge, between the Dark Ages and the modern world, and the build-up of evidence about early pig products which we can read in the works of several distinguished Italian food historians.

Small artisan workshops today carry on making salumi in a way which gives their products a claim to *tipicità*, typicalness, a quality which implies a genuine product in terms of raw material and its treatment, characteristic of a particular place or area. Not as easy as you might think, if a traditional method is used with meat from a very different race of animal, even if fed with traditional things (roots, cereals, nuts rather than milk products and industrial animal food), or a rare breed that is perhaps different from the original pigs of a particular place but gets a similar food and treatment—cutting the meat with a knife, for example, rather than putting it through a grinder; pounding, slicing, chopping with traditional tools rather than modern machinery; or combining the two, employing old-fashioned ways of *maturazione* and *stagionatura*, maturing and curing, but not disdaining the benefits of refrigeration, cold storage, and rapid transport to points of sale. Add to this confusing array of parameters wholly personal choices of seasonings—spices, local wines, and herbs, some of them as innovative as vanilla—and the final insistence on the highest quality.

Alongside this, with a discriminating worldwide market avid for Italian salumi, modern methods of production are inevitable but not necessarily regrettable—the uncertain hygiene of the not very well scrubbed kitchen table and the clinical purity of the stainless steel laboratory are both sides of the same coin. The empirical, intuitive understanding of the roles of environment, temperature, and ingredients can result in failure as well as success. Some believe that science can help us identify the microbes, bacteria, and enzymes—the "good bugs," that help send off the "bad bugs," and which encourage fermentation and bestow flavour, texture, and keeping qualities on a homemade product—and introduce them as "starters" into industrially made salami, so getting the best of both worlds. This can be compared to scientific investigations into what goes on during the maturing of genuine BALSAMIC VINEGAR, *aceto balsamico tradizionale di Modena*, but this is done to authenticate and protect the real thing, and not in an attempt to replicate it. Postmodern magic bullets, bonging away at the genetic mix of pig, the nutritional components of its feed, the high-tech preparation of all the salumi, and the computer-controlled maturing and curing, might seem like rocket science, but could be the shape of things to come, though perhaps Giotto's pig twinkling down from Fiesole might have had a merrier life.

SAMBUCA (O). See DIGESTIVI; ELDER.

SAMPHIRE, *finocchio marino, erba San Pietro, Crithmum maritimum*, rock samphire, is not to be confused with glasswort or marsh samphire, *salicornia, Salicornia europaea*, a chenopodium, the one we are used to seeing at the fishmonger's in Great Britain, with a pleasantly salty, slightly acidic taste. Rock samphire grows everywhere on Italy's coastline, on rocky outcrops or buildings, a decorative member of the Umbelliferae family, and has a much more aromatic flavour. It has pretty pale yellow flowers, and fleshy leaves which can be eaten raw or cooked, and are often pickled in salt or vinegar. Both plants can be eaten raw when young and tender, or boiled and eaten with oil and vinegar.

SAND SMELT, *latterini*, are tiny little fish, like baby sardines, anchovies, or twaite shad, white or transparent, about 5 to 10 millimetres long, of the Perciformes order (to which the barracuda also belongs). The name *latterini* belongs to another small fish of the same family, Atherinidae, distinguished by its two dorsal fins. The name *nunnatu* "not-born" has a long history—one ancient Greek term for these tiny fish was *aphye*, which means exactly the same. It was in fact once thought that they developed from sea-foam rather than as offspring of larger fish. A larger fish, fully grown at 5 centimetres, is called *rossetto* (*Aphia minuta*, one of the goby family, a quite different order). All these minute creatures, whatever the name, can be deep fried like whitebait and served with a squeeze of lemon, but the Sicilian recipe immortalised by Andrea Camilleri is even better:

When the Commissario Montalbano was comfortably seated at his usual table in the trattoria San Calogero the proprietor, Calogero, approached him with a conspiratorial air.

"Dottore, I've got some *nunnatu.*"

"But isn't it forbidden to fish them?" [Fishing *nunnatu* is prohibited between 1 December and 30 April.]

"Of course, but sometimes they're allowed to take on board the odd case."

"So why are you being so conspiratorial?"

"Because everybody wants some and there aren't enough to go round."

"How will you do them for me? With lemon?"

"No way, dottore, they meet their fate in *polpettine.*"

There was quite a wait, but it was worth it. The *polpettine*, flat, crispy little fritters, were spangled with hundreds of tiny black dots, the eyes of newborn baby fishes. Montalbano ate them with reverence, knowing that devouring them was a sort of murder, a massacre of the innocents. As self-punishment, he did without a second course. But he was hardly out of the trattoria when, as sometimes happened, the voice of his hypersensitive conscience made itself heard.

"Self-punishment? You hippocrite Montalbano! Wasn't it just to avoid indigestion? You know how many *polpettine* you got through? Eighteen!"

Be that as it may, Montalbano went down to the port and strolled as far as the lighthouse, enjoying the sea breezes. (Camilleri, 2001, p. 82)

These exquisite little fritters, seasoned with garlic, parsley, and wild fennel and a little parmesan, in a batter lightened with beaten egg whites, are cooked quickly in hot olive oil.

SANGUINACCIO. *See* PIG'S BLOOD.

SAOR is a Venetian way of pickling fish, in which well-salted, fried sardines or other fish are layered in a pot or jar with thinly sliced onions which have been cooked in olive oil and boiled up with vinegar, or vinegar and wine, sometimes with a little sugar (with the addition in winter of dried fruit soaked in white wine, and pine nuts, said to provide useful calories). Prepared this way, fish will keep up to a week or more. This Venetian speciality is enjoyed in the intense summer heat as a cold and refreshing snack, especially on the night of 19 July, when the feast of the Redentore is celebrated on the Lagoon. The Venetian name derives from a Germanic language (German *sauer*, English *sour*), like the French *hareng saur*, pickled herring. A similar procedure, a name derived from the Spanish *in escabeche*, is used in Liguria, *scabeccio*, and the south of Italy, SCAPECE, often for vegetables as well as fish. From being a useful way of preserving food it has developed into a delicious recipe in its own right.

SAR, *sarago maggiore, sargo,* is one of the Diplodus subdivisions of bream, bigger than the other saragos, with fainter vertical stripes, and tasty flesh. It is good grilled or fried, often with bay leaves and garlic.

SARDEGNA. *See* SARDINIA.

SARDINE, *sarda, sardina,* is the same as pilchard (we confuse ourselves by having two different names for the same fish), one of the Clupeidae, which includes sprat, *papalina*, a freshwater sardine (*see* SARDINE, FRESHWATER), twaite shad, *cheppia, alosa*, anchovy, *acciuga, alice*, and of course herring, *arringa*, which is not found fresh in Italian waters, but is known in its dried and salt form. All these sardine-like creatures look similar, though varying in flavour, and can be cooked in the same way, so problems of identification need not inhibit us when cooking them, using some of the many recipes suggested for anchovies.

SARDINE, FRESHWATER,

agone, sardelle, alaccia, Alosa agone (not to be confused with *alaccia*, SHAD, *Alosa alosa*), is one of the Clupeidae, the sardine family, which embraces sardines, herrings, and pilchards, but the freshwater sardine is not found in northern waters, and so, unlike herring and pilchard, does not have an English version of its name for us to look up and use. This particular member of the sardine family is a freshwater fish who lives in the subalpine lakes, and has various names in Italy—*sarda* in Lake Iseo, *agone* in Lake Garda and Lake Maggiore—and when salted and dried, used to be a staple food of fishing communities all the year round. Around Lake Como they are sun- and wind-dried, and in this form are called *missultitt* and when dry roasted in an unoiled pan are skinned and prepared and eaten as a delicacy, as antipasto or to season polenta. Platina found *sardelle* in Lake Albano and liked them stewed with butter, parsley, and spices. He also liked those from Lake Garda, fried and seasoned with bitter orange juice. A 17th-century writer praised the *sarde* in Lake Iseo for their beauty, a silvery steel blue with a greenish blue back, and their whiteness and flavour—not as big as those in Benaco (Lake Garda) but more tasty. Most recipes for sardines or anchovies can be used with this agreeable fish.

SARDINIA, *Sardegna,* is the second

largest island in the Mediterranean sea, equidistant from the south of France, Liguria, and Lazio. History and geography formed a past that was harsh and far from kind to the inhabitants of this beautiful but hostile land, where foreign dominion and battles against climate and terrain left no time or energy for constructive politics or culture. Courage and independence have always been there, and perhaps we can read it in the food better than anywhere else. Sardinian politicians have been defined as *"pocos, locos y mal unidos,"* and it was not until the experience of World War I that a sense of national unity prevailed over the lawlessness and poverty. Folklore and superstition rather than culture surrounded much of everyday life. The politician Emilio Lussu saw that foreign dominion by a series of absentee rulers, from pre-Roman times onwards, had left a legacy of introspective resentment and distrust.

But today, almost a century later, unforeseen economic and political factors have drawn tourists and developers to the once unspoilt coastline, and industrial conglomerates have exploited the empty spaces inland and the cheap labour market. So now a coastal cuisine is flourishing, even though in the past Sardinians have mistrusted the sea and the pirates and invaders borne in on it—though one might remember the mariner Domenico Millelire, who saw off the French Revolutionary forces when they attempted to attack Sardinia from both the north and the south. Hoping to use the large island in the south, Maddalena, as a spearhead, the navy landed huge and seemingly invincible amounts of artillery on the smaller island of San Stefano, but Millelire sneaked up and landed a few cannon behind their backs and blasted them out of the water. A setback for their leader, the arrogant young Buonaparte. But Sardinians were not primarily maritime folk, and the fish recipes of the coastal waters were not in the past as important as those of Liguria and the Tuscan littoral. Many recipes are similar to those of Liguria and Spain, but the similarities could simply represent what all fishing communities do with smaller, less prestigious fish when it comes to making stews and soups. The *burrida* (not the same as *bourride* or the Ligurian fish stew) is a cold dish made from *gattuccio*, one of the dogfish family, which are skinned, cleaned, reserving the liver, cut in slices, simmered in salt water, then left to marinate for some hours in a sauce made from the liver and walnuts pounded in a mortar, cooked with chopped parsley and garlic, then diluted with vinegar. This is reminiscent of medieval and Renaissance sauces, but need not necessarily be derived from them, when the raw materials are local and plentiful. The peasant tradition of using available nuts and herbs is more plausible than the transmission of courtly Spanish or Roman sauces. A version of *cassola* is made with available fish which could include John Dory, squid, octopus, crabs of several kinds, star gazer, gurnard, scorpion fish, various bream, and grey mullet, cooked with some subtlety, separately in salted water, then kept to one side and eventually united in a sauce of finely chopped onion and garlic cooked in olive oil with chilli and the inevitable tomato, reduced down in the fishes' cooking water. Sometimes the fish are added to the sauce in the order in which they need to cook, and finished off together. Red mullet are gutted (or not) and scaled, coated with flour, and fried in olive oil. They are then marinated in a sauce of a great deal of chopped garlic, simmered in oil, to which is added some chopped skinned tomatoes and hot chilli, and then some white wine vinegar and a handful of chopped parsley, and eaten cold. Octopus are simmered in salted water until half cooked, then finished in oil and white wine with garlic and black olives, and served hot or cold with chopped parsley. Trout from inland waters are cleaned, dried, and stuffed with a mixture of chopped parsley, rosemary, and garlic, sprinkled with olive oil and baked. Bream can be cleaned, then slashed along the back and sides and desalted fillets of anchovy inserted into the cuts. The fish is then sprinkled with olive oil and baked in a hot oven, and when done, the cooking juices and residue in the pan are diluted with a little white wine to make a sauce. *Muggine*, grey mullet, are prepared around Cabras by cooking briefly in very salty water, then dried and completely covered with marsh samphire, locally known as *ziba*, whose saltiness and possibly also soda content help it to keep, as well as imparting flavour. *Bottarga* or salted and cured mullet roe, along with that of tunny, is a delicacy used in many ways, shaved onto slices of bread as an appetizer, marinated in oil and lemon and used as a spread, or grated into pasta and rice dishes. The roes in their enclosing membrane are salted in a temperate atmosphere, then pressed and air dried in cool surroundings and matured for some months.

There are several recipes for combining shellfish and their cooking liquid with a form of pasta unique to Sardinia, *fregula*, or *fregola*, which resembles but is by no means the same as couscous. Coarse semolina is rubbed by hand in a flat shallow dish, *scivedda*, with enough salted water to form little balls, bigger than couscous grains, about the size of peppercorns; these are then dried out in the sun or a low oven until hard and golden, and can then be cooked either in broth or water and finished with an appropriate sauce. Local lobster, after sautéing in chopped onion, tomato, and basil, are served on a bed of *fregula* cooked in the resultant liquid. Another version uses shellfish of various kinds.

Inland, the cooking, based on subsistence agriculture and grazing, was and still is simple and elemental, with grilled and roast meat (mainly game, pork, and lamb, with sucking pig a speciality) seasoned with pungent herbs, including myrtle, bay, sage, rosemary, and mint. Meat and game is often roasted in a pit full of smouldering embers, covered with the same, and layers of fragrant myrtle, *a carraxiu*. A series of boned animals or birds stuffed inside each other makes a festive dish, and more realistically, innards and offal are used in imaginative ways, for example, the black puddings or sausages made from the blood of lambs or goats, and *zurrette*, where the blood is seasoned with sharp cheese, salt, and pepper, mixed with fried cubes of *lardo* and bits of bread, stuffed into the animal's stomach, and simmered in salt water. *Sanguinacci di maiale* is a sweet version, made with pig's blood, sugar, cinnamon, and anise, stuffed into the large intestine, and cooked, sometimes sliced and fried or roasted. *Sa cordula* is made from the hearts, livers, and spleens of kids or lambs cut into strips, seasoned and held together with their cleaned and twisted intestines and sprigs of herbs, put on a spit, then grilled or fried, often eaten with a dish of young peas, or sometimes stewed instead with the peas and some tomato. The organs can be cubed, put on spits interspersed with bits of bacon and herbs, then all wound up in the intestines and roasted until crisp and golden. The intestines of milk-fed lamb have a milky residue which gets lost when they are scrubbed clean, so intrepid souls prefer to eat them as they are, just wiped clean, grilled, frieds or stewed, as in the PAJATA of Rome. This tradition of eating up every bit of the animal still exists; many still buy direct from the producer, and make use of everything

There is plentiful game, including *mouflon*, or *muflone*, a native breed of wild sheep, now cherished in nature reserves. When an old family friend was bringing a baby *muflone* as a present for his goddaughter, the writer Grazia Deledda, he was robbed by bandits and arrived without horse, purse, or overcoat, but still clutching the wild lamb, which she said was the best present she had ever had: "All the wide wild airs of the mountains and the unsettling mysteries of the forest entered the house with this graceful creature, still untamed but with a natural timidity and sweetness. The farmyard animals gathered round, drawn by the odour of the wild, and intimations of the scrub and the hidden lairs among the rocks, but the lit-tle animal took fright and leapt to the top of the woodpile," to be rescued by the kindly old man.

Deledda's childhood in the wild country around Nuoro gave her a taste for the legends and folklore of Sardinia, a background to the evocative food she sometimes mentions, like the *gattò* or *durke de mendula*, a sort of almond brittle made of sliced and toasted almonds mixed with orange zest and honey, cooked in the oven and then sliced into lozenge shapes. Walnuts and hazelnuts get the same treatment—*durke de nuke* and *de nizzola*. The harmonious blending of these elemental flavours seemed to express the essence of Sardinia. So did the rituals and activities around bread-making. Deledda remembers these in a short story, "*Il pane*," in which she recalls the hardships of getting up before dawn in the cold midwinter to start the day's bread-making, a domestic tradition, stronger than the power of religion or the law, that obliged even girls in a comfortably off middle-class household to learn, toil, and suffer, making the range of breads that are still one of the glories of Sardinian food. (To escape from this, she resolved, at the age of 12, to get married as soon as possible.) But her affectionate childhood memories are of the welcome heat in the stone-flagged kitchen, the elderly *infornatrice* who went from house to house giving her expert attention to the oven and the bread, watching over the huge flat *focacce*, quick to swell, burst open, and burn if not bashed into submission with the baker's peel that tossed and turned and smote them "like maternal caresses on the fat bottoms of naughty babies." (The bashing was to get rid of pockets of air, as with babies.) The best known of the flatbreads is the *pane carasau* or *carta da* (or *di*) *musica*. When it has puffed up into two thin layers, this flatbread can be whipped out of the oven, the layers separated with a sharp knife, and put back to dry out. Sometimes folded during cooking, these would keep for a long time, the staple food of shepherds away from home for long periods. They could be eaten with olive oil and cheese, torn into pieces to drop into soups, or softened in boiling water and eaten covered with tomato sauce and a poached egg (*pane fratau*). There are many versions of this oven-baked flat-bread, long-lasting or to be eaten fresh. Festive breads were made in intricate patterns for special occasions, complicated sculptural fantasies, made by the women of every family, rich or poor, using knives, scissors, and rollers, with designs appropriate to each occasion. A thin, highly decorated bread for weddings, *pane de kojuados noos*, often heart- or crescent-shaped, is stamped and perforated with intricate patterns, then glazed to accentuate the decoration. Easter breads are adorned with lambs, birds, flowers. In Oristano, the *pane di Villaurbana* is made from a stiff dough which is cut, snipped, and pinched into elaborate shapes, then dunked in boiling water to get a firm glaze. This has traditionally been a family occupation, one from which the watchful 13-year-old Deledda, who wanted to work with words, was glad to escape. As a writer living in Rome, she recalled the hardships and expertise of the bread-making experience, and in the short story "*Il pane*" recalls a supernatural explanation of one of the hazards—a batch of sour-dough starter that went wrong and ruined the whole day's production. (*Il dono di natale*, Biblioteca Sarda, vol. V 35. http://sardinia.net/BibliothecaSarda)

In the story, a mean and avaricious woman, Donna Barbara, was visited on baking day by a fair-haired, blue-eyed child dressed in red rags who begged for a taste of fresh bread. Donna Barbara scraped together the scraps and leavings from the bread-making, and her servant made a mean little *focaccia* which she put into the oven; there it miraculously swelled and grew, too good to give away. The next one did the same, and Barbara again kept it for herself. By this time, the Christ Child had vanished, and the amazing loaves, indeed the whole batch, were found to be acidic and inedible. "*Così fu castigata Dama Barbara per il suo cattivo cuore*" (Thus was the lady Barbara punished for her hardness of heart). *S'oriattu* is another bread mentioned by Deledda, made from fine rye flour, treated in a complex series of transformations in order to get the stuff to rise, described with loving attention to detail in *Il pane* (INSOR, 2000, p. 285).

Other dishes from inland share the intricate skills of the bread-makers. The various shapes of pasta are constructed to hold the rich sauces of pork, lamb, or cheese. *Maccarones a ferritus* are made from sheets of thin egg pasta, sometimes coloured with saffron, cut into finger-length ribbons or small squares, which are twisted round a metal rod to make rugged hollow tubes. These can also be made by taking lumps of the pasta mixture and shaping them by hand, twisting and stretching them around the *ferritus* or rod. They are often served with the juices from a piece of braised lamb or pork, the meat which is served later as a *secondo piatto*. Sometimes these juices are mixed with fresh ricotta to make a creamy sauce. *Malloreddus* or *maccarones caidos*, or *ciciones alla sassarese*, are a sort of gnocchi made from a hard wheat semolina and salt water, sometimes mixed with saffron and oil. The mixture is not rolled out wafer thin like the sophisticated *tagliatelle* of the north of Italy, but stretched into worm-like lengths which are then cut into small pieces and formed, with equally impressive skills, into little shell shapes, ridged on the outside by rolling and pressing onto a cheese grater, coarse strainer, or other ridged surface. They are often served with a sauce made of onion and *lardo* softened in oil and cooked with chopped pork, many herbs, and tomatoes, and served with grated pungent pecorino.

The vast areas of grazing land nourish sheep and goats from which an ocean of milk flows into both small- and large-scale production of a whole range of cheeses, from the pungent *pecorino romano*, in worldwide demand (especially in the United

States, which buys a good 60 percent of the total production), to fresh delicate little innovative creations like *bonassai* and *biancospino*, developed to meet new consumer tastes. *Pecorino romano* is a hard mature table or grating sheep's cheese with a pungency that goes better with many of the robust dishes of Lazio and Sardinia than the more subtle, more expensive parmesan. A larger percentage is now made in Sardinia than in Lazio, both of them protected and controlled with a DOC and DOP. A nice little earner. These and *pecorino fiore sardo* make up over 60 percent of cheese production. European Economic Community quotas are not always helpful, and exports fluctuate with the value of the euro, the cost of the milk, and competition from other cheeses. A balance is being achieved between industrial production (now one-third of the total), cheeses made in cooperatives, and artisan manufacture, bearing in mind that cheap products from the rest of Europe can only be met by exploiting the history and ecological and environmental factors that make the cheeses of Sardinia so special. With legal definitions and accurate labelling, the price/quality equation could work, and the battle might be won, with white-robed boffins and rugged peasants in close harmony.

The local *pecorino sardo* has its own DOC and DOP, which is considered by some to smother rather than enhance the identities of *caciotta* and *semicotto*, now described as *pecorino sardo dolce* and *pecorino sardo maturo*, but with labelling which serves to distinguish it from the industrial product. *Fiore sardo* also has its DOP, and is traditionally made from raw milk from native sheep, just as shepherds have been doing for thousands of years up on the remote pastures, to produce a rich hard cheese. Fresh ricotta is a by-product of the production of pecorino and is used in stuffings for pasta, and added to pasta sauces; a smoked matured version is widespread, *ricotta mustia* is specially fine, and there is a salted ricotta, which is matured for

some weeks. Ricotta thickened with egg yolks and flavoured with honey, saffron and orange zest makes a filling for *pardulas*, little open tarts. There are fresh and matured goat's cheeses; *caprino a pasta cruda*, a raw milk cheese, made and matured by small producers in traditional ways; and *semicotto caprino*, a delicate cheese, eaten fresh or matured for several months. Cow's milk is used in some pulled cheeses; *peretta* is a pearshaped cheese eaten fresh; *casizolu* was made, unusually, by women, from milk of the special *razza sardo-modicana*, a breed of semiwild cattle, obtained from a cross between a reddish autochthonous cow, the ancient *podolico*, and Modicana bulls from Ragusa in Sicily, with glowing coats ranging from bright red or deep mahogany to dark brown. These sturdy animals were bred in the 19th century for their strength as beasts of burden, and although numbers have declined (now to about 3,000), they are at last enjoying a more tranquil existence, grazing placidly in a semiwild state on the wild myrtle and camomile of the Mediterranean scrub around Montiferru, prized for their tasty flesh and fragrant milk, and ability to survive in these conditions. The milk is treated as soon as it comes from the cow, then, at precisely the right moment of coagulation, day or night, the curds are cooked and worked by hand in punishingly hot water, and are then squeezed and shaped and formed to a smooth and shining consistency, and nurtured like fragile newborn infants in swaddling clothes, then hung to dry and finally eaten fresh, or matured for a month or even longer. The cheese retains the delicate aromas of the grass and herbs on which the cows feed, uncontaminated by pesticides or artificial foodstuffs. Changed social conditions now make it possible for men to work round the clock at this demanding task, but in the past they would have been away with their flocks while women saw to the bread and the task of curing pork products, as well as this special cheese.

The *salumi* of Sardinia are excellent, but tend to be eclipsed in the public mind by the ubiquitous roast sucking pig, and since most are for autoconsumption, there is not a big market for characteristic products that can get to claim *tipicità*, that untranslatable word for something individual and characteristic of a specific place or region. People go on making cured pig and sheep salami and sausages for family and friends, with variations of technique and seasoning, but few can claim any weird local peculiarity. A cured sausage found all over the island, *salsiccia sarda stagionata*, is made from lean pork meat cut with a knife and seasoned according to local tastes, with herbs, garlic, chilli, cinnamon, or fennel seeds. A fresh sausage, *salsiccia fresca,* is made with local pork, cut not ground, in natural casings of intestines treated with red wine and vinegar; that from Irgoli in the province of Nuoro is widely available. *Sa supressada* is a large flat salame made from prime lean cuts of pork and diced cured back fat. An emphasis on indigenous breeds of pig, and their protection from cheap imports, is helping to establish a market. Hams from local pigs and wild boar are sought after. Less noble parts go into a mixture of meats from a pig's head, *testa in cassetta*, with aromatics and wine, which is cooked and eaten cold.

Apart from latecomers like tomatoes and chillies, which have infiltrated themselves, fresh and dried, into many dishes that existed before their arrival, there are cardoons, artichokes, eggplants, cauliflowers, and many kinds of wild herbs and vegetables which are cooked in a variety of original ways. Tender young peas are simmered with chopped onion softened in oil, moistened with broth, and flavoured and coloured with saffron. Trimmed artichoke hearts are cooked in olive oil with parsley and garlic and finished cooking with cubed potatoes. Round tomatoes of the appropriate size are cut in half, emptied of juice and seeds, lightly seasoned with salt and chopped basil; then into each one is inserted a lightly poached egg. The closed tomatoes are dipped in beaten egg, then breadcrumbs, and fried quickly in olive oil. Organic saffron is cultivated around San Gavino Monreale in the province of Cagliari, where the soil and climate are ideal, and its colour and perfume go into many dishes—pasta, *fregula cun cocciula*, desserts like *casadinas* and *pardulas*, many broths and stews.

SAUSAGES, FRESH AND CURED. *See* SALSICCIA, LUCANICA.

SAVOIARDI, sponge fingers or ladyfingers, are a light sponge made with egg yolks beaten to a froth with sugar to which flour is added, then incorporated with the whites, whisked to a stiff foam, piped into elongated biscuit shapes, sprinkled with sugar, and cooked until golden in a low oven. Today they are flavoured with vanilla, but in the past anise seeds, cinnamon, and candied citron were used. They accompany creams and soft desserts, and can be dunked in wine or hot chocolate, and used as a base for trifles and other puddings. Perhaps the most flagrant flaunting of this luxury biscuit is in a painting from the late 1640s by Giovanna Garzoni of one of the pet lap dogs of the grand duchess Vittoria della Rovere in her villa at Poggio Imperiale in the Florentine countryside. This pampered creature sits toying with an uneaten crumbled biscuit and half a sponge finger alongside a delicate china bowl of milk on a deep pink silk cloth spread over a low table. The two flies on the sponge finger add to the casual immediacy of the scene—the smiling pug who has never known hunger taking this aristocratic food for granted. A contemporary recipe from Bartolomeo Stefani in Mantua uses six eggs beaten with sugar for half an hour to a pale foam, a little flour folded in, baked in paper cases or little tins.

Other artists at the Medici court painted sponge fingers alongside luxury goods, rich textiles, luscious fruit, and musical instruments. Cristoforo Munari provides some vivid images. The name *savoiardi* must relate to the House of Savoy, at that time of considerable political importance, though it is worth noting that in Naples, with different allegiances, Corrado calls his version *biscotti alla bugnè* and gives another recipe, *biscotti all'africana*, made with egg yolks beaten to a white foam with sugar, mixed with whipped egg whites, flavoured with a touch of candied citron, but with no flour, and baked in long thin paper cases—Africa being less remote than Savoy.

SAVORY, summer savory, *santoreggia, Satureja hortensis,* winter savory, *santoreggia salvatica, Saturja montana,* is traditionally used to flavour beans, perhaps because of its many healthy properties, for it is both antispasmodic, digestive, carminative, and stimulant, all you need in a dish of beans. In Tuscan folk medicine, it is used as an infusion in the bathwater of infants learning to walk, to strengthen their little legs. This is a herb that is good dried as well as fresh.

SCALLOP, *cappasanta, pellegrina, conchiglia di San Giacomo, ventaglio,* is the familiar pilgrims' shell, the concave half of this useful and delicious bivalve a convenient thing for a holy person travelling light, a container for alms, food, and drink, and a badge of recognition, on the journey to Santiago de Compostela in Spain, when pilgrims wore them on their staffs. The best part to eat is the muscle, *noce,* which holds the two shells together in an iron grip (the creature gets around from the momentum got by opening and closing the shells, by means of this tenacious cylinder of tender—if not overcooked—and delicate flesh). Either prize the scallop open with a knife as you

would an oyster, or put it on an iron pan or grid with a fierce heat, or, as Scappi recommends, repeatedly plunge a net full of them into boiling water, seasoned with salt and pepper, until they open, and then eat them still warm with more pepper; this sounds like the Venetian version, which disdains the use of oil and lemon juice with a sprinkling of parsley. Or the extracted muscle can be dusted in flour, fried in olive oil, and served with a sauce of bitter orange juice, sugar, and pepper; or marinated in oil, fennel flowers, and pepper, and cooked over a grill wrapped in paper, *en papillote.* The shells make pretty serving dishes, which can be an incentive to overelaborate, dishing precooked scallops up with a crust of parmesan and breadcrumbs and so forth, a temptation to be resisted.

SCAMORZA MOLISANA is a pulled cow's milk cheese, a "lite" version of *caciocavallo,* eaten fresh or smoked, usually grilled. When the climate is unfavourable for the slow maturing of *caciocavallo,* small producers make it for immediate sale and consumption, so avoiding the risk of loss and deterioration of the precious cheeses. With its low fat content and pleasant flavour, grilled *scamorza* is becoming a popular substitute for meat. It is made in many parts of the south and now also in northern Italy.

SCAMPI, Dublin Bay prawns, *Nephrops norvegicus,* are one of the lobster family, and although the creature is not common in Mediterranean waters, excellent ones are found in the Adriatic, and the name, loosely used, is familiar on Italian menus. The delicate flavour requires simple treatment, plain boiling and eating with oil and lemon, or grilling. The shells and debris, boiled, make a nice broth with which to make a scampi risotto.

SCAPECE is way of pickling fish or vegetables similar to CARPIONE and SAOR and the Spanish *escabeche*. A Sicilian recipe for eggplants involves finishing deep-fried eggplants in a sauce of fried onions, wine vinegar, and tomato sauce, with sugar, pepper, mint, and *caciocavallo* cheese. SOTTACETI) is the name given to many products simply pickled in vinegar.

SCAPPI, BARTOLOMEO

(d. 1577). Until recently, little was known about the life of Bartolomeo Scappi, private cook to Pope Pius V and author of a monumental work published under the title *Opera* in 1570 by Michele Tramezzino in Venice. His origins were always considered controversial: some were convinced he came from Bologna (the family name can be traced here) while others believed he came from Venice (distinct traces of dialect in the text). June di Schino and Furio Luccichenti (2000) managed by patient detective work to research and publish all the missing information in 2004, showing he came from the town of Dumenza in Lombardy, as indicated by the inscription on the stone plaque found in the nearby church of Luino. Subsequently, Scappi's wills were found amongst the notary public documents in various archives, showing that cooks had their own association (the Confraternity of Cooks) and religious institution (the Church of the Cooks). Bartolomeo left money to these institutions, and in the absence of a wife and children, the rest of his money went to his relatives. These new facts and further studies help us to understand his life and contribute towards an initial biography. He was active during the pontificates of seven popes (1534–1576): Paul III, Julius III, Marcello II (only 22 days), Paul IV, Pius IV, Pius V, and Gregorius XIII.

Scappi first refers to his stay in Venice in the service of Cardinal Grimani. Then he describes "the dinner offered in Trastevere by Cardinal Lorenzo Campeggio to his majesty the Emperor Charles V" in April 1536. This may be one of the lengthiest repasts of the times, as it comprised 13 services of 789 elaborate dishes. Subsequently, he served Cardinal du Bellay, and a collation served by eight stewards and eight carvers after a theatrical performance is described in detail. He was also in the service of Pietro Bembo and Andrea Cornaro. Cardinal Rodolfo Pio di Carpi is cited several times, and Scappi describes a collation prepared at his vineyard on the Quirinal. Pius IV was not adverse to the simple pleasures of the table, and Scappi mentions that His Holiness drank barley water and ate frogs fried with garlic and parsley. The pope, however, issued an edict to restrict and regulate banquets in 1563. Scappi appears in the papal roles in 1566; he created the traditional enthronement banquet for Pius V, and only planned the second one.

Pope Pius V, Michele Ghisleri (1566–1572), was in all respects an intransigent ascetic who maintained an austere and abstemious attitude towards food, drink, and the table, for which he laid aside a miserly sum. In 1567, while prostrate from habitual fasting, he threatened to excommunicate anyone who dared to strengthen the simple broth he sipped to sustain himself. The only concession he made was ass's milk, as he was convinced it helped his suffering from gallstones. Towards the end of his career, Scappi acquired the title of *mazziere* required for supervising pontifical ceremony and was nominated knight and Lateran count palatine. The *Book of the Dead* of St. Peter's Archives in the Vatican testifies he died on the 13 April 1577 and was buried in the cemetery of the Church of the Cooks.

His major work, considered a *Summa*, is both vast in content and precise in detail, and goes beyond the confines of a mere cookery book to become an important reference for the 16th-century Roman papal court. The 900-page treatise is divided into six sections called "books," the first of which deals with the qualities the ideal cook should possess: he should be a man of sobriety and a careful supervisor—quick, patient, imaginative, and well-mannered, utterly devoted to duty and to his master. Information is provided about the right choice of foods and the various techniques for cooking and preserving. The layout of the Renaissance kitchen and the various kinds of equipment are also described. The second book deals with all varieties of meats, poultry and game and fowl. Here we find one of the very first recipes for *gallo d'India*, the turkey, as well as one for cooking guinea pigs and dormice—typical ancient Roman fare, still to be found in Calabria today. There are also instructions for the preparation of veal, bull, lamb, boar, buffalo, and stag testicles. The subject of the third book is fish and the many ways of preparing it. Seven pages are dedicated to the highly prized sturgeon and the numerous ways of frying, braising, grilling, and baking it. Scappi illustrates Renaissance specialities such as *schinale*, the cured back of the fish, and *moronella*, the salted sturgeon's belly referred to by the steward of Reverend Cardinal Pole of England. Turbot, John Dory, lampreys, eels, and oysters receive the same attention as minor fish and sea foods such as sardines, anchovies, sea slugs, and clams. The fourth book offers the complete presentations of numerous sumptuous banquets of the times and lists seasonal menus. It is curious to note that several banquets were dedicated solely to one food, for example, two complete dinners of veal (with a list of 24 alternative dishes); one based on fresh water, salted fish, and salads; a menu only of sturgeon; a dinner of butter, cheese, and eggs. The fifth book teaches how to make all sorts of pastry: pasta, pies, tarts, *pasticci*, many of which are feasible to make and delicious to taste. The final book covers food for the sick and convalescent. Nourishing broths tend to be predominant, for example the strong capon soup, which was given to Cardinal Andrea Cornaro, or vegetable *minestra* made

with red chickpea, stuffed lettuce, or borage. There are also numerous recipes for less bland dishes like marzipan cake, liver sausage, stewed kid's heads, frog, tortoise (*terra non turtle di acqua*) potage, pumpkin pie, pheasant.

The recipes are highly innovative for the times, as they not only describe the ingredients but explain in specific detail each phase of the cooking procedures and the presentation of every dish. Scappi's *Opera* can be considered a complete compendium from every point of view.

A careful reading between the lines, revealing Scappi's cosmopolitan experience, shows how well acquainted he was with the various traditions. Although his *Opera* mainly mirrors the aristocratic cuisine of the 16th century, Scappi offers several gleanings of more simple fare. He says, for example, that several fish recipes, like turbot potage, are exactly the same as the fishermen of Chioggia make, hence "they are the very finest." Examples of Venetian cuisine can be traced in recipes for turnip broth or the capon consommé so enjoyed by Cardinal Pietro Bembo. There are also abundant references to Roman fare of the times: veal meatloaf, fried *ferlingotti* (*maccheroni*), apostolic broth (a herb and parsley soup), freshwater shrimps, fritters and biscuits to go with Malvasia wine, and *torta bianca reale*, a cake enjoyed by Pope Julius III.

Scappi recalls his northern homeland in several meat soup recipes, and refers especially to the fish from Lombardy. He says that the finest freshwater fish comes from Lake Garda and recommends the pike from Lake Como and tench from Lake Maggiore. He sums up his wide experience in one sentence, saying that the Milanese like to cook trout cut in pieces but "we the cooks of Rome prefer it whole." The 28 engraved plates, which include a rarely found medallion portrait of the author, are of exceptional value, as they provide the most comprehensive picture of the Renaissance kitchen. Twenty-six full-page illustrations depict the structure and organization of the kitchens, such as the main one with a lofted ceiling with hooked chains to hang *lardo* and dried meats. Running water and a row of bubbling pots on the fire are visible on each side, and in the foreground we can see a table for rolling pastry with a pastry wheel identical to ones today and a butcher's block with cleaver and a leg of meat. Among the wide range of cooking receptacles of every shape and size, principally made of tin-lined copper, there is a gigantic iron cauldron which could contain 700 litres of water. The manoeuvring of such an enormous pot was complex and hazardous and required it to be removed with a chain mechanism on wheels, and then pulled on ropes by at least four men. An essential element for travelling, outdoor cooking was frequent and well planned, as can be seen by the cloth-covered wooden tent, the wicker baskets containing crockery, the spits, and the suspended cooking vessels. A specially designed saddle for the gastronome shows the space below the seat to keep food hot and lateral metal-lined compartments for keeping wine flasks and beverages cool. The vast assortment of knives remind us of the important and theatrical role of the carver, and the wide diversity of cooking utensils and implements indicate how advanced the cuisine of the times was from a technological point of view. There is an ingeniously designed, multiple-level clockwork spit turned at different speeds according to the weight, the size of the meat, and the distance from the heat. A single double plate illustrates the ritual presentation for inspection of hot and cold foods to be sent up on a revolving wheel to the cardinals in conclave for the election of a new pope after the death of Paul III.

(JdS)

SCHIACCIATA. *See* FESTIVITY AND FOOD.

SCORPION FISH, *scorfano rosso*, is one of the *rascasses*, whose incomparable flavour is indispensable in fish stews and soups, and whose dramatic appearance, bright orange red, with a big fierce mouth and staring eyes, make it an essential ingredient of many dramatic still life paintings of fish. In 1708, the painter Giuseppe Maria Crespi came to Livorno and so impressed the grand duke Ferdinand that he was asked to paint, in only two days, two still lifes, one of game and one of fish. The painter sent for a variety of wild birds and fish, which he rendered with astonishing verve and speed, passing the material for recycling to the courtiers, who must have recognised at once in the confusion of fish all the ingredients needed for Livorno's celebrated fish stew, CACCIUCCO, with in the centre a large red fish gasping its last breath on a sombre shore. In a series of paintings by Felice Boselli, a huge scorpion fish dominates the composition, with humble fishermen quite eclipsed by the great red fish, surely a comment not just on its beauty but its important gastronomic role.

SEA BASS, *spigola, branzino, lupo*, one of the Serranidae, is found in both fresh and salt waters. Platina maybe fished for them in the Tiber, at the bottom of Pomponio Leto's garden in Trastevere, and the two of them enjoyed this fine fish grilled with a green sauce, or simmered, with a white sauce of *banco-mangiare*. Pliny had written of the excellence of a fish caught *inter duos pontes*, between the Ponte Milvio and today's Ponte Sant'Angelo, and Platina thought that this must have been the *spigola*, but Laurioux has established that Pomponio was right in calling it *alaccia* or shad (Laurioux, 2006, p. 208). Today they are much esteemed for their firm white flesh, and extensively farmed, which meets the demand with a less tasty fish than the wild ones.

Sea bass live in both fresh and salt water, often entering rivers. (Shutterstock)

SEA BREAM, *pagro,* have silvery pink backs and sides, but not as pink as DEN- TEX. The flesh is similar, not quite as firm, and the size varies from quite small to over 50 centimetres. They can be cooked the same way as GILT-HEAD BREAM. *See also* BREAM.

SEA URCHIN, *riccio di mare,* is a sea creature (*Paracentrotus lividus* is the best known in Italy) beneath whose sharp deep purple spines lurk five orange corals or go- nads which when extracted can be eaten raw with a drop of lemon. The delicate but in- tense flavour is much loved by people of Ital- ian descent in California, where a large and very good sea urchin can be found. Japanese reastaurants in the United States use these fine creatures for sushi. They can also be in- corporated into a sauce for spaghetti, espe- cially in Sicily, Puglia, and Calabria, where they are plentiful. A version of this sauce prepared by his cleaning lady, Adelina, plunges Andrea Camilleri's fictional detec- tive Montalbano into a moral dilemma in the middle of a very sensitive case—whether to take the phone off the hook while the pasta boils and miss an important contact, or risk ruining the meal.

SENAPE. *See* MUSTARD.

SESAME, *sesamo, Sesamum indicum,* has been used as a source of oil since 1000 BC, but Dalby (2003) points out that we have no archeo-botanical evidence for its use before that, so earlier texts may have been referring to linseed oil. The seeds are what matter in Italian cuisine, where they have been used since Roman times, mainly with bread and confec- tionery, although the oil, having little flavour when refined, is often used to dilute other oils, legally or fraudulently. The unrefined oil of toasted sesame seeds has an agreeable nutty flavour, but as Mattioli pointed out, it is rather rich and sticky, and olive oil in all its varieties is preferred in Italy today.

Sesame originated in India, and can only be grown in hot parts of Italy, but the use of the seeds is widespread. A recipe from Sicily for hake baked in a sauce of toasted sesame seeds ground with white wine, parsley, garlic, and chilli might be a legacy of the earlier Arab presence. Apicius used sesame seeds to flavour honey-sweetened cookies and pan- cakes, and they figure in Sally Grainger's re- construction of an account in Cato, which she adapted as a possible version of the much earlier "cheese and sesame sweetmeats fried in hottest oil and rolled in sesame seeds" offered at a banquet offered by Philoxenus in Sicily in around 400 BC. She mixed semolina cooked in milk with ricotta and honey, deep fried little balls of the mixture, then rolled them in melted honey and toasted sesame seeds (Dalby and Grainger, p. 54). In Sicily today, *mafalda* is a yeasted bread, made of finely milled semolina, flavoured with malt, which is made into twisted or braided rolls and strewn with sesame seeds before baking. There are today many mixtures of nuts and sugar or honey, cooked to a brittle crunchi- ness, which include sesame seeds. The *cubaita* of Sicily (Simeti, 1989, p. 98) involves cook- ing sesame seeds in boiling sugar and honey until fragrant, then adding chopped pista- chios and toasted almonds, flattening the cooled mixture with a half lemon, and cut- ting into lozenges.

SFORMATO is Italy's pragmatic stress-free answer to the soufflé—a cooked and puréed ingredient mixed into breadcrumbs or a béchamel, with the addition of eggs, cheese, and seasonings, to make a savoury pudding baked in the oven, often in a *bagno maria*, or cooked in a mould and then turned out (hence the name "unmoulded") and usually served warm or tepid. The eggs make the mixture rise agreeably, but this is not a mark of success, for it will subside gracefully as it cools. A *sformato* can be made with spinach, artichokes, eggplants, or almost any combination of vegetables and meat or fish. This idea of a mould or baked pudding is older than its present name; the traditional Milanese *scarpazza* is usually made with spinach cooked, squeezed dry, chopped, seasoned in butter and spices, and mixed with breadcrumbs soaked in milk, instead of béchamel, cream, and eggs, and cooked in the oven in a buttered dish lined with breadcrumbs. It is similar in name and content to the *scarpazzone* of Emilia, or the *erbazzone* of Reggio Emilia.

SHAD, *alaccia*, belongs to that broad church the herring family, of which the best-known kinds in Europe are the allice shad, *Alosa alosa*, and the twaite shad, *Alosa fallax*; their flesh is delicious and their bones are highly unpleasant, for which reason this fish is often cooked with sorrel, whose acid helps to deconstruct them. Scappi reminds us of how they come up the big rivers to spawn, those caught in the Tiber being the best of all (to the enjoyment of Platina and Pomponio Leto a century earlier), and gives three ways of cooking them, including a delicious sweet/sour marinade of vinegar, cooked grape must, wine, and spices, in which they will keep for several days after salting, flouring, and frying in oil. There is a small fish of the same family, *agone* or confusingly *alaccia* or *sarda*, which can be found in some of the north Italian lakes, and can be cooked like SARDINES.

Shallots exemplify many of the favorable qualities of both onions and garlic, and can be used as a substitute for either one. (Shutterstock)

SHALLOT, *scalogna, Allium cepa* or *ascalonicum*, is one of the onion family, whose bulbs are bunched together, rather than single. The flavour is between garlic and onion, but on the whole milder. Early authorities warned of its tendency to induce melancholy and horrid feelings, which can be mitigated by boiling first and then serving with chopped sage and parsley. The predominance of the shallot in French cuisine is not found in Italian cooking.

SHARKS belong to the same order as dogfish; there are several edible fishes in this group available in Italy, of which the best known are smooth hound *palombo*, which is good cooked with peas.

SHEEP, *ovino*, is officially classified in two main groups: *agnello* and *ovino adulto*. The main subdivisions of the adult group are *agnellone*, a young sheep between six and ten months old, *castrato*, and *pecora*; *agnello* is the legal name for lamb or young sheep on a predominantly milk diet weighing not more than 10 kilos, but commercially the important division is between *agnello* and *agnellino da latte* or *abbacchio*, a baby lamb fed only on its mother's milk and just three to four weeks old, a delicacy enjoyed in Rome and Lazio, whence the name has spread. *Abbacchio al forno con patate* is baby lamb, perfumed with rosemary and garlic, cooked in a slow oven with chunks of potato anointed with lard, until the potatoes are golden and the meat is ready to fall off the bone. *Abbacchio a scottadito* is simply baby lamb cutlets cooked on a grid over charcoal, basted with lard, until slightly blackened on the outside and still slightly pink within, eaten straightaway with the fingers. Belli devoted a sonnet to the care this takes: *"Er lardo acceso sbrodola e borbotta / mannanno in giù tante goccette ardente, / che, una qua, una là, tutte uguarmente / vanno a investi' la carne in sin che è cotta"* (The kindled lard mutters and splutters everywhere, / tossing up so many ardent droplets, / here and there, that it evenly / anoints the meat as it cooks). An audaciously blasphemous comparison with the investiture of St. Peter ends the sonnet, with the Holy Spirit compared to the sparks flying upwards from the lard.

Young lambs up to 10 weeks old will have had a more adventurous diet, but still mainly milk, giving pale pink flesh, with plenty of pure white fat, which will keep the meat moist while roasting, which, unlike *abbacchio*, usually leaves the meat lightly cooked and still pink.

The season for young lamb coincides with the arrival of the first artichokes, and there are several regional recipes which take advantage of this. In a Roman recipe for lambs' offal and artichokes, *coratella con carciofi*, the bitterness of the artichokes offsets the sweetness of the meat: the lungs, heart, and liver are cut into small pieces and fried in lard, starting with the lungs, adding the heart, and finally the liver, and the young artichokes, which have been trimmed of their hard outer leaves and cooked separately in lard, with a little water if they show signs of burning. The liver cooks in a few minutes, and at this point the dish can be moistened with marsala, dry white wine, or lemon juice, and eaten very hot.

In a Ligurian recipe, pieces of lamb are browned with garlic and chopped parsley, to which is then added a glass of white wine, which is partly evaporated over a high heat. The meat is removed, and some prepared Ligurian artichokes are cooked in the pan juices for a while, then the lamb is put back in, and when both are cooked, the mixture is thickened with a mixture of beaten egg and lemon juice, stirred in carefully off the heat to avoid curdling.

Castrato is a castrated and fattened young male sheep, sold in Great Britain as "lamb," although more mature than the Italian idea of lamb. Paradoxically, baby milk-fed lambs are plentiful in Italy as surplus of the cycle of rearing sheep for wool and milk rather than for mature meat, but virtually impossible to find in the United States or Great Britain. Common food like baby lamb was thus of little interest to Corrado in 18th-century Naples, who preferred kid for aristocratic tables, but has some delightful recipes for *castrato*, a more prestigious meat: a whole leg of lamb larded with ham, cloves, and little pieces of cinnamon, simmered in water and white wine, bay leaves, lemon, coriander, salt, and pepper, and served cold with a sauce of anchovies pounded up with parsley and marjoram, diluted with oil, lemon juice, and vinegar. Scappi, when writing of loin of *castrato*, distinguishes between young and old, and says that the best is from sheep fed on the mountains, not the plains "The mountain sheep are sweeter, / but the valley sheep are fatter, / we there deem'd it meeter / to carry off the latter," as Thomas Love Peacock said of lamb from the Welsh Marches ("The War Song of Dinas Vawr").

He recommends a preliminary simmering in broth, then grilling or spit or oven roasting the joint in a crust of breadcrumbs seasoned with fennel. This to us strange technique of giving a joint of meat a boil before roasting helps to firm it up so that it can be larded more effectively.

SHEEPSHEAD BREAM, *sarago pizzuto*, with a snout rather like a beak and dark vertical stripes, is not as fine as other bream but can go into fish soups.

SHELLFISH AND CRUSTACEANS include: crabs, lobsters (*aragosta, astice* etc.), shrimp (prawns; *canocchia, gambero, scampo, mazzancolla*), scallops (*capasante*), cockles (*cappa liscia*), palourdes (*vongole*), squid, octopus (*polpo, calamaro, seppia, totano, moscardino*, etc.), oysters, and sea urchins. Razor-shells (*cannolicchio, cappalunga*), another type of crustacean, live buried in the sand on the seashore, and are quite distinctive in appearance, as indicated in this fragment from a Greek mime by the ancient Sicilian author Sophron: "Whatever are these long shells?" "Oh, those are razor-shells, a delicacy sweet of flesh, a joy to widows." The joke is that the creature which lives inside the shell has a distinctly phallic shape—and indecently protrudes in the course of cooking. Whether for this reason or another, razor-shell was considered by classical physicians a useful food in treating gynaecological illnesses.

(AKD)

SHERBET. *See* ICE CREAM.

SHRIMP is the name in the United States for what are called prawns in Great Britain, where shrimp is the name given to tiny ones. They have various names in Italy: *gambero rosso* are bright red with a violet head; *gambero rosa* is smaller and pink; *mazzancolla*, the name in Lazio for the *gambero imperiale*, is pink and plump with a delicate flavour, often grilled in the shell, after marinating in chopped garlic, oil, and parsley; *gamberello* is the common prawn or shrimp; *gamberetto grigia* is a very small greyish brown shrimp (*see* GAMBERO).

SICILIA. *See* SICILY.

SICILY, *Sicilia.* In a country rich in food traditions, no region is richer than Sicily, even though Italians have been slow to realise the fact and Sicilians slower still.

Sicily is the second largest of the Italian islands. Its dependencies include Pantelleria to the south, more than half way to the African coast; and the Aeolian Islands, Stromboli and others, to the north.

Neither in history nor in language can Sicily be treated simply as a region of Italy. The Sicilian language is a permanent record of the adventurous history and culture of the island. Sometimes described as a dialect of Italian, it is in fact quite individual in its sounds and vocabulary. Sicilian now has a growing presence in gastronomic talk, in print and on the Internet. Some local dishes have never had Italian names. For these reasons, Sicilian names are generally used in this article (but *see* CALABRIA), but two difficulties must be noted. first, dialect variations around Sicily often affect the names of foods. Second, Sicilian orthography is not fixed, and variant spellings, on a kind of spectrum between standard Italian and the versions given here, will certainly be encountered.

The most significant minorities, excluding modern migrants, are the speakers of Albanian (or Arbëreshë) and Siceliot Greek (or Griko), both of whom have lived in Sicily for many centuries. These have their own gastronomic specialities and their own names for them.

At the beginning of written history, three indigenous peoples (their cultures and languages apparently different from those of Italy) were already sharing their island with colonisers from west and east. From the east came the Greeks, whose cities, mostly coastal, spread around the northern, eastern, and southern coasts; eventually there were also Greek cities some way inland. From the west came the Phoenicians, whose well-established colony of Carthage (in modern Tunisia) was the jumping-off point for further settlement on the coasts of Sicily, Sardinia, and Spain as well as North Africa.

When the enthusiasts for European food traditions trace Sicilian *canestratu* back to the cheese-making activities (carefully described in the *Odyssey*) of the one-eyed monster and shepherd Polyphemos, they are doing just what classical Greeks used to do: the Greeks, likewise, assumed that Odysseus's adventure with the Cyclops took place in Sicily. Whatever the truth in that legend, it is certain that in the 5th and 4th centuries BC, when Greek culture flourished in Sicily, the island was already able to boast of its food (by 400 BC, Sicilian salt pork and cheese were being exported to Greece) and food talk was on the menu. Epicharmos, an early 5th-century native of Syracuse and author of comedies, returned insistently to gastronomic topics. He provides the first Sicilian literary menu, in the shape of this reminiscence by a shipwrecked, but not starving, mariner:

In the morning, just at dawn, we used to barbecue plump little anchovies, some baked pork, and octopus, and drink down some sweet wine with them.
"Oh, you poor fellows!'
"Hardly a bite, you see."
"What a shame!"
And there would be nothing the rest of the day but a fat red mullet, and a couple of bonitos split down the middle, and wood-pigeons to match, and *rascasses* . . . (*Comicorum Graecorum fragmenta*, ed. G. Kaibel, vol. 1, pt. 1)

Mithaikos, the first celebrity chef, is said to have migrated (perhaps in the late 5th century) from his native Syracuse to Greece, where he popularised Sicilian luxury, wrote a cookery book, and was expelled from Sparta. Archestratos, the first real food writer of Europe, born in Gela, travelled the Greek world around 350 BC "to satisfy his stomach and even lower appetites" (according to a disapproving later author) and recorded his culinary discoveries in a poem, *Hedypatheia*. All

these writings now survive only in fragments. The Syracusan court in the 4th century was home to Philoxenos of Kythera, a dithyrambic poet and (if it is the same man) a banqueting poet; also to Aristippos of Kyrene, philosopher of hedonism and conscientious gourmand.

Archestratos decried "Sicilian cooks," but he praised their raw materials, specifically the tunny of the north coast and the swordfish caught off Cape Pelorus at the northeastern extremity of the island. Later, Sicily was one of the granaries of the Roman Empire. One of the greatest wines of Italy in Julius Caesar's time, Mamertine, came from the island, presumably from the hills behind Messina. There was more wine from Tauromenium (Taormina) and a sweet wine called Alintium. There was fine honey from the slopes of Hybla, and good hunting, too; but there seems little else to say of Sicily's gastronomy under the Romans. The continual fighting and the forced population movements of the last centuries BC had been too traumatic, perhaps.

Under Arab and then Norman domination, Palermo was the rich capital of a wealthy state. Once again, the island was an exporter of cheese; Sicilian cheese is called for in two recipes, apparently Egyptian, from a medieval Arabic cookbook. Later, subject to a series of mostly unenlightened monarchies, Sicily underwent a long decline in the late medieval and early modern periods, until, after several abortive rebellions, the island joined the new kingdom of Italy in 1860.

Meanwhile, in an anonymous 16th-century survey (*Descrittione dell'isola di Sicilia*, 1546), the island is praised not only for coastal fisheries and fruit but also for river fish and game. Since then, deforestation has put an end to Sicilian venison and wild boar and has altered the summer climate to the detriment of rivers and their fish. Fruit-growing has, if anything increased, especially that of the citrus fruits, a big export item. Of the two resources singled out by Archestratos 2,350 years ago, the tunny fishery and cannery is on the decline, but remains a major industry; the swordfish, too, continues to sacrifice itself to Sicilian gastronomes.

Sicilian landscapes have changed vastly over time, with the successive introduction of vines, olives, almonds, peaches, citrus fruits, and prickly pears. The 16th-century fruits of Sicily, listed in the aforementioned survey as typical of Val Demone, were acorns, olives, grapes, chestnuts, almonds, walnuts, pine nuts, hazelnuts, figs, pears, cherries, apples, plums, peaches, and mulberries. If one lists the typical and finest ingredients in Sicilian food today, and names them in Sicilian, the list of fruits must certainly include oranges (*aranci*) from Ribera and elsewhere, lemons (*lumiuni*), and the late mandarins (*mannarinni*) of Ciaculli; chestnuts, hazelnuts, pistachios, and almonds (*mènnuli*), a significant export crop and the basis of the classic Sicilian "blancmange," *bianuomanciuri*; figs (*fici*), including the *bifara* variety, which retains a classical Latin name; grapes (*racini*), such as those of Mazzarrone and Canicattì, and raisins (*passulina*); peaches (*pèrsici*), including the late *ncuppata* variety; table olives (*alivi*), notably those of Valle del Belice; prickly pears (Italian *ficodindia*, Sicilian *ficurigna*), once a kind of dietary staple. Among vegetables there will be artichokes (*cacòcciuli*) from Palermo and the purple artichokes of Ramacca; local varieties of cauliflower and broccoli (*vruoccoli*), such as *sparaceddu* and *bastardu*; tomatoes (*pummaroru*), including local kinds such as *costoluto* and *buttigghieddu*; aubergines (*mulinciani*), the basis—alongside seafood—of the traditional *capunata*, and squashes (*cucuzzi*), used not only for their flesh but for fried stuffed squash flowers (*sciuriddi*). There will also be capers and caper fruits (*cucunci*) from Pantelleria and from Salina, one of the Aeolian Islands. Fine honey (*mele*) comes from Agrigento and the valleys near Trapani and (as in ancient times) from the Monti Iblei. The last two districts also produce olive oil (*uog-

ghiu*), as do the slopes of Etna and Valle del Belice.

The cheeses of Sicily (*càciu, furmàggiu, tuma*) are numerous. They are made from sheep's, goat's and cow's milk, and include the famous, and apparently ancient, *canestratu*, usually of sheep's milk, with furrowed rind. Matured and salted, *canestratu* becomes *primusali*. There are several other local versions of sheep's milk cheeses (*pecurinu*) and of cow's milk cheeses (*provula, cosacavaddu*); there are goat's milk cheeses, including the small *padduni*, and there are local ricottas from sheep's milk and cow's milk. Cheeses named for their shape include *vastedda* (shaped like the bread of the same name) and the small *tumazzu*, as well as the big round *tuma*. The rustic Polyphemos praised his beloved Galateia as "whiter than a fresh cheese" in the eleventh idyll of Theokritos, and as "softer than curds" in Ovid's reworking of the same idea (*Metamorphoses* 13.796); in modern Sicily, a young woman may be *culu-ri-tumma*, possessor of a backside as shapely as a cheese.

Among typically Sicilian breads there is *mafalda*, made from semolina flour, sprinkled with sesame seeds, baked golden brown, and formed into shapes—crosses, crowns, snakes, and even the eyes of Santa Lucia. Much use is made of filled bread, such as *mulateddi*, rolls filled with minced pork, and *guastedde*, which, as sold in Palermo, are filled with fried calf's spleen and lung. In some districts, Christmas Eve is called *serata re mpanati*, eve of the filled loaves. As these examples show, the Sicilian names of bread may double as names for other things: *guastedda* or *vastedda*, just mentioned, originally a Latin word, in Sicilian is also the name of a cheese; *cuddura*, originally a Greek word, in Sicilian is a ring-shaped loaf and also an almond sweet; *scacciata* is a filled loaf and also a cheese.

Sicily is as enthusiastic about pasta as is mainland Italy. Some types are familiar, including *maccheroni* (*maccaruna*) and vermicelli (*virmiceddi*). The island has its own pastas, too, such as *taccuna*, coloured with cuttlefish ink. Some are named differently in different districts, notably the spiral type, variously called *maccaruna i casa, busiati, gnocculi,* and the hollow *cavatieddi, cavati, cavatuna, gnucchitieddi;* these are a local speciality at Ragusa, where they have yet another name, *gnucchitti,* and are eaten with a tomato or meat sauce and pecorino cheese. Alternative staples map the successive influences on Sicilian food. Greeks introduced lentils (*linticchi*) and broad beans (*favi*). Arabs brought couscous (*cùscusu*), regarded now as a typical dish of Trapani in western Sicily; the Arabs also brought rice to Sicily, widely used, as in the popular *arancini di risu* (*see* RICE), croquettes named after their orange colour. Under Spanish domination came potatoes (*patati*), used, for example, in *cazzilli,* potato croquettes.

Sicilian cattle, sheep, and goats are best occupied when producing the milk for cheese, though meat plays its part in the diet—and especially sausages (*sasizza*), meatballs (*purpetti*), and offal, as in *zuzzu,* a Catana speciality, made from pork trotters, tail, ears, and snout; the tasty *stigghiola,* grilled stuffed lamb intestines, sold as street food in Palermo; and *turcinuna,* an equivalent from Ragusa, in which the intestines are baked in a casserole. As a local rhyme profoundly says, "*La stigghiola 'un è sasizza, La palumma non è jizza*" (A *stigghiola* isn't a sausage, a pigeon is not a snail). In coastal towns, seafood is perhaps more prominent than meat. Swordfish (*pisci spata*) is prized; so is tunny (*tunnu*). It is difficult to avoid two signature dishes of Sicilian gastronomy, *pasta chî sardi* and *sardi a beccaficu.* In the latter, the sardines are not combined with figpeckers, but are split, stuffed, and presented so that they look like these little birds. Small fry has many names—*cincina, muccu, nunnata, nannatu*—and several popular recipes; red mullet fry (*russuliddu, sparacanaci*) is good, too. Sicily (along with Sardinia) produces the powerfully flavoured *bottarga,* grey mullet roe or tunny roe, typically grated over pasta and eggs.

Among sweets there are many local specialities, from the chocolate (*ciocculatu*) of Modica, by way of *cassatelle* of Agira, *cannoli* of Piana degli Albanesi, and *sfogliatella* of Trapani, to *testa di turcu* of Castelbuono; more generally, there are fig cake (*nfigghiulata*), almond biscuits (*viscotta di mènnula*), candied fruits (*frutta candita*), and dried chestnuts (*pastiddi, cruzzitteddi*). The traditional ice cream cake called *cassata* is known more specifically as *cassata alla siciliana* to distinguish it from the ice cream which goes by this name elsewhere in Italy. Marzipan (*pasta riali*) and the beloved marzipan fruits (*frutta marturana*), shaped and coloured with natural dyes, are named after the convent at Palermo which once claimed a kind of monopoly on their making. Sesame was already insistently named as a flavouring in the banquet poem of Philoxenos; nowadays sesame gives its flavour to Sicilian nougats, variously called *cubbaita, giuggiulena,* and in Albanian *xhurxhullet,* all of which names hint at an Arabic origin. The sweet *cuccia di Santa Lucia* is supposed to preserve the memory of a famine in 1646, relieved by the arrival of a shipload of wheat on Saint Lucia's day. Other specialities, like *mustazzoli,* used to be made once a year for Carnevale or on saints' days but have now become year-round treats.

According to one recent source, Sicily's favourite drink is *seltz al limone,* made with fresh lemon juice with salt added. Other soft drinks typical of the island incorporate mandarin juice, tamarind pulp, and anise (in the drink called *zammù*), while Catana continues to favour almond milk.

There is plenty of wine, nonetheless. A recent survey identified 28 autochthonous grape varieties worthy of use. Employing some of these and some more widespread varieties, the DOC wines of Sicily are almost equally numerous (21 when last counted). They will not all be listed here. Historically, the wines of the volcanic slopes of Etna and those of Faro from around Messina deserve mention: they must in some sense descend from the Tauromenian and Mamertan wines liked by the Romans, and Etna was noted in a 1596 survey of Italian wines, but modern vintages scarcely match their ancient reputation. Still, whites of Etna are worth tasting. So are the cherry-reds from Vittoria in the southeast: Cerasuolo di Vittoria is Sicily's first successful contender for the title of DOCG, conferred in summer 2006. Among wines that lack these titles, the reds and whites branded Corvo still deserve drinking. The neighbouring islands are best known for their excellent sweet whites, Moscato di Pantelleria, Passito di Pantelleria, and Malvasia delle Lipari. The favoured grape of Pantelleria is a muscat with a local Arabic name, *zibibbo*; under the same name some cheaper sweet whites are made and bottled in Sicily. Better known internationally than any of these are the wines of Marsala, essentially an invention of John Woodhouse, who began to ship his fortified wines from Marsala in 1773. Marsala suffered a long decline in the 20th century, which its producers have made a sustained effort to reverse. Within Italy, at least, they have had some success.

Naturally, Sicily shares much of its food culture with that of mainland Italy, including such popular ingredients as tomato purée (*strattu*), garlic (*agghiu*), and pasta. Yet Sicilian gastronomy preserves a great deal from the adventurous history of the island, including foods that are forgotten or despised elsewhere. Flour ground from grass peas (Italian *cicerchia*, Sicilian *chiecchiri* [*Lathyrus sativus*]) can still be found at Sicilian markets and is the basis of a local polenta known as *frascatula*, which may (if you find it) be eaten hot with a little oil, or allowed to cool and solidify. *Vinu cuottu*, grape syrup, an excellent flavouring, scarcely differs from the *defritum* or *caroenum* prized by classical Roman cooks. Greeks, Romans, Byzantines, Arabs, Normans, and Angevins have all left their traces. Some dishes now fashionable originate in the cheap but nourishing food of the poor, like *pani cuottu*, bread soup, *maccu di favi*, bean

soup, and *pasta ccu l'agghiu e l'uogghiu*, spaghetti with a sauce of garlic and olive oil, with grated *caciocavallo* cheese. Simple dishes such as *nsalata ri cipudda e pummaroru*, onion and tomato salad, seem as just as typical of Sicily as the complex festival sweets. The classical poet Philoxenos imagined Polyphemos as a gatherer of wild herbs; the rich local flora still provides wild asparagus (*spàraci*), wild artichoke (*cucuzzeddi i carduna*), and numerous wild greens, from purslane (*purciddana*) to mustard (*sinapi*), used as potherbs with salutary effect. In fact, so long as festivals are celebrated in moderation, Sicily, like Crete, now provides an exemplar of the fashionable Mediterranean diet. (AKD)

SILPHIUM. *See* ASAFOETIDA.

SILTER is a mild cow's cheese made in the lower Val Camonica in the province of Brescia in Lombardy from the milk of the *bruno Alpina* breed. Traditionally it was made by the shepherds in summer, up in their mountain shelters (the name derives from a Celtic word from which we get "shelter"), and it is the alpine pasture and the maturing in these airy open refuges which give the cheese its special qualities. The gentle aromatic flavour intensifies as the cheese matures. The artisan production is carried out on the uplands and in the valleys, from the milk of *bruno Alpina* cows, a lower yield but more tasty, and though experts can detect the difference in location, it is always a sought-after table cheese.

SKATE, *razza commune. See* RAY.

SLOW FOOD arose as a response to outrage. Think of this—approaching the Pantheon from the north, a visitor threads

along the narrow streets which lead to it at an angle, gradually glimpsing the mighty columns, a bit of the pediment, then the whole imposing structure, at one time the biggest building in the known world. Emerging later from the splendours of the interior, awed and uplifted by innovative engineering and overwhelming space, the visitor sees before his unbelieving eyes the two golden arches of a fast food chain, aping the empire that once conquered the world with a squalid little fast food empire of its own. The one at the bottom of the Spanish Steps was the first, maybe the worst, but by no means the last. A protest movement was born. Fast food has always been around Italy, from the street food of Pompeii to the fry-ups in Belli's Testaccio, but the universal imposition of bland international crowd fodder, alien to the rich gastronomic traditions of Italy, using ingredients nutritionally baleful and of doubtful origin, was more than thinking gastronomes could stomach. A return to the long slow meals, prepared slowly and carefully from scrupulously sourced ingredients, could be an effective response to the tyrannies of international food industries, agribusiness, and the dictates of an alien bureaucracy. Small producers on the verge of perishing for lack of support could be rescued from extinction by making their products known to a wider clientele; support for quality, sustainability, biodiversity, could be organised and publicised worldwide. And so it came to pass; having begun as a gut reaction to a local threat, the Slow Food movement has at the time of writing attracted 70,000 members worldwide and is an organisation that spans the globe. It actively encourages small producers by giving them a forum and publicity at the Salone del Gusto and smaller events; it encourages the agritourism which attracts visitors away from conventional tourist trails (and their all too predictable exploitation), and in the course of people getting around and eating regional foods, it stimulates a demand back home for more of the same, encouraging importers and retailers to stock things like *lardo di Colonnato* or mountain cheeses from which a few years ago they would have recoiled in horror. Guidebooks, gastronomic itineraries, and other works are published by Slow Food, and a glossy magazine is circulated to members.

Lovers of Italian food are sometimes perplexed by the diversity of information available now that Slow Food has gone global, and the expense of following up the amazing wealth of things on offer; remote and rare products do not come cheap, and the costs of sourcing, publicising, and marketing them catapults some foods from basic local subsistence fare to the luxuries of international high gastronomy.

SMALL BIRDS, *uccellini, uccelletti,* are, with the exception of QUAILS, little wild birds such as thrush, *tordi,* sparrows, *passeri,* larks, *allodole,* ortolans, *ortolani,* figpeckers or warblers, *beccafichi,* blackbirds, *merli,* much loved throughout Italy, hunted, or when protected, imported from abroad, and enjoyed spit or oven roasted, or braised. *Osei e polenta* is a speciality of Lombardy; in Bergamo they are seasoned with crushed juniper berries, put on spits, with alternating cubes of *lardo,* and sage leaves, and fried in a pan in butter, the resultant juices making a rich sauce for the polenta with which they are served. In Brescia they are spit roast, with cubes of loin of pork, and the juices collected in a basting tin. In Tuscany they are cooked *in intingolo,* fried in butter with garlic and sage and finished with red wine and tomato purée.

Uccelli scappati are fakes, tender morsels of liver or meat, sometimes wrapped in pancetta, seasoned in the same way, and when cooked on a spit looking somewhat like little birds.

SMOOTH HOUND. *See* SHARK.

A man ladles out a generous helping of snails at the annual Feast of San Giovanni in Rome. (Hulton Archive/Getty Images)

SNAIL, *lumaca di terra, chiocciola,* is a gastropod mollusc of which there are various kinds, the best known in Italy being *Helix pomata,* the large ones we call Roman snails, though those enjoyed in Rome and Lazio are the smaller, *lumache di vigna,* or *di San Giovanni,* which are eaten on the night of 24 June, the Feast of San Giovanni, a dangerous time, when witches and demons disguised as evil black beasts roamed the streets with evil intent, and fearful souls once flocked to the basilica of San Giovanni in Laterano, for the saint's protection. Belli wrote a cynical sonnet advising us to wear a couple of cloves of garlic instead, good pagan protection. Now it is a popular festival, when the warm summer night is full of the sound of cheerful Romans crowding the streets, taverns, and public places, noisy with music and loud with cries for these excellent little snails, cooked in a dense tomato sauce, perfumed with garlic, anchovies, pennyroyal, salt, pepper, and a hot chilli, after the lengthy and not

very appealing process of getting rid of the slime, and the preliminary cooking in several changes of salty, acidulated water. These orchard or garden snails, full of life in spring and autumn, *lumache corridore,* unlike those withdrawn into their shells in full summer, *lumache dormiglione,* need a day or two confined in a well-aired container from which there is no escape, with some harmless soaked breadcrumbs and vine leaves to "purge" them of any things they might have eaten which could be poisonous to humans.

Italo Calvino uses this image of confined and threatened snails in *Il barone rampante,* where young Cosimo frees the snails imprisoned by his sinister sister, Battista, the *monaca della casa,* in a barrel in the cellar. Her gastronomic ingenuity was equalled only by her cruelty, to both ingredients and those unhappy enough to have to eat her cooking; family meals were thus fraught with tensions, and the escaping snails prefigured Cosimo's wild dash to the freedom of the treetops, away from the confinement and tyranny of family life and authoritarian rule:

> It was on the fifteenth of June 1767 that Cosimo Piovasco di Rondò, my brother, sat down for the last time in our company. I remember it as if it were today. We were in the dining room of our villa in Ombrosa, the windows framed the thick foliage of the large elm tree in the park. . . . "I said I don't want them, and I don't want them!" said Cosimo, pushing the dish of snails away from him. (Calvino, 1962, p. 18.)

There is more to snail gastronomy than eating the creatures with garlic butter, after laboriously putting them back into the shells from which they were earlier laboriously extracted. The many regional Italian recipes after the preliminary purging, desliming, and a first boiling in acidulated water cook the snails for several hours in a mixture of aromatic herbs, garlic, and a reduced tomato sauce; in Bobbio in the Piacentine hills, they finish cooking with chopped onion, celery, carrots, and red wine, and are eaten with polenta. In Liguria, the sauce is aromatised with many herbs, and also dried and soaked *funghi porcini*.

SOFFRITTO is a mixture of chopped

vegetables, usually onion, celery, carrot, garlic, herbs, especially parsley, and often diced *lardo* or PANCETTA, which are cooked gently in oil or butter to become the foundation of many complex structures, adding flavour and richness at the start of soups, stews, and braised dishes. It is not quite the same as a BATTUTO, creamed cured pork fat into which a similar mixture of finely chopped aromatics is incorporated, but the principle is the same—starting a dish off with a rich concentration of flavour, involving herbs, vegetables, and fat. Many recipes will be specific about the composition of the *soffritto*, adding perhaps a particular herb, or anchovies, or tomato in some form or other, using butter or oil instead of fat.

SOLE, *sogliola*, *sfoglia*, is greatly prized in

expensive international cuisine, and it is a relief to read the various regional recipes of Italy with their confusion of regional names; in Ancona the sole is grilled, and anointed generously with olive oil and finally a handful of parsley during the last minutes of cooking; from Abruzzo comes a recipe in which the skinned fish is simmered in a shallow pot with olive oil, lemon juice, parsley, garlic, and a little water, and finished with stoned black olives and slices of lemon. Scappi treated sole like TURBOT, which was more esteemed then, and has recipes for *sfoglia*, *linguattola*, *pesce passera*, all flat fish if not soles, which could be simmered slowly like turbot in a broth of white wine, verjuice, olive oil, mild spices, and a little water, served with fried onions, a method he learned from the fishermen of Chioggia and

Venice, who prepared them better than any cook, probably because the fish were so fresh; he goes on to suggest thickening the broth with ground almonds and adding prunes and dried cherries. From Naples comes one of Corrado's inventive recipes, flat fish simmered in wine with bay leaves and spices, the fillets served garnished with anchovy fillets and a sauce of pounded pistachio nuts thinned with oil and lemon juice. Thanks to Anna del Conte (2001, p. 94) and Massimo Alberini, we have a dish from Caorle, near Venice, in which prepared sole are marinated in an emulsion of oil, lemon, and chopped basil leaves and baked a short time in the oven, with the marinade and coarsely chopped pine nuts added for the last 5 minutes.

SOPPRESSATA is a salame made in

various regions of Italy to different recipes. A version from the district around Fabriano in the Marche is known as *soppressato* and is a spreading salame, with a high percentage of fat to keep it soft; it is lightly smoked, and seasoned with salt, pepper, and garlic. It is similar to the *ciaùscolo* of the province of Macerata, which is flavoured with a fortified wine. In the past, the mixture of prime cuts of pork and a high percentage of fat was chopped with a massive knife to make a creamy mass (similar to the rhythmic chopping with a cleaver in the meat markets of Zue Gou province to make the ineffable filling for dumplings). The authorities at IN-SOR see this paté-like texture (*inconsapevole nutella suina*, unimaginable pork nutella) as a legacy from the Celts who were driven up into the rugged Appenines from the pleasant Adriatic coast over 2,000 years ago, but with the warning that today's war on fat threatens the true texture of this delectable product, creamy but with a certain bite to it (INSOR, *Salumi*, 2002, p. 482).

The *soppressata* of Brescia is made from leaner meat, well spiced, with strips of a fatty cut along its length. That from Calabria includes a higher proportion of fat and hot or mild chilli, described by travellers as something between *ciccioli* and *lardo*, an indication of the high fat content. This product, with its DOC differs from the *soppressata* of Reventino in Calabria, where the coarsely chopped raw pork is mixed with a pungent local sauce made from red peppers, and matured after smoking with aromatic wood, a unique version of the genre. Still in Calabria, the *soppressata di San Nicola da Crissa* is a version flavoured with salt, pepper, chilli, and wild fennel seeds, and benefiting from the microclimate of this area in the province of Vibo Valentia, where the quality of the air, the local pigs, and generations of skill create a unique version of this salame. Campania has its own varieties, in which the fat is either inserted as a strip, or as small dice, in a mixture of lean meat flavoured with chilli and fennel. Back up north in the Veneto and Lombardy are yet more kinds, including the *soppressa delle valli del Pasubio* near Vicenza, depending on the diet of chestnuts and potatoes fed to local pigs, and the technique of chopping the meat and fat rather than putting it all through a mincer.

SORB APPLES, or service fruit, *Sorbus domestica, sorba*, are of the Rosaceae family, and seem acid and unpromising until bletted, either on straw or hung up in bunches, when they become soft and fragrant. They make a preserve which Castelvetro said was good for dysentery.

SORBET, *sorbetto. See* ICE CREAM.

SORREL, *acetosa, romice, Rumex acetosa,* an acid member of the dock family, exists in many varieties, all of which have the characteristic sharpness which makes sorrel sauce such a good foil to rich meat or fish. The young leaves can also be eaten raw in salads, which is what Castelvetro recommended, and Platina, too, would eat them on their own, at the beginning of a meal, for their healthy properties. The tannin content and the acidic oxalate of potash make sorrel good for the digestion; an appetite stimulant, mildly diuretic and laxative; and a cure for dysentery, as is *acetosella* (*Oxalis acetosella*), a less agreeable acid plant used medicinally, with which it is sometimes confused. Corrado uses sorrel in an unusual mixture of herbs and vegetables for a *zuppa alla santè* in which finely sliced celery, chicory, parsnips, lettuce, onion, chervil, and sorrel and a mixture of unspecified herbs are softened in butter and finished in chicken or meat broth. The fresh green acidity of raw sorrel was a good substitute for lemon juice at a time when lemons were expensive luxuries. This may not have meant much to Corrado's rich patrons, but it reminds us of the role of the acidic wild and cultivated herbs in popular Italian cooking.

SOTTACETI are vegetables pickled in VINEGAR, usually served as part of a first course or antipasto. They are now home-made and produced industrially or by small traditional producers. Everything depends on the quality of the vinegar and the things pickled in it; if the mushrooms or peppers or whatever are fresh and flavourful, the vinegar light and aromatic, perhaps mitigated with a good olive oil, *sottaceti* can be delicious, but they are often too assertive to go with the more delicate salumi, or subtle wines.

SOUP and STEW are easygoing, almost interchangeable words in English, used to describe many recipes, anything from a thick to a runny dish, with a huge range of ingredients. In Italy, we find more precise definitions which vary from one region to another: *brodo, minestra, minestrina, minestrone, potaggio, pottaggetto, sopa, zuppa, zuppa di pesce* (with a

multitude of different kinds, depending on the region, like *brodetto* from the Marche). The name *minestra* is derived from the patriarchal custom of dishing up, *minestrare*, the first course into bowls by the head of the family. Many have names of their own, like the basic vegetable *acqua cotta* and the hearty RIBOL-LITA of Tuscany; the pungent fish soup of Livorno, CACCIUCCO; the fish dishes of Liguria, BURIDDA and CIUPPIN; and the *sburrita* of the island of Elba (salt cod perfumed with chilli and *nepitella*). *See also* ZUPPA.

SOURNESS, *agro*, or acidity, *àcido*, is one of the four fundamental tastes, sweet, salt, bitter, and sour (leaving aside considerations of *umami*, the fifth taste, whose combination of monosodium glutamate, sodium inosinate, and guanylate is to be found in PARMESAN CHEESE). Sourness is found in organic acids in various things, citric acid in citrus fruits, malic acid in other fruit, phosphoric acid in cheese, and fatty acids in meat and dairy fat, lactic acid in fermented milk products, and amino acids found in protein. These all affect the flavour of food, and are used in Italian cooking in various ways to enhance flavours or provide contrasts, like the squeeze of lemon over a fatty fish, or the chopped lemon and parsley in a baked trout, the lemon served with a dish of lightly cooked spinach, tossed in oil, eaten at room temperature, or a salad of sliced orange or lemon, seasoned with salt and sugar, to go with a rich roast. The acidity of many berries was exploited in sauces and relishes, while sourness was also obtained from VERJUICE or *agresto*, the fresh or fermented juice of unripe grapes and wine vinegar.

The coagulation and curdling of milk produces lactic acid, which is antibacterial and so helps preserve the product. Junket, *gioncata*, was a way of transforming perishable milk into a state where it could be transported and sold, as a slightly acidic, refresh-

ing treat, drained and served in little rush baskets, from which it got its name. This acidity is helpful when cooking meat in milk or milk products, as in the recipe for *maiale al latte*, pork in milk, in which the milk, as it curdles, tenderises the meat and forms a dense, slightly grainy sauce. One version marinates a loin of pork in dry white wine overnight, then browns it in butter, seasoned with salt and pepper, and simmers it, immersed in milk, with sage, rosemary, and nutmeg, in a covered pot until tender, serving the reduced sauce over the sliced meat. A variation is to marinate the pork in a mixture of white wine vinegar, olive oil, garlic, rosemary and juniper berries for 24 hours and then cover with milk and cook slowly until tender.

Some herbs and vegetables can contribute sourness to a salad or sauce; sorrel, *acetosa*, is the best known of these. *See* VINEGAR.

SOUTHERNWOOD, *abrotano*, *Artemisia abrotanum*, is one of the Compositae, the same family as wormwood, *assenzio* and tarragon, *dragoncello*. It has an aromatic bitterness, reminiscent of lemon and camphor, found in the essential oil and in the glycoside components, which are used as a tonic and stimulant in many liqueurs, fortified wines, and *amari*, bitter drinks (*see* APERITIVI), and unlike wormwood, *artemisia absinthium*, the major component of absinthe, does not have a horrible effect on the nervous system. Wormwood is still used in small quantities in many commercial liqueurs and aperitifs, and gave its name to one of them, *vermouth*. Many rustic grappas were flavoured with it. It is there in one of the *Tacuina sanitatis*, in which a red-robed man, perhaps a physician, is shown plucking its greeny-grey leaves. Southernwood is a safer alternative and can be used in cooking in small amounts, with rich meat and in tisanes and homemade liqueurs, and a splash of vermouth in sauces can have the same effect. Mattioli said its *non ingrato odore* made it a common flavouring for bread and *focaccie*.

SPAGHETTI. *See* PASTA.

SPECK

SPECK is a speciality of the Alto Adige; it is made with the same part of the pig as ham, but cured in a different way. Confusion arises when the same name is applied to pure cured fat, as was the case in the past. The version which earned itself a DOP (*see* DOC) is made by marinating the prepared ham in an aromatic brine flavoured with black pepper, pimento, garlic, juniper berries, and a little sugar, turning it every so often. After a fortnight it is taken out, dried, and lightly smoked for two or three weeks, then hung in a cool place for four to five months. A less rigorously defined version is also made, and there is a peasant tradition of speck made at home for consumption rather than commerce, with every family using their own recipes and methods. In Sauris, in the province of Udine, the *speck di Sauris* is made by dry salting a boned ham, then smoking it for some weeks over aromatic woods like beech, pine, and juniper, before hanging it to dry in a cold, airy atmosphere.

SPELT

SPELT, *Triticum aestivum* subspecies *spelta*, is not the same as emmer wheat, *farro*, with which it is sometimes confused. It grew well in the northern parts of the Roman Empire, and the unripe grains are still used in soups. Today it is appreciated for all the qualities that have been bred out of commercial wheat; it is much tastier, and is protected by its hard outer covering from insects and so spared the use of pesticides. This makes it good to use in traditional Italian recipes, whether for spelt or emmer. Its nutritional content is good, it can be easier to digest than wheat, and it works well as a bread flour as well as a grain. *Frikeh*, parched green wheat, well known in the Middle East, could be made from spelt or emmer as well as wheat, and is becoming popular in Britain and elsewhere.

SPEZZATINO

SPEZZATINO is a dish of small pieces of meat cooked in a small amount of liquid, usually from the less tender cuts of beef, pork, lamb, or mutton, with agreeable amounts of cartilage and connective tissue which are given time cook down to an unctuous gravy. The name is from *spezzettare*, to cut into small pieces. In Milan, *spezzatino di vitello misto* or *de parte mista* was traditionally the name of the cut of meat you would buy to make this dish, as well as the name of the recipe. The pieces of meat are dusted in flour and fried in butter and diced pancetta with onion, celery, and carrot, allowed to absorb some dry white wine, and left to cook very slowly until coated in a dense sauce. There are versions which add tomatoes or potatoes. Artusi has a dish using veal shanks, but he calls it *stufatino di muscolo* and a recipe for veal breast cut up on the bone, which uses the instruction *spezzettate*, cut up, for this, while calling the recipe a *stufatino* (*see* STUFATO). Milan also has a *stufato* and a STRACOTTO, both made with large pieces of mature beef, larded, and cooked for three or four hours, tightly covered, until meltingly tender, in a very little liquid. (But *see* BRASATO for more enlightenment and confusion.)

SPICES

SPICES, *spezie*, once used in large amounts in the cooking of the rich and important, are now used sparingly, the main ones being peppercorns (black and white), cinnamon, cloves, and nutmeg. In medieval and Renaissance Italy, the extremely expensive spices, exotic and of distant and often unknown origin, were status symbols, bringing prestige and much pleasure to wealthy consumers. They were never ever used to disguise the taste of tainted meat. Those who were rich enough to enjoy spices could certainly have afforded good-quality meat, fresh or hung to perfection, all the year round. (Contrary to popular belief, animals were not universally slaughtered at the beginning of winter; many were kept in stalls.) At a time when refrigeration and the industrial processing of meat did not exist, there was less rather than more risk of meat going off or becoming contaminated; beasts came to market, were slaughtered, butchered, bought, taken home, and cooked on the same day, or skilful techniques of preservation were applied, such as salting, drying, smoking, or pickling, that were healthier by far than the bacteria-ridden habitat of our sordid domestic fridges or industrial processing plants. Anyway, tainted meat is so horrible that wasting spices on it would have been a nonsense.

Spices were coming into Europe along well-established trading routes long before the Crusades, and knowledge of Arab gastronomy and medicine had been filtering up from southern Italy and Spain from the fertile areas that benefited from Arab agriculture and agronomy, as well as from trade contacts between Venice and Genoa and the Middle East. Arab medicine, based on the accumulated wisdom of ancient Greek and Roman writers, was rooted in the humoral theory, which linked gastronomy and medicine indissolubly together; pleasure in flavour and sensations on a plate could not be dissociated from the effect that foodstuffs and seasonings had on the body and soul of the eater (*see* ARAB INFLUENCE). When Martino said you need to spice a dish to suit the tastes of your master, he meant not just to please, but to care for his health and state of mind, which would depend on his temperament, the combination of the four humours that was special to him. So spices were not used indiscriminately, but selectively and with care, in mixtures, chosen to delight, soothe, care, and heal, of *spezie forte* (strong

spices) or *spezie dolce* (mild, or sweet, spices). In a 14th-century manuscript (Biblioteca Casanatense 225), probably by an unknown Venetian, published by Ludovico Frati in 1899, the unknown author specifies three spice mixtures. One is *spezie fine* (fine spices, for general use), made up of pepper, cinnamon, ginger, cloves, and saffron. His strong mixture included pepper, long pepper, nutmeg, and cloves. The mild mixture used cloves, ginger, cinnamon, and mace, but no pepper. Most of his recipes for sauces used one or other of these mixtures together with other spices to suit the particular recipe, such as cardamom, cubebs, grains of paradise, and GALANGAL, which figure in a *salsa saracinesca*. The spices that were seeds of native plants—coriander, cumin, anise, fennel, celery, lovage, mustard, parsley, and many more—were part of a local, humbler tradition, without the prestige of vast expense and exotic flavours, but they crept in, too, together with fresh and dried herbs, and as time wore on became harbingers of the new cuisine (offspring of the New Learning of the Renaissance) that Martino was to pioneer, and Scappi to develop with brilliance. Tastes changed throughout Europe, but some time before French cuisine began to abandon heavy spicing, Italian cooks were already seasoning their food more simply, often with just a dusting of cinnamon and pepper and a herb or two. Scappi's monumental work of 1570 included the new, light recipes pioneered by Martino and the old, rich, favourites of state banquets and international power dining—the peacock in its feathers, and the heavy (and delicious) game stews and civets. He insists that spices should be less than a year old and in good condition, and gives the recipe for a general spice mixture consisting of 4 ounces of cinnamon, 2 ounces of cloves, 1 ounce of ginger, 1 ounce of nutmeg, half an ounce each of grains of paradise and saffron, and 1 ounce of sugar. Most of his recipes specify different combinations of spices, as well as sometimes using some of this mixture, but they are subtle, and restrained, and also include fresh herbs. His sauces are light, fruity, acidic, but well sugared, and cinnamon is the predominant spice.

In 18th-century Naples, at a time when French fashions were predominant, styles of eating, menus, table arrangements, and service (as we can see in the elegant engraved plans, and lists of menus, in Corrado's *Il cuoco galante*) were unequivocally French, but the dishes served were unashamedly Neapolitan, with a Spanish influence, and firmly rooted in local traditions. Spices insinuate themselves into many of his sauces, while the French names, *Roberta, Ramolata*, give them credence. His sauce *Alla Spagnola* is made by simmering in Burgundy some sliced onion, garlic, bay leaves, red chillies, cinnamon, and cloves—a pungent brew, a long way from the meaty, slow, dense, long-cooked French *Espagnole*.

Changes in taste over the centuries have made the use of spices unfashionable, and earlier generations of Italian food historians wrote piously of the *uso e abuso* of spices in the past, as if their lavish use was a moral and gastronomic aberration. The fact that a generous dose of spices makes food taste wonderful is accepted by Anglo-Saxon and North American cooks, more open to a multiplicity of traditions, but not welcomed in the country where their use was once a subtle and successful contribution to European culture.

The polarities of Italian cooking—freshness and simplicity on the one hand, complexity and intricacy on the other, include a use of spices which is sometimes not acknowledged; *tortellini in brodo* involve a multiplicity of ingredients, procedures, and flavourings, into which light spicing might have crept. Many varieties of SALUMI, cured meats, are acclaimed for the absence of additional flavourings, *niente aromi*, even when, as in the case of a cured mountain ham from the Appenines, pepper is used as a preservative on the exposed end of the bone. The intense, almost perfumed flavour of *culatello* owes nothing to the addition of spices, only the salt and possibly sugar used in the curing process, but some coarser cuts of meat are improved by spices such as cinnamon and cloves, which are used in *cotecchino* and the various cured salami using fennel, local herbs, garlic, and, in the south, much chilli. Spices are used more often than is admitted, especially in the food industry, in sweet and savoury preparations, and their link with past traditions lurks in many a deceptively simple but exquisite recipe.

SPIGOLA. *See* SEA BASS.

SPINACH, *spinaci, Spinaci oleracea*, is

from the Chenopodium family, and is one of the best loved and most versatile vegetables in Italy. Cooked in water or in its own juices, which are plentiful, a big bundle of spinach is dramatically reduced to a small amount of densely flavoured deep green leaves, ready to be drained, chopped, and treated in various ways, or served as they are with oil, salt, pepper, and a squeeze of lemon. Some shops and market stalls sell round balls of freshly cooked and chopped spinach to take away, as Scappi described in 1570. The cooked leaves can be chopped and heated through in oil or butter, flavoured with chopped garlic, pine, nuts, raisins, and spices (nutmeg and cinnamon go well). This can be a dish on its own, or enriched with cheese and eggs and baked in a tart or pie crust. In the past, this basic mixture was often seasoned with sugar and served with rosewater and cinnamon.

Spinach is the base of various stuffings enclosed in pasta. Florence has a version in which the mixture is cooked as it is, without the wrapping, *ravioli* or *gnocchi ignudi*, naked dumplings, their modesty veiled in a light coating of flour; these light, cork-shaped gnocchi are made of cooked and chopped spinach, ricotta, parmesan, and egg, in a delicate balance, which if disturbed by over rapid boiling in their cooking water, will disintegrate into an ignominious mass. All being well, they cook in a few minutes and float to the top of the pot, to be gently removed and drenched in melted butter and more parmesan.

A SFORMATO of spinach is a wonderful way of enjoying this vegetable without the richness of pastry; bound with béchamel it has a creaminess, the eggs cause it rise sufficiently, and the combination of flavours is more intense than in a soufflé.

Spinach was probably not known to the Greeks and Romans; it was brought to Europe by Arab settlers, who would have known and grown various forms of it in the Middle East, but documentary evidence is sparse. The ancient world did have some familiarity with other Chenopodia, atriplex or orache, wild and cultivated, and various kinds of beets, though these were not a crop of much importance, "familiar but not much relished," as Dalby puts it. However, Grainger has recreated some good recipes from Apicius in which present-day spinach, or beets, or fat hen, or nettles, can be used: a *patina* of nettles or spinach is made by chopping and draining the raw green stuff, then cooking it in a mixture of fish sauce, pepper, and olive oil; it is drained again and mixed with beaten eggs, then cooked as one would a *frittata*, to be eaten tepid in wedges. Arab horticultural skills made spinach and orache better known in the south of Spain, where Ibn al Awam, who wrote a book on agriculture in the second half of the 12th century, reported that crops of spinach and orache were being grown throughout autumn and winter. Spinach adapted well to Italian conditions and tastes; Platina wrote of *bieta,* and *atriplice,* comparing them to "what peasants call *spinacio,*" so we can assume that by the 1460s the kitchens of Italy were using the orache and spinach illustrated in the *Tacuina Sanitatis* (illustrated health handbooks produced in northern Italy in the late 15th century, based on earlier Arab writings), and a century later Mattioli upbraided with characteristic irritation contemporaries who confused spinach with the various types of orache he described and illustrated. He was, as always, accurate in his remarks on cooking them—without water, since they steam in their own juices. Beets, chard, or spinach beets, *Beta vulgaris,* were around in Platina and Martino's time and were used like spinach, particularly to colour food. The expressed juice, along with other herbs, tinged *frittatas,* broths, and tart fillings a bright green hue. A mixture of chopped green leaves went into the famous *Torta Bolognese,* well mixed with grated soft cheese and eggs, and cooked between pastry crusts; an *herbolata di maio* was an open "springtime" tart, in which egg whites, milk, and cheese were mixed with the strained juices of pounded beets, marjoram, sage, mint, and parsley, some finely chopped herbs, and plenty of butter, precooked until the mixture thickens, then finished on a pastry crust. Scappi wrote of a *minestra volgarmente chiamata vivarole,* a version of today's *straciatella* in which the beaten eggs and cheese are stirred into boiling broth coloured with chopped beets, parsley, mint, and marjoram; he has a *minestra* of beets, borage, and bugloss finely chopped and cooked in a little meat or chicken broth, and one of spinach, which he comments "is nowadays available all the year round in Rome." Spinach was served at banquets, often with raisins, herbs, and bitter orange juice—well on the way to becoming the versatile vegetable of today.

SPLEEN. *See* OFFAL.

SPREMUTA is freshly squeezed fruit juice, usually orange or lemon, that can be enjoyed in a bar or made at home using manual or electrical equipment. It does not come from a carton or bottle, and is not diluted with water—a virtue in the past when water supplies were likely to be contaminated, but fruit juice was benign.

SQUID is one of the molluscs, growing up to 50 centimetres long, equipped with fins and eight tentacles, and comes in various shapes and sizes: *calamaro, calamaretto, seppia, seppietta, totano*, all of which can be cooked in a variety of ways, stewed, stuffed, fried, grilled, and as companions of other fish in the many different fish stews of Italy. The general rule is that when cooked fresh and very quickly, grilled and served with olive oil and lemon, they are meltingly tender, but if stale and overcooked, they become rubbery, not a pleasure to eat. Stewed until just done, a few minutes, they make a simple cold dish, with oil or other dressing. Cooked slowly, in a rich sauce, sometimes with young peas, whose texture and flavour lend themselves to the qualities of squid, they achieve a different tenderness. Bloodless these creatures might be, but they are not without intelligence, according to Davidson, and Platina noticed how the male squid will rush to defend a female when attacked (the female did not reciprocate). Platina had read his Pliny and Apicius and knew of the classical dressing of pepper, rue, honey, and oil for squid, and the use of asafoetida and pepper for octopus, probably disdained by his friend Martino, who held that octopus were horrible whatever you did to them.

STEFANI, BARTOLOMEO

published his *L'arte di ben cucinare* in Mantua in 1662, dedicated to Ottavio Gonzaga, one of the ducal family, at one time ambassador to Duke Carlo II. In his introduction he explains how he learnt the craft from his uncle Giulio Cesare Tirelli in their hometown of Bologna. Tirelli had had a distinguished career in Venice and many of the courts of

Italy, and had worked for a time in the English royal court, before coming back to Bologna in his old age, so his nephew got the benefit of this wide experience as well as the traditions of his native city. "*Ancora imparo,*" I am still learning, was Stefani's advice to the cook's assistants, which probably reflects his early training. This seems at first sight a slight book compared with the magisterial volumes of his contemporaries; self-deprecating, mildly humorous, he says that his words had a baptism of kitchen grease before they met with the ink on the printing press, and are to intended to please the taste buds rather than the intellect. He covers fish, meat, fowl, tarts, and pastries and preserved and candied fruits and flowers, but not in the meticulous detail of Scappi. The best parts of this engaging work are the recipes in which Stefani seems to be giving us his own original variations on vegetable dishes, tarts, sauces, and relishes. Then come descriptions of banquets and less elaborate meals, ending with the extremely grandiose banquet he masterminded for one of the visits of Queen CHRISTINA of Sweden to Italy in November 1655. Here we can get the measure of Stefani's not inconsiderable powers, as organiser, and as the skilled hands that made the elaborate pastry and sugar work, the sugar paste flowers, and the marzipan fruit, with their lifelike colouring, the butter sculpture, and the garlands of fresh flowers. This event in Mantua set the tone for later Roman banquets in honour of Christina, whose love of pomp and ceremony was much greater than her appreciation of food. The sophisticated skills that were to produce the baroque banquets in her honour in Rome a decade later were already in evidence in Emilia.

It is a relief to turn to slightly less pretentious meals, like the *Convito per otto signori*, for eight gentlemen, served at a square table, with, instead of the procession of dishes placed upon a long narrow one, a large platter placed in the middle, surrounded by smaller ones with up to eight complementary dishes around it. (ROSSETTI is eloquent on this "German style" of dining.) Each course had several of these sequences of large and small offerings. One began with a young sow's udder, precooked until soft, then spit roasted, basted with butter, and served with a *salsa reale*, and surrounded by a decorative border of pieces of calves' liver *cotto con diligenza* (a subtle point—badly cooked liver is horrible), deep-fried brains, sweetbreads, ornamental festoons of marzipan, and alternating slices of bitter orange and lemons, with side dishes of *coppa*, *mortadella* from Bologna, and bowls of orange relish. This is made from the juice and pulp of semisweet oranges, apples, and sugar, boiled together, stirring all the time, and seasoned with musk, cloves, and cinnamon—good with small game birds and delicate roasts, Stefani said. Small helpings would have been advisable, since this was followed by a *boglione*, a version of the *bollito misto* of the region, in which a calf's tail and feet were cooked with *erba brusca*, pennyroyal, marjoram, borage, and salad burnet, adding chickens and a boiling sausage later, and topping up the cooking liquid as it reduced with quantities of cream, served, not with cooked vegetables, as some do, for they look disturbingly like candied fruits, but with calves' eyes and small poussins, seasoned with spices. The accompanying calves' feet and heads in an amber jelly, decorated round the rim of the dish with red jelly, must have been soothing, along with deep-fried zucchini blossoms sprinkled with sugar. The gentlemen went on to consume seven more big dishes with their *rinforzi* and then onwards towards a final assault on cheeses, hot apple tarts, ricotta with sugar, cinnamon and perfumed water, refreshing raw celery, cardoons and artichokes, sweetened whipped cream, asparagus, fresh fruit, and the usual sugared comfits and candied fruits.

The reader's suspension of disbelief is rewarded by Stefani's description of many of these dishes, both ingredients and methods, which are included in the menus; interesting because they might be his own versions of standard recipes, like the ornate pies or tarts, or ways of cooking fish. *Orata*, gilt-head bream, which he says wears a golden crown on its head as a mark of its excellence, can be cooked in many ways, which he presents, including the simple stewing in butter between two plates, seasoned with nutmeg and lemon juice, and the more elaborate version, simmered in oil, *malvasia*, saffron, and spices, then served hot with oil, powdered aromatic herbs, and bitter orange juice. A huge trout from Lake Garda is put into a well-buttered fish kettle, covered with more butter and spices, and cooked in the oven until half done, then finished with a scattering of prawns, truffles, oysters, pistachios, and stewed celery, and smothered in a sauce made from desalted tunny pounded with cooked prawn meat, diluted with *malvasia* and some of the buttery cooking juices, passed through a sieve, "*per darla poi la perfettione della cottura*" (to bring it to the peak of perfection). This creamy, lightly fishy sauce reminds us of *vitello tonnato*. The description is that of a dedicated cook, with a sureness of touch and a pride in his work; Stefani's comments on cooking veal tripe show that he is giving his version of two recipes, seeing no point in mentioning others, roast or in pies, "*poiche à me non sodisfanno*" (because I find them unsatisfactory). Some of his vegetable recipes have a section to themselves entitled "*Modo gentile e straordinario per formare vivande diverse molto delicate di varii erbaggi*" (pleasing and unusual ways of preparing various really delicate dishes from various green stuff). One of these is a dish of mange-tout peas simmered in broth, or water if a nonmeat day, and served on slices of bread fried in butter, the whole bathed in the cooking liquid, which the bread will soak up, and then seasoned with parmesan and cinnamon or crushed peppercorns. A lean version would be to place the pea pods on slices of toast dressed with a sauce of pounded pine nuts, lemon juice, and sugar, to soak up some of the cooking liquid and a dressing of light olive oil, which must, he stresses, be from Liguria or Tuscany, to be served hot with a dusting of pepper and cinnamon. A curiosity are *aventani*, or egg-plants, which are cultivated in monastery gardens. Stefani is careful to soak them in water, when peeled and cut into chunks, to get rid of the bitterness; they are then cooked in oil and served with a sauce of toasted almonds (important not to burn them) diluted with bitter orange juice and seasoned with sugar and nutmeg. If cooked in butter, the seasoning would be parmesan and cinnamon. Cauliflower or broccoli are carefully trimmed into separate florets, freshened by a soak in cold water, then plunged into boiling water or broth for a brief time, and then turned in melted butter and finished in a sauce of pounded pistachios mixed with egg yolks and some broth and lemon juice, and served hot on slices of bread fried in butter. As a cold salad, they can be dressed with oil, lemon, salt, and pepper. Not a hint of the southern ways of seasoning with garlic, chillies, and anchovies.

Desserts show a change in the composition of that ancient dish BIANCOMANGIARE, which in Stefani's modern version is made with creamy milk thickened with rice flour, cooked carefully away from the smoke and grime of the chimney, seasoned with sugar, musk, and citron blossom water, and then put into moulds moistened with rosewater. The old-fashioned way, using chicken breasts, is described as *alla spagnuola*. Another very modern dish is a version of *crème brulée* made from milk, cream, and eggs, seasoned with musk, brought rapidly to the boil, then left to set in a cool place, and then covered with sugar and browned under a red hot shovel. There is a delicate custard mixture of milk, cream, and eggs cooked in a *bagno maria*, ideal for invalids. He has a custard recipe, *crema*, for a mixture of milk, butter,

eggs (more yolks than whites), white wheat flour, and sugar flavoured with musk, rose-water, and candied citron blossoms. When this has thickened and cooled, it can be cut into slices, dusted in flour, and dipped into beaten egg and fried, just like *crema fritta* in Emilia today. Robert May's *The Accomplisht Cook* of 1685 includes creams and custards made with egg whites or yolks and cream, sometimes thickened with rice flour. These light perfumed dishes of milk and cream were clearly a European fashion, common to noble households who enjoyed this use of the milder spices, cinnamon and nutmeg (mace in England), and the new perfumes MUSK and AMBERGRIS, both of which gave an enigmatic, sexy whiff of violets. The *neve* and *latte miele* of Scappi, nearly a century earlier, can be seen in retrospect as forerunners of this move towards softer, gently sweet dishes, long before the pallid preferences of Rousseau's Julie.

Some of Stefani's sauces have a lightness that is a long way from the heavy medieval ones, pungent with many spices, dried fruit, and vinegar. His *salsa di butiro* prefigures *hollandaise*: melted butter and egg yolks are seasoned with nutmeg, a very small flavouring of cloves, sugar, and lemon juice, with optional musk or ambergris. He does not mention the method, so we do not know if smoothness was desired or achieved. This recipe was recommended for asparagus, artichokes, and simply cooked cutlets. A sauce for roasts is made of candied citron flowers pounded in a mortar, diluted with lemon juice, flavoured with sugar and powdered cinnamon, strained, and served cold. Juniper berries steeped in white wine are simmered slowly in a covered pot with *malvasia*, vinegar and sugar, whole cloves, and cinnamon, and the reduced liquid made a sauce for little game birds. Stefani has been dismissed as perfunctory, and for using material already largely known from other works. What redeems this are the fresh flashes of insight and individual observations.

Later editions of the work contain recipes and menus for less elaborate meals than the great banquets, structured for smaller budgets. At one point Stefani has a remark about how fresh things like peas, asparagus, and artichokes can be got out of season—all you need is rapid transport and plenty of money, "valorosi destrieri, e buona borsa," to seek them on the coasts of Naples and Sicily, the Ligurian Riviera, Gaeta, and even the Venetian hinterland. (So even then out of season luxuries were sought after.) Then follows an overview of where to find the luxury products from each region and city, a fascinating summary of the good things of the time, citrus fruits from Naples and Sicily and huge citrons from Salò, the crisp white cardoons and fennel of Bologna, not to mention its renowned *mortadella*, the musk- and garlic-scented salami of Florence, its *marzolino* cheese, the *provatura* of Rome, among its many delicacies, and of course the *cervellati* of Milan, the incomparable cheeses of Lodi and Piacenza, while Ferrara excels in its variety of fish and of course its wild boars and sturgeon caviar, the delicate sausages of Modena, raw or cooked, and finally a paragraph in praise of the giant carp or *bulbari* found in the waters around Mantua, some weighing as much as 60 or 70 pounds, while giants of 150 pounds or more could be captured by intrepid fishermen by exploding quantities of small mortars underwater, enclosed in airtight wooden cases, which made "*un rimbombo così strano*" (such a strange rumbling) that it drove the troubled monsters from their lairs. Special fish for special occasions. And on that happy note he ends: "*Vivete felici. Il fine*" (Go well. The end)

STEW is a convenient word, along with SOUP, that we apply sloppily to a wide range of dishes which in Italy all have names of their own, often with regional differences; STUFATO, *stufatino*, SPEZZATINO, BRASATO, STRACOTTO, *in umido*, LESSO, not to mention the many *alla* recipes, a sad reflection on the Anglo-Saxon repertoire, but a source of endless pleasure and some confusion to lovers of Italian cooking. When Ada Boni came to explain the classic Roman dish CODA ALLA VACCINARA, she explained that it is cooked "*come una specie di umido*," a dense dark sort of stew, but the more economical version was called *a lesso*, cooked in a copious liquid to yield broth for the *minestra*. She deplored the "*melancolia di questo eterno bollito*," a piece of beef simmered until all the flavour has passed into the copious broth, with the consequent need for various stratagems to reinvest it with anything like interest. Then there is a host of in-between things that imply rich juices, sauces, and concentrated liquids: RAGÙ, *intingolo*, and the like. The boiled meats, the *bollito misto* of Emilia, and the *lesso misto* of Milan, are not strictly speaking stews, providing sumptuous broth and a selection of meats to be eaten separately, similar to the *lesso*.

STOCKFISH, *stoccafisso,* is cod or ling or other white fish preserved without salt by drying. The action of enzymes continues after drying, and helps develop the characteristic pungent flavour. The whole fish, beheaded and gutted, is dried and dehydrated to the consistency of a hard lump of wood, which it resembles on the outside, an unearthly almost translucent white within. When soaked, which takes some days, it almost doubles in weight. In Italy it is not usually subjected to the chemical intervention of lye or limewater, as in the Low Countries and the notorious *lutefisk* of Norway, where the alkali in the caustic soda in which the fish has a short bath, and a long recovery, makes it both white and jellied when cooked. However, some traditional Venetian recipes use *lissia*, wood ash tied in piece of cloth, boiled in water, allowed to cool (once used by washerwomen to clean and whiten linen, reminding us of the French *lessive*, laundry)—by now a forgotten procedure, but a useful technique to apply to an obdurate fish when it was in daily use. Prolonged soaking after this chemical intervention leaves the stockfish white and ready to be trimmed and boned and tidied up in preparation for cooking; some confusion might now arises since stockfish is called "*bacalà*" in the Veneto and northern parts of Italy. The celebrated recipe *Bacalà alla visentina* is for stockfish, not *baccalà*, which needs longer soaking and cooking time; most versions of this recipe use milk and olive oil as the cooking medium, seasoned with anchovies, garlic, and parsley, sometimes butter and onions as well, and the various methods used produce either a thick creamy emulsion, best mopped up with potatoes or runny polenta, or a final result swimming in aromatic oil, the milk completely absorbed, sometimes thickened with flour and parmesan. Cooking time, on top of the stove, or right at the edge of a kitchen fire, in a covered pot, with the liquid emitting a slow heaving bubble from time to time (*pipar* is the untranslatable verb) goes on for up to five hours. A Lenten version, from times when dairy products were forbidden as well as meat, uses almond milk instead of milk and butter, and livens things up with spices (cinnamon, nutmeg, and mace) and sultanas and pine nuts. A 19th-century poet wrote lovingly of *Bacalà del Capussin*, explaining how the monks used to bake pieces of the prepared stockfish (after bringing it to just below the boil) in a pastry crust, along with anchovies, sultanas, pine nuts, chopped candied citron, spices (cinnamon, nutmeg, pepper), mushrooms, and a few truffles, liberally dotted with the best butter.

Moving south, red tides of tomatoes flood over stockfish, with basil instead of parsley, onions and celery, red and white wine, *peperoncino*, and grated lemon peel, in *Stoccafisso alla Basso Porto*, from Livorno. From the Marche comes a recipe with chopped rosemary added to the aromatics, which include chopped celery and carrot, layered with the fish in a pot with a discreet quantity of peeled and sliced firm tomatoes, covered with a layer of sliced potatoes, and cooked in milk and white wine. Genoa has traditional recipes which include capers and green and small black olives, as well as the anchovies and garlic we have come to expect, and the tomatoes of course. In a recipe from Messina, the pieces of soaked and prepared stockfish are first fried with onion, celery, and carrot in oil, then finished in a lot of tomato, whose fruitiness is enhanced by pears, as well as sultanas and pine nuts, then towards the end of cooking capers, local green olives, and a handful of chopped celery leaves are added, and finally the dense sauce is enriched with a slurp of olive oil before serving. Naples has a simple dish, *Baccalà alla pizzaiola*, in which prepared salt cod is simmered a short while with black peppercorns and bay leaves, drained and dried and put in a dish, covered with breadcrumbs, chopped parsley, capers, peeled and diced fresh tomatoes, a good amount of dried oregano, and plenty of pepper, covered with olive oil and left to mature in a medium oven for half an hour or so.

It can be seen that the "red" dishes are less subtle than the "white" ones, but that both depend on the finest quality fish, without which all this painstaking care would be wasted. In Italy, the brand "Ragno" is the one to look out for, but elsewhere it is more difficult to find.

STRACCIATELLE is one of the many names—from the *stracciatelle* of Rome to the *zanzarèle* of the Veneto (recalling the *zanzarelle* of Martino in the 1460s), the *sansarelis* or *cianciarelis* of Friuli (perhaps all linked to the word for rags, *cenci*), and the *grattinato* of Pisa (from *grattare*, to grate, nothing to do with a *gratin*)—for a mixture of stale breadcrumbs, cheese, and eggs swirled into boiling broth, creating ragged streaks in the clear liquid. A sophisticated version in *Leaves from the Walnut Tree* (Taruschio, 1995, p. 31) seasons the egg and breadcrumb mixture

with lemon zest and nutmeg before giving an evocative description of how the chicken broth is prepared.

STRACOTTO is another name for a slow-cooked meat dish, meaning "very well cooked." When applied to pasta, it means you have overcooked it, a *peccato mortale*. The *stracotto di Brianza* is made from a large piece of beef, well larded with strips of pork fat and carrot, rolled in seasonings, browned in butter and oil, and cooked in a sealed pot for several hours. Wine is added at this point, the meat is cooked an hour or so more, then more wine goes in, and some more cooking follows, to yield a rich tender meat and juices which are ideal as a sauce for many of the stuffed pasta dishes of the region.

STRAWBERRY, *fragola*, *Fragaria vesca*, is a cultivated descendant of the wild strawberry, *fragolina di bosco*, but not as delicious. They were known in the ancient world but not used medicinally, so more was written about them by poets than physicians, as Pisanelli commented in 1611, when they had become a new and prized garden fruit. His contemporary Castelvetro envied the British for having an autumn crop as well as one in June. From visual evidence, it is possible that an improved strawberry, crossed with one brought from North America in the 16th century, *F. virginiana*, was cultivated in the Low Countries before being enthusiastically adopted in Italy, for it appears in a work by Lucas van Valkenborch in the 16th century, as well as early Italian genre scenes inspired by Netherlands artists. While Vincenzo Campi has three kinds of cherry and a dish of mulberries in his *Fruitseller*, in the Brera in Milan, there are no strawberries to be seen, although in 1570 Scappi records serving them sprinkled with sugar, as part of the first course of Roman banquets, from May until high summer. Giovanna Garzoni painted a bowl of

them in the 1650s, in varying stages of ripeness, halfway between the gross fruit of today and the indigenous little wild ones. Her patrons, the Medici dukes, already possessed paintings featuring strawberries; one from the 1620s by an unknown Roman has a bowl of strawberries among summer fruit and luxuries like asparagus and artichokes, and a decade later Jan Fyt showed a bowl of them overturned by a marauding monkey. Strawberries and blackberries are part of a characteristic composition by Jan Davids de Heem later in the century, commissioned by the Medici.

The first modern strawberry was produced in France in the 18th century, a hybrid of *virginiana* and *F. chiloensis*, from South America, and most fruit grown today in Italy are descended from these. Today strawberries are cultivated in the north, where the climate is more suitable. They are mainly eaten fresh, with wine, lemon juice, or sugar, not drowned in cream. Dressed with salt, olive oil, and *aceto balsamico tradizionale di Modena*, strawberries make a wonderful salad.

STREET FOOD. *See* SLOW FOOD, FAST FOOD.

STREGA. *See* DIGESTIVI.

STRUTTO. *See* LARD.

STUFATO is a piece of meat covered and cooked slowly with aromatics, not a stew in the sense we know it, using meat cut up into small pieces. The traditional *stufato* of Milan is a large piece of mature beef larded and marinated in red wine and aromatics overnight before cooking in a closed pot for hours on end. The marinating is what distinguishes the *stufato* of the north from a BRASATO or STRACOTTO elsewhere. The *garofo-*

lato of Rome is similar; the long slow cooking of a lump of very mature beef, *girello*, traditionally seasoned with cloves, yields a dense sauce that could then be used to dress pasta and finish tripe in the Roman way. The Roman *stufatino*, according to Ada Boni, is made from slices of shin of beef first browned in a *battuto*—or as she calls it, *pesto*—then cooked very slowly in wine and water until tender. The name *stufato* is derived from *stufa*, or stove, in the sense of a heating rather than cooking stove, where a tightly closed pot could be left to barely simmer for a very long time. *Forno* is the kitchen stove. A *brasato* is a similar process, not quite identical, more like a pot roast.

STURGEON, *storione*, is not fished in

Italy today, but was once a prestigious catch in the major rivers, as the fish, which live in the sea, came upriver to spawn. The deltas of the Po and Ticino were renowned for their sturgeon until early in the 20th century, and Artusi writes of sturgeon as both desirable and available. Farmed or imported sturgeon can still be bought, however, and traditional recipes are still published.

Acipenser sturio is one of a family of fish with a cartilaginous spine without vertebrae, a smooth skin without scales, but with flake-like bony appendages along back and side, like armour. All the sturgeons are the source of caviar (*caviare*) of different qualities, a firm, delicious flesh, and bladders from which fish glue or gum is obtained. Caviar was imported from the Baltic, but was also processed in Italy; Martino gives a recipe, and Messisbugo in 16th-century Ferrara listed the necessary kitchen equipment for making it. Often compared with veal, sturgeon can be cooked like veal. It went in and out of favour in the ancient world.

Pliny, perhaps after a bad experience, claims that the sturgeon (Latin *acipenser*) had lost all its former popularity in his time (the 1st century AD). However that may be, its

early reputation—for which the comic playwright Plautus (2nd century BC) and the statesman Cicero provide evidence—was regained soon after Pliny's time, when the dietary writer Sammonicus Serenus and the antiquarian Macrobius both, in their different ways, praise sturgeon as a food while the Greek author Athenaeus describes the flutes and wreaths that celebrated the arrival of an *acipenser* at a Roman banquet.

Martino cooked properly hung sturgeon in equal quantities of fresh water, white wine, and white vinegar, simmered slowly, preferably whole, not in pieces, something his master (Trevisan) insisted on, which implies having a cooking pot big enough (for a medium-sized fish presumably, since a big specimen could be over a metre and a half long), and served with a white sauce flavoured with ginger or garlic. Scappi begins his section on fish with 27 entries for sturgeon, the most important one of all. His first recipe is simple, the one he prefers: the sturgeon, "*che piu tosto sia frolletta*" (which needs to be hung a bit), is cut into pieces and the spinal cord removed, then put into cold salted water and simmered slowly, carefully skimmed, for an hour more or less, depending on the size of the fish, and served hot with parsley. Both these recipes were innovatively simple, but Scappi gives some old-fashioned versions, where the fish is stewed, in a covered fish kettle, with water, white wine, verjuice, sugar, cinnamon, cloves, nutmeg, ginger, crushed peppercorns, and dried fruit, together with some onions, and pork cheek or sausages when permitted. Between these polarities, he gives a range of delicious ways of using sturgeon; one, a *pottaggio*, is a lighter, more delicate dish, similar to some of today's fish soups, in which pieces of sturgeon, skinned and briefly fried in good olive oil or butter, are cooked with chopped onions softened in oil, then topped up with water, flavoured with white wine and verjuice, a little cinnamon, ginger, pepper, and sufficient saffron to give a yellow tinge to the bunch of chopped green herbs added just before serving, *"accommodando però tal vivanda che abbia un poco del'agretto, & facendosi che il brodo conferisca con l'occhio, cioè non sia troppo verde ne troppo giallo"* (but adjusting the dish to achieve a slight sharpness, and judging the colour of the broth by eye, so that it is neither too green nor too yellow)—a key statement which sums up the by now well-established new cuisine with its light, slightly acidic freshness, and the insistence on the eye as final arbiter of its fresh, delicate greeny-yellow appearance. This new approach, pioneered by Martino a century before, and given intellectual status by his friend Platina, was alive and well and flourishing in Rome a generation before the so-called innovations of La Varenne in Paris in 1651. This is not to claim that 17th-century French cuisine merely copied that of Italy, but that the innovators, as in so many of the arts, were Italian, and that the French debt to them has perhaps been played down by a somewhat partisan view of the later supremacy of French cooking.

Vincenzo Cervio, in his book published in Rome in 1593, regarded carving as a performance art, and his treatment of the sturgeon was typical. It was too big to brandish in the air as one would a joint of meat, but he could hold the dish on which the huge fish was displayed in his left hand, in full view of the assembled company, and with a sharp knife in his right hand, deftly detach the prized flesh from the back of the neck, toss it onto a serving dish, and present it, together with the eyes and the flaps of fatty white flesh beneath the gills on each cheek, neatly salted, to his master. The main body of the fish could then be impaled on a carving fork and rapidly sliced into portions, alternating the unctuous belly meat with the leaner flesh near the tail, salted and sauced, and passed to the waiting guests.

Corrado has a lovely recipe for thin slices from a big sturgeon, spread with butter and a stuffing of minced sturgeon, herbs, spices, capers and anchovies, rolled up and grilled, basted with meat stock, and served with a sauce of truffles and lemon juice. His own invention involves cooking a whole sturgeon, coated with butter, chopped herbs, and onions, wrapped in veal caul and spit roasted, then the caul removed and the fish given a crust of breadcrumbs basted with butter and lemon juice, which will also make a sauce to pour over the crisp covering. (AKD)

SUCKING PIG (or suckling pig) is a

baby pig, weighing as little as 3 or 4 kilos, fed only on its mother's milk, *maialino*, *porcetto*, *porcellino di latte*, or *lattonzolo*. Cooked whole with aromatic herbs and stuffing, it is called *porchetto* (not the same thing as PORCHETTA), or *porcetto* or *porceddu* in Sardinia, where the piglet is stuffed with aromatic herbs (myrtle, thyme, wild fennel, bay), covered with more of the same, and left to absorb the flavours for several hours, then, the herbs removed, slowly spit roasted over embers of beech and oak, perfumed with aromatic herbs, and basted with the drippings from a lump of cured pork fat. It is also roasted in a pit, a traditional outdoor ritual.

Martino's recipe for cooking a baby pig involves splitting it open along the spine, then making a stuffing of its liver, chopped up with bacon, garlic, herbs, saffron, cheese and eggs, and turning the creature inside out, so that the stuffing is contained neatly inside the skin and flesh, while the rib cage is on the outside. This is then stitched up to keep the stuffing in, and the *porchetta* (which is what he calls it, though from the context it has to be a sucking pig) is slowly roasted on the spit, basted from time to time with a sprig of rosemary or sage dipped in a mixture of vinegar, pepper, and saffron.

SUGAR, *Saccarum officinarum*, *zucchero*, in

its refined form has sweetness but virtually

no flavour, unlike honey, which it eventually overtook. In the past, sugar was an expensive luxury, used mainly for medicinal purposes, or in the cuisine of the rich, sprinkled like a spice over food before serving, acting more as a catalyst or flavour-enhancer than a sweetener. Cane sugar was first processed in north India and probably brought to Europe after Alexander the Great's expedition there, but although known to the Greeks and Romans, was little used, honey being the most common sweetener. Sugar cane was cultivated in the Arab world, including the south of Spain and Sicily, from the 8th century, and was used in Italy during the Middle Ages, where it was sold by the *speziale* or pharmacist, who made up medicines and supplied expensive spices and sweetmeats such as comfits, sugar-coated nuts and seeds, and exotic commodities like rice. Sugar was available in various qualities, which must have had different flavours, but the whiter the better was the general opinion. Platina felt that the ancients missed out by using sugar as medicine, when it gave such a pleasure as a condiment, improving even the most insipid food, and quotes the proverb *"Nullum genus edulii addito saccharo insipidius reddi"* (There is no kind of food that is not improved by sugar)—except tripe, added Pisanelli a century later, who thought it made it taste like fresh cow's dung. Sugar or honey went into many of the sweet/sour dishes and sauces of the Middle Ages, but by the Renaissance, Martino was using it more sparingly, with fewer spices, and more herbs; his roast chicken is typical of the new cuisine—the carved bird is sprinkled with bitter orange juice, rosewater, cinnamon, and sugar, a last-minute sparkle just before serving. Scappi's work of 1570 also uses sugar sparingly, even though by then it cost less. He recommends having fine and coarse sugar in stock, and explains the need to examine the top of the sugar cone for impurities. A small amount is included in his all-purpose spice mixture. (*See* SPICES.)

Portuguese adventurers opened up the possibility of producing sugar in their colonies as early as the 15th century, which led to the horrendous triangle of trade in goods with East Africa, in exchange for slaves to work the plantations of the West Indies, and the consequent flood of cheap sugar and comfortable profits into Europe. By the 17th century, overproduction had brought the price down, thus encouraging the use of sugar in confectionery and cookery. The most spectacular development was on the banqueting table, where the skills and technology of sculptors and artists could be applied to the creation of centrepieces and ornaments of cast and spun sugar. Queen Christina of Sweden had little interest in eating and drinking but feasted her eyes, and enormous ego, on the magnificent displays of sugar work produced for the banquets arranged to celebrate her visit to Rome in 1668. Her keen mind focused with pleasure on the complex symbolism, and huge cost, of these *trionfi*. Pierre Paul Sévin made drawings of them which show the statues and mythological groups that beguiled the froward Christina. They are now in the Nationalmuseum in Stockholm and, thanks to the researches of June di Schino, can be matched to contemporary descriptions of some of these banquets. When Pope Clement IX invited Christina to a banquet in his palace on the Quirinale on 9 December 1668, the artist who masterminded the event was Gian Lorenzo Bernini. Sévin's colour sketch of this event gives some idea of the luxurious pomp of the spectacle, with its to us hilarious attention to precedence and ritual, with the Holy Father's table set on a dais several inches higher than that of the queen, a lesser mortal stationed well left of centre of the *baldacchino* as well as visibly inferior (for a heretic Protestant who might be seduced into the Catholic faith, this placement was a subtle political gesture). Christina stubbornly demonstrated her independence of the ritual and protocol she enjoyed yet possibly despised, taking her own initiative and insisting on various outrageous breaches of protocol, snatching the major-domo's embroidered napkin and presenting it to the pope herself, then refusing to take her place until he was seated (in an armchair of considerably more splendour than her own, which was not even gilded) and by not going down on her knees when the pope proposed the first toast, to her, but attempting to get in first, still standing, with her toast to him. The spectacle of a wacky Nordic heretic with an ambivalent attitude to power does not concern us here, but the sugar *trionfi* are of immense importance. Italy led the rest of Europe in this field, with the skills and technology to develop this new artistic medium and display a similar disquieting ambiguity—in rendering symbols of power in a friable, perishable material, the antithesis of the massive travertine blocks of Bernini's Four Rivers fountain in the Piazza Navona, or his marble Apollo and Daphne in the Borghese Gallery, both themes that graced dining tables and sideboards, the white of the sugar contrasting with the coloured jellies and gilded pastries, and the crimson damask hangings (Latini, 1993, vol. 1, p. 483). The gross exuberance of medieval banqueting, with its garish painted wooden structures and large creatures cooked and then displayed in their skins or feathers, stags and peacocks prancing to the sound of trumpets, gave way to a more sophisticated art form, with visual displays of great refinement, soft music, subtle perfumes, all combining to enhance the gastronomic experience. The collaboration between sculptors, artists, pastry cooks, and confectioners drew on a pool of skills without any distinction between the fine arts and the entertainment industry, with artists of the calibre of Bernini masterminding firework displays and fountains, and theatrical performances, and submitting sketches for sugar *trionfi*. We do not know if these sugar sculptures were taken apart and eaten by the guests, or taken away as sou-

venirs, or recycled on future occasions. Their fragility might have made them as ephemeral as the food they accompanied. In his work *Lo scalco alla moderna*, published in Naples in 1692, Antonio Latini lists every possible variety of table ornament, made from pastry, marzipan, jelly, and pleated linen, as well as sugar, but without any instructions on how to make them, these skills presumably taken for granted. A large foldout engraving shows how a banquet table would be presented, with purely ornamental items, the *trionfi* displayed so that the guests could admire them from every angle, interspersed with decorated dishes of food and place settings with elaborately folded napkins. A hundred years later, still in Naples, Vincenzo Corrado published in his *Cuoco Galante*, a series of diagrams of table settings in the French manner, a refined, delicate rococo layout, a complete contrast to the full-blown baroque of Landi's magnificent banquets. The sugar work is still present, in the long *parterre* which goes the length of the oval table, its mirrored surface decorated with curlicues of moulded sugar, with various compartments filled with coloured sugar "sand" and at either end filigree baskets of sugar, holding marzipan fruits with a soft bloom of powdered sugar and exquisite flowers fashioned from sugar paste and with lifelike colouring. His *Il credenziere di buon gusto* of 1778 has an even more elaborate table setting for the dessert course, which by then was served separately, often in a different room or on a terrace. Three square, mirrored, flat surfaces, each bordered with a sugar *parterre*, had a complex mythological group in its centre, also of sugar, and there was a massive *baldacchino* in the middle one, over another group in a simulated bosky glade, the whole surrounded by swags of fruit suspended between obelisks and statues. Corrado does not specify how much of this is made of sugar, but we know that by the 1750s biscuit porcelain was being made, at Vincennes and later Sèvres, which had all of the soft glow of sugar work, for beautiful and more durable table centrepieces and ornaments. The heroic splendour of Bernini gave way to the sweet pastoral themes of Boucher, including an endearing chubby *putto, The Little Confectioner,* in which the sugar sweetmeats are now as inedible as they are enticing.

Though still expensive sugar was now plentiful enough to be generally available for ICE CREAM–making, so popular in 17th-century Naples that Latini tiptoed carefully around the situation in his chapter on ices and sorbets, being careful not to offend the ice cream–makers by appearing to disclose the secrets of their trade. By Corrado's time, there were no such inhibitions, and ice cream–making is described in detail, along with many other things needing plenty of sugar, from cakes, biscuits, and pastries to preserves of all kinds, candied fruit and nuts, and syrups. From then onwards, cane sugar became a plentiful commodity, and when sugar production from sugar beets became widespread, it got even cheaper. The persistence of traditional styles of confectionery and sweets in Italy, even when industrially manufactured, and their modest consumption, might account for the fact that Italy today has, along with Spain, the lowest sugar consumption in Europe, half that of Great Britain and a fraction of that of the United States and Scandinavian countries.

The uses of sugar in confectionery were specified in recipe books and commercial handbooks, and familiar to both domestic and professional cooks. The list that follows gives modern and, where appropriate, traditional names, with their English equivalents, for the different stages in the boiling of sugar—used before a predictable quality of raw sugar, and the thermometers to measure it, were generally available. Much still depends on experience; hand and eye as well as thermometer are necessary for the domestic cook.

Velatura, light syrup

Filo sottile, manuscristo, 105° C, thread, *manus Christi*

Filo forte, 107° C, thread

Piuma, 111.5° C, soft ball

Piuma forte, 112.5° C, soft ball

Piccola palla, 117.5° C, soft ball

Grande palla, 121° C, firm ball

Piccolo cassé, 132° C, soft crack

Gran cassé, caramello, 145° C, hard crack

Caramello, 145° C, light caramel, butterscotch

Caramello forte, 180° C, dark caramel

SUNFLOWER, *girasole,* one of the Compositae, was introduced into Italy from the Americas in the mid–16th century, possibly via Spain. Its striking beauty made the sunflower a botanical treasure before its utility became known, and the grand duke Cosimo III of Tuscany commissioned Bartolomeo Bimbi to record in a life-size portrait—a huge example of a double flower, glowing amongst its sombre foliage against the fitful light of a stormy evening sky. Later the seeds (in fact not seeds but fruit) of the ornamental plant became valued as a source of oil, and were roasted and salted as a pleasant snack. The oil, high in polyunsaturated fatty acids, is a healthy alternative to other oils. It is good for cooking, when a mild flavour is needed, but not for deep frying, for it deteriorates at the high heat required. Its cultivation, for the seeds as animal fodder, and as a source of oil, is now widespread in Italy.

SUPPLÌ. *See* ARANCINI, RISOTTO.

SWEET CICELY, anise chervil, *finocchiella, cerfoglio anisato, Myrrhis odorosa,* is one of the Umbelliferae, a pretty feathery leaf with a delicate anise flavour, used in salads, stuffings, *frittatas*, and also in fruit salads, refreshing long drinks, and liqueurs.

SWEET OR BELL PEPPER,

peperone, came to Italy from the New World in the second half of the 16th century but took some time to get from the ornamental garden to the kitchen. Peppers belong to the *Capsicum annuum* group, which has the ability to reproduce itself in a variety of forms and flavours and so gives us both the small hot chilli pepper and the glorious range of mild fleshy varieties. This puzzled the early naturalists, who at first viewed the exotic New World plants with suspicion, thinking them decorative but probably poisonous. In 1572, Costanzo Felici sent his friend Ulisse Aldrovandi some seeds from an unfamiliar plant he thought might be similar to the *melanciano*, eggplant, but with fruit rather like a tomato, the red kind, not the yellow one in sections. Plant them and see what comes up, he suggested. Meanwhile, hot chilli peppers had caught on more quickly; a cheap and delicious substitute for expensive peppercorns, they were already a common sight in windowboxes, according to Mattioli. The *peparoli* Corrado in the late 18th century calls *rustico volgar cibo,* common rustic fare, might be sweet or hot peppers, and his recipes could work well with either; the significant thing is that they were not mainstream, even in late 18th-century Naples, even to a lover of the vegetable world. Today sweet or bell peppers are widely cultivated and fit into the gastronomy of most regions. They are abundant in Basilicata, Calabria, Lombardy, Piedmont, and Umbria. A summer-ripened product, full of flavour, crisp and juicy, they are now having to compete with forced, year-round crops from all over the world, many of them tasteless. Some of the best ways of preparing Italian peppers are the simplest—grilled or scorched over a gas flame to blacken the outer skin, which can then be removed, revealing the bright slightly softened flesh underneath. This can then be cooked lightly in olive oil, retaining some crispness, or marinated in oil and lemon juice, with garlic, anchovies, and olives, to taste, or finished cooking with onions, garlic, and tomatoes, to make *peperonata*. Peppers go well with pasta, and can be stuffed with many different fillings, roasted with a selection of vegetables, pickled, dried, or cooked along with meat or chicken, like the *pollo in padella* of Rome.

SWEETBREADS, *animelle*, the thymus gland of young animals, found in the neck, or the pancreas, located near the stomach, are delicacies. They are usually cooked first in water or aromatic broth, and can then be coated in flour, egg, and breadcrumbs and fried, or turn up in a FRITTO MISTO or sautéed in butter. Their firm texture and pleasant pallid hue, obtained by careful soaking, trimming, and blanching, lend them to delicate seasonings—cream and truffles— or turning in butter, finished in a dish of peas and ham, or cooked with ham and marsala and combined with a dish of sliced young artichokes simmered in oil. In the past, they went into pies, tarts, and exotic stuffings. Scappi prepared and chopped them with bone marrow, cheese, suet, herbs, sugar, spices, and some raisins, all bound with egg yolks and put into casings or wrapped in caul, and poached, fried, or grilled.

SWORDFISH, *pesce spada*, is a big fish, up to 3 metres long, with a long snout like a sword, usually sold in steaks. These can be pan-fried, grilled, put on skewers, or cooked in a variety of sauces. The dramatic appearance of its warlike head make it a good focal point for a fishmonger's display. It has a firm, meaty texture, the belly being fattier and tenderer than the back, which lends itself to recipes for veal, thin slices en-

closing a variety of fillings. Marinated in a mixture of lemon juice, oil, and herbs like mint, oregano, and wild fennel, the slices can be floured and fried briskly, and very thin slices can also be marinated and eaten raw, as a *carpaccio*. *Pesce spada* has been fished and eaten for centuries, especially in the Straits of Messina, and there are many lively Sicilian recipes, and a recent popular song from Domenico Modugno, celebrating the devotion to each other of pairs of swordfish, the male refusing to desert his wounded companion, and being slaughtered in his turn.

In spite of its being known in the ancient world, it is hard to find references to this great fish in early writers. Platina and Scappi make no mention, but the latter's recipes for tunny and sturgeon would apply to any big fish cut into portions, and he does mention in particular the need to cook the head of a tunny fish at once before it goes off—*"havendo il piu horrendo odore che qualunque testa d'altro pesce"* (having a more horrendous smell than the head of any other fish)—which is what we are told of the swordfish today. Latini, working in Naples towards the end of the 17th century, mentions the huge amounts of swordfish caught at Messina and Naples

and says they can be cooked like sturgeon, *"in adobbo, o in piccatiglio, o in polpettoni, o in altri pottaggi."* These names are difficult to translate, but they are evidence of a Spanish influence. Latini's *adobo* is a way of cooking swordfish with cloves of garlic, vinegar, sage, rosemary, and spices. He fried slices of swordfish, dusted in flour, in good oil or butter, and decorated the rim of the serving dish with asparagus tips, slices of lemon, and glistening pomegranate seeds. A century later, also in Naples, Corrado described complex recipes: a cut from the belly larded with herbs, simmered in a fish broth with butter, bay leaves, and onion, and served with a herb sauce; or chunks larded with capers, anchovies, and strips of truffle, cooked in fish broth, and served with tomato sauce. Today *alla ghiotta* or *a ghiotta* is a recipe for cooking slices of swordfish in a sauce of finely chopped onion cooked in oil with celery, tomato, capers, and green olives; a more complicated version from Messina, *agghiotta di pesce spada alla messinese*, puts floured and fried slices of swordfish in a dish with fresh young peas and a sauce similar to the foregoing one, but including anchovies, garlic, basil, and bay leaves.

t

TABLE MANNERS are in some ways different in Italy; there is a robust elegance in the way food gets from plate to mouth, from the necessary slurping of pasta to the neat handling of a lamb chop (not to take it up in the fingers, for the teeth to get at the last tasty morsels, is a *peccato mortale*, a mortal sin, as a friend once reproached me). The knife is used to cut things up, then put neatly to one side, and the fork is taken in the right hand and, helped with a lump of bread in the left, conveys food to the mouth. The bread does not sit, buttered, in neat slices on a plate; it is broken up into serviceable pieces on the tablecloth, sometimes balanced on the rim of one's plate. It is used to mop as well as push, for another mortal sin is to leave the juices uneaten. During a family meal, one might wipe knife and fork clean before the next course, although restaurants offer fresh cutlery. The use of napkins to mop the mouth and hands of the eater goes back a long way, to the refinements of the Renaissance banquet (*see* BANQUET), where beautifully laundered and perfumed napkins were presented to guests and changed frequently throughout the meal. Right at the beginning there was the ritual of hand washing, not in a communal bowl, which would have defeated the purpose of getting guests to table with hands hygienic enough to dip into the communal dishes without fear of contamination, but in water poured from a vessel over the hands, which were then wiped on clean embroidered towels. Hence the numbers of basins and ewers in household inventories. The vigorous use of napkins by Italians is a sensible response to eating with gusto. But gusto can be delicately done—Emilio Lancellotti remembered an elegant couple in the family's Michelin-starred restaurant; each ordered the superb roast squab, which came to the table in a small pool of rich cooking juices; the young woman wore a terrifyingly vulnerable lime green silk outfit, which remained immaculate at the end of the meal, while the pigeon had been deftly reduced to a neat pile of bare bones at the edge of an almost pristine plate.

A painting by Annibale Carracci, *The Bean Eater*, is a complicated take on table manners, for the man, battered straw hat still on his head, eating back-eyed beans with a spoon, is unmistakably slurping, and his hands are far from clean, but he wears a fresh shirt with a frilled collar, and the table is laid with a nice white cloth, the wine from a jug is in a clear glass goblet, the bread is white and freshly baked, and the spring onion, beans, and fractured vegetable tart or *foccacia*, could denote a Lenten meal, rather than an uncouth one. It is a puzzle, too, to ponder on who might want to hang this on his wall, a rich patron enjoying some vicarious low life, or a more humble client. The huge painting by VERONESE, *The Wedding at Cana*, provides many glimpses of aristocratic dining in the 17th century; the two-pronged fork used to spear sticky preserved fruit served at the final course of a banquet can also be seen in use as a toothpick, as indeed was intended, for perfumed toothpicks, *stecchi profumati*, were listed in menus of the time. Guests can also be seen calling for wine, or for dishes of their choice from those presented along the length of the table, allowing us to see in action the rather static sequence of courses in printed accounts of such feasts in a sometimes confusing sequence of servants carrying dishes, with courtiers, musicians, animals, and buffoons in attendance. The custom of eating food with a knife or spoon meant that the fingers were constantly used to select morsels from a dish and convey them to the mouth; this hands-on approach added a sensual dimension to eating, where touch anticipates texture and flavour, while the mingled aromas of spices and perfumed waters stimulated the appetite. The knife was used to cut food into bite-sized lumps, speared on its point, to pass to fellow diners or into one's own mouth. A much earlier fresco by Ghirlandaio in Santa Maria Novella in Florence shows a group of fashionable young women enjoying the comfits and cookies at the end of a meal, their elegant fingers toying with the profusion of crumbs on the damask tablecloth.

The cheap engraved prints that were the tourist postcards of 19th-century Naples show street urchins devouring long strands of spaghetti held aloft in their grubby fingers; a performance art encouraged by the corrupting small change of wealthy visitors, insensitive to the degrading imperatives of hunger and poverty. Pasta is eaten today with a fork, spearing short pasta on it, or twirling long threads around it, a reminder of the small amount of sauce needed to cling to pasta, but not form a pool in which it wallows, getting soggy as it cools.

The tolerated presence of small children in restaurants gives them the chance to learn about food and table manners from an early age. They hopefully learn respect for food and how to eat it, as fond relatives and long-suffering waiters guide and restrain them.

TAILS. *See* CODA ALLA VACCINARA, OFFAL, PIG'S EXTREMITIES.

TALEGGIO is one of the category of cheeses that used to be called *stracchino*, made for centuries in areas of Lombardy, and the name it has today arose from the need to distinguish and define, and treasure, a version of *stracchino* with particular characteristics. This is now enshrined in its DOP (*see* DOC), and the area of production is defined as the provinces of Bergamo, Brescia, Como, Cremona, Milan, and Pavia, with some made in Novara in Piedmont and Treviso in the Veneto. It is a square or rectangular cheese, soft and buttery, with a sweet, delicate flavour, developing to a tangy piquancy as it matures. Some versions are still matured in mountain caves, wafted by draughts of cold humid air, although most are usually made in cheese factories in the valleys, where adjustments can be made to achieve results similar to those in the olden days from unpasteurised milk and wild lactic ferments. Industrial conditions now guarantee a consistent quality of this cheese, much loved and widely used in Milan and the surrounding area. As well as being a delicious table cheese, *taleggio* can be sliced over polenta to melt into a fragrant cream, or added to a risotto or *frittata*, or as a filling for pasta. Renzo, the hero of *I Promessi Sposi*, stopped during an epic flight from Milan: "he saw a bush hung outside a hovel some way outside a small hamlet, and asked for a bite to eat; he was offered some *stracchino* and good wine, and accepted the cheese." What Manzoni meant by *stracchino* is a mystery; he might have researched his 16th-century cheeses and come up with a historic example, or he might have been more preoccupied with making a link with the past, using a timeless local product to emphasise continuity, as he was trying to do in his use of language. Some claim that this was an early sighting of gorgonzola; others that we have here a genuine rustic *taleggio*. The same mystery surrounds the cheese that the archbishop of Milan mentioned in his will in 868, important enough to be a legacy, which might have been one of these manifestations of *stracchino*.

TANSY, *tanaceto, Tanacetum vulgare,* has bitter leaves, unpleasant in large amounts, but giving a pungent bitterness to stuffings and both sweet and savoury dishes. (*See* COSTMARY.)

TARALLO is a kind of CIAMBELLA (*see* BREADS, RING-SHAPED), circular, braided, or twisted, twice-cooked to a friable crispness, often flavoured with fennel, cumin, or chilli, common in Puglia and Campania, enjoyed as a snack or with wine. The INSOR publication *Pane* quotes the saying *"Tutto finisce a tarallucci e vino"* when a dispute or divergence of opinion is resolved with an amicable glass of wine (INSOR, 2000, p. 237).

TARRAGON, *dragoncello, estragone, targone, Artemisia dranunculus,* is one of the many artemisias, which include wormwood (notorious for its horrible effects when taken by addicts of absinthe) and southernwood; tarragon has some of their acrid pungency, but a more refined sweetness of flavour. The French tarragon is more subtle and tasty than the Russian kind.

Associated today with classic French cuisine, tarragon is still grown and used in Italy, though not perhaps as much as in the past. It is said to have been introduced in Siena as a gift from Charlemagne (probably another gastro-myth), but it is certainly grown and

used in the Tuscan countryside, to flavour roast potatoes, salads, and *frittatas*, a more widespread use than conventional cookery books disclose.

Vincenzo CORRADO used it a lot, in surprising ways, more subtle than the French manner, usually as part of a mixture, for stuffing blanched lettuce leaves, modestly named *alla Corradina*, which included spring onions, peas, parsley, tarragon, and sorrel, softened in butter and bound with blanched brains, parmesan, and egg, the stuffed and rolled lettuce leaves then cooked in chicken broth and served with a *coulis* of chicken breasts. Or blanched cauliflower florets finished in butter and a mixture of finely chopped onion, parsley, tarragon, sorrel, salt, and pepper, served with some reduced beef gravy. This combination of sorrel and tarragon crops up several times in Corrado, but is used with discretion.

Corrado was keenly interested in local resources and regional products, and noted that in his time (18th-century Naples), the lowly parsnip had made a comeback and appeared on princely tables; in one recipe, peeled, the hard core removed, and blanched in salt water, they were finished in butter, herbs, and spices and served in a *coulis* of ham and chopped tarragon. He seasoned a salad of cooked lettuce with a sauce of tarragon pounded with anchovies and capers, diluted with oil and vinegar.

A modern tarragon sauce is made by pounding or blending a handful each of parsley and tarragon with garlic, salt, breadcrumbs, oil, and vinegar. Tarragon has always been used to flavour vinegar, and also goes into many herbal liqueurs.

TART. *See* PIE.

TEA, *tè,* is an infusion made from the leaves of *Camellia sinensis*. The plant is the same throughout the world, and the enor-

ILLUSTRAZIONE del POPOLO

Supplemento della "GAZZETTA DEL POPOLO"

BAR
NATANTE

A pagina 15 il romanzo poliziesco "La perla del mandarino,, di R. Austin Freeman

A couple of Italian swimmers drink their afternoon tea using a floating table. Illustration by Aldo Molinari in *Illustrazione del Popolo*, August 7, 1932. (Mary Evans Picture Library)

mous variations in flavour are due to the variety of conditions in which it is grown, and the way the leaves and young leaf shoots are harvested and processed. Various methods of drying, fermenting, and storing give very different results. The caffeine content is a stimulant in both green and black teas, something that neither cheers nor inebriates. The custom of drinking tea was brought to Europe by the Dutch and the Portuguese, and rapidly spread to the rest of Europe. In Italy in the 17th century, tea joined coffee and chocolate as expensive, exotic nonalcoholic drinks, with rituals of preparation and consumption that created new forms of ceramic pots and cups, to be seen in still life paintings, which put tea drinking as a leisure activity in the context of luxurious worldly goods. But it never caught on the way it did in England and the United States, perhaps because a tradition of less expensive herbal teas, infusions, and cordials had always existed in Italy. Unlike coffee and chocolate,

it was never used as a flavouring in other dishes, although innovatory uses in ices or frothy sauces are now to be found.

The name of the Palazzo Te, or del Te, in Mantua is derived from its location, originally a lowly hut, *tezeto*, or *teieto*, shortened to Te, on what was virtually an island on the edge of swampy ground on the edge of the city.

TENCH, *tinca,* is one of the CARP family, a large freshwater fish which likes a muddy habitat, but if healthily farmed can have a tasty flesh, enjoyed in spite of the many bones. Small tench can be floured and fried, the larger ones cleaned, washed, stuffed, and baked. A recipe from Lake Iseo stuffs tench with a mixture of breadcrumbs, parmesan, herbs, and spices and bakes them surrounded by bay leaves, covered in breadcrumbs, and kept moist underneath with a little broth, the breadcrumbs forming a crisp topping. Martino went one better, with a complex procedure which involved scaling and boning the tench, turning it inside out, with the skin side inside, into which an aromatic stuffing of the roe, fat, and liver of the fish, mixed with garlic, herbs, spices (including saffron), dried fruit, and pine nuts, all bound with egg, is placed, and the creature wrapped round with thread and very carefully roasted over a grid, basted with a *salamora* of oil, vinegar, salt, pepper, and saffron. Scappi has a similar recipe, and both cooks describe how this method can also be inflicted on a suckling pig. The stuffing enclosed in the soft but impermeable skin must have been like a "pudding" in its belly, a savoury accompaniment to the carefully grilled fish. Scappi calls the scaled skin, fins removed, *cotica*, the word used for the skin of the piglet, which becomes soft and glutinous when cooked in this way. The soft, pliable, fatty skin of the tench might just possibly be the forerunner of the later ubiquitous pudding cloth, often erroneously described as a

British gift to the world. Another use for the carefully prepared skin of the tench is to leave it attached to the head and tail of a nice big fish, remove the bones and flesh (quite a procedure), chop the flesh up with some salt tunny fish and aromatics, stuff the skin with this mixture, sew it up, and grill, wrapped in sage leaves or sprigs of rosemary, basted with the *salamora* which will serve as its sauce. Cut into slices, tench can be fried in oil until almost done, then finished along with fresh young peas cooked in a rich broth and served with a handful of chopped herbs. CORRADO offers a sophisticated stuffing which includes anchovies, capers, pistachio nuts, and spices. Clearly a fish worth taking trouble over.

TESTICLES. *See* OFFAL.

THYME, *garden, timo, Thymus vulgaris; wild, serpillo, Thymus pulegioides; golden, serpillo dorato, Thymus serpyllum "Aureum"* are just some of the varieties of thyme available. This is a herb that is as effective dried as it is fresh, and indeed the pungent thyme that grows wild in hot dry areas seems dried compared with the gently fresh green herb familiar to us in cool damp countries. Its uses vary accordingly—dried in stews, with roasts, grilled fish and meat, or the young leaves in salads, stuffings, soups, and sauces, with a particular affinity with mushrooms. Thyme is also a preservative, and is sometimes used in the making of cheese and salami. The essential oils have antiseptic and invigorating properties, due to the phenols thymol and carvacrol, and infusions of thyme are good for coughs, sore throats, and gastric troubles, as Mattioli reminds us; an infusion of thyme leaves sweetened with thyme honey clears up catarrh and can sort out both lethargy and hyperactive bad temper. In his *Commentaries,* we catch an endearing glimpse of the old botanist in rare good humour picking wild thyme on the rocky hillsides of Gorizia, perhaps a living proof of these beneficial effects.

Costanzo Felici was familiar with the use of thyme in winter salads and the dried or fresh leaves pounded with oil in sauces, as described by Virgil in his *Bucolics.*

TIELLA. *See* PUGLIA.

TIMBALLO is a tall cylindrical container, *timbale* in French, and gives its name to any dish cooked in it, usually enclosed in a pastry or pasta lining, which is then unmoulded. The contents can be short or stuffed pasta in a rich sauce, sometimes a *besciamella,* with the addition of many delicacies like truffles, sweetbreads, artichoke bottoms. This is also called a *pasticcio,* and for the social significance of the most famous one in fiction, *see* PASTA, BAKED.

TIRAMISÙ is one of the many variations on the trifle (*see* ZUPPA INGLESE); when potent with strong espresso coffee, chocolate, and alcohol (often rum) it is indeed a pick-me-up of considerable force, though coming at the end of a lavish meal could well become a knockout. It is said to have been invented quite recently in Treviso, though there are so many versions that it is perhaps unwise to become dogmatic about its origins. Some recipes use zabaglione as the custard/cream element; others deploy a mixture of whipped cream and *mascarpone,* often with whipped egg yolks and sugar combined with the well-beaten whites; some use powdered cocoa; others grated bitter chocolate; some omit the coffee; the alcohol can be rum, brandy, or any of the Italian flavoured liqueurs. The sponge fingers are soaked in the coffee and brandy or rum and layered with whatever cream is used and the chocolate or cocoa, and the final layer of cream decorated with chocolate and, in one inspired version, some chocolate-covered coffee beans. At its best, in small quantities, a fine dessert, otherwise a gross, overrated indulgence.

TOFEJA is the name of special shape of terra cotta cooking pot and the dish that is cooked in it, from the Canavese in Piedmont. The neck is narrower than the base—the same principle as the Tuscan bean pot. The recipe involves *borlotti* beans simmered slowly with pig's extremities, herbs, vegetables, and spices, to give an unctuous, fragrant result.

TOMA is the name attached to many cheeses made in alpine and prealpine valleys, mainly in Piedmont, with quite a range of characteristics and sizes. A DOC has been conferred on the name *toma piemontese*, which might function as a supportive structure for many other excellent cheeses deserving protection. *Toma di Lanzo* is made in the Valle di Lanzo and the surrounding area; full cream milk from cows of the Valdostana breed is pasteurised and after mild heat and coagulation is allowed to sink to the bottom of the vat and rest, then removed and drained, shaped, pressed, turned, and salted, and after a month is left to mature for about three more, producing a young cheese, pleasantly mild at first, becoming more piquant as it matures. Many versions are still made on a small scale in small dairy farms all over the area. *Toma di Balme* is made with freshly milked milk from Valdostana or sometimes Bruno Alpina cows, which is skimmed and the curd worked more vigorously.

Pantaleone di Confienza wrote that some *toma* cheeses have a not very agreeable taste when young, and, after maturing in somewhat unhygienic conditions (in hay, cereals, and flour) undergo such unpleasant fermentations that the acrid result is, he said, ideal for the poor, too horrible to eat to excess, and piquant enough to avoid the use of salt and pepper. Harsh words, for today the *Toma del Maccagno*, in Biella, is made traditionally by straining the milk through ferns, lichen, and nettles, is eventually laid to ripen under layers of mountain grasses, and is much prized for its flavour.

TOMATO, *pomodoro, Solanum lycopersicum,* sometimes also called *Lycopersicum esculentum,* is one of the Solanaceae or nightshade family, which includes peppers, potatoes, and eggplants. Tomatoes came from the New World in the early 16th century, but it took some time for this beautiful but curious plant, at first regarded with suspicion as a pretty but probably poisonous novelty, to become the most widely consumed vegetable in Italy, where the annual consumption today averages 10 kilos per head.

The main tomato producing areas are Sicily, Calabria, Sardinia, Puglia, Campania, and Emilia-Romagna. Of the over 300 varieties grown today, there are two kinds. First are those destined for industrial use, paste, *doppio concentrato,* the strained and pasteurised juice, *passata,* the deseeded and chopped pulp, *polpa,* and whole peeled *pelati,* as well as the ubiquitous dried tomatoes. Then there is a much smaller percentage of tomatoes for domestic use, cooking or raw in salads, with a growing section of consumers looking for flavour rather than the uniformity and long shelf life of the supermarkets. The lumpen, segmented tomatoes, picked only when ripe, keep only a week or so, compared with the more commercial kinds. Many families still make and bottle their own sauces, in spite of the proliferation of tomato products in the shops. Tomatoes grown for flavour, plucked when ripe on the branch, and used fresh, in moderate quantities, surpass commercial products; but the tasteless fresh ones, fast-ripening and with the required long shelf life, are inferior to good tinned varieties. The cook has many choices.

Tomatoes reached Europe through Spain, where curiosity about products from Mexico and Peru went along with a ruthless exploitation of the more tangible resources of the newly discovered continent. Gold and silver filled the coffers of the overstretched empire, and strange things infiltrated their way into the larders and gardens of Europe. Cocoa, vanilla, chilli peppers, beans, and "Indian corn" gradually became assimilated. Perhaps the resemblance of the flowers to those of the familiar eggplants (introduced centuries earlier by the Arabs), or the terrain and climate, made Spain a more welcome environment. Tomatoes probably arrived in Seville, along with descriptions of Aztec food by scholarly priests like Sahagun. Trade connections with Italy may have brought them to Naples (for a long time under Spanish rule) and Sardinia. When Mattioli published his great commentaries on Dioscorides in 1568, he wrote of *pomi d'oro* as being similar to eggplant, and cooked and eaten in much the same way, implying that it was edible as well as ornamental, and went on to say that the seeds of eggplants were very like those of *siliquastro* or *pepe d'India*, which we now know as *peperoncino*, chillies—"India" being the faraway newly discovered lands in South America. Mattioli was not making any connection between chillies and tomatoes, but he does point out that chillies were already well known for their pungency and in common use.

Mattioli's contemporary the physician and naturalist Costanzo Felici wrote in the late 1560s in his *Letter on Salads* of a *pevere rosso* or *pevere d'India* cultivated in pots on windowsills, and mentions tomatoes as well, *pomo d'oro* or *pomo del Perù*, of an intense yellow or vivid red, which can be cooked like eggplants, but *"al mio gusto è più presto bello che buono"* (to my taste better to look at than

to eat). In 1572, he sent his friend the naturalist and physician Ulisse Aldrovandi a few rare seeds from Pesaro, from a plant with stems and leaves rather like an eggplant and a lobed fruit similar to the red tomato. "Try it out and then give me your opinion." There was a void between popular use and refined cookery books. Scappi's *Opera* of 1570 has no tomato recipes. Latini gives recipes which allow one to infer that both chillies and tomatoes were in common use, Corrado does the same, and Cavalcanti confirms this. Artusi strikes the moderate balance one would expect from him.

Early images of tomatoes are hard to find, apart from herbals and botanical illustration. There is a sighting in an anonymous still life painted towards the end of the 16th century in Rome. They sit alongside some chilli peppers, both of them new and perhaps viewed with suspicion, segregated from the rest of the fruit and vegetables in the bottom right-hand corner. There are more images from Naples and Madrid, where Spanish culture prevailed and tomatoes were more welcome. In Fano by the late 18th century Carlo Magini has tomatoes on a kitchen table along with red mullet, onion, garlic, wine, oil, and a little packet of spices, which might indicate a *brodetto*.

In 19th-century Naples, the street food vendors created a sort of visual pun, topping the pyramid of grated parmesan ready to strew over dishes of *maccheroni* with a tomato, echoing the dollop of bright red *alacca* used on ice cream cornets.

The bright colour and sweet fruitiness, balanced by just enough acidity, eventually conquered the kitchens of Italy, with tomatoes creeping into ancient historic dishes which might have been better without them. In the past, fruit like apples, quinces, pomegranates, sour grapes (verjuice), bitter oranges, lemons, and many kinds of dried fruit had done what tomatoes now do, but without their garish colour.

TONGUE. *See* OFFAL, PIG'S HEAD.

TORRONE, nougat, is a syrup of cooked honey and sugar mixed with ground and whole nuts, and sometimes candied fruits; it can be brittle, or soft like the *cubbaita* of Sicily and Calabria. We should be wary of assuming an Arabic derivation of the word, for this way of using locally available nuts and honey is followed all over Italy in many areas that were not influenced by Arab gastronomy (*see* WALNUTS).

TORTA (pie, tart, cake). *See* PIE.

TORTELLINI. *See* EMILIA-ROMAGNA; PASTA ALIMENTARE; PASTA, STUFFED.

TRENTINO–ALTO ADIGE

is a combination of two different regions, lumped together for administrative reasons, with different gastronomic traditions. The Süd Tirol, Alto Adige, retains its Austrian language and food preferences, but having said that, it helps to go further back to pre-Roman times when a population of Celts or possibly Etruscans were exploiting the natural resources of the Dolomites. Roman occupation lead eventually to a native language based on vulgar Latin and the languages of these early peoples, surviving today as Ladino, in the Alta Badia, where a way of life based on survival techniques in that dazzlingly beautiful but harsh environment overrides today's imposed cultural divisions. The communal use of land and dwellings, the sharing of work and resources, was never totally extinguished by feudalism, and today both areas are at last enjoying increased prosperity from tourism and light industries. In the past, there was a disturbing contrast between the subsistence food of the majority of the population, and the obligatory luxury and pomp of the nobility, prelates, and reigning monarchs who made their way to and fro through the passes connecting Italy with the rest of Europe. The Council of Trent, which lasted from 1545 until 1563, brought the rich and powerful, and their cooks, to the city of Trento. Echoes of this are found in the works of Scappi, Cervio, and Geigher, who would have known of the hedonistic cuisine and its rituals, even if not present themselves, and these glory years left a mark on the local cuisine, while local usage and products may have filtered through to the papal court, as when Scappi wrote *"delle volte in Roma si porta certo orzo di terra tedesca rotto, il quale ha del gialetto, ed'esso si fa orzata e minestre"* (sometimes there arrives in Rome a kind of cracked barley from German lands, a sort of yellowish colour, used to make soups and barley water). A reminder of how even the grandest tables used what we now consider humble ingredients. Cabbages, fresh and preserved as sauerkraut, and root vegetables, later potatoes, and the *canederi*, or *knoderl*, dumplings ranging in size from huge to tiny, made usually from breadcrumbs, eggs, and a variety of flavourings and additions (liver, herbs, cheese, or sweet ingredients). *Smacafam*, "hunger-beater," is a kind of *focaccia* made with maize flour, richly seasoned with garlic, onion, and a local version of *luganega*, a spiced fresh sausage. The *lamon* bean is renowned for its thin skin and melting interior. Game, especially hare, is cooked in recipes that the 16th-century cardinals would have found familiar: a long marinade in wine and vinegar, highly spiced, with onions, raisins, and pine nuts. Local plants and herbs perfume the milk of animals, hence their cheese; some mountain cheeses are recent and some of ancient origin, like the *schlander* of Silandro, the *ziger* of the Dolomites round Belluno, the *formaggio grigio* or *graukäse*, a pungent young cheese from the eastern Alto Adige, *almkäse*, another young mountain cheese, or the hard *solandro magro*, similar to a *grana* cheese, and not needing to compete with the *grana padano* made all over the province of Trento, or the *vezzena*, a hard cheese preferred above all others by the emperor Franz Josef. Salami of various kinds are enjoyed cooked and raw, some made from lesser parts like pig's tongue and head, *mortandela*, others, like *carne salada*, made of pieces of beef salted with spices and dried, to become, according to Tanara, *"incorruttibile companatico,"* an incorruptible companion to bread. *Speck* comes from all over Alto Adige in many versions, all salted, spiced, dried, and smoked in various ways.

Rye bread is made in many shapes and textures, with the addition of flour from millet and oats, mixtures of several grains, seeds like cumin and poppy, and sometimes crushed almonds in a sweet bread, rich with butter and milk, from Bolzano. Polenta and potatoes go into frugal warming dishes, with today a wider range of pasta and well-known Italian recipes alongside local food to meet the tastes of tourists. And so the serried ranks of brightly dressed cardinals are superseded by the colourful leisure-wear of secular visitors, exploring the "cathedrals of rock," with their changing colours, and in their turn widening gastronomic horizons.

TRIFLE. *See* ZUPPA INGLESE.

TRIFOLATI. *See* FUNGHETTO, AL.

TRIONFI. *See* BANQUETS, SUGAR.

TRIPE, *trippa,* means to us the various stomachs of the cow and other ruminant animals, which when washed scrupulously and given long and inspired treatment can be-

come a dish of sumptuous delicacy. A revelation after the horrible chewy boiled tripe eaten with vinegar in the north of England. *Trippa* or *trippe* can also mean in some regions a part of the intestines of young lamb or veal, or indeed as a slightly vulgar expression to refer to one's insides, as in "guts." Tripe is recognised—in spite of revulsion at its appearance, cleaned and boiled, lying on butchers' stalls like bundles of dirty dishcloths—as nutritionally and gastronomically desirable. A high protein and mineral content, low fat, and, when properly cooked, a pleasing texture make the many regional recipes a delight to discover. Italian uses of offal have always been sophisticated, and banish the current view that tripe is an inferior ingredient, food for the poor; it featured on banquet menus in the past, and is on many restaurant menus today. The saying *"giovedì gnocchi, venerdì baccalà, sabato trippa"* puts tripe in place for Saturday night carousing, as Belli's sonnet implies (*see* LAZIO). His young tearaway would probably have enjoyed *trippa alla romana*, tripe which after its preliminary simmering in aromatic vegetables and broth, is cut up and finished in a sauce, traditionally from a rich beef stew, but nowadays often made with tomato, and seasoned with *menta romana* and pecorino. *Trippa alla milanese*, *busecca*, is stewed for a long time in a rich beef broth with pancetta, carrots, onion, celery, garlic, and parsley, and seasoned with sage leaves.

TRIPPA. *See* TRIPE.

TROTTERS AND FEET. *See* OFFAL, PIG'S EXTREMITIES.

TROUT, *trota,* are wild freshwater fish of the salmon family, though those on sale today are mainly farmed, usually rainbow trout.

Scappi writes of trout:

Large trout are cooked in Milan in this way—scaled, gutted, and cut into slices two fingers thick. Wash them and place in a copper pan they call a *caldaro* with a wide bottom, packing the pieces in side by side, for if they are put in on top of each other they might fall apart when you come to take them out, then put in enough white wine to cover them a good two fingers deep and enough salt and let them simmer very gently, removing the white scum that comes to the surface, and when the pieces can be seen to rise, with certain round blobs on them like a woman's nipples, then they are done, and can be carefully taken out one by one and laid to dry on a board; cooked this way they will keep for three days, more or less depending on the season and the weather, and they are served cold covered with parsley, and sauces on the side. They can also be cooked this way in salt, water, vinegar and wine, and when they are skimmed add crushed spices. But we cooks here in Rome [*noi altri cuochi di Roma*] take medium sized trout, scale them and gut them, and cook them as they are, whole, in wine, vinegar and spices, and when they are done we take them out, and if to be served hot, keep them warm in white cloths. We also make various *pottaggi* of them like the recipe for sea bass (Scappi, bk. 3, p. 127).

A recipe for trout from the Alta Val Taro in the hills around Parma, quoted in Capacchi, finishes prepared trout, floured and fried in butter, in a sauce of chopped garlic and parsley and hot red chilli, fried, then moistened with dry white wine and some tomato concentrate diluted in fish broth. Trout can also be cooked *in cartoccio*, wrapped in paper or kitchen foil, with aromatics.

TRUFFLE, *tartufo*, is known in Italy as the white, *Tuber magnatum*, *tartufo d'Alba*, named for the town of Alba in Piedmont, where the best are found, and the black, *Tuber melanosporum*, *tartufo di Norcia*, which is less tasty, but works well in stuffings for fowl and meat, and is sometimes included in the mixture for up-market salami. Both kinds are also found in other regions. Their esteem as a luxury product has pushed up the price of this once less costly ingredient to a point where an international truffle market, festivals, and the creations of chefs, exploiting the prestige and rare qualities of truffles, have made them almost unaffordable. Sometimes to experience a white truffle at its best it is worth the expense of going to a good Italian restaurant for the quality of the truffle and the cooking. But at home, a very small white truffle, shaved over fresh egg pasta tossed in butter with a little parmesan, makes a splendid feast. This small shaving of truffle improves many a humble meal; a dish of *ribollita* floats on a higher plane, and sautéed sweetbreads, scrambled eggs, or a *frittata* are transformed. Truffles go well with risotto, polenta, and various kinds of gnocchi, and supremely well with potatoes and fondue. Truffles grow wild, usually in symbiosis with various trees, and are hunted by men with dogs or pigs, who respond with enthusiasm to the feral odours of the tuber. A police sniffer dog once nearly caused the arrest of a renowned restaurateur, as described in Franco Taruschio's *Leaves from the Walnut Tree*, when Italian customs officers, fully armed, tried to impound a suitcase full of truffles, but soon relaxed, impressed by such entrepreneurism. The appeal of the odour of truffles is nature's way of getting certain animals to eat them and so spread spores through their droppings, which is why a sow will respond eagerly to a steroid compound called androstenone, found in men's armpits and the saliva of the male pig. Another factor in the appeal of truffles is the presence of UMAMI, and probably why the combination of truffle and parmesan is so agreeable. There are also attempts to cultivate truffles commercially in many European countries. Castelvetro might have been the first to introduce to the British a mysterious sonnet by Petrarch, with its reference to a gift of truffles to a friend, contrasting darkness and light, and the self-generated treasures hidden in the dark womb of the earth. More light-heartedly he talks of the surprise of an aristocratic German at the sight of Italian noblemen walking their estates in the company of a pig—all explained with much merriment and some confusion over *tartufo* and *der Teufel*.

TUNNY or tuna, *tonno* and *alalonga*

(*Thunnus spp.*, especially *T. thynnus*, bluefin tuna, and *T. alalunga*, longfin tuna), is one of the greatest of Italian fish, rightly placed first in Platina's survey of seafood (*De Honesta Voluptate et Valetudine*, bk. 10). Platina believed, wrongly, that some tunny originate in the river Po; he reported a specimen he had seen caught that was "two cubits across," a monster indeed. Though not the most delicate of gastronomic specialities, tunny is a versatile food and is very important economically in Italy.

Ancient and modern authorities are unanimous that the best cut of tunny is the underbelly, now known in Italian as *ventresca*. Fresh tunny is often eaten in steaks—much better, thin steaks of *ventresca*, which can be lightly grilled. Tunny is also commonly stewed in a tomato sauce.

Tinned tuna is used in many ways. The Tuscan beans-and-tuna dish, *fagioli toscani col tonno*, may count as a local equivalent of *Gascon cassoulet*. A Roman recipe, a version of which is described by David Downie (2002, p. 248), uses tinned tuna as a stuffing for red peppers—but it had better be tinned *ventresca*, and helped along with a couple of anchovies. An unusually meaty fish, tuna is even employed (in mayonnaise with capers, gherkins, and parsley) as a sauce for stewed veal in the traditional *vitello tonnato*; but per-

haps tuna mayonnaise, an Italian invention, has rather too many uses.

The tunny is a long-distance migrator, following the coasts of the western Mediterranean and entering the Atlantic by way of the Straits of Gibraltar. During the annual migration, at various points on these coasts, large numbers of tunny are easily trapped with a system of nets, Italian *tonnare*. There are fewer such traps than there used to be, but they are still numerous on the coasts of Sicily and other parts of Italy. The main net diverts the swimming fish into a series of enclosures, *isole*, the last of which is the death chamber, *camera della morte*. Here they are killed, a bloody business, and difficult at first; the fish that are not among the first to be taken gradually become exhausted, sometimes killing one another in their desperate struggle to escape. The "harvest" is highly seasonal, and the majority of the fish caught are destined to be tinned or otherwise preserved. Dried tuna fillets are a speciality, known as *mosciame*. The roe, salted and dried, is well worth tasting, though not as good as grey mullet roe: it is known as *bottarga di tonno* (*see* BOTARGO).

Tunny is a very ancient Mediterranean product, and the catch has been practised for thousands of years—certainly since Neolithic times. Tunny, usually salted or pickled, was well known and prized in the Roman Empire and before. In the 4th century BC, Aristotle reported that salted or pickled tunny from Cadiz was traded by Carthaginians; after the fall of Carthage, this trade continued under Roman control, and meanwhile along the Tyrrhenian coast of Italy there were watchtowers, so that the migrating shoals of tunny would not be missed.

(AKD)

TURBOT, *rombo chiodato*, is one of the

most prized of the flatfish, *rombi*, of which brill, *rombo liscio*, is another, with *rombo di rena* and *rombo giallo* also to be found. It can be cooked whole or as fillets, taking care not to overdo it, or the firm white flesh can deteriorate in flavour. Butter is an appropriate cooking medium, and tarragon or sage are good seasonings. Platina described this laconically as "always too big for the frying pan," but unlike Brillat-Savarin, who had to fall back on a laundry kettle, he suggests simmering it gently, suspended in a large cauldron on a board or shallow basket, so that it can be removed without breaking. Scappi had no qualms about cutting a huge turbot into pieces; for his recipe, *see* SOLE.

TURKEY, *tacchino* (*Melagris galloparvo*), was brought to Europe from the New World, where the Aztecs had domesticated it in Mexico. At first known as *gallo* or *pollo d'India*, it soon supplanted the tough and stringy peacock, being a plumper, more succulent bird, as well as being a modern fowl, innovative, and different from the conventional banqueting fare of past times. In Florence, at the end of the 17th century, the Accademia della Crusca alternated little procedural squabbles and deep discussions of the State of the Language with much guttling, *stravizzi*, when *galli d'India* were served on one occasion by a member wishing to impress his disgruntled colleagues. Modernity in thought, word, and deed. A contemporary versifier at the feast rated turkey well above peacock:

> *Egli della cucina è l primo onore,*
> *Delle tavole è re, ché la sua carne*
> *È di sustanza e d'egregio sapore . . .*
> *Sia arrosto o lesso, è d'un piatto*
>   *ornamento*
> *È buon di fuora e l ripien ch'egli ha*
>   *dentro.*

First in honour in the kitchen,
King of the table, whose meat
Is substantial, and well-flavoured . . .
Whether roast or stewed, it is a fine
    dish
Both the outer flesh and the stuffing
    within.

Camporesi reminds us that the name *tacchino* is derived from dialect usage, based on the creature's onomatopoeic gobbling sound, "tac, tac," hence *tacco* in Florence and *tòch* in Emilia. *Pitto* is another name for turkey in the Veneto. There are no images of turkeys in the farmyard scenes in the *Tacuinum Sanitatis* (an illustrated health handbook from 15th-century northern Italy), or guinea fowls, but Aldrovandi had pictures of both of them done for his collection of images of plants and animals in Bologna in the early 16th century.

Kitchen scenes from the Low Countries show turkeys at about the time Scappi was telling us how to cook them. Joachim Beuckelaer included one in *Christ in the House of Martha and Mary* in 1570, and a century later Evaristo Baschenis included both a plucked turkey and a guinea fowl in a melancholy still life in which the unappetizing birds are more of a *memento mori* than an invitation to a meal. Jacopo Chimenti da EMPOLI shows a turkey with tail feathers splayed in a still life, as decorative if not as bright as the traditional peacock's plumage. This painter had a reputation for greed, and may well have set up these lavish still life subjects in order to consume them later ("Empoli" has been understood as a pun on "*empimi*," fill me up). This work would have appealed to Florentine tastes, as the plump and more tractable bird was a welcome change from peacock. The Genoese liked them, too, as we can see in a kitchen scene by Bernardo Strozzi, in which a decorative servant is plucking a swan, before embarking on two turkeys, hanging up with wing feathers outstretched.

Turkey recipes from Italy are varied, perhaps because they are not exclusively eaten at Christmas or Thanksgiving, although they often are a festive food. A dish from Vicenza, *Paèta rosta co'l malgaragno*, included in a collection of recipes in Venetian dialect (Zuliani, p. 185) involves basting the bird with pomegranate juice while it roasts. The sweet/sour effect is obtained by including some of the bitter white supporting structure of the juice-covered pips, strained out of the squeezed juice before using. The author quotes a local proverb: *"Quando a novembre el vin no xe più mosto, la paeta xe pronta par el rosto!"* (In November when wine's no longer must, the turkey's ready for a roast!) That would be the feast of San Martino on 11 November. Carol Field writes of a recipe from the Abruzzo, where the Sagra del Pitone (turkey) is celebrated with a turkey roasted with a generous amount of garlic and rosemary, and split in two lengthways halfway through cooking, so that the insides, which are turned outwards, as when roasting a sucking pig, get browned as well as the breast.

Because turkeys are not exclusively a Christmas food, Italy has more recipes using parts of the bird; some particularly delicious ones use the breasts in many imaginative ways. Carol Field describes a simple but beautiful recipe she found in Florence in which flattened slices of turkey breast are covered with pieces of parsley and garlic *frittata* and slices of *mortadella*, rolled up, fried in butter and oil, and finished by simmering slowly in milk, then sliced to reveal the delicate colours within.

TURNIP, *rapa, Brassica campestris* var. *rapa,* is another brassica of the Crucifer family, and within this broad category are many sizes, colours, and consistencies of roots. Some of these have edible tops as well. *Navone, Brassica campestris* var. *napus,* could also be called a kind of turnip; it gave its name to the Scottish *neep,* which is what they call a swede, but is not. However, the different kinds of turnip seen in markets, mainly in the north, can be cooked in similar ways, regardless of category. Boil the root first to soften it and get rid of any rank taste, then finish in rich broth, or olive oil, with herbs and flavourings. *Rape armate,* "turnips in full armour," was the heavily humorous name ap-

Turnips and greens at an Italian farmers' market. (Shutterstock)

plied in the 15th century to a dish of boiled turnips, sliced and layered with slices of cheese, butter, and spices, and baked quickly for about 20 minutes. The ponderous joke was that the more tasty the reinforcements, the more vulnerable the turnips became to the greedy—their protection provoking their doom. This recipe works well with tender young turnips or root vegetables of any kind.

TUSCANY, Toscana, has a coastline to the east, below LIGURIA, and is separated from EMILIA-ROMAGNA by the Apennines, with the MARCHE to the west, and UMBRIA and LAZIO to the south. In Tuscany today, roads and motorways snake alongside rivers, through the heart of the region, whereas in the past the main routes to the north were the Via Aurelia along the coast to Genoa and beyond, or up north from Rome along the Via Salaria to join the

Via Emilia heading towards the Po Valley and the barbarian north. Etruscans flourished before the arrival of the Romans, with a cuisine based on vegetables and spelt, but making use of meat and milk products of sheep, goats, and cattle.

Tuscany's city-states cherished the arts while squabbling brutally amongst themselves throughout the Middle Ages and Renaissance. But a reputation for gastronomic and aesthetic purity has become attached to them, idealised and romanticised by generations of historians and writers. Although attitudes to Florentine culture and traditions have been fatally skewed, and now mass tourism does its worst, the carefully preserved historic inner city, a tough, austere, proud, self-contained background for the genius of Giotto and Masaccio, which was later home to the pleasure-loving cardinals and the effete courtiers painted by Bronzino, can still be experienced, surrounded by the unchanging landscape. Pontormo could stroll from one side of the city to the other, greeting friends and sometimes beguiled by his friend Bronzino to eat fried fish in local taverns (later regretted). Michelangelo could drop into Santa Maria Novella on his way to work in the sacristy of San Lorenzo to gaze at Masaccio's *Crucifixion*. We can be blinded by this kaleidoscopic flurry of genius to the hard-nosed realities of what paid for it all—wealth from wool and luxury goods, traded by businessmen and landowners with a keen sense of profit and loss that was applied equally to commerce and a form of self-government that it would be an exaggeration to call democracy. Divine proportion and double-entry bookkeeping went hand in hand.

Unlike many regions of Italy which have different geographical identities and food ways, other cities, Lucca, Pisa, Pistoia, and Siena share a typical Tuscan gastronomy—simple, even austere, based on pulses, vegetables, fine cheese, and superb meat and bread. Livorno has similar characteristics, but adds

to these some typical seafood recipes. The Tuscan countryside is as hard to work as it is beautiful to be in. When systems of landholding changed in the 1960s, there was a movement away from the land; the sharecropping culture, *mezzadria*, which had kept a balance between landscape and productivity for centuries, meeting the needs of often rapacious landowners and those less fortunate who toiled for pitifully small reward, disappeared, and now a higher standard of living can be got working in light industries and in towns. The white oxen which pulled the ploughs within living memory have nearly all gone, tractors have taken over, farmhouses crumble, terraces are levelled, motorways rumble. After the war, the local wild boars somehow got crossed with a more prolific foreign breed (could this be the hunting lobby?), and now they rampage in hordes through a terrain unused to such excesses. When the young vines of a world-class Chianti are destroyed by massed wild pigs overnight the answer is high wire fences and subtle changes in the landscape. But in spite of all the changes, the classic ingredients and recipes survive and flourish. Pulses and beans are of high quality, and the white *cannellini*, *toscanelli*, or *zolfini* are the glory of dishes like *fagioli al fiasco* and *fagioli all'uccelletto*. These have a special resonance for early admirers of Elizabeth David, who introduced us to both the recipes and the *fiaschetto*, a type of earthenware cooking pot, glazed inside, porous on the outside, based on the shape of the traditional Chianti flask, which she used to sell in her shop. There was an elegant flask shape with a narrow neck, and a flatter, potbellied version, with a small opening, so that the beans and aromatics within could simmer very gently for many hours, in the ashes of a dying fire, or suspended over a low heat, without drying out. This frugal way of cooking—low heat, minimal evaporation, simple ingredients—is characteristic of Tuscan food. When served *all'uccelletto*, the cooked beans are finished off in sauce made of garlic lightly coloured in oil with sage, to which a few chopped fresh tomatoes are added; the sweetness and acidity of the tomatoes helps the beans keep their shape. The name might be because many small birds are cooked with a similar seasoning, and this is an agreeable way of enjoying the flavour without the expense, or maybe that it used to be the traditional accompaniment to roast small birds.

Other pulses enjoyed in Tuscany are chickpeas, lentils, and dried broad beans, all of which were cultivated by Michelangelo on his estates, and sent to him in Rome, along with *marzolino* cheeses and Trebbiano wine. *"Compera niuna di quelle cose, quali puoi prendere da e' tuoi terreni,"* as Alberti said (don't spend money on stuff that you can get from your own land). The menus Michelangelo jotted on the back of a letter indicate as much refinement as austerity (*see* MICHELANGELO).

Machiavelli's writings were influenced by his role as landowner, as well as his experiences of the tortuous world of local and European politics, and it was while in enforced exile on his farm in San Casciano Val di Pesa that he wrote *Il principe*. He spent the days looking after his estate, chatting with passers-by, or in the local tavern, and his evenings reading from classical authors, thus absorbing peasant cunning and wisdom and the lessons of history. He had served the government of Florence in missions all over Europe, and experienced the anguish of the power struggles of the French and Spanish in Italy, the destruction of the network of small city-states, and the misery of a countryside perpetually pillaged by mercenary armies. Like Michelangelo, he knew what it was like to restore a ravaged landscape, hide provisions from enemies, and be constrained to spend money on grain for new crops. When he wrote that a ruler should rather have a reputation for parsimony than liberality, he might have had cynical memories of the papal banquets masterminded by Scappi, and

the deliberately low-key wedding festivities of the Medici, when conspicuous consumption would have sent out all the wrong messages. By being mean and tight-fisted with his or her own resources, a ruler could avoid the brutal oppressiveness of the bankrupt spendthrift. Michelangelo would have agreed with that.

An earlier Florentine, Dante, had equally harsh views on the folly of profligacy, consigning to the torments of his *Inferno* a group of 12 idle rich young men from Siena who, not unreasonably sickened with politics and fearing the imminent end of the world, decided to eat and drink up their resources in a short wild flurry of indulgence. The *brigata spendereccia*, Spendthrift Brigade, got through 216,000 *fiorini* in a few months, and early commentators on Dante remembered them well, claiming that they introduced *biancomangiare* and *frittelle ubaldine*, which is absurd, and first had the idea of larding or stuffing roast pheasants and partridges with cloves, which was not true, but served to smear the Sienese, denounced by killjoy Dante as even more effete than the French, and quite capable of chucking expensive cloves on the barbecue, and growing them in their gardens, *"zoè, mise tal uso tra glutti e gu-*

Onde l'altro lebbroso, che m'intese,
rispuose al detto mio: "Tra'mene Stricca
che seppe far le temperate spese,
e Niccolò che la costuma ricca
del garofano prima discoverse
ne l'orto dove tal seme s'appicca."

Where the other leper replied to my question saying: "We exclude Stricca, who spent modestly, and Nicolò [Salimbene], who first discovered the extravagant use of cloves, in the place where they flourish."

luxi," as Jacopo della Lana put it in the 14th century (a reference to Siena, the ambience where this "gluttony and greed" flourished, a city not much loved by Florence after her defeat by the Sienese at Montaperti in 1260).

Confusingly, Dante excluded from the torments of canto 29 the two Salimbene brothers, Stricca, whose *temperate spese*, moderate expenditure, was a redeeming feature, and Niccolò, whose *costuma ricca* of using cloves was perhaps pardonable because of their medicinal virtues.

It seems strange to name and shame and then let these two individuals off the hook, while the rest of the *brigata* are languishing in torment along with dishonest alchemists. Perhaps if they really were the first foodies to commission a cookbook to record their exploits, as a 19th-century commentator claims, they deserved this fate.

The theme of 12 gluttons resurfaced in the 16th century; Vasari described a group of 12 artists and poets who formed a sort of creative dining club in Florence, La compagnia del Paiuolo, where every member had to provide gastronomic and aesthetic contributions to a meal, with penalties for duplication and plagiarism, and applause for ingenuity. The instigator, Gianfrancesco Rustici, an architect and sculptor with private means and manic inventiveness, convened them all to an event which took place in what appeared to be a giant bathtub, complete with steam, with a huge upraised handle from which hung a chandelier. The guests were obliged to step into this *trompe l'oeil* tank, within which were seats round a table, from which some ingenious device caused a tree to rise, with each person's food suspended in bowls from its boughs; up and down it rose and fell though several courses. This was quite eclipsed, however, by the contribution of Andrea del Sarto; an octagonal temple like the Baptistery, with columns made from sausages, with bases and capitals carved out of parmesan, pediments of sugar work, a marble floor of multicoloured meat brawn,

and inside a lectern with a huge folio made of sheets of lasagne, with music and letters formed from whole peppercorns, and a choir complete with choristers impersonated by various roast birds. Domenico Pulico contributed a *porchetta* got up as an elephant, somehow fostering a brood of real-life chickens who were supposed to clear the table. This is of course a rather galumphing prefiguration of the baroque feasts that were later set up to tease and delight the great and the good.

A century earlier, in June 1469, the wedding of Piero di Cosimo de' Medici's son Lorenzo to Clarice Orsini was celebrated with a deliberately low-key feast, a populist political event, a family celebration shared with all citizens, although on a huge and expensive scale. Piero di Marco Parenti, who was one of the guests, wrote: "*Le vivande furono accomodate a nozze più tosto che a conviti splendidissimi: per questo credo che facessi de industria, per dare esemplo agli altri a servare quella modestia e mediocrità che si richiede nelle nozze*" (The food was appropriate to a wedding rather than a splendid banquet), and I think this was deliberate, to set an example to others of the restraint and moderation that a wedding requires). So the 400 citizens who were invited, as well as the important guests, had a relatively simple meal starting with savoury morsels, then boiled meats, followed by a roast, ending with sweet biscuits and comfits, and ending with sticky candied and preserved fruits. In addition, refreshments were offered to respectable passers-by on a table on the ground floor *loggia*, and also in the house of the bridegroom's uncle, so that it could be seen that Piero di Cosimo de' Medici, first citizen, included all his fellow Florentines in this modest family celebration. Modest it may have been, but the quantity of provisions that flooded into the city from as far away as Pisa and Arezzo and the surrounding countryside to fuel the three days of celebration was colossal, to feed the many rather than the few, with a nod towards the sumptuary laws, and gifts to every citizen of joints of veal and dishes of brawn.

The marriage of Piero's daughter Nannina to Bernardo, son of Giovanni Rucellai in June 1466, was also both lavish, and in the end economical, for the not inconsiderable expense was for what amounted to a politically motivated public spectacle: food, entertainment, music, and dancing in and around a structure erected in the piazza opposite the Rucellai home, with an outdoor kitchen manned by 50 cooks operating in a nearby street, feeding over 500 people as well as the 170 elite on the top tables. The food was generous in quantity but not overelaborate; the first meal of the three-day event began with boiled tongue and capons with *bramangiere* (BIANCOMANGIARE), followed by roast meats and chickens, fragrant with sugar and rosewater, then in the evening dishes of cold meat and fish in jelly, and another big roast. This was not the refined banquet of course after course for the select few, but mass provision of splendid, rich fare without too much elaboration, something for the amazed citizens to remember for years. The total expense of 6,638 florins was offset by the bride's dowry and gifts from friends and dependents. Michele di Bernardo Fei da Volterra gave two calves, a barrow load of capons, and a *mozzarella di bufala*, while two unnamed peasants gave two hares, one live and one dead, and some brought cherries, cheese, ricotta, and junkets. The sweetmeats, spices, and candles cost as much as erecting the structure and its awning.

The various uses of spices in Siena are not all extravagant, and many are medicinal. Herbs are the main seasonings in the cuisine of rural Tuscany, and a recent addition to the Giardino dei semplici of the Botanical Museum in Florence is a group of beds containing the typical culinary and medicinal plants of the different zones, the coast, the rolling green inland area, and the dryer hilly and mountainous region. The botanical gardens were begun in 1545 by Cosimo I de' Medici and by the 18th century were world famous. Collecting plants of medicinal and scientific interest was part of the broad sweep of Medici interests, good housekeeping that Machiavelli and Michelangelo would have approved of, though accompanied by political decline, bringing increased agricultural prosperity and productivity, the establishment of new industries, and the encouragement of scientific knowledge (Duke Leopoldo gave Galileo discreet support throughout his troubles). We can enjoy this urge to collect and describe in the works of artists commissioned by the dukes, the huge "group portraits" of fruit by BIMBI, the delicate plant studies of LIGOZZI, and the small miniature studies of fruit and vegetables painted by GARZONI on vellum. The use of plants for healing had been going on for centuries, and the survival of an ancient pharmacy contemporary with Dante gives us an insight into the wider uses of plants we tend not to think of as medicinal, like Niccolò's cloves. The Farmacia di Santa Maria Novella still produces cordial waters, liqueurs, soothing cosmetic lotions, and *pasticche* which used to claim miraculous sedative powers and have a comforting herbal taste. This might be the pharmacy once owned by Matteo Palmieri, who had an administrative post and business interests in Florence in the 15th century, and combined this with managing his estates and property like a good Tuscan, keeping in touch with his roots and enjoying the produce of his farms. His death was commemorated by a huge painting of the Assumption of the Virgin in the church of San Pier Maggiore, commissioned by his widow, and it illustrates beautifully the Florentine spirit, with its intense spiritual preoccupations: it shows the angels, powers, and principalities in concentric circles above and Matteo with Niccolosa, his wife, kneeling below, against the backdrop of a typically Tuscan landscape, showing in detail the land, mills, bridges, and farm buildings owned by them, source of their worldly wealth. A similar scene of calm rural life is on the walls of the Palazzo Publico in Siena, where Ambrogio Lorenzetti's frescos of Good and Bad Government show the benefits of a firm and just rule alongside images of the reverse, disorder and mayhem on the streets, and bands of pillaging warriors and lawless vagrants in a dismal, unkempt countryside, where ruined farms and broken bridges lie among ruined crops and wasted pastures. The Good Government landscape is peaceful but busy, with prosperous farms with red tiled roofs, neat hedges, immaculate dry stone walls and terraces, orchards, vineyards, and olive groves, animated with people tending them. The road is neat and smooth, full of people leading heavily laden mules or driving a *cinta senese* pig to market, talking placidly as they go, the only violent action being huntsmen on horseback chasing across the stubble of an empty wheat field, something for the pot, not murder and mayhem. It might have been political propaganda or love for the Tuscan landscape that made Lorenzetti the first landscape artist since classical times; he also produced two small works, now in the Pinoteca, of a fortified town overlooking the sea, and a castle in typical Tuscan surroundings.

Francesco Datini was also a rich businessman who cherished his roots in the Tuscan soil; he made his money, a great deal of it, in banking and commerce, with branches in Avignon as well as various Italian cities, then came back home to Prato to make even more from the woollen industry and investments in land. He hoarded his papers obsessively and left them on his death to the charitable institution, Il Ceppo, that he had founded to care for orphaned children. By the 17th century, they were tucked away on a deserted staircase and forgotten for 200 years, leaving an incomparable treasure trove for economic and social historians to wallow in. His name today identifies an institute for serious economic history, the Istituto Datini, while popular works about his daily life have

information about food and drink. There was a large household to feed, a *famiglia* consisting of servants, slaves, employees, relatives, and dependents, and visiting friends. Datini was parsimonious, tight-fisted, yet also generous and a touch greedy. He and his guests ate well, mainly his own produce, but Datini insisted on buying the best quality veal and fowls, and much freshwater fish from the Arno and the Bisenzio, eels from Comacchio, local frogs, as well as salt fish, parmesan cheese, and the local *marzolini*, best at lambing time. Vegetables and herbs, fresh country eggs, broad beans that "melt before they even touch the fire," as a grateful friend said, chickpeas that he bossily told his long-suffering wife Margherita how to cook— soak overnight, boil in water, stirring often, then finish simmering in a larger pot with salt and olive oil. The warnings of his physician, Maestro Lorenzo, went unheeded—to avoid rich fatty meat and ducks and geese, "beware of pies," eat vegetables like asparagus and capers dressed with vinegar to encourage urination; even fruit needed some restraint: melons and cherries before a meal, "but by God after a meal let them be." Spices and sugared comfits and preserves were good for you and health giving, and he bought them in quantities from *speziali* in Florence. Margherita gave bowls of comfits to friends in childbirth in the ritual procession of neighbours to succour and comfort the new mother. CHICKENS had a value incomprehensible to us, who see them as merely cheap industrial white meat; to Datini and his physician they were medicinal, something to help cure the infirm and elderly, and sustain women in childbed. On 19 September 1473, Caterina, the wife of Ser Girolamo da Colle, gave birth to their son Giovanni, and his detailed account of the expenses of her pregnancy (which was difficult) include quite a sum for the purchase and feeding of chickens to cherish her through the ordeal (Musacchio, 1999, p. 40). When she went into labour, he went and bought a fat pigeon, some sweetmeats, and three fresh eggs. One can see a restorative chicken in a painting of the birth of the Virgin by Giusto de' Menabuoi in 1367; it is being brought to the mother, while midwife and wet-nurse busy themselves with the babe. Francesco Datini sent three pairs of guinea fowl to a sick servant in 1396, "and look to it that you eat them, for you could eat nought better or more wholesome, and I will go on procuring them for you."

Another benefit of stable civic life was the great hospital of Santa Maria della Scala in the centre of Siena, between the Piazza del Duomo and the city walls. This was famous throughout Europe for its professionalism and quality of care. Studies of its written records, along with archaeological evidence, give some idea of how the kitchens were organised and provisioned during the second half of the 14th century, when Lorenzetti's frescoes were already complete (Belli, Grassi, Sordini, 2004). It is not hard to imagine the mules in his landscape entering the vast hospital premises along what had once been a public street, now swallowed up in the hospital, to unload their provisions in the storage area of the five kitchens which fed the monastic community of monks and nuns, the community's infirmary, the hospital for the poor and sick, and the private kitchen of the rector and his staff. The products listed in the archive material might have come from those tranquil woods and fields, some of the extensive and lucrative properties of the order, the biggest landowner of the region. The care of the sick, the poor, pilgrims, and orphans was curative and medicinal, and in this food was all-important. The archives tell us a lot about the daily provisioning of this vast civic institution, and although they do not reveal the number of mouths to feed, or the recipes used, we can deduce a varied diet, and a consistent use of spices for both gastronomic and medicinal purposes. These included anise, fennel, coriander, cumin, cloves, cinnamon, pepper, ground and whole, nutmeg,

saffron, mustard, and ginger, along with several spice mixtures. Spices had always been used by physicians, and this puts the Spendthrift Brigade in perspective, for they were only enjoying what was both costly and good for you, though in a gluttonous context. Santa Maria's archives show that spices were bought from a number of apothecaries in Siena, as well as being used by the hospital dispensary, to heal and comfort the poor and the sick, so one could assume that there was also a market in the city for them, and that the many spiced biscuits and cakes still associated with Siena were widely enjoyed for both health and pleasure. An inventory of the *spezzaria degl'infermi*, the hospital's dispensary for the sick, is full of equipment for pounding spices, distilling perfumed waters, making sugared pills. SUGAR was above all medicinal, and sometimes used as a condiment to aid digestion, sprinkled on food before serving. It was bought in large quantities for the sick, white and powdered, whole in "sugar cones" of varying kinds. A contemporary cookery manuscript, *Anonimo Toscano*, has a *vivanda da fare bon stomacho* made of the pulp of stewed quinces cooked with almond milk and seasoned with sweet spices and plenty of sugar, combining pleasure and health in the most agreeable way. PANFORTE did not originate in Siena but was made all over Italy, being a good way to combine dried fruit, nuts, spices, sugar, and honey, a pleasant and healthy item at the end of a meal. CANTUCCI are crisp spicy biscuits, and *ricciarelli* are lozenge-shaped soft little cookies made of ground almonds, sugar, beaten egg whites, and lemon or orange zest. Sugar was used in preserving fruit as jam, as jelly, candied, and in syrup; much of the hospital's massive revenues went into buying this beguiling drug. The comfits listed as *draggeia bianca* were made by laboriously coating spices or seeds or nuts with molten sugar, layer after layer, and the tiny little pellets tasted so good they must have comforted weary pilgrims and lost children (*see* CONFETTI). Today's *confetti*, sugared almonds, are made in the same way and now distributed for weddings and First Communion celebrations. This benign use of enjoyable medicaments is a corrective to Dante's mean-spirited remarks about the Sienese and their use of spices.

Herbs and garlic were grown in the hospital kitchen gardens, and bread was baked on the premises from flour and grain coming in from its domains. Seasonal vegetables, beets, spinach, salads, roots, and much cabbage were used, along with plenty of anonymous fresh greenery, eaten lightly cooked with salt, pepper and oil, enlivened with herbs, and throughout the year pulses, chickpeas, lentils, black-eyed beans, dried broad beans and peas, lupines, and vetches were used, staples during Lent and lean or fast days, their cooking liquid a substitute for the meat and chicken broth of meat days. A dish of green vegetables and herbs, *herbetella*, from *Anonimo Toscano* is a mass of whatever greens are to hand ("*ogni bona herba che tu poy havere*"), like beets, spinach, cabbage, anything fresh and young, partly cooked, drained, chopped, pounded with sage, marjoram, mint, and parsley, mixed with egg, and cooked in lard in a frying pan; a version for Lent leaves out the fat and eggs, using olive oil and salt instead, cooked nice and dry and served sprinkled with spices.

The hospital storerooms had ample amounts of cured sausages, hams, and salami, salt tongues with great slabs of *lardo* (cured pork fat or bacon), pots of dripping, jars of *strutto* (what we call lard). An inventory of 22 April 1356 notes 71 pairs of cured pork fat weighing 70 pounds each, and 115 pairs of cured ham, the weights and quantities all carefully noted—beady-eyed stock-taking, but generous provision for the establishment.

The *lardo* might have been the renowned cured pork fat *lardo di Colonnata* (*see* LARDO), whose excellence depends on the breed of pig, what it fed on, and the special composition of the marble troughs in which the fat is

cured. The sausages and salami are usually both well spiced. FINOCCHIONA or *sbriciolona* is flavoured with fennel seeds; *buristo* or *biroldo* is a PIG'S BLOOD sausage with cooked head meat and pork rind, seasoned with garlic, lemon peel, parsley, salt, and pepper—the version from Siena includes pine nuts and sultanas. From Prato comes the *mortadella di Prato*, a lightly cured then cooked spiced mixture of lean and fat cuts, flavoured and coloured with the lurid *alchermes*, pepper, cinnamon, and coriander, to be eaten fresh. The various salami have more or less seasoning, depending on the quality of pork they are made from—*salame toscano*, finely minced lean pork with larger dice of hard fat, needs only salt, pepper, and garlic macerated in wine, while the *sanbudello* from Arezzo, made of lower grade meat and lungs, heart, and liver, all coarsely chopped, is enhanced with garlic, cloves, and wild fennel. The hams in the inventory would have been from the sprightly black pig with a light patch or collar trotting purposefully along in Lorenzetti's painting in its native landscape. This animal is well equipped for the roving outdoor life, with a long snout to root out things to eat, small floppy ears to protect its eyes while doing this, and strong straight legs to cope with the gradients; its meat is marbled with fat rather than being encased in great slabs of it, and this leaner but well-lubricated meat makes hams to rival those from the black pigs of Spain. This black *cinta senese* race has a protective consortium to ensure its once precarious survival.

Tuscany has other fine hams, from wild boar and from pigs raised locally; *prosciutto toscano* is made throughout the region, and is seasoned with pepper and local herbs. *Tonno del Chianti* is traditionally made in the summer from surplus young pigs, *lattonzoli*, which cannot be fattened up for the winter; the boned joints are salted for a few days and then cooked for a long time with bay leaves in sharp young white wine that is also surplus to requirements, and which had best be used up before it gets any worse. The cooked pieces of meat are then preserved in sunflower or olive oil, which is perhaps how these tender pink morsels got the name *tonno*, tunny, which they are not.

The local cheeses brought for Nannina's wedding were probably fresh young ones or pecorino, *marzolino*, or *caciotta*, and these are still made in the same way today, dependent as in the past on the breeds of animals, their food and pasture, the techniques of the cheese-maker, and the maturing process. Michelangelo had them sent to him in Rome, local delicacies to impress friends and patrons. Italians do the same now, and we are at the moment in the midst of what INSOR (2001) *Formaggi* calls a *fermentazione tumultuosa*, like the coagulating milk in the Tuscan peasant's vat, where after years of stagnation, expensive artisan cheeses now rival and surpass their cheap industrial imitations. Pecorino, sheep's milk cheese (*see* PECO-RINO), is the unifying factor in cheesemaking across the whole of central Italy, and though the name is recent (*cacio*, cheese, was the usual term), distinguished by local descriptions of a variety of sheep's milk cheeses. *Pecorino Toscano DOP* defines what goes into them, and how they are made. But it has been suggested that the blanket DOP (*see* DOC) might erode these separate identities. Slow Food lists over seven special types of pecorino, as well as the DOP, including the *pecorino delle crete senesi*, made in an area of bleak clay soil south of Siena, where what little plant life grows makes amazingly fragrant feeding for the hardy sheep that roam there, and *pecorino della Garfagnana*, from an area in the province of Lucca where sheep of the Massese race roam wild, grazing on the local plants, to give a pale, fresh cheese, eaten young, or *pecorino di Pienza* and *pecorino senese*. *Pecorino baccellone* is a fresh young sheep's cheese, unripened, and delicious with the first tender young broad beans of the season. *Marzolino del Chianti*, although a lighter, younger cheese, was rated by Platina the equal of parmesan. It is made from unpasteurized milk from the evening and morning milkings and coagulated with wild artichoke flowers, and gets its name from the fragrant milk of March, which makes a particularly prized version.

Tuscan bread, saltless but flavourful, is the perfect foil to Tuscan food, which is tasty and salty. The cured meats and salami, the rich stews and roasts need just this combination of firmness and rigour. Where others fill up on rice or pasta, Tuscans eat bread, the bedrock of every meal, often transforming a simple snack of cheese and salami and a bit of greenery into a perfect gastronomic experience; the varied pasta sauces of some regions give way to the things put on bread, from the simple *panunta* or *fett'unta* (stale or dry bread toasted and rubbed with a peeled garlic clove, then anointed with rich olive oil) to more elaborate *crostini*. When stale, Tuscan bread has a varied afterlife, used in soups like *ribollita*, *pappa col pomodoro* (a version of *pancotto*), and is often the base line for a rich stew or broth, where toasted or fried bread is placed at the bottom of each bowl or the serving dish, or in salads like *panzanella*, where stale bread, softened in water and squeezed dry, is a base for tomatoes, onions, garlic, basil, and other herbs, maybe anchovies and of course good Tuscan olive oil. The bread keeps its texture and character while absorbing the liquids. Elizabeth Romer has a lyrical description of a farmer's wife preparing *panzanella* which conveys the immediacy and freshness of the dish (1993, p. 108). *Stiacciata* is a Tuscan version of *focaccia*, sprinkled with salt and oil before cooking, sometimes rosemary. *Pan di ramerino* is a sweet enriched bread or bun with raisins and rosemary. A version is made at Carnevale time in Florence, with eggs, lard, sugar, and orange peel, often with whole black grapes embedded in the dough. *Castagnacio* is one of these sweetish flatbreads, made with chestnut flour, sometimes with the addition of a little sugar, pine nuts, raisins, or rosemary; the stiff batter is baked or fried like a fritter and has the same addictive nuttiness as the chickpea *farinata* of Genoa.

Pasta and rice dishes exist, though; *pappardelle con la lepre* is made with broad ribbons of pasta, often with a gently ruffled edge to hold the sauce, which is either the strained liquid in which pieces of hare have been cooked, or better still the meat removed from the bone and added to the juices to make a thick rich sauce. There are gnocchi and ravioli, and the ineffable *gnocchi ignudi* or *strozza preti alla fiorentina*, the cork-shaped blobs of "filling" of spinach, eggs, and ricotta clad only in the flour in which they are dusted, which rise to the surface of gently simmering water in a few minutes and are then fully dressed in copious parmesan and butter. This Florentine version of spinach or chard dumplings is made without flour in the mixture (which would make them heavy and lumpish), and needs careful handling to avoid ignominious disintegration.

Meat dishes range from the superb *lombatina alla fiorentina*, loin steaks of beef from *chianina* cattle, grilled over a wood fire, cuts of pork cooked in various ways, like *arista*, loin roasted with garlic and rosemary, lamb and mutton grilled or cooked with beans, to the offal dishes traditionally served around the markets of Florence. Sant'Ambrogio, not far from Santa Croce, is a less tourist-ridden market than San Lorenzo, where the many tripe dishes, made from a bewildering selection of tripe, looking like old rags on offer on the market stalls, and classics like CIBREO, a stew of chicken innards, including livers, cockscombs, and testicles, an economical use of humble parts superbly cooked at the restaurant of the same name, earthier by far than the *delicato e gentile* version offered by ARTUSI, with a thickening of egg yolks, lemon, and broth. Traditionally, beef from hard-working cattle is tough and needs long slow cooking, in dishes like PEPOSO, and *stracotto*, where a joint of beef is larded with garlic and pancetta, marinated in red wine

and aromatics, and cooked slowly until the meat falls apart. Another Tuscan speciality, *buristo, mallegato,* or *biroldo*, is a sausage made from the coarsely chopped cooked head meat and skin together with cooked hard fat, with a certain amount of blood, seasoned with herbs and lemon zest (some versions include pine nuts, candied citron, and raisins, cooked in the pig's stomach), and eaten as it is or sliced and fried.

Freshwater fish from lakes and streams, and fish from the Maremma coast are used in memorable recipes like *triglie alla livornese*, with red mullet. Eels are cooked in many ways, fried, then pickled in a very pungent sauce with chillies *alla grossetana*, or *alla fiorentina*, covered in breadcrumbs and baked in olive oil with garlic and sage leaves. Livorno was a new trading port on the coast, created by the Medici dukes to replace the silted-up port attached to Pisa, with concessions allowing freedom of religion, as well as free trade, welcoming immigrants and refugees from all over, ex–galley slaves and pirates, Huguenots, Moors, and Jews from Spain, with their gastronomic cultures, and well-seasoned food—Arab couscous, Jewish *roschette*. Livorno had none of the culture and history of the ancient inland cities, no connections with the hinterland; it was brash and braw and had a cuisine to match, using chillies, garlic, and tomatoes with enthusiasm, usually with the less expensive fish, as in *cacciucco*, a hearty fisherman's stew, now a delicacy. Salt and dried cod, another staple of mariners, were used in subsistence and luxury dishes. The ubiquitous tomato is used with subtlety in *baccalà all livornese*, where prepared salt cod is cooked slowly in olive oil and garlic and finished in a reduced tomato sauce made with more garlic, chopped onion, basil, parsley, and tomato; a dense, concentrated dish bringing out the pungency of the ingredients. A reminder that tomatoes were late-comers is the recipe from Livorno for *polpette* of *baccalà*, in which pounded cooked salt cod is mixed with garlic pounded with anchovies and parsley, soaked breadcrumbs, pepper, and parmesan, bound with egg yolks, made into small balls, rolled in flour, then beaten egg, then breadcrumbs, and deep fried.

TWAITE SHAD, *alosa*, or *cheppia*, another of the Clupeidae, with spots along its side, to distinguish it from SHAD, is a salt water sardine, which makes its way into lakes and rivers, where it spawns, and is then at its best, although the bones are a nuisance. It is similar to the freshwater sardine *sardina*, which lives in subalpine lakes all the time.

TWO-BANDED BREAM,

sarago fasciato, is smaller than other members of the bream family, with faint yellowish horizontal stripes and large dark vertical ones, especially by the head and tail; another tasty fish, and sometimes used in the Tuscan dish *Paraghi e Saraghi*, in which small bream are gutted, boned, and stuffed with rosemary and *prosciutto crudo*, threaded onto spits with alternating slices of bread and sage leaves, and grilled over a bright fire, basted with oil, white wine, and their cooking juices. Perhaps easier grilled or baked, and a welcome reminder of how good fish can be with a different range of flavours from the inevitable lemon and parsley.

u

UDDERS. *See* OFFAL.

UMAMI is an oriental word for a universal concept—deliciousness, and now that the substance responsible for it, and the receptors in brain and mouth that perceive it, have been identified, a mention here is justified, for many key condiments in Italian cooking have the *umami* effect—flavour enhancer. To the four tastes, sweet, sour, salty, and bitter, is now joined a scientifically ascertained fifth, *umami*. As long ago as 1908, a Japanese scientist, Kikunae Ikeda, isolated in his laboratory monosodium glutamate (MSG), one of the main elements in kombu seaweed, and went on to achieve both fame and fortune by manufacturing and marketing this industrial version of *umami* on a worldwide scale. Scepticism about the commercial promotion of MSG by his company Ajinomoto need not blind us to its uses. A discreet amount of this harmless powder can enhance many dishes in most cuisines, but an understanding of where it is found naturally is even more useful. An instinctive, pragmatic use of ingredients which we now know to contain *umami* was happening in the past, and can be perceived today in Italian cuisine. Shitake mushrooms, kombu, and dried bonito flakes, along with miso paste, are important ingredients in Japan's miso soup; all contain *umami* without resorting to MSG. We can get a similar buzz of flavour and tastiness by combining different sources of *umami* that enhance other ingredients, and

this is what was going on in ancient Roman cooking; the *garum* and *liquamen*, table condiments and cooking ingredients used since the 5th century BC, were made of fish, often anchovies and their blood and guts, fermented in salt to yield by enzymic proteolysis a clear, amber-coloured liquid, with a horrible smell and a pleasant saltiness which improved the flavour of everything it was added to. It was extensively used by Apicius and his contemporaries in sweet and savoury dishes, along with honey or grape must, vinegar, and the mysterious "lost" flavouring *silphium.* Overproduction or misuse of the terrain where it flourished in Libya caused this plant, whose resinous sap might have been similar to the asafoetida we use as substitute, to disappear forever, after the emperor Nero had devoured the last surviving specimen. Dalby and Grainger, in *The Classical Cookbook,* use this and Southeast Asian fish sauce (*nam pla* or *nuoc mam*) in their recreations of ancient recipes with great success, achieving the *umami* effect—for example, the combination of asafoetida, fish sauce, red wine vinegar, and raisin wine with mint and pennyroyal in a sauce for cucumbers (1996, p. 118), or a sweet custard with pears seasoned with honey, fish sauce, raisin wine, cumin, and black pepper (p. 125). A recipe for mushrooms, sliced and cooked down quickly in a mixture of oil, fish sauce, and honey, leaving them in a thick shiny glaze, seasoned with black pepper and fresh lovage, seems to do the job, bringing out the "mushroominess" of the *funghi* with a careful balance of sweet/salty/pungent. Boletus mushrooms are cooked in Rome today sliced in oil with garlic, and served with a sauce of salted anchovies melted in butter.

The food historian Sally Grainger (2006) has examined culinary and literary sources and demonstrated the possibility that *liquamen* (a cooking sauce used mainly by chefs) and *garum* (a table sauce more likely to be known to gourmets) and *allec*, a paste made from the residue of producing these, were in use in classical times. But there does not seem to be much evidence for continuity in the manufacture and use of *garum* and *liquamen* after the decline of the Roman Empire, and although salt fish was valued and used a lot throughout the Middle Ages, *garum* had no equivalent either then or in the Renaissance. Early cookery manuscripts and texts rarely mention ANCHOVIES as seasoning, but some historians point out that while the poor had to be content with salt fish as seasoning, expensive spices, sugar, and citrus fruit were used instead with prodigality by the rich, who disdained the crude harshness of a rustic condiment, which might have come into disrepute for its harsh taste and poor quality and its coarse associations. Vincenzo Corrado, in his sophisticated 18th-century Neapolitan cuisine, used anchovies in a sauce he called *tornagusto*, "taste reviver," a mixture of hot green chillies, oregano, peppermint, fresh fennel seeds, garlic, and anchovies, pounded together and thinned with vinegar, lemon juice, and olive oil—a vibrant assault on jaded aristocratic palates. A milder sauce, *di bottariche*, was made of cured grey mullet roe, *bottarga*, pounded with candied orange and lime peel, spices, fragrant vinegar, lemon juice, and oil. In another, truffles are sliced, softened in butter along with anchovies, and moistened with some meat *jus* and a little lemon juice. A sauce *alla galante* combines *bottarga*, anchovies, pistachio nuts, mint, and truffles with tarragon vinegar, lemon juice, and oil, seasoned with spices. A *coulis* of anchovies pounded with toasted al-

monds and breadcrumbs soaked in broth is sharpened with a little lemon juice. These condiments, all with *umami* qualities, are offered as modern sauces, not as antiquarian curiosities, and it is hard to tell if they represent survivals from the remote past or are the product of Corrado's lively imagination, but he certainly does not use anchovies as often as Apicius does *garum*. In Rome today, the slightly bitter juicy stems of *puntarelle* are dressed with a sauce of pounded anchovies, garlic, vinegar, and oil, and anchovies are an ingredient in the pasta sauce *alla putanesca*. In Sicily, *pasta con acciughe e mollica* is spaghetti dressed with a pungent sauce of anchovies and tomato paste and garlic, topped with chopped parsley and toasted breadcrumbs; there is a more ancient version without the tomatoes, using raisins, pine nuts, garlic, parsley, oregano, and salted anchovies, and in both we can see *umami* at work (Simeti, 1989, p. 148). Botarga melted into olive oil is a classic Sardinian sauce for spaghetti, where the pungent cured roe brings out the flavours of the oil and pasta.

Salted anchovies are not the same as fish sauce, but they do have a keen pungency which combines with other things to enhance flavour, as in some pizza seasonings, like a version of *pizza alla napoletana*, with its usual cheese and tomato, but also oregano and anchovies. The Ligurian *acciugata* at its simplest is made by dissolving fillets of salted anchovies in tepid oil, sometimes with the addition of capers and tomato *passato*. The BAGNA CAUDA of Piedmont is similar. But although many homes in the past had a jar of homemade salted anchovies to hand, or bought them in as needed from the large tins in provision stores to use in a variety of ways, it would be an exaggeration to see this as continuity with *garum* and *liquamen*.

One of the richest sources of *umami* is parmesan cheese, often used as a condiment; the combination of that and fresh tomatoes as a pasta sauce or a pizza topping is *umami* in action. But long before the tomato became ubiquitous, similar effects were got by sprinkling grated parmesan on food as a last-minute seasoning, perhaps with pepper and herbs. Parmesan or pecorino in *pesto* serves the same purpose. Scappi's idea of a "plain" poached egg was to serve the egg anointed with sugar, bitter orange juice, and grated parmesan on bread fried in butter, then dusted with salt, sugar, and cinnamon. Parmesan is added to vegetable dishes like *sformato* to add flavour; it goes into the spinach and ricotta filling for gnocchi or *tortelloni*; it is essential in *melanzane alla parmigiana* where the melting mozarella and tomato sauce need the boost of flavour from plenty of parmesan. Parmesan goes into stuffings, and cured salami, and is an incomparable cheese to take at the end of a meal—the almost crystalline graininess is not salt but a concentrated form of *umami*.

The amino acids and peptides that occur in aged cheeses and cured hams are full of flavour, and so wrapping a fish in a few thin slivers of Parma ham makes a good seasoning, and the cured ham and parmesan, with a sage leaf, that enliven slices of veal in *saltimbocca alla romana* are using the power of *umami*, while the chopped bacon or cured lard that go into the seasonings at the start of a stew or pot roast are exploiting the flavoursome changes that happen in the curing and fermentation of meat and fat. Tossing the rind of parmesan cheese into a soup goes beyond frugality—it adds flavour, and the use of ham bones and off-cuts in vegetable or meat recipes is another way of doing this. Parmesan ice cream sounds bizarre, but what the cheese is doing is bringing out the flavour of the custard base and the honey or brown sugar used to sweeten it. The ambiguity of historic recipes that are both sweet and savoury now begins to make sense; it was not the yucky-ness of Trimalchio's dormice in honey and poppy seeds but the insensitivity of a vulgar host and an incompetent cook in getting the balance of sweet/salty all wrong that was mocked in the *Satyricon*. The

small amount of chocolate put into Mexico's *mole poblano* or the game stews of France and Italy add flavour, not chocolaty-ness. Today's food industry showers salt into sweet products and sugar into savoury dishes with reckless abandon, revealed only in the small print.

Another way of getting the *umami* effect was to season a dish just before serving with sugar, cinnamon, and bitter orange juice; this improves roast chicken, meat, and many fish recipes. Martino did this with many simple dishes in which the sugar acts as a catalyst rather than a sweetener. He used rosewater to the same effect, more as a condiment than a perfume. (This may have been a legacy from the early influence of Arab court cookery, or due to contacts with contemporary Middle Eastern practise.)

Italian cuisine today and in the past shows how enhanced flavour can be obtained using natural sources of *umami*, even if not properly understood, with better results than a synthetic powder. An understanding of the instinctive combination of *umami*-bearing ingredients in Italian cuisine helps to appreciate the legacy of the past.

UMBRIA has no coastline; it is a secret world of little hill towns, gentle rolling countryside, with pinkish white tones on the dry uplands, and a gentle green, the green heart of Italy, below. Pilgrims, travellers, and invading armies have always passed through Umbria on their way to somewhere else, helping themselves to the good things, before pushing on south through LAZIO to Rome, or east to the MARCHE and west to TUSCANY. Commodities and products circulated, and with them the reputation of Umbria; *norcineria*, cured pig products, were made with rare skill by the people of Norcia, and at pig-killing time they travelled all over central Italy to organise and take part in the making of cured and fresh sausages and salami.

Umbrian Salami

The *corallina romana di Norcia* is made in the provinces of Perugia and Terni, and also around Rome, where tastes and microclimate favour this salame made from finely ground cuts of lean pork interspersed with cubes of prime-quality back fat, flavoured with wine and garlic. Not much to choose between this and the *salame di Fabbriano* in the Marche; something they both have in common, as well as the skills of the *norcino*, is the use of the *budello gentile* (the colon end of the large intestine of the animal), which needs a longer cure but confers special qualities on the product. In his sonnet *"Er giro delle pizzicarie"* Belli described the food store of the *pizzicagnolo*, Biaggio alla Ritonna, in the Piazza della Rotonda (Piazza del Pantheon) with its Easter displays of columns of cheeses and curtains of these prized salami, some from Umbria, with a mountain of hams topped with a huge sculpture of Moses made of lard, towering over a grotto of sausages within which can be seen the Madonna and Child carved in butter. Many symbolic images of the Easter meal show hard-boiled eggs and quality salami, so we can deduce that these salami, made in January, are meant to be at their prime for Easter, before the atmosphere changes with the coming of spring, and the prized contents risk deterioration. The *mortadella umbra* originated in Preci in the province of Perugia, where it is said that the *norcini* were so skilled at cutting up pigs that the nearby Benedictine monks in the abbey of Sant' Eutizio use to call them in to perform delicate surgery on their patients. This Umbrian salame is not like the cooked *mortadella* of Bologna, but a flattened salame with a strip of hard white back fat down the centre, depending on a simple seasoning of salt and pepper to the finely cut prime quality meat. It is popular in Lazio and Abruzzo where it as also made. Smaller salami are made with different combinations of meat and fat, often perfumed with truffles. A humbler product is the *maz-zafegato*, made with liver and the coarser parts of pork, seasoned with salt, pepper, sugar, pine nuts, raisins, and orange peel, the sugar being more to assist the curing process than as a sweetener. There is also a version made with salt, pepper, and pine nuts; both can be eaten raw or cooked. *Barbozza* is made from the pig's cheeks, trimmed and sewn up, flavoured with garlic, salt, and pepper. The renown of all these salami and the cured ham of Norcia lies in the quality of the pigs and what they have been fed on, as well as the handling of the meat, often still an artisan craft. Rarely do they rummage in a semiwild state among oak woods and wallow in muddy waters, as in the past, but small producers, encouraged by a growing interest in local produce, are finding a return to the old ways can be profitable.

Meat Cookery

Meat, farmed and wild, was traditionally spit roasted or grilled, and the skills remain, giving local meat and game, perfumed with herbs and wood smoke, a special quality; a mere recipe cannot convey the character of a cuisine that is based so firmly in *terroir* and the unique qualities of local produce. Pieces of pork tenderloin (fillet), marinated in a mixture of chopped thyme, rosemary, garlic, salt, and pepper, are wrapped in pieces of caul and alternated with bay leaves on a spit, then roasted, turning frequently, before a moderate fire, and depend on a truffle-loving foraging pig and fresh wild herbs, and a masterly control of the heat. The local *porchetta* is usually cooked in the communal bread oven, boned and stuffed with its lightly cooked and chopped innards, and garlic and herbs, including wild fennel and other wild herbs, another unrepeatable combination. Even the universal *alla cacciatora* style comes in a version unique to Umbria, omitting the overubiquitous tomato and using a mixture of rosemary, sage, thyme, and garlic, in which the chicken pieces are fried golden in oil, along with slices of lemon, then finished, uncovered, in a little dry white wine. Game, particularly pigeons, are stewed and spit roasted, often perfumed with truffles; hare, wild boar, and small birds are pungent with herbs. Saint Francis was given one by a fisherman on Lake Piediluco; it nestled in his comforting hands and refused to fly away, until calm enough to seize its freedom—a living being, not an ingredient.

Freshwater Fish

Although landlocked, Umbria has fine fish from rivers and ponds and from the vast inland water of Lake Trasimeno. Fishing has changed a lot in the past half century; artificial fibres replace the old nets and the old ways of making and mending them, motor power replaces oars and sails, and refrigeration makes it possible to keep a valuable catch in good condition, and at the same time reach wider markets, while the repressive social and political conditions which added to the hardships of the fishermen have changed. And so has the fish population, sometimes afflicted by pollution, or by changes, often manmade, some of them accidental, in the introduction of new species. Hardship and want made for frugal behaviour, and subtle skills in manipulating the permitted, and illicit, quotas of fish, getting hold of fruit and vegetables from the countryside, sometimes in exchange, sometimes more furtively. Living on the edge of hardship called for a careful cuisine, and fisherfolk made tasty dishes from the lesser fish—stews, eked out with rice, often using local herbs and vegetables, or simply fried or grilled; many prestigious fish, eels or pike, or carp, were for sale, and only enjoyed on special occasions. Today, lakeside restaurants offering traditional food use old recipes, but are able to be more lavish with ingredients. Some of the frugal habits, using the innards and intestines instead of throwing them away, or cooking a fish like pike ungutted, after scorching the skin over the fire and re-moving it before salting and cooking in various ways, are out of use. *Regina*, the local name for carp, is cooked *in porchetta*, with a *battuto* of *lardo*, or fat from a ham, chopped with the herbs, salt, pepper, and garlic and rubbed into incisions in the scaled and gutted fish, which after marinating for 12 hours is roasted in a wood-fired oven anointed with its *unzione*, an emulsion of olive oil and lemon, until crisp and golden. Spit roasted skinned chunks of *capitone*, large eel, have an *unzione* of oil, vinegar, salt, and bay leaves. Small eel are cooked *in umido*, skinned and marinated in salt and lemon juice, then stewed with a mixture of fried garlic, parsley, salt, and pepper, moistened with white wine, and finished with tomato sauce. Peas from Bettona are the best to use in a dish of stewed tench, starting with chopped onion and celery fried in oil, topped up with chopped fresh tomatoes, and simmered together until peas and fish are done. The fish stew, *tegamaccio*, is traditionally made in a wide earthenware cooking pot, in which a *soffritto* of chopped onion, celery, garlic, parsley, and chilli are cooked in oil; then pieces of eel are cooked gently, next some white wine is added, and the other fish are put in according to the time it will take them to cook, and finished off with fresh tomatoes, the pan shaken from time to time but never stirred.

Massimo Montanari's pursuit of references to food in Italian culture caught a touching anecdote concerning Saint Francis of Assisi; ill and without appetite, he was urged to eat, and eventually admitted to a wish for *pesce squalo*, a fish of the shark family, maybe dogfish, which was at that time of year hard to find, but no sooner had he uttered the words than a man appeared with a basket of the fish and some freshwater prawns, which the saint ate up with pleasure.

Fresh Cheeses

Cheeses include a pungent artisan pecorino from Norcia, made with a coagulant made by the shepherds, dried in the wood smoke in the chimney, which contributes to the aromas from the wood fires over which the cheeses are cooked in whey before their final ripening, enhancing the flavour of the milk, already fragrant from local grazing and forage. The resultant whey is made into the *ricotta salata di Norcia*, whose lovely firm but not desiccated texture and characteristic flavour is due to the careful handling by the artisan producer of the reheating of the ricotta in its whey. There are many different fresh young *caciotta* cheeses, some flavoured with herbs; the best known is *caciotta di tartufo*, which has a more than local market. Ricotta, *ravigiolo*, and mozzarella are also made in Umbria.

Grains and Pulses

On his travels with a disciple, Saint Francis would beg for food from the towns and villages they passed through, and one day they arranged to meet by a well outside a town, to share the offerings. The saint was amused when his companion, a charismatic and good-looking young man, came up with a range of freshly baked treats, a contrast to his own dry crusts. Perhaps some of these were the sourdough breads of Strettura, in the province of Terni, or that from Montebibico, where the water and the use of various local grains today gives this artisan, wood-baked bread a special character. Or perhaps they were one of the ritual breads of Umbria, made for special saints' days and in many shapes and sizes, like the little, sweet *ciambelle* made by the nuns in the convent of Sant'Antonio Abate in Norcia, and threaded into garlands to put round the necks of the animals under the protection of this benign saint, who has a small defenceless piglet as his emblem. Many local flatbreads or buns had the image of their saint stamped into them, or in relief. The *crescia al testo* from Gubbio and the surrounding district is made on a heavy disk made from clay and shingly river gravel, ground together and baked like brick or tile. It is heated over the coals until

white hot, and then a flour, oil, and water dough, unleavened and rolled out thin, is placed upon it and covered with a metal lid with some of the hot coals on it, to cook quickly with heat above and below. When cooked, the "pizza" is cut in half and opened up to receive a filling of cooked greens and herbs, or a *frittata*, or cheese and salame. A delicacy Saint Francis would not have met is *brustengolo*, a rich cake-like bread made with maize flour enriched with olive oil, sugar, pine nuts, walnuts, hazelnuts, sultanas, and sliced apples, flavoured with a slug of *mistrà*, an anise-flavoured liqueur, and grated lemon peel.

Grains and pulses grow in the fertile soil—*farro* (emmer wheat), the famous lentils from Castelluccio, expensive but worth it, with their earthy, meaty taste that needs no help, just salt and the exquisite local oil. Wheat is grown for both handmade and industrial pasta. Truffles, black and white, are one of the glories of the region, and in spite of the high price, are used in many local recipes, for example, a simple sauce for spaghetti made by dissolving some boned salted anchovies in garlic-flavoured olive oil, adding grated black truffles, and serving over the well-drained pasta (an economical version ekes out the costly truffles with mature *trompettes de mort*). A sauce for a dish of sloppy polenta is made of local sausages from Sangemini, crumbled and fried in oil, finished with some dry white wine, and perfumed with shavings of black truffles, served with parmesan and black pepper. Truffles go into a stuffing for a boned rabbit—mixed meats of turkey breast, lean pork, and beef, with the rabbit's liver cooked in garlic and rosemary, all chopped together with plenty of grated truffles, then roasted in a medium oven, basted from time to time with white wine, and served cold or tepid with the hot sauce. Wild herbs and vegetables, including wild rocket, hop shoots, *crispigni* (*grespino*), *rapacciole* (wild mustard), *papaine* (young poppy plants), and the shoots of clematis, *striguli*, are cooked and eaten as *contorni* or as ingredients in sauces and stuffings and put into flatbreads and folded pizzas. A sauce for fresh *tagliatelle* is made from chopped fresh herbs—garlic, wild fennel, mint, sage, bay, basil, rosemary, thyme, parsley, chervil, marjoram, and parsley, with the tips of some wild asparagus, cooked in oil and butter in which a boned and salted anchovy has been dissolved.

Pasta made at home is robust. *Stringozzi* are said to look like boot laces, which is how they got their name; they are made from a pasta made with white of egg, flour, and salt, rolled not too thin, then cut into narrow strips, and usually served with a sauce of wild asparagus tips, garlic, and chilli. *Picchiarelli* make the title of a book on the traditional cooking of Umbria, *I picchiarelli della Malanotte* (Cardillo Violati and Majnardi, 1990), which is untranslatable, but might be construed as "Fisticuffs at the Bad Night Out" (Malanotte is the name of a restaurant in Sangemini). It highlights the *picchiarelli* made there from a flour-and-water dough, from which pieces are taken and rolled in the hands to make long irregular strands of pasta about 4 millimetres thick, and served with a hefty sauce of minced veal and pork cooked with the usual chopped onion, carrot, and celery, wild mushrooms sweated in oil, finished in a dense tomato sauce, and served with abundant parmesan and pecorino. Other recipes from the restaurant include artichoke slices cooked in oil with parsley and pennyroyal, then sieved, and mixed with the local ricotta to make a filling for ravioli. Wild asparagus, cooked and chopped, also go with ricotta in a filling for pasta.

Gluttony and Godliness

Gola e preghiera, the title of a selection of recipes from the notebooks of Maria Vittoria DELLA VERDE, a nun in 17th-century Perugia (Casagrande 1989), gives more insights into the cuisine of the time than into traditions of monastic austerity.

Solitude and a benign landscape made Umbria a welcoming site for religious orders escaping from the clamour and corruption of Rome. Saint Benedict sought tranquillity here and founded an order centred on work and prayer, with a simple diet based on the trinity of bread, olive oil, and wine, and centuries later Saint Francis abandoned both worldly wealth and the corporate life of the by then rich and mighty international monastic corporations to preach a renunciation of power and riches. But it was within, although apart from, the city life of Perugia that Maria Vittoria della Verde, a nun in an enclosed order, left us, in her private notebooks, a collection of recipes, often using quite rich and expensive ingredients. Her *strozzapreti* are classic— a soft dough of flour and breadcrumbs, made into short cylindrical lengths, shaped on a curved cheese grater, which leaves indentations to hold the sauce, cooked gently in simmering salted water, and served at once before they get soggy and glutinous; there is a plentiful use of local herbs; plump squabs are stuffed with a mixture of creamed back fat, herbs, and spices, interspersed with sharp whole grapes, first simmered in broth to firm them up, then spit roasted carefully, to avoid burning the breasts, and served sprinkled with rosewater, with cinnamon and sliced bitter oranges, a time-consuming and sophisticated cuisine. Tench are cooked in the traditional way, scorched black to remove the skin and fins, then gutted and stuffed with either garlic, or raisins and prunes, plus salt, fennel, and rosemary, salted and fried in very hot oil. Chickpeas, carefully soaked, are simmered with charcoal-infused water, then finished with herbs and cooked chestnuts. A plain dish of spinach, well washed and cooked in its own liquid, is squeezed dry and cooked briefly in oil with raisins; carrots are served in a sweet/sour sauce. There is a rich spiced *panforte*, then a universal sweetmeat. Umbria clings to its gastronomic traditions, as unspoilt as its many secluded small towns and villages.

V

VALERIANELLA. *See* LAMB'S LETTUCE.

VALLE D'AOSTA, in the northwest, is the smallest of the Italian regions, tucked away between France, Switzerland, and PIEDMONT. It follows the river Doria Baltea, with 20 or so valleys leading into it. In the past, its strategic mountain passes were penetrated by waves of settlers, including Celts and Ligurians; the Romans valued its strategic possibilities, and set about augmenting and fortifying them, building roads, aqueducts and bridges. Hannibal's elephants suffered getting over the passes, but would have had an even worse time in today's tunnels. Until they superseded the arduous mountain passes, pilgrims and armies struggled against terrain and weather, and the great charitable hospices at the great and small passes of Saint Bernard are monuments to his zeal to convert the local pagans and succour benighted travellers. Saint Anselm was born in Aosta in the 11th century and grew up among the greatest mountains of Europe, as well as powerful monastic communities. He rebelled against parental pressures to conform to the life of the minor nobility into which he was born, and took himself off to the grey skies of Normandy, where he became archbishop of Bec before becoming archbishop of Canterbury, mildly but firmly opposing from its verdant water meadows the venal and tyrannical monarchs of England with their designs on church revenues and autonomy. It is perhaps Anselm's early experience of sublimity and independence that formed his powerful philosophy, his opposition to slavery, and his personal authority. *Fides quaerens intellectum* might have been a concept born among the immense beauties of nature and the rugged individuality of the people of the region. Subsequent settlers or dynasties of rulers, squabbling on the international scene for control of these routes, failed to diminish the independence of the native inhabitants, who now enjoy some of the highest standards of living and employment in Italy, thanks to hydroelectric power and tourism, miraculously preserving the delicate balance between immemorial land usage and new activities. The cuisine reflects this, with local delicacies, cheese, and cured meats used in many recipes which depend on the climate and amenities of the high mountain pastures, with influences from adjoining areas.

Perhaps the best known product of the region is FONTINA—not the only cheese made in the Valle d'Aosta, but as one of the best loved in Italy, needing to be described, before looking at its use in recipes. Unskimmed milk from separate morning and evening milkings is heated, but not pasteurised, and coagulated with natural rennet, and the subsequent curds are then reheated and allowed to settle before draining, pressing, salting, and maturing in a humid atmosphere, before the final ageing. During this process, the cheeses need constant attention, turning and scraping away surface mould.

When made with summer milk from fragrant mountain pastures, this melting cheese with small "pheasant's eye" holes is a delicacy, although the bulk of production can be made all year round, not all of it on those uplands.

The herbs and forage which perfume the milk, hence the cheese, as well as flavouring the celebrated *Lardo d'Arnad* (*see* LARDO), are used in cooking and the preparation of liqueurs and cordials. The local breed of cattle (used for work and milk and eaten when too old for either) traditionally found their apotheosis in good meat broth, simmered for hours over the welcoming open fires, a basis for the hearty soups and stews, like the simple *pane e bouillon,* made of meat broth into which dark rye bread rolls are crumbled along with diced *fontina,* or the more elaborate preparations such as *soupe paisanne,* a sort of savoury bread pudding made by layering in a dish slices of stale bread covered with slices of *fontina* and tomato, soaking the lot in meat broth, and baking in the oven until the cheese has melted. An even heartier dish is made by combining layers of rye bread fried in butter with an unctuous risotto based on the meat broth and the inevitable slices of *fontina,* perfumed with cinnamon, anointed with more butter, and baked until all bubbling and golden. *Zuppa di Valtellina* is equally hearty, not a soup as we know it, but true to the origins of the word, which means to absorb or sop up (*inzuppare*); cabbage leaves are cooked in meat broth, seasoned with cinnamon and nutmeg, then layered with slices of rye bread, *fontina,* crumbled cooked *cotechino,* and freshly ground pepper, the whole soaked in the broth and some white wine, baked in the oven, and served with melted butter poured over. The rich versions of polenta seem almost restrained beside these, made as they are with plentiful butter and *fontina* or served with a *carbonade* of quickly cooked beef and onions, moistened with red wine. The real, slow-cooked *carbonade* is made from local beef

marinated in salt and aromatics (in the past, salt or cured meats), then cut up and browned in butter and oil and cooked, uncovered, with sliced onions browned in the same fat, in red wine, for hours on end, with local herbs and juniper berries, as well as spices. Joints of rabbit fried in olive oil and *lardo,* with chopped celery and onions, then simmered with white wine seasoned with garlic, sage, and rosemary and finished off with a slug of grappa, seem quite delicate in comparison. Veal cutlets and beef steaks cannot escape their swaddling clothes of *fontina* beneath an outer garment of crisp buttery breadcrumbs. But the more economical use of *fontina* to add richness to a traditional dish of meat and vegetables is the *soça a la cogneintze,* from Cogne, where meats preserved in salt with garlic and herbs are cooked with potatoes, cabbage, and leeks in broth, and when done layered in an ovenproof dish with slices of *fontina,* finished in the oven to melt the cheese, and served with melted butter flavoured with sage leaves. Here the virtue of *fontina* to melt into a dish, adding a creamy softness without going stringy, is seen at its best. The popularity of this cheese has spawned many imitators, with cunningly similar names, but inferior in every way, so look for the *marchio* or trademark showing the name against a profile of the Matterhorn, which can only be used by cheeses inspected and approved by the Consorzio which applies the DOP (*see* DOC) standards and specification. Its use in *fonduta* is widespread, with several different recipes, but the general idea is to melt cubed *fontina* in a little milk or cream, and beat in butter and egg yolks to get a rich smooth mass, to be eaten hot.

Other cheeses are *brossa,* a runny ricotta traditionally eaten with polenta, and *salignoùn,* a fresh rich ricotta with the addition of cream, strongly flavoured with chilli, herbs, and garlic; *séras* is another local ricotta. *Reblec* is a small fresh cream cheese made by small producers for their own use, but a version of it is made on larger scale by commercial cheese-makers. *Toma di Gressoney* is a particularly fine *toma* with complex flavours that develop with aging, a process promoted by Slow Food, encouraging the renewal of an almost obsolete production. *Fromadzo* from the lower Valle d'Aosta is another similar cheese made from semiskimmed milk; that from the alpine area of Valle d'Aosta with its DOP is a more perfumed version, often using aromatic plants.

GAME is a natural resource which is not just used for roasts and stews, but cured in various ways; *mocetta*, the salted and dried "ham" of chamois or mountain goat, is seasoned with spices and local herbs, then dried, and is now a tourist attraction rather than subsistence food. It can also be made from deer, wild boar, donkey, or beef cattle. Vittorio Emanuele II is said to have enjoyed the local *bocon du diable*, a slice of toasted rye bread, perfumed with garlic, spread with honey, and adorned with *lardo d'Arnad* or slivers of *mocetta.*

Other cured meats are *lardo d'Arnad*, fat from the necks and shoulders of pigs, cured in salt, spices, and herbs, once depending on the tasty fat of local breeds of pig foraging among chestnut woods, but now, responding to increased demand, from pigs sourced elsewhere. Until recently, the aromatised pieces of fat were cured in containers of impervious chestnut wood, but now, for reasons of hygiene, glass or ceramic is used. This delicacy, in defiance of prejudice against animal fat, is increasingly enjoyed thinly sliced as an antipasto, on its own, or with other things.

Jambon de Bosses is a dry-salted ham, flavoured with local herbs—sage, rosemary, thyme, bay leaves, juniper berries, and garlic, massaged into the meat for two or three weeks, then hung to dry for a year or so in cool alpine haylofts, with the exposed bone and flesh liberally covered in coarsely ground black pepper. Such is the demand that pigs from elsewhere are brought to feed on the local pastures, sometimes fattened with the by-

products of cheese-making, and still qualify for a DOP.

Less noble parts go into fresh and cured sausages and salami, and *boudin*, blood sausages which are highly flavoured mixtures of blood, cured fat, and vegetables as unexpected as potatoes and beetroot, both of which cut the richness and have beneficial preservative qualities. *Teteun*, udders, usually cow's, can become a delicacy after prolonged treatment—wrung dry, salted, and seasoned with herbs and spices, then cooked until tender and served rolled up and sliced, with an interesting flavour and texture similar to tongue. A reminder that *zinna* or *poppa*, cooked in various painstaking ways described by Scappi, was considered banquet fare in the past.

Wild fruit and berries, chestnuts, and mushrooms are all of superb quality. The dessert *montebianco* is made from chestnuts cooked in milk, flavoured in various ways, and topped with peaks of whipped cream. Chestnuts are so good that they are often part of mixed antipasti, served with butter or *lardo d'Arnad*.

In the past, bread was made to last, usually wholemeal or rye, and as it kept it got harder and harder, cut up with the help of a structure like a guillotine, and edible only when soaked in broth or milk. With improved communications and ways of storing, this is now a thing of the past, but love for this dense and flavourful staple lives on in many recipes which can be made with artisan rye bread.

VANILLA, *vaniglia, Vanilla planifolia*, is today one of the characteristic odours of Italy; it scents the air around bars and *pasticcerie*, and finds its way into ice cream, liqueurs, and cosmetics, as well as all kinds of cakes and biscuits, vanquishing the more ancient perfumes of rosewater and orange flower water. The genuine aroma comes from the cured seed pod of the vanilla plant, a native of Mexico, now cultivated mainly in Madagascar and Réunion, but a much cheaper synthetic version, vanillin, is made from various substances, and although less subtle and complex is widely used commercially. "Poodle-faking cheap brandy and whisky," as Tom Stobart puts it, and we have all met the sickly reek from the overuse of vanillin in cheap liqueurs. Vanilla and cocoa were introduced into Europe from the New World by the mid-16th century, and the Aztec practice of using vanilla (along with many other things) to flavour hot chocolate drinks became popular. But it was some time before the wide range of exotic flavourings available to the confectioner gave way to today's ubiquitous and unimaginative use of vanilla and lemon peel. Musk, ambergris, cinnamon, and a whole range of spices were deployed by Corrado in the late 18th century, with only occasional use of vanilla. It became more popular in the 19th century after improved ways of pollinating the flowers were developed, making large-scale cultivation possible, followed within a few decades by the development of synthetic vanilla, which is now widely available. Best results are from the whole vanilla bean, used in a container of sugar to impart its flavour, infused whole in milk or cream for sauces and ice cream, or pounded up or processed with other ingredients. If the claims that vanilla has mind-bending properties have anything in them, the idea that it can create feelings of security and well-being, soothing the child within us, especially when used with chocolate, another psychotropic substance, leaves one with respect for the ancient Aztec traditions of offering vanilla in cocoa beverages whipped up with chilli and herbs, taken by royal personages communicating with their gods.

Today, innovative chefs are flavouring savoury food (especially shellfish) and sauces with real vanilla, and sweet dishes with chilli, reverting to ancient ways in a spirit of innovation.

Vasselli's recipes often used flowers. (Shutterstock)

VASSELLI, GIOVAN FRANCESCO (dates unknown), published in 1647, the year before he died, a work entitled *Apicio overo Il maestro de' Conviti*, which he dedicated to the Senate, or ruling body, of Bologna. This is all about elaborate aristocratic dining, with detailed descriptions of banquets interspersed with recipes for dishes somewhat different from the run-of-the-mill grand roasts and set pieces listed in the menus—a subtle choice, therefore, of elegant and refined sauces, salads, relishes, and perfumed waters and vinegars, taking for granted expertise in the nuts and bolts of the well-known recipes of contemporary writers, and concentrating on the finer points. For example, chicken livers are cut small and lightly poached in chicken broth, then thickened with raw livers pounded with pistachios, marzipan, Naples biscuits, and preserved citron, and finished with egg yolks, lemon juice, and musk-flavoured rosewater. Another of these *minestre reale* sounds familiar: testicles, wattles, and crests of young cockerel, simmered, then chopped, slightly sweetened and thickened with pounded pistachios, almond milk, cream, lemon juice, and musk rosewater—a version of CIBREO almost perfumed out of existence. Vasselli's salads are a response to the fashionable taste for what had once been derided as "animal food" and were by then refined delicacies. A salad of young garlic shoots and bulbs chopped with the tender tops of pennyroyal and dressed with salt, oil, and vinegar was slumming in

style; and one of trimmed and finely chopped spring onions, with sprigs of thyme, soaked first in chilled water, then dressed with oil, cinnamon flavoured vinegar, and borage flowers must have been a delight to the eye as well as a delicate relish, a far cry from the uncouth *mangiafagioli* of Annibale Carracci half a century earlier, with his bunch of spring onions to munch with a rustic dish of beans. We find an early mention of the pale leaves of forced chicory (endive), which are soaked in water to get rid of some of the bitterness, then dried and served, if entertaining foreign notables, decorated with gold leaf, borage flowers, and capers, as well as the usual dressing of oil, vinegar, salt, sugar, and lemon blossom–flavoured vinegar. The ingredients for a *mescolanza fina*, by then well known, were grown in many gardens, but it takes the care of a good gardener, says Vasselli, to select the fresh young tips of each plant and get a nice balance of flavours. A revival of this *misticanza*, as they called it, was pioneered in the 1990s by the Lancellotti restaurant not far from Bologna, and the time taken tending the plants, plucking the young leaves, and washing and preparing the salad amounted to several hours a day. Vasselli understood this: *"Quest'insalata è cosa tanto nota, che tutti ormai la fanno raccogliere, e seminare ne'loro orti. Il coglierla però Wna, non è cosa tanto comune a tutti; ma solo de'buoni Giardinieri"* (This salad is so well known that by now everyone grows it in their gardens. But it takes a good gardener to gather a really delicate selection, a rare gift; Vasselli, p. 60). Angelo had this gift; his skills were unsurpassed. Depending on the time of year, the *misticanza* would include chicory, salad burnet, tarragon, *erba stella*, rocket, sorrel, lemon balm, borage, young lettuce, the tips of thyme, pennyroyal, and basil, together with petals from any flower in season, borage, bugloss, rosemary, sage, orange, and citron, with a seasoning of young garlic shoots, chives, and spring onions. The combined properties of all these herbs should enhance and balance each other.

Salads were so modish that Vasselli gave versions made with meat, chicken, and fish. The huge pike, *bulbari*, for which the lakes around Mantua are famous, were gutted, scaled, marinated in oil, fennel seeds, sugar, and salt, and grilled using this mixture, and some Malvasia, to baste them; when cooked, they were put in an *adobo* of cinnamon-flavoured vinegar, saffron, pepper, nutmeg, cloves, sage, rosemary, and a little crushed garlic, and served on a big dish decorated with slices of citron and sprigs of parsley and basil. There is a salad of cold beef, that has been larded with cloves and pennyroyal and stewed slowly until tender, then part of it sliced thinly and the rest chopped very fine and dressed with a little oil, vinegar, and crushed pepper, arranged on a dish *in conformità del tuo genio*, and decorated with shavings of parmesan, the sliced meat, raisins cooked in sweet wine, capers from Genova, and borage flowers.

Vasselli had the organisational skills to source, prepare, and serve the grandiose baroque banquets he describes, but he also had the delightful gift of improvisation and a touch of self-mockery. The splendid feast offered in Bologna by Cornelio Malvasio to his boss, Francesco d'Este, duke of Modena, along with his wife, sister, aunt, and four brothers, and their retinue—a seamless succession of 16 dishes from the kitchen, followed by fruit, cheeses, and sweetmeats, all cluttered up with sugar *trionfi* and pleated napkins and table decorations—was luxurious in the extreme, and it is only at the end of the event, when the ducal party were already leaving for Modena, that the delayed consignment of live fish from Lake Garda arrived—huge trout, carp, and tench. Vasselli rose to the occasion and presented them in silver and gold basins as a farewell offering, and they were duly trundled all the way to Modena at the request of the grateful recipient. If only poor Vatel could have improvised his way out of the apparent late delivery of fish to Chantilly which precipitated his suicide in 1671.

Vasselli concludes the work with an account of what might have been the earliest ever cookbook launch party. At the end of an imposing wedding banquet, the guests were treated to a mock debate on Parnassus in which the god Apollo heard polite criticisms of Vasselli's work from an eminent *scalco*, Matteo Belloni, and an equally decorous defence from Vittorio Lancellotti, another colleague, both of whom had learned their trade at the nearby court of Alessandro, duke of Mirandola, and who must have come all the way from Rome to celebrate with their frail and elderly friend the publication of his book. The debate ends with Apollo graciously praising the author and conferring immortality upon the publication, a fate envied by cookery writers ever since.

VEAL, *vitello*, is a young milk-fed calf, and its meat is valued and cooked to perfection in Italy, especially in the north, where these very young animals are part of the structure of cattle breeding, for milk and its by-products and for the meat of the adult animals. It makes more sense, economically, to sell as meat young animals surplus to requirements than to feed them at some expense. In the south, where cows and oxen used to be beasts of burden, their meat did not get into the pot until the animals were too old to be of use, and there rich and sumptuous recipes for various cuts of BEEF flourish, depending on slow cooking to tame their obdurate fibres. Pinelli's engravings of hordes of bulls being driven to market show huge fierce beasts rampaging through the streets of Rome, or other proud creatures, pulling carts of hay as high as houses. Anglo-Saxons and people from the American continent appreciate the qualities of fine cuts of mature beef, despising the blandness of veal, as well they might, for the industrial production of suspiciously white, tender, but tasteless veal flesh is often all we can get. Veal properly reared is a pale pink, with a small amount of white fat and a delicate flavour, firm but not soggy.

Sanato, a speciality of Piedmont, is veal of the *razza piemontese* fed on milk only for as long as a year, thus a big child, with plenty of tender pale flesh, which can be cooked like milk-fed veal. *Roston* is a recipe from Albi in which a fillet of *sanato* is pot roasted for several hours with rosemary and sliced onion, celery, and carrot, to which are added *funghi porcini* towards the end, moistened from time to time with white wine, and perfumed with white truffles just before serving. Recipes from the north are imaginative; *vitello tonnato* from Piedmont is a way of serving slices of cold, succulent, pot roasted loin of veal, spread or fashionably dribbled with a sauce made of good mayonnaise mixed with the best possible canned tunny fish and some of the cooking liquids, light and creamy and subliminally fishy, decorated with capers. A version of this from Lombardy serves the veal hot, pot roasted, after larding with garlic and prepared salted anchovies, with a sauce made by stirring some tunny into the cooking liquid, passing it through a sieve, then thickening the sauce with butter and flour. Another way with veal, OSSOBUCO ALLA MILANESE, is made from slices of leg of veal cut through the bone, marrow and all. SALTIMBOCCA ALLA RO-MANA is made with thin slices of veal upon each of which a fresh sage leaf is placed, then a slice of *prosciutto crudo*, secured with a toothpick. Martino had a more subtle version, in which the flattened slices of veal are sprinkled with pulverised salt and fennel seeds, then spread with a mixture of cured fat pounded with marjoram and parsley and a few spices, rolled up and spit roasted gently so that they do not dry up. This is similar to the *uccelli* or *uccellini scappati* of Emilia, where thin slices of veal or pork are covered with pancetta or *prosciutto crudo*, rolled up, secured with toothpicks, and fried in butter. A version from Lombardy alternates on a skewer cubes of veal liver, lean veal, or pork, interleaved with sage leaves and cubes of cured fat, to be fried in butter, and finished in white wine.

Corrado and Scappi were concerned with calves fed only on their mothers' milk; Scappi gave recipes for this *vitella mongana*, milk-fed veal available from April through July, but which could be had all year round in Rome from small establishments keeping cattle in stalls and feeding them milk and cheese by-products, and he mentions *vitella campareccia*, a more mature calf grazing with its mother outdoors.

Scappi gave us over 35 recipes for the different parts of milk-fed veal, which reflects the taste of his rich patrons rather than local Roman usage, which relied on mature or elderly beef. Corrado did the same 200 years later, extolling the virtues of this luxury meat to his Neapolitan contemporaries: "Of all the exquisite, health-giving and nourishing food that can be prepared from quadrupeds that of milk-fed veal is in my opinion the best, there being no part of the animal that cannot be seasoned and tastefully prepared, so I shall take upon myself the task of expounding the visual and gustatory delights of every part, starting with the head" (Corrado 1778, p. 1)—which he did in some detail: 15 for the head, 16 for brains, 13 ways with tongue, 7 ways of dealing with innards, 15 for the various cuts of breast, 14 for the rump, 4 more for the top rump, 6 for the loin, and for the chops, while kidneys have 4, ears 5, feet 6, the exquisite sweetbreads 9, and finally the liver 12. All of them are delicious—some familiar but many of some originality, like the whole calf's liver, stuffed with a mixture of chopped kidney, liver, bone marrow, chopped ham, grated parmesan, beaten eggs, and spices, wrapped in cured ham, cooked in the oven, and served sliced, with a sauce of truffles and butter. A boned piece of leg of veal can be stuffed

with a mixture of chopped lean meat, cured ham, herbs, spices, pine nuts and pistachios, and sliced truffles, cooked, covered, in the oven, moistened with good reduced meat *jus*, and served with a sauce of garlic, chopped onions, and spring onions cooked with ham, butter, mushrooms, truffles, and spices, diluted with the cooking juices, vinegar, and lemon juice.

Veal offal is delicate, and the liver is particularly prized. *Fegato alla veneziana* (*see* LIVER) is a delicacy cooked faster than it takes to describe. The liver is also cooked whole with a stuffing of herbs. BRAINS are a delicacy, as are SWEETBREADS, and veal intestines are a Roman speciality, *la pajata*.

VEGETARIANISM fits comfortably into Italian culture, conditioned perhaps by the many days of abstinence from flesh and dairy products required by the Church, and the voluptuous profusion of delicious fruit and vegetables which abounds. Vegetarian food is not easy to identify in menus, but it is there all the same, and both conviction and pragmatic vegetarians can find appropriate dishes from *tagliolini* with fresh herbs to *melanzane alla parmigiana* and the many vegetable *sformati*. Some early monastic orders were vegetarian, and ate well on an austere diet of pulses and vegetables; in fact, the great trinity of wheat, vine, and olive was the foundation of the Benedictine order, providing the staples of bread, oil, and wine, often enhanced with cheese from the flocks of cows and sheep which were also part of the monastic economy, along with fish from the streams and ponds, and herbs and vegetables from the kitchen garden.

Giacomo CASTELVETRO was nothing if not pragmatic in his attitude to vegetarianism. He needed patrons and a pension, so his mission to persuade the British to eat less meat and sweet things and more fruit and vegetables was expressed with tact and discretion. Exiled in England in the early 17th century, he sensed a budding interest in a new, lighter cuisine and the cultivation of new edible plants in kitchen gardens and orchards, as the many surviving domestic cookery manuscripts confirm. His account through the seasons of the vegetables and fruit of his native Italy offers simple cooking methods and seasonings but is by no means meat-free. Finely sliced cabbage can be simmered in meat broth until half done, then finished off with a mixture of fresh herbs and garlic chopped into hard bacon fat, and served with freshly grated parmesan and pepper—rich and tasty. But so is the "lean" version, where a hearted cabbage is parboiled, quartered, and finished off in butter in the oven or on a low heat. Lyrical over asparagus, versatile with artichokes, Castelvetro entices us gently away from meat with no doctrinal pressure whatsoever.

A century and a half later, Vincenzo COR-RADO wrote beguilingly of the Pythagorean diet made fashionable by philosophers and antiquarians. Both Voltaire and Rousseau, with their unique blends of theory and dyspepsia, had endorsed varying degrees of vegetarianism, and in 1781 Corrado, the urbane and sophisticated cleric, explained the voluptuous delights of vegetable cuisine to the hedonistic pleasure-seekers of 18th century Naples in *Del Cibo Pitagorico ovvero Erbaceo per uso de' nobili, e de' letterati, opera meccanica dell' Oritano Vincenzo Corrado*.

The "nobility and the intellectuals" for whose use this book was intended were a long way from the rural and urban poor, who had been enjoying simple vegetable-based food for millennia. Corrado provided his aristocratic readers with versions of the *coulis*, purées or sauces, and jus of fashionable French cuisine, but deployed them in an inventive and original way. Zucchini *farsite alla Paolina* are carefully hollowed out and stuffed with a mixture of anchovies, pine kernels, chopped herbs, a touch of garlic, and fish (tunny or swordfish), cooked in fish stock, and served with haricot beans cooked

with oil, salt, garlic, herbs, and spring onions, and puréed with anchovies and fillets of white fish to make a gentle creamy sauce.

Artichoke hearts precooked in salty acidulated water are finished in oil with pepper, chopped parsley, and *bottarga* and served with peeled prawns and a sauce made of their shells and trimmings cooked with herbs, butter, and spices, thickened with a little flour, then passed through a sieve.

Writers on CUCINA POVERA are sometimes unkindly scornful of modern "innovative" vegetarian cookery, but Corrado was there already, exuberantly inventive and unashamedly luxurious, naming the more outrageous recipes modestly after himself—*alla Corradina*. One example among many is dried beans cooked in water with bay leaves, and served with a sauce made from ripe sorb apples, *bottarga*, anchovies, chillies, garlic, oregano, and basil pounded together and diluted with olive oil, lemon juice, vinegar, and fish stock.

VENETO is a large region in the northeast of Italy, with a varied landscape and many gastronomic traditions. There are mountainous areas in the north, stretching down from the Dolomites to the prealpine ranges in the southwest, with rich pastures and grazing, and a fertile rolling central part, abutting on EMILIA-ROMAGNA in the south, with abundant agriculture and livestock, with a coastline, the Po delta, and lagoons on the Adriatic, and Venice and its characteristic cuisine. A love of POLENTA is common to all, described by Anna del Conte as a "golden thread running through the cooking of northern Italy," wonderful when enriched with butter and cheese or eaten with meat and fish, but a nutritional disaster when it was the subsistence food of the poor. Rice has been cultivated since the 16th century, and the whole region has an abundance of imaginative risotto recipes. A survivor of this early high-quality rice cultivation is the *riso di Grumolo delle ab-badesse,* grown in a small village halfway between Vicenza and Padua, begun in the 16th century by Benedictine nuns who cleared the land, tamed the water into canals, and grew rice on a large scale, copied later by the local nobility (*Slow Food,* 2002, p. 148). Dried and salt cod (*see* BACCALÀ) are loved and eaten by everyone in the Veneto, although we can get confused by the nomenclature—*baccalà* is their name for stockfish, so the wonderful creamy *baccalà alla vicentina* is in fact made with this, the dried unsalted fish, but pragmatic attempts to recreate that and similar recipes with salt cod can be made to work. Beans are another staple and are used fresh and dry. Cattle and sheep are reared on the fertile rolling plains, as well as the alpine areas, and cured meats and cheeses are numerous.

Vegetables include fine asparagus, especially the fat pinkish blanched spears from Bassano. Bunches of mixed wild shoots, *bruscandoli,* might include wild and woodland asparagus, hops, and other edible young shoots, with a bitterness that is a contrast to the delicate sweetness of the cultivated varieties (*see* WILD GREENS). The tender young peas from the lagoon and those grown inland are much prized in springtime, and prepared with rice and pasta in many imaginative ways. Radicchio, a variety of chicory (*see* ENDIVE) whose shoots are forced and blanched, is renowned—the *rossa di Treviso* is grilled or roasted, while the *rossa di Verona* and the *variegata di Chioggia* are enjoyed in salads. The round and rosy *radicchio di Castelfranco* is used in risottos, where its bitterness makes an agreeable contrast with the blandness of the rice and the mellowness of local cheeses. Small purple artichokes are a speciality of an island in the lagoon, Sant'Erasmo, which gives its name to those produced on other islands and the mainland, where the well-drained, saline soil is fertilised with crab and other shell debris which counteracts the acidity.

Cheeses are made in the mountains and on the plain and include the well-known *asiago.* This delicate table cheese, also good for cooking, becomes more pungent with age. ASIAGO has its DOP (*see* DOC), and is one of the best loved and widely made cheeses in the region, varying between the huge amounts made in large-scale *caseifici* and that from small producers up in the high pastures above Vicenza. The kinds and qualities vary a lot, which is why Slow Food has given particular attention to some specially excellent varieties, like *asiago stravecchio d'allevo di malga,* which is made from the milk of cows of the *rendene* race, adapted over centuries to the pasture and conditions of the area around the commune of Asiago; it is well matured, acquiring added piquancy and depth as it ages. Other kinds of *asiago* are the young *asiago pressato,* fresh and creamy, matured for only a month or so, and the *asiago d'allevo,* which, as the name implies, needs cherishing at every stage of it life, and comes as *mezzano, stagionato,* and *stravecchio. Montasio,* also made in Friuli–Venezia Giulia, it is a fresh table cheese, and used in cooking, getting stronger as it matures. *Vezzena* shares its location with the uplands of Trentino; that made from the milk of cows grazing on the grass and herbs of summer is the one Slow Food goes for, and this keeps its herby creaminess even when matured for some time. *Morlac* or *morlacco* is a cheese from the upland pastures of Monte Grappa; a fine version of it is made from the milk of indigenous cows, *burline,* grazing on fragrant grass and flowers, whose aroma survives the heavy salting of this unpasteurized cheese from skimmed or semiskimmed milk, a subsistence rather than a gastronomic cheese (the cream was taken off for butter) whose flavour went with the everyday food of mountain folk, coarse bread and polenta.

Salami of many kinds are made from all the lesser parts of pigs and other animals, and the more refined cuts, to produce a wide range of cured and cooking sausages and hams.

Horse meat is used more than in other regions, and although we might wish to disregard the myth that the taste derives from a particularly brutal battle between Goths and Lombards in the 6th century, when the surviving populace thought up ways of dealing with all the good meat on the carcasses of slaughtered horses, there is also a tradition of disposing of beasts of burden unfit for work: horses trudging along the route between Genoa, Cremona, and Venice, and ending up at Saonara, the last place on *terraferma*, too tired for the return journey, were slaughtered for food. The *bresaola di cavallo* is a local speciality, and there are also salami from the same area. The *luganega* of Treviso is a cooking sausage using the lesser parts of the pig, sometimes with blood and guts as well, generously spiced with various spice mixtures, and although named for Lucania, a long way away in Basilicata, this traditional use of well-seasoned bits and pieces probably does date back to Roman soldiers on service in Lucania in the 3rd century BC, who brought back home both the delicacy (cured spicy sausages) and the recipe, which we can find in Apicius (Grocock and Grainger, 2006, p. 153).

Fish from the sea and lagoon, the Po delta, and inland rivers and still waters, are cooked in many different ways, with the combination of frugality and opulence characteristic of the region. *Sarde in saor*, a way of preserving even the cheapest little fish of the catch, is a delicacy, and a similar treatment given to carp, trout, and other freshwater fish—first fried, then doused in a pickle of wine or vinegar and flavourings—is both sumptuous and economical. But this is only one of dozens of ways of enjoying sardines or small young fish. Many go into the delicate *antipasti di pesce*, along with shellfish of various kinds, lightly poached, delicate in colour and flavour, dressed only with salt and pepper, oil and lemon. There are as many ways of preparing *bisati* or eels—roast, grilled, basted only with their own rich fat, or the richness mitigated by simmering in a

sauce of red or white wine and aromatics, thickened at the end with flour browned golden in butter. *Brusiolo* is a way of cooking young squid on the remote island of San Piero in Volta, simmered for hours with oil, onion, rosemary, salt, and a little tomato purée and water, loosened with a little white wine from time to time, and served as a sauce for plain boiled rice. Squid, cooked to melting tenderness in its ink, and eaten with polenta, is a rich contrast to the simply grilled or fried expensive fish like *branxin* or *orada* (sea bass), turbot, or monkfish. Sea bass or trout can also be baked on a bed of sliced lemon, anointed with oil and salt and pepper. Trout can be stuffed with sage and parsley butter, covered in white wine and seasoned with salt and pepper, and baked; when done, a slug of grappa is poured over and set alight. Eels, snails, and freshwater fish are inland delicacies, as well as small freshwater sardines, the *agone* of Lake Garda, and the *cavedano*, which is often fried, then finished in a dish of fresh young peas.

Lake Garda to the west has been a place of delight since Roman times, and its charms, and the poetry in praise of them, have been an inspiration to later cultures. Ovid and Virgil were from those parts and delighted in the landscape, while even Dante mitigated the gloom of his Inferno with a lyrical description in canto 20 of the charms of Benaco. Men of letters liked to seek out references to its gastronomic delights as well as literary and visual ones; MANTEGNA frolicked with his friend the disreputable epigrapher Felice Feliciano among the orange and lemon groves in his search for Roman inscriptions, which he later incorporated in his paintings, along with the golden fruit, among swags of foliage inspired by Roman sculpture. PLATINA described the renown of the *carpione*, a fish of the Salmonidae family, unique to Lake Garda, which our antiquaries might well have enjoyed whilst celebrating their discoveries. SCAPPI described their flesh as whiter than trout, and explained how they are cooked round Lake Garda, first salted, then deep fried in oil, and put into hot vinegar or a *salamoia*, then packed in boxes with some of the fragrant fronds of bay and myrtle that so enchanted Mantegna, a luxury distributed far and wide. Luca Pacioli's *Summa de arithmetica*, first published in 1494, has this in the colophon of a reprint of 1523: *"Novamente impressa in Toscolano su la riva dil Benacense et unico carpionista laco; amenissimo sito"* (Newly reissued in Tusculum on the shores of Benaco, most charming site and unique home of *carpioni*). The mathematical monk, inventor of double-entry bookkeeping and a system of proportion based on the circle and the square, was also enthusiastic about Roman inscriptional letters, and their geometric construction, and seems to have shared a delight in the lake and its less abstract amenities.

The Renaissance flourished in the Veneto, where the enthusiasm for classical culture was fed by this abundance of classical remains and artefacts. Palladio was a protégé of the poet and philosopher Giangiorgio Trissino, and under his influence became the architect who best defined the new style. Both had a sense of contemporary vernacular culture, in literature and architecture. Palladio's buildings belonged in their surroundings in the same way Trissino hoped a rejuvenated, non-Tuscan language would convey classical themes in straightforward Italian. Palladio wrote in a clear, matter-of-fact Italian, as he might have spoken it, with a humane concern for the everyday life going on in and around his buildings, unlike the heavy theorising, in Latin, of Vitruvius, Alberti, and Serlio. His villas were the icing on a rich organic homemade cake; not just an idealised version of life in the ancient world but a practical form of investment in land and property by the nobles of Vicenza, Verona, and Venice, combining land reclamation and estate management with high culture, and organising farm buildings and the appurtenances of a country house into a harmonious visual and functional whole. Palladio's *Quattro libri dell'architettura* is a clear exposition of the fundamentals of classical architecture, but when he comes to describe these country villas, he writes of the realities of everyday life, not of little gems in an idyllic landscape. He delights us with practical details of how to combine efficient farming with an elegant summer retreat, making it clear that the workforce who ran the estate should also have convenient and pleasant quarters, that animals and farming equipment should be housed in decent spaces, that the necessary dovecotes were placed in decorative towers and turrets, the cattle kept downwind of the princely apartments, but not too far away to escape scrutiny, the kitchens with top lighting in the lower ground floor, grain stored in the attics behind the portico, above the frescoed *piano nobile*, and the functional and noble elements of the villa linked by pillared covered walkways or *loggias* to protect master and servants from driving rain or summer heat. Water and fresh air were important—look at the cattle and where they drink, he said: the strong healthy ones had the benefit of clear flowing streams, and another way you can tell if the water is any good is if it makes good bread, and if pulses cook quickly in it (*"quell'acqua è tenuta perfetta che fa buon pane, e nella quale i legumi presto si cuoceno"*). One villa near Treviso exploited a spring in the rocks; it was channelled into a fountain, which fed a pool full of carp, then flowed downhill to supply the kitchen with running water, then on to the gardens, and finally filled cattle troughs on the public highway. Not too far from Catullus's "crystal brook high on a mountain top that gushes forth from a mossy rock and after tumbling headlong down a steep valley sweeps straight across the highway thronged with people—welcome refreshment to the traveller in his weary sweat, when the sultry heat cracks the parched soil" (Dalby, *Empire of Pleasures*, 2000, p. 88)—a passage which might have been known to Palladio and his patrons.

Roads, canals and waterways linked these inland investments, and this combination of sea-based wealth and productive husbandry created a prosperous region. The great banquet scenes by VERONESE show the flamboyant display of wealth that these rich merchant princes enjoyed. It is claimed that the cuisine of Veneto is one of the most refined in Italy, a legacy of this sophistication, and it is not hard to imagine feasts described by Scappi (his work was published in the same year, 1570, as the *Quattro libri*, in a clear and rational Italian very like that of Palladio), served amidst the bustle and ostentation of these vast canvases. And some of his recipes for the humble pulses prudently stashed away in Palladian attics are equally subtle. Chickpeas, soaked in tepid water with a little lye to loosen the outer skins, are well rinsed, then mixed with oil, salt, and a little flour, and simmered slowly, covered in fresh water four fingers deep, along with sprigs of rosemary and sage, whole garlic cloves, and pepper. Dried beans are cleaned and rinsed, then partly cooked in water, drained, and finished with fresh water, dried chestnuts, a mixture of flour, salt, and oil, sage, whole garlic cloves, cinnamon, saffron, and sometimes rice. Dried broad beans are given the usual soaking, then simmered with salt, oil, and water, and finished with lightly fried chopped onions and fresh herbs, pepper, and saffron. Not *cucina povera*, as the use of expensive spices and saffron indicates, but the cuisine of a rich landowner living off the land. Today's *risi e fasioi* is in this robust tradition: soaked beans are stirred into some chopped onion and pancetta browned in butter and oil, then simmered with broth; when soft, rice is added and cooked slowly until done, then the dish is doused with a slug of grappa and plenty of pepper, and eaten tepid. *Riso alla pilota* (*see* RICE) is a hearty dish of rice cooked by the evaporation method, which involves less care and attention than a classic risotto and is said to have been made by workers known as *piloti*, busy husking and winnowing rice, who poured it into a pot of boiling water, in a mound like a pyramid, gave it a good boil, then clapped the lid on, sealed it hermetically, and left it to cook while they carried on toiling. The mound of rice, preferably *vialone* or *arborio*, with the grains separate and firm, is a total reversal of the risotto technique, in which al dente grains wallow in a dense creamy liquid, thickened by the starch particles loosened by the bashing of the grains against the side of the pan during cooking. A hearty sauce of fried onions and a crumbled fatty local sausage completes the dish of *riso alla pilota*. *Risi e bisi*, a springtime recipe, is made with fresh young peas and a small-grained risotto rice like *vialone nano*; a pea for every grain of rice is the aspiration, and shelling them a labour of love. (They creep into one of Donna Leon's crime stories, where a very early springtime dish of *risi e bisi* prepared by Commisario Brunetti's wife Paola affirms the wholesomeness of his domestic life, a contrast to the murky worlds of Venetian crime.) Some recipes cook the peas first, for about 10 minutes, before adding the rice, which will take another 20 minutes—confusing, for very fresh young peas do not usually need 30 minutes cooking, so what you do has to depend on the age and tenderness of the peas. A broth made from their shells, sometimes with meat or chicken stock, puréed and strained, adds colour and flavour. Diced pancetta and chopped onion are cooked in oil or butter, together with a handful of parsley, finely chopped, and the peas and rice are then cooked in this (in whatever seems the appropriate sequence) with the broth, and served with parmesan, with a result that can be soupy or more solid according to taste. A traditional family recipe from Venice seems the ideal treatment (Zuliani 1978, p. 63); the peas are partly cooked on their own in the chopped onion and pancetta, very quickly to keep their green colour, and then added to the rice, which has been simmering separately in chicken broth; finely chopped parsley is stirred in right at the end, along with some parmesan, to achieve a really bright fresh green colour (overcooked peas acquire a slightly khaki hue). Another rice and pulse dish from the same source involves cooking rice in a purée of well-cooked dried beans, and some of their liquid, finished with chopped onion, oil, butter, parsley, and freshly ground black pepper, the bean liquid absorbed by the rice into a creamy mass. Alternatively, the rich bean purée is eaten tepid alongside piping hot *riso in cagnon*, plain boiled rice into which plenty of butter and cheese have been stirred. This combination is described by the authors: *"In çerte famegie venessiane, sto 'riso in cagnon' i lo dopara par zontarlo (servire a parte e caldo) a un puré de fasioi fredo. El contrasto fra el puré fredo e i risi caldi el xe de una delicatessa che non ve digo!"* (Some Venetian families serve this rice dish hot alongside a cool bean purée. The contrast between the hot rice and the cold beans is unspeakably delicate!; Zuliani, p. 67). *Pasta e fagioli* is another classic of the Veneto; nutritionally this combination of beans, pasta and vegetables is just about perfect—for manual labourers—and for us, taken in small quantities. Cooked with care, using Lamon beans from Belluno, and home-made egg pasta, it is a delicacy. The soaked beans are simmered with a nice meaty ham bone, or leg (some versions include bacon rind, a pig's trotter, and chopped *lardo*), and a *soffritto* of onion, garlic, celery, bay leaves, and parsley cooked in oil and butter, oil, and pasta are added towards the end, with some of the beans crushed to thicken the brew. Some recipes are at pains to eliminate excess fat, a noble aspiration, but maybe somewhat misplaced. Commercial short pasta works well; *borlotti* beans are suitable; the combination of ingredients is best not enshrined in dogma, but allowed to depend on resources. *Minestrone grasso alla bellunese* omits the pasta and adds celery, carrots, tomato, potatoes, parsley, and basil.

Polenta is comfort food combined with visual pleasure; it can be a filling dish, eaten in large helpings with small amounts of something well flavoured, or as an accompaniment to dishes like a rich dark deep meat or game stew, or one of the many pungent or creamy dishes of salt or dried cod. It can be enriched with butter and cheese and baked, perhaps grilled or fried, cut into small shapes and cooked as gnocchi, and added to bread and cakes. The *zaleti* of Venice are small biscuits made with corn meal. Pietro Longhi's painting of 1740, *La Polenta*, conveys the love, almost reverence, of the populace for this staple. Two rather pale moon-faced women serve the thick yellow mass from a copper pan onto a clean towel, watched by two men, with the more robust complexions of an outdoor life, gazing with rapture at this reassuring sight; the man on the left breathes in the delectable aroma with half-closed eyes, and his companion on the right plays a primitive musical instrument, barely distinguishable from the long pole used by one of the women in her constant stirring of the polenta—a glimpse of low life that appealed to the clients who bought Longhi's paintings of aristocratic flummery, for they, too, shared similar tastes in food. (The malnutrition attendant on this nutritionally inadequate ingredient might account for the unhealthy looks of the women.)

With beans, rice, and polenta prepared in so many inventive ways, it is not surprising that pasta does not get much of a look in, although noodles and dumplings were often made at home. The exception is *bigoli*, at one time made by most families with a soft wheat, buckwheat, or wholemeal flour dough, with or without eggs; this is then made into *bigoli* in a piece of equipment operated by a sort of screw press which forces the pasta through a perforated disk at the bottom of a metal cylinder to give a mass of twisted, ridged strands—compared by Ranieri da Mosto (Da Mosto, 1969, p. 126) to the snake-like locks of the Gorgon's head. The virtue of this method is that it produces a rough surface which is ideal for holding the rich sauces traditionally prepared for *bigoli*. The simplest is *agio e ogio*, a cold uncooked mixture of olive oil and garlic pounded with parsley and plenty of coarsely ground pepper, used in generous abundance (worlds away from the *oglio, aglio, peperoncino* of Lazio). The *bigoli in salsa* of Venice are served with a sauce of finely sliced onions melted in oil without changing colour (adding water from time to time to prevent this), into which some deboned and desalted *sarde* or—this is where confusion might arise—anchovies have been mixed until melted into the sauce. Another sauce for *bigoli* is made from the innards of a stewed duck, chopped together with the fried liver and moistened with some of the duck broth, in which the dark version of *bigoli* will have been cooked. There are also gnocchi and stuffed pasta recipes, as varied as the *casunziei ampezzani*, substantial ravioli stuffed with grated turnips and beetroot, or the *casonzei* from Belluno with their filling of spinach and cheese. A traditional rhyme includes pasta making among the activities of a diligent housewife (see panel).

A painting by Giovanni Bellini in the National Gallery in London, *The Madonna of the Meadow*, painted around 1500, has a background glimpse of life in the fertile inland areas of the *terraferma*, with mountains in the blue distance, gentle rolling hills, fortified castles perched upon them, and cattle, sheep, and goats watched over by caring humans. Traditional beef recipes are for mature animals too old to work, tasty but needing long slow cooking, but the poultry were renowned for their plump tenderness; the chickens of Padua, the turkeys of Vicenza, the pigeons of Treviso, and the ducks, geese, and guinea fowl of the entire region were used in recipes like the *paeta rosta al magaragno*, roast turkey basted with pomegranate juice, or pot roasted turkey cooked with butter and sage, and finished in pomegranate juice, served

La sa stizar el fuogo
la sa lavar squele
la fa ben papardele
la stìa ben fen in prò
la sa ingrassar un bo
la mena a pascolo i puorci
la sa ben vender e comprare

She knows how to stoke the fire
how to wash the clouts
make good noodles
how to fatten up an ox
take the pigs to graze
and how to buy and sell.*

*From a dialect wedding verse, *Mariazo* (Coltro, 1983, p. 17)

with the liver and giblets, which have been chopped small and cooked slowly in oil and pomegranate juice, served, jointed, on a dish decorated with glowing pomegranate seeds—a reminder of an ancient Persian dish, *fesenjan*, a *khoresh* of pheasant in which the sweetness and astringency of the pomegranate juice is balanced by the gentle bitterness of walnuts and spices. Merchants and mariners might have enjoyed this on their travels, or met it in the deep south of Italy, where Arab influences survived. A farmyard chicken, fat and plump and all ready for the first beans of the season, makes a rich dish for high summer; the beans are cooked separately (*borlotti* or *cannellini*, not green beans) and seasoned with a sauce made of the chopped up innards of the bird, fried with garlic, onion, salt anchovies, parsley, basil, rosemary, and *sopressa*, a local salami, moistened with white wine and well seasoned with pepper. The carved chicken, oven roasted or pot roasted, is served in a big dish over the seasoned beans. Goose is a festive dish throughout the region, often stuffed with puréed cooked apples and chestnuts, seasoned, and bound with egg, and served with sliced apples fried in butter and more chestnuts. Ducks, wild and tame, have flourished in the aquatic habitat of the lagoons, and grown fat in inland farmyards, and recipes are rich and sumptuous. They are often cooked stuffed with a rich mixture which might include the chopped innards, fried with garlic and herbs, mixed with the chopped liver, breadcrumbs, pine nuts, and raisins. This rich treatment of a luxury bird was not everyday food, but was a treat at the many *sagre* or local festivities; the feast of the Redentore was celebrated in Venice with fireworks on the Giudecca and everyone enjoying stuffed roast duck from outdoor tables. Once they would have been the wild ducks, *osei*, of the Lagoon, but there were never enough of them to go round, what with being offered as tribute to doges and popes and hard to catch as well. The Carpaccio painting of what is sometimes described as a bird hunt on the lagoon, but might be a fishing expedition with trained cormorants, gives some idea of the enthusiasm for the pleasures of the chase.

Meat and cheeses and agricultural prosperity are celebrated by Bellini, while Carpaccio was evoking the polyglot, multiracial world of Venice, flaunting its access to luxury goods from the far and near east, and the bustling canals and open spaces, noisy with commerce and fragrant with the most elusive and expensive of all their wares—spices. Venice dominated the whole region, while looking east and growing wealthy and powerful through trade and aggressive seamanship. The fishermen who long ago found a perilous sort of security on lumps of mud protruding from the lagoon evolved over centuries into statesmen and explorers operating from a proud city of amazing beauty. The spices that were part of Venice's trading wealth did not fall in a cloud over every dish; always expensive, they were deployed with restraint, and today only a faint reminder of their use can be found, for example, in the *peverata*, although the historic use of spices

survives more in sausages and preserved meats than in cooking. An anonymous manuscript of the 14th century, *Libro per cuoco*, now in the Casanatense Library in Rome (Anonimo Veneziano), gives an idea of the use of spices in sauces and complex cooked dishes. Spice mixtures made up by the cook or *speziale*, druggist, would be to suit the taste of the master of the house; usually *dolce* or *fine*, mild, or *forte*, strong. Much has been written about the exoticism and mystery of these substances, but by the time they got to the (locked) kitchen cupboard they were down-to-earth, if expensive, ingredients, chosen and used for the immediate pleasures of aroma and taste and their practical medicinal properties. Recipe 74 for sweet spices has cloves, cinnamon, ginger, and mace pounded together in a mortar. The strong spices are cloves, pepper, long pepper, and nutmeg. The sweet spices went into a delicate sauce for chicken made by mixing fairly sharp pomegranate juice with a sweet wine and flavouring it with sweet spices, anise seeds, and rosewater. In contrast, a potent, harsh, black sauce for wild boar uses long pepper, *melegueta* pepper (grains of paradise), and ginger pounded with bread toasted black as sin and soaked in vinegar, and some of the meat to give it body, diluted with some of the meat broth. The world of Saracens and Turks, trading and dining partners rather than enemies, is evoked in a mild sauce, *savore tartaresco perfettissimo*, for roast piglet, made of peeled garlic cloves blanched in boiling water pounded with almonds, cooked egg yolks, ginger, cloves, cinnamon, and sugar, diluted with vinegar. A *salsa sarasinesca* is made of almonds pounded with raisins, ginger, cinnamon, cloves, grains of paradise, nutmeg, cardamom, and *galangal*, diluted with verjuice. Lovers of Middle Eastern food might perhaps find more pleasure and familiarity in these recipes than would a modern Venetian. Today there are few dishes using spices in a significant way; even the traditional *peverada*, made of bone marrow cooked in butter and then in broth with breadcrumbs, heavily seasoned with a lot of freshly ground black pepper and sometimes cinnamon, with a handful of parmesan as a knockout blow at the end, is a shadow of those medieval delicacies. One version of it, served with roast guinea fowl, adds parsley, garlic, and anchovies. The *pearà*, a sauce to go with boiled meats of various kinds, uses the same thickening of breadcrumbs pounded with bone marrow cooked in butter and simmered in some of the beef broth with salt and pepper to make a creamy sauce, described as *"del tutto sconsigliabile per i stomachi deboli"* (Da Mosto, p. 264), and no wonder, for a medieval cook would have countered this dull richness with a selection of digestive spices and a hint of acidity to the benefit of all concerned. The move away from strong spices began early; by the beginning of the 17th century Giacomo Castelvetro, resident for many years in Venice, was seasoning his vegetable recipes with salt, pepper, oil, and bitter orange juice, and only occasionally used "strong spices" as well. Venice was then in commercial and political decline, and tastes had changed. The English housewives Castelvetro was trying to persuade to eat less meat were in fact using the mild spices like cinnamon and nutmeg plentifully. What is interesting is that he was describing the everyday food of ordinary folk, simple, fresh, and unpretentious. Although a native of Modena, Castelvetro had lived long enough in Venice to be familiar with the vegetable glories of the republic, and maybe appreciated them more than the British ambassador, Sir Dudley Carleton, who had rescued him from the dreaded *piombi* after he was grabbed by the Inquisition. Castelvetro left town in a hurry, and Carleton was glad to be transferred to the Hague, for a more vibrant diplomatic career; his letters are void of any insights into Venetian life, which bored him, while Castelvetro, who loved it, gives us some unforgettable vignettes of market women trimming artichoke bottoms, ladies growing

climbing beans in their window boxes, and the entrepreneurial landowners round Verona cultivating asparagus on an industrial scale, for their great pleasure and profit.

Another resident who left town in a hurry, Giacomo Casanova, exploited the gastronomic possibilities of his imprisonment in the *piombi* by demanding the best oil from Lucca for his salads, which he then used for an illicit lamp to illuminate his night-time excavations, throwing the salad away as being inedible without its dressing. When he needed to convey a long knife to a fellow prisoner, he achieved the risky undertaking by trying to conceal it in a large book, disguising the protruding end by using the book as a sort of tray on which to balance an overflowing bowl of *pasta in brodo* swimming with butter, swathed in a cloth to protect the book; the deliberately orchestrated confusion of this performance rendered the jailor who had to carry this perilous burden quite incapable of detecting the ruse. We can only speculate that the dish might have been *bigoli* in a duck broth.

It was centuries after Carpaccio painted his colourful paintings, crowded with everyday life and exotic glimpses of other races and their imported luxuries, that his name was given to a colourful and intriguing dish, a rare example of an "invention" that really can be pinned down to a particular time and place—Harry's Bar in the 1960s or thereabouts, where Giuseppe Cipriani devised his *carpaccio*, a lean and pleasant offering for the countess Amalia Nani Mocenigo, who for health reasons was on a strict diet which had to include raw meat. Wafer-thin slices of prime tender beef, trimmed of any scrap of fat or sinews, were served raw with a sprinkling of salt and a decorative swirl of a light mayonnaise flavoured with mustard and Worcester sauce (spices creeping in by the back door). The warm red of the beef in his recipe reminded Cipriani of the deep reds in the paintings in a stunning exhibition in the Palazzo Ducale in 1963 of works by

Carpaccio, a name to conjure with, which is what everyone has been doing ever since, naming anything raw, from beef to fish to vegetables, given this elegant treatment.

It would be churlish to make too much of the similarity with *carne al'Albese*, an ancient speciality of Alba in Piedmont, where similar slices, or a mound of finely chopped raw beef, are served with a light dressing of oil and lemon juice, often graced with shavings of parmesan and white truffles.

VENISON. *See* DEER.

VERDURA, greenery, means any edible green plant, wild or cultivated. But the "greenery" we admire in landscapes is "verde." "Verde" can also mean fresh or young when applied to vegetables and fruit, or rare when applied to meat. *See* WILD GREENS.

VERJUICE, *agresto*, is obtained from the fresh or fermented juice of unripe grapes, giving a sour flavour in cooking. It was used as a cooking medium, and as an addition to sauces, being as plentiful as vinegar in wine-producing areas. It gives a fresh, light acidity which is less biting than vinegar, and was remembered rather smugly by Platina, recalling a simple chicken dish, *pollo in agresto*, that he had enjoyed at the house of Poggio Bracciolini, in the years he spent studying in Florence—an example of the new cuisine of the Renaissance (offspring of the New Learning of the Renaissance)—in which fried chicken was finished in freshly squeezed unripe grape juice and chopped herbs. Illustrations in the various *Tacuina sanitatis*, health handbooks produced in northern Italy in the late 15th century, show an idyllic early summer scene, with two men sitting under a pergola of vines, contentedly crushing bunches of grapes to make this refreshing condiment. Verjuice has recently seen

something of a revival in North America, where it is used in many imaginative ways. The juice of ripe grapes is less acid, and used to make MUST and *sapa*, which are both sweet and are mentioned elsewhere. *See also* SOURNESS.

VERMICELLI. *See* PASTA, HISTORY; PASTA SHAPES.

VERONESE, Paolo Caliari (1528–1588), known as Veronese, worked in Venice from 1551 until his death in 1588. SCAPPI too had been in Venice in the service of Cardinal Grimani from 1528 to 1535. Later, working in Rome, he might have heard of the magnificent banquet Grimani held in Venice in 1542 for the nephew of Pope Paul III. Veronese was only 13 years old then, still working in Verona, but by the time he had established himself in Venice, with a large number of wealthy patrons, many of them clerics, he would have become familiar with similar banquets enjoyed by the Venetian nobility. The contract for the most grandiose of his banquet scenes was signed in 1562, *The Wedding Feast at Cana*, a vast panoramic canvas across one end of the refectory of Palladio's church of San Giorgio Maggiore. The painting is now in the Louvre, after the villainous theft of it by Napoleon. What strikes us, as food historians, is the depiction of a contemporary feast, with participants in modern dress, a version of a Bible story which vaunts the wealth and splendour of aristocratic Venetian life, in which the miracle of turning water into wine passes almost unnoticed in the thronging bustle of serving and eating, the passing of dishes, the reaching out for goblets, the snuffling of domestic pets, the cries of pages and waiters, and the band, not strumming tactfully in the background, but center stage, a small chamber orchestra with Titian himself playing the cello. The discipline and decorum of Scappi's menus

dissolves into an ordered chaos, a missing dimension is brought to our understanding of one of the greatest cookery books of the modern world. Not that this, and the four banquet scenes painted by Veronese ten years later, tell us as much as we could have wished about the exact appearance of the food.

The Last Supper in the Academia in Venice illustrates a Bible story in modern dress and gives a glimpse of a banquet towards the end (half-concealed by a pillar, a guest deftly handles one of the perfumed toothpicks which came with the sticky candied fruits in the final course). Wines and food are being called for by guests and master of ceremonies; dishes from the kitchen on the right, or from the tall stepped *credenza* with its rows of silver and gold plate just visible on the left, are being passed round in a flurry of movement and noise. The idealised architectural fantasy in the background is a foil to the realism of the meal; one wonders how the musicians ever made themselves heard. This secular modernity got Veronese into trouble with the Inquisition in 1573, but, unrepentant, he simply renamed the work *Feast in the House of Levi*, and carried on as before. A head count indicates that more than 20 guests were being attended by 30 or more servants of various ranks.

Long family lunches in Italy can go on for many hours; food and drink arrive slowly, with a similar slow rhythm, but without the burdens of protocol. But it is quite another thing to try to imagine the impact of Scappi's or Messisbugo's banquets or figure out how the participants managed to handle the sequence of dishes; typically 136 dishes over 17 courses, excluding a few salads to start with, and sugared comfits and preserved fruits to round things off. Perhaps one should think of them as *tapas*—when a group share exquisite small portions of many things, sipping drinks and chatting, with always the option of doing without or asking for something else instead. Dishes were brought to table with ceremony and

placed there, sometimes overlapping, but could then be passed around, while calls for the different wines on offer were dealt with by a flurry of pages and waiters. Veronese shows us this ebb and flow of people and food, the scuffles between pages and servants, the presence of pets, with a tough tabby cat giving two wary greyhounds a very bad time, in the foreground of *Feast in the House of Levi*. The contents of the overlapping plates and dishes are none too clear in the paintings, but we can get all that from Messisbugo and Scappi, and the paintings mitigate the fearsome precision of the printed accounts. To Veronese's sense of movement and ordered confusion we can add the sounds of the musicians he placed in the foreground, some of it so ravishing that *"ogn'uno pareva essere di quivi alle superne parti passato"* (everyone felt transported from here to higher things), as Messisbugo said of the performance by M. Alphonso dalla Viola with six voices, six viols, a lyre, a lute, a guitar, a trombone, a large flute, a medium-sized flute, a German flute, a sourdine, and two plucked instruments.

Veronese's massive *Wedding Feast at Cana*, looted by Napoleon from Palladio's refectory in S. Giorgio Maggiore in Venice and now in the Louvre, shows the musicians in the foreground, between us and the table; the players, in an almost indecipherable foreshortening, are also hard at work, intent on a single sheet of music, concentrating on each other—they are indeed in a world apart. The conversation of the guests hums all around them; the activities of the dogs (prestigious possessions, status symbols comparable to the musical instruments), of officials and servants, and of the pensive, preoccupied master of ceremonies, exhausted at the end of several hours of intense effort, monitoring every move and directing operations, are all part of the sound and movement. We are at the dessert course: the shallow plates and bowls contain comfits, seeds, spices, or nuts coated in sugar, and fruit in syrup—hence the perfumed toothpicks, which had a dual purpose, essential at the end of the meal, and useful for spearing sticky things.

The precise details of the dishes served up in these vast canvases are unclear, but they must have been as fashionable as the rich costumes and music. Fortunately, lesser painters, like the BASSANO family, or Vicenzo CAMPI, give us more information.

VIGNAROLA is a currently fashionable Roman dish made only in the early spring when the ingredients are tiny, tender, and at their freshest. We are told that there is no point in even thinking of making this at any other time of year, or even, Romans would assure you, in any other place. Markets often sell the ingredients ready prepared, but in fact the pleasure of handling these prime ingredients is part of the enjoyment in making the dish. Sliced spring onions are softened but not browned in olive oil and some diced pancetta; then in go the first young broad beans and peas, shelled, together with some small baby artichokes, quartered or sliced (they are so immature that the choke is nonexistent), and after simmering for 10 minutes, the leaves from the hearts of a romaine lettuce are added, with a little white wine, and once this has evaporated, the vegetables are covered and simmered very slowly until soft. This is usually served as an antipasto. *La bazzoffia*, a more liquid version from the Pontine Marshes in southern Lazio, is served over poached eggs on a slice of bread, and seasoned with grated pecorino. *Scafata alla moda di Cori*, also from the Pontine Marshes, includes diced new potatoes and water to make a more liquid soup. It is possible that the name *vignarola* is fairly recent, for there are many similar versions of this dish, without a specific name, using fresh peas, or artichokes, or young broad beans, on their own, cooked with chopped onion in diced pancetta or *guanciale*; in fact, too rigid a definition would exclude other young vegetables, the shoots of wild asparagus, immature wild figs, green garlic leaves, baby carrots, young spinach, anything that the *vignarole*, the young women who hoed and weeded the vineyards in the early spring, would make with what they found growing there. In recent years, this has become trendy enough for one of our brazen young telly chefs to take it to his heaving bosom in an accessible version, but earlier works on traditional Roman food mention neither the recipe nor the name, and one could see *vignarola* as a quite recent variation on the truly Roman *fave al guanciale*, which depends on the special quality of the broad beans of Lazio—something like the way *tiramisù* is a variation on trifle.

VINCISGRASSI. *See* MARCHE.

VINEGAR, *aceto*, perhaps the most ubiquitous source of sourness, is still made in large quantities on a domestic scale, and is available in a wide range of good-quality commercial products. Wine becomes vinegar thanks to certain microorganisms, bacterial acids, which get to work on the alcohol in the wine, turning it, in the presence of oxygen, into an acid; this all happens when a "vinegar mother" taken from an earlier batch is added to the selected wine and the subsequent processes of maturing, clarification, and filtering take place. The industrial process is different, but controlled by stringent legislation, and authenticated before point of sale, producing something more consistent but perhaps less individual than the cherished homemade vinegars many Italian families make whenever they have the materials to hand. Vinegar is used in marinades, in pickling and preserving, and, with restraint, in salads, where oil is the most important seasoning, applied with a generous hand, salt with caution, and vinegar in miserly quantities. The exception is a salad of *puntarelle* (*see*

ENDIVE) which is dressed with salted anchovies mashed up with garlic in red wine vinegar and little or no oil.

Flavoured vinegars are made by infusing aromatic substances in vinegar, such as tarragon, basil, and chillies; BALSAMIC VINEGAR is the misleading name for a substance that is not a vinegar at all, even though vinegar may sometimes play a small part in its inception.

In the past, vinegar was valued for its medicinal as well as its culinary uses, and combined with water and flavourings, made a healthy drink. *Posca*, vinegar and water, was what Andrew Dalby describes as "the regular beverage of the classical Roman army on bad days." The Romans mixed vinegar with honey to make a sort of aperitif (as they did with wine, to make *mulsum*) with digestive properties, as well as a nice taste.

Vinegar or wine in a marinade tenderises and flavours meat; when put into a stew early on and allowed to evaporate, and when added towards the end of cooking, vinegar can sharpen or modify the taste of the dish, like the squeeze of lemon or bitter orange juice, or the decorative pips of pomegranates, added just before serving.

A way of preserving that most perishable of food, fish, is to pickle it in brine or vinegar in various ways. From being a necessity some of these methods have became a pleasure, like *sardelle in saor*, where fried sardines are matured in a sauce of sliced onions cooked in olive oil, and finished in white wine vinegar. Many freshwater and sea fish were treated in similar ways in the past, changing an ephemeral food to an even more delicious commodity which would keep for some time. Scappi gives a recipe for pike, carefully scaled, cleaned, and salted, then floured and fried slowly in oil, and when cooked, immersed briefly in a bath of boiling vinegar, flavoured with salt, sugar, and spices, or left in the solution, where it would keep for up to 10 days.

VIOLET. *See* FLOWERS.

VIOLINO DI CAPRA is made from the thigh, from knee to hip, of GOAT (also lamb, kid, or chamois), including the bone, but trimmed of skin, fat, and sinews. It is marinated for about 10 days in white wine, salt, pepper, juniper berries, and bay leaves, followed by a couple of months first in a dry, well-ventilated spot, then in an enclosed cold place. It does not look all that much like a violin, but is small enough to be carved with a sharp knife held like a violin bow, to the delight of gastro-tourists visiting Valtellina or Valchiavenna in Lombardy, its place of origin.

VITELLO TONNATO.
See VEAL.

VONGOLA(E). *See* PALOURDE.

W

WAFER, *cialda,* is best known today in the form of an ICE CREAM cone or cornet, but claims that this was "invented" in North America during the early years of the 20th century are flying in the face of history, for the delectable crisp thin wafer has been made in many European countries since the 15th century. A mixture of fine flour, powdered sugar, egg yolk, milk, and butter, nowadays perfumed with vanilla, is poured into a patterned round iron disk, hinged to a similar one, which then is then closed and put over the fire, and turned to cook on both sides. It can then be turned out and served hot, sprinkled with sugar, flat or rolled into cylinders, suitable for filling with mixtures of sweetened cream or ricotta, or dunked in appropriate drinks. The metal disks, *ferri, pinze* or *goffriere,* used to make them were traditionally decorated with sacred designs, or more secular coats of arms and emblems, to create festive wafers for banquets and celebrations.

Maria Vittoria DELLA VERDE, a generation later, has a less coherent, more hands-on description, from her convent kitchen, with tips about the consistency of the batter (flavoured with anise), the way to oil the irons with bacon rind, or three hen feathers dipped in oil, or how to hold the wafer up to the light to see if the texture is right.

Waffles, with their characteristic honeycomb texture, cooked between two textured hot metal plates, are part of the same family, though more common in the Netherlands and the United States.

Costanzo FELICI described wafers in the 1560s (Felici, 1986, p. 116):

S'intride parimente questa farina molto liquida e flussibile, che poi a poco a poco si cuoce fra ferri caldi segnati e fatti a posta, in forma rotonda, sottile como la carta e chiamasi nevola o cialda; overo al medemo modo s'intride aggiongendovi mele o zuccaro e cuocesi fra li medemi ferri e chiamasi cialdone quali si reducono in canelli.

This flour can also be worked as a fluid, liquid mixture which is cooked a little at a time between patterned hot metal disks, round in shape, made specially for this purpose, it is thin as paper and called *nevola* or *cialda.* They can be made in the same way adding honey or sugar, cooked in the same irons, which are rolled into cylinders and called *cialdone.*

WALLFLOWER. *See* FLOWERS.

WALNUT, *noce,* fruit of *Juglans regia,* is sometimes mistakenly translated as "nut", which is confusing when it is used empirically to indicate the size of an ingredient, like a lump of butter, a meatball, or a dumpling (*see* NUT). There are many different kinds of

Walnut trees grow throughout Italy and are valued for their wood and oil, in addition to their nuts. (Shutterstock)

walnut in Italy—the large *noce di Sorrento*, from Campania, famous for the quality of its walnuts, the medium-sized *premice* or *cinciallegra*, used mostly for oil, and the *noce di Benevento*, *noce Feltrina*, *albina*, *di montagna*, *vellana*, *regina*, *malecia*, *Putignao*, *lobrecina*, and *cardella*. This ancient tree is widespread throughout Italy, valued for its wood, and its oil, which was both medicinal and a substitute for olive oil, and was also used in lamps and as furniture polish, while the leaves, dried and fresh, had curative value, used in potions and as poultices, while the nuts are usually eaten dried, the bitter outer membrane removed, today mainly in sweet cakes, breads and biscuits, but also in sauces and stuffings. It is not surprising that a tree with such qualities has been an object of veneration for centuries, associated with the revelries and cults held around the summer solstice. The great walnut tree of Benevento was the centre of persistent pagan practise: gatherings of witches from all over the world took to the skies and landed beneath it, disguised as wild boars, goats, and cats—something the Lombards seemed to encourage, hence the ritual destruction of the tree in the 7th century by the Catholic bishop Barbato, at the time of the defeat of Romualdo by Constance II. (The evidence for this legend comes from later records, when the persecution of witches was gathering strength in 17th-century Europe.) The tree lived on in folk memory, and there must have been many others to replace it, so the coincidence of the feast day of San Giovanni Battista on 24

June with the summer solstice on 21 June was exploited by the Church; the wanton revels that would not go away were sanitised and brought under some kind of control, and young women who on Midsummer's Eve might have been rolling in the dew to promote fecundity were virtuously gathering green walnuts, barefoot and bareheaded, using only a wooden knife, for the making of NOCINO. The green walnuts were picked before the shell and its contents became hard and dry, split into four, and macerated in pure alcohol with sugar, spices, usually cinnamon, nutmeg, and mace, and lemon peel, and left to mature at least until the autumn. This is one of the many ancient liqueurs, part witches-brew, part tonic, part digestivo, part of a long tradition of homemade potions prepared by women, benign domestic medicine using the properties of the walnut tree to heal and restore the parts that academic medicine did not reach. The leaves are dried and used in infusions and poultices, to cure gastroenteritis, gout, heal wounds and sores, and help dispel anaemia; the pounded shells and juice restored fading and falling hair; and the kernels are a good source of vitamins (A, B1, B2, PP, B5), with plenty of glucids and proteins, copper and zinc. Many of the oldest surviving trees are in convents, where trees were cherished for these nutritional and therapeutic qualities. In the notebooks of the Perugian nun Maria Vittoria della Verde, there is a recipe for preserving green walnuts in honey, as one would make candied fruits; she said they should be gathered on the feast of San Barnaba with the moon in the right quarter, around 11 June, and repeatedly soaked to get rid of the bitterness. Her recipe for *panmelato*, a rich version prepared for the prioress five days before the feast of San Tommaso (16 December), is a mixture of pounded walnuts, and stale breadcrumbs soaked in sweet wine, cooked with grape must flavoured with candied orange peel, then baked in the oven on an oiled tin, and afterwards, while still hot, soaked in a syrup of honey boiled to "pearl" stage, flavoured with cloves, pepper, and cinnamon. The honey bread was then and put up in boxes, layered with bay leaves. She has a strange recipe for mushrooms, first given a boil, drained, cut up, and layered in an earthenware dish with chopped garlic, fennel seeds, and chopped walnuts, seasoned with salt and pepper and a generous amount of olive oil, then baked in a hot oven. She also gives a version of *agliata*, the universally popular sauce made with shelled and skinned walnuts pounded with garlic and spices (cloves, pepper, fennel), basil, and breadcrumbs, thinned with fresh verjuice, to have with roast meat. (*Agliata* today is a garlic sauce made by incorporating olive oil into crushed cloves of garlic in a mortar, sometimes with the addition of breadcrumbs moistened with vinegar, to have with boiled fish; the walnuts have vanished, and now the result is more like the aïoli of the south of France.) Scappi's version of a walnut sauce uses a slightly smaller quantity of almonds as well, both carefully peeled, and the garlic is parboiled for a milder effect; all are pounded with breadcrumbs soaked in either meat or fish broth, depending on what the sauce is for, seasoned with ginger, and the whole diluted with the same broth, but not strained, so that the crunch of the nuts remains. A version of this he calls *nosella* is prepared in the same way, but with a higher proportion of walnuts, then cooked in some more broth, and seasoned with mild spices, saffron, and chopped rosemary, mint, and marjoram—good with frogs, snails, and fish poached in water. Scappi also used walnuts in a stuffing for boiled fowl or meat. A Renaissance cookery manuscript in the Morgan Library in New York has a recipe for what we would now call a white pudding—although tinged with saffron—made with pounded peeled walnut kernels, garlic, chopped veal fat, grated parmesan, raisins, and eggs, cooked in veal intestines; suitable also for stuffing chickens or joints of veal.

Martino gave a recipe for a mixture of pounded walnuts, garlic, parmesan cheese, chopped veal suet, marjoram, mint, parsley, pepper, and saffron, bound with eggs, wrapped in blanched cabbage leaves, and simmered in broth. In Liguria today, a walnut sauce, *tocco de noxe,* is made with skinned walnut kernels pounded with soaked white breadcrumbs and garlic in a mortar, then mixed with grated parmesan, olive oil, a little chopped marjoram, and some *prescinsoeua* (slightly soured milk clotted with rennet) or ricotta; it is served with pasta and in particular *pansotti*. Ada Boni mentions a custom in central Italy of preparing homemade fettucine for the evening meal on Christmas Eve, the *vigilia di Natale,* served with crushed walnuts, sugar, cinnamon, and breadcrumbs, a lingering survival of the ancient use of walnuts in a pasta sauce, and the use of cinnamon and sugar as a flavour enhancer, so widespread in the past. This is similar to the *lasagne di Natale* of the Veneto, where sheets of lasagne are layered with chopped walnuts, sugar, cinnamon, and butter, and baked in the oven.

Walnuts are often served as dessert, as they were in Roman times, when they were also enjoyed at wedding ceremonies. One of those restless mosaic floors with *trompe l'oeil* foodstuff scattered all over has a little mouse nibbling a walnut. Apicius used them in a *patina*, a sort of upside-down flan or custard, in which roasted nuts—almonds, pine kernels, and walnuts—are ground in a mortar with honey, peppercorns, fish sauce, and some rich dessert wine, then mixed with eggs and milk and baked in the oven or cooked in a frying pan, and served turned out on a dish. Scappi began serving the new season's walnuts for dessert in late July, shelled, with the bitter skins removed, soaked in red wine, or roasted and seasoned with salt, sugar, and pepper. By mid-August he was serving fresh young hazelnuts, shelled and laid on vine leaves, tender young almonds, cracked open, also on vine leaves, and walnuts in red wine.

Walnuts are used extensively today in biscuits and confectionery. The *cavallucci* of Siena are made with blanched walnuts and flour, mixed into a sugar syrup with diced candied orange peel, anise, and spices, especially cinnamon, shaped into characteristic flat ovals, and baked in a low oven.

The *copeta* of Valtellina is a traditional sweetmeat made of chopped walnuts and figs mixed with honey and sandwiched between wafers, and used to be the forfeit paid on the eve of the feast of the Epiphany by folk who failed to greet friends in the street with the cry *"Gabinatt!"* A similar mixture of honey and walnuts, flavoured with anise, is the *copata* of Tuscany, the *cupeta* of Puglia, and the *cubbaita* of Sicily, made with sesame seeds and crushed nuts boiled up with honey and sugar for the Feast of All Souls, although of much more ancient origin, for the name probably derives from the Arabic *khabasa*, a verb which means to mix or mingle, which is what medieval Arab recipes specify—mixtures of ground nuts are mixed into a syrup of sugar and rosewater, sometimes with a coarse wheat flour rather like semolina, spread thin, and when set, put between wafers or thin flatbread, as in the *khabis al-lauz*, a version made from almonds, rolled up in a soft pancake. (Charles Perry gently but firmly demolished the myth of the derivation of our word "lozenge" from *lauz*, almond, for although at one time this sweetmeat was thought to have been cut into diamond shapes, it was in fact was neatly flattened or rolled into a cylinder, as the recipes clearly say.)

Walnuts sometimes appear in religious art for their symbolism, the shell being the hard wood of the Cross, and the soft meat within the redeeming power of divine love for humankind.

WATER, *acqua*, flat or fizzy mineral water, *acqua minerale*, is an indispensable part of Italian meals, and is also taken in bars, with drinks, with espresso coffee, and with snacks—sparkling, *gassosa, con gas* or *gaz*, or plain, *naturale*. It comes, on request at the start of a meal with the basket of bread, and serves to quench the thirst and regulate consumption of wine during the meal. Although national brands of mineral water are everywhere, most regions have their own local product, with labels that make impressive reading, listing all the minerals that are so good for one. In many places the tap water will be good, too, and if not it will be labelled *non potabile*, a sign to look for on taps and fountains in the streets. Water is a precious element in Italian life, from the wells of Venice, sweet and clear from deep beneath the mud and slime, to the copious fountains of Rome, and the natural springs of many rural areas, the natural cascades of Tivoli contrasting with the complex magical waterworks of the Villa d'Este. The aqueducts of ancient Rome, miracles of civil engineering, brought water from the surrounding hills to the city, and later their ruins, snaking across the Campagna, were a reminder of imperial power and the immense resources of the state. When Pope Sixtus V set about restoring Rome after the Sack, in the white heat of the Counter-Reformation, his great project of urban renewal placed fountains, fed by restored aqueducts, at the end of every vista, with obelisks and monuments celebrating the renewed power of the papacy, not out of benevolence, but as a grandiose gesture to hammer home the impact of the political and temporal powers of the Church. This was reinforced by inscriptions above every fountain in majestic capital letters based on those of ancient Rome, but with a subtle baroque sinuousness, indicating the triumph of the papacy over pagan and Protestant influences (Mosley, 2007). The complexities of the public and secret history of water in Rome are told by Cesare D'Onofrio in his work *Le fontane di Roma* (1986).

The magic of the fountains is still potent, even to the citizens washing their cars at the *Fontanone*, the Acqua Paola on the Giani-colo, the tourists fecklessly tossing coins into the Trevi fountain, or the market people washing fruit in the great basin in the Campo dei Fiori. Abundant water in a hot city is a blessing and a delight.

WATER BUFFALO, *bufalo, bufala,*

a native of southern Asia, and now spread round the world, was brought to Europe during the late Roman Empire and has been at home in central Italy ever since, prized for the MOZZARELLA cheese made from its milk, though its meat is also enjoyed, cooked the same way as beef. Pliny wrote of the bison of northern Europe and Asia, and the water buffaloes of the Indian sub-continent. The Jews in Imperial Rome cele-brated the New Year with a feast of buffalo meat and cabbage. Maybe the Lombards brought their own beasts as well, as some believe.

The water buffalo belongs to the same group of bovine ruminants as bison, but with an adaptability to watery places which makes it the ideal—in fact the only—livestock suited for the once unhealthy Pon-tine Marshes near Rome. Resistance to dis-ease and an ability to survive on unpromising vegetation, patience under duress (as beast of burden), and a fond attachment to its young are just some of the characteristics of the water buffalo. An 18th-century naturalist describe its love of water: "Water seems to be their ideal element, they gambol together as they swim, dipping, twisting and turning, on side and back, or drift lazily with the cur-rent, without moving a limb." But when de-prived of water, they can turn nasty—galloping furiously towards the nearest stream, destroying everything in their way. Having no sweat glands, buffaloes need to cool down in water and mud, as do pigs.

Water buffaloes can be intensively farmed, or reared in semifree conditions, fed organically. Those no longer free to wallow

in the wild are provided with artificial lakes and shelters from the sun. In the past, each cow would come when called at milking time, answering to her name, but now the buffaloes are identified by microchip tags im-posed by Eurocrats who don't respond to names, and automatic milking machines are widely used. Buffaloes are reared mainly in the provinces of Salerno, Caserta, Frosinone, and Latina, and although they are now ex-ploited mainly for the making of mozzarella cheese, the meat, similar to beef, is con-sumed fresh locally, and also cured to make a fine version of *bresaola*, and some salami. It has all the qualities of beef—tenderness, tastiness—but is leaner, and with a higher percentage of proteins and iron.

WATERMELON, *cocomero, anguria,*

Citrullus lanatus or *vulgaris*, a separate genus of the cucumber family, has, apart from minerals and trace elements, a sweet red flesh which is a pleasant thirst-quenching fruit (*see* MELON). As an alternative to a tainted water supply, they were a popular street refreshment, and the subject of many engravings by Pinelli of Roman and Neapolitan life, for a freshly cut water-melon, free from flies and dust, is healthy enough, whatever the health police might say. The red flesh within the hard green outer skin is of such pleasing colour and texture that painters exploited this in many compositions of aristocratic snacks, where, unlike the melon, a more prestigious fruit which is usually shown cut into neat sections, the watermelon is hacked into craggy lumps, spilling juice and black seeds—abundant, careless refreshment.

WEDGE SHELL, *tellina*, sometimes

known as *vongola*, is one of the bivalves. It is good with pasta, as in *spaghetti alle vongole*, or as a soup, in which the little molluscs, opened in a big pot over a high flame, are strained and finished in olive oil in which garlic and chilli have been lightly coloured but not scorched, some white wine, and plenty of chopped parsley. *Tellina* is also known as *arsella* in Tuscany, where a soup is made from it called *Zuppa di Telline.*

WEEVER, *tracin: tracina ragno, tracina drago* (greater weever), *tracina raggiata,* are ocean fish which are all good to eat, but the venomous spines on their backs and heads need to be avoided. The firm flesh is good grilled or in fish soups.

WHEAT, *frumento,* is divided for practical purposes today into strong, durum wheat, *grano duro, Triticum durum,* and soft, *grano tenero, Triticum aestivum.* Both kinds are grown in Italy. The durum wheat grows mainly in the south and is mostly used for pasta, and the soft mostly for bread, unlike in Great Britain, where we prefer strong flour. Rich in protein and amino acids, wheat eaten as bread is a healthy staple, and when matched with beans and pulses, the balance of nutrients gets even better. Think of Tuscan stewed beans and the local unsalted bread, dressed with olive oil and eaten with vegetables or salad herbs as a perfect archetypal balanced meal. But to feed the Roman masses, wheat was imported from Sicily, "the Republic's granary," as Cato put it, and as far afield as Egypt and Africa, even though some varieties were grown in Italy.

Wheat grains in their most primitive form can be cooked whole after soaking for several days, as in Mary Taylor Simeti's mouth-watering account of *cuccia,* a dish prepared on 13 December for the Feast of Saint Lucy, who protected eyesight and brought the promise of light on the darkest day of the year (Simeti, 1989, p. 17). Wheat berries are boiled until tender, then mixed with *most cotto,* creamed ricotta, candied citron, and bits of dark chocolate, and flavoured with vanilla. If you eliminate the chocolate and vanilla, this is a link with a very distant past, when a Christian saint was recruited to legitimise a much earlier offering. Later legends say that this was the date of the arrival of ships full of grain in Palermo to relieve a famine in the year 1600, and the starving populace could not wait for the grain to become bread but boiled it up and ate it dressed with olive oil. (How they managed the necessary prolonged soaking is not explained.) *Cuccia* is best made with soft white winter wheat grains; the hard summer wheat toughens even after cooking.

When the ripe wheat was harvested by hand, the grains had a different time of it; cut with a sickle, the handfuls of grain were gathered into sheaves and stacked in groups, stooks, and left to mature in the open sometimes for weeks, exposed to damp, heat, and local microorganisms which produced changes in the grain which affected flavour and the response of the flour to yeast. Now that everything is done by machinery, however, the characteristics of the flour are different.

WHEY. *See* CHEESE, RICOTTA.

WHITEFISH, *coregoni,* or pollan, were introduced into Italy from German lakes in the mid–19th century and are now found in the northern Italian lakes and the volcanic lakes of Lazio. Legends surround this relative newcomer, and many people claim that this not very exciting fish is unique to their lake, either a survival from some prehistoric denizen, or released into the lake from some titanic cloudburst, or, in the case of Lake Bracciano, in northern Lazio, brought by Pope Sixtus V when he set up an improved water supply for the new fountains gracing Rome's urban renewal. But a boring fish, redeemed perhaps by a liberal dosage of herbs and lemon juice.

WILD ASPARAGUS. *See* ASPARAGUS.

WILD BOAR, *cinghiale*, still roams the mountainous areas of north and central Italy and the south, where forage of various kinds and ponds and streams provide it with a congenial habitat. With agricultural land falling into disuse in many areas, there is now scope for rearing semiwild boars in fenced-in areas, for the production of meat and salami. The enormous damage they can do, rootling and rampaging in cultivated areas, makes it advisable to fence them out as well. The meat is like rare-breed pork and can be cooked in the same way, according to the different categories, depending on the age of the animal: *porcastro*, *cinghialotto* (or *cinghialetto*), *giovane*, *maturo*, and *adulto*—milk-fed baby, young (under a year), mature, and adult. Scappi uses the term *rufalotto* for a young animal. Most dishes lend themselves to *contorni* and flavourings reminiscent of the wild boar's environment—juniper and myrtle berries, wild mushrooms, chestnut purée, tart jellies from wild fruit.

Wild boar were enjoyed in the ancient world and, when brought home in triumph from the hunt, dominated the feasts of the great. The ferocity, strength, and courage of the wild animal called for similar powers in its hunters, useful attributes in warriors, statesmen, and prelates, so the head of the beast, vanquished in combat, had a symbolic function—eating it might convey these qualities to the revellers, as well as celebrate their prowess, but this had also to be an appropriately sumptuous gastronomic experience. The boar's head was borne in, decorated with garlands of flowers, an orange in its mouth, and with rich spicy sauces to accompany the different parts. In Scappi's recipe, the head had been skinned, thoroughly cleaned, simmered in a deep pot with wine, water, and vinegar seasoned with salt, crushed pepper, and heads of dried fennel,

then served hot or cold. He describes how to dish up the snout, ears, cheeks, brain, tongue, and eyes. The rest of the beast could be cooked like pork or goat, having removed the hard calloused outer skin and hair (pork has a soft smooth skin, so the *cotenna* or rind is invaluable in enriching and thickening the cooking juices). The whole boar was sometimes skinned, spit roasted, stitched back in its bristly pelt, and brought to table with much pomp.

A recipe from Rome for *cinghiale in agrodolce*, sweet-sour wild boar, first skins the joint, then leaves it for a day or two in a marinade of white wine and vinegar simmered with the usual carrots, onions, celery, herbs, and spices, and then cooled. Then the meat is removed, dried, and browned in lard with some more chopped vegetables, diced bacon, and ham, and when they are all a good dark colour, a glass of white wine is tipped in and allowed to evaporate, the meat is topped up with water or broth, adding more spices to taste, and cooked covered for several hours until done. The sauce is then skimmed of fat, reduced if necessary, and finished with some lightly caramelised sugar dissolved in vinegar, a little dark chocolate, some of the broth, soaked raisins and stoned bitter cherries, pine nuts, and chopped candied peel.

A much simpler recipe from "a green and secret valley joining Umbria and Tuscany" recorded by Elizabeth Romer in 1984 explains how, after a local boar hunt, the farmer's wife would select the loin of a young animal, cut it into chunks, and brown it in olive oil with bay leaves and garlic, then add a glass of white wine and simmer slowly until tender, topping up with wine as needed. This method yields a tender, pale, aromatic meat, gentler than the treatment needed for an older beast.

The meat of young and old wild boar is used in *salumi* of various kinds, especially in Tuscany, where it is got by hunting, from farmed animals, and from a considerable im-

Nettle tops are a popular boiled green in Italy. Because of their sting, many cooks throw out the first water and boil them a second time. (Shutterstock)

port of carcass meat from abroad, mainly destined for restaurants and for cured hams. Hams are cured in the Chianti area, and salami and fresh sausages are made all over Tuscany by small artisan producers when the hunting season is in full swing, especially in Sinalunga and San Gimignano.

WILD GARLIC. *See* GARLIC.

WILD GREENS, *verdure selvatiche, erbe spontanee,* are still gathered for domestic and commercial use. *Verdura* is a useful name that can mean any kind of green stuff, and also vegetables in general, cultivated as well as wild. *Erbe* are not just herbs, but plants of many kinds; *erbe aromatiche* are the fragrant herbs used in cooking. The concept of a *cucina della nonna* is to some extent focussed on the role of wise old women with instinctive and inherited wisdom, who have for centuries fed and dosed families with a wide range of wild roots, shoots, buds, and leaves for medicinal or gastronomic use. As the *nonnas* become extinct, a new generation of young chefs and ecologically minded enthu-

siasts are rediscovering the virtues and pleasures of wild plants, and using them in traditional and innovative ways. The revival of the *mischianza* or *misticanza* is by now a well-known phenomenon. These green things can sometimes be found in country markets, and cultivated versions of them are widely available, like the comfortably domesticated "wild" rocket, *diplotaxis tenuifolia, rucola, rugola, ruchetta selvatica,* with its sharp mustardy taste and characteristic bitterness.

From the moment the first shoots of the various kinds of dandelion, *dente di leone, tarassaco,* appear towards the end of winter, people can be seen in meadows, on roadsides, and in urban green spaces stooping to gather the bitter leaves, with their agreeable taste and health-giving properties (tonic, laxative, diuretic, digestive). They are used raw in mixed salads, can be cooked in soups and stews, and make a pungent but delicious tepid salad, mixed with slivers of fried *lardo* or pancetta and its tasty fat.

Apart from wild herbs, used as seasoning, there are many wild plants which appear in regional cooking, and can often be found in country markets. The bewildering proliferation of local names makes it difficult to say what they are; rather than worry about identification, it is safer to ask how to cook and eat them, an effective way of discovering local recipes. Wild fennel—the bulbs or fronds—has a more pungent taste then cultivated varieties, and makes a wonderful addition to cooked dishes as well as salads. In a recipe cooked by a friend from the Marche, rabbit joints, together with its liver and giblets, are cooked in a covered pan, after frying with pancetta and garlic, and absorbing some dry white wine, with olives, capers, wild fennel, and wild mushrooms. Sorrel leaves are available all year round in most regions; raw or cooked, they give a sharp acidity to salads and sauces. The tips of the young shoots of wild hops and clematis and asparagus are eaten in salads and *frittatas.* The tender young leaves of nettles, *ortiche,* gathered with care, are used in soups, risottos, and *frittatas*. Wild beets, *bietola selvatica*; good King Henry, *bono Enrico*, *spinaccio selvatico*; mallow, *malva*; *aggretti*, sometimes called *barba di prete*, or *barba di becco*; *lampascioni*, samphire, *cretamo*, *finocchio di mare*; wild chicory, *cicoria commune*; wild endive, *radicchio selvatico*, are just a few of the wild plants to be found.

The *pansôti* of Liguria are large plump ravioli with a filling of steamed greens of various kinds, a mixture which is improved by including some wild greens. The *prebôggion* of the region is a mixture of herbs and wild plants used for this dish and many others, including, depending on the season and the locality, sorrel, borage, wild chicory, chervil, lovage, pimpernel, dandelion, and thistle. The climate of Liguria, with its sunshine and sea breezes, is particularly favourable to wild aromatic plants and herbs.

WINE, *vino*, is the national beverage and almost the national occupation: there are 1.2 million wine-growers in Italy. Dry whites and reds (*vino bianco*, *vino rosso*), as varied as the land and climate, are necessary companions to Italian cuisine, wherever practised; most often, their destiny is to accompany food. Sweet wines, white and red (*semisecco*, *abboccato*, *amabile*, *dolce*, in order of increasing sweetness) and sparkling wines (*frizzante*, gently fizzy; *spumante*, sparkling) make up a range with more individuality and more potential surprises than those of any other country. Which wine for which food and occasion?

Italians drink only half as much wine as they did a century ago—beer and spirits help to keep up their alcohol intake—and they are drinking less of it year by year. At 60 to 70 litres per head, they still drink more wine than almost anyone else in the world. Much of the wine drunk in Italy is made in Italy, and a large proportion of that, difficult to quantify because statistics are never complete, is made somewhere very close to where it is consumed.

Vines and wine were familiar in Italy at the dawn of recorded history. The god known by the traditional Latin name of Liber Pater (Father Liber) presided over wine, festivity, and drunkenness. Liber afterwards coalesced with the Greek god Dionysos, who was better known in Latin by his alternate name Bacchus, but this was by no means a smooth process: the Roman Senate in 193 BC puritanically forbade the nocturnal mountain festivals in which Italian women were learning from their Greek counterparts to celebrate the mysteries of Bacchus. After this, the mysteries were still celebrated, but more privately. In the *Fresco of the Mysteries*, in a house outside Pompeii, initiation into these mysteries is depicted; Bacchus and Silenus are present alongside other divine and human participants.

For Etruscans, and after them for Romans of the republic and empire, it was normal to drink wine with meals. Romans took honeyed wine (*mulsum*) or spiced wine (*conditum*) before a dinner party; they drank wine with the main course. Wine was sometimes poured through a linen *saccus* to strain and at the same time flavour it; aromatics such as bitter almonds and anise seeds might be placed in the *saccus*, or the wine was poured through a *saccus nivarius*, containing snow. Some people disapproved of all this, considering it a sophistication that reduced the wine's natural flavour and nutritional quality. It was usual to drink wine mixed with water, but it was recognised that unmixed wine might be salutary when correctly prescribed by physicians. Wine was an important element in the prescriber's armoury, part of the regimen prescribed for many patients.

Romans had a belief that "in the old days" women were not allowed to drink wine, and that the kiss given by an early

Roman husband to his wife on returning home in the evening was a way of assuring himself that this rule had been kept; some also believed that while men used to recline at table, women, in the old days, sat demurely at the foot of a husband's or father's couch. These were myths. Art and literature combine to show that in Roman dining, as in Etruscan, both men and women had always reclined and engaged in dinner conversation (and seduction) on fairly equal terms.

In Roman gastronomy, the most general geographical distinction among wines divided the *transmarine*, "overseas," from the *cis mare nata* "laid down on this side of the sea." The sea in question was the strait separating southern Italy from Greece; even if they reached Rome by sea, the wines of Sicily, Spain, and Gaul were not classed as *transmarina*. The legions, the urban poor, and the great majority of slaves tasted real wine only on lucky days. For those who could not afford it, there were various cheaper alternatives. Farm slaves drank *lora*, secondary wine made by macerating already pressed grapes in water (*acquarello* and *graspia* in later Italian). Soldiers were sometimes given wine, sometimes (in central and northern Europe) beer, and sometimes *posca*, which was vinegary wine mixed with water and flavoured with pennyroyal and other herbs.

Old or young, sweetened or dry, ancient wine tasted very different from modern. There were no fortified wines, since alcoholic distillation was not practised. Wines were fermented in half-buried earthenware vats (*dolia*) fumigated and sealed with pine resin; they were transported in earthenware amphorae or in vast, bulging ox skins. The wine called Raeticum, from the hills north of Verona, must have tasted different from all other Italian vintages, since it was matured in wooden barrels. It was a favourite of the emperor Augustus; 2,000 years ahead of his time, he liked the taste of oak.

Italy's huge number of varieties and variety names (the two are seldom coterminous) is now slowly diminishing. Appellation regulations favour local varieties, but in limited number, and even some of those that are approved are losing ground to the predictable and marketable Cabernet Sauvignon, Sauvignon Blanc, Chardonnay, Pinot Noir, and Merlot. Hundreds of varieties are grown mainly or exclusively in Italy: among the most widespread are Barbera and Nebbiolo from Piedmont, Garganega from Veneto, Montepulciano from Abruzzi, and the local heroes Sangiovese and Lambrusco, scions of the subspecies *Vitis vinifera* ssp. *sylvestris*. Italy shares with other countries some familiar and historic varieties, including not only Malvasia, Trebbiano, and Moscato but also Cannonau (Guarnaccia, Grenache, Garnacha), Riesling Italico (Welschriesling), Riesling Renano (Rheinriesling), and Traminer.

With speedier transport and the general growth in international trade, far more Italian wines reached non-Italian palates in the 19th and 20th centuries. Oddly enough, marsala was the harbinger. Developed scarcely 230 years ago by John Woodhouse on the basis of the traditional strong dry whites of southwestern Sicily, marsala was a new fortified wine to replace those once known to the English as Wine Greek, Wine Corse, and Vernage. Its reputation has fluctuated. The producers of marsala nowadays struggle, or fail to struggle, against the popular image of a cheap, sweet, often flavoured cooking wine; good marsala is hard to find.

With three further exceptions, the Italian wines that have gained an international reputation in modern times have been dry whites and dry reds. One of those exceptions consists of the flavoured wine aperitifs, Martini and the like, in which a great deal of Italian wine is swallowed up. The other two are Asti Spumante and Lambrusco (*frizzante*), white and red, respectively, light, easy to drink, and drunk in enormous quantities. They have been so popular—like Chianti, the most widely known Italian dry red—that they have produced a marketing problem for Italian wine exporters similar to the one that marsala producers created for themselves—Italian wines came to be equated with cheap plonk. The problem was worsened by Italian and European farming policy in the 1950s and 1960s, which assumed that demand for wine would increase and that consumer taste would level downwards. Generous subsidies encouraged low-quality, high-volume production to match these expectations, and it is taking a long time to reverse the effects.

It was only in the 1960s that Italy introduced an official system of wine appellations (DOC, Denominazione di Origine Controllata). Even more recently, a supposedly higher level has been introduced (DOCG, Denominazione di Origine Controllata e Garantita), and 24 appellations have so far been admitted to this upper group, but the G does not make them any better than their rivals. Although they have done a lot of good, the DOC regulations are very far from perfect. Some of the finest Italian wines can't or won't fit into them; producers intent on high quality may well choose either to ignore them or to label their finest wines *Vino da Tavola*. Valpolicella and Chianti are among wine appellations whose DOC(G) guarantees practically nothing, and the producer's name is a better guide.

Many Italians seldom buy by the bottle; they get their wine locally, direct from producers, after tasting. However, knowledge of the geographical range of Italian wines is spreading rapidly. Shops, restaurants, and supermarkets offer much more choice than in the recent past, though they will still favour wines from their own region—Italian restaurateurs abroad will often do the same. In Britain, the United States, Australia, and several other countries, a great variety of Italian wines can be found on sale, or can be ordered from wine merchants and importers.

The Internet is increasing the range available, and it makes searching and ordering easier than ever before. Even so, nothing substitutes for the opportunity to taste before buying: all such opportunities are to be seized.

Wine is also an important ingredient in Italian cooking. Many recipes specify the one to use, and it is in most cases safe to say that a regional dish will be cooked with a typical regional wine, so "a glass of red or white" wine in a recipe can be interpreted as using one of the light *vini dei castelli* in Rome and Lazio, or a hearty Barolo in Piemonte. Many risottos are good with wine added at the beginning to enhance the flavour and cut the richness of the final result, as with the use of white in one version of the classic *risotto alla milanese*. In sweet dishes, dessert wines or Marsala are often used. ZABAGLIONE, or *zabaione*, is a heady mixture of egg yolks and sugar beaten to a foam into which Marsala or a rich sweet wine is incorporated, and then heated, still beating, over a *bain-marie* until it starts to thicken, and served hot.

It might be local "plonk," but wine in a dish is treated with care, never put into a sizzling hot preparation of meat and vegetables at the start of cooking without first cooling the mixture with a little cold water to avoid scorching the wine and ruining the flavour. When it has been added, to a stew or braised dish for example, it is allowed to evaporate completely, *sfumare*, to become absorbed into the overall amalgam of seasonings; the dish can then be topped up with water where needed and allowed to go on cooking; if more wine is added, the same procedure is followed. This is very different from tipping a bottle of wine into a stew and letting it get on with it. The Italian way is to aim at a dense concentration of flavour, and it works brilliantly in *ossobuco alla milanese* using white wine, and a *stracotto*, or the Roman *coda alla vaccinara*, using red. This is wine as flavouring rather than cooking medium. It is important to interpret a recipe carefully, to avoid too liquid a result. Large amounts of wine are used to marinate some dishes using obdurate cuts of beef, and are then added to the later cooking process (*see* STEW). Wine used to finish a dish is usually a splash to dislodge the tasty cooking residues, like the white wine added at the end of frying *saltimbocca alla romana. See also* GRAPES.

(AKD)

WORMWOOD. *See*

SOUTHERNWOOD.

Y

YEAST, *lievito*, is the raising agent used in making bread; it releases gases which are contained by the resilient gluten in the dough, creating lightness and flavour. There are several kinds of raising agents, natural yeasts, beer or brewer's yeast (now usually an industrial product, sold as dry cakes or granules), and chemical yeast (baking powder). Most Italian breads are made using a combination of these, but the key element is usually a saltless sour dough starter, left from the previous day's bake, called *lievito madre, crescente, criscenti, criscolo, biga* or *pasta acida*, which was the main and often only raising agent in the past. This is sometimes mixed with flour and water, kept around after baking day, and added to the next batch of bread, maybe reinforced with other forms of yeast.

The other kind of yeast is a *lievito naturale*, a starter made from water, flour, and wild yeast spores in vegetables, unsulfured grapes, or the skins of untreated fruit, or yoghurts, or simply from spores in the air. The process of creating this is described in detail in the INSOR publication (INSOR, 2000, *Pane*, p. 39, n. 15); it takes many days, allowing a mixture of flour, best wholemeal, *integrale*, and water, perhaps with the addition of honey, olive oil, and grape must, to ferment slowly and gradually, topped up with more flour and water, left in a warm place to mature, and eventually, working and waiting, brought to the ideal condition for use. This process, unlike the alcoholic fermentation of beer yeast, produces a lactic acid fermentation which contributes to the flavour and aroma of the bread but above all makes for better keeping qualities and greater digestibility, all the more so if the flour used has not been deprived of enzymes in the wheat germ and the outer coating of the grain. The lactic acid bacteria in sour dough that react with the yeast and the surrounding microsystem produce flavours that industrially made, fast-working yeast cannot achieve, but the acidity of some sour dough starters can be less than pleasant, and the true art of the baker lies in manipulating these different yeasts, along with the changes that happen when baking the dough. In this Italian bakers excel, although the authors of *Pane* (INSOR, 2000) wryly acknowledge the supremacy of the bread of San Francisco, where the unique presence of the yeast *Saccaromices exiguis* and the lactic acid *Saccaromices San Francisco* function together in amicable symbiosis with spectacular results. (But Carol Field points out that the San Francisco bacillus is in fact also found in Milan.) Another good thing about slow-working sour dough is that it makes many of the beneficial things in whole wheat bread, *pane integrale*, more accessible to our digestive systems, while the speeded-up version can effectively cancel out all the minerals and vitamins we hoped we were getting from the dietary fibre, and even inhibit their absorption. An excessive bran content combined with fast-working industrial yeast can be as inimical as the "pure, white, and deadly" products of the Chorleywood process.

Size matters, too; in a large loaf weighing several pounds, cooked slowly in a wood-fired oven, the inner crumb stays below 60–70 degrees, and some of the microbes and enzymes in the yeast spores remain active, and continue to enhance the flavour and nutritional content of the bread as it keeps.

Every home where bread was made regularly had a *madia*, a wooden trough with sloping sides and a hinged lid, with storage space underneath. The dough was kneaded in the trough and left to rise; the manipulation and shaping of the risen dough was done on its flat lid. The baked loaves were kept in the cupboard below, and after every baking, a lump of the dough would be put on one side in the *madia*, where microorganisms in the atmosphere would aid and abet the maturing and fermenting that made each family's sour dough a special unique thing. This sanctuary for the sour dough was a sacred spot, and often the magic powers of the yeast would be used to aid the growth of a stunted child, by placing the little mite in the *madia* for a short while. In the south, women often shared this natural yeast, giving some to a neighbour for her baking, and receiving some of the precious bread in return.

Another form of leavening, for cakes and biscuits, comes in little packets, *bustine*, sometimes flavoured with vanilla. This is really baking powder, usually a mixture of acidic and alkaline chemicals, including bicarbonate of soda, cream of tartar, and other substances (McGee, 2004, p. 533). These mild acids and alkalis react together to make carbon dioxide, which creates bubbles in the mixture without one's having to wait for some time, as one does with a yeast-raising agent. These handy little packets can be bought in most delis.

YOGHURT. *See* MILK.

Z

ZABAGLIONE or *zabaione* is a pale delicate froth of egg yolks beaten up with sugar in a bowl over a pan of hot but not boiling water to thicken it slightly. It is usually flavoured with Marsala, though other dessert wines of character are also used—*vin santo, moscato* or even foreigners like Madeira or sherry. Cinnamon can be added. It is best made to order and served warm from the bowl. This is one of the many whipped desserts, sometimes including milk, like syllabubs and possets, in which a transient froth is flavoured with wine. The name occurs as early as 1570 in one of Scappi's recipes for a *ginestrata over zambaglione con rossi d'uove fresche*, flavouring the mixture with a muscat Malvasia and cinnamon, and enriching it with light chicken broth and butter. We find recipes in Latini (vol. 2, 1694, p. 163) from the late 17th century for versions which include pistachios and butter, as well as strong sweet wines, cinnamon, and flavoured waters; *"questo si mantiene l'huomo senza mangiare per un giorno"* (this will keep a man going for a whole day without eating).

ZAMPONE MODENA is made by putting a filling similar to that of COTECHINO into the carefully prepared boned hind foot of a PIG, which retains much of the glutinous properties of the skin and cartilage to augment the already lipsticking texture of the mixture. The contents and procedure are stipulated in its IGP (*see* DOC), and today *zampone Modena* is made in a wide area from Modena to Bergamo by way of Rimini and Milan. The seasonings vary, but can include cinnamon, nutmeg, pepper, and cloves; every artisan maker has special skills and secrets used to achieve a rich but not heavy texture from this unpromising mix of ingredients. What began as a way of using up NERVETTI (*gnervítt*), which are not nerves but cartilage and sinews from the knee and leg of VEAL, and the skin, ears, and snout of the pig, and all the bits inappropriate for more refined SALUMI, has evolved into a luxurious product, with the proportion of weird bits considerably smaller today than in the past. The meltingly glutinous qualities of *zampone* go well with LENTILS, POLENTA, mashed potatoes, or SPINACH. The partially cooked kind does not keep more than a month beyond manufacture in the autumn, and has traditionally been the focus of gluttons impatiently waiting for the end of summer, marked by the feast of San Michele on 29 September, when this delicacy inaugurated the delights of winter eating. Careful, slow cooking, with the zampone wrapped in swaddling clothes, in water barely bubbling, for three or four hours, produces a soft savoury sausage which must be eaten hot, on the spot, for once cooled and reheated it loses both flavour and texture.

ZEPPOLE are deep-fried sweet fritters, characteristic of central and southern Italy and Sardinia. The *sfinci* of Sicily are similar; both are made either of a yeasted dough, or a mixture like choux pastry, some enriched with eggs and butter. Formed into little rings or twisted shapes, they are deep fried and coated with icing sugar, or honey, in the case of *sfinci*. Overkill can be achieved with a filling of custard, or creamed ricotta.

ZIMINO, or *in zimino*, is a Florentine way of cooking *baccalà*, salt cod, or *seppie*, cuttlefish. The distinguishing ingredient is spinach or Swiss chard. The leaves are wilted, then sliced into coarse strips. The cod is soaked and trimmed of bones and skin and fried golden in olive oil in which a chopped onion, garlic, and plenty of chopped parsley have been cooked; some skinned and chopped tomatoes come next, then the spinach is added, and the mixture is left to simmer for a while. *Il libro del baccalà* quotes an early health manual: *"Si può dar loro un gentile zimino per tornagusta"* (You could give them [invalids] a nice *zimino* to revive the appetite; Cerini di Castegnate, Livio, 1986, p. 112). Artusi has a version made with tench, in which the fishes' heads make a sauce with the usual chopped vegetables, which is poured over the fried fish, and the spinach is then added to soak up the flavours; a light Lenten dish, not too rich and certainly tasty enough to cheer a jaded palate. There are similar recipes from Liguria, including one without fish described by Plotkin, using tiny young artichokes and peas cooked in softened onions and pancetta and some dry white wine, served with torn-up basil leaves stirred in after cooking. From Sardinia comes a fish soup called *ziminu* and in complete contrast, a dish of freshly killed calf's offal with the same name from Sassari.

ZUCCA. *See* MARROW, PUMPKIN.

ZUCCHERO. *See* SUGAR.

Zucchini flowers, usually sold attached to young squash, are delicious sauteed in butter, or stuffed, battered, and deep fried. (Shutterstock)

ZUCCHINI (USA), *zucchina* (Italian usage), *courgette* (Great Britain and France), baby marrow, *Cucurbita pepo*, is not really a baby, but a small member of this family, which came to Europe from the New World. The noun can be masculine or feminine, but North Americans prefer the version zucchini. It has a pleasanter texture and flavour than the larger marrows, a sweet freshness that demands careful cooking. There are many recipes that exploit these qualities— zucchini can be sautéed lightly in oil or butter, thinly sliced, dipped in flour or batter and deep fried, baked, roasted on a hot griddle, stuffed, or fried and finished in a sauce of tomatoes and oregano. Zucchini flowers, often sold still attached to the immature little marrows, can be fried gently in butter, added to *frittatas*, or stuffed, enclosed in batter, and deep fried. The stuffing can be a melting cheese like mozzarella, with the addition of herbs and anchovies, or ricotta with herbs. The standard *frittata* of Rome is made with zucchini sliced in rounds and cooked quickly in olive oil before adding the eggs to make a deep, soft dish served tepid or at room temperature, cut in wedges. Elizabeth David liberated us from the tyranny of watery, stringy, rank-tasting boiled marrow by writing enthusiastically about this expensive unknown Italian vegetable that no market gardener dared grow and no greengrocer dared stock. Even before the publication of her *Italian Food* in 1954, she was writing enthusiastically about *zucchine* in the *Spectator*, a rare case of a single-handed small revolution that introduced a new ingredient into our larders.

ZUCCOTTO is a *semifreddo*, one of

the many soft ICE CREAMS that are served chilled rather than frozen solid. There is no documentary evidence for claims that this is a typical Florentine speciality, and the profusion, today and in the past, of similar confections, all related to the methods of making ZUPPA INGLESE, found all over Italy, make this unlikely. *Zuccotto* is made in a domed mould which is lined with sponge fingers or langue de chat biscuits soaked in *alchemes* or rum and usually filled with a soft mixture of whipped cream, sometimes flavoured with vanilla or chocolate, often incorporating candied fruits, or fruit preserves, or chestnuts, covered with a final layer of soaked sponge. It is unmoulded after chilling, to make a semispherical or domed shape, vaguely resembling a squash or pumpkin, from which it gets its name, *zucca* being a colloquial word for head, and by extension for someone none too bright or turnip-headed. It can also be filled with a creamed ricotta filling not light-years away from that within the *cassata siciliana*, another dessert made in a domed container, in which a layer of sponge encloses a rich ricotta cream, and the unmoulded creation is then decorated with an extravagantly baroque array of bright green pistachio icing studded with candied fruits. This dessert used to be a speciality made by skilled convent pastry cooks, perhaps heirs to the rich Arab tradition of sweetmeats enjoyed in Sicily long before the convolutions of Sicilian baroque. Simeti (1989, p. 249) reminds us how at the Ponteleone ball in Palermo, Lampedusa's Gattopardo admired a version of it called *trionfi della gola*, and chose to eat the profane *minni di virgini*, having disdained fashionable fancy French pastries for these traditional Sicilian delicacies. A *trionfo della gola*, "triumph of gluttony," was a cone-shaped cake (p. 251)

made up of layers of pastry or sponge cake and light creams supporting lumps of *zuccata*, candied pumpkin, and brilliant green pistachios, perfumed with jasmine and cinnamon. This was the sort of cake that if well chilled could have been one of the great family of *semifreddi*.

The claimed resemblance of a modern *zuccotto* to Brunelleschi's dome might be a recent and understandable *campanalismo*, a typically austere Tuscan version of a wild southern extravagance. Artusi has a recipe in which the sponge fingers line a dome-shaped mould into which is poured custard and jam, "in summer this can be put on ice," he said, but he calls it *zuppa inglese* and makes no territorial claims.

ZUPPA is a SOUP or BROTH that is

served over slices of bread or toast to soak up (*inzuppare*) the liquid. Sometimes toast or croutons are floated on the surface, often

An Italian woman samples her soup with much delight in *Sketch*, a photo by Mario Nunes Vais. (Alinari/Art Resource, NY)

with an accompanying sauce or garnish. It can mean any soup or *minestra in brodo*, without rice or pasta, but usually with bread, and to list them all would make a book-length entry. On the Adriatic coast, BRODETTO is the name given to a *zuppa di pesce*. The name for *zuppa inglese*, trifle, refers to the liqueur-soaked layers of cake or biscuit in the many versions of this dessert.

The idea of a rustic soup, often of vegetables or pulses, is what lurks behind the name, implying a lack of refinement, given an ironic twist by Corrado, who, tongue in cheek, served *zuppe* in a sophisticated aristocratic setting, using the pulses and vegetables of the peasant food of Campania in inventive and delicious ways, not fooling us for one moment with French names or fashions. His banquet menus always have two *zuppe* and two *potaggi* or two *terrine*. The *zuppe* included tomato soup with basil (an early sighting), one of chickpeas and pasta, lentils and fennel, and one called *fantastica*, in which chopped herbs—parsley, thyme, borage, and tarragon—are simmered with slices of toast in a beef and game stock, then served with a swirl of puréed white beans; one can visualise the fantastic beauty of these rococo twists and spirals of green and white. Chickpeas were cooked in a fish broth, seasoned with thyme and garlic, pounded in a mortar, diluted with broth, and served with toasted bread decorated with whole chickpeas. Corrado, who had explored the regional cuisines of Italy in his youth, and was no slave to French gastronomy, served hearty bean soup from Florence, and a Milanese cabbage soup at his grand banquets. A century later, Artusi was more squeamish, and could not bring himself to include these plebeian brews in his book, but in his more refined *zuppe* he kept to the same distinction, the use of bread defining the soup. *Acquacotta* is a humble soup characteristic of the Maremma in Tuscany, made from simple ingredients—onions, garlic, sweet peppers, celery, tomatoes, softened in olive oil, then finished cook-ing in plain water, flavoured maybe with chilli, and poured over slices of toasted Tuscan bread, with an egg poached in the liquid slid onto each slice, served with grated pecorino.

ZUPPA INGLESE, trifle, literally "English soup," is unlikely to have been an English invention, in spite of its popularity there now and in the past. From dunking cake or biscuits in a dessert wine, it was but a short step to layering them in a dish, soaked in wine, liqueurs, or fruit and dousing them with custard or cream. The custard is made with egg yolks and milk, thickened with flour, which prompted Artusi to mention the superior lightness and elegance of the Florentine way with creams, a lighter, runnier, flour-free egg custard served in little cups. The cake element can be *pan di spagna*, sponge cake cut in slices, or *savoiardi*, sponge fingers. Artusi didn't much care for *zuppa inglese* and praised instead a much lighter *zuppa tartara* made with alternating layers of sponge fingers soaked in cordial or *alchemes*, peach or apricot jam, and a cream of ricotta thinned with milk or liqueur and beaten smooth with cinnamon and sugar. Messisbugo's *tartara* was an egg custard (*see* CUSTARD).

The origins of our word "trifle," a whim or a thing of small importance, point to the emergence in England as early as the 16th century of a light ephemeral concoction, like flummery and syllabub. But there were similar developments in Italy before then, where *zuppa* indicates something less ethereal, more like "sops" (hence the name soup) where slices of bread are toasted or fried then allowed to absorb a liquid, savoury or sweet, often enriched with eggs. Messisbugo in 1557 has a recipe for *zuppa dorata reale* which seems to combine the best of a bread and butter pudding (another English favourite) with an ancestor of the *zuppa inglese* as we know it. A rich sauce of almonds toasted and ground with spices, diluted with bitter orange juice or verjuice, thickened with egg yolks, and sweetened with sugar, is layered with slices of bread dipped in egg and fried in butter and raisins softened in wine and rosewater, finished with powdered sugar and cinnamon. His *zuppa magra inglese* is made of stewed parsley roots in a broth thickened with egg and poured over slices of bread. The Englishness of all this is more likely to be the root vegetable than the method. Sabban and Serventi recount with the necessary scepticism a legend about its invention in Siena in 1552 to beguile Cosimo de' Medici into diplomatic intervention on the city's behalf, who then took the recipe back to Florence, where visiting Brits took to it, hence the name.

Today there are many regional variations, from the rather hefty version of EMILIA-ROMAGNA, using the vivid red of *alchermes* to colour half of the sponge and sometimes flavouring half of the custard with chocolate, to the Roman version which includes diced candied fruits and is covered with meringue and lightly cooked in the oven to firm up the egg whites. Corrado has two recipes which resemble trifle in his chapter on *budin,* puddings. One, *alla Spagnola*, is a rich custard flavoured with musk, spread over slices of sponge cake, and served with a crust of caramelised sugar; the other, his own invention, is a dense mixture of strained whipped cream and sweetened egg yolks flavoured with cinnamon and vanilla, chopped pistachios and orange zest, piled over slices of sponge cake, dusted with sugar, and cooked lightly in the oven, to be served hot. Modern variations on *zuppa inglese* include TIRAMISÙ, though enthusiasts claim it to be the recent invention of a restaurant in Treviso.

Italy

SWITZERLAND

AUSTRIA

Mt. Blanc
15,771 ft.

TRENTINO-
ALTO
ADIGE

VALLE
D'AOSTA

FRIULI-
VENEZIA
GIULIA

SLOVENIA

Trento

LOMBARDY

VENETO

CROATIA

Turin

Milan

Venice

PIEDMONT

Po R.

Cuneo

Parma

EMILIA-
ROMAGNA

Bologna

BOSNIA AND
HERZEGOVINA

Genoa

LIGURIA

FRANCE

Rimini

MONACO

TUSCANY

SAN MARINO

LIGURIAN
SEA

Pisa

Florence

Siena

MARCHE

ADRIATIC

Perugia

Elba

UMBRIA

Pescara

Corsica
(FRANCE)

Tiber R.

Viterbo

ABRUZZO

SEA

Maddalena
Island

Rome

LAZIO

MOLISE

Foggia

Bari

Nuoro

Naples

CAMPANIA

PUGLIA

Sorrento

BASILICATA

SARDINIA

Oristano

TYRRHENIAN SEA

CALABRIA

Crotone

EOLIE
ISLANDS

IONIAN
SEA

Palermo

Messina

M

E

Mt. Etna
10,899 ft.

D

I

T

E

Catania

R

R

A

SICILY

N

E

A

Pantelleria
Island

N

S

E

A

AFRICA

MALTA

0   100 miles

0   100 km

Bibliography

Albala, Kenneth. 2002. *Eating Right in the Renaissance*. Berkeley: University of California Press.

———. 2007. *The Banquet*. Champaign: University of Illinois Press.

Alberini, Massimo. 1966. *Storia del pranzo all'italiana*. Milan: Rizzoli.

———. 1992. *Storia dell cucina italiana*. Casale Monferato: Piemme.

Anderson, Burton. 1994. *Treasures of the Italian table*. New York: William Morrow.

Artusi, Pellegrino. 1970. *La scienza in cucina e l'arte di mangiar bene*. With an introduction and notes by Piero Camporesi. Turin: Einaudi. (The best way to enjoy Artusi, with Camporesi's informative notes and background information.)

Balinska, Maria. 2006. *The Bagel: A Cultural History*. New Haven: Yale University Press.

Ballarini, Giovanni. 2002. *Storia sociale del maiale*. Parma: Editrice PPS. (The pig and pork products, in the past, present and future.)

———. 2003. *Piccola storia della grande salumeria italiana*. Milan: EDRA.

———. 2005. *Cibo e cultura nell'eccelenza di Parma*. CD. Parma: Provincia di Parma.

Ballerini and Parzen, see Martino.

Bartolotti, Luisa. 1989. *A tavola con i Malatesti*. Rimini: Panozzo. (Many local publishers and museums produce little gems like this.)

———, ed. 1993. *Il codice di cucina*. Rimini: Panozzo.

Bastianich, Lidia. 1980. *Lidia's Italian Table*. New York: HarperCollins.

———. 2003. *La cucina di Lidia*. New York: Random House.

———. 2004. *Lidia's Family Table*. New York: Barnes and Noble.

———. 2007. *Lidia's Italy*. New York: Random House.

Batali, Mario. 2002. *Babbo Cookbook*. New York: Clarkson Potter.

———. 2005. *Molto Italiano*. New York: Ecco.

Belli, Maddalena, Francesca Grassi, and Beatrice Sordini. 2004. *La cucina di un ospedale del trecento*. Pisa: Pacini.

Benedetti, Benedetto. 1986. *L'aceto balsamico*. Spilamberto: Consorteria dell'aceto balsamico.

———. 1999. *L'aceto balsamico del ducato di ModenaI*. Modena: Il Fiorino.

Benporat, Claudio. 1990. *Storia della gastronomia italiana*. Milan: Mursia. (Based firmly on texts from early cookery manuscripts to Artusi, with commentaries and much quoted material.)

———. 1996. *Cucina italiana nel quattrocento*. Florence: Olschki. (The complete texts of three versions of Martino, with illuminating commentaries.)

———. 2001. *Feste e bancchetti*. Florence: Olschki. (A discussion of the role of the banquet in 14th- and 15th-century Italy, with contemporary accounts and menus.)

Bergström, Ingemar. 1985. *Anonimo Meridionale, Due libri di cucina.* Stockholm: Almqvist & Wiksell.

Biasin, Gian-Paolo. 1993. *The Flavours of Modernity: Food and the Novel.* Princeton, N.J.: Princeton University Press.

Birri, Flavio, and Carla Coco. 2000. *Cade a fagiolo.* Venice: Marsilio.

Bizzarri, Giulio, and Eleonora Bronzoni, eds. 1986. *Libro contenente la maniera di cucinare . . .* Bologna: Il lavoro editoriale.

Black, William. 2003. *Al dente.* London: Corgi Books.

Blumental, Heston. 2006. *In Pursuit of Perfection.* London: Bloomsbury.

Bober, Phyllis Pray. 1999. *Art, Culture and Cuisine.* Chicago: University of Chicago Press.

Boni, Ada. 1982. *La Lombardia in Cucina.* Milan: Martello.

———. 1983. *La cucina romana.* Rome: Newton Compton.

———. n.d. *Il talismano della felicità.* Rome: Colombo.

Bourcard, Francesco de. 1857. *Usi e Costumi di Napoli.* Naples.

Bozzi, Ottorina Perna. 1969. *Vecchia Milano in cucina.* Milan: Martello.

———. 1982. *La Lombardia in cucina.* Milan: Martello.

Buford, Bill. 2006. *Heat.* New York: Knopf.

Calvino, Italo. 1962. *Il barone rampante.* Turin: Einaudi.

Camilleri, Andrea. 1999. *Gli arancini di Montalbano.* Milan: Mondadori.

———. 2000. *La Forma dell'Aqua.* Palermo: Sellerio.

———. 2001. *L'odore della notte.* Palermo: Sellerio.

Camporesi, Piero. 1980. *Alimentazione, folclore, società.* Parma: Pratiche Editrice.

———. 1985. *Le officine dei sensi.* Milan: Garzanti.

Capacchi, Guglielmo. 1989. *La cucina popolare parmigiana.* Parma: Artegrafica Silva.

Capatti, Alberto, and Massimo Montanari. 1999. *La cucina italians: Storia di una cultura.* Rome: Laterza. (Stimulating arguments and interpretations as well as facts.)

Cardillo Violati, Leda, and Carlo Majnardi. 1990. *I picchiarelli della Malanotte.* Foligno: Edizioni dell'Arquata. (A model of how to investigate and publish local food traditions.)

Carluccio, Antonio, and Priscilla Carluccio. 1997. *Complete Italian Food.* London: Quadrille.

Carnacina, Luigi, and Luigi Veronelli. 1977. *La cucina rustica regionale.* 4 vols. Milan: Rizzoli.

Casagrande, Giovanna. 1989. *Gola e preghiera.* Foligno: Edizioni dell'Arquata.

Castelvetro, Giacomo. 1989. *The Fruit, Herbs and Vegetables of Italy.* Translated by Gillian Riley. London: Viking.

Casale, Gerardo. 1991. *Giovanna Garzoni 'Insigne miniatrice' 1600–1670.* Milan: Jandi Sapi.

Cavalcanti, Ippolito. 1847. *Cucina teorico-pratica.* Naples: De' Gemelli.

Cavanna, Guelfo. 1914. *I doni di Nettuno.* Florence.

Cerini di Castegnate, Livio. 1986. *Il libro del baccalà.* Milan: Longanesi.

Clauser, Marina, and Paolo Luzzi. 2002. *Piante medicinali di uso popolare della tradizione Toscana.* Florence: Museo di storia naturale, Università di Firenze.

Coe, Sophie D., and Michael D. Coe. 1996. *The True History of Chocolate.* London: Thames and Hudson.

Coltro, Dino. 1983. *La cucina tradizionale veneta.* Rome: Newton Compton.

Contini, Mary. 2002. *Dear Francesca.* London: Ebury Press.

Corrado, Vincenzo. 1972. *Il cuoco galante.* Sala Bolognese: Arnaldo Forni. Facsimile of 1778 edition.

————. 1991. *Del cibo pitagorico ovvero erbaceo per uso de' nobili e de' letterati.* Sala Bolognese: Arnaldo Forni. Facsimile of 1781 edition.

Da Confienza, Pantaleone. 1990. *Trattato dei Laticini.* Translated and edited by Emilio Faccioli. Milan: Grana Padano.

Dalby, Andrew. 2000. *Empire of Pleasures.* London: Routledge. (The best account of the pleasures of Roman gastronomy.)

————. 2000. *Dangerous Tastes: The Story of Spices.* London: British Museum Press.

————. 2003. *Food in the Ancient World from A to Z.* London: Routledge.

Dalby, Andrew, and Sally Grainger. 1996. *The Classical Cookbook.* London: British Museum Press.

Da Mosto, Ranieri. 1969. *Il Veneto in cucina.* Milan: Martello.

David, Elizabeth. 1954; 1963. *Italian Food.* London: Penguin.

————. 1987. *Italian Food.* Illus. ed. London: Barrie and Jenkins.

Davidson, Alan. 1972. *Mediterranean Seafood.* London: Penguin.

————. 2006. *The Oxford Companion to Food.* Oxford: Oxford University Press.

De la Mata, Juan. 1992. *Arte de reposteria.* Burgos: La Olmeda. Facsimile of 1747 edition.

Del Conte, Anna. 1989. *Secrets from an Italian Kitchen.* London: Bantam.

————. 2001; 2004. *Gastronomy of Italy.* London: Pavillion. (Indispensable combination of recipes and short descriptions of ingredients and methods.)

————. 2006. *Amaretto, Apple cake and Artichokes: The Best of Anna del Conte.* London: Vintage Books.

Dèttore, Mariapaola. 1979. *Il pane dall'antipasto al dolce.* Milan: Garzanti.

Di Corato, Riccardo. 1978. *928 condimenti d'Italia.* Milan: Sonzogno.

————. 1979. *838 frutti e verdure d'Italia.* Milan: Sonzogno.

Di Schino, June. 2000. *Tre banchetti in onore di Cristina di Svezia.* Rome: Accademia Italiana della Cucina.

————, ed. 2005. *I fasti del banchetto barocco.* Rome: Diomeda Centro Studi.

Di Schino, June, and Furio Luccichenti, eds. 2004. *Bartolomeo Scappi cuoco nel Roma del cinquecento.* Rome: private publication. (Ground-breaking research into Scappi and his career.)

Downie, David. 2002. *Cooking the Roman Way.* New York: HarperCollins.

Et coquatur ponendo . . . 1996. Prato: Istituto Internazionale di Storia Economica "F. Datini." (Descriptions of texts and manuscripts with commentaries by experts from Laurioux to Milham.)

Evitascandalo, Cristoforo. 1609. *Libro dello scalco.* Rome: Vullietti.

Faccioli, Emilio. 1962. *L'eccellenza e il trionfo del porco.* Milan: Mazzotta.

————. 1992. *L'arte della cucina in Italia.* Turin: Einaudi. (A pioneering work, with selections from, as well as complete, historical gastronomic texts.)

Felici, Costanzo. 1982. *Lettere a Ulisse Aldrovandi.* Edited by Giorgio Nonni. Urbino: Quattro Venti.

————. 1986. *Dell'insalata e piante she in qualunque modo vengono per cibo del'homo.* Urbino: Quattro Venti.

Field, Carol. 1985. *The Italian Baker.* New York: HarperCollins.

⸻. 1990. *Celebrating Italy.* New York: Morrow. (The most erudite and stimulating work on Italian festive food, with recipes and detailed bibliography.)

⸻. 1997. *In Nonna's Kitchen.* New York: HarperCollins.

⸻. 2004. *Italy in Small Bites.* New York: Morrow.

Flandrin, J.-L., and M. Montanari. 1997. *Storia dell'alimentazione.* Rome: Laterza.

Firpo, Luigi, ed. 1974. *Gastronomia del rinascimento.* Turin: Utet.

Fort, Matthew. 2004. *Eating Up Italy.* London: Fourth Estate.

Francesconi, Jeanne Carola. 1965. *La cucina napoletana.* Naples: Fausto Fiorentino.

Gaudentio, Francesco. 1990. *Il panunto toscano.* Edited by Guido Gianni. Sala Bolognese: Arnaldo Forni. Originally published 1705.

Giarmoleo, Giuseppe. 1998. *La pasta al museo.* Rome: Museo Nazionale delle paste alimentari.

Giusti, Giovanna Galardi. 2001. *Dolci a Corte.* Livorno: Sillabe.

Gowers, Emily. 1993. *The Loaded Table.* Oxford: Oxford University Press.

Grainger, Sally. 2006. *Cooking Apicius.* Totnes, England: Prospect Books.

Grande enciclopedia illustrata della gastronomia. 2000. Milan: Camuzzi. (The best reference book, with helpful illustrations and recipes.)

Gray, Patience. 1987. *Honey from a Weed.* New York: Harper Collins.

Grieve, M., and C. E. Leyel. 1979. *A Modern Herbal.* Reprint. London: Jonathan Cape.

Grocock, Christopher, and Sally Grainger. 2006. *Apicius: A Critical Edition and Translation.* Totnes, England: Prospect Books. (The only decent translation, with insights from a hands-on cook.)

Guberti, Brenda, Electra Stamboulis, and Mario Turci. 1998. *Buono come . . . la piadina di Romagna.* Rimini: Panozzo.

Hazan, Marcella. 1980. *The Classic Italian Cookbook.* London: Macmillan.

⸻. 1997. *Marcella Cucina.* London: Macmillan.

Hollingsworth, Mary. 2005. *The Cardinal's Hat.* London: Profile Books.

Ignoto napoletano. n.d.; c. 17th century. *Brieve e nuovo modo di farsi ogni sorte di sorbette con facilità.* Naples: Cristofaro Migliaccio. (Only one copy has survived of this battered little ice cream maker's handbook.)

INSOR (Istituto nazionale di sociologia rurale). 2000. *Atlante dei prodotti tipici: Il pane.* Rome: Agra.

⸻. 2001. *Atlante dei prodotti tipici; I formaggi.* Rome: Agra.

⸻. 2002. *Atlante dei prodotti tipici: I salumi.* Rome: Agra.

Kasper, Lynne Rossetto. 1992. *The Splendid Table.* New York: Morrow.

Knauer, Elfriede R. 2003. "Fishing with Cormorants." *Apollo,* September.

Lampedusa, Giuseppe Tomasi di. 1960. *Il gattopardo.* Milan: Feltrinelli.

La natura morta al tempo di Caravaggio. 1995. Naples: Electa.

Landi, Giulio. n.d. *Trattato dei latticini.* Edited by Emilio Faccioli. Milan: Grana Padano.

Latini, Antonio. 1992. *Autobiografia.* Edited by Furio Luccichenti. Rome: private publication.

⸻. 1993. *Lo scalco alla moderna.* 2 vols. Milan: Appunti di Gastronomia. Facsimile of 1692, 1694 volumes, Naples: Parrino and Mutii.

Laurioux, Bruno. 1997. *Le règne de Taillevet.* Paris: Publications de la Sorbonne.

———. 2002. *Manger au moyen âge.* Paris: Hachette.

———. 2005. *Une histoire culinaire du Moyen Age.* Sciences, Techniques et Civilisation du Moyen Âge à l'Aube des Lumières, 8. Paris: Honoré Champion.

———. (2006) *Gastronomie, humanisme et societé à Rome au milieu du xv siècle.* Florence: Galluzzo. (The last word on the gastronomic culture of humanism.)

L'economia domestica. 1995. Edited by Giovanni Aliberti and Gabriele De Rosa. Pisa/Rome: Istituto Luigi Sturzo.

Leemann, Pietro. 1991. *Alta cucina vegetariana.* Milan: Giorgio Bernardini Editore.

Liberati, Francesco. 1974. *Il perfetto maestro di casa.* Sala Bolognese: Arnaldo Forni. Facsimile of 1668 edition, Rome, Bernabò.

Locatelli, Giorgio. 2006. *Made in Italy: Food and Stories.* London: Fourth Estate.

Lussu, Emilio. 1976. *Il cinghilae del diavolo.* Turin: Einaudi.

Mafai, Miriam. 1987. *Pane nero.* Milan: Mondadori.

Magnoni, Grazia Bravetti. 1997. *La cucina dell'arzdora.* Rimini: Panozzo.

Maioli, Giorgio, and Giancarlo Roversi. 1993. *Civilta della tavola a Bologna.* Sala Bolognese: Arnaldo Forni.

Malacarne, Giancarlo. 2000. *Sulla mensa del principe, alimentazione e banchetti alla corte dei Gonzaga.* Modena: Il Bulino edizioni d'arte.

Marchese, Pasquale. 1989. *L'invezione della forchetta.* Soveria Manelli: Rubbettino.

Martínez Montiño, Francisco. 1982. *Arte de cocina.* Barcelona: Tusquets Editores. Facsimile of 1678 edition, Barcelona.

Martino, Maestro. 2001. *Libro de arte coquinaria.* Edited by Luigi Ballerini and Jeremy Parzen. Milan: Guido Tomasi.

———. 2005. *The Art of Cooking.* Translated by Jeremy Parzen. Edited by Luigi Ballerini. Berkeley: University of California Press.

———. 2006. *Libro de arte coquinaria.* CD. Text with translation by Gillian Riley. Oakland, Calif.: Octavo.

Mattioli, Andrea. 1967. *I discorsi.* Rome: Roberto Peliti. Facsimile of 1568 edition, Venice.

McGee, Harold, 1992. *The Curious Cook.* London: HarperCollins.

———. 2004. *On Food and Cooking.* New York: Scribner.

Messisbugo, Cristoforo. 1960. *Banchetti compositioni di vivande.* Ferrara: Bughait & Hucher. Facsimile of 1549 ed.

———. 1980. *Libro novo.* Sala Bolognese: Arnaldo Forni. Facsimile of 1557 ed., Venice, Heredi di Gioanne Padoano.

Metz, Vittorio. 1972. *La cucina di Gioachino Belli.* Rome: Edizioni del Gattopardo.

Molinari Pradelli, Alessandro. 1997. *La cucina della Liguria.* Rome: Tascabili Economici Newton.

Montanari, Massimo. 1988. *Alimentazione e cultura nel medioevo.* Rome/Bari: Laterza.

———. 1989. *Convivio: Storia e cultura dei piaceri della tavola dall' antichità al medioevo.* Rome/Bari: Laterza.

———. 1993. *La fame e l'abbondanza: Storia del'alaimentazione in Europa.* Rome/Bari: Laterza.

Moravia, Albert. 1957. *La Ciociara.* Milan: Tascabili Bompiani.

Mosley, James. 1964. "Trajan Revived," *Motif.* London: Lund Humphries.

Musacchio, Jacqueline Marie. 1999. *The Art and Ritual of Childbirth in Renaissance Italy.* New Haven, Conn.: Yale University Press.

Newby, Eric. 1975. *Love and War in the Appenines*. London: Michael Joseph.

Nigro, Salvatore. 1998. *L'orologio di Pontormo*. Milan: Rizzoli.

Oliver, Jamie. 2005. *Jamie's Italy*. London: Michael Joseph.

————. 2007. *Cook with Jamie*. London: Michael Joseph.

Pantaleone da Confienza. 1990. *Trattato dei Laticini*. Translated and edited by Emilio Faccioli. Milan: Grana Padano.

Pederiali, Giuseppe. 1985. *Padania Felix*. Reggio Emilia: Diabasis.

Pellegrino, Artusi. 1970. *La scienza in cucina e l'arte di mangiar bene*. Edited with an introduction by Piero Camporesi. Turin: Einaudi.

Perry, Charles. 2001. *Medieval Arab Cookery*. Totnes, England: Prospect Books.

Pisanelli, Baldassare. (1611) *Trattato della natura de'cibi et del bere*. Venice: Domenico Imbetti.

Platina, Bartolomeo. 1998. *De honesta voluptate et valetudine* [On right pleasure and good health]. Translated with notes by Mary Ella Milham. Tempe, Ariz.: Medieval and Renaissance Texts and Studies. (Awesome scholarship, but a less than perfect translation.)

Plotkin, Fred. 1997. *Recipes from Paradise*. New York: Little, Brown.

Porcaro, Giuseppe. 1985. *Sapore di Napoli*. Naples: Adriano Gallina.

Redon, O., Saban, F., Serventi, S. (1994) *A tavola nel medioevo*, Rome/Bari: Laterza.

Roden, Claudia. 1989. *The Food of Italy*. London: Chatto and Windus.

————. 1997. *The Book of Jewish Food*. London: Viking.

Romer, Elizabeth. 1993. *The Tuscan Year*. London: Weidenfeld and Nicolson.

Rosselli, Giovanni de'. 1973. *Opera nova chiamata Epulario*. Rome: Bimo. Facsimile of 1518 edition.

Rossetti, Giovanni Battista. 1991. *Dello scalco*. Sala Bolognese: Arnaldo Forni. Facsimile of 1584 edition, Ferrara: Domenico Mammarello.

Sabban, Françoise, and Silvano Serventi. 1996. *A tavola nel rinascimento*. Rome/Bari: Laterza.

Scappi, Bartolomeo. 1981. *Opera*. Sala Bolognese: Arnaldo Forni. Facsimile of 1570 edition. (One of the greatest cookery texts, still relevant and delicious.)

Serventi, Silvano, and Françoise Sabban. 2000. *La Pasta: Storia e cultura di un cibo universale*. Rome/Bari: Laterza.

The Silver Spoon. 2005. London: Phaidon. English translation of the classic first published in 1950 as *Il cucchiaio d'argento*.

Simeti, Mary Taylor. 1989. *Sicilian Food*. London: Jill Norman Century. (Brilliant combination of cultural history and recipes.)

Simeti, Mary Taylor, and Maria Grammatico. 1994. *Bitter Almonds*. London: Bantam.

Slow Food. 2002. *Formaggi d'Italia*. Bra: Slow Food.

————. 2005. *L'Italia dei presidi*. Bra: Slow Food.

Smith, Delia. 2004. *The Delia Collection: Italian*. London: Ted Smart BBC Books.

Sotti, M. L., and M. T. Della Beffa. 1989. *Le piante aromatiche*. Milan, Giorgio Mandadori.

Spurling, Hilary. 1986. *Elinor Fettiplace's Receipt Book*. London: Viking Salamander.

Strong, Roy. 2002. *Feast: A History of Grand Eating*. London: Jonathan Cape.

Taruschio, Ann, and Franco Taruschio. 1993. *Leaves from the Walnut Tree*. London: Pavillion.

————. 1995. *Bruschetta, Crostoni and Crostini*. London: Pavillion.

————. 2000. *100 Great Pasta Dishes*. London: Kyle Cathie.

Teti, Vito. 1978. *Il pane, la beffa e la festa*. Florence: Guaraldi.

Valerio, Nico. 1988. *Mangiare italiano: I piatti ricchi della cucina povera*. Milan: Mondadori.

————. 1989. *La tavola degli Antichi*. Milan: Mondadori.

Vasselli, Gio. Francesco. 1998. *L'Apicio overo il maestro de' conviti. L'Apicio overo il maestro de' conviti*. Sala Bolognese: Arnaldo Forni. Facsimile of 1647 edition, Bologna: Del Dozza.

Wardrop, James. 1963. *The Script of Humanism*. Oxford: Clarendon Press.

Wright, Clifford A. 1992. *Cucina Paradiso: The Heavenly Food of Sicily*. New York: Simon & Schuster.

Zuliani, Mariù Salvatori de. 1978. *A tola co i nostri veci*. Milan: Franco Angeli.

Zanlari, Andrea. 1996. *A tavola con i Farnese*. Parma: Public Promo Service.

Index